SIGNS OF LIFE
IN THE U.S.A.

Readings on Popular Culture for Writers

THIRD EDITION

SIGNS OF LIFE
IN THE U.S.A.

Readings on Popular Culture for Writers

SONIA MAASIK
University of California, Los Angeles

JACK SOLOMON
California State University, Northridge

Bedford/St. Martin's   Boston ■ New York

We dedicate this book to our dear friends, Susie and Charlie.

For Bedford/St.Martin's
Developmental Editor: John E. Sullivan III
Production Editor: Bridget D. Leahy
Production Supervisor: Catherine Hetmansky
Marketing Manager: Karen Melton
Editorial Assistant: Katherine Gilbert
Production Assistant: Coleen O'Hanley
Copyeditor: Rosemary Winfield
Text Design: Anna Post George
Cover Design: Hannus Design Associates
Cover Art: Cover illustration by Pierre-Paul Pariseau
Composition: Pine Tree Composition, Inc.
Printing and Binding: Haddon Craftsmen, Inc.

President: Charles H. Christensen
Editorial Director: Joan E. Feinberg
Director of Editing, Design, and Production: Marcia Cohen
Managing Editor: Elizabeth M. Schaaf

Library of Congress Catalog Card Number: 99–65147

For information, write: Bedford/St. Martin's, 75 Arlington Street, Boston, MA
02116 (617-399-4000)

ISBN: 0–312–19582–6

Acknowledgments

Melissa Algranati, "Being an Other," from *Becoming American, Becoming Ethnic:
College Students Explore Their Roots,* edited by Thomas Dublin. Copyright
© 1996 by Melissa Algranati. Reprinted by permission of the author.
Gigi Anders and the Editors of *Deaf Life,* "Beauty and the Battle," from *Deaf
Life Magazine,* July 1995. Originally appeared in March 3–5 issue of *USA
Weekend.* Copyright © 1995 by Gigi Anders. Reprinted by permission of
the author.

*Acknowledgments and copyrights are continued at the back of the book on pages
812–18, which constitute an extension of the copyright page. It is a violation of the law
to reproduce these selections by any means whatsoever without the written permission of
the copyright holder.*

PREFACE FOR INSTRUCTORS

When the first edition of *Signs of Life in the U.S.A.* appeared, the study of popular culture was still embroiled in the "culture wars" of the early 1990s, a struggle for academic legitimacy in which the adherents of cultural studies ultimately prevailed. Since then, more and more scholars and teachers have come to recognize the importance of understanding what Michel de Certeau has called "the practice of everyday life" and the value of using popular culture as a thematic ground for educating students in critical thinking and writing. Once excluded from academic study on the basis of a naturalized distinction between "high" (or academically approved) and "low" (or mass) culture that contemporary cultural analysis has shown to be historically contingent, popular culture has come to be an accepted part of the curriculum, widely studied in freshman composition classrooms as well as in upper-division undergraduate courses and graduate seminars.

But recognition of the important place that popular culture has assumed in our society has not been restricted to the academy. Increasingly, Americans are coming to realize that American culture and popular culture are coming to be synonymous and that whether we are looking at our political system, our economy, or simply our national consciousness, the power of popular culture to shape our lives is strikingly apparent. Sometimes this realization has been fraught with controversy, as when in the aftermath of a spate of schoolyard slayings in the late 1990s a host of politicians and pundits pointed their fingers at violent entertainment as the culprit behind the violence. At other times, the growing influence of popular culture has been received more enthusiastically, as in the widespread belief that the Internet is a medium of economic and educational reform and revival. But whether the recognition is tinged with controversy or splashed with enthusiasm, at no time in our history have Americans been more aware of the place of popular culture in their lives.

For this reason, we believe that learning to think and write critically about popular culture is even more important today than it was when we published the first edition of this book. As the boundary between "culture" and popular culture blurs and even disappears, it is all the more essential that our students understand how popular culture works and how it generates meaning. This is why we continue to make semiotics the guiding methodology behind *Signs of Life in the U.S.A.* Semiotics leads us, and our students, to take an analytic stance toward popular culture, one that avoids the common pitfalls of uncritical celebration or simple scapegoating.

The reception of the first two editions of *Signs of Life in the U.S.A.* has demonstrated that the semiotic approach to popular culture has indeed found a place in America's composition classrooms. Composition instructors have seen that students feel a certain sense of ownership toward the products of popular culture — and that using popular culture as a focus can help students overcome the sometimes alienating effects of traditional academic subject matter. At the same time, the semiotic method has helped instructors lead their students to analyze critically the popular cultural phenomena that they enjoy writing about and so learn the critical thinking and writing skills that their composition classes are designed to impart.

The Book's Organization

Reflecting the broad academic interest in cultural studies, we've assumed an inclusive definition of popular culture. This definition can be seen in the book's organization. Its two sections — Cultural Productions and Cultural Constructions — highlight the essential cultural connection between the things we do and the things we believe. The five chapters in the first section focus on the marketing and consumption of the products of mass culture and mass production, from sport utility vehicles to TV shows, movies, and blockbuster novels. The five chapters in the second part of the book may seem a bit more sobering, but they are inextricably linked to the text's first half. In addressing gender issues, race relations, marginal subcultures, American icons, and spatial semiotics, these chapters show how ideologies work to construct us as consumers and producers.

The Critical Method: Semiotics

Signs of Life departs from some textbook conventions in that it makes explicit an interpretive approach, semiotics, that can guide students' analyses of popular culture. We've made this approach explicit because it has struck us that while students enjoy assignments that ask them to look at popular cultural phenomena, they often have trouble distinguishing between an argued interpretive analysis and the simple expression of an opinion. Some textbooks, for example, suggest assignments that involve analyzing a TV program or film, but they don't always tell a student how to do that. The semiotic method provides that guidance.

At the same time, semiotics reveals that there's no such thing as a pure, ideologically neutral analysis, even in freshman composition. Anthologies typically present analysis as a "pure" category: they present readings that students are asked to analyze but articulate no conceptual framework and neither explore nor define theoretical assumptions and ideological positions. Being self-conscious about one's point of view, however, is an essential part of academic writing, and we can think of no better place for students to learn that lesson than in a writing class.

We've found through experience that a semiotic approach is especially well suited to this purpose. As a conceptual framework, semiotics teaches students to formulate cogent, well-supported interpretations. It emphasizes the examination of assumptions and the way language shapes our apprehension of the world. And because it focuses on *how* beliefs are formulated within a social and political context (rather than just judging or evaluating those beliefs), it's ideal for discussing sensitive or politically charged issues. As an approach used in literature, media studies, anthropology, art and design coursework, sociology, law, and market research (to name only some of its more prominent field applications), semiotics has a cross-disciplinary appeal that makes it ideal for a writing class of students from a variety of majors and disciplines. We recognize that semiotics has a reputation for being highly technical or theoretical: be assured that *Signs of Life* does not require students or instructors to have a technical knowledge of semiotics. In fact, we've provided clear and accessible introductions that explain what students need to know.

We also recognize that adopting a theoretical approach may be new to some instructors, so we've designed the book to allow instructors to be as semiotic with their students as they wish. The book does not obligate instructors or students to spend a lot of time with semiotics — although we do hope you'll find the approach intriguing and provocative.

The Editorial Apparatus

With its emphasis on popular culture, *Signs of Life* should generate lively class discussion and inspire many kinds of writing and thinking activities. The general introduction provides an overall framework for the book by acquainting students with the semiotic method they can use to interpret the topics raised in each chapter. It is followed by a section on

Writing about Popular Culture that not only provides a brief introduction to writing about popular culture but additionally features three sample student essays that demonstrate different approaches to writing critical essays on pop culture topics. Each chapter starts off with a frontispiece, a provocative visual image related to the chapter's topic, and an introduction that suggests ways to "read" the topic, presents model interpretations, and links the issues raised by the reading selections. Every chapter introduction contains three types of boxed questions designed to stimulate student thinking on the topic. The Exploring the Signs questions invite students to reflect on an issue in a journal entry or other prewriting activity, whereas the Discussing the Signs questions trigger class activities such as debates, discussions, or small-group work. Reading the Net questions invite students to explore the chapter's topic on the Internet, both for research purposes and for texts to analyze.

The readings themselves are followed by two sorts of assignments. The Reading the Text questions help students comprehend the selections by asking them to identify important concepts and arguments, explain key terms, and relate main ideas to each other and to the evidence presented. The Reading the Signs questions are writing and activity prompts designed to produce clear analytic thinking and strong persuasive writing; they often make connections among reading selections from different chapters. Most assignments call for analytic essays, while some invite journal responses, in-class debates, group work, or other creative activities. We've also included a Glossary of semiotic terms, which can serve as a ready reference of key terms and concepts used in the chapter introductions. Finally, the instructors manual (*Editors' Notes to Accompany Signs of Life in the U.S.A.*) provides suggestions for organizing your syllabus, encouraging student response to the readings, and using popular culture and semiotics in the writing class.

What's New in the Third Edition

Few subjects move so quickly as does the pace of popular culture, and the third edition of *Signs of Life* reflects this essential mutability through its substantial revision of the second edition. First, we have updated our readings, adding selections that focus on issues and trends important in the late 1990s. With forty-two new readings, our third edition represents a fifty-five percent turnover from the second. At the same time, we have updated the exemplary topics in our introductions used to model the critical assignments that follow and have readjusted the focus of some chapters to reflect changing conditions. For instance, we have changed our former chapter on "Cultural Outlaws" to one on cultural "otherness" (Chapter 8, "Life on the Margins: Representing the 'Other' in American Culture"), focusing on some of the many subcultures that live on the margins of American society, including outlaws but also the deaf, gays and lesbians, and the emerging group of American schoolchildren who feel marginalized on their school campuses. We have also added two entirely new chapters. One, "It Was a Dark and Stormy Night: The Codes of Popular Literature" (Chapter 5), explores the place of popular literature in our culture, especially as it affects American literacy, and the other, "Popular Spaces: Interpreting the Built Environment" (Chapter 10), looks at the way that the built environment reflects and constructs American values and ideologies.

We have also moved our section on Writing about Popular Culture to the front of the book, following the Introduction, to make it handier for student use. This section contains two new student-written essays prompted by the second edition of *Signs of Life,* as well as a student essay from the second edition that pursues a semiotic analysis of the movie *Cool Hand Luke.* In this essay, the student writer uses insights from one of the text's readings, Robert B. Ray's "The Thematic Paradigm" (p. 299), to write a critical analysis that proposes his own political interpretation of the film's ideology. In the other essays, one student analyzes the relationships between science fiction entertainment and social trends, and one takes a personal approach to the tattoo and body piercing fads.

Finally, we have added more visual images to the third edition of *Signs of Life* to underscore the power of the image in contemporary American life and to offer further subjects for discussion and analysis.

Even as we revise this text to reflect current trends, popular culture continues to evolve. The inevitable gap between the pace of editing and publishing, on the one hand, and the flow of popular culture, on the other, need not affect its use in the classroom, however. The readings in the text, and the semiotic method we propose, are designed to show students how to analyze and write critical essays about any topic they choose. They can, as one of our student writers does, choose a topic that appeared before they were born, or they can turn to the latest box office or prime-time hit to appear after the publication of this edition of *Signs of Life.* To put it another way, the practice of everyday life may itself be filled with evanescent fads and trends, but it is not itself a fad. As the vital texture of our lived experience, popular culture provides a stable background against which students of every generation can test their critical skills.

Acknowledgments

The vastness of the terrain of popular culture has enabled many users of the second edition of this text to make valuable suggestions for the third edition. We have incorporated many such suggestions and thank all our reviewers for their comments on our text: Glen Scott Allen, Towson State University; Lori Anderson, Skidmore College; Scott Beal, University of

Michigan; Wendy Bentley, Central Piedmont Community College; Valerie A. Booth, University of Delaware; Liane Bryson, San Diego State University; Julie A. Cary, University of Kentucky; Ann M. Ciasullo, University of Kentucky; Robert Cousins, Utah Valley State College; Robin DeRosa, Tufts University; Edward A. Dougherty, Elmira College; Christine Farris, Indiana University at Bloomington; Priscilla Finley, Elmira College; Karin Fuog, Eastern Connecticut State University; Victoria Gaydosik, East Central University; David C. Hoffman, University of Iowa; Laura Lane, University of North Florida; Donald E. Levin, Marygrove College; Elizabeth Charlton McConnell, Emerson College; Sharon Merritt, Santa Clara University; Robert Michalski, Santa Clara University; Steve Pierson, Purdue University; Cheli Reutter, University of California, Riverside; Lynne Schaeffer, Marygrove College; Siobhan Senier, University of Maine at Farmington; Philip Serrato, University of California, Riverside; Allison Singley, Gettysburg College; Diana Slampyak, University of California, Riverside; Terry L. Spaise, University of California, Riverside; Megan Sullivan, Boston University; Tad Wakefield, University of California, Riverside; Pamela Washington, University of Central Oklahoma; Jeremy Webster, University of Tennessee; Terry Williams, San Diego State University. If we have not included something you'd like to work on, you may still direct your students to it, using this text as a guide, not as a set of absolute prescriptions. The practice of everyday life includes the conduct of a classroom, and we want all users of the third edition of *Signs of Life in the U.S.A.* to feel free to pursue that practice in whatever way best suits their interests and aims. In addition, we are grateful to Martha Sayles (California State University, Northridge) and Miriam Hardin (Lehigh University) for supplying sample student essays, and to Meredith Kurz (California State University, Northridge) and Deborah Banner (University of California, Los Angeles) for their useful contributions to the instructor's manual.

We'd like to thank Jim Moyle for his constant good fellowship and his generous open-door policy, which allowed us to go online through a snowy winter.

And once again, we wish also to thank the people at Bedford/St. Martin's who have enabled us to make this third edition a reality, from Chuck Christensen and Joan Feinberg, who have now been at the helm through five of our textbook projects, to John Sullivan, our editor on this edition, whose ability to devote himself entirely to the needs and crotchets of the authors he assists reminds us of the legendary Maxwell Perkins. Bridget Leahy ably guided our manuscript through the rigors of production, while Katherine Gilbert handled the innumerable details that crop up during textbook development. In addition, Coleen O'Hanley and Rosemary Winfield contributed their intelligence and superb competence to the production of this book.

CONTENTS

PART TWO

CULTURAL CONSTRUCTIONS   *435*

6. WE'VE COME A LONG WAY, MAYBE:
Gender Codes in American Culture   *437*

10. POPULAR SPACES: *Interpreting the Built Environment*   *733*

POPULAR SIGNS

Or, Everything You've Always Known about
American Culture (But Nobody Asked)

The Truth Is Out There

Maybe it all began with *The X-Files*.
Or maybe it began with *E. T.*
Or maybe it started at Roswell.
Wherever or whenever it began, something uncanny is going on in America's popular imagination. A lurking suspicion that we are not alone, that other creatures besides ourselves exist in the universe, has taken hold. More profound, perhaps, is the growing suspicion that our government knows something about all this that it isn't telling us—indeed, that it is covering up.

That, at least, is the message one gets when contemplating the continued national fascination with the murky aftermath of the Roswell incident and the explosive popularity of TV programs like Fox's *The X-Files*. With movies like *Independence Day, Men in Black*, and *Mars Attacks!* bringing in large audiences, not to mention the continuing *Star Wars* saga and its many spinoffs and now prequel, it is clear that aliens are haunting the popular imagination. And there are no signs that the fascination will disappear soon.

Have you ever wondered why so many people seem caught up in extraterrestrial fervor, or why almost twenty years after his first appearance, E.T. himself could appear as part of the 1999 Super Bowl telecast?

Have you ever wondered, for that matter, why the Super Bowl itself is such a big deal?

Such questions belong to the growing academic field known as cultural studies, a branch of knowledge that seeks to analyze and understand the things people do in the course of their everyday lives, especially within the realm of popular culture. Within the university, the study of popular culture is a fairly recent development. Traditionally, academics have regarded popular culture as being too trivial for serious study, and thus the passing trends of everyday life have largely been excluded from the typical college curriculum.

But when you think about it, there is only one world after all, the everyday world within which we do what we do, from the way we entertain ourselves to the way we educate ourselves. And with the advent of cultural studies into university curricula, that old, artificial wall between everyday life and the ivory tower is at last coming down. Today, more and more instructors are deciding that America's popular culture—a field that embraces not only the way we entertain ourselves and the products we consume but the whole fabric of contemporary behavior and belief—is worth studying and writing about. This has been especially true in composition classrooms, which are now leading the way in incorporating popular culture into academic study, both because of the inherent interest value of the subject and because of its profound familiarity to most students. Your own expertise in popular culture means not only that you may know more about a given topic than your instructor but that you may use that knowledge as a basis for learning the critical thinking and writing skills that your composition class is charged to teach you. This book is designed to show you how to do that—how to write about American popular culture as you would write about any other academic subject.

We have prepared *Signs of Life in the U.S.A.*, in other words, because we believe that you are already a sophisticated student of American culture. Think of all you already know. Just list all the bands you can name and all the various categories they fall into: Is the lounge scene still around? Frat metal? Has "emotional core" music emerged from the shadows? Where's hip hop these days? Or the indie set? Face it, you're an expert. So isn't that a good place to start learning how to write college essays—with what you know already? We all write best when we can write from our strengths, and this book is intended to let you tap into your own storehouse of information and experience as you learn to write college essays.

Signs of Life in the U.S.A., then, is designed to let you exploit your knowledge of popular culture so that you may grow into a better writer about any subject. You can interpret the popularity of programs like *The X-Files*, for example, in the same manner as you would interpret, say, a short story because *The X-Files*, too, constitutes a kind of *sign*. A sign is something, *anything*, that carries a meaning. A stop sign, for instance, means exactly what it says—"Stop when you approach this intersection"—and also carries the implied message of "or risk getting a ticket." Words, too, are signs: you read them to figure out what they mean. You were trained to read such signs, but that training began so long ago that you may well take your ability to read for granted. But all of your life you have been encountering, and interpreting, other sorts of signs that you were never formally taught to read. You know what they mean anyway. Take the way you wear your hair. When you get your hair cut, you are not simply removing hair: you are making a statement, sending a message about yourself. It's the same for both men and women. For men, think of the different messages you'd send if you got a buzz cut to match a goatee, like Mark McGwire, or grew your hair out long, like Fabio, or shaved your head. What does a woman communicate when she adopts Rachel's hairdo from *Friends* or chooses instead Gwyneth Paltrow's sleek style? Why was your hair short last year and long this year (or long last year and short this year)? Aren't you saying something with the scissors? In this way, you make your hair style into a sign that sends a message about your identity. You are surrounded by such signs. Just look at your classmates.

The world of signs could be called a kind of text, the text of

America's popular culture. We want you to think of *Signs of Life in the U.S.A.* as a window onto that text. What you read in the essays and introductions included in this book should lead you to study and analyze the world around you for yourself. Let the readings guide you to your own interpretations, your own readings, of the text of America.

Windows 2000

We have chosen ten "windows" in this edition of *Signs of Life in the U.S.A.*, each of which looks out onto a separate, but often interrelated, segment of the American scene. In some cases, we have put some of the scenery directly into this book, as when we include actual ads in our chapter on advertising. In other cases, where it is impossible to put something directly into a textbook, like a TV show or a movie, we have included essays that help you think about specific programs and films and assignments that invite you to go out and interpret a TV show or movie of your own choosing.

Each chapter contains an introduction designed to alert you to the kinds of signs you will find there, as well as advice on how to go about interpreting them. The readings that follow offer positions and interpretations of their own, as well as texts and contexts for your further analysis. Shelby Steele's provocative essay on Malcolm X, for example, argues that Malcolm X was an essentially conservative figure and that Spike Lee's film about him presents us with a myth rather than a man. To make your own judgment on the matter, you might want to read a biography of Malcolm X and compare it with the movie. Then you could write an essay stating your position. Will you agree or disagree with Steele? Only by looking closely into the matter will you be able to decide.

We have divided *Signs of Life in the U.S.A.* into two sections that reflect the twofold structure of American popular culture. The first section, Cultural Productions, explores America's dedication to the production of consumer goods and services, from clothes to movies and television shows. The second section, Cultural Constructions, surveys the many ways in which culture, through the use of ideology, shapes our sense of reality and of ourselves, from the way culture constructs our racial and gender identities to the way it governs our experience of our spatial environment. These two sections, which are complementary to each other, thus introduce both the entertainment and the ideological sides of popular culture—and show how the two sides are mutually interdependent. Indeed, one of the major lessons you can learn from this book is how to find the ideological underpinnings of some of the most apparently innocent entertainments and consumer goods.

The first section of *Signs of Life in the U.S.A.* accordingly begins with a chapter on "Consuming Passions: The Culture of American Consumption" because America is a consumer culture, and so the environment within which the galaxy of popular signs functions is, more often than not, a consumerist one. This is true not only for obvious consumer products like blue jeans and sport utility vehicles but for such traditionally nonconsumer items as political candidates and college campuses as well, both of which are often marketed these days like any other consumer product. It is difficult to find anything in contemporary America that is not affected in one way or another by our consumerist ethos or by consumerism's leading promoter, the advertiser. Thus, the second chapter, "Brought to You B(u)y: The Signs of Advertising," explores the world of advertising, for advertising provides the grease, so to speak, that lubricates the engine of America's consumer culture. Because television (including MTV) and film are the sources of many of our most significant cultural products, we include a chapter on each in this section. And we include a chapter on popular literature that analyzes the cultural codes to be found in literary entertainment.

The book's second section begins with a chapter on the ways culture constructs our gender identities and then moves to a chapter on the ways it shapes our racial and ethnic identities. Subsequent chapters explore the cultural construction of "otherness"—from the outlaw to people with AIDS—and of America's favorite cultural icons—figures like Michael Jordan—who also play a major role in America's consumer world. The concluding chapter explores the cultural construction of the built environment, from Disney World to the workplace, and from the ghetto to the open road.

Throughout, the book invites you to go out and select your own "texts" for analysis (an advertisement, a film, a fashion fad, a political opinion, a building, and so on). Here's where your own experience is particularly valuable because it has made you familiar with many different kinds of popular signs and their backgrounds, with the particular popular cultural *system* or environment to which they belong.

The ten "windows" you will find in *Signs of Life in the U.S.A.* are all intended to reveal the common intersections of entertainment and ideology that can be found in contemporary American life. Often what seems to be simply entertainment, like a TV show, is actually quite political, while what seems purely political, like a gender conflict, can be cast as entertainment as well—as in movies like *Thelma and Louise*. The point is to see that little in American life is "merely" entertainment; indeed, just about everything we do has a meaning, often a profound one.

The Semiotic Method

To find this meaning—to interpret and write effectively about the signs of popular culture—you need a method, and it is part of the purpose of this book to introduce such a method to you. Without a methodology for interpreting signs, writing about them could become little more than descriptive reviews or opinion pieces. There is nothing wrong with writing descriptions and opinions, but one of your tasks in your writing class is to learn how to write academic essays—that is, analytical essays that present theses or arguments that are well supported by evidence. The method we draw on in this book—a method that is known as *semiotics*—is especially well suited for analyzing popular culture. Whether or not you're familiar with this word, you are already practicing sophisticated semiotic analyses every day of your life. Reading this page is an act of semiotic decoding (words and even letters are signs that must be interpreted), but so is figuring out just what your classmate *means* by wearing a particular shirt or dress. For a semiotician (one who practices semiotic analysis), a shirt, a haircut, a television image—anything at all—can be taken as a sign, as a message to be decoded and analyzed to discover its meaning. Every cultural activity for the semiotician leaves a trace of meaning, a kind of blip on the semiotic Richter scale, that remains for us to read, just as a geologist "reads" the earth for signs of earthquakes, volcanos, and other geological phenomena.

Many who hear the word *semiotics* for the first time assume that it is the name of a new, and forbidding, subject. But in truth, the study of signs is neither very new nor forbidding. Its modern form took shape in the late nineteenth century and early twentieth century through the writings and lectures of two men. Charles Sanders Peirce (1839–1914) was an American philosopher and physicist who first coined the word *semiotics,* while Ferdinand de Saussure (1857–1913) was a Swiss linguist whose lectures became the foundation for what he called *semiology.* Without knowing of each other's work, Peirce and Saussure established the fundamental principles that modern semioticians or semiologists— the terms are essentially interchangeable—have developed into the contemporary study of semiotics.

The application of semiotics to the interpretation of popular culture was pioneered in the 1950s by the French semiologist Roland Barthes (1915–1980) in a book entitled *Mythologies*. The basic principles of semiotics had already been explored by linguists and anthropologists, but Barthes took the matter to the heart of his own contemporary France, analyzing the cultural significance of everything from professional wrestling to striptease, from toys to plastics.

It was Barthes, too, who established the political dimensions of semiotic analysis. Often, the subject of a semiotic analysis—a movie, say, or a TV program—doesn't look political at all; it simply looks like entertainment. In our society (especially in the aftermath of the Watergate and Monicagate scandals), *politics* has become something of a dirty word, and to *politicize* something seems somehow to contaminate it. So you shouldn't feel alarmed if at first it feels a little odd to search for a political meaning in an apparently neutral topic. You may even think that to do so is to "read too much" into that topic. But Barthes's point—and the point of semiotics in general—is that all social behavior is political in the sense that it reflects some personal or group interest. Such interests are encoded in what are called *ideologies,* or worldviews that express the values and opinions of those who hold them. Politics, then, is just another name for the clash of ideologies that takes place in any complex society where the interests of all those who belong to it constantly compete with one another.

Sometimes the political values of a popular entertainment or entertainer are quite clear—no one is in any doubt about Charlton Heston's politics—but sometimes they are concealed behind images that don't look political at all. Consider, for example, the depiction of the "typical" American family in the classic TV sitcoms of the fifties and sixties, particularly all those images of happy, docile housewives. To most contemporary viewers, those images looked "normal" or natural at the time that they were first broadcast—the way families and women were supposed to be. The shows didn't seem at all ideological. To the contrary, they seemed a retreat from political rancor to domestic harmony. But to a feminist semiotician, the old sitcoms were in fact highly political because the happy housewives they presented were really images designed to *convince* women that their place is in the home, not in the workplace competing with men. Such images—or signs—did not reflect reality; they reflected, rather, the interests of a patriarchal, male-centered society. If you think not, then ask yourself why there were shows called *Father Knows Best, Bachelor Father,* and *My Three Sons,* but no *My Three Daughters*? And why did few of the women in the shows have jobs or ever seem to leave the house? Of course, there was always *I Love Lucy,* but wasn't Lucy the screwball character that her husband Ricky had to rescue from one crisis after another?

Such are the kinds of questions that semiotics invites us to ask. They may be put more generally. When analyzing any popular cultural phenomenon, always ask yourself questions like these: "Why does this thing look the way it does? Why are they saying this? Why am I doing this? What are they really saying? What am I really doing?" In short, take nothing for granted when analyzing any image or activity.

Take, for instance, the reason you may have joined a health club (or decided not to). Did you happen to respond to a photo ad that showed you a gorgeous girl or guy (with a nice-looking guy or girl in the background)? On the surface of the ad, you simply see an image showing— or *denoting*—a patron of the club. You may think: "I want to look like that." But there's probably another dimension to the ad's appeal. The ad may *show* you someone with a nice body, but what it is suggesting—or *connoting*—is that this club is a good place to pick up a hot date. That's why that other figure appears in the background. That's supposed to be *you.* The one in the foreground is the sort of person you're being promised you'll find at the club. The ad doesn't say this, of course, but that's what it wants you to think because that's a more effective way of getting you to join. Suggestion, or connotation, is a much more powerful stimulant than denotation, but it is often deliberately masked in the signs you are presented with every day. Semiotics, one might say, reveals all the denotative smoke screens around you.

Health club membership drives, you may think, aren't especially political (though actually they are when you think of the kinds of bodies that they are telling you are desirable to have), but the powerful effect of a concealed suggestion is used all the time in actual political campaigns. The now infamous Willie Horton episode during the 1988 presidential campaign provides a classic instance. What happened was that some Republican supporters of George Bush's candidacy ran a series of TV ads featuring the photographic image of one Willie Horton, a convicted rapist from Massachusetts who murdered someone while on parole. On the surface, the ads simply showed, or denoted, this fact. But they connoted racial hatred and fear (Willie Horton is black) and were very effective in prompting white voters to mistrust Massachusetts governor Michael Dukakis and to vote instead for George Bush.

Signs, in short, often conceal some interest or other, whether political, or commercial, or whatever. And the proliferation of signs and images in an era of electronic technology has simply made it all the more important that we learn to decode the interests behind them.

Semiotics, accordingly, is not just about signs and symbols: it is equally about ideology and power. This makes semiotics sound rather serious, and often the seriousness of a semiotic analysis is quite real. But reading the text of modern life can also be fun, for it is a text that is at once popular and accessible, a "book" that is intimately in touch with the pulse of American life. As such, it is constantly changing. The same sign can change meaning if something else comes along to change the environment in which it originally appeared. Take all those extraterrestrials.

Interpreting Popular Signs

Let's say that you want to analyze America's popular fascination with aliens. How would you go about it? What you first need to do is to set aside any personal opinions you have concerning the existence or nonexistence of extraterrestrials. That isn't your subject: your subject is the place of extraterrestrials in the popular imagination. To put this another way, your task is to analyze the current social significance of the widespread popularity of books, movies, and TV shows that feature "close encounters of the third kind."

The first step in drafting your analysis is to sketch the overall context within which "aliens" appear in American popular culture—that is, the interrelated network of books (fiction and nonfiction), magazine articles, movies, TV shows, and even Internet websites that feature extraterrestrial topics. This is one of the key elements of a semiotic interpretation: the establishing of a set of associated phenomena. For from a semiotic perspective, the meaning of a sign largely lies in its relations to other signs, both in its *similarities* to them and in its *differences*. In other words, when looking at a popular cultural sign, you will want to ask "What is this thing like?" and "How is it different from some of the things that it resembles?" By asking such questions, you are identifying the *system* in which a sign works, and it is in the context of such a system that you may pursue your interpretation.

Let's return to extraterrestrials to see what this means in practice. Taken alone, any given TV show or movie featuring aliens doesn't mean very much. Consider *E.T.* In one sense, it was just an entertaining flick that made a few people a lot of money. But seen in relation to other alien-featured entertainments, *E.T.* becomes a cultural sign. To see how, let's build up the system within which it functions. Our first question in building this system is "What does *E.T.* resemble?" And the first answer that occurs to us, given that the starring role was played by an alien being, is that the film resembles many other products of science fiction, for science fiction has been the traditional genre in which aliens appear. So let's consider for a moment the history of science fiction to see what clues it might give us to the current ways in which aliens are featured in popular entertainment.

The history of science fiction extends back into the nineteenth century with authors such as Jules Verne helping to invent the genre, but in many ways H. G. Wells's science fiction classic *The War of the Worlds* is a more useful place to begin. Not only did it establish a certain paradigm for the extraterrestrial imagination, but it earned a special place in American media history thanks to Orson Welles's notorious radio broadcast of the novel in the 1930s, a broadcast that panicked thousands of listeners who didn't realize it was just a dramatization and not a news bulletin.

The War of the Worlds is the story of an alien invasion from Mars, an invasion that is nearly successful due to Martian technical superiority but that ultimately fails because the Martians are annihilated by an earthly illness against which they have no immunity. (*Mars Attacks!* made a joke of this by having the Martians succumb to the broadcasting of some really bad pop music.) The pattern that this story establishes—the hostile invasion of Earth by technologically superior aliens—has governed much of the science fiction of the twentieth century when it comes to imagining contacts between Earth and other planets.

But now consider what this pattern resembles—that is, with what it in turn might be associated. Are there any other ways in which human beings have imagined visitations to Earth by extraterrestrial beings who are superior to us but are not gods? Think about it a moment.

Here's what we've come up with. Long before the invention of science fiction, extraterrestrial visitations have been described in the Western tradition in basically two ways: either as visits by angels or as invasions by devils. Like space aliens, angels and devils have powers beyond merely mortal power (for one thing, they can hover in the atmosphere, just like flying saucers), but they are not gods. Neither are they human. They are, rather, different kinds of beings who, also like space aliens, have their origins in a realm among the stars (devils, after all, are fallen angels and so originally come from the heavens as well).

In one of the classics of English literature, John Milton's *Paradise Lost*, both kinds of visitation are imagined: the benign arrival of winged angels and the malignant invasion of Satan, shown literally flying to Earth to wreak as much havoc as he can on the newborn human race. As we consider these precedents to science fiction stories, it is useful to know that Arthur C. Clark, one of science fiction's preeminent writers, made the link between angels, devils, and space invaders explicit in a novel called *Childhood's End*. In that novel, extraterrestrial invaders who *look* just like our traditional image of the devil take over Earth, but, ironically, their visitation is actually angelic in purpose because it is intended to help human beings evolve to a higher state of existence. (We can also note how Ray Walston, an actor who gained fame by playing the Visitor from Hell in *Damn Yankees,* was later recast as a Martian in the 1960s TV series *My Favorite Martian*.)

By comparing such stories—Milton's, Clark's, Wells's—we can lay down a foundation for our systematic interpretation: that contacts between humans and extraterrestrial beings historically have been imagined either as demonic invasions or as angelic visitations. At this point, we can do a little research to see whether anyone else has made a similar connection, and, sure enough, logging on to the UFO Popular Culture website **(http://www.ufomind.com/misc/1997/jul/d10-002.shtml)** reveals that the connection has been made, and more than once. From a religious minister who declares that aliens are "fallen angels from another earthly dimension rather than another planet" to the author of a book entitled *Angels and Aliens*, interpreters of the extraterrestrials are drawing parallels between angels, demons, and aliens.

The next question to ask is "In what form do aliens appear in a given story: as angels or demons?" When we look at *The War of the Worlds*, the alien contact clearly takes a demonic form. Now, in pursuing a semiotic interpretation, we might ask "*Why* demons and not angels?" And to answer this question, we can look around at what else may have been going on when the novel was written as well as when it was later broadcast on American radio. One thing we can find is that, when *The War of the Worlds* was published in 1898, England was getting more and more worried about Germany (World War I broke out only sixteen years later), and when it was broadcast in America in the 1930s, World War II was only a few years away. At a time of concern about the alien "other" (in the latter case, the Germans), we hypothesize, the popular imaginations of English and American audiences were especially likely to envision alien contacts as dangerous and destructive. To put this another way, we can argue that science fiction can function as a substitute, or metaphor, for real-world worries and anxieties. As evidence for our hypothesis, we can point to the science fiction of the 1950s, a period when cold war fears were at their height. The sci-fi of this period tended to feature demonic-invasion stories like *Invasion of the Body Snatchers*, a film that has been often interpreted as a metaphor for cold war fears of Soviet infiltration.

Whenever alien invasions assume a demonic form, we can also note how the authorities—the police, the military, and the government—are depicted as protectors, as the only barrier between us and the alien invaders. And once again we can find a real-world parallel for this popular sign, for in the 1950s the American government, military, and police enjoyed especially high levels of social esteem.

Thus, we can find two relevant patterns in the past as we attempt to unravel the meaning of today's depictions of alien invasions. The first is that in times of international anxiety, the sci-fi imagination tends to cast the alien as a demon; and the second is that when aliens are demonized, the local authorities are heroicized. So when a story comes along that contradicts this dual pattern, that itself is significant, drawing our attention to an entirely different set of interpretive possibilities. Which brings us back to *E.T.*

The most popular movie of its time (it took *Jurassic Park* and *Titanic* to break its box office records), *E.T.*, like so many other science fiction plots, featured an alien who comes to Earth. But now let's ask another question: "How was *E.T.* different from other science fiction stories featuring alien encounters?" The answer is pretty clear, for unlike stories like *The War of the Worlds* or even the more benign *Childhood's End*, the extraterrestrial in *E.T.* is not an invader. He is not threatening. In fact, he is rather cute and cuddly, angelic even, albeit in an unconventional way. At the same time, in *this* story it is the earthly authorities—the police and the military—who are dangerous and threatening, even evil. Rather than protecting us, the authorities are out to hide the truth from us by capturing E.T. and removing him from view.

The background story for *E.T.* is the real-world controversy over what did, or did not, happen near Roswell, New Mexico, on July 4, 1947. For those who believe that something did happen, the story runs that a group of extraterrestrials (who look a lot like E.T.) crash-landed on Earth and were captured by U.S. Air Force personnel (or at least their bodies were collected by them). The story holds that the United States still has these bodies but that a Pentagon conspiracy is covering up the whole incident. (Recall how in the introductory sequence to *The X-Files* a flying saucer appears and then the words "government denies knowledge.")

It is not germane to a semiotic analysis to debate what did or did not happen at Roswell. What matters is the way the story *reverses* the pattern established by *The War of the Worlds*, a reversal that officially entered popular culture in a big way with Spielberg's *E.T.* This is our crucial *difference* that can lead us to an interpretation of the current place of extraterrestrials in the popular imagination.

The difference is that these days, when close encounters of the third kind are imagined, the aliens are often viewed as innocent, or angelic, while it is the official authorities who are demonic (even when the aliens are also demonic, as in *Mars Attacks!*, the authorities appear as either villainous hypocrites or complete idiots). Can we associate *this* phenomenon—that is, the demonization of authority and the benign depiction of aliens—with anything else going on in American culture? The answer is yes—because if you think about it, there are a lot of other indications in contemporary American culture that governmental authority (or any kind of authority, for that matter) is no longer as widely trusted or respected as it once was and that anyone who feels oppressed by that authority is an innocent victim of it in one way or another. From the populist anti-Washington appeal of Jesse Ventura to far-right beliefs that the U.S. government is part of a conspiratorial "new world order," American society is sending plenty of signals about its mistrust of official authority. The stubborn belief that the government is covering up a conspiracy behind the John F. Kennedy assassination (consider Oliver Stone's *JFK*, or *The X-Files* episode that suggests, albeit ambiguously, that the character known as the Cigarette Smoking Man had a hand in Kennedy's death) is another such sign, as is the continuing controversy over military exposure to chemical agents in the Gulf War. This mistrust is also reflected in declining voter participation rates (you know the attitude: "Since they're all crooks, why vote?") and in the rise of such antigovernment political parties as the Libertarians. And nowhere is this disaffection from authority more widespread than among the young, who tend to see themselves as authority's victims. It is no accident, then, that *E.T.* features a group of children who rescue the childlike alien from brutal grownups.

When you consider this cultural tendency to mistrust authority in relation to our current extraterrestrial imagination, an interpretation begins to emerge. In short, the shift from a sci-fi imagination in which aliens are seen as dangerous invaders and governments as protectors to one in which governments are conspiratorial tyrannies and aliens innocent victims reflects a cultural shift in which all forms of authority are coming into question, especially among the youthful audiences of such entertainments. Television shows like *The X-Files*, which want to attract young viewers (with its sly reference to Generation X, it isn't called *The X-Files* for nothing), accordingly exploit this distrust of official authority and so maintain their popularity—and profitability.

There is yet another angle to consider as we examine the system in which the extraterrestrial imagination functions today. Briefly put, we live in an era in which science enjoys a great deal of social prestige. At the same time, large numbers of people who no longer subscribe to traditional (and authoritative) religious faiths find themselves searching for spiritual alternatives. The extraterrestrial provides the perfect resolution for such a cultural contradiction. Belonging at once to the realm of science, especially astronomy, and belief (indeed, we talk of "believing" or "not believing" in the existence of extraterrestrials), the alien appeals to two cultural trends simultaneously, blending the prestige of scientific inquiry with the spiritual appeal of the supernatural in a tidily popular package. (We find support for this interpretation on the Web in the complaint by the religious pastor of Roswell's Calvary Chapel that "People are looking to UFOs as a replacement for God.")

Our analysis could continue (and indeed, conducting a semiotic analysis is a bit like peeling an onion: there is always another layer one might consider), but we'll stop here. The point simply is that entertainments featuring extraterrestrials aren't *just* entertainments. They are signs, indicators of the larger social and cultural forces and trends behind them. The task of a semiotic analysis is to uncover those forces to find the meaning behind the everyday things we do and say.

The Classroom Connection

The interpretive analysis we have sketched out is, in essence, no different from the more conventional interpretive analyses you will be asked to perform in your college writing career. It is in the nature of all interpretations to make connections and mark differences to go beyond the surface of a text or issue toward a meaning. The skills you already have as an interpreter of the popular signs around you—of images, objects, and forms of behavior—are the same skills that you develop as a writer of critical essays that present a point of view and an argument to defend it.

Because most of us tend to identify closely with our favorite popular cultural phenomena and have strong opinions about them, it can be more difficult to adopt the same sort of analytic perspective toward popular culture than we do toward, say, texts assigned in a literature class. Still, that is what you should do in a semiotic interpretation: you need to set your opinions aside to pursue an interpretive argument with evidence to support it. Note how in our interpretation of *E.T.* we didn't say whether we like the movie: our concern was what it might mean within a larger cultural context. It is not difficult to express an opinion, but that isn't the goal of analytic writing. Analytic writing requires the martialing of supporting evidence, just like a lawyer needs evidence to argue a case. So by learning to write analyses of our culture, by searching for supporting evidence to underpin your intepretive take on modern life, you are also learning to write critical arguments.

"But how," you (and perhaps your teacher) may ask, "can I know that a semiotic interpretation is right?" Good question: it is commonly asked by those who fear that a semiotic analysis might "read too much into" a subject. But then, it can be asked of the writer of any interpretive essay, and the answer in each case is the same. No one can ever absolutely *prove* the truth of any argument in the social sciences; what you do is *persuade* your audience through the use of pertinent evidence. In writing analyses about popular culture, that evidence comes from your knowledge of the system to which the object you are interpreting belongs. The more you know about the system, the more convincing your interpretations will be. And that is true whether you are writing about *The X-Files* or about more traditional academic subjects.

But often our interpretations of popular culture involve issues that are larger than those involved in music or entertainment. How, for instance, are we to analyze fully the widespread belief—as reflected in the classic sitcoms mentioned earlier—that it is more natural for women to stay at home and take care of the kids than it is for men to do so? Why, in other words, is the concept of "housewife" so easy to accept, while the idea of a "househusband" may seem odd? How, in short, can we interpret some of our most basic values semiotically? To see how, we need to look at those value systems that semioticians call *cultural mythologies*.

Of Myths and Men

As we have seen, in a semiotic analysis we do not search for the meanings of things in the things themselves. Rather, we find meaning in the way we can relate things together, either through association or differentiation. We've done this with the place of aliens in popular culture, but what about doing it with beliefs? This book asks you to explore the implications of social issues like gender norms that involve a great many personal beliefs and values that we do not always recognize *as* beliefs and values. Rather, we think of them as truths (one might think, "Of course it's odd for a man to stay home and take care of the house!"). But from a semiotic perspective, our values too belong to systems from which they take their meaning. Semioticians call these systems of belief *cultural mythologies*.

A cultural mythology, or *myth* for short, is not some fanciful story from the past. Indeed, if you find this word confusing because of its traditional association with such stories, you may prefer to use the phrase *value system*. Consider the value system that governs our traditional thinking about gender roles. Have you ever noticed how our society presumes that it is primarily the role of women—adult daughters—to take care of aging and infirm parents? If you want to look at the matter from a physiological perspective, it might seem that men would be better suited to the task: in a state of nature, men are physically stronger and so would seem to be the natural protectors of the aged. And yet, though our cultural mythology holds that men should protect the nuclear family, it tends to assign to women the care of extended families. It is culture that decides here, not nature.

But while cultural myths guide our behavior, they are subject to change. You yourself may have already experienced a transitional phase in the myths surrounding courtship behavior. In the past, the gender myths that formed the rules of the American dating game held that it is the role of the male to initiate proceedings (*he* calls) and for the female to react (*she* waits by the phone). Similarly, the rules once held that it is invariably the responsibility of the male to plan the evening and pay the tab. These rules are changing, aren't they? Can you describe the rules that now govern courtship behavior?

A cultural mythology, or value system, then, is a kind of lens that governs the way we view our world. Think of it this way: say that you were born with rose-tinted eyeglasses permanently attached over your eyes but you didn't know they were there. Because the world would look rose-colored to you, you would presume that it *is* rose-colored. You wouldn't wonder whether the world might look otherwise through different lenses. But in the world there are other kinds of eyeglasses with different lenses, and reality does look different to those who wear them. Those lenses are cultural mythologies, and no culture can claim to have the one set of glasses that sees things as they really are.

The profound effect our cultural mythologies have on the way we view reality, on our most basic values, is especially apparent today when the myths of European culture are being challenged by the worldviews of the many other cultures that have taken root in American soil. Where, for example, European American culture upholds a profoundly individualistic social mythology, valuing individual rights before those of the group, traditional Chinese culture believes in the primacy of the family and the community over the individual. Maxine Hong Kingston's short story "No Name Woman" poignantly demonstrates how such opposing ideologies can collide with painful results in its tale of a Chinese woman who is more or less sacrificed to preserve the interests of her village. The story, from *The Woman Warrior*, tells of a young woman who gives birth to a baby too many months after her husband's departure to America for it to be her husband's child. Her husband and most of the village's other young men had left for America to earn the money that keeps the impoverished villagers from starving. They may be away for years and so need to be assured that their wives will remain faithful to them in their absence lest they refuse to go at all. The unfortunate heroine of the tale—who, to sharpen the agony, had probably been more the victim of rape than the instigator of adultery—is horribly punished by the entire village as an example to any other wives who might disturb the system and ends in a tragic suicide.

That Kingston wrote "No Name Woman" as a self-consciously "hyphenated" Asian-American, as one whose identity fuses both Chinese and Euro-American values, reveals the fault lines between conflicting mythologies. On the one hand, as an Asian, Kingston understands the communal values behind the horrific sacrifice of her aunt, and her story makes sure that her Euro-American readers understand this too. But on the other hand, as an American and as a feminist, she is outraged by the violation of an individual woman's rights on behalf of the group (or mob, which is what the village becomes in the story). Kingston's own sense of personal conflict in this clash of mythologies—Asian, American, and feminist—offers a striking example of the inevitable conflicts that America itself will face as it changes from a monocultural to a multicultural society.

To put this another way, from the semiotic perspective, *how* you interpret something is very much a product of *who* you are; for culture is just another name for the frames that shape our values and perceptions. Traditionally, American education has presumed a monocultural perspective, a "melting pot" view that no matter what one's cultural background, truth is culture-blind. Langston Hughes took on this assumption many years ago in his classic poem "Theme for English B," where he writes, "I guess I'm what/I feel and see and hear," and wonders whether "my page will be colored" when he writes. "Being me, it will not be white," the poet suggests, but while he struggles to find what he holds in common with his white instructor, he can't suppress the differences. In essence, that is the challenge of multicultural education itself: to identify the different cultural codes that inform the mythic frameworks of the many cultures that share America while searching for what holds the whole thing together.

That meaning is not culture-blind, that it is conditioned by systems of ideology and belief that are codified differently by different cultures, is a foundational semiotic judgment. Human beings, in other words, construct their own social realities, and so who gets to do the constructing becomes very important. Every contest over a cultural code is, accordingly, a contest for power, but the contest is usually masked because the winner generally defines its mythology as the "truth," as what is most "natural" or "reasonable." Losers in the contest become objects of scorn and are quickly marginalized, declared "unnatural," or "deviant," or even "insane." The stakes are high as myth battles myth, with "truth" itself as the highest prize.

This does not mean that you must abandon your own beliefs when conducting a semiotic analysis, only that you cannot take them for granted and must be prepared to argue for them. We want to assure you that semiotics will not tell you what to think and believe. It *does* assume that what you believe reflects some cultural system or other and that no cultural system can claim absolute validity or superiority. The readings and chapter introductions in this book contain their own values and ideologies, and if you wish to challenge those values you can begin by exposing the myths that they may take for granted.

To put this another way, everything in this book reflects a political point of view, and if you hold a different one it is not enough to simply presuppose the innate superiority of your own point of view—to claim that one writer is being "political" while you yourself are simply telling the truth. This may sound heretical precisely because human beings operate within value systems whose political invisibility is guaranteed by the system. No mythology, that is to say, begins by saying, "This is just a political construct or interpretation." Every myth begins, "This is the truth." It is very difficult to imagine, from within the myth, any alternatives. Indeed, as you read this book, you may find it upsetting to see that some traditional beliefs—such as the "proper" roles of men and women in society—are socially constructed and not absolute. But the outlines of the myth—the bounding (and binding) frame—best appear when challenged by another myth, and this challenge is probably nowhere more insistent than in America, where so many of us are really "hyphenated" Americans, citizens combining in our own persons two (or more) cultural traditions.

Getting Started

Mythology, like culture, is not static, however, and so the semiotician must always keep his or her eye on the clock, so to speak. History, time itself, is a constant factor in a constantly changing world. Since the first and second editions of this book, American popular culture has moved on. In this edition, we have tried to reflect those changes, but inevitably, further changes will occur in the time it takes for this book to appear on your class syllabus. That such changes occur is part of the excitement of the semiotic enterprise: there is always something new to consider and interpret. What does not change is the nature of semiotic interpretation: whatever you choose to analyze in the realm of American popular culture, the semiotic approach will help you understand it.

It's your turn now. Start asking questions, pushing, probing. That's what critical writing is all about, but this time *you're* part of the question. Arriving at answers, conclusions, is the fun part here, but answers aren't the basis of analytic thinking: questions are. You always begin with a question, a query, a hypothesis, something to explore. If you already knew the answer, there would be no point in conducting the analysis. We leave you to it to explore the almost infinite variety of questions that the readings in this book raise. Many come equipped with their own answers, but you may (indeed will and should) find such "answers" raise further questions. To help you ask those questions, keep in mind the two elemental principles of semiotics that we have explored so far:

1. The meaning of a sign can be found not in itself but in its *relationships* (both differences and similarities) with other signs

within a *system*. To interpret an individual sign, then, you must determine the general system in which it belongs.

2. What we call social *reality* is a human construct, the product of a cultural *mythology* or *value system* that intervenes between our minds and the world we experience. Such cultural myths reflect the values and ideological interests of its builders, not the laws of nature or logic.

Perhaps our first principle could be more succinctly phrased as "Everything is connected," and our second simply as, "Question authority." Think of them that way if it helps. Or just ask yourself whenever you are interpreting something, "What's going on here?" In short, question *everything*. And one more reminder: Signs are like weather vanes; they point in response to invisible historical winds. We invite you now to start looking at the weather.

WRITING ABOUT POPULAR CULTURE

Throughout this book, you will find readings on popular culture that you can use as models for your own writing or as subjects to which you may respond, assignments for writing critical essays on popular culture, and semiotic tips to help you analyze a wide variety of cultural phenomena. As you approach these readings and assignments, you may find it helpful to review the following suggestions for writing critical essays—whether on popular culture or on any subject—as well as some examples of student essays written in response to assignments based on *Signs of Life in the U.S.A.* Mastering the skills summarized and exemplified here should prepare you for writing the kinds of papers you will be assigned through the rest of your college career.

As you prepare to write a critical essay on popular culture, remember that you are already an expert in your subject. Being an expert doesn't necessarily mean spending years of studying in a library; simply by actively participating in everyday life, you have accumulated a vast store of knowledge about what makes our culture tick. Just think about all you know about movies, or the thousands on thousands of ads you've seen, or even the many unwritten "rules" governing courtship behavior among your circle of friends. All of these help form the fabric of contemporary American culture—and, if you've ever had to explain to a younger sibling why her latest outfit was inappropriate for work or why his comment to a blind date struck the wrong chord, you've already played the role of expert.

Because popular culture is part of everyday life, however, you may take for granted this knowledge: it might not seem that it can "count" as material for a college-level assignment, and you might not think to include it in an essay. Thus, it can be useful to spend some time, before you start writing, to generate your ideas freely and openly: your goal at this point is to develop as many ideas as possible, even ones that you might not actually use in your essay. Writing instructors call this process *prewriting,* and it's a step you should take when writing on any subject in any class, not just in your writing class. This textbook includes many suggestions for how you can develop your ideas; even if your instructor doesn't require you to use all of them, you can try them on your own.

Developing Ideas about Popular Culture

The first step in developing your ideas for an essay about any topic is to make sure you understand accurately the reading selections that your instructor has assigned. You want to engage in *active* reading—that is, you want not simply to get the "drift" of a passage but to understand the nuances of how the author constructs his or her argument. With any selection, it can be helpful to read at least twice: first, to gain a general sense of the author's ideas and, second, to study more specifically how those ideas are put together to form an argument. Ask yourself questions, such as the following, that enable you to evaluate the selection:

- What is the author's primary argument? Can you identify a thesis statement, or is the thesis implied?
- What words or key terms are fundamental to that argument? If the fundamental vocabulary of the selection is unfamiliar to you, be sure to check a dictionary or encyclopedia for their meaning.
- What evidence does the author provide to support the argument?
- What underlying assumptions shape the author's position? Does the author consider alternative points of view (counterarguments)?
- What style and tone does the author adopt?
- What is the genre of the piece? You need to take into account what kind of writing you are responding to, for different kinds have different purposes and goals. A personal narrative, for instance, expresses the writer's experiences and beliefs, but you shouldn't expect it to present a fully demonstrated argument.
- Who is the intended readership of this selection, and does it affect the author's reasoning or evidence?

Signs of Life in the U.S.A. frequently asks you to respond to a reading selection in your journal, sometimes directly and sometimes indirectly, as in suggestions that you write a letter to the author of a selection. In doing so, you're taking an important first step in articulating your response to the issues and to the author's presentation of them. In asking you to keep a journal or a reading log, your instructor will probably be less concerned with your writing style than with your comprehension of assigned readings and your thoughtful responses to them. Let's say you're asked to write your response to a reading selection; we'll take for an example Emily Prager's "Our Barbies, Ourselves" in Chapter 9. You should first think through exactly what Prager is saying — what her point is — using the questions listed. Then consider how you feel about it. If you agree with Prager's belief that the Barbie doll perpetuates outmoded ideas about women, why do you feel that way? Can you think of other objects (or even people) who seem to exemplify those same ideas? What alternative ways of designing a doll can you imagine? Note that the purpose of imagining your own doll is not so you'll actually produce one; it's so you think through alternatives and explore the implications of Prager's and your own thoughts. Or say you're irritated by Prager's argument: Again, why do you feel that way? What would you say to her in response? What, perhaps in your own experience as a child, might show that she's wrong? Your aim in jotting all this down is not to produce a draft of an essay. It's to play with your own ideas, see where they lead, and even just help you decide what your ideas are in the first place.

Often we or your instructor may ask you to brainstorm ideas or to freewrite in response to an issue. These are both strategies you can use in your journal or on your own as you start working on an essay. Brainstorming is simply amassing as many relevant (and even some irrelevant) ideas as possible. Let's say your instructor asks you to brainstorm a list of popular toys used by girls and boys in preparation for an essay about the gendered designs of children's toys. Try to list your thoughts freely, jotting down whatever comes to mind. Don't censor yourself at this point. That is, don't worry if something is really a toy or a game, or if it is used by both boys and girls, or if it really is an adult toy. Later on you can throw out ideas that don't fit. What you'll be left with is a rich list of examples that you can then study and analyze. Freewriting works much the same way and is particularly useful when you're not sure of how you feel about an issue. Sit down and just start writing or typing, and don't stop until you've written for at least ten or fifteen minutes. Let your ideas wander around your subject, working associatively, following their own path. As with brainstorming, you may produce some irrelevant ideas, but you may also come to a closer understanding of how you really feel about an issue.

Sometimes your instructor may invite you to create your own topic. Where should you start? Let's say you decide to analyze an aspect of the film industry but can't decide on a focus. Here, the Internet might help. You could explore a search engine such as Yahoo!, specifically its Movies and Films index. There you'll find dozens of subcategories, such as History, Theory and Criticism, Cultures and Groups, and Trivia. Each of these subcategories has many sites to explore: History, for instance, includes the Archives of the Lindy Hop as well as The Bill Douglas Centre for the History of Cinema and Popular Culture, a wonderful compendium of 25,000 books, posters, and other movie-related memorabilia. With so many sites to choose from, you're bound to find something that interests you. The Net, in effect, allows you to engage in electronic brainstorming and so arrive at your topic.

One cautionary note: in using the Internet to brainstorm, be sure to evaluate the appropriateness of your sources. Many sites are commercial and therefore are intended more to sell a product or image than to provide reliable information. In addition, since anyone with the technological knowhow can set up a website, some sites (especially personal home pages) amount to little more than personal expression and need to be evaluated for their reliability, accuracy, and authenticity. Scrutinize the sites you use carefully: Is the author an authority in the field? Does the site identify the author, at least by name and e-mail address (be wary of fully anonymous sites)? Does the site contain interesting and relevant links? If you find an advocacy site, one that openly advances a special interest, does the site's bias interfere with the accuracy of its information? Asking such questions can help ensure that your electronic brainstorming is fruitful and productive. If you are not sure of the validity of a website, you might want to check with your instructor.

Not all prewriting activities need be solitary, of course. In fact, *Signs of Life* includes lots of suggestions that ask you to work with other students, either in your class or from across campus. We do that because much academic work really is collaborative and collegial. When a scientist is conducting research, for instance, he or she often works with a team, may present preliminary findings to colloquia or conferences, and may call or e-mail a colleague at another school to try out some ideas. There's no reason you can't benefit from the social nature of academic thinking as well. But be aware that such in-class group work is by no means "busy work." The goal, rather, is to help you to develop and shape your understanding of the issues and your attitudes toward them. If you're asked to study a men's fashion magazine with three classmates, for instance, you're starting to test Diane Barthel's thesis in "A Gentleman and a Consumer" (Chapter 2), seeing how it applies or doesn't apply and benefiting from your peers' insights.

Let's say you're asked to present to the class a semiotic reading of a childhood toy. By discussing a favorite toy with your class, you are articulating, perhaps for the first time, what it meant (or means) to you and so are taking the first step toward writing a more formal analysis of it in an essay (especially if you receive feedback and comments from your class).

Similarly, if you stage an in-class debate over whether Batman is a gay character, you're amassing a wonderful storehouse of arguments, counterarguments, and evidence to consider when you write your own essay that either supports or refutes Andy Medhurst's thesis in "Batman, Deviance, and Camp" (Chapter 9). As with other strategies to develop your ideas, you may not use directly every idea generated in conversation with your classmates, but that's okay. You should find yourself better able to sort through and articulate the ideas that you do find valuable.

Developing Strong Arguments about Popular Culture

We expect that students will write many different sorts of papers in response to the selections in this book. You may write personal experience narratives, opinion pieces, research papers, formal pro-con arguments, and many others. We'd like here to focus on writing analytic essays because the experience of analyzing popular culture may seem different than that of analyzing other subjects. Occasionally we've had students who feel reluctant to analyze popular culture because they think that analysis requires them to trash their subject, and they don't want to write a "negative" essay about what may be their favorite film or TV program. Or a few students may feel uncertain because "It's all subjective." Since most people have opinions about popular culture, they say, how can any one essay be stronger than another?

While these concerns are understandable, they needn't be an obstacle in writing a strong analytic paper—whether on popular culture or any other topic. First, we often suggest that you set aside your own personal tastes when writing an analysis. We do so not because your preferences are not important; recall that we often ask you to explore your beliefs in your journal, and we want you to be aware of your own attitudes and observations about your topic. Rather, we do so because an analysis of, say, *The Mummy* is not the same as a paper that explains "why I like (or dislike) this movie." Instead, an analysis would explain how it works, what cultural beliefs and viewpoints underlie it, what its significance is, and so forth. And such a paper would not necessarily be positive or negative; it would seek to explain how the elements of the film work together to have a particular effect on its audience. If your instructor asks you to write a critical analysis or a critical argument, he or she is requesting neither a hit job nor a celebration of your topic.

As a result, the second concern, about subjectivity, becomes less of a problem. That's because your analysis should center around a clear argument about that movie. You're not simply presenting a personal opinion about it; rather, you're presenting a central insight about how the movie works, and you need to demonstrate it with logical, specific evidence. It's that evidence that will take your essay out of the category of being "merely subjective." You should start with your own opinion, but you want to add to it lots of proof that shows the legitimacy of that opinion. Does that sound familiar? It should, because that's what you need to do in any analytic essay, no matter what your subject matter happens to be.

When writing about popular culture, students sometimes wonder what sort of evidence they can use to support their points. Your instructor will probably give you guidelines for each assignment, but we'll provide some general suggestions here. Start with your subject itself. You'll find it's useful to view your subject—whether it's an ad, a film, or anything else—as a text that you can "read" closely. That's what you would do if you were asked to analyze a poem: you would read it carefully, studying individual words, images, rhythm, and so forth, and those details would support whatever point you wanted to make about the poem. Read your pop culture subject with the same care. Let's say your instructor asks you to analyze an advertisement. Look at the details: Who appears in the ad, and what is their expression? What props are used, and what is the "story" that the ad tells? Is there anything missing from this scene that you would expect to find? Your answers to such questions could form the basis of the evidence that you use in your essay.

If your instructor has asked you to write a semiotic analysis, you can develop evidence as well by locating your subject within a larger system. Recall that a system is the larger network of related signs to which your subject belongs and that identifying it helps to reveal the significance of your subject. This may sound hard to do, but it is through identifying a system that you can draw on your own vast knowledge of popular culture. And that may sound abstract, but it becomes very specific when applied to a particular example. If you were to analyze platform shoes, for instance, it would help to locate them within the larger fashion system— specifically, other choices of footwear. How do the signals sent by wearing a pair of platforms differ from those sent by wearing, say, a pair of Doc Martens? How does the history of platform shoes, specifically their popularity in the 1970s, affect their current appeal? Can you associate the retro look of platforms with any other fashion and popular cultural trends? Teasing out such differences and associations can help you explain the shoes' social and cultural signficance.

You can strengthen your argument as well if you know and use the history of your subject. That might sound like you have to do a lot of library research, but often you don't have to: you may already be familiar with the social and cultural history of your subject. If you know, for instance, that the baggy pants so popular among teens in the mid-1990s were a few years before ubiquitous among street gang members, you know an important historical detail that goes a long way toward explaining their significance. Depending on your assignment, you might want to expand on your own historical knowledge and collect other data about your topic, perhaps through surveys and interviews. If you're analyzing gendered patterns of courtship rituals, for instance, you could interview some people from different age groups, as well as both genders, to get a sense of how such patterns have evolved over time. The material you gather through such an interview will be raw data, and you'll want to do more than just "dump" the information into your essay. See this material instead as an original body of evidence that you'll sort through (you probably won't use every scrap of information), study, and interpret in its own right.

Reading Essays about Popular Culture

In your writing course, it's likely that your instructor will ask you to work in groups with other students, perhaps reviewing each other's rough drafts. You'll find many benefits to this activity. Not only will you receive more feedback on your own in-progress work, but you will see other students' ideas and approaches to an assignment and develop an ability to evaluate academic writing. For the same reasons, we're including three sample student essays that satisfy assignments about popular culture. You may agree or disagree with the authors' views, and you might think you'd respond to the assigned topics differently: that's fine. We've selected these essays because they differ in style, focus, and purpose and thus suggest different approaches to their assignments—approaches that might help you as you write your own essays about popular culture. We've annotated the essays to point out argumentative, organizational, and rhetorical strategies that we found effective. As you read the essays and the annotations, ask why the authors chose these strategies and how you might incorporate some of the same strategies in your own writing.

Essay 1: Personal Experience Essay

Some assignments may allow you to respond to a topic by discussing your own personal experiences and observations. Such assignments enable you to draw on a wealth of details and specific evidence that you have close to hand, and they also enable you to develop your own voice as a writer (because the subject is your own experience, you will want to use the first-person form of address). Dana Mariano, a student at Lehigh University in Bethlehem, Pennsylvannia, wrote the following essay, "Patrons of the Arts," about a recent trend that many young people have embraced despite their parents' disapproval: tattooing and body piercing. Mariano was not required to base her discussion on a close reading of the selections. But notice that she combines her own tale of visiting a tattoo parlor with a full and rich consideration of the system into which her visit can be interpreted—thus fulfilling one of the central tenets of the semiotic approach.

Patrons of the Arts

The glow from Tattoo 46's neon sign reflected onto the
dashboard of my car and attracted most of the flies from the
surrounding area. As I walked into Tattoo 46, I asked myself
a very logical question: "What the hell am I doing here?" I
was not a biker, a World War II veteran, or a criminal; I was
simply an eighteen-year-old girl who wanted a tattoo. Actually, I had wanted a tattoo since I was in the eighth grade,
and now I was finally old enough to get one.

   I looked around the waiting room of Tattoo 46 and saw
plastered on the walls a potpourri of tattoos that ranged from
fire-breathing dragons to roses to cartoon characters. I could
hear a faint buzz coming from a room in the back that was
shut off with a curtain that looked like a bedspread from the
sixties. Luckily, I already knew exactly what tattoo I wanted,
so I did not have to search for the perfect one from the
plethora of tattoos on the walls. I planned to get my tattoo
of a Hawaiian flower and get it tattooed onto my lower
stomach.

   A burly, gray-haired man, who reminded me so much of
Jerry Garcia, walked out from another back room and asked,
"So, let me guess. You are here to get your belly-button
pierced."

   "Actually, I would like it if you could do a tattoo of this,"
I said as I handed him the picture of the tiny narcissus flower
my friend Samantha had drawn for me.

   "Yeah, I can do this," he said. "Do you have any ID?"

   "Sure, here it is," I said triumphantly as I showed him my
driver's license.

   "Well, well, well. Happy Birthday. So, are you ready to
roll?" he asked.

   "As ready as I'll ever be," I replied with a voice that
lacked any semblance of confidence.

   As I walked into the small room, I saw all over the walls
pictures of tattooed and pierced people. Most of these people
had body piercings in regions where I had only heard people
could get them, but I never thought it was truly physically possible. I heard a man scream from the other room, and once
again I asked myself, "What the hell am I doing here?" I was a
medium-height, blonde, Abercrombie-wearing, sorority type

of girl. Why would I get a tattoo or anything other than my ears pierced?

Looking at society today, one realizes that a variety of people are now getting tattoos and body piercings. These body adornments, which were once an accessory for rebels, punks, bikers, and freaks, are now commonly seen on models, actors, people in the business world, and even teachers. Today, one cannot walk down the street without seeing someone sporting a tattoo, eyebrow ring, tongue ring, or labret (pierced lower lip).

> **Dana broadens her focus to a general cultural trend.**

These people are proud to show off their personal artwork. Tattooing and body piercing was once a symbol of nonconformity in society; now it almost seems to be a form of conformity. The question is, why have so many decided to pierce their bodies in weird areas and adorn their bodies with tattoos? What exactly has happened to polite society?

Celebrities and rock stars have always influenced the way people believe they should look. With many models, rock icons, sports figures, actors, and actresses getting their bodies tattooed and pierced, the public wants to follow in their footsteps. Even the most feminine and revered actresses and models are tattooing themselves with small flowers and butterflies or getting their belly-buttons pierced as a symbol of sexuality. Sports figures such as Dennis Rodman cannot stop with just one tattoo and body piercing. For many, body piercing and tattooing becomes a strange addiction. Society has always looked at these types of people as role models. If they can pierce and tattoo, why shouldn't the public?

> **She analyzes her subject, drawing on popular culture to describe the semiotic system in which tattoos and body piercing exist.**

If one looks at the type of people who are piercing themselves, one sees that many are in their thirties and forties, the baby-boomers who are in the midlife-crisis age range. Many baby-boomers have reached the midlife-crisis age and need something to show a sense of rebellion against society. Also, many baby-boomers did not feel that having a tattoo or body piercing was appropriate until now because of its new appeal in polite society and the mainstream.

My mother is one of the people in this category. She got a tattoo five years ago. One could say that she was going through a midlife crisis. She lost one hundred pounds, grew her once-short hair rather long, and bought a very cute red convertible. The last thing on her agenda of making a new woman was to get a tattoo of a butterfly on her lower stomach. Now she is through her midlife crisis, and she feels a sense of youth from her tattoo. She has even said when she dies she wants there to be a hole in her dress where her tattoo is. She wants everyone to be able to see her personal work of art.

Dana provides an alternative explanation, which adds depth to her analysis.

Another explanation for this trend is the *National Geographic* syndrome. In other parts of the world, tattooing and piercing have been common practices for thousands of years. In many non-Western cultures and societies, body art is an indicator of nobility and the upper class. In India, when a woman gets married, she is covered with patterns in henna, a type of die. This body art is considered a sacred symbol of beauty for an Indian woman. Since the world is becoming more and more aware of other cultures, we can see other cultures' ways and are far more accepting of them. The globalization of the world has truly opened up society to be more accepting of one another's cultures, views, and even body adornments.

She offers a third explanation and follows it with an extended example.

A compelling reason for the act seems to be to establish identity. This is why many people my age get body piercings and tattoos. Many teenagers are scared of getting lost in the crowd, and that is why they resort to such measures. It is so hard to stand out in a diverse society; teenagers today go to any measure they can to get more attention. My friend Deanna, who is the valedictorian of my class, recently got her eyebrow pierced. She is one of the people who did this as a form of rebellion and to make a departure from her girly, brainy persona. She did this a few days before graduating high school.

"So, do you think all the parents will be thrilled to see my beautiful eyebrow ring?" Deanna asked with a sly grin.

Dialogue dramatizes the point and makes it personal and immediate.

"Oh, you know they are going to love it. I am sure that you will make the school so proud sporting your eyebrow ring," I said in one of my more sarcastic tones.

"Do you know that the principal already asked me to take it out for graduation? He said he doesn't want me to give the school a bad look," Deanna said with a hint of pride.

"You aren't going to take it out, are you?" I asked.

"Are you kidding me? Of course not. I refuse to allow people to remember me as perfect little Deanna. I would look like I was the principal's pet, even though I was at one time. I have worked so hard to move away from the old Deanna. This eyebrow ring represents a new more independent Deanna," she firmly stated.

Whatever the reason, many people have decided to adorn their bodies with tattoos and piercings. Today's diverse society makes it harder and harder for a person to get noticed, so many have changed their appearance so they can stand out in the crowd. The abundance of body piercing and tattooing has also changed the way society looks at beauty. It was once considered ugly and manly for a woman to have a tattoo. Today, it is considered sexy and erotic if a woman has a small, feminine tattoo on her body. The abundance of tattooing and body piercing has certainly changed the way that society views these things that were once considered proper only for freaks.

As I lay on the cold metal table, I tried to decide whether I truly wanted this tattoo or not. I pulled down my pants and watched my tattoo artist get out a new needle. I was going to do this. I had no idea why, but I was going to get the tattoo I always wanted. There is no rational explanation for why I wanted a tattoo; I just did.

> **Dana returns to the introduction's dramatic scene, signaling closure to the narrative.**

"So why are you getting a tattoo?" my tattoo artist asked.

"I don't know." I said. "I just want one."

Essay 2: Critical Reading of a Film

Your instructor may ask you to read one of the selections in this text and then to apply the author's general ideas to a new example, either one provided by the assignment or one that you select. Such an assignment asks you to work closely with two "texts"—the reading selection and a pop cultural example—and requires you to articulate the relationship you see between the two. In essence, such an assignment asks you to use the reading selection as a critical framework for analyzing the particular example. In this essay, William Martin-Doyle of Harvard University applies Robert B. Ray's theory of heroic archetypes in American cinema ("The Thematic Paradigm," p. 299) to a film of his own choice, *Cool Hand Luke.* His instructor explained to his class, "A really good essay will not simply say *why* Ray's theory does or does not apply but will go further and speculate what that relevance or irrelevance *means.*" As you read Martin-Doyle's essay, look for how the student fulfills both tasks.

Cool Hand Luke:
The Exclusion of the
Official Hero in
American Cinema

William sums
up Ray's defini-
tion of hero and
presents his
argument that
Cool Hand Luke
(CHL) departs
from Ray's
archetypal
pattern.

In his article "The Thematic Paradigm," Robert B. Ray
contends that the two heroic types of outlaw and official are
the stock figures of American cinema. The author implies that
by the acceptance of the two characters' juxtaposition in popular culture, Americans are revealing a type of immaturity:
"The parallel existence of these two contradictory traditions
evinced the general pattern of American mythology: the denial
of the necessity for choice" (para. 15). This contention is well
rooted: movies such as *Shane,* for example, illustrate Ray's
point quite effectively, presenting the viewer with the story of
a gunslinger and a farmer joining forces to combat evil and defend the American way. Movies have come a long way since
Shane, though. Films display their coming-of-age by making
choices far more often than they used to. This new decisiveness does not necessarily reflect a responsible adulthood,
however; when a choice is made, it is now frequently for the
outlaw hero. This trend is easily seen in the movie *Cool Hand
Luke* (1967).

The paragraph
doesn't just give
a plot summary
but explains plot
details in terms
of the ideologies
Ray describes.

The movie tells the story of an individualist who is
sentenced to two years working on a chain gang for his
rebellion against authority. To avoid alienating the viewer with
the story of an inhuman criminal, the makers of the movie
choose a crime that panders to the audience, in the form of
"malicious destruction of municipal property": cutting the
heads off parking meters while bored and drunk. In this way,
lawbreaking is romanticized as the vice of a man who refuses
to conform. Luke's individualism and powerful personality
initially alienate the other prisoners, but he soon becomes their
idol; through him they live vicariously. After attempting to
live in the suffocating atmosphere of the prison camp, Luke
begins his escape efforts. He is repeatedly recaptured, with
mounting consequences for each attempt. The authorities, as
symbolized by the nameless man who supervises the chain
gang's work from behind the mask of his sunglasses, attempt
to break Luke's spirit. They degrade and beat him for every attempt, and they finally kill him after his third try, but Luke's

refusal to conform, expressed through his escapes, is made into a victory for individuality.

    Cool Hand Luke's unreserved depiction of the legal system as a brutally unjust entity signals a definite departure from movies that contain both of Ray's stock hero types. Ray asserts that "by customarily portraying the law as the tool of villains . . . this mythology betrayed a profound pessimism about the individual's access to the legal system" (para. 11). The law, confusingly, is also the tool of the official hero. This is a puzzling situation in many movies, as order is the very basis for the character of the official hero. That the support for the "Good Good Boys" (para. 3) should come from an institution that the audience for some reason views with suspicion suggests that the official hero character is only a substitute for the outlaw hero in most people's minds: the renegade is the ideal. The presence of both types in a film might indicate a certain confusion in the viewer about what he or she really values. Ray, however, indicates that American cinema is typified by the presence of the two. *Cool Hand Luke* represents a departure from that "duplicity" (para. 22). There is no confused romanticizing of two conflicting ideals: instead, the clear choice is Newman's outlaw. Everywhere in the movie, the forces of law and order are portrayed as a tool for oppression rather than for the protection of everyday citizens, a group to which one might assume the average audience member belongs.

William presents more fully Ray's definition of heroes and moves to the essay's assertion that *CHL* fails to fulfill this pattern.

    Ray writes of the pervasive theme of the reluctant hero, the man who is eventually forced by outside pressures into promoting the greater good; he is "the private man attempting to keep from being drawn into action on any but his own terms. In this story, the reluctant hero's ultimate willingness to help the community satisfied the official values" (para. 17). In this way, the reluctant hero represents a synthesis of the official and the outlaw hero, rendering a somewhat contradictory picture, almost of a man with a split personality. Once again, *Shane* epitomizes this concept, as the mysterious stranger is drawn into aiding the brave settlers in their struggle against the ranchers, despite his initial desire to lay aside his guns and lead a peaceful life. In contrast, *Cool Hand Luke* presents no such capitulation to the moral pressure of helping others. Luke's only priority is to live his life his own way, not to

Here and in the next two paragraphs, William analyzes specific cinematic details that demonstrate the kind of hero Luke is.

aid the other prisoners. There is no plot device of the hero righteously leading a rebellion against the armed guards for subjecting them to life in the chain gang. Luke never consciously tries to become a leader, and the other prisoners' admiration for him never fosters a sense of responsibility in him for their well-being. His strong personality induces others to become attached to him, yet he never feels any reciprocal ties. Indeed, the only strong emotional bond that he has during the entire movie is the one to his sickly mother, who comes to visit him at one point. Later in the movie, word of her death arrives, and Luke is cut off from any emotional tie, making him a complete loner. Even this instance is used as an example of the cruelty of the established authority, as Luke is confined in a wooden box the size of a closet for several days just so that he won't get any ideas about escaping to go to the funeral. This measure does force Luke to the edge, but his response is not that of Ray's stereotypical hero, who exhibits traits of both the official and the outlaw hero. His response is straightforward, in keeping with his character. He doesn't combat injustice in general, helping the greater good of the other prisoners; instead, he makes his first attempt at escape (a perfectly understandable, yet hardly selfless action). In this way, the character of Luke remains consistent: he begins as an outlaw, and he never strays from that image.

The conspicuous lack of an official hero is accented by George Kennedy's character Dragune, who at first seems like he might play that role. A prisoner who has been serving time for several years, he has become a sort of leader among the prisoners, who listen to him because of his strength and his outspokenness. A bit of a blowhard, he defends the status quo, holding forth on the value of order in the prisoners' lives: "We got rules here. In order to learn 'em, you gotta do more work with your ears than with your mouth." Ray states that the official hero's motto is "You cannot take the law into your own hands" (para. 12), and this is clearly Dragune's own personal opinion. Luke, on the other hand, obviously has no use for society's impositions; during his first night, he says, "I ain't heard that much worth listening to. Just a lot of guys laying down a lot of rules and regulations." When conflict arises between Dragune and Luke, it first appears that the viewpoint of the authority will triumph over Luke's

William doesn't limit his analysis to Luke; he studies other characters as well.

championing of the individual. They box, as is the custom for two prisoners with irreconcilable differences, and Dragune easily beats Luke senseless. This physical triumph of authority quickly turns into a moral victory for Luke, however, as Dragune is forced to leave the ring when he realizes that the only way that Luke will ever stay on the ground after a knockdown is if Dragune kills him. After this turning point, Dragune soon becomes Luke's friend and eventually his disciple.

Luke's tenacity is simultaneously the strong point of his personality, the very trait that makes him worthy of admiration, and his fatal flaw. This character will never give up, no matter the pain he must endure, whether the situation is in the boxing ring against a man who heavily outweighs him, in a bet that he can eat fifty eggs in an hour, or in his repeated attempts at escape, for which he is punished with escalating viciousness. These escape attempts are the main outlet for his rebellion, and they are always initially successful. Despite the fact that he is always later apprehended, he always makes his escapes in grand fashion, confounding the authorities who attempt to chase him. The escapes are therefore victories of a kind against the establishment, symbolic of his death grip on his own identity. After the first recapture, the captain of the camp debases Luke and reflects to the other prisoners: "What we've got here is failure to communicate. Some men, you just can't reach." In this world of polar extremes, there can be no communication between the outlaw hero and the forces of conformity that would normally be wielded by an official hero. It is officialdom's failure to reach Luke, to "get his mind right," that gives the outlaw his victory. His death is imbued with nobility as the car that takes him away, dying, crushes the supervisor's sunglasses that have come to be the recurring metaphor for the rule of the law.

Cool Hand Luke represents a shift away from the standards presented in Ray's article, as illustrated by *Shane,* in which American movies have a conflicting duality of protagonists. *Cool Hand Luke* has instead made the choice for the outlaw hero. This is a definite shift away from earlier movies that emphasized the official hero, such as Jimmy Stewart films, and war movies, which celebrated the triumph of the ultimate official body, the United States government. Despite the fact that the movie was a product of the late 1960s, a time

> William locates *CHL* in the context of American film history, including films that both predate and postdate *CHL*.

of political and social unrest, *Cool Hand Luke*'s decision still has relevance in this decade. The rejection of society in its present form, as represented by the official hero, is still visible in the progression to modern hits like *Natural Born Killers* and *Pulp Fiction,* which glorify serial killers and organized crime hit men. Ray implies that Americans' failure to make a choice when it comes to their movies is a societal problem. In *Cool Hand Luke,* the choice has been made, but a new problem is reflected in that choice. Any country is based on the idea that there must be rules to govern acceptable and unacceptable behavior; the constant deprecation of those rules therefore signals an extreme dissatisfaction with present society. Such dissatisfaction is a normal reaction against the perceived failure of authority, as exemplified by problems such as the Vietnam War, Watergate, and the national economy. Dissatisfaction isn't necessarily a bad thing, but expressing discontent without hinting at the possibility of a real solution is troubling.

The essay moves toward its conclusion by suggesting the social implications of the ideology presented in CHL.

The problem with the choice of the outlaw hero lies in the fact that the outlaw doesn't confront issues and deal with them in a mature fashion. Instead, he runs away as Luke did or uses force until there is nothing left to face. In short, the choice of the outlaw hero exposes the fact that Americans are indulging in a form of moral escapism: they dislike their present circumstances, yet are too scared to face up to them.

William concludes with a sharp statement of his view of those implications.

Essay 3: Open-Ended Analytic Assignment

Your instructor may assign an open-ended topic, one that allows you to select your own focus and subject matter. If you receive such an assignment, first brainstorm possible topics that interest you, for you'll produce the best writing if you're excited about your topic. Many students feel tempted to choose a broad subject (for instance, images of African Americans in modern media), assuming they will have more to say about it, but with such a broad and unwieldy topic you can have trouble deciding where to start. Aim for a more specific topic, preferably one that you discuss with your instructor. The following essay, by Mike Nordberg of Lehigh University, is entitled "Science Fiction: A Mirror to Our Universe," but notice that Mike doesn't attempt to discuss all science fiction; instead, he narrows his focus to the *Star Trek* phenomenon. Note that Mike grounds his argument about science fiction in a rich array of details that constitute the semiotic system in which *Star Trek* and its many spin-offs can be interpreted.

Science Fiction: A Mirror to Our Universe

"Space, the final frontier. These are the voyages of the
Starship *Enterprise.* Its continuing mission, to explore strange
new worlds. To seek out new life and new civilizations. To
boldly go where no man, er . . . um . . . where no one has gone
before." This opening monologue to the TV series *Star Trek*
and *Star Trek: The Next Generation* is one of the most
recognizable in television history. It has existed in nearly the
same form since the original series debuted in 1966. However,
as one can see above, it has not gone completely unchanged.
As the world around *Star Trek* transformed during those thirty
years, the program itself adjusted to the changing world
around it. And yet this is one of science fiction's great
strengths. Behind all the action, technical wizardry, and
stunning special effects, there exists an ideal stage to comment
on present-day culture. This is because the way we as a society
view the future reveals a great deal about how we live in the
present. Indeed, science fiction is often a mirror of the real
world where present-day issues are discussed in a futuristic
setting.

 Many controversial issues have been addressed in the four
television series — *Star Trek, Star Trek: The Next Generation,
Star Trek: Deep Space Nine,* and *Star Trek: Voyager* — and
nine movies that make up the *Star Trek* universe. Producer
Gene Roddenberry created a fantastic world where humankind
has overcome war, greed, and poverty while still leaving room
for a moral dilemma or two to creep in. This formula makes
for not only interesting and profitable programming but also
excellent social commentary when the problems faced in the
show have parallels to current events. Take, for example, the
original series episode, "Let That Be Your Last Battlefield." In
that episode, the crew of the *Enterprise* comes across a species
with two distinct races. One is black on the right side of their
bodies and white on the left; the other race is the opposite,
white on the right and black on the left. The black-and-white
race persecutes and enslaves the white-and-black race. The
hatred and constant war between the races leads to the destruction of their world. Because this episode was aired in the
time of Dr. Martin Luther King Jr.'s work for desegregation,
it sent a clear message about the senselessness of racism.

Marginal notes:

Mike grabs
the reader's
attention with
catchy, familiar
phrases that are
humorously
qualified.

Mike states his
thesis.

He presents spe-
cific supporting
evidence.

Likewise, in the episode "A Private Little War," the evil Klingons supply firearms to one faction of a primitive, usually peaceful, race. To keep the Klingons from gaining control of the planet, Captain Kirk gives guns to the other faction, thus restoring the balance of power. This was a perfect analogy to the Vietnam War that was raging at the time.

This tradition of social commentary continued in *Star Trek: The Next Generation.* For instance, the episode "The Outcast" addresses the always delicate topic of homosexuality but with an intriguing twist. In the show, the *Enterprise* travels to a world where all the inhabitants are androgynous. There, the outcasts are the ones who show tendencies toward being female or male and attracted to the opposite sex. Whoever has this "deformity" is dealt with through brainwashing. *Star Trek* has also covered issues such as terrorism, capital punishment, genetic engineering, medical ethics, and drug abuse.

Mike draws additional evidence from the system of sci-fi TV.

Of course, social criticism is not limited solely to *Star Trek. Babylon 5,* a science fiction show created by television veteran J. Michael Straczynski, has garnered an audience almost as loyal and fanatical as that of *Star Trek* (Sharkey 20). The show presents a somewhat darker vision of the future than *Star Trek* where humans are not the dominant species in the galaxy. In her article "A Man with a Five-Year Plan," Betsy Sharkey notes, "Set in 2261, the society Straczynski has created allows him to explore the most volatile issues of today—race, culture, life, death, God, religion, truth—outside the boundaries that traditionally define and divide us" (20). Consider the episode "The Geometry of Shadows." Here, a race known as the Drazi begins a ritualistic though seemingly pointless conflict between two groups identified by green and purple scarves. However, the faction that one belongs to is determined simply by what color scarf is pulled out of a barrel. The show makes an obvious correlation to present-day gang violence, where one's affiliation may be determined by nothing more than the color of a bandana, but does so without raising the question of race. In Sharkey's words, "When those at odds are Centauris and Narns, it allows the debate to be conducted without devisiveness" (20). There are countless more examples. *The Terminator* and *2001: A Space Odyssey* comment on our world by describing a society that is increasingly being run by computers. The list goes on and on,

He supports his thesis by citing authoritative sources.

with today's issues repeatedly manifesting themselves in our fantasies of the future.

Science fiction not only tells us where we are; it also shows us where we have been. As stated earlier, how society views the future depends on how it functions in the present. Consequently, science fiction programs that deal with the future adapt to the time in which they exist. Just compare the original *Star Trek* series of the 1960s with the *Star Trek* series of the 1980s and 1990s. The repressive gender roles that were still prevalent in the 1960s were quite evident in the original series. In their book *Deep Space and Sacred Time: Star Trek in the American Mythos,* anthropologists Jon G. Wagner and Jan Lundeen note that while women were "usually depicted as twenty-third-century airheads and alien temptresses stuffed into 'tin-foil bikinis' in the original series, a woman finally commands a starship in *Star Trek: Voyager*" (61). The long-awaited female captain was not the only change seen in the politically correct 1990s. While the original series had a racially diverse cast for the time, women and minorities were rarely seen in command decisions. Beginning with *Star Trek: Deep Space Nine* in 1993, that pattern changed. Creators Rick Berman and Michael Piller eventually cast Avery Brooks, an African American, to play the lead character. Said Rick Berman, "Michael Piller and I had discussed at length that we were not going to limit the casting of the lead to a white male. We had decided that we were going to be as open-minded as possible even to the thought of casting a woman" (Dillard 167). A woman was eventually cast as in the show's first officer role. As stated earlier, a female captain finally became a reality in *Star Trek: Voyager,* with a Native American first officer to boot. The uniforms worn on the various series also provide a glimpse of society's changing view of women in the workplace. The original series had women wearing miniskirts in the twenty-third century. By the time of *Star Trek: The Next Generation,* women were wearing the same professional outfits as men. In fact, in the first season of *Star Trek: The Next Generation,* many men wore a miniskirt-like tunic as a sort of tongue-in-cheek parody of the original women's uniforms.

So how do they do it? That is to say, how does a television program like *Star Trek* or *Babylon 5* remain so popular while at the same time treating such controversial

Mike draws support from the history of science fiction TV programming.

He includes more specific details.

Mike refers to
the history of
satire and
fantasy writing
to contextualize
contemporary
science fiction's
treatment of
controversial
issues.

issues? During the Enlightenment, great philosophers like
Voltaire used the art of satire to criticize certain aspects of the
world in which they lived. If they had openly expressed their
radical ideas, they could have faced serious personal danger.
In *Don Quixote*, Cervantes cleverly disguised his views of the
Catholic church within the satire of the story. In her book, *Star
Trek: Where No One Has Gone Before*, author and *Star Trek*
enthusiast J. M. Dillard commented,

> In the great tradition of Jonathan Swift and *Gulliver's
> Travels*, Roddenberry and the many writers who con-
> tributed to the *Star Trek* universe were able to attain a
> level of social commentary that was ahead of its time —
> all because the series used the trappings of the fantastic
> as a backdrop. (42)

It would have been nearly impossible for any other kind
of television show to air a program that dealt with racism in
the way that *Star Trek* did in the turbulent 1960s. As Dillard
put it, "This was strong stuff in the sixties. . . . So *Star Trek*
used its science-fiction guise to make the statements more
palatable" (42). In this way, *Star Trek* and all of science fiction
became the twentieth-century version of classic satire.

Mike further
contextualizes
Star Trek by
relating it
to cultural
mythologies.

However, satire does not begin to describe the immense
influence that science fiction has had on popular culture. Wagner and Lundeen went so far as to say, "*Star Trek* has become
part of the twentieth-century American mythology" (61). They
describe myths as "the narratives that structure [a culture's]
worldview and give form and meaning to the disconnected
data of everyday life" (61). One needs only to look at the over
thirty-year history of *Star Trek* and compare that to the three
decades of American culture that have gone on around it to see
just how much this one television show has structured our
worldview. As Dillard commented,

> *Star Trek*'s special spin—born of the volatile era in
> which it was conceived—was that these morality tales
> could encourage viewers to think along the lines of such
> then-radical liberal beliefs as "All men are good, no
> matter what the color of their skin" and "No good
> comes of getting involved in other people's internal
> wars." (42)

Indeed, this is the strength of all kinds of science fiction. No
other kind of program is in a more ideal position to comment

on our world. Oddly, or perhaps expectedly, science fiction does this from a platform that is usually out of this world.

Sources

Bing, Jonathan, et al. "Deep Space and Sacred Time: *Star Trek* in the American Mythos." *Publishers Weekly.* 2 Nov 1998: 61. Online. ProQuest Direct. Available: http://proquest .umi.com. 25 Nov 1998.

Dillard, J. M. *Star Trek: "Where No One Has Gone Before."* New York: Pocket Books, 1994.

Sharkey, Betsy. "A Man with a Five-Year Plan." *Mediaweek.* 21 Oct 1996: 20, 24, 28. Online. ProQuest Direct. Available: http://proquest.umi.com. 25 Nov 1998.

Wagner, Jon G., and Jan Lundeen. *Deep Space and Sacred Time: Star Trek in the American Mythos.* Westport, Conn.: Praeger, 1998.

CULTURAL PRODUCTIONS

CHAPTER ONE

CONSUMING PASSIONS

The Culture of American Consumption

If you were given a blank check to purchase anything—and everything—you wanted, what would you buy? Try making a list, and then annotate that list with brief explanations for why you want each item. Did you come by your desires entirely on your own, or have you been influenced by what other people desire or what others have encouraged you to desire?

Now consider the things you do own. Make another list and annotate it too. Why did you buy this item or that? Which were presents that reflect someone else's tastes and desires? What compromises did you have to make in choosing one item over another? How often did price or quality affect your decisions? How often did style or image? How often did you consider what others would think of your purchase?

Such questions are a good place to begin a semiotic analysis of American consumer culture—for every choice you make in the products you consume, from clothing to furniture to cars to electronics and beyond, is a sign, a signal you send to the world about yourself. Those aren't just a pair of shoes you're wearing: they're a statement about your identity. That's not just a collection of CDs: it's a message about your worldview. Indeed, your music collection may say more about you than anything else you own.

To read the signs of American consumption, it is best to start with yourself because you've already got an angle on the answers. But be careful and be honest. Remember, a cultural sign gets its meaning from the system in which it appears. Its significance does not lie in its usefulness but rather in its symbolism, in the image it projects, and that image is socially constructed. You didn't make it by yourself. To decode your own possessions, you've got to ask yourself what you are trying to say with them and what you want other people to think about you. And you've got to remember the difference between fashion and function.

To give you an idea of how to go about analyzing consumer objects and behavior, let's look at a very simple product that on the surface seems completely functional and meaningless. Let's look at coffee.

Interpreting the Culture of American Consumption

At first, coffee may not seem like a subject you can interpret. After all, it's just a beverage that you might drink when waking up or studying or chatting with friends. Its function is obvious; its physical appearance, downright innocuous. But remember that a semiotic analysis looks beyond your subject's use — what you do with it — to its wider cultural and social significance.

Let's consider those wider significances. As tea is to the British, coffee is to America — the defining beverage of our culture, consumed at breakfast, lunch, dinner, and all hours in between. As our own cultural myths have it, coffee took the place of tea in American life after the Boston Tea Party and so, at first, assumed a patriotic significance. But beyond this more or less nationalistic signification, coffee connotes a number of other meanings in American consumer culture, bearing a different image depending on the context and on the consumer. As we look at a few of those images of coffee here, ask yourself which appeals the most to you. Which images have less appealing cultural associations, and why?

Discussing the Signs of Consumer Culture

On the board, list in categories the fashion styles worn by members of the class. Be sure to note details, such as styles of shoes, jewelry, watches, or sunglasses, as well as broader trends. Then discuss what the clothing choices say about individuals. What messages are people sending about their personal identity? Do individual students agree with the class's interpretations of their clothing choices? Can any distinctions be made by gender, age, or ethnicity? Then discuss what the fashion styles worn by the whole class say: Is a group identity projected by class members?

The Mrs. Olson Scenario

The traditional image of coffee in America associated coffee drinking with men and breakfast. The Mrs. Olson campaign that promoted Folgers coffee in the 1960s is paradigmatic of this association. It dramatized the serving of coffee as a housewifely duty, as Mrs. Olson's neighbor served her spouse and he brooded behind his newspaper before going to work. Note how in this symbolic scenario, coffee is a relatively solitary drink. Rather than talking, the man behind the newspaper drinks and reads; if he talks at all, it's in distracted mumbles. Such an image is part of a larger cultural mythology that assigns behavioral roles on the basis of gender. Women are assigned the task of brewing and serving the morning coffee, while men are cast as judges. Rather than sitting as equals conversing together in a domestic environment, husband and wife are shown in a hierarchical relationship with the man holding the power. Indeed, the whole strategy of the Mrs. Olson ads was to convince young wives that the key to a successful marriage was serving hubbie a successful cup of morning coffee—Folgers, of course.

Truck Stops and Coffee Shops

A second traditional image of coffee, related to the first in its reliance on traditional gender codes, had a typical location—the truck stop. You've seen this scenario—a lone truckdriver, head hung over his plate of biscuits and gravy, flirting, perhaps, with a tired waitress. Here coffee means caffeine: it's not just the big rig that's tanking up. The coffee's quality is unimportant; what matters is the jolt. This image, too, is masculine and solitary. It also suggests haste—got to get back on the road.

A closely related image was found in the office coffee break, which suggests both haste (you've got only ten minutes) and masculinity, insofar as it takes place in the traditionally masculine space of an office or workplace. While women certainly are no longer excluded from the office, the traditional scene showed them generally in a subordinate role as secretaries or as those responsible for brewing the coffee. Fast-food coffee—the 7-11 or McDonald's big slurp grabbed on the way to work—is also part of this associational complex in which coffee connotes haste, work, and the fast and demanding pace of adult life.

For travelers and retirees, among others, the coffee shop image may be the most familiar. In a coffee shop, coffee serves as a background beverage to mediocre meals (airline coffee fits this category as well). The meal may be eaten at leisure, but coffee in this scenario is a drink one orders with the hash browns or the apple pie without caring much about the way it tastes. The image sometimes suggests elderly or palateless coffee drinkers passing the time.

Common Grounds

Recently, yet another cultural image for coffee has been revived, an image born of the coffeehouse tradition. Unlike the coffee shop, where coffee is a background drink, in the coffeehouse the center of attention is not simply the coffee—*good* coffee, that is—but also a certain experience that goes along with drinking it. The coffeehouse tradition goes back centuries in English cultural life and continues to flourish in American intellectual and artistic circles. It is worth remembering in this context that the international insurance firm, Lloyds of London, began in an eighteenth-century English coffeehouse and that Joseph Addison and Richard Steele launched *The Spectator* in 1711 to bring "philosophy out of . . . libraries, schools and colleges to dwell in . . . coffee-houses."

The American coffeehouse tradition has maintained the English focus on good conversation (borrowing also from the tradition of the French coffee bar). Conversation, whether for business purposes or intellectual exploration, is the desired "product" at the coffeehouse. But while such conversation in eighteenth-century England was definitely associated with masculinity, it has become gender-neutral in America. Where American women once tended to meet in tea shops, they now flock to such coffee bar chains as Starbucks, places where women as well as men can be seen conversing together. In this code, the image of coffee strongly differs from images in the Mrs. Olson and truck stop scenarios.

This difference is probably behind the popularity of coffeehouses among college students today. But here another difference comes into play. Coffee bars, with their shining chrome-and-glass surfaces and $200 cappucino makers for sale, tend to be most popular among the middle-aged set. College hangouts, on the other hand, tend to resemble the coffeehouse environments of the beat fifties: self-consciously shabby sites designed for late-night conversation, poetry readings, and alternative music. Here battered old sofas and cheap tables and chairs contrast strongly with the upscale image of the chain coffee sites. Connectedness

---

Exploring the Signs of Consumer Culture

"You are what you buy." In your journal, freewrite on the importance of consumer products in your life. How do you respond to being told your identity is equivalent to the products you buy? Do you resist the notion? Do you recall any instances when you have felt lost without a favorite object? How do you communicate your sense of self to others through objects, whether clothing, books, food, home decor, cars, or something else?

is what matters in the student coffeehouse, the sense of generational belonging and relationship. We know of one such coffeehouse near our own university campus, appropriately called Common Grounds. The pun refers both to what is served there as a product (coffee) and what is offered there as an experience (a place for people to connect). The fact that such places are springing up all over America signifies a certain shift in the interpretation of coffee by the American student population. Do you find yourself drawn to coffeehouses of this kind? Why or why not? What do you think of the people who spend their time there? Is there a definite image such people project? Why would they (and you) choose one place over another?

The Franchise

The resurgence of the student coffeehouse has not gone unnoticed, however, and strenuous efforts have been made to lure young consumers away from their more bohemian coffee haunts into the sanitized and standardized realm of the upscale coffee bar. No coffee emporium has been more assiduous or more successful in this endeavor than the Starbucks franchise, which has managed to do for coffee what McDonald's did for the hamburger a generation ago. Carefully targeting the Gen X market by sponsoring such youth events as the Lilith Fair, turning its coffee bars into sites for live performances of alternative rock music (complete with tie-ins to local alternative rock radio stations), and teaming up with such bookstore chains as Barnes and Noble, Starbucks has successfully overcome the distinction between the "common grounds" coffeehouse and the chromium coffee bar. (If you think this was not deliberate, a visit to the Starbucks website—**http://www.starbucks.com**—will show the company promoting itself as being "in the tradition of the coffeehouse.") Also promoting itself as a champion of environmental activism, Starbucks has done an end-run around the usual image of corporate capitalism as well. The result has been a spectacular capturing of the national coffee market that can also be read as a sign of American culture.

That sign teaches us a lesson about the way corporate capitalism works in contemporary consumer culture. Basically, it tells us that the marketing divisions of large consumer product corporations are, in effect, filled with semioticians (though they wouldn't necessarily use this word) who conduct painstaking analyses of the lifestyles and desires of their targeted markets to get them to buy their products. The emphasis, to put this another way, is less on the production of the product than on the reading of the market and the creation of an image with which that market will identify. Thanks to its sponsorship of Lilith Fair, for example, the Starbucks mermaid is known to millions of young consumers. Add to that the tee shirts, coffee mugs, CDs, and other paraphernalia that sport

the Starbucks logo, and you can see how Starbucks isn't just about coffee, any more than McDonald's is just about hamburgers. Starbucks has
successfully transformed itself into a lifestyle signifier that has crossover
appeal beyond the divisions of age, class, and gender.

Note, then, that whether we are talking truck stops or coffee bars,
the actual cup of joe is not important to a semiotic analysis. What matters
is the overall cultural system—the social context in which that substance
is consumed. The residue from boiling ground coffee beans in water is
not meaningful in itself. What is meaningful is the social and cultural
context in which we consume that residue and the way we relate to
other people when we do so.

If you find coffee consumption and its significance out of your line,
think of any current consumer trend and question it. What messages are
people sending when they buy the thing? What images do they project?
How does the fad relate to other cultural trends? Such are the questions
that you must ask as a reader of consuming images, probing everything
that you may find in the marketplace of goods and services and taking
care never to be satisfied with the answer "because this product is *better*
than that" or, more simply, "just because . . ."

Disposable Decades

When analyzing a consumer sign, you will often find yourself referring to particular decades in which certain popular fads and trends were
prominent, for the decade in which a given style appears may be an essential key to the system that explains it. Have you ever wondered why
American cultural trends seem to change with every decade, why it is so
easy to speak of the sixties or the seventies or the eighties and immediately recognize the popular styles that dominated each decade? Have you
ever looked at the style of a friend and thought, "Oh, she's so seventies"?
Can you place an Earth Shoe at the drop of a hat or a Nehru jacket? A
change in the calendar always seems to herald a change in style in a consuming culture. But why?

The decade-to-decade shift in America's pop cultural identity goes
back a good number of years. It is still easy, for example, to distinguish
F. Scott Fitzgerald's Jazz Age twenties from John Steinbeck's wrathful
thirties. The fifties, an especially connotative decade, raise images of
ducktail haircuts and poodle skirts, drive-in culture and Elvis, family sitcoms and white-bread innocence, while the sixties are remembered for
acid rock, hippies, the student movement, and back-to-the-land com-
munes. We remember the seventies as a pop cultural era divided between
disco, Nashville, and preppiedom, with John Travolta, truckers, and
Skippy and Muffy as dominant pop icons. The boom-boom eighties gave
us Wall Street glitz and the yuppie ascendancy. Indeed, each decade since

the First World War—which, not accidentally, happens to coincide roughly with the rise of modern advertising and mass production—seems to carry its own consumerist style.

It's no accident that the decade-to-decade shift in consumer styles coincides with the advent of modern advertising and mass production because it was mass production that created a need for constant consumer turnover in the first place. Mass production, that is, promotes stylistic change because with so many products being produced, a market must be created to consume all of them, and this means constantly consuming *more.* To get consumers to keep buying all the new stuff, you have to convince them that the stuff they already have has gone out of style. Why else, do you think, do fashion designers completely redesign their lines each year? The new designs aren't functional improvements; they are inducements to go out and replace what you already have to avoid appearing to be out of fashion.

Mass production, in other words, creates consumer societies based on the constant production of new products that are intended to be disposed of with the next product year. But something happened along the way to the establishment of our consumer culture: we began to value consumption more than production. Listen to the economic news: consumption, not production, is relied on to carry America out of its economic downturns. When Americans stop buying, our economy grinds to a halt. Consumption lies at the center of our economic system now, and the result has been a transformation in the very way we view ourselves.

A Tale of Two Cities

It has not always been thus in America, however. Once, Americans prided themselves on their productivity. In 1914, for example, the poet Carl Sandberg boasted of a Chicago that was "Hog butcher for the world, Tool maker, Stacker of Wheat, Player with Railroads and the Nation's Freight Handler." One wonders what Sandberg would think of the place today. From the south shore east to the industrial suburb of Gary, Indiana, Chicago's once-proud mills and factories rust in the winter wind. The broken windows of countless tenements stare blindly at the Amtrak commuter lines that transport the white-collared brokers of the Chicago Mercantile Exchange to the city center, where trade today is in commodity futures, not commodities. Even Michael Jackson, Gary's most famous export, rarely goes home.

Meanwhile, a few hundred miles to the northwest, Bloomington, Minnesota, buzzes with excitement. For there stands the Mall of America, a colossus of consumption so large that it contains within its walls a seven-acre Knott's Berry Farm theme park, with lots of room to spare. You can find almost anything you want in the Mall of America, including all the

---

Reading Consumer Culture on the Net

Log onto one of the many home shopping networks or catalogues. You might try the Internet Shopping Network (http://
www.isn.com), imall (http://www.imall.com), the Internet
Mall (http://www.internet-mall.com), or Shop at Home
(http://www.shopathome.com). Analyze both the products
sold and the way they are marketed. Who is the target audience
for the network you're studying, and what images and values are
used to attract this market? How does the marketing compare
with nonelectronic sales pitches, such as displays in shopping malls
and magazine or TV advertising? Does the electronic medium affect your own behavior as a consumer? How do you account for
any differences in electronic and traditional marketing strategies?

---

latest Michael Jackson CDs, but most of what you will find won't have
been manufactured in America. Jackson himself is under contract with
Sony. The proud tag "Made in the USA" is an increasingly rare item.

It's a long way from Sandberg's Chicago to the Mall of America, a
trip that traverses America's shift from a producer to a consumer economy. This shift is not simply economic; it is behind a cultural transformation that is shaping a new mythology within which we define ourselves,
our hopes, and our desires.

Ask yourself right now what your own goals are in going to college.
Do you envision a career in law or medicine or banking and finance? Do
you want to be a teacher, an advertising executive, or a civil servant? Or
maybe you are preparing for a career on the Internet. If you've considered any of these career examples, you are contemplating what are
known as service jobs. While essential to a society, these jobs don't actually produce anything. If you've given thought to going into some facet
of manufacturing, on the other hand, you are unusual because America
offers increasingly fewer opportunities in that area and little prestige. The
prestige jobs are in law and medicine and, increasingly, in digital marketing operations like Amazon.com, a fact that it is easy to take for granted.
But ask yourself: Does it have to be so?

Simply to ask such questions is to begin to reveal the outline of a
cultural mythology based in consumption rather than production. For
one thing, while law and medicine require specialized training available
to only a few, doctors and lawyers also make a lot of money and so are
higher up on the scale of consumption. Quite simply, they can buy more
than others can. It is easy to presume that this would be the case anywhere, but in the former Soviet Union physicians — most of whom were

women—were relatively low on the social scale. Male engineers, on the other hand, were highly valued for their role in facilitating military production. In what was a producer rather than a consumer culture, it was the producers who roosted high on the social ladder.

And as for the Internet, the big excitement these days is over the retail potential of the Web. Computer makers and chip manufacturers—who, after all, do produce something—find themselves being eclipsed by companies like eBay and America Online, companies that do not produce anything but, rather, are efficient media for consumption.

To live in a consumer culture is not simply a matter of shopping, however; it is also a matter of *being*. For in a consumer society, you are what you consume, and the entire social and economic order is maintained by the constant encouragement to buy. The ubiquity of television and advertising in America is a direct reflection of this system, for these media deliver the constant stimulus to buy in avalanches of consuming images. Consider how difficult it is to escape the arm of the advertiser. You may turn off your TV set, but a screen awaits you at the check-out counter of your supermarket, displaying incentives to spend your money. If you rush to the restroom to hide, you may find advertisements tacked to the stalls. If you shop on the Internet, advertisements greet you on your monitor. Resistance is useless. Weren't you planning to do some shopping this weekend anyway?

When the Going Gets Tough, the Tough Go Shopping

In a cultural system where our identities are displayed in the products we buy, it accordingly is appropriate for us to pay close attention to what we consume and why. From the cars we drive to the clothes we wear, we are enmeshed in a web of consuming images. As students, you are probably freer to choose the particular images you wish to project through the products you consume than most other demographic groups in America. This claim may sound paradoxical: After all, don't working adults have more money than starving students? Yes, generally. But the working world places severe restrictions on the choices employees can make in their clothing and grooming styles, and even automobile choice may be restricted (real estate agents, for example, can't escort their clients around town in Volkswagen Beetles). Corporate business wear, for all its variations, still revolves around a central core of necktied and dark-hued sobriety, regardless of the gender of the wearer. And even though long hair for men returned into fashion in the nineties, few professions outside the entertainment industry allow it on the job. On campus, on the other hand, you can be pretty much whatever you want to be, which is why your own daily lives provide you with a particularly rich field of consumer signs to read and decode.

So go to it. By the time you read this book, a lot will have changed. The nineties themselves will be over without yet having achieved a distinctive identity. Was it the decade of the Net? The SUV? Talk radio and talk TV? Look around yourself. Start reading the signs.

The Readings

As this chapter's lead essay, Laurence Shames's "The More Factor" provides a mythological background for the discussions of America's consuming behavior that follow. Shames takes an historical approach to American consumerism, relating our frontier history to our ever-expanding desire for more goods and services. Anne Norton follows with a semiotic analysis of shopping malls, mail-order catalogues, and the Home Shopping Network, focusing on the ways in which they construct a language of consumption tailored to specific consumer groups. Thomas Hine's interpretation of the packaging that contains America's most commonly consumed products shows how packages, too, constitute complex sign systems intended for consumer "readings," while Stuart Ewen's analysis of the "hard-body" trend explores the cultural significance of the way we package our own bodies. Fred Davis next surveys the history of blue jeans and how they have been transformed from an emblem of labor to one of leisure, and Joan Kron studies the way we use home furnishings to reflect our sense of identity. Finally, David Goewey concludes the chapter with his semiotic analysis of the SUV trend.

LAURENCE SHAMES

The More Factor

||||||||||||||||||||||||||||||||||||||||||||||||||||||||

A bumper sticker popular in the 1980s read, "Whoever dies with the most toys wins." In this selection from The Hunger for More: Searching for Values in an Age of Greed *(1989), Laurence Shames shows how the great American hunger for more — more toys, more land, more opportunities — is an essential part of our history and character, stemming from the frontier era when the horizon alone seemed the only limit to American desire. The author of* The Big Time: The Harvard Business School's Most Successful Class and How It Shaped America *(1986) and the holder of a Harvard M.B.A., Shames is a journalist who has contributed to such publications as* Playboy, Vanity Fair, Manhattan, inc., *and* Esquire. *He currently is working full-time on writing fiction and screen plays, with his most recent publications including* Florida Straits *(1992),* Sunburn *(1995), and* Welcome to Paradise *(1999).*

1

Americans have always been optimists, and optimists have always liked to speculate. In Texas in the 1880s, the speculative instrument of choice was towns, and there is no tale more American than this.

What people would do was buy up enormous tracts of parched and vacant land, lay out a Main Street, nail together some wooden sidewalks, and start slapping up buildings. One of these buildings would be called the Grand Hotel and would have a saloon complete with swinging doors. Another might be dubbed the New Academy or the Opera House. The developers would erect a flagpole and name a church, and once the workmen had packed up and moved on, the towns would be as empty as the sky.

But no matter. The speculators, next, would hire people to pass out handbills in the Eastern and Midwestern cities, tracts limning the advantages of relocation to "the Athens of the South" or "the new plains Jerusalem." When persuasion failed, the builders might resort to bribery, paying people's moving costs and giving them houses, in exchange for nothing but a pledge to stay until a certain census was taken or a certain inspection made. Once the nose count was completed, people were free to move on, and there was in fact a contingent of folks who made their living by keeping a cabin on skids and dragging it for pay from one town to another.

The speculators' idea, of course, was to lure the railroad. If one could create a convincing semblance of a town, the railroad might come through it, and a real town would develop, making the speculators staggeringly rich. By these devices a man named Sanborn once owned Amarillo.[1]

But railroad tracks are narrow and the state of Texas is very, very wide. For every Wichita Falls or Lubbock there were a dozen College Mounds or Belchervilles,[2] bleached, unpeopled burgs that receded quietly into the dust, taking with them large amounts of speculators' money.

Still, the speculators kept right on bucking the odds and depositing empty towns in the middle of nowhere. Why did they do it? Two reasons — reasons that might be said to summarize the central fact of American economic history and that go a fair way toward explaining what is perhaps the central strand of the national character.

The first reason was simply that the possible returns were so enormous as to partake of the surreal, to create a climate in which ordinary logic and prudence did not seem to apply. In a boom like that of real estate when the railroad barreled through, long shots that might pay one hundred thousand to one seemed worth a bet.

The second reason, more pertinent here, is that there was a presumption that America would *keep on* booming — if not forever, then at least longer than it made sense to worry about. There would always be another gold rush, another Homestead Act, another oil strike. The next generation would always ferret out opportunities that would be still more lavish than any that had gone before. America *was* those opportunities. This was an article not just of faith, but of strategy. You banked on the next windfall, you staked your hopes and even your self-esteem on it, and this led to a national turn of mind that might usefully be thought of as the habit of more.

A century, maybe two centuries, before anyone had heard the term *baby boomer,* much less *yuppie,* the habit of more had been instilled as the operative truth among the economically ambitious. The habit of more seemed to suggest that there was no such thing as getting wiped out in America. A fortune lost in Texas might be recouped in Colorado. Funds frittered away on grazing land where nothing grew might flood back in as silver. There was always a second chance, or always seemed to be, in this land where growth was destiny and where expansion and purpose were the same.

The key was the frontier, not just as a matter of acreage, but as idea. Vast, varied, rough as rocks, America was the place where one never quite came to the end. Ben Franklin explained it to Europe even before the Revolutionary War had finished: America offered new chances to those "who, in their own Countries, where all the Lands [were] fully oc-

---

1. For a fuller account of railroad-related land speculation in Texas, see F. Stanley, *Story of the Texas Panhandle Railroads* (Borger, Tex.: Hess Publishing Co., 1976).

2. T. Lindsay Baker, *Ghost Towns of Texas* (Norman, Okla.: University of Oklahoma Press, 1986).

cupied . . . could never [emerge] from the poor Condition wherein they were born."[3]

So central was this awareness of vacant space and its link to economic promise that Frederick Jackson Turner, the historian who set the tone for much of the twentieth century's understanding of the American past, would write that it was "not the constitution, but free land . . . [that] made the democratic type of society in America."[4] Good laws mattered; an accountable government mattered; ingenuity and hard work mattered. But those things were, so to speak, an overlay on the natural, geographic America that was simply *there,* and whose vast and beckoning possibilities seemed to generate the ambition and the sometimes reckless liberty that would fill it. First and foremost, it was open space that provided "the freedom of the individual to rise under conditions of social mobility."[5]

Open space generated not just ambition, but metaphor. As early as 1835, Tocqueville was extrapolating from the fact of America's emptiness to the observation that "no natural boundary seems to be set to the efforts of man."[6] Nor was any limit placed on what he might accomplish, since, in that heyday of the Protestant ethic, a person's rewards were taken to be quite strictly proportionate to his labors.

Frontier; opportunity; more. This has been the American trinity from the very start. The frontier was the backdrop and also the raw material for the streak of economic booms. The booms became the goad and also the justification for the myriad gambles and for Americans' famous optimism. The optimism, in turn, shaped the schemes and visions that were sometimes noble, sometimes appalling, always bold. The frontier, as reality and as symbol, is what has shaped the American way of doing things and the American sense of what's worth doing.

But there has been one further corollary to the legacy of the frontier, with its promise of ever-expanding opportunities: given that the goal—a realistic goal for most of our history—was *more,* Americans have been somewhat backward in adopting values, hopes, ambitions that have to do with things *other than* more. In America, a sense of quality has lagged far behind a sense of scale. An ideal of contentment has yet to take root in soil traditionally more hospitable to an ideal of restless striving. The ethic of decency has been upstaged by the ethic of success. The concept of growth has been applied almost exclusively to things that can be measured, counted, weighed. And the hunger for those things that are unmeasurable but fine—the sorts of accomplishment that cannot be

---

3. Benjamin Franklin, "Information to Those Who Would Remove to America," in *The Autobiography and Other Writings* (New York: Penguin Books, 1986), 242.

4. Frederick Jackson Turner, *The Frontier in American History* (Melbourne, Fla.: Krieger, 1976 [reprint of 1920 edition]), 293.

5. Ibid., 266.

6. Tocqueville, *Democracy in America.*

undone by circumstance or a shift in social fashion, the kind of serenity that cannot be shattered by tomorrow's headline—has gone largely unfulfilled, and even unacknowledged.

2

If the supply of more went on forever, perhaps that wouldn't matter   15
very much. Expansion could remain a goal unto itself, and would continue to generate a value system based on bulk rather than on nuance, on quantities of money rather than on quality of life, on "progress" itself rather than on a sense of what the progress was for. But what if, over time, there was less more to be had?

That is the essential situation of America today.

Let's keep things in proportion: The country is not running out of wealth, drive, savvy, or opportunities. We are not facing imminent ruin, and neither panic nor gloom is called for. But there have been ample indications over the past two decades that we are running out of more.

Consider productivity growth—according to many economists, the single most telling and least distortable gauge of changes in real wealth. From 1947 to 1965, productivity in the private sector (adjusted, as are all the following figures, for inflation) was advancing, on average, by an annual 3.3 percent. This means, simply, that each hour of work performed by a specimen American worker contributed 3.3 cents worth or more to every American dollar every year; whether we saved it or spent it, that increment went into a national kitty of ever-enlarging aggregate wealth. Between 1965 and 1972, however, the "more-factor" decreased to 2.4 percent a year, and from 1972 to 1977 it slipped further, to 1.6 percent. By the early 1980s, productivity growth was at a virtual standstill, crawling along at 0.2 percent for the five years ending in 1982.[7] Through the middle years of the 1980s, the numbers rebounded somewhat—but by then the gains were being neutralized by the gargantuan carrying costs on the national debt.[8]

Inevitably, this decline in the national stockpile of more held consequences for the individual wallet.[9] During the 1950s, Americans' average

---

7. These figures are taken from the Council of Economic Advisers, *Economic Report of the President,* February 1984, 267.

8. For a lucid and readable account of the meaning and implications of our reservoir of red ink, see Lawrence Malkin, *The National Debt* (New York: Henry Holt and Co., 1987). Through no fault of Malkin's, many of his numbers are already obsolete, but his explanation of who owes what to whom, and what it means, remains sound and even entertaining in a bleak sort of way.

9. The figures in this paragraph and the next are from "The Average Guy Takes It on the Chin," *New York Times,* 13 July 1986, sec. 3.

hourly earnings were humping ahead at a gratifying 2.5 percent each year. By the late seventies, that figure stood just where productivity growth had come to stand, at a dispiriting 0.2 cents on the dollar. By the first half of the eighties, the Reagan "recovery" notwithstanding, real hourly wages were actually moving backwards—declining at an average annual rate of 0.3 percent.

Compounding the shortage of more was an unfortunate but crucial demographic fact. Real wealth was nearly ceasing to expand just at the moment when the members of that unprecedented population bulge known as the baby boom were entering what should have been their peak years of income expansion. A working man or woman who was thirty years old in 1949 could expect to see his or her real earnings burgeon by 63 percent by age forty. In 1959, a thirty-year-old could still look forward to a gain of 49 percent by his or her fortieth birthday.

But what about the person who turned thirty in 1973? By the time that worker turned forty, his or her real earnings had shrunk by a percentage point. For all the blather about yuppies with their beach houses, BMWs, and radicchio salads, and even factoring in those isolated tens of thousands making ludicrous sums in consulting firms or on Wall Street, the fact is that between 1979 and 1983 real earnings of all Americans between the ages of twenty-five and thirty-four actually declined by 14 percent.[10] The *New York Times,* well before the stock market crash put the kibosh on eighties confidence, summed up the implications of this downturn by observing that "for millions of breadwinners, the American dream is becoming the impossible dream."[11]

Now, it is not our main purpose here to detail the ups and downs of the American economy. Our aim, rather, is to consider the effects of those ups and downs on people's goals, values, sense of their place in the world. What happens at that shadowy juncture where economic prospects meld with personal choice? What sorts of insights and adjustments are called for so that economic ups and downs can be dealt with gracefully?

Fact one in this connection is that, if America's supply of more is in fact diminishing, American values will have to shift and broaden to fill the gap where the expectation of almost automatic gains used to be. Something more durable will have to replace the fat but fragile bubble that had been getting frailer these past two decades and that finally popped—a tentative, partial pop—on October 19, 1987. A different sort of growth—ultimately, a growth in responsibility and happiness—will have to fulfill our need to believe that our possibilities are still expanding.

20

---

10. See, for example, "The Year of the Yuppie," *Newsweek,* 31 December 1984, 16.

11. "The Average Guy."

The transition to that new view of progress will take some fancy stepping, because, at least since the end of World War II, simple economic growth has stood, in the American psyche, as the best available substitute for the literal frontier. The economy has *been* the frontier. Instead of more space, we have had more money. Rather than measuring progress in terms of geographical expansion, we have measured it by expansion in our standard of living. Economics has become the metaphor on which we pin our hopes of open space and second chances.

The poignant part is that the literal frontier did not pass yesterday: it has not existed for a hundred years. But the frontier's promise has become so much a part of us that we have not been willing to let the concept die. We have kept the frontier mythology going by invocation, by allusion, by hype.

It is not a coincidence that John F. Kennedy dubbed his political program the New Frontier. It is not mere linguistic accident that makes us speak of Frontiers of Science or of psychedelic drugs as carrying one to Frontiers of Perception. We glorify fads and fashions by calling them Frontiers of Taste. Nuclear energy has been called the Last Frontier; solar energy has been called the Last Frontier. Outer space has been called the Last Frontier; the oceans have been called the Last Frontier. Even the suburbs, those blandest and least adventurous of places, have been wryly described as the crabgrass frontier.[12]

What made all these usages plausible was their being linked to the image of the American economy as an endlessly fertile continent whose boundaries never need be reached, a domain that could expand in perpetuity, a gigantic playing field that would never run out of room and on which the game would get forever bigger and more filled with action. This was the frontier that would not vanish.

It is worth noting that people in other countries (with the possible exception of that other America, Australia) do not talk about frontier this way. In Europe, and in most of Africa and Asia, "frontier" connotes, at worst, a place of barbed wire and men with rifles, and at best, a neutral junction where one changes currency while passing from one fixed system into another. Frontier, for most of the world's people, does not suggest growth, expanse, or opportunity.

For Americans, it does, and always has. This is one of the things that sets America apart from other places and makes American attitudes different from those of other people. It is why, from *Bonanza* to the Sierra Club, the notion or even the fantasy of empty horizons and untapped resources has always evoked in the American heart both passion and wist-

---

12. With the suburbs again taking on a sort of fascination, this phrase was resurrected as the title of a 1985 book — *Crabgrass Frontier: The Suburbanization of America,* by Kenneth T. Jackson (Oxford University Press).

fulness. And it is why the fear that the economic frontier—our last, best version of the Wild West—may finally be passing creates in us not only money worries but also a crisis of morale and even of purpose.

3

It might seem strange to call the 1980s an era of nostalgia. The 30 decade, after all, has been more usually described in terms of coolness, pragmatism, and a blithe innocence of history. But the eighties, unawares, were nostalgic for frontiers; and the disappointment of that nostalgia had much to do with the time's greed, narrowness, and strange want of joy. The fear that the world may not be a big enough playground for the full exercise of one's energies and yearnings, and worse, the fear that the playground is being fenced off and will no longer expand—these are real worries and they have had consequences. The eighties were an object lesson in how people play the game when there is an awful and unspoken suspicion that the game is winding down.

It was ironic that the yuppies came to be so reviled for their vaunting ambition and outsized expectations, as if they'd invented the habit of more, when in fact they'd only inherited it the way a fetus picks up an addiction in the womb. The craving was there in the national bloodstream, a remnant of the frontier, and the baby boomers, described in childhood as "the luckiest generation,"[13] found themselves, as young adults, in the melancholy position of wrestling with a two-hundred-year dependency on a drug that was now in short supply.

True, the 1980s raised the clamor for more to new heights of shrillness, insistence, and general obnoxiousness, but this, it can be argued, was in the nature of a final binge, the storm before the calm. America, though fighting the perception every inch of the way, was coming to realize that it was not a preordained part of the natural order that one should be richer every year. If it happened, that was nice. But who had started the flimsy and pernicious rumor that it was normal?

Reading the Text

1. Summarize in a paragraph how, according to Shames, the frontier functions as a symbol of American consciousness.
2. What connections does Shames make between America's frontier history and consumer behavior?
3. Why does Shames term the 1980s "an era of nostalgia" (para. 30)?

---

13. Thomas Hine, *Populuxe* (New York: Alfred A. Knopf, 1986), 15.

Reading the Signs

1. Shames asserts that Americans have been influenced by the frontier belief "that America would *keep on* booming" (para. 8). Do you feel that this belief continues to be influential into the twenty-first century? Write an essay arguing for your position.
2. Shames claims that, because of the desire for more, "the ethic of decency has been upstaged by the ethic of success" (para. 14) in America. In class, form teams that either agree or disagree with this position, and debate the validity of Shames's claim.
3. Read or review Joan Kron's "The Semiotics of Home Decor" (p. 94) and Stuart Ewen's "Hard Bodies" (p. 79). How are Martin J. Davidson and Raymond H—— influenced by the frontier myth that Shames describes?
4. In groups, discuss whether street gang members share the desire for "more" that Shames claims is a distinctly American trait. Then write an essay in which you argue whether you believe gangs can be called "typically American."

ANNE NORTON

The Signs of Shopping

ıı

> *Shopping malls are more than places to shop, just as mail-order catalogues are more than simple lists of goods. Both malls and catalogues are coded systems that not only encourage us to buy but, more profoundly, help us to construct our very sense of identity, as in the J. Peterman catalogue that "constructs the reader as a man of rugged outdoor interests, taste, and money." In this selection from* The Republic of Signs *(1993), Anne Norton (b. 1954), a professor of political science at the University of Pennsylvania, analyzes the many ways in which malls, catalogues, and home shopping networks sell you what they want by telling you who you are. Norton's other books include* Alternative Americas *(1986) and* Reflections on Political Identity *(1988).*

Shopping at the Mall

The mall has been the subject of innumerable debates. Created out of the modernist impulse for planning and the centralization of public activity, the mall has become the distinguishing sign of suburban decentralization, springing up in unplanned profusion. Intended to restore something of the lost unity of city life to the suburbs, the mall has come to export styles and strategies to stores at the urban center. Deplored by modernists, it is regarded with affection only by their postmodern foes. Ruled more by their content than by their creators' avowed intent, the once sleek futurist shells have taken on a certain aura of postmodern playfulness and popular glitz.

The mall is a favorite subject for the laments of cultural conservatives and others critical of the culture of consumption. It is indisputably the cultural locus of commodity fetishism. It has been noticed, however, by others of a less condemnatory disposition that the mall has something of the mercado, or the agora, about it. It is both a place of meeting for the young and one of the rare places where young and old go together. People of different races and classes, different occupations, different levels of education meet there. As M. Pressdee and John Fiske note, however, though the mall appears to be a public place, it is not. Neither freedom of speech nor freedom of assembly is permitted there. Those who own and manage malls restrict what comes within their confines. Controversial displays, by stores or customers or the plethora of organizations and agencies that present themselves in the open spaces of the mall, are not permitted. These seemingly public spaces conceal a pervasive private authority.

The mall exercises its thorough and discreet authority not only in the regulation of behavior but in the constitution of our visible, inaudible, public discourse. It is the source of those commodities through which we speak of our identities, our opinions, our desires. It is a focus for the discussion of style among peripheral consumers. Adolescents, particularly female adolescents, are inclined to spend a good deal of time at the mall. They spend, indeed, more time than money. They acquire not simple commodities (they may come home with many, few, or none) but a well-developed sense of the significance of those commodities. In prowling the mall they embed themselves in a lexicon of American culture. They find themselves walking through a dictionary. Stores hang a variety of identities on their racks and mannequins. Their window displays provide elaborate scenarios conveying not only what the garment is but what the garment means.

A display in the window of Polo provides an embarrassment of semiotic riches. Everyone, from the architecture critic at the *New York Times* to kids in the hall of a Montana high school, knows what *Ralph Lauren* means. The polo mallet and the saddle, horses and dogs, the broad lawns of Newport, Kennebunkport, old photographs in silver frames, the evocation of age, of ancestry and Anglophilia, of indolence and the Ivy League, evoke the upper class. Indian blankets and buffalo plaids, cowboy hats and Western saddles, evoke a past distinct from England but nevertheless determinedly Anglo. The supposedly arcane and suspect arts of deconstruction are deployed easily, effortlessly, by the readers of these cultural texts.

Walking from one window to another, observing one another,   5
shoppers, especially the astute and observant adolescents, acquire a facility
with the language of commodities. They learn not only words but a
grammar. Shop windows employ elements of sarcasm and irony, strategies of inversion and allusion. They provide models of elegant, economical, florid, and prosaic expression. They teach composition.

The practice of shopping is, however, more than instructive. It has
long been the occasion for women to escape the confines of their homes
and enjoy the companionship of other women. The construction of
woman's role as one of provision for the needs of the family legitimated
her exit. It provided an occasion for women to spend long stretches of
time in the company of their friends, without the presence of their husbands. They could exchange information and reflections, ask advice, and
receive support. As their daughters grew, they would be brought increasingly within this circle, included in shopping trips and lunches with their
mothers. These would form, reproduce, and restructure communities of
taste.

The construction of identity and the enjoyment of friendship outside the presence of men was thus effected through a practice that constructed women as consumers and subjected them to the conventions of
the marketplace. Insofar as they were dependent on their husbands for
money, they were dependent on their husbands for the means to the
construction of their identities. They could not represent themselves
through commodities without the funds men provided, nor could they,
without money, participate in the community of women that was realized in "going shopping." Their identities were made contingent not
only on the possession of property but on the recognition of dependence.

Insofar as shopping obliges dependent women to recognize their dependence, it also opens up the possibility of subversion.[1] The housewife
who shops for pleasure takes time away from her husband, her family,
and her house and claims it for herself. Constantly taught that social
order and her private happiness depend on intercourse between men and
women, she chooses the company of women instead. She engages with
women in an activity marked as feminine, and she enjoys it. When she
spends money, she exercises an authority over property that law and custom may deny her. If she has no resources independent of her husband,
this may be the only authority over property she is able to exercise.
When she buys things her husband does not approve—or does not

---

1. Nuanced and amusing accounts of shopping as subversion are provided in John
Fiske's analyses of popular culture, particularly *Reading the Popular* (Boston: Unwin
Hyman [now Routledge], 1989), pp. 13–42.

know—of she further subverts an order that leaves control over property in her husband's hands.[2]

Her choice of feminine company and a feminine pursuit may involve additional subversions. As Fiske and Pressdee recognize, shopping without buying and shopping for bargains have a subversive quality. This is revealed, in a form that gives it additional significance, when a saleswoman leans forward and tells a shopper, "Don't buy that today, it will be on sale on Thursday." Here solidarity of gender (and often of class) overcome, however partially and briefly, the imperatives of the economic order.

Shoppers who look, as most shoppers do, for bargains, and sales-   10
people who warn shoppers of impending sales, see choices between commodities as something other than the evidence and the exercise of freedom. They see covert direction and exploitation; they see the withholding of information and the manipulation of knowledge. They recognize that they are on enemy terrain and that their shopping can be, in Michel de Certeau's[3] term, a "guerrilla raid." This recognition in practice of the presence of coercion in choice challenges the liberal conflation of choice and consent.

Shopping at Home

Shopping is an activity that has overcome its geographic limits. One need no longer go to the store to shop. Direct mail catalogues, with their twenty-four-hour phone numbers for ordering, permit people to shop where and when they please. An activity that once obliged one to go out into the public sphere, with its diverse array of semiotic messages, can now be done at home. An activity that once obliged one to be in company, if not in conversation, with one's compatriots can now be conducted in solitude.

The activity of catalogue shopping, and the pursuit of individuality, are not, however, wholly solitary. The catalogues invest their commodities with vivid historical and social references. The J. Peterman catalogue, for example, constructs the reader as a man of rugged outdoor interests, taste, and money.[4] He wears "The Owner's Hat" or "Hemingway's Cap," a leather flight jacket or the classic "Horseman's Duster," and

---

2. See R. Bowlby, *Just Looking: Consumer Culture in Dreiser, Gissing, and Zola* (London: Methuen, 1985), p. 22, for another discussion and for an example of the recommendation of this strategy by Elizabeth Cady Stanton in the 1850s.

3. **Michel de Certeau** (1925–1986)   French social scientist and semiologist who played an important role in the development of contemporary cultural studies. — EDS.

4. I have read several of these. I cite *The J. Peterman Company Owner's Manual No. 5,* from the J. Peterman Company, 2444 Palumbo Drive, Lexington, Ky. 40509.

various other garments identified with the military, athletes, and European imperialism. The copy for "The Owner's Hat" naturalizes class distinctions and, covertly, racism:

> Some of us work on the plantation.
> Some of us own the plantation.
> Facts are facts.
> This hat is for those who own the plantation.[5]

Gender roles are strictly delineated. The copy for a skirt captioned "Women's Legs" provides a striking instance of the construction of the gaze as male, of women as the object of the gaze:

> just when you think you see something, a shape you think you recognize, it's gone and then it begins to return and then it's gone and of course you can't take your eyes off it.
>   Yes, the long slow motion of women's legs. Whatever happened to those things at carnivals that blew air up into girls' skirts and you could spend hours watching.[6]

"You," of course, are male. There is also the lace blouse captioned "Mystery": "lace says yes at the same time it says no."[7] Finally, there are notes of imperialist nostalgia: the Sheapherd's Hotel (Cairo) bathrobe and white pants for "the bush" and "the humid hell-holes of Bombay and Calcutta."[8]

> It may no longer be unforgivable to say that the British left a few good things behind in India and in Kenya, Singapore, Borneo, etc., not the least of which was their Englishness.[9]

As Paul Smith observes, in his reading of their catalogues, the *Banana Republic* has also made capital out of imperial nostalgia.[10]

The communities catalogues create are reinforced by shared mailing lists. The constructed identities are reified and elaborated in an array of

---

5. Ibid., p. 5. The hat is also identified with the Canal Zone, "successfully bidding at Beaulieu," intimidation, and LBOs. Quite a hat. It might be argued against my reading that the J. Peterman Company also offers the "Coal Miner's Bag" and a mailbag. However, since the descriptive points of reference on color and texture and experience for these bags are such things as the leather seats of Jaguars, and driving home in a Bentley, I feel fairly confident in my reading.

6. Ibid., p. 3. See also pp. 15 and 17 for instances of women as the object of the male gaze. The identification of the gaze with male sexuality is unambiguous here as well.

7. Ibid., p. 17.

8. Ibid., pp. 7, 16, 20, 21, 37, and 50.

9. Ibid., p. 20.

10. Paul Smith, "Visiting the Banana Republic," in *Universal Abandon?* ed. Andrew Ross for *Social Text* (Minneapolis: University of Minnesota Press, 1988), pp. 128–48.

semiotically related catalogues. One who orders a spade or a packet of seeds will be constructed as a gardener and receive a deluge of catalogues from plant and garden companies. The companies themselves may expand their commodities to appeal to different manifestations of the identities they respond to and construct. Smith and Hawken, a company that sells gardening supplies with an emphasis on aesthetics and environmental concern, puts out a catalogue in which a group of people diverse in age and in their ethnicity wear the marketed clothes while gardening, painting, or throwing pots. Williams-Sonoma presents its catalogue not as a catalogue of things for cooking but as "A Catalog for Cooks." The catalogue speaks not to need but to the construction of identity.

The Nature Company dedicates its spring 1990 catalogue "to trees," 15 endorses Earth Day, and continues to link itself to *The Nature Conservancy* through posters and a program in which you buy a tree for a forest restoration project. Here, a not-for-profit agency is itself commodified, adding to the value of the commodities offered in the catalogue.[11] In this catalogue, consumption is not merely a means for the construction and representation of the self, it is also a means for political action. Several commodities are offered as "A Few Things You Can Do" to save the earth: a string shopping bag, a solar battery recharger, a home newspaper recycler. Socially conscious shopping is a liberal practice in every sense. It construes shopping as a form of election, in which one votes for good commodities or refuses one's vote to candidates whose practices are ethically suspect. In this respect, it reveals its adherence to the same ideological presuppositions that structure television's Home Shopping Network and other cable television sales shows.

Both politically informed purchasing and television sales conflate the free market and the electoral process. Dollars are identified with votes, purchases with endorsements. Both offer those who engage in them the possibility to "talk back" to manufacturers. In television sales shows this ability to talk back is both more thoroughly elaborated and more thoroughly exploited. Like the "elections" on MTV that invite viewers to vote for their favorite video by calling a number on their telephones, they permit those who watch to respond, to speak, and to be heard by the television. Their votes, of course, cost money. On MTV, as in the stores, you can buy as much speech as you can afford. On the Home Shopping Network, the purchase of speech becomes complicated by multiple layers and inversions.

Each commodity is introduced. It is invested by the announcer with a number of desirable qualities. The value of these descriptions of the commodities is enhanced by the construction of the announcer as a

---

11. *The Nature Company Catalog,* The Nature Company, P.O. Box 2310, Berkeley, Calif. 94702, Spring 1990. See pp. 1–2 and order form insert between pp. 18 and 19. Note also the entailed donation to Designs for Conservation on p. 18.

mediator not only between the commodity and the consumer but between the salespeople and the consumer. The announcer is not, the format suggests, a salesperson (though of course the announcer is). He or
she is an announcer, describing goods that others have offered for sale.
Television claims to distinguish itself by making objects visible to the
eyes, but it is largely through the ears that these commodities are constructed. The consumer, in purchasing the commodity, purchases the
commodity, what the commodity signifies, and, as we say, "buys the
salesperson's line." The consumer may also acquire the ability to speak
on television. Each purchase is recorded and figures as a vote in a rough
plebiscite, confirming the desirability of the object. Although the purchase figures are announced as if they were confirming votes, it is, of
course, impossible to register one's rejection of the commodity. Certain
consumers get a little more (or rather less) for their money. They are invited to explain the virtue of the commodity—and their purchase—to
the announcer and the audience. The process of production, of both the
consumers and that which they consume, continues in this apology for
consumption.

The semiotic identification of consumption as an American activity,
indeed, a patriotic one, is made with crude enthusiasm on the Home
Shopping Network and other video sales shows. Red, white, and blue
figure prominently in set designs and borders framing the television
screen. The Home Shopping Network presents its authorities in an office
conspicuously adorned with a picture of the Statue of Liberty.[12] Yet the
messages that the Home Shopping Network sends its customers—that
you can buy as much speech as you can afford, that you are recognized
by others in accordance with your capacity to consume—do much to
subvert the connection between capitalism and democracy on which this
semiotic identification depends.

Reading the Text

1. What does Norton mean when she claims that the suburban shopping
   mall appears to be a public place but in fact is not?
2. What is Norton's interpretation of Ralph Lauren's Polo line?
3. How is shopping a subversive activity for women, according to Norton?
4. How do mail-order catalogues create communities of shoppers, in Norton's view?
5. What are the political messages sent by the Home Shopping Network, as
   Norton sees them, and how are they communicated?

---

12. This moment from the Home Shopping Network was generously brought to
my attention, on videotape, by Peter Bregman, a student in my American Studies class
of fall 1988, at Princeton University.

Reading the Signs

1. Visit a local shopping mall, and study the window displays, focusing on stores intended for one group of consumers (teenagers, for instance, or children). Then write an essay in which you analyze how the displays convey what the stores' products "mean."
2. Bring a few product catalogues to class, and then in small groups compare the kind of consumer "constructed" by the catalogues' cultural images and allusions. Do you note any patterns associated with gender, ethnicity, or age group? Report your group's conclusions to the whole class.
3. Interview five women of different age groups on their motivations and activities when they shop in a mall. Then use the results of your interviews as evidence in an essay in which you support, complicate, or refute Norton's assertion that shopping constitutes a subversive activity for women.
4. Watch an episode of the Home Shopping Network (your school's media library may be able to provide you access to cable TV), and write a semiotic analysis of the ways in which products are presented to consumers.
5. Select a single mail-order catalogue, and write a detailed semiotic interpretation of the identity it constructs for its market.
6. Visit the website for a major store chain (for instance, **http://www .thegap.com**), and study how it "moves" the consumer through it. How does the site induce you to consume?

THOMAS HINE

What's in a Package

‖‖

What's in a package? According to Thomas Hine (b. 1947), a great deal, perhaps even more than what is actually inside *the package. From the cereal boxes you find in the supermarket to the perfume bottles sold at Tiffany's, the shape and design of the packages that contain just about every product we consume have been carefully calculated to stimulate consumption. Indeed, as Hine explains in this excerpt from* The Total Package: The Evolution and Secret Meanings of Boxes, Bottles, Cans, and Tubes *(1995), "for manufacturers, packaging is the crucial final payoff to a marketing campaign." The architecture and design critic for the* Philadelphia Inquirer, *Hine has also published* Populuxe *(1986), on American design and culture, and* Facing Tomorrow *(1991), on past and current attitudes toward the future.*

When you put yourself behind a shopping cart, the world changes. You become an active consumer, and you are moving through environments—the supermarket, the discount store, the warehouse club, the home center—that have been made for you.

During the thirty minutes you spend on an average trip to the supermarket, about thirty thousand different products vie to win your attention and ultimately to make you believe in their promise. When the door opens, automatically, before you, you enter an arena where your emotions and your appetites are in play, and a walk down the aisle is an exercise in self-definition. Are you a good parent, a good provider? Do you have time to do all you think you should, and would you be interested in a shortcut? Are you worried about your health and that of those you love? Do you care about the environment? Do you appreciate the finer things in life? Is your life what you would like it to be? Are you enjoying what you've accomplished? Wouldn't you really like something chocolate?

Few experiences in contemporary life offer the visual intensity of a Safeway, a Krogers, a Pathmark, or a Piggly Wiggly. No marketplace in the world—not Marrakesh or Calcutta or Hong Kong—offers so many different goods with such focused salesmanship as your neighborhood supermarket, where you're exposed to a thousand different products a minute. No wonder it's tiring to shop.

There are, however, some major differences between the supermarket and a traditional marketplace. The cacophony of a traditional market has given way to programmed, innocuous music, punctuated by enthusiastically intoned commercials. A stroll through a traditional market offers an array of sensuous aromas; if you are conscious of smelling something in a supermarket, there is a problem. The life and death matter of eating, expressed in traditional markets by the sale of vegetables with stems and roots and by hanging animal carcasses, is purged from the supermarket, where food is processed somewhere else, or at least trimmed out of sight.

But the most fundamental difference between a traditional market and the places through which you push your cart is that in a modern retail setting nearly all the selling is done without people. The product is totally dissociated from the personality of any particular person selling it—with the possible exception of those who appear in its advertising. The supermarket purges sociability, which slows down sales. It allows manufacturers to control the way they present their products to the world. It replaces people with packages.

Packages are an inescapable part of modern life. They are omnipresent and invisible, deplored and ignored. During most of your waking moments, there are one or more packages within your field of vision. Packages are so ubiquitous that they slip beneath conscious notice, though many packages are designed so that people will respond to them even if they're not paying attention.

Once you begin pushing the shopping cart, it matters little whether you are in a supermarket, a discount store, or a warehouse club. The important thing is that you are among packages: expressive packages intended to engage your emotions, ingenious packages that make a product useful, informative packages that help you understand what you want and what you're getting. Historically, packages are what made self-service retailing possible, and in turn such stores increased the number and variety of items people buy. Now a world without packages is unimaginable.

Packages lead multiple lives. They preserve and protect, allowing people to make use of things that were produced far away, or a while ago. And they are potently expressive. They assure that an item arrives unspoiled, and they help those who use the item feel good about it.

We share our homes with hundreds of packages, mostly in the bathroom and kitchen, the most intimate, body-centered rooms of the house. Some packages—a perfume flacon, a ketchup bottle, a candy wrapper, a beer can—serve as permanent landmarks in people's lives that outlast homes, careers, or spouses. But packages embody change, not just in their age-old promise that their contents are new and improved, but in their attempt to respond to changing tastes and achieve new standards of convenience. Packages record changing hairstyles and changing lifestyles. Even social policy issues are reflected. Nearly unopenable tamper-proof seals and other forms of closures testify to the fragility of the social contract, and the susceptibility of the great mass of people to the destructive acts of a very few. It was a mark of rising environmental consciousness when containers recently began to make a novel promise: "less packaging."

For manufacturers, packaging is the crucial final payoff to a marketing campaign. Sophisticated packaging is one of the chief ways people find the confidence to buy. It can also give a powerful image to products and commodities that are in themselves characterless. In many cases, the shopper has been prepared for the shopping experience by lush, colorful print advertisements, thirty-second television minidramas, radio jingles, and coupon promotions. But the package makes the final sales pitch, seals the commitment, and gets itself placed in the shopping cart. Advertising leads consumers into temptation. Packaging *is* the temptation. In many cases it is what makes the product possible.   10

But the package is also useful to the shopper. It is a tool for simplifying and speeding decisions. Packages promise, and usually deliver, predictability. One reason you don't think about packages is that you don't need to. The candy bar, the aspirin, the baking powder, or the beer in the old familiar package may, at times, be touted as new and improved, but it will rarely be very different.

You put the package into your cart, or not, usually without really having focused on the particular product or its many alternatives. But sometimes you do examine the package. You read the label carefully, looking at what the product promises, what it contains, what it warns. You might even look at the package itself and judge whether it will, for example, reseal to keep a product fresh. You might consider how a cosmetic container will look on your dressing table, or you might think about whether someone might have tampered with it or whether it can be easily recycled. The possibility of such scrutiny is one of the things that make each detail of the package so important.

The environment through which you push your shopping cart is extraordinary because of the amount of attention that has been paid to the packages that line the shelves. Most contemporary environments are landscapes of inattention. In housing developments, malls, highways, office buildings, even furniture, design ideas are few and spread very thin. At the supermarket, each box and jar, stand-up pouch and squeeze bottle, each can and bag and tube and spray has been very carefully considered. Designers have worked and reworked the design on their computers and tested mock-ups on the store shelves. Refinements are measured in millimeters.

All sorts of retail establishments have been redefined by packaging. Drugs and cosmetics were among the earliest packaged products, and most drugstores now resemble small supermarkets. Liquor makers use packaging to add a veneer of style to the intrinsic allure of intoxication, and some sell their bottle rather than the drink. It is no accident that vodka, the most characterless of spirits, has the highest-profile packages. The local gas station sells sandwiches and soft drinks rather than tires and motor oil, and in turn, automotive products have been attractively repackaged for sales at supermarkets, warehouse clubs, and home centers.

With its thousands of images and messages, the supermarket is as visually dense, if not as beautiful, as a Gothic cathedral. It is as complex and as predatory as a tropical rain forest. It is more than a person can possibly take in during an ordinary half-hour shopping trip. No wonder a significant percentage of people who need to wear eyeglasses don't wear them when they're shopping, and some researchers have spoken of the trance-like state that pushing a cart through this environment induces. The paradox here is that the visual intensity that overwhelms shoppers is precisely the thing that makes the design of packages so crucial. Just because you're not looking at a package doesn't mean you don't see it. Most of the time, you see far more than a container and a label. You see a personality, an attitude toward life, perhaps even a set of beliefs.

The shopper's encounter with the product on the shelf is, however, only the beginning of the emotional life cycle of the package. The package is very important in the moment when the shopper recognizes it either as an old friend or a new temptation. Once the product is brought home, the package seems to disappear, as the quality or usefulness of the product it contains becomes paramount. But in fact, many packages are still selling even at home, enticing those who have bought them to take them out of the cupboard, the closet, or the refrigerator and consume their contents. Then once the product has been used up, and the package is empty, it becomes suddenly visible once more. This time, though, it is trash that must be discarded or recycled. This instant of disposal is the time when people are most aware of packages. It is a negative moment, like the end of a love affair, and what's left seems to be a horrid waste.

The forces driving package design are not primarily aesthetic. Market researchers have conducted surveys of consumer wants and needs, and consultants have studied photographs of families' kitchen cupboards and medicine chests to get a sense of how products are used. Test subjects have been tied into pieces of heavy apparatus that measure their eye movement, their blood pressure or body temperature, when subjected to different packages. Psychologists get people to talk about the packages in order to get a sense of their innermost feelings about what they want. Government regulators and private health and safety advocates worry over package design and try to make it truthful. Stock-market analysts worry about how companies are managing their "brand equity," that combination of perceived value and consumer loyalty that is expressed in advertising but embodied in packaging. The retailer is paying attention to the packages in order to weed out the ones that don't sell or aren't sufficiently profitable. The use of supermarket scanners generates information on the profitability of every cubic inch of the store. Space on the supermarket shelf is some of the most valuable real estate in the world, and there are always plenty of new packaged products vying for display.

Packaging performs a series of disparate tasks. It protects its contents from contamination and spoilage. It makes it easier to transport and store goods. It provides uniform measuring of contents. By allowing brands to be created and standardized, it makes advertising meaningful and large-scale distribution possible. Special kinds of packages, with dispensing caps, sprays, and other convenience features, make products more usable. Packages serve as symbols both of their contents and of a way of life. And just as they can very powerfully communicate the satisfaction a product offers, they are equally potent symbols of wastefulness once the product is gone.

Most people use dozens of packages each day and discard hundreds of them each year. The growth of mandatory recycling programs has made people increasingly aware of packages, which account in the United States for about forty-three million tons, or just under 30 percent of all refuse discarded. While forty-three million tons of stuff is hardly insignificant, repeated surveys have shown that the public perceives that far more than 30 percent—indeed, nearly all—their garbage consists of packaging. This perception creates a political problem for the packaging industry, but it also demonstrates the power of packaging. It is symbolic. It creates an emotional relationship. Bones and wasted food (13 million tons), grass clippings and yard waste (thirty-one million tons), or even magazines and newspapers (fourteen million tons) do not feel as wasteful as empty vessels that once contained so much promise.

Packaging is a cultural phenomenon, which means that it works dif-   20
ferently in different cultures. The United States has been a good market for packages since it was first settled and has been an important innovator of packaging technology and culture. Moreover, American packaging is part of an international culture of modernity and consumption. At its deepest level, the culture of American packaging deals with the issue of surviving among strangers in a new world. This is an emotion with which anyone who has been touched by modernity can identify. In lives buffeted by change, people seek the safety and reassurance that packaged products offer. American packaging, which has always sought to appeal to large numbers of diverse people, travels better than that of most other cultures.

But the similar appearance of supermarkets throughout the world should not be interpreted as the evidence of a single, global consumer culture. In fact, most companies that do business internationally redesign their packages for each market. This is done partly to satisfy local regulations and adapt to available products and technologies. But the principal reason is that people in different places have different expectations and make different uses of packaging.

The United States and Japan, the world's two leading industrial powers, have almost opposite approaches to packaging. Japan's is far more elaborate than America's, and it is shaped by rituals of respect and centuries-old traditions of wrapping and presentation. Packaging is explicitly recognized as an expression of culture in Japan and largely ignored in America. Japanese packaging is designed to be appreciated; American packaging is calculated to be unthinkingly accepted.

Foods that only Japanese eat—even relatively humble ones like refrigerated prepared fish cakes—have wrappings that resemble handmade paper or leaves. Even modestly priced refrigerated fish cakes have beautiful wrappings in which traditional design accommodates a scannable bar code. Such products look Japanese and are unambiguously intended to do so. Products that are foreign, such as coffee, look foreign, even to the point of having only Roman lettering and no Japanese lettering on the can. American and European companies are sometimes able to sell their packages in Japan virtually unchanged, because their foreignness is part of their selling power. But Japanese exporters hire designers in each country to repackage their products. Americans—whose culture is defined not by refinements and distinctions but by inclusiveness—want to think about the product itself, not its cultural origins.

We speak glibly about global villages and international markets, but problems with packages reveal some unexpected cultural boundaries. Why are Canadians willing to drink milk out of flexible plastic pouches that fit into reusable plastic holders, while residents of the United States are believed to be so resistant to the idea that they have not even been given the opportunity to do so? Why do Japanese consumers prefer packages that contain two tennis balls and view the standard U.S. pack of three to be cheap and undesirable? Why do Germans insist on highly detailed technical specifications on packages of videotape, while Americans don't? Why do Swedes think that blue is masculine, while the Dutch see the color as feminine? The answers lie in unquestioned habits and deep-seated imagery, a culture of containing, adorning, and understanding that no sharp marketer can change overnight.

There is probably no other field in which designs that are almost a century old—Wrigley's gum, Campbell's soup, Hershey's chocolate bar—remain in production only subtly changed and are understood to be extremely valuable corporate assets. Yet the culture of packaging, defined by what people are buying and selling every day, keeps evolving, and the role nostalgia plays is very small.

For example, the tall, glass Heinz ketchup bottle has helped define the American refrigerator skyline for most of the twentieth century (even though it is generally unnecessary to refrigerate ketchup). Moreover, it provides the tables of diners and coffee shops with a vertical accent and a token of hospitality, the same qualities projected by candles and vases of flowers in more upscale eateries. The bottle has remained a fixture of American life, even though it has always been a nuisance to pour the thick ketchup through the little hole. It seemed not to matter that you have to shake and shake the bottle, impotently, until far too much ketchup comes out in one great scarlet plop. Heinz experimented for years with wide-necked jars and other sorts of bottles, but they never caught on.

Then in 1992 a survey of consumers indicated that more Americans believed that the plastic squeeze bottle is a better package for ketchup than the glass bottle. The survey did not offer any explanations for this change of preference, which has been evolving for many years as older people for whom the tall bottle is an icon became a less important part of the sample. Could it be that the difficulty of using the tall bottle suddenly became evident to those born after 1960? Perhaps the tall bottle holds too little ketchup. There is a clear trend toward buying things in larger containers, in part because lightweight plastics have made them less costly for manufacturers to ship and easier for consumers to use. This has happened even as the number of people in an average American household has been getting smaller. But houses, like packages, have been getting larger. Culture moves in mysterious ways.

The tall ketchup bottle is still preferred by almost half of consumers, so it is not going to disappear anytime soon. And the squeeze bottle does contain visual echoes of the old bottle. It is certainly not a radical departure. In Japan, ketchup and mayonnaise are sold in cellophane-wrapped plastic bladders that would certainly send Americans into severe culture shock. Still, the tall bottle's loss of absolute authority is a significant change. And its ultimate disappearance would represent a larger change in most people's visual environment than would the razing of nearly any landmark building.

But although some package designs are pleasantly evocative of another time, and a few appear to be unchanging icons in a turbulent world, the reason they still exist is because they still work. Inertia has historically played a role in creating commercial icons. Until quite recently, it was time-consuming and expensive to make new printing plates or to vary the shape or material of a container. Now computerized graphics and rapidly developing technology in the package-manufacturing industries make a packaging change easier than in the past, and a lot cheaper to change than advertising, which seems a far more evanescent medium. There is no constituency of curators or preservationists to protect the endangered package. If a gum wrapper manages to survive nearly unchanged for ninety years, it's not because any expert has determined that it is an important cultural expression. Rather, it's because it still helps sell a lot of gum.

So far, we've been discussing packaging in its most literal sense: designed containers that protect and promote products. Such containers have served as the models for larger types of packaging, such as chain restaurants, supermarkets, theme parks, and festival marketplaces. . . . Still, it is impossible to ignore a broader conception of packaging that is one of the preoccupations of our time. This concerns the ways in which people construct and present their personalities, the ways in which ideas are presented and diffused, the ways in which political candidates are selected and public policies formulated. We must all worry about packaging ourselves and everything we do, because we believe that nobody has time to really pay attention. 30

Packaging strives at once to offer excitement and reassurance. It promises something newer and better, but not necessarily different. When we talk about a tourist destination, or even a presidential contender, being packaged, that's not really a metaphor. The same projection of intensified ordinariness, the same combination of titillation and reassurance, are used for laundry detergents, theme parks, and candidates alike.

The imperative to package is unavoidable in a society in which people have been encouraged to see themselves as consumers not merely of toothpaste and automobiles, but of such imponderables as lifestyle, government, and health. The marketplace of ideas is not an agora, where people haggle, posture, clash, and come to terms with one another. Rather, it has become a supermarket, where values, aspirations, dreams, and predictions are presented with great sophistication. The individual can choose to buy them, or leave them on the shelf.

In such a packaged culture, the consumer seems to be king. But people cannot be consumers all the time. If nothing else, they must do something to earn the money that allows them to consume. This, in turn, pressures people to package themselves in order to survive. The early 1990s brought economic recession and shrinking opportunities to all the countries of the developed world. Like products fighting for their space on the shelf, individuals have had to re-create, or at least represent, themselves in order to seem both desirable and safe. Moreover, many jobs have been reconceived to depersonalize individuals and to make them part of a packaged service experience.

These phenomena have their own history. For decades, people have spoken of writing resumes in order to package themselves for a specific opportunity. Thomas J. Watson Jr., longtime chairman of IBM, justified his company's famously conservative and inflexible dress code—dark suits, white shirts, and rep ties for all male employees—as "self-packaging," analogous to the celebrated product design, corporate imagery, and packaging done for the company by Elliot Noyes and Paul Rand. You can question whether IBM's employees were packaging themselves or forced into a box by their employer. Still, anyone who has ever dressed for success was doing a packaging job.

Since the 1950s, there have been discussions of packaging a candidate to respond to what voters are telling the pollsters who perform the same tasks as market researchers do for soap or shampoo. More recently, such discussions have dominated American political journalism. The packaged candidate, so he and his handlers hope, projects a message that, like a Diet Pepsi, is stimulating without being threatening. Like a Weight Watchers frozen dessert bar, the candidate's contradictions must be glazed over and, ultimately, comforting. Aspects of the candidate that are confusing or viewed as extraneous are removed, just as stems and sinew are removed from packaged foods. The package is intended to protect the candidate; dirt won't stick. The candidate is uncontaminated, though at a slight remove from the consumer-voter.

People profess to be troubled by this sort of packaging. When we say a person or an experience is "packaged," we are complaining of a sense of excessive calculation and a lack of authenticity. Such a fear of unreality is at least a century old; it arose along with industrialization and rapid communication. Now that the world is more competitive, and we all believe we have less time to consider things, the craft of being instantaneously appealing has taken on more and more importance. We might say, cynically, that the person who appears "packaged" simply doesn't have good packaging.

Still, the sense of uneasiness about encountering packaged people in a packaged world is real, and it shouldn't be dismissed. Indeed, it is a theme of contemporary life, equally evident in politics, entertainment, and the supermarket. Moreover, public uneasiness about the phenomenon of packaging is compounded by confusion over a loss of iconic packages and personalities.

Producers of packaged products have probably never been as nervous as they became during the first half of the 1990s. Many of the world's most famous brands were involved in the merger mania of the 1980s, which produced debt-ridden companies that couldn't afford to wait for results either from their managers or their marketing strategies. At the same time, the feeling was that it was far too risky to produce something really new. The characteristic response was the line extension — "dry" beer, "lite" mayonnaise, "ultra" detergent. New packages have been appearing at a rapid pace, only to be changed whenever a manager gets nervous or a retailer loses patience.

The same skittishness is evident in the projection of public personalities as the clear, if synthetic, images of a few decades ago have lost their sharpness and broken into a spectrum of weaker, reflected apparitions. Marilyn Monroe, for example, had an image that was, Jayne Mansfield notwithstanding, unique and well defined. She was luscious as a Hershey's bar, shapely as a Coke bottle. But in a world where Coke can be sugar free, caffeine free, and cherry flavored (and Pepsi can be clear!), just one image isn't enough for a superstar. Madonna is available as Marilyn or as a brunette, a Catholic schoolgirl, or a bondage devotee. Who knows what brand extension will come next? Likewise, John F. Kennedy and Elvis Presley had clear, carefully projected images. But Bill Clinton is defined largely by evoking memories of both. As our commercial civilization seems to have lost the power to amuse or convince us in new and exciting ways, formerly potent packages are recycled and devalued. That has left the door open for such phenomena as generic cigarettes, President's Choice cola, and H. Ross Perot.

This cultural and personal packaging both fascinates and infuriates.   40
There is something liberating in its promise of aggressive self-creation, and something terrifying in its implication that everything must be subject to the ruthless discipline of the marketplace. People are at once passive consumers of their culture and aggressive packagers of themselves, which can be a stressful and lonely combination.

Reading the Text

1. How does Hine compare a supermarket with a traditional marketplace?
2. What does Hine mean when he asserts that modern retailing "replaces people with packages" (para. 5)?

3. How does packaging stimulate the desire to buy, according to Hine?
4. How do American attitudes toward packaging compare with those of the Japanese, according to Hine?

Reading the Signs

1. Bring one product package to class, preferably with all students bringing items from the same product category (personal hygiene, say, or snack food or drinks). Give a brief presentation to the class in which you interpret your own package. After all the students have presented, compare the different messages the packages send to consumers.
2. Visit a popular clothing store, such as the Gap or Banana Republic, and study the ways the store uses packaging to create, as Hine puts it, "a personality, an attitude toward life" (para. 15). Be thorough in your investigations, studying everything from the bags in which you carry your purchases to perfume or cologne packages to clothing labels. Use your findings as evidence for an essay in which you analyze the image the store creates for itself and its consumers.
3. In your journal, write an entry in which you explore your motives if you have ever purchased a product because you liked the package. What did you like about the package, and how did it contribute to your sense of identity?
4. Visit a store with an explicit political theme, such as the Body Shop or the Nature Company, and write a semiotic analysis of some of the packaging you see in the store.
5. Study the packages that are visible to a visitor to your home, and then write an analysis of the messages those packages might send to a visitor. To develop your ideas, you might read or reread Joan Kron's "The Semiotics of Home Decor" (p. 94).

STUART EWEN

Hard Bodies

|||||||||||||||||||||||||||||||||||||||||||||||||||||||||||||||||

In this selection from All Consuming Images: The Politics of Style in Contemporary Culture *(1988), Stuart Ewen (b. 1945) analyzes the way our bodies themselves can be signs of cultural desire. Focusing on the body sculpting popular among urban professionals in recent years, Ewen argues that the "hard-body" fad reflects a postindustrial transformation of the body into a kind of industrial product, something you "build" every day at the gym. Health clubs thus can be seen as factories that produce the sorts of bodily objects that America*

*values, with Nautilus machines standing in as the tools of mass pro-
duction. Ewen documents the pulse of American culture as a professor
of media studies in the Department of Communications at Hunter
College, and he also serves as professor in the Ph.D. programs in history and sociology at the City University of New York Graduate Center. He is the author of numerous books and articles on American popular and consumer culture, including* Channels of Desire: Mass
Images and the Shaping of American Consciousness *with Elizabeth Ewen (1982),* Captains of Consciousness: Advertising and
the Social Roots of the Consumer Culture *(1976), and* PR! A
Social History of Spin *(1996).*

Writing in 1934, the sociologists George A. Lundberg, Mirra Ko-
marovsky, and Mary Alice McInerny addressed the question of "leisure"
in the context of an emerging consumer society. Understanding the
symbiotic relationship between mass-production industries and a con-
sumerized definition of leisure, they wrote of the need for society to
achieve a compatibility between the worlds of work and daily life. "The
ideal to be sought," they proposed, "is undoubtedly the gradual oblitera-
tion of the psychological barrier which today distinguishes work from
leisure."[1]

That ideal has been realized in the daily routine of Raymond H——,
a thirty-four-year-old middle-management employee of a large New
York City investment firm. He is a living cog in what Felix Rohatyn has
termed the new "money culture," one in which "making things" no
longer counts; "making money," as an end in itself, is the driving force.[2]
His days are spent at a computer terminal, monitoring an endless flow of
numerical data.

When his workday is done, he heads toward a local health club for
the relaxation of a "workout." Three times a week this means a visit to
the Nautilus room, with its high, mirrored walls, and its imposing assembly line of large, specialized "machines." The workout consists of exercises for his lower body and for his upper body, twelve "stations" in all.
As he moves from Nautilus machine to Nautilus machine, he works on
his hips, buttocks, thighs, calves, back, shoulders, chest, upper arms, fore-
arms, abdomen, and neck, body part by body part.

At the first station, Raymond lies on the "hip and back machine,"
making sure to align his hip joints with the large, polished, kidney-
shaped cams which offer resistance as he extends each leg downward
over the padded roller under each knee. Twelve repetitions of this, and
he moves on to the "hip abduction machine," where he spreads his legs

---

1. George A. Lundberg et al., *Leisure: A Suburban Study* (1934), p. 3.
2. *New York Times,* 3 June 1987, p. A27.

outward against the padded restraints that hold them closed. Then leg extensions on the "compound leg machine" are followed by leg curls on the "leg curl machine." From here, Raymond H—— proceeds to the "pullover/torso arm machine," where he begins to address each piece of his upper body. After a precise series of repetitions on the "double chest machine," he completes his workout on the "four-way neck machine."

While he alternates between different sequential workouts, and different machines, each session is pursued with deliberate precision, following exact instructions. 5

Raymond H—— has been working on his body for the past three years, ever since he got his last promotion. He is hoping to achieve the body he always wanted. Perhaps it is fitting that this quintessential, single, young, urban professional—whose life has become a circle of work, money culture, and the cultivation of an image—has turned himself, literally, into a piece of work. If the body ideal he seeks is *lean,* devoid of fatty tissue, it is also *hard.* "Soft flesh," once a standard phrase in the American erotic lexicon, is now—within the competitive, upscale world he inhabits—a sign of failure and sloth. The hard shell is now a sign of achievement, visible proof of success in the "rat race." The goal he seeks is more about *looking* than *touching*.

To achieve his goal, he approaches his body piece by piece; with each machine he performs a discrete task. Along the way he also assumes the job of inspector, surveying the results of each task in the mirrors that surround him. The division of labor, the fragmentation of the work process, and the regulating function of continual measurement and observation—all fundamental to the principles of "scientific management"—are intrinsic to this form of recreation. Like any assembly line worker, H—— needs no overall knowledge of the process he is engaged in, only the specific tasks that comprise that process. "You don't have to understand *why* Nautilus equipment works," writes bodybuilder Mike Mentzer in the foreword to one of the most widely read Nautilus manuals. "With a tape measure in hand," he promises, "you will see what happens."[3]

The body ideal Raymond H—— covets is, itself, an aestheticized tribute to the broken-down work processes of the assembly line. "I'm trying to get better definition," H—— says. "I'm into Nautilus because it lets me do the necessary touchup work. Free weights [barbells] are good for building up mass, but Nautilus is great for definition."[4] By "definition," H—— is employing the lingo of the gym, a reference to a body surface upon which each muscle, each muscle group, appears segmented and distinct. The perfect body is one that ratifies the fragmentary process of its construction, one that mimics—in flesh—the illustrative qualities of a schematic drawing, or an anatomy chart.

Surveying his work in the mirror, H—— admires the job he has done on his broad, high pectorals, but is quick to note that his quadriceps "could use some work." This ambivalence, this mix of emotions, pursues him each time he comes for a workout, and the times in between. He is never quite satisfied with the results. The excesses of the weekend-past invariably leave their blemish. An incorrectly struck pose reveals an overmeasure of loose skin, a sign of weakness in the shell. Despite all efforts, photogenic majesty is elusive.

The power of the photographic idiom, in his mind's eye, is rein-   10
forced, again and again, by the advertisements and other media of style visible everywhere. The ideal of the perfectly posed machine—the cold, hard body in response—is paraded, perpetually, before his eyes and ours. We see him, or her, at every glance.

An advertisement for home gym equipment promises a "Body By Soloflex." Above is the silent, chiaroscuro portrait of a muscular youth, his torso bare, his elbows reaching high, pulling a thin-ribbed undershirt

---

3. Ellington Darden, *The Nautilus Bodybuilding Book* (1986), pp. viii–ix.
4. Style Project, interview I-13.

up over his head, which is faceless, covered by shadow. His identity is situated below the neck, an instrumentally achieved study in brawn. The powerful expanse of his chest and back is illuminated from the right side. A carefully cast shadow accentuates the paired muscle formations of his abdominal wall. The airbrush has done its work as well, effecting a smooth, standardized, molded quality, what John Berger has termed "the skin without a biography." A silent, brooding hulk of a man, he is the unified product of pure engineering. His image is a product of expensive photographic technology, and expensive technical expertise. His body—so we are informed—is also a technical achievement. He has reached this captured moment of perpetual perfection on a "machine that fits in the corner" of his home. The machine, itself, resembles a stamping machine, one used to shape standardized, industrial products. Upon this machine, he has routinely followed instructions for "twenty-four traditional iron pumping exercises, each correct in form and balance." The privileged guidance of industrial engineering, and the mindless obedience of work discipline, have become legible upon his body; yet as it is displayed, it is nothing less than a thing of beauty, a transcendent aspiration.

This machine-man is one of a generation of desolate, finely tuned loners who have cropped up as icons of American style. Their bodies, often lightly oiled to accentuate definition, reveal their inner mechanisms like costly, open-faced watches, where one can see the wheels and gears moving inside, revealing—as it were—the magic of time itself. If this is eroticism, it is one tuned more to the mysteries of technology than to those of the flesh.

In another magazine advertisement, for Evian spring water from France, six similarly anatomized figures stand across a black and white two-page spread. From the look of things, each figure (three men and three women) has just completed a grueling workout, and four of them are partaking of Evian water as part of their recovery. The six are displayed in a lineup, each one displaying a particularly well-developed anatomical region. These are the new icons of beauty, precisely defined, powerful machines. Below, on the left, is the simple caption: "Revival of the Fittest." Though part of a group, each figure is conspicuously alone.

Once again, the modern contours of power, and the structures of work discipline, are imprinted upon the body. In a world of rampant careerism, self-absorption is a rule of thumb. If the division of labor sets each worker in competition with every other, here that fragmentation is aestheticized into the narcissism of mind and body.

Within this depiction, sexual equality is presented as the meeting 15 point between the anorectic and the "nautilized." True to gender distinctions between evanescent value and industrial work discipline, the three women are defined primarily by contour, by the thin lines that their willowy bodies etch upon the page. Although their muscles are toned, they strike poses that suggest pure, disembodied form. Each of the men, situated alternately between the women, gives testimony on behalf of a particular fraction of segmented flesh: abdomen, shoulders and upper arms, upper back. In keeping with the assembly line approach to muscle building, each man's body symbolizes a particular station within the labor process.

Another ad, for a health and fitness magazine, contains an alarmingly discordant statement: "Today's women workers are back in the sweat shop." There is a basis to this claim. In today's world, powerful, transnational corporations search the globe looking for the cheapest labor they can find. Within this global economy, more and more women—from Chinatown to Taiwan—are employed at tedious, low-paying jobs, producing everything from designer jeans to computer parts.

Yet this is not the kind of sweatshop the ad has in mind. The photographic illustration makes this clear. Above the text, across the two-page color spread, is the glistening, heavily muscled back of a woman hoisting a chrome barbell. Her sweat is self-induced, part of a "new woman" lifestyle being promoted in *Sport* magazine, "the magazine of the new vitality." Although this woman bears the feminine trademark of blonde, braided hair, her body is decidedly masculine, a new body aesthetic in the making. Her muscles are not the cramped, biographically induced muscles of menial labor. Hers is the brawn of the purely symbolic, the guise of the middle-class "working woman."

While the text of the advertisement seems to allude to the real conditions of female labor, the image transforms that truth into beauty, rendering it meaningless. Real conditions are copywritten into catchy and humorous phrases. The harsh physical demands of women's work are reinterpreted as regimented, leisure-time workouts at a "health club." Real sweat is reborn as photogenic body oil.

The migration of women into the social structures of industrial discipline is similarly aestheticized in an ad for Jack LaLanne Fitness Centers. A black and white close-up of a young woman wrestling with a fitness "machine" is complemented by the eroticized grimace on her face. Once again, the chiaroscuro technique accentuates the straining muscles of her arms. The high-contrast, black and white motif may also suggest the "night and day" metamorphosis that will occur when one commits to this particular brand of physical discipline.

In large white letters, superimposed across the shadowy bottom of [20] the photograph, are the words: "Be taut by experts." With a clever play on words the goal of education moves from the mind to the body. Muscle power is offered as an equivalent substitute for brain power. No problem. In the search for the perfectly regulated self, it is implicit that others will do the thinking. This woman, like the Soloflex man, is the product of pure engineering, of technical expertise:

We were building bodies back when you were building blocks. . . .
We know how to perfectly balance your workout between swimming, jogging, aerobics and weight training on hundreds of the most
advanced machines available. . . . Sure it may hurt a little. But remember. *You only hurt the one you love.* [Emphasis added.]

These advertisements, like Raymond H———'s regular visits to the
Nautilus room, are part of the middle-class bodily rhetoric of the 1980s.
Together they mark a culture in which self-absorbed careerism, conspicuous consumption, and a conception of *self* as an object of competitive
display have fused to become the preponderant symbols of achievement.
The regulated body is the nexus where a cynical ethos of social Darwin-
ism, and the eroticism of raw power, meet.

Reading the Text

1. Write a one-paragraph description of the hard-body style.
2. How, according to Ewen, is the body treated like a machine in the hard-
   body exercise regimen?
3. Why does Raymond H——— exercise so much?
4. Why does Ewen say that "the goal [Raymond H———] seeks is more
   about *looking* than *touching*" (para. 6)?

Reading the Signs

1. Ewen accuses those who follow the hard-body trend of conceiving the
   self as "an object of competitive display" (para. 21). To what extent do
   you find his accusation valid? To support your argument, draw on your
   own habits of exercising and those of your friends.
2. In class, discuss the tone Ewen adopts in his essay. How does that tone affect your response to his argument?
3. Break your class into two groups according to gender. In each group,
   brainstorm ideal body types for both men and women, and then rank
   them according to the group's preferences. Compare the results of the
   two groups: How are they gender-related?
4. Interview three or four people who are working out in your school or
   local gym, asking them about the results they want to achieve through
   their exercising. Using Ewen's argument about hard bodies as your
   model, analyze the results of your interviews.
5. Does the TaeBo fad represent a continuation of or departure from the
   hard-body style? To develop your ideas, you might interview TaeBo fans
   or visit a web site such as **http://www.taebo.com**.

FRED DAVIS
Blue Jeans

Blue Jeans are almost certainly America's greatest contribution to fashion history, and in this analysis, which originally appeared in his book Fashion Culture and Identity *(1992), Fred Davis (1925–1992) shows how this staple of the American wardrobe has become a symbol of many of our most enduring, and contradictory, cultural values. At once an emblem of democratic populism and elite status symbol, blue jeans are part of an American dialectic, Davis argues, in which "status and antistatus, democracy and distinction," are in a constant flux, moving with the tides of history itself. A former professor of sociology at the University of California at San Diego, Davis authored such books as* Yearning for Yesterday: A Sociology of Nostalgia *(1979) and* Illness, Interaction, and the Self *(1972).*

The new clothes [jeans] express profoundly democratic values. There are no distinctions of wealth or status, no elitism; people confront one another shorn of these distinctions.
>   —CHARLES A. REICH,
>   *The Greening of America*

Throughout the world, the young and their allies are drawn hypnotically to denim's code of hope and solidarity—to an undefined vision of the energetic and fraternal Americanness inherent in them all.
>   —KENNEDY FRASER,
>   "That Missing Button"

Karl Lagerfeld for Chanel shapes a classic suit from blue and white denim, $960, with denim bustier, $360, . . . and denim hat, $400. All at Chanel Boutique, Beverly Hills.
>   —Photograph caption in *Los Angeles Times Magazine*
>   for article "Dressed-Up Denims," April 19, 1987

Since the dawn of fashion in the West some seven hundred years ago, probably no other article of clothing has in the course of its evolution more fully served as a vehicle for the expression of status ambivalences and ambiguities than blue jeans. Some of the social history supporting this statement is by now generally well known.[1] First fashioned in the mid-nineteenth-century American West by Morris Levi Strauss, a

---

1. Excellent, sociologically informed accounts of the origins and social history of blue jeans are to be found in Belasco (n.d.) and Friedmann (1987).

Bavarian Jewish peddler newly arrived in San Francisco, the trousers then as now were made from a sturdy, indigo-dyed cotton cloth said to have originated in Nimes, France. (Hence the anglicized contraction to *denim* from the French *de Nimes.*) A garment similar to that manufactured by Levi Strauss for goldminers and outdoor laborers is said to have been worn earlier in France by sailors and dockworkers from Genoa, Italy, who were referred to as "genes"; hence the term *jeans.* The distinctive copper riveting at the pants pockets and other stress points were the invention of Jacob Davis, a tailor from Carson City, Nevada, who joined the Levi Strauss firm in 1873, some twenty years after the garment's introduction.

More than a century went by, however, before this working man's garment attained the prominence and near-universal recognition it possesses today. For it was not until the late 1960s that blue jeans, after several failed moves in previous decades into a broader mass market, strikingly crossed over nearly all class, gender, age, regional, national, and ideological lines to become the universally worn and widely accepted item of apparel they are today. And since the crossover, enthusiasm for them has by no means been confined to North America and Western Europe. In former Soviet bloc countries and much of the Third World, too, where they have generally been in short supply, they remain highly sought after and hotly bargained over.

A critical feature of this cultural breakthrough is, of course, blue jeans' identity change from a garment associated exclusively with work (and hard work, at that) to one invested with many of the symbolic attributes of leisure: ease, comfort, casualness, sociability, and the outdoors. Or, as the costume historians Jasper and Roach-Higgins (1987) might put it, the garment underwent a process of cultural authentication that led to its acquiring meanings quite different from that with which it began. In bridging the work/leisure divide when it did, it tapped into the new, consumer-goods-oriented, postindustrial affluence of the West on a massive scale. Soon thereafter it penetrated those many other parts of the world that emulate the West.

But this still fails to answer the questions of why so rough-hewn, drably hued, and crudely tailored a piece of clothing should come to exercise the fascination it has for so many diverse societies and peoples, or why within a relatively short time of breaking out of its narrow occupational locus it spread so quickly throughout the world. Even if wholly satisfactory answers elude us, these questions touch intimately on the twists and turns of status symbolism. . . .

To begin with, considering its origins and longtime association with 5 workingmen, hard physical labor, the outdoors, and the American West, much of the blue jeans' fundamental mystique seems to emanate from populist sentiments of democracy, independence, equality, freedom, and fraternity. This makes for a sartorial symbolic complex at war, even if rather indifferently for nearly a century following its introduction, with class distinctions, elitism, and snobbism, dispositions extant nearly as much in jeans-originating America as in the Old World. It is not surprising, therefore, that the first non–"working stiffs" to become attached to blue jeans and associated denim wear were painters and other artists, mainly in the southwest United States, in the late 1930s and 1940s (Friedmann 1987). These were soon followed by "hoodlum" motorcycle gangs ("bikers") in the 1950s and by New Left activists and hippies in the 1960s (Belasco n.d.). All these groups (each in its own way, of course) stood strongly in opposition to the dominant conservative, middle-class, consumer-oriented culture of American society. Blue jeans, given their origins and historic associations, offered a visible means for announcing such antiestablishment sentiments. Besides, jeans were cheap, and, at least at first, good fit hardly mattered.

Whereas by the late 1950s one could in some places see jeans worn in outdoor play by middle-class boys, until well into the 1960s a truly ecumenical acceptance of them was inhibited precisely because of their association with (more, perhaps, through media attention than from firsthand experience) such disreputable and deviant groups as bikers and hippies. Major sales and public relations campaigns would be undertaken by jeans manufacturers to break the symbolic linkage with disreputability and to convince consumers that jeans and denim were suitable for one and all and for a wide range of occasions (Belasco n.d.). Apparently such efforts helped; by the late 1960s blue jeans had achieved worldwide popularity and, of greater relevance here, had fully crossed over the occupation, class, gender, and age boundaries that had circumscribed them for over a century.

What was it—and, perhaps, what is it still—about blue jeans? Notwithstanding the symbolic elaborations and revisions (some would say perversions) to which fashion and the mass market have in the intervening years subjected the garment, there can be little doubt that at its crossover phase its underlying symbolic appeal derived from its antifashion significations: its visually persuasive historic allusions to rural democracy, the common man, simplicity, unpretentiousness, and, for many, especially Europeans long captivated by it, the romance of the American West with its figure of the free-spirited, self-reliant cowboy.[2]

But as the history of fashion has demonstrated time and again, no vestmental symbol is inviolable. All can, and usually will be, subjected to

---

2. This is not to put forward some absurd claim to the effect that everyone who donned a pair of jeans was swept up by this imagery. Rather, it is to suggest that it was such imagery that came culturally to be encoded in the wearing of blue jeans (Berger 1984, 80–82), so that whether one wore them indifferently or with calculated symbolic intent, imitatively or in a highly individual manner, they would "on average" be viewed in this light.

the whims of those who wish to convey more or different things about their person than the "pure" symbol in its initial state of signification communicates. Democratic, egalitarian sentiments notwithstanding, social status still counts for too much in Western society to permanently suffer the proletarianization that an unmodified blue-jean declaration of equality and fraternity projected. No sooner, then, had jeans made their way into the mass marketplace than myriad devices were employed for muting and mixing messages, readmitting evicted symbolic allusions, and, in general, promoting invidious distinctions among classes and coteries of jean wearers. Indeed, to the extent that their very acceptance was propelled by fashion as such, it can be said an element of invidiousness was already at play. For, other things being equal and regardless of the "message" a new fashion sends, merely to be "in fashion" is to be one up on those who are not as yet.[3]

Elite vs. Populist Status Markers

Beyond this metacommunicative function, however, the twists, inversions, contradictions, and paradoxes of status symbolism to which blue jeans subsequently lent themselves underscore the subtle identity ambivalences plaguing many of their wearers. In a 1973 piece titled "Denim and the New Conservatives," Kennedy Fraser (1981, 92) noted several such, perhaps the most ironic being this:

> Some of the most expensive versions of the All-American denim theme have come bouncing into our stores from European manufacturers. The irresistible pull of both European fashion and denim means that American customers will pay large sums for, say, French blue jeans despite the galling knowledge that fashionable young people in Saint-Tropez are only imitating young people in America, a country that can and does produce better and cheaper blue jeans than France.

---

3. From this perspective, assumed by such important French critics as Barthes (1983) and Baudrillard (1984), all fashion, irrespective of the symbolic content that animates one or another manifestation of it, gravitates toward "designification" or the destruction of meaning. That is to say, because it feeds on itself (on its ability to induce others to follow the fashion "regardless"), it soon neutralizes or sterilizes whatever significance its signifiers had before becoming objects of fashion. Sheer display displaces signification; to take the example of blue jeans, even people hostile to their underlying egalitarian message can via fashion's mandate wear them with ease and impunity and, contrary to the garment's symbolic anti-invidious origins, score "status points" by doing so. This argument is powerful but in my view posits, in a manner similar to the claim that fashion is nothing more than change for the sake of change, too complete a break between the symbolic content of culture and the communication processes that embody and reshape it.

By 1990 a nearly parallel inversion seemed about to occur in regard   10
to the garment's post-1950s image as leisure wear, although for destination other than fields and factories. With the introduction of men's fall
fashions for the year featuring "urban denim," a spokesman for the Men's
Fashion Association said (Hofmann 1990): "It's not just about cowboys
and country and western anymore. It used to be that denim meant play
clothes; now men want to wear it to the office the next day."

Framing the garment's status dialectic was the contest of polarities,
one pole continuing to emphasize and extend blue jeans' "base-line"
symbolism of democracy, utility, and classlessness, the other seeking to
reintroduce traditional claims to taste, distinction, and hierarchical division. (Any individual wearer, and often the garment itself, might try to
meld motifs from both sides in the hope of registering a balanced, yet appropriately ambivalent, statement.)

Conspicuous Poverty: Fading and Fringing

From the "left" symbolic (and not altogether apolitical) pole came
the practice of jean fading and fringing. Evocative of a kind of conspicuous poverty, faded blue jeans and those worn to the point of exposing
some of the garment's warp and woof were soon more highly prized,
particularly by the young, than new, well-blued jeans. Indeed, in some
circles worn jeans commanded a higher price than new ones. As with
Chanel's little black dress, it cost more to look "truly poor" than just ordinarily so, which new jeans by themselves could easily accomplish. But
given the vogue that fading and fringing attained, what ensued in the
marketplace was predictable: Jeans manufacturers started producing pre-
faded, worn-looking, stone- or acid-washed jeans.[4] These obviated, for
the average consumer if not for the jeans connoisseur disdainful of such
subterfuge, the need for a long break-in period.

Labeling, Ornamentation, and Eroticization

From the "right" symbolic pole emerged a host of stratagems and
devices, all of which sought in effect to de-democratize jeans while capitalizing on the ecumenical appeal they had attained: designer jeans,
which prominently displayed the label of the designer; jeans bearing factory sewn-in embroidering, nailheads, rhinestones, and other decorative
additions; specially cut and sized jeans for women, children, and older
persons; in general, jeans combined (with fashion's sanction) with items

---

4. A yet later variation on the same theme was "shotgun washed" jeans manufactured by a Tennessee company that blasted its garments with a twelve-gauge shotgun
(Hochswender 1991).

of clothing standing in sharp symbolic contradiction of them, e.g., sports jackets, furs, dress shoes, spiked heels, ruffled shirts, or silk blouses.

Paralleling the de-democratization of the jean, by the 1970s strong currents toward its eroticization were also evident. These, of course, contravened the unisex, de-gendered associations the garment initially held for many: the relative unconcern for fit and emphasis on comfort; the fly front for both male and female; the coarse denim material, which, though it chafed some, particularly women, was still suffered willingly. Numerous means were found to invest the jean and its associated wear with gender-specific, eroticized meaning. In the instance of women—and this is more salient sociologically since it was they who had been de-feminized by donning the blatantly masculine blue jeans in the first place—these included the fashioning of denim material into skirts, the "jeans for gals" sales pitches of manufacturers, the use of softer materials, cutting jeans so short as to expose the buttocks, and, in general, the trans-mogrification of jeans from loose-fitting, baggy trousers into pants so snugly pulled over the posterior as to require some women to lie down to get into them. So much for comfort, so much for unisexuality! Inter-estingly, in the never-ending vestmental dialectic on these matters baggy jeans for women again became fashionable in the mid-1980s.

Designer Jeans

Of all of the modifications wrought upon it, the phenomenon of de- 15 signer jeans speaks most directly to the garment's encoding of status am-bivalences. The very act of affixing a well-known designer's label—and some of the world's leading hautes couturiers in time did so—to the back side of a pair of jeans has to be interpreted, however else it may be seen, along Veblenian lines, as an instance of conspicuous consumption; in effect, a muting of the underlying rough-hewn proletarian connota-tion of the garment through the introduction of a prominent status marker.[5] True, sewing an exterior designer label onto jeans—a practice designers never resort to with other garments—was facilitated psycho-logically by the prominent Levi Strauss & Co. label, which had from the

---

5. Everyone, without exception, whom I interviewed and spoke with in the course of my research on fashion (designers, apparel manufacturers, buyers, persons from the fashion press, fashion-conscious laypersons) interpreted designer jeans in this light. Most felt that status distinctions were the *only* reason for designer jeans because, except for the display of the designer label, they could detect no significant difference between designer and nondesigner jeans. Not all commentators, however, are of the opinion that the prominent display of an outside label can be attributed solely to invidi-ous status distinctions. Some (Back 1985) find in the phenomenon overtones of a mod-ernist aesthetic akin, for example, to Bauhaus design, exoskeletal building construction, action painting, and certain directions in pop art wherein the identity of the creator and the processual markings of his/her creation are visibly fused with the art work itself.

beginning been sewn above the right hip pocket of that firm's denim jeans and had over the years become an inseparable part of the garment's image. It could then be argued, as it sometimes was, that the outside sewing of a designer label was consistent with the traditional image of blue jeans. Still, Yves Saint Laurent, Oscar de la Renta, or Gloria Vanderbilt, for that matter, are not names to assimilate easily with Levi Strauss, Lee, or Wrangler, a distinction hardly lost on most consumers.

But as is so characteristic of fashion, every action elicits its reaction. No sooner had the snoblike, status-conscious symbolism of designer jeans made its impact on the market than dress coteries emerged whose sartorial stock-in-trade was a display of disdain for the invidious distinctions registered by so obvious a status ploy. This was accomplished mainly through a demonstration of hyperloyalty to the original, underlying egalitarian message of denim blue jeans. As Kennedy Fraser (1981, 93) was to observe of these countercyclicists in 1973:

> The denim style of the more sensitive enclaves of the Village, the West Side, and SoHo is the style of the purist and neo-ascetic. Unlike the "chic" devotee of blue jeans, this loyalist often wears positively baggy denims, and scorns such travesties as embroideries and nail-heads. To underline their association with honesty and toil, the denims of choice are often overalls.

Not long after, the "positively baggy denims" of which Fraser speaks—this antifashion riposte to fashion's prior corruption of denim's 1960s-inspired rejection of status distinctions—were themselves, with that double reflexive irony at which fashion is so adept, assimilated into the fashion cycle. Then those "into" denim styles could by "dressing down" stay ahead of—as had their older, first-time-around denim-clad siblings of the sixties—their more conformist, "properly dressed" alters.

Conclusion

And so . . . do the dialectics of status and antistatus, democracy and distinction, inclusiveness and exclusiveness pervade fashion's twists and turns; as much, or even more, with the workingman's humble blue jeans as with formal dinner wear and the evening gown.

But such is fashion's way. If it is to thrive it can only feed off the ambiguities and ambivalences we endure in our daily lives and concourse, not only over those marks of social status considered here but equally over such other key identity pegs as age, gender, and sexuality, to mention but the most obvious. Were it the case, as some scholars have maintained, that fashion's sole symbolic end was registering and re-registering invidious distinctions of higher and lower, or better and lesser—that is, distinctions of class and social status—it would hardly have enough "to talk about"; certainly not enough to account for its having thrived in

Western society for as long as it has. But, as we have already seen . . . , it does have more to say: about our masculinity and femininity, our youth and age, our sexual scruples or lack thereof, our work and play, our politics, national identity, and religion. This said, one need not take leave of what has engaged us here, that rich symbolic domain that treats of the deference and respect we accord and receive from others (what Max Weber meant by *status*), in order to appreciate that fashion is capable of much greater subtlety, more surprises, more anxious backward glances and searching forward gazes than we credit it with.

WORKS CITED

Back, Kurt W. 1985. "Modernism and Fashion: A Social Psychological Interpretation," in Michael R. Solomon, ed., *The Psychology of Fashion*. Lexington, Mass.: Heath.

Barthes, Roland. 1983. *The Fashion System*. Translated by Matthew Ward and Richard Howard. New York: Hill and Wang.

Baudrillard, Jean. 1984. "La Mode ou la féerie du code." *Traverses* 3 (October): 7–19.

Belasco, Warren A. n.d. "Mainstreaming Blue Jeans: The Ideological Process, 1945–1980." Unpublished.

Berger, Arthur Asa. 1984. *Signs in Contemporary Culture*. New York: Longman.

Fraser, Kennedy. 1981. *The Fashionable Mind*. New York: Knopf.

Friedmann, Daniel. 1987. *Une Histoire du blue jean*. Paris: Ramsay.

Hochswender, Woody. 1991. "Patterns." *New York Times*, Jan. 8.

Hofmann, Deborah. 1990. "New Urbanity for Denim and Chambray." *New York Times,* Sept. 24.

Jasper, Cynthia R., and Mary Ellen Roach-Higgins. 1987. "History of Costume: Theory and Instruction." *Clothing and Textile Research Journal* 5, no. 4 (Summer): 1–6.

Reich, Charles A. 1970. *The Greening of America*. New York: Crown.

Reading the Text

1. Why, according to Davis, were jeans linked with "disreputability" (para. 6) until the mid-1960s?
2. In Davis's view, what enabled jeans to "crossover" (para. 2) from being disreputable to fashionable?
3. Summarize in your own words the ambivalence between "democracy and distinction" (para. 17) or "left" (para. 12) and "right" (para. 13) that Davis ascribes to jeans since the 1960s.
4. How does Davis interpret the advent of designer jeans?

Reading the Signs

1. Bring an issue of a current fashion magazine for men or women (such as *Elle* or *Details*), and study the jeans ads in small groups. Do you find that today's jeans ads use the democratizing or dedemocratizing symbolism that Davis describes? How can you account for your observations?

2. This selection, originally published in 1992, takes its analysis through the 1980s. Using Davis's categories of democracy and distinction, write your own update of jeans through the 1990s. For evidence of the system in which jeans operate, you can rely on advertisements, videos, film, web sites of jeans manufacturers, and other popular media.

3. Write an argumentative essay in response to the contention that, rather than having a social or cultural significance as Davis presumes, jeans are worn simply for comfort and budgetary reasons.

4. In your journal, brainstorm a list of brands of jeans, and then note which you currently wear, would like to wear, or would never consider wearing. Reflect on the image associated with each brand. How does image affect your taste in attire?

5. Observe students at your school congregating in a public place (say, the student union building), and note the predominant fashion styles. Then write a semiotic interpretation of the fashion trends you observe.

JOAN KRON

The Semiotics of Home Decor

ıı

Just when you thought it was safe to go back into your living room, here comes Joan Kron with a reminder that your home is a signaling system just as much as your clothing is. In Home-Psych: The Social Psychology of Home and Decoration *(1983), from which this selection is taken, Kron takes a broad look at the significance of interior decoration, showing how home design can reflect both an individual and a group identity. Ranging from a New York entrepreneur to Kwakiutl Indian chiefs, Kron further discusses how different cultures use possessions as a rich symbol system. The author of* High Tech: The Industrial Style and Source Book for the Home *(1978) and of some five hundred articles for American magazines, she is particularly interested in fashion, design, and the social psychology of consumption. Currently an editor-at-large at* Allure *magazine, Kron has recently published* Lift: Wanting, Fearing, and Having a Face-Lift *(1998).*

On June 7, 1979, Martin J. Davidson entered the materialism hall of fame. That morning the thirty-four-year-old New York graphic design entrepreneur went to his local newsstand and bought fifty copies of the *New York Times* expecting to read an article about himself in the Home section that would portray him as a man of taste and discrimination. Instead, his loft and his life-style, which he shared with singer Dawn Bennett, were given the tongue-in-cheek treatment under the headline: "When Nothing But the Best Will Do."[1]

Davidson, who spent no more money renovating his living quarters than many of the well-to-do folks whose homes are lionized in the *Times*'s Thursday and Sunday design pages — the running ethnographic record of contemporary upper-middle-class life-style — made the unpardonable error of telling reporter Jane Geniesse how much he had paid for his stereo system, among other things. Like many people who have not been on intimate terms with affluence for very long, Davidson is in the habit of price-tagging his possessions. His 69-cent-per-bottle bargain Perrier, his $700 Armani suits from Barney's, his $27,000 cooperative loft and its $150,000 renovation, his sixteen $350-per-section sectionals, and his $11,000 best-of-class stereo. Martin J. Davidson wants the world to know how well he's done. "I live the American dream," he told Mrs. Geniesse, which includes, "being known as one of Barney's best customers."[2]

Davidson even wants the U.S. Census Bureau's computer to know how well he has done. He is furious, in fact, that the 1980 census form did not have a box to check for people who live in cooperatives. "If someone looks at my census form they'll think I must be at the poverty level or lower."[3] No one who read the *Times* article about Martin Davidson would surmise that.

It is hard to remember when a "design" story provoked more outrage. Letters to the editor poured in. Andy Warhol once said that in our fast-paced media world no one could count on being a celebrity for more than fifteen minutes. Martin Davidson was notorious for weeks. "All the Martin Davidsons in New York," wrote one irate reader, "will sit home listening to their $11,000 stereos, while downtown, people go to jail because they ate a meal they couldn't pay for."[4] "How can one man embody so many of the ills afflicting our society today?"[5] asked another offended reader. "Thank you for your clever spoof," wrote a third reader. "I was almost convinced that two people as crass as Martin Davidson and Dawn Bennett could exist."[6] Davidson's consumption largesse was even memorialized by Russell Baker, the *Times*'s Pulitzer Prize–winning humorist, who devoted a whole column to him: "While

---

1. Jane Geniesse, "When Nothing But the Best Will Do," *New York Times,* June 7, 1979, p. C1ff.

2. Ibid.

3. Author's interview with Martin Davidson.

4. Richard Moseson, "Letters: Crossroads of Decadence and Destitution," *New York Times,* June 14, 1979, p. A28.

5. Letter to the Editor, *New York Times,* June 14, 1979, p. C9.

6. Letter to the Editor, ibid.

simultaneously consuming yesterday's newspaper," wrote Baker, "I consumed an article about one Martin Davidson, a veritable Ajax of consumption. A man who wants to consume nothing but the best and does."[7] Counting, as usual, Davidson would later tell people, "I was mentioned in the *Times* on three different days."

Davidson, a self-made man whose motto is "I'm not taking it with   5
me and while I'm here I'm going to spend every stinking penny I make," couldn't understand why the *Times* had chosen to make fun of him rather than to glorify his 4,000-square-foot loft complete with bidet, Jacuzzi, professional exercise gear, pool table, pinball machine, sauna, two black-tile bathrooms, circular white Formica cooking island, status-stuffed collections of Steiff animals, pop art (including eleven Warhols), a sound system that could weaken the building's foundations if turned up full blast, and an air-conditioning system that can turn cigarette smoke, which both Davidson and Bennett abhor, into mountain dew—a loft that has everything Martin Davidson ever wanted in a home except a swimming pool and a squash court.

"People were objecting to my life-style," said Davidson. "It's almost as if there were a correlation between the fact that we spend so much on ourselves and other people are starving. No one yells when someone spends $250,000 for a chest of drawers at an auction," he complained. "I just read in the paper that someone paid $650,000 for a stupid stamp. Now it'll be put away in a vault and no one will ever see it."[8]

But Dawn Bennett understood what made Davidson's consumption different. "It's not very fashionable to be an overt consumer and admit it,"[9] she said.

What Are Things For?

As anyone knows who has seen a house turned inside out at a yard sale, furnishing a home entails the acquisition of more objects than there are in a spring housewares catalog. With all the time, money, and space we devote to the acquisition, arrangement, and maintenance of these household possessions, it is curious that we know so little about our relationships to our possessions.

"It is extraordinary to discover that no one knows why people want goods," wrote British anthropologist Mary Douglas in *The World of*

---

7. Russell Baker, "Observer: Incompleat Consumer," *New York Times,* June 9, 1979, p. 25.

8. Author's interview with Martin Davidson.

9. Author's interview with Dawn Bennett.

Goods.[10] Although no proven or agreed-upon theory of possessiveness in human beings has been arrived at, social scientists are coming up with new insights on our complicated relationships to things. Whether or not it is human nature to be acquisitive, it appears that our household goods have a more meaningful place in our lives than they have been given credit for. What comes across in a wide variety of research is that things matter enormously.

Our possessions give us a sense of security and stability. They make us   10
feel in control. And the more we control an object, the more it is a part of us. If it's *not mine,* it's *not me.*[11] It would probably make sense for everyone on the block to share a lawn mower, but then no one would have control of it. If people are reluctant to share lawn mowers, it should not surprise us that family members are not willing to share TV sets. They want their own sets so they can watch what they please. Apparently, that was why a Chicago woman, furious with her boyfriend for switching from *The Thorn Birds* to basketball, stabbed him to death with a paring knife.[12]

Besides control, we use things to compete. In the late nineteenth century the Kwakiutl Indian chiefs of the Pacific Northwest made war with possessions.[13] Their culture was built on an extravagant festival called the "potlatch," a word that means, roughly, to flatten with gifts. It was not the possession of riches that brought prestige, it was the distribution and destruction of goods. At winter ceremonials that took years to prepare for, rival chiefs would strive to outdo one another with displays of conspicuous waste, heaping on their guests thousands of spoons and blankets, hundreds of gold and silver bracelets, their precious dance masks and coppers (large shields that were their most valuable medium of exchange), and almost impoverishing themselves in the process.

Today our means of competition is the accumulation and display of symbols of status. Perhaps in Utopia there will be no status, but in this

---

10. Mary Douglas and Baron Isherwood, *The World of Goods* (New York: Basic Books, 1979), p. 15. A number of other social scientists have mentioned in recent works the lack of attention paid to the human relationship to possessions: See Coleman and Rainwater, *Social Standing,* p. 310. The authors observed that "the role of income in providing a wide range of rewards — consumption — has not received sufficient attention from sociologists." See Carl F. Graumann, "Psychology and the World of Things," *Journal of Phenomenological Psychology,* Vol. 4, 1974–75, pp. 389–404. Graumann accused the field of sociology of being thing-blind.

11. Lita Furby, "Possessions: Toward a Theory of Their Meaning and Function Throughout the Life Cycle," in Paul B. Baltes (ed.), *Life-Span Development and Behavior,* Vol. 1 (New York: Academic Press, 1978), pp. 297–336.

12. " 'Touch That Dial and You're Dead,' " *New York Post,* March 30, 1983, p. 5.

13. Ruth Benedict, *Patterns of Culture* (Boston: Houghton Mifflin [1934], 1959); Frederick V. Grunfeld, "Homecoming: The Story of Cultural Outrage," *Connoisseur,* February 1983, pp. 100–106; and Lewis Hyde, *The Gift* (New York: Vintage Books, [1979, 1980], 1983), pp. 25–39.

world, every human being is a status seeker on one level or another—
and a status reader. "Every member of society," said French anthropologist Claude Lévi-Strauss, "must learn to distinguish his fellow men according to their mutual social status."[14] This discrimination satisfies
human needs and has definite survival value. "Status symbols provide the
cue that is used in order to discover the status of others, and, from this,
the way in which others are to be treated," wrote Erving Goffman in his
classic paper, "Symbols of Class Status."[15] Status affects who is invited to
share "bed, board, and cult,"[16] said Mary Douglas. Whom we invite to
dinner affects who marries whom, which then affects who inherits what,
which affects whose children get a head start.

Today what counts is what you eat (gourmet is better than greasy
spoon), what you fly (private jet is better than common carrier), what
sports you play (sailing is better than bowling), where you matriculate,
shop, and vacation, whom you associate with, how you eat (manners
count), and most important, where you live. Blue Blood Estates or Hard
Scrabble zip codes? as one wizard of demographics calls them. He has figured out that "people tend to roost on the same branch as birds of a
feather."[17] People also use status symbols to play net worth hide-and-
seek. When *Forbes* profiled the 400 richest Americans,[18] its own in-house
millionaire Malcolm Forbes refused to disclose his net worth but was delighted to drop clues telling about his status entertainments—his bal-
looning, his Fabergé egg hunts, his châteaux, and his high life-style. It is
up to others to translate those obviously costly perks into dollars.

A high price tag isn't the only attribute that endows an object with
status. Status can accrue to something because it's scarce—a one-of-a-
kind artwork or a limited edition object. The latest hard-to-get item is
Steuben's $27,500 bowl etched with tulips that will be produced in an
edition of five—one per year for five years. "Only one bowl will bloom
this year,"[19] is the headline on the ad for it. Status is also found in objects
made from naturally scarce materials: Hawaii's rare koa wood, lapis lazuli,
or moon rock. And even if an object is neither expensive nor rare, status
can rub off on something if it is favored by the right people, which
explains why celebrities are used to promote coffee, cars, casinos, and
credit cards.

---

14. Edmund Leach, *Claude Lévi-Strauss* (New York: Penguin Books, 1980), p. 39.
15. Erving Goffman, "Symbols of Class Status," *British Journal of Sociology,* Vol. 2,
December 1951, pp. 294–304.
16. Douglas and Isherwood, *World of Goods,* p. 88.
17. Michael J. Weiss, "By Their Numbers Ye Shall Know Them," *American Way,*
February 1983, pp. 102–106 ff. "You tell me someone's zip code," said Jonathan
Robbin, "and I can predict what they eat, drink, drive, buy, even think."
18. "The Forbes 400," *Forbes,* September 13, 1982, pp. 99–186.
19. Steuben Glass advertisement, *The New Yorker,* April 4, 1983, p. 3.

If you've been associated with an object long enough you don't even   15
have to retain ownership. Its glory will shine on you retroactively. Perhaps that is why a member of Swiss nobility is having two copies made of
each of the Old Master paintings in his collection. This way, when he
turns his castle into a museum, both his children can still have, so to
speak, the complete collection, mnemonics of the pictures that have been
in the family for centuries. And the most potent status symbol of all is not
the object per se, but the *expertise* that is cultivated over time, such as the
appreciation of food, wine, design, or art.

If an object reflects a person *accurately,* it's an index of status. But *symbols* of status are not always good indices of status. They are not official
proof of rank in the same way a general's stars are. So clusters of symbols
are better than isolated ones. Anyone with $525 to spare can buy one
yard of the tiger-patterned silk velvet that Lee Radziwill used to cover
her dining chair seats.[20] But one status yard does not a princess make. A
taxi driver in Los Angeles gets a superior feeling from owning the same
status-initialed luggage that many of her Beverly Hills fares own. "I have
the same luggage you have," she tells them. "It blows their minds," she
brags. But two status valises do not a glitterati make. Misrepresenting your
social status isn't a crime, just "a presumption," said Goffman. Like wearing a $69 copy of a $1,000 watch that the mail-order catalog promises
will make you "look like a count or countess on a commoner's salary."[21]

"Signs of status are important ingredients of self. But they do not ex-
haust all the meanings of objects for people," wrote sociologists Mihaly
Csikszentmihalyi and Eugene Rochberg-Halton in *The Meaning of
Things: Domestic Symbols of the Self.*[22] The study on which the book was
based found that people cherished household objects not for their status-
giving properties but especially because they were symbols of the self and
one's connections to others.

The idea that possessions are symbols of self is not new. Many people
have noticed that *having* is intricately tied up with *being.* "It is clear that
between what a man calls *me* and what he simply calls *mine,* the line is
difficult to draw," wrote William James in 1890.[23] "Every possession is
an extension of the self," said Georg Simmel in 1900.[24] "Humans tend to

20. Paige Rense, "Lee Radziwill," *Celebrity Homes* (New York: Penguin Books,
1979), pp. 172–81.

21. *Synchronics* catalog, Hanover, Pennsylvania, Fall 1982.

22. Mihaly Csikszentmihalyi and Eugene Rochberg-Halton, *The Meaning of Things:
Domestic Symbols and the Self* (New York: Cambridge University Press, 1981), p. 18.

23. William James, *Principles of Psychology,* Vol. 1 (New York: Macmillan, 1890),
p. 291.

24. Georg Simmel, *The Philosophy of Money,* trans. Tom Bottomore and David
Frisby (Boston: Routledge & Kegan Paul, 1978), p. 331.

integrate their selves with objects," observed psychologist Ernest Beaglehole some thirty years later.[25] Eskimos used to *lick* new acquisitions to
cement the person/object relationship.[26] We stamp our visual taste on
our things making the totality resemble us. Indeed, theatrical scenic designers would be out of work if Blanche DuBois's boudoir could be furnished with the same props as Hedda Gabler's.

Csikszentmihalyi and Rochberg-Halton discovered that "things are
cherished not because of the material comfort they provide but for the
information they convey about the owner and his or her ties to others."[27] People didn't value things for their monetary worth, either. A
battered toy, a musical instrument, a homemade quilt, they said, provide
more meaning than expensive appliances which the respondents had
plenty of. "What's amazing is how few of these things really make a difference when you get to the level of what is important in life,"[28] said
Csikszentmihalyi. All those expensive furnishings "are required just to
keep up with the neighbors or to keep up with what you expect your
standard of living should be."

"How else should one relate to the Joneses if not by keeping up with   20
them," asked Mary Douglas provocatively.[29] The principle of reciprocity
requires people to consume at the same level as one's friends.[30] If we accept hospitality, we have to offer it in return. And that takes the right
equipment and the right setting. But we need things for more than
"keeping level" with our friends. We human beings are not only tool-
makers but symbol makers as well, and we use our possessions in the
same way we use language — the quintessential symbol — to *communicate*
with one another. According to Douglas, goods make the universe
"more intelligible." They are more than messages to ourselves and others, they are "the hardware and the software . . . of an information system."[31] Possessions speak a language we all understand, and we pay close
attention to the inflections, vernacular, and exclamations.

---

25. Ernest Beaglehole, *Property: A Study in Social Psychology* (New York: Macmillan, 1932).

26. Ibid., p. 134.

27. Csikszentmihalyi and Rochberg-Halton, p. 239.

28. Author's interview with Mihaly Csikszentmihalyi.

29. Douglas and Isherwood, *World of Goods,* p. 125. Also see Jean Baudrillard, *For
a Critique of the Political Economy of the Sign,* trans. Charles Levin (St. Louis, MO: Telos
Press, 1981), p. 81. Said Baudrillard: "No one is free to live on raw roots and fresh
water. . . . The vital minimum today . . . is the standard package. Beneath this level,
you are an outcast." Two classic novels on consumption are (1) Georges Perec, *Les
Choses* (New York: Grove Press, [1965], 1967). (2) J. K. Huysmans, *Against the Grain
(A Rebours)* (New York: Dover Publications, [1931], 1969).

30. Douglas and Isherwood, *World of Goods,* p. 124.

31. Ibid., p. 72.

The young husband in the film *Diner* takes his things very seriously. How could his wife be so stupid as to file the Charlie Parker records with his rock 'n' roll records, he wants to know. What's the difference, she wants to know. What's the difference? How will he find them otherwise? Every record is sacred. Different ones remind him of different times in his life. His things *take* him back. Things can also *hold* you back. Perhaps that's why Bing Crosby's widow auctioned off 14,000 of her husband's possessions—including his bed. "'I think my father's belongings have somehow affected her progress in life,'" said one of Bing's sons.[32] And things can tell you where you stand. Different goods are used to rank occasions and our guests. Costly sets of goods, especially china and porcelain, are "pure rank markers. . . . There will always be luxuries because rank must be marked," said Douglas.[33]

One of the pleasures of goods is "sharing names."[34] We size up people by their expertise in names—sports buffs can converse endlessly about hitters' batting averages, and design buffs want to know whether you speak spongeware, Palladio, Dansk, or Poggenpohl. All names are not equal. We use our special knowledge of them to show solidarity and exclude people.

In fact, the social function of possessions is like the social function of food. Variations in the quality of goods define situations as well as different times of day and seasons. We could survive on a minimum daily allotment of powdered protein mix or grains and berries. But we much prefer going marketing, making choices, learning new recipes. "Next to actually eating food, what devout gastronomes seem to enjoy most is talking about it, planning menus, and remembering meals past," observed food critic Mimi Sheraton.[35] But it's not only experts who thrive on variety. Menu monotony recently drove a Carlsbad, New Mexico, man to shoot the woman he was living with. She served him green beans once too often. "Wouldn't you be mad if you had to eat green beans all the time?" he said.[36] If every meal were the same, and if everyone dressed alike and furnished alike, all meanings in the culture would be wiped out.[37]

The furnishings of a home, the style of a house, and its landscape are all part of a system—a system of symbols. And every item in the system has meaning. Some objects have personal meanings, some have social

---

32. Maria Wilhelm, "Things Aren't Rosy in the Crosby Clan as Kathryn Sells Bing's Things (and not for a Song)," *People,* May 31, 1982, pp. 31–33.

33. Douglas and Isherwood, *World of Goods,* p. 118.

34. Ibid., p. 75.

35. Mimi Sheraton, "More on Joys of Dining Past," *New York Times,* April 9, 1983, p. 48.

36. "Green Beans Stir Bad Blood," *New York Times,* March 26, 1983, p. 6.

37. Douglas and Isherwood, *World of Goods,* p. 66.

meanings which change over time. People understand this instinctively and they desire things, not from some mindless greed, but because things are necessary to communicate with. They are the vocabulary of a sign language. To be without things is to be left out of the conversation. When we are "listening" to others we may not necessarily agree with what this person or that "says" with his or her decor, or we may misunderstand what is being said; and when we are doing the "talking" we may not be able to express ourselves as eloquently as we would like. But where there are possessions, there is always a discourse.

And what is truly remarkable is that we are able to comprehend and manipulate all the elements in this rich symbol system as well as we do— for surely the language of the home and its decor is one of the most complex languages in the world. But because of that it is also one of the richest and most expressive means of communication.

Decor as Symbol of Self

One aspect of personalization is the big I—Identity. Making distinctions between ourselves and others. "The self can only be known by the signs it gives off in communication," said Eugene Rochberg-Halton.[38] And the language of ornament and decoration communicates particularly well. Perhaps in the future we will be known by our computer communiqués or exotic brainwaves, but until then our rock gardens, tabletop compositions, refrigerator door collages, and other design language will have to do. The Nubian family in Africa with a steamship painted over the front door to indicate that someone in the house works in shipbuilding, and the Shotte family on Long Island who make a visual pun on their name with a rifle for a nameplate, are both decorating their homes to communicate "this is where our territory begins and this is who we are."

Even the most selfless people need a minimum package of identity equipment. One of Pope John Paul I's first acts as pontiff was to send for his own bed. "He didn't like sleeping in strange beds," explained a friend.[39] It hadn't arrived from Venice when he died suddenly.

Without familiar things we feel disoriented. Our identities flicker and fade like ailing light bulbs. "Returning each night to my silent, pictureless apartment, I would look in the bathroom mirror and wonder who I was," wrote D. M. Thomas, author of *The White Hotel*, recalling the sense of detachment he felt while living in a furnished apartment dur-

---

38. Eugene Rochberg-Halton, "Where Is the Self: A Semiotic and Pragmatic Theory of Self and the Environment." Paper presented at the 1980 American Sociological Meeting, New York City, 1980, p. 3.

39. Dora Jane Hamblin, "Brief Record of a Gentle Pope," *Life,* November 1978, p. 103.

ing a stint as author-in-residence at a Washington, D.C., university. "I missed familiar things, familiar ground that would have confirmed my identity."[40]

Wallpaper dealers wouldn't need fifty or sixty sample books filled with assorted geometrics, supergraphics, and peach clamshells on foil backgrounds if everyone were content to have the same roses climbing their walls. Chintz wouldn't come in forty flavors from strawberry to licorice, and Robert Kennedy, Jr.'s, bride Emily wouldn't have trotted him around from store to store "for ten hours" looking for a china pattern[41] if the home wasn't an elaborate symbol system—as important for the messages it sends to residents and outsiders as for the functions it serves.

In the five-year-long University of Chicago study[42] into how modern Americans relate to their things, investigators Mihaly Csikszentmihalyi and Rochberg-Halton found that we all use possessions to stand for ourselves. "I learned that things can embody self," said Rochberg-Halton. "We create environments that are extensions of ourselves, that serve to tell us who we are, and act as role models for what we can become."[43] But what we cherish and what we use to stand for ourselves, the researchers admitted, seemed to be "scripted by the culture."[44] Even though the roles of men and women are no longer so tightly circumscribed, "it is remarkable how influential sex-stereotyped goals still remain."[45] Men and women "pay attention to different things in the same environment and value the same things for different reasons," said the authors.[46] Men and children cared for action things and tools; women and grandparents cared for objects of contemplation and things that reminded them of family. It was also found that meaning systems are passed down in families from mothers to daughters—not to sons.

Only children and old people cared for a piece of furniture because it was useful. For adults, a specific piece of furniture embodied experiences and memories, or was a symbol of self or family. Photographs which had the power to arouse emotions and preserve memories meant the most to grandparents and the least to children. Stereos were most important to the

30

40. D. M. Thomas, "On Literary Celebrity," *The New York Times Magazine,* June 13, 1982, pp. 24–38, citation p. 27.

41. "Back Home Again in Indiana Emily Black Picks Up a Freighted Name: Mrs. Robert F. Kennedy, Jr.," *People,* April 12, 1982, pp. 121–23, citation p. 123.

42. Eugene Rochberg-Halton, "Cultural Signs and Urban Adaptation: The Meaning of Cherished Household Possessions." Ph.D. dissertation, Department of Behavioral Science, Committee on Human Development, University of Chicago, August 1979; and Mihaly Csikszentmihalyi and Eugene Rochberg-Halton, *The Meaning of Things: Domestic Symbols of the Self* (New York: Cambridge University Press, 1981).

43. Author's interview with Eugene Rochberg-Halton.

44. Csikszentmihalyi and Rochberg-Halton, *Meaning of Things,* p. 105.

45. Ibid., p. 112.

46. Ibid., p. 106.

younger generation, because they provide for the most human and emotional of our needs—release, escape, and venting of emotion. And since
music "seems to act as a modulator of emotions," it is particularly important in adolescence "when daily swings of mood are significantly greater
than in the middle years and . . . later life."[47] Television sets were cherished more by men than women, more by children than grandparents,
more by grandparents than parents. Plants had greater meaning for the
lower middle class, and for women, standing for values, especially nurtur-
ance and "ecological consciousness."[48] "Plateware," the term used in the
study to cover all eating and drinking utensils, was mentioned mostly
by women. Of course, "plates" are the tools of the housewife's trade. In
many cultures they are the legal possession of the women of the house.

The home is such an important vehicle for the expression of identity
that one anthropologist believes "built environments"—houses and
settlements—were originally developed to "*identify a group*—rather than
to provide shelter."[49] But in contemporary Western society, the house
more often identifies a person or a family instead of a group. To put no
personal stamp on a home is almost pathological in our culture. Fear of
attracting attention to themselves constrains people in crime-ridden areas
from personalizing, lack of commitment restrains others, and insecurity
about decorating skill inhibits still others. But for most people, painting
some sort of self-portrait, decoratively, is doing what comes naturally.

All communications, of course, are transactions. The identity we express is subject to interpretation by others. Will it be positive or negative?
David Berkowitz, the "Son of Sam" murderer, didn't win any points
when it was discovered he had drawn a circle around a hole in the wall
in his apartment and written "This is where I live."[50] A person who fails
to keep up appearances is stigmatized.

Reading the Text

1. Summarize how, according to Kron, our possessions act as signs of our
   identity.
2. How do our living places work to create group identity?
3. Why did *New York Times* readers object to the consumption habits of
   Martin J. Davidson?

---

47. Ibid., p. 72.

48. Ibid., p. 79.

49. Amos Rapoport, "Identity and Environment," in James S. Duncan (ed.),
Housing and Identity: Cross-Cultural Perspectives (London: Croom Helm, 1981), pp. 6–35,
citation p. 18.

50. Leonard Buder, "Berkowitz Is Described as 'Quiet' and as a Loner," *New York
Times,* August 12, 1977, p. 10.

Reading the Signs

1. In a small group, discuss the brand names of possessions that each of you owns. Then interpret the significance of each brand: What do the brands say about each of you? About the group?
2. With your class, brainstorm factors other than possessions that can communicate a person's identity. Then write your own essay in which you compare the relative value of possessions to your own sense of identity with the additional factors your class brainstormed.
3. Write an essay in which you argue for or against Kron's claim that "To put no personal stamp on a home is almost pathological in our culture" (para. 32).
4. Analyze semiotically your own apartment or a room in your house, using Kron's essay as a critical framework. How do your possessions and furnishings act as signs of your identity?
5. How would Joan Kron explain the body culture as described by Stuart Ewen ("Hard Bodies," p. 79)?

DAVID GOEWEY

"Careful, You May Run Out of Planet": SUVs and the Exploitation of the American Myth

If you think that a car is just a car and that a sport utility vehicle is just a bigger car, then David Goewey's (b. 1955) semiotic analysis of the SUV craze could be something of an eyeopener for you. Situating America's love affair with the automobile, in general, and the SUV, in particular, within an historical context, Goewey reveals how the sport utility vehicle is a full-fledged myth machine, symbolically incorporating many of America's ideological values and contradictions within its several tons of heavy metal. An actor and teacher, Goewey wrote this essay, which won the Oliver Evans Undergraduate Essay prize at California State University, Northridge, as a term paper in a class on popular culture.

"For centuries man had fantasized about the glories of independent travel," wrote the thirteenth-century scientist and philosopher Roger Bacon. Although writing during the Middle Ages, Bacon predicted, with uncanny accuracy, that humanity "shall endow chariots with incredible speed, without the aid of any animal" (Pettifer and Turner 9). Bacon's prescient forecast conjured a vision that became a twentieth-century American fact of life: the ubiquitous automobile. By 1872, French inventor Amédée Bollée had developed steam-powered demonstration models (Flink 6), and within the next thirty-five years the United States dominated the world market for gasoline-powered automobiles (Pettifer and Turner 15). In the new century America itself—with a vast geography, scattered settlements, and relatively low population density— seemed best suited to the spread of a romanticized car culture (Flink 43). America, in short, took to the roads with relish.

The automobile quickly entered American popular culture. Tin Pan Alley devoted no fewer than six hundred songs to the pleasures of motoring (Pettifer and Turner 17). The futurist art movement, furthermore, appropriated the automobile as a specific symbol of modernity itself (Wernick 80), representative of speed, progress, and technology. As a token, the car embodied escapist fantasy (Pettifer and Turner 239), allowing the individual to conquer time and space. But it was America's unique values of freedom, individualism, and the pursuit of happiness that became manifested in the automobile—values that imbued the car with definitive mythic significance (Robertson 191).

Now, at the end of the twentieth century, the vehicle that combines the most potent mix of American mythologies is the sport utility vehicle (SUV)—hybrid passenger cars/light trucks with four-wheel drive. With sales expected to exceed one million units in 1998, the SUV is the fastest-growing segment of the automobile market (Storck 79). However, as a social phenomenon, SUVs contain both practical and mythic contradictions. For example, these vehicles are designed for rugged, off-road motoring, yet a mere 10 percent of drivers ever leave surface streets or highways (Storck 99). With their muscular styling and dominant height and weight, SUVs are almost ludicrously masculine in design, yet women account for 40 percent of sales (Storck 79). Furthermore, while SUV advertising campaigns often pose the vehicle in rural settings of woodlands or along lakesides, the SUV is anything but nature-friendly with its thirsty gasoline tank and lower emission standards (Pope 14). In short, the modern SUV represents a preeminent symbol of American popular culture.

A semiotic analysis of the contradictions inherent in the SUV phenomenon, as well as its historical and socioeconomic significance, therefore, reveals the intriguing ironies that underscore America's predominant ideology. American culture's faddish preoccupation with the SUV may be seen as deeply embedded in a national identity. Furthermore, a close look at the SUV trend also reveals America's understanding of reality and fantasy and its conflicting attitude toward human survival and environmental protection. As a cultural signifier, the SUV both reveals and reflects the principal components of America's popular mythology.

The most obvious ironies are perhaps best observed in the SUV model names chosen by the manufacturers. Many vehicle names are directly evocative of America's western frontier mythology, such as the

Jeep Wrangler or the Isuzu Rodeo. Others are linked to the Western European tradition of the exploration and settlement of foreign lands, such as the Ford Explorer or the Land Rover Discovery. Indeed, the GMC Yukon blends both American western imagery and the European exploratory drive and thus embodies the American notion of a frontier: remote, extremely wild, and to the average person unknown.

The fascination with the American frontier, which today's automakers so effectively exploit, is directly tied to America's historical beginnings. The idea of the frontier as both sacred and menacing is a principal tenet in the nation's mythology. The first Europeans, after all, encountered a daunting wilderness. Mayflower passenger William Bradford described a "hideous and desolate wilderness . . . represent[ing] a wild and savage hue" (Robertson 45). The Europeans, steeped in fairy-tale traditions of the forest as the dark dwelling place of witches and cannibals, therefore considered the woods intrinsically evil (Robertson 49). The forests were godless and had to be tamed before they could be inhabitable, leveled before they could be considered usable. The Native Americans, likewise, were viewed as the personification of this savage wasteland and therefore had to be subjugated along with the wilderness to ensure the spread of civilization (Robertson 50). And the early Americans' religious convictions justified this expansion.

The notion that Americans were on a God-given mission to subdue this newfound jungle and expand Western civilization "into the limitless wilderness" (Robertson 44) became institutionalized in American mythology by the Jacksonian policy of Manifest Destiny. Americans were believed to be ordained by God to carry the noble virtues of democracy, freedom, and civilization westward across the continent (Robertson 72). This relentless expansionism, then, was suffused with religious significance and mission. The frontier was seen as the demarcation between order and disorder, between goodness and evil. To challenge the frontier, therefore, took supreme courage and zeal, and men like Daniel Boone, George Rogers Clark, and Andrew Jackson became outstanding western heroes (Robertson 80).

Corollary to this idea of an expansive frontier was the belief in the ever-abundant opportunities and riches available to whoever was brave and ambitious enough to pursue them. This idea of "more" was contingent on the belief in a limitless frontier and served as a motivating factor in the pursuit of happiness and the drive to succeed. Expansion, in a sense, became an end in itself (Shames 33–34). However, in late twentieth-century America, the concept of more has suffered a practical setback. Diminishing economic expectations from the 1960s through the 1980s, including a shrinking productivity rate, a decrease in real earnings, and a growing national debt, all contributed to challenge the mythic notion of the frontier as fruitful with economic possibilities (Shames 34–36).

It is perhaps not coincidental, then, that the sport utility vehicle craze began in earnest in the early 1980s (Storck 79). In reaction to "the fear that the world may not be . . . big enough" (Shames 37), the decade's penchant for conspicuous consumption can be seen as a challenge to that anxiety. And the introduction of large, powerful vehicles into the mass market, with names like the Ford Bronco and the Chevy Blazer, may represent the reassertion of a courageous American defiance in response to threatened frontiers.

Furthermore, the growth of the SUV market through the 1990s, with this segment comprising 23 percent of total auto sales (Storck 79), suggests the adaptability of the SUV's mythic significance. The expanding economy of the Clinton years—based on the globalization of economic interests and the consequent resurrection of expanding frontiers—recasts the SUV as a celebratory metaphor for power and control. The SUV, in this context, represents the resurgence of the conquering American.

The GMC Yukon, named for a region far from the American mainstream, can be seen to embody the cultural notion of the wild frontier as fearsome and therefore in need of civilization. And the vehicle is certainly well designed for the rugged task of settlement. Weighing in at over 5,300 pounds (with passengers), measuring over 16½ feet in length and just under 6 feet in height, the GMC Yukon is among the largest SUVs on the market (Storck 27). Its massive size arguably manifests the expansive idea of America's western frontier.

However, the GMC Yukon's heftiness necessarily affects its miles-per-gallon ratio. The average rounds off at a measly 13 miles per gallon (Storck 27), less than half what the U.S. government requires for passenger cars. And with a fuel tank capacity of 30 gallons and an estimated full tank mileage of under 400 miles, the GMC Yukon can be seen vehemently to declare the concept of more. Furthermore, juxtaposing the GMC Yukon with its namesake suggests an egregious symmetry. The Yukon Territory, north of British Columbia, Canada, abuts Prudhoe Bay. Exploratory oil drilling there in 1967 uncovered the largest oilfield in North America, with an estimated capacity of about 10 billion barrels (Yergin 571). The American myth of an ever-expansive frontier, then, is powerfully manifested in the heavyweight GMC Yukon, which locates and justifies its own mass production in the fact of a naturally oil-abundant Yukon Territory.

Another popular SUV that contains a doubly potent signifier within the manufacturer's title is the Jeep Cherokee. Considered the original SUV, the Jeep Cherokee dates all the way back to 1948. As a result, owners take a measure of purist's pride, believing their SUV is the one that started it all (Storck 41). But a closer look at this SUV's mythohistorical connections may provide the owners' pride with a deeper significance.

The Jeep Cherokee prototype—the General Purpose Vehicle, which was shortened to Jeep—was introduced during World War II in response to a U.S. Army–sponsored competition among automakers. It was first developed by the Bantam Motor Company, and the design was then completed by the Willys-Overland Company. The Ford Motor Company also assisted in the mass production of what was soon considered the "backbone of all Allied military transport" and the "crowning success of the war" (Flink 276). No doubt drawing on their heroic wartime performance, surplus military jeeps were sold stateside and helped to introduce a market for four-wheel drive, recreational vehicles (Flink 276).

The usefulness and durability of four-wheel-drive vehicles, however, was recognized even earlier during World War I, and many automakers, including Packard, Peerless, and Nash motor companies, vied for government contracts. Manufacturers found that luxury car chassis were easily converted to 2 or 3 ton truck bodies (Flink 78)—a literal blending of automobiles and trucks that clearly prefigures the modern SUV. Along with the Jeep's victorious wartime service, then, the SUV conveys such powerful militaristic connotations as morally righteous patriotism, overwhelming industrial ingenuity and might, and the imperative conquest of evil.

An interesting link between automobility and the American frontier was provided approximately forty years earlier by a Civil War hero. On his retirement in 1903, Civil War veteran General Nelson A. Miles, who had successfully hunted Chief Joseph and the Nez Perce to ground in 1877 and to whom the Apache war leader Geronimo surrendered in 1886 (Josephy 416, 429), foresaw the military promise of motor vehicles. He urged Secretary of War Elihu Root to "replace five regiments of calvary" with troops on bicycles and in motor vehicles (Flink 74), believing that the horse was now obsolete. General Miles's foresight was ironic in light of the Jeep Cherokee's double significance.

The Jeep Cherokee's militaristic connotations become oppressive when considering the grotesquely racist misapplication of a Native American tribal name to a motor vehicle. Although the word *Cherokee* is a misnomer derived from the Choctaw definition for cave dwellers and actually has no meaning in the language of those to whom it is applied, it is nevertheless used to designate at least one group of Native Americans, the United Keetoowah Band of Cherokee, in Oklahoma (Josephy 323). This original misnaming indicates the indeterminability of language, especially in the traumatic context of Native American history. And while it may be argued that such indeterminacy freely allows a manufacturer's use of the name to sell a product, the word *Cherokee* nevertheless denotes a group of people still thriving today despite oppression.

In the 1820s, despite the fierce allegiance to tradition held by many Cherokee, a large number of them succumbed to the ongoing

15

proselytizing efforts of Moravian missionaries to become the "most acculturated of southern tribes" (Josephy 320). The Cherokee learned the English alphabet and even innovated a Cherokee alphabet based on the English model. In 1828, this led to the remarkable publication, in English and Cherokee, of a native newspaper (Josephy 320). Cherokee efforts to assimilate into what could be seen even then as a dominant culture, in other words, were vigorous.

Nevertheless, also in 1828, President Andrew Jackson undertook an aggressive campaign of ethnic cleansing against the Cherokee. Capitalizing on white racism to pass anti-Cherokee legislation, and with the discovery of gold on Cherokee territory, Jackson made physical removal of the tribe a national issue (Josephy 325). This culminated in the infamous and tragic Trail of Tears, the forced march west to Oklahoma of eighteen thousand Cherokee men, women, and children under the armed escort of General Winfield Scott and seven thousand U.S. Army troops (Josephy 331).

The manufacturers of the Jeep Cherokee clearly ignore this dismal   20
chapter in U.S. history and instead evoke superficially positive components of a mythic American past. Drawing on traditional viewpoints of the western frontier as the border between civilization and wilderness (Robertson 92) and oblivious to the fact that the Cherokee were an enforced western tribe, the Jeep Cherokee manufacturer exploits mythic identifications of Native Americans with the fearsome and violent "imagery and logic of the frontier" (Robertson 106).

The Jeep Cherokee manufacturer also mines the symbol of the quintessential American hero, the cowboy. Pitted against the frontier, the cowboy was directly descended from the backwoodsmen and pathfinders who pioneered west to the Ohio River Valley and beyond to the Northwest Passage. As the frontier pushed on, the continent's western plains and mountains became the wilderness that was next in need of subjugation and control. The cowboy, and his close companions in the American mythic imagination of the Wild West, the U.S. Calvary, became the defenders of civilization and the champions of progress (Robertson 161–62). As such, they symbolized law and order in a lawless land. Both the cowboy and the U.S. Calvary were the good guys risking themselves to save civilization from the bad guys, most notably the wildly violent Indians (Robertson 162).

The Jeep Cherokee, then, is a multilayered symbol indeed. This SUV appropriates the token of a victorious American struggle over the frontier, won by American cowboys and calvarymen, and combines it with the morally righteous conquest over evil achieved during World War II. The modern driver who slips behind the wheel of a Jeep Cherokee assumes the militaristically heroic mantle that is suffused within the vehicle's legend and manifested in the control available in the "tight and precise steering, easy maneuverability . . . and taut overall feel from the firm suspension" (Storck 41). Detached from historical truths, however, the SUV's "excellent visibility all around" and "superior driving position" (Storck 41), qualities essential to success in battle, capitalize on these military/frontier connotations and at the same time sublimate factual battlefield horrors into an aggressive game of on-the-road cowboys and Indians.

The SUV, with its rugged militaristic symbolism, magnifies the traditional association of the automobile as a masculine token. Yet women account for a sizable share of the SUV market (Storck 79). This appeal, in fact, extends and amplifies a traditional relationship between women and motor vehicles. The introduction of the automobile may well have affected the scope of women's societal role more than that of men. Unlike the horse and buggy, for instance, the automobile demanded skill over physical strength to operate, and so women were offered mobility and parity that driving a team of horses denied them (Flink 162).

However, middle-class women by the 1920s were still traditionally tied to the home, for the most part, although electrical household appliances had nevertheless increased leisure time. The refrigerator, for example, permitted the bulk buying of a week's worth of perishable food at one stop, leaving time for socializing or an afternoon movie matinee (Flink 164). The added spare time, combined with automobility's enhanced sense of individual freedom (Robertson 191), afforded women at least temporary escape from the confines of the home that defined their routine (Flink 163).

As the automobile helped to change women's role from that of home-based providers of food and clothing into consumers of mass-produced goods, car designers soon recognized the potential of the female market. Such comfort features as plush upholstery, heaters, and automatic transmissions were planned with women in mind (Flink 163). And advertising executives, quick to determine that women were disproportionately the nation's consumers (Marchand 66), began to target automobile ads at them. One of the most famous advertisements, for the Jordan Motor Company's Playboy automobile, began "Somewhere west of Laramie there's a broncho-busting, steer-roping girl" (Pettifer and Turner 130), clearly utilizing the familiar western imagery of freedom and control.

This relationship between women and their automobiles has grown even more complex in recent years. First, the car didn't so much redefine women's fundamental domestic role as increase the scope of its domain. Also, it is reasonable to assume that the automobile facilitated women's introduction into the workplace by easing transportation between the home and job. And yet in 1997, economic equality still eludes the American workforce: working women earn less than 75 percent of men's average income (Jones et al. 49). A woman's job, furthermore, may include not only doing outside work but ferrying children to and from school and activities and shopping for the family. A subsequent feeling of disempowerment, then, may find relief behind the wheel of a physically powerful and symbolically potent SUV.

Advertisers evidently think so. They still acknowledge a woman's buying power and capitalize on the appeal SUVs hold for many female drivers. One current SUV advertisement aimed at women, promoting the Subaru Forester, both stresses its inherent power and rugged potential and notes the female-friendly design of this smaller vehicle. The larger photo in a recent two-page spread in *Time* shows the Forester kicking up a dust trail as it barrels down a dirt track. The accompanying smaller picture presents a casually dressed young woman easily tying a kayak to the SUV's roof. The ad's dominant image is a rough and careless strength. And while the woman in the ad is proportionally submissive, she is capably preparing for an exciting outdoor adventure. The double message suggests a sense of diminishment that is compensated for with images of ability, ease, and the casual transference of power.

Perhaps the most logical and disarming association carmakers and advertisers exploit when designing and promoting an SUV is the vehicle's connection to nature. As previously noted, implicit within the SUV's frontier imagery is a confrontational attitude toward the wilderness. Accordingly, automakers design—and advertisers sell—SUVs capable of handling the roughest terrain. And indeed, much of the appeal of SUVs is their promise of providing access to the farthest reaches of the globe. As a marketing gimmick, for instance, Land Rover cosponsors and participates in the annual Camel Trophy relay, pitting various SUVs against the jungle wilds of Borneo and South America. Besides the obvious British imperialistic connotations such a race implies, the challenge of maneuvering a Land Rover Discovery "over garbage can sized rocks" or "through streams where the entire vehicle is submerged" (Storck 6) positions the competitor in a naturally inharmonious contest.

Advertisers take a dual approach when exploiting the adversarial relationship between SUVs and nature. In some print ads this relationship is clothed in benign natural imagery, often with a warning text. The Mitsubishi Montero Sport, for example, pictures a gleaming silver vehicle perched prominently on the rocky shoreline of a wooded lakesite. The tall stand of evergreen trees are at a safe distance; the water surface is without a ripple. The bold black headline proclaims, "It Came to Comfort Earth," and the text goes on to inform the reader that "the planet wasn't exactly designed for your comfort."

So the Montero Sport offers a wondrous solution to an uncomfortable world. The proximity of nature to the vehicle in the photo is remote, suggesting that the mere presence of the Montero Sport is enough to keep nature at bay. Furthermore, the SUV's silver color combines with the headline to imply that the Montero Sport carries an otherworldly salvation. Nature and its uncomfortability, therefore, are controlled by the SUV's omnipresence, and the driver is safe to the vehicle's "car-like . . . civility."

Ads for the luxury Infiniti QX4 portray a similar oppositional message but with a more active approach. A silver SUV is pictured once again, but this time bolting through the shallow water of black-rock lakeshore. The landpoint jutting into the water directly behind the QX4, as though in pursuit, is in silhouette and resembles a large black serpent lagging just behind. The text's message cautions: "careful, you may run out of planet." Although the threat is clear, the presentation is nevertheless one of SUV power in opposition to nature. Indeed, the QX4 appears to be riding atop the water, and the text ends with the admonishment, "resist the urge to circumnavigate the globe."

So while the Infiniti ad sells the promise of adventure, at the same time it positions the SUV's representational power as necessary and inevitable. The QX4 is vigorously slashing through the water on its way to points unknown because it has to; the natural environment is dangerous, hostile to civilization, and quite capable of destroying it if not met with even more superior power. And as if to drive home the point, both the Montero Sport and the Infiniti QX4 ads present a silver SUV as the symbol of modernity, thereby drawing on the traditional American mythology of progress in opposition to a hostile wilderness.

The design and marketing of SUVs are based on traditional American attitudes toward nature and the wilderness. The vehicles are at the same time built for access to the natural world and yet sold by exploiting that relationship as confrontational. The SUV, in other words, makes easily available a world that is threatening to the driver and its occupants. And yet underlying these contradictions, and compounding them, is the very real impact that SUVs make on the environment.

The GMC Suburban, big sister to the aforementioned GMC Yukon, asserts itself with a 42 gallon capacity fuel tank. With a curb-side weight pushing five thousand pounds and amenities like air conditioning, the Suburban's gas mileage is generously estimated at about 16 miles to the gallon (Storck 29). While the GMC Suburban is admittedly the largest SUV model on the market, poor gas mileage ratios are the norm for these vehicles. Where the Environmental Protection Agency has determined that automobiles must meet a fuel economy standard of 27.5 miles a gallon, light trucks, which include all SUVs, currently need only to clear 20.7 miles a gallon. And many don't even achieve that (Bradsher).

The world oil industry may keep billions of barrels in their inventories on any given day (Yergin 686), leading to the understandable public perception that supplies are unlimited. But fossil fuels are still a nonrenewable resource. Moreover, American gasoline use is expected to rise by 33 percent within the next fifteen years, indicating that fuel conservation is not much of an issue with consumers (Bradsher).

But perhaps the more pressing problem, and one that is directly exacerbated by the SUV craze, is the threat of global warming from the increased burning of fossil fuels. Carbon dioxide levels in the atmosphere have risen by about 25 percent in the last century and appear to coincide with a worldwide increase in the use of petroleum. Various cataclysmic effects are predicted as a result, including rising sea levels from melting ice caps, the spread of tropical diseases to normally temperate regions, and extreme weather fluctuations (McKibben 9, 18). Yet the booming SUV market belies any overwhelming concern on the part of American consumers. In fact, the vehicle's popularity in the face of such dire predictions seems the latest manifestation of an established confrontational relationship to nature.

As the world does indeed become more dangerous, the apparent protection that SUVs afford becomes more desirable, and the need to control the uncontrollable becomes more acute. Driving a five thousand pound, resource-devouring behemoth not only justifies the impact on the environment, as a means of revenge against an enemy, but it acts as a means of celebration—the exultation of victory over the savage beast of nature. The SUV, in its design and presentation, seeks to make safely available what it can ultimately dominate; as such, it attempts to reduce the entire world to the state of a drive-through wildlife nature preserve. At the end of the twentieth century, the SUV perfectly embodies an American mythology of conquest and control.

America's love affair with the sport utility vehicle shows the abiding power of traditional beliefs. The expansion of the frontiers continues despite facts that suggest there is nowhere left to go. This joyful faith in "more" feeds on the challenge of less. Indeed, a sport utility vehicle is the triumphant representation of denial—denial of the past, the present, and the future. American mythology is continuously reinvented and thereby endures in this pop cultural symbol.

WORKS CITED

Bradsher, Keith. "Light Trucks Increase Profits But Foul Air More Than Cars." *New York Times* 30 Nov. 1997, national ed., sec. 1:1+.
Flink, James J. *The Automobile Age.* Cambridge: MIT, 1988.
Jones, Barbara, Anita Blair, Barbara Ehrenreich, Arlie Russell Hochschild, Jeanne Lewis, and Elizabeth Perle McKenna. "Giving Women the Business." *Harper's* Dec. 1997: 47–58.
Josephy, Alvin M., Jr. *Five Hundred Nations: An Illustrated History of North American Indians.* New York: Knopf, 1994.
Marchand, Roland. *Advertising the American Dream: Making Way for Modernity 1920–1940.* Berkeley: University of California Press, 1985.
McKibben, Bill. *The End of Nature.* New York: Anchor, 1989.
Pettifer, Julian, and Nigel Turner. *Automania: Man and the Motorcar.* Boston: Little, Brown, 1984.
Pope, Carl. "Car Talks—Motown Walks." *Sierra Magazine* Mar./Apr. 1996: 14+.

Robertson, James Olvier. *American Myth, American Reality*. New York: Hill & Wang, 1980.

Shames, Laurence. "The More Factor." *Signs of Life in the USA: Readings on Popular Culture for Writers*. Ed. Sonia Maasik and Jack Solomon. Boston: Bedford, 1994.

Storck, Bob. *Sport Utility Buyer's Guide '98*. Milwaukee: Pace, 1998.

Wernick, Andrew. "Vehicles for Myth." *Signs of Life in the USA: Readings on Popular Culture for Writers*. Ed. Sonia Maasik and Jack Solomon. Boston: Bedford, 1994.

Yergin, Daniel. *The Prize: The Epic Quest for Oil, Money and Power*. New York: Simon & Schuster, 1991.

Reading the Text

1. What significance does Goewey see in the names automakers give to SUVs?
2. In your own words, explain why Goewey considers the popularity of SUVs to be full of "ironies" (para. 5) and "contradictions" (para. 4).
3. How does Goewey account for the SUV's appeal to women?
4. In Goewey's view, why does the imagery associated with SUVs have an adversarial relationship with nature?
5. Chart how Goewey uses the semiotic method. How does he explicate the system to which SUVs belong and the cultural mythologies that such vehicles evoke?

Reading the Signs

1. Write a journal entry in which you interpret how your own car (or that of a friend or relative) acts as a sign. What messages does it send about your identity?
2. Using Goewey's approach as a model, interpret a different category of automobile—small two-seaters such as the Mazda Miata.
3. Collect automobile advertisements from several popular magazines, and analyze how the cars are promoted as signs. What slogans are used to catch your interest? What values and ideologies are linked to particular makes and models?
4. Interview several people who drive SUVs on why they prefer this type of vehicle. Use your findings as a basis for an essay in which you support, refute, or complicate Goewey's thesis. Be sure to keep in mind that Goewey acknowledges that he is analyzing unconscious, not deliberate, motivating factors.

CHAPTER TWO

BROUGHT TO YOU B(U)Y

The Signs of Advertising

Are you wearing jeans? What brand? Gap? Levi's? Bugle Boys? Tommy Hilfiger? The brand matters, doesn't it? Because those aren't just jeans you're wearing: they're a statement, they project an image. In the last chapter we looked at the many ways in which the products you buy make statements, but there is another part of the story to tell. You often have an assistant on hand to help you choose the images that you want your belongings to project: this assistant is an advertiser, whose primary interest is that you buy a particular product.

Advertising: it's not just show and tell. Just think of the many ways jeans alone are pitched in America. Take Levi's as an example. How are they packaged for the marketplace? What sorts of images are associated with them today? Take care to be up to date because those images change rapidly as the trends of popular culture change. In the 1980s, for example, Levi's were promoted as hip urban wear in TV spots set on city streets, where they were associated with the blues as "Levi's 501 Blues." These commercials were notable for the way they took a fashion that had been associated with rural and wilderness settings in the 1960s—the back-to-the-land movement—and redefined them as a part of the back-to-the-city trend of the 1980s. The significance of this shift, once more, lay in a *difference*—in the vast gap between Walden Pond and Wall Street. But that was then and this is now. Look at a Levi's display in your local department store. With what are they associated today? Do these associations make you want to go out and buy a pair?

Interpreting the Signs of Advertising

Let's say you are assigned the task of writing a semiotic analysis of an advertisement, and you choose a print ad for blue jeans—in particular, an ad campaign for Calvin Klein jeans that drew a lot of political as well as consumer attention in 1995. (To see a collection of such ads on the Internet, you can go to **http://pobox.upenn.edu/~davidtoc/ calvin.html.**) One representative ad in the campaign featured a boy and a girl, both epitomes of the waif look—straight, bleached hair, very thin bodies. They stand next to an ordinary ladder with a simple paneled wall for a backdrop. The boy is shirtless; the girl wears a revealing white tank top. Both figures thrust their pelvises forward in provocative poses, and the girl's makeup suggests that her eyes have been blackened. Finally, both models appear to be in their early adolescence, perhaps fourteen years old.

To interpret this ad, you need first, as always in a semiotic analysis, to suspend your opinion of the actual object of your analysis—in this case, Calvin Klein jeans. What you are studying is the image with which the object is associated. To analyze that image, you will want to study the details of the ad itself and the cultural system in which the ad functions, looking for both associations and differences. Let's begin by considering the cultural system.

We can note, for example, that Calvin Klein's advertisers have long used youthful sexuality to promote jeans, starting with a fifteen-year-old Brooke Shields in 1979 who cooed that nothing came between her and her Calvins. Similarly, Jordache in the 1970s made quite clear the connection between sexual satisfaction and skin-tight denim attire, while in the early 1990s Guess? jeans featured such models as Claudia Schiffer posed in such a way that it wasn't always clear whether the ad was for blue jeans or Maidenform. In short, advertisers have long been using sexual imagery to sell jeans; the question is "Why?"

Discussing the Signs of Advertising

Bring to class a print ad from a newspaper or magazine, and in small groups discuss your semiotic reading of it. Be sure to ask, "Why am I being shown this or being told that?" How do the characters in the ad function as signs? What sort of people don't appear as characters? What cultural myths are invoked in this ad? What relationship do you see between those myths and the intended audience of the publication? Which ads do your group members respond to positively and why? Which ads doesn't your group like?

The answer to this question may seem obvious. After all, sex is a potent attention-getter and so is frequently used to sell all sorts of products. But as we continue to consider the cultural system in which blue jeans advertisements signify, it is important to note how, at least at first, sex could not have been used to sell jeans. This is because from the first appearance of jeans in America in the nineteenth century up through the 1950s, denim clothing was associated with manual labor. Miners, steel workers, and cowboys wore jeans, a clothing staple that was designed for durability and comfort, not for fashion and style. When, by the 1950s, jeans had become popular as leisure as well as work wear, the association was still with comfort over style, especially for women. If a woman wanted to wear sexy pants, she put on pedal pushers or capris. It is true that, among such marginalized subcultures as motorcycle gangs, jeans had already begun to assume a new meaning as a symbol of defiance, but, by and large, jeans still signified comfort wear for work or leisure.

The change came in the 1960s, when middle-class youth (following the lead of the 1950s bikers) adopted blue jeans as one of their symbols of rebellion against the bourgeois values of their parents. At first, however, the significance of the symbol came from the old system. That is, by wearing denim, middle-class kids sought to identify themselves with the working class. But as jeans became more and more fashionable, they changed their meaning—and this is something that happens all the time in popular cultural consumption. Thanks to changing circumstances, the same object assumes a different meaning. In the case of blue jeans, as millions of young people adopted the new fashion, the old significance was forgotten. Consumers saw jeans less as a sign of working-class solidarity and more as fashion necessities that helped launch the sexual revolution that swept America in the middle to late sixties. By the 1970s, then, jeans had become associated with fashion and sex, not work, and manufacturers responded with sexy new designs and marketing campaigns.

So far our analysis of the Calvin Klein campaign has revealed a good deal about America's popular cultural history in the postwar era. But even though the Klein ads reflect the sexualization of blue jeans that began in the 1960s, the public response to the way the 1995 CK ads made use of sex was so negative that Calvin Klein canceled them after a few months. Klein's retreat was especially significant because the Brooke Shields campaign attracted a lot of criticism in its time, but never severe enough to cause a retraction. What then is the difference between the two ad campaigns, and what can we learn from it?

By looking more closely at the details of the 1995 ad itself, we can see that every detail counts—the lighting, the use of color (or lack of it), the copy that may (or may not) accompany the ad, and the posing of the models. If we consider the ad in question, we find two pale and rather glum-looking teenagers, provocatively dressed and posed. The ad is also in black and white, a detail that enhances the stark, even sinister tone of the scene, which at the time was referred to as "heroin chic." This contrasts sharply with the 1979 Brooke Shields campaign. Those ads were in color and featured a well-known child fashion model and movie star who appears in her ads as a girl in charge of her sexuality and her world. The anonymous children in the later ad, on the other hand, don't look like they're in charge at all. There's a hint that, if anything, they're in bondage, offering themselves to the gaze of some sleezy voyeur. This suggestion comes from the makeup that hints at beatings and the pairing of the two figures against a plain, even harsh, background that evokes the aura of a low-budget child pornography video.

One might object that we are "reading too much into the ad." But a look at the ad's public reception—the social context in which it is meaningful—suggests that this interpretation may not be so far-fetched after all. The ad (and others like it in the same CK campaign) met with an immediate and vocal public protest, as well as published reviews that pointed out the ads' pornographic style. It wasn't the sexuality that caused all the trouble—as we've seen, that's been a staple of blue jeans advertising for years—it was the suggestion of child abuse and exploitation. And this, in turn, raises another set of questions for semiotic analysis.

That is, why would Calvin Klein use such images? Here we can look for a new set of associations, relating this time to teenaged sexuality in the 1990s, as well as to pornography and child abuse. One association we can make is to a movie called *Kids,* which appeared shortly before the appearance of the Klein ads. This film also featured a rather stark and quasi-pornographic depiction of youthful sexuality, and so it could be argued that Klein may have been simply trying to piggyback onto the popularity of the film to attract young consumers.

This interpretation might have some truth to it, but we think that there is more to the matter. First of all, we need to consider this ad's relation to another Klein ad that was also pulled in response to a public outcry, an ad selling not jeans but underwear. This ad featured a teenaged male model provocatively posed (and made-up) in briefs. Now, this ad violated two taboos. The first taboo, which it shared with the image of the boy and the girl, is its open depiction of child sexuality. The second taboo is its unusually explicit (unusual, that is, for mainstream culture) appeal to the homoerotic gaze. By considering such taboos, and their violation, we can move toward our full interpretation of the ads.

Let's begin with taboo against depicting child sexuality. In our culture, by law as well as moral precept, any sexual approach to a child (someone under eighteen years of age) is a form of child abuse. Until recently, the subject of child abuse—of which child pornography is a particularly ugly example—was not something Americans liked to think about. It happened, but we didn't talk about it. In the past few years the topic has been put on the front burner of American consciousness, however, and not only among oversensitive adults. Consider the subject of one of Pearl Jam's earliest hits, "Jeremy," a song that tells the story of a mistreated child. Or of Ten Thousand Maniacs' "What's the Matter Here," an unambiguous description of suburban child abuse. The pop singer Fiona has made a career out of dramatizing the way she was sexually abused as a child. In short, what was once unspoken now appears on the pop charts, and with that shift in consciousness has come a greater sensitivity to potentially abusive images. The depiction of these two black-eyed waifs sporting the "abandoned" look that was often found in late nineties fashion photography is thus more likely to provoke an accusation of child exploitation than it was in the days when such subjects weren't part of public consciousness.

Oddly enough, given all the resistance to his exploitation of teen sexuality, in 1999 Clavin Klein went even further by posting a billboard in Times Square featuring *little* children in underwear. The campaign immediately made the national news, but the uproar was so intense this time that it was canceled within a matter of hours. Still, the billboard did go up, albeit briefly, which itself illustrates the way that pedophilia—which has traditionally been among the most taboo of pornographic fetishes—is now such a part of popular cultural discourse that it can at least be tried out for marketing purposes.

We can expand the scope of our survey of fashion advertising to note that a great many advertisements in the nineties feature models whose expressions could be described as everything from waiflike and abandoned to tormented and abused. Take a look at any contemporary fashion magazine. Note how often the women, in particular, appear as if they're about to be attacked. And even when things aren't that extreme, consider the serious expressions they often have on their faces. In conventional fashion advertising—just look at a mail-order catalog—

Exploring the Signs of Advertising

Select one of the products advertised in the "Portfolio of Advertisements" (pp. 210–21), and design in your journal an alternative ad for that product. Consider what different images or cast of characters you could include. What different myths—and thus different values—could you use to pitch this product? Then freewrite on the significance of your alternative ad. If you have any difficulty imagining an alternative image for the product, what does that say about the power of advertising to control our view of the world? What does your choice of imagery and cultural myths say about you?

everyone looks happy. But high fashion imagery in the nineties seemed to require some hint at sadomasochism. In such an environment, the Calvin Klein ads can be associated with a trend in which sex and suffering have been bonded—the traditional formula for pornography.

The Calvin Klein ads with homoerotic overtones refer us to a different cultural change. That is, while mainstream American society is still openly hostile to homosexuality, youth culture is not. The popularity of such gender benders as Marilyn Manson and Dennis Rodman points to a widespread trend among American youth to experiment with sexual codes, challenge tradition, and violate taboos. Knowing this, the Calvin Klein advertisers may have thought that explicitly homoerotic advertising could help expand sales in the youth market.

At this point, we can sketch out a thesis, which is that the Calvin Klein campaign used images hinting at teenage sexuality and homoeroticism to sell to a youth culture that embraced such images—but that it miscalculated the response of the adult audience who would see such ads as child pornography, both heterosexual and homosexual. The body of our essay would then be devoted to defending this thesis.

Note the process by which we came to our thesis. We didn't begin with it. Rather, in our prewriting stage, we began by looking around for sets of associations to similar signs, as well as for significant differences. By building several systems of associated and differentiated signs, we arrived at a conclusion. But in writing a paper presenting and defending our thesis, we wouldn't order our ideas according to the sequence in which we thought of them; we would reverse the order. That is, we would present our thesis first, then use the body of the essay to defend and develop that thesis. The evidence we would use to defend our argument has already been suggested in our overview of both the details of the ad and the systems in which it functions. We would point, for example, to the *difference* between the image of Brooke Shields's confidently empowered sexuality and the vulnerable and brutalized images in the more recent ad to support our contention that the image is not simply one of teen sexuality innocently designed for teen viewers. We would also point to a *system* of fashion advertisements that feature quasi-pornographic or sadomasochistic images with which the ads can be associated, as well as to a subcultural tendency toward gender bending and sexual experimentation. We would also point to the *difference* between Calvin Klein's response to past criticism (he's never backed down before) and his decision to pull this campaign: the suggestion here is of a recognition that things may have gone too far.

Having assembled the evidence, we can now present a larger conclusion based on our thesis—that America is going through a period of cultural fascination with such traditionally forbidden forms of sexual expression as pedophilia, sadomasochism, and homoeroticism, an obsession strong enough to cause advertisers to exploit it in a never-ending struggle to move the goods and protesters to denounce just how far advertisers are willing to go. This larger conclusion would come at the end of our essay rather than at the beginning. By building on the foundation provided by our introductory thesis, we can develop our argument rather than simply repeat it at the end. This is one of the secrets of effective academic argumentation: you want to begin with a working thesis and defend that thesis in the body of your essay, but your conclusion shouldn't simply restate your thesis. Rather, your conclusion should suggest an enlargement of your thesis, a sense of development instead of simple repetition.

The Semiotic Foundation

Having outlined a semiotic analysis of a particular advertisement, we turn now to a semiotic overview of the overall logic of advertising. Indeed, there is perhaps no better field for semiotic analysis than advertising, for ads work characteristically by substituting signs for things, and by reading those signs you can discover the values and desires that advertisers seek to exploit.

It has long been recognized that advertisements substitute images of desire for the actual products. Coca Cola ads, for example, don't really sell soda: they sell images of fun, popularity, or sheer celebrity, promising a gratifying association with the likes of Paula Abdul or Whitney Houston if you'll only drink "The Real Thing." Automobile commercials, for their part, are notorious for selling not transportation but fantasies of power, prestige, sexual potency, or even generational solidarity, as a Mercedes-Benz commercial featuring the crooning voice of the late Janis Joplin demonstrates in its appeal to baby-boom consumers most likely to recognize her old song, "Lord, Won't You Buy Me a Mercedes-Benz."

By substituting desirable images for concrete needs, modern advertising seeks to transform desire into necessity. You *need* food, for example, but it takes an ad campaign to convince you through attractive images that you need a Big Mac. Your job may require you to have a car, but it's an ad that persuades you that a Jeep Cherokee is necessary for your happiness. If advertising worked otherwise, it would simply present you with a functional profile of a product and let you decide whether it will do the job.

From the early twentieth century, advertisers have seen their task as the transformation of desire into necessity. In the twenties and thirties, for example, voluminously printed advertisements created elaborate story lines designed to convince readers that they needed this mouthwash to attract a spouse or that caffeine-free breakfast drink to avoid trouble on the job or in the home. In such ads, products were made to appear not only desirable but absolutely necessary. Without them, your very survival as a socially competent being would be in question.

Many ads still work this way, particularly "guilt" ads that prey on your insecurities and fears. Deodorants are typically pitched in such a fashion, playing on our fear of smelling bad in public. Can you think of any other products whose ads play on guilt or shame? Do you find them to be effective?

The Commodification of Desire

Associating a logically unrelated desire with an actual product (as in pitching beer through sexual come-ons) can be called the "commodification" of desire. In other words, desire itself becomes the product that the advertiser is selling. This marketing of desire was recognized as early as the 1950s in Vance Packard's *The Hidden Persuaders*. In that book, Packard points out how by the 1950s America was well along in its historic shift from a producing to a consuming economy. The implications for advertisers were enormous. Since the American economy was increasingly dependent on the constant growth of consumption, as the introduction to Chapter 1 of this text discusses, manufacturers had to find ways to convince people to consume ever more goods. So they turned to the advertising mavens on Madison Avenue, who responded with advertisements that persuaded consumers to replace perfectly serviceable products with "new and improved" substitutions within an overall economy of planned design obsolescence.

America's transformation from a producer to a consumer economy also explains that while advertising is a worldwide phenomenon, it is nowhere so prevalent as it is here. Open a copy of the popular French picture magazine *Paris Match*. You'll find plenty of paparazzi photos of international celebrities but almost no advertisements. Then open a copy of *Vogue*. It is essentially a catalog, where scarcely a page is without its ad. Indeed, advertisers themselves call this plethora of advertising "clutter" that they must creatively "cut through" each time they design a new ad campaign. The ubiquity of advertising in our lives points to a society in which people are constantly pushed to buy, as opposed to economies like Japan's that emphasize constant increases in production. And desire is what loosens the pocketbook strings.

While the basic logic of advertising may be similar from era to era, the content of an ad, and hence its significance, differs as popular culture changes. Looking at ads from different eras tells the tale. Advertising in the 1920s, for instance, focused especially on its market's desires for improved social status. Ads for elocution and vocabulary lessons, for example, appealed to working- and lower-middle-class consumers who were invited to fantasize that buying the product or service could help them enter the middle class. Meanwhile, middle-class consumers were invited to compare their enjoyment of the sponsor's product with that of the upper-class models shown happily slurping this coffee or purchasing that vacuum cleaner in the ad. Of course, things haven't changed *that* much since the twenties. Can you think of any ads that use this strategy today? How often are glamorous celebrities called in to make you identify with his or her "enjoyment" of a product? Have you heard ads for vocabulary-building programs that promise you a "verbal advantage" in the corporate struggle?

One particularly amusing ad from the twenties played on America's fear of communism in the wake of the Bolshevik revolution in Russia. "Is your washroom breeding Bolsheviks?" asks a print ad from the Scot paper towel company. The ad's lengthy copy explains how it might be doing so. If your company restroom is stocked with inferior paper towels, it says, discontent will proliferate among your employees and lead to subversive activities. R.C.A. Victor and Campbell's Soup, we are assured, are no such breeding grounds of subversion, thanks to their contracts with Scot. You, too, can fight the good fight against communism by buying Scot towels, the ad suggests. To whom do you think this ad was directed? What did they fear?

Populism versus Elitism

American advertising tends to swing in a pendulum motion between the status-conscious ads that dominated the twenties and the more populist approach of decades like the seventies, when country music and truck-driving cowboys lent their popular appeal to Madison Avenue. This swing between elitist and populist approaches in advertising reflects a basic division within the American dream itself, a mythic promise that at once celebrates democratic equality *and* encourages you to rise above the crowd to be better than anyone else. Sometimes Americans are more attracted to one side than to the other, but there is bound to be a shift back to the other side when the thrill wears off. Thus, the populist appeal of the seventies (even disco had a distinct working-class flavor: recall John Travolta's character in *Saturday Night Fever*) gave way to the elitist eighties, and advertising followed. Products such as Gallo's varietal wines, once considered barely a step up from jug wine, courted an upscale market through ads that featured classy yuppies serving it along with their salmon and asparagus, while Michelob light beer promised its fans that they "could have it all." Status advertising was all the rage in that glitzy, go-for-the-gold decade. Do ads work this way today? Or has the pendulum shifted back to populism and democratic equality? Can you think of any ads that might be a sign of such a shift?

Determining whether the dominant tone of advertising at any given time is populist or elitist is one way of using advertisements as a kind of weather vane of shifting cultural trends. They help you know which way the wind blows. But a lot of other things in an ad can help you get a sense of the cultural environment in which they appear. We've looked at one such cultural weather signal in our analysis of a Calvin Klein jeans ad. But a culture is complex, and all sorts of contradictory cultural trends may occur at any given time. To see how, let's look now at an ad campaign that ran at the same time as the Klein ad and that, far from raising controversy, has shaped up as one of the most successful advertising gambits of the 1990s.

Pink Rabbits

Consider the Energizer battery ad series that features a pink mechanical bunny who beats his drum as he storms through a sequence of mock advertisements to show how he "keeps going and going and going" on an Energizer battery. The ad's apparent point is to tell you how long an Energizer battery lasts, but it could have done that by simply presenting battery test statistics (a dull though still usable advertising strategy). So what is the ad really doing?

First, it helps to know that when the pink bunny commercials initially appeared, a chief competitor, Duracell, already had for some time been running ads that featured contests between battery-operated toys that "demonstrated" the long-lasting superiority of Duracell products. That's part of the system in which the Energizer ad functions. So, here comes that bunny. How does his appearance relate to the Duracell ads? Does it suggest that the Energizer people have come up with a better *battery* or a better *ad*?

Now let's expand the system. When that bunny suddenly interrupts a startlingly realistic "commercial" for "Chateau Marmoset" wine, for instance, it reminds us of the rather pretentious campaign that Gallo had pitched to the yuppie market. In spoof after spoof, the Energizer ads invite us to relate them to the commercial system as a whole—to the en-

---

Reading Advertising on the Net

Advertising typically reflects the moods, values, and interests of the decade in which it is produced. Visit *Advertising Age*'s Fifty Best Commercials page (**http://adage.com/news_and _features/special_reports/commercials**), a compendium of blockbuster ads from the 1950s to the present. How have the advertising techniques changed through the decades? What do those changes say about the tone and interests of each decade?

tire terrain of American advertising. So what effects do *these* comparisons have?

Think about it. When you're sick of something, don't you like to see a good parody of it? It appears, then, that the Energizer spoofs are appealing to a certain disgust in its intended audience, a weariness with Madison Avenue gimmicks. Isn't that what the ads are doing, playing to your skepticism of advertising?

In short, in a skeptical climate, the Energizer bunny tells us, really clever advertisers (like the creators of the Joe Isuzu campaign that played on consumer skepticism of extravagant claims in automotive advertising) come up with new ways of making us identify with their product. Gladly recognizing spoof ads as reflections of their own frustration with silly and manipulative advertising, viewers find themselves identifying with the creators and sponsors of spoof commercials. And thus they buy a product not because it is better but because they feel good about the way it was presented to them (so good that, in the case of the Energizer bunny, they went out in large numbers to buy pink bunny toys and other spin-off paraphernalia). So nothing has really changed: once again a sign has been substituted for a thing, commodifying the consumer desire to be free of commodified desire.

We can go further. The Energizer bunny campaign can be referred to a larger system beyond the advertising world, to a social complex where citizen-consumers are becoming increasingly fed up (and with good reason) with the cynicism of the powerful in America, whether politicians or advertisers. As such, our bunny serves as a cultural barometer, pointing toward the same social forces that produced Ross Perot's campaigns for the presidency in 1992 and 1996 and the increasing popularity of registering as an Independent rather than as a Democrat or Republican. But the fact that our barometric reading comes from an *ad* is itself a sign of just how entrenched the current system is. For as the bunny tells us, the powerful are always one step ahead. In response to voter frustration, political incumbents run their campaigns as if they were political "outsiders," while advertisers, detecting a growing consumer immunity to advertising, run anticommercial commercials. The system remains the same; only the strategies change.

So in reading an ad, always ask, "Why am I being shown *this* or being told *that*?" Cast yourself as the director of an ad, asking yourself what you would do to pitch a product, and then look at what the advertiser has done. Pay attention to the way an ad's imagery is organized. Every detail counts. Why are these colors used, or why is the ad in black and white? Why are cute stuffed animals chosen to pitch toilet paper? What are those people *doing* in that perfume commercial? Why the cowboy hat in an ad for jeans? How does the slogan "Just Do It" sell Nikes? Look too for what the ad *doesn't* include: Is it missing a clear view of the product itself or an ethnically diverse cast of characters? In short, when interpreting an ad, transform it into a text, and read it as you would a poem or an editorial or any piece of rhetoric—for in its mandate to persuade, advertising constitutes the most potent rhetoric of our times.

The Readings

Our selections in this chapter include interpretations and analyses of the world of advertising, as well as advertisements for you to interpret yourselves. The chapter begins with an historical perspective: Roland Marchand's "The Parable of the Democracy of Goods" shows how advertisers in the 1920s played on the unconscious desires of their market by exploiting the fundamental myths of American culture. Jack Solomon follows with a semiotic analysis of the culture of American advertising, exploring the underlying value systems that cause us to respond to advertisements in the ways that we do. The next two readings address gender issues: Diane Barthel's analysis of the images of men in ads complements Gloria Steinem's insider's view of what goes on behind the scenes at women's magazines. Three readings that explore the truth claims of advertising follow, with John E. Calfee defending advertisers as efficient communicators of useful information, Patricia J. Williams questioning the truthfulness of advertising imagery, and Fern Schumer Chapman warning consumers about web sites that masquerade as information providers but that are really marketing devices. James B. Twitchell concludes the readings portion of this chapter with his analysis of a culture that has become so saturated by advertising that it might as well be called "Adcult USA." Finally, we include a portfolio of print ads for you to decode for yourselves.

R O L A N D   M A R C H A N D

The Parable of the Democracy of Goods

||||||||||||||||||||||||||||||||||||||||||||||||||||||||||||

Advertisements do not simply reflect American myths; they create them, as Roland Marchand (d. 1997) shows in this selection from Advertising the American Dream *(1985). Focusing on elaborate advertising narratives, he describes "The Parable of the Democracy of Goods," which pitches a product by convincing middle-class consumers that, by buying this toilet seat or that brand of coffee, they can share an experience with the very richest Americans. The advertising strategies Marchand analyzes date from the 1920s to 1940s, and new "parables" have since appeared that reflect more modern times, but even the oldest are still in use today. A former professor of history at the University of California, Davis, Marchand was also the author of* The American Peace Movement and Social Reform, 1898– 1918 *(1973) and* Creating the Corporate Soul: The Rise of Public Relations and Corporate Imagery in American Big Business *(1998).*

As they opened their September 1929 issue, readers of the *Ladies' Home Journal* were treated to an account of the care and feeding of young Livingston Ludlow Biddle III, scion of the wealthy Biddles of Philadelphia, whose family coat-of-arms graced the upper right-hand corner of the page. Young Master Biddle, mounted on his tricycle, fixed a serious, slightly pouting gaze upon the reader, while the Cream of Wheat Corporation rapturously explained his constant care, his carefully regulated play and exercise, and the diet prescribed for him by "famous specialists." As master of Sunny Ridge Farm, the Biddles's winter estate in North Carolina, young Livingston III had "enjoyed every luxury of social position and wealth, since the day he was born." Yet, by the grace of a modern providence, it happened that Livingston's health was protected by a "simple plan every mother can use." Mrs. Biddle gave Cream of Wheat to the young heir for both breakfast and supper. The world's foremost child experts knew of no better diet; great wealth could procure no finer nourishment. As Cream of Wheat's advertising agency summarized the central point of the campaign that young Master Biddle initiated, "every mother can give her youngsters the fun and benefits of a Cream of Wheat breakfast just as do the parents of these boys and girls who have the best that wealth can command."[1]

---

1. *Ladies' Home Journal,* Sept. 1929, second cover; *JWT News Letter,* Oct. 1, 1929, p. 1, J. Walter Thompson Company (JWT) Archives, New York City.

While enjoying this glimpse of childrearing among the socially distinguished, *Ladies' Home Journal* readers found themselves schooled in
one of the most pervasive of all advertising tableaux of the 1920s—the
parable of the Democracy of Goods. According to this parable, the wonders of modern mass production and distribution enabled every person to
enjoy the society's most significant pleasure, convenience, or benefit.
The definition of the particular benefit fluctuated, of course, with each
client who employed the parable. But the cumulative effect of the constant reminders that "any woman can" and "every home can afford" was
to publicize an image of American society in which concentrated wealth
at the top of a hierarchy of social classes restricted no family's opportunity
to acquire the most significant products.[2] By implicitly defining "democracy" in terms of equal access to consumer products, and then by depicting the everyday functioning of that "democracy" with regard to one
product at a time, these tableaux offered Americans an inviting vision of
their society as one of incontestable equality.

In its most common advertising formula, the concept of the Democracy of Goods asserted that although the rich enjoyed a great variety of
luxuries, the acquisition of their *one* most significant luxury would provide anyone with the ultimate in satisfaction. For instance, a Chase and
Sanborn's Coffee tableau, with an elegant butler serving a family in a
dining room with a sixteen-foot ceiling, reminded Chicago families that
although "compared with the riches of the more fortunate, your way of
life may seem modest indeed," yet no one—"king, prince, statesman, or
capitalist"—could enjoy better coffee.[3] The Association of Soap and
Glycerine Producers proclaimed that the charm of cleanliness was as
readily available to the poor as to the rich, and Ivory Soap reassuringly
related how one young housewife, who couldn't afford a $780-a-year
maid like her neighbor, still maintained a significant equality in "nice
hands" by using Ivory.[4] The C. F. Church Manufacturing Company
epitomized this version of the parable of the Democracy of Goods in an
ad entitled "a bathroom luxury everyone can afford": "If you lived in
one of those palatial apartments on Park Avenue, in New York City,
where you have to pay $2,000 to $7,500 a year rent, you still couldn't
have a better toilet seat in your bathroom than they have—the Church
Sani-white Toilet Seat which you can afford to have right now."[5]

Thus, according to the parable, no discrepancies in wealth could prevent the humblest citizens, provided they chose their purchases wisely,

---

2. *Saturday Evening Post,* Apr. 3, 1926, pp. 182–83; Nov. 6, 1926, p. 104; Apr. 16,
1927, p. 199; Scrapbook 54 (Brunswick-Balke-Collender), Lord and Thomas Archives,
at Foote, Cone and Belding Communications, Inc., Chicago.

3. *Chicago Tribune,* Nov. 21, 1926, picture section, p. 2.

4. *Los Angeles Times,* July 14, 1929, part VI, p. 3; *Tide,* July 1928, p. 10; *Photoplay
Magazine,* Mar. 1930, p. 1.

5. *American Magazine,* Mar. 1926, p. 112.

from retiring to a setting in which they could contemplate their essential equality, through possession of an identical product, with the nation's millionaires. In 1929, Howard Dickinson, a contributor to *Printers' Ink,* concisely expressed the social psychology behind Democracy of Goods advertisements: "'With whom do the mass of people think they want to foregather?' asks the psychologist in advertising. 'Why, with the wealthy and socially distinguished, of course!' If we can't get an invitation to tea for our millions of customers, we can at least present the fellowship of using the same brand of merchandise. And it works."[6]

Some advertisers found it more efficacious to employ the parable's negative counterpart—the Democracy of Afflictions. Listerine contributed significantly to this approach. Most of the unsuspecting victims of halitosis in the mid-1920s possessed wealth and high social position. Other discoverers of new social afflictions soon took up the battle cry of "nobody's immune." "Body Odor plays no favorites," warned Lifebuoy Soap. No one, "banker, baker, or society woman," could count himself safe from B.O.[7] The boss, as well as the employees, might find himself "caught off guard" with dirty hands or cuffs, the Soap and Glycerine Producers assured readers of *True Story.* By 1930, Absorbine Jr. was beginning to document the democratic advance of "athlete's foot" into those rarefied social circles occupied by the "daintiest member of the junior set" and the noted yachtsman who owned "a railroad or two" (Fig. 1).[8]

The central purpose of the Democracy of Afflictions tableaux was to remind careless or unsuspecting readers of the universality of the threat from which the product offered protection or relief. Only occasionally did such ads address those of the upper classes who might think that their status and "fastidious" attention to personal care made them immune from common social offenses. In 1929 Listerine provided newspaper readers an opportunity to listen while a doctor, whose clientele included those of "the better class," confided "what I know about *nice* women."[9] One might have thought that Listerine was warning complacent, upper-class women that they were not immune from halitosis—except that the ad appeared in the *Los Angeles Times,* not *Harper's Bazaar.* Similarly, Forhan's toothpaste and the Soap Producers did not place their Democracy of Afflictions ads in *True Story* in order to reach the social elite. Rather, these tableaux provided enticing glimpses into the lives of the wealthy while suggesting an equalizing "fellowship" in shared

5

---

6. *Printers' Ink,* Oct. 10, 1929, p. 138.

7. *Tide,* Sept. 15, 1927, p. 5; *American Magazine,* Aug. 1929, p. 93; *True Story,* June 1929, p. 133; *Chicago Tribune,* Jan. 11, 1928, p. 16; Jan. 18, 1928, p. 15; Jan. 28, 1928, p. 7; *Photoplay Magazine,* Feb. 1929, p. 111.

8. *True Story,* May 1928, p. 83; June 1929, p. 133; *American Magazine,* Feb. 1930, p. 110; *Saturday Evening Post,* Aug. 23, 1930, p. 124.

9. *Los Angeles Times,* July 6, 1929, p. 3.

FIGURE 1   A negative appeal transformed the Democracy of Goods into the Democracy of Afflictions. Common folk learned from this parable that they could inexpensively avoid afflictions that beset even the yachting set.

susceptibilities to debilitating ailments. The parable of the Democracy of Goods always remained implicit in its negative counterpart. It assured readers that they could be as healthy, as charming, as free from social offense as the very "nicest" (richest) people, simply by using a product that anyone could afford.

Another variation of the parable of the Democracy of Goods employed historical comparisons to celebrate even the humblest of contemporary Americans as "kings in cottages." "No monarch in all history ever saw the day he could have half as much as you," proclaimed Paramount Pictures. Even reigning sovereigns of the present, Paramount continued, would envy readers for their "luxurious freedom and opportunity" to enter a magnificent, bedazzling "palace for a night," be greeted with fawning bows by liveried attendants, and enjoy modern entertainment for a modest price (Fig. 2). The Fisher Body Corporation coined the phrase "For Kings in Cottages" to compliment ordinary Americans on their freedom from "hardships" that even kings had been forced to endure in the past. Because of a lack of technology, monarchs who traveled

FIGURE 2   Of course, real kings had never shared their status with crowds of other "kings." But the parable of the Democracy of Goods offered a brief, "packaged experience" of luxury and preference.

in the past had "never enjoyed luxury which even approached that of the present-day automobile." The "American idea," epitomized by the Fisher Body Corporation, was destined to carry the comforts and luxuries conducive to human happiness into "the life of even the humblest cottager."[10]

Even so, many copywriters perceived that equality with past monarchs might not rival the vision of joining the fabled "Four Hundred" that Ward McAllister had marked as America's social elite at the end of the nineteenth century. Americans, in an ostensibly conformist age,

10. *Saturday Evening Post,* May 8, 1926, p. 59; *American Magazine,* May 1932, pp. 76–77. See also *Saturday Evening Post,* July 18, 1931, pp. 36–37; Aug. 1, 1931, pp. 30–31; *Better Homes and Gardens,* Mar. 1930, p. 77.

hungered for exclusivity. So advertising tableaux celebrated their ascension into this fabled and exclusive American elite. Through mass production and the resulting lower prices, the tableaux explained, the readers could purchase goods formerly available only to the rich—and thus gain admission to a "400" that now numbered millions.

The Simmons Company confessed that inner-coil mattresses had once been a luxury possessed only by the very wealthy. But now (in 1930) they were "priced so everybody in the United States can have one at $19.95." Woodbury's Soap advised the "working girl" readers of *True Story* of their arrival within a select circle. "Yesterday," it recalled, "the skin you love to touch" had been "the privilege of one woman in 65," but today it had become "the beauty right of every woman."[11] If the Democracy of Goods could establish an equal consumer right to beauty, then perhaps even the ancient religious promise of equality in death might be realized, at least to the extent that material provisions sufficed. In 1927 the Clark Grave Vault Company defined this unique promise: "Not so many years ago the use of a burial vault was confined largely to the rich. . . . Now every family, regardless of its means, may provide absolute protection against the elements of the ground."[12] If it seemed that the residents of Clark vaults had gained equality with the "400" too belatedly for maximum satisfaction, still their loving survivors could now share the same sense of comfort in the "absolute protection" of former loved ones as did the most privileged elites.

The social message of the parable of the Democracy of Goods was 10 clear. Antagonistic envy of the rich was unseemly; programs to redistribute wealth were unnecessary. The best things in life were already available to all at reasonable prices. But the prevalence of the parable of the Democracy of Goods in advertising tableaux did not necessarily betray a concerted conspiracy on the part of advertisers and their agencies to impose a social ideology on the American people. Most advertisers employed the parable of the Democracy of Goods primarily as a narrow, nonideological merchandising tactic. Listerine and Lifebuoy found the parable an obvious, attention-getting strategy for persuading readers that if even society women and bankers were unconsciously guilty of social offenses, the readers themselves were not immune. Simmons Mattresses, Chevrolet, and Clark Grave Vaults chose the parable in an attempt to broaden their market to include lower-income groups. The parable emphasized the affordability of the product to families of modest income while attempting to maintain a "class" image of the product as the preferred choice of their social betters.

---

11. *Saturday Evening Post,* Nov. 10, 1928, p. 90; *True Story,* Aug. 1934, p. 57. See also *Chicago Tribune,* Oct. 8, 1930, p. 17; *American Magazine,* Aug. 1930, p. 77; *Woman's Home Companion,* May 1927, p. 96.

12. *American Magazine,* Feb. 1927, p. 130.

Most advertisers found the social message of the parable of the Democracy of Goods a congenial and unexceptionable truism. They also saw it, like the other parables prevalent in advertising tableaux, as an epigrammatic statement of a conventional popular belief. Real income was rising for nearly all Americans during the 1920s, except for some farmers and farmworkers and those in a few depressed industries. Citizens seemed eager for confirmation that they were now driving the same make of car as the wealthy elites and serving their children the same cereal enjoyed by Livingston Ludlow Biddle III. Advertisers did not have to impose the parable of the Democracy of Goods on a contrary-minded public. Theirs was the easier task of subtly substituting this vision of equality, which was certainly satisfying *as a vision,* for broader and more traditional hopes and expectations of an equality of self-sufficiency, personal independence, and social interaction.

Perhaps the most attractive aspect of this parable to advertisers was that it preached the coming of an equalizing democracy without sacrificing those fascinating contrasts of social condition that had long been the touchstone of high drama. Henry James, writing of Hawthorne, had once lamented the obstacles facing the novelist who wrote of an America that lacked such tradition-laden institutions as a sovereign, a court, an aristocracy, or even a class of country gentlemen. Without castles, manors, and thatched cottages, America lacked those stark juxtapositions of pomp and squalor, nobility and peasantry, wealth and poverty that made Europe so rich a source of social drama.[13] But many versions of the parable of the Democracy of Goods sought to offset that disadvantage without gaining James's desired "complexity of manners." They dressed up America's wealthy as dazzling aristocrats, and then reassured readers that they could easily enjoy an essential equality with such elites in the things that really mattered. The rich were decorative and fun to look at, but in their access to those products most important to comfort and satisfaction, as the magazine *Delineator* put it, "The Four Hundred" had become "the four million."[14] Advertisers left readers to assume that they could gain the same satisfactions of exclusiveness from belonging to the four million as had once been savored by the four hundred.

While parables of consumer democracy frequently used terms like "everyone," "anyone," "any home," or "every woman," these categories were mainly intended to comprise the audience of "consumer-citizens" envisioned by the advertising trade, or families economically among the nation's top 50 percent. Thus the *Delineator* had more in mind than mere alliteration when it chose to contrast the old "400" with the new "four million" rather than a new "one hundred and twenty million." The

---

13. Henry James, *Hawthorne,* rev. ed. (New York, 1967 [c. 1879]), p. 55.
14. *Printers' Ink,* Nov. 24, 1927, p. 52.

standard antitheses of the Democracy of Goods parables were "mansion" and "bungalow." Advertising writers rarely took notice of the many millions of Americans whose standard of living fell below that of the cozy bungalow of the advertising tableaux. These millions might overhear the promises of consumer democracy in the newspapers or magazines, but advertising leaders felt no obligation to show how their promises to "everyone" would bring equality to those who lived in the nation's apartment houses and farmhouses without plumbing, let alone those who lived in rural shacks and urban tenements.

In the broadest sense, the parable of the Democracy of Goods may be interpreted as a secularized version of the traditional Christian assurances of ultimate human equality. "Body Odor plays no favorites" might be considered a secular translation of the idea that God "sends rain on the just and on the unjust" (Matt. 5:45). Promises of the essential equality of those possessing the advertised brand recalled the promise of equality of access to God's mercy. Thus the parable recapitulated a familiar, cherished expectation. Far more significant, however, was the parable's insinuation of the capacity of a Democracy of Goods to redeem the already secularized American promise of political equality.

Incessantly and enticingly repeated, advertising visions of fellowship in a Democracy of Goods encouraged Americans to look to similarities in consumption styles rather than to political power or control of wealth for evidence of significant equality. Francesco Nicosia and Robert Mayer describe the result as a "deflection of the success ethic from the sphere of production to that of consumption." Freedom of choice came to be perceived as a freedom more significantly exercised in the marketplace than in the political arena. This process gained momentum in the 1920s; it gained maturity during the 1950s as a sense of class differences was nearly eclipsed by a fascination with the equalities suggested by shared consumption patterns and "freely chosen" consumer "lifestyles."[15]

Reading the Text

1. Summarize in your own words what Marchand means by the "parable of the Democracy of Goods" (para. 2).
2. What is the "Democracy of Afflictions" (para. 5), in your own words?
3. In class, brainstorm examples of current ads that illustrate the parable of the democracy of goods and the democracy of afflictions.

---

15. Francesco M. Nicosia and Robert N. Mayer, "Toward a Sociology of Consumption," *The Journal of Consumer Research* 3 (1976): 73; Roland Marchand, "Visions of Classlessness; Quests for Dominion: American Popular Culture, 1945–1960," in *Reshaping America: Society and Institutions, 1945–1960,* ed. Robert H. Bremner and Gary W. Reichard (Columbus, Ohio, 1982), pp. 165–70.

Reading the Signs

1. Does the parable of the democracy of goods work to make society more egalitarian, or does it reinforce existing power structures? Write an essay arguing for one position or the other, focusing on particular ads for your support.
2. Bring to class a popular magazine of your own choosing. In groups, study your selections. In which magazines is the myth of the democracy of goods most common? Do you find any relationship between the use of this myth and the intended audience of the magazines?
3. Obtain from your college library an issue of *Time* magazine dating from the 1920s, and compare it with a current issue. In what ways, if any, have the social messages communicated in the advertising changed? Try to account for any changes you identify.
4. Compare and contrast the myth of the democracy of goods with the frontier myth that Laurence Shames describes in "The More Factor" (p. 55). Consider how the two myths shape our consuming behavior; you may also want to show how the myths appear in some current ads.

JACK SOLOMON

Masters of Desire: The Culture of American Advertising

||||||||||||||||||||||||||||||||||||||||||||||||||||||||||||

Advertising campaigns come and go, as do the products they promote, but what does not change so quickly are the cultural patterns that advertisers rely on to work their magic. For as Jack Solomon (b. 1954) argues in this excerpt from The Signs of Our Time *(1988), advertising does not work in a vacuum: it plays on deeply held cultural values and desires to stimulate consumption. To analyze an ad, then, is to analyze the culture in which it appears. A professor of English at California State University, Northridge, Solomon is also the author of* Discourse and Reference in the Nuclear Age *(1988) and the coeditor (with Sonia Maasik) of* California Dreams and Realities *(1999) and of this textbook.*

Amongst democratic nations, men easily attain a certain equality of condition; but they can never attain as much as they desire.

—ALEXIS DE TOCQUEVILLE

On May 10, 1831, a young French aristocrat named Alexis de Tocqueville arrived in New York City at the start of what would become one of the most famous visits to America in our history. He had come to observe firsthand the institutions of the freest, most egalitarian society of the age, but what he found was a paradox. For behind America's mythic promise of equal opportunity, Tocqueville discovered a desire for *unequal* social rewards, a ferocious competition for privilege and distinction. As he wrote in his monumental study, *Democracy in America*:

> When all privileges of birth and fortune are abolished, when all professions are accessible to all, and a man's own energies may place him at the top of any one of them, an easy and unbounded career seems open to his ambition.... But this is an erroneous notion, which is corrected by daily experience. [For when] men are nearly alike, and all follow the same track, it is very difficult for any one individual to walk quick and cleave a way through the same throng which surrounds and presses him.

Yet walking quick and cleaving a way is precisely what Americans dream of. We Americans dream of rising above the crowd, of attaining a social summit beyond the reach of ordinary citizens. And therein lies the paradox.

The American dream, in other words, has two faces: the one communally egalitarian and the other competitively elitist. This contradiction is no accident; it is fundamental to the structure of American society. Even as America's great myth of equality celebrates the virtues of mom, apple pie, and the girl or boy next door, it also lures us to achieve social distinction, to rise above the crowd and bask alone in the glory. This land is your land and this land is my land, Woody Guthrie's populist anthem tells us, but we keep trying to increase the "my" at the expense of the "your." Rather than fostering contentment, the American dream breeds desire, a longing for a greater share of the pie. It is as if our society were a vast high-school football game, with the bulk of the participants noisily rooting in the stands while, deep down, each of them is wishing he or she could be the star quarterback or head cheerleader.

For the semiotician, the contradictory nature of the American myth of equality is nowhere written so clearly as in the signs that American advertisers use to manipulate us into buying their wares. "Manipulate" is the word here, not "persuade"; for advertising campaigns are not sources of product information, they are exercises in behavior modification. Appealing to our subconscious emotions rather than to our conscious intellects, advertisements are designed to exploit the discontentments fostered by the American dream, the constant desire for social success and the material rewards that accompany it. America's consumer economy runs on desire, and advertising stokes the engines by transforming common objects—from peanut butter to political candidates—into signs of all the things that Americans covet most.

But by semiotically reading the signs that advertising agencies manu-   5
facture to stimulate consumption, we can plot the precise state of desire in the audiences to which they are addressed. Let's look at a representative sample of ads and what they say about the emotional climate of the country and the fast-changing trends of American life. Because ours is a highly diverse, pluralistic society, various advertisements may say different things depending on their intended audiences, but in every case they say something about America, about the status of our hopes, fears, desires, and beliefs.

We'll begin with two ad campaigns conducted by the same company that bear out Alexis de Tocqueville's observations about the contradictory nature of American society: General Motors' campaigns for its Cadillac and Chevrolet lines. First, consider an early magazine ad for the Cadillac Allanté. Appearing as a full-color, four-page insert in *Time,* the ad seems to say "I'm special—and so is this car" even before we've begun to read it. Rather than being printed on the ordinary, flimsy pages of the magazine, the Allanté spread appears on glossy coated stock. The unwritten message here is that an extraordinary car deserves an extraordinary advertisement, and that both car and ad are aimed at an extraordinary consumer, or at least one who wishes to appear extraordinary compared to his more ordinary fellow citizens.

Ads of this kind work by creating symbolic associations between their product and what is most coveted by the consumers to whom they are addressed. It is significant, then, that this ad insists that the Allanté is virtually an Italian rather than an American car, an automobile, as its copy runs, "Conceived and Commissioned by America's Luxury Car Leader—Cadillac" but "Designed and Handcrafted by Europe's Renowned Design Leader—Pininfarina, SpA, of Turin, Italy." This is not simply a piece of product information, it's a sign of the prestige that European luxury cars enjoy in today's automotive marketplace. Once the luxury car of choice for America's status drivers, Cadillac has fallen far behind its European competitors in the race for the prestige market. So the Allanté essentially represents Cadillac's decision, after years of resisting the trend toward European cars, to introduce its own European import—whose high cost is clearly printed on the last page of the ad. . . .

American companies manufacture status symbols because American consumers want them. As Alexis de Tocqueville recognized a century and a half ago, the competitive nature of democratic societies breeds a desire for social distinction, a yearning to rise above the crowd. But given the fact that those who do make it to the top in socially mobile societies have often risen from the lower ranks, they still look like everyone else. In the socially immobile societies of aristocratic Europe, generations of fixed social conditions produced subtle class signals. The accent of one's voice, the shape of one's nose, or even the set of one's chin, immediately communicated social status. Aside from the nasal bray and uptilted head of the Boston Brahmin, Americans do not have any native sets of personal status signals. If it weren't for his Mercedes-Benz and Manhattan townhouse, the parvenu Wall Street millionaire often couldn't be distinguished from the man who tailors his suits. Hence, the demand for status symbols, for the objects that mark one off as a social success, is particularly strong in democratic nations—stronger even than in aristocratic societies, where the aristocrat so often looks and sounds different from everyone else.

Status symbols, then, are signs that identify their possessors' place in a social hierarchy, markers of rank and prestige. We can all think of any number of status symbols—Rolls-Royces, Beverly Hills mansions, even Shar Pei puppies (whose rareness and expense has rocketed them beyond Russian wolfhounds as status pets and has even inspired whole lines of wrinkle-faced stuffed toys)—but how do we know that something *is* a status symbol? The explanation is quite simple: when an object (or puppy!) either costs a lot of money or requires influential connections to possess, anyone who possesses it must also possess the necessary means and influence to acquire it. The object itself really doesn't matter, since it ultimately disappears behind the presumed social potency of its owner. Semiotically, what matters is the signal it sends, its value as a sign of power. One traditional sign of social distinction is owning a country estate and enjoying the peace and privacy that attend it. Advertisements for Mercedes-Benz, Jaguar, and Audi automobiles thus frequently feature drivers motoring quietly along a country road, presumably on their way to or from their country houses.

Advertisers have been quick to exploit the status signals that belong   10
to body language as well. As Hegel observed in the early nineteenth century, it is an ancient aristocratic prerogative to be seen by the lower orders without having to look at them in return. Tilting his chin high in the air and gazing down at the world under hooded eyelids, the aristocrat invites observation while refusing to look back. We can find such a pose exploited in an advertisement for Cadillac Seville in which we see an elegantly dressed woman out for a drive with her husband in their new Cadillac. If we look closely at the woman's body language, we can see her glance inwardly with a satisfied smile on her face but not outward toward the camera that represents our gaze. She is glad to be seen by us in her Seville, but she isn't interested in looking at *us!*

Ads that are aimed at a broader market take the opposite approach. If the American dream encourages the desire to "arrive," to vault above the mass, it also fosters a desire to be popular, to "belong." Populist commercials accordingly transform products into signs of belonging, utilizing such common icons as country music, small-town life, family picnics, and farmyards. All of these icons are incorporated in GM's "Heartbeat of America" campaign for its Chevrolet line. Unlike the Seville commercial, the faces in the Chevy ads look straight at us and smile. Dress is casual; the mood upbeat. Quick camera cuts take us from rustic to suburban to urban scenes, creating an American montage filmed from sea to shining sea. We all "belong" in a Chevy.

Where price alone doesn't determine the market for a product, advertisers can go either way. Both Johnnie Walker and Jack Daniel's are better-grade whiskies, but where a Johnnie Walker ad appeals to the buyer who wants a mark of aristocratic distinction in his liquor, a Jack Daniel's ad emphasizes the down-home, egalitarian folksiness of its product. Johnnie Walker associates itself with such conventional status symbols as sable coats, Rolls-Royces, and black gold; Jack Daniel's gives us a Good Ol' Boy in overalls. In fact, Jack Daniel's Good Ol' Boy is an icon of backwoods independence, recalling the days of the moonshiner and the Whisky Rebellion of 1794. Evoking emotions quite at odds with those stimulated in Johnnie Walker ads, the advertisers of Jack Daniel's have chosen to transform their product into a sign of America's populist tradition. The fact that both ads successfully sell whisky is itself a sign of the dual nature of the American dream. . . .

Populist advertising is particularly effective in the face of foreign competition. When Americans feel threatened from the outside, they tend to circle the wagons and temporarily forget their class differences. In the face of the Japanese automotive "invasion," Chrysler runs populist commercials in which Lee Iacocca joins the simple folk who buy his cars as the jingle "Born in America" blares in the background. Seeking to capitalize on the popularity of Bruce Springsteen's *Born in the USA* album, these ads gloss over Springsteen's ironic lyrics in a vast display of flag-waving. Chevrolet's "Heartbeat of America" campaign attempts to woo American motorists away from Japanese automobiles by appealing to their patriotic sentiments.

The patriotic iconography of these campaigns also reflects the general cultural mood of the early to mid-1980s. After a period of national anguish in the wake of the Vietnam War and the Iran hostage crisis, America went on a patriotic binge. American athletic triumphs in the Lake Placid and Los Angeles Olympics introduced a sporting tone into the national celebration, often making international affairs appear like one great Olympiad in which America was always going for the gold. In response, advertisers began to do their own flag-waving.

The mood of advertising during this period was definitely upbeat.   15 Even deodorant commercials, which traditionally work on our self-doubts and fears of social rejection, jumped on the bandwagon. In the guilty sixties, we had ads like the "Ice Blue Secret" campaign with its connotations of guilt and shame. In the feel-good Reagan eighties, "Sure" deodorant commercials featured images of triumphant Americans throwing up their arms in victory to reveal—no wet marks! Deodorant commercials once had the moral echo of Nathaniel Hawthorne's guilt-ridden *The Scarlet Letter*; in the early eighties they had all the moral subtlety of *Rocky IV,* reflecting the emotions of a Vietnam-weary nation eager to embrace the imagery of America Triumphant. . . .

Live the Fantasy

By reading the signs of American advertising, we can conclude that America is a nation of fantasizers, often preferring the sign to the substance and easily enthralled by a veritable Fantasy Island of commercial illusions. Critics of Madison Avenue often complain that advertisers create consumer desire, but semioticians don't think the situation is that simple. Advertisers may give shape to consumer fantasies, but they need raw material to work with, the subconscious dreams and desires of the marketplace. As long as these desires remain unconscious, advertisers will be able to exploit them. But by bringing the fantasies to the surface, you can free yourself from advertising's often hypnotic grasp.

I can think of no company that has more successfully seized upon the subconscious fantasies of the American marketplace—indeed the world marketplace—than McDonald's. By no means the first nor the only hamburger chain in the United States, McDonald's emerged victorious in the "burger wars" by transforming hamburgers into signs of all that was desirable in American life. Other chains like Wendy's, Burger King, and Jack-In-The-Box continue to advertise and sell widely, but no company approaches McDonald's transformation of itself into a symbol of American culture.

McDonald's success can be traced to the precision of its advertising. Instead of broadcasting a single "one-size-fits-all" campaign at a time, McDonald's pitches its burgers simultaneously at different age groups, different classes, even different races (Budweiser beer, incidentally, has succeeded in the same way). For children, there is the Ronald McDonald campaign, which presents a fantasy world that has little to do with hamburgers in any rational sense but a great deal to do with the emotional desires of kids. Ronald McDonald and his friends are signs that recall the Muppets, *Sesame Street,* the circus, toys, storybook illustrations, even *Alice in Wonderland.* Such signs do not signify hamburgers. Rather, they are displayed in order to prompt in the child's mind an automatic association of fantasy, fun, and McDonald's.

The same approach is taken in ads aimed at older audiences—teens, adults, and senior citizens. In the teen-oriented ads we may catch a fleeting glimpse of a hamburger or two, but what we are really shown is a teenage fantasy: groups of hip and happy adolescents singing, dancing, and cavorting together. Fearing loneliness more than anything else, adolescents quickly respond to the group appeal of such commercials. "Eat a

Big Mac," these ads say, "and you won't be stuck home alone on Saturday night."

To appeal to an older and more sophisticated audience no longer so   20
afraid of not belonging and more concerned with finding a place to go
out to at night, McDonald's has designed the elaborate "Mac Tonight"
commercials, which have for their backdrop a nightlit urban skyline and
at their center a cabaret pianist with a moon-shaped head, a glad manner,
and Blues Brothers shades. Such signs prompt an association of McDonald's with nightclubs and urban sophistication, persuading us that
McDonald's is a place not only for breakfast or lunch but for dinner too,
as if it were a popular off-Broadway nightspot, a place to see and be seen.
Even the parody of Kurt Weill's "Mack the Knife" theme song that Mac
the Pianist performs is a sign, a subtle signal to the sophisticated hamburger eater able to recognize the origin of the tune in Bertolt Brecht's
Threepenny Opera.

For yet older customers, McDonald's has designed a commercial
around the fact that it employs a large number of retirees and seniors. In
one such ad, we see an elderly man leaving his pretty little cottage early
in the morning to start work as "the new kid" at McDonald's, and then
we watch him during his first day on the job. Of course he is a great success, outdoing everyone else with his energy and efficiency, and he returns home in the evening to a loving wife and a happy home. One
would almost think that the ad was a kind of moving "help wanted" sign
(indeed, McDonald's *was* hiring elderly employees at the time), but it's
really just directed at consumers. Older viewers can see themselves
wanted and appreciated in the ad—and perhaps be distracted from the
rationally uncomfortable fact that many senior citizens take such jobs because of financial need and thus may be unlikely to own the sort of home
that one sees in the commercial. But realism isn't the point here. This is
fantasyland, a dream world promising instant gratification no matter what
the facts of the matter may be.

Practically the only fantasy that McDonald's doesn't exploit is the
fantasy of sex. This is understandable, given McDonald's desire to present
itself as a family restaurant. But everywhere else, sexual fantasies, which
have always had an important place in American advertising, are beginning to dominate the advertising scene. You expect sexual come-ons in
ads for perfume or cosmetics or jewelry—after all, that's what they're
selling—but for room deodorizers? In a magazine ad for Claire Burke
home fragrances, for example, we see a well-dressed couple cavorting
about their bedroom in what looks like a cheery preparation for sadomasochistic exercises. Jordache and Calvin Klein pitch blue jeans as props
for teenage sexuality. The phallic appeal of automobiles, traditionally an
implicit feature in automotive advertising, becomes quite explicit in a
Dodge commercial that shifts back and forth from shots of a young man
in an automobile to teasing glimpses of a woman—his date—as she
dresses in her apartment.

The very language of today's advertisements is charged with sexuality. Products in the more innocent fifties were "new and improved," but everything in the eighties is "hot!"—as in "hot woman," or sexual heat. Cars are "hot." Movies are "hot." An ad for Valvoline pulses to the rhythm of a "heat wave, burning in my car." Sneakers get red hot in a magazine ad for Travel Fox athletic shoes in which we see male and female figures, clad only in Travel Fox shoes, apparently in the act of copulation—an ad that earned one of *Adweek's* annual "badvertising" awards for shoddy advertising.

The sexual explicitness of contemporary advertising is a sign not so much of American sexual fantasies as of the lengths to which advertisers will go to get attention. Sex never fails as an attention-getter, and in a particularly competitive, and expensive, era for American marketing, advertisers like to bet on a sure thing. Ad people refer to the proliferation of TV, radio, newspaper, magazine, and billboard ads as "clutter," and nothing cuts through the clutter like sex.

By showing the flesh, advertisers work on the deepest, most coercive   25
human emotions of all. Much sexual coercion in advertising, however, is a sign of a desperate need to make certain that clients are getting their money's worth. The appearance of advertisements that refer directly to the prefabricated fantasies of Hollywood is a sign of a different sort of desperation: a desperation for ideas. With the rapid turnover of advertising campaigns mandated by the need to cut through the "clutter," advertisers may be hard pressed for new ad concepts, and so they are more and more frequently turning to already-established models. In the early 1980s, for instance, Pepsi-Cola ran a series of ads broadly alluding to Steven Spielberg's *E.T.* In one such ad, we see a young boy, who, like the hero of *E.T.*, witnesses an extraterrestrial visit. The boy is led to a soft-drink machine where he pauses to drink a can of Pepsi as the spaceship he's spotted flies off into the universe. The relationship between the ad and the movie, accordingly, is a parasitical one, with the ad taking its life from the creative body of the film. . . .

Madison Avenue has also framed ad campaigns around the cultural prestige of high-tech machinery. This is especially the case with sports cars, whose high-tech appeal is so powerful that some people apparently fantasize about *being* sports cars. At least, this is the conclusion one might draw from a Porsche commercial that asked its audience, "If you were a car, what kind of car would you be?" As a candy-red Porsche speeds along a rain-slick forest road, the ad's voice-over describes all the specifications you'd want to have if you *were* a sports car. "If you were a car," the commercial concludes, "you'd be a Porsche."

In his essay "Car Commercials and *Miami Vice*," Todd Gitlin explains the semiotic appeal of such ads as those in the Porsche campaign. Aired at the height of what may be called America's "myth of the entrepreneur," these commercials were aimed at young corporate managers who imaginatively identified with the "lone wolf" image of a Porsche speeding through the woods. Gitlin points out that such images cater to the fantasies of faceless corporate men who dream of entrepreneurial glory, of striking out on their own like John DeLorean and telling the boss to take his job and shove it. But as DeLorean's spectacular failure demonstrates, the life of the entrepreneur can be extremely risky. So rather than having to go it alone and take the risks that accompany entrepreneurial independence, the young executive can substitute fantasy for reality by climbing into his Porsche — or at least that's what Porsche's advertisers wanted him to believe.

But there is more at work in the Porsche ads than the fantasies of corporate America. Ever since Arthur C. Clarke and Stanley Kubrick teamed up to present us with HAL 9000, the demented computer of *2001: A Space Odyssey,* the American imagination has been obsessed with the melding of man and machine. First there was television's *Six Million Dollar Man,* and then movieland's *Star Wars, Blade Runner,* and *Robocop,* fantasy visions of a future dominated by machines. Androids haunt our imaginations as machines seize the initiative. *Time* magazine's "Man of the Year" for 1982 was a computer. Robot-built automobiles appeal to drivers who spend their days in front of computer screens — perhaps designing robots. When so much power and prestige is being given to high-tech machines, wouldn't you rather be a Porsche?

In short, the Porsche campaign is a sign of a new mythology that is emerging before our eyes, a myth of the machine, which is replacing the myth of the human. The iconic figure of the little tramp caught up in the cogs of industrial production in Charlie Chaplin's *Modern Times* signified a humanistic revulsion to the age of the machine. Human beings, such icons said, were superior to machines. Human values should come first in the moral order of things. But as Edith Milton suggests in her essay "The Track of the Mutant," we are now coming to believe that machines are superior to human beings, that mechanical nature is superior to human nature. Rather than being threatened by machines, we long to merge with them. *The Six Million Dollar Man* is one iconic figure in the new mythology; Harrison Ford's sexual coupling with an android is another. In such an age it should come as little wonder that computer-synthesized Max Headroom should be a commercial spokesman for Coca-Cola, or that Federal Express should design a series of TV ads featuring mechanical-looking human beings revolving around strange and powerful machines.

Fear and Trembling in the Marketplace

While advertisers play on and reflect back at us our fantasies about   30
everything from fighter pilots to robots, they also play on darker imaginings. If dream and desire can be exploited in the quest for sales, so can nightmare and fear.

The nightmare equivalent of America's populist desire to "belong," for example, is the fear of not belonging, of social rejection, of being different. Advertisements for dandruff shampoos, mouthwashes, deodorants, and laundry detergents ("Ring Around the Collar!") accordingly exploit such fears, bullying us into consumption. Although ads of this type are still around in the 1980s, they were particularly common in the fifties and early sixties, reflecting a society still reeling from the witch-hunts of the McCarthy years. When any sort of social eccentricity or difference could result in a public denunciation and the loss of one's job or even liberty, Americans were keen to conform and be like everyone else. No one wanted to be "guilty" of smelling bad or of having a dirty collar.

"Guilt" ads characteristically work by creating narrative situations in which someone is "accused" of some social "transgression," pronounced guilty, and then offered the sponsor's product as a means of returning to "innocence." Such ads, in essence, are parodies of ancient religious rituals of guilt and atonement, whereby sinning humanity is offered salvation through the agency of priest and church. In the world of advertising, a product takes the place of the priest, but the logic of the situation is quite similar.

In commercials for Wisk detergent, for example, we witness the drama of a hapless housewife and her husband as they are mocked by the jeering voices of children shouting "Ring Around the Collar!" "Oh, those dirty rings!" the housewife groans in despair. It's as if she and her husband were being stoned by an angry crowd. But there's hope, there's help, there's Wisk. Cleansing her soul of sin as well as her husband's, the housewife launders his shirts with Wisk, and behold, his collars are clean. Product salvation is only as far as the supermarket. . . .

If guilt looks backward in time to past transgressions, fear, like desire, faces forward, trembling before the future. In the late 1980s, a new kind of fear commercial appeared, one whose narrative played on the worries of young corporate managers struggling up the ladder of success. Representing the nightmare equivalent of the elitist desire to "arrive," ads of this sort created images of failure, storylines of corporate defeat. In one ad for Apple computers, for example, a group of junior executives sits around a table with the boss as he asks each executive how long it will take his or her department to complete some publishing jobs. "Two or three days," answers one nervous executive. "A week, on overtime," a tight-lipped woman responds. But one young up-and-comer can have everything ready tomorrow, today, or yesterday, because his department uses a Macintosh desktop publishing system. Guess who'll get the next promotion?

For other markets, there are other fears. If McDonald's presents senior citizens with bright fantasies of being useful and appreciated beyond retirement, companies like Secure Horizons dramatize senior citizens' [35] fears of being caught short by a major illness. Running its ads in the wake of budgetary cuts in the Medicare system, Secure Horizons designed a series of commercials featuring a pleasant old man named Harry—who looks and sounds rather like Carroll O'Connor—who tells us the story of the scare he got during his wife's recent illness. Fearing that next time Medicare won't cover the bills, he has purchased supplemental health insurance from Secure Horizons and now securely tends his roof-top garden. . . .

The Future of an Illusion

There are some signs in the advertising world that Americans are getting fed up with fantasy advertisements and want to hear some straight talk. Weary of extravagant product claims and irrelevant associations, consumers trained by years of advertising to distrust what they hear seem to be developing an immunity to commercials. At least, this is the semiotic message I read in the "new realism" advertisements of the eighties, ads that attempt to convince you that what you're seeing is the real thing, that the ad is giving you the straight dope, not advertising hype.

You can recognize the "new realism" by its camera techniques. The lighting is usually subdued to give the ad the effect of being filmed without studio lighting or special filters. The scene looks gray, as if the blinds were drawn. The camera shots are jerky and off-angle, often zooming in for sudden and unflattering close-ups, as if the cameraman was an amateur with a home video recorder. In a "realistic" ad for AT&T, for example, we are treated to a monologue by a plump stockbroker—his plumpness intended as a sign that he's for real and not just another actor—who tells us about the problems he's had with his phone system (not AT&T's) as the camera jerks around, generally filming him from below as if the cameraman couldn't quite fit his equipment into the crammed office and had to film the scene on his knees. "This is no fancy advertisement," the ad tries to convince us, "this is sincere."

An ad for Miller draft beer tries the same approach, recreating the effect of an amateur videotape of a wedding celebration. Camera shots shift suddenly from group to group. The picture jumps. Bodies are poorly framed. The color is washed out. Like the beer it is pushing, the ad is supposed to strike us as being "as real as it gets."

Such ads reflect a desire for reality in the marketplace, a weariness with Madison Avenue illusions. But there's no illusion like the illusion of reality. Every special technique that advertisers use to create their "reality effects" is, in fact, more unrealistic than the techniques of "illusory" ads. The world, in reality, doesn't jump around when you look at it. It doesn't appear in subdued gray tones. Our eyes don't have zoom lenses, and we don't look at things with our heads cocked to one side. The irony of the "new realism" is that it is more unrealistic, more artificial, than the ordinary run of television advertising.

But don't expect any truly realistic ads in the future, because a realis- 40 tic advertisement is a contradiction in terms. The logic of advertising is entirely semiotic: it substitutes signs for things, framed visions of consumer desire for the thing itself. The success of modern advertising, its penetration into every corner of American life, reflects a culture that has itself chosen illusion over reality. At a time when political candidates all have professional image-makers attached to their staffs, and the President of the United States can be an actor who once sold shirt collars, all the cultural signs are pointing to more illusions in our lives rather than fewer — a fecund breeding ground for the world of the advertiser.

Reading the Text

1. Describe in your own words the paradox of the American dream, as Solomon sees it.
2. In Solomon's view, why do status symbols work particularly well in manipulating American consumers?
3. What is a "guilt" (para. 32) ad, according to Solomon, and how does it affect consumers?
4. Why, according to Solomon, has McDonald's been so successful in its ad campaigns?
5. What relationship does Solomon see between the "new realism" (para. 37) of some ads and the paradoxes of the American dream?

Reading the Signs

1. Bring to class a general-interest magazine, such as *Time*, or *Better Homes and Gardens*, and in small groups study the advertising. Do the ads tend to have an elitist or a populist appeal? What relationship do you see between the appeal you identify and the magazine's target readership? Present your findings to the class.
2. Watch an episode of a popular prime-time TV program, such as *ER* or *The X-Files*, focusing your attention on the advertising that sponsors the show. Then write an essay in which you interpret these ads. Do the ads reveal a particular vision of the American dream, and if so, how might the vision be related to the show's audience?
3. Visit your college library, and locate an issue of a popular magazine from earlier decades, such as the 1930s or 1940s. Then write an essay in which you compare and contrast the advertising found in that early issue with that in a current issue of the same publication. What similarities and differences do you find in the myths underlying the advertising, and what is their significance?

4. In class, brainstorm a list of status symbols common in advertising today. Then discuss what groups they appeal to and why. Can you detect any patterns based on gender, ethnicity, or age?
5. The American political scene has changed since the late 1980s, when this essay was first published. In an analytic essay, argue whether you believe the populist/elitist paradox that Solomon describes still affects American advertising and media. Be sure to base your discussion on specific media examples.

D I A N E   B A R T H E L

A Gentleman and a Consumer

|||||||||||||||||||||||||||||||||||||||||||||||||||||||

It's not only women who are pressured to conform to unattainable standards of physical appearance: men are victims, too. Diane Barthel (b. 1949), in this selection from Putting on Appearances: Gender and Advertising *(1988), surveys the various images men are expected to live up to as presented in advertisements in men's magazines. From the cowboy to the corporate jungle fighter, from the playboy to the polo player, men are urged to adopt traditionally aggressive male gender roles. At the same time, Barthel points out, they are to become obsessed with their appearance—a role that, ironically, is traditionally considered feminine. A professor of sociology at the State University of New York, Stony Brook, Barthel is also the author of* Amana: From Pietist Sect to American Community *(1984) and* Historic Preservation: Collective Memory and Historical Identity *(1996).*

There are no men's beauty and glamour magazines with circulations even approaching those of the women's magazines. The very idea of men's beauty magazines may strike one as odd. In our society men traditionally were supposed to make the right appearance, to be well groomed and neatly tailored. What they were *not* supposed to do was to be overly concerned with their appearance, much less vain about their beauty. That was to be effeminate, and not a "real man." Male beauty was associated with homosexuals, and "real men" had to show how red-blooded they were by maintaining a certain distance from fashion.

Perhaps the best-known male fashion magazine is *GQ* founded in 1957 and with a circulation of 446,000 in 1986. More recently, we have seen the launching of *YMF* and *Young Black Male*, which in 1987 still

[had] few advertising pages. *M* magazine, founded in 1983, attracts an audience "a cut above" that of *GQ*.[1]

Esquire magazine, more venerable (founded in 1933), is classified as a general interest magazine. Although it does attract many women readers, many of the columns and features and much of the advertising are definitely directed toward attracting the attention of the male readers, who still make up the overwhelming majority of the readership.

The highest circulations for men's magazines are for magazines specializing either in sex (*Playboy*, circulation 4.1 million; *Penthouse*, circulation nearly 3.8 million; and *Hustler*, circulation 1.5 million) or sports (*Sports Illustrated*, circulation 2.7 million).[2] That these magazines share an emphasis on power—either power over women or over other men on the playing field—should not surprise. In fact, sociologist John Gagnon would argue that sex and sports now represent the major fields in which the male role, as defined by power, is played out, with physical power in work, and even in warfare, being less important than it was before industrialization and technological advance.[3]

If we are looking for comparative evidence as to how advertisements   5
define gender roles for men and women, we should not then see the male role as defined primarily through beauty and fashion. This seems an obvious point, but it is important to emphasize how different cultural attitudes toward both the social person and the physical body shape the gender roles of men and women. These cultural attitudes are changing, and advertisements are helping to legitimate the use of beauty products and an interest in fashion for men, as we shall see. As advertisements directed toward women are beginning to use male imagery, so too advertisements for men occasionally use imagery resembling that found in advertisements directed toward women. We are speaking of two *modes,* then. As Baudrillard[4] writes, these modes "do not result from the differentiated nature of the two sexes, but from the differential logic of the system. The relationship of the Masculine and the Feminine to real men and women is relatively arbitrary."[5] Increasingly today, men and women use both modes. The two great terms of opposition (Masculine and Feminine) still, however, structure the forms that consumption takes; they provide identities for products and consumers.

Baudrillard agrees that the feminine model encourages a woman to please herself, to encourage a certain complacency and even narcissistic

1. Katz and Katz, *Magazines,* pp. 703–5.

2. Ibid.

3. John Gagnon, "Physical Strength: Once of Significance," in Joseph H. Pleck and Jack Sawyer, eds., *Men and Masculinity* (Englewood Cliffs, N.J.: Prentice-Hall, 1974), pp. 139–49.

4. **Jean Baudrillard** (b. 1929)   French semiologist.—EDS.

5. Baudrillard, *La société de consommation,* pp. 144–47.

solicitude. But by pleasing herself, it is understood that she will also please others, and that she will be chosen. "She never enters into direct competition. . . . If she is beautiful, that is to say, if this woman is a woman, she will be chosen. If the man is a man, he will choose his woman as he would other objects/signs (HIS car, HIS woman, HIS eau de toilette)."[6]

Whereas the feminine model is based on passivity, complacency, and narcissism, the masculine model is based on exactingness and choice.

> All of masculine advertising insists on rule, on choice, in terms of rigor and inflexible minutiae. He does not neglect a detail. . . . It is not a question of just letting things go, or of taking pleasure in something, but rather of distinguishing himself. To know how to choose, and not to fail at it, is here the equivalent of the military and puritanical virtues: intransigence, decision, "virtus."[7]

This masculine model, these masculine virtues, are best reflected in the many car advertisements. There, the keywords are masculine terms: *power, performance, precision.* Sometimes the car is a woman, responding to the touch and will of her male driver, after attracting him with her sexy body. "Pure shape, pure power, pure Z. It turns you on." But, as the juxtaposition of shape and power in this advertisement suggests, the car is not simply other; it is also an extension of the owner. As he turns it on, he turns himself on. Its power is his power; through it, he will be able to overpower other men and impress and seduce women.

> How well does it perform?
> How well can you drive? (Merkur XR4Ti)

> The 1987 Celica GT-S has the sweeping lines and aggressive stance that promise performance. And Celica keeps its word.

> Renault GTA:
> Zero to sixty to zero in 13.9 sec.
> It's the result of a performance philosophy where acceleration and braking are equally important.
> There's a new Renault sports sedan called GTA. Under its slick monochromatic skin is a road car with a total performance attitude. . . . It's our hot new pocket rocket.

In this last example, the car, like the driver, has a total performance attitude. That is what works. The slick monochromatic skin, like the Bond Street suit, makes a good first impression. But car, like owner, must have what it takes, must be able to go the distance faster and better than the competition. This point is explicitly made in advertisements in which the

---

6. Ibid.
7. Ibid.

car becomes a means through which this masculine competition at work is extended in leisure. Some refer directly to the manly sport of auto-racing: "The Mitsubishi Starion ESI-R. Patiently crafted to ignite your imagination. Leaving little else to say except . . . gentlemen, start your engines." Others refer to competition in the business world: "To move ahead fast in this world, you've got to have connections. The totally new Corolla FX 16 GT-S has the right ones." Or in life in general. "It doesn't take any [Japanese characters] from anyone. It won't stand for any guff from 300ZX. Or RX-7. Introducing Conquest Tsi, the new turbo sport coupe designed and built by Mitsubishi in Japan." Or Ferrari, which says simply, "We are the competition." In this competition be-tween products, the owners become almost superfluous. But the adver-tisements, of course, suggest that the qualities of the car will reflect the qualities of the owner, as opposed to the purely abstract, apersonal qual-ity of money needed for purchase. Thus, like the would-be owner, the BMW also demonstrates a "relentless refusal to compromise." It is for "those who thrive on a maximum daily requirement of high perfor-mance." While the BMW has the business attitude of the old school ("aggression has never been expressed with such dignity"), a Beretta sug-gests what it takes to survive today in the shark-infested waters of Wall Street. In a glossy three-page cover foldout, a photograph of a shark's fin cutting through indigo waters is accompanied by the legend "Discover a new species from today's Chevrolet." The following two pages show a sleek black Beretta similarly cutting through water and, presumably, through the competition: "Not just a new car, but a new species . . . with a natural instinct for the road . . . Aggressive stance. And a bold tail lamp. See it on the road and you won't soon forget. Drive it, and you never will."

And as with men, so with cars. "Power corrupts. Absolute power corrupts absolutely" (Maserati). Not having the money to pay for a Maserati, to corrupt and be corrupted, is a source of embarrassment. Advertisements reassure the consumer that he need not lose face in this manly battle. Hyundai promises, "It's affordable. (But you'd never know it.)"

> On first impression, the new Hyundai Excel GLS Sedan might seem a trifle beyond most people's means. But that's entirely by de-sign. Sleek European design, to be exact.

Many advertisements suggest sexual pleasure and escape, as in "Pure 10 shape, pure power, pure Z. It turns you on." Or "The all-new Chrysler Le Baron. Beauty . . . with a passion for driving." The Le Baron may ini-tially suggest a beautiful female, with its "image of arresting beauty" and its passion "to drive. And drive it does!" But it *is* "Le Baron," not "La Baronness." And the advertisement continues to emphasize how it "*at-tacks* [emphasis mine] the road with a high torque, 2.5 fuel-injected engine. And its turbo option can blur the surface of any passing lane." Thus the object of the pleasure hardly has to be female if it is beautiful or sleek. The car is an extension of the male that conquers and tames the (female) road: "Positive-response suspension will calm the most demanding roads." The car becomes the ultimate lover when, like the Honda Prelude, it promises to combine power, "muscle," with finesse. Automobile advertisements thus play with androgyny and sexuality; the pleasure is in the union and confusion of form and movement, sex and speed. As in any sexual union, there is ultimately a merging of identities, rather than rigid maintenance of their separation. Polymorphous perverse? Perhaps. But it sells.

Though power, performance, precision as a complex of traits find their strongest emphasis in automobile advertisements, they also appear as selling points for products as diverse as shoes, stereos, and sunglasses. The car performs on the road, the driver performs for women, even in the parking lot, as Michelin suggests in its two-page spread showing a male from waist down resting on his car and chatting up a curvaceous female: "It performs great. And looks great. So, it not only stands out on the road. But in the parking lot. Which is one more place you're likely to discover how beautifully it can handle the curves" (!).

As media analyst Todd Gitlin points out, most of the drivers shown in advertisements are young white males, loners who become empowered by the car that makes possible their escape from the everyday. Gitlin stresses the advertisements' "emphasis on surface, the blankness of the protagonist; his striving toward self-sufficiency, to the point of displacement from the recognizable world."[8] Even the Chrysler advertisements that coopt Bruce Springsteen's "Born in the USA" for their "Born in America" campaign lose in the process the original political message, "ripping off Springsteen's angry anthem, smoothing it into a Chamber of Commerce ditty as shots of just plain productive-looking folks, black and white . . . whiz by in a montage-made community." As Gitlin comments, "None of Springsteen's losers need apply — or rather, if only they would roll up their sleeves and see what good company they're in, they wouldn't feel like losers any longer."[9]

This is a world of patriarchal order in which the individual male can and must challenge the father. He achieves identity by breaking loose of the structure and breaking free of the pack. In the process he recreates the order and reaffirms the myth of masculine independence. Above all, he demonstrates that he knows what he wants; he is critical, demanding, and free from the constraints of others. What he definitely does not want,

8. Todd Gitlin, "We Build Excitement," in Todd Gitlin, ed., *Watching Television* (New York: Pantheon, 1986), pp. 139–40.
9. Ibid.

and goes to some measure to avoid, is to appear less than masculine, in any way weak, frilly, feminine.

Avoiding the Feminine

Advertisers trying to develop male markets for products previously associated primarily with women must overcome the taboo that only women wear moisturizer, face cream, hair spray, or perfume. They do this by overt reference to masculine symbols, language, and imagery, and sometimes by confronting the problem head-on.

There is not so much of a problem in selling products to counteract balding—that traditionally has been recognized as a male problem (a bald woman is a sexual joke that is not particularly amusing to the elderly). But other hair products are another story, as the March 1987 GQ cover asks, "Are you man enough for mousse?" So the advertisements must make their products seem manly, as with S-Curl's "wave and curl kit" offering "The Manly Look" on its manly model dressed in business suit and carrying a hard hat (a nifty social class compromise), and as in college basketball sportscaster Al McGuire's testimonial for Consort hair spray:

> "Years ago, if someone had said to me, 'Hey Al, do you use hair spray?' I would have said, 'No way, baby!'"
> "That was before I tried Consort Pump."
> "Consort adds extra control to my hair without looking stiff or phony. Control that lasts clean into overtime and post-game interviews . . ."
> Grooming Gear for Real Guys. *Consort.*

Besides such "grooming gear" as perms and hair sprays, Real Guys use "skin supplies" and "shaving resources." They adopt a "survival strategy" to fight balding, and the "Fila philosophy"—"products with a singular purpose: performance"—for effective "bodycare." If they wear scent, it smells of anything *but* flowers: musk, woods, spices, citrus, and surf are all acceptable. And the names must be manly, whether symbolizing physical power ("Brut") or financial power ("Giorgio VIP Special Reserve," "The Baron. A distinctive fragrance for men," "Halston—For the privileged few").

As power/precision/performance runs as a theme throughout advertising to men, so too do references to the business world. Cars, as we have seen, promise to share their owner's professional attitude and aggressive drive to beat out the competition. Other products similarly reflect the centrality of business competition to the male gender role. And at the center of this competition itself, the business suit.

>At the onset of your business day, you choose the suit or sport
>coat that will position you front and center . . .
>
>The Right Suit can't guarantee he'll see it your way. The wrong
>suit could mean not seeing him at all.

Along with the Right Suit, the right shirt. "You want it every time you
reach across the conference table, or trade on the floor, or just move
about. You want a shirt that truly fits, that is long enough to stay put
through the most active day, even for the taller gentleman." The businessman chooses the right cologne—Grey Flannel, or perhaps Quorum.
He wears a Gucci "timepiece" as he conducts business on a cordless telephone from his poolside—or prefers the "dignity in styling" promised
by Raymond Weil watches, "a beautiful way to dress for success."

Men's products connect status and success; the right products show
that you have the right stuff, that you're one of them. In the 1950s
C. Wright Mills[10] described what it took to get ahead, to become part of
the "power elite":

>The fit survive, and fitness means, not formal competence . . . but
>conformity with the criteria of those who have already succeeded. To
>be compatible with the top men is to act like them, to look like
>them, to think like them: to be of and for them—or at least to dis-
>play oneself to them in such a way as to create that impression. This,
>in fact, is what is meant by "creating"—a well-chosen word—"a
>good impression." This is what is meant—and nothing else—by
>being a "sound man," as sound as a dollar.[11]

Today, having what it takes includes knowing "the difference between dressed, and well dressed" (Bally shoes). It is knowing that "what
you carry says as much about you as what you put inside it" (Hartmann
luggage). It is knowing enough to imitate Doug Fout, "member of one
of the foremost equestrian families in the country."

>Because of our adherence to quality and the natural shoulder
>tradition, Southwick clothing was adopted by the Fout family years
>ago. Clearly, they have as much appreciation for good lines in a
>jacket as they do in a thoroughbred.

There it is, old money. There is no substitute for it, really, in business or
in advertising, where appeals to tradition form one of the mainstays guar-
anteeing men that their choices are not overly fashionable or feminine,
not working class or cheap, but, rather, correct, in good form, above

---

10. **C. Wright Mills** (1916–1962) American sociologist.—EDS.
11. C. Wright Mills, *The Power Elite* (New York: Oxford University Press, 1956),
p. 141.

criticism. If, when, they achieve this status of gentlemanly perfection, then, the advertisement suggests, they may be invited to join the club.

When only the best of associations will do

Recognizing style as the requisite for membership, discerning men prefer the natural shoulder styling of Racquet Club. Meticulously tailored in pure wool, each suit and sportcoat is the ultimate expression of the clubman's classic good taste.

Ralph Lauren has his Polo University Club, and Rolex picks up on the polo theme by sponsoring the Rolex Gold Cup held at the Palm Beach Polo and Country Club, where sixteen teams and sixty-four players competed for "the pure honor of winning, the true glory of victory":

It has added new lustre to a game so ancient, its history is lost in legend. Tamerlane is said to have been its patriarch. Darius's Persian cavalry, we're told, played it. It was the national sport of 16th-century India, Egypt, China, and Japan. The British rediscovered and named it in 1857.

The linking of polo and Rolex is uniquely appropriate. Both sponsor and sport personify rugged grace. Each is an arbiter of the art of timing.

In the spring of 1987, there was another interesting club event—or nonevent. The prestigious New York University Club was ordered to open its doors to women. This brought the expected protests about freedom of association—and of sanctuary. For that has been one of the points of the men's club. It wasn't open to women. Members knew women had their place, and everyone knew it was not there. In the advertisements, as in the world of reality, there is a place for women in men's lives, one that revolves around: [20]

Sex and Seduction

The growing fascination with appearances, encouraged by advertising, has led to a "feminization" of culture. We are all put in the classic role of the female: manipulable, submissive, seeing ourselves as objects. This "feminization of sexuality" is clearly seen in men's advertisements, where many of the promises made to women are now made to men. If women's advertisements cry, "Buy (this product) and he will notice you," men's advertisements similarly promise that female attention will follow immediately upon purchase, or shortly thereafter. "They can't stay away from Mr. J." "Master the Art of Attracting Attention." She says, "He's wearing my favorite Corbin again." Much as in the advertisements directed at women, the advertisements of men's products promise that they will do the talking for you. "For the look that says come closer." "All the French you'll ever need to know."

Although many advertisements show an admiring and/or dependent female, others depict women in a more active role. "I love him—but life in the fast lane starts at 6 A.M.," says the attractive blonde tying on her jogging shoes, with the "him" in question very handsome and very asleep on the bed in the background. (Does this mean he's in the slow lane?) In another, the man slouches silhouetted against a wall; the woman leans aggressively toward him. He: "Do you always serve Tia Maria . . . or am I special?" She: "Darling, if you weren't special . . . you wouldn't be here."

The masculine role of always being in charge is a tough one. The blunt new honesty about sexually transmitted diseases such as AIDS appears in men's magazines as in women's, in the same "I enjoy sex, but I'm not ready to die for it" condom advertisement. But this new fear is accompanied by old fears of sexual embarrassment and/or rejection. The cartoon shows a man cringing with embarrassment in a pharmacy as the pharmacist yells out, "Hey, there's a guy here wants some information on Trojans." ("Most men would like to know more about Trojan brand condoms. But they're seriously afraid of suffering a spectacular and terminal attack of embarrassment right in the middle of a well-lighted drugstore.") Compared with such agony and responsibility, advertisements promising that women will *want* whatever is on offer, and will even meet the male halfway, must come as blessed relief. Men can finally relax, leaving the courting to the product and seduction to the beguiled woman, which, surely, must seem nice for a change.

Masculine Homilies

A homily is a short sermon, discourse, or informal lecture, often on a moral topic and suggesting a course of conduct. Some of the most intriguing advertisements offer just that, short statements and bits of advice on what masculinity is and on how real men should conduct themselves. As with many short sermons, many of the advertising homilies have a self-congratulatory air about them; after all, you do not want the consumer to feel bad about himself.

What is it, then, to be a man? It is to be *independent.* "There are   25
some things a man will not relinquish." Among them, says the advertisement, his Tretorn tennis shoes.

It is to *savor freedom.* "Dress easy, get away from it all and let Tom Sawyer paint the fence," advises Alexander Julian, the men's designer. "Because man was meant to fly, we gave him wings" (even if only on his sunglasses).

It is to live a life of *adventure.* KL Homme cologne is "for the man who lives on the edge." Prudential Life Insurance preaches, "If you can dream it, you can do it." New Man sportswear tells the reader, "Life is more adventurous when you feel like a New Man."

It is to *keep one's cool.* "J. B. Scotch. A few individuals know how to keep their heads, even when their necks are on the line."

And it is to stay one step *ahead of the competition.* "Altec Lansing. Hear what others only imagine." Alexander Julian again: "Dress up a bit when you dress down. They'll think you know something they don't."

What is it, then, to be a woman? It is to be *dependent.* "A woman   30
needs a man," reads the copy in the Rigolletto advertisement showing a young man changing a tire for a grateful young woman.

The American cowboy as cultural model was not supposed to care for or about appearances. He was what he was, hard-working, straightforward, and honest. He was authentic. Men who cared "too much" about how they looked did not fit this model; the dandy was effete, a European invention, insufficient in masculinity and not red-blooded enough to be a real American. The other cultural model, imported from England, was the gentleman. A gentleman did care about his appearance, in the proper measure and manifestation, attention to tailoring and to quality, understatement rather than exaggeration.[12]

From the gray flannel suit of the 1950s to the "power look" of the 1980s, clothes made the man fit in with his company's image. Sex appeal and corporate correctness merged in a look that spelled success, that exuded confidence.

Whether or not a man presumed to care about his appearance, he did care about having "the right stuff," as Tom Wolfe and *Esquire* call it, or "men's toys," as in a recent special issue of *M* magazine. Cars, motorcycles, stereos, sports equipment: these are part of the masculine appearance. They allow the man to demonstrate his taste, his special knowledge, his affluence: to extend his control. He can be and is demanding, for only the best will do.

He also wants to be loved, but he does not want to appear needy. Advertisements suggest the magic ability of products ranging from cars to hair creams to attract female attention. With the right products a man can have it all, with no strings attached: no boring marital ties, hefty mortgages, corporate compromises.

According to sociologist Barbara Ehrenreich, *Playboy* magazine did   35
much to legitimate this image of male freedom. The old male ethos, up to the postwar period, required exchanging bachelor irresponsibility for married responsibility, which also symbolized entrance into social adulthood.[13] The perennial bachelor, with his flashy cars and interchangeable women, was the object of both envy and derision; he had fun, but . . . he

---

12. See Diane Barthel, "A Gentleman and a Consumer: A Sociological Look at Man at His Best," paper presented at the annual meeting of the Eastern Sociological Society, March 1983, Baltimore.

13. Barbara Ehrenreich, *The Hearts of Men: American Dreams and the Flight from Commitment* (New York: Anchor Books, 1983).

was not fully grown up. There was something frivolous in his lack of purpose and application.

This old ethos has lost much of its legitimacy. Today's male can, as Baudrillard suggests, operate in both modes: the feminine mode of indulging oneself and being indulged and the masculine mode of exigency and competition. With the right look and the right stuff, he can feel confident and manly in boardroom or suburban backyard. Consumer society thus invites both men and women to live in a world of appearances and to devote ever more attention to them.

Reading the Text

1. Define in your own words what Barthel means by the "feminine" (para. 6) and "masculine" (para. 7) modes.
2. Why, according to Barthel, are men's magazines less popular than women's magazines?
3. Summarize what Barthel claims it means "to be a man" (para. 25) in magazine advertising.
4. How are women typically portrayed in men's magazine ads, according to Barthel?

Reading the Signs

1. Buy a copy of one of the men's magazines that Barthel mentions in her essay, and study the advertising. Do the ads corroborate Barthel's claim that men today are allowed to demonstrate both their "masculine" and "feminine" sides?
2. Write an essay in which you apply Barthel's analysis of car advertising to an automotive category she doesn't mention—sport utility vehicles. To what extent have the keywords "power," "performance," and "precision" influenced the ads you find? To develop your ideas, read or reread David Goewey's "'Careful, You May Run Out of Planet': SUVs and the Exploitation of the American Myth" (p. 105).
3. Have each class member bring a copy of a men's or women's magazine to class. Form same-sex groups, and give each group a few magazines designed for the opposite sex. Analyze the gender roles depicted in the magazines, and report to the class the group's findings.
4. Barthel claims that "the growing fascination with appearances" has led to a "feminization" (para. 38) of our culture. Read or review Holly Devor's "Gender Role Behaviors and Attitudes" (p. 447), and use her essay as a critical framework to critique Barthel's claim.
5. In class, brainstorm images of masculinity and femininity, and write your results on the board. Then compare the class's list to the gender traits that Barthel claims are common in advertising. Discuss with your class the possible origins of your brainstormed images.

GLORIA STEINEM
Sex, Lies, and Advertising

One of the best-known icons of the women's movement, Gloria Steinem (b. 1934) has been a leader in transforming the image of women in America. As a cofounder of Ms. *magazine, in which this selection first appeared, Steinem has provided a forum for women's voices for more than twenty years, but as her article explains, it has not been easy to keep this forum going. A commercial publication requires commercials, and the needs of advertisers do not always mesh nicely with the goals of a magazine like* Ms. *Steinem ruefully reveals the compromises* Ms. *magazine had to make over the years to satisfy its advertising clients, compromises that came to an end only when* Ms. *ceased to take ads. Steinem's most recent book is* Moving Beyond Words *(1994), and her many other publications include* Revolution from Within *(1992), a personal exploration of the power of self-esteem. Currently the president of Voters for Choice and a consulting editor for* Ms., *Steinem continues to combine her passion for writing and activism as an unflagging voice in American feminism.*

Goodbye to cigarette ads where poems should be.
Goodbye to celebrity covers and too little space.
Goodbye to cleaning up language so *Ms.* advertisers won't be boycotted by the Moral Majority.
In fact, goodbye to advertisers *and* the Moral Majority.
Goodbye to short articles and short thinking.
Goodbye to "post-feminism" from people who never say "post-democracy."
Goodbye to national boundaries and hello to the world.
Welcome to the magazine of the post-patriarchal age.
The turn of the century is *our turn!*

That was my celebratory mood in the summer of 1990 when I finished the original version of the exposé you are about to read. I felt as if I'd been released from a personal, portable Bastille. At least I'd put on paper the ad policies that had been punishing *Ms.* for all the years of its nonconforming life and still were turning more conventional media, especially (but not only) those directed at women, into a dumping ground for fluff.

Those goodbyes were part of a letter inviting readers to try a new, ad-free version of *Ms.* and were also a homage to "Goodbye to All That," a witty and lethal essay in which Robin Morgan bade farewell to the pre-feminist male Left of twenty years before. It seemed the right tone for the birth of a brand-new, reader-supported, more international form of *Ms.,* which Robin was heading as editor-in-chief, and I was serving as consulting editor. Besides, I had a very personal kind of mantra running through my head: *I'll never have to sell another ad as long as I live.*

So I sent the letter off, watched the premiere issue containing my exposé go to press, and then began to have second thoughts: Were ad policies too much of an "inside" concern? Did women readers already know that magazines directed at them were filled with editorial extensions of ads—and not care? Had this deceptive system been in place too long for anyone to have faith in changing it? In other words: Would anybody give a damn?

After almost four years of listening to responses and watching the ripples spread out from this pebble cast upon the waters, I can tell you that, yes, readers do care; and no, most of them were not aware of advertising's control over the words and images around it. Though most people in the publishing industry think this is a practice too deeply embedded ever to be uprooted, a lot of readers are willing to give it a try— even though that's likely to mean paying more for their publications. In any case, as they point out, understanding the nitty-gritty of ad influence has two immediate uses. It strengthens healthy skepticism about what we read, and it keeps us from assuming that other women must want this glamorous, saccharine, unrealistic stuff.

Perhaps that's the worst punishment ad influence has inflicted upon us. It's made us feel contemptuous of other women. We know we don't need those endless little editorial diagrams of where to put our lipstick or blush—we don't identify with all those airbrushed photos of skeletal women with everything about them credited, *even their perfume* (can you imagine a man's photo airbrushed to perfection, with his shaving lotion credited?)—but we assume there must be women out there somewhere who *do* love it; otherwise, why would it be there?

Well, many don't. Given the sameness of women's magazines resulting from the demands made by makers of women's products that advertise in all of them, we probably don't know yet what a wide variety of women readers want. In any case, we do know it's the advertisers who are determining what women are getting now.

The first wave of response to this exposé came not from readers but from writers and editors for other women's magazines. They phoned to say the pall cast by anticipated or real advertising demands was even more widespread than rebellious *Ms.* had been allowed to know. They told me how brave I was to "burn my bridges" (no critic of advertising would ever be hired as an editor of any of the women's magazines, they said) and generally treated me as if I'd written about organized crime instead of practices that may be unethical but are perfectly legal. After making me promise not to use their names, they offered enough additional horror stories to fill a book, a movie, and maybe a television series. Here is a

5

typical one: when the freelance author of an article on moisturizers observed in print that such products might be less necessary for young women—whose skin tends to be not dry but oily—the article's editor was called on the carpet and denounced by her bosses as "anti-moisturizer." Or how about this: the film critic for a women's magazine asked its top editor, a woman who makes millions for her parent company, whether movies could finally be reviewed critically, since she had so much clout. No, said the editor; if you can't praise a movie, just don't include it; otherwise we'll jeopardize our movie ads. This may sound like surrealism in everyday life, or like our grandmothers advising, "If you can't say something nice, don't say anything," but such are the forces that control much of our information.

I got few negative responses from insiders, but the ones I did get were bitter. Two editors at women's magazines felt I had demeaned them by writing the article. They loved their work, they said, and didn't feel restricted by ads at all. So I would like to make clear in advance that my purpose was and is to change the system, not to blame the people struggling within it. As someone who has written for most women's magazines, I know that many editors work hard to get worthwhile articles into the few pages left over after providing all the "complementary copy" (that is, articles related to and supportive of advertised products). I also know there are editors who sincerely want exactly what the advertisers want, which is why they're so good at their jobs. Nonetheless, criticizing this ad-dominant system is no different from criticizing male-dominant marriage. Both institutions make some people happy, and both seem free as long as your wishes happen to fall within their traditional boundaries. But just as making more equal marital laws alleviates the suffering of many, breaking the link between editorial and advertising will help all media become more honest and diverse.

A second wave of reaction came from advertising executives who were asked to respond by reporters. They attributed all problems to *Ms.* We must have been too controversial or otherwise inappropriate for ads. I saw no stories that asked the next questions: Why had non-women's companies from Johnson & Johnson to IBM found our "controversial" pages fine for their ads? Why did desirable and otherwise unreachable customers read something so "inappropriate"? What were ad policies doing to *other* women's media? To continue my marriage parallel, however, I should note that these executives seemed only mildly annoyed. Just as many women are more dependent than men on the institution of marriage and so are more threatened and angry when it's questioned, editors of women's magazines tended to be more upset than advertisers when questioned about their alliance. . . .

Then came the third wave—reader letters which were smart, 10 thoughtful, innovative, and numbered in the hundreds. Their dominant themes were anger and relief: relief because those vast uncritical oceans of food/fashion/beauty articles in other women's magazines weren't necessarily what women wanted after all, and also relief because *Ms.* wasn't going to take ads anymore, even those that were accompanied by fewer editorial demands; anger because consumer information, diverse articles, essays, fiction, and poetry could have used the space instead of all those oceans of articles about ad categories that had taken up most of women's magazines for years. . . .

Last and most rewarding was the response that started in the fall. Teachers of journalism, advertising, communications, women's studies, and other contemporary courses asked permission to reprint the exposé as a supplementary text. That's another reason why I've restored cuts, updated information, and added new examples—including this introduction. Getting subversive ideas into classrooms could change the next generation running the media.

The following pages are mostly about women's magazines, but that doesn't mean other media are immune.

Sex, Lies, and Advertising

Toward the end of the 1980s, when glasnost was beginning and *Ms.* magazine seemed to be ending, I was invited to a press lunch for a Soviet official. He entertained us with anecdotes about the new problems of democracy in his country; for instance, local Communist leaders who were being criticized by their own media for the first time, and were angry.

"So I'll have to ask my American friends," he finished pointedly, "how more subtly to control the press."

In the silence that followed, I said: "Advertising." 15

The reporters laughed, but later one of them took me aside angrily: How dare I suggest that freedom of the press was limited in this country? How dare I imply that *his* newsmagazine could be influenced by ads?

I explained that I wasn't trying to lay blame, but to point out advertising's media-wide influence. We can all recite examples of "soft" cover stories that newsmagazines use to sell ads, and self-censorship in articles that should have taken advertised products to task for, say, safety or pollution. Even television news goes "soft" in ratings wars, and other TV shows don't get on the air without advertiser support. But I really had been thinking about women's magazines. There, it isn't just a little content that's designed to attract ads; it's almost all of it. That's why advertisers—not readers—had always been the problem for *Ms.* As the only women's magazine that didn't offer what the ad world euphemistically describes as "supportive editorial atmosphere" or "complementary copy" (for instance, articles that praise food/fashion/beauty subjects in order to "support" and "complement" food/fashion/beauty ads), *Ms.* could never attract enough ads to break even.

"Oh, *women*'s magazines," the journalist said with contempt. "Everybody knows they're catalogs—but who cares? They have nothing to do with journalism."

I can't tell you how many times I've had this argument since I started writing for magazines in the early 1960s, and especially since the current women's movement began. Except as moneymaking machines—"cash cows," as they are so elegantly called in the trade—women's magazines are usually placed beyond the realm of serious consideration. Though societal changes being forged by women have been called more far-reaching than the industrial revolution by such nonfeminist sources as the *Wall Street Journal*—and though women's magazine editors often try hard to reflect these changes in the few pages left after all the ad-related subjects are covered—the magazines serving the female half of this country are still far below the journalistic and ethical standards of news and general-interest counterparts. Most depressing of all, this fact is so taken for granted that it doesn't even rate an exposé.

For instance: If *Time* and *Newsweek,* in order to get automotive and GM ads, had to lavish editorial praise on cars and credit photographs in which newsmakers were driving, say, a Buick from General Motors, there would be a scandal—maybe even a criminal investigation. When women's magazines from *Seventeen* to *Lear's* publish articles lavishing praise on beauty and fashion products, and crediting in text describing cover and other supposedly editorial photographs a particular makeup from Revlon or a dress from Calvin Klein because those companies also advertise, it's just business as usual.

When *Ms.* began, we didn't consider *not* taking ads. The most important reason was to keep the price of a feminist magazine low enough for most women to afford. But the second and almost equal reason was to provide a forum where women and advertisers could talk to each other and experiment with nonstereotyped, informative, imaginative ads. After all, advertising was (and is) as potent a source of information in this country as news or TV or movies. It's where we get not only a big part of our information but also images that shape our dreams.

We decided to proceed in two stages. First, we would convince makers of "people products" that their ads should be placed in a women's magazine: cars, credit cards, insurance, sound equipment, financial services—everything that's used by both men and women but was then advertised only to men. Since those advertisers were accustomed to the division between editorial pages and ads that news and general-interest magazines at least try to maintain, such products would allow our editorial content to be free and diverse. Furthermore, if *Ms.*

could prove that women were important purchasers of "people products," just as men were, those advertisers would support other women's magazines, too, and subsidize some pages for articles about something other than the hothouse worlds of food/fashion/beauty. Only in the second phase would we add examples of the best ads for whatever traditional "women's products" (clothes, shampoo, fragrance, food, and so on) that subscriber surveys showed *Ms.* readers actually used. But we would ask those advertisers to come in *without* the usual quid pro quo of editorial features praising their product area; that is, the dreaded "complementary copy."

From the beginning, we knew the second step might be even harder than the first. Clothing advertisers like to be surrounded by editorial fashion spreads (preferably ones that credit their particular labels and designers); food advertisers have always expected women's magazines to publish recipes and articles on entertaining (preferably ones that require their products); and shampoo, fragrance, and beauty products in general insist on positive editorial coverage of beauty aids—a "beauty atmosphere," as they put it—plus photo credits for particular products and nothing too depressing; no bad news. That's why women's magazines look the way they do: saccharine, smiley-faced and product-heavy, with even serious articles presented in a slick and sanitized way.

But if *Ms.* could break this link between ads and editorial content, then we should add "women's products" too. For one thing, publishing ads only for gender-neutral products would give the impression that women have to become "like men" in order to succeed (an impression that *Ms.* ad pages sometimes *did* give when we were still in the first stage). For another, presenting a full circle of products that readers actually need and use would allow us to select the best examples of each category and keep ads from being lost in a sea of similar products. By being part of this realistic but unprecedented mix, products formerly advertised only to men would reach a growth market of women, and good ads for women's products would have a new visibility.

Given the intelligence and leadership of *Ms.* readers, both kinds of products would have unique access to a universe of smart consultants whose response would help them create more effective ads for other media too. Aside from the advertisers themselves, there's nobody who cares as much about the imagery in advertising as those who find themselves stereotyped or rendered invisible by it. And they often have great suggestions for making it better.

As you can see, we had all our energy, optimism, and arguments in good working order.

I thought at the time that our main problem would be getting ads with good "creative," as the imagery and text are collectively known. That was where the women's movement had been focusing its efforts, for instance, the National Organization for Women's awards to the best ads, and its "Barefoot and Pregnant" awards for the worst. Needless to say, there were plenty of candidates for the second group. Carmakers were still draping blondes in evening gowns over the hoods like ornaments that could be bought with the car (thus also making clear that car ads weren't directed at women). Even in ads for products that only women used, the authority figures were almost always male, and voice-overs for women's products on television were usually male too. Sadistic, he-man campaigns were winning industry praise; for example, *Advertising Age* hailed the infamous Silva Thin cigarette theme, "How to Get a Woman's Attention: Ignore Her," as "brilliant." Even in medical journals, ads for tranquilizers showed depressed housewives standing next to piles of dirty dishes and promised to get them back to work. As for women's magazines, they seemed to have few guidelines; at least none that excluded even the ads for the fraudulent breast-enlargement or thigh-thinning products for which their back pages were famous.

Obviously, *Ms.* would have to avoid such offensive imagery and seek out the best ads, but this didn't seem impossible. The *New Yorker* had been screening ads for aesthetic reasons for years, a practice that advertisers accepted at the time. *Ebony* and *Essence* were asking for ads with positive black images, and though their struggle was hard, their requests weren't seen as unreasonable. . . .

Let me take you through some of our experiences—greatly condensed, but just as they happened. In fact, if you poured water on any one of these, it would become a novel:

■ Cheered on by early support from Volkswagen and one or two other 30 car companies, we finally scrape together time and money to put on a major reception in Detroit. U.S. carmakers firmly believe that women choose the upholstery color, not the car, but we are armed with statistics and reader mail to prove the contrary: a car is an important purchase for women, one that is such a symbol of mobility and freedom that many women will spend a greater percentage of income for a car than will counterpart men.

But almost nobody comes. We are left with many pounds of shrimp on the table, and quite a lot of egg on our face. Assuming this near-total boycott is partly because there was a baseball pennant play-off the same day, we blame ourselves for not foreseeing the problem. Executives go out of their way to explain that they wouldn't have come anyway. It's a dramatic beginning for ten years of knocking on resistant or hostile doors, presenting endless documentation of women as car buyers, and hiring a full-time saleswoman in Detroit—all necessary before *Ms.* gets any real results.

This long saga has a semi-happy ending: foreign carmakers understood better than Detroit that women buy cars, and advertised in *Ms.;* also years of research on the women's market plus door-knocking began to pay off. Eventually, cars became one of our top sources of ad revenue.

Even Detroit began to take the women's market seriously enough to put car ads in other women's magazines too, thus freeing a few more of their pages from the food/fashion/beauty hothouse.

But long after figures showed that a third, even half, of many car models were being bought by women, U.S. makers continued to be uncomfortable addressing female buyers. Unlike many foreign carmakers, Detroit never quite learned the secret of creating intelligent ads that exclude no one and then placing them in media that overcome past exclusion. Just as an African American reader may feel more invited by a resort that placed an ad in *Ebony* or *Essence,* even though the same ad appeared in *Newsweek,* women of all races may need to see ads for cars, computers, and other historically "masculine" products in media that are clearly directed at them. Once inclusive ads are well placed, however, there's interest and even gratitude from women. *Ms.* readers were so delighted to be addressed as intelligent consumers by a routine Honda ad with text about rack-and-pinion steering, for example, that they sent fan mail. But even now, Detroit continues to ask: "Should we make special ads for women?" That's probably one reason why foreign cars still have a greater share of the women's market in the U.S. than of the men's.

■ In the *Ms.* Gazette, we do a brief report on a congressional hearing into coal tar derivatives used in hair dyes that are absorbed through the skin and may be carcinogenic. This seems like news of importance: newspapers and newsmagazines are reporting it too. But Clairol, a Bristol-Myers subsidiary that makes dozens of products, a few of which have just come into our pages as ads *without* the usual quid pro quo of articles on hair and beauty, is outraged. Not at newspapers or newsmagazines, just at us. It's bad enough that *Ms.* is the only women's magazine refusing to provide "supportive editorial" praising beauty products, but to criticize one of their product categories on top of it, however generically or even accurately—well, *that* is going too far.

We offer to publish a letter from Clairol telling its side of the story. 35 In an excess of solicitousness, we even put this letter in the Gazette, not in Letters to the Editors, where it belongs. Eventually, Clairol even changes its hair-coloring formula, apparently in response to those same hearings. But in spite of surveys that show *Ms.* readers to be active women who use more of almost everything Clairol makes than do the readers of other women's magazines, *Ms.* gets almost no ads for those dozens of products for the rest of its natural life.

■ Women of color read *Ms.* in disproportionate numbers. This is a source of pride to *Ms.* staffers, who are also more racially representative than the editors of other women's magazines (which may include some beautiful black models but almost no black decisionmakers; Pat Carbine hired the first black editor at *McCall's,* but she left when Pat did). Nonetheless, the reality of *Ms.*'s staff and readership is obscured by ads filled with enough white women to make the casual reader assume *Ms.* is directed at only one part of the population, no matter what the editorial content is.

In fact, those few ads we are able to get that feature women of color—for instance, one made by Max Factor for *Essence* and *Ebony* that Linda Wachner gives us while she is president of Max Factor—are greeted with praise and relief by white readers, too, and make us feel that more inclusive ads should win out in the long run. But there are pathetically few such images. Advertising "creative" also excludes women who are not young, not thin, not conventionally pretty, well-to-do, able-bodied, or heterosexual—which is a hell of a lot of women.

■   Our intrepid saleswomen set out early to attract ads for the product category known as consumer electronics: sound equipment, computers, calculators, VCRs, and the like. We know that *Ms.* readers are determined to be part of this technological revolution, not to be left out as women have been in the past. We also know from surveys that readers are buying this kind of stuff in numbers as high as those of readers of magazines like *Playboy* and the "male 18 to 34" market, prime targets of the industry. Moreover, unlike traditional women's products that our readers buy but don't want to read articles about, these are subjects they like to see demystified in our pages. There actually *is* a supportive editorial atmosphere.

"But women don't understand technology," say ad and electronics executives at the end of our presentations. "Maybe not," we respond, "but neither do men—and we all buy it."

"If women *do* buy it," counter the decisionmakers, "it's because ⁴⁰ they're asking their husbands and boyfriends what to buy first." We produce letters from *Ms.* readers saying how turned off they are when salesmen say things like "Let me know when your husband can come in."

Then the argument turns to why there aren't more women's names sent back on warranties (those much-contested certificates promising repair or replacement if anything goes wrong). We explain that the husband's name may be on the warranty, even if the wife made the purchase. But it's also true that women are experienced enough as consumers to know that such promises are valid only if the item is returned in its original box at midnight in Hong Kong. Sure enough, when we check out hair dryers, curling irons, and other stuff women clearly buy, women don't return those warranties very often either. It isn't the women who are the problem, it's the meaningless warranties.

After several years of this, we get a few ads from companies like JVC and Pioneer for compact sound systems—on the grounds that women can understand compacts, but not sophisticated components. Harry Elias, vice president of JVC, is actually trying to convince his Japanese bosses that there is something called a woman's market. At his invitation, I find myself speaking at trade shows in Chicago and Las Vegas trying to persuade JVC dealers that electronics showrooms don't have to be locker rooms. But as becomes apparent, however, the trade shows are part of the problem. In Las Vegas, the only women working at technology displays are seminude models serving champagne. In Chicago, the big attraction is Marilyn Chambers, a porn star who followed Linda Lovelace of *Deep Throat* fame as Chuck Traynor's captive and/or employee, whose pornographic movies are being used to demonstrate VCRs.

In the end, we get ads for a car stereo now and then, but no VCRs; a welcome breakthrough of some IBM personal computers, but no Apple or no Japanese-made ones. Furthermore, we notice that *Working Woman* and *Savvy,* which are focused on office work, don't benefit as much as they should from ads for office equipment either. . . .

■ Then there is the great toy train adventure. Because *Ms.* gets letters from little girls who love toy trains and ask our help in changing ads and box-top photos that show only little boys, we try to talk to Lionel and to get their ads. It turns out that Lionel executives *have* been concerned about little girls. They made a pink train and couldn't understand why it didn't sell.

Eventually, Lionel bows to this consumer pressure by switching to a   45
photograph of a boy *and* a girl—but only on some box tops. If trains are associated with little girls, Lionel executives believe, they will be devalued in the eyes of little boys. Needless to say, *Ms.* gets no train ads. If even 20 percent of little girls wanted trains, they would be a huge growth market, but this remains unexplored. In the many toy stores where displays are still gender divided, the "soft" stuff, even modeling clay, stays on the girls' side, while the "hard" stuff, especially rockets and trains, is displayed for boys—thus depriving both. By 1986, Lionel is put up for sale.

We don't have much luck with other kinds of toys either. A *Ms.* department, Stories for Free Children, edited by Letty Cottin Pogrebin, makes us one of the very few magazines with a regular feature for children. A larger proportion of *Ms.* readers have preschool children than do the readers of any other women's magazine. Nonetheless, the industry can't seem to believe that feminists care about children—much less have them.

■ When *Ms.* began, the staff decided not to accept ads for feminine hygiene sprays and cigarettes on the same basis: they are damaging to many women's health but carry no appropriate warnings. We don't think we should tell our readers what to do—if marijuana were legal, for instance, we would carry ads for it along with those for beer and wine—but we should provide facts so readers can decide for themselves. Since we've received letters saying that feminine sprays actually kill cockroaches and take the rust off metal, we give up on those. But antismoking groups have been pressuring for health warnings on cigarette ads as well as packages, so we decide we will accept advertising if the tobacco industry complies.

Philip Morris is among the first to do so. One of its brands, Virginia Slims, is also sponsoring women's tennis tournaments and women's public opinion polls that are historic "firsts." On the other hand, the Virginia Slims theme, "You've come a long way, baby," has more than a "baby" problem. It gives the impression that for women, smoking is a sign of progress.

We explain to the Philip Morris people that this slogan won't do well in our pages. They are convinced that its success with *some* women means it will work with *all* women. No amount of saying that we, like men, are a segmented market, that we don't all think alike, does any good. Finally, we agree to publish a small ad for a Virginia Slims calendar as a test, and to abide by the response of our readers.

The letters from readers are both critical and smart. For instance: 50
Would you show a photo of a black man picking cotton next to one of an African American man in a Cardin suit, and symbolize progress from slavery to civil rights by smoking? Of course not. So why do it for women? But instead of honoring test results, the executives seem angry to have been proved wrong. We refuse Virginia Slims ads, thus annoying tennis players like Billie Jean King as well as incurring a new level of wrath: Philip Morris takes away ads for *all* its many products, costing *Ms.* about $250,000 in the first year. After five years, the damage is so great we can no longer keep track.

Occasionally, a new set of Philip Morris executives listens to *Ms.* saleswomen, or laughs when Pat Carbine points out that even Nixon got pardoned. I also appeal directly to the chairman of the board, who agrees it is unfair, sends me to another executive—and *he* says no. Because we won't take Virginia Slims, not one other Philip Morris product returns to our pages for the next sixteen years.

Gradually, we also realize our naïveté in thinking we could refuse all cigarette ads, with or without a health warning. They became a disproportionate source of revenue for print media the moment television banned them, and few magazines can compete or survive without them; certainly not *Ms.*, which lacks the support of so many other categories. Though cigarette ads actually inhibit editorial freedom less than ads for food, fashion, and the like—cigarette companies want only to be distant from coverage on the dangers of smoking, and don't require affirmative praise or photo credits of their product—it is still a growing source of sorrow that they are there at all. By the 1980s, when statistics show that women's rate of lung cancer is approaching men's, the necessity of taking cigarette ads has become a kind of prison.

Though I never manage to feel kindly toward groups that protest our ads and pay no attention to magazines and newspapers that can turn them down and still keep their doors open—and though *Ms.* continues to publish new facts about smoking, such as its dangers during pregnancy—I long for the demise of the whole tobacco-related industry. . . .

■   General Mills, Pillsbury, Carnation, Del Monte, Dole, Kraft, Stouffer, Hormel, Nabisco: you name the food giant, we try to get its ads. But no matter how desirable the *Ms.* readership, our lack of editorial recipes and traditional homemaking articles proves lethal.

We explain that women flooding into the paid labor force have   55 changed the way this country eats; certainly, the boom in convenience foods proves that. We also explain that placing food ads *only* next to recipes and how-to-entertain articles is actually a negative for many women. It associates food with work—in a way that says only women have to cook—or with guilt over *not* cooking and entertaining. Why not advertise food in diverse media that don't always include recipes (thus reaching more men, who have become a third of all supermarket shoppers anyway) and add the recipe interest with specialty magazines like *Gourmet* (a third of whose readers are men)?

These arguments elicit intellectual interest but no ads. No advertising executive wants to be the first to say to a powerful client, "Guess what, I *didn't* get you complementary copy." Except for an occasional hard-won ad for instant coffee, diet drinks, yogurt, or such extras as avocados and almonds, the whole category of food, a mainstay of the publishing industry, remains unavailable to us. Period. . . .

■ By the end of 1986, magazine production costs have skyrocketed and postal rates have increased 400 percent. Ad income is flat for the whole magazine industry. The result is more competition, with other magazines offering such "extras" as free golf trips for advertisers or programs for "sampling" their products at parties and other events arranged by the magazine for desirable consumers. We try to compete with the latter by "sampling" at what we certainly have enough of: movement benefits. Thus, little fragrance bottles turn up next to the dinner plates of California women lawyers (who are delighted), or wine samples lower the costs at a reception for political women. A good organizing tactic comes out of this. We hold feminist seminars in shopping centers. They may be to the women's movement what churches were to the civil rights movement in the South—that is, *where people are.* Anyway, shopping center seminars are a great success. Too great. We have to stop doing them in Bloomingdale's up and down the East Coast, because meeting space in the stores is too limited, and too many women are left lined up outside stores. We go on giving out fancy little liquor bottles at store openings, which makes the advertisers happy—but not us.

Mostly, however, we can't compete in this game of "value-added" (the code word for giving the advertisers extras in return for their ads). Neither can many of the other independent magazines. Deep-pocketed corporate parents can offer such extras as reduced rates for ad schedules in a group of magazines, free tie-in spots on radio stations they also own, or vacation junkets on corporate planes.

Meanwhile, higher costs and lowered income have caused the *Ms.* 60/40 preponderance of edit over ads—something we promised to readers—to become 50/50: still a lot better than most women's magazines' goals of 30/70, but not good enough. Children's stories, most poetry, and some fiction are casualties of reduced space. In order to get variety into more limited pages, the length (and sometimes the depth) of articles suffers. Though we don't solicit or accept ads that would look like a parody in our pages, we get so worn down that some slip through. Moreover, we always have the problem of working just as hard to get a single ad as another magazine might for a whole year's schedule of ads.

Still, readers keep right on performing miracles. Though we haven't been able to afford a subscription mailing in two years, they maintain our guaranteed circulation of 450,000 by word of mouth. Some of them also help to make up the advertising deficit by giving *Ms.* a birthday present of $15 on its fifteen anniversary, or contributing $1,000 for a lifetime subscription—even those who can ill afford it.

What's almost as angering as these struggles, however, is the way the media report them. Our financial problems are attributed to lack of reader interest, not an advertising double standard. In the Reagan-Bush era, when "feminism-is-dead" becomes one key on the typewriter, our problems are used to prepare a grave for the whole movement. Clearly, the myth that advertisers go where the readers are—thus, if we had readers, we would have advertisers—is deeply embedded. Even industry reporters rarely mention the editorial demands made by ads for women's products, and if they do, they assume advertisers must be right and *Ms.* must be wrong; we must be too controversial, outrageous, even scatalogical to support. In fact, there's nothing in our pages that couldn't be published in *Time, Esquire,* or *Rolling Stone*—providing those magazines devoted major space to women—but the media myth often wins out. Though comparable magazines our size (say, *Vanity Fair* or the *Atlantic*) are losing more money in a single year than *Ms.* has lost in sixteen years, *Ms.* is held to a different standard. No matter how much never-to-be-recovered cash is poured into starting a magazine or keeping it going, appearances seem to be all that matter. (Which is why we haven't been able to explain our fragile state in public. Nothing causes ad flight like the smell of nonsuccess.)

My healthy response is anger, but my not-so-healthy one is depression, worry, and an obsession with finding one more rescue. There is hardly a night when I don't wake up with sweaty palms and pounding heart, scared that we won't be able to pay the printer or the post office; scared most of all that closing our doors will be blamed on a lack of readers and thus the movement, instead of the real cause. ("Feminism couldn't even support one magazine," I can hear them saying.)

We're all being flattened by a velvet steamroller. The only difference is that at *Ms.,* we keep standing up again.

Do you think, as I once did, that advertisers make decisions based on rational and uniform criteria? Well, think again. There is clearly a double standard. The same food companies that insist on recipes in women's magazines place ads in *People* where there are no recipes. Cosmetics companies support the *New Yorker,* which has no regular beauty columns, and newspaper pages that have no "beauty atmosphere."

Meanwhile, advertisers' control over the editorial content of 65 women's magazines has become so institutionalized that it is sometimes written into "insertion orders" or dictated to ad salespeople as official policy—whether by the agency, the client, or both. The following are orders given to women's magazines effective in 1990. Try to imagine them being applied to *Time* or *Newsweek.*

■ Dow's Cleaning Products stipulated that ads for its Vivid and Spray 'n Wash products should be adjacent to "children or fashion editorial"; ads for Bathroom Cleaner should be next to "home furnishing/family" features; with similar requirements for other brands. "If a magazine fails for ½ the brands or more," the Dow order warned, "it will be omitted from further consideration."

■ Bristol-Myers, the parent of Clairol, Windex, Drano, Bufferin, and much more, stipulated that ads be placed next to "a full page of compatible editorial."

■ S. C. Johnson & Son, makers of Johnson Wax, lawn and laundry products, insect sprays, hair sprays, and so on, insisted that its ads *"should not be opposite extremely controversial features or material antithetical to the nature/copy of the advertised product."* (Italics theirs.)

■ Maidenform, manufacturer of bras and other women's apparel, left a blank for the particular product and stated in its instructions: "The creative concept of the _____ campaign, and the very nature of the product itself appeal to the positive emotions of the reader/consumer. Therefore, it is imperative that all editorial adjacencies reflect that same positive tone. The editorial must not be negative in content or lend itself contrary to the _____ product imagery/message (e.g., *editorial relating to illness, disillusionment, large size fashion, etc.*)." (Italics mine.)

■ The De Beers diamond company, a big seller of engagement rings, 70 prohibited magazines from placing its ads with "adjacencies to hard news or anti-love/romance themed editorial." . . .

■ Kraft/General Foods, a giant with many brands, sent this message with an Instant Pudding ad: "urgently request upbeat parent/child activity editorial, mandatory positioning requirements—opposite full page of positive editorial—right hand page essential for creative—minimum 6 page competitive separation (i.e., all sugar based or sugar free gelatins, puddings, mousses, creames [sic] and pie filling)—Do not back with clippable material. Avoid: controversial/negative topics and any narrow targeted subjects."

■ An American Tobacco Company order for a Misty Slims ad noted that the U.S. government warning must be included, but also that there must be: "no adjacency to editorial relating to health, medicine, religion or death."

■   Lorillard's Newport cigarette ad come with similar instructions, plus:
"Please be aware that the Nicotine Patch products are competitors. The
minimum six page separation is required."

Quite apart from anything else, you can imagine the logistical nightmare this creates when putting a women's magazine together, but the
greatest casualty is editorial freedom. Though the ratio of advertising to
editorial pages in women's magazines is only about 5 percent more than
in *Time* or *Newsweek,* that nothing-to-read feeling comes from all the
supposedly editorial pages that are extensions of ads. To find out what
we're really getting when we pay our money, I picked up a variety of
women's magazines for February 1994, and counted the number of pages
in each one (even including table of contents, letters to the editors, horo-
scopes, and the like) that were not ads and/or copy complementary to
ads. Then I compared that number to the total pages. Out of 184 pages,
McCall's had 49 that were nonad or ad-related. Of 202, *Elle* gave readers
48. *Seventeen* provided its young readers with only 51 nonad or ad-
related pages out of 226. *Vogue* had 62 out of 292. *Mirabella* offered readers 45 pages out of a total of 158. *Good Housekeeping* came out on top,
though only at about a third, with 60 out of 176 pages. *Martha Stewart
Living* offered the least. Even counting her letter to readers, a page devoted to her personal calendar, and another one to a turnip, only seven
out of 136 pages had no ads, products, or product mentions. . . .

Within the supposedly editorial text itself, praise for advertisers'   75
products has become so ritualized that fields like "beauty writing" have
been invented. One of its practitioners explained to me seriously that
"It's a difficult art. How many new adjectives can you find? How much
greater can you make a lipstick sound? The FDA restricts what companies can say on labels, but we create illusion. And ad agencies are on the
phone all the time pushing you to get their product in. A lot of them
keep the business based on how many editorial clippings they produce
every month. The worst are products [whose manufacturers have] their
own name involved. It's all ego."

Often, editorial becomes one giant ad. An issue of *Lear's* featured an
elegant woman executive on the cover. On the contents page, we learn
she is wearing Guerlain makeup and Samsara, a new fragrance by Guerlain. Inside, there just happen to be full-page ads for Samsara, plus a
Guerlain antiwrinkle skin cream. In the article about the cover subject,
we discover she is Guerlain's director of public relations and is responsible for launching, you guessed it, the new Samsara. . . .

When the *Columbia Journalism Review* cited this example in one of
the few articles to include women's magazines in a critique of ad influence, Frances Lear, editor of *Lear's,* was quoted at first saying this was a
mistake, and then shifting to the defense that "this kind of thing is done
all the time."

She's right. Here's an example with a few more turns of the screw.
Martha Stewart, *Family Circle*'s contributing editor, was also "lifestyle and

entertaining consultant" for Kmart, the retail chain, which helped to underwrite the renovation of Stewart's country house, using Kmart products; *Family Circle* covered the process in three articles not marked as ads; Kmart bought $4 million worth of ad pages in *Family Circle,* including "advertorials" to introduce a line of Martha Stewart products to be distributed by Kmart; and finally, the "advertorials," which at least are marked and only *look* like editorial pages, were reproduced and distributed in Kmart stores, thus publicizing *Family Circle* (owned by the New York Times Company, which would be unlikely to do this kind of thing in its own news pages) to Kmart customers. This was so lucrative that Martha Stewart now has her own magazine, *Martha Stewart Living* (owned by Time Warner), complete with a television version. Both offer a happy world of cooking, entertaining, and decorating in which nothing critical or negative ever seems to happen.

I don't mean to be a spoilsport, but there are many articles we're very unlikely to get from that or any other women's magazine dependent on food ads. According to Senator Howard Metzenbaum of Ohio, more than half of the chickens we eat (from ConAgra, Tyson, Perdue, and other companies) are contaminated with dangerous bacteria; yet labels haven't yet begun to tell us to scrub the meat and everything it touches—which is our best chance of not getting sick. Nor are we likely to learn about the frequent working conditions of this mostly female work force, standing in water, cutting chickens apart with such repetitive speed that carpal tunnel syndrome is an occupational hazard. Then there's Dole Food, often cited as a company that keeps women in low-level jobs and a target of a lawsuit by Costa Rican workers who were sterilized by contact with pesticides used by Dole—even though Dole must have known these pesticides had been banned in the U.S.

The consumerist reporting we're missing sometimes sounds familiar. Remember the *Ms.* episode with Clairol and the article about potential carcinogens in hair dye? Well, a similar saga took place with L'Oréal and *Mademoiselle* in 1992, according to an editor at Condé Nast. Now, editors there are supposed to warn publishers of any criticism in advance, a requirement that might well have a chilling effect.

Other penalties are increasing. As older readers will remember, women's magazines used to be a place where new young poets and short story writers could be published. Now, that's very rare. It isn't that advertisers of women's products dislike poetry or fiction, it's just that they pay to be adjacent to articles and features more directly compatible with their products.

Sometimes, advertisers invade editorial pages—literally—by plunging odd-shaped ads into the text, no matter how that increases the difficulty of reading. When Ellen Levine was editor of *Woman's Day,* for instance, a magazine originally founded by a supermarket chain, she admitted, "The day the copy had to rag around a chicken leg was not a happy one."

The question of ad positioning is also decided by important advertisers, a rule that's ignored at a magazine's peril. When Revlon wasn't
given the place of the first beauty ad in one Hearst magazine, for instance, it pulled its ads from *all* Hearst magazines. In 1990 Ruth Whitney, editor in chief of *Glamour,* attributed some of this pushiness to "ad
agencies wanting to prove to a client that they've squeezed the last drop
of blood out of a magazine." She was also "sick and tired of hearing that
women's magazines are controlled by cigarette ads." Relatively speaking,
she was right. To be as controlling as most advertisers of women's products, tobacco companies would have to demand articles in flat-out praise
of smoking, and editorial photos of models smoking a credited brand. As
it is, they ask only to be forewarned so they don't advertise in the same
issue with an article about the dangers of smoking. But for a magazine
like *Essence,* the only national magazine for African American women,
even taking them out of one issue may be financially difficult, because
other advertisers might neglect its readers. In 1993, a group called
Women and Girls Against Tobacco, funded by the California Department of Health Services, prepared an ad headlined "Cigarettes Made
Them History." It pictured three black singers—Mary Wells, Eddie
Kendricks, and Sarah Vaughan—who died of tobacco-related diseases.
Essence president Clarence Smith didn't turn the ad down, but he didn't
accept it either. When I talked with him in 1994, he said with pain, "the
black female market just isn't considered at parity with the white female
market; there are too many other categories we don't get." That's in
spite of the fact that *Essence* does all the traditional food-fashion-beauty
editorial expected by advertisers. According to California statistics,
African American women are more addicted to smoking than the female
population at large, with all the attendant health problems.

Alexandra Penney, editor of *Self* magazine, feels she has been able to
include smoking facts in health articles by warning cigarette advertisers in
advance (though smoking is still being advertised in this fitness magazine). On the other hand, up to this writing in 1994, no advertiser has
been willing to appear opposite a single-page feature called "Outrage,"
which is reserved for important controversies, and is very popular with
readers. Another women's magazine publisher told me that to this day
Campbell's Soup refuses to advertise because of an article that unfavorably
compared the nutritional value of canned food to that of fresh food—fifteen years ago.

I don't mean to imply that the editors I quote here share my objections to ad demands and/or expectations. Many assume that the women's
magazines at which they work have to be the way they are. Others are
justifiably proud of getting an independent article in under the advertising radar, for instance, articles on family violence in *Family Circle* or a series on child sexual abuse and the family courts in *McCall's.* A few insist
they would publish exactly the same editorial, even if there were no ads.

But it's also true that it's hard to be honest while you're still in the job. "Most of the pressure came in the form of direct product mentions," explained Sey Chassler, who was editor in chief of *Redbook* from the sixties to the eighties and is now out of the game. "We got threats from the big guys, the Revlons, blackmail threats. They wouldn't run ads unless we credited them.

What could women's magazines be like if they were as editorially free as good books? as realistic as the best newspaper articles? as creative as poetry and films? as diverse as women's lives? What if we as women— who are psychic immigrants in a public world rarely constructed by or for us—had the same kind of watchful, smart, supportive publications on our side that other immigrant groups have often had?

We'll find out only if we take the media directed at us seriously. If readers were to act in concert in large numbers for a few years to change the traditional practices of *all* women's magazines and the marketing of *all* women's products, we could do it. After all, they depend on our consumer dollars—money we now are more likely to control. If we include all the shopping we do for families and spouses, women make 85 percent of purchases at point of sale. You and I could:

- refuse to buy products whose ads have clearly dictated their surroundings, and write to tell the manufacturers why;

- write to editors and publishers (with copies to advertisers) to tell them that we're willing to pay *more* for magazines with editorial independence, but will *not* continue to pay for those that are editorial extensions of ads;

- write to advertisers (with copies to editors and publishers) to tell them that we want fiction, political reporting, consumer reporting, strong opinion, humor, and health coverage that doesn't pull punches, praising them when their ads support this, and criticizing them when they don't;

- put as much energy and protest into breaking advertising's control over what's around it as we put into changing the images within it or protesting harmful products like cigarettes;

- support only those women's magazines and products that take us seriously as readers and consumers;

- investigate new laws and regulations to support freedom from advertising influence. The Center for the Study of Commercialism, a group founded in 1990 to educate and advocate against "ubiquitous product marketing," recommends whistle-blower laws that protect any members of the media who disclose advertiser and other commercial conflicts of interest, laws that require advertiser influence to be disclosed, Federal Trade Commission involvement, and denial of income tax exemptions for advertising that isn't clearly identified—as well as conferences, citizen watchdog groups, and a national clearinghouse where examples of private censorship can be reported.

Those of us in the magazine world can also use this carrot-and-stick technique. The stick: If magazines were a regulated medium like television, the editorial quid pro quo demanded by advertising would be against the rules of the FCC, and payola and extortion would be penalized. As it is, there are potential illegalities to pursue. For example: A magazine's postal rates are determined by the ratio of ad pages to editorial pages, with the ads being charged at a higher rate than the editorial. Counting up all the pages that are *really* ads could make an interesting legal action. There could be consumer fraud cases lurking in subscriptions that are solicited for a magazine but deliver a catalog.

The carrot is just as important. In twenty years, for instance, I've found no independent, nonproprietary research showing that an ad for, say, fragrance is any more effective placed next to an article about fragrance than it would be when placed next to a good piece of fiction or reporting. As we've seen, there are studies showing that the greatest factor in determining an ad's effectiveness is the credibility and independence of its surroundings. An airtight wall between ads and edit would also shield corporations and agencies from pressures from both ends of the political spectrum and from dozens of pressure groups. Editors would be the only ones responsible for editorial content—which is exactly as it should be.

Unfortunately, few agencies or clients hear such arguments. Editors often maintain the artificial purity of refusing to talk to the people who actually control their lives. Instead, advertisers see salespeople who know little about editorial, are trained in business as usual, and are usually paid on commission. To take on special controversy editors might also band together. That happened once when all the major women's magazines did articles in the same month on the Equal Rights Amendment. It could happen again—and regularly.

Meanwhile, we seem to have a system in which everybody is losing. The reader loses diversity, strong opinion, honest information, access to the arts, and much more. The editor loses pride of work, independence, and freedom from worry about what brand names or other critical words some sincere freelancer is going to come up with. The advertiser loses credibility right along with the ad's surroundings, and gets more and more lost in a sea of similar ads and interchangeable media.

But that's also the good news. Because where there is mutual interest, there is the beginning of change.

If you need one more motive for making it, consider the impact of U.S. media on the rest of the world. The ad policies we tolerate here are invading the lives of women in other cultures—through both the con tent of U.S. media and the ad practices of multinational corporations imposed on other countries. Look at our women's magazines. Is this what we want to export?

Should *Ms.* have started out with no advertising in the first place? The odd thing is that, in retrospect, I think the struggle was worth it. For all those years, dozens of feminist organizers disguised as *Ms.* ad saleswomen took their courage, research, slide shows, humor, ingenuity, and fresh point of view into every advertising agency, client office, and lion's den in cities where advertising is sold. Not only were sixteen years of *Ms.* sustained in this way, with all the changeful words on those thousands of pages, but some of the advertising industry was affected in its imagery, its practices, and its understanding of the female half of the country. Those dozens of women themselves were affected, for they learned the art of changing a structure from both within and without, and are now rising in crucial publishing positions where women have never been. *Ms.* also helped to open nontraditional categories of ads for women's magazines, thus giving them a little more freedom—not to mention making their changes look reasonable by comparison.

But the world of advertising has a way of reminding us how far there   95 is to go.

Three years ago, as I was finishing this exposé in its first version, I got a call from a writer for *Elle.* She was doing an article on where women parted their hair: Why, she wanted to know, did I part mine in the middle?

It was all so familiar. I could imagine this writer trying to make something out of a nothing assignment. A long-suffering editor laboring to think of new ways to attract ads for shampoo, conditioner, hairdryers, and the like. Readers assuming that other women must want this stuff.

As I was working on this version, I got a letter from Revlon of the sort we disregarded when we took ads. Now, I could appreciate it as a reminder of how much we had to disregard:

> We are delighted to confirm that Lauren Hutton is now under contract to Revlon.
>
> We are very much in favor of her appearing in as much editorial as possible, but it's important that your publication avoid any mention of competitive color cosmetics, beauty treatment, hair care or sun care products in editorial or editorial credits in which she appears.
>
> We would be very appreciative if all concerned are made aware of this.

I could imagine the whole chain of women—Lauren Hutton, preferring to be in the Africa that is her passion; the ad executive who signed the letter, only doing her job; the millions of women readers who would see the resulting artificial images; all of us missing sources of information, insight, creativity, humor, anger, investigation, poetry, confession, outrage, learning, and perhaps most important, a sense of connection to each other; and a gloriously diverse world being flattened by a velvet steamroller.

I ask you: Can't we do better than this?   100

Reading the Text

1. What does Steinem mean by "complementary copy" (para. 17)?
2. Summarize the relationship that Steinem sees between editorial content and advertising in women's magazines.
3. According to Steinem, what messages about gender roles does complementary copy send readers of women's magazines?

Reading the Signs

1. Steinem asserts that virtually all content in women's magazines is a disguised form of advertising, by what it either says or doesn't say. Test her hypothesis by writing a detailed analysis of a single issue of a magazine such as *Cosmopolitan, Jane,* or *Elle.* Do you find instances of complementary copy? How do you react as a potential reader of such a magazine?
2. Explore whether Steinem's argument holds for men's magazines such as *Maxim* or *GQ.* If you identify differences, how might they be based on different assumptions about gender roles?
3. Have each member of the class bring in a favorite magazine. In small groups, study the relationship between ads and articles. Which magazines have the most complementary copy? How can you account for your findings?
4. Do advertisers infringe on the freedom of the press? Write a journal entry in which you explore this issue.

JOHN E. CALFEE

How Advertising Informs to Our Benefit

||||||||||||||||||||||||||||||||||||||||||||||||||||||||||

> *Most cultural analysts of advertising don't like it very much, to put it mildly. George Orwell called it "the rattling of a stick inside a swill bucket," but John E. Calfee disagrees. In this article from* Consumers' Research Magazine *(1998), Calfee argues that advertising performs a valuable public service by providing us with useful information that we might otherwise not receive. He cites, for example, the Kellogg's All-Bran campaign that successfully broadcast the heretofore ignored*

recommendation from the National Cancer Institute for people to eat more fiber. The author of Fear of Persuasion: A New Perspective on Advertising and Regulation *(1997), Calfee is a resident scholar at the American Enterprise Institute and is the author (with James K. Glassman) of* Fear of Persuasion: A New Perspective on Advertising and Regulation *(1998).*

A great truth about advertising is that it is a tool for communicating information and shaping markets. It is one of the forces that compel sellers to cater to the desires of consumers. Almost everyone knows this because consumers use advertising every day, and they miss advertising when they cannot get it. This fact does not keep politicians and opinion leaders from routinely dismissing the value of advertising. But the truth is that people find advertising very useful indeed.

Of course, advertising primarily seeks to persuade and everyone knows this, too. The typical ad tries to induce a consumer to do one particular thing—usually, buy a product—instead of a thousand other things. There is nothing obscure about this purpose or what it means for buyers. Decades of data and centuries of intuition reveal that all consumers everywhere are deeply suspicious of what advertisers say and why they say it. This skepticism is in fact the driving force that makes advertising so effective. The persuasive purpose of advertising and the skepticism with which it is met are two sides of a single process. Persuasion and skepticism work in tandem so advertising can do its job in competitive markets. Hence, ads represent the seller's self-interest, consumers know this, and sellers know that consumers know it.

By understanding this process more fully, we can sort out much of the popular confusion surrounding advertising and how it benefits consumers.

How Useful Is Advertising?

Just how useful is the connection between advertising and information? At first blush, the process sounds rather limited. Volvo ads tell consumers that Volvos have side-impact air bags, people learn a little about the importance of air bags, and Volvo sells a few more cars. This seems to help hardly anyone except Volvo and its customers. But advertising does much more. It routinely provides immense amounts of information that benefits primarily parties other than the advertiser. This may sound odd, but it is a logical result of market forces and the nature of information itself.

The ability to use information to sell products is an incentive to create   5
new information through research. Whether the topic is nutrition, safety, or more mundane matters like how to measure amplifier power, the necessity of achieving credibility with consumers and critics requires much

of this research to be placed in the public domain and that it rest upon some academic credentials. That kind of research typically produces results that apply to more than just the brands sold by the firm sponsoring the research. The lack of property rights to such "pure" information ensures that this extra information is available at no charge. Both consumers and competitors may borrow the new information for their own purposes.

Advertising also elicits additional information from other sources. Claims that are striking, original, forceful, or even merely obnoxious will generate news stories about the claims, the controversies they cause, the reactions of competitors (a price war? a splurge of comparison ads?), the reactions of consumers, and the remarks of governments and independent authorities. Probably the most concrete, pervasive, and persistent example of competitive advertising that works for the public good is price advertising. Its effect is invariably to heighten competition and reduce prices, even the prices of firms that assiduously avoid mentioning prices in their own advertising.

There is another area where the public benefits of advertising are less obvious but equally important. The unremitting nature of consumer interest in health, and the eagerness of sellers to cater to consumer desires, guarantee that advertising related to health will provide a storehouse of telling observations on the ways in which the benefits of advertising extend beyond the interests of advertisers to include the interests of the public at large.

A Cascade of Information

Here is probably the best documented example of why advertising is necessary for consumer welfare. In the 1970s, public health experts described compelling evidence that people who eat more fiber are less likely to get cancer, especially cancer of the colon, which happens to be the second leading cause of deaths from cancer in the United States. By 1979, the U.S. Surgeon General was recommending that people eat more fiber in order to prevent cancer. Consumers appeared to take little notice of these recommendations, however. The National Cancer Institute decided that more action was needed. NCI's cancer prevention division undertook to communicate the new information about fiber and cancer to the general public. Their goal was to change consumer diets and reduce the risk of cancer, but they had little hope of success given the tiny advertising budgets of federal agencies like NCI.

Their prospects unexpectedly brightened in 1984. NCI received a call from the Kellogg Corporation, whose All-Bran cereal held a commanding market share of the high-fiber segment. Kellogg proposed to use All-Bran advertising as a vehicle for NCI's public service messages. NCI thought that was an excellent idea. Soon, an agreement was reached in which NCI would review Kellogg's ads and labels for accuracy and value before Kellogg began running their fiber-cancer ads.

The new Kellogg All-Bran campaign opened in October 1984. A typical ad began with the headline, "At last some news about cancer you can live with." The ad continued: "The National Cancer Institute believes a high fiber, low fat diet may reduce your risk of some kinds of cancer. The National Cancer Institute reports some very good health news. There is growing evidence that may link a high fiber, low fat diet to lower incidence of some kinds of cancer. That's why one of their strongest recommendations is to eat high-fiber foods. If you compare, you'll find Kellogg's All-Bran has nine grams of fiber per serving. No other cereal has more. So start your day with a bowl of Kellogg's All-Bran or mix it with your regular cereal."

The campaign quickly achieved two things. One was to create a regulatory crisis between two agencies. The Food and Drug Administration thought that if a food was advertised as a way to prevent cancer, it was being marketed as a drug. Then the FDA's regulations for drug labeling would kick in. The food would be reclassified as a drug and would be removed from the market until the seller either stopped making the health claims or put the product through the clinical testing necessary to obtain formal approval as a drug.

But food advertising is regulated by the Federal Trade Commission, not the FDA. The FTC thought Kellogg's ads were non–deceptive and were therefore perfectly legal. In fact, it thought the ads should be encouraged. The Director of the FTC's Bureau of Consumer Protection declared that "the [Kellogg] ad has presented importance public health recommendations in an accurate, useful, and substantiated way. It informs the members of the public that there is a body of data suggesting certain relationships between cancer and diet that they may find important." The FTC won this political battle, and the ads continued.

The second instant effect of the All-Bran campaign was to unleash a flood of health claims. Vegetable oil manufacturers advertised that cholesterol was associated with coronary heart disease, and that vegetable oil does not contain cholesterol. Margarine ads did the same, and added that vitamin A is essential for good vision. Ads for calcium products (such as certain antacids) provided vivid demonstrations of the effects of osteoporosis (which weakens bones in old age), and recounted the advice of experts to increase dietary calcium as a way to prevent osteoporosis. Kellogg's competitors joined in citing the National Cancer Institute dietary recommendations.

Nor did things stop there. In the face of consumer demand for better and fuller information, health claims quickly evolved from a blunt tool to a surprisingly refined mechanism. Cereals were advertised as high in fiber and low in sugar or fat or sodium. Ads for an upscale brand of bread noted: "Well, most high-fiber bran cereals may be high in fiber, but often only one kind: insoluble. It's this kind of fiber that helps promote regularity. But there's also a kind of fiber known as soluble, which most high-fiber bran cereals have in very small amounts, if at all. Yet diets high in this kind of fiber may actually lower your serum cholesterol, a risk factor for some heart diseases." Cereal boxes became convenient sources for a summary of what made for a good diet.

Increased Independent Information

The ads also brought powerful secondary effects. These may have been even more useful than the information that actually appeared in the ads themselves. One effect was an increase in media coverage of diet and health. *Consumer Reports,* a venerable and hugely influential magazine that carries no advertising, revamped its reports on cereals to emphasize fiber and other ingredients (rather than testing the foods to see how well they did at providing a complete diet for laboratory rats). The health-claims phenomenon generated its own press coverage, with articles like "What Has All-Bran Wrought?" and "The Fiber Furor." These stories recounted the ads and the scientific information that prompted the ads; and articles on food and health proliferated. Anyone who lived through these years in the United States can probably remember the unending media attention to health claims and to diet and health generally.

Much of the information on diet and health was new. This was no coincidence. Firms were sponsoring research on their products in the hope of finding results that could provide a basis for persuasive advertising claims. Oat bran manufacturers, for example, funded research on the impact of soluble fiber on blood cholesterol. When the results came out "wrong," as they did in a 1990 study published with great fanfare in the *New England Journal of Medicine,* the headline in *Advertising Age* was "Oat Bran Popularity Hitting the Skids," and it did indeed tumble. The manufacturers kept at the research, however, and eventually the best research supported the efficacy of oat bran in reducing cholesterol (even to the satisfaction of the FDA). Thus did pure advertising claims spill over to benefit the information environment at large.

The shift to higher fiber cereals encompassed brands that had never undertaken the effort necessary to construct believable ads about fiber and disease. Two consumer researchers at the FDA reviewed these data and concluded they were "consistent with the successful educational impact of the Kellogg diet and health campaign: consumers seemed to be making an apparently thoughtful discrimination between high- and low-fiber cereals," and that the increased market shares for high-fiber non-advertised products represented "the clearest evidence of a successful consumer education campaign."

Perhaps most dramatic were the changes in consumer awareness of diet and health. An FTC analysis of government surveys showed that when consumers were asked about how they could prevent cancer through their diet, the percentage who mentioned fiber increased from 4 percent before the 1979 Surgeon General's report to 8.5 percent in 1984 (after the report but before the All-Bran campaign) to 32 percent in 1986 after a year and a half or so of health claims (the figure in 1988 was 28 percent). By far the greatest increases in awareness were among women (who do most of the grocery shopping) and the less educated: up from 0 percent for women without a high school education in 1984 to 31 percent for the same group in 1986. For women with incomes of less than $15,000, the increase was from 6 percent to 28 percent.

The health-claims advertising phenomenon achieved what years of effort by government agencies had failed to achieve. With its mastery of the art of brevity, its ability to command attention, and its use of television, brand advertising touched precisely the people the public health community was most desperate to reach. The health claims expanded consumer information along a broad front. The benefits clearly extended far beyond the interests of the relatively few manufacturers who made vigorous use of health claims in advertising.

A Pervasive Phenomenon

Health claims for foods are only one example, however, of a pervasive phenomenon—the use of advertising to provide essential health information with benefits extending beyond the interests of the advertisers themselves. Advertising for soap and detergents, for example, once improved private hygiene and therefore, public health (hygiene being one of the underappreciated triumphs in twentieth century public health). Toothpaste advertising helped to do the same for teeth. When mass advertising for toothpaste and tooth powder began early in this century, tooth brushing was rare. It was common by the 1930s, after which toothpaste sales leveled off even though the advertising, of course, continued. When fluoride toothpastes became available, advertising generated interest in better teeth and professional dental care. Later, a "plaque reduction war" (which first involved mouthwashes, and later toothpastes) brought a new awareness of gum disease and how to prevent it. The financial gains to the toothpaste industry were surely dwarfed by the benefits to consumers in the form of fewer cavities and fewer lost teeth. 20

Health claims induced changes in foods, in nonfoods such as toothpaste, in publications ranging from university health letters to mainstream newspapers and magazines, and of course, consumer knowledge of diet and health.

These rippling effects from health claims in ads demonstrated the most basic propositions in the economics of information. Useful information initially failed to reach people who needed it because information producers could not charge a price to cover the costs of creating and disseminating pure information. And this problem was alleviated by advertising, sometimes in a most vivid manner.

Other examples of spillover benefits from advertising are far more common than most people realize. Even the much-maligned promotion of expensive new drugs can bring profound health benefits to patients and families, far exceeding what is actually charged for the products themselves. The market processes that produce these benefits bear all the classic features of competitive advertising. We are not analyzing public service announcements here, but old-fashioned profit-seeking brand advertising. Sellers focused on the information that favored their own products. They advertised it in ways that provided a close link with their own brand. It was a purely competitive enterprise, and the benefits to consumers arose from the imperatives of the competitive process.

One might see all this as simply an extended example of the economics of information and greed. And indeed it is, if by greed one means the effort to earn a profit by providing what people are willing to pay for, even if what they want most is information rather than a tangible product. The point is that there is overwhelming evidence that unregulated economic forces dictate that much useful information will be provided by brand advertising, and only by brand advertising. Of course, there is much more to the story. There is the question of how competition does the good I have described without doing even more harm elsewhere. After all, firms want to tell people only what is good about their brands, and people often want to know what is wrong with the brands. It turns out that competition takes care of this problem, too.

Advertising and Context

It is often said that most advertising does not contain very much information. In a way, this is true. Research on the contents of advertising typically finds just a few pieces of concrete information per ad. That's an average, of course. Some ads obviously contain a great deal of information. Still, a lot of ads are mainly images and pleasant talk, with little in the way of what most people would consider hard information. On the whole, information in advertising comes in tiny bits and pieces. 25

Cost is only one reason. To be sure, cramming more information into ads is expensive. But more to the point is the fact that advertising plays off the information available from outside sources. Hardly anything about advertising is more important than the interplay between what the ad contains and what surrounds it. Sometimes this interplay is a burden for the advertiser because it is beyond his control. But the interchange between advertising and environment is also an invaluable tool for sellers.

Ads that work in collaboration with outside information can communicate far more than they ever could on their own.

The upshot is advertising's astonishing ability to communicate a great deal of information in a few words. Economy and vividness of expression almost always rely upon what is in the information environment. The famously concise "Think Small" and "Lemon" ads for the VW "Beetle" in the 1960s and 1970s were highly effective with buyers concerned about fuel economy, repair costs, and extravagant styling in American cars. This was a case where the less said, the better. The ads were more powerful when consumers were free to bring their own ideas about the issues to bear. The same process is repeated over again for all sorts of products. Ads for computer modems once explained what they could be used for. Now a simple reference to the Internet is sufficient to conjure an elaborate mix of equipment and applications. These matters are better left vague so each potential customer can bring to the ad his own idea of what the Internet is really for.

Leaning on information from other sources is also a way to enhance credibility, without which advertising must fail. Much of the most important information in advertising—think of cholesterol and heart disease, antilock brakes and automobile safety—acquires its force from highly credible sources other than the advertiser. To build up this kind of credibility through material actually contained in ads would be cumbersome and inefficient. Far more effective, and far more economical, is the technique of making challenges, raising questions and otherwise making it perfectly clear to the audience that the seller invites comparisons and welcomes the tough questions. Hence the classic slogan, "If you can find a better whiskey, buy it."

Finally, there is the most important point of all. Informational sparseness facilitates competition. It is easier to challenge a competitor through pungent slogans—"Where's the beef?" "Where's the big saving?"—than through a step-by-step recapitulation of what has gone on before. The bits-and-pieces approach makes for quick, unerring attacks and equally quick responses, all under the watchful eye of the consumer over whom the battle is being fought. This is an ideal recipe for competition.

Reading the Text

1. Describe in your own words the benefits of advertising according to Calfee.
2. Summarize the history of Kellogg's advertising campaign for All-Bran. What does Calfee see as the significance of this ad campaign?
3. How does Calfee defend the fact that, in his own words, "information in advertising comes in tiny bits and pieces" (para. 25)?
4. According to Calfee, how do competitive market forces help ensure that information in advertising benefits the consumer?

Reading the Signs

1. In class, form teams, and debate Calfee's proposition that "Advertising Informs to Our Benefit." To prepare, collect and analyze advertisements
   that support your team's position.
2. While Calfee focuses on the advertising of health and nutrition products, he
   implies that all advertising can be beneficial to consumers. Read or reread
   Patricia J. Williams's "The Fiction of Truth in Advertising" (below), and
   write an essay supporting, refuting, or complicating Calfee's claim that advertising is an efficient medium for transmitting accurate information.
3. Study health- and diet-related ads, which abound in publications such as
   Better Homes and Gardens or *Shape*. Use them as the evidence in an essay
   that demonstrates, refutes, or modifies Calfee's claim that ads serve the
   "interests of the public at large" (para. 7).
4. Research the history of cigarette advertising in twentieth-century America.
   Use your findings as the basis of an argumentative essay on whether the tobacco industry has been a source of beneficial information to consumers.
5. In your journal, reflect on Calfee's claim that consumers "miss advertising
   when they cannot get it" (para. 1).

PATRICIA J. WILLIAMS
The Fiction of Truth in Advertising

‖‖‖‖‖‖‖‖‖‖‖‖‖‖‖‖‖‖‖‖‖‖‖‖‖‖‖‖‖‖‖‖‖‖‖‖‖‖‖

In The Alchemy of Race and Rights *(1991), from which this selection is taken, Patricia J. Williams (b. 1951) explores the relationship between the law and everyday life, focusing particularly on the
ways that race and gender can complicate American social relations. In
this passage, Williams brings her legal training to bear on advertising.
Notions of "truth" are increasingly absent from modern advertising,
she finds, as she reflects on the dehumanizing and disenfranchising effect of media fictions. Educated at Harvard Law School, she currently
is professor of law at Columbia Law School and has written widely on
civil rights issues and legal ethics. Currently serving on the Board of
Governors of the Society of American Law, Williams is also on the
Board of Scholars of* Ms. *magazine and is a contributing editor of the*
Nation. *Her recent publications include* The Rooster's Egg *(1997)
and* Seeing a Color-Blind Future: The Paradox of Race *(1998).*

When I first started teaching consumer protection a decade ago, the
mathematics of false advertising was simple. If the box or brochure said

"100% cotton," you merely took the item in question and subtracted it from the words: Any difference was the measure of your legal remedy. Sometimes you had to add in buyer's expertise or multiply the whole by seller's bad faith, but generally the whole reason people even took a class in consumer protection was that you didn't have to learn logarithms. Today, however, advertisers almost never represent anything remotely related to the reality of the product—or the politician—they are trying to sell; misrepresentation, the heart of false-advertising statutes, is very hard to prove. Increasingly, television ads are characterized by scenarios that neither mention the product nor contain a description of any sort. What fills the sixty seconds are "concepts" and diffuse images—images that used to be discursive, floating in the background, creating a mellow consumerist backdrop—which now dominate and direct content. Nothing is promised, everything evoked: warm fuzzy camera angles; "peak" experiences; happy pictures, mood-shaping music; almost always a smarmy, soft-peddling overvoice purring "This magic moment has been brought to you by. . . ."

An example, in the form of an anecdote: About a year ago, I was sitting at home, installed before the television set. I was preparing for a class in consumer protection. The next day's assignment was false advertising, and I was shopping for an advertisement whose structure I could use as a starting point for discussion. An ad for Georges Marciano clothing flashed on the screen and dragged me in, first with the music, South African music of haunting urgency, the echoing simultaneity of nonlinear music, the syncopation of quickening-heartbeat percussive music, dragging the ear. In the picture, a woman with long blond hair and sunglasses ran from a crowd of photographers and an admiring public. The film was black and white, a series of frames jaggedly succeeding each other, like a patchwork of secretly taken stills. Sliced into the sequence of her running away were shots of the blond and her manager/bodyguard/boyfriend packing. He packed the passports and the handgun, she packed the Georges Marciano jeans. The climax came when she burst into a room of exploding flashbulbs—a blazing bath of white light.

The effect of this particular visual and aural juxtaposition was the appearance of the music as being inside the woman's head or her heart. The music was primal, dangerous, desperate. The woman's crisis of adoration framed the burning necessity of this profound music, and the soaring universality of sound became white, female, privatized. The pulsing movement of the music elevated this event of narcissistic voyeurism to elemental importance. The music overflowed boundaries. Voices merged and surged; mood drifted and soared in the listening. African voices swelled and rose in the intricate music of knowledge, the wisdom of rhythm, the physics of echoing chasms bounded in intervals, the harmonic bells of voices striking each other in excitement and the wind, black African voices making music of the trees, of groundhogs, of whistling birds and pure chortling streams. It was generous shared music, open and eternal.

The pictures presented sought privacy. The chase was an invasion; the photographers pursued her private moments; she resisted even as her glamour consented. The viewer was drawn into desire to see her never-quite-revealed face, swept along by the urgency of her running to privacy, even as we never quite acknowledged her right to it. Thus the moment of climax, the flashing of cameras in her face (and ours, so completely have we identified with her), was one of release and relief. The music acted against the pictures. The mind resolved it queerly. The positive magnetic boundlessness of the music was turned into negative exposure. The run for privacy became an orgasmic peep show, the moment of negative exposure almost joyful.

In my lap, my textbook lay heavy, unattended pages drifting open to the Lanham Act:[1]   5

> *False designations of origin and false descriptions forbidden:*
>   . . . any person who shall affix, apply, or annex, or use in connection with any goods or services . . . a false designation of origin, or any false description or representation, including words or other symbols tending falsely to describe or represent the same, and shall cause such goods or services to enter into commerce, and any person who shall with knowledge of the falsity of such . . . description or representation cause or procure the same to be transported or used in commerce . . . or used, shall be liable to a civil action . . . by any person who believes that he is or is likely to be damaged by the use of any such false description or representation.[2]

I have recounted this story at some length, not just for its illustrative contrast between the sight and the sound of an advertisement, but also because the relationship between the music and the pictures can serve as a metaphor for the tension between the political and marketplace dynamic that is my larger subject. I think that the invisible corruption of one by the other has consequences that are, ultimately, dehumanizing.

Ours is not the first generation to fall prey to false needs; but ours is the first generation of admakers to realize the complete fulfillment of the consumerist vision through the fine-tuning of sheer hucksterism. Surfaces, fantasies, appearances, and vague associations are the order of the day. So completely have substance, reality, and utility been subverted that products are purified into mere wisps of labels, floating signifiers of their former selves. "Coke" can as easily add life plastered on clothing as poured in a cup. Calculating a remedy for this new-age consumptive pandering is problematic. If people like—and buy—the enigmatic emptiness used to push products, then describing a harm becomes elu-

---

1. **Lanham Act**   U.S. statute enacted in 1947 that revised trademark laws. —EDS.
2. §243(a), Lanham Act, 15 U.S.C.S. §21125(a) (1988).

sive. But it is elusive precisely because the imagery and vocabulary of advertising have shifted the focus from need to disguise. With this shift has come—either manipulated or galloping gladly behind—a greater public appetite for illusion and disguise. And in the wake of that has come an enormous shift of national industry, national resources, and national consciousness.

Some years ago, when I first started teaching, most of my students agreed that a nice L. L. Bean Baxter State Parka delivered without a label saying "L. L. Bean" was a minor default indeed. Today I have to work to convince them that the absence of the label is not a major breach of contract; I have to make them think about what makes the parka "an L. L. Bean": its utility or its image? Its service to the wearer or its impact on those around the wearer? If masque becomes the basis of our bargains, I worry that we will forget the jazzy, primal King Lear-ish essence of ourselves from which wisdom springs and insight grows. I worry that we will create new standards of irrelevance in our lives, reordering social relations in favor of the luxurious—and since few of us can afford real luxury, blind greed becomes the necessary companion.

On a yet more complicated level, I worry that in accustoming ourselves to the emptiness of media fictions, we will have reconstructed our very notion of property. If property is literally the word or the concept used to describe it, then we have empowered the self-willed speaker not just as market actor but as ultimate Creator. If property is nothing more than what it evokes on the most intimate and subjective levels, then the inherence of its object is denied; the separateness of the thing that is property must be actively obliterated in order to maintain the privately sensational pleasantry of the mirror image. A habituated, acculturated blindness to the inherent quality of the people and things around us grows up, based on our safety from having to see. Our interrelationships with these things is not seen; their reasons for being are rendered invisible.

At the simplest level of market economics, the modern algebra of advertising deprives society of a concept of commodities as enduring. Sales of goods are no longer the subject of express or long-term promissory relationships—there is at best an implied warranty of merchantability at the fleeting moment of contract and delivery. Contract law's historic expectation interest[3] becomes even more thoroughly touch and go, in the most virulent tradition of caveat emptor. It is an unconscious narrowing of expectation to the extent that we lose our expectations. Thus, in some way, Coke and Pepsi lead us to obliterate the future, not just with empty calories but with empty promises. The illusion of a perky, sexy self is meaningless as to the reality of a can of corn syrup: But this substitution,

10

---

3. The "expectation interest" in contract law is the promisee's "interest in having the benefit of his bargain by being put in as good a position as he would have been in had the contract been performed." §344(a), *Restatement of the Law, Contracts (2d)*.

this exchange of images, is a harm going beyond wasted money, tooth decay, or defeated notions of utility. The greater harm is that it is hypnotic, and culturally addictive.

In theory, contract doctrine is the currency of law used to impose economic order on human beings for certain purposes; defenses to contract formation such as fraud, duress, and undue influence are, I think, a theoretical attempt to impose an ordered humanity on economics. Increasingly, however, the day-to-day consumer purchases that form most of what is governed by contract have been characterized by a shift in popular as well as legal discourse: Contract is no longer a three-party transliterative code, in which law mediates between profit and relationship, and in which property therefore remains linked to notions of shared humanity. Instead, consumerism is locked into a two-party, bipolar code that is little more mediative than a mirror. Money reflects law and law reflects money, unattached to notions of humanity. The neat jurisprudence of interpretive transposition renders the whole into a system of equations in which money = money, words = words (or law = law). The worst sort of mindless materialism arises. The worst sort of punitive literalism puts down roots.

Some time ago, my friend and colleague Dinesh Khosla traveled to Costa Rica for a conference. On his way back to the United States, he found himself in the airport behind throngs of Costa Ricans pushing five or six huge suitcases apiece. Dinesh stopped often to assist several different people; each time he was surprised by how light the suitcases felt. After this much of the story, I already imagined its end, filling the suitcases with media images of feathery coca leaves and dusty white powders. But I was wrong; it turned out that these travelers were all wealthy Costa Ricans going to Miami for the sole purpose of shopping. They planned to load up the suitcases with designer clothes and fancy consumables and cart them back home. I was reminded of the Sufi tale of the customs official who for years scrutinized the comings and goings of a man famed as a smuggler. For years he subjected each parcel to thorough searches, but all he ever found was straw. Many years later when they were both retired, he asked the smuggler where he had hidden the contraband all that time. The man replied: "I was smuggling straw." Dinesh's account made the conspicuous luxury of North American commodities into a similar form of invisible contraband, a sinfully expensive and indulgent drug.

One last anecdote: A little way down Broadway from the 14th Street subway station in Manhattan, there is a store called the Unique Boutique. Yards from the campus of New York University, it is a place where stylish coeds shop for the slightly frumpy, punky, slummy clothes that go so well with bright red lipstick and ankle-high black bootlets. One winter day I saw a large, bright, fun-colored sign hanging in the window: "Sale! Two-dollar overcoats. No bums, no booze." Offended, and not wanting to feel how offended I was, I turned my head away toward the street. There, in the middle of the intersection of Broadway and Washington Place, stood a black man dressed in the ancient remains of a Harris Tweed overcoat. His arms were spread-eagled as if to fly, though he was actually begging from cars in both directions. He was also drunk and crying and trying to keep his balance. Drivers were offended, terrified of disease or of being robbed. Traffic slowed as cars described wide avoiding arcs around him and his broad-winged pleading.

So the sign was disenfranchising the very people who most needed two-dollar overcoats, the so-called bums. Moreover, it was selling the image of the disenfranchised themselves. The store is a trendy boutique aimed at NYU's undergraduate population. It was selling an image of genteel poverty, of casual dispossession. It attracted those who can afford to slum in style: yet it simultaneously exploited the slum itself. It was segregationist in the same way that "whites only" signs are. And it was not just segregationist along race and class lines; it also stole the images of those who had nothing and styled it as a commodity (slumminess) to be sold to those who have much. It was the ultimate in short-term consumerist redundance: Clothes do not just make the man, they would admit him into the clothing store itself.

In discussing the tension between liberty and authority, John Stuart   15
Mill observed that self-government means "not the government of each by himself but of each by all the rest." Mill feared what he called the "tyranny of the majority" and cautioned,

> Protection . . . against the tyranny of the magistrate is not enough; there needs protection also against the tyranny of prevailing opinion and feeling; against the tendency of society to impose, by other means than civil penalties, its own ideas and practices as rules of conduct on those who dissent from them . . . how to make the fitting adjustment between individual independence and social control—is a subject on which nearly everything remains to be done.[4]

The tyranny of the majority has survived in liberal political theory as a justification for all manner of legislative restraint, particularly economic restraint. But what Mill did not anticipate was that the persuasive power of the forum itself would subvert the polis, as well as the law, to the extent that there is today precious little "public" left, just the tyranny of what we call the private. In this nation there is, it is true, relatively little force in the public domain compared to other nations, relatively little intrusive governmental interference. But we risk instead the life-crushing disenfranchisement of an entirely owned world. Permission must be sought to walk upon the face of the earth. Freedom becomes contractual and therefore obligated; freedom is framed by obligation; and obligation is paired not with duty but with debt.

---

4. John Stuart Mill, *On Liberty,* ed. David Spitz (New York: Norton, 1975), p. 6.

Reading the Text

1. What relationship does Williams see between products and their advertising images?
2. Why does Williams find the legal designation of "false advertising" (para. 5) almost irrelevant in today's marketing world?
3. How, according to Williams, has our notion of "property" (para. 9) been altered by modern advertising?

Reading the Signs

1. Williams assumes that the fleeting relationship between product and image in advertising is a recent phenomenon. Visit your college library, and survey some popular magazines published at the beginning of this century. What sort of relationship between product and image do you see in advertising? What does the relationship you find say about social values? To develop your ideas, consult Roland Marchand's "The Parable of the Democracy of Goods" (p. 129).
2. Compare the "image of the disenfranchised" (para. 14) Williams mentions to grunge fashion in the 1990s. Is grunge similarly "segregationist" (para. 14)?
3. Read or review Gloria Steinem's "Sex, Lies, and Advertising" (p. 160), and write an essay in which you explain how the business practices of the magazine industry illustrate Williams's concluding point: "Freedom becomes contractual and therefore obligated; freedom is framed by obligation; and obligation is paired not with duty but with debt" (para. 15).
4. Write a semiotic analysis of the Georges Marciano commercial that Williams describes.

FERN SCHUMER CHAPMAN
Web of Deceit

||||||||||||||||||||||||||||||||||||||||||||||||||||

How can you "separate information from infomercials on the Net?" Fern Schumer Chapman asks this question in her analysis of the way that marketers disguise advertising and market research campaigns as entertainment and information sites on the Web. And the answer is . . . often you can't, for even if you surf the Web with a healthy dose of skepticism, Internet advertisers and marketers are ever devising new ways of camouflaging advertising as information. So is resistance useless, or is it time to wise up and take action against this "web of deceit"? A Chicago-based freelance writer, Chapman is a regular contributor to magazines like PC World *and* Fortune.

How to Separate Information from Infomercials on the Net

Last February a new site opened its doors in a corner of the World Wide Web. The site was called *Circuit Breaker* (**www.circuitbreak .com**), and it advertised itself as an entertainment guide for the San Francisco Bay Area. It was hip and colorful—even earned a mention in *USA Today* as a hot site. In reality, it was something more troubling. Among *Circuit Breaker*'s many links were a few simple interactive games. To play, you had to supply a little information about yourself. Name. (Sure.) E-mail address. (Why not?) Are you 21? (Hmm.) Do you smoke? (Hey, what's going on here?) *Circuit Breaker* turned out to be sponsored by the Brown & Williamson Tobacco Corporation—the company that brings you Lucky Strike cigarettes. Nowhere on the site was this information disclosed. (The company's name is now displayed, but you will find no mention of Lucky Strike.)

The Center for Media Education, a group that monitors unethical practices in cyberspace, threatened to report the site to the Federal Trade Commission. Brown & Williamson officials insisted *Circuit Breaker* was a legitimate entertainment site, part of a test to see if the company could reach its target audience over the Web. And Web watchers became more convinced than ever of one unnerving fact: The Web ain't what it used to be. "The Web started with defense, math, and science people," explains Janice Norton of Hands of Time Animation & Design, interactive advertising specialists in Sherman Oaks, California. "And now marketers have taken over."

And taken over they have. Everywhere you go on the Web, you will find marketers lurking. Some disguise their efforts as innocent entertainment sites. Some are cementing influential partnerships with media groups you trust, the better to sell you their wares. And most are using the unique interactive ability of the Web to gather information about you even as they try to sell you goods and services.

Stealth Marketing

On the Web, what looks like objective information may be anything but. The Web is rife with "stealth sites," which appear to offer unbiased content but are really marketing material in disguise.

Cafe Herpe (**www.cafeherpe.com**), for instance, appears merely to   5 provide frank information about a common virus. It has attractive graphics, a quiz that tests knowledge of the subject, links to support groups, even an art gallery of romantic paintings. The gallery page proclaims, "Art must be shared, or it grows stale. Sensing this, we opened *Cafe Herpe,* which we designed as an ideal environment to house our collection."

Who, you might ask, is "we"? If you scroll down to the bottom of the home page, you'll find that the site is copyrighted by SmithKline Beecham. To many people, that name means nothing—it's not a household name like Pepsi or Nike. SmithKline Beecham is in fact a pharmaceutical company that makes Famvir, a drug to fight herpes. You can find out all about Famvir if you click on the link that takes you to the *Cafe Herpe Espresso Bar.* In short, the site is not just an online version of a coffee shop where you can get information in a relaxed atmosphere—it's a virtual soft-sell product brochure. But you'll be hard-pressed to find any mention that the site's sponsor manufactures the product it's endorsing.

A Word from Our Sponsor

Sites like *Circuit Breaker* and *Cafe Herpe* are basically the work of single companies. But a more common form of marketing on the Web brings two companies together: the content provider and the marketer— a.k.a. the sponsor.

Because media companies find it hard to produce interesting online publications and still turn a profit, many have reached out to advertisers in a way that might be frowned upon in the world of print. More and more sites are pulling in corporate sponsors to fund their editorial. In some cases, these sponsors are in a business that is directly related to the content they sponsor.

For example, Procter & Gamble recently joined forces with Time Warner to create *ParentTime,* a site dedicated to parenting issues and advice (found on Pathfinder's site at **www.pathfinder.com**). As with some stealth sites, the only notice that P&G is involved appears in the fine print. But maybe you're enough of a consumer to recognize that many of the products advertised are from P&G. If readers don't make the connection between *ParentTime* and its sponsor, they won't realize that the site is also a marketing vehicle for P&G—on the surface it looks like an electronic magazine.

ParentTime articles range from "Taking the Sting Out of Diaper Rash" to "The Magic of Reading," providing an excellent resource for parents. Depending on when you visit *ParentTime* (ads rotate in and out), you may find a link to P&G's Pampers Parenting Institute near the diaper rash story. At the Institute's site, you can get more information about bringing up baby, plus a directory of P&G's Pampers products. This kind of marketing marriage isn't necessarily unscrupulous, but it's more than just an online magazine. "The public isn't necessarily aware that one of the major news organizations they trust is partnering with P&G to jointly create editorial content online," says Jeff Chester, executive director of the Center for Media Education.

"Procter & Gamble has no influence over *ParentTime*'s content," says

Paula McDonald, director of marketing and sales for *ParentTime*. According to McDonald, P&G partnered with Time Warner to create a site that would attract potential buyers of P&G products. To *ParentTime*'s credit, the site doesn't review or recommend products sold by its sponsor. But some websites are sponsored by marketers who stand to profit from the reviews appearing there.

Salon Magazine (**www.salonmag.com/**) is a literary website in the spirit of magazines like the *New Yorker*. It covers current events and social issues and reviews books and recordings. The review sections are clearly sponsored by Borders Books & Music, with a line at the top of the page indicating so. In fact, you can click on a link to order a reviewed book or CD—directly from Borders. The link on *Salon*'s review page does not reveal that Borders, the company that makes the site possible, is also the merchant. You won't know that you're ordering from Borders until you go to make a purchase. This lack of disclosure makes the reviews suspect. But David Talbott, editor and CEO of *Salon,* insists that the reviews are impartial. "Borders completely appreciates the need for editorial separation," he says.

Do consumers care when the lines between editorial and advertising blur? A Chicago doctor, who asked that his name not be used, says he felt "duped" when he was attracted to a site offering educational materials about infectious diseases. When he visited the site, he discovered that the material was produced by a pharmaceutical company with the purpose of hawking its antibiotics. "When I realized that, I immediately clicked off the site," he says. "[The drug maker's] sponsorship discredited the information," he explains.

You Are Being Watched

One of the most chilling aspects of the marketing explosion on the Web, however, is that salespeople are doing more than just disguising ads as editorial so they can hawk products at you. They lure you to their site, and while you're there, they gather detailed information. Sites like *Circuit Breaker* can obtain information about you instantly by getting you to register. Children surfing the Web are especially susceptible to fun-looking sites that request information about their families for purposes of marketing. Advertisers can also get a detailed picture of what interests you by gathering data about where you click when you're online. They do this by sending out cookies—miniature programs that track your activity. Once they've got this data and your registration information, they can use it to target ads at you or even send junk mail to your house. This type of information gathering is probably the most common marketing activity on the Web. "The new online business model is based on capturing and controlling the most personal information," says Chester.

Consumers are accustomed to media that is carefully regulated and   15
harmless. And if they assume the Internet is merely an electronic form of
other media, offering on a computer screen the same objectivity of, say,
newspapers and magazines, they will be easily duped. How would you
feel about the magazine you're reading right now if you knew it was taking notes as you turned the pages and reporting back to advertisers?

While many websites, such as news sites, remain unbiased, others
take advantage of users' assumptions that the Web is just another form of
media. They may pretend to be journalistic, or fail to disclose their marketing slant. And few can resist the temptation to gauge how well their
marketing efforts are working.

Who's Watching the Watcher?

The problem is, the Web is still new, and regulators are just learning
about potential abuses. In the absence of enforceable guidelines, marketers are free to reach out in ways that aren't possible or allowed in print
or on television. Moreover, just about anyone can be a publisher on
the Web. In traditional media like magazines and TV, the producer
of the publication or show controls the advertisers' access to the audience. The Web has no go-between—advertisers can take their messages
directly to the site visitors. When print or television marketers do produce their own content—so-called advertorials and infomercials—strict
industry guidelines require them to label the material as an ad. But as yet
no guidelines for such disclosure are in force on the Web.

Seth Goldstein, whose company, SiteSpecific, markets brands on the
Web, acknowledges the effect that groups like his are having on Web
content. "We're reaching a time when you won't be able to separate
what's [editorial] and what's advertising," he says.

Finding Credible Content

There's certainly nothing criminal about the strategies that companies employ to lure Web surfers, but consumers need to know whether a
site's information is objective. "If users want objectivity, they have to be
willing to pay for it," says Cebra Graves, the editor of *Morningstar.Net*
(www.morningstar.net), a site that helps people build and track stock
and mutual fund portfolios. If users paid for the information they got on
the Web, it could even up the score with marketers. No longer would
advertisers be the only source of revenue for groups that want to publish
on the Web. But so far, visitors haven't been all that willing to pay subscription fees. According to a study by NetSmart Research, only 8 percent of Web surfers surveyed are willing to pay.

What you may not realize is that you are already paying for much of 20 the material you find on the Web. The currency you use is your own personal information, rather than cash. Essentially, you pay for the sites that you visit by revealing who you are and what you'll buy. To keep drawing ad dollars, sites must prove to advertisers that they attract a targeted audience with plenty of disposable income. With cookies in one hand and registration forms in the other, sites try to reel you in and find out about you.

Morningstar.Net has made a concerted effort not to mingle advertising with editorial content, but Graves certainly understands how a site could succumb to the pressures. "The theory," he says, "is that the more we know about you, the more we can target the advertising to you. But it's hard to draw the line between the content provider and someone selling you something."

Regulating the Market

In February 1997, the American Society of Magazine Editors drew up guidelines for Web content. Essentially, the online guidelines invoke the same principles that apply to editorial content, ads, and special advertising sections in print publications. The proposed guidelines state, "It is the responsibility of each online publication to make clear to readers which online content is editorial and which is advertising and to prevent any juxtaposition that gives the impression that editorial material was created for or influenced by advertisers."

Frank Lalli, president of the ASME board and managing editor of *Money* magazine, says ASME has enforced print guidelines very successfully, and he feels that publishers understand the importance of distinguishing between editorial and advertising. Now, he says, ASME will find out if it can regulate the Web. "Publications that serve their readers build a loyal audience, and it is that loyal audience that becomes their stock-in-trade," says Lalli.

The FTC says its regulations regarding unfair marketing practices apply to the Web, but so far the agency has turned its attention mainly to flagrant cases of fraud, such as credit repair schemes and pyramid scams. In a speech last March, Commissioner Roscoe B. Starek said regulating online advertising poses unprecedented problems because of the Web's international scope — rules and regulations vary greatly from country to country. "My concern is that once governments begin to regulate or try to enforce their own laws against advertising on the Internet, we may be left with a Net containing only that which violates no country's laws," he said.

The fact is, policing the Web is nearly impossible; no government is 25 staffed or equipped to do the job. Without the security of law and its enforcement on your side, you'll have to take an active role in keeping marketers in check. Always ask questions as you browse. Who published this information? Who is paying for it? Look for disclaimers like "sponsored by." Does knowing who's behind the site affect the way you interpret the information it provides? If you find yourself the subject of slippery marketing tactics, simply leave the site. And you can always refuse to give out personal information. You can also opt to turn away all cookies at the door.

When you venture into the open market of the Web, you need a healthy sense of consumerism. A magnifying glass for reading the fine print may become your most useful Web browsing tool. Look closely before you answer any questions or buy anything. And keep an eye on your wallet.

Getting Past the Hype

You want the best information you can get from the Web. But everywhere you go, sites are rife with marketing. Here are a few tips to help you deflect and fight the Web's increasing commercialism.

- Don't believe everything you read. Your mother said it long ago, and it still holds true. Sometimes it's hard to tell the editorial matter from the marketing pitch.

- Get more than one opinion. If you read a glowing review, look for other discussion of the same product. On the Web, you can't tell what influences might creep into a review.

- Find sites you trust. Once you build a relationship with a website, you'll have confidence in its information, just as you do with magazines and newspapers.

- Assume your name is for sale. When you're asked to fill out an online registration form, chances are that information will be used to pitch something to you.

- Don't sell out. If a site asks you to register, think twice before you sign up. Personal information is a commodity on the Web, so spend it at sites you like. Don't just give it away.

- Know where you're going and where you've been. If you click on a banner or some other link, you may be transported to an advertiser's site. Before clicking the mouse, hold the cursor over the link and check the status bar. It may tell you where you're heading, so you won't be surprised when you get there.

- See the entire picture. If a website is the creation of a corporate sponsor, it may reveal this fact only at the bottom of the page. So scroll down.

■ Blow the whistle. If you think a website has crossed the line between content and advertising without telling its visitors, complain. Send e-mail to the site, to the Federal Trade Commission (**consumerline@ftc.gov**), or to the Center for Media Education (**cme@cme.org**).

Reading the Text

1. What is a "stealth" (para. 4) website, according to Chapman? How do website editors and sponsors defend their practices?
2. What does Chapman consider the most dangerous consequence of stealth advertising on the Internet?
3. What are the differences between the regulation of print and television advertising and of Internet advertising?
4. What recommendations does Chapman offer to avoid being fooled by supposedly informative and objective websites?

Reading the Signs

1. In your journal, describe the advertising, both obvious and stealth, you have seen on the Internet, and reflect on its effect on you. Do you feel like you have been a victim of unfair advertising practices?
2. Write an imaginary dialogue between Chapman and John E. Calfee ("How Advertising Informs to Our Benefit," p. 180). Alternately, adopt the perspective of one of these authors, and write a critique of the other's position.
3. Write an essay that argues for or against the tighter regulation of advertising on the Internet.
4. Visit several of the websites that Chapman mentions. To what extent do you find that the term *stealth advertising* applies to these sites?
5. Write an essay in which you reflect on the advertising's effect on the public's access to information. To develop your ideas, consult John E. Calfee ("How Advertising Informs to Our Benefit," p. 180) and Gloria Steinem ("Sex, Lies, and Advertising," p. 160).

JAMES B. TWITCHELL
Plop, Plop, Fizz, Fizz

iiiiiiiiiiiiiiiiiiiiiiiiiiiiiiiiiiiiiiiiiiiiiiiiiii

When Colonel Sanders, the Jolly Green Giant, and Tony the Tiger are among America's best-known celebrities, and most people not only know the meaning of Fahrvergnugen *but can pronounce it as well, you know that advertising is not only a sideshow in American culture: it is becoming American culture. That, at least, is James B. Twitchell's (b. 1943) thesis in his book* Adult USA: The Triumph of Advertising in American Culture *(1996), from which this selection is taken. Giving this new culture a name — "adcult" — Twitchell surveys the many ways in which advertising has saturated our lives, arguing that it has been able to do so not because of the nefarious schemes of Madison Avenue insiders but because, quite simply, "Human beings like things," which is why we call the things we buy "goods" and not "bads." The author of numerous books of literary and cultural criticism, Twitchell's publications include* Lead Us Into Temptation: The Triumph of American Materialism *(1999),* For Shame: The Loss of Common Decency in American Culture *(1997), and* Carnival Culture: The Trashing of Taste in America *(1992).*

We live in the age of advertising, and in the spirit of the endeavor I call this new culture Adcult. I don't intend to defend it (well, maybe just a little) but to explain how American—and, increasingly, world—culture is carried on through the boom-box noise and strobe lights of commercialism. Much of what we share, and what we know, and even what we treasure is carried to us each second in a plasma of electrons, pixels, and ink created by multinational agencies dedicated to attracting our attention for entirely nonaltruistic reasons.

Once they gain our attention, they essentially rent it to other companies for the dubious purpose of selling us something we've longed for all our lives, although we've not heard of it before. The condition of modern selling is not so much information trading, as it was in the nineteenth century, as it is information glutting. Adcult is there when we blink, it's there when we listen, it's there when we touch, it's even there to be smelled in scented strips when we open a magazine. If we have no attention span, as academic Cassandras claim, it may be because by adolescence most of us are exhausted.

No treatment of advertising can proceed further without the familiar litany of statistics, the one usually invoked by well-meaning Commissions to Frighten Parents about how commercialism is choking Junior to death. But it may show the opposite: just how unimportant advertising has become. No matter. Here is a bit of how it goes. In 1993 companies spent more than $140 billion on advertising; in 1915 that figure was about $1 billion. The A. C. Nielsen Company reports that two- to five-year-olds average more than twenty-eight hours of television a week—forty school days a year—in front of the flickering screen.

Assuming they reach maturity with consciousness intact, the current crop of teenagers will have spent years watching commercials. No one has done the numbers on what happens if you factor in radio, magazine, newspaper advertisements, and billboards, but today's teens probably have spent the equivalent of a decade of their lives being bombarded by bits of advertising information. In 1915 a person could go entire weeks without observing an ad. The average adult today sees some three thousand every day.

Barely a space in our culture is not already carrying commercial mes-   5
sages. Look anywhere. Schools? Channel One. Movies? Product placement. Ads invade our urinals, telephones (while we're on hold), taxis (alphanumeric displays), fax machines, catalogs, the wall facing the Stair-Master at the gym, T-shirts, doctors' offices, grocery carts, parking meters, golf tees, inner-city basketball backboards, elevators (piped-in with the Muzak) . . . ad nauseam (yes, even airline barf bags).

We have to shake magazines like a rag doll to free the pages of the "blown-in" inserts and then wrestle out those sewn in before we can begin to read. We now have to fast-forward through some five minutes of advertising on rented videotapes.

President Clinton's inaugural parade featured a Budweiser float. At the Smithsonian the Orkin Pest Control Company sponsored an exhibit on exactly what it advertises it kills: insects. Is there a blockbuster museum show not decorated with corporate logos? Public Broadcasting is littered with "underwriting announcements," which look and sound almost exactly like what PBS claims they are not. Athletes sport as many advertising decals as Indy 500 cars, which look like billboards, which themselves are looking more and more like television, eternally blinking on and off. One of the most popular games in the 1980s was called Adverteasing. To play you matched the jingle or slogan with the product's brand name. Why was it so popular? It was one of the few games the whole family could play and the kiddies would win. When Junior goes to see *Barney and Friends* at Madison Square Garden, he passes, from streetside to seat, ninety-eight separate ads for cigarettes. The interesting question would be where is commercial speech *not* "heard."

One inescapable conclusion from such commercial saturation is that—exempting classified and supermarket ads—more than 99 percent of advertising does no "work." The martini has more effect on the schoolmarm than on the town drunk, and most of us are ad-inebriated

by adolescence. The American Association of Advertising Agencies—
the "Four A's," an industry self-promotion group—estimates that of the
three thousand ads we consume each day, we notice only eighty and
have some sort of reaction to only twelve. Video Storyboard Tests, a
company that conducts "recall testing," reports that a startling 40 percent
of the twenty thousand consumers surveyed each year cannot think of a
single memorable commercial.

No one knows how often provocation, or even recall, leads to a sale,
but manufacturers spend a relatively small amount of their money on advertising anyway. Believe it or not, if advertising really sold products,
there would be even more. Today advertising is clearly done for many
more reasons than increasing sales. In fact, no one really knows why
some companies advertise in the first place. Clearly, there is a comfort
value for the producer, the salespeople, and the postdecision consumer.
And there is the unmentionable to consider: we like being advertised to.
We like being told that "You deserve a break today," "You, you're the
one," and that "You are special to us," although we may know it's not
true. Not only does it make us feel important but perhaps, as Swift said,
"Happiness is the possession of being perpetually well-deceived." Deception is the reality of Adcult.

The billions of dollars spent to keep us well deceived are huge, but   10
the percentages are not. A generation ago Fairfax Cone of Foote, Cone
& Belding ran the numbers to defend the industry against charges that it
was adding to the costs of goods. The cost of advertising Coca-Cola, he
reckoned, added about 0.006 cents per can, about a penny for each 35
cents of the cost of producing frozen foods, about 18 cents per $3,000 to
the cost of a car, and so on. The economies of mass production more
than offset those expenses, he contended.

Where the social cost of advertising is felt, however, is not in achieving the economies of scale but in the cultural ramifications of delivering
the pitch. In giving value to objects, advertising gives value to our lives.
With Fast-Moving Consumer Goods (FMCGs) especially, we consume
the advertising more often than we do the goods. As Burt Manning,
chief executive officer (CEO) of J. Walter Thompson, has commented
apropos of the great variety of beer advertising, "People don't drink beer,
they drink its advertising" (Vadehra 1993, 16). This is certainly true of
bottled water, which in taste tests is regularly ranked as less pleasing than
New York City tap water.

Although advertising cannot create desire, it can channel it. And
what is drawn down that channel, what travels with the commercial, is
our culture. Adcult has its greatest power in determining what travels
with the commercial. For what is carried in and with advertising is what
we know, what we share, what we believe in. It is who we are. It is us.

The simple fact is that advertising is too serious not to study. There is
no point pretending it does not exist and no point thinking that if we

hector it with criticism it will change or go away. I mentioned to a colleague that if I were to go into a class and whistle just the first notes of the McDonald's "You Deserve a Break Today" all my students could continue the tune. But they couldn't complete what is arguably the most famous nineteenth-century sentence: "My heart leaps up when I behold . . ." To which my erstwhile departmental chairman replied, "Then you should be spending more time teaching Wordsworth." The point is well taken and speaks not only to the role of higher education but to the more general subject of teaching values in school. Most academics consider advertising valueless. Why study trash? After all, it's what we throw away.

But take a trip sometime through a college dormitory and look at what is on the walls. Adolescents decorate their walls with the aspirational images of their future. A decade ago or so they could buy poster-size reproductions of the works of great masters to thumbtack to the dorm wall. Now a company called Beyond the Wall sells students ads from Nike, Citizen Watch, Bain de Soleil, Valvoline, Sony, and the rest blown up to poster size at $10 a copy. Such posters are the mezzotints of modern life, the art of materialism. Japanese school kids have textbooks on America that are nothing more than ads. The books have proved so popular that a series of adult picture books shows General Motors ads from the 1950s. No surprise: consuming ads is how all of us have spent most of our time.

Beyond the Wall may call its jumbo ads poster art, but many of us   15
resolutely consider such commercial speech junk. Ironically, much inspiration for modern art comes from wall posters that were regularly pasted over with newer images. Junk has its place in aesthetics; one hallmark of cultural garbage is that an item becomes a throwaway commodity only *after* being used. Like the word *weed,* with which it shares many interesting traits, *junk* is a matter of perception. It is not a specific item or class of items per se. Rather it is what we call certain objects as we are on our way to root them out. Often the weeds become so interesting, or so indomitable, that we call them wildflower gardens instead.

Something like this is happening in academia with advertising. Since the mid-1980s we have come to appreciate the power and purpose of commercialism. Although only a few institutions of higher learning offer courses on advertising in the liberal arts curriculum (there should be more, starting in elementary school with simple lessons in persuasive techniques), and a few books have been written on the subject, academic libraries are already starting to preserve ad agency archives as if they were repositories of important history. They are. The Smithsonian has the records of N. W. Ayer; Duke University has the Benton & Bowles and J. Walter Thompson collections; for a while Northwestern had the Foote, Cone & Belding (once Lord & Thomas) papers, which have now gone to the University of Wisconsin, which also holds some of the papers of Bruce Barton (one of the *B*s in BBDO). It may well be that the study of advertising will proceed from the library to the classroom rather than the reverse. The Thompson collection at Duke, for instance, is the most-used archive at the university.[1]

A few years ago, in a tenderhearted and well-meaning way, an English professor at the University of Virginia, E. D. Hirsch, published a book called *Cultural Literacy,* with the daunting subtitle *What Every American Needs to Know.* Hirsch's thesis is compelling. If we want to get together, we first need to share a culture. We could be forgiven for guessing that a white-bred professor at a white-bread university would prescribe a cultural matrix of white bread. And in fact that's what Hirsch's prescription to the body politic is. Little wonder his book became a best-seller. Book publishing is one of the few media left that maintains the myth that Western culture is still print based. People who buy books like to be told that what they know is worth knowing and *should* be known by all.

I took a much-shortened list of what "every American needs to know" to my class of juniors and seniors at a large state-supported university. I made up the list by choosing the lower righthand entries from each page in Hirsch's appendix, cleverly entitled "What Literate Americans Know," so it is an almost random sample of the really important stuff. I asked them to briefly define or explain the following:

ampersand	Auschwitz	biochemical pathways
Bundestag	Neville Chamberlain	complex sentence
cyclotron	dog in the manger	Elysian Fields
federalism	Indira Gandhi	D. W. Griffith
Hoover Dam	installment buying	Joseph and his brothers
Leibnitz	Ferdinand Magellan	Herman Melville
National Guard	nucleotide	paradox
planets	prosecution	Reign of Terror
sacred cow	Shawnee Indians	Battle of Stalingrad
taproot	topsoil	vector
Winnie the Pooh	Richard Wright	Zurich

Of course, they are soon bored doing this. Who cares about this school stuff? they seem to say. I ask them to continue the process, only with these entries:

---

1. Adcult even has its own museum. Although a full-scale advertising museum really belongs in Manhattan, the only museum devoted solely to the cause—the American Advertising Museum—is in Portland, Oregon, the hotbed of advertising. Perhaps it is appropriate that the museum should be housed in a warehouse on the almost West Coast, because so many agencies have long deserted Madison Avenue for SoHo and Manhattan for Minneapolis.

Just do it	Uh huh	Colonel Sanders
Morris	Feel really clean	Heartbeat of America
Mmmm mmmm good	Kills bugs dead	Mrs. Olsen
Fahrvergnugen	Quality is job 1	Why ask why?
Two scoops!	Because I'm worth it	Tony the Tiger
Have it your way	99 44/100% pure	Master the moment
57 Varieties	Speedy	Never had it, never will
White knight	Jolly Green Giant	Mountain grown
Mr. Whipple	Do you know me?	Be all you can be
Betty Crocker	Still going	Snap, Crackle, Pop
Aunt Jemima	We try harder	That's Italian

They are so excited they are shouting entries for me to consider. Clearly they like this Adcult version, partly because it is thrilling to think that what they know has any value but also because they realize that they really share something. Blacks and whites, males and females, front row and back row do have a common culture. Professor Hirsch is correct. There is a cohesive power in the remembrance of things past. It does link us together. Let Proust have his madeleines. We have ads. Some of my students are embarrassed, of course, that cultural junk food is what they share. Perhaps they realize there is nothing behind this knowledge, no historical or cultural event, no reason to know it. Yet it is precisely the recognition of jingles and brand names, precisely what high culturists abhor, that links us as a culture. More than anything this paper-thin familiarity is what gives Adcult its incredible reach and equally incredible shallowness. It is a culture without memory and hence without depth. Ironically, concepts in advertising explain the phenomenon: the further the reach (cost per thousand) the shallower the effect (recall of individual product).

If academic culture has been slow to acknowledge the power of Ad- 20 cult, its upstart rival, popular culture, has eagerly embraced it. Advertising is no longer treated with grudging respect in the press; it is front page. The national newspapers, the *New York Times* and the *Wall Street Journal,* give advertising almost daily coverage in their financial and marketplace sections. When RJR Nabisco fired an ad agency, the story made page one of the *Times.* In fact, the *Times* recently paid the ultimate high-culture tribute by referring to two BBDO copywriters as "auteurs." Advertising stories regularly appear on the first page of the *Journal's* Marketplace section. When an occasional ad jumps loose of Adcult and perplexes popular culture, such as happened some years ago with the man-in-pajamas ad for Benson & Hedges, the press devotes tons of newsprint to explaining it.

As might be expected, the gaudy step-cousin, *USA Today,* a

newspaper unabashedly dedicated to the proposition that advertising is what the Gannett chain is all about, continually runs ad stories free of any critical taint. And the line between press release and news story is often invisible. For instance, in its June 21, 1985, weekend edition, *USA Today*'s front page announced an inside story on the latest Clint Eastwood movie. What was inside? An advertising supplement paid for by Warner Bros. Advertisements have even started to appear on the front pages of the inside sections of *USA Today,* in the upper "ears" of the pages.

After the Super Bowl an annual feeding frenzy of the print media is to critique not the boring game but the exciting new ad campaigns. *USA Today* even wires up a select audience to test responses. For a while the paper even ran a feature called "AD-ing It Up with Elliot and Cox" in which two reporters discussed recent campaigns in a mock Siskel-Ebert debate, replacing the thumbs up or down with "play it or zap it."

Daily newspapers are not alone. Tina Brown's revived *New Yorker* dedicated almost an entire issue—including cartoons—to detailing the Stolichnaya Vodka campaign (Lubow 1994). Leslie Savan, of the raucous *Village Voice,* not only writes an occasional edgy column on advertising but almost received a Pulitzer for it. And *Advertising Age,* once a professional journal, appears on newsstands in the company of other newsweeklies, which also cover advertising.

Although television is the pure advertising-supported medium, few programs have discussed its influence. Admittedly, *Entertainment Tonight* routinely covers advertising-related show-biz stories—the celebrity commercial shoots and their new campaigns. And advertising outtakes figure prominently in the blooper genre mastered by the avuncular Ed McMahon and the ever youthful Dick Clark. Advertising parodies are the staples of *Saturday Night Live* and *In Living Color.* Occasionally PBS runs a *Nova*esque show on advertising, as it recently did (in the *Smithsonian Presents* format) of the work done by Grey Advertising for Mitsubishi's new sports car, the 3000GT. But network television offers surprisingly little coverage of advertising. It's coming: Barbara Lippert of *Adweek* expresses her opinions on *Business This Morning,* a syndicated CBS program, Bob Garfield of *Advertising Age* has taped a pilot for CNBC, and in the flurry of interest about new channels possible with fiberoptic cable an advertising-only channel is on its way.

To be sure, television shows about advertising are made difficult by copyright clearance problems. The boilerplate in performers' contracts stipulates the number of runs and the venues for which they will receive the payments known as residuals. This explains why most shows about commercials feature animated spots. Tony the Tiger and his animated colleagues have no residual rights. But television has also been slow to consider advertising as a subject for the same reason that dairy farmers drink proportionally less milk. After all, advertising is what television *is.*

What is lacking on television, and what I predict is soon to come, is a serious discussion of ads with participants from agencies, sponsors, media, and academia. The French already have a hugely popular half-hour weekly show in which intellectuals chat up the most recent ads. Each Sunday night millions of viewers watch a program called *Culture Pub*. For almost fifteen years Parisians have gathered for the annual *Nuit des Publivores* to watch nightlong screenings of as many as five hundred uninterrupted commercials. Perhaps this could be expected of a culture that produced such popcult commentators as Roland Barthes and Jean Baudrillard. Doubtless the Yale School of Advertising is even now taking shape. But not just media snobs say that the best things on television are the commercials; the ordinary viewer would agree.

WORKS CITED

Lubow, Arthur. "Annals of Advertising: This Vodka Has Legs." *New Yorker,* September 12, 1994, pp. 62–87.
Vadehra, David. "My, How TV Sports Have Changed." *Advertising Age,* August 16, 1993, p. 16.

Reading the Text

1. What does Twitchell mean by the term "Adcult" (para. 1)?
2. What evidence does Twitchell give to show how advertising has saturated American life?
3. How have the popular news media responded to "the power of Adcult" (para. 20), in Twitchell's view?
4. Characterize Twitchell's tone. What effect does it have on the persuasiveness of his argument?

Reading the Signs

1. Twitchell asserts that, because ads actually do little to sell products, "no one really knows why some companies advertise in the first place" (para. 9). Write an essay in which you explain why you believe products are so widely advertised. For evidence, you may use current ad campaigns or your friends' consumption habits.
2. Write an essay supporting, refuting, or complicating Twitchell's claim that advertising has so saturated American life that we are now an "ad culture."
3. Brainstorm advertising slogans other than those that Twitchell mentions, and present your list to the class. Does your list trigger the same reaction that Twitchell's did when he read it to his students? Discuss the implications of your class's response.
4. Adopting the perspective of E. D. Hirsch, write a response to Twitchell's claim that "cultural junk food" (para. 19) is what binds Americans together. To develop your ideas, you might refer to Hirsch's *Cultural Literacy* (1987).
5. Read Vance Packard's *The Hidden Persuaders* (1957), and compare and contrast his view of American advertising with that of Twitchell.

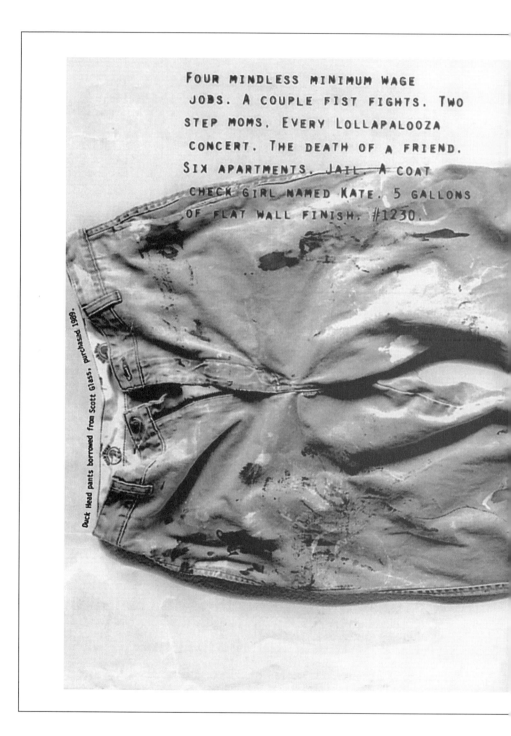

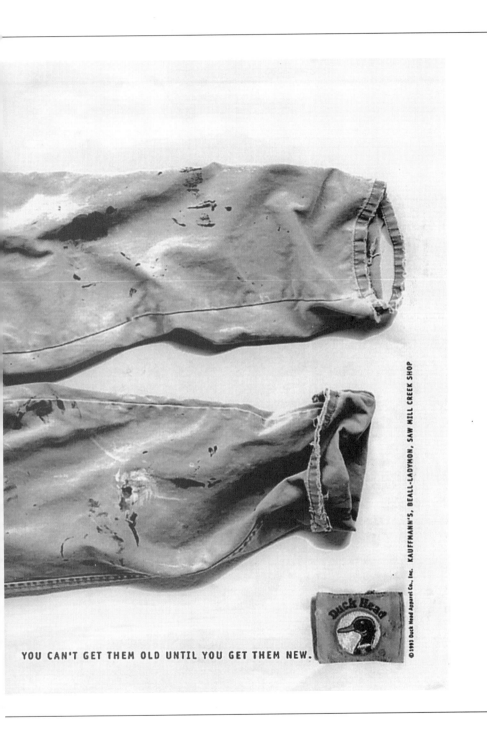

YOU CAN'T GET THEM OLD UNTIL YOU GET THEM NEW.

© 1993 Duck Head Apparel Co., Inc.   KAUFFMANN'S, BEALL-LADYMON, SAW MILL CREEK SHOP

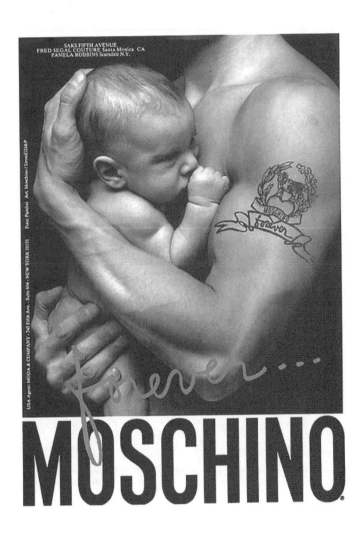

forever...

MOSCHINO

Who says guys are afraid of commitment? He's had the same backpack for years.

When it comes to choosing a lifelong companion, lots of guys pick one of our backpacks. Each one comes with a lifetime guarantee not to rip, tear, break, or ask for a ring.

what would you do?

ask people

to judge me by my

ability

not my

disability

cindy bolas, colorado

Reading the Signs

1. Have the class vote for the ads contained in the Portfolio that are most effective and least effective in persuading the target audience to purchase the products. Then discuss the significance of the results. What strategies does the class consider more persuasive? Do you see any gender-related patterns in the class's votes?

2. In what ways does the Altoids ad use retro humor to attract its audience? Why do you think the audience would respond to such humor?

3. How does using Kermit the Frog as an advertising character ring a new change on the popular Got Milk campaign? To whom does this advertisement most appeal?

4. Write a semiotic interpretation of the Duck Head ad. Be sure to analyze details such as the copy, the typeface, and the condition of the pants. How do those details relate to the ad's probable audience and to the fashion system to which the pants belong?

5. Do a semiotic reading of the imagery in the Volkswagen advertisement. What sort of narrative does the scene suggest, and what is the significance of that narrative for the intended market?

6. Divide the class in two and have each group brainstorm the connotations attached to the male image in the Moschino ad and those attached to the baby's image. Have each group put their results on the board. Then as a group discuss why Moschino might have decided to combine these two images in an ad for their product line.

7. How does the Joe Boxer campaign's use of humor contribute to the product's image?

8. Together, the text and imagery of the Eastpak ad tell a story about the male figure who owns the packpack. What is the story? Do you think the ad is intended to appeal to men, women, or both? Why the same food displayed in each photograph? Use your observations to formulate an argument about the strategies this ad uses to appeal to consumers.

9. Advertisers call the Esprit ad a "message" ad. Discuss that message and why you think the advertiser found it a useful strategy to sell clothing.

10. How does the Gardenburger ad use gender roles to create a visual argument, and what is that argument?

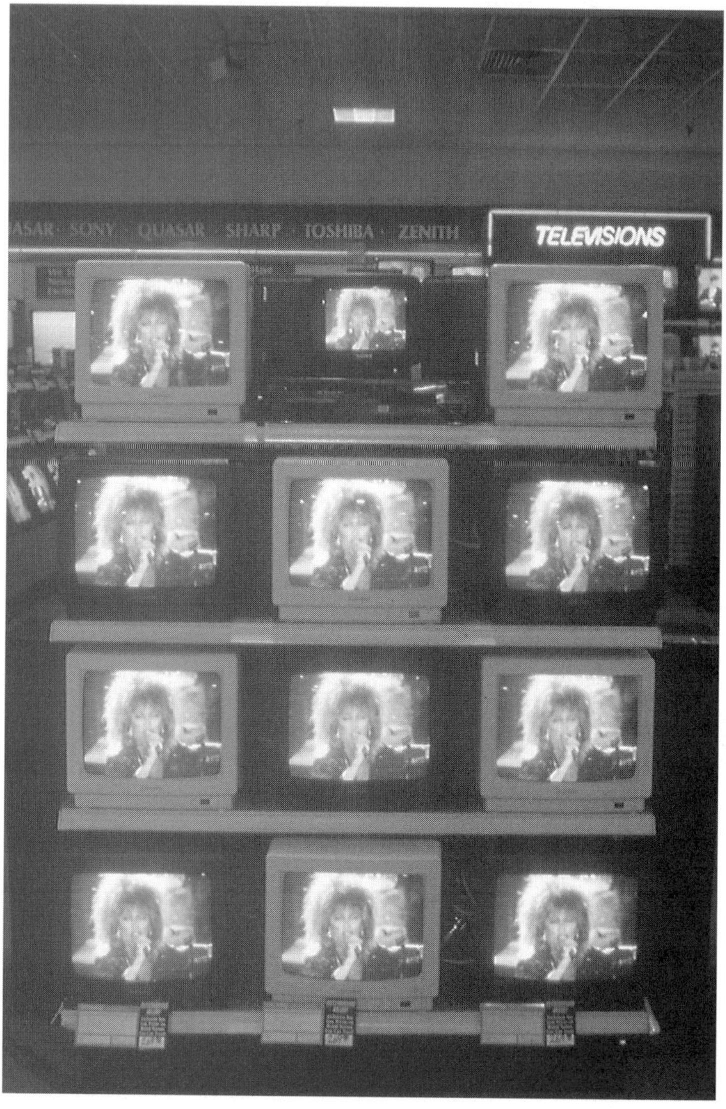
SONY · QUASAR · SHARP · TOSHIBA · ZENITH
TELEVISIONS

CHAPTER THREE

VIDEO DREAMS

The Signs of Music and Television

Writing Television

Writing about television is an assignment students often receive in their composition classes, so this chapter's topic ought to come as no surprise to you. Indeed, in high school you may have been asked to write about a favorite TV program or music video, perhaps in a summary writing exercise, a descriptive essay, or an opinion piece on why such-and-such a program is your favorite show. But in college you will be asked to write critical interpretations of popular entertainment. In doing so, you will rely on your skills in description and summary, of course, but now your purpose is to go beyond these writing tasks and to focus on constructing interpretive arguments about the cultural significance of your topic.

Television offers an especially rich field of possible writing topics, ranging from an historical survey of a whole category of TV programming (such as the Western or detective show) to an interpretive analysis of a single episode or video. Some topics, especially if you choose an historical approach (in a decade-by-decade analysis, for instance, of the role that situation comedies allowed women), will require research. Comparing, say, the female leads in *Father Knows Best, I Love Lucy, The Mary Tyler Moore Show, Murphy Brown,* and *Ally McBeal* will reveal a great deal about the cultural contexts in which those programs appeared and so enable you to construct a thesis about the role of women in American society over the past forty years. The interpretation of a single television episode requires less research (though you will want to consider the cultural context in which the show appears), focusing instead on a close reading of every significant detail in the program you've chosen to analyze. To suggest what such analyses might look like, we'll first sketch out an interpretive reading of a single TV program episode and then take a semiotic look at one of the hottest television categories of the 1990s, the prime-time cartoon sitcom.

Interpreting the Televising of America

From the mid- to late 1990s, *Friends*, a program that supplanted *Beverly Hills 90210* and *Melrose Place* as a favorite among teen and twenty-something viewers, remained at or near the top of the Nielsen ratings. Outlasting *Seinfeld* and, at least on occasion, outdistancing *ER*, *Friends* firmly established itself as one of those television programs—like *Bonanza* in the 1960s, *Happy Days* in the 1970s, and *The Cosby Show* in the 1980s—that help to define a decade. The enduring popularity of the show thus leads us to our prime semiotic question: Why *Friends*? Why did *this* show so appeal to the cultural taste of its times?

As with all semiotic analyses, your first step when preparing to write an analysis of a TV program is to suspend your aesthetic opinions of the show—that is, whether you like it or not. It also doesn't matter whether *Friends* is as popular today as it was when we wrote this introduction. It may well be that the popularity of *Friends* has declined or that the show may even be off the air: one of the constants of popular culture is its rapid turnover of fads and trends. What you are working toward is a critical opinion—what you think a program's underlying social significance may be. This process is also different from describing what you think the show's *explicit* message is. Many programs have clearly presented "messages"—indeed, the episode of *Friends* we'll examine here has a "message" of this sort. What you'll be looking for is the message beyond the message, so to speak—the implicit signals the show is sending. To see

---

Exploring the Signs of Music Videos

In your journal, explore the impact music videos have had on you. How have videos shaped your desires and expectations about life? How were your actions and behavior influenced by MTV? What videos were especially meaningful to you? What did you think about them when you were younger, and how do you see them now? (If you didn't watch MTV, you might focus instead on other types of television programs.)

what we mean, consider a single episode of *Friends* that focuses, typically, on relationships.

This episode aired fairly early in the history of *Friends,* but we want to look at it anyway both because it bears an especially rich cultural significance and because it was an especially famous episode. Since you may not remember our sample episode even if you saw it, we'll summarize the story briefly. As with most sitcoms, this episode's plot is rather loosely constructed—the main point is to deliver as many punch lines as possible within a half-hour time slot—but it does have a main plot and two subplots. The main plot centers on the plans of Carol and Susan to get married in a lesbian wedding. Ross, Carol's former husband, isn't too thrilled with the idea and at first glumly refuses to attend the ceremony. Eventually, he comes around and is even the one to get the wedding back on track when Carol confides to him that her parents' refusal to attend is threatening the whole event. In the end, the wedding happily takes place with Ross giving his former wife away to Susan. End of main plot.

The first subplot concerns Phoebe, a masseuse. An elderly client of Phoebe's named Mrs. Adelman dies on the massage table, and her spirit, instead of ascending to wherever, lodges inside Phoebe. Throughout the episode, young blonde Phoebe accordingly turns into a stereotypical eighty-two-year-old Jewish woman at unpredictable times (rather in the way that Gary Trudeau's *Doonesbury* character Boopsie used to turn into Hunk Ra). Mr. Adelman explains his deceased spouse's lingering on in this way as her desire to "see everything" before she died. A tall order, no doubt, but everything is resolved when Phoebe attends the lesbian wedding and the spirit of Mrs. Adelman blurts out, "Now I've seen everything!" and flits off to wherever, leaving Phoebe back to Phoebe. End of first subplot.

The second subplot concerns Rachel's mother, who shows up for a visit, only to reveal that she is leaving her husband (Rachel's father) because she married him not for love but merely for the economic security he provided. Mom seems to want the kind of swinging life she sees Rachel living, a plot line that offers all sorts of opportunities to make this middle-aged parent look silly. The episode ends without this subplot being resolved, leaving room for future developments.

All right, let's analyze this episode. First, we need to select those details that seem most suggestive, prodding us to an interpretive hypothesis. Being selective is an important step in your analysis because not every detail of a TV show is necessarily semiotically interesting, and not every semiotically interesting detail will necessarily contribute to your emerging argument. In the interpretation we are developing here, for example, we are leaving out the Phoebe/Mrs. Adelman subplot. One could argue that it is intended as a spoof of New Age spiritualism, but its sheer goofiness suggests to us that it is simply a marker of Phoebe's zaniness and is included more or less just for laughs.

A part of the show we do want to note, though, is its overall premise—the comic dramatization of a group of twentysomething men and women whose paths cross in a Manhattan apartment. Here, the characters' occupations, which run the gamut from a fledgling soap opera actor to a coffee shop waitress, are significant. Being a waitress, especially if you grew up in a comfortable middle-class or upper-middle-class household, isn't very exciting, is it? And yet that's what Rachel, one of *Friends*' central characters, does for a living. Do you see a set of associations emerging here—a cultural system that would give these details their meaning? We do.

First, we can associate *Friends* with a large number of programs that appeared in the mid-nineties, all featuring attractive twentysomething characters living and loving together in urban apartments—shows like *Melrose Place*, *Central Park West*, MTV's *Real World*, and the post–high school episodes of *Beverly Hills 90210*. Often the characters are the children of far more prosperous parents and are beginning their struggles in a difficult economic environment. Thus they must band together with a large number of roommates; otherwise, they wouldn't be able to make the rent in the sort of fashionable urban neighborhoods the shows feature. And they tend to put most of their energies into relationships, both with their friends and their lovers.

Do you see an image emerging here? It is, of course, the standard stereotype of Generation X, that middle-class generation supposedly resigned to a less prosperous life than their parents enjoyed and compensating for it by caring more about relationships than about material prosperity. Whether or not such a generation ever really existed or exists today, its image was much coveted in the mid-1990s as a potential market by advertisers and their clients, which helps explain why so many TV shows of the *Friends* variety appeared at that time.

A look at the Rachel subplot of our episode of *Friends* makes it quite clear that its sponsors' target market was indeed stereotypically Gen X. As a waitress and the daughter of an upper-middle-class family, Rachel has chosen the emotional fulfillment of living with her "friends" over the economic security she could have had by marrying Barry, an orthodontist. When Rachel's mother visits, Rachel and her friends worry that she'll bother them all with her disapproval of this choice. But mom surprises everyone—first, by fussing over how wonderful it is that Rachel earns her living as a waitress and, second, by revealing that her own husband was her "Barry." Mom confides that she's now bored and wants to live the sort of life Rachel has chosen, giving up economic security for emotional satisfaction.

The significance of this reversal points to a certain fantasy, which is what television is best at providing. As Marshall McLuhan once put it, the medium is the *massage* (not message), and the massage here is the presentation of a materially diminished life as emotionally more fulfilling than a materially enhanced one. Twentysomething viewers who had good reason to be worried about their economic prospects in a downsized, restructured America could watch themselves dramatized in *Friends* as happy, emotionally well-connected comrades whose strong bonding looks like a potent compensation for the prosperity that is being denied them. And by emotionally connecting themselves with the show, such viewers may connect to the products that sponsor the show as well and buy them. That, at least, is what the sponsors hope.

Of course, the show doesn't make explicit that it is playing on fantasies of emotional connectedness. If this were obvious, viewers might feel insulted and bolt (after all, most members of Generation X loathe the term and the stereotype). If viewers bolt, nothing gets sold. So another, at once more attractive and obvious message is provided through the main plot of this episode that can distract us from the fact that TV shows exist to sell things.

Recall how the main plot presents the announcement and fulfillment of a lesbian marriage. The explicit message here is that society should be tolerant of such nontraditional unions. A number of signs point to this message, from Ross's switch from troubled doubt to hearty support for Carol's wedding to the image of Susan's Marine Corps father cheerfully giving her away. And even though the wedding provides the opportunity for a lot of sitcom wisecracks from some of the male characters who wonder whether it's worth the trouble to flirt with any of the women at such an affair, the sheer *ordinariness* of the scene sends the signal that this is no big deal, just two people who love each other getting married. The ease with which the marriage is dramatized, the lack of preachiness, and the relaxed acceptance of what is still somewhat controversial suggests that viewers of *Friends* are just like the characters—loving, supportive, tolerant, progressively nonjudgmental people.

To underscore this message of emotional and political solidarity between show and audience, the director of this episode of *Friends* cast Candace Gingrich, the real-life lesbian sister of then–Speaker of the House Newt Gingrich—a well-known icon of American conservatism at the time—as the minister who performs the wedding ceremony. The show thus invites us to identify with Candace and all those other nice people at the wedding. As if to further underscore the sense of emotional community the show promotes between its characters and its audience, a tease for the NBC 11:00 P.M. news promised a story on the "controversial" topic of that night's episode of *Friends*. Viewers accordingly were invited to compare their progressive acceptance of the lesbian marriage with that hostile world represented by Newt Gingrich. Take that, Newt.

The main plot of our episode thus complements our semiotic interpretation of the program as a whole. Just as *Friends* in general presents a Gen X image that invites its viewers to join the fantasy, so too does this individual episode invite its audience to identify with the particular "message" of the story. Either way, we're all just "friends," helping each other and finding satisfaction in bonding and emotional commitment.

The tone of our interpretation may disturb you. After all, you may want to ask, like the Elvis Costello song, "Just what's wrong with peace, love, and understanding?"—that is, with the promotion of social tolerance and emotional commitment? Nothing at all. But here we have to look at the context in which *Friends* appears. Like all commercial programming, it is not presented as a public service. It is not there for free. It is on television because it has sponsors, and its sponsors are concerned only with attracting an audience that will buy its products. To see something of what those sponsors are thinking, we need only look at a few of the ads that were broadcast along with this episode.

Among the ads that night were ads for Miller Lite, Coors, McDonald's, and Mercedes-Benz cars. The beer ads presented images attractive to people in their late teens and early twenties—especially a Coors ad that featured young men and women dressed in plaid shirts, shorts, and Doc Martens. You got it; the media stereotype of Gen X grunge wear. Given the program's popularity, those were pretty expensive ads, and their purpose was to share the fantasy the show offers to get their audiences to buy beer, hamburgers, and Mercedes. We'll let you judge the merits of beer and hamburgers, but consider the ad for Mercedes-Benz. In Chapter 2 of this book, we remark how advertising stokes desire, and indeed, the Mercedes ad made the car look quite desirable. But isn't there a contradiction here? While twentysomethings are being dramatized as finding greater satisfaction in relationships than in things, here we find one of the most expensive of those things being presented as fulfilling in itself. Is some sort of cruel joke going on?

Our analysis of this episode of *Friends* thus leads to our argument. The thesis for the paper we could now write is that, through a semiotic reading of *Friends,* we can discover the way in which corporate America provides its targeted markets with feel-good fantasies intended primarily to get them to buy products, while having the perhaps unintentional effect of distracting its viewers from certain grim social and economic realities. That the episode of *Friends* was set in New York City, one of the most racially mixed cities on Earth, and managed to show not a single nonwhite face could be used as further support of such a thesis insofar as the show provides an entertaining distraction from New York's ongoing racial tensions. But that wouldn't make us feel very good, would it?

Son of Bart

The enduring popularity of *Friends* through the end of the 1990s indicates that the cultural forces behind its creation were still in place years after its initial appearance. But, as is always the case in the history of popular culture, other, sometimes conflicting cultural trends were emerging even as *Friends,* and the shows with which it can be associated, were making their run. Indeed, as a number of cultural commentators have pointed out, contemporary TV programming is explicitly designed to appeal to a highly segmented marketplace, with some segments of that market being preferred to others. Thus shows like *Seinfeld*, which in spite of its top Nielsen ratings never attracted the number of viewers that shows like *The Beverly Hillbillies* pulled in before the viewing audience became so divided, could command unprecedented advertising fees due to the relative affluence of its core audience (generally the eighteen to forty-nine age group). For this reason, in what is called *niche programming,* the networks tend to target their programs at those audiences that they believe constitute the most lucrative markets (Fox TV's targeting of the youth market is thus a sign of the spending power of young Americans), while ignoring others (the neglect of elderly audiences in prime-time television is notorious). Analyzing the audience of a particular TV program is, accordingly, both an economic and a cultural exploration. This makes all the more interesting the emergence, at the end of the decade, of a very different kind of show from the sort *Friends* represents. This was the prime-time cartoon sitcom—shows like *Family Guy* and *South Park.* And with this difference we can begin our analysis.

The prime-time cartoons of the late 1990s owed their existence to the smash success of *The Simpsons*, a program that, when it appeared some ten years earlier, was definitely unique. What made *The Simpsons* unique was not the fact that it was an animated series that had made it to prime-time (both *The Flintstones* and *The Rocky and Bulwinkle Show* had done that in the 1960s) but rather the self-ironizing attitude that it projected. This was the key difference that made the show significant, for where *The Flintstones* was essentially an animated sitcom little different in tone and content from such earlier nonanimated sitcoms featuring working-class characters as *The Jackie Gleason Show* and *The Life of Reilly*, *The Simpsons* self-consciously presented itself *as* a television sitcom whose purpose was to mock not only television sitcoms as such but America's whole fascination with television culture and its products. Whether spoofing the polite and domesticated world of such classic TV sitcoms as *Father Knows Best* and *Leave It to Beaver* or mocking the rituals surrounding the Superbowl, *The Simpsons*, led by wise-talking Bart, constituted the first *postmodern* television series to attract a mass audience. Since the shows that have followed in its path also reflect postmodern attitudes, we need to look briefly at postmodernism to see how it constitutes the *system* within which the new prime-time cartoons function as cultural signs.

The Postmodern System

Postmodernism is, in effect, both an historical period and an attitude. As an historical period, it refers to the culture that has emerged in the wake of the media age, one obsessed with electronic imagery and the products of mass culture. (Indeed, according to philosophers like Jean Baudrillard, images—or what Baudrillard calls "simulacra"—are the only reality left in the postmodern era.) As an attitude, postmodernism rejects the values of the past, not in favor of any new values but only to ironize value systems as such. In the postmodern worldview, the traditional distinctions we make between things—valuing high culture over low culture, morality over immorality, creativity over imitation—tend to get flattened out. What was once viewed in terms of an oppositional hierarchy—for instance, creative originality is opposed to imitation and is superior to it—is reconceived and deconstructed. Thus postmodern artists tend to repeat existing cultural images in their work, as Andy Warhol's tomato soup canvas repeats an existing cultural image, rather than come up with new ones. In a similar vein, postmodern filmmakers frequently allude to existing films in their work, as in the final scene of Tim Burton's *Batman*, which directly alludes to Alfred Hitchcock's *Vertigo*, or Oliver Stone's *Natural Born Killers*, which recalls *Bonnie and Clyde* and echoes various popular cultural images from movies, television, and cartoon books. Such allusions to, and repetitions of, existing cultural images in postmodern art is called *double coding* because of the way the postmodern artifact at once refers to existing cultural codes while simultaneously recasting them in new contexts. (For instance, the end of *Batman*, while alluding to the conclusion of *Vertigo*, is still quite different from it and has quite a different significance.)

To put this another way, the postmodern style reflects a worldview that holds that it is no longer possible or desirable to create new images; rather, one surveys the vast range of available images that mass culture has to offer and repeats them, but with a difference. Consider what Madonna does with the image of Marilyn Monroe in her video "Material Girl," a half-serious, half-parodic remake of Monroe's film *Gentlemen Prefer Blondes*. In the video, Madonna both resembles Marilyn Monroe and doesn't. Her image recycles an existing cultural icon, but with a new spin. It's the same, and not the same, simultaneously.

This sense of parody, of repetition with a difference, is all there in *The Simpsons*, where Homer Simpson's ineradicable afternoon shadow repeats Fred Flintstone's, but Homer is hardly Fred. At the same time, while *The Flintstones* basically reflected the middle-class values of its core audience, *The Simpsons* mocks those values by placing itself at an ironic distance from them. A postmodern *Flintstones*, *The Simpsons* is at once a repetition and a divergence. It points to the values implicit in the traditional sitcom only to subvert them. For instance, if the traditional sitcom reflected the cultural belief that parents, in the end, should have the final word, *The Simpsons* gives us Bart, and so much for "father knows best."

The irreverent, value-mocking prime-time cartoons of the late 1990s all reflect this postmodern obsession with existing cultural images (the characters from *Family Guy* appeared in an ad sequence run during the

1999 Super Bowl that explicitly referred to the film *The Full Monty*) and disdain for conventional etiquette and morality (hence the stir *South Park* has caused among parents and educators). Born of the popular success of *The Simpsons*—and, we should add, *Beavis and Butthead*, MTV's contribution to the pantheon of media-savvy, trash-talking cartoon heroes—the new run of prime-time cartoons can be taken as a sign of an emerging cultural ethos that differs significantly from that reflected in *Friends*.

So what is that difference? Answering that question can help us understand the cultural significance of the "sons of Bart" beyond the fact that they are postmodern productions that reflect an ironic disdain for traditional values. Recall the central fantasy and appeal of *Friends*—that young Gen Xers can get together in warm, emotionally satisfying relationships that can take the place of the economic expectations that earlier generations enjoyed. Now consider *South Park*. The fantasy here is a kind of social and moral chaos in which dim-witted children wreak havoc on everything and everyone. Cruelty, not coziness, is the dominant emotion, with gross-out humor getting the most laughs (*Ren and Stimpy* is almost certainly part of the show's heritage). To analyze the success of such shows, one needs to look at their audiences. (Close readings of particular episodes will largely turn up the same low jokes.) So we'll ask you: What is the audience for these programs? Is it different in any way from the ongoing audience for shows like *Friends* and *Melrose Place*? If so, does this difference point to a new "post–Gen X" generation (Pepsi's Generation Next!) with a whole new mood and attitude?

Altered States

We'll leave the answering of such questions to you. Our point is that whether you are considering a show like *Friends* or one like *The Simpsons* or any other sort of show, you can find a cultural message behind the entertaining façade shown on the screen. The façade is the fantasy, which distracts its viewers from the ways in which television programmers use their programs to achieve their primary ends—which are, in effect, to get us to go out and buy the products that sponsor the shows. That is why TV shows reflect the attitudes and desires of their core audiences and why interpreting TV reveals what those attitudes and desires are.

By blurring the line between fiction and reality (a process accelerated by the advent of "docudrama" style shows like *America's Most Wanted*—and skewered in a film like *Natural Born Killers*), television has profoundly affected the very way that we perceive our world. If television were to vanish today—no more shows, no more prime time—its effects would live on in the way it has altered our sense of reality. We expect instant visual access to every corner of the Earth because of TV, and we want to get to the point quickly. It is often claimed that our attention spans have been shortened in a universe of televised sound bites, but at the same time our desire for information has been expanded (inquiring minds want to know). Indeed, the television age has equally been an information age.

In semiotic terms, the ubiquity of television and video in our lives represents a shift from one kind of sign system to another. As Marshall McLuhan pointed out almost forty years ago in *The Gutenberg Galaxy*, Western culture since the fifteenth century has defined itself around the printed word—the linear text that reads from left to right and top to bottom. The printed word, in the terminology of the American founder of semiotics, Charles Sanders Peirce, is a *symbolic* sign, one whose meaning is entirely arbitrary or conventional. A symbolic sign means what it does because those who use it have decided so. Words don't look like what they mean. Their significance is entirely abstract.

Not so with a visual image like a photograph (or TV picture), which does resemble its object and is not entirely arbitrary. Though a photograph is not literally the thing it depicts and often reflects a good deal of staging and manipulation by the photographer, we often respond to it as if it were an innocent reflection of the world. Peirce called such signs *icons*, referring by this term to any sign that resembles what it means. The way you interpret an icon, then, differs from the way you interpret a symbol or word. The interpretation of words involves your cognitive capabilities; the interpretation and reception of icons is far more sensuous, more a matter of vision than cognition. The shift from a civilization governed by the paradigm of the book to one dominated by television accordingly involves a shift in the way we "read" our world, as the symbolic field of the printed page yields to the iconic field of the video screen.

The shift from a symbolic, or word-centered, world to an iconic universe filled with visual images carries profound cultural implications. Such implications are not necessarily negative. The relative accessibility of video technology, for example, has created opportunities for personal expression that have never existed before. It is very difficult to publish a book, but anyone can create a widely reproducible video simply by possessing a camcorder. The rapid transmissibility of video images speeds up communication and can bond groups of linguistically and culturally diverse people together, as MTV speaks to millions of people around the nation and world at once in the language of dance and music.

At the same time, video images may be used to change consciousness and stimulate political action. Look at it this way: TV has a visceral power that print does not. Words abstractly describe things; television shows you concrete images. The world pretty much ignored the famine in sub-Saharan Africa in the early 1980s, for example, until the TV cameras arrived to broadcast its images of starvation. Television, in short, bears the potential to awake the apathetic as written texts cannot.

But there is a price to be paid for the new modes of perception that the iconic world of TV has stimulated. For while one *can* read the signs of TV and video actively and creatively, and one can be moved to action by a video image, the sheer visibility of icons tempts one to receive them uncritically. Icons look so much like the realities they refer to that it is easy to forget that icons, too, are signs—images that people construct that carry ideological meanings.

Just think of all those iconic images of the classic fifties-era sitcoms. *Leave It to Beaver, Father Knows Best, The Ozzie and Harriet Show,* and so on have established an American mythology of an idyllic era by the sheer persuasiveness of their images. In fact, the fifties were not such idyllic years. Along with the McCarthyite hysteria of the cold war and the looming specter of nuclear war and contamination from open-air nuclear testing, there were economic downturns, the Korean War, and a grow-ing sense that American life was becoming sterile, conformist, and mate-rialistic—though it wasn't until the sixties that this uneasiness broke into the open. Few fathers in the fifties had the kind of leisure that the sitcom dads had, and the feminist resurgence in the late sixties demonstrated that not all women were satisfied with the housewifely roles assigned them in every screenplay. And yet, those constructed images of white middle-class contentment and security have become so real in the American imagination that they can be called on in quite concrete ways. *Leave It to Beaver* is not simply the sort of thing that shows up in Trivial Pursuit games: the image of the show has become a potent political weapon. Conservative campaigners point to the classic sitcoms as exemplars of the "family values" that America is losing, apparently forgetting that many a modern sitcom, from *The Cosby Show* to *Roseanne,* often reflect strikingly similar images of family solidarity. After all, the whole point of *Leave It to Beaver* was to show every week how "the Beav" might screw something up and create a family crisis and then to have the whole matter resolved in time for the closing commercials. While it may take several episodes to do the trick, how was *Roseanne* different?

Discussing the Signs of Television

In class, choose a current television program, and have the entire class watch one episode (either watch the episode as "homework" or ask someone to tape it and then watch it in class). Interpret the episode semiotically. What values and cultural myths does the show project? What do the commercials broadcast during the show say about the presumed audience for it? Go beyond the episode's surface appeal or "message" to look at the particular images it uses to tell its story, always asking, "What is this pro-gram *really* saying?"

The Audience Is the Authority

One thing that has changed in the relatively brief history of television is the emergence of cable TV. The proliferation of cable companies and channels has fostered a more finely targeted programming schedule by which producers can focus on narrowly defined audiences, from nature lovers to home shoppers. In one respect, the fine-tuning of audiences simply reflects a fine-tuning of marketing: specially defined audiences can be targeted for specially defined marketing campaigns. In this sense, the advent of cable repeats the same history as that of traditional commercial television, which became a medium primarily for the pitching of goods and services. But the proliferation of channels bears the potential to upset television's commercial monopoly. When NBC, CBS, ABC, and their affiliates ruled the airways, programming decisions for an entire nation were made by a tiny group of executives. Aside from the Nielsen ratings, viewers had little chance to let programmers know what they wanted to see. While certainly no revolution has occurred in the wake of cable, there has been some movement toward audience participation in viewing.

The phenomenal success of MTV provides a good example of the increasing power of the television audience. In its early years, rock music appeared on TV in such programs as *American Bandstand* and *The Monkees*. In each case, a rock act had to be toned down considerably before it could be televised (Elvis was ordered not to bump and grind to avoid being banned from the TV screens of the fifties). What amounted to censorship worked because the venues for the televising of rock were often adult-oriented (consider how the Beatles and the Rolling Stones first appeared to American audiences on the adult variety program *The Ed Sullivan Show*). MTV, on the other hand, is an entirely youth-oriented network. Though it too exists to promote products—through both the videos it displays and the commercials it runs—MTV must conform to the tastes of its audience to succeed.

By linking popular music to video imagery, MTV has also created a new type of pop star: singer-choreographers like Madonna, who has created something of an industry among academic critics eager to interpret her work. Some see her as a postmodern feminist heroine who has challenged, through one phase after another, America's sexual mores. Others see her as an irresponsible promoter of teen sexuality whose message to young women is that their bodies are all that matter. Whatever one thinks of her, her preeminent place in American pop culture of the eighties and nineties fairly screams for analysis.

In recent years, Madonna has joined a number of gender-bending pop culture icons—from Marilyn Manson to Dennis Rodman—who challenge the codes that govern sexual identity itself. Thus, where in the past Madonna played with the codes of feminine sexuality in her imper-

---

Reading Music on the Net

Many popular musicians and groups boast their own website or host special "concert" events on the Internet. Find the site of a favorite artist by using a search engine such as Yahoo (**http://www.yahoo.com/Entertainment/Music/Artists**) or trying the Ultimate Band List (**http://american.recordings.com/wwwofmusic**), a huge list of music-related websites. Then study your artist's site, and analyze the images created for him or her. How is the artist "packaged" on the Net, and does that packaging differ from that used in other media? What sort of relationship is established between the artist and you, the fan, and how does the electronic medium affect that relationship?

---

sonations of Marilyn Monroe, she has more recently adopted the bisexual, cross-dressing persona of Marlene Dietrich—complete with top hat, tux, and tails. "Boys will be girls and girls will be boys" pretty much sums up Madonna's current performance philosophy, and by the time you read these pages, she is likely to have moved on yet again as she continues to surf the wave of American popular culture.

The Readings

We begin the readings in this chapter with two essays by Steven D. Stark. The first explores the cultural division between the two most successful sitcoms of the 1990s—the suburban and middle-class *Home Improvement* and the urban *Seinfeld*—while the second situates *The Oprah Winfrey Show* in a system of daytime talk shows that function as a kind of "group therapy for the masses." Two feminist analyses follow, with Laura Stempel Mumford critiquing the common "paternity plot" found in daytime soap operas and Susan Douglas focusing on *NYPD Blue* and *ER*, arguing that behind these shows' progressive surface lies a less-than-enlightened ideological reality. Jimmie L. Reeves, Mark C. Rogers, and Michael Epstein then take on *The X-Files*, situating the explosively popular series within a history of cult favorites from *Star Trek* to *Twin Peaks*. Walter Kirn next tackles Generation X, the first generation to grow up with MTV. And the chapter concludes with Tricia Rose's semiotic decoding of such MTV "Bad Sistas" as Salt 'N' Pepa and MC Lyte.

STEVEN D. STARK

A Tale of Two Sitcoms

Through much of the 1990s, Oprah Winfrey, Jerry Seinfeld, and Tim Allen ranked among Hollywood's most successful television stars. But the success of The Oprah Winfrey Show, Seinfeld, *and* Home Improvement — *as Steven D. Stark (b. 1951) argues in these two excerpts from his book* Glued to the Set: The Sixty Television Shows and Events That Made Us What We Are Today *(1997) — was no mere accident. Each program, in its way, reflected the attitudes and desires of its core audience — housewives for* Oprah, *men with the sensibilities of "11- to 15-year-old boys" for* Seinfeld, *and Middle American suburbanites for* Home Improvement. *Finding in television a mirror image not of American realities but of American needs and desires, Stark provides a model for understanding the cultural significance of the tube. A contributor to such publications as the* Atlantic Monthly *and the* New York Times Magazine, *Stark is also a commentator for National Public Radio.*

The popular shows of a decade are usually a lot alike. In many ways *Dallas* and *Dynasty* were indistinguishable, and it would take Wyatt Earp himself to discern great differences between *Wagon Train* and *Gunsmoke*. In the late seventies *Happy Days, Laverne and Shirley,* and *Three's Company* often seemed to form one long seamless web.

Yet sometimes, in eras of cultural conflict or confusion, no one type of show can accurately capture the public mood. In the early 1970s, for example, *All in the Family* made a hero of a conservative traditionalist while *The Mary Tyler Moore Show* romanticized the life of a single career woman blazing new ground. In their own ways, both shows reflected their times and both were popular — often with the same viewers.

In much the same fashion, popular programming in the nineties offered a contrast, as it struggled with an emerging question which had no clear answer: What does it mean to be a man in a postfeminist age? Two very different situation comedies which hit Number 1 in that decade tried to provide an answer. On the one hand, there was ABC's *Home Improvement* — the top-rated show for the 1993–94 season. And then, there was NBC's *Seinfeld* — which hit Number 1 the following season.

Even the reaction to both shows provided a sharp contrast. Critics regularly lavished *Seinfeld* with praise for its postmodern plots; its technical innovations were hailed as breakthroughs; and the show was always an Emmy contender in several categories. Novelist Jay McInerney went so far in a 1996 issue of *TV Guide* to ask, "Is Seinfeld the Best Comedy

Ever?" By comparison, *Home Improvement* was perhaps the quietest Number 1 in TV history, eliciting a few critical comments and winning little more than a slew of (what else?) People's Choice awards, in which the public does the voting.

There were indeed surface similarities between the two shows. Both starred male comedians, who took their standup nightclub acts and transformed them for television. Both comedians wrote best-selling books once they hit it big, and both shows featured subplots about television itself. Both presented memorable supporting players, like Kramer of *Seinfeld*, or next-door neighbor Wilson of *Home Improvement,* whose full face is never shown over his fence. Both ran in prime time and in syndication over roughly the same period with similar ratings—though the one time *Seinfeld* was matched directly against *Home Improvement* in 1992–93, *Seinfeld* got plastered in the ratings.

Yet the differences between the shows were more revealing. *Home Improvement* was set in suburban Detroit, in the white-bread heartland. Though actually filmed in L.A., *Seinfeld* was a New York show which roughly approximated the lifestyles of influential New York critics and Madison Avenue types. *Home Improvement* was solidly suburban middle class; *Seinfeld* was a portrait of life in yuppie Upper Manhattan.

Home Improvement was a rather traditional family sitcom about a wife, three kids, and a bumbling Dad; the *Seinfeld* family of friends featured no children and no workplace either, at least in the traditional sense. With its "morality tale" quality, *Home Improvement* was a cousin of *Leave It to Beaver* and *My Three Sons*—an anachronism in an era when wisecracking shows like *Friends* or *Murphy Brown* dispensed with nuclear families altogether.

By contrast, *Seinfeld* was closer to Jack Benny, or even Milton Berle. That was a remarkable turnaround for a medium which for much of its bland and homogeneous entertainment life took single Jews like Seinfeld, changed their names, converted them to Christianity, married them off to attractive WASP housewives, and moved them to the suburbs. New York *Newsday* once called *Seinfeld* "the most fully realized schlemiel in the history of television."

What encouraged programmers to take these chances was the way that cable television had atomized the viewing audience. Because of cable competition, network television was not the mass medium in 1995 that it was in 1975; it took far fewer viewers to make a hit. *Seinfeld* won the 1994–95 ratings race with a rating that two decades earlier wouldn't have even placed in the Top Twenty-five. Such a disintegration of the network audience meant that the networks no longer had to program for as large a mass to make money, and shows like *Seinfeld*—which appealed to upscale viewers—often were the result. By 1995, half the sitcoms on TV seemed to feature singles living in cities like New York, if only because these series appealed to viewers similarly situated who, in turn, appealed to advertisers because they have lots of discretionary income.

Yet even though television was finally acknowledging the nation's diversity, that didn't mean that shows like *Seinfeld* were realistic national self-portraits either. After all, the more that television sitcoms have moved in the direction of "realism," the less authentic they have often become. For all the praise that *All in the Family* received, Archie Bunker was a parody; even the witty comedy of *Mary Tyler Moore* hardly reflected a workplace anyone could recognize with honest assurance. Similarly, no one—not even an Upper East Sider—has hours every day to spend chatting with friends in a diner. Yet critics were fond of praising the realism of *Seinfeld*. "Men probably laughed louder than women at the episode in which Elaine discovered that her nipple was exposed on her Christmas card photo," wrote McInerney. "This stuff happens to all of us." Oh, really?

Seinfeld did have considerable strengths, however. The show was genuinely funny, a rare treat on prime-time television. Some of the series episodes, like the one on the "soup Nazi" or on losing a car in a parking lot, were inspired, and the supporting cast of Elaine, Kramer, and George was exceptional. "It's about nothing, everything else is about something; this, it's about nothing," said George in pitching his and Jerry's sitcom proposal to a network, as *Seinfeld* became a show within a show. Already some of its lines have become pop culture classics: "I'm Cosmo Kramer, the Assman!"; "Not that there's anything wrong with that"; and "Master of your Domain."

Seinfeld was also a hit because it appealed to men more than did many other sitcoms, as it reflected a new adolescent sensibility sweeping America in the 1990s. Along with the comedy of David Letterman, the cartoon series *Beavis and Butthead,* megamovies like *Jurassic Park,* and syndicated radio talkmeisters Howard Stern and Don Imus, *Seinfeld* often echoed the world of 11- to 15-year-old boys. The radio style of Stern and Imus, for example, was that of the narcissistic class cutup in seventh grade: Both sat in a playhouse-like radio studio with a bunch of guys and horsed around for hours talking about sex, sports, and politics, all the while laughing at their own loutish, subversive jokes.

Seinfeld shared a similar sensibility, albeit softened somewhat for television. Like a group of 14-year-olds, the men on *Seinfeld* seemed not to hold real regular jobs, the better to devote time to "the gang." (One woman, Elaine, was allowed to tag along with the boys, much like those younger sisters who are permitted to hang out with their brothers.) Not only was every man in Seinfeld's gang unmarried and pushing fortysomething, but it also was difficult to imagine any having a real relationship with any woman but his mother. Note how much more often parents of adult children appeared here than on other shows.

Or compare *Seinfeld* to its predecessor in its NBC Thursday night time slot, *Cheers*. If the men on that show didn't spend much time at work either, they did hang out in a traditional domain of adults—the tavern—and the hero, Sam Malone, spent many of his waking hours chasing women. Seinfeld, by contrast, was better known for sitting in a restaurant eating french fries with his pals. One of the most celebrated risqué *Seinfeld* episodes was about (what else?) masturbation, while others dealt with urinating in the shower or on couches. That's usually big stuff in the seventh grade, but not much beyond.

The *Seinfeld* evocation of early male adolescence did reflect deeper cultural strains. This country has always venerated "bad boys," from Huck Finn to Holden Caulfield. Moreover, many psychologists consider that preteen stage of life, when one is acutely aware of being powerless, as the time when individuals are most subversive of the society at-large. That sentiment fit a nineties cultural mood, as America became full of the defiant, oppositional anger that often characterizes the early adolescent—witness the tearing down of public figures with the ready help of the tabloid press, and the flocking to antiestablishment talk radio whereon the humor grew more derisive by the day. In a similar vein, one could imagine the whole *Seinfeld* cast of perpetual adolescents on the Clinton White House staff working with George Stephanopolous or Craig Livingstone. Yet boys will be boys: Maybe that's why much of the country viewed the Clinton administration's missteps as benignly as they viewed George Costanza's.

Because this country has always had tendencies that remind observers of a 14-year-old boy, no one would blame *Seinfeld* alone for society's failure to grow up and take care of its real children; its current ambivalence about paternal authority; or its vulgarity and exhibitionist inclinations. Yet the show definitely played a role, along with its cultural cousins. In much the same way that *Roseanne* had domesticated tabloid television for the masses, *Seinfeld* did the same for sophomoric talk radio, as embodied by fellow Manhattanites Stern and Imus.

By contrast, *Home Improvement* had the gentle ring of mainstream truth. It's no accident that 14- to 30-year-olds in a *TV Guide* poll voted Jill and Tim the TV parents most like their own. Naturally, that state of affairs sometimes drew the critics' ire. "'Home Improvement' is a reactionary return, after 'Roseanne' and 'Married with Children' and all those Census Bureau reports, to the semi-extinct idea of a nuclear family whose members actually like each other," wrote Chuck Eddy in a review of the show for *millennium pop*.

Unlike *Seinfeld, Home Improvement* was about grown-ups. Take the premiere episode: Tim (the Toolman) Taylor, host of a cable show called *Tool Time*, wants to rewire his dishwasher to make it more powerful but ends up breaking it. When he tries to comfort his wife after she doesn't get a job, he inadvertently ends up making her feel worse. In just such a fashion *Home Improvement* was built around that preoccupation central to the zeitgeist of the nineties: If television once told us *Father Knows Best*, this show probed what it meant to be the best father and husband in an age of feminism and embattled male identity.

When Matt Williams and David McFadzean were developing ideas for this show, they were both reading the work of noted linguist Deborah Tannen on male-female communication. "Her book deals with the fact that men and women speak different languages," Williams once remembered. "That right there is the piston that drives this television series. Jill and Tim will never do the same thing the same way, and both sides are valid." On another occasion, Williams noted:

> The biggest challenge for us is to take absurd situations, or extreme points of view or actions, and root them in some kind of truth. . . . If we do our job correctly, those are the things the audience will never think twice about, because we've rooted them in some kind of behavioral truth.

And so the show went in the 1990s, quietly drawing better in rural than urban areas yet still doing well among professionals. Like Jerry Seinfeld, Tim Allen's persona became a new cultural icon—the postfeminist handyman. His was a sitcom prototype with the qualities that many Americans in the 1990s held dear—low-key, predictable, intelligent but not particularly well-educated, with a little dirt under his fingernails. If he'd been a politician in the nineties, he would have had little in common with Bill Clinton or Newt Gingrich—Washington insiders and policy preachers to the core. (Colin Powell would be another story.) For different reasons, Taylor also would have had little to talk about with Seinfeld, who never would have tuned in to *Tool Time,* much less own a hammer. (Like many Manhattanites, Seinfeld always seemed to prefer the movies to television anyway.)

Here, then, were two conflicting strains in the American character: *Seinfeld,* a popular urban show about eccentric individualism and the flight from adulthood, versus *Home Improvement,* a popular suburban show about commitment and ultimately about family. The forces which create "the buzz" in this country—the press, the public relations establishment, and Madison Avenue—simply loved *Seinfeld,* which tells us as much about their makeup and tastes as about the show itself. We also had our Seinfeld-esque White House.

The guess here, however, is that *Home Improvement* was still a better reflection of who we are, despite major social changes over decades. In the not-so-grand tradition of television, viewers still feel more comfortable with the Cleavers, the Andersons, and the Bradys than they do with the *Seinfeld* alternative. Viewers want happy, traditional families, even when they realize that a TV family and setting is idealized—or perhaps *especially* when they realize it. The perfect man for the nineties? It's OK to have that fling with the "bad boy"—who, after all, has always been part of the greater American family. But when it's time to settle down, he isn't the guy you're going to want to bring into your living rooms and bedrooms, night after night.

Reading the Text

1. How, according to Stark, did *Home Improvement* and *Seinfeld* reflect television's divergent response to the question "What does it mean to be a man in a postfeminist age?" (para. 3)?
2. In Stark's view, how did *Seinfeld* evoke "early male adolescence" (para. 15), and what was the appeal of this emphasis?
3. What were the audience niches that *Seinfeld* and *Home Improvement* targeted?
4. How do *Seinfeld* and *Home Improvement* reflect "two conflicting strains in the American character" (para. 21)?

Reading the Signs

1. In your journal, reflect on your response to *Seinfeld* and *Home Improvement*. Have you been a fan of either show, and why or why not?
2. *Seinfeld* inspired many imitators, such as *Men Behaving Badly*. Survey a current list of prime-time sitcoms, and write an analysis of a show that focuses on male characters. Which of the "two conflicting strains in the American character" does your show reflect, or does it reflect a different strain?
3. Stark reports that when *Seinfeld* was shown head to head with *Home Improvement* in 1992 to 1993, *Seinfeld* "got plastered in the ratings" (para. 5). Using Stark's analysis of the two programs as a basis for your argument, write an essay explaining why you think *Home Improvement* outscored *Seinfeld*.
4. At a time of national debate over the behavior of adolescent "bad boys" (para. 15), especially in the wake of numerous school shootings, finding humor in bad boy behavior may have cultural ramifications. Conduct an in-class debate on the social effects of the glorification of adolescent rebelliousness in popular culture.

STEVEN D. STARK

The Oprah Winfrey Show *and the Talk-Show Furor*

||||||||||||||||||||||||||||||||||||||||||||||||||||||||||||||||

Start with these two basic premises:

1. Oprah Winfrey is probably the most celebrated and powerful black woman in U.S. history.
2. Oprah Winfrey is the undisputed leader of a television genre which has been more vehemently attacked by the Establishment than any other in television history.

You don't have to be an Albert Einstein to recognize that these two propositions are related.

The modern daytime talk show—created by Phil Donahue in the late 1960s, revolutionized by Oprah in the 1980s, and then transmogrified in the 1990s by everyone from Ricki Lake to Jenny Jones—is the newest genre to sweep television. On an average mid-nineties weekday, *The Oprah Winfrey Show* was watched by ten million Americans, mostly women, and the 20 or so other daytime talk shows in 1995 had a combined daily audience of around 50 million viewers—though many people undoubtedly watched a whole slew of these shows each day. Though these numbers were high, they pale when compared to those of the combined audiences that watch the violence of prime-time action shows or the local news.

Yet the talk-show genre was absolutely vilified by critics—blamed for everything from the culture's preoccupation with victimization to the general decline of civic discourse. Daytime talk generated a well-publicized crusade (led by two U.S. senators and former Secretary of Education William Bennett) to purify the medium, not to mention a dozen or so critical books and hundreds of negative articles which joined these Washington officials in calling the new genre a "case study of rot" and "the pollution of the human environment."

Admittedly daytime talk shows are not for the squeamish or children—though one hopes that Bennett and his minions were as concerned about the millions who live full-time in economic and social surroundings far more squalid than anything on *The Maury Povich Show*. The shows typically involve from two to six guests talking about their personal experiences, followed by boos, applause, tears, questions, and shouts from a studio audience modeled roughly on Howdy Doody's Peanut Gallery. A typical week of mid-nineties programming on these shows was likely to include such topics as:

Leathermen Love Triangles

Bisexuals

Abusive Boyfriends

Men Engaged to Three Pregnant Women

Clueless Men

Women Who Marry Their Rapists

Runaway Teens

Secret Crushes

This was the genre where a man was surprisingly "confronted" with a secret admirer on *Jenny Jones,* found the admirer was a man, and killed him after the show for humiliating him on national television. (The show was never broadcast due to the shooting.) "Rather than being mortified, ashamed, or trying to hide their stigma," two sociologists wrote of this genre, "guests willingly and eagerly discuss their child-molesting, sexual quirks, and criminal records in an effort to seek 'understanding' for their particular disease."

These shows obviously offer a distorted vision of America, thrive on feeling rather than thought, and worship the sound-bite rather than the art of conversation. Yet it's not like television hasn't been walking down these same paths in other forms every day for the past 50 years. If daytime talk has been preoccupied with sex, race, and family dysfunction, it may be because there is still so little discussion of those rather significant topics elsewhere on television, even in the nineties. All movements have their crazies. Yet when Oprah Winfrey can rank in a poll as the celebrity Americans believe to be most qualified to be president (far more than Bill Bennett, by the way), something significant is going on.

Just as vaudeville was the root of much early American television, the circus and carnival with their freak shows influenced talk shows. Like any new television genre, these talk shows were a mixture of old programming types—many of which once dominated the daytime. Morning and afternoon talk, geared mostly to women, has a long TV history, beginning with Arthur Godfrey and with Art Linkletter's *People Are Funny*. From the soap opera, these new shows borrowed a feminine style of disclosure and a focus on issues considered to be of particular relevance to women, like family and relationships. Game shows were a rich source: From programs like *The Price Is Right* the new talk shows learned how to involve an audience of ordinary people. From games like *Strike It Rich* and *Queen for a Day* they learned about the entertainment value of debasing "contestants" who will tell their sob story for money or fleeting fame. And from *Family Feud* they learned that conflict sells in the daytime. Throw in a smattering of TV religion (the televised confession and revelation so prominent on these shows), melodrama (Will the runaway teenager's father take her back?), and the news sensibility of Barbara Walters, once an early-morning mainstay on *Today,* and the pieces were in place for a profitable genre—especially because daytime talk shows are so inexpensive to stage.

Like other popular forms of programming, these shows also mirrored their times. Phil Donahue created the genre because network television wasn't reflecting the serious concerns of many of its women viewers. It began in 1967, at the dawn of the women's movement, when this Midwestern Catholic started a new type of daytime talk show in Dayton, Ohio, hosting for that first show atheist Madalyn Murray O'Hair. Donahue's story was simple: "The average housewife is bright and inquisitive," he said, "but television treats her like a mental midget." His approach was to take TV talk out of its preoccupation with entertainment celebrities, and tackled instead (often with only one guest an hour) "difficult" women's issues that television wasn't addressing—sexism, artificial insemination, impotence, and homosexuality—combined with more-traditional topics, like bathroom fixtures. "He flies in the face of TV tradition, which used to be that you didn't risk offending anyone," Steve Allen, former host of *The Tonight Show,* said. Donahue also brilliantly added an active studio audience, usually composed almost entirely of women (though not by design—they're just the ones who showed up), which not only served as a kind of Greek chorus for the guests, but also asked many of the show's most penetrating questions.

For his part, Donahue the rebel frequently bounced about the crowd, microphone in hand, smashing the barrier between host and audience. It didn't hurt the show's populist appeal that it came to stations independently through syndication, rather than from a paternalistic network. In its heyday, *Donahue* also originated from Chicago—in the nation's heartland—rather than among the elites in New York. The more the women's movement progressed, however, the more well-educated women left home for the workplace, and found other outlets for their interests. That left Donahue and his imitators with a growing audience of less-affluent, homebound women who often were full of anger and confusion, ignored as they were by more elite media. The women's movement first made Donahue, and then took away the cream of his audience who were interested in more serious topics.

Still, for over a decade he had the field to himself before along came a certain Oprah Winfrey in 1984. She was an empathetic black woman and former coanchor of the local news in Baltimore. Oprah's advantage over Donahue was that, seeming to resemble her audience, she used that similarity to create a talk show which made the political more personal. Her program was infused with a therapeutic sensibility: Though Oprah did some politics, like her celebrated show in Forsyth County, Georgia, in 1987 (when white racists were on the march), she was more likely to do a show on abusive boyfriends, recovering alcoholics, or competitive sisters. The cause of many of the problems discussed on her show was not so much men, but the so-called rigid confines of traditional family. "What we are witnessing with the proliferating talk show is a social revolution which has at its core the demystification of the family," Michael Arlen, former TV critic for the *New Yorker,* would tell a reporter much later. Say goodbye to Ozzie and Harriet!

Oprah's style was different, too. If Donahue was, at heart, a journalist exposing issues, Oprah ran what she called a "ministry"—the "church" being a branch of pop psychology which held that revealing problems, improving self-esteem, and receiving empathy could cure just about anything, and empower women besides. Oprah hugged her guests, wept openly, and personally said good-bye to each member of the studio audience after a show. Even in 1996, Oprah spoke far more often on her shows than other hosts did. She confessed on the air that she had been sexually abused by relatives as a child, and in later years that she had smoked cocaine. On a show about dieting, she told the audience about the night she ate hot-dog buns drowned in syrup.

Oprah's race and street sass ("Hey, Girl!") also made her more authentically hip, at least to her audience, than almost anyone else on television. Oprah would call her success an alternative to the "Twinkies and Barbie and Ken dolls" that make up so much of television. "Racism remains the most difficult subject in America, and it is only really on the talk show that the raw hatred and suspicion that the races feel for each other is vented," Arlen had told that reporter. As a host who could walk the narrow line between the races, Oprah offered reassurance which others couldn't hope to match. That cultural bilingualism also allowed her to put together an audience coalition of the sort that Jesse Jackson could only dream about.

With rock-and-roll in the 1950s, black artists had been swept aside so that more-acceptable white singers could "cover" their songs. With daytime talk, the opposite occurred: Oprah's show soon wiped out *Donahue* in the ratings — and everyone else, too. By 1994, *Working Woman* put Oprah's net worth at over $250 million. By then the show itself was grossing almost $200 million a year, had 55 percent more viewers than *Donahue* (its closest competitor), and enjoyed higher ratings on many days than *Today, Good Morning America,* and the *CBS Morning News* combined.

Understandably, Oprah's success bred imitators. Since other hosts couldn't hope to match her in identifying with the audience personally (Ricki Lake was a notable exception, as she went after younger viewers), they tried to win viewers by topping her with their list of sensationalistic topics and revelations. As TV news became ever more tabloid, these shows pushed the envelope even further. By 1992, even Donahue was tackling topics like "Safe Sex Orgies" and "What Happens When Strippers Get Old?" Other shows borrowed from the confrontational style of talk shows once run by Mort Downey Jr. and turned Oprah's group hug into a daily talk riot with topics like "Wives Confront the Other Woman."

By the mid-1990s, an average day on these other shows revealed   15
subjects like "Married Men Who Have Relationships with Their Next-Door Neighbors," "Mothers Who Ran Off with Their Daughter's Fiancé," and "Drag Queens Who Got Makeovers." A 1995 study of these programs, done by a team of researchers at Michigan State University, found that a typical one-hour show had:

> four sexual-activity disclosures, one sexual-orientation disclosure, three abuse disclosures, two embarrassing-situation disclosures, two criminal-activity disclosures and four personal-attribute disclosures, for a total of 16 personal disclosures. . . .

These entertainment programs were selling more, however, than just their guests' disclosures or the "hot" topics which seemed to come straight out of the supermarket tabloids. They also purported to offer group therapy for the masses, at a price everyone could afford. As psychotherapist Murray Nossel once told a reporter, America is "the country that popularized psychoanalysis. Freud's theory of the psyche is that repression brings depression, whereas expression is liberating. Emotionally to cathart in America, to reveal one's darkest secrets, is a desired social good in and of itself." Critics would have a field day pointing out the dangers of trying to provide such "therapy" on television, but that played right into the notion that elites were trying to keep the masses away from something that had once exclusively been available only to the well-to-do. After all, if daytime talk shows thrived on the violation of taboos, that was, in part, to stick a finger in the eye of those members of the Establishment who looked down on a television pursuit favored by the downscale.

The supporters of these shows also felt that they regularly received too little credit for tackling issues which mainstream television had traditionally ignored, like race and family dysfunction. "If people didn't get up there and talk about incest," Lee Fryd, director of media relations for the *Sally Jessy Raphael* show once told a reporter, "it would never come to light." If these shows often presented what many considered a freak parade, others would argue that they had helped bring nonconformists further into the mainstream. Joshua Gamson, a cultural critic, once wrote:

> The story here is not about commercial exploitation but just about how effective the prohibition on asking and telling is in the United States, how stiff the penalties are, how unsafe this place is for people of atypical sexual and gender identities. You know you're in trouble when Sally Jessy Raphael (strained smile and forced tear behind red glasses) seems your best bet for being heard, understood, respected, and protected. That for some of us the loopy, hollow light of talk shows seems a safe, shielding haven should give us all pause.

On the other hand, the values of these talk shows were oddly traditional—one reason why they posted such strong ratings with Bible Belt females who considered themselves conservative. The parade of guests was almost always hooted down by the studio audience, which embodied a rather conventional view of morality (albeit one heavily tempered by empathy for victims). The parade of "trash," to use one critic's words, was also a way for those at home to feel better about themselves, since their lives were rarely as hopeless as what they could find here on the screen. Like so much else on TV, what these shows offered was a form of reassurance.

If these talk shows had a larger political consequence, it came with the administration of Bill Clinton, who accomplished little but empathized with everybody. He ran a kind of talk-show presidency—forged in the 1992 campaign with his appearance on *Donahue,* and continuing in that year into a second debate with George Bush and H. Ross

Perot which did away with journalist-questioners and substituted an inquiring studio audience like Oprah's. One of Clinton's principal contributions to our culture was to take the language and zeitgeist of the talk
show and bring it into mainstream politics. After all, the "I feel your
pain" trademark of his presidency first gained cultural prominence as a
talk-show staple: The whole point of talk shows like Oprah's is to encourage "audience-victims" to "feel their pain" as a way of empowering
themselves to strike back against those who seem more powerful.

Such a stance was undoubtedly a big reason why women, over time,   20
supported Clinton so strongly. In fact, by 1996, the talk-show style and
its celebration of victims was on display throughout both political conventions: There was Liddy Dole's Winfreyesque "among the delegates"
talk to the Republican convention, Al Gore's speech recounting his
dying sister's final moments, and the endless parade of the disease-
afflicted. Our politics had been Opracized.

Yet if the nineties has been a decade tending to elevate feeling over
thought and encourage a no-fault approach to behavior, the talk shows
were hardly the only culprit, no matter what Bill Bennett thought. Few
cultural movements of this magnitude proceed from the bottom up
rather than the other way around. As Michiko Kakutani would point out
in another context in the *New York Times,* the cult of subjectivity en-
veloping America came as much from Oliver Stone, with his fantasies
about JFK, and from "inventive" biographers like Joe McGinniss, as they
came from Ricki Lake. Invective was as much a calling card of CNN's
Crossfire as it was of Montel and Jerry Springer.

By late 1995, however, in response to criticisms by Bennett and others (and as ratings for the "confrontational" shows dropped by as much as
a third), Oprah changed her mix of guests and topics too, moving away
from tabloid psychology and toward less-conventional, more-"educational" subjects like anorexia and planning for old age. "She said to us
that after 10 years and 2,000 shows of mostly dysfunctional people, she
felt it was time to start focusing on solutions," said Tim Bennett, Oprah's
production-company president. At the same time, *The Rosie O'Donnell
Show* rose to daytime prominence by essentially taking the old fifties' upbeat variety formula, popularized by Arthur Godfrey, and repackaging it
with a likable female host, celebrity guests, and a nineties' zeitgeist.

But were even these small shifts something of a betrayal of a large
portion of the talk show audience? What was always most striking about
this form of "entertainment"—and what made it so different from anything else on television—was its never-ending portrait of despair and
alienation. If the downtrodden who populated these shows popularized
deviancy or celebrated the cheap confessional, they did it mostly as a
plaintive cry for help. Yet Oprah had been there to bless them at the end
of every weekday. "They are the people you'd ignore if you saw them in
line at the supermarket instead of on TV," Wendy Kaminer, a cultural

analyst, once wrote, but that was precisely the point. Talk television was yet another step in the 1990s' trend to democratization of the medium — this time to include the real have-nots. That may be why the elites responded with their usual rejoinder to let them eat cake.

Reading the Text

1. What does Stark mean when he says that *The Oprah Winfrey Show* and its imitators "offer group therapy for the masses" (para. 16)?
2. What evidence does Stark provide to support his view that talk shows have had a special appeal to women?
3. Why does Stark say that talk shows are "oddly traditional" (para. 18), despite their often lurid content?
4. Explain what Stark means by saying that Bill Clinton "ran a kind of talk-show presidency" (para. 19).

Reading the Signs

1. In your journal, reflect on your responses to talk shows. If you enjoy sensationalized programming, explore why; if you avoid it, discuss the reasons for your distate.
2. In competing with *The Oprah Winfrey Show*, talk-show hosts such as Jerry Springer and Sally Jessy Raphael have upped the ante with "sensationalistic topics and revelations" (para. 14). In an essay, argue for or against the social value of sensationalized talk shows.
3. Write an argumentative essay supporting, refuting, or complicating Stark's assertion that talk shows have helped to bring about the "democratization" (para. 23) of television.
4. Watch an episode of *The Oprah Winfrey Show*, and write an essay in which you offer your own analysis of its appeal. To develop your support, you might interview some avid fans of the program.
5. Write a letter to talk-show critics such as William Bennett, supporting or refuting their desire to "purify" television.

L A U R A   S T E M P E L   M U M F O R D

Plotting Paternity: Looking for Dad on the Daytime Soaps

In recent years, feminist analysts of daytime soap operas have reinter-preted this oft-maligned television genre to argue that its focus on such domestic matters as marriage and childbirth serves a progressive purpose by validating the lives and concerns of the home-centered women who constitute the soaps' most loyal audience. But Laura Stempel Mumford isn't so sure. Analyzing the pervasiveness of the "paternity plot" in the promiscuous world of the daytime soap opera, Mumford argues that this obsession with the question of who is the father of whom functions, in the end, as a "mythic" reaffirmation of the patriarchal status quo by making certain that fatherhood, not motherhood, remains the key marker of social identity. An independent scholar and writer, Mumford writes about TV, women's fiction, feminist theory, and style.

As anyone familiar with the genre knows, the attribution of paternity is something of an obsession on daytime soap operas. In fact, if the frequency of unplanned pregnancies (often from a single sexual encounter), the prominence of storylines involving secrets or mistakes over paternity, and the importance characters attach to discovering who has fathered a particular child are any evidence, the preoccupation with questions and mysteries about paternity is almost a defining characteristic of the genre. Every single daytime soap opera, as well as each prime-time serial, deals with the issue of paternity on a regular basis, and the most heavily freighted single piece of information on any given show is commonly the knowledge of paternity. From a feminist perspective, the issue seems almost overdetermined—so much so that, if it is possible to describe soap operas as being "about" any one thing, they are about paternity.

The predominance of this subject, which is presented through what I call the *paternity plot,* raises a number of questions about how and why women viewers enjoy soap operas, and about the genre's political and ideological role. In particular, it is a paradigmatic example of the methods by which soap operas provide competent viewers with an opportunity for pleasurable anticipation and utopian, woman-centered fantasy, while ultimately containing and managing the disruptive aspects of that fantasy through the inevitable reestablishment of patriarchal order. . . .

The [paternity] plot itself rests on a simple premise: a woman character becomes pregnant but does not know or will not reveal the father's identity. The storyline generally begins at or just before conception, but such a beginning may only be implicit, since some paternity plots, particularly the ones involving the sudden appearance of previously unknown

adult children, only erupt many years after the fact. Other characters—
usually including but never limited to the men who might have fathered
her child—become involved in the pregnancy or with the child, depending on the stage at which the mystery becomes known. According
to their relationships to the woman and in keeping with their functions
as "good" or "evil" figures, these characters attempt to discover, repress,
or reveal the pregnancy's origin. Predictable soap opera complications
ensue and varying lengths of time may pass between conception and revelation, but the identity of the true father eventually becomes public
knowledge. There are numerous variations on this basic plot, the most
common of which revolve around the woman's engagement or marriage
to a man other than the lover responsible for her pregnancy, that lover's
marriage or engagement to another woman, or—in the case of adult
children—rivalry between legitimate or acknowledged offspring and
their newly discovered (putative) sibling.[1]

The paternity plot is so pervasive that examples can be chosen almost
at random, but one should be enough to suggest the mechanisms by
which it is typically worked out. In the spring of 1994, *All My Children*
revealed that Dimitri Marrick had unknowingly fathered a son in Hun-
gary by one of his family's servants, Corvina Lane, over 20 years earlier.
Corvina had raised the child, Anton, as her brother, and while Anton
had been living in Pine Valley for some months, his true identity was
only discovered when Dimitri's brother and sister-in-law Edmund and
Maria, honeymooning at the Marrick's Hungarian estate, found a cryptic
old unsent letter from Corvina to Dimitri and confronted Corvina about
her secret. Although they soon informed Dimitri of his real relationship
with Anton, for whom he had always felt a special but heretofore unex-
plained fondness, Corvina strenuously objected to telling Anton that she
and Dimitri were his parents, leaving the four characters who were in the
know struggling to keep the information away, not only from Anton,
but from his conniving fiancee, Kendall.

Typically, the Marrick family history is a tangle of stories about mys-   5
terious paternity and maternity: Kendall is the previously unknown
daughter of Dimitri's estranged wife, Erica Kane, and the discovery that
Edmund is Dimitri's brother was itself the center of an elaborate, Gothic-
style paternity plot. Such complex family trees and the tension and suspense that surround them may be relatively rare in real life, but the ubiq-

---

1. Other critics have, of course, noted the predominance of storylines about paternity, although none have made a sustained argument about the subject's importance
to the genre. See, among many others, Ellen Seiter, "Promise and Contradiction: The
Daytime Television Serial," *Film Reader* 5 (1982): 154; Christine Geraghty, *Women and
Soap Opera: A Study of Prime Time Soaps* (Cambridge, UK: Polity Press, 1991), pp.
68–69; and Patricia Mellencamp, *High Anxiety: Catastrophe, Scandal, Age, and Comedy*
(Bloomington: Indiana University Press, 1992), pp. 242–43.

uitousness of the paternity plot makes them typical of kinship relations on soap operas, where most members of a family like the Marricks have been involved in some kind of paternity mystery.

Significantly, however, while the immediate effects of such mysteries are profound, it is also rare for such a dispute to resonate very far beyond the revelation of the true father. Although post-revelation resentment occasionally lasts a few weeks (or a few months on prime-time shows), the tension is focused on the actual news about paternity, and it is a rare soap opera character who continues to harbor negative feelings beyond the moment of confrontation and acknowledgment. (For example, although much drama surrounded the revelation itself, once *All My Children*'s Adam Chandler acknowledged Hayley Vaughan as his daughter, Hayley adjusted quickly to the new relationship, and soon began characterizing the manipulative Adam as a good father.) When such resentment does last longer, it tends to be a function of the resentful character's already well-established "evil," selfish, or spiteful nature. (On *One Life to Live*, Tina Lord's transformation from an evil and conniving character to a more sympathetic one was marked in part by her shift from resentment to acceptance of the identity of her father, the late Victor Lord.) Despite the fact that it initially threatens to destroy the family structure, then, the paternity mystery is in practice only a temporary disruption of family life, one whose long-term effects consist almost entirely of the realignment of specific family ties, rather than the undermining of essential family or community frameworks. . . .

On the surface, such storylines seem to fit easily into the daytime soaps' fixation on their characters' private lives. As Tania Modleski has pointed out, soap operas' preoccupation with private questions—family, love, sex, loyalty, jealousy—reassures the traditional daytime audience of home-centered women that their focus on the private world is not merely legitimate, but fascinating.[2] By presenting not only women, but men who are as bound up with private concerns as the most stereotypical housewife, these programs glamorize those interests and reassure viewers that such men do—or could—exist. (Janice Radway makes an analogous point about the male heroes of romance novels, who can be seen at their first appearance to express a "feminine" sensitivity that she suggests contrasts with the men in romance readers' daily lives.)[3] This characterization of the shows' bias toward the private explains their almost exclusive focus on the family, and the elision of public and private explains the fact that every member of the soap opera community eventually discovers the secrets of paternal identity.

2. Tania Modleski, *Loving with a Vengeance: Mass-Produced Fantasies for Women* (New York: Methuen, 1982), pp. 88, 108.

3. Janice Radway, *Reading the Romance: Women, Patriarchy, and Popular Literature* (Chapel Hill: University of North Carolina Press, 1984), p. 148.

Still, we might expect that, for home-centered women viewers, issues of *maternity* would be far more compelling than issues of paternity. And indeed, there are cases in which maternity is in question—often involving babies switched at birth—although it is not a common plot device. For example, many years ago on *One Life to Live,* well-meaning friends told a former prostitute that her baby had died and gave the child to a former nun, who did not know that her baby *had* died. (Although paternity plots figure prominently on this show, the writers of *One Life to Live* also seem to be unusually interested in cases of mistaken or unknown maternity. Two separate maternity mysteries were featured during 1989 alone, one a particularly complicated storyline involving the recovery by Viki Lord Buchanan of a daughter born to her twenty-five years earlier, the other a version of the standard baby-switching plot. Viki's story was especially complex because her multiple personality disorder and resultant partial amnesia meant that she was unaware of the existence of her daughter Megan.) Like paternity mysteries, maternity mysteries are always resolved through the absolute identification of the mother and/or child, yet the very rarity of this plot twist highlights the extent to which uncertainties and anxieties about *men's* position within the family are manipulated and reversed in soap operas.

Why, however, does paternity figure so prominently in a genre directed primarily at women? A simple but inadequate explanation, of course, is that mainstream, mass-media-generated popular culture reflects the prevailing political and social ethos of the culture in which it is produced, in this case patriarchal interests that privilege the father's role and identity over the mother's. But a consideration of the differences between soap opera presentations of uncertain maternity and paternity may help to illuminate the choice to emphasize the latter.

First of all, the paternity plot is narratively both far simpler and far 10 richer in potential complications than one centered on mistaken or unknown maternity. For a child's father to be unknown, no intentional act of deception is needed. It is only necessary for a woman character to have had or appear to have had sex with more than one man around the time of conception. Although the woman herself may be actively plotting to conceal the information, or to pin the pregnancy on an "innocent" man, there are many other possible explanations, including an unreported rape, a secret love affair, or that time-honored soap staple, the sudden return of a long-lost husband or lover. This is largely a narrative consideration, but it helps to explain why such a theme would prove popular among soap opera writers. While simplicity of premise is not necessarily the overriding concern, extremely complicated plots do not often become staples. Since a daily serial quickly exhausts new story ideas, this wide range of possible explanations and the suspense inherent in them makes paternity an excellent subject for a continuing serial in which additional storylines must constantly be introduced. Questions about a character's paternity can be introduced at any time, even "retro-fitted" years later.[4]

In contrast, the physical facts of reproduction make maternity a relatively less abundant source of either suspense or mystery. For a child's *mother* to be unknown, someone must act—and act after the child's birth—to confuse or obscure things. Although it is not possible for the error to be innocent, and thus not part of an explicit plot to confound iden-tity or custody, it cannot be truly inadvertent. And because maternal iden-tity itself cannot usually be as mysterious as paternity, it is far more difficult to introduce the idea of questionable maternity after the fact and there are probably fewer potential permutations to a maternity-centered plot. While such secrets are not unheard of, it is far more difficult for a woman to hide a pregnancy than for a man to conceal a sexual liaison, and it is far easier to prove, whether through eyewitness testimony or medical examination that a woman has given birth than that a man has fathered a child. . . .

On the soaps, as in real life, paternity is more than a biological fact. It means inheritance of name and property, defines kinship patterns, and seems to carry the weight of loyalty, family traits, and even day-to-day behavior. On soap operas, the assimilation of all family members into the family of the father is so complete that, for example, a woman who mar-ries into a family often takes on whatever traits are typical of the new family. (On countless occasions on *General Hospital*, for instance, Monica Quartermaine has been referred to as a "real" Quartermaine, although she carries that name and identity only through her marriage to Alan.)

The fact that inheritance of wealth and property is so frequently the key to attributions and misattributions of paternity suggests that for so many soap opera women, the power to name the father represents a con-crete form of economic power. Although the attribution of paternity is often presented in terms of love, it is also often a question of money: If he thinks (or knows) this child is his, he'll have to marry me and give my child his name, money, and position. Or, from the child's point of view, the concealment of my father's identity has denied me access to money and power that are mine by right.

But the correct assignment of name and kinship position appears to be even more important, for questionable or misattributed paternity oc-curs even among soap opera characters of relatively modest means. When we remember soap operas' focus on private life and their construction of a closely knit community, the reason for this becomes clear: If the family is the most important structure in the world of the soaps, a character's

---

4. Mimi White argues that this kind of "retrofitting" is an important characteristic of soap opera narrative. See her "Women, Memory, and Serial Melodrama: Rewrit-ing/Reviewing History," paper delivered at the second annual conference, Console-ing Passions: Television, Video, and Feminism, Los Angeles, April 1993, from which my later page references come.

relationship to a particular family is a central pole of his or her identity. Despite the use of workplace settings and the relatively recent introduction of exotic mystery and suspense plots, romantic and family relationships and conflicts remain the storyline staples, and such conflicts make the exact definition of a character's position in the family crucial. Just how important it is for soap opera characters to know their precise kinship positions is underlined by the occasional threat of brother-sister incest posed by unknown or misattributed paternity—as occurred, for instance, not only in the *Young and the Restless* Cole-Victor storyline, but when, in 1989, Cricket Blair and her half-brother Scott Grainger fell in love on the same show, and several years earlier, on *All My Children,* between Erica Kane and her half-brother Mark Dalton.[5]

In the soap opera world, the power to define another person's family   15
position is often the only power women are permitted to exercise with impunity, and the only exertion of power that generates even short-term satisfaction. Although women characters wield other forms of power—through money, ownership of property or businesses, political influence, and so on—these women are usually villainesses, and they have often acquired financial or political power through marriage, divorce, or, more commonly, widowhood. "Good" women—even those who are wealthy and/or fully employed outside the home—exert power indirectly, primarily through family ties and most often by their private influence on other family members. This makes the ability to name and thereby control the father and define the family a crucial route to autonomy, however limited and temporary it may be.

The same larger context that identifies women's reproductive role as passive also defines soap opera women as dependent creatures. Women characters almost never achieve money, success, or political power through their own exertions, and if they do, it becomes insignificant in contrast to their unhappy personal lives. (Erica Kane is an archetypal example of this.) With few exceptions, women who would in the real world be seen as highly successful (such as prominent doctors and lawyers) expend all of their emotional energy sorting out their marriages, and seem to get little satisfaction and almost no public acclaim for their hard-won careers. In contrast, the men who seem so caught up in personal concerns continue at the same time to advance in their careers and to receive recognition and rewards for their performance in the public sphere. . . .

But as I've already suggested, the attribution of paternity is not only a function of power and money, for fatherhood is more than a social or economic role. Daytime soaps also posit an almost mystical bond between biological parents, and most notably, between father and child. (In

---

5. Mimi White calls this the "romantic incest plot" in "Women, Memory, and History," p. 36. See also Louise Spence, "Family, Limits, and Desire: Incest on Daytime Soap Operas," paper presented at the third annual conference, Console-ing Passions: Television, Video, and Feminism, Tucson, April 1994.

the words of *The Young and the Restless*'s Nikki Reed Newman Abbott, "Once you've had children with someone, you're just naturally interested in what happens to them. . . . It's human nature.")[6] Western culture tends to promote the idea that *mothers* and children experience such a bond, and recent feminist theory has paid particular attention to the mother-child relationship.[7] But the focus of the soap opera paternity plot is, fittingly for a mainstream product of patriarchal culture, the profound feelings that *fathers* experience. A man's discovery that he has fathered a child arouses a powerful sense of love and attachment, frequently drawing him to the child's mother—often regardless of his previous feelings for her or his ties to any other woman—and almost always drawing him to the newly recognized child. (In contrast, for example, to Dimitri Marrick's affection for Anton, which preexisted his discovery of their biological relationship, Erica expressed great concern over the fact that her realization that Kendall was her daughter did *not* prompt an upsurge of maternal emotion.) The soap opera assertion of the power exerted by all family ties is evident here, but such a plot invests paternal feelings with a special kind of significance and weight. For instance, the child may be presented as forcing a couple to admit their love for one another, but such "love" is frequently indistinguishable from lack of interest or even dislike before the pregnancy. Shared parenthood is sometimes even capable of overcoming all other considerations, including infidelity or other betrayals, and couples not only get married and stay together because of a child, they often stay *happily* married—or as happily married as the exigencies of the soaps permit.

The positing of this special bond between fathers and their children may be an important source of pleasurable fantasy for women viewers all too aware that, if the statistics on child-support payments are any indication, men in the "real" world do not universally feel (much less express) such attachment. Thus, it is possible to see the soap opera version of fatherhood as a particularly "feminized" one. Needless to say, however, the depth of fathers' feelings toward their children is never the route to a feminist transformation of the soap opera family into one characterized by equal parenting or a sharing of domestic responsibilities. Although soap opera men are obsessed with private concerns, this obsession never extends to an interest in the maintenance work that family life requires. (Of course, few soap opera women not clearly marked as working class actually perform this work either, and such domestic labor as is performed on-screen is usually done by housekeepers or other domestic helpers. Nevertheless, soap opera women are presented as bearing primary responsibility for the domestic routine through their planning of

---

6. All quotations are my transcriptions from program broadcasts.

7. See, for example, Nancy Chodorow, *The Reproduction of Mothering: Psychoanalysis and the Sociology of Gender* (Berkeley: University of California Press, 1978); and the writings of Adrienne Rich and Sarah Ruddick, among others.

parties, dinners, and holiday gatherings, and their direct supervision of household staff.) . . .

The mystique of the father-child bond is also demonstrated when a woman lies about a pregnancy or about her child's paternity in an attempt to force a man to marry her. Such situations usually rest on the woman's desire to make a man fall in love with her (although sometimes marriage alone is the goal), and her conviction that this will happen is one of the most stubborn feelings on the soaps. On *All My Children,* for instance, Natalie Hunter, pregnant by her recently deceased husband, claimed that her stepson and former lover Jeremy was actually the father, and insisted beyond all reason that his feelings for the child would lead inevitably to love for her. As always, a blood test resolved everything, but until that moment, no other arguments could persuade her that her belief was groundless — including Jeremy's obvious hatred of her, his commitment to another woman, and his suspicion (correct, as the audience knew) that he and Natalie had not actually had sex. Such insistence clearly draws on the folk convention that intense hatred is actually a cover for love. The fact is that this sometimes turns out to be true for soap opera characters makes it even more significant that "true love" never follows from a woman's lies about pregnancy or paternity.

These twists will all be familiar to any regular soap opera viewer. But the fact that, year after year, soap opera women intentionally misattribute paternity brings us back to the question of why a television genre directed primarily at women should emphasize fatherhood rather than motherhood. One plausible explanation is simply that these plots offer viewers an opportunity for the vicarious experience of power, permitting women simultaneously to acknowledge and to manage feelings of powerlessness and emotional deprivation, a function Janice Radway suggests is also performed by romance novels.[8] In contrast to the traditional male-dominated family of real life, where power resides in the husband/father, the soap opera family confers very real power on women: the power to name, or to misname, the father. While they are unable to act directly concerning their pregnancies, soap opera women hold the key to family relations and are therefore in a position, however briefly, to define the most important structure in the social world of these shows. Although their control over this structure may be temporary, and is always resolved by incontrovertible biological fact, these women exert a form of power denied to their male counterparts and thus offer the traditional soap opera viewer an opportunity to imagine a world in which women like themselves (i.e., centered on the family) are in control of the central fact of family life.

But this focus on paternity also provides evidence that, however much they may appear to be shaped by women's interests, soap operas

20

---

8. See, for example, Radway, *Reading the Romance,* p. 141.

are no more radical or woman-centered than any other form of mass-media commercial entertainment. Regardless of the degree of immediate disruption it may cause, the paternity plot always ends with restoration of family order. In fact, that very restoration demonstrates the strength of the traditional family, presented in soap operas as a structure able to withstand all assaults and to triumph in the face of the greatest threats.[9] Thus, despite the suggestions of critics like Modleski that the active villainesses of soap operas represent a significant departure from traditional portrayals of female passivity, both the constant eruption of the paternity theme and the meaning and prominence given to the inevitable identification of the father continually undermine whatever progressive or woman-centered message we might see in "evil" women shaping the circumstances of their lives. This, then, is the paternity plot's main role in soap operas' vivid restatement of patriarchal ideology.

But that role entails more than the simple repetition of the principle of male dominance. Viewers must have developed competence in understanding and predicting events on the programs to appreciate fully the intricacies of soap opera plots. In fact, it seems likely that a good deal of viewers' pleasure arises from the recognition that they are superior in knowledge to the shows' characters, a superiority that is especially evident in the presentation of the paternity plot, where regular viewers usually know (or can guess) the father's identity long before the father himself. Given the narrative importance of individual storylines' movement toward closure, this advantageous position is usually crucial to suspense, but at the same time, the very familiarity that aids in building this suspense includes a knowledge of how paternity plots are conventionally resolved. For experienced viewers, then, the pleasure of watching the mystery unfold must inevitably exist in tension with the realization that it will not remain a mystery for long. And most important for my reading of the paternity plot, that familiarity includes the recognition that whatever family-shaping power the woman has exerted will end when some particular man is finally identified as her baby's father.

It is, of course, profoundly ironic that women viewers should enjoy watching programs that recapitulate what some feminist theorists see as the first stage in women's oppression. As Hilary Radner points out, however, "to say that something is pleasurable for women does not ultimately justify this practice as feminist."[10] The fact that soap operas reenact as fact what in real life could until recently never be more than a myth—the absolute identity of the father—makes them a particularly striking

---

9. Contrast Ien Ang's comment that "[f]amily is not actually romanticized in soap operas; on the contrary, the imaginary ideal of the family as safe haven in a heartless world is constantly shattered," *Watching "Dallas,"* p. 69.

10. Hilary Radner, "Quality Television and Feminine Narcissism: The Shrew and the Covergirl," *Genders* 8 (Summer 1990): 123.

example of the way in which popular cultural forms restate and thereby indirectly reinforce the patriarchal status quo. (Perhaps the inevitable reiteration of the father's identity and power also helps to explain the popularity soaps have attained among male viewers.)

But I do not want to suggest that viewing soap operas is simply an exercise in masochism, for there is an important utopian aspect to the repeated reworkings of the paternity plot. I use "utopian" here in the same sense as Janice Radway (who has in turn adopted it from Fredric Jameson), to refer to an "oppositional moment" that permits readers—or in this case, viewers—to participate in a brief fantasy about a more satisfying world.[11] Although many other parts of the viewing experience contribute to women's pleasure in the soaps, I think that the paternity plot itself—or at least that part of it that precedes the final and absolute establishment of paternal identity—constitutes a significant aspect of the enjoyment. The pleasure it produces resides partly in the hope such a plot holds out that women *can* define the family structure, *can* attribute paternity with impunity, *can* name the father according to their own desires and without reference to blood tests. The centrality of the paternity plot also means that, even as the identity of one father is established, viewers can look forward to the eruption of another paternity mystery down the road—another opportunity, however short-lived, for utopian pleasure. If this is so, then the fantasies viewers spin about the shows they watch may be the most radical aspect of them.

However, as Radway repeatedly cautions, while its enjoyment depends on the (often unconscious) recognition of a basic dissatisfaction with things as they are, such a moment of opposition may in fact stand in the way of garnering support for a movement for social change, since it provides a temporary fulfillment of desires unmet in daily life. And the paternity plot's implication in this process goes far beyond its power to distract women from their complaints by offering a fictional substitute for social action. In my view, it is in fact one of the chief methods through which soap operas repress the very resistance women enjoy—not only by incorporating what might be a feminist or protofeminist utopian fantasy into an essentially conservative narrative, but by defusing and ultimately canceling out that fantasy through its inevitable resolution in favor of the father-centered family.

In what has been in part an effort to claim the soap opera as a genre worth taking seriously, feminist critics have tended to argue that its narrative or formal disruptions are sites at which the "feminine" successfully undermines the dominant, or to insist that the serial form and its attention to women's private concerns are themselves inherently progressive. Instead, I would argue that the genre of the soap opera is able simultane-

---

11. Radway, *Reading the Romance,* pp. 214–15.

ously to vent and to contain those concerns. Laura Mulvey has questioned the common assumption that contradiction automatically undermines ideology, pointing out that "[n]o ideology can even pretend to totality: it must provide an outlet for its own inconsistencies."[12] Her identification of 1950s melodramas as a "safety valve" for the contradictions inherent in the dominant ideology suggests a way of talking about television soap operas.

Mulvey's claim that "[i]deological contradiction is actually the overt mainspring and specific content of melodrama"[13] can, I think, be adapted to soap operas—with an important qualification. In soap operas, contradiction and disruption are raised as content but are then repeatedly smoothed over, resulting in a narrative that maintains rather than undermines the dominant ideology. While these shows allow for the play of women's fantasies—particularly through the workings of the paternity plot—and may therefore provide a pleasurable utopian dream-space, that space is finally both carefully managed and ultimately closed off by the reassertion of the conservative, male-centered ideology the genre promotes.

Reading the Text

1. Write a paragraph in which you outline the typical soap opera paternity plot, as Mumford describes it.
2. How does the paternity plot ultimately reassert a "conservative, male-centered ideology" (para. 27), according to Mumford?
3. In what ways do soap operas and romance novels offer women an experience of power that they lack in their everyday lives?
4. How does Mumford explain the greater appeal that paternity plots have in comparison to maternity plots?

Reading the Signs

1. If you watch daytime soap operas, reflect in your journal why they appeal to you.
2. Write an essay in which you support, refute, or complicate Mumford's assertion that the daytime soap opera "maintains rather than undermines the dominant ideology" (para. 27) of patriarchal society.
3. Read or reread Steven D. Stark's "*The Oprah Winfrey Show* and the Talk-Show Furor" (p. 241), and compare the way Winfrey's talk show and the soap opera appeal to female audiences. What myths and values does each evoke?

---

12. Laura Mulvey, "Notes on Sirk and Melodrama," in Gledhill, *Home Is Where the Heart Is,* p. 75.
13. Mulvey, "Notes on Sirk and Melodrama," p. 75.

4. In class, list current plot lines on daytime soap operas. What do these plots indicate about the desires, interests, and fantasies of their viewers?
5. Write an argumentative essay that supports or challenges the proposition that soap operas' appeal lies in their camp humor.

SUSAN DOUGLAS
Signs of Intelligent Life on TV

ΙΙΙΙΙΙΙΙΙΙΙΙΙΙΙΙΙΙΙΙΙΙΙΙΙΙΙΙΙΙΙΙΙΙΙΙΙΙΙΙΙΙΙΙΙΙΙΙΙ

Do you look for television programming that reflects an enlightened view of American women? Susan Douglas (b. 1950) does, and in this essay that originally appeared in Ms. *she reports her findings, which are mixed, at best. Although popular TV dramas like* ER *and* NYPD Blue *appear to present characters and plotlines that defy gender stereotypes, Douglas still finds the telltale signs of cultural bias against women in such programs—especially a bias against strong, professional women. When not watching TV, Douglas is a professor of communication studies at the University of Michigan and media critic for* The Progressive. *She is the author of* Where the Girls Are: Growing Up Female with the Mass Media *(1994) and* Inventing American Broadcasting, 1899–1922 *(1987).*

When the hospital show *ER* became a surprise hit, the pundits who had declared dramatic television "dead" were shocked. But one group wasn't surprised at all.

Those of us with jobs, kids, older parents to tend to, backed-up toilets, dog barf on the rug, and friends/partners/husbands we'd like to say more than "hi" to during any diurnal cycle don't have much time to watch television. And when we do—usually after 9:38 P.M.—we have in recent years been forced to choose between Diane Sawyer interviewing Charles Manson or Connie Chung chasing after Tonya [Harding] and Nancy [Kerrigan]. People like me, who felt that watching the newsmagazines was like exposing yourself to ideological smallpox, were starved for some good escapist drama that takes you somewhere else yet resonates with real life and has ongoing characters you care about.

When *NYPD Blue* premiered in the fall of 1993 with the tough-but-sensitive John Kelly, and featuring strong, accomplished women, great lighting, bongo drums in the sound track, and male nudity, millions sighed with relief. When *ER* hit the air, we made it one of the tube's highest rated shows. Tagging farther behind, but still cause for hope, is another hospital drama, *Chicago Hope.*

All three shows acknowledge the importance of the adult female audience by featuring women as ongoing characters who work for a living and by focusing on contemporary problems in heterosexual relationships (no, we haven't yet achieved everyday homosexual couples on TV). More to the point, hound-dog-eyed, emotionally wounded yet eager-to-talk-it-through guys are center stage. So what are we getting when we kick back and submerge ourselves in these dramas? And what do they have to say about the ongoing project of feminism?

For those of you who don't watch these shows regularly, here's a   5
brief précis: *NYPD Blue* is a cop show set in New York City and has producer Steven Bochco's signature style—lots of shaky, hand-held camera work, fast-paced editing (supported by the driving, phallic backbeat in the sound track), and multiple, intersecting plots about various crimes and the personal lives of those who work in the precinct. Last season there were more women in the show; and last season there was John Kelly.

This year, the show is more masculinized. Watching Bobby Simone, played by Jimmy Smits, earn his right to replace Kelly was like witnessing a territorial peeing contest between weimaraners. Bobby had to be as sensitive and emotionally ravaged as Johnny, so in an act of New Age male one-upmanship, the scriptwriters made him a widower who had lost his wife to breast cancer. But Bobby had to be one tough customer too, so soon after we learn of his wife's death, we see him throwing some punks up against a fence, warning them that he will be their personal terminator unless they stop dealing drugs.

ER has the same kind of simultaneous, intersecting story lines, served up with fast-tracking cameras that sprint down hospital corridors and swirl around operating tables like hawks on speed. And there are the same bongo drums and other percussive sounds when patients are rushed in for treatment. *Chicago Hope* is *ER* on Valium: stationary cameras, slower pace, R&B instead of drumbeats. It's also *ER* on helium or ether, kind of a *Northern Exposure* goes to the hospital, with more offbeat plots and characters, like a patient who eats his hair or a kid whose ear has fallen off.

Whenever I like a show a lot—meaning I am there week in and week out—I figure I have once again embraced a media offering with my best and worst interests at heart. Dramatic TV shows, which seek a big chunk of the middle- and upper-income folks between 18 and 49, need to suck in those women whose lives have been transformed by the women's movement (especially women who work outside the home and have disposable income) while keeping the guys from grabbing the remote. What we get out of these twin desires is a blend of feminism and antifeminism in the plots and in the female characters. And for the male characters we have an updated hybrid of masculinity that crossbreeds decisiveness, technical expertise, and the ability to throw a punch or a basketball, with a soft spot for children and a willingness to cry.

On the surface, these shows seem good for women. We see female cops, lawyers, doctors, and administrators, who are smart, efficient, and successful. But in too many ways, the women take a backseat to the boys. In *NYPD Blue,* for example, we rarely see the women actually doing their jobs. The overall message in the three shows is that, yes, women can be as competent as men, but their entrance into the workforce has wrecked the family and made women so independent and hard-hearted that dealing with them and understanding them is impossible. Despite this, they're still the weaker sex.

In *ER* it is Carol Hathaway (Julianna Margulies), the charge nurse,   10
who tried to commit suicide. It is Dr. Susan Lewis (Sherry Stringfield) who is taken in by an imposter who claims to be a hospital administrator. Dr. Lewis is also the only resident who has trouble standing up to white, male authority figures: she is unable to operate while the head cardiologist watches her. In *Chicago Hope,* a psychiatrist prevails upon a female nurse to dress up like Dorothy (ruby slippers, pigtails, and all) because a patient refusing surgery is a *Wizard of Oz* junkie. Even though she points out that no male doctor would be asked to do anything like it, the shrink insists she continue the masquerade because the patient's life is at stake. Here's the crucial guilt-shifting we've all come to know and love — this patient's illness is somehow more her responsibility than anyone else's. Her humiliation is necessary to save him.

The Ariel Syndrome — Ariel was the name of Walt Disney's little mermaid, who traded her voice for a pair of legs so that she could be with a human prince she'd seen from afar for all of ten seconds — grips many of the women, who have recurring voice problems. Watch out for female characters who "don't want to talk about it," who can't say no, who don't speak up. They make it even harder for the women who do speak their minds, who are, of course, depicted as "bitches."

One major "bitch" is the wife of *ER*'s Dr. Mark Greene (Anthony Edwards). He's a doctor who's barely ever home, she's a lawyer who lands a great job two hours away, and they have a seven-year-old. Those of us constantly negotiating about who will pick up the kids or stay late at work can relate to this. The problem is that *ER* is about *his* efforts to juggle, *his* dreams and ambitions. We know this guy, we like him, we know he's a great doctor who adores his wife and child. Her, we don't know, and there's no comparable female doctor to show the woman's side of this equation. As a result, when conflicts emerge, the audience is primed to want her to compromise (which she's already done, so he can stay at the job he loves). When she insists he quit his job and relocate, she sounds like a spoiled child more wedded to a rigid quid pro quo than to flexibility, love, the family. It's the conservative view of what feminism has turned women into — unfeeling, demanding blocks of granite.

One of the major themes of all three shows is that heterosexual relationships are a national disaster area. And it's the women's fault. Take *NYPD Blue.* Yes, there's the fantasy relationship between Andy Sipowicz

(Dennis Franz) and Sylvia Costas (Sharon Lawrence), in which an accomplished woman helps a foul-mouthed, brutality-prone cop with really bad shirts get in touch with his feelings and learn the pleasures of coed showering. While this affair has become the emotional anchor of the show, it is also the lone survivor in the ongoing gender wars.

It looks like splitsville for most of the show's other couples. Greg Medavoy (Gordon Clapp) infuriates Donna Abandando (Gail O'Grady) by his behavior, which includes following her to see whom she's having lunch with. She's absolutely right. But after all the shots of Greg looking at her longingly across the office (again, we're inside his head, not hers), the audience is encouraged to think that she should give the guy a break. By contrast, her explanations of why she's so angry and what she wants have all the depth and emotional warmth of a Morse code message tapped out by an iguana. Of course Greg doesn't understand. She won't help him.

In this world, female friendships are nonexistent or venomous. And   15 there is still worse ideological sludge gumming up these shows. Asian and Latina women are rarely seen, and African American women are also generally absent except as prostitutes, bad welfare moms, and unidentified nurses. In the *ER* emergency room, the black women who are the conscience and much-needed drill sergeants of the show don't get top billing, and are rarely addressed by name. There is also an overabundance of bad mothers of all races: adoptive ones who desert their kids, abusive ones who burn their kids, and hooker ones (ipso facto bad). Since the major female characters—all upper-middle class—don't have kids, we don't see their struggles to manage motherhood and work. And we certainly don't see less privileged moms (the real majority in the U.S.), like the nurses or office workers, deal with these struggles on a lot less money.

One of the worst things these shows do, under a veneer of liberalism and feminism, is justify the new conservatism in the U.S. The suspects brought in for questioning on *NYPD Blue* are frequently threatened and sometimes beaten, but it's O.K. because they all turn out to be guilty, anyway. Legal representation for these witnesses is an unspeakable evil because it hides the truth. After a steady diet of this, one might assume the Fourth Amendment, which prohibits unreasonable search and seizure, is hardly worth preserving.

So why are so many women devoted to these shows? First off, the women we do see are more successful, gutsy, more fully realized than most female TV characters. But as for me, I'm a sucker for the men. I want to believe, despite all the hideous evidence to the contrary, that some men have been humanized by the women's movement, that they have become more nurturing, sensitive, and emotionally responsible. I want to believe that patriarchy is being altered by feminism. Since I get zero evidence of this on the nightly news, I want a few hours a week when I can escape into this fantasy.

Of course, we pay a price for this fantasy. TV depicts "real men" being feminized for the better and women masculinized for the worse.

The message from the guys is, "We became the kind of men you feminists said that you wanted, and now you can't appreciate us because you've forgotten how to be a 'real' woman." It's a bizarre twist on the real world, where many women have changed, but too many men have not. Nevertheless, in TV land feminism continues to hoist itself with its own petard. Big surprise.

Reading the Text

1. What does Douglas mean by saying that "watching the newsmagazines was like exposing yourself to ideological smallpox" (para. 2), and what attitude toward the media does this comment reveal?
2. Why, according to Douglas, are professional women attracted to programs such as *ER* and *NYPD Blue*?
3. What, according to Douglas, is the overt message about gender roles communicated by the TV shows she discusses? What is the hidden message?
4. How are non-Caucasian women presented in *ER* and *NYPD Blue*, according to Douglas, and what is her opinion about their presentation?
5. How does Douglas view the "new conservatism in the U.S." (para. 16)?

Reading the Signs

1. Watch an episode of *ER* or *NYPD Blue,* and write an argumentative essay in which you support, refute, or modify Douglas's belief that the show, despite superficial nods at feminism, perpetuates traditional gender roles.
2. In class, brainstorm TV shows that portray women as professionals or in other responsible, intelligent roles. Then, using Douglas's argument as your starting point, discuss whether the shows really adopt a feminist or an antifeminist stance in portraying female characters.
3. In your journal, discuss your favorite prime-time TV show, exploring exactly what you find attractive about the program.
4. Apply Douglas's argument to the films Sandra Tsing Loh discusses in "The Return of Doris Day" (p. 357). To what extent is the good-girl motif that Loh describes symptomatic of the covert antifeminism that Douglas decries?
5. Watch a TV show that focuses on young adult characters. Do you see evidence of the covert antifeminism that Douglas describes? What does the treatment of female characters say about the show's presumed audience? Use your findings as evidence in an analytical essay about how the show depicts women.
6. Do you see any evidence of covert antifeminism in advertising? Write an essay in which you explore the depiction of women in advertising, focusing perhaps on ads in a woman's magazine such as *Elle* or *Vogue*. To develop your argument, consult Gloria Steinem's "Sex, Lies, and Advertising" (p. 160).

JIMMIE L. REEVES,
MARK C. RODGERS,
AND MICHAEL EPSTEIN

Rewriting Popularity: The Cult Files

||||||||||||||||||||||||||||||||||||||||||||||||||

Like Star Trek *before it,* The X-Files *has become a full-fledged cult classic, complete with Internet bulletin boards, fan conventions, and marketing tie-ins like clothing lines and coffee mugs. In this essay, which originally appeared in* Deny All Knowledge: Reading the X-Files *(1996), Jimmie L. Reeves, Mark C. Rodgers, and Michael Epstein analyze the popularity of* The X-Files *(and other cult TV programs) in the context of an historical survey of the postwar history of television. This history was marked, the authors argue, by a shift from mass-marketed programming to the "niche" approach in which TV shows are designed for selected audiences with particular market appeal to potential sponsors. Michael Epstein and Mark C. Rodgers are Ph.D. candidates in American culture at the University of Michigan; Jimmie L. Reeves is an assistant professor of communication at Texas Tech University and is the author (with Dick Campbell) of* Cracked Coverage: Television News, the Anti-Cocaine Crusade, and the Reagan Legacy *(1994).*

I also know that your publishing house is owned by Warden-White, Inc., a subsidiary of McDougall-Kessler, which makes me suspect a covert agenda on the behalf of the military-industrial-entertainment complex.

—MULDER, in "Jose Chung's *From Outer Space*"

In our chart of the family tree of cult TV, diehard supporters of the Dallas Cowboys and rabid followers of the World Wrestling Federation are positioned as their beer-swilling uncles. Their homebound aunts organize weekday routines around the intrigues of *Days of Our Lives* or *All My Children.* Rush Limbaugh's Ditto Heads and Jerry Garcia's Dead Heads are their first cousins. Offspring of the Trekkie clan, their siblings include disciples of *Twin Peaks, Mystery Science Theater 3000,* and *Beavis and Butthead.* Because of their fondness of Fox's *The X-Files,* they call themselves "X-Philes" — and because of their high profile on the express lane of the information superhighway, they have generated a great deal of media attention, putting stars Gillian Anderson (Dana Scully) and David Duchovny (Fox Mulder) on the covers of *People, TV Guide,* and a host of other magazines that hope to cash in on the cult.

There is, indeed, a lot of cash in them thar *Files*/Philes. Directly connecting the marketing of *X-Files* paraphernalia to the *Star Trek* gold rush, *People* observes that "Like *Star Trek, X-Files* has spawned novels, comic books, T-shirts (emblazoned with the show's motto, The Truth Is Out There), coffee mugs and Internet bulletin boards" (Gliatto and Tomashoff, 74). Moreover, in reporting the franchising frenzy, the popular press often describes the consumers of *X-Files* merchandise in predatory terms. For instance, *TV Guide* opens its cover story on "20 Things You Need to Know about *The X-Files*" with a rather unflattering comparison: "Fans of *The X-Files* crave information the way mutant flukes crave human flesh" (Nollinger, 18). In the tradition of William Shatner's famous "get a life" renunciation of Trekkies on *Saturday Night Live,* Duchovny publicly keeps his distance from these voracious creatures who hunger for his image, if not his flesh. As item 10 of the *TV Guide* article reports, Duchovny believes that the "Internet enthusiasts have a tendency to sometimes get a little out of control": "During one discussion, perplexed fans tried to figure out why Scully never adjusts the car seat after the much taller Mulder has been driving. 'That was probably the last time I ever looked at the Internet, because that kind of frightened me,' Duchovny says, 'I didn't want to see myself scrutinized in such a fashion.'" However, creator and executive producer Chris Carter is more honest—or at least more self-conscious—about his own entanglement in promoting X-mania. In a bit of soul-searching that appears in the liner notes of *Songs in the Key of X,* Carter reverses the predator/prey roles assigned by *TV Guide:* "Here I go searching for context and corollary, reason and rationale—writer's crampons. Why an '*X-Files*' record, album, or CD? Why indeed. Have we succumbed to the swinish flu of grubbing moneymakers who see dollar signs like a fever dream, an endless sea of swag stamped with the eponymous 'X'; the spiders to the flies of the New World Wide Web Order, for whom mammon is its own impenetrable logic, a one-word syllogism?"

As authors of this article, we have asked ourselves the same question, and arrived at roughly the same "Yes, but" answer. Yes, we too are implicated, like it or not, in exploiting the *X-Files* phenomenon; but, like Carter, we evade feelings of guilt by thinking of ourselves as altruistic arachnoids who are on a mission to make the snares of the web—and their attachments to larger entrapments—visible to the flies. Weaving our own account of cult TV's significance around Carter's acknowledgment that "mammon" is the "impenetrable logic" underlying this peculiar programming trend, we enlist the *Star Trek/X-Files* genealogy to explore the political and textual economies of what Agent Mulder has described as the "military-industrial-entertainment complex." Without endorsing Mulderesque conspiracy theories involving ominous Men in Black or sinister chain-smoking operatives, we want to make it clear that the current prominence of cult TV is still no harmless freak show in the carnival of American popular culture. Instead, it is a phenomenon that speaks powerfully of a divisive system of taste distinctions that both supports and masks the radical inequities of the age by dividing the audience into "insiders" and "outsiders." . . .

Fordism, TV I, and *Star Trek*

Yet, as we also hope to demonstrate, *The X-Files* differs from most other cult television shows in that it represents a step back toward the inclusiveness of TV I. A shorthand term for the broadcasting system that emerged in the 1950s, triumphed in the 1960s, and was slowly displaced in the 1970s, the term "TV I" refers to what has also been studied as "network era television." A period dominated by a three-corporation oligopoly, TV I played a central ideological role in promoting the ethic of consumption, naturalizing the nuclear family ideal, selling suburbanization, sustaining cold war paranoia, publicizing the Civil Rights movement, and managing social upheaval. Put another way, TV I was one of the chief products and producers of Fordism—a "rigid" economic order (named for Henry Ford) that drove the general prosperity of the postwar boom through an expansive manufacturing economy of assembly-line production and mass consumption.

As an expression of Fordism, television popularity during this period   5 was defined in terms of audience size as measured in the brute numbers of ratings and shares. Consequently, the prime-time schedule was dominated by Westerns, situation comedies, and crime shows, all designed to attract the largest possible undifferentiated viewership. Of course, many have condemned programming during TV I as "mass culture" or a "vast wasteland," but, whatever its faults, the "least objectionable programming" (or more cynically, "lowest common denominator") philosophy made sense—and also astounding profits—for the three major networks. At the same time, the definition of popularity underlying this programming philosophy resulted in the prime-time schedule evolving into a nightly showcase for what David Thorburn calls "consensus narrative," stories that attempt to speak for, and to, the core values of American culture (167–68).

Star Trek, like the Super Bowl, the *Tonight Show,* and *60 Minutes,* is a relic of TV I. Unlike these other cultural institutions, however, *Star Trek* was initially considered to be an "unpopular" failure by its home network. NBC premiered *Star Trek* on September 8, 1966, and nationwide broadcasts of the original network episodes were not able to attract large (enough) audiences: in its initial run of two and one-half seasons, *Star Trek* never made it into the top twenty highest-rated shows and frequently finished last in its timeslot against ABC's and CBS's offerings (Alexander, 366). In retrospect, though, as the harbinger of a radically new type of popularity—a type of popularity that would govern television programming in the postnetwork era—*Star Trek* is significant for three related reasons: its prototype status in the history of cult TV; the fanaticism of its avid followers; and its place in the syndication of revolution of the 1970s.

What separated *Star Trek* from its peers and its predecessors and even now establishes it as classic cult TV is audience engagement. . . . According to our scheme, nearly all entertainment programs attract three different kinds of viewers who can be categorized in terms of engagement: casual viewers, devoted viewers, and avid fans.

■   Casual viewers will attend to a show if they happen to be watching TV but do not experience the show as a "special event." For the casual viewer, the show is part of the flow of television and not something that requires rapt attention nor prompts adjustments in the viewer's schedule of activities in order to tune in. Because of the limited range of viewing options during TV I, casual viewing was, probably, the dominant type of engagement with prime-time programming in the 1950s and 1960s.

■   Devoted viewers will make arrangements to watch every episode of their favorite show. For the devoted viewer, a favorite show is a "special event" that disrupts the flow of television and inspires more intense levels of identification and attention than typical television fare. However, though the devoted viewer may read occasional articles about the show or talk about it with their friends, their involvement with the show falls short of fanaticism. Because of the drastically expanded range of viewing options, devoted viewing is probably more common now than in the network era. In fact, it could be argued that the serialization of prime time (as exemplified by shows like *Dallas, Hill Street Blues, ER*) is at least partially attributable to the heightened competition for viewer attention in the TV II era—a competition that has encouraged the networks to develop programming forms that inspire devoted rather than casual engagement.

■   Avid fans will not only take special pains to watch every episode of   10 the show but, today, will tape the episodes so that they can review them or even archive them. The show is not only a special event but also a major source of self-definition, a kind of quasi-religious experience. Avid fans enthusiastically purchase or consume ancillary texts related to the program and often join interpretive communities that have formed around the show, such as fan clubs, online discussion groups, and APAs (American Press Association). Though the availability of such groups in cyberspace has made the recruitment process somewhat easier, it is still difficult for a new show to build "cult" interpretive communities from scratch. Therefore, most new shows hoping to cultivate a cult following tend to appeal to existing interpretive communities, particularly the large umbrella of sci-fi fandom which has in place an infrastructure of fanzines, newsgroups, and conventions. In TV I, daytime serials and professional sports programming may be considered as antecedents to cult television in that they cultivated the kind of enthusiastic viewer engagement that is characteristic of the avid fan. . . .

As early as spring 1967, before *Star Trek* had completed its first season, it was becoming clear to both cast and crew that the series had developed a fan base unlike that of other, more highly rated prime-time shows. The first indication that there was something strikingly different about the *Star Trek* audience was the volume of mail that arrived at the studio after each episode aired (Nichols, 188). The deluge—which, according to some cast members, was measured in rooms full of mail—seemed far out of proportion to the total estimated number of viewers reported by Nielsen each week (Nichols, 162; Takei, 247). In addition to the typical fan requests for photos and autographs, a sizable number of the first generation of *Star Trek* fans wrote longer letters that detailed their opinions, suggestions, complaints, and questions about a character, an episode, or the direction of the show in general.

This extraordinary audience engagement quickly caught the attention of the show's creator, Gene Roddenberry. As recently published letters from the Roddenberry archives suggest, Roddenberry took fan letters seriously and made a practice of responding to the more salient comments of fans and critics alike (see, e.g., Alexander, 307–8). Roddenberry was impressed by the caliber of the people who were writing what he considered the best letters, many of whom were college students, professionals, and scientists. As NBC's pressure to cancel the series grew more intense, Roddenberry turned to a small cadre of these discriminating fans in order to save his brainchild. While keeping his distance publicly, *Star Trek*'s creator carried out a covert strategy of inviting fan leaders to the studio, underwriting some of the costs of fan club activities, orchestrating a letter-writing campaign to the network, and even appearing incognito at fan pickets of NBC (Alexander, 301–14; Takei, 264). In the short term, the strategy resulted in the series being renewed for a second season; in the long term, even though the next year Roddenberry lost the battle to keep his show on the air, he ultimately won the war by galvanizing fan demand for future incarnations of *Star Trek*.

United in their affinity for the *Star Trek* universe and buoyed by the apparent impact they had on Roddenberry and NBC, the loyal Trek fans of the late 1960s continued to stay active even after the series closed production. Fan groups founded "zines" devoted to fan-authored *Star Trek* stories, convened fan meetings that would later be called conventions, and continued to petition the television establishment to revive the series. Active fan interest helped speed *Star Trek* reruns into syndication within months of cancellation, notwithstanding the show's short run of 79 episodes (Alexander, 377). By December 1971, *Star Trek* was airing in more than one hundred local television markets in the United States and seventy more internationally (Beerman, 1, 69). By 1977, after eight years in syndication, *Star Trek* was aired in 134 American markets and 131 overseas, was aired 308 times a week, and was the number one offnetwork show for men ages 18 to 49 (Alexander, 447). In daily reruns, Roddenberry's "Wagon Train of the stars" finally got the exposure it needed to attract a huge number of new viewers, many of whom found it easy and appealing to become active participants in the established fan culture as "Trekkies" or "Trekkers." The result was that *Star Trek* fandom became even more vibrant and pervasive (see, e.g., Jenkins 19–22, 185–86,

193–94). In short, the extraordinary audience engagement generated by *Star Trek* in the 1960s had been transformed into a full-fledged cult by the mid-1970s—and in the process, Paramount became the preeminent syndicator in the industry, completely altering the marketing structure for offnetwork series television and ushering in a new economics of popularity associated with the systematic fragmentation of television's mass audience into lifestyle sectors, psychographic segments, and niche markets.

Post-Fordism, TV II, and *The X-Files*

In the 1970s, as Fordism's manufacturing economy was traumatized by the end of the Vietnam War, oil embargoes, inflation, and deindustrialization, a new economic order emerged—an order that David Harvey identifies as "flexible accumulation" (141–72) and others simply call "post-Fordism." As the name implies, flexible accumulation departs drastically from the rigidities of the Fordist order. Displacing the long-term stabilities of Fordism with the instabilities of short-term engagement, flexible accumulation promotes a fundamental shift in collective norms and beliefs toward the values of an entrepreneurial culture based on old-fashioned competitive individualism. Oriented on windfall profits, hit-and-run marketing, and "paper entrepreneurialism," these values emphasize (in Harvey's words) "the new, the fleeting, the ephemeral, the fugitive, and the contingent in modern life, rather than the more solid values implanted under Fordism" (171). On the supply side, flexible accumulation has been marked by expansions of the service sector (most notably, in the private health-care, banking, real estate, fast-food, and entertainment industries), accelerations in the pace of product innovation, reductions in turnover time, and—most significantly for this essay—explorations of highly specialized market niches. On the demand side, it has entailed what Mike Davis terms "overconsumptionism" (156). Indeed, the relationship between Fordism's classic consumerism and post-Fordism's fashionable overconsumptionism is roughly analogous to the relationship between what we have described as TV I's casual viewing and cult TV's avid fanship.

Just as TV I was one of the chief products and producers of Fordism, TV II exhibits a complicated product/producer relationship with post-Fordism. In other words, TV II's combination satellite and cable distribution system, augmented by remote controls, personal computers, and video cassette recorders, in conforming to the grand logic of flexible accumulation has also played a decisive role in naturalizing that logic and promoting the values of its overconsumptionism. Ironically, in the transformation from TV I to TV II, the three networks that dominated the first three decades of television found themselves caught in roughly the same vulnerable situation experienced by Hollywood's major studios during the chaotic years attending the arrival of broadcast TV—that is, the networks, like the major studios before them, were forced to witness the disturbing spectacle of their audiences fragmenting and dissipating before their very eyes. Where once ABC, NBC, and CBS commanded over 90 percent of the audience, today the major network audience has decreased to about 60 percent.

Several developments in the 1970s prepared the way for the new television order. In sync with the syndication revolution, a new paradigm in programming strategy emerged in the early 1970s. Whereas the "lowest common denominator" philosophy had defined popularity in terms of brute ratings, the emergent philosophy reshaped popularity in terms of the quest for "quality demographics"—a giant step toward the "niche audience" strategies of the 1980s and 1990s. One of the earliest manifestations of this emergent view of popularity was CBS's "rural purge" in 1971, the cancellation of highly rated shows (most notably *Mayberry*

R.F.D. and *Hee Haw*) because they did not attract segments of the population that were most valued by advertisers. According to Jane Feuer, the cancellation of the "hayseed" comedies signaled the industry's reconceptualization of the audience not as "an aggregate or mass" but as a "differentiated mass possessing identifiable demographic categories": "'Popularity' came to mean high ratings with the eighteen- to forty-nine-year-old urban dweller, rather than popularity with the older rural audience" (152). The emergent regime of popularity, in Feuer's estimation, is largely responsible for the reinvention of the sitcom genre by Norman Lear and MTM Productions in the 1970s.

In the early 1980s, this "quality demographic" view of popularity also sponsored the narrative innovations of *Magnum, P.I.* Celebrated by Horace Newcomb as a new form of episodic storytelling, *Magnum* is a "cumulative narrative." Like the traditional series and unlike the traditional "open-ended" serial, each installment of a cumulative narrative has a distinct beginning, middle, and end; however, unlike the traditional series and like the traditional serial, one episode's events can greatly affect later episodes. As Newcomb puts it, "Each week's program is distinct, yet each is grafted onto the body of the series, its characters' pasts" ("*Magnum,*" 24). In its straddling of the series and serial forms, *Magnum* stands as an important noncult antecedent to *The X-Files.*

In addition to the refinement of cumulative narrative, the networks' pursuit of sophisticated viewers with money to burn has provided economic incentive for supporting other narrative innovations that are often labeled "postmodern." This incentive, combined with television's maturation as a storytelling medium and the parallel maturation of the "television generation," has made TV II an era when talented producers are rewarded for exploring and blurring generic boundaries. This revisioning (or blurred visioning) of the American television experience can be discerned in the hybridization of the cop show, the tabloidization of the news, and the carnivalization of the Super Bowl—but it is most clearly manifested in the current prominence of cult TV.

By the 1990s, two general types of cult television shows had emerged. The first type, in the tradition of *Star Trek,* is comprised of prime-time network programs that failed to generate large ratings numbers but succeeded in attracting substantial numbers of avid fans. *Twin Peaks* is the most outstanding recent example of this category. By contrast, shows of the second type first appear on cable or in fringe timeslots and are narrowly targeted at a niche audience. Comedy Central's *Mystery Science Theater 3000* and MTV's *Beavis & Butthead* exemplify this category of cult programming that was never intended to appeal to a mass audience.

In many ways, *The X-Files* represents a new model of cult television, due to its placement on Fox. Fox, at least at the time that *The X-Files* was introduced, was in a mediate position between the network prime-time model and the cable/fringe/syndication market. While Fox had little possibility of creating a ratings juggernaut like *Roseanne* or *Home Improve-*

ment, it still could not afford to run a show like *Mystery Science Theater 3000* that attracted such a small (though fanatically devoted) audience. Although Fox would have been perfectly happy if *The X-Files* were a top ten show, they initially conceived of the program as a candidate for cult status, hoping that (like *Star Trek* and *Star Trek: The Next Generation*) the relatively small avid viewership of the program would gradually build to a respectably large audience. This strategy has proven successful, as *The X-Files* is now among the most popular shows on Fox and is well on its way to becoming a genuine mass hit.

Fox has also taken advantage of *The X-Files'* cult success in other ways. Active fans consume ancillary products, and so Fox has licensed a wide variety of *X-Files* merchandise, ranging from novels and comic books to coffee mugs and clothing. Fox has also used the show to promote some of its other media holdings. In Britain, first-run episodes of the series appear only on Sky One, part of Rupert Murdoch's satellite network. Fox also attempted to use *The X-Files* to promote Delphi, its online service; Delphi became the official online home of *The X-Files,* and writers and producers were encouraged to frequent the discussion areas related to the show. By using the show's cult status to multiply its revenue streams, Fox has taken away some of the pressure on *The X-Files* to be a ratings hit. . . .

Despite being on the brink of mass success, *The X-Files* still shares a number of characteristics with other cult programs, particularly in its narrative structure and audience engagement. *The X-Files* has been especially canny in courting several preexisting fan cultures. Most importantly, the show's generic migrations allow it to appeal to a variety of subgroups within sci-fi fandom. The omnipresent discussion of UFOs and aliens brings its own particular group of fans to the show, as does the incorporation of high-tech, hard science elements in the plotlines of episodes like "Roland," "Ghost in the Machine," and "Soft Light." The frequent plots dealing with serial killers and/or the supernatural draw in fans from the horror/dark fantasy fan groups that exist on the margins of sci-fi fandom. Dana Scully, clearly patterned after Agent Starling in *Silence of the Lambs,* represents in many ways the traditional scientist hero of classic sci-fi. She is an expert in one scientific area, forensic pathology, but has a mastery of the scientific method that allows her to venture outside her specialty. *The X-Files* has also aggressively courted the fans of television's most spectacular cult failure, *Twin Peaks.* Beyond the obvious connection through David Duchovny, who played the transvestite DEA agent Dennis/Denise Bryson in *Twin Peaks,* both shows have at their center a brilliant if quirky FBI agent who believes in the supernatural. A number of actors have appeared in both series: *Twin Peaks*'s Michael Horse (Deputy Hawk), Michael J. Anderson (Man from Another Place), and Kenneth Welsh (Windom Earle) appeared in the *X-Files* episodes "Shapes," "Humbug," and "Revelations," respectively. Don Davis (*Twin Peaks*'s Major Garland Briggs) appeared in "Beyond the Sea" as Scully's father, now a naval captain rather than an air force major.

Judging by the amount of carryover between the two fan communities, *The X-Files* has been at least moderately successful in courting the *Twin Peaks* audience. There are several examples of fan fiction crossovers between the two programs, the most notable being Peggy Mei-Ling Li's "Out of the Woods." The alt.tv.x-files newsgroup frequently contains rumors about possible *Twin Peaks/X-Files* crossovers, which probably represent more wishful thinking than anything else. *Wrapped in Plastic,* the premiere *Twin Peaks* fanzine, devoted an entire issue to *The X-Files* and features a regular column that reports on the show.

Of course, *The X-Files* shares some other properties of previous cult shows. It is both difficult and uncommon to be able to deal with a series in holistic fashion because of the sheer breadth of the narrative. The engagement of the fan audience with cult television, however, through reviewing and discussion, goes far beyond the hour the program is on the air. This leads to a focus on minutia within the program between episodes. Fan fascination with *The X-Files* is generally either fixed on certain elements of the program (as exemplified by the David Duchovny Estrogen Brigade, a fan group infatuated with the male star) or on particular episodes (often the current ones, although fans will often cite earlier episodes or scenes when references are made to them in new episodes). Though the series is less quirky and quotable than *Twin Peaks,* fans of *The X-Files* do remember certain scenes (Scully eating the cricket in "Humbug") or certain lines (an archive of Mulderisms and Scullyisms exists online).

Obviously, Chris Carter and the other producers of *The X-Files* [25] learned from the failures of *Twin Peaks,* particularly in terms of taking a different narrative strategy. Serial elements are important in a cult show because they reward regular viewers and give reasons for reviewing earlier episodes. At the same time, programs that are continuously serial may alienate new viewers who lack knowledge of events in previous episodes. Once the initial luster of *Twin Peaks* wore off, the show began to hemorrhage viewers; because it was a continuous serial, it was difficult to recruit new viewers to replace the deserters.

The X-Files, like *Magnum,* walks an intermediate path between the episodic series and the open-ended serial, one that is for the most part episodic but in which certain ongoing plotlines carry across episodes and even seasons. Consequently, *The X-Files* qualifies as a cumulative narrative (or what Marc Dolan [34] terms a "sequential series"). *The X-Files* has dealt with the problem of recruiting new viewers by presenting self-contained installments that feature only minor references to continuous plotlines, like the appearances of Mr. X in "Soft Light" or the Lone Gunmen in "Fearful Symmetry." At the same time, the program continues to tell a serial story in the linked episodes that deal with UFOs, the government conspiracy, and the disappearance of Samantha Mulder. These episodes (the pilot, "Deep Throat," "Fallen Angel," "E.B.E.," and "The Erlenmeyer Flask" from season one; "Little Green Men," "Duane

Barry"/"Ascension," "One Breath," "Colony"/"Endgame," and "Anasazi" from season two; "The Blessing Way"/"Paper Clip," "Nisei"/ "731," and "Piper Maru"/"Apocrypha" from season three), while each somewhat self-contained, form a sort of mini-serial within the series.

By shifting gears between the serial and the episodic, *The X-Files* self-consciously rewards avid fans by drawing on the continuity of previous episodes, hence validating their diligent viewing, while at the same time welcoming new audience members since most of the plotlines don't rely on previous knowledge of the series. In fact, *The X-Files* is even able to switch gears within the same episode. In "F. Emasculata," the mysterious Cancer Man argues with Mulder about whether the FBI should have made a public disclosure about the deadly plague carried by two ex-convicts. While fans of the show will read this exchange in light of their knowledge of the history of the interaction between Mulder and Cancer Man, the episode is constructed so the interchange is still comprehensive and not alienating to first-time viewers.

WORKS CITED

Alexander, David. *"Star Trek" Creator: The Authorized Biography of Gene Roddenberry.* New York: Rock, 1994.

Dolan, Marc. "The Peaks and Valleys of Serial Creativity: What Happened to/on *Twin Peaks.*" In *Full of Secrets: Critical Approaches to "Twin Peaks,"* edited by David Lavery, 30–50. Detroit: Wayne State Univ. Press, 1994.

Feuer, Jane. "Genre Study and Television." In *Channels of Discourse, Reassembled: Television and Contemporary Criticism,* edited by Robert C. Allen, 138–59. Chapel Hill: Univ. of North Carolina Press, 1992.

Gliatto, Tom, and Craig Tomashoff. "X-Ellence." *People Weekly,* Oct. 9, 1995, 73–78.

Harvey, David. *The Condition of Postmodernity: An Inquiry into the Origins of Cultural Change.* Oxford: Basil Blackwell, 1989.

Jenkins, Henry. *Textual Poachers: Television Fans and Participatory Culture.* New York: Routledge, 1992.

Newcomb, Horace. "*Magnum:* The Champagne of TV?" *Channels of Communications* (May/June 1985): 23–26.

Nichols, Nichelle. *Beyond Uhura: "Star Trek" and Other Memories.* New York: Putnam, 1994.

Nollinger, Mark. "Twenty Things You Need to Know about *The X-Files.*" *TV Guide,* Apr. 6, 1996, 18–29.

Takei, George. *To the Stars.* New York: Pocket Books, 1994.

Thorburn, David. "Television as an Aesthetic Medium." *Critical Studies in Mass Communication* 4, no. 2 (June 1987): 161–73.

Reading the Text

1. Define in your own words what the authors mean by the terms "Fordism," "TV I," and "TV II" (para. 4).
2. How do cult TV shows differ from ordinary programs, according to Reeves, Rodgers, and Epstein?

3. What were the technological changes that enabled the shift from TV I to TV II, in the authors' view?

4. In your own words, how does *The X-Files* combine features of the episodic series and the open-ended serial?

Reading the Signs

1. If you are an *X-Files* fan, write a journal entry in which you explore the show's appeal to you. If you dislike the program, discuss the reasons for your response.

2. Cult TV is part of the niche programming strategies that target specific audience demographics rather than attempt to appeal to all viewers. Write an essay in which you discuss the social implications of the "quest for 'quality demographics'" (para. 16) that such programming fosters.

3. Write an essay in which you compare and contrast the appeal of *Star Trek* and of *The X-Files*.

4. In class, brainstorm names of other cult TV shows. To what extent does your list demonstrate the features of cult programming that the authors describe? Does your list suggest modifications or additions to the authors' criteria for such programming?

WALTER KIRN

Twentysomethings

||||||||||||||||||||||||||||||||||||||||||||||||||||||||

They've been called "slackers," "Generation X," and "the first generation in American history that expects to do worse than its parents." And "they" may be you. In this wicked look at "twentysomething" culture — "a sluggish mainstream underground that sold out even before it could drop out" — Walter Kirn (b. 1962) rips apart the movies, TV shows, fashions, and attitudes of what may be your generation, accusing it of being made up of "mopey" consumers whose greatest contribution to culture is "the glum 'Seattle Sound.'" Kirn pulls no punches in this media and cultural review; in fact, he practically begs you to respond. The book review editor at New York *magazine, Kirn has also published a novel,* She Needed Me *(1992), and a collection of short stories,* My Hard Bargain *(1990).*

The pathology of the new kids is familiar: impatience, distrust of authority, malaise, and a wistful, ironic sense of longing for defunct ideals and lost horizons. Minus the rebelliousness and hedonism that lent punch to earlier youth movements, this is almost the same set of traits shared by Hemingway's post–World War I "lost generation," Kerouac's Beats, and Hoffman's hippies. What distinguishes the most recent brood of disaffected youth—variously identified as "twentysomethings," "slackers," and "the first generation in American history that expects to do worse than its parents"—is not its desolation but the curiously lame, detached self-consciousness of its popular culture. Examples include TV shows such as *Melrose Place* and *The Heights,* magazines from *Details* to *Pulse,* bands such as R.E.M. and its countless psychedelic-lite imitators, and all movies starring Bridget Fonda that use the word "single" in their titles. The merits of the individual works vary widely, but taken together they evoke an oddly soulless counterculture, a sluggish mainstream underground that sold out even before it could drop out.

The mopey inertia of twentystuff culture is, in a way, no surprise. A generation whose defining collective experience is its lack of defining collective experiences, whose Woodstock was watching *The Partridge Family* with a couple of friends and whose great moral dilemma is "paper or plastic?" is unlikely to produce a crop of quick-witted passionate radicals. That would require adversaries; but the twentysomethings' one true nemesis—the media monster that babysat them through their loveless youths—has managed to convince them that it's their buddy, a partner in self-realization.

Consider *Melrose Place,* a show about a group of mildly disillusioned, urban young people, manufactured by Aaron Spelling, the same man who, with *The Love Boat* and *Dynasty,* did much of the initial illusioning. The program has all the twentystuff hallmarks, from a mailing address for a premise (in twentystuff narratives, zip code is destiny) to therapy-speak dialogue ("I think it's really good that you're feeling these things that you're talking about"). It's basically an ensemble coping drama, with stressors-of-the-week—career troubles, problem pregnancies—replacing storylines. The show ends when everyone has aired their issues, exchanged supportive hugs. Conflicts are not resolved, they're extinguished, flash fires of emotion brought under control by pouring words on them.

The same goes for the . . . movie *Singles,* a cut above *Melrose* in craftsmanship and acting but identical in its tone of plucky pathos. Once again, the lazy organizing principle is physical location, a grungy, Seattle apartment building populated by pure-hearted young folks saddled with dead-end jobs and ingrown dreams. Jaded and wary, with uncertain prospects, these white-kid nouvelle losers struggle for intimacy, fail, and then try again and provisionally succeed. In this twentystuff soap opera, public causes exist to be gestured at ("Think Globally, Act Locally," reads a bumper sticker), but private life is all the life there is, the world having shrunk to the cramped dimensions of one's wacky, sad, starter apartment with its sardonic, cheap, recycled furnishings. Indeed, it is this notion of recycling—both of material and cultural goods—that's the essence of the twentystuff esthetic. In *Singles,* casual friends are recycled into pseudo-family members, then into lovers, then back into friends. Portentous seventies rock 'n' roll is recycled into the glum "Seattle sound." Last night's takeout is this morning's breakfast and yesterday's philosophical fads (in this case, a paperback copy of *The Fountainhead* toted around by Bridget Fonda) are today's amusements. Resigning one's self to living off the table scraps of the American century is what twentystuff culture is all about. It's about recycling anger into irony, pain into poses.

Just check out an issue of *Details* magazine, a monthly lifestyle guide   5
for wannabe desolation angels. In a recent issue that also happens to feature an interview with recycled guru Allen Ginsberg—adopted bard of all postwar youthquakes—the bedrooms of arty young single males are inspected for hidden fashion statements ("What your crib says about you"). Paolo, described as a "sound engineer/motorcycle racer," takes obvious pride in his wacky scavenging, in the fragments he has shored against his ruin: "I found the dentist's chair on the street; the sofa is the back seat of a van." Then there's Craig, a "graphic designer/DJ" (the cute juxtapositions never end), who boasts: "The trunk's from a thrift shop, the cowhide rug was a gift." The implication, of course, is that one can never be too aware of the ironic signals one is sending, even while alone, in private. According to the twentystuff credo, one's life is a self-directed TV series (*Wayne's World! Wayne's World!*), and one is always spiritually on-camera.

That's sad, I think. Not funny-sad, just sad. Consumers tricked into thinking they're producers, entombed in their own bemused self-consciousness, acting at life instead of taking action, the devotees of twentystuff may be a lost generation, indeed.

Reading the Text

1. What, according to Kirn, are the characteristics of "twentysomethings" (para. 1) in television programs today?
2. What does Kirn mean by saying "resigning one's self to living off the table scraps of the American century is what twentystuff culture is all about" (para. 4)?
3. How does Kirn explain the "pathology" (para. 1) that he attributes to the twentysomething generation?

Reading the Signs

1. Kirn neglects to mention that many of the shows he criticizes were written and produced by people who were far from twentysomething. How does this omission affect the credibility of his argument?

2. Take Kirn up on his challenge: check out an issue of *Details* magazine. Is it, as Kirn claims, "a monthly lifestyle guide for wannabe desolation angels" (para. 5)? Write an essay in which you support, refute, or modify his characterization of this magazine and its readership.
3. Watch an episode of one of the TV shows that Kirn discusses—you may find them in syndication—and write your own analysis of it. How does it function as a sign of the twentysomething generation, in your view?
4. In class, discuss Kirn's tone. How does it affect your response to his essay?
5. Kirn can be accused of stereotyping a generation. In a journal entry, explore the implications of such stereotyping. Is it based in reality? What difference does it make if a generation—as opposed to, say, an ethnic group—is stereotyped? If you are part of the generation Kirn attacks, how does his article make you feel? How does his stereotyping compare with images of "baby boomers"?

TRICIA ROSE

Bad Sistas

|||||||||||||||||||||||||||||||||||||||||||||||||||||||||||||

Female rappers tell male rappers where to get off when it comes to sexual harassment and exploitation, don't they? Such is the manifest message of rap videos from such performers as Salt 'N' Pepa and MC Lyte. But as Tricia Rose (b. 1962) argues in this selection from Black Noise: Rap Music and Black Culture in Contemporary America *(1994), the tendency of such raps to situate women in the context of sexual courtship rituals undermines their surface meaning. Wouldn't it be even more subversive to perform raps that have nothing to do with sexual relations at all, Rose implies? An associate professor of history and Africana studies at New York University, Rose is coeditor, with Andrew Ross, of* Microphone Fiends: Youth Music and Youth Culture *(1994).*

Courting Disaster

Raps written by women that specifically concern male-female relationships almost always confront the tension between trust and savvy; between vulnerability and control. Some raps celebrate their sisters for "getting over" on men, rather than touting self-reliance and honesty. For example, in Icey Jaye's "It's a Girl Thang," she explains how she and her friends find ways to spend as much of their dates' money as possible and mocks the men who fall for their tricks. Similarly, in the video for Salt

'N' Pepa's "Independent" Salt accepts several expensive gifts from a string of dates who hope to win her affection with diamond necklaces and rings. In raps such as these, women are taking advantage of the logic of heterosexual courtship in which men coax women into submission with trinkets and promises for financial security. Nikki D's "Up the Ante for the Panty" and B. W. P.'s "We Want Money" are more graphic examples of a similar philosophy. However, for the most part, when they choose to rap about male-female relations, women rappers challenge the depictions of women in many male raps as gold diggers and address the fears many women share regarding male dishonesty and infidelity.

MC Lyte and Salt 'N' Pepa have reputations for biting raps that criticize men who manipulate and abuse women. Their lyrics tell the story of men taking advantage of women, cheating on them, taking their money, and leaving them for other unsuspecting female victims. These raps are not mournful ballads about the trials and tribulations of being a heterosexual woman. Similar to women's blues, they are caustic, witty, and aggressive warnings directed at men and at other women who might be seduced by them in the future. By offering a woman's interpretation of the terms of heterosexual courtship, these women's raps cast a new light on male-female sexual power relations and depict women as resistant, aggressive participants. Yet, even the raps that explore and revise women's role in the courtship process often retain the larger patriarchal parameters of heterosexual courtship.

Salt 'N' Pepa's single "Tramp" is strong advice, almost boot camp, for single black women. "Tramp" is not, as Salt 'N' Pepa warn, a "simple rhyme," but a parable about courtship rituals between men and women:

> Homegirls attention you must pay to what I say
> Don't take this as a simple rhyme
> Cause this type of thing happens all the time
> Now what would you do if a stranger said "Hi"
> Would you dis him or would you reply?
> If you'd answer, there is a chance
> That you'd become a victim of circumstance
> Am I right fellas? tell the truth
> Or else I'll have to show and prove
> You are what you are I am what I am
> It just so happens that most men are TRAMPS.[1]

In the absence of any response to "Am I right fellas?" (any number of sampled male replies easily could have been woven in here), Salt 'N' Pepa "show and prove" the trampings of several men who "undress you with their eyeballs," "think you're a dummy, on the first date, had the nerve to tell me he loves me" and of men who always have sex on the

---

1. Salt 'N' Pepa, "Tramp," *Hot, Cool & Vicious* (Next Plateau Records, 1986).

mind. Salt 'N' Pepa's parable defines promiscuous *males* as tramps, and thereby inverts the common belief that male sexual promiscuity is a status symbol. This reversal undermines the degrading "woman as tramp" image by stigmatizing male promiscuity. Salt 'N' Pepa suggest that women who respond to sexual advances made by these men are victims of circumstance. In this case, it is predatory, disingenuous men who are the tramps.

The music video for "Tramps" is a comic rendering of a series of social club scenes that highlight tramps on the make, mouth freshener in hand, testing their lines on the nearest woman. Dressed in the then-latest hip hop street gear, Salt 'N' Pepa perform the song on television, on a monitor perched above the bar. Because they appear on the television screen, they seem to be surveying and critiquing the club action, but the club members cannot see them. There are people dancing and talking together (including likeable men who are coded as "nontramps"), who seem unaware of the television monitor. Salt 'N' Pepa are also shown in the club, dressed in very stylish, sexy outfits. Salt 'N' Pepa act as decoys, talking and flirting with the tramps to flesh out the dramatization of tramps on the prowl. They make several knowing gestures at the camera to reassure the viewer that they are unswayed by the tramps' efforts.

The tramps and their victims interact only with body language. The club scenes have no dialogue; we hear only Salt 'N' Pepa lyrics over the musical tracks for "Tramp," which serve respectively as the video's narrative and the club's dance music. Viewing much of the club action from Salt 'N' Pepa's authoritative position—through the television monitor—we can safely observe the playful but cautionary dramatization of heterosexual courtship. One tramp who is rapping to a woman, postures and struts, appearing to ask something like the stock pick-up line: "what is your zodiac sign, baby?" When she shows disgust and leaves her seat, he repeats the same body motions and gestures on the next woman who happens to sit down. Near the end of the video, a frustrated "wife" enters the club and drags one of the tramps home, smacking him in the head with her pocketbook. Salt 'N' Pepa are standing next to the wife's tramp in the club, shaking their heads as if to say "what a shame." Simultaneously, they are pointing and laughing at the husband from the television monitor. At the end of the video, a still frame of each man is stamped "tramp," and Salt 'N' Pepa revel in having identified and exposed them. They then leave the club together, without men, seemingly enjoying their skill at exposing the real intentions of these tramps.

Salt 'N' Pepa are "schooling" women about the sexual politics of the club scene, by engaging in and critiquing the drama of heterosexual courtship. The privileged viewer is a woman who is directly addressed in the lyrics and presumably can empathize fully with the visual depiction and interpretation of the scenes. The video's resolution can be interpreted as a warning to both men and women. Women: Don't fall for

5

these men either by talking to them in the clubs or believing the lies they'll tell you when they come home. Men: You will get caught eventually, and you'll be embarrassed. Another message suggested by the video for "Tramp" is that women can go to these clubs, successfully play along with "the game" as long as the power of female sexuality and the terms of male desire are understood and negotiated.

However, "Tramp" does not interrogate "the game" itself. "Tramp" implicitly accepts the larger dynamics and power relationships between men and women. Although the tramps are embarrassed and momentarily contained at the end of the video, in no way can it be suggested that these tramps will stop hustling women and cheating on their wives. More important, what of women's desire? Not only is it presumed that men will continue their dishonest behavior, but women's desire for an idealized monogamous heterosexual relationship is implicitly confirmed as an unrealized (but not unrealizable?) goal. In their quest for an honest man, should not the sobering fact that "most men are tramps" be considered a point of departure for rejecting the current courtship ritual altogether?

Salt 'N' Pepa leave the club together, seemingly pleased by their freedom and by their ability to manipulate men into pursuing them "to no end." But the wife drags her husband home—she is not shocked but rather frustrated by what appears to be frequent dishonest behavior. What conclusion is to be drawn from this lesson? Do not trust tramps, separate the wheat from the tramps, and continue in your quest for an honest, monogamous man. "Tramp" is courtship advice for women who choose to participate in the current configuration of heterosexual courtship, it does not offer an alternative paradigm for such courtship, and in some ways it works inside of the very courtship rules that it highlights and criticizes. At best, "Tramp" is an implicit critique of the club scene as a setting for meeting potential mates as well as of the institution of marriage that permits significant power imbalances clearly weighted in favor of men.

MC Lyte has a far less comedic response to Sam, a boyfriend whom she catches trying to pick up women. MC Lyte's underground hit "Paper Thin" is one of the most scathingly powerful raps about male dishonesty and infidelity and the tensions between trust and vulnerability in heterosexual relations. Lyte has been burned by Sam, but she has turned her experience into a black woman's anthem that sustains an uncomfortable balance between brutal cynicism and honest vulnerability:

> When you say you love me it doesn't matter
> It goes into my head as just chit chatter
> You may think it's egotistical or just very free
> But what you say, I take none of it seriously. . . .

> I'm not the kind of girl to try to play a man out
> They take the money and then they break the hell out.

No that's not my strategy, not the game I play
I admit I play a game, but it's not done that way.
Truly when I get involved I give it my heart

I mean my mind, my soul, my body, I mean every part.
But if it doesn't work out—yo, it just doesn't.
It wasn't meant to be, you know it just wasn't.
So, I treat all of you like I treat all of them.
What you say to me is just paper thin.[2]

Lyte's public acknowledgment that Sam's expressions of love were   10
paper thin is not a source of embarrassment for her but a means of empowerment. She plays a brutal game of the dozens on Sam while wearing
her past commitment to him as a badge of honor and sign of character.
Lyte presents commitment, vulnerability, and sensitivity as assets, not indicators of female weakness. In "Paper Thin," emotional and sexual
commitment are not romantic, Victorian concepts tied to honorable but
dependent women; they are a part of her strategy, part of the game she
plays in heterosexual courtship.

"Paper Thin's" high-energy video contains many elements present in
hip hop. The video opens with Lyte, dressed in a sweatsuit, chunk jewelry, and sneakers, abandoning her new Jetta hastily because she wants to
take the subway to clear her head. A few members of her male posse,
shocked at her desire to leave her Jetta on the street for the subway, follow
along behind her, down the steps to the subway tracks. (Her sudden decision to leave her new car for the subway and her male posse's surprised reaction seem to establish that Lyte rarely rides the subway anymore.) Lyte
enters a subway car with an introspective and distracted expression. Once
in the subway car, her DJ K-Rock, doubling as the conductor, announces
that the train will be held in the station because of crossed signals. While
they wait, Milk Boy (her female but very masculine-looking bodyguard)
spots Sam at the other end of the car, rapping heavily to two stylish
women, and draws Lyte's attention to him. Lyte, momentarily surprised,
begins her rhyme as she stalks toward Sam. Sam's attempts to escape fail;
he is left to face MC Lyte's wrath. Eventually, she throws him off the train
to the chorus of Ray Charles's R&B classic, "Hit the Road Jack," and
locks Sam out of the subway station and out of the action. The subway car
is filled with young black teenagers, typical working New Yorkers and
street people, many of whom join Lyte in signifying on Sam while they
groove on K-Rock's music. MC Lyte's powerful voice and no-nonsense
image dominate Sam. The taut, driving music, which is punctuated by
sampled guitar and drum sections and an Earth Wind and Fire horn section, complement Lyte's hard, expressive rapping style.

---

2. MC Lyte, "Paper Thin," *Lyte as a Rock* (First Priority Records, 1988).

It is important that "Paper Thin" is set in public and on the subway, the quintessential mode of urban transportation. Lyte is drawn to the subway and seems comfortable there. She is also comfortable with the subway riders in her video; they are her community. During musical breaks between raps, we see passengers grooving to her music and responding to the drama. By setting her confrontation with Sam in the subway, in front of their peers, Lyte moves a private problem between lovers into the public arena and effectively dominates both spaces.

When her DJ, the musical and mechanical conductor, announces that crossed signals are holding the train in the station, it frames the video in a moment of communication crisis. The notion of crossed signals represents the inability of Sam and Lyte to communicate with one another, an inability that is primarily the function of the fact that they communicate on different frequencies. Sam thinks he can read Lyte's mind to see what she is thinking and then feed her all the right lines. But what he says carries no weight, no meaning. His discourse is light, it's paper thin. Lyte, who understands courtship as a game, confesses to being a player, yet expresses how she feels directly and in simple language. What she says has integrity, weight, and substance.

After throwing Sam from the train, she nods her head toward a young man standing against the subway door, and he follows her off the train. She will not allow her experiences with Sam to paralyze her but instead continues to participate on revised terms. As she and her new male friend walk down the street, she raps the final stanza for "Paper Thin" that sets down the new courtship ground rules:

> So, now I take precautions when choosing my mate
> I do not touch until the third or fourth date
> Then maybe we'll kiss on the fifth or sixth time that we meet
> Cause a date without a kiss is so incomplete
> And then maybe, I'll let you play with my feet
> You can suck the big toe and play with the middle
> It's so simple unlike a riddle . . .

Lyte has taken control of the process. She has selected her latest companion; he has not pursued her. This is an important move, because it allows her to set the tone of the interaction and subsequently articulates the new ground rules that will protect her from repeating the mistakes she made in her relationship with Sam. Yet, a central revision to her courtship terms involves withholding sexual affection, a familiar strategy in courtship rituals for women that implicitly affirms the process of male pursuit as it forestalls it. Nonetheless, Lyte seems prepared for whatever takes place. Her analysis of courtship seems to acknowledge that there are dishonest men and that she is not interested in negotiating on their terms. Lyte affirms her courtship rules as she identifies and critiques the terms of men such as Sam. In "Paper Thin" she has announced that her desire will

15

govern her behavior and *his* ("you can suck my big toe and then play with the middle") and remains committed to her principles at the same time.

As "products of an ongoing historical conversation," "Paper Thin" and "Tramp" are explicitly dialogic texts that draw on the language and terms imbedded in long-standing struggles over the parameters of heterosexual courtship. These raps are also dialogic in their use of black collective memory via black music. Salt 'N' Pepa's "Tramp" draws its horns and parts of its rhythm section from the 1967 soul song of the same name performed by Otis Redding and Carla Thomas. Otis's and Carla's "Tramp" is a dialogue in which Carla expresses her frustration over Otis's failure in their relationship while he makes excuses and attempts to avoid her accusations.[3] Salt 'N' Pepa's musical quotation of Otis's and Carla's "Tramp" set a multilayered dialogue in motion. The musical style of Salt 'N' Pepa's "Tramp" carries the blues bar confessional mode of many rhythm and blues songs updated with rap's beats and breaks. Salt 'N' Pepa are testifying to Carla's problems via the music, at the same time providing their contemporary audience with a collective reference to black musical predecessors and the history of black female heterosexual struggles.

Lyte's direct address to Sam ("when you say you love it doesn't matter") is her half of a heated conversation in which Sam is silenced by her, but nonetheless present. Lyte's announcement that she "admits playing a game but it's not done that way" makes it clear that she understands the power relationships that dictate their interaction. Lyte encourages herself and by extension black women to be fearless and self-possessed ("sucker you missed, I know who I am") in the face of significant emotional losses. Her game, her strategy, have a critical sexual difference that lays the groundwork for a black female-centered communal voice that revises and expands the terms of female power in heterosexual courtship.

The dialogic and resistive aspects in "Tramps" and "Paper Thin" are also present in the body of other women rappers' work. Many female rappers address the frustration heterosexual women experience in their desire for intimacy with and commitment from men. The chorus in Neneh Cherry's "Buffalo Stance" tells men not to mess with her, and that money men can't buy her love because it's affection that she's lookin' for; "Say That Then" from West Coast female rappers Oaktown 3-5-7, give no slack to "Finger popping, hip hoppin' wanna be bed rockin'" men; Monie Love's "It's a Shame" is a pep talk for a woman breaking up with a man who apparently needs to be kicked to the curb; Ice Cream Tee's "All Wrong" chastises women who allow men to abuse

---

3. See Atlantic Records, *Rhythm and Blues Collection 1966–1969*, vol. 6. In the liner notes for this collection, Robert Pruter refers to "Tramp" as a dialogue between Carla and Otis, in which Carla's "invectives" are insufficiently countered by Otis. It should be pointed out that the Otis and Carla "Tramp" is a remake of (an answer to?) Lowell and Fulsom's version made popular in 1966.

them; Monie Love's "Just Don't Give a Damn" is a confident and harsh rejection of an emotionally and physically abusive man; and MC Lyte's "I Cram to Understand U," "Please Understand," and "I'm Not Havin' It" are companion pieces to "Paper Thin."

This strategy, in which women square off with men, can be subverted and its power diminished. As Laura Berlant suggests, this mode of confrontational communication can be contained or renamed as the "female complaint." In other words, direct and legitimate criticism is reduced to "bitching" or complaining as a way of containing dissent. Berlant warns that the "female complaint . . . as a mode of expression is an admission and recognition both of privilege and powerlessness . . . circumscribed by a knowledge of woman's inevitable delegitimation within the patriarchal public sphere." Berlant argues that resistance to sexual oppression must take place "in the patriarchal public sphere, the place where significant or momentous exchanges of power are perceived to take place," but that the female complaint is devalued, marginalized, and ineffective in this sphere. Berlant offers an interpretation of "Roxanne's Revenge," an early and popular rap record by black female rapper Roxanne Shante, as an example of the pitfalls of the "female complaint." Attempts were made to contain and humiliate Roxanne on a compilation record that included several other related answer records. Berlant says that "Roxanne's Revenge" is vulnerable to "hystericization by a readily available phallic discourse (which) is immanent in the very genre of her expression."[4]

Berlant is making an important point about the vulnerability of women's voices to devaluation. No doubt women's angry responses have long been made to appear hysterical and irrational or whiny and childlike. I am not sure, though, that we can equate attempts to render women's voices as "complaint" with the voices themselves. To do so may place too much value on the attempts to contain women. "Roxanne's Revenge" gave voice to a young girl's response to real-life street confrontations with men. She entered into black male-dominated public space and drew a great deal of attention away from the UTFO song to which she responded. More importantly, "Roxanne's Revenge" has retained weight and significance in hip hop since 1985 when it was released. This has not been the case for UTFO, the UTFO song, or any of the fabricated responses on the compilation record. Much of the status of the original UTFO song "Roxanne Roxanne" is a result of the power of Roxanne Shante's answer record. What Berlant illustrates is the ways in which Roxanne's "female complaint" needed to be labeled as such and then contained precisely because it was threatening. It did not go

4. Laura Berlant, "The Female Complaint," *Social Text,* Fall, 237–59, 1988.

unnoticed, because it was a compelling voice in the public domain that captured the attention of male and female hip hop fans. The compilation record is clearly an attempt at containing her voice, but it was in my estimation an unsuccessful attempt. Furthermore, such attempts at circumscription will continue to take place when partial, yet effective, attacks are made, whether in the form of the female complaint or not. Nonetheless, Berlant's larger argument, which calls for substantial female public sphere presence and contestation, is crucial. These public sphere contests must involve more than responses to sexist male speech; they must also entail the development of sustained, strong female voices that stake claim to public space generally.

Reading the Text

1. What are the standard themes of female rap videos, according to Rose?
2. How, according to Rose, do many women's rap videos inadvertently subvert the messages of female empowerment that they intend to send?
3. What does Rose believe are the explicit and implicit messages of Salt 'N' Pepa's "Tramp" video, and how does she feel about those messages?
4. In your own words, summarize Rose's interpretation of MC Lyte's "Paper Thin."

Reading the Signs

1. Using Rose's article as your critical framework, compare and contrast a male and female rap video. What gender roles do you see in each, and what response is a viewer likely to have to them? To develop your ideas, read or reread Holly Devor's "Gender Role Behaviors and Attitudes" (p. 447).
2. In your journal, brainstorm a list of attributes that you would like to give your gender in a video of your own design. Then write a "screenplay" for your own rap video, being sure to incorporate your preferred attributes. Share your screenplay with your class.
3. Watch a current video by either one of the artists Rose discusses or another female rapper. Then write an analysis of your video, examining whether it perpetuates, in Rose's words, "the larger patriarchal parameters of heterosexual courtship" (para. 2).
4. Rose, Susan Douglas ("Signs of Intelligent Life on TV," p. 260), and Laura Stempel Mumford ("Plotting Paternity: Looking for Dad on the Daytime Soaps," p. 249) discuss the ways in which popular culture perpetuates traditional gender roles even while it may present a superficially feminist slant. In class, discuss this phenomenon, exploring the reasons behind it. Do you see any evidence that this pattern may change in the twenty-first century? Do you wish to see it change, and why or why not?

CHAPTER FOUR

THE HOLLYWOOD SIGN

The Culture of American Film

"The Envelope, Please!"

In the 1999 Oscar sweepstakes, five films were nominated for Best Picture. All five dealt with historical subjects.

To refresh your memory of the seventy-first annual Academy Awards nominations, three of the films—*Life Is Beautiful, Saving Private Ryan,* and *The Thin Red Line*—were set during World War II, while the remaining two—*Elizabeth* and *Shakespeare in Love*—took place during the Elizabethan era. When one considers that the hands-down champion of 1998's Academy Awards, *Titanic,* was also an historical movie, a definite pattern emerges, a pattern worth analyzing as you approach your study of the cultural significance of the products of the Hollywood film industry.

Interpreting the Culture of American Film

When analyzing a movie or a group of movies, you must first suspend any personal feelings or aesthetic judgments that you may have toward your subject. As with any semiotic analysis, your object is to interpret the cultural significance of your topic, not to express an evaluative opinion. Thus, you may find it more rewarding to interpret those films that promise to be culturally meaningful rather than simply to choose your favorite flick. Determining whether a movie is culturally meaningful in the prewriting stage, of course, may be something of a hit-or-miss affair: you may find that your first choice does not present you with any particularly interesting grounds for interpretation. That's why it can be helpful to consider those factors—such as enormous popularity or widespread critical attention—that seem to set off a particular movie as being special. Academy Award candidates are also pretty reliable as cultural signs.

For this introduction, then, we have chosen the historical connection that seems to link 1999's five nominees for best picture into a meaningful pattern. Our choice does not mean you couldn't consider other movies or other possible patterns; you could examine, for example, the fact that two popular movies over the same period—*The Water Boy* and *Varsity Blues*—were student-athlete films. The point here is not that you want to determine in advance the meaning of your topic; that's what you want to discover in the course of your analysis. Rather, we only want to suggest that when choosing a film, it is useful to begin with a sense of the *meaningfulness* of your topic, whatever its meaning might be. A five-for-five focus on history in the Academy Awards best film category, for instance, definitely suggests that something meaningful is going on. And the question for a semiotic analysis is, "What is that meaning?"

As always with a semiotic analysis, you need to construct the *system* in which your subject signifies, which often means looking at its historical background. In researching the history of your topic, you will want to mark the various ways in which the film (or films) you are analyzing can be both *associated* with other films and *differentiated* from them because it is in within this system of associations and differences that you can discern a meaning. To see how this works in practice, let's look at the background of the historical movie.

First we need to define just what we mean by "historical movies." Many movies (Westerns, for example, or any "period" film) involve historical subjects, but some that are set in the past focus on individual characters. The main interest of the film, in other words, is in the fictional story, not the historical situation behind it that serves as a setting rather than a subject. In historical movies, on the other hand, the historical

---

Exploring the Signs of Film

In your journal, list your favorite movies. Then consider your list: What does it say about you? What cultural myths do the movies tend to reflect, and why do you think those myths appeal to you? What signs particularly appeal to your emotions? What sort of stories about human life do you most respond to?

situation *is* the subject, with the individual characters serving as the dramatic means through which history is presented, as in a movie like *How the West Was Won*. Although such movies may include actual figures from history who are interesting in their own right, the historical film always makes the past itself a major part of its subject matter.

Since armed conflict provides one of the most dramatic possibilities for cinematic storytelling, it is not surprising that wars have provided the subject matter for a great many of Hollywood's historical films, from *All Quiet on the Western Front* and *Gone with the Wind* (both of which won the Oscars for best film in the thirties) to *Platoon* and *Braveheart*, which are more recent Academy Award–winning warrior films. Of course, a war movie doesn't have to win the Oscar to be important, and some also-rans, like *M*A*S*H* and *Apocalypse Now*, have gone on to become Hollywood classics. The point is simply that Hollywood has often made one war or another the subject of its more popular movies (some 581 films deal with World War II alone), and so the success of films like *Saving Private Ryan* and *The Thin Red Line* in one sense simply signifies business as usual.

In addition to focusing on combat, films use history as their subject in many other ways. Monumental individuals who were major historical figures in their own right have supplied Hollywood with a rich supply of such subjects, and celebrated films that have featured them include *Lawrence of Arabia*, *Patton*, *Gandhi*, and *Malcolm X*. The fact that two of these films involve heroes who became famous through their participation in a war (T. E. Lawrence in World War I, George Patton in World War II) shows how easily these two categories of historical filmmaking—war and the monumental individual—can be combined.

Stop the presses! A significant link between the seventy-first Academy Awards nominees and two of the most popular forms of the historical film—combat and the monumental individual—has just appeared because three of those movies (*Saving Private Ryan*, *The Thin Red Line*, and *Life Is Beautiful*) were set during World War II, while the other two, *Shakespeare in Love* and *Elizabeth*, concerned the lives of monumental individuals. This *association* can help us to push further our interpretation of the basic facts that we have just considered.

For one thing, the fact that 1999's nominees present us with two "monument" movies signifies business as usual just as it did for the three war films. This point is not trivial because it reminds us of the motivation behind all mainstream Hollywood productions—to make money. This is why there is so little real innovation in the film industry: with so much money at stake, the studios generally go with tried-and-true formulas, and war and historical monument films offer just such a formula. It is easy to take this for granted, but the very obviousness of the point raises another question: "Why are movies that feature historical 'monuments' and/or warfare such safe bets for the studios?"

We'll hazard a few speculative answers to this question. First, war is highly dramatic, action-packed, and emotional. Drama, action, and emotion are all characteristics of entertaining stories, and so it is no wonder that war films should be entertaining. At the same time, a war story, if told in a certain way, can be a source of patriotic affirmation, something that can be very appealing to audiences looking for reassurance during wartime. *Guadalcanal Diary* (1943) is one such movie, described in *Halliwell's Film Guide* as "Standard war propaganda, with good action scenes," while John Wayne's *The Green Berets* is another, though by the time it was made the popularity of both the Vietnam War and the patriotic war film as such was waning, as we explore a little further in a moment.

For their part, stories about monumental individuals may be dramatic, action-packed, emotional, and patriotic, but that is not their main appeal. Rather, movies about historical giants often play off the ancient human tendency to hero worship — our fascination with people who are somehow larger than life. This basic human tendency has been updated in recent years in the cult of the celebrity, which has led to a number of movies whose subjects are the lives of particular celebrity figures, many of whom come from the entertainment industry itself — movies like *The Doors* and *The Buddy Holly Story*. Such movies, while not taking heroes off their pedestals, still tend to make them figures we can relate to by telling their stories in human terms. By seeing their personal experiences and struggles dramatized, we can see what we share with them, which in turn can reassure us of the validity and value of our own lives. This humanization of the hero on the silver screen, of course, is only a fantasy, but it is a fantasy with a potent appeal in an era of mass culture, where reality seems to offer little more than a sense of our increasing insignificance next to the stellar figures who dominate the news.

The personalizing of history in the historical monument film can be associated with many of the other ways in which contemporary popular culture seeks to personalize the lives of those celebrated individuals who are otherwise so distant from us. From the "Up Close and Personal" segments that are now such an integral part of the coverage of the Olympic Games to the ubiquitous talk shows that pretend to bring the stars into your own living room, American media cut the rich and famous down to size so they can fit into the kind of saleable packages that television sponsors desire. You will not really ever be invited into George Clooney's living room, but seeing him let his hair down, so to speak, on *The Tonight Show* makes you feel as if you might, and so you watch the show.

Such a cutting down to size occurs in *Shakespeare in Love*, which ended up taking the Oscar for best picture after a spirited competition with *Saving Private Ryan*. By turning the awesome and distant figure of William Shakespeare into a sort of Gen X-er with writer's block and complicated relationships, the movie puts a human face on one of history's greatest monuments. This isn't the guy whose writing you had to memorize in school: he's the Elizabethan equivalent of a budding screen-writer, who, with his little goatee, is the sort of fellow that young audiences can relate to. Whether or not the film accurately depicts the sort of man William Shakespeare was, it turned out to be a pretty good formula for a successful date movie.

War and Peace

But what about a movie like *Saving Private Ryan*, a war film that focuses on the experience of ordinary men rather than on historical monuments? What might it say about the era in which it appeared? To answer this question, we can return to the system to which war films belong, looking this time not for associations but for the *differences* that distinguish *Saving Private Ryan* from the others and that point to its special significance.

As a combat film focused on the D-Day invasion at Normandy, *Saving Private Ryan* especially recalls *The Longest Day* (1962), a John Wayne vehicle that surveys the invasion from a number of points of view but that, like most World War II films made prior to the 1970s, questions neither the war effort itself nor the military spirit necessary to the conduct of warfare. An earlier John Wayne movie, *Sands of Iwo Jima* (1949), did feature a character who questioned the military values of his officer father, but he is converted to them by the end of the film. Such films do not attempt to glamorize combat but, rather, seek to show how military sacrifices are needed to defend the nation.

Movies whose message is to underscore the meaningfulness of war's sacrifices strongly contrast with films like *Catch-22* (1970). Based on Joseph Heller's novel of the same title, *Catch-22* represents a sharp turn away from the patriotic war film. Set during World War II, the movie emphasizes the absurdity and violence of all war, and while not quite challenging America's role in World War II, it skewers the military mentality. Produced when the Vietnam War was tearing the country apart, *Catch-22* (like *M*A*S*H* after it) was a protest film that marked the beginning of a popular rejection of American militarism.

By the later 1970s, this rejection had become something of a fad. The Vietnam War replaced World War II as a subject for movie making, with films like *Apocalypse Now* and *The Deer Hunter* seizing the stage. *Apocalypse Now* went beyond the satirical comedy of *Catch-22* to launch a frontal attack on American military authority while openly demonizing the American war effort in Vietnam. Making its audience more sympathetic with the crazed renegade Kurtz (famously played by Marlon Brando) than with the cold-blooded military officers who send Willard out to kill him, *Apocalypse Now* depicts the insanity of war in all its gory intensity without attempting to redeem it through acts of heroic sacrifice or moments of romantic consolation.

In the 1980s, however, the American mood shifted again. With Ronald Reagan leading the way, American popular culture went on a patriotic binge, celebrating militarism in movies like *Top Gun, The Right Stuff,* and *An Officer and a Gentleman,* all of which made the military life seem quite glamorous, if arduous. Along with the popularity of Marine-style haircuts and the brief cult of Oliver North, such films reflected a general cultural celebration of the American military that exactly contradicted the mood of the late sixties and seventies, and they even departed from the somber realities of earlier war movies in which militarism is not quite so attractive.

It is in the context of these three types of war movies—what we might call the "patriotic," the "protest," and the "militaristic"—that we can assess the cultural significance of a movie like *Saving Private Ryan.* Opening with a screen-filling image of the American flag and a framing scene in which an American veteran revisits Normandy with his family, the movie at first suggests that it will honor the tradition of the patriotic film. But when things turn violent in a flashback to 1944, the film begins to look as if it might be a protest movie after all. For with its unusually gritty and gorily realistic attempt to recreate the conditions on Omaha Beach during the D-Day invasion, the movie departs from the conventions of the patriotic film, which show men dying in combat but never panicking and not with so much blood. By providing a glimpse into the horrific, and occasionally unheroic, conditions of actual combat, *Saving Private Ryan* hints that it means to question whether war is worth such sacrifices.

But you don't cast Tom Hanks in protest films (not, at least, after *Forrest Gump*), and *Saving Private Ryan* was not one because after the invasion scene, the movie settled down to dramatize the efforts of a basically decent squad of American soldiers, following basically decent orders, to do their duty and rescue one of their own. Concluding with a return to the present, the movie suggests that the sacrifices were justified after all, especially through a parting shot of the American flag, which, through its red-white-and-blue symbolism, reassures the audience that it is still flying precisely because of the efforts of the men whose story we have just been told.

So *Saving Private Ryan* had a lot in common with the traditional patriotic war film after all. But it still wasn't quite the same thing because after enduring the seemingly endless battle sequence at the beginning, audiences were unlikely to forget the blood and guts behind the glory. At the same time, the movie was completely different from the 1980s-style militaristic movie, which was all glory, so to speak. In some respects, then, *Saving Private Ryan* created its own category of war movie: neither patriotic, protesting, nor militaristic, it combined elements of patriotism and protest to create a new kind of film that was, as it turns out, especially in keeping with the time when it was produced. For by the

||||||||||||||||||||||||||||||||||||||||||||||||||||||||||||||||||||||||||||||||||||||||||||||||||||||||||||||||||||||||||||||||||||||||||||||||||||||||||||||||||||||||||||||||||||||

Discussing the Signs of Film

In any given year, one film may dominate the Hollywood box office, becoming a blockbuster that captures that public's cinematic imagination. In class, discuss which film would be your choice as this year's top hit. Then analyze the film semiotically. Why has *this* film so successfully appealed to so many moviegoers?

late 1990s, American culture itself seemed to combine, in a sometimes uneasy alliance, both the iconoclasm of the 1960s and 1970s and the patriotism of an earlier time. On the one hand, Americans were no longer disposed to dismiss or gloss over the flaws in their collective history, as they had once been, but neither were they inclined to flagellate themselves for those flaws. They were willing to admit to and cinematically revisit past sins — as the production of films like *Amistad* demonstrates — but they weren't in a mood to condemn themselves or their history — as the box-office failure of *Beloved* suggests. In such a climate, the historical compromise of *Saving Private Ryan* was a perfect cultural fit.

Movies as Metaphors

Our brief interpretational survey of the Oscar crop for 1999 is intended to demonstrate how the semiotic analysis of a film (or group of films) can uncover the cultural significance of the movies that entertain us. But while war movies are rather somber, just about any kind of movie can offer a rich field of possibilities for cultural analysis. Indeed, even a grade-B horror flick can be a cultural signifier.

Consider, for instance, the original Godzilla movies. If we study only their plots, we would see little more than horror stories featuring a reptilian monster rather like the dragons of medieval literature. But Godzilla was no mere dragon transported to the modern world. The dragons that populate the world of medieval storytelling were often metaphors for the Satanic serpent in the Garden of Eden, but Godzilla was a wholly different sort of metaphor. Created by Japanese filmmakers, Godzilla was originally a metaphor for the nuclear era. A mutant creation of nuclear poisoning, Godzilla rose over her Japanese audiences like a mushroom cloud, symbolizing the potential for future mushroom clouds both in Japan and around the world in the cold war era.

For their part, American movie makers in the 1950s had their own metaphors for the nuclear era. Whenever some "blob" threatened to consume New York or some especially toxic slime escaped from a laboratory, the suggestion that science—especially nuclear science—was threatening to destroy the world filled the theater along with the popcorn fumes. And if it wasn't science that was the threat, cold war filmmakers could scare us with communists, as films like *Invasion of the Body Snatchers* metaphorically suggested.

In such ways, an entire film can be a kind of metaphor, but you can find many smaller metaphors at work in the details of a movie as well. Early filmmakers, for example, used to put a table cloth on the table in dining scenes to signify that the characters at the table were good, decent people (you can find such a metaphor in Charlie Chaplin's *The Kid*, where an impoverished tramp who can't afford socks or a bathrobe still has a nice tablecloth on the breakfast table). Sometimes a director's metaphors have a broad political significance, as at the end of the James Dean classic *Giant*, where the parting shot presents a tableau of a white baby goat standing next to a black baby goat, which is juxtaposed with the image of a white baby standing in a crib side by side with a brown baby. Since the human babies are both the grandchildren of the film's protagonist (one of whose sons has married a Mexican woman, the other an Anglo), the goats are added to underscore metaphorically the message of racial reconciliation that the director wanted to send.

Movies as Archetypes

While filmmakers always have some plan in mind when making their films, there is often another element to a movie of which they may not be conscious. This is the *archetypal* dimension, through which a film can be seen to repeat what may be very ancient story or character patterns (see Linda Seger's essay in this chapter, p. 308, for more on archetypes). All those male buddy films from the last three decades, for example—from *Butch Cassidy and the Sundance Kid* to *Lethal Weapon* to *Men in Black*—hark back to male bonding stories as old as *Gilgamesh* (from the third millennium B.C.) and the *Iliad*. Cruella de Vil from *101 Dalmatians* is sister to the Wicked Witch of the West, Sleeping Beauty's stepmother, Hansel and Gretel's gingerbread temptress, and every other witch or crone dreamed up by the patriarchal imagination, while all those sea monsters, from Jonah's "whale" to Jaws, are part of the same archetypal phylum. Each time a movie hero struggles to return home after a long journey—Dorothy to Kansas, Lassie to Timmie—a story as old as *Exodus* and the *Odyssey* has been retold. And Sigourney Weaver can't do in the Alien without recalling St. George or Beowulf.

In short, films are filled with archetypal patterns as old as storytelling, and you can learn much about the nature of the human imagination simply by identifying the various archetypes in a given film. Some archetypes, however, like the recurrent appearance of what Robert B. Ray calls the "outlaw hero" and the "official hero" in American cinema (see the first selection in this chapter, p. 299), have a more local significance whose meaning bears on the particular culture in which they appear. Americans, for example, with their frontier past and car culture present, have made the beckoning open road one of their most prominent archetypal symbols (*Easy Rider* and *Route 66* are prime examples), while the more geographically fixed and historically aristocratic societies of Europe have made the stationary space of the castle or cathedral (think of King Arthur's Camelot or *The Hunchback of Notre Dame*) archetypal symbols of their own.

Since archetypal symbols are part of a society's collective unconscious, both filmmakers and audiences may not be consciously aware of them, but they have their cultural effects all the same. A heavy dosage of male bonding films, for instance, can send the unspoken cultural message that a man can't really make friends with a woman, that women are simply the sexual reward for manly men. Too many witches can send the message that there are too many bitches. In other words, archetypes are not necessarily innocent, and analyzing those archetypes that are most prominent in the movies can reveal much about the cultural mood in which they are presented.

Reading a film, then, is much like reading a novel. Both are texts filled with intentional and unintentional signs and archetypes. Both are cultural signifiers. The major difference is in their medium of expression. Literary texts are cast entirely in written words; films combine verbal language, visual imagery, and sound effects. Thus, we perceive literary and cinematic texts differently, for the written sign is perceived in a linear fashion that relies on one's cognitive and imaginative powers, while a film primarily targets the senses: one sees and hears (and sometimes even smells!). That film is such a sensory experience often conceals its

---

Reading Film on the Net

Most major films now released in the United States receive their own website. You can find them listed in print ads for the film (check your local newspaper), or visit a list of links to the major film studios at **http://www.afionline.org/cinemedia**. Select a current film, find the web address, log on, and analyze the film's site semiotically. What images are used to attract your interest in the film? What interactive strategies, if any, are used to increase your commitment to the film? If you've seen the movie, how does the Net presentation of it compare with your experience viewing it either in a theater or on video?

textuality. One is tempted to sit back and go with the flow, to say that it's only entertainment and doesn't have to "mean" anything at all. But as cinematic forms of storytelling overtake written forms of expression, the study of movies as complex texts bearing cultural messages and values is becoming more and more important. Our "libraries" are increasingly to be found in theaters and minimalls, where the texts of Hollywood can be read for eight dollars a view or rented for two dollars a night. There's a lot to read out there.

The Readings

The readings in this chapter address the various myths that pervade Hollywood films, starting with Robert B. Ray's analysis of the ways in which America's "official" and "outlaw" heroes appear both in the cinema and in American history and culture. Linda Seger follows with a screenwriter's how-to-do-it guide for the creation of the kind of archetypal characters that made *Star Wars* one of the most popular movies of all time. Susan Bordo's critique of the "just-do-it" culture behind movies like *Braveheart* comes next, offering an alternative approach to the film from that proposed in the introduction to Chapter 8 of this book, along with a plea for more movies like *Babe*. The next three selections tackle racial issues, beginning with Shelby Steele's analysis of Malcolm X, the man and the movie, which offers a surprising take on a one-time outlaw hero who is rapidly becoming an official one. Todd Boyd then situates the "gangsta" film within a history of gangster movies, focusing on the politics of such films as *Boyz N the Hood* and *American Me*, while Jessica Hagedorn surveys a tradition of American filmmaking in which Asian women are presented as either tragic or trivial. Sandra Tsing Loh follows with a tongue-in-cheek report on the return of another mythic figure to American cinema, the Good Girl, exemplified by everyone from that "mother of all modern Good Girls," Doris Day, to that savior of virtual culture, Sandra Bullock. And Michael Parenti concludes the chapter with a social-class-based approach to the codes of American cinema, noting the class biases inherent in such popular hits as *Pretty Woman*.

ROBERT B. RAY
The Thematic Paradigm

||||||||||||||||||||||||||||||||||||||||||||||||||||||

Usually we consider movies to be merely entertainment, but as Robert Ray (b. 1943) demonstrates in this selection from his book A Certain Tendency of the Hollywood Cinema *(1985), American films have long reflected fundamental patterns and contradictions in our society's myths and values. Whether in real life or on the silver screen, Ray explains, Americans have always been ambivalent about the value of civilization, celebrating it through official heroes like George Washington and Jimmy Stewart, while at the same time questioning it through outlaw heroes like Davy Crockett and Jesse James. Especially when presented together in the same film, these two hero types help mediate America's ambivalence, providing a mythic solution. Ray's analyses show how the movies are rich sources for cultural interpretation, they provide a framework for decoding movies as different as* Lethal Weapon *and* Malcolm X. *Robert Ray is a professor and director of film and media studies at the University of Florida at Gainesville. His most recent publication is* The Avant Garde Finds Andy Hardy *(1995).*

The dominant tradition of American cinema consistently found ways to overcome dichotomies. Often, the movies' reconciliatory pattern concentrated on a single character magically embodying diametrically opposite traits. A sensitive violinist was also a tough boxer (*Golden Boy*); a boxer was a gentle man who cared for pigeons (*On the Waterfront*). A gangster became a coward because he was brave (*Angels with Dirty Faces*); a soldier became brave because he was a coward (*Lives of a Bengal Lancer*). A war hero was a former pacifist (*Sergeant York*); a pacifist was a former war hero (*Billy Jack*). The ideal was a kind of inclusiveness that would permit all decisions to be undertaken with the knowledge that the alternative was equally available. The attractiveness of Destry's refusal to use guns (*Destry Rides Again*) depended on the tacit understanding that he could shoot with the best of them, Katharine Hepburn's and Claudette Colbert's revolts against conventionality (*Holiday, It Happened One Night*) on their status as aristocrats.

Such two-sided characters seemed particularly designed to appeal to a collective American imagination steeped in myths of inclusiveness. Indeed, in creating such characters, classic Hollywood had connected with what Erik Erikson has described as the fundamental American psychological pattern:

> The functioning American, as the heir of a history of extreme contrasts and abrupt changes, bases his final ego identity on some tentative combination of dynamic polarities such as migratory and sedentary, individualistic and standardized, competitive and co-operative, pious and free-thinking, responsible and cynical, etc. . . .
>
> To leave his choices open, the American, on the whole, lives with two sets of "truths."[1]

The movies traded on one opposition in particular, American culture's traditional dichotomy of individual and community that had generated the most significant pair of competing myths: the outlaw hero and the official hero.[2] Embodied in the adventurer, explorer, gunfighter, wanderer, and loner, the outlaw hero stood for that part of the American imagination valuing self-determination and freedom from entanglements. By contrast, the official hero, normally portrayed as a teacher, lawyer, politician, farmer, or family man, represented the American belief in collective action, and the objective legal process that superseded private notions of right and wrong. While the outlaw hero found incarnations in the mythic figures of Davy Crockett, Jesse James, Huck Finn, and all of Leslie Fiedler's "Good Bad Boys" and Daniel Boorstin's "ring-tailed roarers," the official hero developed around legends associated with Washington, Jefferson, Lincoln, Lee, and other "Good Good Boys."

An extraordinary amount of the traditional American mythology adopted by Classic Hollywood derived from the variations worked by American ideology around this opposition of natural man versus civilized man. To the extent that these variations constituted the main tendency of American literature and legends, Hollywood, in relying on this mythology, committed itself to becoming what Robert Bresson has called "the Cinema."[3] A brief description of the competing values associated with this outlaw hero–official hero opposition will begin to suggest its pervasiveness in traditional American culture.

1. *Aging:* The attractiveness of the outlaw hero's childishness and   5
propensity to whims, tantrums, and emotional decisions derived from America's cult of childhood. Fiedler observed that American literature celebrated "the notion that a mere falling short of adulthood is a guarantee of insight and even innocence." From Huck to Holden Caulfield, children in American literature were privileged, existing beyond society's confining rules. Often, they set the plot in motion (e.g., *Intruder in the Dust, To Kill a*

---

1. Erik H. Erikson, *Childhood and Society* (New York: Norton, 1963), p. 286.

2. Leading discussions of the individual-community polarity in American culture can be found in *The Contrapuntal Civilization: Essays Toward a New Understanding of the American Experience,* ed. Michael Kammen (New York: Crowell, 1971). The most prominent analyses of American literature's use of this opposition remain Leslie A. Fiedler's *Love and Death in the American Novel* (New York: Stein and Day, 1966) and A. N. Kaul's *The American Vision* (New Haven: Yale University Press, 1963).

3. Robert Bresson, *Notes on Cinematography,* trans. Jonathan Griffin (New York: Urizen Books, 1977), p. 12.

Mockingbird), acting for the adults encumbered by daily affairs. As Fiedler also pointed out, this image of childhood "has impinged upon adult life itself, has become a 'career' like everything else in America,"[4] generating stories like *On the Road* or *Easy Rider* in which adults try desperately to postpone responsibilities by clinging to adolescent life-styles.

While the outlaw heroes represented a flight from maturity, the official heroes embodied the best attributes of adulthood: sound reasoning and judgment, wisdom and sympathy based on experience. Franklin's *Autobiography* and *Poor Richard's Almanack* constituted this opposing tradition's basic texts, persuasive enough to appeal even to outsiders (*The Great Gatsby*). Despite the legends surrounding Franklin and the other Founding Fathers, however, the scarcity of mature heroes in American literature and mythology indicated American ideology's fundamental preference for youth, a quality that came to be associated with the country itself. Indeed, American stories often distorted the stock figure of the Wise Old Man, portraying him as mad (Ahab), useless (Rip Van Winkle), or evil (the Godfather).

2. *Society and Women:* The outlaw hero's distrust of civilization, typically represented by women and marriage, constituted a stock motif in American mythology. In his *Studies in Classic American Literature,* D. H. Lawrence detected the recurring pattern of flight, observing that the Founding Fathers had come to America "largely to get *away.* . . . Away from what? In the long run, away from themselves. Away from everything."[5] Sometimes, these heroes undertook this flight alone (Thoreau, *Catcher in the Rye*); more often, they joined ranks with other men: Huck with Jim, Ishmael with Queequeg, Jake Barnes with Bill Gorton. Women were avoided as representing the very entanglements this tradition sought to escape: society, the "settled life," confining responsibilities. The outlaw hero sought only uncompromising relationships, involving either a "bad" woman (whose morals deprived her of all rights to entangling domesticity) or other males (who themselves remained independent). Even the "bad" woman posed a threat, since marriage often uncovered the clinging "good" girl underneath. Typically, therefore, American stories avoided this problem by killing off the "bad" woman before the marriage could transpire (*Destry Rides Again, The Big Heat, The Far Country*). Subsequently, within the all-male group, women became taboo, except as the objects of lust.

The exceptional extent of American outlaw legends suggests an ideological anxiety about civilized life. Often, that anxiety took shape as a

---

4. Leslie A. Fiedler, *No! In Thunder* (New York: Stein and Day, 1972), pp. 253, 275.

5. D. H. Lawrence, *Studies in Classic American Literature* (New York: Viking/Compass, 1961), p. 3. See also Fiedler's *Love and Death in the American Novel* and Sam Bluefarb's *The Escape Motif in the American Novel: Mark Twain to Richard Wright* (Columbus: Ohio State University Press, 1972).

romanticizing of the dispossessed, as in the Beat Generation's cult of the bum, or the characters of Huck and "Thoreau," who worked to remain idle, unemployed, and unattached. A passage from Jerzy Kosinski's *Steps* demonstrated the extreme modern version of this romanticizing:

> I envied those [the poor and the criminals] who lived here and seemed so free, having nothing to regret and nothing to look forward to. In the world of birth certificates, medical examinations, punch cards, and computers, in the world of telephone books, passports, bank accounts, insurance plans, wills, credit cards, pensions, mortgages and loans, they lived unattached.[6]

In contrast to the outlaw heroes, the official heroes were preeminently worldly, comfortable in society, and willing to undertake even those public duties demanding personal sacrifice. Political figures, particularly Washington and Lincoln, provided the principal examples of this tradition, but images of family also persisted in popular literature from *Little Women* to *Life with Father* and *Cheaper by the Dozen*. The most crucial figure in this tradition, however, was Horatio Alger, whose heroes' ambition provided the complement to Huck's disinterest. Alger's characters subscribed fully to the codes of civilization, devoting themselves to proper dress, manners, and behavior, and the attainment of the very things despised by the opposing tradition: the settled life and respectability.[7]

3. *Politics and the Law:* Writing about "The Philosophical Approach   10
of the Americans," Tocqueville noted "a general distaste for accepting any man's word as proof of anything." That distaste took shape as a traditional distrust of politics as collective activity, and of ideology as that activity's rationale. Such a disavowal of ideology was, of course, itself ideological, a tactic for discouraging systematic political intervention in a nineteenth-century America whose political and economic power remained in the hands of a privileged few. Tocqueville himself noted the results of this mythology of individualism which "disposes each citizen to isolate himself from the mass of his fellows and withdraw into the circle of family and friends; with this little society formed to his taste, he gladly leaves the greater society to look after itself."[8]

This hostility toward political solutions manifested itself further in an ambivalence about the law. The outlaw mythology portrayed the law, the sum of society's standards, as a collective, impersonal ideology im-

---

6. Jerzy Kosinski, *Steps* (New York: Random House, 1968), p. 133.

7. See John G. Cawelti, *Apostles of the Self-Made Man: Changing Concepts of Success in America* (Chicago: University of Chicago Press, 1965), pp. 101–23.

8. Alexis de Tocqueville, *Democracy in America,* ed. J. P. Mayer, trans. George Lawrence (Garden City, N.Y.: Anchor/Doubleday, 1969), pp. 430, 506. Irving Howe has confirmed Tocqueville's point, observing that Americans "make the suspicion of ideology into something approaching a national creed." *Politics and the Novel* (New York: Avon, 1970), p. 337.

posed on the individual from without. Thus, the law represented the very thing this mythology sought to avoid. In its place, this tradition offered a natural law discovered intuitively by each man. As Tocqueville observed, Americans wanted "To escape from imposed systems . . . to seek by themselves and in themselves for the only reason for things . . . in most mental operations each American relies on individual effort and judgment" (p. 429). This sense of the law's inadequacy to needs detectable only by the heart generated a rich tradition of legends celebrating legal defiance in the name of some "natural" standard: Thoreau went to jail rather than pay taxes, Huck helped Jim (legally a slave) to escape, Billy the Kid murdered the sheriff's posse that had ambushed his boss, Hester Prynne resisted the community's sexual mores. This mythology transformed all outlaws into Robin Hoods, who "correct" socially unjust laws (Jesse James, Bonnie and Clyde, John Wesley Harding). Furthermore, by customarily portraying the law as the tool of villains (who used it to revoke mining claims, foreclose on mortgages, and disallow election results—all on legal technicalities), this mythology betrayed a profound pessimism about the individual's access to the legal system.

If the outlaw hero's motto was "I don't know what the law says, but I do know what's right and wrong," the official hero's was "We are a nation of laws, not of men," or "No man can place himself above the law." To the outlaw hero's insistence on private standards of right and wrong, the official hero offered the admonition, "You cannot take the law into your own hands." Often, these official heroes were lawyers or politicians, at times (as with Washington and Lincoln), even the executors of the legal system itself. The values accompanying such heroes modified the assurance of Crockett's advice, "Be sure you're right, then go ahead."

In sum, the values associated with these two different sets of heroes contrasted markedly. Clearly, too, each tradition had its good and bad points. If the extreme individualism of the outlaw hero always verged on selfishness, the respectability of the official hero always threatened to involve either blandness or repression. If the outlaw tradition promised adventure and freedom, it also offered danger and loneliness. If the official tradition promised safety and comfort, it also offered entanglements and boredom.

The evident contradiction between these heroes provoked Daniel Boorstin's observation that "Never did a more incongruous pair than Davy Crockett and George Washington live together in a national Valhalla." And yet, as Boorstin admits, "both Crockett and Washington were popular heroes, and both emerged into legendary fame during the first half of the 19th century."[9]

---

9. Daniel J. Boorstin, *The Americans: The National Experience* (New York: Random House, 1965), p. 337.

The parallel existence of these two contradictory traditions evinced   15
the general pattern of American mythology: the denial of the necessity
for choice. In fact, this mythology often portrayed situations requiring
decision as temporary aberrations from American life's normal course. By
discouraging commitment to any single set of values, this mythology fostered an ideology of improvisation, individualism, and ad hoc solutions
for problems depicted as crises. American writers have repeatedly attempted to justify this mythology in terms of material sources. Hence,
Irving Howe's "explanation":

> It is when men no longer feel that they have adequate choices in their
> styles of life, when they conclude that there are no longer possibilities
> of honorable maneuver and compromise, when they decide that the
> time has come for "ultimate" social loyalties and political decisions—
> it is then that ideology begins to flourish. Ideology reflects a harden-
> ing of commitment, the freezing of opinion into system. . . . The
> uniqueness of our history, the freshness of our land, the plenitude of
> our resources—all these have made possible, and rendered plausible,
> a style of political improvisation and intellectual free-wheeling.[10]

Despite such an account's pretext of objectivity, its language betrays an
acceptance of the mythology it purports to describe: "honorable maneuver and compromise," "hardening," "freezing," "uniqueness," "fresh-
ness," and "plenitude" are all assumptive words from an ideology that
denies its own status. Furthermore, even granting the legitimacy of the
historians' authenticating causes, we are left with a persisting mythology
increasingly discredited by historical developments. (In fact, such invali-
dation began in the early nineteenth century, and perhaps even before.)

The American mythology's refusal to choose between its two heroes
went beyond the normal reconciliatory function attributed to myth by
Lévi-Strauss. For the American tradition not only overcame binary oppositions; it systematically mythologized the certainty of being able to do
so. Part of this process involved blurring the lines between the two sets of
heroes. First, legends often brought the solemn official heroes back down
to earth, providing the sober Washington with the cherry tree, the prudent Franklin with illegitimate children, and even the upright Jefferson
with a slave mistress. On the other side, stories modified the outlaw
hero's most potentially damaging quality, his tendency to selfish isolationism, by demonstrating that, however reluctantly, he would act for
causes beyond himself. Thus, Huck grudgingly helped Jim escape, and
Davy Crockett left the woods for three terms in Congress before dying
in the Alamo for Texas independence. In this blurring process, Lincoln, a
composite of opposing traits, emerged as the great American figure. His
status as president made him an ex officio official hero. But his Western

10. *Politics and the Novel*, p. 164.

origins, melancholy solitude, and unaided decision-making all qualified him as a member of the other side. Finally, his ambivalent attitude toward the law played the most crucial role in his complex legend. As the chief executive, he inevitably stood for the principle that "we are a nation of laws and not men"; as the Great Emancipator, on the other hand, he provided the prime example of taking the law into one's own hands in the name of some higher standard.

Classic Hollywood's gallery of composite heroes (boxing musicians, rebellious aristocrats, pacifist soldiers) clearly derived from this mythology's rejection of final choices, a tendency whose traces Erikson detected in American psychology:

> The process of American identity formation seems to support an individual's ego identity as long as he can preserve a certain element of deliberate tentativeness of autonomous choice. The individual must be able to convince himself that the next step is up to him and that no matter where he is staying or going he always had the choice of leaving or turning in the opposite direction if he chooses to do so. In this country the migrant does not want to be told to move on, nor the sedentary man to stay where he is; for the life style (and the family history) of each contains the opposite element as a potential alternative which he wishes to consider his most private and individual decision.[11]

The reconciliatory pattern found its most typical incarnation, however, in one particular narrative: the story of the private man attempting to keep from being drawn into action on any but his own terms. In this story, the reluctant hero's ultimate willingness to help the community satisfied the official values. But by portraying this aid as demanding only a temporary involvement, the story preserved the values of individualism as well.

Like the contrasting heroes' epitomization of basic American dichotomies, the reluctant hero story provided a locus for displacement. Its most famous version, for example, *Adventures of Huckleberry Finn,* offered a typically individualistic solution to the nation's unresolved racial and sectional anxieties, thereby helping to forestall more systematic governmental measures. In adopting this story, Classic Hollywood retained its censoring power, using it, for example, in *Casablanca* to conceal the realistic threats to American self-determination posed by World War II.

Because the reluctant hero story was clearly the basis of the Western, American literature's repeated use of it prompted Leslie Fiedler to call the classic American novels "disguised westerns."[12] In the movies, too, this story appeared in every genre: in Westerns, of course (with *Shane* its most schematic articulation), but also in gangster movies (*Angels with*

---

11. *Childhood and Society,* p. 286.
12. *Love and Death in the American Novel,* p. 355.

Dirty Faces, Key Largo), musicals (*Swing Time*), detective stories (*The Thin Man*), war films (*Air Force*), screwball comedy (*The Philadelphia Story*), "problem pictures" (*On the Waterfront*), and even science fiction (the Han Solo character in *Star Wars*). *Gone with the Wind,* in fact, had two selfish heroes who came around at the last moment, Scarlett (taking care of Melanie) and Rhett (running the Union blockade), incompatible only because they were so much alike. The natural culmination of this pattern, perfected by Hollywood in the 1930s and early 1940s, was *Casablanca.* Its version of the outlaw hero–official hero struggle (Rick versus Laszlo) proved stunningly effective, its resolution (their collaboration on the war effort) the prototypical Hollywood ending.

The reluctant hero story's tendency to minimize the official hero's role (by making him dependent on the outsider's intervention) suggested an imbalance basic to the American mythology: Despite the existence of both heroes, the national ideology clearly preferred the outlaw. This ideology strove to make that figure's origins seem spontaneous, concealing the calculated, commercial efforts behind the mythologizing of typical examples like Billy the Kid and Davy Crockett. Its willingness, on the other hand, to allow the official hero's traces to show enables Daniel Boorstin to observe of one such myth, "There were elements of spontaneity, of course, in the Washington legend, too, but it was, for the most part, a self-conscious product."[13]

The apparent spontaneity of the outlaw heroes assured their popularity. By contrast, the official values had to rely on a rational allegiance that often wavered. These heroes' different statuses accounted for a structure fundamental to American literature, and assumed by Classic Hollywood: a split between the moral center and the interest center of a story. Thus, while the typical Western contained warnings against violence as a solution, taking the law into one's own hands, and moral isolationism, it simultaneously glamorized the outlaw hero's intense self-possession and willingness to use force to settle what the law could not. In other circumstances, Ishmael's evenhanded philosophy paled beside Ahab's moral vehemence, consciously recognizable as destructive.

D. H. Lawrence called this split the profound "duplicity" at the heart of nineteenth-century American fiction, charging that the classic novels evinced "a tight mental allegiance to a morality which all [the author's] passion goes to destroy." Certainly, too, this "duplicity" involved the mythology's pattern of obscuring the necessity for choosing between contrasting values. Richard Chase has put the matter less pejoratively in an account that applies equally to the American cinema:

> The American novel tends to rest in contradictions and among extreme ranges of experience. When it attempts to resolve contradic-

---

13. *The Americans: The National Experience,* p. 337.

tions, it does so in oblique, morally equivocal ways. As a general rule it does so either in melodramatic actions or in pastoral idylls, although intermixed with both one may find the stirring instabilities of "American humor."[14]

Or, in other words, when faced with a difficult choice, American stories resolved it either simplistically (by refusing to acknowledge that a choice is necessary), sentimentally (by blurring the differences between the two sides), or by laughing the whole thing off.

Reading the Text

1. What are the two basic hero types that Ray describes in American cinema?
2. How do these two hero types relate to America's "psychological pattern" (para. 2)?
3. Explain why, according to Ray, the outlaw hero typically mistrusts women.

Reading the Signs

1. In "Malcolm X" (p. 328), Shelby Steele offers his reading of Malcolm X as a cinematic hero. Review Steele's selection, and compare his analysis with Ray's discussion of heroes. To what extent does Ray's essay shed light on Malcolm's status as a hero?
2. Read Gary Engle's "What Makes Superman So Darned American?" (p. 677) and Andy Medhurst's "Batman, Deviance, and Camp" (p. 686), and write an essay in which you explain which type of heroes Superman and Batman are to their audiences.
3. What sort of hero is Arnold Schwarzenegger in the *Terminator* films? Write an essay in which you apply Ray's categories of hero to the Schwarzenegger character, supporting your argument with specific references to one or more films.
4. In class, brainstorm on the blackboard official and outlaw heroes you've seen in movies. Then categorize these heroes according to characteristics they have in common (such as race, gender, profession, or social class). What patterns emerge in your categories, and what is the significance of those patterns?
5. Rent one of the *Alien* films, and discuss whether Sigourney Weaver fits either of Ray's two categories of hero.
6. Cartoon television series like *The Simpsons* and *South Park* feature characters that don't readily fit Ray's two types of hero. Invent a third type of hero to accommodate such characters.

---

14. Richard Chase, *The American Novel and Its Tradition* (Garden City, N.Y.: Anchor/Doubleday, 1957), p. 1.

LINDA SEGER

Creating the Myth

||||||||||||||||||||||||||||||||||||||||||||||||||||||

To be a successful screenwriter, Linda Seger suggests in this selection from Making a Good Script Great *(1987), you've got to know your archetypes. Seger reveals the secret behind the success of such Hollywood creations as* Star Wars's *Luke Skywalker and tells you how you can create such heroes yourself. In this "how to" approach to the cinema, Seger echoes the more academic judgments of such semioticians of film as Umberto Eco—the road to popular success in mass culture is paved with cultural myths and clichés. A script consultant and author who has given professional seminars on filmmaking around the world, Seger has also published* When Women Call the Shots: The Developing Power and Influence of Women in Television and Film *(1997).*

All of us have similar experiences. We share in the life journey of growth, development, and transformation. We live the same stories, whether they involve the search for a perfect mate, coming home, the search for fulfillment, going after an ideal, achieving the dream, or hunting for a precious treasure. Whatever our culture, there are universal stories that form the basis for all our particular stories. The trappings might be different, the twists and turns that create suspense might change from culture to culture, the particular characters may take different forms, but underneath it all, it's the same story, drawn from the same experiences.

Many of the most successful films are based on these universal stories. They deal with the basic journey we take in life. We identify with the heroes because we were once heroic (descriptive) or because we wish we could do what the hero does (prescriptive). When Joan Wilder finds the jewel and saves her sister, or James Bond saves the world, or Shane saves the family from the evil ranchers, we identify with the character, and subconsciously recognize the story as having some connection with our own lives. It's the same story as the fairy tales about getting the three golden hairs from the devil, or finding the treasure and winning the princess. And it's not all that different a story from the caveman killing the woolly beast or the Roman slave gaining his freedom through skill and courage. These are our stories—personally and collectively—and the most successful films contain these universal experiences.

Some of these stories are "search" stories. They address our desire to find some kind of rare and wonderful treasure. This might include the search for outer values such as job, relationship, or success; or for inner values such as respect, security, self-expression, love, or home. But it's all a similar search.

Some of these stories are "hero" stories. They come from our own experiences of overcoming adversity, as well as our desire to do great and special acts. We root for the hero and celebrate when he or she achieves the goal because we know that the hero's journey is in many ways similar to our own.

We call these stories *myths*. Myths are the common stories at the root   5 of our universal existence. They're found in all cultures and in all literature, ranging from the Greek myths to fairy tales, legends, and stories drawn from all of the world's religions.

A myth is a story that is "more than true." Many stories are true because one person, somewhere, at some time, lived it. It is based on fact. But a myth is more than true because it is lived by all of us, at some level. It's a story that connects and speaks to us all.

Some myths are true stories that attain mythic significance because the people involved seem larger than life, and seem to live their lives more intensely than common folk. Martin Luther King, Jr., Gandhi, Sir Edmund Hillary, and Lord Mountbatten personify the types of journeys we identify with, because we've taken similar journeys—even if only in a very small way.

Other myths revolve around make-believe characters who might capsulize for us the sum total of many of our journeys. Some of these make-believe characters might seem similar to the characters we meet in our dreams. Or they might be a composite of types of characters we've met.

In both cases, the myth is the "story beneath the story." It's the universal pattern that shows us that Gandhi's journey toward independence and Sir Edmund Hillary's journey to the top of Mount Everest contain many of the same dramatic beats. And these beats are the same beats that Rambo takes to set free the MIAs, that Indiana Jones takes to find the Lost Ark, and that Luke Skywalker takes to defeat the Evil Empire.

In *Hero with a Thousand Faces,* Joseph Campbell traces the elements   10 that form the hero myth. "In their own work with myth, writer Chris Vogler and seminar leader Thomas Schlesinger have applied this criteria to *Star Wars*. The myth within the story helps explain why millions went to see this film again and again."

The hero myth has specific story beats that occur in all hero stories. They show who the hero is, what the hero needs, and how the story and character interact in order to create a transformation. The journey toward heroism is a process. This universal process forms the spine of all the particular stories, such as the *Star Wars* trilogy.

The Hero Myth

1. In most hero stories, the hero is introduced in ordinary surroundings, in a mundane world, doing mundane things. Generally, the hero begins as a nonhero; innocent, young, simple, or humble. In *Star Wars,* the first time we see Luke Skywalker, he's unhappy about having to do

his chores, which consists of picking out some new droids for work. He wants to go out and have fun. He wants to leave his planet and go to the Academy, but he's stuck. This is the setup of most myths. This is how we meet the hero before the call to adventure.

2. Then something new enters the hero's life. It's a catalyst that sets the story into motion. It might be a telephone call, as in *Romancing the Stone,* or the German attack in *The African Queen,* or the holograph of Princess Leia in *Star Wars.* Whatever form it takes, it's a new ingredient that pushes the hero into an extraordinary adventure. With this call, the stakes are established, and a problem is introduced that demands a solution.

3. Many times, however, the hero doesn't want to leave. He or she is a reluctant hero, afraid of the unknown, uncertain, perhaps, if he or she is up to the challenge. In *Star Wars,* Luke receives a double call to adventure. First, from Princess Leia in the holograph, and then through Obi-Wan Kenobi, who says he needs Luke's help. But Luke is not ready to go. He returns home, only to find that the Imperial Stormtroopers have burned his farmhouse and slaughtered his family. Now he is personally motivated, ready to enter into the adventure.

4. In any journey, the hero usually receives help, and the help often comes from unusual sources. In many fairy tales, an old woman, a dwarf, a witch, or a wizard helps the hero. The hero achieves the goal because of this help, and because the hero is receptive to what this person has to give.

There are a number of fairy tales where the first and second son are sent to complete a task, but they ignore the helpers, often scorning them. Many times they are severely punished for their lack of humility and unwillingness to accept help. Then the third son, the hero, comes along. He receives the help, accomplishes the task, and often wins the princess.

In *Star Wars,* Obi-Wan Kenobi is a perfect example of the "helper" character. He is a kind of mentor to Luke, one who teaches him the Way of the Force and whose teachings continue even after his death. This mentor character appears in most hero stories. He is the person who has special knowledge, special information, and special skills. This might be the prospector in *The Treasure of the Sierra Madre,* or the psychiatrist in *Ordinary People,* or Quint in *Jaws,* who knows all about sharks, or the Good Witch of the North who gives Dorothy the ruby slippers in *The Wizard of Oz.* In *Star Wars,* Obi-Wan gives Luke the light saber that was the special weapon of the Jedi Knight. With this, Luke is ready to move forward and do his training and meet adventure.

5. The hero is now ready to move into the special world where he or she will change from the ordinary into the extraordinary. This starts the hero's transformation, and sets up the obstacles that must be surmounted to reach the goal. Usually, this happens at the first Turning Point of the story, and leads into Act Two development. In *Star Wars,* Obi-Wan and Luke search for a pilot to take them to the planet of

Alderan, so that Obi-Wan can deliver the plans to Princess Leia's father. These plans are essential to the survival of the Rebel Forces. With this action, the adventure is ready to begin.

6. Now begin all the tests and obstacles necessary to overcome the enemy and accomplish the hero's goals. In fairy tales, this often means getting past witches, outwitting the devil, avoiding robbers, or confronting evil. In Homer's *Odyssey,* it means blinding the Cyclops, escaping from the island of the Lotus-Eaters, resisting the temptation of the singing Sirens, and surviving a shipwreck. In *Star Wars,* innumerable adventures confront Luke. He and his cohorts must run to the *Millennium Falcon,* narrowly escaping the Stormtroopers before jumping into hyperspace. They must make it through the meteor shower after Alderan has been destroyed. They must evade capture on the Death Star, rescue the Princess, and even survive a garbage crusher.

7. At some point in the story, the hero often hits rock bottom. He often has a "death experience," leading to a type of rebirth. In *Star Wars,* Luke seems to have died when the serpent in the garbage-masher pulls him under, but he's saved just in time to ask R2D2 to stop the masher before they're crushed. This is often the "black moment" at the second turning point, the point when the worst is confronted, and the action now moves toward the exciting conclusion.

8. Now, the hero seizes the sword and takes possession of the treasure. He is now in charge, but he still has not completed the journey. Here Luke has the Princess and the plans, but the final confrontation is yet to begin. This starts the third-act escape scene, leading to the final climax.

9. The road back is often the chase scene. In many fairy tales, this is the point where the devil chases the hero and the hero has the last obstacles to overcome before really being free and safe. His challenge is to take what he has learned and integrate it into his daily life. He *must* return to renew the mundane world. In *Star Wars,* Darth Vader is in hot pursuit, planning to blow up the Rebel Planet.

10. Since every hero story is essentially a transformation story, we need to see the hero changed at the end, resurrected into a new type of life. He must face the final ordeal before being "reborn" as the hero, proving his courage and becoming transformed. This is the point, in many fairy tales, where the Miller's Son becomes the Prince or the King and marries the Princess. In *Star Wars,* Luke has survived, becoming quite a different person from the innocent young man he was in Act One.

At this point, the hero returns and is reintegrated into his society. In *Star Wars,* Luke has destroyed the Death Star, and he receives his great reward.

This is the classic "Hero Story." We might call this example a *mission* or *task myth,* where the person has to complete a task, but the task itself is not the real treasure. The real reward for Luke is the love of the Princess and the safe, new world he had helped create.

A myth can have many variations. We see variations on this myth in James Bond films (although they lack much of the depth because the hero is not transformed), and in *The African Queen,* where Rose and Allnutt must blow up the *Louisa,* or in *Places in the Heart,* where Edna overcomes obstacles to achieve family stability.

The *treasure myth* is another variation on this theme, as seen in *Romancing the Stone.* In this story, Joan receives a map and a phone call which forces her into the adventure. She is helped by an American bird catcher and a Mexican pickup truck driver. She overcomes the obstacles of snakes, the jungle, waterfalls, shootouts, and finally receives the treasure, along with the "prince."

Whether the hero's journey is for a treasure or to complete a task, the elements remain the same. The humble, reluctant hero is called to an adventure. The hero is helped by a variety of unique characters. S/he must overcome a series of obstacles that transform him or her in the process, and then faces the final challenge that draws on inner and outer resources.

The Healing Myth

Although the hero myth is the most popular story, many myths involve healing. In these stories, some character is "broken" and must leave home to become whole again.

The universal experience behind these healing stories is our psychological need for rejuvenation, for balance. The journey of the hero into exile is not all that different from the weekend in Palm Springs, or the trip to Hawaii to get away from it all, or lying still in a hospital bed for some weeks to heal. In all cases, something is out of balance and the mythic journey moves toward wholeness.

Being broken can take several forms. It can be physical, emotional, or psychological. Usually, it's all three. In the process of being exiled or hiding out in the forest, the desert, or even the Amish farm in *Witness,* the person becomes whole, balanced, and receptive to love. Love in these stories is both a healing force and a reward.

Think of John Book in *Witness.* In Act One, we see a frenetic, insensitive man, afraid of commitment, critical and unreceptive to the feminine influences in his life. John is suffering from an "inner wound" which he doesn't know about. When he receives an "outer wound" from a gunshot, it forces him into exile, which begins his process of transformation.

At the beginning of Act Two, we see John delirious and close to death. This is a movement into the unconscious, a movement from the rational, active police life of Act One into a mysterious, feminine, more intuitive world. Since John's "inner problem" is the lack of balance with his feminine side, this delirium begins the process of transformation.

Later in Act Two, we see John beginning to change. He moves from his highly independent life-style toward the collective, communal life of his Amish hosts. John now gets up early to milk the cows and to assist with the chores. He uses his carpentry skills to help with the barn building and to complete the birdhouse. Gradually, he begins to develop relationships with Rachel and her son, Samuel. John's life slows down and he becomes more receptive, learning important lessons about love. In Act Three, John finally sees that the feminine is worth saving, and throws down his gun to save Rachel's life. A few beats later, when he has the opportunity to kill Paul, he chooses a nonviolent response instead. Although John doesn't "win" the Princess, he has nevertheless "won" love and wholeness. By the end of the film, we can see that the John Book of Act Three is a different kind of person from the John Book of Act One. He has a different kind of comradeship with his fellow police officers, he's more relaxed, and we can sense that somehow, this experience has formed a more integrated John Book.

Combination Myths

Many stories are combinations of several different myths. Think of *Ghostbusters,* a simple and rather outrageous comedy about three men saving the city of New York from ghosts. Now think of the story of "Pandora's Box." It's about the woman who let loose all manner of evil upon the earth by opening a box she was told not to touch. In *Ghostbusters,* the EPA man is a Pandora figure. By shutting off the power to the containment center, he inadvertently unleashes all the ghosts upon New York City. Combine the story of "Pandora's Box" with a hero story, and notice that we have our three heroes battling the Marshmallow Man. One of them also "gets the Princess" when Dr. Peter Venkman finally receives the affections of Dana Barrett. By looking at these combinations, it is apparent that even *Ghostbusters* is more than "just a comedy."

Tootsie is a type of reworking of many Shakespearean stories where a woman has to dress as a man in order to accomplish a certain task. These Shakespearean stories are reminiscent of many fairy tales where the hero becomes invisible or takes on another persona, or wears a specific disguise to hide his or her real qualities. In the stories of "The Twelve Dancing Princesses" or "The Man in the Bearskin," disguise is necessary to achieve a goal. Combine these elements with the transformation themes of the hero myth where a hero (such as Michael) must overcome many obstacles to his success as an actor and a human being. It's not diffi-cult to understand why the *Tootsie* story hooks us.

Archetypes

A myth includes certain characters that we see in many stories. These characters are called *archetypes*. They can be thought of as the original "pattern" or "character type" that will be found on the hero's journey. Archetypes take many forms, but they tend to fall within specific cate-gories.

Earlier, we discussed some of the helpers who give advice to help the hero — such as the *wise old man* who possesses special knowledge and often serves as a mentor to the hero.

The female counterpart of the wise old man is the *good mother*. Whereas the wise old man has superior knowledge, the good mother is known for her nurturing qualities, and for her intuition. This figure often gives the hero particular objects to help on the journey. It might be a protective amulet, or the ruby slippers that Dorothy receives in *The Wiz ard of Oz* from the Good Witch of the North. Sometimes in fairy tales it's a cloak to make the person invisible, or ordinary objects that become extraordinary, as in "The Girl of Courage," an Afghan fairy tale about a maiden who receives a comb, a whetstone, and a mirror to help defeat the devil.

Many myths contain a *shadow figure*. This is a character who is the opposite of the hero. Sometimes this figure helps the hero on the jour-ney; other times this figure opposes the hero. The shadow figure can be the negative side of the hero which could be the dark and hostile brother in "Cain and Abel," the stepsisters in "Cinderella," or the Robber Girl in "The Snow Queen." The shadow figure can also help the hero, as the whore with the heart of gold who saves the hero's life, or provides bal-ance to his idealization of woman.

Many myths contain *animal archetypes* that can be positive or negative figures. In "St. George and the Dragon," the dragon is the negative force which is a violent and ravaging animal, not unlike the shark in *Jaws*. But in many stories, animals help the hero. Sometimes there are talking don-keys, or a dolphin which saves the hero, or magical horses or dogs.

The *trickster* is a mischievous archetypical figure who is always caus-ing chaos, disturbing the peace, and generally being an anarchist. The trickster uses wit and cunning to achieve his or her ends. Sometimes the trickster is a harmless prankster or a "bad boy" who is funny and enjoy-able. More often, the trickster is a con man, as in *The Sting,* or the devil, as in *The Exorcist,* who demanded all the skills of the priest to outwit him. The "Till Eulenspiegel" stories revolve around the trickster, as do the Spanish picaresque novels. Even the tales of Tom Sawyer have a trickster motif. In all countries, there are stories that revolve around this figure, whose job it is to outwit.

"Mythic" Problems and Solutions

We all grew up with myths. Most of us heard or read fairy tales when we were young. Some of us may have read Bible stories, or stories from other religions or other cultures. These stories are part of us. And the best way to work with them is to let them come out naturally as you write the script.

Of course, some filmmakers are better at this than others. George Lucas and Steven Spielberg have a strong sense of myth and incorporate it into their films. They both have spoken about their love of the stories from childhood, and of their desire to bring these types of stories to audiences. Their stories create some of the same sense of wonder and excitement as myths. Many of the necessary psychological beats are part of their stories, deepening the story beyond the ordinary action-adventure.

Myths bring depth to a hero story. If a filmmaker is only thinking   45
about the action and excitement of a story, audiences might fail to connect with the hero's journey. But if the basic beats of the hero's journey are evident, a film will often inexplicably draw audiences, in spite of critics' responses to the film.

Take *Rambo* for instance. Why was this violent, simple story so popular with audiences? I don't think it was because everyone agreed with its politics. I do think Sylvester Stallone is a master at incorporating the American myth into his filmmaking. That doesn't mean it's done consciously. Somehow he is naturally in sync with the myth, and the myth becomes integrated into his stories.

Clint Eastwood also does hero stories, and gives us the adventure of the myth and the transformation of the myth. Recently Eastwood's films have given more attention to the transformation of the hero, and have been receiving more serious critical attention as a result.

All of these filmmakers—Lucas, Spielberg, Stallone, and Eastwood—dramatize the hero myth in their own particular ways. And all of them prove that myths are marketable.

Application

It is an important part of the writer's or producer's work to continually find opportunities for deepening the themes within a script. Finding the myth beneath the modern story is part of that process.

To find these myths, it's not a bad idea to reread some of Grimm's   50
fairy tales or fairy tales from around the world to begin to get acquainted

with various myths. You'll start to see patterns and elements that connect with our own human experience.

Also, read Joseph Campbell and Greek mythology. If you're interested in Jungian psychology, you'll find many rich resources within a number of books on the subject. Since Jungian psychology deals with archetypes, you'll find many new characters to draw on for your own work.

With all of these resources to incorporate, it's important to remember that the myth is not a story to force upon a script. It's more a pattern which you can bring out in your own stories when they seem to be heading in the direction of a myth.

As you work, ask yourself:

Do I have a myth working in my script? If so, what beats am I using of the hero's journey? Which ones seem to be missing?

Am I missing characters? Do I need a mentor type? A wise old man? A wizard? Would one of these characters help dimensionalize the hero's journey?

Could I create new emotional dimensions to the myth by starting my character as reluctant, naive, simple, or decidedly "un-heroic"?

Does my character get transformed in the process of the journey?

Have I used a strong three-act structure to support the myth, using the first turning point to move into the adventure and the second turning point to create a dark moment, or a reversal, or even a "near-death" experience?

Don't be afraid to create variations on the myth, but don't start with the myth itself. Let the myth grow naturally from your story. Developing myths are part of the rewriting process. If you begin with the myth, you'll find your writing becomes rigid, uncreative, and predictable. Working with the myth in the rewriting process will deepen your script, giving it new life as you find the story within the story.

Reading the Text

1. How does Seger define the "hero myth" (para. 10)?
2. In your own words, explain what Seger means by "the healing myth" (para. 29).
3. What is an "archetype" (para. 37) in film?

Reading the Signs

1. Linda Seger is writing to aspiring screenwriters. How does her status as an industry insider affect her description of heroic archetypes?

2. Compare Seger's formulation of heroes with Robert B. Ray's in "The Thematic Paradigm" (p. 299). To what extent do Seger and Ray adequately explain the role of women in movies?

3. Review Michael Parenti's "Class and Virtue" (p. 366), and then write an essay identifying the myths behind the modern stories *Pretty Woman* and *Indecent Proposal.*

4. Rent a videotape of *Titanic,* and write an essay in which you explain the myths and archetypal characters the film includes. How might archetypal and mythic patterns explain the film's success?

5. Seger recommends that aspiring screenwriters read Grimm's fairy tales for inspiration. Read some Grimm's tales, and then write an argument for or against the suitability of such tales as inspiration for films today.

6. What myths about American history, race, and gender do you see in *Gone with the Wind*? Brainstorm these myths in class, and then use your list of myths to write an essay in which you explain why the film has become an American classic.

SUSAN BORDO

Braveheart, Babe, *and the Contemporary Body*

"Just do it," Nike commands, and, as Susan Bordo (b. 1947) observes in this selection from Twilight Zones: The Hidden Life of Cultural Images from Plato to O.J. *(1997), a good part of American society has obeyed. Situating movies like Mel Gibson's* Braveheart *in a cultural system in which the "notion that all that is required to succeed . . . is to stop whining, lace up your sneakers, and forge ahead" has become the mantra of a nation of body-mad consumers, Bordo laments the ease with which traditional American self-reliance has been transformed into the freedom to buy what everyone else is buying. Why can't more people be like Babe? Bordo wonders. The little pig can't keep up with the collies but uses his head to come up with a better way to herd sheep—and in so doing, she suggests, offers an allegorical model for our own capacities to change the world. Bordo is the Otis A. Singletary Professor in the Humanities at the University of Kentucky, and the author of many books including* The Male Body: A New Look at Men in Public and in Private *(1999),* Unbearable Weight: Feminism, Western Culture, and the Body *(1993), and* Twilight Zone: The Hidden Life of Cultural Images from Plato to O.J. *(1997).*

Braveheart and "Just Do It"

I was stunned when Mel Gibson's *Braveheart* won the Oscar for best picture of the year. I know Hollywood loves a "sweeping" epic, and I liked the innovative use of mud and the absence of hairbrushes for the men (a commitment to material realism not matched in the commercial-perfect shots of the movie's heroines). But as interesting as it was to see Mel in unkempt cornrows, I didn't think it would add up to an Academy Award. Usually we require at least the semblance of an idea from our award-winning epics. *Braveheart* is a one-liner (actually a one-worder)— and an overworked one. "Your heart is free. Have the courage to follow 'er," the young William Wallace is told by his father's ghost at the start of the film. And he does, leading an animal-house army of howling Scotsmen against the yoke of cruel and effete British tyrants. "Freedom!" he screams, as he is disemboweled in the concluding scene, refusing to declare allegiance to British rule. Between these two scenes, "free," "freedom," and "freemen" were intoned reverently or shrieked passionately. And that was about it for "content."

"Live free or die." That slogan does have historical and ideological resonance for Americans. But it's clearly not the collective fight against political tyranny that counts in the movie; it's the courage to *act* and the triumph of the undauntable, unconquerable action hero. Yes, Gibson makes William Wallace a fluent linguist, educated in Latin, well traveled, a man who uses his brain to plot battle strategy. But this is just a ploy to create the appearance of masculine stereotype busting. It's *doing,* not thinking, that reveals a man's worth in the film, whose notion of heroics is as tough-guy as they come. In the last scene Wallace endures public stretching, racking, and evisceration so that Scotland will know he died without submitting, and Gibson (who directed the film as well as starred in it) makes the torture go on for a long, painful time. Wallace's resistance is really the point of the film. Braveheart has his eyes on a prize, and his will is so strong, so powerful, that he is able to endure anything to achieve it. The man has the right stuff.

This macho model of moral fortitude has a lot of living currency today—and for the first time, we now see it as applying to women as well as men. Undiluted testosterone drives *Braveheart.* Its band of Scottish rebels is described in a voice-over as fighting "like warrior-poets," an unmistakable nod to the mythopoetic men's movement to reclaim masculinity. King Longshank's son is a homosexual, and this is clearly coded in the film as signifying that he lacks the equipment to rule. But the movie's women, within the limits of their social roles, are as rebellious and brave-hearted as the men and enjoy watching a good fight too. (In an early scene Wallace's girl's eyes light up as he and a fellow Scot have sport throwing bricks at each other's heads.) I think this is Gibson's idea of feminism—that one doesn't have to be male in order to be a real man—and it is an idea that is widely shared today, with "power" and "muscle" feminism the culturally approved way of advancing the cause of women.

That women have just as much guts, willpower, and *balls* as men, that they can put their bodies through as much wear and tear, endure as much pain, and remain undaunted, was a major theme of the coverage of the 1996 Summer Olympics. Not since Leni Riefenstahl's *Olympiad* of 1936 has there been such a focus on the aesthetics of athletic perfection. But *this* version of beauty, like Riefenstahl's and like those stressed in the numerous photo-articles celebrating the Olympic body, has little to do with looking pretty. It's about strength, yes, and skill, but even more deeply it's about true grit. "Determined, defiant, dominating," the bold caption in the *New York Times Magazine* describes Gwen Torrence. (The same words, applied to rebellious wives or feminist politicos, have not been said so admiringly.) As in *Braveheart,* the ability to rise above the trials of the body is associated with the highest form of courage and commitment. Mary Ellen Clark's bouts of vertigo. Gail Devers's Graves' disease. Gwen Torrence's difficult childbirth. Amy Van Dyken's asthma. *Life* magazine describes these as personal tests of mettle sent by God to weed out the losers from the winners. And when gymnast Kerri Strug performed her second vault on torn tendons, bringing her team to victory in the face of what must have been excruciating pain, she became the unquestionable hero of the games (and set herself up with ten million dollars in endorsement contracts).

It's not the courage of these athletes I'm sniping at here; I admire   5
them enormously. What bothers me is the message that is dramatized by the way we tell the tales of their success, a message communicated to us mortals too in commercials and ads. Nike has proven to be the master manipulator and metaphor maker in this game. Don't moan over life's problems or blame society for holding you back, Nike instructs us. Don't waste your time berating the "system." Get down to the gym, pick up those free weights, and turn things around. If it hurts, all the better. No pain, no gain. "Right after Bob Kempainen qualified for the marathon, he crossed the finish line and puked all over his Nike running shoes," Nike tells us in a recent advertisement. "We can't tell you how proud we were." A Nike commercial, shown during the games: "If you don't lose consciousness at the end, you could have run faster." Am I the only one who finds this recommendation horrifying in its implications? But consciousness apparently doesn't figure very much in our contemporary notion of heroism. What counts, as in *Braveheart,* is action. *Just Do It.* This is, of course, also what Nike wants us to do when we approach the cash register. (The call to *act* sends a disturbing political message as well. Movies like *Braveheart,* as a friend of mine remarked after we'd seen the film, seem designed to provide inspiration for the militia movement.)

The notion that all that is required to succeed in this culture is to stop whining, lace up your sneakers, and forge ahead, blasting your way through social limitations, personal tribulations, and even the laws of nature, is all around us. . . . Commercials and advertisements egg us on: "Go for It!" "Know No Boundaries!" "Take Control!" Pump yourself up with our product—a car, a diet program, hair-coloring, sneakers—and take your destiny into your own hands. The world will open up for you like an oyster. Like the Sector watch advertisement, AT&T urges us to "Imagine a world without limits" in a series of commercials shown during the 1996 Summer Olympics; one graphic depicts a young athlete pole-vaulting over the World Trade Center, another diving down an endless waterfall. And, indeed, in the world of these images, there are no impediments—no genetic disorders, no body-altering accidents, not even any fat—to slow down our progress to the top of the mountain. All that's needed is the power to *buy*.

The worst thing, in the *Braveheart*/Nike universe of values, is to be bossed around, told what to do. This creates a dilemma for advertisers, who somehow must convince hundreds of thousands of people to purchase the same product while assuring them that they are bold and innovative individualists in doing so. The dilemma is compounded because many of these products perform what Foucault and feminist theorists have called "normalization." That is, they function to screen out diversity and perpetuate social norms, often connected to race and gender. This happens not necessarily because advertisers are consciously trying to promote racism or sexism but because in order to sell products they have to either exploit or create a perception of personal *lack* in the consumer (who buys the product in the hope of filling that lack). An effective way to make the consumer feel inadequate is to take advantage of values that are already in place in the culture. For example, in a society where there is a dominant (and racialized) preference for blue-eyed blondes, there is a ready market for blue contact lenses and blonde hair-coloring. The catch is that ad campaigns promoting such products also reglamorize the beauty ideals themselves. Thus, they perpetuate racialized norms.

But people don't like to think that they are pawns of astute advertisers or even that they are responding to social norms. Women who have had or are contemplating cosmetic surgery consistently deny the influence of media images.[1] "I'm doing it for me," they insist. But it's hard to account for most of their choices (breast enlargement and liposuction being the most frequently performed operations) outside the context of current cultural norms. Surgeons help to encourage these mystifications. Plastic surgeon Barbara Hayden claims that breast augmentation today is

---

1. See Marcene Goodman, "Social, Psychological, and Developmental Factors in Women's Receptivity to Cosmetic Surgery," *Journal of Aging Studies* 8, no. 4 (1994): 375–96.

"as individual as the patient herself"; a moment later in the same article another surgeon adds that the "huge 1980s look is out" and that many stars are trading their old gigantibreasts for the currently stylish smaller models![2]

I'm doing it for me. This has become the mantra of the television talk show, and I would gladly accept it if "for me" meant "in order to feel better about myself in this culture that has made me feel inadequate as I am." But people rarely mean this. Most often on these shows, the "for me" answer is produced in defiant refutation of some cultural "argument" (talk-show style, of course) on topics such as "Are Our Beauty Ideals Racist?" or "Are We Obsessed with Youth?" "No, I'm not having my nose (straightened) (narrowed) in order to look less ethnic. I'm doing it *for me.*" "No, I haven't had my breasts enlarged to a 38D in order to be more attractive to men. I did it *for me.*" In these constructions "me" is imagined as a pure and precious inner space, an "authentic" and personal reference point untouched by external values and demands. A place where we live free and won't be pushed around. It's the *Braveheart* place.

But we want to both imagine ourselves as bold, rebellious Brave-   10
hearts *and* conform, become what our culture values. Advertisers help us enormously in this self-deception by performing their own sleight-of-hand tricks with rhetoric and image, often invoking, as *Braveheart* does, the metaphor and hype of "political" resistance: "Now it's every woman's right to look good!" declares Pond's (for "age-defying" makeup). "What makes a woman revolutionary?" asks Revlon. "Not wearing makeup for a day!" answers a perfectly made-up Claudia Schiffer (quickly adding, "Just kidding, Revlon!"). A recent Gap ad: "The most defiant act is to be distinguished, singled out, marked. Put our jeans on." The absurdity of suggesting that everyone's donning the same (rather ordinary-looking) jeans can be a "defiant" and individualistic act is visually accompanied by two photos of female models with indistinguishable bodies.

Power as Agency: Masking Reality

From evisceration at the hands of tyrants to defiance through dungarees may seem like a large leap. And in real terms, of course, it is. But we live in a world of commercial rhetoric that brooks no such distinctions. And not only commercial rhetoric. "Just Do It" is an ideology for our time, an idea that bridges the gulf between right and left, grunge and yuppie, chauvinist and feminist. The left wing didn't like "Just Say No,"

---

2. Quoted in Sally Ogle Davis, "Knifestyles of the Rich and Famous," *Marie Claire,* May 1996, p. 46.

perhaps because it came from Nancy Reagan, perhaps because it was aimed at habits they didn't want to give up themselves. It isn't that easy, they insisted. The neighborhoods, the culture, social despair. . . . But the mind-over-matter message of "Just Do It," with its "neutral" origins (the brain of an ad woman) and associations with jogging, nice bodies, and muscle-lib for women, has roused no protests.

In a recent interview rock star Courtney Love urged "liberals" to "breed" in order to outpopulate the Rush Limbaughs of the world. "It's not that hard," she said. "It's nine months. You know, just do it."[3] But right-wing ideologues like Limbaugh, who celebrate bootstrapping and Horatio Alger and scorn (what they view as) the liberal's creation of a culture of "victims," also advocate "just doing it."[4] And so too do celebrities like Oprah when they present themselves as proof that "anyone can make it if they want it badly enough and try hard enough." The implication here—which Oprah, I like to believe, would blanch at if she faced it squarely—is that if you *don't* succeed, it's proof that you *didn't* want it badly enough or try hard enough. Racism and sexism? Just so many hurdles to be jumped, personal challenges to be overcome. And what about the fact that in a competitive society someone *always has to lose*? We won't think about that, it's too much of a downer. Actually, in the coverage of the 1996 Olympics, everything short of "getting the gold" was constructed as losing. The men's 4 × 100 relay team, which won the silver medal, was interviewed by NBC after, as the commentator put it, their "defeat"! How can everyone be a winner if "winning" is reserved only for those who make it to the absolute pinnacle?

As far as women's issues go, "power feminists" are telling us that we're past all those tiresome harangues about "the beauty system" and "objectification" and "starving girls." What's so bad about makeup, anyway? Isn't it my right to go for it? Do what I want with my body? Be all that I can be? Just a few years back "third-wave" feminist Naomi Wolf wrote a best-selling book, *The Beauty Myth* (1991), which spoke powerfully and engagingly to young women about a culture that teaches them they are nothing if they are not beautiful. But in a wink of the cultural zeitgeist, she declares in her latest, *Fire with Fire* (1993), that all that

---

3. Interview with Amanda de Cadenet, *Interview,* August 1995.

4. Rush Limbaugh, in his tirades against feminists and the academic left, has apparently not noticed that among these groups too the "victim" is *not* politically correct but passé. In the 1990s postmodern academics look around and see not "oppressive" systems (which would be old-fashioned and "totalizing," so very "sixties") but "resistance," "subversion," and "creative negotiation" of the culture. (These academics may balk at being lined up on the side of *Braveheart* and Nike; they might be surprised at how often the trope of cultural "resistance" appears in automobile ads.) In exalting the creative power and efficacy of the individual, the right and left—polarized around so many other issues—seem to be revelers at the same party.

bitching and moaning has seen its day. Now, according to the rehabili-
tated Wolf, we're supposed to stop complaining and—you guessed it—
"Just Do It." Wolf, in fact, offers Nike's commercial slogan as her symbol
for the new feminism, which as she describes it is about "competition...
victory...self-reliance...the desire to win."[5] Wolf is hardly alone in her
celebratory mood. Betty Friedan has also said she is "sick of women wal-
lowing in the victim state. We have empowered ourselves." A 1993
Newsweek article—most of its authors women—sniffs derisively at an in-
stallation of artist Sue Williams, who put a huge piece of plastic vomit on
the floor of the Whitney Museum to protest the role of aesthetic ideals in
encouraging the development of eating disorders. That kind of action
once would have been seen as guerrilla theater. In 1993, *Newsweek* writers sneered: "Tell [the bulimics] to get some therapy and cut it out."[6]

Getting one's body in shape, of course, has become the exemplary
practice, symbol, and means of empowerment in this culture. "You
don't just shape your body," as Bally Fitness tells us. "You shape your
life." As a manufacturer of athletic shoes, Nike—like Reebok and
Bally—is dedicated to preserving the connection between having the
right stuff and strenuous, physical activity. "It's about time," they declare
disingenuously in a recent ad, "that the fitness craze that turned into the
fashion craze that turned into the marketing craze turned back into the
fitness craze." But despite Nike's emphasis on fitness, in contemporary
commercial culture the rhetoric of taking charge of one's life has been
yoked to everything from car purchases to hair-coloring, with physical
effort and discipline often dropping out as a requirement. Even plastic
surgery is continually described today—by patients, surgeons, and even
by some feminist theorists—as *an act* of "taking control," "taking one's
life into one's own hands" (a somewhat odd metaphor, under the circumstances). . . .

Babe: **A Real Metaphor for Our Lives...**

And so I come to *Babe,* which did not win the Academy Award but   15
which moved and haunted me for weeks after I saw it. For a long time I
tried to put my finger on just why that was. As I've said, I generally
bristle against the triumphant success story. And *Babe,* like *Braveheart* (and
Rocky), is a success story, a tale of individual empowerment and personal
triumph against enormous odds, of questing, self-transformation, and,
you might even say, transcendence of the body. A little pig, seemingly

---

5. Naomi Wolf, *Fire with Fire* (New York: Random House, 1993), 45.

6. Friedan quote and "Tell them to get some therapy" in Debra Rosenberg, Stanley Holmes, Martha Brant, Donna Foote, and Nina Biddle, "Sexual Correctness,"
Newsweek, October 25, 1993, p. 56.

destined to be dinner, dreams of becoming a sheepdog—and he succeeds! Crowds cheer and tears flow. And so did mine (dry at the end of *Braveheart* and *Rocky*).

When I tried to explain to a more cynical friend why I loved the film, I grasped impotently at the available takes on the film then circulating in magazines and among intellectuals. "Allegory of social prejudice," that sort of thing. But I knew that wasn't exactly what did it for me, and when my friend pressed on, amazed that I could be so taken by what she saw as a sentimental fantasy, I realized that sentimental—in the sense of wrenching emotion while falsifying reality—was precisely what I found *Babe* not to be and that this was a large part of the reason why it moved me so powerfully. *Braveheart,* apparently based on real events, seemed like a slick commercial to me from start to finish. But *Babe*—a fable with talking animals—was for me a moment of reality in a culture dominated by fantasy.

Babe, on the face of it, seems far removed from the land of Stair-Masters, liposuction, and face-lifts—and it is certainly nothing like a Nike commercial. Babe's personal triumph takes place in a world that—as the film never lets us forget—permits such moments only for a very few. On the farm most of the animals eke their joy humbly from the circumscribed routines and roles allotted to them—and they are the lucky ones, the safe ones. The others—those who are destined to be eaten—tremble on little islands of temporary peace, the vulnerability and perishability of their existence always hovering before them. Death for them will not be accompanied by the dignifying hoopla of the big battle or the knowledge that they have made a statement for history. They will have no control over when death comes, and they will be unable to make the "why" of it more meaningful than the fact that others are luckier and more powerful and more arrogant than they are. This is a world in which those who can "just do it" are a privileged few. A world in which "agency" is real but limited and "empowerment" possible but hardly an everyday affair. A world in which the notion that we are "in charge," "in control," "at the reins" is strictly an illusion. Existence is precarious for the animals on the farm, as it is materially for many people, and as it is existentially for all of us, whether we recognize it or not. We can try to avoid this recognition with illusions of "agency," fantasies of staying young forever, and the distractions of "self-improvement," but it only lies in wait for us.

It is very important to the emotional truth of the film that Babe himself learns about the fragility of his safety. When he decides to go on anyway, it is not as a hopeful hero-to-be, dreaming of glory, but out of the simple fact that despite "the way things are" in the awful world he has learned about, there is still the unanswerable, unbreakable bond between him and the Boss. The men in *Braveheart* are bonded too. But, as Gibson directs it, the relationship amounts to a fraternity handshake, a pledge of affiliation; they're all pumped up, looking out over the grandeur of the countryside, ready to take up arms together. The bond between Babe and the Boss is established in a very different sort of exchange, in which each, in a Kierkegaardian leap of faith, bravely lets down his defenses in a moment of simple caring for and trust in the other. The taciturn and reserved farmer, trying to get depressed Babe to eat and obeying some wild impulse of inspiration, leaps up and performs an unrestrained, goofy hornpipe for him. Babe watches and, although he has heard "the way things are" from Fly, his surrogate-mother (pigs get eaten, even by the Boss and his wife), cedes final authority to the reasons of the heart. He eats.

Babe's world is the one we live in; heroic moments are temporary and connections with others are finally what sustain us. This is a reality we may be inclined to forget as we try to create personal scenarios that will feel like Olympic triumphs and give us the power and "agency" over our bodies and lives that the commercials promise. But we still feel the emotional tug of abandoned dreams of connection and intimacy and relationships that will feed us in the open-hearted way that the Boss feeds little Babe and Babe's eating feeds *him*. My cynical friend disliked the movie for—as she saw it—idealizing parent-child relations through scenes such as this (and Babe's relationship with his surrogate mother, the Border collie Fly). But unlike the Gerber's commercials that feature mother and child ensconced in an immaculate nursery, cocooned together by the accoutrements of cozy furniture, perfectly tended plants, good hair and skin, *Babe*'s images of caring and intimacy do not work through sugarcoating but by keeping the dark realities always on the horizon. They are the reason we need to take care of one another.

Babe is, of course, a success story. But unlike *Rocky, Flashdance,* 20 *Braveheart,* and the many other fantasies of empowerment in which socially underprivileged heroes and heroines rise above their circumstances and transform themselves through discipline, will, and dazzling physical prowess, *Babe* is a fable about the power of "difference," of nonassimilation. The polite little pig, who talks to the sheep rather than snap and bark, turns out to be a better herder than the bossy Border collies! And in a significant way he transforms the culture and the values of the world he lives in. (It is suggested both at the beginning and the end of the film that attitudes toward pigs were never the same after Babe won the competition.) The *Rocky* model of success, like the "power feminism" model, is one of "making it" in a world that remains unchanged while the hero or heroine's body transforms itself to meet—and perhaps even surpass—the requirements of that world. This is what we celebrate when female athletes demonstrate that they can develop the strength and power of men, when "special" Olympians cross the finish lines in their competitions, when those who have struggled to lose weight finally squeeze into those size eight Calvin Kleins; the "outsider" is included by showing that he or she can "do it" too—on the terms of the culture. When the media celebrates such successes (and I do not deny that they are cause for celebration, as dramas of individual will, courage, and dedication), it usually leaves those cultural terms unquestioned.

Babe illustrates a different kind of success, one in which the "it" (of "Just Do It," "making it," "going for it") is interrogated and challenged. Those collies own the world (their own little world, that is) by virtue of their physical prowess and aggression, which—until Babe comes along—are the dominant values of that world. No one could have imagined that sheepherding could be done in any other way. How many of us have found ourselves struggling to prove our worth in worlds which do not value us or our contributions? Often, the pressure to conform is overwhelming. Babe, unable to transform his waddly little body and unwilling to transform his empathic little soul into a mean, lean, fighting machine, represents the possibility of resisting that pressure—and transforming "the way things are." In a culture in which people are shamed for their "defects" and differences and seek safety in conformity, this may be a fantasy. But it is a precious one, one more worthy of our imaginations and ambitions—and our children's, surely—than "Just Do It!"

Babe is a fable and presents its message through the conventions of that genre, not through gritty realism. A glorious triumph is the reward for the "alternative" values that the little pig represents. Few of us experience such definitive or resounding validation of our efforts. But it is not necessary to win the big race in order to transform "the way things are." All of us, in myriad small ways, have the capacity to do this, because nothing that we do is a self-contained, disconnected, isolated event. Seemingly minor gestures of resistance to cultural norms can lay deep imprints on the lives of those around us. Unfortunately, gestures of capitulation do so as well. Consider the message sent by the mother who anxiously monitors her own weight and ships her daughter off to Jenny Craig at the first sign that her child's body is less than willowy, or the father who teases his wife (perhaps in front of their daughter) for being "out of shape." I don't mean to sound harsh; these responses may reflect personal insecurity, concern about the social acceptability of loved ones, panic over a child's future. But when we demonstrate seamless solidarity with our culture of images, we make its reign over the lives of those we love just a little bit stronger. And we unwittingly promote for them a life on the cultural treadmill.

I have learned a great deal about the extremes of that treadmill existence from my students' journals and from conversations with them in my office. Yes, my students know that as long as they keep up their daily hours at the gym, they can feel pumped up, look like Madonna, and burn enough calories so perhaps they will not have to throw up after dinner. But how, they wonder, can they possibly keep it up their entire lives? They know there is no equilibrium there, that the conditions of their feeling all right about themselves are *precarious*. Here is where *Babe* does speak to the situation of those who try to stop those breasts from sagging, thighs from spreading, wrinkles from forming. The parable not only makes visible more basic struggles that our obsession with appearance masks but also presents us with a metaphor for the *pathos* of that seemingly "superficial" obsession. The little pig performs in the final competition without any solid assurance of a happy ending. Even as he herds the sheep into the pen, he has not been told, in so many words, that he will be spared the carving knife. He wins the sheepherding trials, and, as is customary, the farmer utters the standard words "real" dogs hear at the end of their runs. "That'll do, Pig. That'll do." A formality usually—but in the context of Babe's long struggle, these words say more, both to Babe and to the viewer. They represent, I believe, an acknowledgment that so many of us fervently long for in our lives—and are so rarely given. So many of us feel like Babe, trying our hardest to become something valued and loved, uncertain about whether we will ever be granted the right to simply exist. "That'll do. That'll do." These are words to break the heart. Enough. You've worked hard enough. I accept you. You can rest.

Reading the Text

1. What, according to Bordo, are the different kinds of success dramatized in *Braveheart* and *Babe*?
2. Describe in your own words what Bordo means by "the *Braveheart*/Nike universe of values" (para. 7).
3. What are Bordo's objections to the phrase "Just Do It" (para. 5)?
4. Why does Bordo prefer *Babe* to *Braveheart*?
5. How does Babe represent alternative values, in Bordo's view?
6. Chart Bordo's construction of the *system* in which she analyzes *Braveheart* and *Babe*.

Reading the Signs

1. In your journal, reflect on whether you have been influenced by the Just-Do-It philosophy.
2. Compare and contrast Bordo's interpretation of *Braveheart* with that in the Introduction to Chapter 8, "Life on the Margins: Representing the 'Other' in American Culture" (p. 599). Which reading of the film do you find more persuasive, and why?
3. In class, brainstorm two lists of recent films—those that encourage what Bordo terms the Just-Do-It philosophy and those that encourage viewers to change, not overpower, the world. Analyze your results. Do the lists differ in length or in the commercial success of their titles? Can you account for any differences you find?

4. Compare and contrast Bordo's discussion of the Just-Do-It philosophy with Stuart Ewen's description of "Hard Bodies" (p. 79).
5. In an essay, support, refute, or complicate Bordo's criticism of power feminism.
6. Bordo contends that "I'm doing it for me" has become the "mantra of the television talk show" (para. 9). Watch one such show, and write an essay evaluating the validity of Bordo's contention. To develop your ideas, read or reread Steven D. Stark's "*The Oprah Winfrey Show* and the Talk-Show Furor" (p. 241).

SHELBY STEELE
Malcolm X

<hr>

iiiiiiiiiiiiiiiiiiiiiiiiiiiiiiiiiiiiiiiiiiiiiiiiiiii

One of the most independent-minded and widely read of America's writers on racial relations, Shelby Steele (b. 1946) has never been afraid to take a controversial position. In this reading of Spike Lee's Malcolm X, *Steele goes beyond a critique of the film, which he feels oversimplifies the life and meaning of Malcolm X, to take on the myth of Malcolm X itself. At a time when Malcolm X is being celebrated as an icon of radical black nationalism, Steele argues that Malcolm was a profoundly conservative man whose appeal lies precisely in his cultural conservatism. From his beliefs in the family-building responsibilities of black women to his abhorrence of tobacco and alcohol, Malcolm X actually endorsed many of America's most traditional values—a side to his character that is often ignored. For Steele, who wishes to understand Malcolm X, not debunk him, all the mythmaking about the man does little to help us interpret his full cultural significance—a task that Steele begins here. Shelby Steele is currently a research fellow at Stanford University's Hoover Institute and the author of* The Content of Our Character: A New Vision of Race in America *(1990), which won a National Book Critics Circle Award, and* A Dream Deferred: The Second Betrayal of Black Freedom in America *(1998).*

When asked recently what he thought of Malcolm X, Thurgood Marshall is reported to have said, "All he did was talk." And yet there is a kind of talk that constitutes action, a catalytic speech that changes things as irrevocably as do events or great movements. Malcolm X was an event, and his talk transformed American culture as surely, if not as thoroughly, as the civil rights movement, which might not have found the moderation necessary for its success had Malcolm not planted in the American consciousness so uncompromised a vision of the underdog's rage.

Malcolm staked out this territory against his great contemporary and foil, Martin Luther King, Jr. Sneering at King's turn-the-other-cheek Christianity, he told blacks, "Don't ask God to have mercy on him [the white man]; ask God to judge him. Ask God to do onto him what he did onto you. Ask God that he suffer as you suffered." To use the old Christian categories, Malcolm was the Old Testament to King's New Testament. Against the moral nobility of the civil rights movement, he wanted whites to know that he was not different from them; that he, too, would kill or die for freedom. "The price of freedom is death," he often said.

Like all true revolutionaries, Malcolm had an intimate relationship with his own death. By being less afraid of it than other men, he took on power. And this was not so much a death wish as it was the refusal of a compromised life. These seemed to be his terms, and for many blacks like myself who came of age during his era, there was nothing to do but love him, since he, foolishly or not, seemed to love us more than we loved ourselves.

It is always context that makes a revolutionary figure like Malcolm X a hero or a destroyer. Even when he first emerged in the late fifties and early sixties, the real debate was not so much about him (he was clear enough) as about whether or not the context of black oppression was severe enough to justify him. And now that Malcolm has explosively reemerged on the American scene, those old questions about context are with us once again.

Spike Lee has brought Malcolm's autobiography to the screen in one   5
of the most thoroughly hyped films in American history. Malcolm's life is available in airport bookstalls. Compact discs and videotapes of his "blue-eyed devil" speeches can be picked up at Tower Records. His "X" is ubiquitous to the point of gracing automobile air fresheners. Twenty-seven years after his death, in sum, he is more visible to Americans than he was during his life. Of course Americans will commercialize anything; but that is a slightly redundant point. The really pressing matter is what this says about the context of race relations in America today. How can a new generation of blacks—after pervasive civil rights legislation, Great Society programs, school busing, open housing, and more than two decades of affirmative action—be drawn to a figure of such seething racial alienation?

The life of Malcolm X touched so many human archetypes that his story itself seems to supersede any racial context, which is to say that it meshes with virtually every context. Malcolm X is a story. And so he meets people, particularly young people, in a deeply personal way. To assess whether or not he is a good story for these times, I think we have to consider first the nature of his appeal.

Let me say—without, I hope, too many violins—that when I was growing up in the 1950s, I was very often the victim of old-fashioned racism and discrimination. These experiences were very much like the literal experience of being burned. Not only did they hurt, they also caused me to doubt myself in some fundamental way. There was shame in these experiences as well, the suspicion that by some measure of human worth I deserved them. This, of course, is precisely what they were designed to make me feel. So right away there was an odd necessity to fight and to struggle for both personal and racial dignity.

Those were the experiences that enabled me to hear Malcolm. The very soul of his legend was the heroic struggle that he was waging against racial doubt and shame. After a tortuous childhood and an early life of crime that left him shattered, he reconstructed himself—against the injuries of racial oppression—by embracing an ideology of black nationalism. Black nationalism offered something very important to Malcolm, and this quickly became his magnificently articulated offering to other blacks. What it offered was a perfectly cathartic distribution of love and hate. Blacks were innocent victims, whites were evil oppressors, and blacks had to distribute their love and hate accordingly. But if one focuses on the called-for hatred of whites, the point of Malcolm's redistribution of emotion will be missed. If Malcolm was screaming his hatred of whites, his deeper purpose was to grant blacks a license to give themselves what they needed most: self-love.

This license to love and to hate in a way that soothed my unconscious doubts was nothing less than compelling by the time I reached college. Late at night in the dorm, my black friends and I would turn off the lights for effect and listen to his album of speeches, *The Ballot or the Bullet,* over and over again. He couldn't have all that anger and all that hate unless he really loved black people, and, therefore, us. And so he massaged the injured part of ourselves with an utterly self-gratifying and unconditional love.

With Martin Luther King, by contrast, there were conditions. King 10 asked blacks—despised and unloved—to spread their meager stock of love to all people, even to those who despised us. What a lot to ask, and of a victim. With King, we were once again in second place, loving others before ourselves. But Malcolm told us to love ourselves first and to project all of our hurt into a hatred of the "blue-eyed devil" who had hurt us in the first place.

In Malcolm's deployment of love and hate there was an intrinsic logic of dignity that was very different from King's. For King, racial dignity was established by enlarging the self into a love of others. For Malcolm, dignity came from constriction, from shrinking to the enemy's size, and showing him not that you could be higher than he was, but that you could go as low. If King rose up, Malcolm dropped down. And here is where he used the hatred side of his formula to lay down his two essential principles of black dignity: the dehumanization of the white man and the threat of violence.

What made those principles essential to the dignity of blacks for Malcolm was that they followed a tit-for-tat logic—the logic by which, in his mind, any collective established its dignity against another collective. And both these principles could be powerfully articulated by Malcolm because they were precisely the same principles by which whites had oppressed blacks for centuries. Malcolm dehumanized whites by playing back, in whiteface, the stereotypes that blacks had endured. He made them animals—if they like their meat rare, "that's the dog in 'em." In the iconography of his Black Muslim period, whites were heathen, violent, drooling beasts who lynched and raped. But he often let his humor get the best of him in this, and most blacks took it with a grain of salt.

What made Malcolm one of the most controversial Americans of this century was the second principle in his logic of dignity: the threat of violence. "If we have a funeral in Harlem, make sure they have one downtown, too." "If he puts his hand on you, send him to the cemetery." Tit-for-tat logic taken to its logical conclusion. In fact, Malcolm's focus on violence against whites was essentially rhetorical. Like today's black street gangs, his Black Muslims were far more likely to kill each other than go after whites. Yet no one has ever played the white hysteria over black violence better than Malcolm.

He played this card very effectively to achieve two things. The first was to breach the horrible invisibility that blacks have endured in America. White racism has always been sustained by the white refusal or reluctance to see blacks, to think about them as people, to grant them the kind of place in the imagination that one would grant, say, to the English or even the Russians. Blacks might be servile or troublesome, but never worthy of serious, competitive consideration. Against this Malcolm sent a concrete message: We are human enough to want to kill you for what you have done to us. How does it feel to have people you have never paid much attention to want to kill you? (This was the terror Richard Wright captured so powerfully in *Native Son*: Your humble chauffeur may kill your daughter. And that novel, too, got attention.) Violence was a means to black visibility for Malcolm, and later for many other militants.

Today this idea of violence as black visibility means that part of Malcolm's renewed popularity comes from his power as an attention-getting figure. If today's "X" is an assertion of self-love, it is also a demand to be seen. This points to the second purpose of Malcolm's violent rhetoric: to restore dignity to blacks in an almost Hegelian sense. Those unwilling to kill and to die for dignity would forever be a slave class. Here he used whites as the model. They would go to war to meet any threat, even when it was far removed. Many times he told his black audiences that whites would not respect them unless they used "any means necessary" to seize freedom. For a minority outnumbered ten to one, this was not rational. But it was a point that needed to be made in the name of

15

dignity. It was something that many blacks needed to feel about themselves, that there was a line that no one could cross.

Yet this logic of dignity only partly explains Malcolm's return as an icon in our own day. I believe that the larger reason for his perdurability and popularity is one that is almost never mentioned: that Malcolm X was a deeply conservative man. In times when the collective identity is besieged and confused, groups usually turn to their conservatives, not to their liberals; to their extreme partisans, not to their open-minded representatives. The last twenty-five years have seen huge class and cultural differences open up in black America. The current bromide is that we are not a monolith, and this is profoundly true. We now have a black governor and a black woman senator and millions of black college graduates and so on, but also hundreds of thousands of young blacks in prison. Black identity no longer has a centrifugal force in a racial sense. And in the accompanying confusion we look to the most conservative identity figure.

Malcolm was conservative through and through. As a black nationalist, he was a hard-line militarist who believed in the principle of self-mastery through force. His language and thinking in this regard were oddly in line with Henry Kissinger's description of the world as a brutal place in which safety and a balance of power is maintained through realpolitik. He was Reaganesque in his insistence on negotiating with whites from a position of strength—meaning the threat of violence. And his commitment (until the last year of his life) to racial purity and separatism would have made him the natural ally of David Duke.

In his personal life, moreover, Malcolm scrupulously followed all the Islamic strictures against alcohol, tobacco, drugs, fornication, and adultery, and his attitude toward women was decidedly patriarchal: As a Black Muslim minister he counseled that women could never be completely trusted because of their vanity, and he forbade dancing in his mosque. In his speeches he reserved a special contempt for white liberals, and he once praised Barry Goldwater as a racial realist. Believing entirely in black self-help, he had no use for government programs to uplift blacks, and sneered at the 1964 Civil Rights Bill as nothing more than white expedience.

Malcolm X was one of the most unabashed and unqualified conservatives of his time. And yet today he is forgiven his sexism by black feminists, his political conservatism by black and white liberals, his Islamic faith by black Christians, his violent rhetoric by nonviolent veterans of the civil rights struggle, his anti-Semitism by blacks and whites who are repulsed by it, his separatism by blacks who live integrated lives, and even the apparent fabrication of events in his childhood by those who would bring his story to the screen. Malcolm enjoys one of the best Teflon coatings of all time.

I think one of the reasons for this is that he was such an extreme   20
conservative, that is, such an extreme partisan of his group. All we really
ask of such people is that they love the group more than anything else,
even themselves. If this is evident, all else is secondary. In fact, we demand conservatism from such people, because it is a testament of their
love. Malcolm sneered at government programs because he believed so
much in black people: They could do it on their own. He gave up all his
vices to intensify his love. He was a father figure who distributed love
and hate in our favor. Reagan did something like this when he called the
Soviet Union an "evil empire," and he, too, was rewarded with Teflon.

The point is that all groups take their extreme partisans more figura-
tively than literally. Their offer of unconditional love bribes us into loving them back rather unconditionally, so that our will to be literal with
them weakens. We will not see other important black leaders of the
1960s—James Farmer, Whitney Young, Andrew Young, Medgar Evers
(a genuine martyr), Roy Wilkins, John Lewis—gracing the T-shirts of
young blacks who are today benefiting more from their efforts than from
Malcolm's. They were too literal, too much of the actual world, for
iconography, for the needs of an unsure psyche. But Malcolm, the hater
and the lover, the father figure of romantic blackness, is the perfect icon.

It helps, too, that he is dead, and therefore unable to be literal in our
own time. We can't know, for example, if he would now be supporting
affirmative action as the reparation that is due to blacks, or condemning
it as more white patronization and black dependency. In a way, the revival of Malcolm X is one of the best arguments I know of for the validity of the deconstructionist view of things: Malcolm is now a text. Today
we *read* Malcolm. And this—dare I say—is one quality he shares with
Christ, who also died young and became a text. He was also an Odyssean
figure who journeyed toward self-knowledge. He was a priest and a
heretic. For many whites he was a devil and for many blacks a martyr.
Even those of my generation who grew up with him really came to
know him through the autobiography that he wrote with Alex Haley.
Even in his time, then, he was a text, and it is reasonable to wonder if he
would have the prominence he has today without that book.

How will the new epic movie of his life—yet another refracting
text—add to his prominence? Clearly it will add rather than subtract. It
is a film that enhances the legend, that tries to solidify Malcolm's standing
as a symbol of identity. To this end, the film marches uncritically
through the well-known episodes of the life. It is beautifully shot and su-
perbly acted by a cast that seemed especially inspired by the significance
of the project. And yet it is still, finally, a march. Spike Lee, normally
filled with bravado, works here like a TV docudramatist with a big budget, for whom loyalty to a received version of events is more important
than insight, irony, or vision. Bruce Perry's recent study of Malcolm's

life, *Malcolm: A Life of the Man Who Changed Black America,* which contradicts much of the autobiography, is completely and indefensibly ignored.

Against Lee's portrayal of Malcolm's father as a stalwart Garveyite
killed by the Klan, Perry reveals a man with a reputation for skirt-chasing
who moved from job to job and was often violent with his children. Lee
shows the Klan burning down Malcolm's childhood home, while Perry
offers considerable evidence to indicate that Malcolm's father likely
burned it down himself after he received an eviction notice. Lee offers a
dramatic scene of the Klan running Earl Little and his family out of Nebraska, yet Malcolm's mother told Perry that the event never happened.
The rather heroic cast that Malcolm (and Lee) gave to his childhood is
contradicted by Perry's extensive interviews with childhood friends, who
portray Malcolm as rather fearful and erratic. Lee's only response to
Perry's work was simply, "I don't believe it."

It was Spike Lee's unthinking loyalty to the going racial orthodoxy, I   25
believe, that led him to miss more than he saw, and to produce a film
that is finally part fact, part fiction, and entirely middlebrow. That racial
orthodoxy is a problem for many black artists working today, since its
goal is to make the individual artist responsible for the collective political
vision. This orthodoxy arbitrates the artist's standing within the group:
The artist can be as individual as he or she likes as long as the group view
of things is upheld. The problem here for black artists is that their racial
identity will be held hostage to the practice of their art. The effect of this
is to pressure the work of art, no matter what inspired it, into a gesture of
identification that reunites the artist and the group.

In this sense Lee's *Malcolm X* might be called a reunion film, or a
gesture of identification on his part toward the group. Thus his loyalist,
unquestioning march through Malcolm's mythology. It is certainly
ironic, given the debate over whether a white man could direct this film,
that Spike Lee sees his hero as only a black man with no more than black
motivations. Human motivations like doubt, fear, insecurity, jealousy,
and love, or human themes like the search for the father, betrayal, and
tragedy, are present in the film because they were present in Malcolm's
story, but Lee seems unaware of them as the real stuff of his subject's life.
The film expresses its identification with much racial drama, but in a
human monotone.

Thus many of the obvious ironies of Malcolm's life are left hanging.
If black nationalism resurrected Malcolm in prison, it also killed him in
the end. This was a man who put all his faith in the concept of a black
nation, in the idea that blackness, in itself, carried moral significance, and
yet it was black nationalist fingers pulling the triggers that killed him.
Even on its surface this glaring irony points to the futility of cultish racial
ideologies, to the collective insecurities that inspire them, and to the
frightened personalities that adhere to them as single-mindedly as Malcolm did. But doesn't this irony also underscore the much more com-

mon human experience of falling when we grip our illusions too tightly, when we need them too much? It should not embarrass Lee to draw out the irony of Malcolm being killed by blacks. He was. And there is a lesson in it for everyone, since we are all hurt by our illusions. To make his gesture of identification, however, Lee prefers to sacrifice the deeper identification that his entire audience might have with his subject.

He also fails to perform the biographer's critical function. Clearly Malcolm had something of the true believer's compulsion to believe blindly and singularly, to eradicate all complexity as hypocrisy. All his life he seemed to have no solid internal compass of his own to rely on in the place of ideology—which is not to say that he didn't have brilliance once centered by a faith. But in this important way he was very unlike King, who, lacking Malcolm's wounds, was so well centered that he projected serenity and composure even as storms raged around him. Out of some underlying agitation Malcolm searched for authorities, for systems of belief, for father figures, for revelations: West Indian Archie, Elijah Muhammad, the Black Muslim faith, Pan Africanism, and finally the humanism of traditional Islam. All this in thirty-nine years! What else might have followed? How many more fathers? How many more -isms?

Moreover, once Malcolm learned from these people, faiths, and ideologies—or had taken what he could from them—he betrayed them all, one after another. There was always this pattern of complete, true-believing submission to authority and then the abrupt betrayal of it. There was something a little narcissistic in this, as though his submissions were really setups for the victories that he would later seize. And with each betrayal-victory there was something of a gloat—his visit to West Indian Archie when he was broken, his telling Mike Wallace on national television about Elijah Muhammad's infidelities. Betrayal was triumph for Malcolm, a moving beyond some smallness, some corruption, some realm that was beneath him.

The corruption at the heart of Malcolm's legend is that he looked   30 bigger than life because he always lived in small, cultish worlds, and always stood next to small people. He screamed at whites, but he had no idea of how to work with them to get things done. King was the man who had to get things done. I don't think that it is farfetched to suggest that finally Malcolm was afraid of white people. While King stared down every white from Bull Connor to the Kennedys, Malcolm made a big deal out of facing off with Elijah Muhammad, whom he had likely propped up for the purpose. His proclivity for little people who made him look big suggests that his black nationalism covered his fear of hard, ordinary work in the American crucible. Up against larger realities and bigger people, he might have felt inadequate.

Lee's film, as beautifully executed as it is, refuses to ask questions about Malcolm's legend. A quick look behind the legend, however, shows that Malcolm's real story was, in truth, tragedy. And the understanding of this grim truth would have helped the film better achieve the racial protest it is obviously after. Malcolm was hurt badly by oppression early in his childhood. If his family was not shattered in the way he claimed, it was shattered nevertheless. And this shattering had much to do with America's brutal racial history. He was, in his pain, a product of America. But his compensations for the hurt only extended the hurt. And the tragedy was the life that this extraordinary man felt that he needed to live, that Malcolm Little had to become Malcolm X, had to be a criminal, then a racial ideologue, and finally a martyr for an indefinable cause. Black nationalism is a tragedy of white racism, and can sometimes be as ruinous as the racism itself.

And so it is saddening to witness the reemergence of this hyped-up, legendary Mr. X, this seller of wolf tickets and excuses not to engage American society. This Malcolm is back to conceal rather than to reveal. He is here to hide our fears as he once hid his own, to keep us separated from any helpful illumination. Had the real Malcolm, the tragic Malcolm, returned, however, it would have represented a remarkable racial advancement. That Malcolm might have given both blacks and whites a way to comprehend our racial past and present. In him we all could have seen the damage done, the frustrations borne, and the fruitless heroism of the American insistence on race.

Reading the Text

1. How has the image of Malcolm X evolved since the 1950s, according to Steele?
2. Summarize in a paragraph Steele's opinion of the film *Malcolm X.*
3. Why does Steele see Malcolm X as a fundamentally conservative figure? What evidence does he offer in support of his thesis?
4. What does Steele mean by saying that "This Malcolm is back to conceal rather than to reveal" (para. 32)?

Reading the Signs

1. Rent a videotape of *Malcolm X,* and write your own critique of it.
2. Do you agree with Steele's assertion that Malcolm X is a popular figure because of his conservatism? Write an essay in which you provide your own explanation of the popularity of Malcolm X (the movie and the character). Why were the 1990s the decade in which he made a comeback in American popular consciousness?
3. How would Paul C. Taylor ("Funky White Boys and Honorary Soul Sisters," p. 549) explain the popularity of Malcolm X? In what ways would his perspective on race in America contradict or extend Steele's analysis?

4. Read *The Autobiography of Malcolm X,* and write an essay in which you compare the book's vision of Malcolm X with his portrayal in the film.
5. Drawing on Robert B. Ray's "The Thematic Paradigm" (p. 299), write an essay in which you analyze Malcolm X as an American hero.

TODD BOYD

So You Wanna Be a Gangsta?

Before there were "gangstas" there were gangsters, and as Todd Boyd points out in this selection from Am I Black Enough for You? *Popular Culture from the 'Hood and Beyond (1997), both have played their part in American and cinematic history. From the Italian gangsters of* Scarface *and the* Godfather *films to the Latino and African American gangstas of* American Me *and* Boyz N the Hood, *the gang movie has provided a dramatic setting for an ongoing contest in which the American underclass both resists and embraces the values of mainstream society. An assistant professor of critical studies in the School of Cinema-Television at the University of Southern California, Boyd is coeditor (with Aaron Baker) of* Out of Bounds: Sports, Media, and the Politics of Identity *(1997) and has written for such journals as* Wide Angle, Cinéaste, Filmforum, *and* Public Culture.

The gangster film and the Western are two of the most important genres in the history of Hollywood, especially with respect to articulation of the discourse of American history and masculinity. Whereas the Western concentrated on the mythic settling of the West and a perceived notion of progression, it was primarily concerned with the frontier mentality of the eighteenth through the late nineteenth century. The gangster genre, on the other hand, is about the evolution of American society in the twentieth century into a legitimate entity in the world economy.

Though the Western covertly articulated the politics of oppression against Native Americans during the settling of the West, the gangster genre focused on questions of ethnicity—e.g., Italian, Irish—and how these are transformed over time into questions of race—Black, Latino, etc. This ideological shift provided an interesting representation of the significant position that race has come to occupy in the discourse of American society. We must look at the transformation of the linguistic sign "gangster" and its slow transition to its most recent embodiment as "gangsta" as an instructive historical metaphor. . . .

Americans have always had a fascination with the underworld society populated by those who openly resisted the laws of dominant society and instead created their own world, living by their own rules. Gangsters have in many ways been our version of revolutionaries throughout history. Whereas Europe has always had real-life political revolutionaries, twentieth-century American discourse, upheld by police and government activity, seems to have found ways of perverting for the public the political voices that exist outside the narrow traditions of allowed political expression.

The displacement of these political voices by the forces of oppression has created a renegade space within American culture that allows for the expression of gangster culture. Gangsters indeed function as somewhat revolutionary in comparison to the rest of society, as demonstrated by their open defiance of accepted societal norms and laws, existence in their own environment, and circulation of their own alternative capital. This allows them to remain part of the larger society but to fully exist in their own communities at the same time. This lifestyle has been a consistent media staple throughout the twentieth century, particularly in film.

From as early as D. W. Griffith's *Musketeers of Pig Alley* (1912) and [5] the celebrated studio films of the 1930s—e.g., *Little Caesar* (1930), *Public Enemy* (1931), and *Scarface* (1932)—through the epic treatment rendered in the first two *Godfather* films (1972, 1974), the gangster has enjoyed a vivid screen life. What is important here is that these criminals, as they are deemed by the dominant society, are defined as deviant primarily because of issues of ethnicity, as opposed to issues of race, though to some extent all definitions of ethnicity in this context are inevitably influenced by a subtle definition of race.

This emphasis on ethnicity as it functions in opposition to the standard "white Anglo-Saxon Protestant" is summarized in the first two *Godfather* films. As the United States, both at and immediately after the turn of the century, increasingly became a nation of European immigrants, incoming Italians were consigned to the bottom of the social ladder. In the opening segment of *Godfather II*, Michael Corleone is berated and verbally abused by Senator Geery of Nevada because of his Italian heritage. The word "Italian" is set in opposition to "American" constantly in this segment so as to highlight the ethnic hierarchy which remains a foundational issue in this film. Corleone's ascension to power is complicated by his inability to fully surmount this societal obstacle, at least at this point in the film, and by extension that point in American history—the early 1950s.

It is Francis Ford Coppola's argument that such oppression forced these Italian immigrants into a subversive lifestyle and economy much like that practiced throughout southern Italy, especially in Sicily. Borrowing from their own cultural tradition, some of these new Americans used the underground economy as a vital means of sustenance in the face of ethnic, religious, and cultural oppression. And though their desire, being heavily influenced by the discourse of an "American dream," was to ultimately be fully assimilated into American society, the achievement of this desire was revealed to be at the cost of losing their ethnic and cultural heritage. . . .

At a larger level, the film's historical themes indicate the assimilation of ethnicity into a homogeneous American society, yet foreground the continued rejection of race as a component of the metaphoric "melting pot"—because it is the challenge of race that accelerates the assimilative process of ethnicity.

In the first *Godfather* film, we see this same social dynamic at play regarding ethnicity over race. Near the film's conclusion, we witness the memorable meeting of the "heads of the five families," where the dilemmas of drug trafficking are being discussed by the various Mafia leaders. Vito Corleone is characterized as opposing this potentially lucrative venture for moral reasons, while many of the other members are excited about the possible financial benefits. The chieftain from Kansas City suggests that the Mafia should engage in selling drugs, but only at a distance, leaving the underside of this environment to be experienced by what he describes as the "dark people" because, as he adds, "they're animals anyway, let them lose their souls." His use of the phrase "dark people" and his labeling of them as "animals" clearly reference African Americans, and by extension racialized others in general. This line of dialogue is viewed by many African Americans as prophetic, seeing that the release of *The Godfather* in the early 1970s closely paralleled the upsurge in underworld drug activity throughout African American ghetto communities.

In relation to the assimilation of ethnicity at the expense of race, this 10 line also signifies the way in which the previously mentioned structural hierarchy exists aside from the racial hierarchy, which many African Americans have been unable to transcend because of the difference in skin color. Though Italians through this perverted formulation could be considered inferior to "wasps," those traits that make them different can be easily subsumed when contrasted with the obvious difference of skin color and the history that goes along with being darker. It is in this context that the thematic progression of the *Godfather* films signals the end of the public fascination with the Italian gangster and his ethnically rich underworld.

Furthermore, this line indicates that the drug culture would be an important turning point in the historical discourse specific to the question of race as time moved forward. This line of reasoning has been pursued in numerous texts, most recently through Bill Duke's film *Deep Cover* (1992), which comments on the conspiracy involved in both furnishing and addicting segments of the Black community with drugs as a political maneuver by the government to keep these individuals sedated and oppressed so as to quell any potential political resistance. Mario Van Peebles's film *Panther* (1995) asserts the same theory in connection with the attempted destruction of the Black Panther Party by J. Edgar Hoover and the FBI. In both cases, crime can be seen as affirming capitalism, yet in specifically racial terms.

With this assimilation of ethnicity as signified through the Coppola films, America finds the need to fulfill this otherwise empty space with the next logical descending step on the social ladder, that being race.[1] Two other films from the 1980s effectively mark the shift away from the ethnic gangster to the racialized gangsta. Brian De Palma's remake of *Scarface* (1983) is an obvious rewriting of the genre from the perspective of race. Whereas the main character in the 1932 film was an Italian, in the De Palma version we deal with a racialized Cuban.

Drawing from real political events, De Palma's film begins with the Mariel boat lift of Cuban refugees into south Florida during the latter part of the 1970s, an event which many still consider a lingering legacy of Jimmy Carter's presidency. The film's main character, Tony Montana, is clearly foregrounded as a racialized other. His Cuban identity, broken accent, penchant for garishness, and overall ruthless approach to wealth and human life served as the basis for the popular media representation of Latin American drug dealers that came to dominate the 1980s.

With an increase in drug paranoia from the conservative Reagan and Bush administrations, this form of representation would nearly erase past images of Italian mob figures from the popular memory. While John Gotti was a celebrated folk hero for his stylish media-friendly disposition, individuals such as Carlos Lader Rivas, Pablo Escobar, and Manuel

---

1. The popular 1990 Martin Scorsese film *Goodfellas* is different from the gangster films which preceded it. At the conclusion of this film, the main character, Henry Hill, turns state's evidence on his former colleagues, thus violating one of the most stringent codes of the gangster lifestyle. And though some would argue that this film is a revisionist gangster film, it is sufficiently separated from other examples of the genre so as not to be confused. Scorsese's *Casino* (1995) continues this move to a contemporary gangster epic.

Another example of this revisionist trend would be Barry Levinson's fictional account of the life of Benjamin "Bugsy" Segal, with its emphasis on Segal's mistress, Virginia Hill, and the way in which her influence can be read as substantial, though detrimental, to Segal in the financial decisions that he makes. *Bugsy* (1991) presents a sentimental underworld figure who has been "softened" by this female presence, which goes against the masculinist approach normally associated with the gangster. This rereading of the central character, with an emphasis on the female, adds to my notion of a revisionist trend in the genre, though in this case it is gender, not race, that is the point of transition.

Noriega, who became common sights on the evening news and network news magazine programs, were depicted as threats to the very fabric of our society. To add to this popular form of representation, NBC's series *Miami Vice* drew many of its story lines and criminal figures from this newly accepted version of racialized representation.[2] . . .

The other major filmic event that reflected this obsession with the drug culture and the question of race was Dennis Hopper's *Colors* (1988). Hopper's film offered an intricate look at the gang culture that existed in both South Central and East Los Angeles. Its main characters were two white Los Angeles police officers who were commissioned with the monumental task of eliminating the urban crime being perpetrated by African American and Latino youth. This film tied in neatly with the increasing commentary presented by national news programs about what had begun as a regional situation and was later argued to have spread throughout the country. Using the police, and by extension the rest of white society, as its victims, the film endorsed the racial paranoia concerning criminality that at this time was in full swing.

Colors, for all intents and purposes, made the gangbanger America's contemporary criminal of choice, turning a localized problem into a national epidemic that once again linked crime with specific notions of race. In many ways, *Colors* served the same function for gangsta culture that *Birth of a Nation* served for the early stages of African American cinema. Both films, through their overt racial paranoia, and in both cases using armed militia as an answer to the perceived Black threat—in one case the Ku Klux Klan, in the other a racist police department—inspired a series of African American cinematic responses. This regressive film engendered a public fascination with the newly defined "gangsta."

With the traditional white ethnic gangster film having all but disappeared, the way was clear for the entrance of a new popular villain to be screened across the mind of American society. The ideological link between crime and race would be made worse, and the image of the African American gangbanger would become not only popular in the sense of repeated representation, but financially lucrative as well. In addition to the changing history of the Hollywood gangster film, several other historical factors specific to African American culture would contribute to the emergence and eventual proliferation of the African American "gangsta."

---

2. For a detailed discussion of the drug trade in Los Angeles, see Mike Davis, "The Political Economy of Crack," in *City of Quartz* (New York: Verso, 1990), and for a larger discussion of the role played by the media, the politics of Reagan/Bush, and the drug culture of the 1980s, see Jimmie Reeves and Richard Campbell, *Cracked Coverage* (Durham: Duke Univ. Press, 1994).

From the Black Godfather to the Black Guerrilla Family

The late 1960s and early 1970s saw an increase in underworld activity, especially involving drugs, throughout many lower-class Black communities. In many ways more important than the drugs themselves was the culture that accompanied this underworld lifestyle and the way in which it was represented visually. The garish fashions popularized by Eleganza and Flag Brothers, heavily adorned, ornament-laden Cadillacs, and other materialistic excesses helped to define this cultural terrain as "cool" during this period. . . .

In several of the films that define this period, eventually known as the "Blaxploitation" era of Hollywood (1970–73), the Black protagonist was presented in opposition to a stereotypical white menace who was bent on destroying the African American community, primarily through the influx of drugs and the accompanying culture of violence. For the most part, evil in the films was personified in the form of a corrupt police or mafia figure, if not both at the same time. Thus much of the narrative action appeared in battles between some faction of the white mafia, who had traditionally been in control of the ghetto, albeit from a distance, and the emerging Black underworld figures who were striving to wrest control of this alternative economy from their white counterparts.

It was as if the loosening of societal restrictions gained during the civil rights movement permitted exploitation of the community through control of underworld vices, though the actual control was in the hands of manipulative outsiders, who used the Black gangster as their foil. The Black gangster, whether he was a pimp, dope dealer, or hustler, through these films became a prominent example of what it meant to be an entrepreneur. The tension between outside influence and inside control is represented in many of the films of the period, most notably *Cotton Comes to Harlem, Across 110th Street, Superfly,* and *The Mack.* The African American gangster had become a media staple by the mid-1970s. . . .

Many of the films of this period were based on the dynamics of an African American underworld existence (e.g., *Sweetsweetback's Badass Song, The Mack, Willie Dynamite, Coffy, Cleopatra Jones*), and in conjunction with the popular ghetto literature of Iceberg Slim and Donald Goines, as well as the more esoteric works of author Chester Himes and playwright Charles Gordone, this form of representation remained viable long after this period had passed. In line with Nelson George's argument that "Blaxploitation movies are crucial to the current 70's retro-nuevo phase" (149), this historical period left a series of low-budget films which would eventually be perfect for transfer to the home video format. The "Blaxploitation" films would leave an indelible imprint on African American popular culture as the "gangsta" continued to rise in prominence and position.

A Small Introduction to the "G" Funk Era

With the historical antecedents of the Hollywood gangster film and 1970s Blaxploitation films, along with popular African American literature that explored the culture, the stage was set for the flowering of gangsta culture in the late 1980s and early 1990s. The contemporary manifestation continued to appear in the form of cinema, but also gained increasing visibility in the world of rap music, to the point of establishing its own genre and forming a solid cultural movement. This transition from genre to cultural movement included representations in film, music, and literature, and involved multiple layers of society: communal, political, and corporate. From the regular individuals whose personal narratives drew heavily from gangster culture, to rap artists whose real-life antics coincided with the fictional rhetoric of their lyrics, and finally to the highest levels of government, where questions of moral integrity, community debasement, and freedom of speech were constantly being posed, this cultural movement had a great deal of currency with respect to African Americans in society, especially the African American male. . . .

Though there are glimpses of the gangster lifestyle in a number of films that appeared throughout the late 1980s and especially in the early 1990s, the two films most relevant to an understanding of gangsta culture are John Singleton's *Boyz N the Hood* (1991) and Allen and Albert Hughes's *Menace II Society* (1993). Not to ignore such a popular film as Mario Van Peebles's *New Jack City* (1991) or Abel Ferrera's cult video classic *The King of New York* (1990), but these texts are more directly influenced by the traditional gangster paradigm, in addition to being set in New York City. The filmic representation of gangsta culture draws many of its influences from rap music, and in turn rap music assumes a great deal of identity with the work of Singleton and the Hughes brothers. Contemporary gangsta culture is undoubtedly a West Coast phenomenon.

The other film that holds a vital position in the representation of gangsta culture is Edward James Olmos's *American Me* (1992). This film addresses the culture from a Latino perspective as opposed to an African American one. This is of utmost importance, for while gangsta culture is publicly regarded as an African American entity, much of the culture derives from the close proximity in which African Americans and Latinos coexist in racialized Los Angeles. . . .

Hispanics Causin' Panic

American Me demonstrates that aspects of African American gangsta 25
life and Mexican American gangsta culture are in dialogue with one another, though it can at times be a highly contested dialogue. There are

two distinct instances in the film where a potential clash between the races is openly criticized as being counterproductive to someone's coming to consciousness and ultimate cultural empowerment. As the Mexican mafia (La Eme) smuggles drugs into the prison, we witness a Black inmate who steals the cocaine intended for another inmate. Upon revelation of the culprit, Santana, the leader of La Eme, instructs his soldiers to burn the man as an act of punishment. This triggers a cell-block confrontation that borders on a riot between La Eme and the Black Guerrilla Family (BGF). As the prison guards descend, the riot is aborted, but not without critical commentary. Santana informs the leader of the BGF that the situation was not racially motivated, but simply an action of retribution to forestall any future attempts at hindering their drug-trafficking efforts in prison. In other words, "business, never personal." This is a case in which the interest of underground capitalism supersedes any specific racial agenda.

Yet this scene is important as the setup for a similar situation that occurs later in the film. When La Eme attempts to sever its tie with the traditional Italian Mafia, the move is met with much resistance. Scagnelli, the mob boss, refuses to relinquish his end of the drug business in East L.A. As a result, several members of La Eme rape and murder Scagnelli's son while he is in prison. In response, Scagnelli sends uncut heroin into the barrio, causing several overdoses. This creates a chain reaction of retribution, which eventually culminates in Santana's death at the hands of his own men. At a certain point during this series of events, J.D., the only white member of La Eme, who slowly attempts to wrest control of the gang from Santana, orders a hit on the BGF by using the Aryan Brotherhood, the white gang represented in the film. Santana objects to this action and criticizes J.D. for "sending out the wrong message."

Santana's objection is based on his increasing awareness of racial and social consciousness, which has been facilitated by the politically empowered female character Julie. Julie, like the female character of Ronnie in *Menace,* helps Santana to realize the error of his misguided ways. On several occasions she criticizes his violent philosophy in ways that other characters cannot for fear of death. In a pivotal scene late in the film, Julie exposes Santana's position in all its limitations. After a series of extremely critical remarks about Santana's hypocritical use of crime as a way of arguing for *la raza,* he tells her, "If you were a man, I'd . . ." His incomplete sentence is cut short by Julie's own completion of it: "You'd kill me; no, you'd fuck me in the ass." Having witnessed several scenes in which men were raped because of Santana's power over them, in addition to his rape of Julie, we can feel the magnitude of her statement. She not only criticizes his politics, she has criticized his masculinity by alluding to the latent homosexuality of his supposed gestures of power.

Ultimately, she forces Santana to understand that the power struggles which often take place between those who are marginalized permit the continued oppression of their voices by those in power. Santana even says to J.D., "We spend all our time dealing with the miatas [their slang term for Blacks], and the Aryan Brotherhood, only to be dealing with ourselves." In other words, ideological distractions ultimately leave us in the same place, with no advancement in consciousness or power.

These ideas eventually separate Santana's newfound political consciousness from J.D.'s "business as usual" approach to crime and the underlying destruction of the community. It is not coincidental that J.D.'s whiteness, which is endorsed by Santana early in the film, looms as the final authority once he has ordered the killing of Santana and presumably taken control of the gang. At the beginning of the film, as expressed through the American military oppression of the Mexican American citizens, and at the conclusion, with J.D.'s murdering of Santana, thus destroying any possibility for an overall group consciousness, we can see that racism and white supremacy are the root causes of the chaos that permeates much of the present-day urban landscape. It is this fundamental understanding of race, racism, and complicity in one's own oppression that substantiates the importance of *American Me*. *American Me* engages history and politics to subtly yet convincingly argue that the real root of evil in American society as it relates to oppressed minorities is the bondage of systemic and institutionalized racism. This understanding also distinguishes it as a political statement from the rather limited bourgeois politics of *Boyz N the Hood* and the nihilistically apolitical *Menace II Society*. . . .

Boyz Will Be Boyz

Either they don't know, won't show, or don't care what's going on in the hood.

—DOUGHBOY, *Boyz N the Hood*

While *American Me* serves as an "objective third party" against which   30
to evaluate *Boyz* and *Menace,* the similarities notwithstanding, to engage the culturally specific tenets of Black popular culture we must look at texts which are firmly situated in the domain of African American cinema in order to study the class politics of each film. In this regard, the political position of *Boyz N the Hood* can be defined as either a bourgeois Black nationalist or an Afrocentric model that focuses on the "disappearing" Black male, yet also fits easily into the perceived pathology of the culture in a modernized version of the legendary Moynihan report of the late 1960s. This report regarded the typically broken African American family as a cause of societal dysfunction at the highest level.

Singleton's film was integral to the politically charged period of resurgent Black nationalism in the late 1980s and early 1990s. This cultural resurgence of Black nationalism, most closely associated with the work of Public Enemy, KRS-One, and Sister Souljah, also set the tone for the discourse that informed *Do the Right Thing,* as well as many of the debates that emerged after the film's release.

From the outset it is obvious that Singleton's film is conversant with the Afrocentric discourse that permeates much of Black intellectual and cultural life. The film opens by establishing South Central Los Angeles as its geographical, cultural, and political center. Yet the landscape of Los Angeles is a historically specific one. The film begins in 1984, as we quickly spot several campaign posters that support the re-election of President Ronald Reagan—the obvious contradiction of this image being seen in a community such as South Central, which is the type of community most victimized by the racial and class politics of Reagan's first term. Another contradiction is signaled as a young Black male, while looking at an abandoned dead body lying in an alley, gives this political image "the finger." This young character is identified as being closely associated with gang culture. He declares that both of his brothers have been shot, and in turn they are heroic in his mind because they have yet to be killed. His marginal status allows him to recognize at some level that this supreme image of white male authority is in stark contrast to his own existence.

As we enter the classroom, we are presented with another contradiction. The camera pans the student drawings that cover the wall. These pictures contain images of people being shot, police brutality, and other acts that emphasize the daily violence that defines many of the lives in this poor Black community. These images are contradicted by the speech being delivered by the white teacher about the historical importance of the first European "settlers" or "pilgrims" on American soil. Her lecture is on the reasons this country celebrates the Thanksgiving holiday, yet by implication it also articulates the exploitation of America and Native Americans and the ensuing colonization, which was a helpful instrument in establishing the societal hierarchy that we inhabit today.

The ideology that is being discussed is being put into practice through the attitudes and policies of Ronald Reagan. Reagan clearly felt the need to return to some form of these earlier examples of oppression in the course of his presidential career, as his repeated attacks on affirmative action, his support of states' rights, and his overall embrace of positions consistent with right-wing conservatism about race clearly indicated. In a sense, the actions of those who are being celebrated by the teacher, the "pilgrims," have contributed to the conditions of the people depicted in the children's drawings. The film sets up a binary opposition between the conservative politics of America and African Americans' rejection of these oppressive policies. This scene is one of the few in the film in which racism and white supremacy are directly critiqued.

As the scene develops, Tre, the film's main character, confronts his 35 elementary school teacher, asserting that humankind originated in Africa and not in Europe. Yet in his presentation, Tre is criticized not only by his teacher, but by other students as well. The same student who gave Reagan "the finger" completely dissociates himself from Tre's Afrocentric assertion, "We're all from Africa." In response, this child declares, "I ain't from Africa, I'm from Crenshaw Mafia," further linking himself to gang culture through his identification with the set known as "Crenshaw Mafia." The obvious irony of this scene is that gang affiliation is set in direct conflict with one's racial and cultural identity. It is as if being a gangsta supersedes race, as opposed to being a result of racial and class hierarchies in America.

In this same exchange, we can also hear echoes of Tre's father, Furious, and his lessons on life that recur throughout the film. This is once again set in opposition to the words of the aspiring gangsta's older brothers. This exchange leads to a fight between the two children, underscoring the incompatibility of progressive politics and existence in gangsta culture. Yet through the setting of gangsta culture in opposition to nationalist politics, it becomes clear that this bourgeois understanding ignores the fact that gangsters historically are easily transformed into revolutionaries because of their marginal status in society.

Remarks about the plight of the "Black man" dominate much of Furious's commentary in the film. As critic Michael Dyson has alluded, these comments fit well with the male-centered Afrocentric ideals of thinkers such as Jawanza Kanjufu, Haki Madhabuti, and Molefi Asante. *Boyz* uses gangsta culture as an alluring spectacle, which is underscored by the film's exaggeratedly violent trailer, but this spectacle is used to engage an Afrocentric critique that denounces the routine slaying of Black men, whether by other gang members or by the police. *Boyz* makes interesting use of many of the icons of gangsta culture while conducting its Black nationalist critique. The film straddles both areas, opening the door to the ensuing onslaught of gangsta imagery.

In this sense, *Boyz* is much like the imagery connected with one of its co-stars, Ice Cube. As a rapper, Ice Cube has consistently combined signs of gangsta culture with an ideological perspective that emphasizes a perverted Black nationalist agenda, borrowed primarily from the Nation of Islam. Similarly, *Boyz* combines gangsta icons with Afrocentrism, ultimately privileging the ideological critique over the iconography. This strain of political discourse was popular during the late 1980s and early 1990s, with *Boyz* providing a cinematic counterpart to rap music. Singleton's film, though visualizing gangsta culture on a mass scale, is really more acceptable as a political text than as a thesis on the complex gangsta mentality. In many ways, *Boyz* represents the culmination of this politically resurgent period, as the theme of Black nationalism slowly disappeared from most popular forms shortly thereafter.

Though the film is overtly political, it reflects a bourgeois sense of politics. At the conclusion of the film we see a didactic scroll which tells us that Tre and Brandi, the one utopic Black male/female relationship presented in the film, have ventured off to Morehouse and Spelman College in Atlanta respectively, to pursue their middle-class dreams far away from South Central L.A. Morehouse and Spelman have often been thought of as the Black equivalent of Harvard or Yale, the historical breeding ground for bourgeois Blackness. The fact that the two colleges are located in Atlanta, the current "mecca" of Black America, underscores the film's flimsy political position. *Boyz N the Hood* demonizes the landscape of Los Angeles while uncritically offering middle-class Atlanta as a metaphoric space where future generations of African Americans can exist free of the obstacles that are depicted in this film.

Reading the Text

1. What, according to Boyd, has been the cultural and political significance of the gangster underworld in American history and popular culture?
2. How did Hollywood in the late 1960s and early 1970s respond to the emergence of a drug culture in impoverished black communities, in Boyd's analysis?
3. Why does Boyd believe that *Boyz N the Hood* reflects both black nationalist and conventional bourgeois values?
4. How did *American Me* reflect the conflicts between Mexican American and African American gang subcultures?
5. What is the difference, according to Boyd, between race and ethnicity?

Reading the Signs

1. Write an essay supporting, complicating, or refuting the proposition that Hollywood's depiction of gangstas glorifies criminal behavior.
2. Rent a videotape of a film like *Scarface* or *The Godfather,* and write an analysis comparing its treatment of ethnic "others" with the treatment of black gang members in a movie like *Boyz N the Hood.*
3. Write an essay in which you explore the reasons gangsta films and culture are so popular among middle-class white teens. To develop your ideas, consult Nell Bernstein's "Goin' Gangsta, Choosin' Cholita" (p. 562).
4. In class, form teams and debate the proposition that Hollywood exploits the black community in making gang films.
5. Rent a videotape of a film focusing on African Americans that Boyd does not discuss — *Waiting to Exhale.* Then write a response to Boyd in which you address the importance of gender in film analysis.

JESSICA HAGEDORN

Asian Women in Film: No Joy, No Luck

〰〰〰〰〰〰〰〰〰〰〰〰〰〰〰〰〰〰〰〰〰〰〰〰〰〰〰〰

Why do movies always seem to portray Asian women as tragic victims of history and fate? Jessica Hagedorn (b. 1949) asks in this essay, which originally appeared in Ms. *Even such movies as* The Joy Luck Club, *based on Amy Tan's breakthrough novel that elevated Asian American fiction to best-seller status, reinforce old stereotypes of the powerlessness of Asian and Asian American women. A screenwriter and novelist herself, Hagedorn calls for a different kind of storytelling that would show Asian women as powerful controllers of their own destinies. Hagedorn's publications include* Dogeaters *(1990) and* The Gangster of Love, *both novels;* Danger and Beauty *(1993), a collection of poems;* Charlie Chan is Dead: An Anthology of Contemporary Asian American Fiction *(1993); and* Fresh Kill *(1994), a screenplay.*

Pearl of the Orient. Whore. Geisha. Concubine. Whore. Hostess. Bar Girl. Mama-san. Whore. China Doll. Tokyo Rose. Whore. Butterfly. Whore. Miss Saigon. Whore. Dragon Lady. Lotus Blossom. Gook. Whore. Yellow Peril. Whore. Bangkok Bombshell. Whore. Hospitality Girl. Whore. Comfort Woman. Whore. Savage. Whore. Sultry. Whore. Faceless. Whore. Porcelain. Whore. Demure. Whore. Virgin. Whore. Mute. Whore. Model Minority. Whore. Victim. Whore. Woman Warrior. Whore. Mail-Order Bride. Whore. Mother. Wife. Lover. Daughter. Sister.

As I was growing up in the Philippines in the 1950s, my fertile imagination was colonized by thoroughly American fantasies. Yellowface variations on the exotic erotic loomed larger than life on the silver screen. I was mystified and enthralled by Hollywood's skewed representations of Asian women: sleek, evil goddesses with slanted eyes and cunning ways, or smiling, sarong-clad South Seas "maidens" with undulating hips, kinky black hair, and white skin darkened by makeup. Hardly any of the "Asian" characters were played by Asians. White actors like Sidney Toler and Warner Oland played "inscrutable Oriental detective" Charlie Chan with taped eyelids and a singsong, chop suey accent. Jennifer Jones was a Eurasian doctor swept up in a doomed "interracial romance" in *Love Is a Many Splendored Thing.* In my mother's youth, white actor Luise Rainer played the central role of the Patient Chinese Wife in the 1937 film adaptation of Pearl Buck's novel *The Good Earth.* Back then, not many thought to ask why; they were all too busy being grateful to see anyone in the movies remotely like themselves.

Cut to 1960: *The World of Suzie Wong,* another tragic East/West affair. I am now old enough to be impressed. Sexy, sassy Suzie (played by Nancy Kwan) works out of a bar patronized by white sailors, but doesn't seem bothered by any of it. For a hardworking girl turning nightly tricks to support her baby, she manages to parade an astonishing wardrobe in damn near every scene, down to matching handbags and shoes. The sailors are also strictly Hollywood, sanitized and not too menacing. Suzie and all the other prostitutes in this movie are cute, giggling, dancing sex machines with hearts of gold. William Holden plays an earnest, rather prim, Nice Guy painter seeking inspiration in The Other. Of course, Suzie falls madly in love with him. Typically, she tells him, "I not important," and "I'll be with you until you say—Suzie, go away." She also thinks being beaten by a man is a sign of true passion and is terribly disappointed when Mr. Nice Guy refuses to show his true feelings.

Next in Kwan's short-lived but memorable career was the kitschy 1961 musical *Flower Drum Song,* which, like *Suzie Wong,* is a thoroughly American commercial product. The female roles are typical of Hollywood musicals of the times: women are basically airheads, subservient to men. Kwan's counterpart is the Good Chinese Girl, played by Miyoshi Umeki, who was better playing the Loyal Japanese Girl in that other classic Hollywood tale of forbidden love, *Sayonara.* Remember? Umeki was so loyal, she committed double suicide with actor Red Buttons. I instinctively hated *Sayonara* when I first saw it as a child; now I understand why. Contrived tragic resolutions were the only way Hollywood got past the censors in those days. With one or two exceptions, somebody in these movies always had to die to pay for breaking racial and sexual taboos.

Until the recent onslaught of films by both Asian and Asian American filmmakers, Asian Pacific women have generally been perceived by Hollywood with a mixture of fascination, fear, and contempt. Most Hollywood movies either trivialize or exoticize us as people of color and as women. Our intelligence is underestimated, our humanity overlooked, and our diverse cultures treated as interchangeable. If we are "good," we are childlike, submissive, silent, and eager for sex (see France Nuyen's glowing performance as Liat in the film version of *South Pacific*) or else we are tragic victim types (see *Casualties of War,* Brian De Palma's graphic 1989 drama set in Vietnam). And if we are not silent, suffering doormats, we are demonized dragon ladies—cunning, deceitful, sexual provocateurs. Give me the demonic any day—Anna May Wong as a villain slithering around in a slinky gown is at least gratifying to watch, neither servile nor passive. And she steals the show from Marlene Dietrich in Josef von Sternberg's *Shanghai Express.* From the 1920s through the '30s, Wong was our only female "star." But even she was trapped in limited roles, in what filmmaker Renee Tajima has called the dragon lady/lotus blossom dichotomy.

Cut to 1985: There is a scene toward the end of the terribly dishonest but weirdly compelling Michael Cimino movie *Year of the Dragon* (cowritten by Oliver Stone) that is one of my favorite twisted movie moments of all time. If you ask a lot of my friends who've seen that movie (especially if they're Asian), it's one of their favorites too. The setting is a crowded Chinatown nightclub. There are two very young and very tough Jade Cobra gang girls in a shoot-out with Mickey Rourke, in the role of a demented Polish American cop who, in spite of being Mr. Ugly in the flesh—an arrogant, misogynistic bully devoid of any charm— wins the "good" Asian American anchorwoman in the film's absurd and implausible ending. This is a movie with an actual disclaimer as its lead-in, covering its ass in advance in response to anticipated complaints about "stereotypes."

My pleasure in the hard-edged power of the Chinatown gang girls in *Year of the Dragon* is my small revenge, the answer to all those Suzie Wong "I want to be your slave" female characters. The Jade Cobra girls are mere background to the white male foreground/focus of Cimino's movie. But long after the movie has faded into video-rental heaven, the Jade Cobra girls remain defiant, fabulous images in my memory, flaunting tight metallic dresses and spiky cock's-comb hairdos streaked electric red and blue.

> Mickey Rourke looks down with world-weary pity at the unnamed Jade Cobra girl (Doreen Chan) he's just shot who lies sprawled and bleeding on the street: "You look like you're gonna die, beautiful."
> JADE COBRA GIRL: "Oh yeah? [blood gushing from her mouth] I'm proud of it."
> ROURKE: "You are? You got anything you wanna tell me before you go, sweetheart?"
> JADE COBRA GIRL: "Yeah. [pause] Fuck you."

Cut to 1993: I've been told that like many New Yorkers, I watch movies with the right side of my brain on perpetual overdrive. I admit to being grouchy and overcritical, suspicious of sentiment, and cynical. When a critic like Richard Corliss of *Time* magazine gushes about *The Joy Luck Club* being "a fourfold *Terms of Endearment*," my gut instinct is to run the other way. I resent being told how to feel. I went to see the 1993 eight-handkerchief movie version of Amy Tan's best-seller with a group that included my ten-year-old daughter. I was caught between the sincere desire to be swept up by the turbulent mother-daughter sagas and my own stubborn resistance to being so obviously manipulated by the filmmakers. With every flashback came tragedy. The music soared; the voice-overs were solemn or wistful; tears, tears, and more tears flowed onscreen. Daughters were reverent; mothers carried dark secrets.

I was elated by the grandness and strength of the four mothers and the luminous actors who portrayed them, but I was uneasy with the passivity of the Asian American daughters. They seemed to exist solely as receptors for their mothers' amazing life stories. It's almost as if by assimilating so easily into American society, they had lost all sense of self.

In spite of my resistance, my eyes watered as the desperate mother 10 played by Kieu Chinh was forced to abandon her twin baby girls on a country road in war-torn China. (Kieu Chinh resembles my own mother and her twin sister, who suffered through the brutal Japanese occupation of the Philippines.) So far in this movie, an infant son had been deliberately drowned, a mother played by the gravely beautiful France Nuyen had gone catatonic with grief, a concubine had cut her flesh open to save her dying mother, an insecure daughter had been oppressed by her boorish Asian American husband, another insecure daughter had been left by her white husband, and so on. . . . The overall effect was numbing as far as I'm concerned, but a man sitting two rows in front of us broke down sobbing. A Chinese Pilipino writer even more grouchy than me later complained, "Must ethnicity only be equated with suffering?"

Because change has been slow, *The Joy Luck Club* carries a lot of cultural baggage. It is a big-budget story about Chinese American women, directed by a Chinese American man, cowritten and coproduced by Chinese American women. That's a lot to be thankful for. And its box office success proves that an immigrant narrative told from female perspectives can have mass appeal. But my cynical side tells me that its success might mean only one thing in Hollywood: more weepy epics about Asian American mother-daughter relationships will be planned.

That the film finally got made was significant. By Hollywood standards (think white male; think money, money, money), a movie about Asian Americans even when adapted from a best-seller was a risky proposition. When I asked a producer I know about the film's rumored delays, he simply said, "It's still an *Asian* movie," surprised I had even asked. Equally interesting was director Wayne Wang's initial reluctance to be involved in the project; he told the *New York Times,* "I didn't want to do another Chinese movie."

Maybe he shouldn't have worried so much. After all, according to the media, the nineties are the decade of "Pacific Overtures" and East Asian chic. Madonna, the pop queen of shameless appropriation, cultivated Japanese high-tech style with her music video "Rain," while Janet Jackson faked kitschy orientalia in hers, titled "If." Critical attention was paid to movies from China, Japan, and Vietnam. But that didn't mean an honest appraisal of women's lives. Even on the art house circuit, filmmakers who should know better took the easy way out. Takehiro Nakajima's 1992 film *Okoge* presents one of the more original film roles for women in recent years. In Japanese, "okoge" means the crust of rice that sticks to the bottom of the rice pot; in pejorative slang, it means fag hag. The way "okoge" is used in the film seems a reappropriation of the term; the portrait Nakajima creates of Sayoko, the so-called fag hag, is clearly an affectionate one. Sayoko is a quirky, self-assured woman in contemporary Tokyo who does voice-overs for cartoons, has a thing for Frida Kahlo paintings, and is drawn to a gentle young gay man named Goh. But the other women's roles are disappointing, stereotypical "hysterical females" and the movie itself turns conventional halfway through. Sayoko sacrifices herself to a macho brute Goh desires, who rapes her as images of Frida Kahlo paintings and her beloved Goh rising from the ocean flash before her. She gives birth to a baby boy and endures a terrible life of poverty with the abusive rapist. This sudden change from spunky survivor to helpless, victimized woman is baffling. Whatever happened to her job? Or that arty little apartment of hers? Didn't her Frida Kahlo obsession teach her anything?

Then there was Tiana Thi Thanh Nga's *From Hollywood to Hanoi,* a self-serving but fascinating documentary. Born in Vietnam to a privileged family that included an uncle who was defense minister in the Thieu government and an idolized father who served as press minister, Nga (a.k.a. Tiana) spent her adolescence in California. A former actor in martial arts movies and fitness teacher ("Karaticize with Tiana"), the vivacious Tiana decided to make a record of her journey back to Vietnam.

From Hollywood to Hanoi is at times unintentionally very funny. Tiana   15
includes a quick scene of herself dancing with a white man at the Metropole hotel in Hanoi, and breathlessly announces: "That's me doing the tango with Oliver Stone!" Then she listens sympathetically to a horrifying account of the My Lai massacre by one of its few female survivors. In another scene, Tiana cheerfully addresses a food vendor on the streets of Hanoi: "Your hairdo is so pretty." The unimpressed, poker-faced woman gives a brusque, deadpan reply: "You want to eat, or what?" Sometimes it is hard to tell the difference between Tiana Thi Thanh Nga and her Hollywood persona: the real Tiana still seems to be playing one of her B-movie roles, which are mainly fun because they're fantasy. The time was certainly right to explore postwar Vietnam from a Vietnamese woman's perspective; it's too bad this film was done by a Valley Girl.

Nineteen ninety-three also brought Tran Anh Hung's *The Scent of Green Papaya,* a different kind of Vietnamese memento—this is a look back at the peaceful, lush country of the director's childhood memories. The film opens in Saigon, in 1951. A willowy ten-year-old girl named Mui comes to work for a troubled family headed by a melancholy musician and his kind, stoic wife. The men of this bourgeois household are idle, pampered types who take naps while the women do all the work. Mui is male fantasy: she is a devoted servant, enduring acts of cruel mischief with patience and dignity; as an adult, she barely speaks. She scrubs floors, shines shoes, and cooks with loving care and never a complaint. When she is sent off to work for another wealthy musician, she ends up being impregnated by him. The movie ends as the camera closes in on Mui's contented face. Languid and precious, *The Scent of Green Papaya* is visually haunting, but it suffers from the director's colonial fantasy of women as docile, domestic creatures. Steeped in highbrow nostalgia, it's the arty Vietnamese version of *My Fair Lady* with the wealthy musician as Professor Higgins, teaching Mui to read and write.

And then there is Ang Lee's tepid 1993 hit, *The Wedding Banquet*—a clever culture-clash farce in which traditional Chinese values collide with contemporary American sexual mores. The somewhat formulaic plot goes like this: Wai-Tung, a yuppie landlord, lives with his white lover, Simon, in a chic Manhattan brownstone. Wai-Tung is an only child and his aging parents in Taiwan long for a grandchild to continue the family legacy. Enter Wei-Wei, an artist who lives in a grungy loft owned by Wai-Tung. She slugs tequila straight from the bottle as she paints and flirts boldly with her young, uptight landlord, who brushes her off. "It's my fate. I am always attracted to handsome gay men," she mutters. After this setup, the movie goes downhill, all edges blurred in a cozy nest of happy endings. In a refrain of Sayoko's plight in *Okoge,* a pregnant, suddenly complacent Wei-Wei gives in to family pressures—and never gets her life back.

"It takes a man to know what it is to be a real woman."
—SONG LILING in *M. Butterfly*

Ironically, two gender-bending films in which men play men playing women reveal more about the mythology of the prized Asian woman and the superficial trappings of gender than most movies that star real women. The slow-moving *M. Butterfly* presents the ultimate object of Western male desire as the spy/opera diva Song Liling, a Suzie Wong/ Lotus Blossom played by actor John Lone with a five o'clock shadow and bobbing Adam's apple. The best and most profound of these forays into cross-dressing is the spectacular melodrama *Farewell My Concubine,* directed by Chen Kaige. Banned in China, *Farewell My Concubine* shared the prize for Best Film at the 1993 Cannes Film Festival with Jane Campion's *The Piano.* Sweeping through 50 years of tumultuous history in China, the story revolves around the lives of two male Beijing Opera stars and the woman who marries one of them. The three characters make an unforgettable triangle, struggling over love, art, friendship, and politics against the bloody backdrop of cultural upheaval. They are as capable of casually betraying each other as they are of selfless, heroic acts. The androgynous Dieyi, doomed to play the same female role of concubine over and over again, is portrayed with great vulnerability, wit, and grace by male Hong Kong pop star Leslie Cheung. Dieyi competes with the prostitute Juxian (Gong Li) for the love of his childhood protector and fellow opera star, Duan Xiaolou (Zhang Fengyi).

Cheung's highly stylized performance as the classic concubine-ready-to-die-for-love in the opera within the movie is all about female artifice. His sidelong glances, restrained passion, languid stance, small steps, and delicate, refined gestures say everything about what is considered desirable in Asian women—and are the antithesis of the feisty, outspoken woman played by Gong Li. The characters of Dieyi and Juxian both see suffering as part and parcel of love and life. Juxian matter-of-factly says to Duan Xiaolou before he agrees to marry her: "I'm used to hardship. If you take me in, I'll wait on you hand and foot. If you tire of me, I'll . . . kill myself. No big deal." It's an echo of Suzie Wong's servility, but the context is new. Even with her back to the wall, Juxian is not helpless or whiny. She attempts to manipulate a man while admitting to the harsh reality that is her life.

Dieyi and Juxian are the two sides of the truth of women's lives in   20
most Asian countries. Juxian in particular—wife and ex-prostitute—could be seen as a thankless and stereotypical role. But like the characters Gong Li has played in Chinese director Zhang Yimou's films, *Red Sorghum, Raise the Red Lantern,* and especially *The Story of Qiu Ju,* Juxian is tough, obstinate, sensual, clever, oafish, beautiful, infuriating, cowardly, heroic, and banal. Above all, she is resilient. Gong Li is one of the few Asian Pacific actors whose roles have been drawn with intelligence, honesty, and depth. Nevertheless, the characters she plays are limited by the possibilities that exist for real women in China.

"Let's face it. Women still don't mean shit in China," my friend Meeling reminds me. What she says so bluntly about her culture rings painfully true, but in less obvious fashion for me. In the Philippines, infant girls aren't drowned, nor were their feet bound to make them more desirable. But sons were and are cherished. To this day, men of the bourgeois class are coddled and prized, much like the spoiled men of the elite household in *The Scent of Green Papaya.* We do not have a geisha tradition like Japan, but physical beauty is overtreasured. Our daughters are protected virgins or primed as potential beauty queens. And many of us have bought into the image of the white man as our handsome savior: G.I. Joe.

Buzz magazine recently featured an article entitled "Asian Women/ L.A. Men," a report on a popular hangout that caters to white men's fantasies of nubile Thai women. The lines between movies and real life are blurred. Male screenwriters and cinematographers flock to this bar-restaurant, where the waitresses are eager to "audition" for roles. Many of these men have been to Bangkok while working on film crews for Vietnam War movies. They've come back to L.A., but for them, the movie never ends. In this particular fantasy the boys play G.I. Joe on a rescue mission in the urban jungle, saving the whore from herself. "A scene has developed here, a kind of R-rated *Cheers,*" author Alan Rifkin writes. "The waitresses audition for sitcoms. The customers date the waitresses or just keep score."

Colonization of the imagination is a two-way street. And being enshrined on a pedestal as someone's Pearl of the Orient fantasy doesn't seem so demeaning, at first; who wouldn't want to be worshipped? Perhaps that's why Asian women are the ultimate wet dream in most Hollywood movies; it's no secret how well we've been taught to play the role, to take care of our men. In Hollywood vehicles, we are objects of desire or derision; we exist to provide sex, color, and texture in what is essentially a white man's world. It is akin to what Toni Morrison calls "the Africanist presence" in literature. She writes: "Just as entertainers, through or by association with blackface, could render permissible topics that otherwise would have been taboo, so American writers were able to employ an imagined Africanist persona to articulate and imaginatively act out the forbidden in American culture." The same analogy could be made for the often titillating presence of Asian women in movies made by white men.

Movies are still the most seductive and powerful of artistic mediums, manipulating us with ease by a powerful combination of sound and image. In many ways, as females and Asians, as audiences or performers, we have learned to settle for less—to accept the fact that we are either decorative, invisible, or one-dimensional. When there are characters who look like us represented in a movie, we have also learned to view between the lines, or to add what is missing. For many of us, this way of watching has always been a necessity. We fill in the gaps. If a female character is presented as a mute, willowy beauty, we convince ourselves she is an ancestral ghost—so smart she doesn't have to speak at all. If she is a whore with a heart of gold, we claim her as a tough feminist icon. If she is a sexless, sanitized, boring nerd, we embrace her as role model for our daughters, rather than the tragic whore. And if she is presented as an utterly devoted saint suffering nobly in silence, we lie and say she is just like our mothers. Larger than life. Magical and insidious. A movie is never just a movie, after all.

Reading the Text

1. Summarize in your own words Hagedorn's view of the traditional images of Asian women as presented in American film.
2. What is the chronology of Asian women in film that Hagedorn presents, and why do you think she gives us an historical overview?
3. Why does Hagedorn say that the film *The Joy Luck Club* "carries a lot of cultural baggage" (para. 11)?
4. What sort of images of Asian women does Hagedorn imply that she would prefer to see?

Reading the Signs

1. Rent a videotape of *The Joy Luck Club* (or another film featuring Asian characters), and write an essay in which you support, refute, or modify Hagedorn's interpretation of the film.

2. In class, form teams and debate the proposition that Hollywood writers and directors have a social responsibility to avoid stereotyping ethnic characters. To develop your team's arguments, first brainstorm films that depict various ethnicities, and then discuss whether the portrayals are damaging or benign. You might also consult Michael Omi's "In Living Color: Race and American Culture" (p. 526).
3. Study a magazine that targets Asian American readers, such as *Transpacific* or *Yolk*. Then write an essay in which you discuss the extent to which Asian women fit the stereotypes that Hagedorn describes, keeping in mind the magazine's specific readership (businessmen, twentysomethings of both sexes, and so forth).
4. In class, compare the stereotyped roles for Asian women that Hagedorn describes with the good and bad girl archetypes that Sandra Tsing Loh discusses in "The Return of Doris Day" (below). What does your comparison suggest for the roles available for female characters of any race?
5. Watch one of the gender-bending films Hagedorn mentions (such as *M. Butterfly*), and write your own analysis of the gender roles portrayed in the film. To develop your ideas, consult Holly Devor's "Gender Role Behaviors and Attitudes" (p. 447).

SANDRA TSING LOH

The Return of Doris Day

||||||||||||||||||||||||||||||||||||||||||||||||||||||||||||||||||

Madonna is out and Doris Day is in, according to Sandra Tsing Loh's (b. 1962) pop cultural analysis, first published in Buzz *magazine. Bad girls may have ruled the Hollywood roost in the eighties, Loh observes, but the success of actresses like Sandra Bullock shows that good girls are making a comeback in the nineties. A journalist with a B.S. in physics from Cal Tech, Loh writes widely on popular cultural topics and has published* Depth Takes a Holiday: Essays From Lesser Los Angeles *(1996),* Aliens in America *(1997), and* If You Lived Here, You'd Be Home by Now *(1997).*

The seventies and eighties were tough times for us Good Girls. As polite people, we like to do what's expected of us. Unfortunately, what was expected, in our sexual heyday, was for Girls to be . . . anything but Good.

In junior high, I dutifully grappled with whatever icky senior boy that Spin the Bottle sent me. By college, my sisters and I had graduated to smoking pot and swimming nude in the Sierras, sleeping with men on the first date (or before—you're welcome!), and developing evasive "mumble vaguely and give back rubs" routines if forced into a threesome.

We were lost, I tell you. Lost. But not anymore. Recently I was faced with a Nude Hot Tub Situation. It was a tame one by eighties standards. The tub was vast, the night was dark, and my companions were three platonic male friends—thirtysomethings like me stooped with worry, hardly a threat.

"C'mon!" I heard that inner coach urging me. It was the voice born in 1975, when everyone in my junior high had Chemin de Fer jeans and Candie's sandals. *Don't be a drag,* it said. *Take off your clothes and jump in!*

But then, for the first time, I heard another voice. Clear as a bell, it   5 was the soaring soprano of Mary Martin in *South Pacific,* or perhaps Shirley Jones in *Oklahoma!* It sang:

> I've got a guy!
> A really great guy!
> He makes me as high
> As an elephant's eye!

Or something to that effect. It was like a light bulb going on. Suddenly I felt right with my world—fresh, natural, confident, all the pantyshield adjectives. It was so simple, so clear. The wandering days of these breasts were over.

"If you'd known me in my twenties," I lecture my hot tub companions, as though sharing an amazing story from ancient lore, "you would have seen my boobs and seen them often!" I'm in the water now, but demurely covered in my white cotton T-shirt from Victoria's Secret. (A white cotton T-shirt is typical of what we women actually *buy* there.) "But no more." I lift a teacherly finger. "Today, I feel much more liberated keeping my shirt on. I don't have to prove anything anymore. I can turn the world on with a smile!" I hear myself excitedly half-singing, flashing on Mary Tyler Moore.

My treatise is cut short by the arrival of two 24-year-old modern dancers who rip off towels and flash their naked pink everything. The men's attention snaps away with the zing of taut bungee cords. But I don't feel bad. I know it's only I, Goody Two Shoes, who feels that wonderful glowing specialness inside.

I. Good Girls: A Cleaned and Buffed Thumbnail History

Were our moms actually right way back when? Maybe so. Because like it or not, these days Good Girls are back in. Demure behavior is suddenly clever, fashionable, even attractive.

Who *is* the nineties Good Girl? She is: (a) spunky; (b) virginal;   10

(c) busy with purposeful activity. But not obsessively so. Her hormones are in balance. Brave chin up, she works within society's rules, finds much to celebrate in her immediate surroundings, makes the best of her lot. Good Girls don't challenge the status quo.

Good Girls have been around a long time in Western culture. The star of the very first novel in English? A Good Girl! We find her in Samuel Richardson's 1740 opus, *Pamela*. In it, Pamela's resistance to sex charges five-hundred-plus pages of narrative tension; it's so effective a gambit that Good Girls (typically poor but beautiful governesses) become the very foundation of the eighteenth- and nineteenth-century novel.

It is in twentieth-century America, however, that we start to see the rowdy Good Girl. She does more than keep her knees crossed. In fact, if so moved, she may even spread her legs boldly akimbo! (If only to punctuate a funny singalong.)

The forties and fifties brought the U.S. Good Girl her two most sacred boons: World War II, and Rodgers & Hammerstein. The former yielded new busy-but-virginal archetypes like Rosie the Riveter, the Andrews Sisters, and the Chipper Navy Nurse. The latter fleshed out the canon via the Feisty Governess of the past (Anna in *The King and I*), the Chipper Navy Nurse of the semipresent (Nellie Forbush in *South Pacific*), even the boldly innovative Frisky Nun of the future (Julie Andrews in *The Sound of Music*). Indeed, Frisky Nun proved so popular she'd soon hop mediums and become TV's *The Flying Nun* (comical ex-Gidget Sally Field). Even *The Mary Tyler Moore Show*—a milestone in the modern Good Girl's progress—almost had Moore playing a version of Frisky Nun. Laugh no more at winged hats: in the past, Frisky Nun was a female star's emancipated alternative!

The quintessential Good Girl of midcentury America—indeed the mother of all modern Good Girls—was Doris Day. We mean, of course, Nubile Doris Day, in her guise as pert, urban, apartment-dwelling career girl (*Pillow Talk*), as opposed to harangued suburban housewife (*Please Don't Eat the Daisies*). Never mind that Doris typically chucked her career at the end of the film for Rock Hudson; what mattered was that while Doris *was* a Good Girl, she was hardly a nun—in fact, she was quite sexy in her spunky purposefulness.

It was too bad that Doris stayed mainly in the movies, for the most per- 15
fect form for the American Good Girl remains the musical. Here emerges a unique symbiosis: on the one hand, the musical needs the Good Girl's soprano, her can-do optimism, the soaring love songs only she can inspire. On the other, not to put too fine a point on it, the Good Girl needs the musical. The musical could *create* Good Girls where there once were none. Example: where, outside the musical, do you find that rarest of beings—the ethnic Good Girl? Sure, ethnic girls can have hearts o' gold, but in the real world they—can we say it?—tend to be a bit sassy. Happily, the musical has the miraculous power to freshen, sanitize, uplift even ethnicities

who might feel too irked with society to be Good. We see Jewish Good Girls: Tevye's daughters in *Fiddler on the Roof*. (Imagine "Matchmaker, Matchmaker" done in dialogue on a hot afternoon in Queens—another tale entirely.) It also gave us Yentl. Hm. *West Side Story* produces Latina Good Girl Maria (Natalie Wood, but we quibble). *Flower Drum Song* yields that mousy Asian Good Girl whose name no one can remember (not Nancy Kwan, the other one). *The Wiz* even gives us a black Good Girl: Diana Ross (who was never that Good again).

As we move into the late seventies, however, even white Good Girls are hard to come by. There's a general Fall of the Musical (we could discuss Andrew Lloyd Webber, but why?)—and Fall of Filmic Good Girls. We lose our bright, dependable, pony-tailed stars—our June Allysons, Shirley Joneses, Julie Andrewses. We collapse into the nude/seminude group therapy "line" musicals: *Oh! Calcutta!, Pippin,* the exhaustingly confessional *A Chorus Line*. By 1977, we have, God forbid, Liza Minnelli trying to play an ex-WAC in *New York New York*. Liza Minnelli? The eyelashes alone would have scared Our Boys.

And you know why we saw this fall, this demise, this dismal sinking? Because national hope is failing. No one whistles a happy tune. We're moving into bad times for optimism. Bad times for patriotism. Bad times for Good Girls. Forrest Gump drifts out of touch with Jenny . . . and America itself becomes very *dark*.

II. The Enduring Power of Good Girls

If Good Girls are back in the nineties, what does this imply? That we've come full circle? Forgiven Mom and Dad? We're in love with a wonderful guy? More deeply, does the Good Girl's resurgence signal an uplift in national character, a kind of neo-fifties patriotism, a return to what we might call, without irony, American values?

We have no idea—Good Girls are notoriously poor at political analysis. All we know is, we look around and Good Girls seem to be all over the place, winning again.

Look how they flourish, in the very bosom of our society! Good [20] Girls are our great: morning-show hosts (Katie Couric now, Jane Pauley before); figure skaters (Nancy Kerrigan vanquishing Tonya Harding now, Dorothy Hamill vanquishing all those foreigners before); country singers (Reba, Tammy & Co. now; Dolly Parton before); middle-of-the-road pop stars (Whitney Houston, Paula Abdul now; Linda Ronstadt before); goyische straight gals to nervous Jewish comics (Sally to Harry, Helen Hunt to Paul Reiser now; Diane Keaton to Woody Allen before); Peter Pans (Sandy Duncan now-ish, Mary Martin way before); androgynous gals (Ellen DeGeneres now, Nancy Drew's pal boyish George before); astronauts (Sally Ride); Australians (Olivia Newton-John); MTV newspersons (Tabitha Soren); princesses (Di).

Can a video vixen be Good? Absolutely. Look at ex-Aerosmith girl and rising star Alicia Silverstone. You thought she was Drew Barrymore, but she's not. In Amy Heckerling's surprise summer hit *Clueless* (loosely based on Jane Austen's *Emma!*), Silverstone played Cher, a fashion-obsessed virgin ("You see how picky I am about my shoes, and *they* only go on my feet!"). Alicia the person is very spunky, clean, convincingly virginal, attends Shakespeare camp, takes tap-dancing lessons, and loves animals!

Good Girl accessories are in. Look what Hillary Clinton did for the headband—an astounding semiotic statement. Look how she reinvented cookie baking. Too-thin Nancy Reagan in her let-them-eat-cake Adolfo suit is over. Today, posing as a Good Girl—as clever Hillary does— seems powerfully subversive.

Look how even yesterday's swampy girls are cleaning up. Jane Seymour bounced back from whatever seamy B-stuff she was doing to triumph today as Dr. Quinn, Medicine Woman. Consider post-Donald Ivana, her pertness and brave industry recalling the Czech girl skier of yore. Even Sharon Stone seems downright nice. She makes an effort to dress "up" for press briefings and is so polite, modest, funny! (She showed us her home in *In Style*—the essence of nice! Is a *Redbook* cover in her future?)

And why not? Being a Good Girl pays off. Look how well Meg Ryan/Sandra Bullock films are doing. These girls don't titillate by getting naked. Why? They can turn the world on with a smile!

Even the musical is coming back! Via Disney, we have Belle and the   25
Little Mermaid, even Princess Jasmine and Pocahontas. Look how ethnic! Maybe there *is* a place called Hope.

III. The Nastiest Truth of All

But what is the bottom line appeal of the Good Girl? Why do we urban nineties women want to *be* her? It's not as uncalculated as one might think. The Good Girl's draw is that she is the opposite of Bad. And Bad is something we no longer want to be.

You remember Bad Girl—she who reigned in the go-go eighties. Bad Girl is very Bad. Ow. She needs a spanking, she wants it, but beware of giving it to her because ironically it is you (or, more likely, Michael Douglas) who will suffer afterward.

Good Girl's opposite, Bad Girl, has out-of-control hormones. Bad Girl comes from a wildly dysfunctional family; her past makes her do strange, erratic things. Bad Girl tells us something is terribly wrong with society. Bad Girl challenges the status quo. Bad Girl uses sex for everything but love and babies: it's power, self-expression, psychosis, hate, revolt, revenge.

What we have in Bad Girl is Power Slut. Like Madonna in, well, ninety percent of her oeuvre. Joan Collins in *Dynasty*. Glenn Close in *Fatal Attraction*. Sharon Stone in *Basic Instinct*. Demi Moore in *Disclosure*. (Sure those last few are technically nineties, but anything written by Joe Eszterhas is really quite eighties, no?)

Good feminists we, we have saluted Bad Girl/Power Slut's right to   30
exist, to demolish, to flourish in her own dark way. But the nagging question remains: Is this a good behavior model for us? Is Bad Girl's life healthy, happy, productive? Does she get enough love? Even more creepily we ask: Is she aging well?

Because the fact is, even we—once-nubile twentysomething gals who gamboled defiantly topless in the mountain streams of yore—feel ourselves gently softening with age each day. The drama in the bathroom no longer centers around the scale. Forget that—we've gained and lost the same fifteen pounds so often that the cycle has become like an old pal, natural as our monthly period. But our skin! Each new wrinkle tells us there's no going back. No wonder our obsessions have become all Oil of Olay, Clinique moisturizer, antiwrinkle cream!

And while we hate to be unsupportive of our Badder sisters, we can't help noticing that, well, Bad Girlhood seems so bad *for* you. Look at Heidi Fleiss—drawn and witchy and actually too thin at 29. Partying, prostitution, cocaine, and, heck, the eighties don't wear well on a gal. And look at spooky seventysomething *Cosmo* girl Helen Gurley Brown, a.k.a. "the Crypt Keeper in capri pants," as she is known to AM-radio wag Peter Tilden.

Even the indestructible Madonna is looking a bit exhausted. Sure she's a zillionaire and superpowerful and has been on top forever. Her *Sex* book broke every boundary, sold tons. But it must be tough, we secretly think, for Madonna to greet her 5,012th weekend with only those girly dancing boys with the weird hair for company. Sean is off having babies with Robin Wright (a Good Girl, if oddly skinny). Geez: Madonna's going to be 40 soon. If she keeps hanging onto Bad Girl, soon she'll be Old Crone girl. Can we women age with dignity? By what strategy will we engineer fabulous forties, fifties, sixties, and beyond? (My God—a healthy woman of 65 today can expect to live to 83! Almost half our life will be spent being 50 or older!)

As we drift past our midthirties, we begin to question the idea of relentlessly pushing the boundaries of society, psychology, and biology. Will we end up like tart-talking Roseanne? We used to love her. We still do, but it's 1995 now and we are confused. She had a hit show, but still she felt the need for plastic surgery, butt tattoos, Tom Arnold tattoos, a Tom Arnold divorce, she hates her family, belched the anthem, lit her farts (or could if she'd wanted), married her bodyguard and has had a new baby, like, surgically implanted . . . where? Is this feminism? Help!

We will not go like that. (Anyway, we can't afford to.) We women 35 are survivors, and we are battening down our hatches . . . for the future.

IV. The Good Girl Manifesto

Herewith, then, a declaration of our principles:

1. We're no longer promiscuous. Diseases suck. And so do noncommittal men our age (often spoiled for commitment by all that free sex we gave them in the sixties, seventies, and eighties). There's really no point. We can do it ourselves.

2. We're tailing down on booze and drugs. Eight glasses of water a day—better for the skin.

3. We're trying not to be anorexic. That seems very eighties. Then again, we don't want to be fat. As a result, we're just a wee bit bulimic. Sorry! We know this is not good.

4. We're *trying* to envision a future without plastic surgery. We try to keep happy, confident, glowing, nonlifted, fortysomething earth mothers Meryl/Cybill/Susan foremost in our minds. (See Nivea wrinkle cream ad: a blond mom in white feels good about her face, baby splashing in the background.)

5. We're trying to love our parents again. Their mortality weighs heavily upon us. When a parent dies, we peruse the photo album, weep while contemplating their jauntily hopeful forties hats, the huge families they came from. We feel suddenly lonely.

6. Were the forties and fifties really so bad? Gee, we feel nostalgic. We yearn for old love songs and old movies. At least our filmic Good Girl heroines do. (See Meg Ryan in *Sleepless in Seattle,* Marisa Tomei in *Only You.*) Although I must tell you: if I hear Harry Connick Jr. singing "It Had to Be You" again on the soundtrack of one more light romantic comedy, I will kill someone.

7. We're drawn to stuff that seems traditional, even if it isn't. Laura Ashley sheets. Coach bags. *Martha Stewart Living.*

8. We're back to white cotton underpants. (And as Victoria's Secret tells us, cotton is sexy again!)

9. We love our pets—our very own Disney familiars. (If we are starring in a movie, we can be expected to talk to our cat or dog in a very cute way. Starlets who need their tawdry images to be cleaned up can be expected to join PETA.)

10. We believe in true love, but we don't expect to find it in Rock Hudson. That's a dream of the past. Urban Lotharios *never* settle down— we've learned that, unlike Doris, we can't domesticate them through interior design.

That's why we're looking for love in all new places. Maybe we find it via a much younger man (a third of today's women already do). Maybe we find it by falling in love again with the family (like Sandra Bullock does in *While You Were Sleeping*). Maybe we find it in our children, postdivorce.

Consider that the template for the female sitcom today is not single newsgal Mary Tyler Moore, but single mom Murphy Brown, divorced mom Brett Butler, divorced mom Cybill. Exhusbands are reduced to comic characters sticking their heads in the door, like Howard the neighbor on the old *Bob Newhart Show.* In these days, when conception's becoming increasingly immaculate, maybe we have a baby without a guy.

Or maybe, hell, we find love for a few beautiful days with a fiftysomething shaman/photographer called Robert Kincaid with a washboard stomach. Maybe we never see him again after that. But today's Good Girl is tough and prudent—a little bit of love and she says, uncomplainingly, "I'm fine. I'm full. I have plenty."

Then goes outside and, into the air, high above her head, throws not   50
her bra . . . but her hat.

Reading the Text

1. Why, do you think, does Loh begin her essay with a racy hot tub anecdote?
2. Summarize in your own words what Loh means by "Good Girls"
   (para. 1).
3. Why do good girls have such an enduring appeal in American culture, according to Loh?
4. What are bad girls, in Loh's view, and why are they a necessary complement to good girls?
5. Why, according to Loh, were the 1980s a decade in which bad girls
   thrived?
6. What is Loh's tone in this essay, and do you find that her approach to her
   topic makes the essay more or less persuasive?

Reading the Signs

1. If you are female, explore in your journal whether in your childhood you
   were raised to be a "good girl" and whether that upbringing influences
   you today. If you are male, explore in your journal whether you believe
   good girls have a male equivalent: Were you raised to be a "good boy"? If
   so, what traits were you expected to follow? If not, explore whether you
   believe our culture values good boys.
2. In class, brainstorm a list of current female film stars and their chief roles,
   and then discuss whether they are good or bad girls (or neither). Drawing
   on the class discussion, write an essay in which you challenge, support, or
   qualify Loh's contention that the 1990s saw a return of good girls to
   Hollywood.
3. Good girls aren't political enough to explain their return to favor in the
   1990s, Loh claims. Write your own interpretation of why the good girl
   supplanted the bad girl of the 1980s, being sure to base your discussion on
   specific examples from film.
4. Keeping Loh's discussion of good girls in mind, watch an episode of *ER*
   or *NYPD Blue* (or any other "progressive" show), and write an essay that
   discusses the extent to which the female characters in the show fulfill the
   good girl archetype. To develop your ideas, read or reread Susan Douglas's "Signs of Intelligent Life on TV" (p. 260).
5. Rent a videotape of one of the Doris Day films that Loh mentions, and
   write a semiotic analysis of the gender roles portrayed in the film.
6. Study a popular women's fashion magazine such as *Glamour* or *Vogue,*
   and write an analysis of the way women are portrayed in the advertising. To
   what extent do advertisers rely on the good-girl archetype that Loh describes? How can you account for your findings?

MICHAEL PARENTI

Class and Virtue

||||||||||||||||||||||||||||||||||||||||||||||

In 1993, a movie called Indecent Proposal *presented a story in which a billionaire offers a newly poor middle-class woman a million dollars if she'll sleep with him for one night. In Michael Parenti's terms, what was really indecent about the movie was the way it showed the woman falling in love with the billionaire, thus making a romance out of a class outrage. But the movie could get away with it, partly because Hollywood has always conditioned audiences to root for the ruling classes and to ignore the inequities of class privilege. In this selection from* Make-Believe Media: The Politics of Entertainment *(1992), Parenti (b. 1933) argues that Hollywood has long been in the business of representing the interests of the ruling classes. Whether it is forgiving the classist behavior in* Pretty Woman *or glamorizing the lives of the wealthy, Hollywood makes sure its audiences leave the theater thinking you can't be too rich. Michael Parenti is a writer who lectures widely at university campuses around the country. His publications include* Power and the Powerless *(1978),* Inventing Reality: The Politics of the News Media *(1986),* Democracy for the Few *(1988),* Against Empire *(1995),* Dirty Truths *(1996), and* America Besieged *(1998).*

Class and Virtue

The entertainment media present working people not only as unlettered and uncouth but also as less desirable and less moral than other people. Conversely, virtue is more likely to be ascribed to those characters whose speech and appearance are soundly middle- or upper-middle class.

Even a simple adventure story like *Treasure Island* (1934, 1950, 1972) manifests this implicit class perspective. There are two groups of acquisitive persons searching for a lost treasure. One, headed by a squire, has money enough to hire a ship and crew. The other, led by the rascal Long John Silver, has no money—so they sign up as part of the crew. The narrative implicitly assumes from the beginning that the squire has a moral claim to the treasure, while Long John Silver's gang does not. After all, it is the squire who puts up the venture capital for the ship. Having no investment in the undertaking other than their labor, Long John and his men, by definition, will be "stealing" the treasure, while the squire will be "discovering" it.

To be sure, there are other differences. Long John's men are cutthroats. The squire is not. Yet, one wonders if the difference between a bad pirate and a good squire is itself not preeminently a matter of having the right amount of disposable income. The squire is no less acquisitive than the conspirators. He just does with money what they must achieve with cutlasses. The squire and his associates dress in fine clothes, speak an educated diction, and drink brandy. Long John and his men dress slovenly, speak in guttural accents, and drink rum. From these indications alone, the viewer knows who are the good guys and who are the bad. Virtue is visually measured by one's approximation to proper class appearances.

Sometimes class contrasts are juxtaposed within one person, as in *The Three Faces of Eve* (1957), a movie about a woman who suffers from multiple personalities. When we first meet Eve (Joanne Woodward), she is a disturbed, strongly repressed, puritanically religious person, who speaks with a rural, poor-Southern accent. Her second personality is that of a wild, flirtatious woman who also speaks with a rural, poor-Southern accent. After much treatment by her psychiatrist, she is cured of these schizoid personalities and emerges with a healthy third one, the real Eve, a poised, self-possessed, pleasant woman. What is intriguing is that she now speaks with a cultivated, affluent, Smith College accent, free of any low-income regionalism or ruralism, much like Joanne Woodward herself. This transformation in class style and speech is used to indicate mental health without any awareness of the class bias thusly expressed.

Mental health is also the question in *A Woman under the Influence* (1974), the story of a disturbed woman who is married to a hard-hat husband. He cannot handle—and inadvertently contributes to—her emotional deterioration. She is victimized by a spouse who is nothing more than an insensitive, working-class bull in a china shop. One comes away convinced that every unstable woman needs a kinder, gentler, and above all, more *middle-class* hubby if she wishes to avoid a mental crack-up. 5

Class prototypes abound in the 1980s television series *The A-Team*. In each episode, a Vietnam-era commando unit helps an underdog, be it a Latino immigrant or a disabled veteran, by vanquishing some menacing force such as organized crime, a business competitor, or corrupt government officials. As always with the make-believe media, the A-Team does good work on an individualized rather than collectively organized basis, helping particular victims by thwarting particular villains. The A-Team's leaders are two white males of privileged background. The lowest ranking members of the team, who do none of the thinking nor the leading, are working-class palookas. They show they are good with their hands, both by punching out the bad guys and by doing the maintenance work on the team's flying vehicles and cars. One of them, "B.A." (bad ass), played by the African-American Mr. T., is visceral, tough, and purposely bad-mannered toward those he doesn't like. He projects an image of crudeness and ignorance and is associated with the physical side of things. In sum, the team has a brain (the intelligent white leaders) and a body with its simpler physical functions (the working-class characters), a hierarchy that corresponds to the social structure itself.[1]

Sometimes class bigotry is interwoven with gender bigotry, as in *Pretty Woman* (1990). A dreamboat millionaire corporate raider finds himself all alone for an extended stay in Hollywood (his girlfriend is unwilling to join him), so he quickly recruits a beautiful prostitute as his playmate of the month. She is paid three thousand dollars a week to wait around his superposh hotel penthouse ready to perform the usual services and accompany him to business dinners at top restaurants. As prostitution goes, it is a dream gig. But there is one cloud on the horizon. She is lowclass. She doesn't know which fork to use at those CEO power feasts, and she's bothersomely fidgety, wears tacky clothes, chews gum, and, y'know, doesn't talk so good. But with some tips from the hotel manager, she proves to be a veritable Eliza Doolittle in her class metamorphosis. She dresses in proper attire, sticks the gum away forever, and starts picking the right utensils at dinner. She also figures out how to speak a little more like Joanne Woodward without the benefit of a multiple personality syndrome, and she develops the capacity to sit in a poised, wordless, empty-headed fashion, every inch the expensive female ornament.

She is still a prostitute but a classy one. It is enough of a distinction for the handsome young corporate raider. Having liked her because she was charmingly cheap, he now loves her all the more because she has real polish and is a more suitable companion. So suitable that he decides to do the right thing by her: set her up in an apartment so he can make regular visits at regular prices. But now she wants the better things in life, like marriage, a nice house, and, above all, a different occupation, one that would allow her to use less of herself. She is furious at him for treating her like, well, a prostitute. She decides to give up her profession and get a high-school diploma so that she might make a better life for herself— perhaps as a filing clerk or receptionist or some other of the entry-level jobs awaiting young women with high school diplomas.[2]

After the usual girl-breaks-off-with-boy scenes, the millionaire prince returns. It seems he can't concentrate on making money without her. He even abandons his cutthroat schemes and enters into a less lucrative but supposedly more productive, caring business venture with a struggling old-time entrepreneur. The bad capitalist is transformed into a good capitalist. He then carries off his ex-prostitute for a lifetime of bliss. The moral is a familiar one, updated for post-Reagan yuppiedom: A woman can escape from economic and gender exploitation by winning the love and career advantages offered by a rich male. Sexual allure goes only so far unless it develops a material base and becomes a class act.[3]

---

1. Gina Marchetti, "Class, Ideology and Commercial Television: An Analysis of *The A-Team*," *Journal of Film and Video* 39, Spring 1987, pp. 19–28.
    2. See the excellent review by Lydia Sargent, *Z Magazine,* April 1990, pp. 43–45.
    3. Ibid.

Reading the Text

1. What characteristics are attributed to working-class and upper-class film characters, according to Parenti?
2. How does Parenti see the relationship between "class bigotry" and "gender bigotry" (para. 7) in *Pretty Woman*?
3. What relationship does Parenti see between mental health and class values in films?

Reading the Signs

1. Rent a videotape of *Wall Street,* and analyze the class issues that the movie raises.
2. Using Parenti's argument as a critical framework, interpret the class values implicit in a television show such as *Beverly Hills 90210*. Is the show that you've selected guilty of what Parenti calls "class bigotry" (para. 7)?
3. Do you agree with Parenti's interpretation of *Pretty Woman*? Write an argumentative essay in which you defend, challenge, or complicate his claims.
4. Read or review Holly Devor's "Gender Role Behaviors and Attitudes" (p. 447). How would Devor explain the gender bigotry that Parenti finds in *Pretty Woman*?
5. Rent the 1954 film *On the Waterfront,* and watch it with your class. How are labor unions and working-class characters portrayed in that film? Does the film display the class bigotry that Parenti describes?
6. Read or review Michael Omi's "In Living Color: Race and American Culture" (p. 526). Then write a journal entry in which you create a category of cinematic racial bigotry that corresponds to Parenti's two categories of class and gender bigotry. What films that you have seen illustrate your new category?

KAT MARTIN

She set out to unmask a spy,
but uncovered her own burning desire—
for the enemy...

Dangerous Passions

IT WAS A DARK
AND STORMY NIGHT

The Codes of Popular Literature

The Great Divide

When you reach for something to read, what do you grab? A volume of poetry? *The Collected Plays of William Shakespeare*? *War and Peace*? Not likely—not, at least, if you are like most Americans. But it isn't, as English professors often complain, that Americans don't read: they read plenty. It's just that they don't read what English professors typically want them to read. Instead, Americans eagerly snatch up the latest works by authors with names like Stephen King, John Grisham, Tom Clancy, Jackie Collins, and Michael Crichton. We consume, by the millions, books that tell us how to lose weight, make money, lower our cholesterol, make love, learn what we learned in kindergarten, listen to our spouses, or find God. Every celebrity bio or tell-all is a potential gold mine, especially if it comes from such celebrities-of-the-week as Marcia Clark or Monica Lewinsky, for in American publishing, sufficient unto the day is the scandal thereof.

So why all the complaints, usually uttered in academic circles, about American illiteracy? With so many books being consumed in this country, purchased from such booming retailers as Barnes and Noble, Borders, and Amazon.com, Americans can hardly be accused of being unable to read. To be able to read, in the strict sense of the term, is to be literate, so the complaint does not literally refer to literacy. And it usually doesn't refer to the thousands of Americans who, for lack of education, technically cannot read even simple instructions or road signs. Rather, the accusation is based on a distinction that is a subset of the more general distinction between high and low culture that has traditionally been policed by the academy. This is the separation of "literature" from all other sorts of writing, especially popular writing, and, like the distinction between high and low culture, it is a division that has shifted through time.

In the Middle Ages, when the word *literature* first entered the English vocabulary, it simply referred to everything in letters—that is, everything written. What we now think of as high literature—poetry, for instance—was not highly valued in the past, which is why Shakespeare never bothered to preserve the written drafts of his own plays. Dramatic poetry just wasn't as prestigious as other sorts of writing in Shakespeare's time—especially theological and philosophical writing. So a playwright in Elizabethan England had roughly the same status that a television scriptwriter has today—and how often do scriptwriters publish their manuscripts?

Today, of course, the very name Shakespeare signifies the highest sort of literary merit, while philosophy and theology aren't considered literature at all. What has changed is the definition of *literature* itself, which has narrowed in scope to refer generally only to works of the creative imagination—to poems, stories, plays, and novels. But there's a catch: not all poems, stories, plays, and novels get to be called literature. Only those of a certain quality make the grade; the rest is considered hack work—popular stuff to be consumed and forgotten. And thus not all authors get to be considered writers of literature: only a few enter the literary canon (that is, the list of authors who are taught in the schools), while the rest are forgotten. But even that distinction has changed over time.

Consider what has happened to the likes of Ann Radcliffe and Bram Stoker. Ann Radcliffe, along with a writer named Horace Walpole, virtually invented the Gothic novel in the eighteenth century, while Bram Stoker perfected it in the nineteenth century with *Dracula,* still the single most successful Gothic novel of all time. When Radcliffe, Walpole, and Stoker were writing their novels, they were considered popular writers, and their work sold widely. Today, all three have been enshrined in the academic literary canon, while, paradoxically, the literary form they helped invent, the Gothic novel and its horror story successor, is firmly entrenched in the low category of popular fiction. Without Ann Radcliffe, we probably wouldn't have a Stephen King, but he is not taught in the schools.

Still, Stephen King, and the horror fiction he specializes in, have had their revenge, for in a consumer society being defined as literary doesn't really matter much. Being low, or popular, matters more because popular writing is, well, more popular than high literature and so sells better.

|||||||||||||||||||||||||||||||||||||||||||||||||||||||||||||||||||||||||||||||||||||||||||||||||||||||||||||||||||||||||||||||||||||

Exploring the Signs of Popular Literature

In your journal, reflect on the material that you prefer to read in your spare time, whether novels, magazines, comic books, or other texts. What have been your favorite books to read, and why? Why do you prefer some authors, and what pleasure do you gain from reading their work?

And in a capitalist culture, sales are more important than academic approval.

The fact that Americans read so much popular literature, and tend to avoid high literature once they get out of school, thus says something about the nature of modern American culture: in a consumer society, writing that is widely consumed is more valued, at least in dollars and cents, than writing that isn't. Which raises some semiotic questions: Why *do* we consume popular literature? What does it offer us? And what cultural lessons can we draw from an interpretation of popular literary tastes?

Interpreting the Codes of Popular Literature

To answer these questions, we can look at two kinds of popular literature—the horror tale and the detective story—and trace their cultural origins and current meanings. We could consider many other types of popular fiction, from the romance to science fiction to the action-adventure novel, which all share with detective and horror fiction the power to entertain their readers through the escapist pleasures that most popular fiction offers. But an analysis of the particular histories and cultural meanings of the full range of popular writing is beyond the scope of this introduction. Rather, by taking a look at detective and horror fiction, we mean to illustrate how you might conduct your own analysis of the popular writing that most interests you.

Let's start with the horror story. Horror is about as old as it gets when it comes to a literary tradition that is filled with murder and mayhem. Aeschylus's tragic trilogy, the *Oresteia,* for example, is splashed with gore, including a scene in which a man is served a banquet made of the flesh of his own children. Sophocles's *Oedipus the King* concludes with the hero clawing his eyes out (offstage). But despite the antiquity of the horrible, the actual origin of the horror tale is much more recent. That origin can be found in eighteenth-century England, when Ann Radcliffe wrote a novel called *The Mysteries of Udolpho* (1794) and Horace Walpole wrote *The Castle of Otranto* (1765). These novels established what is known as the tradition of the Gothic novel, a tradition better known today through Bram Stoker's *Dracula.*

Most Gothic novels share a standard set of conventional formulas. They tend to be set in France, Italy, or the Balkans (Transylvania is a Balkan region), and they generally feature monstrous aristocrats (Dracula, after all, is a count) or priests who live in dark and gloomy castles or monasteries and commit horrendous crimes that usually involve the violation of fundamental cultural taboos (the protagonist of an eighteenth-century Gothic novel called *The Monk,* for instance, is, in effect, an incestuous necrophiliac).

So what could be the cultural meaning of such tales? There are many possible avenues for approach, but let's begin with a few simple observations. First, most Gothic novels in the English tradition are set outside England in a Catholic country. Second, the hero-villain of the Gothic novel is usually an aristocrat or a priest. And third, the crimes committed by the Gothic villain transcend ordinary criminality through their descent into the realm of the unspeakable, where rape, incest, cannibalism, and worse are the usual fare. Now, what can we make of these facts?

Take the non-English setting of the English Gothic tale. By making the monster someone from the continent, the Gothic novelist was able to distance an English reader from the monster's crimes. Since the crimes are especially revolting (if fascinating) to their readers, such a distancing made it possible for the author to write the worst without offending (or implicating) the reader. Nothing personal—you see, this is the way *other* people (i.e., foreigners) behave, the story implies, thus capitalizing on English xenophobia.

English readers of Gothic fiction could be further distanced from the guilty pleasures of reading such tales by the villains' usually aristocratic status. It is important to note that the Gothic novel came into existence during the era of the French Revolution (*The Mysteries of Udolpho* was written in 1794), when middle-class readers in England were especially well aware of the aristocratic cruelties of pre-Revolutionary France and, therefore, could view the Gothic villain as belonging to a criminal *class* to which they did not belong. This doesn't mean that middle-class readers weren't fascinated by this class (after all, most fans of *Dallas* weren't upper-class oil barons either), but they could still be assured that no one *they* knew (including themselves) behaved in such a fashion and so, once again, could deny any secret pleasure they took in reading about such stuff.

If the Gothic villain was a priest, on the other hand, the Protestantism of the typical English reader came into play. Here the Gothic novel played on the anti-Catholic prejudices of Protestant England and so provided yet another way of distancing the reader from the crimes committed in the tale. (Even when the villain wasn't a priest, most English Gothic novels exploited anti-Catholic feeling by being set in Catholic countries.)

That the Gothic novel revels in the depiction of the most unspeakably taboo behaviors explains why its readers would want to distance themselves from it. From a psychoanalytic point of view, we can say that Gothic fiction appeals to unconscious fantasies that are so repulsive to the conscious mind that few people want to admit to them. But the desires are still there, and the Gothic novel overcomes their repression by foisting them off onto "others." Thus, the desire is put into an acceptable disguise and consumed accordingly.

Dracula demonstrates this point well. Written in the nineteenth century, when discussing sex was especially taboo in English society, *Dracula* doubly disguises itself by presenting a Central European Catholic aristocrat who assaults young women in their beds. Since throat biting in itself isn't explicitly sexual, the surface of the tale is simply horrific. But just under the surface, in an elaborate Gothic code, we find what is, in effect, a seduction or a rape (not to mention an act of cannibalism). English readers didn't admit to wanting to read about seduction or rape (or cannibalism), but they ate up *Dracula* all the same, making it one of England's all-time bestsellers.

At the same time, *Dracula,* with its living-dead villain who pulls his victims into living death with him, reflects a primitive human fear not simply of death but of the dead themselves. Consider stories like "The Monkey's Paw," wherein a family is terrorized by the return to life of the corpse of their beloved son, and our general fear of ghosts, who, if they did exist, one might think we would welcome back, especially if they were the ghosts of friends or loved ones. But the fact that we stand in dreadful awe of the ghost, and of the living corpse, while at the same time eagerly consuming stories about them, shows just how powerful is our compulsion to approach, through popular literature, the forbidden terrain of the dead.

Son of Dracula

This compulsion to trod forbidden ground has been carried forward (one might say with a vengeance) by the horror story, Gothic literature's modern descendant. As developed by such writers as Edgar Allan Poe (who also gave us the classically Gothic "Fall of the House of Usher," which, significantly, includes a corpse who returns to life) and H. P. Lovecraft (who moved the setting from a Balkan castle to a seedy New England mansion—a convention that Stephen King has continued), the American horror story often involves the simply ghoulish: depictions of rotting corpses, violent death, and torture. But as with the Gothic tradition, the modern horror story (cinematic or otherwise) often foists its

||||||||||||||||||||||||||||||||||||||||||||||||||||||||||||||||||||||||||||||||||||||||||||||||||||||||||||||||||||||||||||||||||||||||||||||||||||||||||||||||||||||||||||||

Discussing the Signs of Popular Literature

In class, discuss Americans' general preference for entertaining literature, such as mysteries and romances, over "serious" or "high" literature. Are Americans in danger of losing touch with their cultural traditions, or does the education system prevent that from being a threat? Does it matter whether people read the "classics" anymore? Why or why not?

horrors off on cultural "others," sometimes those made different from their audiences by social class (consider the basic class setup in *Texas Chainsaw Massacre,* in which lower-class ghouls prey on middle-class victims) or physical deformity (like Freddie Krueger in *Nightmare on Elm Street*). Middle-class American audiences (who are presumed to be undeformed) can thus revel in their own darkest fantasies without feeling complicit in the crime just as their English predecessors in the early Gothic tradition could.

The modern American horror story also violates taboos—most especially our taboo against the contemplation and representation of physical mutilation. We are not supposed to be fascinated by what our own Constitution forbids as "cruel and unusual punishment," but the fact that horror stories that absolutely wallow in mutilation fantasies are so popular can be taken as a sign about repressed desires. As represented in horror movies like *Texas Chainsaw Massacre* (and its sequels), *Nightmare on Elm Street* (and its sequels), *Halloween* (and its sequels) or *I Know What You Did Last Summer* (and its sequel), such fantasies often involve cannibalism, corpses that refuse to die, and teenage sexuality. They are especially popular, of course, among teenagers themselves. If you are a fan of stories of this kind, ask yourself what it is that appeals to you in them. Can you find traces of primitive desires that civilization has long since repressed?

Elementary, My Dear Watson

Detective literature also has a long history reflective of the culture in which it was created. By most accounts, the detective story was invented by Edgar Allan Poe in a series of three stories featuring a French detective named Dupin. The tradition was extended in England by Charles Dickens (who left unfinished at his death a novel called *The Mystery of Edwin Drood*) and Wilkie Collins (whose novel *The Moonstone* is considered the first detective novel) and then perfected in the late nineteenth century by Arthur Conan Doyle with the invention of Sherlock Holmes.

In the twentieth century, the detective story has taken two forms. Carrying on the tradition of Dupin and Holmes, one type has come to be called the *genteel* school of detective fiction. Featuring intellectual detectives (like Agatha Christie's Poirot), such stories frequently involve English and European high life (after all, only aristocrats can have butlers) whose crimes are solved by the detective more through intellectual deduction than active investigation (this tradition could be seen at work in the popular television series *Murder, She Wrote*). But in the 1930s a second kind of detective story appeared, one that is now known as the *hard-boiled* school of detective fiction. Invented by numerous little-known writers for such pulp fiction magazines as *Black Mask* and perfected by Dashiel Hammet (who gave us Sam Spade) and Raymond Chandler (the creator of the inimitable Philip Marlowe), the hard-boiled detective story features a lower-middle-class detective who, in the course of an arduous and dangerous investigation, often passes through all levels of society from the lowest depths to the richest heights before he solves the crime. The hard-boiled detective does use his brains, but he also needs his fists and a gun. He is also often no fan of the upper classes (this is especially true of Philip Marlowe) and resents their power and privileges — an attitude that has been perpetuated in such TV detective series as *The Rockford Files* and *Columbo,* which both featured rumpled detectives who liked to run circles around the rich.

So much for history. Now, what cultural meaning can we find in the detective story?

First, we can note that the detective story was invented at just that moment in history when both England and America were becoming urbanized societies. Now, consider the differences between living in a small town or village and in a big city. In a small town, everyone tends to know everyone else and everyone else's business. In such an environment, there are few mysteries. When you walk down the street, you can recognize most of the faces that you meet and know all that you need to know about them. Compare that condition with urban life. As you walk down the street or sit on a bus or subway, you may see literally thousands of faces about which you know nothing (have you ever overheard a fragment of conversation in a crowd and, never hearing the beginning or end, wondered just what was happening with those people?). In a big city, in short, you are "alone in a crowd," surrounded by mysterious people whom you must often instantaneously interpret ("Do I dare stand behind this guy at the ATM?" "Can I trust this person to hold my place in line?") without any certainty that you have "read" them correctly.

It was in such an environment that the literary detective first appeared. A city man (Dupin lived in Paris, Holmes in London), the literary detective is a professional interpreter of human mysteries who, eventually, gets to the bottom of things — unlike the rest of us, who can only touch the surface. The literary detective accordingly satisfies our desires for certainty in an uncertain urban environment. He or she arrives at the final answers that we would like to be able to find in our real lives but must experience vicariously through the detective story. (We get to play detective too in such stories, racing the detective as we try to solve the mystery first, but if we fail, the detective will tell us the answer anyway.) Born of a new living environment, the detective story thus filled a new human need.

But why did it adopt two different sets of conventions in the twentieth century? Here we can note the decade in which the hard-boiled school of detective fiction appeared: the 1930s, the decade of the Great Depression. At such a time, a mass audience was in less of a mood to watch gentlemanly detectives solve mostly gentlemanly mysteries. Financially troubled readers could identify with a lower-middle-class detective with money problems of his own, and it didn't hurt that the upper classes, who could weather the Depression more easily, were sometimes shown as being evil and depraved (the central villain of Raymond Chandler's first novel, *The Big Sleep,* is the pathological daughter of a millionaire). Thus, the hard-boiled detective answered a cultural need brought on by economic turmoil.

The hard-boiled detective story brought in another feature as well that is mostly missing in the genteel school. Sherlock Holmes usually had to contend with English criminals (there are exceptions, of course), and his archenemy was Professor Moriarty, a distinguished scientist. The hard-boiled detective, on the other hand, often contends with exotic or foreign criminals (as in *The Maltese Falcon* and all the Charlie Chan mysteries) and with evil women (particularly in so-called *noir* fiction like James M. Cain's *Double Indemnity* but also in *The Maltese Falcon*). In either case, the villain is an "other," an outsider who threatens accepted society and is brought to heel by the detective. Such stories served to assuage the fears of readers who felt threatened by immigration to the United States (the early twentieth century witnessed the arrival of millions of immigrants who were considered outsiders by Anglo-Saxon America) and by the women's movement, which had achieved the vote for women on the eve of the invention of *noir* detective fiction. Seeing the "other" defeated by an Anglo-Saxon man (there were no women hard-boiled detectives in the early days) enabled readers to achieve a cathartic satisfaction that they may not have been conscious of but that contributed to the popular success of this new kind of detective story.

Of course, the "other" today may be a hard-boiled detective herself, like Sue Grafton's Kinsey Millhone, or himself, like Walter Mosely's Easy Rawlins, showing the flexibility of the hard-boiled genre and how it continues to respond to the needs of its readers. Think of some of your favorite detectives today: What is their race or gender? What sorts of criminals do they stalk? What do their stories say about present-day fears and desires?

Back to the Future

Whatever the genre, popular texts all have in common the way that they reflect back to their readers what they most desire. This is what makes them entertaining. Because popular literature entertains by playing to its readers' often secret desires, it is produced like any other consumer product. Not unlike advertising, its narratives exploit the conscious and unconscious emotional needs of its consumers, providing vicarious substitutes for desired experiences (just consider the typical plot of a Harlequin Romance) rather than innovative ways of thinking about the human experience.

"High" literature, by contrast, tends to challenge its readers (Franz Kafka once remarked that reading a novel should be like getting hit over the head with a hammer), not entertain them. This is one reason those who prefer elite texts often believe that the study of popular literature has no place in the academy. But as we have seen through a brief survey of the cultural history of two popular literary genres, such a study can reveal important cultural messages—sometimes more clearly than "classic" texts can.

This is particularly true of a now-emerging popular literary genre that is appearing on the Internet. With no classical precedents, the authorless narratives called *hypertexts*—open story lines that are posted on the Web for anyone to contribute to—are presenting to literary history a whole new kind of text. Most revolutionary about hypertextual narratives is the way they deconstruct the very notion of an author. Traditionally, an author has been the single person who has, quite literally, *authority* over the text. He or she also has a certain cultural authority as well, often being awarded with such social rewards as fame and, especially in the case of popular authors, money. But hypertexts have no authors in this sense. Many writers, often anonymously, often with pseudonyms (one of the most famous writers on the Web, a cofounder of *Mondo 2000,* is known simply as R. U. Sirius) contribute to hypertextual narratives, making it impossible to determine just who the author is. The English language does not even have a word for it.

Reading Popular Literature on the Net

Visit an online literary magazine or zine, such as *Neon Blue Fiction* (**http://www.clocktowerfiction.com**) or *Boing Boing* (**http://boingboing.net**), and browse its offerings. What advantages does online publication offer to readers as well as to writers? Do you find any disadvantages? Does your behavior as a reader change when you read an online text, and if so, how?

Hypertexts, in short, turn the consumer of a text into a producer as well. The reader is the writer, and vice versa. Since the producer of the text has traditionally held the authority over it—or, to put it another way, the power—the dualistic power relations inherent in reading and writing are changing. It's hard to tell for sure (hypertexts are still quite a new phenomenon), but it does seem certain that the hierarchical model for reading and writing is being democratized. Thanks to the Internet, anyone can become an author. You don't have to persuade a publisher to publish your work, and if you want to, you can become your own publisher, posting whatever you want on your own web site. If you are particularly ambitious, you can publish your own online magazine, or *zine,* for which you serve as the editor as well. Just think: no more rejection slips!

More conventional online magazines that publish popular fiction and poetry, like *Eternity: The Online Journal of the Speculative Imagination* (**http://www.pulpeternity.com**) and *Neon Blue* (**http://www .clocktowerfiction.com**), do have editorial boards that accept or reject submissions, but they too are revolutionizing the way people consume popular literature. The *pulp* in *pulp fiction* originally referred to the cheap paper that popular crime fiction magazines like *Black Mask* were printed on, but digital pulp fiction has no need for paper, ink, or newsstand: the latest issue can be acquired at the touch of a button. And, at least so far, you don't have to pay for it. Whole libraries full of popular literature are waiting on the Web, free of charge, for anyone wishing to browse. The cost-free availability of popular writing on the Internet thus stands to multiply dramatically the numbers of readers who consume it and the number of writings that will be consumed.

Yet another development on the Web is revolutionizing the relationship between the consumer of a story and that story's characters. The traditional model for reading a text is hierarchically dualistic: the text dictates the story to the reader, who "watches" its characters in the course of their textual experiences. But in so-called MUD (multiuser dungeon) sites, participants can log on and not only participate in the creation of an unfolding narrative but participate in the narrative itself as one of its characters. In the fantasy storylines of the MUD domains, the reader-writers *are* the characters. Men play women, and women men. Modern players pretend to be medieval characters, shy computer nerds pretend to be dashing romantic heroes, and everyone gets to be whatever he or she desires—not through the vicarious experience of reading about the fictional lives of others but through direct fictional role playing.

Try to imagine what literary classics would be like if it had always been like this. Bored by *Romeo and Juliet?* Well, if Shakespeare's play had originally been on the Web, you could have just written yourself into it by cutting Romeo (or Juliet) out and putting yourself in his or her place. Tired of *Great Expectations?* You wouldn't be if *you* were its hero, Pip, and your fortune was at stake. The whole thing boggles the imagination, but technology is now making it possible by reinventing what reading can mean in a brave new literary world in which there will be no difference between "high" and "low" literature because there will be no clear differences between readers, writers, and characters. What will we call such stories in the future? It's hard to tell, but whatever we call them, they'll be popular.

The Readings

Amy E. Schwartz begins this chapter with a dual reflection on Sue Grafton's popular series of hard-boiled detective novels and, more generally, on the cultural debate over whether popular literature belongs in American classrooms. The first chapter of Philip K. Dick's *Blade Runner* follows, in which we are introduced to the postnuclear world of Rick Deckard, an android-stalking bounty hunter whose story combines elements of science fiction and the hard-boiled detective novel while anticipating the advent of cyberpunk literature. K. C. Myers's "Roadside Bones," a short story originally published on the Internet, next combines elements of the genteel mystery story, with its scientifically trained protagonist, and science fiction, with its out-of-this-world revelation. Warner Lee then offers up a contemporary retelling of the Dracula legend, producing a kind of hard-boiled Gothic comedy. Matt Zoller Seitz's journalistic feature on John Grisham follows with an explanation for the remarkable popularity of this best-selling author. The next two readings encompass the hard-breathing world of romance literature, beginning with Marilyn M. Lowery's how-to guide to producing romance fiction and followed by a selection from Kat Martin's *Dangerous Passions,* a romantic fantasy that passionately exemplifies the formulas that Lowery describes. We next include Edward Berridge's "Hope I Die before Marcia Gets Old" as an example of what may be found in the zine scene, that democratic netherworld of publication where anyone who wants to can produce his or her own popular journal. And Alison Lurie concludes the chapter with a reflection on popular children's literature, suggesting that children, like adults, prefer those stories that best satisfy their deepest fantasies and desires.

AMY E. SCHWARTZ
The ABCs of Popular Culture

||||||||||||||||||||||||||||||||||||||||||||||||

With the creation of Kinsey Millhone, Sue Grafton provided a female hard-boiled detective with whom women could identify, and in this op-ed article, Amy E. Schwartz describes her own attraction to Grafton's popular heroine. But it is not only Grafton's "alphabet mystery" series that has piqued Schwartz's interest: the whole controversy over the place of popular culture in academic study also intrigues her. Reflecting on the "culture wars" going on between the supporters and opponents of cultural studies, Schwartz observes that if Sue Grafton's writing is any indicator, taking a look at popular culture "is a very sensible thing to do." Amy E. Schwartz is a member of the editorial page staff at the Washington Post.

This week I became a cliché, one of the estimated million-plus readers who have finished reading all the available alphabet mysteries by Sue Grafton (*A is for Alibi, B is for Burglar,* and so forth) and are waiting impatiently for Grafton to finish writing the next one. Like other addicts, I'd been reading as slowly as possible to avoid catching up with Grafton—who is up to *M* in the alphabet but cannot write Kinsey Millhone mysteries as fast as her fans can read them—but you can hold off the inevitable only so long.

It's sheer coincidence that my attainment of this cultural milestone should have coincided with yet another flare-up in the war over what academics should study—and, in particular, whether "cultural studies" of popular non-masterpieces like genre detective series have anything to yield to serious inquiry.

"Popular" is certainly the word for the series of mysteries featuring Millhone, the hard-boiled, twice-divorced female private investigator who spends her days catching murderers and assorted other scoundrels and battling existential angst in a fictional California town called Santa Teresa. Kinsey has netted Grafton staggering sales, a string of imitators (you can't move six inches along a shelf of mysteries in a bookstore without coming across a tough female detective), and the kind of intense fandom that precludes a movie version because no actress lives up to the collective Kinsey fantasy in readers' heads. The attraction isn't difficult to fathom; the books are funny, smart, violent, with good plots and plenty of nutty Southern California landscape. Taking a step back, though, you can also see that Kinsey's adventures are addictively fascinating because so much of the ground she covers is, culturally speaking, brand new.

Someone had to explain to me—I'd reached *I is for Innocent* without getting it—that Kinsey is also a running parody of the Philip Marlowe–Sam Spade male P.I. genre whose protagonists shun intimacy and seek the dark side, a loner sleuth who slouches into a crummy neighborhood dive and then orders herself a glass of white wine. Beyond the obvious humor, such juxtapositions give rise to a fair amount of playful yet intelligent treatment of themes that, in more abstract and solemn forms, inspire serious social commentary and not a little of the new type of academic inquiry. These include the tensions between old and new images of working womanhood, old and new ways to identify uprightness and corruption, and old and new versions of courage and virtue.

Kinsey, for instance, has some trouble with the trappings of dress-up, 5 trappings that her chosen line of work allow her to ignore most but not all of the time. Her friends and colleagues, male and female, give her a lot of grief in the course of the books about her one "black all-purpose dress," which she wears on every occasion that demands something beyond jeans, and about her habit of cutting her own hair at night with nail scissors. It's shtick, sort of, but not really, because Kinsey also spends a lot of time meeting and—this is the point of detective fiction, isn't it?—meticulously casing other women, up and down the social scale, who handle the new and old politics of dress very differently. Murder-mystery plots move forward on an engine of exact observation, the more exact the better, and it's hard to think of a more alert way to be guided through the thicket of behaviors too new to have hardened into norms.

I didn't realize just how much Grafton was doing with these themes, or how deftly, until I came across a scene in *K is for Killer,* where Kinsey heads for San Francisco to interview an obscure porn actor who had appeared with a murdered girl in an X-rated video. Arriving at his house, Kinsey finds herself talking to his roommate Cherie, a luscious blonde who complains cheerfully about the trials of personal hygiene—"You don't wear a lot of makeup, so you probably can't relate to this, but I spend *hours* on myself, and to what end, I ask? Fifteen minutes on the street, and it all evaporates. . . . Oh, well, what's a poor girl to do?"—and then strips off a wig to reveal that she is, in fact, the male porn actor, an after-hours cross-dresser.

Drag queens are anything but original in popular culture these days, of course; what's clever is what Grafton does with hers, turning on a dime to toss out what amounts to a speculation—the first really plausible one I've come across anywhere—as to why pop culture down to even the Steven Spielberg level has fallen on drag queens with such delight. Kinsey finishes the interview, goes home, and changes out of the all-purpose dress, "stripping off my pantyhose with the same relief Cherie had expressed. Once in my jeans and turtleneck, I felt I was back in my own skin again." Of course, Drag queens are hot because most people, like Kinsey, are dabbling around the far edges of the same game, feeling anxious, perhaps, about the degree to which they can change who they are, or who they seem, by switching among the vast number of ways they can now dress.

This is the same territory being mined sometimes brilliantly and sometimes tiresomely by the new academic cultural studies mavens: social clues and ever-migrating social mores, gender roles made complicated but not erased by new opportunities. And if Grafton is any indication, looking at popular as opposed to literary formulations of that new experience is a very sensible thing to do. Unfortunately, scorn at the excesses of some of the no-possible-canon crowd has gotten mixed up with a more generalized scorn at studying these artifacts—the Western, the popular novel, the MTV image—at all. [In 1996] the *New Republic* sent a reporter to a Harvard cultural studies conference where the topics included adolescent girls' reading habits and female sexuality. Perhaps predictably, he covered it with scorn, a standard stance for self-described canon defenders.

[A few weeks later in 1996] the *New Republic* carried a sharp retort by professor Barbara E. Johnson that "Flaubert understood that novel-reading by adolescent girls was a topic worthy of investigation. . . . Kafka depicted the world from an insect's point of view," so why consider such topics silly? But there's another defense, though it won't apply to everything that goes by the name "cultural studies." It's this: In such fascinating, fermenting times, why sweep away the information to be obtained by looking closely at someone who knows this much? You don't have to call Sue Grafton Shakespeare, or go with the crowd that sees no possible difference, to learn a lot from people who can lead a seven-figure readership down an alphabet of addiction.

Reading the Text

1. How, according to Schwartz, do Sue Grafton's novels "parody" (para. 4) and modify the hard-boiled detective novel?
2. What value does Schwartz see in reading popular writers such as Sue Grafton?
3. How does Schwartz situate Sue Grafton's writing in the context of cultural studies?

Reading the Signs

1. Read a Sue Grafton novel, and write an analysis of its appeal to modern readers.
2. Schwartz concludes her selection by referring to the recent culture wars—intellectual debates often symbolized by the publication of E. D. Hirsch's *Cultural Literacy*. Research the debate over culture and the publication of Hirsch's book, and write an essay that argues for your view of

the value of popular literature. You might consult James B. Twitchell's "Plop, Plop, Fizz, Fizz" (p. 202).
3. Conduct an in-class debate on whether popular literature—Stephen King novels, romances, detective fiction, or the ilk—even belongs in the academic canon. To develop your ideas, use Internet search engines to explore the extent to which such literature appears on college-level syllabi—and the extent to which people oppose the study of such literature.
4. Conduct a survey of your peers, and ask them about what books they have read in the last few years (voluntarily, not as an assignment for school). Then write an essay arguing for or against the inclusion of the books your interviewees read in academic study.

PHILIP K. DICK

Selection from Blade Runner

Though William Gibson usually gets the credit for inaugurating the cyberpunk literary movement, the honor might well go to Philip K. Dick (1928–1982), whose science-fiction classic Do Androids Dream of Electric Sheep? *(1968) was the source for Ridley Scott's* Blade Runner, *the archetypal movie of the cyberpunk worldview. In this passage from* Blade Runner *(a 1990 reprinting of* Do Androids Dream of Electric Sheep?*), Dick introduces the postnuclear world of Rick Deckard, a hard-boiled bounty hunter whose job is to locate and terminate renegade androids ("andys"). But in a departure from the movie, we also see a world in which living animals, now rare thanks to nuclear war, have become precious, both as status symbols and signs of empathy and compassion, emotions androids are incapable of feeling. A writer whose life was almost as bizarre as his writings—among other oddities, he believed that he had psychokinetic powers—Dick was the prolific author of scores of stories and novels, including* The Man in the High Castle *(1963) and* Flow My Tears, The Policeman Said *(1975).*

A merry little surge of electricity piped by automatic alarm from the mood organ beside his bed awakened Rick Deckard. Surprised—it always surprised him to find himself awake without prior notice—he rose from the bed, stood up in his multicolored pajamas, and stretched. Now, in her bed, his wife Iran opened her gray, unmerry eyes, blinked, then groaned and shut her eyes again.

"You set your Penfield too weak," he said to her. "I'll reset it and you'll be awake and—"

"Keep your hand off my settings." Her voice held bitter sharpness. "I don't *want* to be awake."

He seated himself beside her, bent over her, and explained softly. "If you set the surge up high enough, you'll be glad you're awake; that's the whole point. At setting C it overcomes the threshold barring consciousness, as it does for me." Friendlily, because he felt well-disposed toward the world—*his* setting had been at D—he patted her bare, pale shoulder.

"Get your crude cop's hand away," Iran said.   5

"I'm not a cop." He felt irritable, now, although he hadn't dialed for it.

"You're worse," his wife said, her eyes still shut. "You're a murderer hired by the cops."

"I've never killed a human being in my life." His irritability had risen, now; had become outright hostility.

Iran said, "Just those poor andys."

"I notice you've never had any hesitation as to spending the bounty   10 money I bring home on whatever momentarily attracts your attention." He rose, strode to the console of his mood organ. "Instead of saving," he said, "so we could buy a real sheep, to replace that fake electric one upstairs. A mere electric animal, and me earning all that I've worked my way up to through the years." At his console he hesitated between dialing for a thalamic suppressant (which would abolish his mood of rage) or a thalamic stimulant (which would make him irked enough to win the argument).

"If you dial," Iran said, eyes open and watching, "for greater venom, then I'll dial the same. I'll dial the maximum and you'll see a fight that makes every argument we've had up to now seem like nothing. Dial and see; just try me." She rose swiftly, loped to the console of her own mood organ, stood glaring at him, waiting.

He sighed, defeated by her threat. "I'll dial what's on my schedule for today." Examining the schedule for January 3, 2021, he saw that a businesslike professional attitude was called for. "If I dial by schedule," he said warily, "will you agree to also?" He waited, canny enough not to commit himself until his wife had agreed to follow suit.

"My schedule for today lists a six-hour self-accusatory depression," Iran said.

"What? Why did you schedule that?" It defeated the whole purpose of the mood organ. "I didn't even know you could set it for that," he said gloomily.

"I was sitting here one afternoon," Iran said, "and naturally I had   15 turned on Buster Friendly and His Friendly Friends and he was talking about a big news item he's about to break and then that awful commer-

cial came on, the one I hate; you know, for Mountibank Lead Cod-
pieces. And so for a minute I shut off the sound. And I heard the building, this building; I heard the—" She gestured.

"Empty apartments," Rick said. Sometimes he heard them at night
when he was supposed to be asleep. And yet, for this day and age a one-
half occupied conapt building rated high in the scheme of population
density; out in what had been before the war the suburbs one could find
buildings entirely empty . . . or so he had heard. He had let the information remain secondhand; like most people he did not care to experience
it directly.

"At that moment," Iran said, "when I had the TV sound off, I was in
a 382 mood; I had just dialed it. So although I heard the emptiness intel-
lectually, I didn't feel it. My first reaction consisted of being grateful that
we could afford a Penfield mood organ. But then I realized how un-
healthy it was, sensing the absence of life, not just in this building but
everywhere, and not reacting—do you see? I guess you don't. But that
used to be considered a sign of mental illness; they called it 'absence of
appropriate affect.' So I left the TV sound off and I sat down at my mood
organ and I experimented. And I finally found a setting for despair." Her
dark, pert face showed satisfaction, as if she had achieved something of
worth. "So I put it on my schedule for twice a month; I think that's a
reasonable amount of time to feel hopeless about everything, about staying here on Earth after everybody who's smart has emigrated, don't you
think?"

"But a mood like that," Rick said, "you're apt to stay in it, not dial
your way out. Despair like that, about total reality, is self-perpetuating."

"I program an automatic resetting for three hours later," his wife said
sleekly. "A 481. Awareness of the manifold possibilities open to me in
the future; new hope that—"

"I know 481," he interrupted. He had dialed out the combination   20
many times; he relied on it greatly. "Listen," he said, seating himself on
his bed and taking hold of her hands to draw her down beside him,
"even with an automatic cutoff it's dangerous to undergo a depression,
any kind. Forget what you've scheduled and I'll forget what I've scheduled; we'll dial a 104 together and both experience it, and then you stay
in it while I reset mine for my usual businesslike attitude. That way I'll
want to hop up to the roof and check out the sheep and then head for
the office; meanwhile I'll know you're not sitting here brooding with no
TV." He released her slim, long fingers, passed through the spacious
apartment to the living room, which smelled faintly of last night's cigarettes. There he bent to turn on the TV.

From the bedroom Iran's voice came. "I can't stand TV before
breakfast."

"Dial 888," Rick said as the set warmed. "The desire to watch TV,
no matter what's on it."

"I don't feel like dialing anything at all now," Iran said.

"Then dial 3," he said.

"I can't dial a setting that stimulates my cerebral cortex into wanting   25
to dial! If I don't want to dial, I don't want to dial that most of all, because then I will want to dial, and wanting to dial is right now the most
alien drive I can imagine; I just want to sit here on the bed and stare at the
floor." Her voice had become sharp with overtones of bleakness as her
soul congealed and she ceased to move, as the instinctive, omnipresent
film of great weight, of an almost absolute inertia, settled over her.

He turned up the TV sound, and the voice of Buster Friendly
boomed out and filled the room. "—ho ho, folks. Time now for a brief
note on today's weather. The Mongoose satellite reports that fallout will
be especially pronounced toward noon and will then taper off, so all you
folks who'll be venturing out—"

Appearing beside him, her long nightgown trailing wispily, Iran shut
off the TV set. "Okay, I give up; I'll dial. Anything you want me to be;
ecstatic sexual bliss—I feel so bad I'll even endure that. What the hell.
What difference does it make?"

"I'll dial for both of us," Rick said, and led her back into the bedroom. There, at her console, he dialed 594: pleased acknowledgment of
husband's superior wisdom in all matters. On his own console he dialed
for a creative and fresh attitude toward his job, although this he hardly
needed; such was his habitual, innate approach without recourse to Penfield artificial brain stimulation.

After a hurried breakfast—he had lost time due to the discussion
with his wife—he ascended clad for venturing out, including his Ajax
model Mountibank Lead Codpiece, to the covered roof pasture whereon
his electric sheep "grazed." Whereon it, sophisticated piece of hardware
that it was, chomped away in simulated contentment, bamboozling the
other tenants of the building.

Of course, some of their animals undoubtedly consisted of electronic   30
circuitry fakes, too; he had of course never nosed into the matter, any
more than they, his neighbors, had pried into the real workings of his
sheep. Nothing could be more impolite. To say, "Is your sheep genuine?" would be a worse breach of manners than to inquire whether a
citizen's teeth, hair, or internal organs would test out authentic.

The morning air, spilling over with radioactive motes, gray and sun-
beclouding, belched about him, haunting his nose; he sniffed involun-
tarily the taint of death. Well, that was too strong a description for it, he
decided as he made his way to the particular plot of sod which he owned
along with the unduly large apartment below. The legacy of World War
Terminus had diminished in potency; those who could not survive the
dust had passed into oblivion years ago, and the dust, weaker now and
confronting the strong survivors, only deranged minds and genetic prop-

erties. Despite his lead codpiece the dust—undoubtedly—filtered in and at him, brought him daily, so long as he failed to emigrate, its little load of befouling filth. So far, medical checkups taken monthly confirmed him as a regular: a man who could reproduce within the tolerances set by law. Any month, however, the exam by the San Francisco Police Department doctors could reveal otherwise. Continually, new specials came into existence, created out of regulars by the omnipresent dust. The saying currently blabbed by posters, TV ads, and government junk mail, ran: "Emigrate or degenerate! The choice is yours!" Very true, Rick thought as he opened the gate to his little pasture and approached his electric sheep. But I can't emigrate, he said to himself. Because of my job.

The owner of the adjoining pasture, his conapt neighbor Bill Barbour, hailed him; he, like Rick, had dressed for work but had stopped off on the way to check his animal, too.

"My horse," Barbour declared beamingly, "is pregnant." He indicated the big Percheron, which stood staring off in an empty fashion into space. "What do you say to that?"

"I say pretty soon you'll have two horses," Rick said. He had reached his sheep, now; it lay ruminating, its alert eyes fixed on him in case he had brought any rolled oats with him. The alleged sheep contained an oat-tropic circuit; at the sight of such cereals it would scramble up convincingly and amble over. "What's she pregnant by?" he asked Barbour. "The wind?"

"I bought some of the highest quality fertilizing plasma available in   35
California," Barbour informed him. "Through inside contacts I have with the State Animal Husbandry Board. Don't you remember last week when their inspector was out here examining Judy? They're eager to have her foal; she's an unmatched superior." Barbour thumped his horse fondly on the neck and she inclined her head toward him.

"Ever thought of selling your horse?" Rick asked. He wished to god he had a horse, in fact any animal. Owning and maintaining a fraud had a way of gradually demoralizing one. And yet from a social standpoint it had to be done, given the absence of the real article. He had therefore no choice except to continue. Even were he not to care himself, there remained his wife, and Iran did care. Very much.

Barbour said, "It would be immoral to sell my horse."

"Sell the colt, then. Having two animals is more immoral than not having any."

Puzzled, Barbour said, "How do you mean? A lot of people have two animals, even three, four, and like in the case of Fred Washborne, who owns the algae-processing plant my brother works at, even five. Didn't you see that article about his duck in yesterday's *Chronicle*? It's supposed to be the heaviest, largest Moscovy on the West Coast." The man's eyes glazed over, imagining such possessions; he drifted by degrees into a trance.

Exploring about in his coat pockets, Rick found his creased, much-   40
studied copy of Sidney's Animal & Fowl Catalogue January supplement.
He looked in the index, found colts (vide horses, offsp.) and presently
had the prevailing national price. "I can buy a Percheron colt from
Sidney's for five thousand dollars," he said aloud.

"No you can't," Barbour said. "Look at the listing again; it's in italics. That means they don't have any in stock; but that would be the price
if they did have."

"Suppose," Rick said, "I pay you five hundred dollars a month for
ten months. Full catalogue value."

Pityingly, Barbour said, "Deckard, you don't understand about
horses; there's a reason why Sidney's doesn't have any Percheron colts in
stock. Percheron colts just don't change hands—at catalogue value,
even. They're too scarce, even relatively inferior ones." He leaned across
their common fence, gesticulating. "I've had Judy for three years and not
in all that time have I seen a Percheron mare of her quality. To acquire
her I had to fly to Canada, and I personally drove her back here myself to
make sure she wasn't stolen. You bring an animal like this anywhere
around Colorado or Wyoming and they'll knock you off to get hold of
it. You know why? Because back before W.W.T. there existed literally
hundreds—"

"But," Rick interrupted, "for you to have two horses and me
none, that violates the whole basic theological and moral structure of
Mercerism."

"You have your sheep; hell, you can follow the Ascent in your indi-   45
vidual life, and when you grasp the two handles of empathy you approach honorably. Now if you didn't have that old sheep, there, I'd see
some logic in your position. Sure, if I had two animals and you didn't
have any, I'd be helping deprive you of true fusion with Mercer. But
every family in this building—let's see; around fifty: one to every three
apts, as I compute it—every one of us has an animal of some sort.
Graveson has that chicken over there." He gestured north. "Oakes and
his wife have that big red dog that barks in the night." He pondered. "I
think Ed Smith has a cat down in his apt; at least he says so, but no one's
ever seen it. Possibly he's just pretending."

Going over to his sheep, Rick bent down, searching in the thick
white wool—the fleece at least was genuine—until he found what he
was looking for: the concealed control panel of the mechanism. As
Barbour watched he snapped open the panel covering, revealing it.
"See?" he said to Barbour. "You understand now why I want your colt
so badly?"

After an interval Barbour said, "You poor guy. Has it always been
this way?"

"No," Rick said, once again closing the panel covering of his electric sheep; he straightened up, turned, and faced his neighbor. "I had a

real sheep, originally. My wife's father gave it to us outright when he emigrated. Then, about a year ago, remember that time I took it to the vet—you were up here that morning when I came out and found it lying on its side and it couldn't get up."

"You got it to its feet," Barbour said, remembering and nodding. "Yeah, you managed to lift it up but then after a minute or two of walking around it fell over again."

Rick said, "Sheep get strange diseases. Or put another way, sheep 50 get a lot of diseases but the symptoms are always the same; the sheep can't get up and there's no way to tell how serious it is, whether it's a sprained leg or the animal's dying of tetanus. That's what mine died of: tetanus."

"Up here?" Barbour said. "On the roof?"

"The hay," Rick explained. "That one time I didn't get all the wire off the bale; I left a piece and Groucho—that's what I called him, then—got a scratch and in that way contracted tetanus. I took him to the vet's and he died, and I thought about it, and finally I called one of those shops that manufacture artificial animals and I showed them a photograph of Groucho. They made this." He indicated the reclining ersatz animal, which continued to ruminate attentively, still watching alertly for any indication of oats. "It's a premium job. And I've put as much time and attention into caring for it as I did when it was real. But—" He shrugged.

"It's not the same," Barbour finished.

"But almost. You feel the same doing it; you have to keep your eyes on it exactly as you did when it was really alive. Because they break down and then everyone in the building knows. I've had it at the repair shop six times, mostly little malfunctions, but if anyone saw them—for instance one time the voice tape broke or anyhow got fouled and it wouldn't stop baaing—they'd recognize it as a *mechanical* breakdown." He added, "The repair outfit's truck is of course marked 'animal hospital something.' And the driver dresses like a vet, completely in white." He glanced suddenly at his watch, remembering the time. "I have to get to work," he said to Barbour. "I'll see you this evening."

As he started toward his car Barbour called after him hurriedly, 55 "Um, I won't say anything to anybody here in the building."

Pausing, Rick started to say thanks. But then something of the despair that Iran had been talking about tapped him on the shoulder and he said, "I don't know; maybe it doesn't make any difference."

"But they'll look down on you. Not all of them, but some. You know how people are about not taking care of an animal; they consider it immoral and anti-empathic. I mean, technically it's not a crime like it was right after W.W.T. but the feeling's still there."

"God," Rick said futilely, and gestured empty-handed. "I *want* to have an animal; I keep trying to buy one. But on my salary, on what a city employee makes—" If, he thought, I could get lucky in my work

again. As I did two years ago when I managed to bag four andys during
one month. If I had known then, he thought, that Groucho was going to
die . . . but that had been before the tetanus. Before the two-inch piece
of broken, hypodermic-like baling wire.

"You could buy a cat," Barbour offered. "Cats are cheap; look in
your Sidney's catalogue."

Rick said quietly, "I don't want a domestic pet. I want what I origi-   60
nally had, a large animal. A sheep or if I can get the money a cow or a
steer or what you have; a horse." The bounty from retiring five andys
would do it, he realized. A thousand dollars apiece, over and above my
salary. Then somewhere I could find, from someone, what I want. Even if
the listing in Sidney's Animal & Fowl is in italics. Five thousand dollars—
but, he thought, the five andys first have to make their way to Earth from
one of the colony planets; I can't control that, I can't make five of them
come here, and even if I could there are other bounty hunters with other
police agencies throughout the world. The andys would specifically have
to take up residence in Northern California, and the senior bounty hunter
in this area, Dave Holden, would have to die or retire.

"Buy a cricket," Barbour suggested wittily. "Or a mouse. Hey, for
twenty-five bucks you can buy a full-grown mouse."

Rick said, "Your horse could die, like Groucho died, without warning. When you get home from work this evening you could find her laid
out on her back, her feet in the air, like a bug. Like what you said, a
cricket." He strode off, car key in his hand.

"Sorry if I offended you," Barbour said nervously.

In silence Rick Deckard plucked open the door of his hovercar. He
had nothing further to say to his neighbor; his mind was on his work, on
the day ahead.

Reading the Text

1. What is the effect of the repetition of the word *dial,* and the inclusion of
   many random numbers, in the first part of the selection?
2. Describe the interaction between Richard Deckard and his wife Iran.
   What does it say about their relationship?
3. Why is animal ownership so important after World War Terminus?
4. Why does Deckard say that "Having two animals is more immoral than
   not having any" (para. 38)?

Reading the Signs

1. Read the rest of the novel, and watch the Ridley Scott film version of *Blade
   Runner.* Write an essay that compares and contrasts the two versions. How
   do you account for any differences you see in their vision of the future?

2. *Blade Runner* is considered a precursor to William Gibian's *Neuromancer,* a work often cited as the original cyberpunk novel. Read *Neuromancer,* and write a semiotic essay analyzing its vision of the future.
3. Much of science fiction is dystopian — that is, it imagines a dysfunctional society that is worse than the present. Write an essay in which you explain why you believe so much science fiction offers a dystopian vision.
4. In class, discuss the significance of animals in this passage. How do the images of animals contrast with the surrounding human environment? What messages is Dick conveying about the human and the natural worlds?
5. The works of Philip K. Dick have developed a cult following. Visit the official website devoted to Dick at **http://www.philipkdick.com**, and read through the many links that provide reviews of his writings, biographical information, and discussions of his philosophy. Then write a semiotic analysis of the Dick website in which you provide your own explanation for Dick's enduring appeal.

K. C. MYERS
Roadside Bones

||||||||||||||||||||||||||||||||||||||||||||||||||||||

Once you had to go to a bookstore, newsstand, or library to get your hands on a story to read, but no more, for with the Internet bulging with online magazines, popular literature is only a click away. K. C. Myers's "Roadside Bones" first appeared in one such magazine, Eternity: The Online Journal of the Speculative Imagination *(http://www.pulpeternity.com), a self-described electronic "pulp" publication. In this story, Myers combines the genres of science fiction and mystery to provide a new slant on the alien invasion tale. This time, E.T. doesn't phone home.*

The sky had just begun to turn pink with Monday morning, but Matt Campbell knew his wife would be up. And probably worrying, as well, since her worthless husband hadn't bothered to call her last night.

He heard the tension in her voice when she answered the phone, changing quickly to annoyance when she heard his voice.

"You were supposed to call me from Pennsylvania last night."

"Sorry, Carly. I never made it to Pennsy."

The tension returned. He pictured her shoving a hand through her   5
thick, red hair. "What happened?"

Matt poked his tongue into his cheek. "I spent the night with another woman."

There was a pause long enough for Matt to worry a little. Then Carly said, "Dead or alive?"

"Both, actually. One was dead, the other was the coroner."

"Where are you, exactly, and what happened?"

"I'm in New Jersey. As far as what happened, you've heard the story   10 a hundred times. Man thinks he can drive from Newark to Allentown without a bathroom break, finds out he can't, heads down an embankment to pee, and finds an abandoned skeleton. It just doesn't usually happen to a Smithsonian forensic pathologist."

She didn't laugh, but Matt could hear her smile in the movement of her voice. "Be sure they send her to us if they can't make an ID."

"You bet."

Matt felt a thrill of excitement when the bones finally arrived on his desk. A new mystery to be solved—and this one was truly his, since he'd found the bones in the first place.

He read the reports forwarded from New Jersey. They'd done everything they could. A narrow-faced, big-eyed girl regarded him from the composite drawing. Sad that no one had missed her.

There were other bits and pieces, but not much. No determined   15 cause of death. No personal effects. A note from the New Jersey coroner said simply, "Weird measurements."

The available evidence didn't make much of a profile. Matt's excitement grew a bit. The puzzle all but dared him to solve it.

He carted the box of bones down the hall to Carly's office. Carly was something of an expert at computerized 3-D reconstructions. The composite from New Jersey probably told most of the story, but Carly could sometimes take things to levels that could only be described as psychic.

Three days later, she had results.

Matt sat down next to Carly, behind her desk, a little closer than he would have if he hadn't had his way with her repeatedly just eight hours before. She casually squeezed his knee, moving the mouse with the other hand.

The portrait she'd generated resembled the other composite, but   20 there were subtle differences: the slant of the eyes, the shape of the nose. Carly rotated the image, turning the head from three-quarters to profile and back to full face, her eyes on Matt, auburn eyebrows raised.

"Can you put hair on her?" Matt said finally.

Carly clicked through a series of hairstyles, finally stopping on straight, pale blond hair that framed Jane Doe's face.

"I like this one," she said.

Matt nodded. There was something right about the waif-like style. "She looks a little different from the New Jersey composite."

Carly enlarged the picture a little.   25

"I took almost twice as many measurements."

"So it's more accurate?"

"It should be," Carly said. "But for some reason. . . ."

Matt's dark eyebrows rose. "Some reason what?"

"I don't know. These bones are, well, strange."   30

Matt remembered the coroner's note. "Strange?"

Carly shook her head. "I don't know."

She shifted the mouse again and a skeletal arm appeared.

"She has very long fingers, long, narrow arm bones. All the bone measurements are odd. Some are too big, some too small. And look at this."

She called the face back to the screen and stripped flesh from the top   35
half.

"I saw this first on the right eye and I thought maybe it was an old injury. But it's on both sockets."

She pointed to odd lumps on the interior curves, next to the nose. "And the sinuses are bizarre."

She leaned back in her chair and looked at Matt, letting go of his knee to cross her arms over her chest.

"The whole skeleton is strange, Matt. But it's not anything you'd notice unless you looked for it."

Matt looked at the face again. The eyes were unnaturally large and   40
tilted, the jaw narrow, the nose tiny. She looked back at him, an odd little lost waif.

He memorized the picture, and wondered.

Matt ran some nonstandard tests on the bones. He brought the results to Carly as she sat eating lunch over a new skull. She took them and glanced at them, then read the sheet carefully from top to bottom. Realization rose to her eyes in stages. Finally she looked up, her face a little pale.

"Matt," she said. "These bones aren't human."

They checked and rechecked the results, but the conclusion was the same. Jane Doe, so obviously, unmistakably human, somehow was not.

At dinner a night later, Carly broke the unspoken rule of not bring-   45
ing work home.

"What do you think it means, Matt?"

She held a fork halfway to her mouth, and her hand shook. Matt just felt tired.

"I think it means," he said, "that whoever is looking for this girl is farther away than we thought."

He said it steadily, as if unaffected by his own words. But it was as close as he could force himself to come to speaking the unspeakable. Carly frowned a little more deeply, and her eyes emptied for a moment.

"I think you may be right," she finally said, and got up to fetch   50
dessert.

They never formally agreed not to tell anyone else, but on the same night, both of them brought home case files. Matt hid the folders in the basement.

At night, he thumbed through the pages and wondered. What had brought Jane Doe here? Who had killed her, and why? Who had loved her? And where, in the star-sprinkled night sky, was her home?

The questions rolled through his head every day, every hour. He sketched the almost-human features on napkins at lunch. He sat on the porch for hours looking at the stars. Sometimes when he made love to Carly, he saw Jane Doe's face.

And Carly knew. For a long time, she said nothing, but sometimes Matt saw her mouth tighten when his thoughts drifted. Sometimes she slammed doors while he stargazed.

Finally, one day, she came to him as he sat at his desk studying star charts. Her hands overflowed with napkins and scraps of paper, covered with sketches of Jane Doe.

"You have to do something, Matt," she said. Her voice quivered.

Matt turned in his chair and looked at her. The pain in her eyes made him ache. "I have to find them," he said.

Carly clutched the papers, and they crinkled against her breast. "Then do it soon."

Matt could have abandoned it then—probably should have—but he had to try one more thing.

His cobbled-together contraption wasn't pretty, but he thought it just might be able to transmit a binary graphics file into outer space. Saturday morning he climbed onto the roof and tied the thing to the chimney with baling wire.

Carly watched as he came down, hair gleaming like burnished copper in the sunlight. She looked not quite angry, not quite despairing, and almost empty.

"It's a transmitter," Matt said.

Her face shifted. Matt hastened down the last two rungs of the ladder to take her arms in his hands. Her lower lip trembled as she looked at him.

"This is the last of it," he said. "If this brings an answer, then it'll be over. If not, then so be it."

"Eight weeks," she said. "It comes down in eight weeks."

Monday morning, Matt took Jane Doe's bones to his office. For a while he sat looking at them. They were gray and lonely.

That night, Matt committed what was surely a federal crime. He dumped the bones into a cardboard box, taped it up with duct tape, and took it home.

There was time to forget, but Matt didn't. He didn't let Carly know that he still looked at Jane Doe's folder every night, or that her bones were in the basement behind the Christmas tree ornaments.

If Matt was pensive from time to time, he blamed it on the dismembered torso that had been given into his care, or the small skeleton which had just been identified, whose parents he'd felt obligated to notify. But as much as these cases touched him, Jane Doe never left his mind.

Eight weeks later, as promised, he took down the transmitter. 70

Time passed. One night they drank too much wine and talked about having children. Finally, Carly went maudlin and drifted off.

Matt plucked the dangling wine glass from her limp hand and set it gently on the table. He kissed her forehead and stepped outside to stare at the stars.

The back yard was filled with moonlight, but there was a new moon tonight. A drifting cloud swallowed it. When the cloud passed, Matt was no longer alone.

The man was tall and thin, dressed in a gray uniform with red pips. His eyes were large and tilted, his hair long, straight, and silver. He had a narrow, jutting chin and a tiny nose. The ageless face could have been twenty or two hundred.

He looked at Matt, blinked, and held out his hand. 75

Matt stood slowly. "Wait here."

Matt went to the basement, moved the Christmas ornaments and hauled out the box. Then he hesitated. Maybe the man thought she was still alive.

But the bones were all Matt had to give. He picked up the box and carried it upstairs.

The man hesitated before he took it. Then he carried the box to the picnic table, laid it down, and opened it. The narrow skull looked up at him. Gently, he touched the cheekbone. Tears flowed in his large eyes. It had never occurred to Matt that aliens might cry.

"I don't know how she died," Matt said. 80

The man looked up. His mouth twitched a little, the thin lips struggling with something unfamiliar. There was so much pain.

"I'm sorry, . . ." Matt ventured.

The man closed the box and cradled it. In a strained, breathy voice, he said, "Daughter."

Matt felt thick through the chest, and a tear moved down his cheek.

"May she rest in peace," he said quietly. 85

The alien smiled, turned, and slowly walked away.

Reading the Text

1. What are Matt and Carly Campbell's professions?
2. Why is Carly so upset about Matt's obsession with the skeleton he found?
3. What does the dialogue suggest about Matt and Carly's relationship?

Reading the Signs

1. When this story first appeared in an online magazine called *Eternity: The Online Journal of the Speculative Imagination,* it was categorized as "science fiction/mystery." In an essay, discuss how "Roadside Bones" combines these two genres.
2. Write an essay analyzing the significance of aliens in this story. To develop your ideas, consult the Introduction to this book.
3. In class, discuss the way Myers maintains the suspense in this story. What narrative techniques keep the reader interested in the mystery?
4. How does the appearance of the aliens in "Roadside Bones" compare to conventional images of aliens? Why do you think Myers depicted his aliens in this way?

WARNER LEE

Cult

IIIIIIIIIIIIIIIIIIIIIIIIIIIIIIIIIIIIIIIIIIIIIIIIIIIIIIIII

Though they drove a stake through his heart at the end of the novel that introduced him to the world (Bram Stoker's Dracula*), Dracula just won't die. And in this contemporary retelling of the Dracula legend, Warner Lee (the pen name of B. W. Battin; b. 1941) presents the king of the vampires in a new light: as a distressed husband with marital difficulties. Combining the hard-boiled detective story with the Gothic/horror tradition, Lee thus introduces a comic new slant on an old tale, which, like its hero, refuses to rest in peace. Lee is the author of numerous horror stories and novels, including* Night Sounds *(1992),* It's Loose *(1990), and* Into the Pit *(1988).*

My name is Edward Long, and I am in a business that does not advertise. Clients hear of me through a friend or on the grapevine. Some have spent weeks trying to find me, not really sure that I truly existed.

I have no office, for being at a known location would put me in jeopardy. I have many enemies, you see, people who would delight in seeing me dead. What I do is illegal and dangerous, so I am very expensive. Thus I only have to work occasionally to earn a comfortable living.

I retrieve people.

Who do not wish to be retrieved.

Usually this means snatching someone from a cult and delivering   5
him or her to the deprogrammers. On one occasion, though, it was much more than that. *Much* more. As you can imagine, a person in my

line of work would have some wild stories to tell. But the one I am going to relate to you now is the most bizarre and frightening one in my collection. I have never told it before, because no one would believe it. I am revealing it now because . . . well, because it's a simmering, volatile thing, and maybe letting it out will enable me to put it to rest.

It began in October two years ago. I had received word from Tom, the bartender at the Buena Vista Lounge, that a man was looking for me. As with my other contacts, Tom had no idea where to find me. I called him periodically from a phone booth, and if anyone had been looking for me, he passed on the information. For this service I slipped him a hundred dollar bill every Christmas, and Tom seemed happy with the arrangement.

The potential client was a middle-aged man. I'd told Tom to let him know that I'd be in the Oasis at eight Tuesday evening. He should wear a fedora, so I could recognize him. Yes, I know it sounds corny, but as I've said, there are a lot of people out there who would like to kill me, and most of them have fanatical organizations behind them.

The Oasis is a place where young people with money can get together and try to experience what it must have been like for people in Humphrey Bogart's era. On the weekends a live dance band plays from an eclectic repertoire that includes Tommy Dorsey's greatest hits and re-arranged Beatles' tunes. This being midweek, there was no band. I sat at a corner table, drinking a beer and keeping an eye on the other patrons.

I first saw him as a reflection in the mirror that ran the length of the bar. A tall, dark-haired man in a gray double-breasted suit. I almost missed the fedora because he was carrying it rather than wearing it. Either he didn't like anything on his head, or he believed in the custom of a gentleman's removing his hat whenever he stepped indoors.

Approaching a vacant table near the bar, he carried himself with an   10
air of superiority, his movements smooth, graceful, elegant. He ordered a Scotch and soda, then unobtrusively surveyed the premises, his eyes passing over me as if he didn't even see me, although I knew he had assessed everyone in the place. When his drink arrived, he left it untouched on the table while he waited.

I called over the waitress. She was new, a buxom young woman with curly blonde hair whose name tag identified her as Kimberly. "Would you ask the gentleman at that table to join me, please," I said. "The one with the hat on the chair beside him."

Kimberly did my bidding, and a moment later the man with the gray fedora was sitting at my table. "Allow me to introduce myself," he said. "I am Miguel La Durca."

His speech contained the hint of an accent, barely discernible, but there. European, I thought. He was extremely fair complected, which seemed to rule out the Indian blood carried by most Latin Americans.

"Are you from Spain?" I asked.

"Yes, Barcelona. I represent a firm that makes computer chips. We   15
are trying to wean your manufacturers away from the Japanese chips in
favor of ours."

"Are you having any luck?"

"Some." He studied me with eyes so deep and dark that looking into
them was like peering into bottomless blackness. "I have need of your
specialty," he said.

"You have someone you want rescued."

"Yes, rescued. A good choice of terms."

"I can be expensive—especially when it involves things that are   20
illegal."

"This, I think, will be illegal."

"A son or daughter?"

"No. My wife."

"And where is your wife at this moment?"

"In the hands of a group called the Church of Seven. Have you   25
heard of it?"

"No. What is it?"

"I think the name refers to Lucifer, which contains seven letters."

"Devil worshipers?"

"Yes. Or something similar. They live in a compound near Foley
Lake. They sleep all day, and at night they hold their disgusting rituals.
I've heard they sacrifice animals, dance naked."

"How did your wife get involved with people like this?"   30

"My wife is English, not Spanish. Since she isn't Catholic, she doesn't
have the teachings of the church to fall back on. She . . ." He frowned,
letting his words trail off. "I am not being totally honest with you. My
wife requires psychiatric help. She ran into some of these people a couple
of months after she checked herself out of a private mental hospital—
over the doctor's objections, I'm afraid. It was a time when she was quite
vulnerable. They prey on people like her, these cultists, people who are
confused, weak, receptive—and who have money to give them."

"How much have they taken from her?"

"Before I could get her access to the accounts cut off, it had passed a
hundred thousand dollars."

"I won't cost you nearly that much," I said.

"How much will you cost me?"   35

"It depends on the situation. Tell me about this compound of theirs."

"It covers several acres in a valley. The buildings themselves are surrounded by a high stone wall. I've noticed surveillance cameras on the
wall, and there are also guards."

"Armed?"

"They don't display any weapons, but I wouldn't be surprised if they
have them."

"Getting someone out of a place like that could be very expensive."   40

"I can afford whatever you charge, Mr. . . ."

"Long."

"Long, yes. No one seemed to know what you were called. In any case, I have money, Mr. Long. You get Sarah back, and I will pay whatever you ask."

"You understand that I may have to force her to come with me."

"She would not accompany you willingly. I only ask that you do not harm her when you kidnap her." 45

Reaching inside his jacket, he produced a photo, which he handed to me. It was a picture of a truly beautiful woman. She had shiny dark hair which hung below her shoulders. Her face might have been just a little too long, but her features were flawless. She had an aristocratic mouth, a knowing smile, eyes that seemed simultaneously sly and innocent, high cheekbones, a nose that curved gracefully to its slightly upraised tip. Everything in balance, nothing too large or too small, too thick or too thin. Although it was the face of a northern European, there was something vaguely exotic in her appearance, something that hinted of warm nights along the Nile or Gypsy caravans. I could certainly see why he wanted her back. She was one of the most stunning women I had ever seen.

"There is one other thing," La Durca said. "You must take her in the daylight."

"Why?"

"They sleep then. At night they are all awake."

"Even so, the darkness could be helpful." 50

He shook his head. "They would kill her before they'd let her go. I can't take that chance. It has to be done while they're sleeping."

I sighed. I didn't like it when clients started making rules. "Have you been inside the place?"

"No, they wouldn't let me in. I hired a private detective, who told me the place is run by a man called Vladimir. He's the high priest. That's his title. I'll give you the detective's report. It may save time."

He produced an envelope, which he slid across the table to me. Kimberly asked if we wanted to order more drinks. La Durca, who hadn't touched his Scotch, said no. I had another beer.

"I'll need a thousand-dollar nonrefundable retainer," I said. "And all 55 that commits me to do is look over the job. If I can do it, there will be a more substantial fee."

Reaching into his inner pocket, the Spaniard said, "I understood those were your terms."

The Church of Seven was an hour-and-a-half drive from the city. I shaved fifteen minutes off that by leaving early enough to beat the morning rush.

It was a pretty day, the sun shining warmly in a cloudless sky, creating the illusion that this year winter might not come. The countryside was New England–like, with small farms nestled among trees whose leaves were turning red and amber and gold. From time to time I passed hand-painted signs that said things like "HOMEMADE CIDER" and "FRESH EGGS."

At first glance, the Church of Seven was just another farm. But on closer inspection, it became clear that nothing had been grown there for years. The fields were covered with weeds and grass; in places bushes and saplings had taken root. A barn and some smaller structures whose use had presumably been agricultural had fallen into disrepair. But then La Durca had said the residents slept all day, so they would not be involved in farming.

The part of the place that was in use was surrounded by a tall stone   60
wall. I spotted the surveillance cameras. The gate was unmarked except for a single sign. In red letters on a white background, it said:

PRIVATE PROPERTY
ADMISSION BY APPOINTMENT ONLY

The gate was made of thick steel bars. It was closed. A wooden guardhouse stood beside it, with a khaki-uniformed security man inside. Through the gate I could see an asphalt drive leading to a two-story farmhouse with a red roof. Though larger than most, it was as unpretentious as any other farmhouse, and the massive gate, the guards, and the security cameras seemed incongruous.

I pulled up to the gate as if I had business there. I was driving my ten-year-old Ford Escort. I have newer, fancier cars, but when I'm looking over a job I prefer something modest and inconspicuous. The guard emerged from his wooden dwelling. Behind him I could see a bank of TV monitors. As he approached my side of the car, I rolled down the window.

"You have an appointment?" the guard asked, his tone making it clear that he knew I didn't. He wasn't wearing a hat, and his blond hair was cut in a flattop. He had a large, boxy face, a square jaw. He looked like a one-time athlete who, no longer the star of his high school, had lapsed into inactivity, losing the muscles but not the weight. On his shoulder was a patch that said "Grigson Security."

"No, I just wanted to ask if the outfit you work for might be hiring."

"Grigson?"   65

"Yeah. I used to work for a security company in Albuquerque, and I thought maybe my experience would help."

The guard shrugged. "Don't know. I don't have anything to do with that. You'd have to talk to Mr. Grigson."

"Where do I find him?"

"In town. At the company's office."

I noticed that two other guards had shown up. They stood inside the   70
gate, watching with bored expressions on their faces. I couldn't see any

weapons, but they wore Ike style uniform jackets, unbuttoned, which could conceal shoulder holsters.

"Do new guys have to start on the graveyard shift, or would my experience count?"

"If you're interested in working here, you won't have to worry about that. The church does its own guarding at night. We're just here during the day."

"I never heard of that before. Usually it's the other way around."

"They're all members of some oddball religion in there," the guard said, inclining his head toward the gate. "As I understand it, they stay up all night and sleep all day. Apparently it's part of their religion that they can't be out while the sun's shining."

"Well, I'll be damned," I said.   75

"It's easy work though. No one ever comes in or goes out. Food's delivered once a week—while they're all asleep. Taylor's Grocery brings it out and puts everything away for them. Other than that nothing ever happens. Some days I spend the whole shift reading a fishing magazine or listening to the radio, and the only people I see are the ones who drive by on the highway."

"I'll talk to Mr. Grigson."

"Office is on 53rd, just north of Stottard. You can't miss it."

"Thanks," I said, and backed away from the gate.

The nearest town was a place called Ridgecrest. It had three traffic   80
lights, two churches, and one grocery store—Taylor's. I bought a few things and struck up a conversation with the checker on my way out.

She said, "They call that place a church, but I don't believe it for a minute. It's one of those groups of weirdos—like the Moonies."

"Some people would say that's a church," I said.

"Well, I certainly wouldn't. A church is an institution that recognizes Jesus as our Lord and Savior."

"Of course," I said. "Do they come into town very often?"

"That's one good thing. We never see them."   85

"Not even to buy groceries?"

"We deliver to them. Every Wednesday morning."

Next I located a road leading to a hill overlooking the compound and spent the rest of the day watching the place. There were four guards. One in the gatehouse, and three who roved the grounds. No one arrived. No one left.

Shortly after nightfall, the lights came on in the former farmhouse, and the guards left. A light stayed on in the gatehouse, and through the window I could see shadows move, indicating that the post was still manned—presumably by a resident of the compound. For some reason, I had not seen the replacement guard arrive, even though I was watching through special nightvision binoculars.

I stayed there for about three hours after the sun went down, never   90 so much as glimpsing a member of the Church of Seven. Just before I left, I thought I saw something slip over the wall and move into the surrounding woods, but I couldn't be sure.

On the way back to town, I considered the private detective's report La Durca had given me. Practically nothing was known about the Church of Seven. It had bought the property from a farmer's estate three years ago and moved in. The PI had spent a day researching the church, finding nothing. He said it appeared to be a publicity shy local organization with only a handful of members, although he could not be sure of the exact number.

The high priest, Vladimir, had authored no books, consented to no interviews, and no photos of him seemed to exist. Unknowns included where he came from, what he'd done before becoming the leader of the church, and whether Vladimir was his real name.

As far as the PI could tell, no one had ever complained to the authorities about the Church of Seven. No one had sued it. No one from its ranks had been arrested.

Strange, I thought.

The word hung there, an invisible passenger that accompanied me all 95 the way back to the city.

The next day I drove to the apartment of Paul Flanders. Paul is a sort of junior partner of mine. We met while working as mercenaries in a Third World country whose name really doesn't matter. We're alike, Paul and I, Vietnam vets who'd been programmed for action by the U.S. Government and never deprogrammed. Unable or unwilling to adapt to the workaday world, we'd become soldiers of fortune, and when we'd grown too old for that life, Paul had tried being a policeman and failed, while I had fared only slightly better in a variety of occupations ranging from bounty hunter to bodyguard.

But now we had found our niche. And we were quite good at it. Probably the best in the world.

I said, "The problem will be what happens once we get inside. We don't know where Sarah might be, which means we'll have to go from room to room until we find her. If we accidentally wake someone up, and he sounds the alarm, we could be in trouble. I don't know how many of them we might be up against."

"You get the plans?" Paul asked.

I handed him the copies I'd obtained at the county courthouse. 100 "They were filed twenty-two years ago," I said. "Who knows what changes might have been made since then?"

"Two stories with a basement," Paul noted, studying the documents. He looked like the aging warrior he was, a big, ruddy-skinned man who appeared at home in a uniform, regardless of whether its origins were Latin American or African or Middle Eastern. His broad shoulders seemed naked without the strap of an Uzi or an AK47.

Running his fingers through the remaining strands of light brown hair, Paul said, "How do we get in?"

I told him the plan, and when I was finished Paul said, "Piece of cake as long as you don't mind committing about half a dozen felonies. How much you going to charge him?"

"A lot," I said.

I met La Durca that evening at the Oasis. He ordered the same 105 drinks, Scotch for him, beer for me.

"I can do it," I said.

"When?"

"Day after tomorrow."

"How much will it cost me?"

"Twenty-five. Half in advance, the rest when I deliver." 110

"And if something goes wrong? Say Sarah has been moved somewhere else."

"You get your money back, except for the thousand dollar retainer."

"You'd like cash, I presume."

I nodded.

"All right, Mr. Long, we have a deal." 115

We shook hands. His flesh was cool, and his grip was unusually firm.

"I'll have the money for you tomorrow night," he said.

After he left, I remained at the table, finished my beer, and ordered another.

"Huh," Kimberly said when she brought me the fresh beer.

"Huh what?" I asked. 120

"Your friend."

"What about him?"

"He always orders Scotch, then never drinks any of it." She picked up La Durca's still full glass.

"Maybe he's a teetotaler," I said, "but he doesn't want to make an issue of it."

"Yeah," Kimberly said, "maybe." 125

I didn't consider the matter further. If the man wanted to buy Scotch he didn't drink it was okay with me.

I met him again the next evening, and the Spaniard presented me with an envelope containing $12,500.

"There's a picnic area on state highway 384, just north of Paddington. I'll meet you there."

"Have you arranged for deprogrammers?" I asked.

"They'll be with me." 130

He again bought Scotch he didn't drink.

The next morning Paul and I were waiting at a bend in the two lane highway leading from Ridgecrest to the Church of Seven. We were using a BMW with fake plates. It was pulled to the side of the road with its hood up. I chose the Beamer because anyone driving anything that expensive would be unlikely to be viewed as a potential lowlife robber-murder-rapist. We also wore suits and ties; we were the image of respectability. When I stepped into the path of the van from Taylor's Grocery, frantically waving my arms, the driver pulled over immediately.

"Car break down?" he asked. He was about eighteen, a skinny kid with pimples. When I stuck the Ingram in his face, he blanched, his eyes widening in fear.

"Scoot over," I said. "I'll drive."

The kid obeyed. To the right was a narrow dirt road leading into the woods. I followed it until we were out of sight from the highway. Paul and I changed into our working clothes—British issue camouflage uniforms. Our gear included tear gas, gas masks, smoke, grenades, and automatic weapons. The guns were primarily for show, to obtain compliance. But they were loaded. We would use them if our lives depended on them.

But then such circumstances seemed quite unlikely. The guards from Grigson Security were not in our league.

We hid in the back of the van while the terrified teenager drove to the Church of Seven. The guard I'd spoken to yesterday was on the gate again.

"Morning, Billy," he said to the teenager. "Andy will ride up with you."

Another guard climbed in with the driver, never even glancing into the cargo area. He was about thirty, a thin man whose dark hair had been trimmed in an uneven home-done barbering job. As the truck started forward, Paul pressed the barrel of his MAC11 against the guard's neck.

"Surprise," Paul whispered.

"Shit," the guard said.

The teenager drove to the rear of the house and stopped. They were out of sight from the gate.

"Do what you'd normally do," I said. "And remember, these Ingrams can fire twelve hundred rounds a minute. You can't run from that—not and get very far. Do you understand?"

The guard and driver said they understood completely.

Two guards were patrolling along the stone wall. I waited until they were out of sight before letting our hostages out of the truck. The guard unlocked the door, and the teenager began carrying cardboard boxes full of groceries into the kitchen.

It was a normal family kitchen, the range and refrigerator from Sears, the wooden table large enough to seat six comfortably, eight in a tight squeeze. I wondered how many people could live here if this was it for cooking facilities. While Paul kept an eye on the teenager, I bound and gagged the guard.

I looked into the boxes the boy was bringing in. They contained mainly canned goods. Beans, peas, corn, soup, beef stew, chili with beans. Perishables were limited to small quantities of milk, cheese, eggs, and two heads of lettuce, which the teenager put in the refrigerator.

"They put the canned stuff away themselves," he said.

I checked the refrigerator's top freezer section. It was empty except for ice cubes.

"Who decides what goes into the order?" I asked.   150

"It's standard," the teenager replied. "It never changes."

I looked into the cabinets. There were a handful of plates, K-Mart quality stuff. In the cabinets beneath the counter I found a couple of frying pans, a few pots, cookware intended for home use, not the sort of thing that would be used to feed a large number of people.

"Something's screwy here," I said to Paul.

"Maybe they don't eat much. It's part of their religion."

I looked at the kid, and he looked back blankly. He had no explana- 155
tions to offer.

"I'm going to tie you up," I told him. "We'll untie you when we leave. As long as you cooperate, no harm will come to you."

"I . . . I'll cooperate," he said.

I bound and gagged the teenager and locked the door we'd entered through. Then I tried the only door leading from the kitchen into the rest of the house. It was locked. With a good quality dead bolt. It took Paul about a minute to pick it. The hostages, gagged and with their hands tied behind them, sat with their backs against the wall, their eyes taking in everything we did.

The rest of the house was absolutely silent and pitch black. We switched on our flashlights. We were in a living room that looked as if it were never used. There were no newspapers or magazines around. The couch, two upholstered chairs, and a reading lamp were arranged haphazardly. A fine layer of dust covered everything.

There was no TV set.   160

No stereo.

No telephone.

"What the hell have we got here?" I whispered to Paul.

"Some very strange people," he replied.

The windows had been covered from the inside with layers of a 165
heavy black material. Absolutely no light came in; the darkness was as absolute as a photographic darkroom's.

Ahead was a hallway. We entered it, moving silently. I gently opened a door on the right, finding an empty room. Paul tried the one on the left; it, too, was empty. As were all the rooms on the ground floor.

We went upstairs. It was as dark here as it had been downstairs. And all the rooms were dusty and empty. Paul and I exchanged looks. The only thing left was the basement.

The entrance to the cellar was sealed with a dead bolt lock, which Paul picked. The door opened onto a set of wooden stairs that extended downward into a blackness so thick and menacing it almost seemed palpable. Paul and I exchanged glances, but we were both soldiers, men of action, unwilling to admit that this whole business was beginning to unnerve us.

As we descended the stairs, the beams of our flashlights poked into the darkness, revealing cobwebs, dust, concrete walls, a cement floor. Odors, dank and musty, assailed my nostrils. And another scent, less well defined. It was reminiscent of the musky animal smell of a menagerie, and at the same time it reminded me of the sour aroma that came from a refrigerator when something inside was starting to go bad.

Some primitive something deep within me was starting to writhe. It 170 wanted out of that place. Desperately.

Paul tapped my arm, pointed. A mountain of canned goods was piled in the corner. All the deliveries from Taylor's Grocery. Never touched. What became of the milk and cheese and vegetables? Were the perishables simply thrown away?

What did the people here eat?

The answer seemed obvious. There *were* no people here. This was some sort of giant deception. The guards, the groceries delivered each week, it was all a hoax. But why? What was the point?

And then I saw something that shot that explanation totally to hell. At the far end of the cellar, people were sleeping. About two dozen of them. Some were on small mattresses. Some were on the hard floor. All of them were dressed in street clothes.

Paul and I stared at each other, neither of us comprehending what 175 we were seeing.

I pulled out the photo of Sarah La Durca and began moving among the sleeping forms. They came in all age groups. I saw a silver-haired man wearing a suit and tie, a lovely blonde woman in an evening gown, a teenage boy in blue jeans, a girl of about ten in a red dress, a man with big, rough-looking hands in worker's overalls. They seemed more drugged than asleep, I realized, for there was no heavy breathing, no snoring, no moans, no rustling of clothing as slumbering bodies shifted position.

They were totally silent.

As still as the subjects of a photograph.

I spotted Sarah lying on a dirty, tattered mattress. She was as beautiful as her picture. She lay with her eyes closed, her white face pointing upward, framed by the lustrous black hair. She wore a blue and red dress, cut in a V in front to reveal the beginning of her cleavage. She was every bit as lovely as in her photo. I picked her up.

She wasn't heavy, but she was a dead weight, as inanimate as a basket 180 of laundry. As I started up the stairs with her, it occurred to me that I might have stumbled on some bizarre mass suicide. Sarah La Durca felt cold, lifeless. Had the cult members come down here to drink poison like their fellow nut cases had done in Guyana?

In the kitchen I found the teenager and the guard where we'd left them, watching us with wide, fear-filled eyes. In the light coming in through the windows, I studied the woman in my arms. She seemed so limp, so —

She wasn't cold anymore, I realized suddenly. I could feel warmth now. She might be drugged, but she wasn't dead.

Paul untied the teenager. After checking to make sure the coast was clear, we slipped out of the building, leaving the bound guard where he was. The sunshine felt good after the dark and eerie cellar. It warmed my flesh, chasing away the basement's cool dankness.

"What the hell kind of a place is this?" Paul asked. His voice had an edge to it I had never heard before.

"I don't know," I said. "Let's just get out of here." 185

Paul opened the side door of the van, and I found myself staring into the barrel of a shotgun. It was held by one of the guards. One of the others appeared from around the corner of the building, aiming a pistol at us.

"Everybody stay exactly where you are," the guard with the shotgun said, climbing out of the van.

"Should I call the cops?" his partner asked.

"No, not yet. I think we should interrogate these scumbags ourselves first. We can learn things the cops can't." I'd seen the type before. Wanted to show how tough he was. A big man with size twelve shoes and mean little eyes.

I did the one thing he wouldn't have expected me to do. I handed 190 him Sarah La Durca. It confused him for a split second, and that was all I needed. Although I am skilled in several forms of the martial arts, there was nothing sophisticated about what I did. I kicked him in the balls. When he doubled over, I kicked him in the face, and that was the end of the fight.

Glancing over my shoulder, I saw that Paul had dispatched the other guard. We took them inside and tied them up. That left only the guard at the gate, and we would have to see that he joined the others. I put Sarah La Durca in the van. The grocery delivery boy was just standing there, afraid to get involved, lest he pick the losing side.

We made him drive us to the gate. The guard was apparently unaware that his colleagues had discovered intruders — a very sloppy way to do things, but then these guys probably earned just slightly better than the minimum wage. Paul and I got out with our Ingrams and politely invited the guard to accompany us to the house. Looking at me, he said, "I guess you didn't ask Mr. Grigson for a job."

"No," I said.

We tied him up along with the teenager and locked them in the house with the other guards. Then we drove to the spot where we'd left the BMW. As Paul was transferring Sarah to the back seat of the car, he said, "Man, she sure is hot."

"Fever?" 195

"I don't know. I mean she's *really* hot, like a furnace. Maybe it's the effects of the drugs—if she was drugged."

I tried not to think of all the ifs as I drove toward Paddington.

"That was the damnedest place I've ever seen," Paul said.

"Yeah," I said, and then we fell silent because we didn't have any answers, which made asking the questions seem pointless.

In the rearview mirror the road behind me appeared misty, although 200 the day was clear and sunny. "Look behind us," I said.

Paul turned around. "Jesus Christ."

"What is it?"

"Her."

I jammed on the brakes.

Sarah La Durca lay in the back seat, steaming. Or maybe she was 205 smoking. Her cheek seemed to shrivel as I watched. All of a sudden she looked middle aged, and in very poor health. She was still recognizable as the beauty I'd carried from the cellar, but only barely.

"What the hell are we going to do?" Paul asked. The car was filling with . . . something. It looked like smoke, but it was odorless.

"Get her to a hospital," I said. "La Durca wants his wife alive."

"What about Paddington?"

"That's at least forty-five minutes away. There's a town just ahead. There's a small hospital. I noticed it the other day."

By the time we slid to a stop outside the emergency entrance of 210 Bolton Community Hospital, Sarah La Durca's flesh had begun to undulate and quiver. We ran inside and grabbed the first two people we saw who had white coats and name tags. As they loaded Sarah on a gurney, a deep crack spread across the flesh of her right hand. Steam erupted from it.

Sarah's eyes flew open, and her mouth formed into the shape of a primal scream, but all that came out was a stream of smoky mist and a muffled croak.

The white-coated figures rolled her inside and disappeared through a large swinging door, telling us to wait there. The emergency room entrance was filled with a grayish-white haze.

Ten minutes later, a doctor came through the swinging door. His eyes were wide, his face drained of color. I asked how Sarah was, but the doctor just stared straight ahead, as if he hadn't heard me.

Finally he said, "She . . . she . . . oh, God."

"She what?" I demanded. "What the hell happened?" 215

"She . . . she . . . spontaneous combustion."

"She burst into flames?" Paul said.

The doctor nodded.

"You mean . . . *poof*?"

"Yes," the doctor said. "Poof. She set the whole bed on fire. We . . . 220 we had to use a fire extinguisher to get it out." He shook his head. "I've got to sit down."

We got out of there.

Miguel La Durca never showed up at Paddington, and it was two days later before he left a message with Tom the bartender saying he wanted to meet me. I left word that I'd see him at the Oasis the following evening. I didn't think he'd ask for his money back. For one thing, I was pretty sure I'd figured out who he was.

"Mr. Long," he said, sitting down at my table.

"Would you like a Scotch and soda?" I asked.

He shook his head. "It is not what I drink."   225

"No," I said.

He studied me with his bottomless dark eyes. "You did not deliver Sarah to me as agreed."

"You didn't expect me to. You didn't even show up at Paddington."

"Still," he said. "I would be within my rights in asking for a refund."

"The woman, Sarah, what was she?"   230

His eyes mocked. "What do you think she was?"

"I think she was a vampire."

"A vampire? Mr. Long, you can't be serious."

"A week ago I would have thought such a notion preposterous. Now I think the Church of Seven was a group of vampires."

"I hope you don't plan to embarrass yourself by saying this in public. 235 I mean, really, Mr. Long. Vampires?"

Ignoring his sarcasm, I said, "Who was she, the woman you had me murder?"

"Murder? If, as you claim, she was a vampire, then she was already dead. How could you have murdered her?"

"Legally it's a gray area. Still, you used me to dispose of her. Who was she? Why did you go to all that trouble to get rid of her?"

He smiled. "All right, Mr. Long. I believe I owe you an explanation. Sarah was my . . . companion, shall we say. We don't exactly get married in the way you do, as I'm sure you understand. She had been my companion for over two hundred years. She was a very domineering woman. She wanted to possess me totally, to control every aspect of my existence."

I noticed that he didn't say "life."   240

He sighed. "Two centuries of that is enough. I tried to get her to go away, but she refused. She saw the relationship as eternal, I think. Think of it, Mr. Long, eternity with a shrew." He shook his head. "Who could be expected to bear such a thing?"

"Why didn't you simply dispatch her yourself?"

"Dispatch her? Mr. Long, Sarah was immortal. How does one dispatch a being who is immortal?"

"She couldn't be stabbed or shot or suffocated?"

"Of course not. She was a vampire."   245

"I was able to kill her—even if I didn't know that's what I was doing."

"Ah, but what you did could only be accomplished in the daylight, and I must sleep in total darkness while the sun shines. It's the only thing that works, exposure to sunlight. The other things you hear about—silver, wooden stakes through the heart, crucifixes—it's all nonsense. The sun kills us. Nothing else. All the rest is pure fiction."

"How about garlic?"

"Garlic does not affect me. I have a reflection in the mirror just like anyone else." He shrugged. "It's all nonsense. Except for the sunlight part."

"Do you live on human blood?"   250

"Of course." He raised his upper lip, displaying a pair of sharply pointed fangs. "I am many times stronger than you are. And I can cloud your mind. If I decided to have you, there would be nothing you could do about it."

It was not a comforting thought. "Is that what happened to the teenager and the guards I left tied up out there?"

"No. Fortunately for them, they managed to free themselves before dark. By the time the police arrived, night had fallen and we had gone. We are through with that place, by the way. We will not use it again." His eyes explored mine.

Did he think I'd planned to go out there and drag all the sleeping vampires into the sunshine? It hadn't occurred to me. Maybe it would have; I don't know.

"Why did you have the food delivered?" I asked, not wanting to   255 dwell on the likelihood of my being a threat.

"If we didn't ever buy food, someone would notice, start to wonder. Even reclusive cultists have to eat."

"Who are you?" I asked.

"Vladimir, the high priest of the Church of Seven."

"There are seven letters in Lucifer, you said."

"Yes."   260

"There are also seven letters in vampire."

"Indeed." He smiled—without showing the fangs, thank goodness. "There are seven letters in other things as well. And I think you know what they are."

I didn't reply to that.

He said, "Although I could technically ask for a refund, the fact is you have accomplished what I wished you to accomplish. Therefore it seems only fair that I pay you the remainder of the agreed upon sum." He tossed an envelope on the table. "And that, Mr. Long, concludes our business."

He rose, nodded once curtly, turned . . . and vanished. I tell myself 265 he simply walked into the shadows in the dimly lit bar. Maybe that's so, but the truth is that one second he was there and the next he was not.

Remaining at the table, I took out a pen and wrote *vampire* on the small paper napkin. Seven letters. Then I wrote another seven letter word: *La Durca.* I rearranged the letters, making another name:

DRACULA

Then I tore up the napkin and left the bar, glancing over my shoulder as I walked through the shadow-filled parking lot to my car.

Reading the Text

1. What is the effect of Lee's use of first-person address in this story? How does it contribute to your sense of Edward Long as a character?
2. To what extent do you trust Edward Long as the narrator?
3. Characterize the tone of the story. How does it effect a reader's response to the content, especially at the end?

Reading the Signs

1. Compare Lee's version of the Dracula legend to a vampire story of your own choice. Possible examples include Bram Stoker's *Dracula* or an Anne Rice work, such as *Interview with a Vampire.*
2. Write an essay in which you analyze the extent to which Lee's story resembles a hard-boiled detective story (read or reread the introduction to this chapter).
3. "The Cult" combines several popular literature genres: hard-boiled mystery, action-adventure tale, and horror story. Write a critical essay describing the effectiveness of their combination.
4. Watch an episode of *Buffy, The Vampire Slayer,* and write an essay analyzing its treatment of the vampire/living dead theme.
5. In class, discuss the humor in this story. Does it add to or detract from the story's effectiveness?

MATT ZOLLER SEITZ
Grisham Succeeds in a Novel Way

‖‖‖

A handful of popular writers, like Stephen King, Michael Crichton, Tom Clancy, and Danielle Steel, have what might be called a literary "Midas touch." John Grisham, the author of such blockbusters as The Firm, The Client, *and* The Pelican Brief, *many of which have been made into successful movies, is a member of this group, and in this journalistic feature article, Matt Zoller Seitz (b. 1968) attempts to explain how he got there. Telling David and Goliath sagas with a Dickensian topspin is part of the formula, Seitz suggests in this admiring portrait of one of America's most successful authors. A 1994 finalist for the Pulitzer Prize in criticism, Seitz is a TV critic for the New Jersey* Star-Ledger *and a film critic for* New York Press.

Ride on any plane or train or bus in America. Walk through any public park or shopping mall. Scan the tables at your favorite greasy spoon or coffeehouse. Any hour of the day or night, anywhere you look, somebody is reading a John Grisham book.

Since the publication of *The Firm,* in 1989, Grisham's work has sold more than 50 million copies. *The Firm, The Pelican Brief,* and *The Client* were made into films that grossed more than $100 million each in North America. *The Client* was spun off into a successful TV series. The latest Grisham-inspired movie, *A Time to Kill,* opened this week on more than 1,500 screens. Along with Stephen King and Michael Crichton, Grisham is the only novelist in America who routinely appears on *Entertainment Weekly* and *Premiere* magazine's lists of Hollywood's most powerful people. But the Grisham phenomenon does not stem solely from savvy marketing and name recognition. It comes from the book-buying public's hunger to read compelling melodramas set in a world they recognize.

Into the Void

In 1988, a few months after the publication of his first novel, *The Bonfire of the Vanities,* Tom Wolfe published a controversial manifesto in the *Atlantic Monthly* titled *Stalking the Billion-Footed Beast.* He lamented the dearth of writers publishing mainstream novels such as *Bonfire*—novels that entertain while seriously examining how people of different races and social classes interact in contemporary society.

Without a trace of false humility, Wolfe suggested that some bright writer out there pick up the gauntlet he had tossed down and become a

Charles Dickens, Victor Hugo, or Sinclair Lewis for the 1990s — a novelist who tells resonant tales about familiar people who live in the real world.

In a startling number of ways, Grisham fits the bill. He's no Victor   5
Hugo, to be sure. No one ever will accuse him of being a masterful prose stylist or a profound thinker. But his work effortlessly straddles the divide between genre fiction and the social novel, and that's quite an accomplishment. With each new book, Grisham's canvas grows in scope, mixing together rich, middle-class, and poor, black and white, men and women, adults and children.

Other successful U.S. authors also write contemporary social novels: Joyce Carol Oates, John Edgar Wideman, Anne Tyler, and Bebe Moore Campbell spring to mind. All are more gifted stylists, more precise thinkers than Grisham. But none regularly works on as broad a narrative canvas as he, and none is as accessible and widely read. To find another best-selling author whose popularity comes close, you have to enter the domain of King, Tom Clancy, Dean R. Koontz, and other genre specialists.

Character and Characters

In *The Rainmaker, A Time to Kill,* and *The Runaway Jury* — and, to a lesser degree, his earlier books — Grisham tells intimate stories about wrenching human conflict unfolding against the troubled backdrop of the New South. His scope is Dickensian, and so are his characters' colorful names: Mitch McDeere, Royce McKnight, Reggie Love, Mark Sway, Thomas Fink, Roy Foltrigg, Billy Ray Cobb, Ethel Twitty, Mrs. Gladys Card, and Colleen Janice Barrow Birdsong. There are plucky urchins, corrupt politicians, intrepid students, dogged cops, dotty old ladies, con men, hit men, massive conspiracies, exploding cars, preposterous escapes, and other stock suspense elements.

But in the end, his fiction is not about cheap thrills or plot contrivance. It's about larger issues. Class. Race. Greed. Political and legal corruption. Sexual conflict. The American South's economic progression from a rural to an industrial to a service economy. And though a lawyer almost always is his protagonist, Grisham's work isn't about being a lawyer: it's about the law's ability (and inability) to change the lives of average Americans for the better. This was evident in his first published novel, *The Firm,* about a hot-shot law student who joins a Memphis, Tenn., law firm that's controlled by the mob. On the surface, it's a paranoid thriller in the tradition of *The Parallax View* and *Klute.* But it's also a powerful story about greed and envy, in which the ambitious son of a Kentucky coal miner sells his soul for professional and social success — then struggles desperately to steal it back.

Class and Action

The Client is equally concerned with class. In it, 11-year-old Memphis "trailer-park kid" Mark Sway—raised in the alternately chivalrous and patronizing Southern style to regard women as inferior to men—learns to love and admire his female attorney (Reggie Love), who has a degree and middle-class aspirations. But he continues to resent his poor, uneducated mother; distrusts the well-dressed, media-savvy federal prosecutor; and loathes the suburban kids who live near his trailer park.

Mark is the exception to Grisham's usual heroes, most of whom are   10
lawyers. Like Love, they are caught between colliding social classes, forced either to save one from the other or to work out meaningful dialogue between the two. This is key to Grisham's strategy. He doesn't put lawyers at the center of his stories because he is a lawyer himself. Rather, he understands that a lawyer—like a cop or a private detective—can rove through society relatively unimpeded, meeting and mingling with all kinds of people.

The Rainmaker, Grisham's 1995 book about a young law school graduate in Memphis who stumbles into the middle of an important lawsuit against a major insurance company, illustrates this concept explicitly. Middle-class hero Rudy Baylor works at a free legal clinic at a senior citizens' home, where his first client is Colleen Birdsong, a.k.a. Miss Birdie, an elderly woman who wants help in disposing of an estate worth $20 million. His second meeting is with a poor couple seeking justice from an insurance company they say wrongfully refused to pay for treatment for their leukemia-stricken son. "I worked in a blue-jean factory for 30 years, joined the union, you know, and we fought the company every day," Dot Black tells Rudy. "Same thing here. Big corporation running roughshod over little people."

David-Goliath Sagas

Grisham has a disarmingly genuine sympathy for "little people." *The Firm* and *The Client* pit handfuls of down-on-their-luck heroes against the combined forces of the mob and the government. In *The Pelican Brief,* a law student and an investigative reporter face off against big business, the Mafia, and the feds. Grisham's bestseller *The Runaway Jury,* about a lawsuit against a giant tobacco company, is told mostly through the point of view of a jury-selection company monitoring the trial. The blasé omnipotence of the selectors is contrasted with the ragtag lives of the average people they spy on. To the surprise of the selectors—and the delight of the reader—the hand-picked jury begins behaving in unexpectedly independent ways. All the high-tech spying and background checks in the world can't predict a person's likelihood of doing the right thing.

But to Grisham's credit, while he likes for the good guys to win, their triumphs are never comforting. In this novelist's universe, there is no such thing as victory; each win comes with an accompanying loss, usually of innocence. The hero of *The Firm* wins independence from those who would try to use him but is condemned to live a nomadic and eternally paranoid existence. The heroine of *The Pelican Brief* and the young hero of *The Client* must disappear into the witness-protection program or risk dying. And the victory of the poor couple over the insurance company in *The Rainmaker* is bittersweet; the corporation declares bankruptcy and no one—not the couple, the lawyer who represented them, or the leukemia charity to whom they intended to donate their winnings—will ever see a dime.

Grisham suggests—persuasively—that it is impossible to bring down big business, corrupt government, organized crime, racism, or other social ills in total, that the best you can hope for is to make a dent. If you manage that, you're lucky. And sometimes, you think you're making a dent, and you haven't accomplished a thing.

The morals of his stories aside, Grisham sells because he understands   15
how to meld thrills with intelligence and idealism with honesty. He is as popular in America today as Charles Dickens was in England more than 100 years ago and with good reason. In book after book, he proves that entertainment is not synonymous with irrelevance, that when art borrows from life, both are enriched.

Reading the Text

1. What, according to Seitz, accounts for John Grisham's extraordinary popularity?
2. What large themes underlie Grisham's novels, in Seitz's description?
3. What is Seitz's opinion of Grisham as a novelist?

Reading the Signs

1. Read a John Grisham novel, and analyze its characters and themes semiotically. Alternately, watch a film based on a Grisham novel, and analyze it.
2. Seitz implies that Grisham is an important writer by comparing him to Charles Dickens. In an argumentative essay, support, challenge, or modify Seitz's judgment. To develop your ideas, consult Amy E. Schwartz's "The ABCs of Popular Culture" (p. 382).
3. This selection originally appeared in the Variety section of the *Minneapolis Star Tribune*. What effect does this journalistic context have on the tone and content of the article?
4. Interview three or four friends or relatives who are Grisham fans, and ask them about the author's appeal to them. Then write your own explanation for Grisham's popularity.

MARILYN M. LOWERY
The Traditional Romance Formula

〰〰〰〰〰〰〰〰〰〰〰〰〰〰〰〰〰〰〰〰〰〰〰〰〰〰〰〰〰

So you want to be a romance writer. Well, here's the formula, as described by Marilyn M. Lowery, author of How to Write Romance Novels That Sell *(1983), from which this selection is excerpted. If it all seems a little cut and dried, that's because it is. Romance fiction works because it establishes a kind of contract with its readers who agree to consume the story so long as it delivers what they want, and what they want, as Lowery suggests, is lots of language like this: "Then they were together, hands exploring, mouths tasting, until their bodies met in passion." Etc., etc., etc. Marilyn Lowery is a romance novelist whose publications include* The Reluctant Duke *(written under the pen name Philippa Castle).*

Romances are based on a traditional formula, which has many variations:

1. A girl, our heroine, meets a man, our hero, who is above her socially and who is wealthy and worldly.
2. The hero excites the heroine but frightens her sexually.
3. She is usually alone in the world and vulnerable.
4. The hero dominates the heroine, but she is fiery and sensual, needing this powerful male.
5. Though appearing to scorn her, the hero is intrigued by her and pursues her sexually.
6. The heroine wants love, not merely sex, and sees his pursuit as self-gratification.
7. The two clash in verbal sparring.
8. In holding to her own standards, the heroine appears to lose the hero. She does not know he respects her.
9. A moment of danger for either main character results in the realization on the part of the hero or heroine that the feeling between them is true love.
10. A last-minute plot twist threatens their relationship.
11. The two finally communicate and admit their true love, which will last forever.

Why is the reader fascinated by this formula? It tells her that she can have the romance she was brought up to believe in; that her life can be exciting and happy; that she is desirable sexually; that true love lasts forever.

The novels also fulfill her sexual fantasies. Throughout each romance she can imagine taming a devilish man who first lusts for her, then respects and loves her. She doesn't mind knowing the outcome of the plot.

In fact, she wants to. It's the satisfying ending she wants to believe in. The formula is unbeatable. . . .

The Heroine's Identity

Who will your heroine be? How old is she? What is her status—orphan, governess, actress, president of a firm? What goal in life is she working toward, or what problem is she trying to sort through? This goal or problem helps to give her an identity and an interest other than the hero. She is a cheerful, spunky person, quite all right without the hero; but he enters, he adds perfection. To appear strong, she must start with a life outside that with the hero, and her goal must not be to find him.

If the heroine has been widowed or divorced, the pain of that experience should usually be out of the way. If the former husband is in the picture, she is over her love for him and feels some other emotion, such as pity. The reader does not want to be reminded of "lost love" but rather of "new love."

An old lover or even the villain, who has earlier raped the heroine, may have affected her psychologically; and sexual tension may result as the hero tries to overcome her resistance. However, the heroine usually is readily able to put a past romance or rape from her mind and approach the future in high spirits.

The Heroine's Vulnerability

The heroine of most romances is vulnerable. She is often much smaller than the hero, tiny against his massive frame. If she is tall, like some of Georgette Heyer's Regency heroines, he is usually taller. The suggestion is always present that he could, if he so desired, rape her; that she is in his power.

A hero is rarely short, but Anne McCaffrey in *Ring of Fear* has been able to portray a short hero who is masculine and masterful:

> I was close enough now to see the light dusting of black hair on his tanned arms and across the muscular plane of his chest, making a thin line down the ridge of the diaphragm muscles, disappearing into the excuse for a bikini he was wearing, which barely covered nature's compensation for his lack of stature.
>
> There was a satisfied expression in his eyes when I jerked mine back from where propriety decreed a well-bred miss ought not to look. He looked suddenly so knowing, so smug, that he was no longer an *objet d'art,* but man, male, masculine. . . .

He soon shows that he is able to rape her if he wishes.

To add to the drama of the heroine's vulnerability, she usually is alone in the world, with few people to depend upon. Also, few people, if any, would ask questions if she were to disappear. This isolation creates suspense.

In Kay Thorpe's *Lord of La Pampa* (Harlequin Presents), the blond heroine from England has not made connections with her dance troupe in Argentina. She signs on as a cocktail waitress, only to learn that she is expected to entertain the men more intimately. The hero rescues her by buying her time then asks her to marry him so he can collect his rightful inheritance. She is alone in the world. What can she do? He reminds her that the nightclub owner has taken her on his payroll:

> ". . . he will expect suitable return. Should it be denied him he may find other ways of extracting a profit. You have heard of the white slave traffic?"

Giving the heroine no choice in the matter keeps the reader sympathetic toward her. The sexual undertones of this scene are obvious, and it is dramatic to think she has just been saved only to be victimized.

If the heroine has a supportive family, its members are usually geographically remote, making it easier for the hero to hire or abduct or marry the heroine. The family may simply be financially unable to help the daughter, as in Richardson's *Pamela* in which the parents lack power to confront the gentleman abductor.

The youthfulness of the heroine can also add to her vulnerability. To the hero's thirty or thirty-five, she can be as young as seventeen, too young to have had a past. This age difference helps to ensure that she is a virgin, and the suggestion is that she is therefore more desirable and, again, more vulnerable.

In some romances, especially contemporaries such as Dell's Candlelight Ecstasy line, the heroine is not a virgin. This fact does not mean that she has experienced the ultimate in love. Her earlier sexual experiences could have been unsatisfactory because of a lack in the husband or lover. Even if her sexual experiences have been satisfactory, no man's lovemaking can compare to that of the hero. . . .

The Complex Hero

The setting and the heroine help to dictate who the hero will be, and he comes rapidly onto the scene. Though he is usually about ten years older than the heroine, this does not always need to be the case. In Jocelyn Day's *Glitter Girl* (Jove Second Chance at Love), the hero and heroine were in school together and knew each other well before the heroine married a wealthy man and moved away. Now she is back in town, where her first love has become financially successful. But does he trust her to love him for himself rather than for his wealth? Here their similar age is effective.

In period pieces, an age difference is more natural than in a contemporary story. Also, in the Harlequin Romance type of story, the young innocent needs someone older on whom to depend. In the racier contemporary, an age difference is no longer necessary. The heroine portrayed as older is more likely to have a career and is less likely to need an older man to direct her. Today, the two leads can come together as equals.

That the hero is wealthy is never what basically attracts the heroine. But, let's face it, a rich man is the man he is because he has had the power to make money, so that power drive is part of what attracts her.

The hero is a combination of Mr. Darcy in *Pride and Prejudice* and Rhett Butler in *Gone with the Wind*. He appears proud, disdainful, certainly sure of himself, strong, and virile. His outer demeanor cloaks a man who is complex and, most important, loving. But his gentle nature has been carefully masked, perhaps because life has jaded him, perhaps because he carries a deep hurt from the past. Here is mystery.

The chemical reaction between hero and heroine is at once apparent to the reader. Laura London describes Katie's meeting the hero in *The Bad Baron's Daughter* (Dell Candlelight Regency):

> He was the most attractive man Katie had ever seen. Once, as a little girl, when Katie's father had been teaching her how to ride, typically on far too large and temperamental a horse for her tiny size, he had sent her to jump a five-barred gate. The horse had refused, sending Katie flying to the ground with a force that drove the air from her lungs. She felt that same breathless confusion now, as the crowd parted to allow her a clear line of sight.

The sensuality of the horse imagery adds to the power of the description.

At this stage of a story, the hero and heroine feel worlds apart. He looks down on her as an utter innocent—or a schemer, for such goodness cannot possibly ring true to him. She, on the other hand, sees the hero as one who scorns her for her youth or lack of position, or some other reason of which she is unaware. 20

His scorn for her is apparent mainly through his smiles, which are *mocking, caustic, ironic, sardonic, superior,* and/or *frustrating*. His sensuous lips are continually curling into one of the above. However, you needn't always define the smile. When Thomas in *The Reluctant Duke* comes to propose to Catherine, he cannot help noticing her younger sister, Julia:

> While this exchange was going on, the Duke raised his quizzing glass to look more closely at this younger sister who appeared so lively. The mother thought she caught a slight smile on his lips, but what it meant she could not tell.

As the romance progresses, the heroine often depends upon the hero, whether wishing to or not. If she is in danger, she is sometimes saved in spite of herself. She usually sees *him* as the danger and often sees another man as the one who can help her. That she has the situation reversed is obvious to the reader.

How can the reader trust the hero, even though the heroine does not? Obviously, we can recognize him anywhere. The more sadistic he acts, the more certain we are that there is a heart of gold (not to mention a bank account) beneath the surface. . . .

No matter how she reacts, the hero must save her from some unfortunate situation, such as a fire or other accident, or he might save her from her own misconceptions. Sometimes he saves her from both. Often, she saves *him* at some point in the story. . . .

Rape and Near-Rape

The most innocent of romances implies that the hero, if he so desires, can rape the heroine. The reader must be aware that the hero is free to do with the heroine as he likes. His size in comparison to hers helps to remind us that he is in control. That he doesn't take advantage of her characterizes him and shows how truly he loves her.

Often the two are entirely alone, as in Barbara Cartland's *Touch a Star* (Jove). During an elaborate Venetian party, the hero takes the heroine to a deserted island on his estate. No help would be forthcoming were she to need it. So the setting in itself creates some suspense while adding to the reader's sexual fantasy.

In Kathleen E. Woodiwiss's *Ashes in the Wind* the heroine, Alaina, fears the hero. "They were in the house alone, and there was no one to stop him if he chose to take her again." Notice that their situation is spelled out for us.

In most romances there is a touch of sadomasochism. The plot in which the husband or lover rapes his wife or loved one and she enjoys it is not uncommon. Woodiwiss gives us such a scene in *Ashes in the Wind,* in which the hero, Cole Latimer, intoxicated, ravishes Alaina, who makes an unsuccessful attempt to stop him. That she desires him, too, is evident. Moreover, since Cole is drunk, he is not in complete control of his actions. This intoxication is a way of including him in a rape scene and minimizing his responsibility so that the heroine—and readers—can remain sympathetic to him. Moreover, we do not blame the heroine for losing her virtue.

Another familiar plot is one in which the hero holds the heroine captive with the constant threat of rape, a threat that she, while claiming to abhor, actually finds exciting, even fascinating. Violet Winspear in *Palace of the Pomegranate* (Harlequin Presents) goes so far as to have her heroine whisked across the Persian sands by the mysterious Kharim Khan. In one scene, after undressing the heroine so she will not get a desert chill, and roughly drying her with a towel, he says:

"You deserve the taste of the whip, my little filly, rather than petting—but come, why be shy with me any more? I know how beautiful you are, and you know that I don't intend to let you go. Be kissed instead of bruised. It is far more pleasant, for you, for me."

As he caresses her, she fights back "with all the desperation of a little   30
animal." This fiery spirit fascinates the hero; and out of such tauntings and strugglings comes an ending of true and lasting love. It is just such animal imagery and the idea that the hero loves the heroine because she is beautiful that cause some to condemn the romance as degrading to women and others to read romances.

Near-rapes by the wrong man are also described in a sensuous manner, but he is described in far different terms than is the hero. The villain's breath is disgusting and his kisses wet in Granbeck's *Maura:*

> His weight was overpowering. She was thrown back to the bed and he fell on her, pinning her arms. His mouth searched wetly. When his lips brushed her cheek, she twisted away. His sour breath sickened her and the intimacy of his body on hers was obscene.

When it is the hero who is drunk and rapes the heroine, Woodiwiss writes about "the brandy taste of his mouth." The touch of the hero's body is desirable even though feared.

The reader must not feel disgusted by the actual rape scene. Early in the "bodice-ripper" romance plot, the heroine is usually raped by the hero; and we must remain sympathetic with both characters. In such scenes, the writer must be especially careful to motivate the actions of the two. These rapes are more acts of passion than of violence, and we mustn't feel as we would while reading about an actual rape.

Though the reader feels good about the scene, the heroine feels guilt and anger. Her emotions make her at odds with the hero, who has caused her to lose control. She will show him she doesn't need him (since she has just shown him that she does). Her pride has been hurt. She also has been reminded of feelings she has not been aware of or has been repressing. Now her confusion of feelings is uppermost in her mind, and she resents the one who has caused such doubt.

Arousing the Reader

Romance writers use strong adjectives and verbs to draw the reader   35
into the love scene. As you write, try adjectives such as *burning, hungering, throbbing, exploding,* or *scalding.* Forget the verb *to be.* Instead, try verbs that convey action or emotion such as *plunged, stroked, caressed, quivered, writhed, pressed, searched, arched,* and *moaned,* to name a few.

When passion subsides and contentment follows, the pace slows and less dynamic verbs take the place of explosive ones. Pacing is important in sex scenes. You as writer may move from short, abrupt sentences to

lyrical metaphors to slower-paced moments in which the couple can lan-
guorously enjoy each other.

Breathless interjections can lend immediacy as in Charlotte Lamb's
Duel of Desire (Harlequin Presents):

> He paused, his breathing rapid and harsh. "Did I hurt you? Darling,
> did I hurt you?"
>
> "No, oh, no," she whispered. Her hands pressed him down to
> her. "Oh, Alex, darling, I want you so much . . ."
>
> He groaned, his body trembling violently. "Deb. . . . Oh, God,
> Deb, I love you like hell . . ."

You will learn to allot little time to sex scenes with a woman other
than the heroine, and your adjectives in such scenes will not be flattering.
She will sound sensuous but not as desirable as the heroine because of
your adjectives and verbs. In Granbeck's *Maura* Beau makes love to Irene:

> Then they were together, hands exploring, mouths tasting, until their
> bodies met in passion. She clawed at his flesh and writhed, to meet
> his body. His hard muscles moved under her hands and his mouth
> stopped her cries until all thoughts were blanketed by exploding
> pleasure.

Similarly, when the wrong man makes love to the heroine, you will
remember to give him less space and see that his sexual prowess does not
compare to that of the hero. . . .

Reading the Text

1. In your own words, summarize the basic formula that Lowery recommends for a romance novel.
2. Describe the typical heroine and hero of romance novels.
3. To what sexual fantasies do romance novels cater, according to Lowery?
4. What stylistic advice does Lowery provide writers of romances?

Reading the Signs

1. If you are a fan of romance novels, reflect in your journal why they appeal
   to you. Alternately, if you dislike romances, interview friends or relatives
   who read romances, and ask them about the pleasure romance reading
   gives them. Discuss in your journal why their movitations for reading may
   differ from yours.
2. In an argumentative essay, support, refute, or modify the contention that
   romance novels are really soft-core pornography. To develop your ideas,
   read or reread the excerpt from Kat Martin's *Dangerous Passions* (p. 425),
   or read one of the romances Lowery mentions.
3. Read or reread Laura Stempel Mumford's "Plotting Paternity: Looking
   for Dad on the Daytime Soaps" (p. 249) and Holly Devor's "Gender Role

Behaviors and Attitudes" (p. 447), and then write an essay that analyzes the extent to which romances reinforce patriarchal gender codes.

4. Both Lowery and Linda Seger ("Creating the Myth," p. 308) direct their comments to aspiring writers of romances and screenplays, respectively. Using their selections as evidence, write an essay that defends or refutes the common charge that much of popular entertainment is conventional and formulaic, not original.

K A T   M A R T I N
Selection from Dangerous Passions

||||||||||||||||||||||||||||||||||||||||||||||||||||||||||||

In this selection from Dangerous Passions *(1998), Kat Martin shows the early stages of a courtship between Elissa, who, posing as a widowed countess intent on discovering a spy known as the Falcon, becomes involved with Lord Wolvermont, Colonel Adrian Kingsland. Here we see the conflicting emotions of fear and attraction that are a staple of the genre play out in the heroine's mind. Combining elements of historical adventure with romantic fantasy, Martin thus creates a world in which her readers' dreams can come true. Kat Martin (www.Katbooks.com) makes her home in Montana's Sapphire Mountains and in Bakersfield, California. She has published over a dozen popular romance novels, including* Wicked Promise *(1998),* Night Secrets *(1999), and* The Silent Rose *(1999).*

Elissa turned once more in front of the cheval glass mirror, studying the sapphire blue taffeta gown trimmed with silver lace she had chosen for her dinner with the colonel. She shouldn't have agreed to go, she knew. Her time here was limited and she had a job to do, but dear lord, he had been so brave!

She would never forget the fierce look on his face when he had stepped between her and the charging boar. There was no doubt he would have laid down his life before he would have let the animal reach her. Her heart had nearly stopped beating and then, when she had seen him covered in blood—she felt a sharp, squeezing pain inside her chest.

Elissa smoothed the front of the gown, a favorite among those Gaby had provided. It set off the blue of her eyes, her friend had said, and the low, square neckline emphasized the swells of her bosom. She had worn it only once, had intended to save it to impress General Steigler.

Elissa's mouth thinned at the thought. Steigler. It was he who had wounded the boar. The general had given no thought to the women back in camp. He'd cared only for his enjoyment in making the kill. And the fact that Colonel Kingsland had risked himself to save them had only gained Steigler's ire. He didn't like being made to look the fool, and though Adrian hadn't done it on purpose, his heroic dispatch of the boar had certainly accomplished the task.

Adrian. She thought of him that way now. She had tried so hard not   5
to and yet it had happened. She was drawn to him more every day though it was obvious their attraction could lead nowhere. Elissa was committed to finding the Falcon, and even if she weren't, the colonel wasn't interested in marriage. Not that she was interested in marrying *him,* of course. Life with an arrogant, domineering man like Wolvermont would probably be unbearable.

Elissa sighed as she drew her long white gloves up over her elbows. She shouldn't have agreed to go tonight, yet she meant to enjoy herself. Life was precious. She was involved in a dangerous business and she wasn't sure where it might end. She would take these few moments for herself. With a last glance in the mirror, she picked up her silver-trimmed sapphire taffeta reticule and headed for the door.

He was waiting at the foot of the stairs, taller than most of the men in the villa, black boots polished to a mirror sheen, gold epaulettes gleaming on the shoulders of his scarlet uniform coat. It took her breath away just to look at him.

"Good evening, my lord."

He smiled and reached for her hand, bent over it and pressed a soft kiss on the back. "I liked it better when you called me Adrian. Do you think you might manage that, at least for tonight?"

"Perhaps I could . . . Adrian."   10

His smile grew broader, and dimples appeared in his cheeks. He took her hand and they left the villa, descending the stairs to a carriage that waited out in front.

"Where are we going?" she asked, once they were settled inside and the carriage rolled over the cobblestone streets. A brass lamp burned on the wall inside, lighting the baron's handsome features, and it occurred to her the freedom a young widow possessed was definitely a thing to be envied.

"There is a restaurant near the center of the city, a favorite of the emperor. The food is supposed to be excellent. I trust you are hungry."

"Ravenous."

His eyes darkened for a moment, then he smiled. "As I have been of   15
late, though food has been the farthest thought from my mind."

Elissa sat up straighter on the bench, her lips parting, ready to demand he take her home, but Adrian caught her hand.

"A jest, my lady. I am sorry if I offended. You are safe with me this night. I give you my word."

She relaxed against the seat. She trusted the colonel to keep his promise. He made no secret of his desire for her and yet she knew without doubt he would not take what she was unwilling to give.

"How is your leg this eve?" she asked. "I noticed you favored it only a little as we walked to the carriage."

"I told you 'twas only a scratch."　　　　20

"A 'scratch' you would not have taken if it hadn't been for Steigler's thoughtlessness."

"True. With the camp so near, he should not have taken the shot." He looked as though he wanted to say something else, but decided against it. Elissa wondered what it might have been.

Watching the baron from beneath her lashes, she found herself comparing the two very different men. The colonel was demanding but he would never force her. She wasn't sure about Steigler. She knew what the general wanted, and that by pretending an interest in him, she was taking a serious risk. Unlike Wolvermont, should the circumstance arise, she feared General Steigler would not hesitate to take what he wanted.

Elissa shivered in the darkness of the carriage.

"You're cold," said the colonel, reaching for the lap robe that rode　25 on the seat at his side.

"No, I—I'm fine, my lord, truly."

Still, he unfolded the robe and draped it over her lap, determined in this as he was in everything else. "Adrian," he corrected softly.

Elissa smiled, oddly comforted by the gesture. "Adrian," she said, and for her acquiescence got another of his charming dimpled smiles.

Reading the Text

1. How does Kat Martin depict the characters of Elissa and Adrian in this passage?
2. Chart the images in this excerpt. How do they contribute to a sense of drama?
3. Characterize the style of the dialogue between Elissa and Adrian.
4. What social class do the characters belong to? What does Martin achieve by setting her story at this social level?

Reading the Signs

1. To what extent does this selection from *Dangerous Passions* illustrate the romance writing techniques that Marilyn M. Lowery recommends in "The Traditional Romance Formula" (p. 418)?
2. Write a semiotic essay that analyzes the gender roles in this passage. To develop your ideas, consult Holly Devor, "Gender Role Behaviors and Attitudes" (p. 447).
3. Rape, or the threat of it, is a common motif in romance novels. In an essay, discuss how this motif affects the romance's appeal to the genre's fans. To develop your ideas, you might read the whole of *Dangerous Passions* or consult Marilyn M. Lowery's "The Traditional Romance

Formula" (p. 418). You might also interview readers of romance about their attitudes toward the rape motif.

4. Romance novels and their readership have received increasing attention in academic research. Write an argumentative essay in which you explain whether romances should be a subject of academic study. To develop your ideas, consult Amy E. Schwartz, "The ABCs of Popular Culture" (p. 382).

EDWARD BERRIDGE

Hope I Die before Marcia Gets Old

‖‖‖

The thing about zines, a fast-growing sector of popular literature made possible by new technologies, is how democratic they are. Anyone with access to a typewriter, photocopier, mimeograph machine, or computer can publish one and become an instant writer and editor with the power to decide what will and what will not be published. In this contribution to BUST, *a zine described as being "for women who are too old for Sassy," Edward Berridge (b. 1966) (*BUST*'s first male contributor) describes what it is like for a Gen Xer to grow old, and it isn't fun. "You are older and poorer and dying," Berridge laments, "but worst of all, you are anonymous." It seems like Berridge needs to publish his own zine. The author of a collection of short stories entitled* The Lives of the Saints *(1995), Berridge is a punk-influenced writer within the Australian grunge scene.*

I would never have thought of myself as part of a generation at all if it were not that whenever I meet someone roughly my own age I can always break the ice with a comment about *The Brady Bunch.* And now we are, as a generation, getting old. Indeed, the aging process is a horrific and irredeemable notion. First, there is the physical deterioration. Men, for example, go soft around the gut. It becomes a major life hassle to maintain tone. You get lines on your face and see your friends losing hair—all those expressions of bodily decay which we know leads to (let's capitalize this, cause it's important) DEATH.

But aging is more than just looking older. There is also that whole trip of *feeling* older. I notice, for instance, that my hangovers are worse these days and I need a day's rest to get over them. I have to exercise constantly to achieve the sort of suppleness I took for granted ten years ago. As you age, time begins to fly. It idles, rolls slowly out on the runway, taxis, picks up speed, and, before you know it, breaks the sound barrier. Suddenly you are older than most popular athletes, actors, musicians, and supermodels—and you realize you will never have their money or lifestyle. As a kid, you didn't resent famous people because you could still kid yourself that you would be like them when you grew up. You knew time was on your side. You had forever to make your move.

No, adulthood for most of us is a bad, bad let-down. You are older and poorer and dying, but worst of all, you are anonymous. You are not photographed, you are not interviewed, nobody cares what you think or what you are wearing. You are the sort of person who gets tickets too far away from the stage to see Madonna or U2. You have to queue up outside nightclubs and restaurants. You are never going to be famous (and I mean real fame, not Andy Warhol's fifteen minutes of fame. If you happen to see an accident and get interviewed, or if you are a game show contestant, that is not fame. That is a mockery of fame). We come to realize that our lives are drab and dirty, not only relative to the celebrity lives we read about but, more importantly, to the people we see on television.

The problem with our generation isn't that we cannot tell the difference between reality and television. Our problem is that we are too acutely aware of the difference. Reality fares badly in comparison, so we watch a lot of TV. Consider *Family Matters:* the main character is a bus driver who lives in a huge, multi-bedroom home. (In reality, lawyers and management consultants live in mansions like that. On television, it's bus drivers.) In the real world, we cannot escape the suspicion that more or less all people are losers, including bus drivers. And one can only imagine that the son of a Minnesota accountant would be the king of losers in Beverly Hills. Yet on television, to be ordinary is to be jolly, affluent, and fulfilled.

So . . . what in fact? Who knows? Having postulated some tenuous   5
connection between us on the grounds of a shared *Brady Bunch* viewing experience, let me apologize for any incoherence. I consider myself more of a writer of fiction than an essayist. Well, in fact, I am not any sort of writer at all. I have cupboards of short stories and rejection slips, but that does not, of course, make a person a writer. I am just a market researcher. But we will all be fifty soon and need each other more than ever.

Reading the Text

1. According to Berridge, what is happening to *The Brady Bunch* generation?
2. What are the reasons that adulthood has been a letdown for Berridge?
3. Why do members of Gen X watch so much television, in Berridge's view?
4. Describe the style of this zine article, noting both diction patterns and sentence construction.

1. Berridge takes it for granted that his generation got its values and hopes from television. In your journal, reflect on the influences in your life that have most shaped your hopes and aspirations.
2. Write an essay analyzing the style of this selection. In what ways is the style suited to a zine, as opposed to, say, an essay for school or even a more established magazine?
3. While *Generation X* apparently refers to people in their twenties, Berridge notes that members of the original Gen X are now in their thirties. In class, devise an alternative term to describe your generational identity. What is the value, if any, of such labels?
4. Berridge assumes that a successful life must include both fortune and fame. Write an essay in which you support, refute, or complicate his assumption.

ALISON LURIE

Reading at Escape Velocity

⁙⁙⁙⁙⁙⁙⁙⁙⁙⁙⁙⁙⁙⁙⁙⁙⁙⁙⁙⁙⁙⁙⁙⁙⁙⁙⁙⁙⁙⁙⁙⁙⁙⁙

Adults aren't the only readers who tend to ignore the literary experts when choosing the books they want to read: children do the same thing all the time, but in this case the "experts" are grown-ups. For, as Alison Lurie (b. 1926) observes in this "Bookend" piece for the New York Times Book Review, *where adults prefer children's books that feature "at least one Wise and Good Grown-Up or Grown-up Equivalent," the kids themselves reach for stories in which children control the action and adults are either out of the loop or "apt to be villains." Indeed, when it comes to literary popularity, the formula for both children and adults is pretty much the same, Lurie concludes, with younger and older readers alike preferring those books that reflect their "real fears and fantasies." The author of ten novels, including* The Last Resort *(1998) and* Foreign Affairs *(1985), which won the Pulitzer Prize for fiction, as well as several books on such topics as clothing and children's literature, Lurie is emeritus Frederic J. Whiton Professor of Literature at Cornell University.*

Have you ever had the feeling that your children are turning into beasts—chimpanzees, maybe, or slovenly, lazy, greedy brown bears? It actually happens in the inventive and wildly popular "Animorphs" series. "All the kids are asking for those books; we can't keep them on the shelves," the clerks in my local bookstore say. Some adults, on the other hand, don't care for the Animorphs: my niece Clarissa, who is a children's librarian in New York City, tells me her system won't purchase them.

There is a big difference between the books that parents and teachers and librarians choose and the books that kids prefer. What grown-ups want is stories in which children are helped by and learn from grown-ups. The lesson may be practical or moral; the adult may be a relative, a teacher, a neighbor, a witch or wizard, an animal or an alien. These kind, wise beings may not appear very often, but the plot turns on their advice or help, and the happy ending wouldn't be possible without them. From Marmee in *Little Women* to Mary Poppins, E. B. White's Charlotte, and Tolkien's Gandalf, these admirable figures guide and care for the younger and less experienced protagonists of the tales in which they appear.

When awards are given for children's books, the books that win tend not only to be admirably well written but also to contain at least one Wise and Good Grown-Up or Grown-Up Equivalent. Back in the 1950s and 60s such books were often set in the historical past (especially in pioneer and Revolutionary War America), and their child protagonists tended to be white. Since cultural diversity was discovered, the settings cover a wider range, and often feature minority children who, with adult guidance, face disasters, overcome obstacles, and learn to be brave, kind, and strong.

The 1997 Newbery winner was E. L. Konigsburg's *View from Saturday*. People who know her earlier work (she won the Newbery 30 years ago for *From the Mixed-Up Files of Mrs. Basil E. Frankweller*) won't be surprised to hear that the book is original, intelligent, and a pleasure to read. It also fits the pattern for prizewinners in several ways. Moral and emotional lessons are taught, and there is a warm relationship between the four sixth graders and the teacher who coaches them to win a state Academic Bowl contest. The sixth graders are diverse in the current manner: one of the children is a WASP, one is Jewish, one East Indian, and one of mixed parentage; two are from one-parent families. But now it's not only the teacher who helps the students; the students help the teacher—making it possible for her to control her class and gain confidence after an automobile accident that has left her a paraplegic. It should be admitted that like Marmee and Gandalf, the four children, who give formal tea parties inspired by *Alice in Wonderland,* sometimes seem a little too wise and good to be true.

The books children choose for themselves typically feature a group   5
of kids who face dangers, have exciting adventures, and help and instruct one another. Any adults who are important in the story are apt to be villains. If there are well-meaning parents and teachers around, they have no idea what really goes on in their absence, like the mother in a classic picture-book version of the genre, Dr. Seuss' *Cat in the Hat*. In these stories, events are often related in the first person by one of the heroes. The

writer who more or less invented the genre was E. Nesbit, whose book *The Story of the Treasure Seekers* (1899) was told by Oswald, one of a family of six children. (In later books Nesbit reduced the number to a more manageable four, and four continues to be the usual number today.)

According to the librarians and booksellers I've consulted, kids who like a book want a sequel, and what they like best are series. This is nothing new: as a child I spent my allowance on Nancy Drew and the Oz books (which at that time were not approved by the public library); my husband was devoted to a series called the Mark Tidd Stories.

The Animorph books, written by K. A. Applegate, follow the preferred pattern. Their heroes are four junior high school students, two male and two female, who are also culturally and socially diverse. There is a sensitive, nature-loving black girl who lives on a farm and a wisecracking Hispanic-American boy from the wrong side of the tracks. But tradition dies hard, and the leader of the Animorphs are two WASP cousins. All the kids can become animals, and they can communicate telepathically when transformed. But if they don't change back in two hours, they are stuck in that morph forever, like their friend Tobias, who in Volume 1 spent too much time as a red-tailed hawk.

Though Tobias misses being human, he is of great help to his friends in their struggle against evil aliens called the Yeerks. The Yeerks, who look like the small gray slugs that eat my tomatoes, wish to conquer Earth. Their method is to crawl into the ears of other beings and take over their minds. There is no outward sign that a person is possessed by a slug, except for an occasional cold emotional falseness. Readers who remember their own adolescence will not be surprised to learn that several people in the kids' world, including the assistant principal at their school, are really Yeerks. So is Jake's brother Tom, who always does the right thing and never gets into trouble. "The Yeerks . . . had already infiltrated human society . . . cops and teachers and soldiers and mayors and TV newspeople. They were everywhere. They could be anyone." One appeal of these books, obviously, is that they give substance to the sense we have all had at one time—perhaps most often in early adolescence—that some people, especially authority figures, are phony. The things they do and say seem false and artificial; very possibly they are under the control of evil alien forces.

Another great attraction of the Animorph books is that they provide thrilling, scientifically convincing descriptions of what it might be like to be an animal. (The idea is not new: several famous earlier instances occur in T. H. White's *Sword in the Stone,* where the wizard Merlin turns the future King Arthur into a variety of beasts, including a hawk, a fish, a hedgehog, and a snake.) The four friends have a wonderful time in most of their morphs, though they are happiest as birds. Since they are independent American kids, however, the one morph that freaks them out is the change into ants, who turn out to have no individuality but are only cells of a colony. As one of the heroes puts it, that experience was "gross beyond belief."

In my local bookstore, by far the largest space on the shelves of the   10
children's section is still devoted to the series by R. L. Stine known as "Goosebumps." The first appeared in 1992, and at last count there were 62 volumes in the series, and 5 more in a new Goosebumps 2000 series, plus over 20 spinoffs with names like the Goosebumps Monster Blood Pack and the Goosebumps 365 Scare-a-Day Calendar. Essentially, Goosebumps is Edgar Allan Poe watered down for modern children. The tone alternates between comic and creepy, and in the best tales the horrors are exaggerated versions of everyday juvenile fears and afflictions. In *The Haunted School,* for instance, a sixth grader named Tommy finds his way into a part of the school building that has been boarded up since 1947, when an evil photographer, taking a class picture, caused all 27 children to vanish.

As it turns out, the class has survived for half a century in an alternate world that is entirely black and white, like an old photograph. By this time most of the kids from 1947 have become insane. A few others remain in the classroom in a hopeless, gray condition that will be familiar to anyone who remembers the longest, most colorlessly boring days of their own education: days when, as they sat at their desks, they thought desperately: "This is driving me crazy. Will I ever get out of this room? Or am I doomed to sit here forever?"

The real fears and fantasies of children appear in the books they like best, just as ours do in the ones we read. The only difference is that in children's books there is almost always a way out. You can fly, these stories say; you can escape from the gray half-life of repetitive boredom, even if your parents didn't.

Reading the Text

1. Summarize in your words the books that children enjoy and the books that adults prefer children to read, according to Lurie.
2. What are the typical characters and plot situations of the Animorphs series, and why do they appeal to children?
3. How have today's children's books come to reflect the influence of multiculturalism?
4. What is the significance of Lurie's title, "Reading at Escape Velocity"?

Reading the Signs

1. In your journal, reflect on your own habits of reading as a child. Which books or authors were your favorites? To what extent were your reading habits influenced by other media, such as comic books, film, or TV?

2. Lurie argues that children prefer books that are escapist, while adults prefer that children read books that teach moral lessons. Write an essay that supports, refutes, or complicates her argument.

3. Conduct a survey among friends and relatives on the books they read as children or buy for their own kids. Then write an essay analyzing your results. What are the reasons children or parents consume the children's literature that they do? Can you think of any explanations that your interviewees don't provide?

4. Read one of the adult-preferred books that Lurie mentions, such as E. L. Konigsburg's *View from Saturday* (you might obtain it from the children's section of your local public library). Then write your own analysis of its appeal. Alternately, select one of the child-preferred books, such as one of the Animorphs series, and analyze its appeal to young readers.

CULTURAL
CONSTRUCTIONS

WE'VE COME A
LONG WAY, MAYBE

Gender Codes in American Culture

Monicagate

In January, 1999, *Time* magazine named Bill Clinton and Kenneth Starr "men of the year" for having had the most impact on the news in 1998.

Time could have chosen Monica Lewinsky—because without Lewinsky, there wouldn't have been any scandal for Kenneth Starr to track down or for Bill Clinton to endure. In one sense, Lewinsky got shortchanged. But in another sense, she got lucky: she didn't pay the price that Clinton paid for getting involved in the stickiest scandal ever to hit the White House, and she even stood to make a profit from it. We mention this scandal not to debate what Lewinsky deserved or didn't deserve. We raise it because her role in the scandal that nearly destroyed a presidency dramatically demonstrates the power and durability of some of America's most fundamental gender codes. That role is what we address here.

So set aside for the moment any opinions you may have about Monicagate—about Bill Clinton, Ken Starr, Paula Jones, Linda Tripp, and the whole supporting cast of the failed attempt to remove the president from office in 1999—and consider the basic structure of the situation. A powerful, married man gets involved with a member of the office staff. Although the woman is a fully consenting adult and although sexual harassment isn't the issue, word gets out anyway. Confronted about the matter, the man denies any wrongdoing, splits hairs, finally admits to making mistakes, and asks forgiveness.

It's the sort of story that happens all the time; it just usually doesn't involve the president of the United States apologizing to an entire nation. But note who was asked to apologize and seek forgiveness: it was not the woman, even though evidence suggested that she went after the man rather than vice versa. Indeed, she was offered rewards in the form of book contract deals and invitations (mostly refused) for modeling assignments, both clothed and unclothed. And many pundits seemed to assume that the whole responsibility should be the man's and that he should bear the brunt of the prosecution.

If you find yourself thinking, "Of course the man is responsible in such cases, especially when the man is so much older than the woman," you are reflecting the power of a gender code. A gender code is a culturally constructed belief system that dictates the appropriate roles and behavior for men and women in society. Though often justified on the basis of appeals to the "natural" differences between the two sexes, gender codes usually reflect cultural values rather than natural facts.

In the early 1990s, for example, a young woman named Shannon Faulkner had to go all the way to the U.S. Supreme Court to gain entrance to the Citadel Military Academy. Although by that time women regularly were being admitted to academies like West Point, the Citadel's admissions policy maintained a lingering cultural belief that women don't really belong in the military. This belief continues to be encoded in the fact that women who *are* in the armed services are not allowed to serve in combat units (former Speaker of the House Newt Gingrich justified this ban by insisting that women couldn't fight in the field because they "got infections"—a classic appeal to nature). By contesting the Citadel's admissions policy, Shannon Faulkner was, in effect, challenging a deeply held gender code, and the fuss made about the whole matter illustrates just how emotional such codes can be. When Faulkner finally won her court case and entered the Citadel, she was followed around by hordes of reporters (who carefully reported on everything from her pushup performance to her weight), and when she finally succumbed to the pressure and left, the campus erupted in an ecstatic celebration.

In the Faulkner incident, then, we find the gender code that holds that it is the role of men, not of women, to be warriors: men are the protectors, women are the ones to be protected (women and children first, as they said on the *Titanic*). This code is reinforced by the traditional belief that men are the aggressive sex, while women are passive. In sexual matters, men, accordingly, are expected to be the pursuers (he calls), while women are the pursued (she waits by the phone). Men gaze (upon women), and women are gazed upon (a gender belief that has been made much of in contemporary film analysis, which considers the way a movie camera represents the gaze of a male viewer).

||||||||||||||||||||||||||||||||||||||||||||||||||||||||||||||||||||||||||||||||||||||||||||||||||||||||||||||||||||||||||||||||||||||||||||||||||

Exploring the Signs of Gender

In your journal, explore the expectations about gender roles that you grew up with. What gender norms were you taught by your family, either overtly or implicitly? Have you ever had any conflicts with your parents over "natural" gender roles? If so, how did you resolve them? Do you think your gender-related expectations today are the same as those you had when you were a child?

We could go on and on. Note, though, how in each case gender roles are arrayed across a system of binary oppositions (men are this, women are the opposite). Indeed, these oppositions are so deeply encoded in our culture that you may find yourself protesting that men *are* aggressive, women *are* passive, men (as the bestseller has it) *are* from Mars, women *are* from Venus. But the fact that these roles can be reversed—indeed, they are being reversed more and more often these days—shows that they reflect cultural values rather than natural facts.

This point takes us back to the Clinton-Lewinsky scandal. Because men often are assumed to be the sexual initiators in our society, suggestions that Monica Lewinsky was herself the initiator were brushed aside in Congress's deliberations on the matter. Clinton was held solely responsible. Because older men are supposed to protect younger women, not expose them to risks, Clinton was also expected to apologize to Lewinsky (which he did), but even though Clinton had to pay the price, few expected Lewinsky to apologize to him. And because it is assumed that women are the ones to be gazed upon, it was Lewinsky who was offered modeling jobs (we're not aware of any comparable offers to Bill Clinton).

Interpreting Gender Codes in American Culture

If you still find yourself feeling uneasy about analyzing gender roles, you are not alone, for our gender codes, like any cultural mythology, provide a framework through which we can understand and experience our world. If that framework is disrupted, our world suffers a dislocation, and we accordingly feel threatened. You may think this isn't so, believing, for instance, that women *shouldn't* be in the military. If that's the case, ask yourself why you feel that way. You might think that, because most women have less physical strength than men, they can't be fighters. But consider that other nations, such as Israel, have long included women in their armed forces, and that today much of military prowess depends on technological know-how, not brute force. If you're concerned about women getting "unfair advantages" in the feminist era (one reason some Americans rooted for the Citadel), wouldn't it seem that allowing them to share the dangerous duty of military combat would actually be the opposite of a privilege?

That many Americans, women as well as men, don't always see it this way shows just how durable our gender codes are. It thus is one of the major tasks of cultural semiotics to expose the outlines of gender myths to reveal just how deeply they influence our lives. Think of how these myths may shape your own behavior. Traditionally, for instance, the myths that govern courtship in America dictate that the man pays the expenses on a date and is responsible for all the logistics, even providing transportation and a destination. But there is no natural reason for this to be so; it's just a cultural expectation, one that has been changing for some time. Ask yourself: Who pays when you date? Who drives? Do you even care? Your answers will help you find your place in today's shifting terrain of gender myths.

In examining the gender myths that influence your own life, you should recognize the difference between the biological category of *sex* and the cultural category of *gender*. Your sex is determined by your chromosomes, but your gender goes beyond your sex to the roles that society has determined are appropriate for you. Your sex, in other words, is your birthright, but the roles you play in society are largely determined by your culture. In everyday life, however, this distinction between the natural category of sex and the cultural category of gender is blurred because socially determined gender roles are regarded as naturally dictated sexual necessities. To return for a moment to one of the codes that was involved in the Clinton-Lewinsky scandal, Western culture traditionally has assumed that women naturally are the attractive sex, designed to be looked at, while men are natural voyeurs, made to do the looking. This myth is related to the belief that the male sex drive is more active than the female's. Both myths are represented in a tradition of European art, which is filled with female nudes but hardly any male ones. Just consider how *Playboy* and *Penthouse* enjoy subscriptions in the millions, while *Playgirl* struggles along in the shadows.

If you think this is obviously the way of nature, consider ancient Greek art, which, from its introduction of the *kouros* (a sculpted figure of a nude male) into art more than two thousand years ago, was at least as interested in the male form as in the female. The example of the Greeks tells us that there is nothing in nature to dictate whose body, male or female, will be considered more attractive. At the same time, the Greeks can show just how much we presume that the roles our gender myths define for us will be heterosexually oriented. For as ancient Greece reminds us, cultures may be homoerotic as well.

Even the standards of beauty that men as well as women are held to are culturally determined. The ideal medieval woman, for example, was short, slender, high-waisted, small-breasted, and boasted a high, domed forehead whose effect she enhanced by shaving her hairline. By the Renaissance, she had filled out considerably, and in the paintings of Peter Paul Rubens could appear positively pudgy by contemporary standards (we even have an adjective, *Rubenesque,* for well-padded feminine beauty). In more recent times, we have seen a shift from the hour-glass figures of the fifties to the aerobically muscled hard bodies of the nineties. You may assume that this is it, the last stop, the one truly beautiful body, but stick around. Wait to see what's fashionable in bodies in the years to come.

Men, too, have seen their bodily ideals change over time. The ideal man of the eighteenth century, for example, was a rather heavyset fellow, rounded in appearance, and with a hint of a double chin, while today's ideal (especially in the corporate world) has square-hewn features and a jutting jaw (cleft if possible: just look at some ads for business-oriented services to see what today's businessman wants to look like). Now think for a moment: What would you look like if you had the choice? Would you look like the ideal of the 1950s or 1960s? Would you be long and lean or buff courtesy of Nautilus?

Backlash

Because of the political stakes involved, the semiotic unmasking of gender myths has not gone unchallenged in America. For once a myth has been identified, it can be questioned or altered. Thus, in the wake of the feminist revival of the seventies, the eighties saw something of a backlash. It became culturally fashionable to embrace a "new traditionalism" that really meant going back to the old mythology that had been questioned the decade before. Indeed, by the late 1980s *Time* had declared that feminism was dead and that Wonder Woman and the ERA were henceforth to be regarded as things of the past, as obsolete as Nehru jackets and Earth shoes.

The media exulted. More and more women, the media exclaimed, were worrying about their "biological clocks" and whether their careers were adequate compensation for the traditional roles they supposedly abandoned. Thanks to an article by Felice Schwartz in the *Harvard Business Review*, a new myth emerged about businesswomen who were now willing to settle for a kind of second-class corporate citizenship (dubbed the *mommy track*) rather than miss out on the joys of motherhood. The postfeminist era, the media declared, had arrived.

According to Susan Faludi's study of the phenomenon, *Backlash,* such declarations were simply part of a nationwide assault on the women's movement, an invention of trends that had little basis in reality but whose effect was to create some of the very anxieties that were eagerly predicted. To convince American women to return home and have children (as women should do, according to the traditional mythology), the media showered us with unsubstantiated stories of yuppie infertility, angst, and fears of spinsterhood. Meanwhile, parenting became a top pop cultural activity—as it remains today. Returning to "traditional values"—in other words, returning to the docile gender roles imposed on women in the fifties and sixties—became the media's new theme. Suddenly everyone wanted to get into the baby game. Can you think of some recent movies or TV shows that exemplify this trend? How have children become our newest media stars?

At the same time, the very word *feminism* itself was demonized. Women around the country, from the college campus to the kitchen, insisted to interviewers that "yes, of course, they were for women's rights, but they were not feminists." Have you ever found yourself making the same declaration? Why? What images come to mind when you think of the word *feminist*? Are those images realistic, or are they, too, myths? And whether you are male or female, what reactions do you get when you do declare that you are a feminist?

Perhaps because of the controversy, the image of feminism in America today is potent. Just consider what happened to Hillary Rodham Clinton during the 1992 presidential campaign. An outspoken feminist with a successful corporate law career of her own, she had gone on record declaring that she was not the type to stay at home and bake cookies. Quite a ruckus ensued, much of which was generated by women who denounced her supposed arrogance and defended their own choice to accept the traditional woman's role as homemaker. The image of the typical feminist, for such women, was that of a privileged, college-educated white woman who sneered at women who weren't as successful as she. And while this image, like so many images, was mostly myth, Bill Clinton deemed it safest to remove his wife from the campaign spotlight until the election was safely won.

Discussing the Signs of Gender

Bring to class a magazine that targets one gender (such as *Maxim* or *Marie Claire*). In small groups, study both the articles and the advertising in your sample magazines, focusing on the gender roles assumed for men and women. List the major roles on the board by magazine title. What patterns do you find? Do some magazines adhere to traditional roles, while others depart from them? How can you account for your findings?

By the end of the decade, however, Hillary Clinton had made a public relations comeback in a manner that was entirely in keeping with traditional gender myths. Publishing her book *It Takes a Village*, the First Lady became the nation's "first mother" by focusing her attention on child rearing, traditionally a female gender role. The media reinforced this image by showing her cope with "the empty nest syndrome" when daughter Chelsea went away to college. And Hillary Clinton won a lot of sympathy in the wake of the Lewinsky scandal as a wronged wife. So popular had Hillary Clinton suddenly become by 1999 that she was seriously considering running for the Senate in the year 2000.

But while America's political culture continues to reinforce the traditional gender codes, America's consumer culture has found a way of taking advantage of women's desires for new, nontraditional gender roles. In campaigns like Virginia Slims' long-running pitch for cigarettes, women are invited to imagine themselves as liberated consumers, free at last to smoke when and where they please. The "new woman" who appears in so many ads today is someone who goes out and buys her own Honda without male advice or chooses a new hair color "just for herself." She purchases Esprit fashions because she is politically aware or Nike sportswear because she believes in herself. But what is really happening? Why would advertisers adopt a "feminist" stance to sell their products? How are they appealing to their market?

The Revenge of the Gorgon

America's consumer culture is perfectly comfortable with the image of the feminist as an avid, if independent, shopper (just look at the heroine of the cartoon strip "Cathy"), but things get dicey when women assert themselves in other ways, especially sexually. Our culture is quite happy with a woman who is sexually *available*, but not when she is a sexual *aggressor*. And when she is both aggressive and bisexual, then America really gets uncomfortable. The horrific nature of the Sharon Stone character in the film *Basic Instinct* is a potent sign of just how America views the image of the sexually predatory, bisexual woman. She becomes, in short, a monster.

Women with their own ideas about sexuality have been viewed this way for a long time. Consider the ancient Greek legend of Perseus and Medusa. Medusa is the name of a monster with the body of a woman, a head curling with writhing snakes, and a stare that reduces men to stone. By cutting off Medusa's head, Perseus became one of the heroes of Greek mythology. But that's only when the tale is read from a traditional perspective. From a feminist perspective, it looks quite different.

For the writhing snakes on Medusa's head suggest other snakes, the two snakes held in the grasp of figurines unearthed in the ruins of the ancient Minoan culture of Crete. Perhaps you've seen her: the image of a goddesslike woman holding two snakes in her hands, standing imperiously in a bare-breasted pose. There is a possibility that the ancient Minoans worshipped her in what may have been a matriarchal, or women-centered, culture. But that culture was eventually overrun by the patriarchal Greeks, and the beautiful Minoan snake goddess vanished. Medusa, as read in a feminist key, is the goddess's patriarchal replacement: a warning to powerful women. For a modern parallel, consider how a woman with "big hair" (say, a snaky perm) is viewed in the male-dominated corporate world. Isn't she, too, pressured to control her locks by a male-defined dress code and forced to appear less sexy in the workplace and, hence, less threatening?

For feminist semioticians, such myths as Medusa's reflect a continuous history of male control, and what men have attempted especially to control is female sexuality. Consider how our culture still encourages young men to "sow their wild oats" but raises its collective eyebrows at the sexually active woman. Indeed, in the traditional sexual mythology, women are offered only three roles: the part of the virginal bride (soon to be a socially approved mother), of the whore, and of the castrating witch (these last two roles may be mixed, as in the figure of Delilah, who is both whore and castrator in the biblical story of Samson's fall). Now, recall *Basic Instinct*. How is the Sharon Stone character like Delilah? Which role does the Michael Douglas character want Stone to play? Is there a "witch" figure in the cast? How, in short, is *Basic Instinct* a veritable display case of America's traditional sexual mythology?

Iron John

Men, too, are influenced by mythic images. Men, as we've seen, are supposed to be warriors (he who flinches is a "coward") and studs (have you ever said "What a stud!" to mean "What a great guy"?). Just think of the typical Big Man on Campus. Is he not likely to be an athlete (the warrior role on a school campus) and a sexual star? What do you think of the guy who avoids athletics and doesn't "score"? How popular is he? With whom?

The men's movement in America, currently led by such writers as Robert Bly, has arisen alongside the women's movement to challenge the traditional masculine gender roles that require men to be aggressive, competitive, and unemotional. In his bestseller *Iron John*, Bly calls for an exploration of both the masculine and the feminine sides of male being. Thus, Bly's drum-beating warrior has a sensitive side, which distinguishes him from the sort of Conan the Barbarian hero America's popular culture continues to admire. How else could we explain the rise of Arnold Schwartzenegger to the top of the Hollywood heap?

Indeed, the images that are shaping your own sense of gender identity are playing now at a theater near you. Start there, or with TV or MTV. What are you being told about your sexual identity? What stars are you supposed to emulate? What images do you avoid? What does a "real man" look like on screen? How about a "real woman"? Do you ever wish that they would just "get real"?

Gender Bending

Probably the most deeply held gender codes in our culture are those that define our sexual orientation. So fundamental are such codes to our sense of personal and social identity that it is still rather controversial even to analyze them. Surely, you may believe, sexual orientation is determined by nature. What has culture to do with it?

But a growing number of scholars engaged in gender studies are questioning the natural determination of sexual orientation. This is especially true for those involved in "queer theory," a movement that deliberately takes a once-pejorative term and subverts it to signify the dismantling of traditional gender norms. For such scholars, the categories of human sexuality, too, are social constructions, inscribing cultural rather than natural divisions. For example, what counts as homosexual behavior in American culture is not necessarily considered homosexual in other cultures, as could be seen when in the early 1980s many of the Haitian men who came down with AIDS denied being homosexual (they were bisexual) because in their cultural code bisexuality and homosexuality are clearly distinguished from each other, as they are not in America.

The most dramatic signs that America's codes governing sexual orientation are shifting can be seen not in the scholarly publications of queer theorists, however, but in the products of popular culture. When *Newsweek* ran a cover story on the new bisexuality in the early 1990s, few protested. Similarly, as you can see in our analysis of an episode of *Friends* in Chapter 3, no great fuss was made when the show dramatized a lesbian marriage in 1996 (a greater fuss occurred a few years earlier when

Reading Gender on the Net

Use search engines such as Yahoo or Infoseek to research what issues are considered "male" and "female" territory on the Internet. Focus your search on a comparison of specific topics, such as "men's rights" and "women's rights." Compare your findings with those of your classmates.

Roseanne featured a lesbian kiss). In popular music, both Boy George and Marilyn Manson have attracted huge followings through their gender-bending antics. And the coming out of Ellen DeGeneres on her sitcom *Ellen* was one of the most-watched television programs in history, an episode that prompted a lot of clucking from the religious right but that was more remarkable for the fact that it aired at all.

We aren't telling you to applaud or to condemn these signifiers of change in American gender codes: we are simply drawing your attention to them. The fact that you may feel strongly about the matter is itself a signifier of the powerful hold our value systems have on us. Gender values take us to the core of our sense of ourselves as individual and social beings, involving religious and moral beliefs that have recently become a central component of our country's political system. And this too is a sign of the essentially political nature of our social codes or mythologies, for if our values weren't political, they wouldn't be entered into the electoral process. So the analysis of gender codes in America isn't simply an academic exercise: it is a social and political activity that will affect you well beyond the classroom.

The Readings

Our chapter begins with Holly Devor's analysis of gender roles and the ways in which men and women manipulate the signs by which we traditionally communicate our gender identity. Deborah Blum follows with an article suggesting that biology *does* play a role in gender identity and that we can best understand the gender gap by looking at both the cultural and the physiological determinants of human behavior. Michael A. Messner's study of the ways in which athletic competition constructs gender identity in America comes next, while Jennifer Scanlon analyzes the effect of children's board games on adolescent girls. Naomi Wolf's indictment of the "beauty myth" that forces otherwise liberated women to feel trapped inside their own bodies follows. Deborah Tannen then looks at the way women are always "marked" in our society: no detail of a woman's appearance, from her hair to her shoes to her name, fails to send a gender-coded message about her, Tannen argues. James William Gibson's analysis of the warrior fantasies that have arisen in the wake of the Vietnam War and the rise of feminism sounds a warning note in the politics of gender identity, and Laura Miller concludes the chapter with a challenge to the widespread assumption that women are second-class citizens on the Net, needing special protection against sexual harassment.

HOLLY DEVOR
Gender Role Behaviors and Attitudes

‖‖‖

"Boys will be boys, and girls will be girls": few of our cultural mythologies seem as natural as this one. But in this exploration of the gender signals that traditionally tell what a "boy" or "girl" is supposed to look and act like, Holly Devor (b. 1951) shows how these signals are not "natural" at all but instead are cultural constructs. While the classic cues of masculinity — aggressive posture, self-confidence, a tough appearance — and the traditional signs of femininity — gentleness, passivity, strong nurturing instincts — are often considered "normal," Devor explains that they are by no means biological or psychological necessities. Indeed, she suggests, they can be richly mixed and varied, or to paraphrase the old Kinks song, "Lola," "Boys can be girls and girls can be boys." Holly Devor is a professor of sociology at the University of Victoria and is the author of Gender Blending: Confronting the Limits of Duality *(1989), from which this selection is excerpted, and* FTM: Female-to-Male Transsexuals in Society *(1997).*

Gender Role Behaviors and Attitudes

The clusters of social definitions used to identify persons by gender are collectively known as "femininity" and "masculinity." Masculine characteristics are used to identify persons as males, while feminine ones are used as signifiers for femaleness. People use femininity or masculinity to claim and communicate their membership in their assigned, or chosen, sex or gender. Others recognize our sex or gender more on the basis of these characteristics than on the basis of sex characteristics, which are usually largely covered by clothing in daily life.

These two clusters of attributes are most commonly seen as mirror images of one another with masculinity usually characterized by dominance and aggression, and femininity by passivity and submission. A more even-handed description of the social qualities subsumed by femininity and masculinity might be to label masculinity as generally concerned with egoistic dominance and femininity as striving for cooperation or communion.[1]

---

1. Eleanor Maccoby, *Social Development: Psychological Growth and the Parent-Child Relationship* (New York: Harcourt, Brace, Jovanovich, 1980), p. 217. Egoistic dominance is a striving for superior rewards for oneself or a competitive striving to reduce the rewards for one's competitors even if such action will not increase one's own rewards. Persons who are motivated by desires for egoistic dominance not only wish the best for themselves but also wish to diminish the advantages of others whom they may perceive as competing with them.

Characterizing femininity and masculinity in such a way does not portray the two clusters of characteristics as being in a hierarchical relationship to one another but rather as being two different approaches to the same question, that question being centrally concerned with the goals, means, and use of power. Such an alternative conception of gender roles captures the hierarchical and competitive masculine thirst for power, which can, but need not, lead to aggression, and the feminine quest for harmony and communal well-being, which can, but need not, result in passivity and dependence.

Many activities and modes of expression are recognized by most members of society as feminine. Any of these can be, and often are, displayed by persons of either gender. In some cases, cross-gender behaviors are ignored by observers, and therefore do not compromise the integrity of a person's gender display. In other cases, they are labeled as inappropriate gender role behaviors. Although these behaviors are closely linked to sexual status in the minds and experiences of most people, research shows that dominant persons of either gender tend to use influence tactics and verbal styles usually associated with men and masculinity, while subordinate persons, of either gender, tend to use those considered to be the province of women.[2] Thus it seems likely that many aspects of masculinity and femininity are the result, rather than the cause, of status inequalities.

Popular conceptions of femininity and masculinity instead revolve around hierarchical appraisals of the "natural" roles of males and females. Members of both genders are believed to share many of the same human characteristics, although in different relative proportions; both males and females are popularly thought to be able to do many of the same things, but most activities are divided into suitable and unsuitable categories for each gender class. Persons who perform the activities considered appropriate for another gender will be expected to perform them poorly; if they succeed adequately, or even well, at their endeavors, they may be rewarded with ridicule or scorn for blurring the gender dividing line.

The patriarchal gender schema currently in use in mainstream North American society reserves highly valued attributes for males and actively supports the high evaluation of any characteristics which might inadvertently become associated with maleness. The ideology underlying the schema postulates that the cultural superiority of males is a natural outgrowth of the innate predisposition of males toward aggression and dominance, which is assumed to flow inevitably from evolutionary and biological sources. Female attributes are likewise postulated to find their

5

---

2. Judith Howard, Philip Blumstein, and Pepper Schwartz, "Sex, Power, and Influence Tactics in Intimate Relationships," *Journal of Personality and Social Psychology* 51 (1986), pp. 102–109; Peter Kollock, Philip Blumstein, and Pepper Schwartz, "Sex and Power in Interaction: Conversational Privileges and Duties," *American Sociological Review* 50 (1985), pp. 34–46.

source in innate predispositions acquired in the evolution of the species. Feminine characteristics are thought to be intrinsic to the female facility for childbirth and breastfeeding. Hence, it is popularly believed that the social position of females is biologically mandated to be intertwined with the care of children and a "natural" dependency on men for the maintenance of mother-child units. Thus the goals of femininity and, by implication, of all biological females are presumed to revolve around heterosexuality and maternity.[3]

Femininity, according to this traditional formulation, "would result in warm and continued relationships with men, a sense of maternity, interest in caring for children, and the capacity to work productively and continuously in female occupations.[4] This recipe translates into a vast number of proscriptions and prescriptions. Warm and continued relations with men and an interest in maternity require that females be heterosexually oriented. A heterosexual orientation requires women to dress, move, speak, and act in ways that men will find attractive. As patriarchy has reserved active expressions of power as a masculine attribute, femininity must be expressed through modes of dress, movement, speech, and action which communicate weakness, dependency, ineffectualness, availability for sexual or emotional service, and sensitivity to the needs of others.

Some, but not all, of these modes of interrelation also serve the demands of maternity and many female job ghettos. In many cases, though, femininity is not particularly useful in maternity or employment. Both mothers and workers often need to be strong, independent, and effectual in order to do their jobs well. Thus femininity, as a role, is best suited to satisfying a masculine vision of heterosexual attractiveness.

Body postures and demeanors which communicate subordinate status and vulnerability to trespass through a message of "no threat" make people appear to be feminine. They demonstrate subordination through a minimizing of spatial use: People appear feminine when they keep their arms closer to their bodies, their legs closer together, and their torsos and heads less vertical than do masculine-looking individuals. People also look feminine when they point their toes inward and use their hands in small or childlike gestures. Other people also tend to stand closer to people they see as feminine, often invading their personal space, while people who make frequent appeasement gestures, such as smiling, also give the appearance of femininity. Perhaps as an outgrowth of a subordinate status and the need to avoid conflict with more socially powerful

---

3. Nancy Chodorow, *The Reproduction of Mothering: Psychoanalysis and the Reproduction of Mothering* (Berkeley: University of California Press, 1978), p. 134.

4. Jon K. Meyer and John E. Hoopes, "The Gender Dysphoria Syndromes: A Position Statement on So-Called 'Transsexualism,'" *Plastic and Reconstructive Surgery* 54 (Oct. 1974), pp. 444–51.

people, women tend to excel over men at the ability to correctly interpret, and effectively display, nonverbal communication cues.[5]

Speech characterized by inflections, intonations, and phrases that
convey nonaggression and subordinate status also make a speaker appear
more feminine. Subordinate speakers who use more polite expressions
and ask more questions in conversation seem more feminine. Speech
characterized by sounds of higher frequencies are often interpreted by listeners as feminine, childlike, and ineffectual.[6] Feminine styles of dress
likewise display subordinate status through greater restriction of the free
movement of the body, greater exposure of the bare skin, and an emphasis on sexual characteristics. The more gender distinct the dress, the more
this is the case.

Masculinity, like femininity, can be demonstrated through a wide   10
variety of cues. Pleck has argued that it is commonly expressed in North
American society through the attainment of some level of proficiency at
some, or all, of the following four main attitudes of masculinity. Persons
who display success and high status in their social group, who exhibit "a
manly air of toughness, confidence, and self-reliance" and "the aura of
aggression, violence, and daring," and who conscientiously avoid anything associated with femininity are seen as exuding masculinity.[7] These
requirements reflect the patriarchal ideology that masculinity results from
an excess of testosterone, the assumption being that androgens supply a
natural impetus toward aggression, which in turn impels males toward
achievement and success. This vision of masculinity also reflects the ideological stance that ideal maleness (masculinity) must remain untainted by
female (feminine) pollutants.

Masculinity, then, requires of its actors that they organize themselves
and their society in a hierarchical manner so as to be able to explicitly
quantify the achievement of success. The achievement of high status in
one's social group requires competitive and aggressive behavior from
those who wish to obtain it. Competition which is motivated by a goal
of individual achievement, or egoistic dominance, also requires of its participants a degree of emotional insensitivity to feelings of hurt and loss in

---

5. Erving Goffman, *Gender Advertisements* (New York: Harper Colophon Books,
1976); Judith A. Hall, *Non-Verbal Sex Differences: Communication Accuracy and Expressive
Style* (Baltimore: Johns Hopkins University Press, 1984); Nancy M. Henley, *Body Politics: Power, Sex and Non-Verbal Communication* (Englewood Cliffs, N.J.: Prentice-Hall,
1979); Marianne Wex, *"Let's Take Back Our Space": "Female" and "Male" Body Language as a Result of Patriarchal Structures* (Berlin: Frauenliteraturverlag Hermine Fees,
1979).

6. Karen L. Adams, "Sexism and the English Language: The Linguistic Implications of Being a Woman," in *Women: A Feminist Perspective,* 3rd ed., ed. Jo Freeman
(Palo Alto, Calif.: Mayfield, 1984), pp. 478–91; Hall, pp. 37, 130–37.

7. Joseph H. Pleck, *The Myth of Masculinity* (Cambridge, Mass.: MIT Press, 1981),
p. 139.

defeated others, and a measure of emotional insularity to protect oneself from becoming vulnerable to manipulation by others. Such values lead those who subscribe to them to view feminine persons as "born losers" and to strive to eliminate any similarities to feminine people from their own personalities. In patriarchally organized societies, masculine values become the ideological structure of the society as a whole. Masculinity thus becomes "innately" valuable and femininity serves a contrapuntal function to delineate and magnify the hierarchical dominance of masculinity.

Body postures, speech patterns, and styles of dress which demonstrate and support the assumption of dominance and authority convey an impression of masculinity. Typical masculine body postures tend to be expansive and aggressive. People who hold their arms and hands in positions away from their bodies, and who stand, sit, or lie with their legs apart — thus maximizing the amount of space that they physically occupy — appear most physically masculine. Persons who communicate an air of authority or a readiness for aggression by standing erect and moving forcefully also tend to appear more masculine. Movements that are abrupt and stiff, communicating force and threat rather than flexibility and cooperation, make an actor look masculine. Masculinity can also be conveyed by stern or serious facial expressions that suggest minimal receptivity to the influence of others, a characteristic which is an important element in the attainment and maintenance of egoistic dominance.[8]

Speech and dress which likewise demonstrate or claim superior status are also seen as characteristically masculine behavior patterns. Masculine speech patterns display a tendency toward expansiveness similar to that found in masculine body postures. People who attempt to control the direction of conversations seem more masculine. Those who tend to speak more loudly, use less polite and more assertive forms, and tend to interrupt the conversations of others more often also communicate masculinity to others. Styles of dress which emphasize the size of upper body musculature, allow freedom of movement, and encourage an illusion of physical power and a look of easy physicality all suggest masculinity. Such appearances of strength and readiness to action serve to create or enhance an aura of aggressiveness and intimidation central to an appearance of masculinity. Expansive postures and gestures combine with these qualities to insinuate that a position of secure dominance is a masculine one.

Gender role characteristics reflect the ideological contentions underlying the dominant gender schema in North American society. That schema leads us to believe that female and male behaviors are the result of socially directed hormonal instructions which specify that females will

8. Goffman; Hall; Henley; Wex.

want to have children and will therefore find themselves relatively help-less and dependent on males for support and protection. The schema claims that males are innately aggressive and competitive and therefore will dominate over females. The social hegemony of this ideology en-sures that we are all raised to practice gender roles which will confirm this vision of the nature of the sexes. Fortunately, our training to gender roles is neither complete nor uniform. As a result, it is possible to point to multitudinous exceptions to, and variations on, these themes. Biologi-cal evidence is equivocal about the source of gender roles; psychological androgyny is a widely accepted concept. It seems most likely that gender roles are the result of systematic power imbalances based on gender discrimination.[9]

Reading the Text

1. List the characteristics that Devor describes as being traditional concep-tions of "masculinity" and "femininity" (para. 1).
2. What relationship does Devor see between characteristics considered mas-culine and feminine?
3. How does Devor explain the cultural belief in the "superiority" (para. 5) of males?
4. How, according to Devor, do speech and dress communicate gender roles?

Reading the Signs

1. In small same-sex groups, brainstorm lists of traits that you consider mas-culine and feminine, and then have each group write their lists on the board. Compare the lists produced by male and female groups. What pat-terns of differences or similarities do you see? To what extent do the traits presume a heterosexual orientation? How do you account for your re-sults?
2. Study the speech patterns, styles of dress, and other nonverbal cues com-municated by your friends during a social occasion, such as a party, trying not to reveal that you are observing them for an assignment. Then write an essay in which you analyze these cues used by your friends. To what extent do your friends enact the traditional gender roles Devor describes?
3. Look through a popular magazine such as *Vogue, Rolling Stone,* or *Maxim* for advertisements that depict men and women interacting with each other. Then write an essay in which you interpret the body postures of the models, using Devor's selection as your framework for analysis. How do males and females typically stand? To what extent do the models enact

---

9. Howard, Blumstein, and Schwartz; Kollock, Blumstein, and Schwartz.

stereotypically masculine or feminine stances? To develop your essay, consult Diane Barthel, "A Gentleman and a Consumer" (p. 149).

4. Devor argues that female fashion traditionally has restricted body movement while male styles of dress have commonly allowed freedom of movement. In class, discuss whether this gender division is still true today, being sure to consider a range of clothing types (e.g., athletic wear, corporate dress, party fashion, and so forth).

DEBORAH BLUM

The Gender Blur: Where Does Biology End and Society Take Over?

‖‖‖

There's an old argument over whether nature or nurture is more important in determining human behavior. Nowhere is this argument more intense than in gender studies, where proponents of the social construction of gender identities are currently exploring the many ways in which our upbringing shapes our behavior. But after watching her two-year-old son emphatically choose to play only with carnivorous dinosaur toys and disdainfully reject the "wimpy" vegetarian variety, Deborah Blum decided that nurture couldn't be all that there was to it. Exploring the role of biology in the determination of human behavior, Blum argues that both nature and nurture have to be taken into account if we are to understand gender differences. A Pulitzer Prize–winning professor of journalism at the University of Wisconsin at Madison, Blum is the author of Sex on the Brain: The Biological Differences between Men and Women *(1997).*

I was raised in one of those university-based, liberal elite families that politicians like to ridicule. In my childhood, every human being—regardless of gender—was exactly alike under the skin, and I mean exactly, barring his or her different opportunities. My parents wasted no opportunity to bring this point home. One Christmas, I received a Barbie doll and a softball glove. Another brought a green enamel stove, which baked tiny cakes by the heat of a lightbulb, and also a set of steel-tipped darts and competition-quality dartboard. Did I mention the year of the chemistry set and the ballerina doll?

It wasn't until I became a parent—I should say, a parent of two boys—that I realized I had been fed a line and swallowed it like a sucker (barring the part about opportunities, which I still believe). This dawned on me during my older son's dinosaur phase, which began when he was about 2½. Oh, he loved dinosaurs, all right, but only the blood-swilling carnivores. Plant-eaters were wimps and losers, and he refused to wear a T-shirt marred by a picture of a stegosaur. I looked down at him one day, as he was snarling around my feet and doing his toddler best to gnaw off my right leg, and I thought: This goes a lot deeper than culture.

Raising children tends to bring on this kind of politically incorrect reaction. Another friend came to the same conclusion watching a son determinedly bite his breakfast toast into the shape of a pistol he hoped would blow away—or at least terrify—his younger brother. Once you get past the guilt part—Did I do this? Should I have bought him that plastic allosaur with the oversized teeth?—such revelations can lead you to consider the far more interesting field of gender biology, where the questions take a different shape: Does love of carnage begin in culture or genetics, and which drives which? Do the gender roles of our culture reflect an underlying biology, and, in turn, does the way we behave influence that biology?

The point I'm leading up to—through the example of my son's innocent love of predatory dinosaurs—is actually one of the most straightforward in this debate. One of the reasons we're so fascinated by childhood behaviors is that, as the old saying goes, the child becomes the man (or woman, of course). Most girls don't spend their preschool years snarling around the house and pretending to chew off their companion's legs. And they—mostly—don't grow up to be as aggressive as men. Do the ways that we amplify those early differences in childhood shape the adults we become? Absolutely. But it's worth exploring the starting place—the faint signal that somehow gets amplified.

"There's plenty of room in society to influence sex differences," says   5
Marc Breedlove, a behavioral endocrinologist at the University of California at Berkeley and a pioneer in defining how hormones can help build sexually different nervous systems. "Yes, we're born with predispositions, but it's society that amplifies them, exaggerates them. I believe that—except for the sex differences in aggression. Those [differences] are too massive to be explained simply by society."

Aggression does allow a straightforward look at the issue. Consider the following statistics: Crime reports in both the United States and Europe record between 10 and 15 robberies committed by men for every one by a woman. At one point, people argued that this was explained by size difference. Women weren't big enough to intimidate, but that would change, they predicted, with the availability of compact weapons. But just as little girls don't routinely make weapons out of toast, women—even criminal ones—don't seem drawn to weaponry in the same way that men are. Almost twice as many male thieves and robbers use guns as their female counterparts do.

Or you can look at more personal crimes: domestic partner murders.

Three-fourths of men use guns in those killings; 50 percent of women do. Here's more from the domestic front: In conflicts in which a woman killed a man, he tended to be the one who had started the fight—in 51.8 percent of the cases, to be exact. When the man was the killer, he again was the likely first aggressor, and by an even more dramatic margin. In fights in which women died, they had started the argument only 12.5 percent of the time.

Enough. You can parade endless similar statistics but the point is this: Males are more aggressive, not just among humans but among almost all species on earth. Male chimpanzees, for instance, declare war on neighboring troops, and one of their strategies is a warning strike: They kill females and infants to terrorize and intimidate. In terms of simple, reproductive genetics, it's an advantage of males to be aggressive: You can muscle your way into dominance, winning more sexual encounters, more offspring, more genetic future. For the female—especially in a species like ours, with time for just one successful pregnancy a year—what's the genetic advantage in brawling?

Thus the issue becomes not whether there is a biologically influenced sex difference in aggression—the answer being a solid, technical "You betcha"—but rather how rigid that difference is. The best science, in my opinion, tends to align with basic common sense. We all know that there are extraordinarily gentle men and murderous women. Sex differences are always generalizations: they refer to a behavior, with some evolutionary rationale behind it. They never define, entirely, an individual. And that fact alone should tell us that there's always—even in the most biologically dominated traits—some flexibility, an instinctive ability to respond, for better and worse, to the world around us.

This is true even with physical characteristics that we've often assumed are nailed down by genetics. Scientists now believe height, for instance, is only about 90 percent heritable. A person's genes might code for a six-foot-tall body, but malnutrition could literally cut that short. And there's also some evidence, in girls anyway, that children with stressful childhoods tend to become shorter adults. So while some factors are predetermined, there's evidence that the prototypical male/female body design can be readily altered.   10

It's a given that humans, like most other species—bananas, spiders, sharks, ducks, any rabbit you pull out of a hat—rely on two sexes for reproduction. So basic is that requirement that we have chromosomes whose primary purpose is to deliver the genes that order up a male or a female. All other chromosomes are numbered, but we label the sex chromosomes with the letters X and Y. We get one each from our mother and our father, and the basic combinations are these: XX makes female, XY makes male.

There are two important—and little known—points about these chromosomal matches. One is that even with this apparently precise system, there's nothing precise—or guaranteed—about the physical construction of male and female. The other point makes that possible. It appears that sex doesn't matter in the early stages of embryonic development. We are unisex at the point of conception.

If you examine an embryo at about six weeks, you see that it has the ability to develop in either direction. The fledgling embryo has two sets of ducts—Wolffian for male, Muellerian for female—an either/or structure, held in readiness for further development. If testosterone and other androgens are released by hormone-producing cells, then the Wolffian ducts develop into the channel that connects penis to testes, and the female ducts wither away.

Without testosterone, the embryo takes on a female form; the male ducts vanish and the Muellerian ducts expand into oviducts, uterus, and vagina. In other words, in humans, anyways (the opposite is true in birds), the female is the default sex. Back in the 1950s, the famed biologist Alfred Jost showed that if you castrate a male rabbit fetus, choking off testosterone, you produce a completely feminized rabbit.

We don't do these experiments in humans—for obvious reasons— 15
but there are naturally occurring instances that prove the same point. For instance: In the fetal testes are a group of cells, called Leydig cells, that make testosterone. In rare cases, the fetus doesn't make enough of these cells (a defect known as Leydig cell hypoplasia). In this circumstance we see the limited power of the XY chromosome. These boys have the right chromosomes and the right genes to be boys; they just don't grow a penis. Obstetricians and parents often think they see a baby girl, and these children are routinely raised as daughters. Usually, the "mistake" is caught about the time of puberty, when menstruation doesn't start. A doctor's examination shows the child to be internally male; there are usually small testes, often tucked within the abdomen. As the researchers put it, if the condition had been known from the beginning, "the sisters would have been born as brothers."

Just to emphasize how tricky all this body-building can get, there's a peculiar genetic defect that seems to be clustered by heredity in a small group of villages in the Dominican Republic. The result of the defect is a failure to produce an enzyme that concentrates testosterone, specifically for building the genitals. One obscure little enzyme only, but here's what happens without it: You get a boy with undescended testes and a penis so short and stubby that it resembles an oversized clitoris.

In the mountain villages of this Caribbean nation, people are used to it. The children are usually raised as "conditional" girls. At puberty, the secondary tide of androgens rises and is apparently enough to finish the construction project. The scrotum suddenly descends, the phallus grows, and the child develops a distinctly male body—narrow hips, muscular build, and even slight beard growth. At that point, the family shifts the child over from daughter to son. The dresses are thrown out. He begins to wear male clothes and starts dating girls. People in the Dominican Republic are so familiar with this condition that there's a colloquial name for it: *guevedoces,* meaning "eggs (or testes) at 12."

It's the comfort level with this slip-slide of sexual identity that's so remarkable and, I imagine, so comforting to the children involved. I'm positive that the sexual transition of these children is less traumatic than the abrupt awareness of the "sisters who would have been brothers." There's a message of tolerance there, well worth repeating, and there are some other key lessons too.

These defects are rare and don't alter the basic male-female division of our species. They do emphasize how fragile those divisions can be. Biology allows flexibility, room to change, to vary and grow. With that comes room for error as well. That it's possible to live with these genetic defects, that they don't merely kill us off, is a reminder that we, male and female alike, exist on a continuum of biological possibilities that can overlap and sustain either sex.

Marc Breedlove points out that the most difficult task may be separating how the brain responds to hormones from how the brain responds to the *results* of hormones. Which brings us back, briefly, below the belt: In this context, the penis is just a result, the product of androgens at work before birth. "And after birth," says Breedlove, "virtually everyone who interacts with that individual will note that he has a penis, and will, in many instances, behave differently than if the individual was a female." 20

Do the ways that we amplify physical and behavioral differences in childhood shape who we become as adults? Absolutely. But to understand that, you have to understand the differences themselves—their beginning and the very real biochemistry that may lie behind them.

Here is a good place to focus on testosterone—a hormone that is both well-studied and generally underrated. First, however, I want to acknowledge that there are many other hormones and neurotransmitters that appear to influence behavior. Preliminary work shows that fetal boys are a little more active than fetal girls. It's pretty difficult to argue socialization at that point. There's a strong suspicion that testosterone may create the difference.

And there are a couple of relevant animal models to emphasize the point. Back in the 1960s, Robert Goy, a psychologist at the University of Wisconsin at Madison, first documented that young male monkeys play much more roughly than young females. Goy went on to show that if you manipulate testosterone level—raising it in females, damping it down in males—you can reverse those effects, creating sweet little male monkeys and rowdy young females.

Is testosterone the only factor at work here? I don't think so. But clearly we can argue a strong influence, and, interestingly, studies have found that girls with congenital adrenal hypoplasia—who run high in testosterone—tend to be far more fascinated by trucks and toy weaponry than most little girls are. They lean toward rough-and-tumble play, too. As it turns out, the strongest influence on this "abnormal" behavior is not parental disapproval, but the company of other little girls, who tone them down and direct them toward more routine girl games.

And that reinforces an early point: If there is indeed a biology to sex 25 differences, we amplify it. At some point—when it is still up for debate—we gain a sense of our gender, and with it a sense of "gender-appropriate" behavior.

Some scientists argue for some evidence of gender awareness in infancy, perhaps by the age of 12 months. The consensus seems to be that full-blown "I'm a girl" or "I'm a boy" instincts arrive between the ages of 2 and 3. Research shows that if a family operates in a very traditional, Beaver Cleaver kind of environment, filled with awareness of and association with "proper" gender behaviors, the "boys do trucks, girls do dolls" attitude seems to come very early. If a child grows up in a less traditional family, with an emphasis on partnership and sharing—"We all do the dishes, Joshua"—children maintain a more flexible sense of gender roles until about age 6.

In this period, too, relationships between boys and girls tend to fall into remarkably strict lines. Interviews with children find that 3 year-olds say that about half their friendships are with the opposite sex. By the age of 5, that drops to 20 percent. By 7, almost no boys or girls have, or will admit to having, best friends of the opposite sex. They still hang out on the same playground, play on the same soccer teams. They may be friendly, but the real friendships tend to be boy-to-boy or girl-to-girl.

There's some interesting science that suggests that the space between boys and girls is a normal part of development; there are periods during which children may thrive and learn from hanging out with peers of the same sex. Do we, as parents, as a culture at large, reinforce such separations? Is the pope Catholic? One of my favorite studies looked at little boys who asked for toys. If they asked for a heavily armed action figure, they got the soldier about 70 percent of the time. If they asked for a "girl" toy, like a baby doll or a Barbie, their parents purchased it maybe 40 percent of the time. Name a child who won't figure out how to work *that* system.

How does all this fit together—toys and testosterone, biology and behavior, the development of the child into the adult, the way that men and women relate to one another?

Let me make a cautious statement about testosterone: It not only has 30 some body-building functions, it influences some behaviors as well. Let's make that a little less cautious: These behaviors include rowdy play, sex drive, competitiveness, and an in-your-face attitude. Males tend to have a higher baseline of testosterone than females—in our species, about seven to ten times as much—and therefore you would predict (correctly, I think) that all of those behaviors would be more generally found in men than in women.

But testosterone is also one of my favorite examples of how responsive biology is, how attuned it is to the way we live our lives. Testosterone, it turns out, rises in response to competition and threat. In the days of our ancestors, this might have been hand-to-hand combat or high-risk hunting endeavors. Today, scientists have measured testosterone rise in athletes preparing for a game, in chess players awaiting a match, in spectators following a soccer competition.

If a person—or even just a person's favored team—wins, testosterone continues to rise. It falls with a loss. (This also makes sense in an evolutionary perspective. If one was being clobbered with a club, it would be extremely unhelpful to have a hormone urging one to battle on.) Testosterone also rises in the competitive world of dating, settles down with a stable and supportive relationship, climbs again if the relationships starts to falter.

It's been known for years that men in high-stress professions—say, police work or corporate law—have higher testosterone levels than men in the ministry. It turns out that women in the same kind of strong-attitude professions have higher testosterone than women who choose to stay home. What I like about this is the chicken-or-egg aspect. If you argue that testosterone influenced the behavior of those women, which came first? Did they have high testosterone and choose the law? Or did they choose the law, and the competitive environment ratcheted them up on the androgen scale? Or could both be at work?

And, returning to children for a moment, there's an ongoing study by Pennsylvania researchers, tracking that question in adolescent girls, who are being encouraged by their parents to engage in competitive activities that were once for boys only. As they do so, the researchers are monitoring, regularly, two hormones: testosterone and cortisol, a stress hormone. Will these hormones rise in response to this new, more traditionally male environment? What if more girls choose the competitive path; more boys choose the other? Will female testosterone levels rise, male levels fall? Will that wonderful, unpredictable, flexible biology that we've been given allow a shift, so that one day, we will literally be far more alike?

We may not have answers to all those questions, but we can ask   35 them, and we can expect that the answers will come someday, because science clearly shows us that such possibilities exist. In this most important sense, sex differences offer us a paradox. It is only through exploring and understanding what makes us different that we can begin to understand what binds us together.

Reading the Text

1. What effect do Blum's opening personal-experience anecdotes have on the persuasiveness of her argument?
2. What evidence does Blum offer to support her contention that males are naturally more aggressive than females?

3. How does testosterone affect human behavior, according to Blum's research?
4. In Blum's view, how do the cultural choices that humans make, such as engaging in sports or other competitive activities, affect hormonal balances?

Reading the Signs

1. In your journal, reflect on the way your upbringing shaped your sense of appropriate gender behavior.
2. Blum's selection challenges the common cultural studies position that gender behavior is socially constructed. Write an essay in which you defend, qualify, or reject Blum's point of view. To develop your ideas, consult Holly Devor's "Gender Role Behaviors and Attitudes" (p. 447).
3. Write an essay describing how you would raise a boy to counteract his tendencies to aggressive behavior. To develop your ideas, consult James William Gibson, "Warrior Dreams" (p. 496).
4. Visit the library, and investigate recent research on the possible genetic basis for homosexuality. Then write an essay in which you extend Blum's argument for the biological basis of gendered behavior to sexual orientation.

MICHAEL A. MESSNER
Power at Play: Sport and Gender Relations

||||||||||||||||||||||||||||||||||||||||||||||||||||

Every little boy should play Little League, right? Sports help to build character, right? Perhaps, but according to Michael A. Messner (b. 1952), the games men play are more than that: they are rituals designed to maintain the ideology and values of a competitive and hierarchical culture. Because masculine identity is rooted in the need to win, athletic competition, according to Messner, causes "men to experience their own bodies as machines . . . and to see other people's bodies as objects of their power and domination." Author of Power at Play: Sports and the Problem of Masculinity *(1992), from which this selection is excerpted, Messner is associate professor in the Department of Sociology and the Program for the Study of Women and Men in Society at the University of Southern California. He is also coeditor of* Men's Lives *(1995) and* Sport, Men, and the Gender Order: Critical Feminist Perspectives *(1990) and coauthor of* Sex, Violence, and Power in Sports: Rethinking Masculinity *(1994).*

> The closer we come to uncovering some form of exemplary mas-
> culinity, a masculinity which is solid and sure of itself, the clearer it
> becomes that masculinity is structured through contradiction: the
> more it asserts itself, the more it calls itself into question.
>
> —LYNN SEGAL, *Slow Motion*

In 1973, conservative writer George Gilder, later to become a central theorist of the antifeminist family policies of the Reagan administration, was among the first to sound the alarm that the contemporary explosion of female athletic participation might threaten the very fabric of
civilization. "Sports," Gilder wrote, "are possibly the single most important male rite in modern society." The woman athlete "reduces the game
from a religious male rite to a mere physical exercise, with some treacherous danger of psychic effect." Athletic performance, for males, embodies "an ideal of beauty and truth," while women's participation represents
a "disgusting perversion" of this truth.[1] In 1986, over a decade later, a
similar view was expressed by John Carroll in a respected academic journal. Carroll lauded the masculine "virtue and grace" of sport, and defended it against its critics, especially feminists. He concluded that in
order to preserve sport's "naturally conserving and creating" tendencies,
especially in the realms of "the moral and the religious, . . . women
should once again be prohibited from sport: They are the true defenders
of the humanist values that emanate from the household, the values of
tenderness, nurture and compassion, and this most important role must
not be confused by the military and political values inherent in sport.
Likewise, sport should not be muzzled by humanist values: it is the living
arena for the great virtue of manliness."[2]

The key to Gilder's and Carroll's chest-beating about the importance
of maintaining sport as a "male rite" is their neo-Victorian belief that
male-female biological differences predispose men to aggressively dominate public life, while females are naturally suited to serve as the nurtu-
rant guardians of home and hearth. As Gilder put it, "The tendency to
bond with other males in intensely purposeful and dangerous activity is
said to come from the collective demands of pursuing large animals. The
female body, on the other hand, more closely resembles the body of
nonhunting primates. A woman throws, for example, very like a male
chimpanzee."[3] This perspective ignores a wealth of historical, anthropo-
logical, and biological data that suggest that the equation of males with

---

1. G. Gilder, *Sexual Suicide* (New York: Bantam Books, 1973), pp. 216, 218.

2. J. Carroll, "Sport: Virtue and Grace," *Theory, Culture and Society* 3 (1986),
pp. 91–98. Jennifer Hargreaves delivers a brilliant feminist rebuttal to Carroll's masculinist defense of sport in the same issue of the journal. See J. Hargreaves, "Where's
the Virtue? Where's the Grace? A Discussion of the Social Production of Gender
through Sport," pp. 109–121.

3. G. Gilder, p. 221.

domination of public life and females with the care of the domestic sphere is a cultural and historical construction.[4] In fact, Gilder's and Carroll's belief that sport, *a socially constructed institution,* is needed to sustain male-female difference contradicts their assumption that these differences are "natural." As R. W. Connell has argued, social practices that exaggerate male-female difference (such as dress, adornment, and sport) "are part of a continuing effort to sustain a social definition of gender, an effort that is necessary precisely *because the biological logic . . . cannot sustain the gender categories.*"[5]

Indeed, I must argue against the view that sees sport as a natural realm within which some essence of masculinity unfolds. Rather, sport is a social institution that, in its dominant forms, was created by and for men. It should not be surprising, then, that my research with male athletes reveals an affinity between the institution of sport and men's developing identities. As the young males in my study became committed to athletic careers, the gendered values of the institution of sport made it extremely unlikely that they would construct anything but the kinds of personalities and relationships that were consistent with the dominant values and power relations of the larger gender order. The competitive hierarchy of athletic careers encouraged the development of masculine identities based on very narrow definitions of public success. Homophobia and misogyny were the key bonding agents among male athletes, serving to construct a masculine personality that disparaged anything considered "feminine" in women, in other men, or in oneself. The fact that winning was premised on physical power, strength, discipline, and willingness to take, ignore, or deaden pain inclined men to experience their own bodies as machines, as instruments of power and domination—and to see other peoples' bodies as objects of their power and domination. . . .

The Costs of Athletic Masculinity

As boys, the men in my study were initially attracted to playing sport because it was a primary means to connect with other people—especially fathers, brothers, and male peers. But as these young males became committed to athletic careers, their identities became directly tied to continued public success. Increasingly, it was not just "being there with the guys" but beating the other guys that mattered most. As their need

---

4. For a critical overview of the biological research on male-female difference, see A. Fausto-Sterling, *Myths of Gender: Biological Theories about Men and Women* (New York: Basic Books, 1985). For an overview of the historical basis of male domination, see R. Lee and R. Daly, "Man's Domination and Woman's Oppression: The Question of Origins," in M. Kaufman, ed., *Beyond Patriarchy: Essays by Men on Pleasure, Power, and Change* (Toronto: Oxford University Press, 1987), pp. 30–44.

5. R. W. Connell, *Gender and Power* (Stanford: Stanford University Press, 1987), p. 81 (emphasis in original text).

for connection with others became defined more abstractly, through their relationships with "the crowd," their actual relationships with other people tended to become distorted. Other individuals were increasingly likely to be viewed as (male) objects to be defeated or (female) objects to be manipulated and sexually conquered. As a result, the socially learned means through which they constructed their identities (public achievement within competitive hierarchies) did not deliver what was most craved and needed: intimate connection and unity with other people. More often than not, athletic careers have exacerbated existing insecurities and ambivalences in young men's developing identities, thus further diminishing their capacity for intimate relationships with others.

In addition to relational costs, many athletes—especially those in "combat sports" such as football—paid a heavy price in terms of health. While the successful operation of the male body-as-weapon may have led, for a time, to victories on the athletic field, it also led to injuries and other health problems that lasted far beyond the end of the athletic career.

It is extremely unlikely that a public illumination of the relational and health costs paid by male athletes will lead to a widespread rejection of sport by young males. There are three reasons for this. First, the continued affinity between sport and developing masculine identities suggests that many boys will continue to be attracted to athletic careers for the same reasons they have in the past. Second, since the successful athlete often basks in the limelight of public adoration, the relational costs of athletic masculinity are often not apparent until after the athletic career ends, and he suddenly loses his connection to the crowd. Third, though athletes may recognize the present and future health costs of their athletic careers, they are likely to view them as dues willingly paid. In short, there is a neat enough fit between the psychological and emotional tendencies of young males and the institution of sport that these costs—if they are recognized at all—will be considered "necessary evils," the price men pay for the promise of "being on top."[6]

---

6. Indeed, "men's liberationists" of the 1970s were overly optimistic in believing that a public illumination of the "costs of masculinity" would induce men to "reject the male role." See, for instance, W. Farrell, *The Liberated Man* (New York: Bantam Books, 1975); J. Nichols, *Men's Liberation: A New Definition of Masculinity* (New York: Penguin Books, 1975). These men's liberationists underestimated the extent to which the costs of masculinity are linked to the promise of power and privilege. One commentator went so far as to argue that the privileges of masculinity were a "myth" perpetrated by women to keep men in destructive success-object roles. See H. Goldberg, *The Hazards of Being Male: Surviving the Myth of Masculine Privilege* (New York: Signet, 1976). For more recent discussions of the need to analyze both the "costs" and the "privileges" of dominant conceptions of masculinity, see M. E. Kann, "The Costs of Being on Top," *Journal of the National Association for Women Deans, Administrators, and Counselors* 49 (1986): 29–37; and M. A. Messner, "Men Studying Masculinity: Some Epistemological Questions in Sport Sociology," *Sociology of Sport Journal* 7 (1990): 136–153.

Competing Masculinities

Boys' emerging identities may influence them to be attracted to sport, but they nevertheless tend to experience athletic careers differently, based upon variations in class, race, and sexual orientation. Despite their similarities, boys and young men bring different problems, anxieties, hopes, and dreams to their athletic experiences, and thus tend to draw different meanings from, and make different choices about, their athletic careers.

RACE, CLASS, AND THE CONSTRUCTION OF ATHLETIC MASCULINITY

My interviews reveal that within a social context stratified by class and by race, the choice to pursue—or not to pursue—an athletic career is determined by the individual's rational assessment of the available means to construct a respected masculine identity. White middle-class men were likely to reject athletic careers and shift their masculine strivings to education and nonsport careers. Conversely, men from poor and blue-collar backgrounds, especially blacks, often perceived athletic careers to be their best chance for success in the public sphere. For nearly all of the men from lower-class backgrounds, the status and respect that they received through sport was temporary—it did not translate into upward mobility.

One might conclude from this that the United States should adopt a public policy of encouraging young lower-class black males to "just say no" to sport. This strategy would be doomed to failure, because poor young black men's decisions to pursue athletic careers can be viewed as rational, given the constraints that they continue to face. Despite the increased number of black role models in nonsport professions, employment opportunities for young black males actually deteriorated in the 1980s, and nonathletic opportunities in higher education also declined. By 1985, blacks constituted 14 percent of the college-aged (18–24 years) U.S. population, but as a proportion of students in four-year colleges and universities, they had dropped to 8 percent. By contrast, black men constituted 49 percent of male college basketball players, and 61 percent of male basketball players in institutions that grant athletic scholarships.[7] For

---

7. W. J. Wilson and K. M. Neckerman, "Poverty and Family Structure: The Widening Gap between Evidence and Public Policy Issues," in S. H. Danzinger and D. H. Weinberg, eds., *Fighting Poverty* (Cambridge: Harvard University Press, 1986), pp. 232–259; F. J. Berghorn et al., "Racial Participation in Men's and Women's Intercollegiate Basketball: Continuity and Change, 1958–1985." *Sociology of Sport Journal* 5 (1988), 107–124.

young black men, then, organized sport appears to be more likely to get them to college than their own efforts in nonathletic activities.

In addition to viewing athletic careers as an arena for career success, there is considerable evidence that black male athletes have used sport as a cultural space within which to forge a uniquely expressive style of masculinity, a "cool pose." As Majors puts it,

> Due to structural limitations, a black man may be impotent in the intellectual, political, and corporate world, but he can nevertheless display a potent personal style from the pulpit, in entertainment, and in athletic competition, with a verve that borders on the spectacular. Through the virtuosity of a performance, he tips the socially imbalanced scales in his favor and sends the subliminal message: "See me, touch me, hear me, but, white man, you can't copy me!"[8]

In particular, black men have put their "stamp" on the game of basketball. There is considerable pride in U.S. black communities in the fact that black men have come to dominate the higher levels of basketball—and in the expressive style with which they have come to do so. The often aggressive "cool pose" of black male athletes can thus be interpreted as a form of masculinity that symbolically challenges the class constraints and the institutionalized racism that so many young black males face.

SEXUAL ORIENTATION AND THE CONSTRUCTION OF ATHLETIC MASCULINITY

Until very recently, it was widely believed that gay men did not play organized sports. Nongay people tended to stereotype gay men as "too effeminate" to be athletic. This belief revealed a confusion between sexual orientation and gender. We now know that there is no neat fit between how "masculine" or "feminine" a man is, and whether or not he is sexually attracted to women, to men, to both, or to neither.[9] Interestingly, some gay writers also believed that gay men were not active in sport. For instance, Dennis Altman wrote in 1982 that most gay men were not interested in sport, since they tended to reject the sexual repression, homophobia, and misogyny that are built into the sportsworld.[10]

The belief that gay men are not interested or involved in sport has proven to be wrong. People who made this assumption were observing

---

8. R. Majors, "'Cool Pose': Black Masculinity and Sports," in M. A. Messner and D. F. Sabo, *Sport, Men, and the Gender Order: Critical Feminist Perspectives* (Champaign, Ill.: Human Kinetics Publishers, 1990), p. 111.

9. See S. Kleinberg, "The New Masculinity of Gay Men, and Beyond," in Kaufman, *Beyond Patriarchy*, pp. 120–138.

10. D. Altman, *The Homosexualization of America* (Boston: Beacon Press, 1982).

the overtly masculine and heterosexual culture of sport and then falsely concluding that all of the people within that culture must be heterosexual. My interview with Mike T. and biographies of gay athletes such as David Kopay suggest that young gay males are often attracted to sport because they are just as concerned as heterosexual boys and young men with constructing masculine identities.[11] Indeed, a young closeted gay male like Mike T. may view the projection of an unambiguous masculinity as even more critical than his nongay counterparts do. As Mike told me, "There are a *lot* of gay men in sports," but they are almost all closeted and thus not visible to public view.

As Mike's story illustrates, gay male athletes often share similar motivations and experiences with nongay athletes. This suggests that as long as gay athletes stay closeted, they are contributing to the construction of culturally dominant conceptions of masculinity. However, Brian Pronger's recent research suggests that many gay male athletes experience organized sport in unique ways. In particular, Pronger's interviews with gay male athletes indicate that they have a "paradoxical" relationship to the male athletic culture. Though the institution itself is built largely on the denial (or sublimation) of any erotic bond between men, Pronger argues, many (but not all) gay athletes experience life in the locker room, as well as the excitement of athletic competition, as highly erotic. Since their secret desires (and, at times, secret actions) run counter to the heterosexist culture of the male locker room, closeted gay male athletes develop ironic sensibilities about themselves, their bodies, and the sporting activity itself.[12] Gay men are sexually oppressed through sport, Pronger argues, but the ironic ways they often redefine the athletic context can be interpreted as a form of resistance with the potential to undermine and transform the heterosexist culture of sport.

THE LIMITS OF MASCULINE RESISTANCES

Men's experience of athletic careers—and the meanings they assign to these experiences—are contextualized by class, race, and sexual orientation. My research, and that of other social scientists, suggests that black male athletes construct and draw on an expressive and "cool" masculinity in order to resist racial oppression. Gay male athletes sometimes construct and draw on an "ironic" masculinity in order to resist sexual oppression.

---

11. See D. Kopay and P. D. Young, *The Dave Kopay Story* (New York: Arbor House, 1977).

12. B. Pronger, "Gay Jocks: A Phenomenology of Gay Men in Athletics," in Messner and Sabo, *Sport, Men, and the Gender Order*, pp. 141–152; and *The Arena of Masculinity: Sports, Homosexuality, and the Meaning of Sex* (New York: St. Martin's Press, 1990).

In other words, poor, black, and gay men have often found sport to be an arena in which they can build a masculinity that is, in some ways, resistant to the oppressions they face within hierarchies of intermale dominance.

But how real is the challenge these resistant masculinities pose to the role that sport has historically played in perpetuating existing differences and inequalities? A feminist perspective reveals the limited extent to which we can interpret black and gay athletic masculinities as liberating. Through a feminist lens, we can see that in adopting as their expressive vehicle many of the dominant aspects of athletic masculinity (narrow definitions of public success; aggressive, sometimes violent competition; glorification of the athletic male body-as-machine; verbal misogyny and homophobia), poor, black, and gay male athletes contribute to the continued subordination of women, as well as to the circumscription of their own relationships and development.

Tim Carrigan, Bob Connell, and John Lee assert that rather than undermining social inequality, men's struggles within class, racial, and sexual hierarchies of intermale dominance serve to reinforce men's global subordination of women. Although strains caused by differences and inequalities among men represent potential avenues for social change, ultimately, "the fissuring of the categories 'men' and 'women' is one of the central facts about a patriarchal power and the way it works. In the case of men, the crucial division is between hegemonic masculinity and various subordinated masculinities."[13] Hegemonic masculinity is thus defined in relation to various subordinated masculinities as well as in relation to femininities. This is a key insight for the contemporary meaning of sport. Utilizing the concept of "multiple masculinities," we can begin to understand how race, class, age, and sexual hierarchies among men help to construct and legitimize men's overall power and privilege over women. In addition, the false promise of sharing in the fruits of hegemonic masculinity often ties black, working-class, or gay men into their marginalized and subordinate status. For instance, my research suggests that while black men's development of "cool pose" within sport can be interpreted as creative resistance against one form of social domination (racism), it also demonstrates the limits of an agency that adopts other forms of social domination (athletic masculinity) as its vehicle.

My research also suggests how homophobia within athletic masculine cultures tends to lock men—whether gay or not—into narrowly defined heterosexual identities and relationships. Within the athletic context, homophobia is closely linked with misogyny in ways that ultimately serve to bond men together as superior to women. Given the extremely

---

13. T. Carrigan, B. Connell, and J. Lee, "Hard and Heavy: Toward a New Sociology of Masculinity," *Theory and Society* 14 (1985): 551–603.

oppressive levels of homophobia within organized sport, it is understandable why the vast majority of gay male athletes would decide to remain closeted. But the public construction of a heterosexual/masculine status requires that a closeted gay athlete actively participate in (or at the very least, tolerate) the ongoing group expressions of homophobia and misogyny—what Mike T. called "locker room garbage." Thus, though he may feel a sense of irony, and may even confidentially express that sense of irony to gay male friends or to researchers, the public face that the closeted gay male athlete presents to the world is really no different from that of his nongay teammates. As long as he is successful in this public presentation-of-self as heterosexual/masculine, he will continue to contribute to (and benefit from) men's power over women.

SPORT IN GAY COMMUNITIES

The fissuring of the category "men," then, as it is played out within the dominant institution of sport, does little to threaten—indeed, may be a central mechanism in—the reconstruction of existing class, racial, sexual, and gender inequalities.[14] Nevertheless, since the outset of the gay liberation movement in the early 1970s, organized sport has become an integral part of developing gay and lesbian communities. The ways that "gay" sports have been defined and organized are sometimes different—even radically different—than the dominant institution of sport in society.

The most public sign of the growing interest in athletics in gay communities was the rapid growth and popularity of bodybuilding among many young, urban gay men in the 1970s and early 1980s. The meanings of gay male bodybuilding are multiple and contradictory.[15] On the one hand, gay male bodybuilding overtly eroticizes the muscular male body, thus potentially disrupting the tendency of sport to eroticize male bodies

20

---

14. One potentially important, but largely unexplored, fissure among men is that between athletes and nonathletes. There are tens of millions of boys who do *not* pursue athletic careers. Many boys dislike sport. Others may yearn to be athletes, but may not have the body size, strength, physical capabilities, coordination, emotional predisposition, or health that is necessary to successfully compete in sports. What happens to these boys and young men? What kinds of adult masculine identities and relationships do they eventually develop? Does the fact of not having been an athlete play any significant role in their masculine identities, goals, self-images, and relationships? The answers to these questions, of course, lie outside the purview of my study. But they are key to understanding the contemporary role that sport plays in constructions of gender.

15. For interesting discussions of bodybuilding, gender, and sexuality, see B. Glassner, *Bodies: Why We Look the Way We Do (and How We Feel about It)* (New York: G. P. Putnam's Sons, 1988); A. M. Klein, "Little Big Man: Hustling, Gender Narcissism, and Homophobia in Bodybuilding," in Messner and Sabo, *Sport, Men, and the Gender Order,* pp. 127–140.

under the guise of aggression and competition. On the other hand, the building of muscular bodies is often motivated by a conscious need by gay men to prove to the world that they are "real men." Gay bodybuilding thus undermines cultural stereotypes of homosexual men as "nelly," effeminate, and womanlike. But it also tends to adopt and promote a very conventional equation of masculinity with physical strength and muscularity.[16] In effect, then, as gay bodybuilders attempt to sever the cultural link between masculinity and heterosexuality, they uncritically affirm a conventional dichotomization of masculinity/male vs. femininity/female.

By contrast, some gay athletes have initiated alternative athletic institutions that aim to challenge conventional views of sexuality and gender. Originally Mike T. had gone into sport to prove that he was "male," and cover up the fact that he was gay. When his career as an Olympic athlete finally ended, he came out publicly, and soon was a very active member of the San Francisco Bay Area gay community. He rekindled his interest in the arts and dance. He also remained very active in athletics, and he increasingly imagined how wonderful it would be to blend the beauty and exhilaration of sport, as he had experienced it, with the emergent, liberating values of the feminist, gay, and lesbian communities of which he was a part. In 1982, his dream became a reality, as 1,300 athletes from twelve different nations gathered in San Francisco to participate in the first ever Gay Games.[17]

Though many of the events in the Gay Games are "conventional" sports (track and field, swimming, etc.), and a number of "serious

---

16. Alan Klein's research revealed that nongay male bodybuilders are also commonly motivated by a need to make a public statement with their muscular bodies that they are indeed "masculine." To the nongay bodybuilder, muscles are the ultimate sign of heterosexual masculinity. But, ironically, as one nongay male bodybuilder put it, "We're everything the U.S. is supposed to stand for: strength, determination, everything to be admired. But it's not the girls that like us, it's the fags!" Interestingly, Klein found that many male bodybuilders who defined themselves as "straight" (including the one quoted above) made a living by prostituting themselves to gay men. See Klein, "Little Big Man," p. 135.

For a thought-provoking feminist analysis of the contradictory relationship between gay male sexuality and masculinity, see T. Edwards, "Beyond Sex and Gender: Masculinity, Homosexuality and Social Theory," in J. Hearn and D. Morgan, eds., *Men, Masculinities, and Social Theory* (London: Unwin Hyman, 1990), pp. 110–123.

17. The Gay Games were originally called the "Gay Olympics," but the U.S. Olympic Committee went to court to see that the word "Olympics" was not used to denote this event. Despite the existence of "Police Olympics," "Special Olympics," "Senior Olympics," "Xerox Olympics," "Armenian Olympics," even "Crab Cooking Olympics," the U.S.O.C. chose to enforce their control legally over the term "Olympics" when it came to the "Gay Olympics." For further discussion of the politics of the Gay Games, see M. A. Messner, "Gay Athletes and the Gay Games: An Interview with Tom Waddell," *M: Gentle Men for Gender Justice* 13 (1984): 13–14.

athletes" compete in the events, overall the Games reflect a value system and a vision based on feminist and gay liberationist ideals of equality and universal participation. As Mike T. said,

> You don't win by beating someone else. We defined winning as doing your very best. That way, everyone is a winner. And we have age-group competition, so all ages are involved. We have parity: If there's a men's sport, there's a women's sport to complement it. And we go out and recruit in Third World and minority areas. All of these people are gonna get together for a week, they're gonna march in together, they're gonna hold hands, and they'll say, "Jesus Christ! This is wonderful!" There's this *discovery*: "I had no idea women were such fun!" and, "God! Blacks are okay—I didn't do anything to offend him, and we became *friends!*" and, "God, that guy over there is in his sixties, and I had no *idea* they were so sexually *active!*"—[laughs].

This emphasis on bridging differences, overcoming prejudices, and building relationships definitely enhanced the athletic experience for one participant I interviewed. This man said that he loved to swim, and even loved to compete, because it "pushed" him to swim "a whole lot better." Yet in past competitions, he had always come in last place. As he put it, "The Gay Games were just wonderful in many respects. One of them was that people who came in second, or third, and *last* got standing ovations from the crowd—the crowd genuinely recognized the thrill of giving a damn good shot, regardless of where you came in, and gave support to that. Among the competitors, there was a whole lot of joking and supportiveness."

In 1986, 3,482 athletes participated in Gay Games II in San Francisco. In 1990, at Gay Games III in Vancouver, 7,200 athletes continued the vision of building, partly through sport, an "exemplary community" that eliminates sexism, homophobia, and racism. Mike T. described what the Gay Games mean to him:

> To me, it's one of those steps in a thousand-mile journey to try and raise consciousness and enlighten people—*not* just people outside the gay community, but within the gay community as well, [because] we're just as racist, ageist, nationalistic, and chauvinistic as anybody else. Maybe it's simplistic to some people, you know, but why does it have to be complicated? Put people in a position where they can experience this process of discovery, and here it is! I just hope that this is something that'll take hold and a lot of people will get the idea.

The Gay Games represent a radical break from past and current conceptions of the role of sport in society. But they do not represent a major challenge to sport as an institution. Alternative athletic venues like the Gay Games, since they exist outside of the dominant sports institution, do not directly confront or change the dominant structure. On the other hand, these experiments are valuable in terms of demonstrating the fact that alternative value systems and structures are possible.[18]

Reading the Text

1. Why, in Messner's view, did conservatives such as George Gilder and John Carroll want to prohibit women from competing in athletic competitions?
2. What does Messner mean when he says that "sports is a social institution that . . . was created by and for men" (para. 3)?
3. What roles do class, race, and sexual orientation play in the construction of athletic masculinity, according to Messner?
4. In what ways, according to Messner, do the Gay Games differ from the Olympic Games?

Reading the Signs

1. In your journal, explore what athletic participation, whether in organized sports such as Little League or in informal activities such as jogging or hiking, has meant to you. Do you believe that the participation has shaped your attitudes about gender roles? If you haven't participated much in sports, what is your attitude toward athletic competition?
2. Write an argumentative essay challenging or supporting George Gilder's position that the female athlete "reduces the game from a religious male rite to a mere physical exercise, with some treacherous danger of psychic effect" (para. 1).
3. In class, outline the racial and gender coding of professional sports. Which ethnicities dominate which sports? In which sports, if any, have women received social acceptance? Then discuss the reasons for the ethnic and gender patterns you have found.
4. Study a magazine such as *Sports Illustrated,* and write an essay in which you explain the extent to which the magazine perpetuates the traditional attitudes toward gender roles that Messner claims sports encourage.
5. In class, form mixed-gender teams and debate Messner's contention that sports encourage homophobia and misogyny.

---

18. During the 1982 Gay Games in San Francisco, the major local newspapers tended to cover the Games mostly in the "lifestyle" sections of the paper, not in the sports pages. Alternative sports demonstrate the difficulties of attempting to change sport in the absence of larger institutional transformations. For instance, the European sport of korfball was developed explicitly as a sex-egalitarian sport. The rules of korfball aim to neutralize male-female biological differences that may translate into different levels of ability. But recent research shows that old patterns show up, even among the relatively "enlightened" korfball players. Korfball league officials are more likely to be male than female. More important, the more "key" roles within the game appear to be dominated by men, while women are partially marginalized. See D. Summerfield and A. White, "Korfball: A Model of Egalitarianism?" *Sociology of Sport Journal* 6 (1989): 144–151.

JENNIFER SCANLON

Boys-R-Us: Board Games and the Socialization
of Young Adolescent Girls

||||||||||||||||||||||||||||||||||||||||||||||||||||

Heart-Throb: The Dream Date Game. Sweet Valley High: Can You
Find a Boyfriend in Time for the Big Date? No, these aren't the titles
of romance novels: they're box games for girls, ages eight and up, and
as Jennifer Scanlon argues in this analysis of games for young girls,
they aren't innocent. For games like these help shape the consciousness
of young girls, telling them what should matter to them (boys) and
what shouldn't (things like intellectual achievement), and that, Scan-
lon suggests, isn't child's play. An associate professor and director of
women's studies at Plattsburgh State University, Scanlon is the author
of Inarticulate Longings: The Ladies' Home Journal, *Gender, and*
the Promises of Consumer Culture (1995) and editor of Significant Contemporary American Feminists *(1999).*

In a 1973 volume of *Ms.* magazine, Letty Cottin Pogrebin introduced a checklist for parents who wanted to buy nonsexist toys for their
children. An acceptable toy would be "respectful of the child's intellect
and creativity, nonracist, moral in terms of the values it engenders, and
nonsexist in the way it is packaged, conceived, and planned for play"
(48). One of the board games she recommended was Life, a Milton
Bradley product, as it encouraged all players to pursue lives of their own,
money of their own, careers of their own.

Now, readers, as the instructions on a game might tell you, advance
twenty years. Enter the 1990s, a mall, Anytown U.S.A. A parent looking
for nonsexist toys for children might, at a Toys-R-Us store, find a few
toys and games that Pogrebin would approve of. The game of Life remains popular, and consumers can find numerous trivia games, memory
games, and games of skill on the shelves. Unfortunately, however, mall
toy stores rely heavily on gender stereotypes for their displays, layout,
advertising, and most importantly, products. This essay looks at four
gender-specific board games directed at young adolescent girls, examines
their messages in light of Pogrebin's now twenty-five-year-old suggestions, and brings to light issues about a much-neglected period in girls'
lives, early adolescence, and a much-neglected area of popular culture or
leisure studies, gender-specific games.

The least gender-specific toys and games in the stores are, arguably,
those in the baby and toddler section. Primary colors predominate in
these toys, and customers purchase chunky trains and boats for baby girls
or boys. Sex-typing occurs quickly as you move either down the aisle or

up in age, as trucks become masculinized, dolls feminized. Pastels replace primary colors in girls' toys, and the packaging, game boards and pieces, even the cover photographs become feminized. For boys' toys, camouflage greens and browns replace soft colors, and war toys and sports equipment fill the shelves. And now you arrive at these four games for young adolescent girls, where the players featured on the game boxes, girls only, dress in feminine clothing and wear heavy make-up and jewelry, even though the suggested starting age for the games is eight.

Heart-Throb: The Dream Date Game, and Sweet Valley High: Can You Find a Boyfriend in Time for the Big Date? are both produced by Milton Bradley, subsidiary of Hasbro, a company with $410 million in annual sales. Hasbro, with no women on its board of directors, produces board games for children and adults as well as a range of other products from teething rings to women's undergarments, baby pacifiers to girls' nightwear. The second two games, Girl Talk: A Game of Truth or Dare, and Girl Talk: Date Line, are produced by Western Publishing Company, which has annual sales of $495 million and produces, among other things, board games for children and adults, gift wrap and novelties, stationery, and books (Dun and Bradstreet 813, 1831).

Not surprisingly, these four games invite girls to enter the consumer marketplace by encouraging players to use products such as clothing and make-up to enhance their looks. Another game for young adolescent girls, Meet Me at the Mall, more blatantly emphasizes the consumer side of things; players run around the mall, visiting stores like The Gap and Benetton, trying to outbuy the competition. For the four games discussed in this [essay], though, players must obtain boyfriends rather than consumer goods. Whether a girl steals one from a friend, wins one through her own matchmaking skills, or reads one in her future, a boyfriend rather than a career or a life remains the player's central goal. . . . 5

Of course, gender is a crucial element in adolescent development for girls and boys. In no other period of life except infancy do so many biological changes occur so quickly, and many of those biological changes are sex-specific (Montemayor et al. 9). Those who study adolescence, however, argue that social expectations, even more than physical changes, shape gender roles (Huston and Alvarez 158). When young people respond to peers and television as socializing influences, they often become increasingly intolerant of deviations from traditional sex role norms; surprisingly enough, peers often promote more traditional roles than do parents. Stereotypical attitudes about girls and boys, while not born in adolescence, often solidify at this age into hard and fast rules rather than simple observations (Montemayor et al. 13; Coleman and Hendry 123; Chandler 150).

The implications of this rigid agenda for girls are dramatic. Studies show that girls' academic and career ambitions actually decline in early adolescence when they internalize the notion that females should achieve less than males. During this period females and males both come to view math, science, and computer skills as male domains (Huston and Alvarez 158, 169). Teachers and educational programs as well as the family encourage such messages. Girls also learn by early adolescence that in order to be defined as successful they must please others, putting the needs of others first. Girls have few illusions about how this translates into real life experiences. Sadly, while cognitive developments that take place in early adolescence can encourage children to look at roles, including gender roles, in a flexible way, social constraints encourage them to limit their thinking and conceptualize gender roles in highly conformist and predictable ways (Huston and Alvarez 173). For girls this translates to the rule that they must get a boyfriend, keep a boyfriend, and learn dependence on males to be successful in life (McRobbie xvii; Newman and Newman 150–51; Chandler x).

While young children repeatedly get these messages at home and in school, they get them from popular culture as well. Widely documented studies of television's influence on gender role socialization reveal the connections between television watching and the likelihood that children and teenagers will have stereotypical beliefs about gender roles (Comstock 160–75). Adolescence heightens sensitivity about gender, and numerous studies demonstrate the extent of gender stereotyping on contemporary television. Males are overrepresented two or three to one in commercial television, and the voice-over in commercials remains male 90 percent of the time. This is significant, of course, as children in the United States watch an average of 40,000 commercials per year (Comstock 188). In addition to television, magazines and fiction addressed to pre-adolescent and adolescent girls stress traditional gender roles, the importance of girls' bodies, and the overwhelming and incessant need to find a boy. Magazines, for example, provide constant reminders that a girl must consciously and continuously cultivate sexual attractiveness, her greatest asset. Magazines, teen formula romance fiction, and other commercial enterprises replay the messages that come, in other forms, through the family and school.

However, unlike family or school, leisure pursuits like reading magazines or playing games do not appear to be coercive. Simply because of this, they demand attention. Associated with freedom, leisure activities for girls often carry heavy ideological messages wrapped in the context of an escape from limits (McRobbie 88). These activities define girlhood in class-, race-, and behavior-specific ways. Three out of four teen fashion magazines in the United States, with a combined circulation of almost four million, portray young American women as white, very feminine, carefree, boy-crazy virgins. A recent issue of *Teen* featured liposuction and plastic surgery as options for those readers dissatisfied with their bodies. *Sassy,* noted for its initial frank discussions of adolescent sexuality, bent to pressure and omitted much of what made it controversial and, not coincidentally, a favorite among many young women craving honest discussion of their needs. These forms of popular culture, rather than an escape from limitations, provide clear and limited definitions of what it means to be a girl.

Board games, another form of popular culture, are a significant aspect 10 of same-sex play for girls. Girls do not play them with boys, nor do they play them to get boys' attention. As the back covers of the games illustrate, girls play in the company of other girls, often in the privacy of one of their bedrooms. The picture on the back of Heart-Throb is typical: four girls in a bedroom, one of them on the bed, the others lounging on the carpeted floor. The game board sits on the floor, and the background features a telephone, a radio/tape player, and a bowl of popcorn. In fact, three of these four covers show a telephone, a radio/tape player, and popcorn, which is, of course, a low-calorie snack. In this sacred space girls learn to define themselves. Real boys do not invade this very feminine scene, but the idea of boys takes up a good deal of space, as each game encourages girls to think about themselves in relation to boys. By playing these board games, girls learn a central rule: they need boys to complete their self-definition.

The four games featured here offer young adolescent girls a wide variety of messages, all of them gender specific. From the uniformly "pretty" boxes to the uniform goal of getting a guy, the games promote traditional gender role behaviors, emphasize clear messages about race, class, and sexual orientation, and encourage play that is decidedly humdrum if not outright insulting to any young adolescent's intelligence. They clearly fail Letty Pogrebin's test for nonsexist toys, but the ways in which they do so and fail young women in the process is worth examining further.

All of these board games promote the idea that the central object in a girl's life is to get a guy. In Sweet Valley High, girls literally race around the school trying to retrieve a boyfriend, a teacher chaperon, and all the accessories needed for a big date. In the process of trying to get it all done first, girls can steal other girls' boyfriends or fight over boyfriends; such behaviors receive rewards.

In Heart-Throb, each player chooses which boy she would like to have ask her out and guesses which boys her competitors will choose. The game pieces include 60 boyfriend cards, each picturing a different boy, and 162 personality cards, which reveal both good and bad qualities of boys. In Girl Talk: Date Line, players match up girl and boy cards they hold in their hands in order to create successful dates. While they travel around the board, trying to set up a date, the players date as well; if they do not secure a date for the imaginary characters they hold in their hands, they themselves must go stag or settle for a blind date.

In Girl Talk: A Game of Truth or Dare, the initial focus seems different. Girls spin a wheel and then must reveal a secret or do a stunt. Many of the stunts are unrelated to getting a boyfriend and include doing situps or sucking a lemon. Others, however, clearly promote the overall gender-enforcing plan and include pretending to put on make-up, calling a boy and telling him a joke, rating your looks from one to ten, or revealing what you would like to change about your looks. Anytime a girl does not complete the required stunt, she must peel off a red zit sticker and wear it on her face for the rest of the game. The game's instructions warn that the zit sticker must be visible: It cannot go under the chin or behind the ear.

The end goal of this game is to collect one of each of the fortune   15
cards, which fit into four categories: Marriage, Children, Career, and Special Moments. However, dependency on boys or men dictates girls' experiences in each of the four categories except Children. Under Marriage, two possible fortunes are "You will marry _____'s boyfriend" or "You will meet your future husband while working together at _____ fast-food restaurant." Under Career, you could receive "After three weeks on your first job as a _____ (profession), you will meet the man that you will eventually marry," or "You will take a job as a carhop just to get a date with a certain boy who drives a _____." Finally, under Special Moments, fortunes include "A tall, dark, and handsome policeman will stop you for speeding and give you a ticket, but will make up for it by asking you for a date," or "While visiting a dude ranch, your horse will bolt and you will be rescued by a ranch hand who looks just like _____ (actor)." In the category of Special Moments, with twenty-four possible cards, seven are specifically about boys, but only one portrays a girl having a special moment with a girlfriend.

Each of these four games portrays girls in strictly feminine terms and boys in strictly masculine terms, with little overlap in traditional definitions. In the Sweet Valley High game, for example, students vote Jessica Most Popular Girl in the school; she is also, not coincidentally, co-captain of the cheerleading squad. Elizabeth, Jessica's sister, receives an award for her newspaper column, a gossip column called "Eyes and Ears." The names used in the Sweet Valley game indicate which girls and boys are popular and which are not. The nerdy and nonmasculine boy is called Winston Egbert; Winston prefers feminine activities like talking and being gentle to masculine qualities like playing football and being aloof. The desirable boys in Sweet Valley, Todd Wilkins and Bruce Patman, do masculine things like skiing and driving expensive sports cars.

Names are used as indicators of appropriate levels of feminine or masculine qualities in Girl Talk: Date Line as well. When players land on a date space, they choose two of the character cards in their hand and set them up for a date. When they put the cards together in a microphone machine, girls discover whether or not the date they choreographed went well. The characters Gert and Homer stand out as nerds in appearance, name, and behavior. Both Gert and Homer wear glasses, but none of the many popular characters wear glasses, and the popular people have names like Nicole and Drew, Stephanie and Matt.

In Girl Talk: Date Line, Homer's personality profile reveals that he loves the computer club and collecting bugs but hates sports and school dances. Boys clearly should love sports, including the sport of pursuing girls at dances, whether or not they actually like to dance. Gert, the girl without make-up and hence without much personality, loves Latin and algebra, hates rock music and gym class. Obviously girls should not have academic aspirations. The attributes of the popular people in Girl Talk: Date Line confirm clear rules about what it means to be a girl or boy. Stacie loves talking on the phone and shopping but hates greasy hair and book reports. Tina loves pizza and make-up but hates computers and report cards. Eric, on the other hand, loves tennis and water skiing, hates shopping malls. Matt loves math and football, hates double-dating (wants to be in control?) and haircuts.

In Heart-Throb, girls and boys behave in gender-specific ways in dating. When the players choose which of the boys in the boyfriend cards they would like to date and which they think the other players will choose, it seems that at last girls are making choices. In actuality, though, the rules state that three boys from the boyfriend cards ask the girls first to dance, then to go on a date, then to go steady. The girls must choose from among the three boys. Players have some very limited choices: They can choose which boy they want, but they cannot choose not to accept a dance, a date, or a steady boyfriend. Refusing the advances of all three boys is not an option, regardless of how uninviting they appear in their personality cards.

These board games clearly promote male privilege, then; they also 20 promote the privileges of race, wealth, and heterosexuality. In the four games, virtually all of the characters are white. In Sweet Valley High, located in California, all of the students are fair-skinned, and the only ones with names that deviate from the most popular or trendy, which include Ken—who does in fact look like Barbie's counterpart—are the names of the nerdy characters, but Winston remains, nevertheless, a Waspy nerd. In Heart-Throb, a game with sixty boyfriend cards, not one of the boys even has an ethnic-sounding name. The only feature that distinguishes a few, and makes them appear somewhat "different," is the appearance of dark sunglasses. In Girl Talk: Date Line, the trendy names include, for the girls, Danielle, Tina, Allison, and Stephanie, and for the boys, Drew, Trent, Eric, and Brad. This game, interestingly enough, features one African-American boy but no African-American girls; one wonders who players match him up with for a date.

In addition to the privilege of race, the characters in these games have the privilege of social class. The Sweet Valley High game goes the furthest with this: One character gets rewarded for giving her housekeeper the day off and making her own bed, another for donating a large sum to charity, a third for taking everyone for a ride in her new sports car. In each of the other games, the girls shown playing the games or the

character pieces in the games dress well, have access to income to buy
clothing and make-up, and have private space all their own. No apartment living for these girls; they relax in their suburban bedrooms with
plush carpet or scoot around town in their very own vehicles.

These board games promote the social control of girls' sexuality as
well, with heterosexuality consistently privileged. In three of the four
games, the only object is either to secure a boyfriend for oneself or secure
one for others. The fourth clearly favors marriage and children as the end
goal in life. Each game encourages competition among girls for boys, as
girls steal others' boyfriends or find warnings in the instructions, as they
do in the Sweet Valley game, that they need to keep an eye on their
thieving girlfriends. Girls play these games together, but rather than promoting positive female culture or solidarity, the games teach girls that
they cannot trust each other when it comes to their primary life definition: boys. The directions in the Sweet Valley game specify that girls can
never have more than one boyfriend at a time; if they pick up a second,
they must discard one. In Girl Talk: Date Line, the directions actually
state in writing that players should not attempt to match up a girl with a
girl or a boy with a boy for a date. According to these games, all girls,
even the nerdy ones, can look forward to a shared future. What the
games encourage players to share, however, is not the ability to laugh,
intelligence, or even stereotypical nurturing qualities; instead, players
share a future that must, apparently at any cost, include a man.

These four games rely on stereotypes about girls that stray far from
the goal of promoting more egalitarian, difference-respecting play experiences. The games suggest that their characters represent the "ordinary"
adolescent in the United States. Virtually all young adolescents, the games
would have us believe, are white, long-haired, fair-haired, blemish-free,
wealthy, heterosexual, and well dressed. The overall message does not
necessarily suggest that all adolescent girls think the same way, because
aside from their desire to secure a boyfriend we or the players learn little
about what interests girls. What ties young adolescent girls together,
through these games, is simply that they must acquire a boyfriend.

Interestingly enough, the stars of these games, the girls featured on
the covers and on the boards and playing pieces, do not closely resemble
the voluptuous and flashy young women of the teen magazines. In fact,
they seem far closer to the "average" than that. It would be a mistake to
think for a moment, though, that they represent anything but a carefully
crafted version of the ideal, of the "average" ideal. Perhaps girls read
fashion magazines and wish they could have the beautiful looks of the
models. Perhaps when they play the board games they wish they could
be the average girl, fit easily into developing peer norms, and blend into
their settings as easily as the girls on the game boxes seem to blend into
theirs. The games present a message just as damaging as that of the magazines, though, because if the game characters represent the norm, the av-

erage, they must represent the attainable. The truth remains that white wealthy heterosexuality is not the norm, not what young girls have in common. Unfortunately, however, most adolescents share a strong desire to meet the established, if largely unattainable, norm.

The final way in which these games fail Letty Pogrebin's test and, in so doing, fail real girls' needs, is that they completely fail to challenge girls' intellects or inspire their creativity. Researchers have revealed that girls' games often provide fewer intellectual challenges than do boys' games. Girls, more restricted in their play than boys in terms of movement and noise, learn to appreciate indoor activities, in smaller groups, and at lower skill levels (Rivers et al. 105–7). The few board games we have focused on match those findings.

The most insulting of the four games is Girl Talk: Date Line. Girls match couples up and then hope that the date takes place. In fact, though, the individual qualities players match up do not determine whether or not the date takes place. Instead, a continuously running cassette tape determines everything. While the game instructs players that if the two individuals seem compatible the date will happen, sheer luck actually determines the course of action. If a player is fortunate enough to put her two characters in the microphone machine when the tape is about to play a successful date scenario, she wins. If not, she loses.

The next two games provide little more of a challenge. In Heart-Throb girls choose which boy they prefer, then they guess which boy their friends will prefer. A simple guessing game, Heart-Throb is packaged as though it contains something of consequence. Girls could easily play the same game, if they wished, using a magazine with pictures of boys in it; they hardly need the game board or pieces. Sweet Valley High is essentially a memory game. Girls have to remember in which classroom the corsage card sits, in which classroom their boyfriend sits. This game hardly differs from any matching game with cards played by young children, except for the ideological messages reinforcing gender and other stereotypes.

Girl Talk: A Game of Truth or Dare is the most sophisticated and potentially challenging of these board games. Girls actually do things in this game; they move around, they talk to each other, they share secrets. Were the end goals not so blatantly sexist, the packaging not so sterotypically feminine, and the zit stickers not so offensive, this might not be a bad game.

Games encourage players to develop particular skills. By encouraging large group play in a variety of settings, many boys' games urge them to achieve success in the world at large. Most girls' games, however, prepare girls for a life in one setting, the home, by emphasizing verbal skills in small groups rather than large ones, and by taking place indoors. Interestingly enough, although the object of many of the girls' games is to secure a boyfriend, the verbal skills emphasized do not apply to him. In other words, girls learn to talk to each other about boys, but they do not learn to communicate with those boys.

Further research may reveal that girls use these games in subversive as well as stereotypical ways or that, like the latest fashions, these trendy games spend more time in closets than they do in the center of girls' play areas. For the many girls who do play them as designated, however, these sex-stereotyped games promote damaging stereotypes, passive rather than active play, and skills that fall short of girls' cognitive abilities. The games assume that all girls share a common future of domestic work, subservience to men, and limited life experience. They also further the likelihood of such a future by failing to encourage intellectual growth. In an advice book for girls published in 1936, Mary Brockman wrote that "boys don't want girls to talk too much or try to appear too wise. . . . [T]hey want girls to know when to sit back and look interested" (173). Apparently, the lesson lives on. These board games, as much a part of the toy-store world of the 1990s as they were of the 1970s, frame a world of limited possibilities for girls.

WORKS CITED

Brockman, Mary. *What Is She Like? A Personality Book for Girls.* New York: Scribner's, 1936.
Chandler, E. M. *Educating Adolescent Girls.* London: Allen, 1980.
Coleman, John C., and Leo Hendry. *The Nature of Adolescence.* New York: Routledge, 1990.
Comstock, George. *Television and the American Child.* San Diego: Academic, 1991.
Dun and Bradstreet. *America's Corporate Families.* Parsippany: Dun and Bradstreet, 1992.
Huston, Aletha, and Mildred Alvarez. "The Socialization Context of Gender Role Development in Early Adolescence." *From Childhood to Adolescence: A Transitional Period?* Ed. Raymond Montemayor, Gerald Adams, and Thomas Gullotta. Newbury Park: Sage, 1990. 156–79.
McRobbie, Angela. *Feminism and Youth Culture: From "Jackie" to "Just Seventeen."* Boston: Unwin Hyman, 1991.
Montemayor, Raymond, Gerald Adams, and Thomas Gullotta, eds. *From Childhood to Adolescence: A Transitional Period?* Introduction. Newbury Park: Sage, 1990.
Newman, Barbara, and Philip Newman. *Adolescent Development.* Columbus: Merrill, 1986.
Pogrebin, Letty Cottin. "Toys for Free Children." *Ms.* Dec. 1973: 48+.
Rivers, Caryl, Rosalind Barnett, and Brace Baruch. *Beyond Sugar and Spice: How Women Grow, Learn, and Thrive.* New York: Putnam, 1979.

Reading the Text

1. What gender values do games like Heart-Throb: The Dream Date Game and Girl Talk: Date Line teach the girls who play them, according to Scanlon?
2. How do race and class figure in the board games that Scanlon analyzes?

3. What is an "ordinary" (para. 23) American adolescent, according to the images projected by board games?
4. How are male identities constructed in the board games Scanlon discusses?

Reading the Signs

1. As a child, did you play with one of the games Scanlon discusses (or with one like them)? If so, write a journal entry reflecting on their influence on you. Did you play with them subversively, or did you follow the rules? If you didn't play such games, reflect on the ways the games you did play may have socialized you.
2. As a class project, design a game that would counteract the gender constructions that Scanlon identifies in her essay.
3. Read or reread Naomi Wolf's "The Beauty Myth" (below), and compare the role of board games in constructing young girls' gender identities with that of the advertising and the beauty industries.
4. Adopting Scanlon's perspective, write a response to Deborah Blum's argument for the biological basis of gender behaviors ("The Gender Blur: Where Does Biology End and Society Take Over?" p. 453).

NAOMI WOLF

The Beauty Myth

||||||||||||||||||||||||||||||||||||||||||||||||||||||||||||||||||

Before Kate Moss there was Twiggy, and before Twiggy, well, women weren't expected to look so slim—not, at least, if we judge by Marilyn Monroe. And for Naomi Wolf (b. 1962), that's exactly the problem. Contemporary standards of feminine beauty have devolved to a point that can only be described as anorexic, and America's young women are paying the price through a near-epidemic of bulimia and anorexia. The most effective way to combat this epidemic, Wolf argues, is to show how what we call "beautiful" is a cultural myth that has been framed for certain purposes—essentially, Wolf believes, to keep women under control by imprisoning them in their bodies. A prominent figure in feminist and neofeminist circles, Naomi Wolf is the author of The Beauty Myth *(1991), from which this selection is excerpted,* Fire with Fire *(1993), and* Promiscuities *(1997).*

At last, after a long silence, women took to the streets. In the two decades of radical action that followed the rebirth of feminism in the early 1970s, Western women gained legal and reproductive rights, pursued higher education, entered the trades and the professions, and overturned ancient and revered beliefs about their social role. A generation on, do women feel free?

The affluent, educated, liberated women of the First World, who can enjoy freedoms unavailable to any woman ever before, do not feel as free as they want to. And they can no longer restrict to the subconscious their sense that this lack of freedom has something to do with—with apparently frivolous issues, things that really should not matter. Many are ashamed to admit that such trivial concerns—to do with physical appearance, bodies, faces, hair, clothes—matter so much. But in spite of shame, guilt, and denial, more and more women are wondering if it isn't that they are entirely neurotic and alone but rather that something important is indeed at stake that has to do with the relationship between female liberation and female beauty.

The more legal and material hindrances women have broken through, the more strictly and heavily and cruelly images of female beauty have come to weigh upon us. Many women sense that women's collective progress has stalled; compared with the heady momentum of earlier days, there is a dispiriting climate of confusion, division, cynicism, and above all, exhaustion. After years of much struggle and little recognition, many older women feel burned out; after years of taking its light for granted, many younger women show little interest in touching new fire to the torch.

During the past decade, women breached the power structure; meanwhile, eating disorders rose exponentially and cosmetic surgery became the fastest-growing medical specialty. During the past five years, consumer spending doubled, pornography became the main media category, ahead of legitimate films and records combined, and thirty-three thousand American women told researchers that they would rather lose ten to fifteen pounds than achieve any other goal. More women have more money and power and scope and legal recognition than we have ever had before; but in terms of how we feel about ourselves *physically,* we may actually be worse off than our unliberated grandmothers. Recent research consistently shows that inside the majority of the West's controlled, attractive, successful working women, there is a secret "underlife" poisoning our freedom; infused with notions of beauty, it is a dark vein of self-hatred, physical obsessions, terror of aging, and dread of lost control.

It is no accident that so many potentially powerful women feel this way. We are in the midst of a violent backlash against feminism that uses images of female beauty as a political weapon against women's advancement: the beauty myth. It is the modern version of a social reflex that has been in force since the Industrial Revolution. As women released themselves from the feminine mystique of domesticity, the beauty myth took

5

over its lost ground, expanding as it waned to carry on its work of social control.

The contemporary backlash is so violent because the ideology of beauty is the last one remaining of the old feminine ideologies that still has the power to control those women whom second-wave feminism would have otherwise made relatively uncontrollable: It has grown stronger to take over the work of social coercion that myths about motherhood, domesticity, chastity, and passivity no longer can manage. It is seeking right now to undo psychologically and covertly all the good things that feminism did for women materially and overtly.

This counterforce is operating to checkmate the inheritance of feminism on every level in the lives of Western women. Feminism gave us laws against job discrimination based on gender; immediately case law evolved in Britain and the United States that institutionalized job discrimination based on women's appearances. Patriarchal religion declined; new religious dogma, using some of the mind-altering techniques of older cults and sects, arose around age and weight to functionally supplant traditional ritual. Feminists, inspired by Betty Friedan, broke the stranglehold on the women's popular press of advertisers for household products, who were promoting the feminine mystique; at once, the diet and skin care industries became the new cultural censors of women's intellectual space, and because of their pressure, the gaunt, youthful model supplanted the happy housewife as the arbiter of successful womanhood. The sexual revolution promoted the discovery of female sexuality; "beauty pornography"—which for the first time in women's history artificially links a commodified "beauty" directly and explicitly to sexuality—invaded the mainstream to undermine women's new and vulnerable sense of sexual self-worth. Reproductive rights gave Western women control over our own bodies; the weight of fashion models plummeted to 23 percent below that of ordinary women, eating disorders rose exponentially, and a mass neurosis was promoted that used food and weight to strip women of that sense of control. Women insisted on politicizing health; new technologies of invasive, potentially deadly "cosmetic" surgeries developed apace to re-exert old forms of medical control of women.

Every generation since about 1830 has had to fight its version of the beauty myth. "It is very little to me," said the suffragist Lucy Stone in 1855, "to have the right to vote, to own property, etcetera, if I may not keep my body, and its uses, in my absolute right." Eighty years later, after women had won the vote, and the first wave of the organized women's movement had subsided, Virginia Woolf wrote that it would still be decades before women could tell the truth about their bodies. In 1962, Betty Friedan quoted a young woman trapped in the Feminine Mystique: "Lately, I look in the mirror, and I'm so afraid that I'm going to look like my mother." Eight years after that, heralding the cataclysmic second wave of feminism, Germaine Greer described "the Stereotype": "To her belongs all that is beautiful, even the very word beauty itself . . . she is a doll . . . I'm sick of the masquerade." In spite of the great revolution of the second wave, we are not exempt. Now we can look out over ruined barricades: A revolution has come upon us and changed everything in its path, enough time has passed since then for babies to have grown into women, but there still remains a final right not fully claimed.

The beauty myth tells a story: The quality called "beauty" objectively and universally exists. Women must want to embody it and men must want to possess women who embody it. This embodiment is an imperative for women and not for men, which situation is necessary and natural because it is biological, sexual, and evolutionary: Strong men battle for beautiful women, and beautiful women are more reproductively successful. Women's beauty must correlate to their fertility, and since this system is based on sexual selection, it is inevitable and changeless.

None of this is true. "Beauty" is a currency system like the gold standard. Like any economy, it is determined by politics, and in the modern age in the West it is the last, best belief system that keeps male dominance intact. In assigning value to women in a vertical hierarchy according to a culturally imposed physical standard, it is an expression of power relations in which women must unnaturally compete for resources that men have appropriated for themselves.

"Beauty" is not universal or changeless, though the West pretends that all ideals of female beauty stem from one Platonic Ideal Woman; the Maori admire a fat vulva, and the Padung, droopy breasts. Nor is "beauty" a function of evolution: Its ideals change at a pace far more rapid than that of the evolution of species, and Charles Darwin was himself unconvinced by his own explanation that "beauty" resulted from a "sexual selection" that deviated from the rule of natural selection; for women to compete with women through "beauty" is a reversal of the way in which natural selection affects all other mammals. Anthropology has overturned the notion that females must be "beautiful" to be selected to mate: Evelyn Reed, Elaine Morgan, and others have dismissed sociobiological assertions of innate male polygamy and female monogamy. Female higher primates are the sexual initiators; not only do they seek out and enjoy sex with many partners, but "every nonpregnant female takes her turn at being the most desirable of all her troop. And that cycle keeps turning as long as she lives." The inflamed pink sexual organs of primates are often cited by male sociobiologists as analogous to human arrangements relating to female "beauty," when in fact that is a universal, nonhierarchical female primate characteristic.

Nor has the beauty myth always been this way. Though the pairing of the older rich men with young, "beautiful" women is taken to be somehow inevitable, in the matriarchal Goddess religions that dominated the Mediterranean from about 25,000 B.C.E. to about 700 B.C.E., the situation was reversed: "In every culture, the Goddess has many lovers. . . . The clear pattern is of an older woman with a beautiful but expendable youth—Ishtar and Tammuz, Venus and Adonis, Cybele and Attis, Isis and Osiris . . . their only function the service of the divine 'womb.'" Nor is it something only women do and only men watch: among the Nigerian Wodaabes, the women hold economic power and the tribe is obsessed with male beauty; Wodaabe men spend hours together in elaborate makeup sessions, and compete—provocatively painted and dressed, with swaying hips and seductive expressions—in beauty contests judged by women. There is no legitimate historical or biological justification for the beauty myth; what it is doing to women today is a result of nothing more exalted than the need of today's power structure, economy, and culture to mount a counteroffensive against women.

If the beauty myth is not based on evolution, sex, gender, aesthetics, or God, on what is it based? It claims to be about intimacy and sex and life, a celebration of women. It is actually composed of emotional distance, politics, finance, and sexual repression. The beauty myth is not about women at all. It is about men's institutions and institutional power.

The qualities that a given period calls beautiful in women are merely symbols of the female behavior that that period considers desirable: *The beauty myth is always actually prescribing behavior and not appearance.* Competition between women has been made part of the myth so that women will be divided from one another. Youth and (until recently) virginity have been "beautiful" in women since they stand for experiential and sexual ignorance. Aging in women is "unbeautiful" since women grow more powerful with time, and since the links between generations of women must always be newly broken: Older women fear young ones, young women fear old, and the beauty myth truncates for all the female life span. Most urgently, women's identity must be premised upon our "beauty" so that we will remain vulnerable to outside approval, carrying the vital sensitive organ of self-esteem exposed to the air.

Though there has, of course, been a beauty myth in some form for as long as there has been patriarchy, the beauty myth in its modern form is a fairly recent invention. The myth flourishes when material constraints on women are dangerously loosened. Before the Industrial Revolution, the average woman could not have had the same feelings about "beauty" that modern women do who experience the myth as continual comparison to a mass-disseminated physical ideal. Before the development of technologies of mass production—daguerreotypes, photographs, etc.— an ordinary woman was exposed to few such images outside the Church. Since the family was a productive unit and women's work complemented men's, the value of women who were not aristocrats or prostitutes lay in their work skills, economic shrewdness, physical strength, and fertility. Physical attraction, obviously, played its part; but "beauty" as we understand it was not, for ordinary women, a serious issue in the marriage marketplace. The beauty myth in its modern form gained ground after the upheavals of industrialization, as the work unit of the family was destroyed, and urbanization and the emerging factory system demanded what social engineers of the time termed the "separate sphere" of domesticity, which supported the new labor category of the "breadwinner" who left home for the workplace during the day. The middle class expanded, the standards of living and of literacy rose, the size of families shrank; a new class of literate, idle women developed, on whose submission to enforced domesticity the evolving system of industrial capitalism depended. Most of our assumptions about the way women have always thought about "beauty" date from no earlier than the 1830s, when the cult of domesticity was first consolidated and the beauty index invented.

For the first time new technologies could reproduce—in fashion plates, daguerreotypes, tintypes, and rotogravures—images of how women should look. In the 1840s the first nude photographs of prostitutes were taken; advertisements using images of "beautiful" women first appeared in mid-century. Copies of classical artworks, postcards of society beauties and royal mistresses, Currier and Ives prints, and porcelain figurines flooded the separate sphere to which middle-class women were confined.

Since the Industrial Revolution, middle-class Western women have been controlled by ideals and stereotypes as much as by material constraints. This situation, unique to this group, means that analyses that trace "cultural conspiracies" are uniquely plausible in relation to them. The rise of the beauty myth was just one of several emerging social fictions that masqueraded as natural components of the feminine sphere, the better to enclose those women inside it. Other such fictions arose contemporaneously: a version of childhood that required continual maternal supervision; a concept of female biology that required middle-class women to act out the roles of hysterics and hypochondriacs; a conviction that respectable women were sexually anesthetic; and a definition of women's work that occupied them with repetitive, time-consuming, and painstaking tasks such as needlepoint and lacemaking. All such Victorian inventions as these served a double function—that is, though they were encouraged as a means to expend female energy and intelligence in harmless ways, women often used them to express genuine creativity and passion.

But in spite of middle-class women's creativity with fashion and embroidery and child rearing, and, a century later, with the role of the suburban housewife that devolved from these social fictions, the fictions' main purpose was served: During a century and a half of unprecedented feminist agitation, they effectively counteracted middle-class women's dangerous new leisure, literacy, and relative freedom from material constraints.

Though these time- and mind-consuming fictions about women's natural role adapted themselves to resurface in the postwar Feminine Mystique, when the second wave of the women's movement took apart what women's magazines had portrayed as the "romance," "science," and "adventure" of homemaking and suburban family life, they temporarily failed. The cloying domestic fiction of "togetherness" lost its meaning and middle-class women walked out of their front doors in masses.

So the fictions simply transformed themselves once more: Since the   20 women's movement had successfully taken apart most other necessary fictions of femininity, all the work of social control once spread out over the whole network of these fictions had to be reassigned to the only strand left intact, which action consequently strengthened it a hundred-fold. This reimposed onto liberated women's faces and bodies all the limitations, taboos, and punishments of the repressive laws, religious injunctions and reproductive enslavement that no longer carried sufficient force. Inexhaustible but ephemeral beauty work took over from inexhaustible but ephemeral housework. As the economy, law, religion, sexual mores, education, and culture were forcibly opened up to include women more fairly, a private reality colonized female consciousness. By using ideas about "beauty," it reconstructed an alternative female world with its own laws, economy, religion, sexuality, education, and culture, each element as repressive as any that had gone before.

Since middle-class Western women can best be weakened psychologically now that we are stronger materially, the beauty myth, as it has resurfaced in the last generation, has had to draw on more technological sophistication and reactionary fervor than ever before. The modern arsenal of the myth is a dissemination of millions of images of the current ideal; although this barrage is generally seen as a collective sexual fantasy, there is in fact little that is sexual about it. It is summoned out of political fear on the part of male-dominated institutions threatened by women's freedom, and it exploits female guilt and apprehension about our own liberation—latent fears that we might be going too far. This frantic aggregation of imagery is a collective reactionary hallucination willed into being by both men and women stunned and disoriented by the rapidity with which gender relations have been transformed: a bulwark of reassurance against the flood of change. The mass depiction of the modern woman as a "beauty" is a contradiction: Where modern women are growing, moving, and expressing their individuality, as the myth has it, "beauty" is by definition inert, timeless, and generic. That this hallucination is necessary and deliberate is evident in the way "beauty" so directly contradicts women's real situation.

And the unconscious hallucination grows ever more influential and pervasive because of what is now conscious market manipulation: powerful industries—the $33-billion-a-year diet industry, the $20-billion cosmetics industry, the $300-million cosmetic surgery industry, and the $7-billion pornography industry—have arisen from the capital made out of unconscious anxieties, and are in turn able, through their influence on mass culture, to use, stimulate, and reinforce the hallucination in a rising economic spiral.

This is not a conspiracy theory; it doesn't have to be. Societies tell themselves necessary fictions in the same way that individuals and families do. Henrik Ibsen called them "vital lies," and psychologist Daniel Goleman describes them working the same way on the social level that they do within families: "The collusion is maintained by directing attention away from the fearsome fact, or by repackaging its meaning in an acceptable format." The costs of these social blind spots, he writes, are destructive communal illusions. Possibilities for women have become so open-ended that they threaten to destabilize the institutions on which a male-dominated culture has depended, and a collective panic reaction on the part of both sexes has forced a demand for counter-images.

The resulting hallucination materializes, for women, as something all too real. No longer just an idea, it becomes three-dimensional, incorporating within itself how women live and how they do not live: It becomes the Iron Maiden. The original Iron Maiden was a medieval German instrument of torture, a body-shaped casket painted with the limbs and features of a lovely, smiling young woman. The unlucky victim was slowly enclosed inside her; the lid fell shut to immobilize the victim, who died either of starvation or, less cruelly, of the metal spikes embedded in her interior. The modern hallucination in which women are trapped or trap themselves is similarly rigid, cruel, and euphemistically painted. Contemporary culture directs attention to imagery of the Iron Maiden, while censoring real women's faces and bodies.

Why does the social order feel the need to defend itself by evading the fact of real women, our faces and voices and bodies, and reducing the meaning of women to these formulaic and endlessly reproduced "beautiful" images? Though unconscious personal anxieties can be a powerful force in the creation of a vital lie, economic necessity practically guarantees it. An economy that depends on slavery needs to promote images of slaves that "justify" the institution of slavery. Western economics are absolutely dependent now on the continued underpayment of women. An ideology that makes women feel "worth less" was urgently needed to counteract the way feminism had begun to make us feel worth more. This does not require a conspiracy; merely an atmosphere. The contemporary economy depends right now on the representation of women within the beauty myth. Economist John Kenneth Galbraith offers an economic explanation for "the persistence of the view of homemaking as a 'higher calling'": the concept of women as naturally trapped within the Feminine Mystique, he feels, "has been forced on us by popular sociology, by magazines, and by fiction to disguise the fact that woman in her role of consumer has been essential to the development of our industrial society. . . . Behavior that is essential for economic reasons is transformed into a social virtue." As soon as a woman's primary social value could no longer be defined as the attainment of virtuous domesticity, the beauty myth redefined it as the attainment of virtuous beauty. It did so to substitute both a new consumer imperative and a new justification for economic unfairness in the workplace where the old ones had lost their hold over newly liberated women.

Another hallucination arose to accompany that of the Iron Maiden: The caricature of the Ugly Feminist was resurrected to dog the steps of the women's movement. The caricature is unoriginal; it was coined to ridicule the feminists of the nineteenth century. Lucy Stone herself, whom supporters saw as "a prototype of womanly grace . . . fresh and fair as the morning," was derided by detractors with "the usual report" about Victorian feminists: "a big masculine woman, wearing boots, smoking a cigar, swearing like a trooper." As Betty Friedan put it presciently in 1960, even before the savage revamping of that old caricature: "The unpleasant image of feminists today resembles less the feminists themselves than the image fostered by the interests who so bitterly opposed the vote for women in state after state." Thirty years on, her conclusion is more true than ever: That resurrected caricature, which sought to punish women for their public acts by going after their private sense of self, became the paradigm for new limits placed on aspiring women everywhere. After the success of the women's movement's second wave, the beauty myth was perfected to checkmate power at every level in individual women's lives. The modern neuroses of life in the female body spread to woman after woman at epidemic rates. The myth is undermining—slowly, imperceptibly, without our being aware of the real forces of erosion—the ground women have gained through long, hard, honorable struggle.

The beauty myth of the present is more insidious than any mystique of femininity yet: A century ago, Nora slammed the door of the doll's house; a generation ago, women turned their backs on the consumer heaven of the isolated multi-applianced home; but where women are trapped today, there is no door to slam. The contemporary ravages of the beauty backlash are destroying women physically and depleting us psychologically. If we are to free ourselves from the dead weight that has once again been made out of femaleness, it is not ballots or lobbyists or placards that women will need first; it is a new way to see.

Reading the Text

1. What is the "secret 'underlife' poisoning" (para. 4) modern women's lives, according to Wolf?
2. Summarize in your own words what Wolf means by "the beauty myth" (para. 5).

3. What relationship does Wolf see between the beauty myth and feminism?
4. How has the beauty myth replaced the myth of "virtuous domesticity" (para. 25), in Wolf's opinion?
5. What are the behaviors that Wolf believes the beauty myth forces women to adopt, and why?
6. What does Wolf see as the significance of the Iron Maiden, both historically and today?

Reading the Signs

1. Discuss in your journal your attitudes toward your own body. To what extent have your attitudes been shaped by contemporary standards of physical attractiveness?
2. Visit a local art museum (or consult a volume of art reproductions), and study the different ways in which women's bodies are represented. How do the images reflect the history of the beauty myth that Wolf presents? Use your findings to support an analytical essay about how women are represented in art.
3. Bring to class a women's fashion magazine such as *Elle* or *Vogue* and in small groups examine the ways in which both advertising and fashion displays portray women. Discuss what the ideal image of female beauty is in your publications.
4. Write an essay in which you support, challenge, or qualify Wolf's belief that the beauty myth constitutes an "Iron Maiden" (para. 24) that torments the lives of modern women.
5. Implicit in Wolf's argument is the assumption that men are not bound by their own version of the beauty myth. In class, form teams, and debate whether men are as trapped by standards of ideal physical attractiveness as women. To develop your ideas, consult Stuart Ewen, "Hard Bodies" (p. 79), and Diane Barthel, "A Gentleman and a Consumer" (p. 149).

DEBORAH TANNEN

There Is No Unmarked Woman

―――

||||||||||||||||||||||||||||||||||||||||||||||||

If you use the pronoun "s/he" when writing, or write "women and men" rather than "men and women," you are not just writing words: you are making a statement that may "mark" you as being a "feminist." In this analysis of the way everything a woman does marks her in some way or other—from writing and speaking to the way she dresses and styles her hair—Deborah Tannen (b. 1945) reveals the asymmetrical nature of gender semiotics in our culture. Wearing makeup or not wearing makeup sends a signal about a woman, whereas a man without makeup sends no signal at all. Tannen's analysis shows how what men do is implicitly considered the norm in society, and so is relatively neutral, while women's difference inevitably marks them, "because there is no unmarked woman." University Professor in Linguistics at Georgetown University, Deborah Tannen is the author of many books, including the best-selling You Just Don't Understand: Women and Men in Conversation *(1986),* Talking from 9 to 5 *(1994),* Gender and Discourse *(1994), and* The Argument Culture *(1998).*

Some years ago I was at a small working conference of four women and eight men. Instead of concentrating on the discussion I found myself looking at the three other women at the table, thinking how each had a different style and how each style was coherent.

One woman had dark brown hair in a classic style, a cross between Cleopatra and Plain Jane. The severity of her straight hair was softened by wavy bangs and ends that turned under. Because she was beautiful, the effect was more Cleopatra than plain.

The second woman was older, full of dignity and composure. Her hair was cut in a fashionable style that left her with only one eye, thanks to a side part that let a curtain of hair fall across half her face. As she looked down to read her prepared paper, the hair robbed her of bifocal vision and created a barrier between her and the listeners.

The third woman's hair was wild, a frosted blond avalanche falling over and beyond her shoulders. When she spoke she frequently tossed her head, calling attention to her hair and away from her lecture.

Then there was makeup. The first woman wore facial cover that   5
made her skin smooth and pale, a black line under each eye and mascara that darkened already dark lashes. The second wore only a light gloss on her lips and a hint of shadow on her eyes. The third had blue bands under her eyes, dark blue shadow, mascara, bright red lipstick and rouge; her fingernails flashed red.

I considered the clothes each woman had worn during the three days of the conference: In the first case, man-tailored suits in primary colors with solid-color blouses. In the second, casual but stylish black T-shirts, a floppy collarless jacket and baggy slacks or a skirt in neutral colors. The third wore a sexy jump suit; tight sleeveless jersey and tight yellow slacks; a dress with gaping armholes and an indulged tendency to fall off one shoulder.

Shoes? No. 1 wore string sandals with medium heels; No. 2, sensible, comfortable walking shoes; No. 3, pumps with spike heels. You can fill in the jewelry, scarves, shawls, sweaters—or lack of them.

As I amused myself finding coherence in these styles, I suddenly wondered why I was scrutinizing only the women. I scanned the eight men at the table. And then I knew why I wasn't studying them. The men's styles were unmarked.

The term "marked" is a staple of linguistic theory. It refers to the way language alters the base meaning of a word by adding a linguistic particle that has no meaning on its own. The unmarked form of a word carries the meaning that goes without saying—what you think of when you're not thinking anything special.

The unmarked tense of verbs in English is the present—for ex-   10
ample, *visit*. To indicate past, you mark the verb by adding *ed* to yield *visited*. For future, you add a word: *will visit*. Nouns are presumed to be singular until marked for plural, typically by adding *s* or *es*, so *visit* becomes *visits* and *dish* becomes *dishes*.

The unmarked forms of most English words also convey "male." Being male is the unmarked case. Endings like *ess* and *ette* mark words as "female." Unfortunately, they also tend to mark them for frivolousness. Would you feel safe entrusting your life to a doctorette? Alfre Woodard, who was an Oscar nominee for best supporting actress, says she identifies herself as an actor because "actresses worry about eyelashes and cellulite, and women who are actors worry about the characters we are playing." Gender markers pick up extra meanings that reflect common associations with the female gender: not quite serious, often sexual.

Each of the women at the conference had to make decisions about hair, clothing, makeup and accessories, and each decision carried meaning. Every style available to us was marked. The men in our group had made decisions, too, but the range from which they chose was incomparably narrower. Men can choose styles that are marked, but they don't have to, and in this group none did. Unlike the women, they had the option of being unmarked.

Take the men's hair styles. There was no marine crew cut or oily longish hair falling into eyes, no asymmetrical, two-tiered construction to swirl over a bald top. One man was unabashedly bald; the others had hair of standard length, parted on one side, in natural shades of brown or gray or graying. Their hair obstructed no views, left little to toss or push back or run fingers through and, consequently, needed and attracted no attention. A few men had beards. In a business setting, beards might be marked. In this academic gathering, they weren't.

There could have been a cowboy shirt with string tie or a three-piece suit or a necklaced hippie in jeans. But there wasn't. All eight men wore brown or blue slacks and nondescript shirts of light colors. No man wore sandals or boots; their shoes were dark, closed, comfortable, and flat. In short, unmarked.

Although no man wore makeup, you couldn't say the men didn't   15
wear makeup in the sense that you could say a woman didn't wear makeup. For men, no makeup is unmarked.

I asked myself what style we women could have adopted that would have been unmarked, like the men's. The answer was none. There is no unmarked woman.

There is no woman's hair style that can be called standard, that says nothing about her. The range of women's hair styles is staggering, but a woman whose hair has no particular style is perceived as not caring about how she looks, which can disqualify her from many positions, and will subtly diminish her as a person in the eyes of some.

Women must choose between attractive shoes and comfortable shoes. When our group made an unexpected trek, the woman who wore flat, laced shoes arrived first. Last to arrive was the woman in spike heels, shoes in hand and a handful of men around her.

If a woman's clothing is tight or revealing (in other words, sexy), it sends a message—an intended one of wanting to be attractive, but also a possibly unintended one of availability. If her clothes are not sexy, that too sends a message, lent meaning by the knowledge that they could have been. There are thousands of cosmetic products from which women can choose and myriad ways of applying them. Yet no makeup at all is anything but unmarked. Some men see it as a hostile refusal to please them.

Women can't even fill out a form without telling stories about them- 20 selves. Most forms give four titles to choose from. "Mr." carries no meaning other than that the respondent is male. But a woman who checks "Mrs." or "Miss" communicates not only whether she has been married but also whether she has conservative tastes in forms of ad- dress—and probably other conservative values as well. Checking "Ms." declines to let on about marriage (checking "Mr." declines nothing since nothing was asked), but it also marks her as either liberated or rebellious, depending on the observer's attitudes and assumptions.

I sometimes try to duck these variously marked choices by giving my title as "Dr."—and in so doing risk marking myself as either uppity (hence sarcastic responses like "Excuse *me*!") or an overachiever (hence reactions of congratulatory surprise like "Good for you!").

All married women's surnames are marked. If a woman takes her husband's name, she announces to the world that she is married and has traditional values. To some it will indicate that she is less herself, more identified by her husband's identity. If she does not take her husband's name, this too is marked, seen as worthy of comment: She has *done* something; she has "kept her own name." A man is never said to have "kept his own name" because it never occurs to anyone that he might have given it up. For him using his own name is unmarked.

A married woman who wants to have her cake and eat it too may use her surname plus his, with or without a hyphen. But this too announces her marital status and often results in a tongue-tying string. In a list (Harvey O'Donovan, Jonathan Feldman, Stephanie Woodbury McGillicutty), the woman's multiple name stands out. It is marked.

I have never been inclined toward biological explanations of gender differences in language, but I was intrigued to see Ralph Fasold bring biological phenomena to bear on the question of linguistic marking in his book *The Sociolinguistics of Language.* Fasold stresses that language and culture are particularly unfair in treating women as the marked case because biologically it is the male that is marked. While two X chromosomes make a female, two Y chromosomes make nothing. Like the linguistic markers *s, es,* or *ess,* the Y chromosome doesn't "mean" anything unless it is attached to a root form—an X chromosome.

Developing this idea elsewhere Fasold points out that girls are born   25
with fully female bodies, while boys are born with modified female bodies. He invites men who doubt this to lift up their shirts and contemplate why they have nipples.

In his book, Fasold notes "a wide range of facts which demonstrates that female is the unmarked sex." For example, he observes that there are a few species that produce only females, like the whiptail lizard. Thanks to parthenogenesis, they have no trouble having as many daughters as they like. There are no species, however, that produce only males. This is no surprise, since any such species would become extinct in its first generation.

Fasold is also intrigued by species that produce individuals not involved in reproduction, like honeybees and leaf-cutter ants. Reproduction is handled by the queen and a relatively few males; the workers are sterile females. "Since they do not reproduce," Fasold said, "there is no reason for them to be one sex or the other, so they default, so to speak, to female."

Fasold ends his discussion of these matters by pointing out that if language reflected biology, grammar books would direct us to use "she" to include males and females and "he" only for specifically male referents. But they don't. They tell us that "he" means "he or she," and that "she" is used only if the referent is specifically female. This use of "he" as the sex-indefinite pronoun is an innovation introduced into English by grammarians in the eighteenth and nineteenth centuries, according to Peter Mühlhäusler and Rom Harré in *Pronouns and People.* From at least about 1500, the correct sex-indefinite pronoun was "they," as it still is in casual spoken English. In other words, the female was declared by grammarians to be the marked case.

Writing this article may mark me not as a writer, not as a linguist, not as an analyst of human behavior, but as a feminist—which will have positive or negative, but in any case powerful, connotations for readers. Yet I doubt that anyone reading Ralph Fasold's book would put that label on him.

I discovered the markedness inherent in the very topic of gender   30
after writing a book on differences in conversational style based on geographical region, ethnicity, class, age, and gender. When I was inter-

viewed, the vast majority of journalists wanted to talk about the differences between women and men. While I thought I was simply describing what I observed—something I had learned to do as a researcher—merely mentioning women and men marked me as a feminist for some.

When I wrote a book devoted to gender differences in ways of speaking, I sent the manuscript to five male colleagues, asking them to alert me to any interpretation, phrasing, or wording that might seem unfairly negative toward men. Even so, when the book came out, I encountered responses like that of the television talk show host who, after interviewing me, turned to the audience and asked if they thought I was male-bashing.

Leaping upon a poor fellow who affably nodded in agreement, she made him stand and asked, "Did what she say accurately describe you?" "Oh, yes," he answered. "That's me exactly." "And what she said about women—does that sound like your wife?" "Oh yes," he responded. "That's her exactly." "Then why do you think she's male-bashing?" He answered, with disarming honesty, "Because she's a woman and she's saying things about men."

To say anything about women and men without marking oneself as either feminist or anti-feminist, male-basher or apologist for men seems as impossible for a woman as trying to get dressed in the morning without inviting interpretations of her character.

Sitting at the conference table musing on these matters, I felt sad to think that we women didn't have the freedom to be unmarked that the men sitting next to us had. Some days you just want to get dressed and go about your business. But if you're a woman, you can't, because there is no unmarked woman.

Reading the Text

1. Explain in your own words what Tannen means by "marked" (para. 9).
2. Why does Tannen say that men have the option of being "unmarked" (para. 9)?
3. What significance does Tannen see in Ralph Fasold's biological explanations of linguistic gender difference?

Reading the Signs

1. Do you agree with Tannen's assumption that men have the luxury of remaining "unmarked" (para. 9) in our society? Do you think it's possible to be purely unmarked? To develop your essay, you might interview some men, particularly those who elect to have an unconventional appearance, and read James William Gibson's "Warrior Dreams" (p. 496).

2. In class, survey the extent to which the males and females in your class are "marked" or "unmarked," in Tannen's terms, studying such signs as clothing and hair style. Do the males tend to have unmarked styles, while the women tend to send a message by their choices? Discuss the results of your survey, and reflect on the validity of Tannen's claims.

3. Interview at least five women who are married, and ask them about their choice of names: Did they keep their "own" name, adopt their husband's, or opt for a hyphenated version? What signals do they want to send about their identity through their names? Use the results of your interviews to write a reflective essay on how our names function as signs, particularly as gender-related signs.

4. What would an unmarked appearance for women be like? Write a speculative essay in which you imagine the features of an unmarked female appearance. Share your essay with your class.

JAMES WILLIAM GIBSON
Warrior Dreams

||||||||||||||||||||||||||||||||||||||||||||||||||||

If you think that Rambo was a joke, James William Gibson has news for you: his popularity was a symptom of an identity crisis that has afflicted American men since the advent of feminism and the U.S. defeat in Vietnam more than a quarter of a century ago. Feeling unmanned by a war lost and by the rewriting of gender codes in the wake of the sexual revolution, millions of American men, as Gibson puts it, "began to dream, to fantasize about the powers and features of another kind of man who could retake and reorder the world." Such fantasy warriors include Rambo, Dirty Harry, and Jack Ryan, fictional role models for the gun-toting legions of a new paramilitary subculture that is quite real, and growing. Paintball, anyone? A professor of sociology at California State University, Long Beach, Gibson is also the author of The Perfect War: Technowar in Vietnam *(1986).*

We couldn't see them, but we could hear their bugles sound the call. The Communist battalions were organizing for a predawn assault. Captain Kokalis smiled wickedly; he'd been through this before. A "human wave" assault composed of thousands of enemy soldiers was headed our way. The captain ordered the remaining soldiers in his command to check their .30- and .50-caliber machine guns. Earlier in the night, the demolitions squad attached to our unit had planted mines and explosive charges for hundreds of meters in front of our position.

And then it began. At a thousand meters, the soldiers emerged screaming from the gray-blue fog. "Fire!" yelled Captain Kokalis. The gun crews opened up with short bursts of three to seven rounds; their bullets struck meat. Everywhere I could see, clusters of Communist troops were falling by the second. But the wave still surged forward. At five hundred meters, Kokalis passed the word to his gunners to increase their rate of fire to longer strings of ten to twenty rounds. Sergeant Donovan, the demolitions squad leader, began to reap the harvest from the night's planting. Massive explosions ripped through the Communist troops. Fire and smoke blasted into the dawn sky. It was as if the human wave had hit a submerged reef; as the dying fell, wide gaps appeared in the line where casualties could no longer be replaced.

But still they kept coming, hundreds of men, each and every one bent on taking the American position and wiping us out. As the Communists reached one hundred meters, Kokalis gave one more command. Every machine gun in our platoon went to its maximum rate of sustained full-automatic frenzy, sounding like chain saws that just keep cutting and cutting

And then it was over. The attack subsided into a flat sea of Communist dead. No Americans had been killed or wounded. We were happy to be alive, proud of our victory. We only wondered if our ears would ever stop ringing and if we would ever again smell anything other than the bittersweet aroma of burning gunpowder . . .

Although an astonishing triumph was achieved that day, no historian   5 will ever find a record of this battle in the hundreds of volumes and thousands of official reports written about the Korean or Vietnam wars. Nor was the blood spilt part of a covert operation in Afghanistan or some unnamed country in Africa, Asia, or Latin America.

No, this battle was fought inside the United States, a few miles north of Las Vegas, in September 1986. It was a purely *imaginary* battle, a dream of victory staged as part of the *Soldier of Fortune* magazine's annual convention. The audience of several hundred men, women, and children, together with reporters and a camera crew from *CBS News,* sat in bleachers behind half a dozen medium and heavy machine guns owned by civilians. Peter G. Kokalis, *SOF*'s firearms editor, set the scene for the audience and asked them to imagine that the sandy brushland of the Desert Sportsman Rifle and Pistol Club was really a killing zone for incoming Communist troops. Kokalis was a seasoned storyteller; he'd given this performance before. When the fantasy battle was over, the fans went wild with applause. Kokalis picked up a microphone, praised Donovan (another *SOF* staff member)—"He was responsible for that whole damn Communist bunker that went up"—and told the parents in the audience to buy "claymores [antipersonnel land mines] and other good shit for the kids." A marvelous actor who knew what his audience wanted, Kokalis sneered, "Did you get that, CBS, on your videocam? Screw you knee-jerk liberals."[1]

The shoot-out and victory over Communist forces conducted at the Desert Sportsman Rifle and Pistol Club was but one battle in a cultural or imaginary "New War" that had been going on since the late 1960s and early 1970s. The bitter controversies surrounding the Vietnam War had discredited the old American ideal of the masculine warrior hero for much of the public. But in 1971, when Clint Eastwood made the transition from playing cowboys in old *Rawhide* reruns and spaghetti westerns to portraying San Francisco police detective Harry Callahan in *Dirty Harry,* the warrior hero returned in full force. His backup arrived in 1974 when Charles Bronson appeared in *Death Wish,* the story of a mild-mannered, middle-aged architect in New York City who, after his wife is murdered and his daughter is raped and driven insane, finds new meaning in life through an endless war of revenge against street punks.

In the 1980s, Rambo and his friends made their assault. The experience of John Rambo, a former Green Beret, was the paradigmatic story of the decade. In *First Blood* (1982), he burns down a small Oregon town while suffering hallucinatory flashbacks to his service in Vietnam. Three years later, in *Rambo: First Blood, Part 2,* he is taken off a prison chain gang by his former commanding officer in Vietnam and asked to perform a special reconnaissance mission to find suspected American POWs in Laos, in exchange for a Presidential pardon. His only question: "Do we get to win this time?" And indeed, Rambo does win. Betrayed by the CIA bureaucrat in charge of the mission, Rambo fights the Russians and Vietnamese by himself and brings the POWs back home.

Hundreds of similar films celebrating the victory of good men over bad through armed combat were made during the late 1970s and 1980s. Many were directed by major Hollywood directors and starred well-known actors. Elaborate special effects and exotic film locations added tens of millions to production costs. And for every large-budget film, there were scores of cheaper formula films employing lesser-known actors and production crews. Often these "action-adventure" films had only brief theatrical releases in major markets. Instead, they made their money in smaller cities and towns, in sales to Europe and the Third World, and most of all, in the sale of videocassettes to rental stores. Movie producers could even turn a profit on "video-only" releases; action-adventure films were the largest category of video rentals in the 1980s.

At the same time, Tom Clancy became a star in the publishing world. His book *The Hunt for Red October* (1984) told the story of the Soviet Navy's most erudite submarine commander, Captain Markus Ramius,

10

and his effort to defect to the United States with the Soviets' premier missile-firing submarine. *Red Storm Rising* (1986) followed, an epic of World War III framed as a high-tech conventional war against the Soviet Union. Clancy's novels all featured Jack Ryan, Ph.D., a former Marine captain in Vietnam turned academic naval historian who returns to duty as a CIA analyst and repeatedly stumbles into life-and-death struggles in which the fate of the world rests on his prowess. All were bestsellers.

President Reagan, Secretary of the Navy John Lehman, and many other high officials applauded Clancy and his hero. Soon the author had a multimillion-dollar contract for a whole series of novels, movie deals with Paramount, and a new part-time job as a foreign-policy expert writing op-ed pieces for the *Washington Post,* the *Los Angeles Times,* and other influential newspapers around the country. His success motivated dozens of authors, mostly active-duty or retired military men, to take up the genre. The "techno-thriller" was born.

At a slightly lower level in the literary establishment, the same publishing houses that marketed women's romance novels on grocery and drug-store paperback racks rapidly expanded their collections of pulp fiction for men. Most were written like hard-core pornography, except that inch-by-inch descriptions of penises entering vaginas were replaced by equally graphic portrayals of bullets, grenade fragments, and knives shredding flesh: "He tried to grab the handle of the commando knife, but the terrorist pushed down on the butt, raised the point and yanked the knife upward through the muscle tissue and guts. It ripped intestines, spilling blood and gore."[2] A minimum of 20 but sometimes as many as 120 such graphically described killings occurred in each 200- to 250-page paperback. Most series came out four times a year with domestic print runs of 60,000 to 250,000 copies. More than a dozen different comic books with titles like *Punisher, Vigilante,* and *Scout* followed suit with clones of the novels.

Along with the novels and comics came a new kind of periodical which replaced the older adventure magazines for men, such as *True* and *Argosy,* that had folded in the 1960s. Robert K. Brown, a former captain in the U.S. Army Special Forces during the Vietnam War, founded *Soldier of Fortune: The Journal of Professional Adventurers* in the spring of 1975, just before the fall of Saigon. *SOF*'s position was explicit from the start: the independent warrior must step in to fill the dangerous void created by the American failure in Vietnam. By the mid-1980s *SOF* was reaching 35,000 subscribers, had newsstand sales of another 150,000, and was being passed around to at least twice as many readers.[3]

---

2. Gar Wilson, *The Fury Bombs,* vol. 5 of *Phoenix Force* (Toronto: Worldwide Library, 1983), 30.

3. *SOF* regularly hired the firm of Starch, Inra, Hopper to study their readership. A condensed version of their 1986 report, from which these figures were taken, was made available to the press at the September 1986 *SOF* convention in Las Vegas.

Half a dozen new warrior magazines soon entered the market. Some, like *Eagle, New Breed,* and *Gung-Ho,* tried to copy the *SOF* editorial package — a strategy that ultimately failed. But most developed their own particular pitch. *Combat Handguns* focused on pistols for would-be gunfighters. *American Survival Guide* advertised and reviewed everything needed for "the good life" after the end of civilization (except birth control devices — too many Mormon subscribers, the editor said), while *S.W.A.T.* found its way to men who idealized these elite police teams and who were worried about home defense against "multiple intruders."

During the same period, sales of military weapons took off. Colt offered two semiautomatic versions of the M16 used by U.S. soldiers in Vietnam (a full-size rifle and a shorter-barreled carbine with collapsible stock). European armories exported their latest products, accompanied by sophisticated advertising campaigns in *SOF* and the more mainstream gun magazines. Israeli Defense Industries put a longer, 16-inch barrel on the Uzi submachine gun (to make it legal) and sold it as a semiautomatic carbine. And the Communist countries of Eastern Europe, together with the People's Republic of China, jumped into the market with the devil's own favorite hardware, the infamous AK47. The AK sold in the United States was the semiautomatic version of the assault rifle used by the victorious Communists in Vietnam and by all kinds of radical movements and terrorist organizations around the world. It retailed for $300 to $400, half the price of an Uzi or an AR-15; complete with three 30-round magazines, cleaning kit, and bayonet, it was truly a bargain.

To feed these hungry guns, munitions manufacturers packaged new "generic" brands of military ammo at discount prices, often selling them in cases of 500 or 1,000 rounds. New lines of aftermarket accessories offered parts for full-automatic conversions, improved flash-hiders, scopes, folding stocks, and scores of other goodies. In 1989, the U.S. Bureau of Alcohol, Tobacco and Firearms (ATF) estimated that two to three million military-style rifles had been sold in this country since the Vietnam War. The Bureau released these figures in response to the public outcry over a series of mass murders committed by psychotics armed with assault rifles.

But the Bureau's statistics tell only part of the story. In less than two decades, millions of American men had purchased combat rifles, pistols, and shotguns and begun training to fight their own personal wars. Elite combat shooting schools teaching the most modern techniques and often costing $500 to over $1,000 in tuition alone were attended not only by soldiers and police but by increasing numbers of civilians as well. Hundreds of new indoor pistol-shooting ranges opened for business in old warehouses and shopping malls around the country, locations ideal for city dwellers and suburbanites.

A new game of "tag" blurred the line between play and actual violence: men got the opportunity to hunt and shoot other men without killing them or risking death themselves. The National Survival Game was invented in 1981 by two old friends, one a screenwriter for the weight-lifting sagas that gave Arnold Schwarzenegger his first starring roles, and the other a former member of the Army's Long Range Reconnaissance Patrol (LRRP) in Vietnam.[4] Later called paintball because it utilized guns firing balls of watercolor paint, by 1987 the game was being played by at least fifty thousand people (mostly men) each weekend on both outdoor and indoor battlefields scattered across the nation. Players wore hard-plastic face masks intended to resemble those of ancient tribal warriors and dressed from head to toe in camouflage clothes imported by specialty stores from military outfitters around the world. The object of the game was to capture the opposing team's flag, inflicting the highest possible body count along the way.

One major park out in the Mojave Desert seventy miles southeast of Los Angeles was named Sat Cong Village. *Sat Cong* is a slang Vietnamese phrase meaning "Kill Communists" that had been popularized by the CIA as part of its psychological-warfare program. Sat Cong Village employed an attractive Asian woman to rent the guns, sell the paintballs, and collect the twenty-dollar entrance fee. Players had their choice of playing fields: Vietnam, Cambodia, or Nicaragua. On the Nicaragua field, the owner built a full-size facsimile of the crashed C-47 cargo plane contracted by Lieutenant Colonel Oliver North to supply the contras. The scene even had three parachutes hanging from trees; the only thing missing was the sole survivor of the crash, Eugene Hasenfus.

The 1980s, then, saw the emergence of a highly energized culture of   20 war and the warrior. For all its varied manifestations, a few common features stood out. The New War culture was not so much military as paramilitary. The new warrior hero was only occasionally portrayed as a member of a conventional military or law enforcement unit; typically, he fought alone or with a small, elite group of fellow warriors. Moreover, by separating the warrior from his traditional state-sanctioned occupations — policeman or soldier — the New War culture presented the warrior roles as the ideal identity for *all* men. Bankers, professors, factory workers, and postal clerks could all transcend their regular stations in life and prepare for heroic battle against the enemies of society.

To many people, this new fascination with warriors and weapons seemed a terribly bad joke. The major newspapers and magazines that arbitrate what is to be taken seriously in American society scoffed at the attempts to resurrect the warrior hero. Movie critics were particularly disdainful of Stallone's Rambo films. *Rambo: First Blood, Part 2* was called

---

4. Lionel Atwill, *Survival Game: Airgun National Manual* (New London, N.H.: The National Survival Game, Inc., 1987), 22–30.

"narcissistic jingoism" by *The New Yorker* and "hare-brained" by the *Wall Street Journal*. The *Washington Post* even intoned that "Sly's body looks fine. Now can't you come up with a workout for his soul?"

But in dismissing Rambo so quickly and contemptuously, commentators failed to notice the true significance of the emerging paramilitary culture. They missed the fact that quite a few people were not writing Rambo off as a complete joke; behind the Indian bandanna, necklace, and bulging muscles, a new culture hero affirmed such traditional American values as self-reliance, honesty, courage, and concern for fellow citizens. Rambo was a worker and a former enlisted man, not a smooth-talking professional. That so many seemingly well-to-do, sophisticated liberals hated him for both his politics and his uncouthness only added to his glory. Further, in their emphasis on Stallone's clownishness the commentators failed to see not only how widespread paramilitary culture had become but also its relation to the historical moment in which it arose.

Indeed, paramilitary culture can be understood only when it is placed in relation to the Vietnam War. America's failure to win that war was a truly profound blow. The nation's long, proud tradition of military victories, from the Revolutionary War through the century-long battles against the Indians to World Wars I and II, had finally come to an end. Politically, the defeat in Vietnam meant that the post–World War II era of overwhelming American political and military power in international affairs, the era that in 1945 *Time* magazine publisher Henry Luce had prophesied would be the "American Century," was over after only thirty years. No longer could U.S. diplomacy wield the big stick of military intervention as a ready threat—a significant part of the American public would no longer support such interventions, and the rest of the world knew it.

Moreover, besides eroding U.S. influence internationally, the defeat had subtle but serious effects on the American psyche. America has always celebrated war and the warrior. Our long, unbroken record of military victories has been crucially important both to the national identity and to the personal identity of many Americans—particularly men. The historian Richard Slotkin locates a primary "cultural archetype" of the nation in the story of a heroic warrior whose victories over the enemy symbolically affirm the country's fundamental goodness and power; we win our wars because, morally, we deserve to win. Clearly, the archetypical pattern Slotkin calls "regeneration through violence" was broken with the defeat in Vietnam.[5] The result was a massive disjunction in American culture, a crisis of self-image: If Americans were no longer winners, then who were they?

---

5. Richard Slotkin, *Regeneration through Violence: The Mythology of the American Frontier, 1660–1860* (Middletown, Conn.: Wesleyan University Press, 1973).

This disruption of cultural identity was amplified by other social   25
transformations. During the 1960s, the civil rights and ethnic pride
movements won many victories in their challenges to racial oppression.
Also, during the 1970s and 1980s, the United States experienced massive
waves of immigration from Mexico, Central America, Vietnam, Cambodia, Korea, and Taiwan. Whites, no longer secure in their power abroad,
also lost their unquestionable dominance at home; for the first time,
many began to feel that they too were just another hyphenated ethnic
group, the Anglo-Americans.

Extraordinary economic changes also marked the 1970s and 1980s.
U.S. manufacturing strength declined substantially; staggering trade
deficits with other countries and the chronic federal budget deficits
shifted the United States from creditor to debtor nation. The post–World
War II American Dream—which promised a combination of technological progress and social reforms, together with high employment rates,
rising wages, widespread home ownership, and ever increasing consumer
options—no longer seemed a likely prospect for the great majority.
At the same time, the rise in crime rates, particularly because of drug
abuse and its accompanying violence, made people feel more powerless
than ever.

While the public world dominated by men seemed to come apart,
the private world of family life also felt the shocks. The feminist movement challenged formerly exclusive male domains, not only in the labor
market and in many areas of political and social life but in the home as
well. Customary male behavior was no longer acceptable in either private relationships or public policy. Feminism was widely experienced by
men as a profound threat to their identity. Men had to change, but to
what? No one knew for sure what a "good man" was anymore.

It is hardly surprising, then, that American men—lacking confidence
in the government and the economy, troubled by the changing relations
between the sexes, uncertain of their identity or their future—began to
dream, to fantasize about the powers and features of another kind of man
who could retake and reorder the world. And the hero of all these
dreams was the paramilitary warrior. In the New War he fights the
battles of Vietnam a thousand times, each time winning decisively. Terrorists and drug dealers are blasted into oblivion. Illegal aliens inside the
United States and the hordes of nonwhites in the Third World are returned by force to their proper place. Women are revealed as dangerous
temptresses who have to be mastered, avoided, or terminated.

Obviously these dreams represented a flight from the present and a
rejection and denial of events of the preceding twenty years. But they
also indicated a more profound and severe distress. The whole modern
world was damned as unacceptable. Unable to find a rational way to face
the tasks of rebuilding society and reinventing themselves, men instead
sought refuge in myths from both America's frontier past and ancient

times. Indeed, the fundamental narratives that shape paramilitary culture and its New War fantasies are often nothing but reinterpretations or re-workings of archaic warrior myths.

In ancient societies, the most important stories a people told about themselves concerned how the physical universe came into existence, how their ancestors first came to live in this universe, and how the gods, the universe, and society were related to one another. These cosmogonic, or creation, myths frequently posit a violent conflict between the good forces of order and the evil forces dedicated to the perpetuation of primordial chaos.[6] After the war in which the gods defeat the evil ones, they establish the "sacred order," in which all of the society's most important values are fully embodied. Some creation myths focus primarily on the sacred order and on the deeds of the gods and goddesses in paradise. Other myths, however, focus on the battles between the heroes and villains that lead up to the founding.[7] In these myths it is war and the warrior that are most sacred. American paramilitary culture borrows from both kinds of stories, but mostly from this second, more violent, type.

In either case, the presence, if not the outright predominance, of archaic male myths at the moment of crisis indicates just how far American men jumped psychically when faced with the declining power of their identities and organizations. The always-precarious balance in modern society between secular institutions and ways of thinking on the one hand and older patterns of belief informed by myth and ritual on the other tilted decisively in the direction of myth. The crisis revealed that at some deep, unconscious level these ancient male creation myths live on in the psyche of many men and that the images and tales from this mythic world of warriors and war still shape men's fantasies about who they are as men, their commitments to each other and to women, and their relationships to society and the state.

Reading the Text

1. How, according to Gibson, did the American defeat in Vietnam lead to the construction of a new kind of "warrior" (para. 20) identity for men?
2. Outline how popular culture helped to shape the warrior image, in Gibson's view.
3. What role does Gibson believe the women's movement play in constructing a new male identity?

---

6. Mircea Eliade, *Myth and Reality,* trans. Willard R. Trask (New York: Harper and Row, 1963).

7. Richard Stivers, *Evil in Modern Myth and Ritual* (Athens: University of Georgia Press, 1982).

4. Explain in your own words how today's "warrior" (para. 20) dreams relate to ancient mythologies.
5. Why does Gibson believe that *Rambo* should be taken seriously?

Reading the Signs

1. Read or reread Michael A. Messner's "Power at Play: Sport and Gender Relations" (p. 460), and compare Messner's argument about the role of sports in the construction of masculine identity with Gibson's analysis of warrior dreams.
2. Gibson suggests that the warrior fantasies found throughout political and popular culture have dangerous real-world implications. Write a critical essay in which you support, complicate, or challenge this suggestion.
3. Using Gibson's argument as your critical framework, write an analysis of militia mentality as described in Peter Doskoch's "The Mind of the Militias" (p. 618).
4. In class, brainstorm current films, TV shows, and video games that are targeted to a male audience. Then discuss the extent to which the warrior dreams that Gibson describes still influence popular culture.

LAURA MILLER

Women and Children First: Gender and the
Settling of the Electronic Frontier

|||||||||||||||||||||||||||||||||||||||||||||||||||||||||||||||||

The Web is often considered a masculine space into which women enter at their peril. Sexual harassment and outright intimidation of women are legion on the Web, right? Wrong, says Laura Miller (b. 1960), in this response to a Newsweek *feature that dwelt on the danger women faced on the Internet. An avid and experienced Internet participant, Miller feels she, and the many women like her who also spend a lot of time in cyberspace, can take care of themselves very well, thank you, and have no need for special protections. Senior editor at* Salon, *an Internet magazine, Miller has published in the* San Francisco Examiner, Wired, Harper's Bazaar, *and the* New York Times Book Review *and is the editor of* The Salon Readers' Guide to Contemporary Authors *(forthcoming).*

When *Newsweek* (May 16, 1994) ran an article entitled "Men, Women and Computers," all hell broke out on the Net, particularly on the on-line service I've participated in for six years, The WELL (Whole Earth 'Lectronic Link). "Cyberspace, it turns out," declared *Newsweek's* Nancy Kantrowitz, "isn't much of an Eden after all. It's marred by just as many sexist ruts and gender conflicts as the Real World.... Women often feel about as welcome as a system crash." "It was horrible. Awful, poorly researched, unsubstantiated drivel," one member wrote, a sentiment echoed throughout some 480 postings.

However egregious the errors in the article (some sources maintain that they were incorrectly quoted), it's only one of several mainstream media depictions of the Net as an environment hostile to women. Even women who had been complaining about on-line gender relations found themselves increasingly annoyed by what one WELL member termed the "cyberbabe harassment" angle that seems to typify media coverage of the issue. Reified in the pages of *Newsweek* and other journals, what had once been the topic of discussions by insiders — on-line commentary is informal, conversational, and often spontaneous — became a journalistic "fact" about the Net known by complete strangers and novices. In a matter of months, the airy stuff of bitch sessions became widespread, hardened stereotypes.

At the same time, the Internet has come under increasing scrutiny as it mutates from an obscure, freewheeling web of computer networks used by a small elite of academics, scientists, and hobbyists to ... well, nobody seems to know exactly what. But the business press prints vague, fevered prophecies of fabulous wealth, and a bonanza mentality has blossomed. With it comes big business and the government, intent on regulating this amorphous medium into a manageable and profitable industry. The Net's history of informal self-regulation and its wide libertarian streak guarantee that battles like the one over the Clipper chip (a mandatory decoding device that would make all encrypted data readable by federal agents) will be only the first among many.

Yet the threat of regulation is built into the very mythos used to conceptualize the Net by its defenders — and gender plays a crucial role in that threat. However revolutionary the technologized interactions of on-line communities may seem, we understand them by deploying a set of very familiar metaphors from the rich figurative soup of American culture. Would different metaphors have allowed the Net a different, better historical trajectory? Perhaps not, but the way we choose to describe the Net now encourages us to see regulation as its inevitable fate. And, by examining how gender roles provide a foundation for the intensification of such social controls, we can illuminate the way those roles proscribe the freedoms of men as well as women.

For months I mistakenly referred to the EFF (an organization   5
founded by John Perry Barlow and Lotus 1-2-3 designer Mitch Kapor to foster access to, and further the discursive freedom of, on-line communications) as "The Electronic Freedom Foundation," instead of by its actual

name, "The Electronic Frontier Foundation." Once corrected, I was struck by how intimately related the ideas "frontier" and "freedom" are in the Western mythos. The *frontier,* as a realm of limitless possibilities and a few social controls, hovers, grail-like, in the American psyche, the dream our national identity is based on, but a dream that's always, somehow, just vanishing away.

Once made, the choice to see the Net as a frontier feels unavoidable, but it's actually quite problematic. The word "frontier" has traditionally described a place, if not land then the limitless "final frontier" of space. The Net, on the other hand, occupies precisely no physical space (although the computers and phone lines that make it possible do). It is a completely bodiless, symbolic thing with no discernable boundaries or location. The land of the American frontier did not become a "frontier" until Europeans determined to conquer it, but the continent existed before the intention to settle it. Unlike land, the Net was created by its pioneers.

Most peculiar, then, is the choice of the word "frontier" to describe an artifact so humanly constructed that it only exists as ideas or information. For central to the idea of the frontier is that it contains no (or very few) other people—fewer than two per square mile according to the nineteenth-century historian Frederick Turner. The freedom the frontier promises is a liberation from the demands of society, while the Net (I'm thinking now of Usenet) has nothing but society to offer. Without other people, news groups, mailing lists, and files simply wouldn't exist and e-mail would be purposeless. Unlike real space, cyberspace must be shared.

Nevertheless, the choice of a spatial metaphor (credited to the science-fiction novelist William Gibson, who coined the term "cyberspace"), however awkward, isn't surprising. Psychologist Julian Jaynes has pointed out that geographical analogies have long predominated humanity's efforts to conceptualize—map out—consciousness. Unfortunately, these analogies bring with them a heavy load of baggage comparable to Pandora's box: open it and a complex series of problems have come to stay.

The frontier exists beyond the edge of settled or owned land. As the land that doesn't belong to anybody (or to people who "don't count," like Native Americans), it is on the verge of being acquired; currently unowned, but still ownable. Just as the idea of chastity makes virginity sexually provocative, so does the unclaimed territory invite settlers, irresistibly so. Americans regard the lost geographical frontier with a melancholy, voluptuous fatalism—we had no choice but to advance upon it and it had no alternative but to submit. When an EFF member compares the Clipper chip to barbed wire encroaching on the prairie, doesn't he realize the surrender implied in his metaphor?

The psychosexual undercurrents (if anyone still thinks of them as   10 "under") in the idea of civilization's phallic intrusion into nature's passive, feminine space have been observed, exhaustively, elsewhere. The classic Western narrative is actually far more concerned with social relationships than conflicts between man and nature. In these stories, the frontier is a lawless society of men, a milieu in which physical strength, courage, and personal charisma supplant institutional authority and violent conflict is the accepted means of settling disputes. The Western narrative connects pleasurably with the American romance of individualistic masculinity; small wonder that the predominantly male founders of the Net's culture found it so appealing.

When civilization arrives on the frontier, it comes dressed in skirts and short pants. In the archetypal 1939 movie *Dodge City,* Wade Hatton (Errol Flynn) refuses to accept the position of marshal because he prefers the footloose life of a trail driver. Abbie Irving (Olivia de Haviland), a recent arrival from the civilized East, scolds him for his unwillingness to accept and advance the cause of law; she can't function (in her job as crusading journalist) in a town governed by brute force. It takes the accidental killing of a child in a street brawl for Hatton to realize that he must pin on the badge and clean up Dodge City.

In the Western mythos, civilization is necessary because women and children are victimized in conditions of freedom. Introduce women and children into a frontier town and the law must follow because women and children must be protected. Women, in fact, are usually the most vocal proponents of the conversion from frontier justice to civil society.

The imperiled women and children of the Western narrative make their appearance today in newspaper and magazine articles that focus on the intimidation and sexual harassment of women on line and reports of pedophiles trolling for victims in computerized chat rooms. If on-line women successfully contest these attempts to depict them as the beleaguered prey of brutish men, expect the pedophile to assume a larger profile in arguments that the Net is out of control.

In the meantime, the media prefer to cast women as the victims, probably because many women actively participate in the call for greater regulation of on-line interactions, just as Abbie Irving urges Wade Hatton to bring the rule of law to Dodge City. These requests have a long cultural tradition, based on the idea that women, like children, constitute a peculiarly vulnerable class of people who require special protection from the elements of society men are expected to confront alone. In an insufficiently civilized society like the frontier, women, by virtue of this childlike vulnerability, are thought to live under the constant threat of kidnap, abuse, murder, and especially rape.

Women, who have every right to expect that crimes against their person will be rigorously prosecuted, should nevertheless regard the notion of special protections (chivalry, by another name) with suspicion. Based as it is on the idea that women are inherently weak and incapable of self-defense and that men are innately predatory, it actually reinforces

15

the power imbalance between the sexes, with its roots in the concept of women as property, constantly under siege and requiring the vigilant protection of their male owners. If the romance of the frontier arises from the promise of vast stretches of unowned land, an escape from the restrictions of a society based on private property, the introduction of women spoils that dream by reintroducing the imperative of property in their own persons.

How does any of this relate to on-line interactions, which occur not on a desert landscape but in a complex, technological society where women are supposed to command equal status with men? It accompanies us as a set of unexamined assumptions about what it means to be male or female, assumptions that we believe are rooted in the imperatives of our bodies. These assumptions follow us into the bodiless realm of cyberspace, a forum where, as one scholar puts it "participants are washed clean of the stigmata of their real 'selves' and are free to invent new ones to their tastes." Perhaps some observers feel that the replication of gender roles in a context where the absence of bodies supposedly makes them superfluous proves exactly how innate those roles are. Instead, I see in the relentless attempts to interpret on-line interactions as highly gendered, an intimation of just how artificial, how created, our gender system is. If it comes "naturally," why does it need to be perpetually defended and reasserted?

Complaints about the treatment of women on line fall into three categories: that women are subjected to excessive, unwanted sexual attention, that the prevailing style of on-line discussion turns women off, and that women are singled out by male participants for exceptionally dismissive or hostile treatment. In making these assertions, the *Newsweek* article and other stories on the issue do echo grievances that some on-line women have made for years. And, without a doubt, people have encountered sexual come-ons, aggressive debating tactics, and ad hominem attacks on the Net. However, individual users interpret such events in widely different ways, and to generalize from those interpretations to describe the experiences of women and men as a whole is a rash leap indeed.

I am one of many women who don't recognize their own experience of the Net in the misogynist gauntlet described above. In researching this essay, I joined America Online and spent an hour or two "hanging out" in the real-time chat rooms reputed to be rife with sexual harassment. I received several "instant messages" from men, initiating private conversations with innocuous questions about my hometown and tenure on the service. One man politely inquired if I was interested in "hot phone talk" and just as politely bowed out when I declined. At no point did I feel harassed or treated with disrespect. If I ever want to find a phone-sex partner, I now know where to look but until then I probably won't frequent certain chat rooms.

Other women may experience a request for phone sex or even those tame instant messages as both intrusive and insulting (while still others maintain that they have received much more explicit messages and inquiries completely out of the blue). My point isn't that my reactions are the more correct, but rather that both are the reactions of women, and no journalist has any reason to believe that mine are the exception rather than the rule.

For me, the menace in sexual harassment comes from the underlying threat of rape or physical violence. I see my body as the site of my heightened vulnerability as a woman. But on line—where I have no body and neither does anyone else—I consider rape to be impossible. Not everyone agrees. Julian Dibble, in an article for the *Village Voice,* describes the repercussions of a "rape" in a multiuser dimension, or MUD, in which one user employed a subprogram called a "voodoo doll" to cause the personae of other users to perform sexual acts. Citing the "conflation of speech and act that's inevitable in any computer-mediated world," he moved toward the conclusion that "since rape can occur without any physical pain or damage, then it must be classified as a crime against the mind." Therefore, the offending user had committed something on the same "conceptual continuum" as rape. Tellingly, the incident led to the formation of the first governmental entity on the MUD.

No doubt the cyber-rapist (who went by the nom de guerre Mr. Bungle) appreciated the elevation of his mischief-making to the rank of virtual felony: all of the outlaw glamour and none of the prison time (he was exiled from the MUD). Mr. Bungle limited his victims to personae created by women users, a choice that, in its obedience to prevailing gender roles, shaped the debate that followed his crimes. For, in accordance with the real-world understanding that women's smaller, physically weaker bodies and lower social status make them subject to violation by men, there's a troubling notion in the real and virtual worlds that women's minds are also more vulnerable to invasion, degradation, and abuse.

This sense of fragility extends beyond interactions with sexual overtones. The *Newsweek* article reports that women participants can't tolerate the harsh, contentious quality of on-line discussions, that they prefer mutual support to heated debate, and are retreating wholesale to women-only conferences and newsgroups. As someone who values on-line forums precisely because they mandate equal time for each user who chooses to take it and forestall various "alpha male" rhetorical tactics like interrupting, loudness, or exploiting the psychosocial advantages of greater size or a deeper voice, I find this perplexing and disturbing. In these laments I hear the reluctance of women to enter into the kind of robust debate that characterizes healthy public life, a willingness to let men bully us even when they've been relieved of most of their tradi-

20

tional advantages. Withdrawing into an electronic purdah where one will never be challenged or provoked, allowing the ludicrous ritual chest-thumping of some users to intimidate us into silence—surely women can come up with a more spirited response than this.

And of course they can, because besides being riddled with reductive stereotypes, media analyses like *Newsweek*'s simply aren't accurate. While the on-line population is predominantly male, a significant and vocal minority of women contribute regularly and more than manage to hold their own. Some of the WELL's most bombastic participants are women, just as there are many tactful and conciliatory men. At least, I think there are, because, ultimately, it's impossible to be sure of anyone's biological gender on line. "Transpostites," people who pose as members of the opposite gender, are an established element of Net society, most famously a man who, pretending to be a disabled lesbian, built warm and intimate friendships with women on several CompuServe forums.

Perhaps what we should be examining is not the triumph of gender differences on the Net, but their potential blurring. In this light, *Newsweek*'s stout assertion that in cyberspace "the gender gap is real" begins to seem less objective than defensive, an insistence that on-line culture is "the same" as real life because the idea that it might be different, when it comes to gender, is too scary. If gender roles can be cast off so easily, they may be less deeply rooted, less "natural" than we believe. There may not actually be a "masculine" or "feminine" mind or outlook, but simply a conventional way of interpreting individuals that recognizes behavior seen as in accordance with their biological gender and ignores behavior that isn't.

For example, John Seabury wrote in the *New Yorker* (June 6, 1994)   25 of his stricken reaction to his first "flame," a colorful slice of adolescent invective sent to him by an unnamed technology journalist. Reading it, he begins to "shiver" like a burn victim, an effect that worsens with repeated readings. He writes that "the technology greased the words . . . with a kind of immediacy that allowed them to slide easily into my brain." He tells his friends, his co-workers, his partner—even his mother—and, predictably, appeals to CompuServe's management for recourse—to no avail. Soon enough, he's talking about civilization and anarchy, how the liberating "lack of social barriers is also what is appalling about the Net," and calling for regulation.

As a newcomer, Seabury was chided for brooding over a missive that most Net veterans would have dismissed and forgotten as the crude potshot of an envious jerk. (I can't help wondering if my fellow journalist never received hate mail in response to his other writings; this bit of e-mail seems comparable, par for the course when one assumes a public profile.) What nobody did was observe that Seabury's reaction—the shock, the feelings of violation, the appeals to his family and support network, the bootless complaints to the authorities—reads exactly like many horror stories about women's trials on the Net. Yet, because Seabury is a man, no one attributes the attack to his gender or suggests that the Net has proven an environment hostile to men. Furthermore, the idea that the Net must be more strictly governed to prevent the abuse of guys who write for the *New Yorker* seems laughable—though who's to say that Seabury's pain is less than any woman's? Who can doubt that, were he a woman, his tribulations would be seen as compelling evidence of Internet sexism?

The idea that women merit special protections in an environment as incorporeal as the Net is intimately bound up with the idea that women's minds are weak, fragile, and unsuited to the rough and tumble of public discourse. It's an argument that women should recognize with profound mistrust and resist, especially when we are used as rhetorical pawns in a battle to regulate a rare (if elite) space of gender ambiguity. When the mainstream media generalize about women's experiences on line in ways that just happen to uphold the most conventional and pernicious gender stereotypes, they can expect to be greeted with howls of disapproval from women who refuse to acquiesce in these roles and pass them on to other women.

And there are plenty of us, as the WELL's response to the *Newsweek* article indicates. Women have always participated in on-line communications, women whose chosen careers in technology and the sciences have already marked them as gender-role resisters. As the schoolmarms arrive on the electronic frontier, their female predecessors find themselves cast in the role of saloon girls, their willingness to engage in "masculine" activities like verbal aggression, debate, or sexual experimentation marking them as insufficiently feminine, or "bad" women. "If that's what women on line are like, I must be a Martian," one WELL woman wrote in response to the shrinking female technophobes depicted in the *Newsweek* article. Rather than regulating so many people to the status of gender aliens, we ought to reconsider how adequate those roles are to the task of describing real human beings.

Reading the Text

1. What images of women on the Net do the mainstream media construct, according to Miller?
2. What does Miller see as the significance of the word "frontier" (para. 5), and how does she relate that word to the Internet?
3. Summarize in your own words the charges that critics make about the gender bias and harassment on the Internet and Miller's response to those charges.
4. Why does Miller state that women should "regard the notion of special protections . . . with suspicion" (para. 15)?

Reading the Signs

1. Log onto a chat room, and see for yourself how gender roles are depicted on the Net. To what extent do you find traditional roles perpetuated or ignored? Use your findings to support an argument for or against Miller's position that women should not be granted special protections on the Internet.

2. Form teams and debate whether regulation should be established to protect Internet users, whether male or female, from harassment, intimidation, or other sorts of abusive language.

3. Read or reread Laurence Shames's "The More Factor" (p. 55). Using his argument as your starting point, write an essay in which you explain the extent to which the Internet appeals to Americans' desire for "more."

4. In your journal, reflect on the controversy Miller mentions over whether online rape is possible. How might one change the traditional definition of rape to include electronic assaults?

5. Interview four or five women on campus who are avid Internet users, asking them about their experiences online. To what extent have they faced the gender-based problems that Miller describes? Use your findings as the basis for an argument about how gender roles are constructed online.

"I think there's a pretty simple reason Jackie
and I are so comfortable with each other.
We see the world as more than just black and white."

©1992 The Cherokee Group

CHER KEE.
Make yourself comfortable.™
Call 1-818-908-9868

Clothes, footwear, and accessories for men, women, and children

CONSTRUCTING RACE

Readings in Multicultural Semiotics

Can Love Be (Color) Blind?

In the 1997-98 season, Fox TV's Ally McBeal fell in love.

So what else is new?

Nothing really, except that Ally's love interest, a series regular named Greg Butters, happened to be black, and as the relationship developed through the 1998-99 season, eyebrows began to rise, not so much because the popular comedy was tackling the issue of interracial romance (*ER*, for one, had done that already) but because it was doing so without making an issue of it. As the producer-creator of the program, David E. Kelley, put it, *Ally McBeal* was a "consciously colorblind show," and so racial consciousness—or tension—just wasn't going to be a part of the story. "Lawyer Ally loves Doctor Greg, and that's all there is to it," the show declared. "Let's not drag race into this."

Was this a sign that America was finally getting over its racial hangups? That the country was entering a new, colorblind era? After all, American popular culture often reflects changing social mores—as *The Mary Tyler Moore Show* signaled a growing mainstream acceptance of the women's movement and *Ellen* indicated that lesbianism was no longer a complete cultural taboo—and so this no-big-deal approach to interracial romance could indeed be taken as a sign that racial attitudes were changing. Otherwise, the plot would have never made it to prime time, where commercial sponsors aren't interested in reaching only the social avante garde: they want big numbers, Nielsen-style.

515

But if *Ally McBeal*'s unusual plot line may have been a sign of change, it did not go unnoticed. Critics of the show's handling of the Ally and Greg romance complained that it was completely unrealistic to depict a black and white romance (especially in a race-conscious city like Boston) without any reference to the difficulties the couple might face, both in public and between themselves. "It's just not authentic," said one critic, who felt that the show should dramatize the problems interracial couples face in America. "What they're doing on *Ally McBeal* is a bold-face lie," said another, while from the other side of the political spectrum, racist postings began to turn up on *Ally McBeal* websites. Indeed, as Kelley himself lamented, "Race not being an issue makes it an issue."

In short, creatively *imagining* a colorblind world is not the same thing as *creating* one. But that has pretty much been the problem all along in America's racial history. From the Declaration of Independence (written, ironically, by a man who owned slaves), which *said* that all of us were equal, to the Fourteenth Amendment, which officially clarified the point, Americans have been trying to imagine a colorblind society. But the issue of race will not go away, and America is not colorblind.

Popular culture, for its part, has been an especially fertile field for the imagining of a colorblind America (consider all those *Lethal Weapon* movies, not to mention *Men in Black,* with their black-and-white buddy pairs) or at least an America where racial intolerance can be put on the table for discussion (as in films like *Guess Who's Coming to Dinner?, In the Heat of the Night,* and *Mississippi Burning*). And in popular music and sports, many of the old racial inequalities have been overthrown, as non-white performers have seized center court, center field, or center stage (indeed, by 1999, hip hop, originally a musical form of black America alone, became America's single most popular musical form). But if America's racial troubles have been somewhat assuaged in the realm of popular entertainment, they are still very much in evidence in our everyday lives—as could be painfully seen when a popular cultural hero named O. J. Simpson stumbled off the stage into the harsh arena of racial reality.

The script for racial conflict in America began to be written when European colonists clashed with the Native American inhabitants of the land and soon started to import African slaves to work the lands that they had conquered. Later conflicts, especially the Mexican-American War, would add a new dimension to the problem, as white Americans moved into territory that belonged to the Republic of Mexico. With a history of interracial interaction so grounded in violence, it's little wonder that America has yet to resolve its racial conflicts.

By the end of the twentieth century, it wasn't supposed to be this way, of course. In the years between the civil rights movement of the sixties and the multicultural initiatives of the eighties, the challenge of racial conflict was supposed to have been answered. A resolution was supposed to be in sight. But, to echo William Butler Yeats's poem "The Second Coming," things fell apart. Not only did the long-standing division between black-and-white America remain, but the division multiplied, bringing other ethnicities into a conflict that now pits race against race in a variety of directions. The traditional black-and-white screen of American racial politics has become technicolor.

It would be nice to be able to claim that a semiotic understanding of racial conflicts in our country will bring a comfortable resolution of them. We can't claim that, of course. There's too much pain, too much emotion, too many irrational forces out there to be overcome by a rational semiotic analysis. Still, as students—particularly in a class designed to train you in critical thinking—you are in an optimal position to analyze America's race relations using the tools of critical reasoning. Semiotics can help you do that because while it does not offer solutions to cultural problems, it can shed light on many of their origins. And we can't begin to solve those problems until we have a clear understanding of what they are.

Interpreting Multicultural Semiotics

The semiotics of race begins with the fundamental semiotic principle that one's world view is determined by one's culture. To put this another way, *what* you believe depends on *who* you are. So let's start with a simple question: "Who are you?" Ask it of a classmate. Of yourself. What's the answer? Did your classmate give her name? Did you? Or did each of you answer differently? Did you say "I am an American"? Or did you say "I am an African American," or an "Asian American," or a "Latino," or a "Native American"? Would you answer "I am a European American" or a "Jewish American"? However you answered the question, can you say why you answered as you did?

To ask how you identify yourself and why you do so as you do is to begin to probe the semiotics of race and culture in America's multicultural society. Some of you may believe that there is a right answer to our question—that it is essential that all Americans think of themselves as

---

Exploring the Signs of Race

In your journal, reflect on the question, "Who are you?" How does your ethnicity contribute to your sense of self? Are there other factors that contribute to your identity? If so, what are they, and how do they relate to your ethnicity? If you don't perceive yourself in ethnic terms, why do you think that's the case?

Americans first and foremost. Others of you may believe just as strongly that your ethnic and cultural identity comes first. In either case, your beliefs reflect a worldview, or cultural mythology, that guides you in your most fundamental thoughts about your identity. Let's look at those myths for a moment.

Say that you feel that all American citizens should view themselves simply as Americans, without all the hyphens and compounds. If so, your feelings reflect a basic cultural mythology best known as the myth of the American "melting pot." This is the belief that America offers all of its citizens the opportunity to blend together into one harmonious whole that will erase the many differences among us on behalf of a new, distinctly American, identity. This belief has led many immigrants to seek to assimilate into what they perceive as the dominant American culture, shedding the specific cultural characteristics that may distinguish them from what they see as the American norm. And it is a belief that stands behind some of the most generous impulses in our culture—at least ideally.

But what if you don't buy this belief? What if, as far as you are concerned, you're proud to belong to a different community, one that differs from the basically Anglo-Saxon culture that has become the dominant, and normative, culture for assimilation? Or what if you and your people have found that you were never really allowed to blend in anyway—that in spite of the promise, the melting pot was never meant for you? If so, how does the myth of the melting pot look to you? Does it look the same as it would to someone who never had any trouble assimilating or never needed to because he or she already belonged to the dominant culture?

To see that the myth of the melting pot looks different depending on who is looking at it is to see why it is so precious to some Americans and so irrelevant to others. It is to realize again the fundamental semiotic precept that our social values are culturally determined rather than inscribed in the marble of absolute truth. This may be difficult to accept, especially if you and your classmates all come from the same culture and hence all hold the same values. But if you know people who are different, you might want to ask them how the myth of the melting pot looks from their perspective. Does it look like an ideal that our nation should strive to achieve? Or does it look like an invitation to cultural submission? It all depends on who's looking.

The failure to recognize that different people view the melting pot differently is one of the major sources of racial misunderstanding and, thus, conflict in America today. On the one hand, we need to realize that many Americans, particularly nonwhites, have felt excluded from full economic and cultural participation in American life and may deeply resent the view that we all should just see ourselves as Americans—with no hyphens. But on the other hand, we also need to realize that many of today's Americans descend from non–Anglo-Saxon European immigrants who embraced the image of the melting pot, prospered, and passed their gratitude on to their descendants. For such Americans, the myth of the melting pot appears to be so benevolent that it doesn't seem right to attack it. A debate that acknowledges the historical reasons for this difference in viewpoint has a better chance to result in some consensus than one that presumes that one side's affection for the melting pot is "racist" or that the other's resentment is "petty" or "un-American."

We Are the People

Such a recognition is difficult to achieve, of course, because of the way that cultural worldviews tend to present themselves in absolute terms. We don't look at our belief systems and say "This is our belief system"; we say "This is the truth." All cultures do this. Even the way cultures form their sense of identity involves a certain reliance on absolutes by assuming that their culture is normative, the right way to be. It's not just Anglo-Saxon America, in other words, that presumes its centrality in the order of things. We can see how groups of people implicitly believe in their privileged place in the world by looking at the names with which they identify themselves. Take the members of the largest Native American tribe in the United States. To the rest of the world, they are known as the Navajos. This is not the name the Navajos use among themselves, however, for the word *Navajo* does not come from their language. In all likelihood, the name was given to them by neighboring Pueblo Indians, for whom the term *Navahu* means "large area of cultivated lands." But in the language of the Navajo, which is quite different from that of the Pueblo, they are not the people of the tilled fields. They are, quite simply, The People, the most common English translation of the word *diné*, the name by which the Navajo know themselves.

Or take the Hmong of Southeast Asia. *Hmong* simply means "person," and so to say "I am a Hmong" implicitly states "I am a person." And even the names of such different nations as Ireland and Iran harbor an ancient sense of normative "peoplehood," for both names are derived from the word *Aryan,* which itself once bore the simple meaning "the people." To be sure, when someone says "I am diné," or "I am Hmong," or "I am Irish," he or she does not mean "I am a human being and the rest of you aren't." Nonetheless, we find inscribed within the unconscious history of these ancient tribal names the trace of a belief found within many a tribal name: the sense that one's own tribe comes first in the order of things. Things are not really so different in America, even though our country's name is derived from the name of a fifteenth-century navigator, Amerigo Vespucci. For in essence, we have tried to make America itself a tribe, and we too conceive of ourselves as a specially favored people. Indeed, our Pledge of Allegiance includes the phrase "one nation, under God," as if America alone enjoyed such a privilege. Just think how often America has tried to define itself as the richest, most powerful, most blessed nation on earth, the center to which all other peoples are to be compared.

But when we try to identify what, precisely, the American tribe is, we run into trouble. With so many races and cultures living together in this land, it is difficult to say just which should have the privilege of becoming the standard by which the others are identified — or if there even should be a standard. And so, as we reach the end of the twentieth century, it may be best to see ourselves as *peoples* rather than The People. By recognizing that cultural absolutes really reflect cultural mythologies, we may level the playing field and rephrase the question, "Who are *we?*"

Culture or Race?

As you consider the cultural bases for your own sense of personal identity, you may object that race stands outside the cultural realm and belongs instead within the natural realm of biology. But even biological issues are subject to cultural interpretation. In 1970, for example, the state of Louisiana passed a law (since repealed) that identified anyone as "black" whose veins flowed with at least a one-thirty-second share of "Negro blood." A woman with a similar share in her blood sued the state in 1982 to have her racial classification changed from "black" to "white," and lost. So what *is* she — what she believes herself to be or what the state defines her to be? Either way, her racial identity is a matter of cultural and political determination, not a natural fact. And with more and more Americans descending from racially mixed families, these are not trivial concerns.

Similarly, the great majority of those who identify themselves as "Indians" or "Native Americans" have considerable amounts of non-Indian blood in their veins. At present, anyone who can demonstrate a 25 percent share of Native American blood will be legally identified as such, but there is political pressure among Native American groups to broaden

---

Discussing the Signs of Race

Demographers predict that, by the middle of the twenty-first century, America will no longer have any racial or ethnic majority population. In class, discuss what effects this may have on Americans' sense of this country's history, culture, and identity.

the blood requirements so as to increase the number of legally identifiable "Indians." Conversely, among Jews, orthodoxy requires that to be identified as a Jew one's mother must be Jewish, and there is resistance to any tampering with this ancient rabbinical definition, even though many individuals with Jewish fathers and non-Jewish mothers consider themselves Jewish.

And so culture, the promptings of ideology rather than biology, makes its voice heard in what may appear to be the most natural of human identifications. But in current racial discourse, culture impinges in quite another way as well. You can see this at work in the very word *multiculturalism*. If taken literally, a call for multicultural education could simply mean an introduction of more Scandinavian or French or Greek or Irish culture into a school curriculum. After all, these groups represent a broad range of cultures whose differences may be far more pronounced than the cultural differences between middle-class American families of African, Latin American, or European ancestry. But the word is not intended to be taken literally, of course. In practice, *multicultural* means "multiracial," and while this codification may strike some as a form of political euphemism, there are some sound reasons, in the context of American history, for so linking culture and race.

Unlike the relatively homogeneous nations of Europe where social divisions have been inscribed largely along class or religious lines, America has been obsessed with racial difference almost from the beginning. Though class divisions are important in America, race defines our sense of social identity. This obsession with racial difference has had its own cultural effects, such that it makes perfect sense to speak, for instance, of African Americans as a culture as well as a race. It makes sense because a history of slavery and racial marginalization have effectively molded a New World culture that can be quite different from the Old World cultures of Africa. The American experience of the descendants of the African people who were dragged in chains to these shores, in other words, has produced a new culture (not without its own local distinctions) that is indeed African American but whose outward signs begin with the color of one's skin.

Culture Matters

With the recent arrival of a new wave of immigrants to American shores—a wave whose potential for effecting widespread cultural change rivals that of the great influx of eastern and southern Europeans at the turn of the century—the confluence of race and culture in American society has produced a new set of social challenges and conflicts. A nation that endured a devastating civil war over the issue of human slavery has traditionally perceived racial conflict in black-and-white terms, but the equations of cultural difference are no longer so neatly balanced. There are too many other races and cultures to consider.

Where the rest of the country, for example, viewed the 1992 Los Angeles riots as a classic expression of black rage against white oppression, those living in L.A. knew that it wasn't this simple. Despite the media's almost exclusive focus on these two groups (*U.S. News & World Report*'s cover read, for instance, "Black vs. White: The New Fears"), a good half of those involved came from the city's largely Central American barrios. And herein lies another distinction. A census form will employ the same ethnic term for people of either Mexican or Central American origin—*Hispanic* or *Latino*—but to use these terms in the context of the L.A. riots is imprecise because L.A.'s more established Chicano (Mexican American) population largely stayed out of the action.

Moreover, the focus on black-white conflict obscured a different sort of conflict. The nation's newspapers and TV screens focused on the Rodney King beating, but how many people outside of L.A. were aware of the Latasha Harlins case? This case, which involved the shooting death of an African American girl by a Korean American shopkeeper, was just as important as the King beating in L.A.'s black community. The King case was the last straw, but the Harlins case, which resulted in the shopkeeper's being sentenced to five years' probation for the killing, really touched a nerve only a few months before the uprising, so much so that Korean American shops were specially targeted for destruction during the unrest.

The simmering conflict between African Americans and Korean Americans is well known to anyone living in New York or Los Angeles, and it provides a particularly good example of what the semiotics of cultural difference is all about. For the racial differences between these groups go hand in hand with cultural differences that are equally potent sources of conflict. The Korean cultural code, for example, holds that it is impolite to make direct eye contact with other people, a practice that many African American customers of Korean American shops have interpreted as a gesture of racial disdain. Similarly, Korean women traditionally are taught to avoid direct physical contact with men and so may drop a man's change on a store counter rather than hand it to him directly. For an African American customer, this may look like another act of disrespect. And, to complicate the cultural confusion further, black immigrants from the West Indies are used to bargaining for their purchases, particularly for produce. Thus, it may be perfectly natural for such a person to haggle over the price of an apple in a Korean-owned grocery. To the owner, however, this looks like the next thing to shoplifting (indeed, Latasha Harlins was shot during an argument that ensued when she offered to pay less for a pint of orange juice than was marked on the bottle).

Of course, larger socioeconomic issues are at work here as well—recent immigrants and long-time black citizens alike are tossed into the same underclass and forced to struggle among themselves for political and economic power—but the cultural issues cannot be dismissed. Sometimes it's the small things that count most (like how one perceives the price of a bottle of orange juice), and a semiotic sensitivity to such differences can head off the larger explosions.

The Multicultural Debate

To explore the outline of a cultural mythology is not the same thing as attacking it, though it may appear that way if it happens to be *your* culture that is under investigation. This is perfectly natural, for not only our values but, as we have seen, our very sense of identity come to us through our cultures. Thus, it can come as a shock to be told that one's cultural worldview is just that: one world view among many. And when a traditionally dominant culture is challenged by other groups intent on winning a share of cultural and political power for themselves, bewilderment can turn into backlash.

Try to think of an instance where your cultural values clashed with someone else's. Can you see why that other person may have felt threatened by your difference of opinion? Do you wish that that other person could just, for once, see things from your point of view? Would it be good to come to some agreement about the matter, or would you prefer to have your own views triumph? If you'd like to find a way to agreement, how would you go about it?

As you consider the particular cultural values that really matter to you, you may well find yourself up against the problem of cultural relativism. Relativism is the position that holds that all values are relative to their social contexts and that there is no single standard by which to judge them. Indeed, opponents of multicultural education often point to the specter of relativism as a point in their favor. "How," they ask, "can

---

Reading Race on the Net

Many Internet sites are devoted to the culture of a particular ethnicity, such as Afronet (**http://www.afronet.com**) or Latinolink (**http://www.latinolink.com**). Visit several such sites, and survey the breadth of information available about different ethnic groups. To what extent can a researcher learn about various ethnicities on the Net? Is there any information that you wish would appear on the Net but could not find? Do you find any material problematic?

we have a civil society if we can't agree on one set of values?" The monocultural position is, in effect, that America has successfully molded the many peoples and cultures in this land together into one harmonious nation (or at least is on its way to such a union) and is now being split apart by the trend toward multiculturalism. But what are the cultural assumptions behind this belief? What sort of culture do the opponents of multicultural education take for granted?

It's not that the opponents of multicultural education necessarily oppose the existence of other cultures in America. Usually, they hold the traditional American value of tolerance for difference even as they argue for a monocultural sense of nationhood. But "tolerance" itself looks tricky when we come to analyze it in cultural terms. It has rarely occurred to the dominant culture in America that people don't want to be "tolerated"—that tolerance assumes a position of social and moral superiority from which one magnanimously chooses to allow other people to exist. From a semiotic perspective, tolerance is absurd in its traditional expression. It is the freedom to found your own country club because you have been blackballed from all the existing ones.

And that is one reason that multiculturalism is threatening to those who oppose it. It doesn't call for more tolerance; it doesn't even call for acceptance (acceptance, too, implies a social superior who is in the position of accepting). Rather, multiculturalism calls for something closer to negotiation, a round-table dialogue presuming the participation of cultural equals who have come together to work out a complex restructuring of society. This negotiation can't take place, however, if everyone at the table presumes that their culture is the one true perspective. The United States has never had to negotiate like this before, and so there is nothing ready made to put on the table for discussion. The first step is simply for all parties to get a chance to tell their story. That is what a multicultural education is about. The next, more challenging step, is to come up with a new story in which everyone can feel—and be—included.

The Readings

This chapter looks at the social construction of racial identity in America, beginning with Michael Omi's survey of how race works as a sign in popular American culture. Benjamin DeMott indicts Hollywood's tendency to mask the grim realities of America's racial history behind "happy faced" images of black-white friendship and solidarity. Paul C. Taylor and Nell Bernstein next offer a pair of readings on popular cultural "crossovers," with Taylor's essay focusing on white performers who excel in black-identified cultural activities like basketball and the blues, while Bernstein reports on the phenomenon of "claiming"—

white teens choosing to identify themselves with nonwhite ethnic groups. An autobiographical reflection by bell hooks on her childhood preference for brown dolls over white follows, after which Melissa Algranati offers a college student's perspective on what it's like to be a Puerto Rican, Egyptian, American Jew in a country that demands clear ethnic identifications. Gloria Anzaldúa's "How to Tame a Wild Tongue" provides a linguistic spin on the nature of racial identity, while Fan Shen analyzes the role his Chinese heritage has played in his experience both as a student and as a professor of freshman composition. And LynNell Hancock concludes the chapter with an exploration of the social and economic implications of online access, or lack thereof, for race relations in America.

MICHAEL OMI

In Living Color: Race and American Culture

‖‖‖‖‖‖‖‖‖‖‖‖‖‖‖‖‖‖‖‖‖‖‖‖‖‖‖‖‖‖‖‖‖‖‖‖‖‖

Though many like to think that racism in America is a thing of the past, Michael Omi argues that racism is a pervasive feature in our lives, one that is both overt and inferential. Using race as a sign by which we judge a person's character, inferential racism invokes deep-rooted stereotypes, and as Omi shows in his survey of American film, television, and music, our popular culture is hardly immune from such stereotyping. Indeed, when ostensibly "progressive" programs like Saturday Night Live *can win the National Ethnic Coalition of Organizations' "Platinum Pit Award" for racist stereotyping in television, and comedians like Andrew Dice Clay command big audiences and salaries, one can see popular culture has a way to go before it becomes colorblind. The author of* Racial Formation in the United States: From the 1960s to the 1980s *(with Howard Winant, 1986, 1994), Michael Omi is a professor of comparative ethnic studies at the University of California, Berkeley. His most recent project is a survey of antiracist organizations and initiatives.*

In February 1987, Assistant Attorney General William Bradford Reynolds, the nation's chief civil rights enforcer, declared that the recent death of a black man in Howard Beach, New York and the Ku Klux Klan attack on civil rights marchers in Forsyth County, Georgia were "isolated" racial incidences. He emphasized that the places where racial conflict could potentially flare up were "far fewer now than ever before in our history," and concluded that such a diminishment of racism stood as "a powerful testament to how far we have come in the civil rights struggle."[1]

Events in the months following his remarks raise the question as to whether we have come quite so far. They suggest that dramatic instances of racial tension and violence merely constitute the surface manifestations of a deeper racial organization of American society—a system of inequality which has shaped, and in turn been shaped by, our popular culture.

In March, the NAACP released a report on blacks in the record industry entitled "The Discordant Sound of Music." It found that despite the revenues generated by black performers, blacks remain "grossly underrepresented" in the business, marketing, and A&R (Artists and

---

1. Reynolds's remarks were made at a conference on equal opportunity held by the bar association in Orlando, Florida. *The San Francisco Chronicle* (7 February 1987).

Repertoire) departments of major record labels. In addition, few blacks are employed as managers, agents, concert promoters, distributors, and retailers. The report concluded that:

> The record industry is overwhelmingly segregated and discrimination is rampant. No other industry in America so openly classifies its operations on a racial basis. At every level of the industry, beginning with the separation of black artists into a special category, barriers exist that severely limit opportunities for blacks.[2]

Decades after the passage of civil rights legislation and the affirmation of the principle of "equal opportunity," patterns of racial segregation and exclusion, it seems, continue to characterize the production of popular music.

The enduring logic of Jim Crow is also present in professional sports. In April, Al Campanis, vice president of player personnel for the Los Angeles Dodgers, explained to Ted Koppel on ABC's *Nightline* about the paucity of blacks in baseball front offices and as managers. "I truly believe," Campanis said, "that [blacks] may not have some of the necessities to be, let's say, a field manager or perhaps a general manager." When pressed for a reason, Campanis offered an explanation which had little to do with the structure of opportunity of institutional discrimination within professional sports:

> [W]hy are black men or black people not good swimmers? Because they don't have the buoyancy. . . . They are gifted with great musculature and various other things. They're fleet of foot. And this is why there are a lot of black major league ballplayers. Now as far as having the background to become club presidents, or presidents of a bank, I don't know.[3]

Black exclusion from the front office, therefore, was justified on the basis of biological "difference."

The issue of race, of course, is not confined to the institutional   5
arrangements of popular culture production. Since popular culture deals with the symbolic realm of social life, the images which it creates, represents, and disseminates contribute to the overall racial climate. They become the subject of analysis and political scrutiny. In August, the National Ethnic Coalition of Organizations bestowed the "Golden Pit Awards" on television programs, commercials, and movies that were deemed offensive to racial and ethnic groups. *Saturday Night Live,* regarded by many media critics as a politically "progressive" show, was

---

2. Economic Development Department of the NAACP, "The Discordant Sound of Music (A Report on the Record Industry)," (Baltimore, Maryland: The NAACP, 1987), pp. 16–17.

3. Campanis's remarks on *Nightline* were reprinted in *The San Francisco Chronicle* (April 9, 1987).

singled out for the "Platinum Pit Award" for its comedy skit "Ching Chang" which depicted a Chinese storeowner and his family in a derogatory manner.[4]

These examples highlight the *overt* manifestations of racism in popular culture—institutional forms of discrimination which keep racial minorities out of the production and organization of popular culture, and the crude racial caricatures by which these groups are portrayed. Yet racism in popular culture is often conveyed in a variety of implicit, and at times invisible, ways. Political theorist Stuart Hall makes an important distinction between *overt* racism, the elaboration of an explicitly racist argument, policy, or view, and *inferential* racism which refers to "those apparently naturalized representations of events and situations relating to race, whether 'factual' or 'fictional,' which have racist premises and propositions inscribed in them as a set of *unquestioned assumptions*." He argues that inferential racism is more widespread, common, and indeed insidious since "it is largely *invisible* even to those who formulate the world in its terms."[5]

Race itself is a slippery social concept which is paradoxically both "obvious" and "invisible." In our society, one of the first things we notice about people when we encounter them (along with their sex/gender) is their *race*. We utilize race to provide clues about *who* a person is and *how* we should relate to her/him. Our perception of race determines our "presentation of *self*," distinctions in status, and appropriate modes of conduct in daily and institutional life. This process is often unconscious; we tend to operate off of an unexamined set of *racial beliefs*.

Racial beliefs account for and explain variations in "human nature." Differences in skin color and other obvious physical characteristics supposedly provide visible clues to more substantive differences lurking underneath. Among other qualities, temperament, sexuality, intelligence, and artistic and athletic ability are presumed to be fixed and discernible from the palpable mark of race. Such diverse questions as our confidence and trust in others (as salespeople, neighbors, media figures); our sexual preferences and romantic images; our tastes in music, film, dance, or sports; indeed our very ways of walking and talking are ineluctably shaped by notions of race.

Ideas about race, therefore, have become "common sense"—a way of comprehending, explaining, and acting in the world. This is made painfully obvious when someone disrupts our common sense understandings. An encounter with someone who is, for example, racially "mixed" or of a racial/ethnic group we are unfamiliar with becomes a

---

4. Ellen Wulfhorst, "TV Stereotyping: It's the 'Pits,'" *The San Francisco Chronicle* (August 24, 1987).

5. Stuart Hall, "The Whites of Their Eyes: Racist Ideologies and the Media," in George Bridges and Rosalind Brunt, eds., *Silver Linings* (London: Lawrence and Wishart, 1981), pp. 36–37.

source of discomfort for us, and momentarily creates a crisis of racial meaning. We also become disoriented when people do not act "black," "Latino," or indeed "white." The content of such stereotypes reveals a series of unsubstantiated beliefs about who these groups are, what they are like, and how they behave.

The existence of such racial consciousness should hardly be surpris-   10
ing. Even prior to the inception of the republic, the United States was a society shaped by racial conflict. The establishment of the Southern plantation economy, Western expansion, and the emergence of the labor movement, among other significant historical developments, have all involved conflicts over the definition and nature of the *color line*. The historical results have been distinct and different groups have encountered unique forms of racial oppression—Native Americans faced genocide, blacks were subjected to slavery, Mexicans were invaded and colonized, and Asians faced exclusion. What is common to the experiences of these groups is that their particular "fate" was linked to historically specific ideas about the significance and meaning of race.[6] Whites defined them as separate "species," ones inferior to Northern European cultural stocks, and thereby rationalized the conditions of their subordination in the economy, in political life, and in the realm of culture.

A crucial dimension of racial oppression in the United States is the elaboration of an ideology of difference or "otherness." This involves defining "us" (i.e., white Americans) in opposition to "them," an important task when distinct racial groups are first encountered, or in historically specific periods where preexisting racial boundaries are threatened or crumbling.

Political struggles over the very definition of who an "American" is illustrates this process. The Naturalization Law of 1790 declared that only free *white* immigrants could qualify, reflecting the initial desire among Congress to create and maintain a racially homogeneous society. The extension of eligibility to all racial groups has been a long and protracted process. Japanese, for example, were finally eligible to become naturalized citizens after the passage of the Walter-McCarran Act of 1952. The ideological residue of these restrictions in naturalization and citizenship laws is the equation within popular parlance of the term "American" with "white," while other "Americans" are described as black, Mexican, "Oriental," etc.

Popular culture has been an important realm within which racial ideologies have been created, reproduced, and sustained. Such ideologies provide a framework of symbols, concepts, and images through which we understand, interpret, and represent aspects of our "racial" existence.

---

6. For an excellent survey of racial beliefs see Thomas F. Gossett, *Race: The History of an Idea in America* (New York: Shocken Books, 1965).

Race has often formed the central themes of American popular culture. Historian W. L. Rose notes that it is "curious coincidence" that four of the "most popular reading-viewing events in all American history" have in some manner dealt with race, specifically black/white relations in the south.[7] Harriet Beecher Stowe's *Uncle Tom's Cabin,* Thomas Ryan Dixon's *The Clansman* (the inspiration for D. W. Griffith's *The Birth of a Nation*), Margaret Mitchell's *Gone with the Wind* (as a book and film), and Alex Haley's *Roots* (as a book and television miniseries), each appeared at a critical juncture in American race relations and helped to shape new understandings of race.

Emerging social definitions of race and the "real American" were reflected in American popular culture of the nineteenth century. Racial and ethnic stereotypes were shaped and reinforced in the newspapers, magazines, and pulp fiction of the period. But the evolution and ever-increasing sophistication of visual mass communications throughout the twentieth century provided, and continue to provide, the most dramatic means by which racial images are generated and reproduced.

Film and television have been notorious in disseminating images of racial minorities which establish for audiences what these groups look like, how they behave, and, in essence, "who they are." The power of the media lies not only in their ability to reflect the dominant racial ideology, but in their capacity to shape that ideology in the first place. D. W. Griffith's aforementioned epic *Birth of a Nation,* a sympathetic treatment of the rise of the Ku Klux Klan during Reconstruction, helped to generate, consolidate, and "nationalize" images of blacks which had been more disparate (more regionally specific, for example) prior to the film's appearance.[8]

In television and film, the necessity to define characters in the briefest and most condensed manner has led to the perpetuation of racial caricatures, as racial stereotypes serve as shorthand for scriptwriters, directors, and actors. Television's tendency to address the "lowest common denominator" in order to render programs "familiar" to an enormous and diverse audience leads it regularly to assign and reassign racial characteristics to particular groups, both minority and majority.

Many of the earliest American films deal with racial and ethnic "difference." The large influx of "new immigrants" at the turn of the century led to a proliferation of negative images of Jews, Italians, and Irish which were assimilated and adapted by such films as Thomas Edison's *Cohen's Advertising Scheme* (1904). Based on an old vaudeville routine, the

---

7. W. L. Rose, *Race and Region in American Historical Fiction: Four Episodes in Popular Culture* (Oxford: Clarendon Press, 1979).

8. Melanie Martindale-Sikes, "Nationalizing 'Nigger' Imagery Through *Birth of a Nation,*" paper prepared for the 73rd Annual Meeting of the American Sociological Association (September 4–8, 1978) in San Francisco.

film featured a scheming Jewish merchant, aggressively hawking his wares. Though stereotypes of these groups persist to this day,[9] by the 1940s many of the earlier ethnic stereotypes had disappeared from Hollywood. But, as historian Michael Winston observes, the "outsiders" of the 1890s remained: "the ever-popular Indian of the Westerns; the inscrutable or sinister Oriental; the sly, but colorful Mexican; and the clowning or submissive Negro."[10]

In many respects the "Western" as a genre has been paradigmatic in establishing images of racial minorities in film and television. The classic scenario involves the encircled wagon train or surrounded fort from which whites bravely fight off fierce bands of Native American Indians. The point of reference and viewer identification lies with those huddled within the circle—the representatives of "civilization" who valiantly attempt to ward off the forces of barbarism. In the classic Western, as writer Tom Engelhardt observes, "the viewer is forced behind the barrel of a repeating rifle and it is from that position, through its gun sights, that he receives a picture history of Western colonialism and imperialism."[11]

Westerns have indeed become the prototype for European and American excursions throughout the Third World. The cast of characters may change, but the story remains the same. The "humanity" of whites is contrasted with the brutality and treachery of nonwhites; brave (i.e., white) souls are pitted against the merciless hordes in conflicts ranging from Indians against the British Lancers to Zulus against the Boers. What Stuart Hall refers to as the imperializing "white eye" provides the framework for these films, lurking outside the frame and yet seeing and positioning everything within; it is "the unmarked position from which . . . 'observations' are made and from which, alone, they make sense."[12]

Our "common sense" assumptions about race and racial minorities in the United States are both generated and reflected in the stereotypes presented by the visual media. In the crudest sense, it could be said that such stereotypes underscore white "superiority" by reinforcing the traits, habits, and predispositions of nonwhites which demonstrate their "inferiority." Yet a more careful assessment of racial stereotypes reveals intriguing trends and seemingly contradictory themes.

While all racial minorities have been portrayed as "less than human," there are significant differences in the images of different groups. Specific racial minority groups, in spite of their often interchangeable presence in

9. For a discussion of Italian, Irish, Jewish, Slavic, and German stereotypes in film, see Randall M. Miller, ed., *The Kaleidoscopic Lens: How Hollywood Views Ethnic Groups* (Englewood, N.J.: Jerome S. Ozer, 1980).

10. Michael R. Winston, "Racial Consciousness and the Evolution of Mass Communications in the United States," *Daedalus,* vol. III, No. 4 (Fall 1982).

11. Tom Engelhardt, "Ambush at Kamikaze Pass," in Emma Gee, ed., *Counterpoint: Perspectives on Asian America* (Los Angeles: Asian American Studies Center, UCLA, 1976), p. 270.

12. Hall, "Whites of Their Eyes," p. 38.

films steeped in the "Western" paradigm, have distinct and often unique qualities assigned to them. Latinos are portrayed as being prone toward violent outbursts of anger; blacks as physically strong, but dim-witted; while Asians are seen as sneaky and cunningly evil. Such differences are crucial to observe and analyze. Race in the United States is not reducible to black/white relations. These differences are significant for a broader understanding of the patterns of race in America, and the unique experience of specific racial minority groups.

It is somewhat ironic that *real* differences which exist within a racially defined minority group are minimized, distorted, or obliterated by the media. "All Asians look alike," the saying goes, and indeed there has been little or no attention given to the vast differences which exist between, say, the Chinese and Japanese with respect to food, dress, language, and culture. This blurring within popular culture has given us supposedly Chinese characters who wear kimonos; it is also the reason why the fast-food restaurant McDonald's can offer "Shanghai Mc-Nuggets" with teriyaki sauce. Other groups suffer a similar fate. Professor Gretchen Bataille and Charles Silet find the cinematic Native American of the Northeast wearing the clothing of the Plains Indians, while living in the dwellings of Southwestern tribes:

> The movie men did what thousands of years of social evolution could not do, even what the threat of the encroaching white man could not do; Hollywood produced the homogenized Native American, devoid of tribal characteristics or regional differences.[13]

The need to paint in broad racial strokes has thus rendered "internal" differences invisible. This has been exacerbated by the tendency for screenwriters to "invent" mythical Asian, Latin American, and African countries. Ostensibly done to avoid offending particular nations and peoples, such a subterfuge reinforces the notion that all the countries and cultures of a specific region are the same. European countries retain their distinctiveness, while the Third World is presented as one homogeneous mass riddled with poverty and governed by ruthless and corrupt regimes.

While rendering specific groups in a monolithic fashion, the popular cultural imagination simultaneously reveals a compelling need to distinguish and articulate "bad" and "good" variants of particular racial groups and individuals. Thus each stereotypic image is filled with contradictions: The bloodthirsty Indian is tempered with the image of the noble savage; the *bandido* exists along with the loyal sidekick; and Fu Manchu is offset by Charlie Chan. The existence of such contradictions, however, does not negate the one-dimensionality of these images, nor does it challenge the explicit subservient role of racial minorities. Even the "good" person

---

13. Gretchen Bataille and Charles Silet, "The Entertaining Anachronism: Indians in American Film," in Randall M. Miller, ed., *Kaleidoscopic Lens,* p. 40.

of color usually exists as a foil in novels and films to underscore the intelligence, courage, and virility of the white male hero.

Another important, perhaps central, dimension of racial minority 25 stereotypes is sex/gender differentiation. The connection between race and sex has traditionally been an explosive and controversial one. For most of American history, sexual and marital relations between whites and nonwhites were forbidden by social custom and by legal restrictions. It was not until 1967, for example, that the U.S. Supreme Court ruled that antimiscegenation laws were unconstitutional. Beginning in the 1920s, the notorious Hays Office, Hollywood's attempt at self-censorship, prohibited scenes and subjects which dealt with miscegenation. The prohibition, however, was not evenly applied in practice. White men could seduce racial minority women, but white women were not to be romantically or sexually linked to racial minority men.

Women of color were sometimes treated as exotic sex objects. The sultry Latin temptress—such as Dolores Del Rio and Lupe Velez—invariably had boyfriends who were white North Americans; their Latino suitors were portrayed as being unable to keep up with the Anglo-American competition. From Mary Pickford as Cho-Cho San in *Madame Butterfly* (1915) to Nancy Kwan in *The World of Suzie Wong* (1961), Asian women have often been seen as the gracious "geisha girl" or the prostitute with a "heart of gold," willing to do anything to please her man.

By contrast, Asian men, whether cast in the role of villain, servant, sidekick, or kung fu master, are seen as asexual or, at least, romantically undesirable. As Asian American studies professor Elaine Kim notes, even a hero such as Bruce Lee played characters whose "single-minded focus on perfecting his fighting skills precludes all other interests, including an interest in women, friendship, or a social life."[14]

The shifting trajectory of black images over time reveals an interesting dynamic with respect to sex and gender. The black male characters in *The Birth of a Nation* were clearly presented as sexual threats to "white womanhood." For decades afterwards, however, Hollywood consciously avoided portraying black men as assertive or sexually aggressive in order to minimize controversy. Black men were instead cast as comic, harmless, and nonthreatening figures exemplified by such stars as Bill "Bojangles" Robinson, Stepin Fetchit, and Eddie "Rochester" Anderson. Black women, by contrast, were divided into two broad character types based on color categories. Dark black women such as Hattie McDaniel and Louise Beavers were cast as "dowdy, frumpy, dumpy, overweight mammy figures"; while those "close to the white ideal," such as Lena

---

14. Elaine Kim, "Asian Americans and American Popular Culture" in Hyung-Chan Kim, ed., *Dictionary of Asian American History* (New York: Greenwood Press, 1986), p. 107.

Horne and Dorothy Dandridge, became "Hollywood's treasured mulattoes" in roles emphasizing the tragedy of being of mixed blood.[15]

It was not until the early 1970s that tough, aggressive, sexually assertive black characters, both male and female, appeared. The "blaxploitation" films of the period provided new heroes (e.g., *Shaft, Superfly, Coffy,* and *Cleopatra Jones*) in sharp contrast to the submissive and subservient images of the past. Unfortunately, most of these films were shoddy productions which did little to create more enduring "positive" images of blacks, either male or female.

In contemporary television and film, there is a tendency to present   30
and equate racial minority groups and individuals with specific social problems. Blacks are associated with drugs and urban crime, Latinos with "illegal" immigration, while Native Americans cope with alcoholism and tribal conflicts. Rarely do we see racial minorities "out of character," in situations removed from the stereotypic arenas in which scriptwriters have traditionally embedded them. Nearly the only time we see young Asians and Latinos of either sex, for example, is when they are members of youth gangs, as *Boulevard Nights* (1979), *Year of the Dragon* (1985), and countless TV cop shows can attest to.

Racial minority actors have continually bemoaned the fact that the roles assigned them on stage and screen are often one-dimensional and imbued with stereotypic assumptions. In theater, the movement toward "blind casting" (i.e., casting actors for roles without regard to race) is a progressive step, but it remains to be seen whether large numbers of audiences can suspend their "beliefs" and deal with a Latino King Lear or an Asian Stanley Kowalski. By contrast, white actors are allowed to play anybody. Though the use of white actors to play blacks in "black face" is clearly unacceptable in the contemporary period, white actors continue to portray Asian, Latino, and Native American characters on stage and screen.

Scores of Charlie Chan films, for example, have been made with white leads (the last one was the 1981 *Charlie Chan and the Curse of the Dragon Queen*). Roland Winters, who played Chan in six features, was once asked to explain the logic of casting a white man in the role of Charlie Chan: "The only thing I can think of is, if you want to cast a homosexual in a show, and you get a homosexual, it'll be awful. It won't be funny . . . and maybe there's something there."[16]

Such a comment reveals an interesting aspect about myth and reality in popular culture. Michael Winston argues that stereotypic images in the visual media were not originally conceived as representations of reality,

---

15. Donald Bogle, "A Familiar Plot (A Look at the History of Blacks in American Movies)," *The Crisis,* Vol. 90, No. 1 (January 1983), p. 15.

16. Frank Chin, "Confessions of the Chinatown Cowboy," *Bulletin of Concerned Asian Scholars,* Vol. 4, No. 3 (Fall 1972).

nor were they initially understood to be "real" by audiences. They were, he suggests, ways of "coding and rationalizing" the racial hierarchy and interracial behavior. Over time, however, "a complex interactive relationship between myth and reality developed, so that images originally understood to be unreal, through constant repetition began to *seem* real."[17]

Such a process consolidated, among other things, our "common sense" understandings of what we think various groups should look like. Such presumptions have led to tragicomical results. Latinos auditioning for a role in a television soap opera, for example, did not fit the Hollywood image of "real Mexicans" and had their faces bronzed with powder before filming because they looked too white. Model Aurora Garza said, "I'm a real Mexican and very dark anyway. I'm even darker right now because I have a tan. But they kept wanting to make my face darker and darker."[18]

Historically in Hollywood, the fact of having "dark skin" made an   35
actor or actress potentially adaptable for numerous "racial" roles. Actress Lupe Velez once commented that she had portrayed "Chinese, Eskimos, Japs, squaws, Hindus, Swedes, Malays, and Japanese."[19] Dorothy Dandridge, who was the first black woman teamed romantically with white actors, presented a quandary for studio executives who weren't sure what race and nationality to make her. They debated whether she should be a "foreigner," an island girl, or a West Indian.[20] Ironically, what they refused to entertain as a possibility was to present her as what she really was, a black American woman.

The importance of race in popular culture is not restricted to the visual media. In popular music, race and race consciousness has defined, and continues to define, formats, musical communities, and tastes. In the mid-1950s, the secretary of the North Alabama White Citizens Council declared that "Rock and roll is a means of pulling the white man down to the level of the Negro."[21] While rock may no longer be popularly regarded as a racially subversive musical form, the very genres of contemporary popular music remain, in essence, thinly veiled racial categories. "R & B" (Rhythm and Blues) and "soul" music are clearly references to *black* music, while Country & Western or heavy metal music are viewed, in the popular imagination, as *white* music. Black performers who want to break out of this artistic ghettoization must "cross over," a

---

17. Winston, "Racial Consciousness," p. 176.

18. *The San Francisco Chronicle,* September 21, 1984.

19. Quoted in Allen L. Woll, "Bandits and Lovers: Hispanic Images in American Film," in Miller, ed., *Kaleidoscopic Lens,* p. 60.

20. Bogle, "Familiar Plot," p. 17.

21. Dave Marsh and Kevin Stein, *The Book of Rock Lists* (New York: Dell Publishing Co., 1981), p. 8.

contemporary form of "passing" in which their music is seen as acceptable to white audiences.

The airwaves themselves are segregated. The designation "urban contemporary" is merely radio lingo for a "black" musical format. Such categorization affects playlists, advertising accounts, and shares of the listening market. On cable television, black music videos rarely receive airplay on MTV, but are confined instead to the more marginal BET (Black Entertainment Television) network.

In spite of such segregation, many performing artists have been able to garner a racially diverse group of fans. And yet, racially integrated concert audiences are extremely rare. Curiously, this "perverse phenomenon" of racially homogeneous crowds takes place despite the color of the performer. Lionel Richie's concert audiences, for example, are virtually all-white, while Teena Marie's are all-black.[22]

Racial symbols and images are omnipresent in popular culture. Commonplace household objects such as cookie jars, salt and pepper shakers, and ashtrays have frequently been designed and fashioned in the form of racial caricatures. Sociologist Steve Dublin in an analysis of these objects found that former tasks of domestic service were symbolically transferred onto these commodities.[23] An Aunt Jemima-type character, for example, is used to hold a roll of paper towels, her outstretched hands supporting the item to be dispensed. "Sprinkle Plenty," a sprinkle bottle in the shape of an Asian man, was used to wet clothes in preparation for ironing. Simple commodities, the household implements which help us perform everyday tasks, may reveal, therefore, a deep structure of racial meaning.

A crucial dimension for discerning the meaning of particular stereo-   40
types and images is the *situation context* for the creation and consumption of popular culture. For example, the setting in which "racist" jokes are told determines the function of humor. Jokes about blacks where the teller and audience are black constitute a form of self-awareness; they allow blacks to cope and "take the edge off" of oppressive aspects of the social order which they commonly confront. The meaning of these same jokes, however, is dramatically transformed when told across the "color line." If a white, or even black, person tells these jokes to a white audience, it will, despite its "purely" humorous intent, serve to reinforce stereotypes and rationalize the existing relations of racial inequality.

Concepts of race and racial images are both overt and implicit within popular culture—the organization of cultural production, the products themselves, and the manner in which they are consumed are deeply

22. *Rock & Roll Confidential,* No. 44 (February 1987), p. 2.
23. Steven C. Dublin, "Symbolic Slavery: Black Representations in Popular Culture," *Social Problems,* Vol. 34, No. 2 (April 1987).

structured by race. Particular racial meanings, stereotypes, and myths can change, but the presence of a *system* of racial meanings and stereotypes, of racial ideology, seems to be an enduring aspect of American popular culture.

The era of Reaganism and the overall rightward drift of American politics and culture has added a new twist to the question of racial images and meanings. Increasingly, the problem for racial minorities is not that of misportrayal, but of "invisibility." Instead of celebrating racial and cultural diversity, we are witnessing an attempt by the right to define, once again, who the "real" American is, and what "correct" American values, mores, and political beliefs are. In such a context, racial minorities are no longer the focus of sustained media attention; when they do appear, they are cast as colored versions of essentially "white" characters.

The possibilities for change—for transforming racial stereotypes and challenging institutional inequities—nonetheless exist. Historically, strategies have involved the mobilization of political pressure against an offending institution(s). In the late 1950s, for instance, "Nigger Hair" tobacco changed its name to "Bigger Hare" due to concerted NAACP pressure on the manufacturer. In the early 1970s, Asian American community groups successfully fought NBC's attempt to resurrect Charlie Chan as a television series with white actor Ross Martin. Amidst the furor generated by Al Campanis's remarks cited at the beginning of this essay, Jesse Jackson suggested that a boycott of major league games be initiated in order to push for a restructuring of hiring and promotion practices.

Partially in response to such action, Baseball Commissioner Peter Ueberroth announced plans in June 1987 to help put more racial minorities in management roles. "The challenge we have," Ueberroth said, "is to manage change without losing tradition."[24] The problem with respect to the issue of race and popular culture, however, is that the *tradition* itself may need to be thoroughly examined, its "common sense" assumptions unearthed and challenged, and its racial images contested and transformed.

Reading the Text

1. Describe in your own words the difference between "overt" and "inferential racism" (para. 6).
2. Why, according to Omi, is popular culture so powerful in shaping America's attitudes toward race?
3. What relationship does Omi see between gender and racial stereotypes?
4. How did racial relations change in America during the 1980s, in Omi's view?

---

24. *The San Francisco Chronicle* (June 13, 1987).

Reading the Signs

1. In class, brainstorm on the blackboard stereotypes, both "good" and "bad," attributed to specific racial groups. Then discuss the possible sources of these stereotypes. In what ways have they been perpetuated in popular culture, including movies, television, advertising, music, and consumer products? What does your discussion reveal about popular culture's influence on our most basic ways of seeing the world?

2. Rent a videotape of *Gone with the Wind,* and view the film. Write a semiotic essay in which you analyze how race operates as a sign in this movie. How, to use Omi's terms, does the film create, reproduce, and sustain racial ideologies in America? What does its racial ideology reveal about its status as a "classic" American film?

3. Rent a videotape of *Malcolm X,* and view the film. Using Omi's essay as your critical framework, write an essay in which you explore how this film may reflect or redefine American attitudes toward racial identity and race relations. To develop your essay, you may want to consult Shelby Steele's "Malcolm X" (p. 328).

4. Buy an issue of a magazine targeted to a specific ethnic readership, such as *Hispanic, Ebony,* or *A.,* and study both its advertising and its articles. Then write an essay in which you explore the extent to which the magazine accurately reflects that ethnicity or, in Omi's words, appeals to readers as "colored versions of essentially 'white' characters" (para. 42).

BENJAMIN DeMOTT

Put on a Happy Face: Masking the Differences
Between Blacks and Whites

||||||||||||||||||||||||||||||||||||||||||||||||||||||

By looking at the movies, you'd think that race relations in the United States were in splendid shape. Just look at Danny Glover and Mel Gibson in the Lethal Weapon *movies, or consider* Driving Miss Daisy. *But according to Benjamin DeMott (b. 1924), things are not so rosy. In fact, DeMott argues in this essay that Hollywood has effectively concealed the true state of American racial politics behind a pleasing facade of black and white happy-faces, and so has inadvertently worked to distract movie audiences from the pressing need to improve our racial climate. A writer whose interests include the media and American racial and class politics, DeMott's books include* Created Equal: Reading and Writing About Class in America *(1985),* The Imperial Middle: Why Americans Can't Think Straight About Class *(1990), and* The Trouble With Friendship: Why Americans Can't Think Straight About Race *(1995).*

At the movies these days, questions about racial injustice have been amicably resolved. Watch *Pulp Fiction* or *Congo* or *A Little Princess* or any other recent film in which both blacks and whites are primary characters and you can, if you want, forget about race. Whites and blacks greet one another on the screen with loving candor, revealing their common humanity. In *Pulp Fiction,* an armed black mobster (played by Samuel L. Jackson) looks deep into the eyes of an armed white thief in the middle of a holdup (played by Tim Roth) and shares his version of God's word in Ezekiel, whereupon the two men lay aside their weapons, both more or less redeemed. The moment inverts an earlier scene in which a white boxer (played by Bruce Willis) risks his life to save another black mobster (played by Ving Rhames), who is being sexually tortured as a prelude to his execution.

Pulp Fiction (gross through July [1995]: $107 million) is one of a series of films suggesting that the beast of American racism is tamed and harmless. Close to the start of *Die Hard with a Vengeance* (gross through July [1995]: $95 million) the camera finds a white man wearing sandwich boards on the corner of Amsterdam Avenue and 138th Street in Harlem. The boards carry a horrific legend: I HATE NIGGERS. A group of young blacks approach the man with murderous intent, bearing guns and knives. They are figures straight out of a national nightmare—ugly, enraged, terrifying. No problem. A black man, again played by Jackson, appears and rescues the white man, played by Willis. The black man and white man come to know each other well. In time the white man declares flatly to the black, "I need you more than you need me." A moment later he charges the black with being a racist—with not liking whites as much as the white man likes blacks—and the two talk frankly about their racial prejudices. Near the end of the film, the men have grown so close that each volunteers to die for the other.

Pulp Fiction and *Die Hard with a Vengeance* follow the pattern of *Lethal Weapon 1, 2,* and *3,* the Danny Glover/Mel Gibson buddy vehicles that collectively grossed $357 million, and *White Men Can't Jump,* which, in the year of the L.A. riots, grossed $76 million. In *White Men Can't Jump,* a white dropout, played by Woody Harrelson, ekes out a living on black-dominated basketball courts in Los Angeles. He's arrogant and aggressive but never in danger because he has a black protector and friend, played by Wesley Snipes. At the movie's end, the white, flying above the hoop like a stereotypical black player, scores the winning basket in a two-on-two pickup game on an alley-oop pass from his black chum, whereupon the two men fall into each other's arms in joy. Later, the black friend agrees to find work for the white at the store he manages.

> WHITE (helpless): I gotta get a job. Can you get me a job?
> BLACK (affectionately teasing): Got any references?
> WHITE (shy grin): You.

Such dialogue is the stuff of romance. What's dreamed of and gained is a place where whites are unafraid of blacks, where blacks ask for and need nothing from whites, and where the sameness of the races creates a common fund of sweet content.[1] The details of the dream matter less than the force that makes it come true for both races, eliminating the constraints of objective reality and redistributing resources, status, and capabilities. That cleansing social force supersedes political and economic fact or policy; that force, improbably enough, is friendship.

Watching the beaming white men who know how to jump, we do   5
well to remind ourselves of what the camera shot leaves out. Black infants die in America at twice the rate of white infants. (Despite the increased numbers of middle-class blacks, the rates are diverging, with black rates actually rising.) One out of every two black children lives below the poverty line (as compared with one out of seven white children). Nearly four times as many black families exist below the poverty line as white families. More than 50 percent of African American families have incomes below $25,000. Among black youths under age twenty, death by murder occurs nearly ten times as often as among whites. Over 60 percent of births to black mothers occur out of wedlock, more than four times the rate for white mothers. The net worth of the typical white household is ten times that of the typical black household. In many states, five to ten times as many blacks as whites age eighteen to thirty are in prison.

The good news at the movies obscures the bad news in the streets and confirms the Supreme Court's recent decisions on busing, affirmative action, and redistricting. Like the plot of *White Men Can't Jump,* the Court postulates the existence of a society no longer troubled by racism. Because black-white friendship is now understood to be the rule, there is no need for integrated schools or a congressional Black Caucus or affirmative action. The Congress and state governors can guiltlessly cut welfare, food assistance, fuel assistance, Head Start, housing money, fellowship money, vaccine money. Justice Anthony Kennedy can declare, speaking for the Supreme Court majority last June, that creating a world of genuine equality and sameness requires only that "our political system and our society cleanse themselves . . . of discrimination."

The deep logic runs as follows: *Yesterday white people didn't like black people, and accordingly suffered guilt, knowing that the dislike was racist and*

---

1. I could go on with examples of movies that deliver the good news of friendship: *Regarding Henry, Driving Miss Daisy, Forrest Gump, The Shawshank Redemption, Philadelphia, The Last Boy Scout, 48 Hours I–II, Rising Sun, Iron Eagle I–II, Rudy, Sister Act, Hearts of Dixie, Betrayed, The Power of One, White Nights, Clara's Heart, Doc Hollywood, Cool Runnings, Places in the Heart, Trading Places, Fried Green Tomatoes, Q & A, Platoon, A Mother's Courage: The Mary Thomas Story, The Unforgiven, The Air Up There, The Pelican Brief, Losing Isaiah, Smoke, Searching for Bobby Fischer, An Officer and a Gentleman, Speed,* etc.

knowing also that as moral persons they would have to atone for the guilt. They would have to ante up for welfare and Head Start and halfway houses and free vaccine and midnight basketball and summer jobs for schoolkids and graduate fellowships for promising scholars and craft-union apprenticeships and so on, endlessly. A considerable and wasteful expense. But at length came the realization that by ending dislike or hatred it would be possible to end guilt, which in turn would mean an end to redress: no more wasteful ransom money. There would be but one requirement: the regular production and continuous showing forth of evidence indisputably proving that hatred has totally vanished from the land.

I cannot tell the reader how much I would like to believe in this sunshine world. After the theater lights brighten and I've found coins for a black beggar on the way to my car and am driving home through downtown Springfield, Massachusetts, the world invented by *Die Hard with a Vengeance* and America's highest court gives way only slowly to the familiar urban vision in my windshield—homeless blacks on trash-strewn streets, black prostitutes staked out on a corner, and signs of a not very furtive drug trade. I know perfectly well that most African Americans don't commit crimes or live in alleys. I also know that for somebody like myself, downtown Springfield in the late evening is not a good place to be.

The movies reflect the larger dynamic of wish and dream. Day after day the nation's corporate ministries of culture churn out images of racial harmony. Millions awaken each morning to the friendly sight of Katie Couric nudging a perky elbow into good buddy Bryant Gumbel's side. My mailbox and millions of demographically similar others are choked with flyers from companies (Wal-Mart, Victoria's Secret) bent on publicizing both their wares and their social bona fides by displaying black and white models at cordial ease with one another. A torrent of goodwill messages about race arrives daily—revelations of corporate largesse, commercials, news features, TV specials, all proclaiming that whites like me feel strongly positive impulses of friendship for blacks and that those same admirable impulses are effectively eradicating racial differences, rendering blacks and whites the same. BellSouth TV commercials present children singing "I am the keeper of the world"—first a white child, then a black child, then a white child, then a black child. Because Dow Chemical likes black America, it recruits young black college grads for its research division and dramatizes, in TV commercials, their tearful-joyful partings from home. ("Son, show 'em what you got," says a black lad's father.) American Express shows an elegant black couple and an elegant white couple sitting together in a theater, happy in one another's company. (The couples share the box with an oversized Gold Card.) During the evening news I watch a black mom offer Robitussin to a miserably coughing white mom. Here's *People* magazine promoting itself under a photo of John Lee Hooker, the black bluesman. "We're these kinds of people, too," *People* claims in the caption. In [a recent] production of

Hamlet on Broadway, Horatio [was] played by a black actor. On *The 700 Club,* Pat Robertson joshes Ben Kinchlow, his black sidekick, about Ben's far-out ties.

What counts here is not the saccharine clumsiness of the inter-   10
changes but the bulk of them—the ceaseless, self-validating gestures of friendship, the humming, buzzing background theme: *All decent Americans extend the hand of friendship to African Americans; nothing but nothing is more auspicious for the African American future than this extended hand.* Faith in the miracle cure of racism by change-of-heart turns out to be so familiar as to have become unnoticeable. And yes, the faith has its benign aspect. Even as they nudge me and others toward belief in magic (instant pals and no-money-down equality), the images and messages of devoted relationships between blacks and whites do exert a humanizing influence.

Nonetheless, through these same images and messages the comfortable majority tells itself a fatuous untruth. Promoting the fantasy of painless answers, inspiring groundless self-approval among whites, joining the Supreme Court in treating "cleansing" as *inevitable,* the new orthodoxy of friendship incites culture-wide evasion, justifies one political step backward after another, and greases the skids along which, tomorrow, welfare block grants will slide into state highway-resurfacing budgets. Whites are part of the solution, says this orthodoxy, if we break out of the prison of our skin color, say hello, as equals, one-on-one, to a black stranger, and make a black friend. We're part of the problem if we have an aversion to black people or are frightened of them, or if we feel that the more distance we put between them and us the better, or if we're in the habit of asserting our superiority rather than acknowledging our common humanity. Thus we shift the problem away from politics—from black experience and the history of slavery—and perceive it as a matter of the suspicion and fear found within the white heart; solving the problem asks no more of us than that we work on ourselves, scrubbing off the dirt of ill will.

The approach miniaturizes, personalizes, and moralizes; it removes the large and complex dilemmas of race from the public sphere. It tempts audiences to see history as irrelevant and to regard feelings as decisive—to believe that the fate of black Americans is shaped mainly by events occurring in the hearts and minds of the privileged. And let's be frank: the orthodoxy of friendship feels *nice.* It practically *consecrates* self-flattery. The "good" Bill Clinton who attends black churches and talks with likable ease to fellow worshipers was campaigning when Los Angeles rioted in '92. "White Americans," he said, "are gripped by the isolation of their own experience. Too many still simply have no friends of other races and do not know any differently." Few black youths of working age in South-Central L.A. had been near enough to the idea of a job even to think of looking for work before the Rodney King verdict, but the problem, according to Clinton, was that whites need black friends.

Most of the country's leading voices of journalistic conscience (editorial writers, television anchorpersons, syndicated columnists) roundly endorse the doctrine of black-white friendship as a means of redressing the inequalities between the races. Roger Rosenblatt, editor of the *Columbia Journalism Review* and an especially deft supplier of warm and fuzzy sentiment, published an essay in *Family Circle* arguing that white friendship and sympathy for blacks simultaneously make power differentials vanish and create interracial identity between us, one by one. The author finds his *exemplum* in an episode revealing the personal sensitivity, to injured blacks, of one of his children.

"When our oldest child, Carl, was in high school," he writes, "he and two black friends were standing on a street corner in New York City one spring evening, trying to hail a taxi. The three boys were dressed decently and were doing nothing wild or threatening. Still, no taxi would pick them up. If a driver spotted Carl first, he might slow down, but he would take off again when he saw the others. Carl's two companions were familiar with this sort of abuse. Carl, who had never observed it firsthand before, burned with anger and embarrassment that he was the color of a world that would so mistreat his friends."

Rosenblatt notes that when his son "was applying to colleges, he   15
wrote his essay on that taxi incident with his two black friends. . . . He was able to articulate what he could not say at the time—how ashamed and impotent he felt. He also wrote of the power of their friendship, which has lasted to this day and has carried all three young men into the country that belongs to them. To all of us."

In this homily white sympathy begets interracial sameness in several ways. The three classmates are said to react identically to the cabdrivers' snub; i.e., they feel humiliated. "[Carl] could not find the words to express his humiliation and his friends *would* not express theirs."

The anger that inspires the younger Rosenblatt's college-admission essay on racism is seen as identical with black anger. Friendship brings the classmates together as joint, equal owners of the land of their birth ("the country that belongs to [all of] them"). And Rosenblatt supplies a still larger vision of essential black-white sameness near the end of his essay: "Our proper hearts tell the truth," he declares, "which is that we are all in the same boat, rich and poor, black and white. We are helpless, wicked, heroic, terrified, and we need one another. We need to give rides to one another."

Thus do acts of private piety substitute for public policy while the possibility of urgent political action disappears into a sentimental haze. "If we're looking for a formula to ease the tensions between the races," Rosenblatt observes, then we should "attack the disintegration of the black community" and "the desperation of the poor." Without overtly mocking civil rights activists who look toward the political arena "to erase the tensions," Rosenblatt alludes to them in a throwaway manner, implying that properly adjusted whites look elsewhere, that there was a time for politicking for "equal rights" but we've passed through it. Now is a time in which we should listen to our hearts at moments of epiphany and allow sympathy to work its wizardry, cleansing and floating us, blacks and whites "all in the same boat," on a mystical undercurrent of the New Age.

Blacks themselves aren't necessarily proof against this theme, as witness a recent essay by James Alan McPherson in the Harvard journal *Reconstruction.* McPherson, who received the 1977 Pulitzer Prize for fiction for his collection of stories *Elbow Room,* says that "the only possible steps, the safest steps . . . small ones" in the movement "toward a universal culture" will be those built not on "ideologies and formulas and programs" but on experiences of personal connectedness.

"Just this past spring," he writes, "when I was leaving a restaurant   20 after taking a [white] former student to dinner, a black [woman on the sidewalk] said to my friend, in a rasping voice, 'Hello, girlfriend. Have you got anything to spare?'" The person speaking was a female crack addict with a child who was also addicted. "But," writes McPherson, when the addict made her pitch to his dinner companion, "I saw in my friend's face an understanding and sympathy and a shining which transcended race and class. Her face reflected one human soul's connection with another. The magnetic field between the two women was charged with spiritual energy."

The writer points the path to progress through interpersonal gestures by people who "insist on remaining human, and having human responses. . . . Perhaps the best that can be done, now, is the offering of understanding and support to the few out of many who are capable of such gestures, rather than devising another plan to engineer the many into one."

The elevated vocabulary ("soul," "spiritual") beatifies the impulse to turn away from the real-life agenda of actions capable of reducing racial injustice. Wherever that impulse dominates, the rhetoric of racial sameness thrives, diminishing historical catastrophes affecting millions over centuries and inflating the significance of tremors of tenderness briefly troubling the heart or conscience of a single individual—the boy waiting for a cab, the woman leaving the restaurant. People forget the theoretically unforgettable—the caste history of American blacks, the connection between no schools for longer than a century and bad school performance now, between hateful social attitudes and zero employment opportunities, between minority anguish and majority fear.

How could this way of seeing have become conventional so swiftly? How did the dogmas of instant equality insinuate themselves so effortlessly into courts and mass audiences alike? How can a white man like myself, who taught Southern blacks in the 1960s, find himself seduced— as I have been more than once—by the orthodoxy of friendship? In the civil rights era, the experience for many millions of Americans was one of discovery. A hitherto unimagined continent of human reality and history came into view, inducing genuine concern and at least a temporary setting aside of self-importance. I remember with utter clarity what I felt at Mary Holmes College in West Point, Mississippi, when a black student of mine was killed by tailgating rednecks; my fellow tutors and I were overwhelmed with how shamefully wrong a wrong could be. For a time, we were released from the prisons of moral weakness and ambiguity. In the year or two that followed—the mid-Sixties—the notion that some humans are more human than others, whites more human than blacks, appeared to have been overturned. The next step seemed obvious: society would have to admit that when one race deprives another of its humanity for centuries, those who have done the depriving are obligated to do what they can to restore the humanity of the deprived. The obligation clearly entailed the mounting of comprehensive *long-term* programs of developmental assistance—not guilt-money handouts—for nearly the entire black population. The path forward was unavoidable.

It was avoided. Shortly after the award of civil rights and the institution, in 1966, of limited preferential treatment to remedy employment and educational discrimination against African Americans, a measure of economic progress for blacks did appear in census reports. Not much, but enough to stimulate glowing tales of universal black advance and to launch the good-news barrage that continues to this day (headline in the *New York Times,* June 18, 1995: "Moving On Up: The Greening of America's Black Middle Class").

After Ronald Reagan was elected to his first term, the new dogma of   25
black-white sameness found ideological support in the form of criticism of so-called coddling. Liberal activists of both races were berated by critics of both races for fostering an allegedly enfeebling psychology of dependency that discouraged African Americans from committing themselves to individual self-development. In 1988, the charge was passionately voiced in an essay in these pages, "I'm Black, You're White, Who's Innocent?" by Shelby Steele, who attributed the difference between black rates of advance and those of other minority groups to white folks' pampering. Most blacks, Steele claimed, could make it on their own—as voluntary immigrants have done—were they not held back by devitalizing programs that presented them, to themselves and others, as somehow dissimilar to and weaker than other Americans. This argument was all-in-the-same-boatism in a different key; the claim remained that progress depends upon recognition of black-white sameness. Let us see through superficial differences to the underlying, equally distributed gift for success. Let us teach ourselves—in the words of the Garth Brooks tune—to ignore "the color of skin" and "look for . . . the beauty within."

Still further support for the policy once known as "do-nothingism" came from points-of-light barkers, who held that a little something might perhaps be done *if* accompanied by enough publicity. Nearly every broadcaster and publisher in America moves a bale of reportage on pro bono efforts by white Americans to speed the advance of black

Americans. Example: McDonald's and the National Basketball Association distribute balloons when they announce they are addressing the dropout problem with an annual "Stay in School" scheme that gives schoolkids who don't miss a January school day a ticket to an all-star exhibition. The publicity strengthens the idea that these initiatives will nullify the social context—the city I see through my windshield. Reports of white philanthropy suggest that the troubles of this block and the next should be understood as phenomena in transition. The condition of American blacks need not be read as the fixed, unchanging consequence of generations of bottom-caste existence. Edging discreetly past a beggar posted near the entrance to Zabar's or H&H Bagels, or, while walking the dog, stepping politely around black men asleep on the sidewalk, we need not see ourselves and our fellows as uncaring accomplices in the acts of social injustice.

Yet more powerful has been the ceaseless assault, over the past generation, on our knowledge of the historical situation of black Americans. On the face of things it seems improbable that the cumulative weight of documented historical injury to African Americans could ever be lightly assessed. Gifted black writers continue to show, in scene after scene—in their studies of middle-class blacks interacting with whites—how historical realities shape the lives of their black characters. In *Killer of Sheep,* the brilliant black filmmaker Charles Burnett dramatizes the daily encounters that suck poor blacks into will-lessness and contempt for white fairy tales of interracial harmony; he quickens his historical themes with images of faceless black meat processors gutting undifferentiated, unchoosing animal life. Here, say these images, as though talking back to Clarence Thomas, here is a basic level of black life unchanged over generations. Where there's work, it's miserably paid and ugly. Space allotments at home and at work cramp body and mind. Positive expectation withers in infancy. People fall into the habit of jeering at aspiration as though at the bidding of physical law. Obstacles at every hand prevent people from loving and being loved in decent ways, prevent children from believing their parents, prevent parents from believing they themselves know anything worth knowing. The only true self, now as in the long past, is the one mocked by one's own race. "Shit on you, nigger," says a voice in *Killer of Sheep.* "Nothing you say matters a good goddamn."

For whites, these words produce guilt, and for blacks, I can only assume, pain and despair. The audience for tragedy remains small, while at the multiplex the popular enthusiasm for historical romance remains constant and vast. During the last two decades, the entertainment industry has conducted a siege on the pertinent past, systematically excising knowledge of the consequences of the historical exploitation of African Americans. Factitious renderings of the American past blur the outlines of black-white conflict, redefine the ground of black grievances for the purpose of diminishing the grievances, restage black life in accordance with the illusory conventions of American success mythology, and present the operative influences on race history as the same as those implied to be pivotal in *White Men Can't Jump* or a BellSouth advertisement.

Although there was scant popular awareness of it at the time (1977), the television miniseries *Roots* introduced the figure of the Unscathed Slave. To an enthralled audience of more than 80 million the series intimated that the damage resulting from generations of birth-ascribed, semi-animal status was largely temporary, that slavery was a product of motiveless malignity on the social margins rather than of respectable rationality, and that the ultimate significance of the institution lay in the demonstration, by freed slaves, that no force on earth can best the energies of American Individualism. ("Much like the Waltons confronting the depression," writes historian Eric Foner, a widely respected authority on American slavery, "the family in 'Roots' neither seeks nor requires outside help; individual or family effort is always sufficient.") Ken Burns's much applauded PBS documentary *The Civil War* (1990) went even further than *Roots* in downscaling black injury; the series treated slavery, birth-ascribed inferiority, and the centuries-old denial of dignity as matters of slight consequence. (By "implicitly denying the brutal reality of slavery," writes historian Jeanie Attie, Burns's programs crossed "a dangerous moral threshold." To a group of historians who asked him why slavery had been so slighted, Burns said that any discussion of slavery "would have been lengthy and boring.")

Mass media treatments of the civil rights protest years carried forward   30
the process, contributing to the "positive" erasure of difference. Big-budget films like *Mississippi Burning,* together with an array of TV biographical specials on Dr. Martin Luther King and others, presented the long-running struggle between disenfranchised blacks and the majority white culture as a heartwarming episode of interracial unity; the speed and caringness of white response to the oppression of blacks demonstrated that broadscale race conflict or race difference was inconceivable.

A consciousness that ingests either a part or the whole of this revisionism loses touch with the two fundamental truths of race in America; namely, that because of what happened in the past, blacks and whites cannot yet be the same; and that because what happened in the past was no mere matter of ill will or insult but the outcome of an established caste structure that has only very recently begun to be dismantled, it is not reparable by one-on-one goodwill. The word "slavery" comes to induce stock responses with no vital sense of a grinding devastation of mind visited upon generation after generation. Hoodwinked by the orthodoxy of friendship, the nation either ignores the past, summons for it a detached, correct "compassion," or gazes at it as though it were a set of aesthetic conventions, like twisted trees and fragmented rocks in nineteenth-century picturesque painting—lifeless phenomena without bearing on the present. The chance of striking through the mask of corporate-underwritten, feel-good, ahistorical racism grows daily more remote. The trade-off—whites promise friendship, blacks accept the status quo—begins to seem like a good deal.

Cosseted by Hollywood's magic lantern and soothed by press releases from Washington and the American Enterprise Institute, we should never forget what we see and hear for ourselves. Broken out by race, the results of every social tabulation from unemployment to life expectancy add up to a chronicle of atrocity. The history of black America fully explains—to anyone who approaches it honestly—how the disaster happened and why neither guilt money nor lectures on personal responsibility can, in and of themselves, repair the damage. The vision of friendship and sympathy placing blacks and whites "all in the same boat," rendering them equally able to do each other favors, "to give rides to one another," is a smiling but monstrous lie.

Reading the Text

1. How does DeMott view current race relations in America, and how have recent Hollywood films presented a distorted view of those relations?
2. How, in DeMott's view, do films represent the wish fulfillment of mainstream America?
3. What does DeMott see as the social effect of fantasy-laden images of happy race relations?
4. What does DeMott mean when he says that "acts of private piety substitute for public policy while the possibility of urgent political action disappears into a sentimental haze" (para. 18)?
5. How does DeMott interpret the depiction of slavery in productions such as *Roots* and *The Civil War*?

Reading the Signs

1. Rent a videotape of one of the films that DeMott discusses in his essay. Then write your own analysis of the race relations depicted in the film. To what extent do you find his claim that the film sugarcoats race relations to be valid?
2. DeMott focuses on black-white relations in this essay. In class, discuss how other ethnicities, such as Latinos or Asian Americans, fit his argument.
3. DeMott is critical of the unrealistic portrayal of race relations in film. In your journal, explore whether you believe this lack of realism has a positive or negative impact on Americans' attitudes toward race.
4. DeMott contends that we can see the same unrealistic friendships between the races in product catalogs and advertising. Select a favorite catalog or magazine and study the models populating the pages. Then write an essay in which you support, refute, or modify his contention.
5. If you were to produce a film that depicts current race relations in Amer-

ica, what sort of film would you create? Write a creative essay describing your ideal film, then share it with your classmates.

6. Keeping DeMott's argument in mind, write an interpretation of race relations as depicted in Spike Lee's *Malcolm X*. To develop your ideas, read or reread Shelby Steele's "Malcolm X" (p. 328).

PAUL C. TAYLOR

Funky White Boys and Honorary Soul Sisters

―――

Can white boys really sing the blues? Or is Eric Clapton just a wannabe who's never paid his dues? For some black critics, the only way that Clapton, and other white performers of black cultural forms, could pay their dues would be to become black, *but Paul C. Taylor (b. 1967) isn't so sure. Reflecting on his own youthful identification of white musicians and athletes whose mastery of black cultural activities qualified them for membership in what he called "The Funky White Boys Club," Taylor explains why many blacks are uncomfortable with funky white boys (and honorary white soul sisters). Taylor is an assistant professor of philosophy at the University of Washington, where he also teaches courses in American ethnic studies.*

Question: What do Stevie Ray Vaughan, Larry Bird, and Phil Woods have in common? Answer: All were charter members of a club that I created when I was growing up. They didn't know this, of course; and the existence of the club says at least as much about me as it does about its members. It speaks, for example, to the existence of an impulse that found expression in other ways—in, for example, the all-star bands that I imagined to unite the likes of Louis Armstrong and Wynton Marsalis, Bird and Branford Marsalis; as well as in my attachment to comic books like The Justice League of America, featuring super-groups composed of heroes who otherwise flew solo. But the club I created wasn't just about me and my need to foster cooperation among my idols and heroes. It was also about something that its members had in common, a commonality indicated by the name they collectively bore: The Funky White Boys Club.

One became eligible for admission to the FWB by being a white person who excelled in a cultural practice that might plausibly be considered part of, or disproportionately shaped by or linked to, black culture. So the late bluesman Vaughan gained entry for his faithful extension of the guitar artistry of Albert King and Jimi Hendrix, Woods was honored for his reverent appropriation of Charlie Parker, and Larry Bird got in just because he was so damn *good* at basketball, never mind his stereotypically "white" playing style and overwhelmingly white team (tellingly, the *Celtics* of Boston). Creating the FWB was my way of marking and celebrating what seemed to me that most anomalous of circumstances: the existence of white people who violated the core assumptions of commonsense racial logic and dared to do things white people weren't supposed to be capable of.

Eventually noticing that the FWB was indeed a boys club, I created a companion female group and inducted Bonnie Raitt and Martina Navratilova as charter members. But due either to a dearth of imagination or a loss of interest, I neglected to name the female group and soon neglected the whole project. That may have been the year when video killed the radio star and MTV was born, giving me more pleasantly mind-numbing ways to spend my time.

The clubs languished in the depths of my memory until fairly recently, when an article in *Vibe* magazine called them to my attention once again.[1] The article was an update on the R&B singer/bassist Teena Marie, a white woman who at one time was the protégée of Rick James. (James is the man who gave us—and, unfortunately, M. C. Hammer— the song "Superfreak" and then acted out the song in a series of encounters with the law. Luckily his, well, eccentricities form no part of our story here and won't be mentioned again.) The text of the piece was arrayed around a series of moody photographs of Marie, one of which bore the caption "honorary soul sister." When I saw this my mind made one of those instant and unmotivated associations that keep psychoanalysts in business and I realized that that should have been the name of the female funky white boys: the honorary soul sisters.

I found the name appropriate not only because, as I then remembered, Marie was one of the early members of the group, but also because the title laid bare the curious nature of the venture I'd undertaken all those years ago, exposing assumptions that the expression "funky white boys" leaves submerged. Why is Teena Marie only an *honorary* soul sister? Why can't she be a real one? Clearly the answer lies in the other title. According to the dominant assumptions of commonsense racial logic, white boys aren't *supposed* to be funky, and white women aren't supposed to be soulful. Teena Marie is just honorary because she's white, and Stevie Ray Vaughan was funky despite being white. There is rather widespread agreement on these assumptions, as evidenced by the frequency with which one still encounters references to the stereotypical white person without rhythm. But it's much less clear what's behind the assumptions. Just what does race have to do with being soulful?

5

---

1. Chuck Eddy, "Teena in Wonderland," *Vibe* Magazine, November 1994.

The *Vibe* article inspired these sorts of questions for me because I read it shortly after concluding an unsatisfactory print debate with another philosopher on a related topic, the question of whether white people can play the blues.[2] His position was that they can, despite claims to the contrary; my position was, and is, that *of course* they can, and that perhaps we'd be better served by looking into the motivation one might have for claiming the contrary. That debate put me in the habit of examining issues of race, culture, and authenticity, so I started to wonder about my youthful conviction that Stevie Ray Vaughan's status as a bluesman was merely honorary. In effect, the issue we'd pursued in the earlier debate was focused and narrowed into this question: What was I doing in those younger days when I created the clubs? Or: What is it about Teena Marie's whiteness that makes her only an *honorary* soul sister?

I'd like to share my thoughts on that topic, as well as on one other. I want to consider also what we should say about the urge to create Funky White Boys clubs. Is it a simple and indefensible racist impulse, relying on essentialist notions of racial characteristics and traits? Or is it something else?

1. Metaphysical Nationalism and the FWB

My clubs started with some rough but fairly reliable generalizations about race and culture. Here's one: By and large, black people tend to participate jointly in distinctive forms of life. This is a claim that sociology can bear out and that history can explain. More important, it is a claim that is neither contradicted nor undermined by the remarkable variety of lives and styles that black people can inhabit. People always say that no two snowflakes are alike, but if they had nothing in common we wouldn't call them both snowflakes. Both are tiny bits of crystalized water, a fact which is prior to all of the very real differences between them. They differ widely within a certain sphere of commonality: there is unity underlying the diversity. The same is true of black people—by which I mean "African-descended peoples in the Americas." Or, alternatively, to paraphrase a definition from W. E. B. Du Bois, "those people who would have had to ride the Jim Crow car in Georgia had they been there in 1940."[3]

By and large, black people speak or at least understand cognate cultural and experiential languages, whatever our many regional, political,

---

2. ". . . So Black and Blue: Response to Rudinow," *Journal of Aesthetics and Art Criticism* 53:3, 313–16, 1995.

3. See W. E. B. Du Bois, *Dusk of Dawn* (1940; New Brunswick: Transaction Press, 1984), 153.

religious, ethnic, or individual differences. This is what struck me as a youth. I knew that my black friends differed from my white friends, that they listened to different music and ate different foods and spoke differently: I had seen it and heard it myself. I knew they aspired to different styles of play on the basketball court after school; I knew that this Bud Powell fellow I'd started listening to was playing in a way that my white piano teachers never mentioned, much less demonstrated.

Knowing these things I drew a conclusion: white people who do   10 things the way we do must have a special status, because most white people don't, or can't. And this conclusion led me to another rough but reliable generalization: By and large, white people are unable to participate in or appreciate black cultural practices. So in the same way that John Turturro's character in Spike Lee's *Do the Right Thing* exempts Magic Johnson and Prince from blackness because they're somehow special, my young mind exempted from whiteness the white people who could participate in black culture. They became honorary black folk, almost. No longer just white boys, but *funky* white boys.

Now, rough but reliable generalizations may suffer one of two fates when stored in an active and curious mind. On the one hand, they may be complicated by additional conditions and have the limits of their reliability precisely marked. This is what happened in my case. When I learned about class differences within and across races, about regional cultural variation and so forth, I realized that whatever I said about The Race was going to be riddled with exceptions and conditions except at a very lofty level of abstraction, and that whatever I said was going to have to answer to the evidence of history and sociology.

On the other hand, the generalizations may be rigidified into necessary truths and the observations which motivate them rendered inevitable. This happens to the points I started with when they are taken up into the framework of a certain kind of cultural nationalism. Cultural nationalism is in part the view that all black people participate in a common form of life, that we share a disposition to enjoy and create the same cultural forms, the same modes of speech and movement, expression and performance. For a cultural nationalist, the possibility of both a vibrant black community and a sane, settled individual black identity rest principally upon one thing: the existence of a coherent, identifiable, *distinct* set of black cultural practices. For the nationalist, "black English" and "black art" and "black music" have to be meaningful expressions, marking some important boundaries. And the behaviors inside the boundaries have to add up to a distinctive culture.

So far the nationalist position is consistent with the mindset that motivated my clubs. But a truly committed nationalist goes farther. A committed nationalist on the model of Molefi Asante hardens my rough generalizations into metaphysical and ethical principles in his search for something deeper and more reliable than the contingencies of history to underwrite the unity of black culture. The metaphysical principle is *essentialism,* which in this context entails that *it is of the nature* of black people, completely apart from considerations of history and sociology, to produce certain forms of life. The list of adjectives used in describing that life ought to be familiar. We favor rhythm over melody, it says; organic unities over dualist bifurcations, blues scales over Greek modes, improvisation over scripting, and so forth and so on. On this view black people naturally and *necessarily* gravitate toward certain cultural forms simply because that's what it is to be black.

The ethical principle has to do with *authenticity,* and like the metaphysical principle from which it follows, hardens a rough generalization into dogma. The generalization, you'll recall, was that white people tend not to be able to participate in or enjoy black cultural practices. Essentialism rigidifies this generalization about how capacities *tend* to be distributed into an airtight claim of necessity, the claim that all black people and only black people can participate in black culture because black cultural practices express the nature of black people. The authenticity principle takes the claim about capacity, about what certain people *can do,* and turns it into a claim about permission, about what certain people *may* do. Not only, it turns out, are white people not able to take part in black culture; they are not even allowed to try. (Perhaps this is the sort of slip that English teachers are trying to help us avoid with their fussiness about the distinction between "may" and "can.")

There is another element to the ethics of committed nationalism, the idea of racial *obligation.* This idea follows also from a plausible generalization, this time the point that if the people who created a culture don't maintain it by continued participation, chances are it will die out. The committed nationalist takes this simple point and turns it into a moral imperative. Black people, he argues, should participate in their culture; those who don't are shirking an obligation to the race. As an added incentive, the nationalist I have in mind is likely to point out that the moral error of opting out of the culture carries with it the prospect of psychological ruin, as the unscrupulous negro loses touch with her true identity and, on Asante's version of this account, "loses her center." The notion of cultural-racial obligation provides some additional support for the exclusionary rhetoric of authenticity: white people are in the same position with regard to their own culture, facing the same psychological and moral dangers, and so should worry about their own ways of life instead of dabbling elsewhere. Instead of interfering with our culture they should be contributing to their own.

Let's get clear on the plausible claims behind (way behind) what I've been calling committed cultural nationalism. For one thing, there are regularities in the practices of black diaspora cultures. For another, it does seem to be a good thing for black people to participate in these cultures, good, that is, for both the people and the practices. The individual participants are able to draw existential sustenance from and take shelter in the symbolic and meaningful practices of their cultures, while the cultures themselves are able to persist and proliferate. (Although in this age of pluralism and global consumer culture there is less danger of a cultural form dying out if its original participants neglect it. Blues music, for example, is more likely to die out these days if white people start to neglect it, since many blacks have already consigned it to the dustbin of history.) The difficulty with committed cultural nationalism is that it tries to find some otherworldly support for these plausible ideas.

In particular, this nationalism tries to find some basis for black cultural continuity that's deeper than culture, than history, than the empirical striving and effort of concrete human beings, and as a result culture turns out not to be very important after all. Perhaps a better name for the view would be *metaphysical nationalism,* because it requires invoking an elaborate and unnecessary metaphysical apparatus to make sense of perfectly natural facts. Sociology, anthropology, history, and politics are more than adequate to account for the continuities that interest the nationalist. We just don't *need* to conjure up an elaborate metaphysics to explain the extent to which black people are, culturally and otherwise, *a* people. To do so is a bit like using an atom bomb to kill a housefly. But questions of explanatory adequacy aside, it is simply more interesting to point out the concrete, historical linkages that connect santeria to West Africa, King Sunny Ade to James Brown, than to trace them all to a single transhistorical essence. It is far more impressive for people to remember their roots themselves and create *themselves* despite the fetters of oppression and forced forgetfulness than it is for them to serve as the vehicles of a transcendent racial essence.

As we saw above, metaphysical nationalism also provides an ontological grounding for racial exclusivism, for the claim that all and *only* black people can participate in black culture. From this perspective Teena Marie is an honorary soul sister because she gets close to the core styles and conventions of R&B. The same holds true for Stevie Ray Vaughan and blues performance. But these performers will never be more than honorary because they're not truly expressing their deepest essences. That is to say, to participate truly and fully in the practice is to express the essence that manifests itself in the practice, and white people simply don't have the essence to express. On this view Vaughan is just imitating Albert King; Phil Woods is just imitating Charlie Parker. And if you listen closely, some people say, you can tell the difference. Never mind that white performers in black idioms or styles are not always mimics, or the possibility that any alleged categorical difference between white and black performances may simply be an overzealous interpretation of stylistic differences between individual performers. And never mind that we could account for any discernible categorical difference that *did* arise by referring to culture, to the lower probability that a white person will be socialized into the communities where the conventions of performance are taught and learned.

As we also saw above, the ethical dimensions of metaphysical nationalism can lead to an exclusivist posture by supporting the claim that even if white people can participate in black styles, they *shouldn't* do so. From this perspective Teena Marie is honorary because she's treading on what is by rights someone else's cultural turf. The honor of (almost-) soul sister status is extended as a grant of permission, and participation without it is immoral. But the frailty of nationalist metaphysics undermines this point as well. Without the metaphysics that link the racial essence to its cultural manifestation there is no reason to assume that the boundaries of culture and the boundaries of race are coextensive. Without the metaphysics there is no reason not to let Bonnie Raitt or Eric Clapton carry on the blues aspect of black culture. And even apart from the historical and sociological considerations I've mentioned above, there seems to be little reason to accept the metaphysics of racial essences. That is, on the evidence of the biological sciences alone, evidence that has been steadily mounting for some time, especially in this century, the idea that race membership as a matter of physiology somehow carries with it interesting moral and cultural traits seems to be a pernicious fiction.

2. Aesthetics Instead of Authenticity

I want to distance both my present self and my thirteen-year-old self   20 from metaphysical nationalism and its excesses. All those years ago I hadn't yet thought out the possible theoretical extensions of the commonsense racial logic I'd accepted. Having done so now, I reject them. Metaphysical nationalism is too timid and narrow; it downplays the wonderful diversity and creativity of African diaspora cultures—with an "s"—and of the concrete, historically located people who've created reggae, R&B, hard bop, and hip-hop. And worst of all for our present purposes, it stands in the way of explaining how we can reasonably make judgments like the ones behind the title of "honorary soul sister." The metaphysical nationalist approach makes these judgments just as inappropriate and ungrounded as any other racist exclusion. Either whites are just naturally incapable or black culture is just naturally off limits.

But having rejected the metaphysical/ethical route to racial exclusivism, I need to offer some other motivation for the urge that led to my imagined clubs. I do this not just to defend myself (although that's always fun) but also, and more importantly, because I want to displace and decenter the dialectic of essentialism-cum-racism. That is, I want to mark off a conceptual space within which we can examine assertions like "white people can't play the blues" without recourse to the vocabularies of essentialism *or* racism. I want us to be able to say something more interesting about the roots of these assertions than that the speaker is a racial essentialist and therefore a racist. This is important to me because I think relatively few of the people who make or presuppose assertions of the sort I have in mind are essentialists or racists. I don't think the FWB was a racist venture, nor do I think that of *Vibe* magazine's decision to use the expression "honorary soul sister." Luckily, there is a way to understand what I was up to, what the *Vibe* magazine people were up to, without slipping into the paralogisms of racial essences. There is a way to explain the urge to withhold or confer the status of funkiness and soulfulness without relying on the bare fact of race.

The approach I have in mind proceeds from yet another plausible and probably familiar idea, especially familiar when it comes to black music, that I'll call *the Elvis Effect*. When white participation in traditionally black avenues of cultural production produces feelings of unease, this is the Elvis Effect. I could as easily call it the Benny Goodman, the Dave Brubeck, or the Vanilla Ice effect, because all follow the same pattern. Black people participate almost exclusively in a cultural practice, mostly untouched by the interest, interference, or acclaim of the white community. A white person finds his or her way into the practice, becomes proficient, and is "discovered" by the white community. The community embraces the practice, but only in the person of the white "pioneer" who introduced it. It snaps up his records or copies his arrangements (or flocks to get cornrows, or lets its jeans sag around its knees), all the while oblivious to the fact that the true pioneers are probably still toiling in obscurity and poverty, and that the black community has probably moved on to something else that has yet to be "discovered."

Of course my brief description of phenomena that produce the Elvis Effect is a crude and over-simple rendering of complex historical events. For one thing it overlooks issues like the extent to which "white" country music and "black" blues grow from common southern roots that grew into people like Elvis as naturally as it did into, say, Muddy Waters; for another, it passes completely over the role of white record companies in preserving and promulgating black musical culture. But it isn't too crude to make the point. How else can we explain the fact that Benny Goodman gets movies made about him, gigs at Carnegie Hall, and the title of the king of swing, while we're still waiting for the movies—the *big* movies—about Duke Ellington and Fletcher Henderson? How else can we account for the fact that Maynard Ferguson and Chet Baker could, decades ago, beat out Dizzy Gillespie, Miles, *and* Clifford Brown in *Downbeat* polls for best trumpeter? (Baker, maybe. But Ferguson?) How else can we explain the phenomenal sales of Vanilla Ice and New Kids on the Block, not to mention Dave Koz?

The Elvis Effect isn't hard to explain. When we talk about black music in the twentieth century we're talking about commodities, market phenomena, so the relative weakness of black consumer power, as a function both of community size and individual wealth and income, is certainly a factor. And then there's the industrial side, the cynical marketing side, of the music business, which gave us Terence Trent D'Arby in much the same way that it gave us Vanilla Ice (the relative merits of each I'll leave up to you). But the most important factor is *the historically racist trajectory* of white American appetites for cultural commodities. That's why in the early days of the blues-based pop styles (soul, rock, and R&B) black musicians often heard their songs on the radio being covered by white performers, or found their pictures effaced from their own album covers to avoid repulsing white consumers. (Both of which are well rendered in Robert Townsend's film, *The Five Heartbeats.*) That's why the Beatles and the rest of the 1960s British invaders were surprised that no one here seemed to understand the homegrown roots of this new rock and roll: that's why we need Eric Clapton to explain Muddy Waters to us—or one reason, anyway. It is too easy for too many people here to assume that nothing of cultural value can come from black folks, or to concede the point but limit the damage by treating the black origins as raw material to be refined by sophisticated whites.

The Elvis Effect is not new. I've just given the name to a phenomenon with which we're all familiar. I bring it up now to make two points. The first is that the familiarity of the Elvis Effect allows it to provide a backdrop for the experience of art in traditionally black idioms. The second is that this backdrop, and the way it mediates the aesthetic experience, can explain what I've been calling the funky white boys urge, the impulse to distinguish white contributions to traditionally black cultural practices.

When I talk about an aesthetic experience I mean an event, the collection of related perceptions and appraisals that emerges from a certain kind of interaction between an observer and an object. On some conceptions of aesthetic experience, like the one John Dewey articulates in his book, *Art as Experience,* the aesthetic experience is more appropriately considered the work of art than the art object itself. The aesthetic experience brings the object to life in what you do with the sounds D'Angelo has recorded for you, what you do with the figures and hues that Picasso has kindly left you—and what they do with, and to, you.

The art object, the painting or the recorded sounds or the novel, is the focus of an aesthetic experience, which—and here we reach the crucial point—works very much like an experience of visual perception and recognition. When you focus your eyes on something, all around the central point of clarity you see a vast fringe that's fuzzy and out of focus. You usually don't notice this fringe, this periphery; that is, after all, what being focused means. But the fringe is there, and it is essential to the coherence of what you see. If you didn't have peripheral vision the objects in plain sight would seem disconnected and isolated, floating free from the rest of the world. Much like this perceptual fringe there is a theoretical fringe that helps us make sense of the sensations that arise from the

25

encounter with the object. The sensations become organized into an experience of a certain *kind* of object, say, a cow, only if you have the concept "cow" available in your cognitive repertoire. Otherwise you've simply encountered a big, smelly beast that makes weird sounds. Perhaps more clearly, you can experience something as a baseball bat only if the right theoretical background is in place to support your perceptual encounter with the stick of wood. If it isn't, if, say, you're from a pre-industrial culture and don't know how to distinguish a baseball from Bisquick, then you've simply encountered a funny stick.

The experience of an artwork follows the same pattern. The work itself is surrounded by a vast range of peripheral experience which stretches out and makes connections with the rest of the world. You may not think about this fringe, this backdrop to experience, but without it the art object doesn't make sense as the kind of thing it's supposed to be, and it can't contribute to the right kind of aesthetic experience. Unless one internalizes the conventions of western painterly representation, one will see only splashes of paint where an art critic sees angels or receding horizons or bowls of fruit. And unless one understands that the conventions of artistic practice undergird the experience of painterly representation, one treats the painting as nothing more than a *picture* when it is so much more, a commentary on a tradition, a manipulation and rejection of themes and approaches created and perfected over time. Unless one can read these in the work, see them along with the work, the work remains opaque. This history is the fringe, the penumbra that makes the experience coherent and complete.

Similarly, unless we appreciate the narrative of the development of jazz composition and improvisation, Ornette Coleman sounds like he never quite finished learning how to play the saxophone. But when we know the history, when we can notice the periphery of the experience, we can hear his interpretation and critique of the techniques of jazz performance. Or: until you can hear the echoes of Marvin Gaye and Prince and southern gospel *and* hip-hop on D'Angelo's album *Brown Sugar,* until you feel the incredible syncretism of the church organ grounded by a thundering jeep beat on the song "Higher," you'll miss the point and miss out on the most satisfying aspects of the experiences promised by encounters with the album—which, incidentally, is precisely what some hip-hop obsessed reviewers did before the album's sales showed them that maybe this guy was onto something.

My claim here is that the Elvis Effect can serve as the periphery for the reception and experience of white performances in black expressive traditions. In the same way that knowing a bit of art history changes the way we appreciate, the way we *see,* a painting, knowing the historically racist trajectory of white American appetites for cultural commodities can change the way one hears Eric Clapton—or the Canadian dancehall dj Snow. Knowledge of the historically racist trajectory of white American

30

appetites for cultural commodities can erect affective obstacles to the reception and enjoyment of otherwise impeccable arrangements of sounds; that knowledge can interfere with and frustrate the pattern of response that would otherwise attend the perception of the music, just as knowing a little more about the context for Picasso's work can and should frustrate the pattern of response that would otherwise lead one to say "my little sister can do *that*."

My point is that the urge to keep Teena Marie at arm's length, to invite her in conditionally as an honorary participant, can be an aesthetic response rather than a moral or a metaphysical one. It can proceed from the realization that "I've heard of Eric Clapton only because he's white," the realization that the dollars I spend on a ticket to his show or to buy his CD will fuel the machine which perhaps without racist intent produces racist outcomes: the realization that if I participate in this process, I'll be partially responsible for the next sister who toils in poverty while the white woman with her style gets the big record deal.

3. Conclusion

What, then, does race have to do with funkiness and soulfulness? Simply this: Race is the principal dynamic in an historical drama that shapes the possibilities for aesthetic experience of traditionally black cultural practices. Less concisely but more simply: Most of us share or are at least acquainted with a cluster of moderately plausible intuitions linking race to cultural production. I've been concerned here with three in particular. One says that there is something answering to the title "black culture," or that there are some things answering to that title. Another says that it is good for black people to perpetuate these cultures. And the last says that white people are either unwilling or unable to participate in these cultures, and that the ones who are willing and who are able differ somehow from the rest. These intuitions, when ossified into a metaphysical nationalism, can support a project something like my honorary soul sisters club, but a project predicated on the view that white people have neither the proper nature nor the moral standing to participate in black culture. This approach can lead to the urge to create funky white boys clubs, but it does so while leaving the undeniable fact of white participation utterly inexplicable, making black and white participants immoral and neurotic, and subordinating history to the dictates of a transcendent racial essence. I've explained these consequences of metaphysical nationalism already, so I'll introduce one more for good measure: it plays into the hands of racism. After all, even if the metaphysical nationalist denies that she's a racist, she has given plenty of ammunition to the white racist. While she's saying that the black essence is linked to rhythm and the like, the white racist can say "You're right, we don't have rhythm; our essence is concerned with other things, like rationality and cognitive powers."

I propose avoiding, instead of inviting, this debate with the racist. Instead of invoking nationalist metaphysics, let's take history and culture seriously. On the view I propose, the three plausible intuitions regarding the existence and worth of black culture and the relation between white participants and the culture are joined by a fourth, which says that white participation tends to exploit and thereby to imperil black culture and its main proponents. This intuition leads to the Elvis Effect, and recognizing that fact enables us to link the other intuitions to the funky white boys club impulse *without* inciting the racist or engaging in an act of metaphysical conjuring. History reports that the fate of black expressive innovation has too often been cooptation without compensation, and it supports the prediction that white participation portends dilution, commercialization, and decay for the culture. Awareness of this history seeps into the reception of white performances and makes a qualitative difference in the aesthetic experience—it seeps in, incidentally, not to distract but to inform, the way the history of painting informs one's appreciation of Picasso's "Les Demoiselles D'Avignon."

This appeal to what we might call a problematized aesthetic response motivates the claim that Stevie Ray Vaughan and Stan Getz are merely honorary. The background to the aesthetic experience is such that what would otherwise be heard as a blues performance is instead experienced as the performance of an honorary bluesman. Teena Marie is honorary not because she lacks the right nature or the moral entitlement to participate in the culture of black music, but because the listener's encounter with the sounds that Marie produces is complicated by the background of commonsense theory that informs the perception and recognition of the sounds.

Some disclaimers are in order. First of all, I am not claiming that the 35 way to understand my particular adolescent urge to designate funky white boys and honorary soul sisters proceeded from an awareness of the historically racist trajectory of white cultural consumption. In the same way that my FWB project didn't rise to the level of definiteness necessary to become metaphysical nationalism, it certainly wasn't definite or politically astute enough to be motivated by the Elvis Effect. It was simply what it was: a youthful effort to occupy an idle mind by following out the consequences of certain familiar and prominent generalizations about race and culture. I am claiming, however, that just as my FWB-urge was neither racist nor essentialist, other similar positions can be neither racist nor essentialist, and that one way to account for such positions is by appeal to the Elvis Effect and the long shadow it can cast over aesthetic experiences.

Second, I don't mean to endorse the claim that white people can only be honorary participants in black culture. I mean only to explain it, or some versions of it. My aim has been to point out only that one can make such claims without being a racist or an essentialist, largely on the basis of certain rough but plausible generalizations about race and culture. Of course, such claims and generalizations are much less plausible now than they were even ten years ago, now that hip-hop culture has penetrated into the deepest and palest recesses of America. And, as it happens, they weren't terribly plausible even then, standing as they did in a tense relationship to the long history of white contribution to and participation in allegedly "black" forms like blues and jazz. But their validity aside, the claims and generalizations are familiar, and as such can be expected to serve as the backdrop to aesthetic experience.

I have a final comment about one of those generalizations, the one concerning what I've labeled "the Elvis Effect." Focusing on the racism of the processes by which black cultural forms have historically found their way into the broader culture moves us past the dialectic of essentialism and authenticity. It shows that there may be concrete political concerns that make racial solidarity an attractive mode of political and cultural practice. It reminds us that anything validly claiming the title "black culture" comes from the concrete strivings of black people rather than from some essence outside of culture. And it reminds us that the strivings of those people take place not in the sociological and historical vacuum often assumed in discussions of racial justice, but in the context of a rich historical drama that is shaped by power relations, by economics and politics. Furthermore, linking judgments like the ones behind the FWB to the background material of economics, history, and politics reminds us that aesthetic experience has a context, one that is as much cultural and political as it is theoretical and art-historical.

Reading the Text

1. What were the criteria for inclusion in Paul C. Taylor's "Funky White Boys Club" (para. 1)?
2. Why did *Vibe* call Teena Marie an "honorary soul sister" (para. 4) rather than a real one?
3. What is the difference between "cultural nationalism" (para. 16) and "metaphysical nationalism" (para. 17)?
4. Define the "Elvis Effect" (para. 22) in your own words.

Reading the Signs

1. Conduct a class debate on whether whites can be authentic performers of African American cultural activities. Be sure to base your arguments on the work of specific artists and performers.
2. Taylor suggests that metaphysical nationalism "plays into the hands of racism" (para. 32) and thus rejects it. Write an essay in which you argue your position on racial exclusivity in popular entertainment and sports.
3. As rap and hip-hop win mainstream acceptance, more white performers

are adopting its styles and rhythms. Write an essay comparing the history of rap and hip-hop with that of rock 'n' roll. To what extent do you believe history will repeat itself?

4. Write an essay arguing for or against the value of preserving one's biological ethnic heritage. To develop your ideas, consult Nell Bernstein ("Goin' Gangsta, Choosin' Cholita," below), bell hooks ("Baby," p. 568), or Gloria Anzaldúa ("How to Tame a Wild Tongue," p. 575).

NELL BERNSTEIN

Goin' Gangsta, Choosin' Cholita

||||||||||||||||||||||||||||||||||||||||||||||||||||

Ever wonder about wannabes—white suburban teenagers who dress and act like nonwhite inner-city gangsters? In this report on the phenomenon of "claiming," Nell Bernstein (b. 1965) probes some of the feelings and motives of teens who are "goin' gangsta" or "choosin' cholita"—kids who try on a racial identity not their own. Their reasons may surprise you. Bernstein is editor of YO!, *a San Francisco area journal of teen life published by the Pacific News Service, and she has published in* Glamour, Woman's Day, Salon, *and* Mother Jones.

Her lipstick is dark, the lip liner even darker, nearly black. In baggy pants, a blue plaid Pendleton, her bangs pulled back tight off her forehead, 15-year-old April is a perfect cholita, a Mexican gangsta girl.

But April Miller is Anglo. "And I don't like it!" she complains. "I'd rather be Mexican."

April's father wanders into the family room of their home in San Leandro, California, a suburb near Oakland. "Hey, cholita," he teases. "Go get a suntan. We'll put you in a barrio and see how much you like it."

A large, sandy-haired man with "April" tattooed on one arm and "Kelly"—the name of his older daughter—on the other, Miller spent 21 years working in a San Leandro glass factory that shut down and moved to Mexico a couple of years ago. He recently got a job in another factory, but he expects NAFTA to swallow that one, too.

"Sooner or later we'll all get nailed," he says. "Just another stab in the back of the American middle class."   5

Later, April gets her revenge: "Hey, Mr. White Man's Last Stand," she teases. "Wait till you see how well I manage my welfare check. You'll be asking me for money."

A once almost exclusively white, now increasingly Latin and black working-class suburb, San Leandro borders on predominantly black East Oakland. For decades, the boundary was strictly policed and practically impermeable. In 1970 April Miller's hometown was 97 percent white. By 1990 San Leandro was 65 percent white, 6 percent black, 15 percent Hispanic, and 13 percent Asian or Pacific Islander. With minorities moving into suburbs in growing numbers and cities becoming ever more diverse, the boundary between city and suburb is dissolving, and suburban teenagers are changing with the times.

In April's bedroom, her past and present selves lie in layers, the pink walls of girlhood almost obscured, Guns N' Roses and Pearl Jam posters overlaid by rappers Paris and Ice Cube. "I don't have a big enough attitude to be a black girl," says April, explaining her current choice of ethnic identification.

What matters is that she thinks the choice is hers. For April and her friends, identity is not a matter of where you come from, what you were born into, what color your skin is. It's what you wear, the music you listen to, the words you use—everything to which you pledge allegiance, no matter how fleetingly.

The hybridization of American teens has become talk show fodder, with "wiggers"—white kids who dress and talk "black"—appearing on TV in full gangsta regalia. In Indiana a group of white high school girls raised a national stir when they triggered an imitation race war at their virtually all-white high school last fall simply by dressing "black." 10

In many parts of the country, it's television and radio, not neighbors, that introduce teens to the allure of ethnic difference. But in California, which demographers predict will be the first state with no racial majority by the year 2000, the influences are more immediate. The California public schools are the most diverse in the country: 42 percent white, 36 percent Hispanic, 9 percent black, 8 percent Asian.

Sometimes young people fight over their differences. Students at virtually any school in the Bay Area can recount the details of at least one "race riot" in which a conflict between individuals escalated into a battle between their clans. More often, though, teens would rather join than fight. Adolescence, after all, is the period when you're most inclined to mimic the power closest at hand, from stealing your older sister's clothes to copying the ruling clique at school.

White skaters and Mexican would-be gangbangers listen to gangsta rap and call each other "nigga" as a term of endearment; white girls sometimes affect Spanish accents; blond cheerleaders claim Cherokee ancestors.

"Claiming" is the central concept here. A Vietnamese teen in Hayward, another Oakland suburb, "claims" Oakland—and by implication blackness—because he lived there as a child. A law-abiding white kid "claims" a Mexican gang he says he hangs with. A brown-skinned girl with a Mexican father and a white mother "claims" her Mexican side, while her fair-skinned sister "claims" white. The word comes up over and over, as if identity were territory, the self a kind of turf.

At a restaurant in a minimall in Hayward, Nicole Huffstutler, 13, sits 15 with her friends and describes herself as "Indian, German, French, Welsh, and, um . . . American": "If somebody says anything like 'Yeah, you're just a peckerwood,' I'll walk up and I'll say 'white pride!' 'Cause I'm proud of my race, and I wouldn't wanna be any other race."

"Claiming" white has become a matter of principle for Heather, too, who says she's "sick of the majority looking at us like we're less than them." (Hayward schools were 51 percent white in 1990, down from 77 percent in 1980, and whites are now the minority in many schools.)

Asked if she knows that nonwhites have not traditionally been referred to as "the majority" in America, Heather gets exasperated: "I hear that all the time, every day. They say, 'Well, you guys controlled us for many years, and it's time for us to control you.' Every day."

When Jennifer Vargas—a small, brown-skinned girl in purple jeans who quietly eats her salad while Heather talks—softly announces that she's "mostly Mexican," she gets in trouble with her friends.

"No, you're not!" scolds Heather.

"I'm mostly Indian and Mexican," Jennifer continues flatly. "I'm 20 very little . . . I'm mostly . . ."

"Your mom's white!" Nicole reminds her sharply. "She has blond hair."

"That's what I mean," Nicole adds. "People think that white is a bad thing. They think that white is a bad race. So she's trying to claim more Mexican than white."

"I have very little white in me," Jennifer repeats. "I have mostly my dad's side, 'cause I look like him and stuff. And most of my friends think that me and my brother and sister aren't related, 'cause they look more like my mom."

"But you guys are all the same race, you just look different," Nicole insists. She stops eating and frowns. "OK, you're half and half each what your parents have. So you're equal as your brother and sister, you just look different. And you should be proud of what you are—every little piece and bit of what you are. Even if you were Afghan or whatever, you should be proud of it."

Will Mosley, Heather's 17-year-old brother, says he and his friends 25 listen to rap groups like Compton's Most Wanted, NWA, and Above the Law because they "sing about life"—that is, what happens in Oakland, Los Angeles, anyplace but where Will is sitting today, an empty Round Table Pizza in a minimall.

"No matter what race you are," Will says, "if you live like we do, then that's the kind of music you like."

And how do they live?

"We don't live bad or anything," Will admits. "We live in a pretty good neighborhood, there's no violence or crime. I was just . . . we're just city people, I guess."

Will and his friend Adolfo Garcia, 16, say they've outgrown trying to be something they're not. "When I was 11 or 12," Will says, "I thought I was becoming a big gangsta and stuff. Because I liked that music, and thought it was the coolest, I wanted to become that. I wore big clothes, like you wear in jail. But then I kind of woke up. I looked at myself and thought, 'Who am I trying to be?'"

They may have outgrown blatant mimicry, but Will and his friends   30 remain convinced that they can live in a suburban tract house with a well-kept lawn on a tree-lined street in "not a bad neighborhood" and still call themselves "city" people on the basis of musical tastes. "City" for these young people means crime, graffiti, drugs. The kids are law-abiding, but these activities connote what Will admiringly calls "action." With pride in his voice, Will predicts that "in a couple of years, Hayward will be like Oakland. It's starting to get more known, because of crime and things. I think it'll be bigger, more things happening, more crime, more graffiti, stealing cars."

"That's good," chimes in 15-year-old Matt Jenkins, whose new beeper—an item that once connoted gangsta chic but now means little more than an active social life—goes off periodically. "More fun."

The three young men imagine with disdain life in a gangsta-free zone. "Too bland, too boring," Adolfo says. "You have to have something going on. You can't just have everyday life."

"Mowing your lawn," Matt sneers.

"Like Beaver Cleaver's house," Adolfo adds. "It's too clean out here."

Not only white kids believe that identity is a matter of choice or   35 taste, or that the power of "claiming" can transcend ethnicity. The Manor Park Locos—a group of mostly Mexican-Americans who hang out in San Leandro's Manor Park—say they descend from the Manor Lords, tough white guys who ruled the neighborhood a generation ago.

They "are like our . . . uncles and dads, the older generation," says Jesse Martinez, 14. "We're what they were when they were around, except we're Mexican."

"There's three generations," says Oso, Jesse's younger brother. "There's Manor Lords, Manor Park Locos, and Manor Park Pee Wees." The Pee Wees consist mainly of the Locos' younger brothers, eager kids who circle the older boys on bikes and brag about "punking people."

Unlike Will Mosley, the Locos find little glamour in city life. They survey the changing suburban landscape and see not "action" or "more fun" but frightening decline. Though most of them are not yet 18, the Locos are already nostalgic, longing for a Beaver Cleaver past that white kids who mimic them would scoff at.

Walking through nearly empty Manor Park, with its eucalyptus stands, its softball diamond and tennis courts, Jesse's friend Alex, the only Asian in

the group, waves his arms in a gesture of futility. "A few years ago, every
bench was filled," he says. "Now no one comes here. I guess it's because
of everything that's going on. My parents paid a lot for this house, and I
want it to be nice for them. I just hope this doesn't turn into Oakland."

Glancing across the park at April Miller's street, Jesse says he knows   40
what the white cholitas are about. "It's not a racial thing," he explains.
"It's just all the most popular people out here are Mexican. We're just
the gangstas that everyone knows. I guess those girls wanna be known."

Not every young Californian embraces the new racial hybridism.
Andrea Jones, 20, an African-American who grew up in the Bay Area
suburbs of Union City and Hayward, is unimpressed by what she sees
mainly as shallow mimicry. "It's full of posers out here," she says. "When
Boyz N the Hood came out on video, it was sold out for weeks. The boys
all wanna be black, the girls all wanna be Mexican. It's the glamour."

Driving down the quiet, shaded streets of her old neighborhood in
Union City, Andrea spots two white preteen boys in Raiders jackets and
hugely baggy pants strutting erratically down the empty sidewalk. "Look
at them," she says. "Dislocated."

She knows why. "In a lot of these schools out here, it's hard being
white," she says. "I don't think these kids were prepared for the backlash
that is going on, all the pride now in people of color's ethnicity, and our
boldness with it. They have nothing like that, no identity, nothing they
can say they're proud of.

"So they latch onto their great-grandmother who's a Cherokee, or
they take on the most stereotypical aspects of being black or Mexican.
It's beautiful to appreciate different aspects of other people's culture—
that's like the dream of what the 21st century should be. But to garnish
yourself with pop culture stereotypes just to blend—that's really sad."

Roland Krevocheza, 18, graduated last year from Arroyo High School   45
in San Leandro. He is Mexican on his mother's side, Eastern European on
his father's. In the new hierarchies, it may be mixed kids like Roland who
have the hardest time finding their place, even as their numbers grow.
(One in five marriages in California is between people of different races.)
They can always be called "wannabes," no matter what they claim.

"I'll state all my nationalities," Roland says. But he takes a greater interest in his father's side, his Ukrainian, Romanian, and Czech ancestors.
"It's more unique," he explains. "Mexican culture is all around me. We
eat Mexican food all the time, I hear stories from my grandmother. I see
the low-riders and stuff. I'm already part of it. I'm not trying to be; I am."

His darker-skinned brother "says he's not proud to be white,"
Roland adds. "He calls me 'Mr. Nazi.'" In the room the two share, the
American flags and the reproduction of the Bill of Rights are Roland's;
the Public Enemy poster belongs to his brother.

Roland has good reason to mistrust gangsta attitudes. In his junior
year in high school, he was one of several Arroyo students who were

beaten up outside the school at lunchtime by a group of Samoans who came in cars from Oakland. Roland wound up with a split lip, a concussion, and a broken tailbone. Later he was told that the assault was "gang-related" — that the Samoans were beating up anyone wearing red.

"Rappers, I don't like them," Roland says. "I think they're a bad influence on kids. It makes kids think they're all tough and bad."

Those who, like Roland, dismiss the gangsta and cholo styles as affectations can point to the fact that several companies market overpriced knockoffs of "ghetto wear" targeted at teens.   50

But there's also something going on out here that transcends adolescent faddishness and pop culture exoticism. When white kids call their parents "racist" for nagging them about their baggy pants; when they learn Spanish to talk to their boyfriends; when Mexican-American boys feel themselves descended in spirit from white "uncles"; when children of mixed marriages insist that they are whatever race they say they are, all of them are more than just confused.

They're inching toward what Andrea Jones calls "the dream of what the 21st century should be." In the ever more diverse communities of Northern California, they're also facing the complicated reality of what their 21st century will be.

Meanwhile, in the living room of the Miller family's San Leandro home, the argument continues unabated. "You don't know what you are," April's father has told her more than once. But she just keeps on telling him he doesn't know what time it is.

Reading the Text

1. How do teens like April Miller define their identity, according to Bernstein?
2. Describe in your own words what "claiming" (para. 14) an ethnic identity means. Why do so many teens "claim" a new ethnicity, according to Bernstein?
3. What relationship does Bernstein see between claiming and the mass media?
4. What does being white mean to many of the kids who claim a nonwhite identity?
5. What does the city signify to the young people whom Bernstein describes?

Reading the Signs

1. In class, stage a conversation between April Miller and her father on her adoption of a Mexican identity, with April defending her choice and her father repudiating it.

2. Write an essay in which you support, challenge, or modify Andrea Jones's assumption that it is media-generated "glamour" that prompts young people to claim a new ethnic identity.

3. Write an argumentative essay in which you explain whether the claiming fad is an expression of racial tolerance or racial stereotyping.

4. Bernstein describes teens claiming the identities of ethnic minorities, but she provides few instances of claiming a white identity. In class, discuss what being white signifies to these teens.

5. Write an essay in which you explore the relationship between claiming and gang membership. To develop your ideas, you might consult Sonia Maasik and Jack Solomon, "Signs of the Street: A Conversation" (p. 609).

b e l l   h o o k s

Baby

||||||||||||||||||||||||||||||||||||||||||||||

Dolls are among the oldest of toys, traditionally given to little girls to help model their future behavior as wives and mothers. But what is a child to think about a doll that isn't of her own race? This dilemma is faced by millions of American girls who aren't white when they are given dolls like white Barbie. Faced with a similar dilemma as a little girl when given a Barbie doll, bell hooks describes in this personal reminiscence how she chose to give her loyalty instead to a brown doll named Baby, who looked a lot more like her. The author of numerous books of cultural criticism, including Black Looks: Race and Representation *(1992),* Killing Rage: Ending Racism *(1995), and* Bone Black *(1996), from which this selection is taken, bell hooks (the pen name of Gloria Watkins, b. 1952) is Distinguished Professor of English at City College of New York.*

We learn early that it is important for a woman to marry. We are always marrying our dolls to someone. He of course is always invisible, that is until they made the Ken doll to go with Barbie. One of us has been given a Barbie doll for Christmas. Her skin is not white white but almost brown from the tan they have painted on her. We know she is white because of her blond hair. The newest Barbie is bald, with many wigs of all different colors. We spend hours dressing and undressing her, pretending she is going somewhere important. We want to make new clothes for her. We want to buy the outfits made just for her that we see in the store but they are too expensive. Some of them cost as much as real clothes for real people. Barbie is anything but real, that is why we like her. She never does housework, washes dishes, or has children to care for. She is free to spend all day dreaming about the Kens of the world. Mama laughs when we tell her there should be more than one Ken for Barbie, there should be Joe, Sam, Charlie, men in all shapes and sizes. We do not think that Barbie should have a girlfriend. We know that Barbie was born to be alone — that the fantasy woman, the soap opera girl, the girl of *True Confessions,* the Miss America girl was born to be alone. We know that she is not us.

My favorite doll is brown, brown like light milk chocolate. She is a baby doll and I give her a baby doll name, Baby. She is almost the same size as a real baby. She comes with no clothes, only a pink diaper, fastened with tiny gold pins and a plastic bottle. She has a red mouth the color of lipstick slightly open so that we can stick the bottle in it. We fill the bottle with water and wait for it to come through the tiny hole in Baby's bottom. We make her many new diapers, but we are soon bored with changing them. We lose the bottle and Baby can no longer drink. We still love her. She is the only doll we will not destroy. We have lost Barbie. We have broken the leg of another doll. We have cracked open the head of an antique doll to see what makes the crying sound. The little thing inside is not interesting. We are sorry but nothing can be done — not even mama can put the pieces together again. She tells us that if this is the way we intend to treat our babies she hopes we do not have any. She laughs at our careless parenting. Sometimes she takes a minute to show us the right thing to do. She too is terribly fond of Baby. She says that she looks so much like a real newborn. Once she came upstairs, saw Baby under the covers, and wanted to know who had brought the real baby from downstairs.

She loves to tell the story of how Baby was born. She tells us that I, her problem child, decided out of nowhere that I did not want a white doll to play with, I demanded a brown doll, one that would look like me. Only grown-ups think that the things children say come out of nowhere. We know they come from the deepest parts of ourselves. Deep within myself I had begun to worry that all this loving care we gave to the pink and white flesh-colored dolls meant that somewhere left high on the shelves were boxes of unwanted, unloved brown dolls covered in dust. I thought that they would remain there forever, orphaned and alone, unless someone began to want them, to want to give them love and care, to want them more than anything. At first they ignored my wanting. They complained. They pointed out that white dolls were easier to find, cheaper. They never said where they found Baby but I know. She was always there high on the shelf, covered in dust — waiting.

Reading the Text

1. What does hooks mean when she says "we know that Barbie was born to be alone" (para. 1)?

2. Why has Baby received more care and protection than other dolls and toys that were in her family?
3. What is the purpose of giving little girls dolls, according to hooks?
4. Describe hooks's style and personal voice in this selection. How do they affect your response to her ideas?

Reading the Signs

1. If you played with dolls as a child, reflect in your journal on the extent to which the ethnicity of the dolls made a difference to you.
2. Read Jennifer Scanlon's "Boys-R-Us: Board Games and the Socialization of Young Adolescent Girls" (p. 472). Write an essay comparing the ways that dolls and board games construct gender roles for girls. You might consult as well Emily Prager's "Our Barbies, Ourselves" (p. 706).
3. Visit a toy store, and study the ethnic identities of the dolls you see there. How many ethnicities are represented? How do you account for your observations?
4. Investigate the ethnic patterns in other forms of children's entertainment and play, such as video games. Then write an essay analyzing the racial ideologies you discover. To develop your ideas, consult Michael Omi's "In Living Color: Race and American Culture" (p. 526).

MELISSA ALGRANATI

Being an Other

‖‖‖‖‖‖‖‖‖‖‖‖‖‖‖‖‖‖‖‖‖‖‖‖‖‖‖‖‖‖‖‖‖‖‖‖‖‖‖

In a country as obsessed with racial identification as America is, Melissa Algranati poses a dilemma. As she puts it, "there are not too many Puerto Rican, Egyptian Jews out there," so the only category left for her on the census form is "other." In this personal essay, Algranati tells the story of how she came to be an "other," a saga of two immigrant families from different continents who eventually came together in a "marriage that only a country like America could create." Algranati is a graduate of the State University of New York at Binghamton and has a master's degree from Columbia University.

Throughout my whole life, people have mistaken me for other ethnic backgrounds rather than for what I really am. I learned at a young age that there are not too many Puerto Rican, Egyptian Jews out there. For most of my life I have been living in two worlds, and at the same time I have been living in neither. When I was young I did not realize that I was unique, because my family brought me up with a healthy balance of Puerto Rican and Sephardic customs. It was not until I took the standardized PSAT exam that I was confronted with the question: "Who am I?" I remember the feeling of confusion as I struggled to find the right answer. I was faced with a bad multiple-choice question in which there was only supposed to be one right answer, but more than one answer seemed to be correct. I did not understand how a country built on the concept of diversity could forget about its most diverse group, interethnic children. I felt lost in a world of classification. The only way for me to take pride in who I am was to proclaim myself as an other, yet that leaves out so much. As a product of a marriage only a country like America could create, I would now try to help people understand what it is like to be a member of the most underrepresented group in the country, the "others."

My father, Jacques Algranati, was born in Alexandria, Egypt. As a Sephardic Jew, my father was a minority in a predominantly Arab world. Although in the minority, socially my father was a member of the upper middle class and lived a very comfortable life. As a result of strong French influence in the Middle Eastern Jewish world, my father attended a French private school. Since Arabic was the language of the lower class, the Algranati family spoke French as their first language. My whole family is polyglot, speaking languages from the traditional Sephardic tongue of Ladino to Turkish and Greek. My grandfather spoke seven languages. Basically, my father grew up in a close-knit Sephardic community surrounded by family and friends.

However, in 1960 my fathers' world came to a halt when he was faced with persecution on an institutional level. As a result of the Egyptian-Israeli conflict, in 1956 an edict was issued forcing all foreign-born citizens and Jews out of Egypt. Although my father was a native-born citizen of the country, because of a very strong anti-Jewish sentiment, his citizenship meant nothing. So in 1960 when my family got their exit visas, as Jews had done since the time of the Inquisition, they packed up and left the country as one large family group.

Unable to take many possessions or much money with them, my father's family, like many Egyptian Jews, immigrated to France. They proceeded to France because they had family who were able to sponsor them. Also, once in France my family hoped to be able to receive a visa to America much sooner, since French immigration quotas to the United States were much higher than those in Egypt. Once in France my family relied on the generosity of a Jewish organization, the United Jewish Appeal. For nine months my father lived in a hotel sponsored by the United Jewish Appeal and attended French school until the family was granted a visa to the United States.

Since my father's oldest brother came to the United States first with his wife, they were able to sponsor the rest of the family's passage over. The Algranati family eventually settled in Forest Hills, Queens. Like

5

most immigrants, my family settled in a neighborhood filled with immigrants of the same background. Once in the United States, my father rejoined many of his old friends from Egypt, since most Egyptian Jewish refugees followed a similar immigration path. At the age of fourteen my father and his group of friends were once again forced to adjust to life in a new country, but this time they had to learn a new language in order to survive. Like many of his friends, my father was forced to leave the comforts and luxuries of his world for the hardships of a new world. But as he eloquently puts it, once his family and friends were forced to leave, there was really nothing to stay for.

Like my father, my mother is also an immigrant; however my parents come from very different parts of the world. Born in Maniti, Puerto Rico, my mom spent the first five years of her life in a small town outside of San Juan. Since my grandfather had attended private school in the United States when he was younger, he was relatively proficient in English. Like many immigrants, my grandfather came to the United States first, in order to help establish the family. After securing a job and an apartment, he sent for my grandmother, and three weeks later my mother and her fourteen-year-old sister came.

Puerto Ricans are different from many other people who come to this country, in the sense that legally they are not considered immigrants. Because Puerto Rico is a commonwealth of the United States, Puerto Ricans are granted automatic U.S. citizenship. So unlike most, from the day my mother and her family stepped on U.S. soil they were considered citizens. The only problem was that the difference in language and social status led "real" Americans not to consider them citizens.

As a result of this unique status, my mother faced many hardships in this new country. From the day my mother entered first grade, her process of Americanization had begun. Her identity was transformed. She went from being Maria Louisa Pinto to becoming Mary L. Pinto. Not only was my mother given a new name when she began school, but a new language was forced upon her as well. Confronted by an Irish teacher, Mrs. Walsh, who was determined to Americanize her, my mother began her uphill battle with the English language. Even until this day my mother recalls her traumatic experience when she learned how to pronounce the word "run":

"Repeat after me, run."

"Rrrrrrrrun."

"No, Mary, run."   10

"Rrrrrrrrun."

No matter how hard my mother tried she could not stop rolling her "r's." After several similar exchanges Mrs. Walsh, with a look of anger on her face, grabbed my mother's cheeks in her hand and squeezed as she repeated in a stern voice, "RUN!" Suffice it to say my mother learned how to speak English without a Spanish accent. It was because of these experiences that my mother made sure the only language spoken in the house or to me and my sister was English. My parents never wanted their children to experience the pain my mother went through just to learn how to say the word "run."

My mother was confronted with discrimination not only from American society but also from her community. While in the United States, my mother lived in a predominantly Spanish community. On first coming to this country her family lived in a tenement in the Bronx. At the age of twelve my mother was once more uprooted and moved to the projects on the Lower East Side. As one of the first families in a predominantly Jewish building, it was a step up for her family.

It was not her environment that posed the biggest conflict for her; it   15
was her appearance. My mother is what people call a "white Hispanic." With her blond hair and blue eyes my mother was taken for everything but a Puerto Rican. Once my mother perfected her English, no one suspected her ethnicity unless she told them. Since she was raised to be above the ghetto, never picking up typical "Hispanic mannerisms," she was able to exist in American society with very little difficulty. Because of a very strong and protective mother and the positive influence and assistance received from the Henry Street Settlement, my mother was able to escape the ghetto. As a result of organizations like Henry Street, my mother was given opportunities such as fresh air camps and jobs in good areas of the city, where she was able to rise above the drugs, alcohol, and violence that consumed so many of her peers.

As a result of her appearance and her upbringing, my mother left her people and the ghetto to enter American society. It was here as an attractive "white" female that my mother and father's two very different worlds merged. My parents, both working on Wall Street at the time, were introduced by a mutual friend. Since both had developed a rather liberal view, the differences in their backgrounds did not seem to be a major factor. After a year of dating my parents decided to get engaged.

Although they were from two different worlds, their engagement seemed to bring them together. Growing up in the midst of the Jewish community of the Lower East Side, my mother was constantly influenced by the beauty of Judaism. Therefore, since my mother never had much connection with Catholicism and had never been baptized, she decided to convert to Judaism and raise her children as Jews. The beauty of the conversion was that no one in my father's family forced her to convert; they accepted her whether she converted or not. As for my mother's family, they too had no real objections to the wedding or conversion. To them the only thing that mattered was that my father was a nice guy who made my mom happy. The most amusing part of the union of these two different families came when they tried to communicate. My father's family is descended from Spanish Jewry where many of them spoke an old Castilian-style Spanish, while my mother's family spoke a very modern Caribbean-style Spanish. To watch them try to communicate in any language other than English was like watching a session of the United Nations.

It was this new world, that of Puerto Rican Jewry, my parents created for me and my sister, Danielle. Resembling both my parents, having my mother's coloring with my father's features, I have often been mistaken for various ethnicities. Possessing light hair and blue eyes, I am generally perceived as the "all-American" girl. Occasionally I have been mistaken for Italian since my last name, Algranati, although Sephardic, has a very Italian flair to it. I have basically lived a chameleon-like existence for most of my life.

As a result of my "otherness," I have gained "acceptance" in many different crowds. From this acceptance I have learned the harsh reality behind my "otherness." I will never forget the time I learned about how the parents of one of my Asian friends perceived me. From very early on, I gained acceptance with the parents of one of my Korean friends. Not only did they respect me as a person and a student, but her father even went so far as to consider me like "one of his daughters." I will always remember how I felt when I heard they made one of their daughters cancel a party because she had invited Hispanics. Even when my friend pointed out that I, the one they loved, was Hispanic they refused to accept it. Even today to them, I will always be Jewish and not Puerto Rican because to them it is unacceptable to "love" a Puerto Rican.

Regardless of community, Jewish or Puerto Rican, I am always confronted by bigots. Often I am forced to sit in silence while friends utter in ignorance stereotypical responses like: "It was probably some spic who stole it," or "You're just like a Jew, always cheap."

For the past three years I have worked on the Lower East Side of Manhattan at the Henry Street Settlement. Basically my mother wanted me to support the organization that helped her get out of the ghetto. Unlike when my mother was there, the population is mostly black and Hispanic. So one day during work I had one of my fellow workers say to me "that is such a collegian white thing to say." I responded by saying that his assumption was only partially correct and asked him if he considered Puerto Rican to be white. Of course he doubted I was any part Hispanic until he met my cousin who "looks" Puerto Rican. At times like these I really feel for my mother, because I know how it feels not to be recognized by society for who you are.

Throughout my life I do not think I have really felt completely a part of any group. I have gone through phases of hanging out with different crowds trying in a sense to find myself. Basically, I have kept my life diverse by attending both Catholic-sponsored camps and Hebrew school at the same time. Similar to my parents, my main goal is to live within American society. I choose my battles carefully. By being diverse I have learned that in a society that is obsessed with classification the only way I will find my place is within myself. Unfortunately, society has not

20

come to terms with a fast-growing population, the "others." Therefore when asked the infamous question: "Who are you?" I respond with a smile, "a Puerto Rican Egyptian Jew." Contrary to what society may think, I know that I am somebody.

Reading the Text

1. Summarize in your own words why Algranati feels like one of the "others" (para. 1).
2. How did the childhood experiences of Algranati's parents differ?
3. How does physical appearance affect strangers' perceptions of ethnic identity, according to Algranati?
4. Why does Algranati say she has never "really felt completely a part of any group" (para. 22)?

Reading the Signs

1. In your journal, reflect on your answer to the question "Who are you?"
2. Write an essay in which you defend or oppose the practice of asking individuals to identify their ethnicity in official documents such as census forms and school applications.
3. Algranati's background includes racial, cultural, and religious differences. Write an essay explaining how you would identify yourself if you were in her shoes.
4. Do you think Algranati would be sympathetic or hostile to people who "try on" different ethnic identities? Writing as if you were Algranati, write a letter to one of the teens who claims a new ethnic identity in Nell Bernstein's "Goin' Gangsta, Choosin' Cholita" (p. 562).
5. In class, brainstorm names of biracial actors, musicians, or models. Then discuss the extent to which the mass media presume that people fit neatly into ethnic categories. What is the effect of such a presumption?

GLORIA ANZALDÚA

How to Tame a Wild Tongue

How would you feel if your teacher scolded you when you tried to tell her how to pronounce your name? That is the opening anecdote in Gloria Anzaldúa's linguistic analysis of Mexican American speech. Showing that the language of Chicanos and Chicanas differs not only from the speech of Anglos but from the speech of other Hispanic groups, Anzaldúa provides a detailed description of the history and significance of her mother tongue. Language is not simply an instrument for communication, she suggests, it is a sign of identity. "So if you really want to hurt me," Anzaldúa concludes, "talk badly about my language." Formerly a lecturer at the University of California, Santa Cruz, Gloria Anzaldúa is a writer and editor whose books include This Bridge Called My Back: Writings by Radical Women of Color *(1983),* Haciendo Caras: Making Face/Making Soul *(1990), and* Borderlands/La Frontera: The New Mestiza *(1987), from which this selection is taken.*

"We're going to have to control your tongue," the dentist says, pulling out all the metal from my mouth. Silver bits plop and tinkle into the basin. My mouth is a mother lode.

The dentist is cleaning out my roots. I get a whiff of the stench when I gasp. "I can't cap that tooth yet, you're still draining," he says.

"We're going to have to do something about your tongue," I hear the anger rising in his voice. My tongue keeps pushing out the wads of cotton, pushing back the drills, the long thin needles. "I've never seen anything as strong or as stubborn," he says. And I think, how do you tame a wild tongue, train it to be quiet, how do you bridle and saddle it? How do you make it lie down?

Who is to say that robbing a people of its language is less violent than war?

— Ray Gwyn Smith[1]

I remember being caught speaking Spanish at recess—that was good for three licks on the knuckles with a sharp ruler. I remember being sent to the corner of the classroom for "talking back" to the Anglo teacher when all I was trying to do was tell her how to pronounce my name. "If you want to be American, speak 'American.' If you don't like it, go back to Mexico where you belong."

"I want you to speak English. *Pa' hallar buen trabajo tienes que saber hablar el inglés bien. Qué vale toda tu educación si todavía hablas inglés con un* 'accent,'"[2] my mother would say, mortified that I spoke English like a Mexican. At Pan American University, I and all Chicano students were required to take two speech classes. Their purpose: to get rid of our accents.

Attacks on one's form of expression with the intent to censor are a violation of the First Amendment. *El Anglo con cara de inocente nos arrancó la lengua.*[3] Wild tongues can't be tamed, they can only be cut out.

---

1. Ray Gwyn Smith, *Moorland Is Cold Country,* unpublished book.

2. *Pa' hallar . . . con un* **'accent.'**   To find a good job you have to know how to speak English well. What good is all your education if you still speak English with an accent?—Eds.

3. *El Anglo . . . la lengua.*   The Anglo with an innocent-looking face made us shut up. Translated literally: "pulled our tongues out."—Eds.

Overcoming the Tradition of Silence

Ahogadas, escupimos el oscuro.
Peleando con nuestra propia sombra
el silencio nos sepulta.[4]

En boca cerrada no entran moscas. "Flies don't enter a closed mouth" is a saying I kept hearing when I was child. *Ser habladora* was to be a gossip and a liar, to talk too much. *Muchachitas bien criadas,* well-bred girls don't answer back. *Es una falta de respeto*[5] to talk back to one's mother or father. I remember one of the sins I'd recite to the priest in the confession box the few times I went to confession: talking back to my mother, *hablar pa' 'tras, repelar. Hocicona, repelona, chismosa,* having a big mouth, questioning, carrying tales are all signs of being *mal criada.*[6] In my culture they are all words that are derogatory if applied to women—I've never heard them applied to men.

The first time I heard two women, a Puerto Rican and a Cuban, say the word "*nosotras,*"[7] I was shocked. I had not known the word existed. Chicanas use *nosotros*[8] whether we're male or female. We are robbed of our female being by the masculine plural. Language is a male discourse.

And our tongues have become
dry   the wilderness has
dried out our tongues   and
we have forgotten speech.
         — IRENA KLEPFISZ[9]

Even our own people, other Spanish speakers *nos quieren poner candados en la boca.*[10] They would hold us back with their bag of *reglas de academia.*[11]

Oyé como ladra: el lenguaje de la frontera[12]

Quien tiene boca se equivoca.[13]
         — MEXICAN SAYING

---

4. *Ahogadas, . . . nos sepulta.*   Drowned, we spit in the dark. / Fighting with our own shadow / the silence buries us.—EDS.

5. *Es una falta de respeto*   It's a lack of respect.—EDS.

6. *mal criada*   Ill-bred.—EDS.

7. *nosotras*   We, female form.—EDS.

8. *nosotros*   We, male form.—EDS.

9. Irena Klepfisz, "*Di rayze aheym* / The Journey Home," in *The Tribe of Dina: A Jewish Women's Anthology,* Melanie Kaye/Kantrowitz and Irena Klepfisz, eds. (Montpelier, VT: Sinister Wisdom Books, 1986), 49.

10. *nos quieren . . . en la boca.*   They want us to put padlocks on our mouths.—EDS.

11. *reglas de academia*   Academic rules.—EDS.

12. *Oyé . . . frontera*   Listen how it barks: the language of the borderlands.—EDS.

13. *Quien . . . equivoca.*   Whoever has a mouth makes mistakes.—EDS.

"*Pocho,* cultural traitor, you're speaking the oppressor's language by speaking English, you're ruining the Spanish language," I have been accused by various Latinos and Latinas. Chicano Spanish is considered by the purist and by most Latinos deficient, a mutilation of Spanish.

But Chicano Spanish is a border tongue which developed naturally. Change, *evolución, enriquecimiento de palabras nuevas por invención o adopción*[14] have created variants of Chicano Spanish, *un nuevo lenguaje. Un lenguaje que corresponde a un modo de vivir.*[15] Chicano Spanish is not incorrect, it is a living language.

For a people who are neither Spanish nor live in a country in which Spanish is the first language; for a people who live in a country in which English is the reigning tongue but who are not Anglo; for a people who cannot entirely identify with either standard (formal, Castillian) Spanish or standard English, what recourse is left to them but to create their own language? A language which they can connect their identity to, one capable of communicating the realities and values true to themselves—a language with terms that are neither *español ni inglés,*[16] but both. We speak a patois, a forked tongue, a variation of two languages.

Chicano Spanish sprang out of the Chicanos' need to identify ourselves as a distinct people. We needed a language with which we could communicate with ourselves, a secret language. For some of us, language is a homeland closer than the Southwest—for many Chicanos today live in the Midwest and the East. And because we are a complex, heterogeneous people, we speak many languages. Some of the languages we speak are: 10

1. Standard English
2. Working class and slang English
3. Standard Spanish
4. Standard Mexican Spanish
5. North Mexican Spanish dialect
6. Chicano Spanish (Texas, New Mexico, Arizona, and California have regional variations)
7. Tex-Mex
8. *Pachuco* (called *caló*)

My "home" tongues are the languages I speak with my sister and brothers, with my friends. They are the last five listed, with 6 and 7 being closest to my heart. From school, the media, and job situations, I've picked up standard and working-class English. From Mamagrande Locha and from reading Spanish and Mexican literature, I've picked up

---

14. *evolución, . . . adopción*   Evolution, enrichment of new words by invention or adoption. —EDS.

15. *un nuevo . . . vivir.*   A new language. A language that matches a way of living. —EDS.

16. *español ni inglés*   Spanish nor English. —EDS.

Standard Spanish and Standard Mexican Spanish. From *los recién llega-dos*,[17] Mexican immigrants, and *braceros*,[18] I learned the North Mexican dialect. With Mexicans I'll try to speak either Standard Mexican Spanish or the North Mexican dialect. From my parents and Chicanos living in the Valley, I picked up Chicano Texas Spanish, and I speak it with my mom, younger brother (who married a Mexican and who rarely mixes Spanish with English), aunts, and older relatives.

With Chicanas from *Nuevo México* or *Arizona* I will speak Chicano Spanish a little, but often they don't understand what I'm saying. With most California Chicanas I speak entirely in English (unless I forget). When I first moved to San Francisco, I'd rattle off something in Spanish, unintentionally embarrassing them. Often it is only with another Chicana *tejana*[19] that I can talk freely.

Words distorted by English are known as anglicisms or *pochismos*. The *pocho* is an anglicized Mexican or American of Mexican origin who speaks Spanish with an accent characteristic of North Americans and who distorts and reconstructs the language according to the influence of English.[20] Tex-Mex, or Spanglish, comes most naturally to me. I may switch back and forth from English to Spanish in the same sentence or in the same word. With my sister and my brother Nune and with Chicano *tejano* contemporaries I speak in Tex-Mex.

From kids and people my own age I picked up *Pachuco*. *Pachuco* (the language of the zoot suiters) is a language of rebellion, both against Standard Spanish and Standard English. It is a secret language. Adults of the culture and outsiders cannot understand it. It is made up of slang words from both English and Spanish. *Ruca* means girl or woman, *vato* means guy or dude, *chale* means no, *simón* means yes, *churro* is sure, talk is *periquiar, pigionear* means petting, *que gacho* means how nerdy, *ponte águila* means watch out, death is called *la pelona*. Through lack of practice and not having others who can speak it, I've lost most of the *Pachuco* tongue.

Chicano Spanish

Chicanos, after 250 years of Spanish/Anglo colonization, have de- 15
veloped significant differences in the Spanish we speak. We collapse two adjacent vowels into a single syllable and sometimes shift the stress in certain words such as *maíz / maiz, cohete / cuete*. We leave out certain consonants when they appear between vowels: *lado / lao, mojado / mojao*.

---

17. *los recién llegados*   The recently arrived. — EDS.
18. *braceros*   Laborers. — EDS.
19. *tejana*   Female Texan. — EDS.
20. R. C. Ortega, *Dialectología Del Barrio*, trans. Hortencia S. Alwan (Los Angeles, CA: R. C. Ortega Publisher & Bookseller, 1977), 132.

Chicanos from South Texas pronounce *f* as *j* as in *jue* (*fue*). Chicanos use "archaisms," words that are no longer in the Spanish language, words that have been evolved out. We say *semos, truje, haiga, ansina,* and *naiden.* We retain the "archaic" *j,* as in *jalar,* that derives from an earlier *h* (the French *halar* or the Germanic *halon* which was lost to standard Spanish in the sixteenth century), but which is still found in several regional dialects such as the one spoken in South Texas. (Due to geography, Chicanos from the Valley of South Texas were cut off linguistically from other Spanish speakers. We tend to use words that the Spaniards brought over from Medieval Spain. The majority of the Spanish colonizers in Mexico and the Southwest came from Extremadura—Hernán Cortés was one of them—and Andalucía. Andalucians pronounce *ll* like a *y,* and their *d*'s tend to be absorbed by adjacent vowels: *tirado* becomes *tirao.* They brought *el lenguaje popular, dialectos y regionalismos.*[21])

Chicanos and other Spanish speakers also shift *ll* to *y* and *z* to *s.*[22] We leave out initial syllables, saying *tar* for *estar, toy* for *estoy, hora* for *ahora* (*cubanos* and *puertorriqueños* also leave out initial letters of some words). We also leave out the final syllable such as *pa* for *para.* The intervocalic *y,* the *ll* as in *tortilla, ella, botella,* gets replaced by *tortia* or *tortiya, ea, botea.* We add an additional syllable at the beginning of certain words: *atocar* for *tocar, agastar* for *gastar.* Sometimes we'll say *lavaste las vacijas,* other times *lavates* (substituting the *ates* verb endings for the *aste*).

We use anglicisms, words borrowed from English: *bola* from ball, *carpeta* from carpet, *máchina de lavar* (instead of *lavadora*) from washing machine. Tex-Mex argot, created by adding a Spanish sound at the beginning or end of an English word such as *cookiar* for cook, *watchar* for watch, *parkiar* for park, and *rapiar* for rape, is the result of the pressures on Spanish speakers to adapt to English.

We don't use the word *vosotros / as* or its accompanying verb form. We don't say *claro* (to mean yes), *imagínate,* or *me emociona,* unless we picked up Spanish from Latinas, out of a book, or in a classroom. Other Spanish-speaking groups are going through the same, or similar, development in their Spanish.

Linguistic Terrorism

Deslenguadas. Somos los del español deficiente.[23] We are your linguistic nightmare, your linguistic aberration, your linguistic *mestisaje,*[24] the

---

21. Eduardo Hernandéz-Chávez, Andrew D. Cohen, and Anthony F. Beltramo, *El Lenguaje de los Chicanos: Regional and Social Characteristics of Language Used by Mexican Americans* (Arlington, VA: Center for Applied Linguistics, 1975), 39.

22. Hernandéz-Chávez, xvii.

23. ***Deslenguadas . . . deficiente.***   Foul-mouthed. We are the ones with deficient Spanish.—Eds.

24. ***mestisaje***   Mongrels.—Eds.

subject of your *burla*.[25] Because we speak with tongues of fire we are culturally crucified. Racially, culturally, and linguistically *somos huérfanos*[26]—we speak an orphan tongue.

Chicanas who grew up speaking Chicano Spanish have internalized the belief that we speak poor Spanish. It is illegitimate, a bastard language. And because we internalize how our language has been used against us by the dominant culture, we use our language differences against each other.

Chicana feminists often skirt around each other with suspicion and   20 hesitation. For the longest time I couldn't figure it out. Then it dawned on me. To be close to another Chicana is like looking into the mirror. We are afraid of what we'll see there. *Pena.* Shame. Low estimation of self. In childhood we are told that our language is wrong. Repeated attacks on our native tongue diminish our sense of self. The attacks continue throughout our lives.

Chicanas feel uncomfortable talking in Spanish to Latinas, afraid of their censure. Their language was not outlawed in their countries. They had a whole lifetime of being immersed in their native tongue; generations, centuries in which Spanish was a first language, taught in school, heard on radio and TV, and read in the newspaper.

If a person, Chicana or Latina, has a low estimation of my native tongue, she also has a low estimation of me. Often with *mexicanas y latinas* we'll speak English as a neutral language. Even among Chicanas we tend to speak English at parties or conferences. Yet, at the same time, we're afraid the other will think we're *agringadas* because we don't speak Chicano Spanish. We oppress each other trying to out-Chicano each other, vying to be the "real" Chicanas, to speak like Chicanos. There is no one Chicano language just as there is no one Chicano experience. A monolingual Chicana whose first language is English or Spanish is just as much a Chicana as one who speaks several variants of Spanish. A Chicana from Michigan or Chicago or Detroit is just as much a Chicana as one from the Southwest. Chicano Spanish is as diverse linguistically as it is regionally.

By the end of this century, Spanish speakers will comprise the biggest minority group in the United States, a country where students in high schools and colleges are encouraged to take French classes because French is considered more "cultured." But for a language to remain alive it must be used.[27] By the end of this century English, and not Spanish, will be the mother tongue of most Chicanos and Latinos.

---

25. ***burla***   Ridicule.—EDS.
26. ***somos huérfanos***   We are orphans.—EDS.
27. Irena Klepfisz, "Secular Jewish Identity: Yidishkayt in America," in *The Tribe of Dina,* Kaye/Kantrowitz and Klepfisz, eds., 43.

So, if you want to really hurt me, talk badly about my language. Ethnic identity is twin skin to linguistic identity—I am my language. Until I can take pride in my language, I cannot take pride in myself. Until I can accept as legitimate Chicano Texas Spanish, Tex-Mex, and all the other languages I speak, I cannot accept the legitimacy of myself. Until I am free to write bilingually and to switch codes without having always to translate, while I still have to speak English or Spanish when I would rather speak Spanglish, and as long as I have to accommodate the English speakers rather than having them accommodate me, my tongue will be illegitimate.

I will no longer be made to feel ashamed of existing. I will have my   25 voice: Indian, Spanish, white. I will have my serpent's tongue—my woman's voice, my sexual voice, my poet's voice. I will overcome the tradition of silence.

> My fingers
> move sly against your palm
> Like women everywhere, we speak in code. . . .
>   —MELANIE KAYE/KANTROWITZ[28]

Reading the Text

1. Why does Anzaldúa blend Spanish and English in her selection?
2. How does Anzaldúa's language contribute to her sense of identity?
3. What are the essential features of Chicano Spanish, according to Anzaldúa?
4. What does Anzaldúa mean by "Linguistic Terrorism" (para. 19)?

Reading the Signs

1. Anzaldúa sees her language in political terms. Write a personal essay in which you explore the significance of your native language to you. If, like Anzaldúa, you too see your language politically, describe an incident that motivated you to feel this way. If you don't view language as she does, consider why your experiences have led you to an alternative view of language.
2. Writing as if you were Gloria Anzaldúa, compose a hypothetical letter to the U.S. English organization, a group that wishes to make English America's official language.
3. In class, discuss the effect of Anzaldúa's blending of English and Spanish and of imagistic and analytic language. How does such blending con-

---

28. Melanie Kaye/Kantrowitz, "Sign," in *We Speak in Code: Poems and Other Writings* (Pittsburgh, PA: Motheroot Publications, Inc., 1980), 85.

tribute to the points she makes? Would the essay have
it were written all in English?

4. How might Anzaldúa respond to the cross-cultural
Bernstein describes ("Goin' Gangsta, Choosin' Cholit
ing Anzaldúa's perspective, write an essay that analyzes ... ...g.

5. How do you think Melissa Algranati ("Being an Other," p. 570) might
respond to Anzaldúa's selection? Write a dialogue between Algranati and
Anzaldúa, and then share your dialogue with your class.

FAN SHEN

The Classroom and the Wider Culture:
Identity as a Key to Learning English Composition

Writing conventions involve more cultural presuppositions and
mythologies than we ordinarily recognize. Take the current practice of
using the first-person singular pronoun "I" when writing an essay.
Such a convention presumes an individualistic worldview, which can
appear very strange to someone coming from a communal culture, as
Fan Shen relates in this analysis of the relation between culture and
composition. Hailing from the People's Republic of China, where the
group comes before the individual in social consciousness, Shen describes
what it was like to move to the United States and have to learn a
whole new worldview to master the writing conventions that he himself
now teaches as a professor of English at Rochester Community and
Technical College. A writer as well as a teacher, Fan Shen has trans-
lated three books from English into Chinese and has written numerous
articles for both English and Chinese publications.

One day in June 1975, when I walked into the aircraft factory where
I was working as an electrician, I saw many large-letter posters on the
walls and many people parading around the workshops shouting slogans
like "Down with the word 'I'!" and "Trust in masses and the Party!" I
then remembered that a new political campaign called "Against Individualism" was scheduled to begin that day. Ten years later, I got back my
first English composition paper at the University of Nebraska–Lincoln.
The professor's first comments were: "Why did you always use 'we' instead of 'I'?" and "Your paper would be stronger if you eliminated some
sentences in the passive voice." The clashes between my Chinese background and the requirements of English composition had begun. At the

center of this mental struggle, which has lasted several years and is still not completely over, is the prolonged, uphill battle to recapture "myself."

In this paper I will try to describe and explore this experience of reconciling my Chinese identity with an English identity dictated by the rules of English composition. I want to show how my cultural background shaped—and shapes—my approaches to my writing in English and how writing in English redefined—and redefines—my *ideological* and *logical* identities. By "ideological identity" I mean the system of values that I acquired (consciously and unconsciously) from my social and cultural background. And by "logical identity" I mean the natural (or Oriental) way I organize and express my thoughts in writing. Both had to be modified or redefined in learning English composition. Becoming aware of the process of redefinition of these different identities is a mode of learning that has helped me in my efforts to write in English, and, I hope, will be of help to teachers of English composition in this country. In presenting my case for this view, I will use examples from both my composition courses and literature courses, for I believe that writing papers for both kinds of courses contributed to the development of my "English identity." Although what I will describe is based on personal experience, many Chinese students whom I talked to said that they had had the same or similar experiences in their initial stages of learning to write in English.

Identity of the Self: Ideological and Cultural

Starting with the first English paper I wrote, I found that learning to compose in English is not an isolated classroom activity, but a social and cultural experience. The rules of English composition encapsulate values that are absent in, or sometimes contradictory to, the values of other societies (in my case, China). Therefore, learning the rules of English composition is, to a certain extent, learning the values of Anglo-American society. In writing classes in the United States I found that I had to reprogram my mind, to redefine some of the basic concepts and values that I had about myself, about society, and about the universe, values that had been imprinted and reinforced in my mind by my cultural background, and that had been part of me all my life.

Rule number one in English composition is: Be yourself. (More than one composition instructor has told me, "Just write what *you* think.") The values behind this rule, it seems to me, are based on the principle of protecting and promoting individuality (and private property) in this country. The instruction was probably crystal clear to students raised on these values, but, as a guideline of composition, it was not very clear or useful to me when I first heard it. First of all, the image or meaning that I attached to the word "I" or "myself" was, as I found out, different from that of my English teacher. In China, "I" is always subordinated to "We"—be it the working class, the Party, the country, or some other collective body. Both political pressure and literary tradition require that "I" be somewhat hidden or buried in writings and speeches; presenting the "self" too obviously would give people the impression of being disrespectful of the Communist Party in political writings and boastful in scholarly writings. The word "I" has often been identified with another "bad" word, "individualism," which has become a synonym for selfishness in China. For a long time the words "self" and "individualism" have had negative connotations in my mind, and the negative force of the words naturally extended to the field of literary studies. As a result, even if I had brilliant ideas, the "I" in my papers always had to show some modesty by not competing with or trying to stand above the names of ancient and modern authoritative figures. Appealing to Mao or other Marxist authorities became the required way (as well as the most "forceful" or "persuasive" way) to prove one's point in written discourse. I remember that in China I had even committed what I can call "reversed plagiarism"—here, I suppose it would be called "forgery"—when I was in middle school: willfully attributing some of my thoughts to "experts" when I needed some arguments but could not find a suitable quotation from a literary or political "giant."

Now, in America, I had to learn to accept the words "I" and "self" as something glorious (as Whitman did), or at least something not to be ashamed of or embarrassed about. It was the first and probably biggest step I took into English composition and critical writing. Acting upon my professor's suggestion, I intentionally tried to show my "individuality" and to "glorify" "I" in my papers by using as many "I's" as possible—"I think," "I believe," "I see"—and deliberately cut out quotations from authorities. It was rather painful to hand in such "pompous" (I mean immodest) papers to my instructors. But to an extent it worked. After a while I became more comfortable with only "the shadow of myself." I felt more at ease to put down *my* thoughts without looking over my shoulder to worry about the attitudes of my teachers or the reactions of the Party secretaries, and to speak out as "bluntly" and "immodestly" as my American instructors demanded.

But writing many "I's" was only the beginning of the process of redefining myself. Speaking of redefining myself is, in an important sense, speaking of redefining the word "I." By such a redefinition I mean not only the change in how I envisioned myself, but also the change in how *I* perceived the world. The old "I" used to embody only one set of values, but now it had to embody multiple sets of values. To be truly "myself," which I knew was a key to my success in learning English composition, meant *not to be my Chinese self* at all. That is to say, when I write in English I have to wrestle with and abandon (at least temporarily) the whole system of ideology which previously defined me in myself. I had to forget Marxist doctrines (even though I do not see myself as a Marxist by choice) and the Party lines imprinted in my mind and familiarize

5

myself with a system of capitalist/bourgeois values. I had to put aside an ideology of collectivism and adopt the values of individualism. In composition as well as in literature classes, I had to make a fundamental adjustment: If I used to examine society and literary materials through the microscopes of Marxist dialectical materialism and historical materialism, I now had to learn to look through the microscopes the other way around, i.e., to learn to look at and understand the world from the point of view of "idealism." (I must add here that there are American professors who use a Marxist approach in their teaching.)

The word "idealism," which affects my view of both myself and the universe, is loaded with social connotations, and can serve as a good example of how redefining a key word can be a pivotal part of redefining my ideological identity as a whole.

To me, idealism is the philosophical foundation of the dictum of English composition: "Be yourself." In order to write good English, I knew that I had to be myself, which actually meant not to be my Chinese self. It meant that I had to create an English self and be *that* self. And to be that English self, I felt, I had to understand and accept idealism the way a Westerner does. That is to say, I had to accept the way a Westerner sees himself in relation to the universe and society. On the one hand, I knew a lot about idealism. But on the other hand, I knew nothing about it. I mean I knew a lot about idealism through the propaganda and objections of its opponent, Marxism, but I knew little about it from its own point of view. When I thought of the word "materialism"—which is a major part of Marxism and in China has repeatedly been "shown" to be the absolute truth—there were always positive connotations, and words like "right," "true," etc., flashed in my mind. On the other hand, the word "idealism" always came to me with the dark connotations that surround words like "absurd," "illogical," "wrong," etc. In China "idealism" is depicted as a ferocious and ridiculous enemy of Marxist philosophy. Idealism, as the simplified definition imprinted in my mind had it, is the view that the material world does not exist; that all that exists is the mind and its ideas. It is just the opposite of Marxist dialectical materialism which sees the mind as a product of the material world. It is not too difficult to see that idealism, with its idea that mind is of primary importance, provides a philosophical foundation for the Western emphasis on the value of individual human minds, and hence individual human beings. Therefore, my final acceptance of myself as of primary importance—an importance that overshadowed that of authority figures in English composition—was, I decided, dependent on an acceptance of idealism.

My struggle with idealism came mainly from my efforts to understand and to write about works such as Coleridge's *Biographia Literaria* and Emerson's "Over-Soul." For a long time I was frustrated and puzzled by the idealism expressed by Coleridge and Emerson—given their ideas, such as "I think, therefore I am" (Coleridge obviously borrowed from Descartes) and "the transparent eyeball" (Emerson's view of himself)—because in my mind, drenched as it was in dialectical materialism, there was always a little voice whispering in my ear "You are, therefore you think." I could not see how human consciousness, which is not material, could create apples and trees. My intellectual conscience refused to let me believe that the human mind is the primary world and the material world secondary. Finally, I had to imagine that I was looking at a world with my head upside down. When I imagined that I was in a new body (born with the head upside down) it was easier to forget biases imprinted in my subconsciousness about idealism, the mind, and my former self. Starting from scratch, the new inverted self—which I called my "English Self" and into which I have transformed myself—could understand and *accept,* with ease, idealism as "the truth" and "himself" (i.e., my English Self) as the "creator" of the world.

Here is how I created my new "English Self." I played a "game" similar to ones played by mental therapists. First I made a list of (simplified) features about writing associated with my old identity (the Chinese Self), both ideological and logical, and then beside the first list I added a column of features about writing associated with my new identity (the English Self). After that I pictured myself getting out of my old identity, the timid, humble, modest Chinese "I," and creeping into my new identity (often in the form of a new skin or a mask), the confident, assertive, and aggressive English "I." The new "Self" helped me to remember and accept the different rules of Chinese and English composition and the values that underpin these rules. In a sense, creating an English Self is a way of reconciling my old cultural values with the new values required by English writing, without losing the former.

An interesting structural but not material parallel to my experiences in this regard has been well described by Min-zhan Lu in her important article, "From Silence to Words: Writing as Struggle" (*College English* 49 [April 1987]: 437–48). Min-zhan Lu talks about struggles between two selves, an open self and a secret self, and between two discourses, a mainstream Marxist discourse and a bourgeois discourse her parents wanted her to learn. But her struggle was different from mine. Her Chinese self was severely constrained and suppressed by mainstream cultural discourse, but never interfused with it. Her experiences, then, were not representative of those of the majority of the younger generation who, like me, were brought up on only one discourse. I came to English composition as a Chinese person, in the fullest sense of the term, with a Chinese identity already fully formed.

Identity of the Mind: Illogical and Alogical

In learning to write in English, besides wrestling with a different ideological system, I found that I had to wrestle with a logical system very different from the blueprint of logic at the back of my mind. By "logical system" I mean two things: the Chinese way of thinking I used to approach my theme or topic in written discourse, and the Chinese critical/logical way to develop a theme or topic. By English rules, the first is illogical, for it is the opposite of the English way of approaching a topic; the second is alogical (nonlogical), for it mainly uses mental pictures instead of words as a critical vehicle.

THE ILLOGICAL PATTERN

In English composition, an essential rule for the logical organization of a piece of writing is the use of a "topic sentence." In Chinese composition, "from surface to core" is an essential rule, a rule which means that one ought to reach a topic gradually and "systematically" instead of "abruptly."

The concept of a topic sentence, it seems to me, is symbolic of the values of a busy people in an industrialized society, rushing to get things done, hoping to attract and satisfy the busy reader very quickly. Thinking back, I realized that I did not fully understand the virtue of the concept until my life began to rush at the speed of everyone else's in this country. Chinese composition, on the other hand, seems to embody the values of a leisurely paced rural society whose inhabitants have the time to chew and taste a topic slowly. In Chinese composition, an introduction explaining how and why one chooses this topic is not only acceptable, but often regarded as necessary. It arouses the reader's interest in the topic little by little (and this is seen as a virtue of composition) and gives him/her a sense of refinement. The famous Robert B. Kaplan "noodles" contrasting a spiral Oriental thought process with a straight-line Western approach ("Cultural Thought Patterns in Inter-Cultural Education," *Readings on English as a Second Language,* Ed. Kenneth Croft, 2nd ed., Winthrop, 1980, 403–10) may be too simplistic to capture the preferred pattern of writing in English, but I think they still express some truth about Oriental writing. A Chinese writer often clears the surrounding bushes before attacking the real target. This bush-clearing pattern in Chinese writing goes back two thousand years to Kong Fuzi (Confucius). Before doing anything, Kong says in his *Luen Yu (Analects),* one first needs to call things by their proper names (expressed by his phrase "Zheng Ming" 正名). In other words, before touching one's main thesis, one should first state the "conditions" of composition: how, why, and when the piece is being composed. All of this will serve as a proper foundation on which to build the "house" of the piece. In the two thousand years after Kong, this principle of composition was gradually formalized (especially through the formal essays required by imperial examinations) and became known as "Ba Gu," or the eight-legged essay. The logic of Chinese composition, exemplified by the eight-legged essay, is like the peeling of an onion: Layer after layer is removed until the reader finally arrives at the central point, the core.

Ba Gu still influences modern Chinese writing. Carolyn Matalene   15
has an excellent discussion of this logical (or illogical) structure and its influence on her Chinese students' efforts to write in English ("Contrastive
Rhetoric: An American Writing Teacher in China," *College English* 47
[November 1985]: 789–808). A recent Chinese textbook for composition lists six essential steps (factors) for writing a narrative essay, steps to
be taken in this order: time, place, character, event, cause, and consequence (*Yuwen Jichu Zhishi Liushi Jiang* [*Sixty Lessons on the Basics of the
Chinese Language*], Ed. Beijing Research Institute of Education, Beijing
Publishing House, 1981, 525–609). Most Chinese students (including
me) are taught to follow this sequence in composition.

The straightforward approach to composition in English seemed to
me, at first, illogical. One could not jump to the topic. One had to walk
step by step to reach the topic. In several of my early papers I found that
the Chinese approach—the bush-clearing approach—persisted, and I
had considerable difficulty writing (and in fact understanding) topic sentences. In what I deemed to be topic sentences, I grudgingly gave out
themes. Today, those papers look to me like Chinese papers with forced
or false English openings. For example, in a narrative paper on a trip to
New York, I wrote the forced/false topic sentence, "A trip to New York
in winter is boring." In the next few paragraphs, I talked about the
weather, the people who went with me, and so on, before I talked about
what I learned from the trip. My real thesis was that one could always
learn something even on a boring trip.

THE ALOGICAL PATTERN

In learning English composition, I found that there was yet another
cultural blueprint affecting my logical thinking. I found from my early
papers that very often I was unconsciously under the influence of a Chinese critical approach called the creation of "yijing," which is totally
non-Western. The direct translation of the word "yijing" is: yi, "mind
or consciousness," and jing, "environment." An ancient approach which
has existed in China for many centuries and is still the subject of much
discussion, yijing is a complicated concept that defies a universal definition. But most critics in China nowadays seem to agree on one point,
that yijing is the critical approach that separates Chinese literature and
criticism from Western literature and criticism. Roughly speaking, yijing
is the process of creating a pictorial environment while reading a piece of
literature. Many critics in China believe that yijing is a creative process of
inducing oneself, while reading a piece of literature or looking at a piece
of art, to create mental pictures, in order to reach a unity of nature, the
author, and the reader. Therefore, it is by its very nature both creative
and critical. According to the theory, this nonverbal, pictorial process

leads directly to a higher ground of beauty and morality. Almost all critics in China agree that yijing is not a process of logical thinking—it is not a process of moving from the premises of an argument to its conclusion, which is the foundation of Western criticism. According to yijing, the process of criticizing a piece of art or literary work has to involve the process of creation on the reader's part. In yijing, verbal thoughts and pictorial thoughts are one. Thinking is conducted largely in pictures and then "transcribed" into words. (Ezra Pound once tried to capture the creative aspect of yijing in poems such as "In a Station of the Metro." He also tried to capture the critical aspect of it in his theory of imagism and vorticism, even though he did not know the term "yijing.") One characteristic of the yijing approach to criticism, therefore, is that it often includes a description of the created mental pictures on the part of the reader/critic and his/her mental attempt to bridge (unite) the literary work, the pictures, with ultimate beauty and peace.

In looking back at my critical papers for various classes, I discovered that I unconsciously used the approach of yijing, especially in some of my earlier papers when I seemed not yet to have been in the grip of Western logical critical approaches. I wrote, for instance, an essay entitled "Wordsworth's Sound and Imagination: The Snowdon Episode." In the major part of the essay I described the pictures that flashed in my mind while I was reading passages in Wordsworth's long poem, *The Prelude*.

> I saw three climbers (myself among them) winding up the mountain in silence "at the dead of night," absorbed in their "private thoughts." The sky was full of blocks of clouds of different colors, freely changing their shapes, like oily pigments disturbed in a bucket of water. All of a sudden, the moonlight broke the darkness "like a flash," lighting up the mountain tops. Under the "naked moon," the band saw a vast sea of mist and vapor, a silent ocean. Then the silence was abruptly broken, and we heard the "roaring of waters, torrents, streams/Innumerable, roaring with one voice" from a "blue chasm," a fracture in the vapor of the sea. It was a joyful revelation of divine truth to the human mind: the bright, "naked" moon sheds the light of "higher reasons" and "spiritual love" upon us; the vast ocean of mist looked like a thin curtain through which we vaguely saw the infinity of nature beyond; and the sounds of roaring waters coming out of the chasm of vapor cast us into the boundless spring of imagination from the depth of the human heart. Evoked by the divine light from above, the human spring of imagination is joined by the natural spring and becomes a sustaining source of energy, feeding "upon infinity" while transcending infinity at the same time. . . .

Here I was describing my own experience more than Wordsworth's. The picture described by the poet is taken over and developed by the reader. The imagination of the author and the imagination of the reader are thus joined together. There was no "because" or "therefore" in the paper. There was little *logic*. And I thought it was (and it is) criticism. This seems to me a typical (but simplified) example of the yijing approach. (Incidentally, the instructor, a kind professor, found the paper interesting, though a bit "strange.")

I am not saying that such a pattern of "alogical" thinking is wrong—in fact some English instructors find it interesting and acceptable—but it is very non-Western. Since I was in this country to learn the English language and English literature, I had to abandon Chinese "pictorial logic," and to learn Western "verbal logic."

If I Had to Start Again

The change is profound: Through my understanding of new meanings of words like "individualism," "idealism," and "I," I began to accept the underlying concepts and values of American writing, and by learning to use "topic sentences" I began to accept a new logic. Thus, when I write papers in English, I am able to obey all the general rules of English composition. In doing this I feel that I am writing through, with, and because of a new identity. I welcome the change, for it has added a new dimension to me and to my view of the world. I am not saying that I have entirely lost my Chinese identity. In fact I feel that I will never lose it. Any time I write in Chinese, I resume my old identity, and obey the rules of Chinese composition such as "Make the 'I' modest," and "Beat around the bush before attacking the central topic." It is necessary for me to have such a Chinese identity in order to write authentic Chinese. (I have seen people who, after learning to write in English, use English logic and sentence patterning to write Chinese. They produce very awkward Chinese texts.) But when I write in English, I imagine myself slipping into a new "skin," and I let the "I" behave much more aggressively and knock the topic right on the head. Being conscious of these different identities has helped me to reconcile different systems of values and logic, and has played a pivotal role in my learning to compose in English.

Looking back, I realize that the process of learning to write in English is in fact a process of creating and defining a new identity and balancing it with the old identity. The process of learning English composition would have been easier if I had realized this earlier and consciously sought to compare the two different identities required by the two writing systems from two different cultures. It is fine and perhaps even necessary for American composition teachers to teach about topic sentences, paragraphs, the use of punctuation, documentation, and so on, but can anyone design exercises sensitive to the ideological and logical differences that students like me experience—and design them so they can be introduced at an early stage of an English composition class? As I pointed out earlier, the traditional advice "Just be yourself" is not clear and helpful to students from Korea, China, Vietnam, or India. From "Be yourself" we are likely to hear either "Forget your cultural habit of writing" or "Write as you would write in your own language." But neither of the two is what the instructor meant or what we want to do. It would be helpful if he or she pointed out the different cultural/ideological connotations of the word "I," the connotations that exist in a group-centered culture and an individual-centered culture. To sharpen the contrast, it might be useful to design papers on topics like "The Individual vs. The Group: China vs. America" or "Different 'I's' in Different Cultures."

Carolyn Matalene mentioned in her article (789) an incident concerning American businessmen who presented their Chinese hosts with gifts of cheddar cheese, not knowing that the Chinese generally do not like cheese. Liking cheddar cheese may not be essential to writing English prose, but being truly accustomed to the social norms that stand behind ideas such as the English "I" and the logical pattern of English composition—call it "compositional cheddar cheese"—is essential to writing in English. Matalene does not provide an "elixir" to help her Chinese students like English "compositional cheese," but rather recommends, as do I, that composition teachers not be afraid to give foreign students English "cheese," but to make sure to hand it out slowly, sympathetically, and fully realizing that it tastes very peculiar in the mouths of those used to a very different cuisine.

Reading the Text

1. Why does Fan Shen say English composition is "a social and cultural experience" (para. 3)?
2. What are the differences between Western and Chinese views of the self, according to Shen?
3. What does Shen mean by the "yijing" (para. 17) approach to writing?
4. In a paragraph, summarize the process by which Fan Shen learned to write English composition essays.

Reading the Signs

1. In your journal, brainstorm ways in which you were brought up either to assert your individuality or to subordinate yourself to group interests (you might consider involvement in sports or school activities). Then stand back, and consider your brainstormed list. To what extent were you raised with a "Western" concept of self? How do your ethnic background and gender affect your sense of self-identity?
2. Compare and contrast Fan Shen's experience in his composition class with your own experiences. How do ethnicity and gender shape a writer's experiences?
3. In class, discuss the extent to which your classes, including your writing

class, assume Western styles of learning and discourse. Then write an essay discussing the results of your discussion, using the "yijing" approach that Fan Shen describes. Read your essay aloud in class.

4. Has anything you have learned in your writing class felt "foreign" to you? Write a list, as Fan Shen did, in which you name features about writing that come "naturally" to you, and then list those that seem "unnatural." Study your lists. Which features seem culturally determined, and which seem linked to your own personality and way of thinking? Can you make such a distinction? How can these lists help you as a writer?

LYNNELL HANCOCK

The Haves and the Have-Nots

As the world gets wired, it gets more and more important to go online if you're going to keep up in a competitive environment. That's why an increasing number of schools are hooking up to the Internet, thus giving their students the earliest possible advantage in the race through cyberspace. As LynNell Hancock (b. 1953) points out, however, not every school can afford the price of admission. If our already economically divided society is not to become even more divided between those who have and those who don't, measures will have to be taken to be sure that everyone has access to the Web. An assistant professor of journalism and director of the Prudential Fellowship for Children and the News at Columbia University, Hancock is also a freelance writer who specializes in public education.

Aaron Smith is a teenager on the techno track. In America's breathless race to achieve information nirvana, the senior from Issaqua, a middle-class district east of Seattle, has the hardware and hookups to run the route. Aaron and 600 of his fellow students at Liberty High School have their own electronic-mail addresses. They can log on to the Internet every day, joining only about 15 percent of America's schoolchildren who can now forage on their own for documents in European libraries or chat with experts around the world. At home, the 18-year-old e-mails his teachers, when he is not prowling the World Wide Web to track down snowboarding conditions on his favorite Cascade mountain passes. "We have the newest, greatest thing," Aaron says.

On the opposite coast, in Boston's South End, Marilee Colon scoots a mouse along a grimy Apple pad, playing a Kid Pix game on an old black-and-white terminal. It's Wednesday at a neighborhood center, Marilee's only chance to poke around on a computer. Her mom, a secretary at the center, can't afford one in their home. Marilee's public-school classroom doesn't have any either. The 10-year-old from Roxbury depends on the United South End Settlement Center and its less than state-of-the-art Macs and IBMs perched on mismatched desks. Marilee has never heard of the Internet. She is thrilled to double-click on the stick of dynamite and watch her teddy-bear creation fly off the screen. "It's fun blowing it up," says the delicate fifth grader, twisting a brown ponytail around her finger.

Certainly Aaron was born with a stack of statistical advantages over Marilee. He is white and middle class and lives with two working parents who both have higher degrees. Economists say the swift pace of high-tech advances will only drive a further wedge between these youngsters. To have an edge in America's job search, it used to be enough to be well educated. Now, say the experts, it's critical to be digital. Employees who are adept at technology "earn roughly 10 to 15 percent higher pay," according to Alan Krueger, chief economist for the U.S. Labor Department. Some argue that this pay gap has less to do with technology than with industries' efforts to streamline their work forces during the recession. . . . Still, nearly every American business from Wall Street to McDonald's requires some computer knowledge. Taco Bell is modeling its cash registers after Nintendo controls, according to Rosabeth Moss Kanter. The "haves," says the Harvard Business School professor, will be able to communicate around the globe. The "have-nots" will be consigned to the "rural backwater of the information society."

Like it or not, America is a land of inequities. And technology, despite its potential to level the social landscape, is not yet blind to race, wealth and age. The richer the family, the more likely it is to own and use a computer, according to 1993 census data. White families are three times as likely as blacks or Hispanics to have computers at home. Seventy-four percent of Americans making more than $75,000 own at least one terminal, but not even one third of all Americans own computers. A small fraction—only about 7 percent—of students' families subscribe to online services that transform the plastic terminal into a telecommunications port.

At least in public schools, the computer gap is closing. More than half the students have some kind of computer, even if it's obsolete. But schools with the biggest concentration of poor children have the least equipment, according to Jeanne Hayes of Quality Education Data. Ten years ago schools had one computer for every 125 children, according to Hayes. Today that figure is one for 12.

Though the gap is slowly closing, technology is advancing so fast, and at such huge costs, that it's nearly impossible for cash-strapped municipalities to catch up. Seattle is taking bids for one company to wire each ZIP code with fiber optics, so everyone—rich or poor—can hook up to video, audio and other multimedia services. Estimated cost: $500 million. Prosperous Montgomery County, Md., has an $81 million plan to put every classroom online. Next door, the District of Columbia public schools have the same ambitious plan but less than $1 million in the budget to accomplish it.

New ideas—and demands—for the schools are announced every week. The '90s populist slogan is no longer "A chicken in every pot" but "A computer on every desk." Vice President Al Gore has appealed to the telecommunications industry to cut costs and wire all schools, a task Education Secretary Richard Riley estimates will cost $10 billion. House Speaker Newt Gingrich stumbled into the discussion with a suggestion that every poor family get a laptop from Uncle Sam. Rep. Ed Markey wants a computer sitting on every school desk within 10 years. "The opportunities are enormous," Markey says.

Enormous, yes, but who is going to pay for them? Some successful school projects have relied heavily on the kindness of strangers. In Union City, N.J., school officials renovated the guts of a 100-year-old building five years ago, overhauling the curriculum and wiring every classroom in Christopher Columbus Middle School for high tech. Bell Atlantic provided wiring free and agreed to give each student in last year's seventh-grade class a computer to take home. Even parents, most of whom are South American immigrants, can use their children's computers to e-mail the principal in Spanish. He uses translation software and answers them electronically. The results have shown up in test scores. In a school where 80 percent of the children are poor, reading, math, attendance and writing scores are now the best in the district. "We believe that technology will improve our everyday life," says principal Bob Fazio. "And that other schools will piggyback and learn from us."

Still, for every Christopher Columbus, there are far more schools like Jordan High School in South-Central Los Angeles. Only 30 computers in the school's lab, most of them 12 to 15 years old, are available for Jordan's 2,000 students, many of whom live in the nearby Jordan Downs housing project. "I am teaching these kids on a system that will do them no good in the real world when they get out there," says Robert Doornbos, Jordan's computer-science instructor. "The school system has not made these kids' getting on the Information Highway a priority."

Having enough terminals to go around is one problem. But another 10 important question is what the equipment is used for. Not much beyond rote drills and word processing, according to Linda Roberts, a technology consultant for the U.S. Department of Education. A 1992 National Assessment of Educational Progress survey found that most fourth-grade math students were using computers to play games, "like Donkey

Kong." By the eighth grade, most math students weren't using them at all.

Many school officials think that access to the Internet could become the most effective equalizer in the educational lives of students. With a modem attached, even most ancient terminals can connect children in rural Mississippi to universities in Asia. A Department of Education report last week found that 35 percent of schools have at least one computer with a modem. But only half the schools let students use it. Apparently administrators and teachers are hogging the Info Highway for themselves.

There is another gap to be considered. Not just between rich and poor, but between the young and the used-to-be-young. Of the 100 million Americans who use computers at home, school or work, nearly 60 percent are 17 or younger, according to the census. Children, for the most part, rule cyberspace, leaving the over-40 set to browse through the almanac.

The gap between the generations may be the most important, says MIT guru Nicholas Negroponte, author of the new book "Being Digital." Adults are the true "digitally homeless, the needy," he says. In other words, adults like Debbie Needleman, 43, an office manager at Wallpaper Warehouse in Natick, Mass., are wary of the digital age. "I really don't mind that the rest of the world passes me by as long as I can still earn a living," she says.

These aging choose-nots become a more serious issue when they are teachers in schools. Even if schools manage to acquire state-of-the-art equipment, there is no guarantee that trained adults will be available to understand them. This is something that tries Aaron Smith's patience. "A lot of my teachers are quite illiterate," says Aaron, the fully equipped Issaqua teenager. "You have to explain it to them real slow to make sure they understand everything." Fast or slow, Marilee Colon, Roxbury's fifth-grade computer lover, would like her chance to understand everything too.

Reading the Text

1. Why does Hancock begin her essay by contrasting Aaron Smith with Marilee Colon, and what effect does that contrast have on her reader?
2. What evidence does Hancock advance to demonstrate that "technology . . . is not yet blind to race, wealth, and age" (para. 4)?
3. According to Hancock, what are some of the problems that impoverished school districts face in trying to bring their students online?
4. Why does MIT professor Nicholas Negroponte say that adults are the "digitally homeless, the needy" (para. 13) in cyberspace?

Reading the Signs

1. In class, propose answers to the question that Hancock raises in her selection: Who is going to pay for making access to the Internet socioeconomically equal?

2. Laura Miller ("Women and Children First," p. 505) accuses mainstream media of insisting "that on-line culture is 'the same' as real life" (para. 24). In an essay, discuss the extent to which that accusation applies to Hancock's selection, which first appeared in *Newsweek.*

3. Read through a cybermagazine such as *Wired,* studying how genders, ethnicities, and age groups are portrayed in both advertising and articles. Then write a semiotic analysis of the publication, explaining the extent to which it portrays a world of "inequalities." To develop your ideas, consult Laura Miller's "Women and Children First" (p. 505).

4. Write an essay in which you support, refute, or complicate the contention "that access to the Internet could be the most effective equalizer in the educational lives of students" (para. 11). You might gather evidence for your position by interviewing students of varying ethnic or socioeconomic backgrounds on their access to cyberspace prior to attending college.

LIFE ON THE MARGINS

Representing the "Other" in American Culture

Being Different

In one of the most popular scenes in the first *Star Wars* movie, Luke Skywalker enters a bar full of intergalactic riffraff, and someone tries to pick a fight with him. What made the scene so funny was that the guy trying to pick the fight looked so grotesque, especially compared to Luke Skywalker's smooth good looks. But while the scene's purpose was mostly comic (it was intended as a parody of stock bar scenes in Westerns), it also made a point that fans of the cult classic *The Twilight Zone* could recognize. Made years earlier, this episode featured a character who was an outcast in her society because she was so "ugly." Only at the end of the episode, when the face of the outcast was finally revealed, did the viewer see that she was really beautiful by human standards and that those who shunned her were hideous. The point of the episode, and to a certain extent of the *Star Wars* scene, is that what we usually take for granted as being "normal"—as opposed to being different or abnormal—can be a very relative matter. What is normal to one group may not be to another, and vice versa.

"Otherness"—the condition of being different from the norm—is a social construct. It begins with the basic judgment we all make about anyone who is "not me" and is then extended under group conditions to anyone who is "not us." In one sense, we are all "others" in our relations to each other as individuals, but the construction of otherness is not so democratic when it comes to social groups. For in this case, the dominant social group does the constructing, with the subordinate groups being the constructed. The dominant group not only defines the "norm" under such circumstances; it also gets to construct the prevailing images of those groups who do not conform to that norm. This power to determine how the "other" is to be represented is especially evident in popular culture, where the face of the "other"—especially the racial other—is often constructed in the form that we call a stereotype. Stereotypes, then, are not simply generalizations applied to every individual within a group; they are also markers of one's marginal social status that can be used to maintain that marginality. Thus, one of the first tasks of any group seeking to overcome its marginal status in America is to contest the stereotypes through which it has been represented in such popular cultural venues as film and television.

In a nation as diverse as the United States, a great many of us are "other" with respect to the dominant culture. American Jews, for example, are "other" in relation to America's Christian identity, southern and eastern Europeans are "other" with respect to the northern European origins of the dominant culture, and non-Europeans are "other" in relation to America's European norms. But people are constructed as social "others" or even outcasts in many other ways. The deaf, for example, live invisibly in the margins of American life, with few mainstream Americans knowing that they have their own language and culture. Some American "others" were born into the mainstream, or norm, but became "other" through, say, a disabling accident, while other Americans are marginalized due to their sexual orientation. Some Americans choose, more or less, to become "other" by rejecting the laws of their society, producing outlaw subcultures as various in their characteristics as motorcycle gangs, rural militias, hackers, and urban street gangs. And in the wake of a spate of campus massacres carried out by disaffected students from West Paducah, Kentucky, to Littleton, Colorado, a new class of American "others" is emerging: racially and religiously mainstream children who feel marginalized by their inability to find a comfortable place for themselves in the social hierarchies of their schools.

Since the ways in which America's dominant culture constructs and represents racial otherness in popular culture is the focus of Chapter 7, this chapter focuses on some of those others who tend to get less attention in multicultural education, especially outlaws, people with AIDS, and the deaf. Such "others" profoundly complicate the more prominent social and cultural divisions in our country and so highlight with special force just how arbitrary the label of "otherness" is. A gay white Anglo-Saxon Protestant, for example, might find himself being thrust further into the margins than a straight non-European; deaf or blind people of any race might find themselves being treated as if they were from another planet by those who share their ethnicity. And then there are those who are multiply marginalized (the late Sammy Davis Jr. joked how being black, Jewish, and blind in one eye made him a triple outcast), including some whose marginalized racial status was complicated by later choices to stand outside the law. Such outlaws are better known these days as gangsters.

Interpreting the "Other" in American Culture

Because of their remarkable influence on popular cultural trends, especially in the case of clothing fashions and popular music, we have chosen those social "others" known as gangsters to interpret in this introduction. Our intention is not to glamorize gangsters or their behavior but rather to provide a semiotic explanation for why popular culture itself has been glamorizing the street outlaw for almost twenty years now by mainstreaming gang fashions (that's where all those baggy pants come from) and, to a certain extent, music (especially in the case of gangsta rap). That the urban street gang subculture has had such an impact on American popular culture is particularly intriguing precisely because of its otherwise marginal social status. How, in short, has this "other" become so influential when "otherness" is usually a mark of powerlessness?

As is often the case in a semiotic analysis, it helps to begin by recalling some history to identify the systematic context through which we can interpret street outlaws. The first question is just when outlaws began to influence popular culture. An article in Chapter 4, Robert B. Ray's "The Thematic Paradigm," suggests that this influence goes back a long way in American history. Describing the "outlaw hero" as an arch individualist who prefers to settle social problems his own way rather than according to the law, Ray refers to such early outlaw heroes as the fictional Huck Finn and the real-life Davy Crockett (Rambo and Dirty Harry would be modern examples) and distinguishes them from the "official heroes" (such as George Washington or Abraham Lincoln) who

---

Exploring the Signs of the "Other"

In your journal, explore the images of hackers and gang members (especially as propagated by films, news, or videos). What is the popular image of hackers and of gangsters? In what ways does the image reflect and influence societal attitudes toward the two groups? Consider the varying treatment that the criminal justice system accords members of the two groups: What role does image play in determining that treatment?

always work within the law. Ray argues that we have always needed outlaw heroes because of a certain ambivalence in American culture. On the one hand, we are a civilized nation that values law and order, but on the other hand, we are still something of a frontier society that values individualistic self-reliance and often mistrusts legal institutions (just think of all those lawyer jokes or the popularity of vigilante movies like *Death Wish*).

But beyond the outlaw hero who plays by his own rules, America has often admired the pure outlaw, criminals like Billie the Kid, Jesse James, and Bonnie and Clyde. Outlaws of this kind tend to have their own followers (Jesse and Frank James were heroes to die-hard Confederates in the post–Civil War South; John Wesley Harding was a sort of latter-day Robin Hood), who see them as representing their cause against official society. Here, of course, things can get relative, and the pure outlaw has never had the same kind of popularity as the outlaw hero, but the point is that America has had a long history of both kinds of hero worship.

So now we can ask, how does the gangster fit into this history? He (and the popular image of gang members is almost always male) certainly isn't an outlaw hero because he makes no pretense of resolving social problems. Monster Cody isn't Dirty Harry. But might he be seen as a kind of Jesse James—a criminal, that is, with a constituency? We think yes. The question is, what constituency? If we can answer that, we have gone a long way toward understanding why the gangster is so influential in American popular culture.

So to whom does the gangster appeal? Part of the answer is easy: to his "'hood." That is, as gangsta rappers like Ice-T, NWA, and Tupac Shakur have tried to make as explicit as possible, the gangster (especially the black gangster) is a kind of urban rebel who defies racial oppression (especially by the police) and, through his defiance, represents the urban underclass in its conflict with the white ruling class. Whether this is true about actual gangbangers, it is a major part of their mythology as it is mediated through popular culture.

But there are two problems with this answer. First of all, few inner-city adults have bought into this mythology: gangs are mostly popular among the young in the inner cities of America. Second, it doesn't explain why the gang subculture is so popular among young middle-class kids of all ethnicities who are not a part of the urban underclass. Why are there so many suburban white "wannabes" strolling around in gang attire, for instance, tagging fences and blasting gangsta rap out of their sound systems? How do street gangs represent *them*?

The key to both problems lies in the word *young,* which constitutes the crucial *difference* that distinguishes gang members from other kinds of outlaw heroes and so establishes their particular cultural meaning. For no matter what the race of the gangster (and he comes in all colors), his constituency is among the young, which was not at all the case for, say, Jesse James. Somehow, American youth of all races and classes have come to identify with the urban outlaw, a popular cultural phenomenon that we can interpret by looking into its history. So when, we now need to ask, did the young first begin to identify with outlaws?

We think that two movies from the 1950s can help us to answer this question: Marlon Brando's *The Wild One* and James Dean's *Rebel Without a Cause*. Both films, which appeared at a time of intense cultural conformity, featured nonconformist heroes, one of whom, as the leader of a motorcycle gang, trashes a town, while the other simply refuses to go along with the emotionally repressive world of his parents. Both Marlon Brando and James Dean became cultural icons because of these films, helping to inaugurate (along with the Beats) a youth rebellion against mainstream (or parental) authority that fully exploded in the social upheavals of the 1960s.

So we can say that in the 1950s, American youth began to identify with outlaws, to valorize social marginality as a way of expressing their resistance to their parents' lifestyles and authority. Many of the young babyboomers who wished to express this defiance came from white middle class families, and so they adopted the codes of socially marginalized subcultures to signify their own sense of alienation from the parental mainstream, or "Establishment." From rock 'n' roll, which originated among socially marginalized African Americans, to drug use (which both the Beats and the hippies made a part of the youth rebellion), what was once the province of the outcast became the symbol of youthful resistance.

Gangsta Chic

It is in this context that we can finally interpret the popular cultural influence of the gangster. Once a hidden, socially marginalized product of poverty and economic inequality, the urban street gang has transcended the traditional boundaries of slum, ghetto, and barrio to become one of America's most prominent, if troubling, subcultures—a subculture whose elaborate linguistic, clothing, and behavioral codes are not only known but admired and emulated by teens around the country regardless of their race, class, or geographical region. Courted by fashion designers, Hollywood producers, recording studios, talk-show hosts, and even civic leaders (in the aftermath of the L.A. riots of 1992, captains of the Bloods and the Crips were treated, some commentators complained, like ambassadors of independent nations), gangsters, homeboys, cholos, gangstas, what-have-you, aren't just thugs anymore. They're cultural heroes for the young of all races.

Thus, codes that once had particular meanings in the subcultures in which they originated have been appropriated and transformed by middle-class kids who are unaware of their original meanings. Ever wear a baseball cap backwards? Everyone does these days, and all it signifies is fashion, but when urban street gangs first began to do that at least twenty years ago, it meant that they were about to go out and kill somebody. Do you wear the baggiest pants you can find? They were first adopted in imitation of prison attire, and were also useful for concealing weapons (for some Latino gangsters, on the other hand, they signified as an updating of the zoot suit). Are there taggers in suburban neighborhoods in your area? Well, tagging began as a means for gangs to mark their territories, and woe be it to the intruder who missed the message.

The widespread adoption of the particular codes of the street gang by middle-class American youth has led not only to their glamorization but to their commodification as well, for whenever a given style, howsoever marginalized in its cultural origins, goes mainstream, you can be sure that the marketers won't be far behind. Hence, gang-inspired fashion (hip hop), music (rap), and violence (exploited in movie after movie, from *Colors* to *Boyz N the Hood*) are, quite simply, big business in a marketplace that extends far beyond the ghettos and barrios where the codes of gang culture originate. Sales of baggy, oversized pants, overalls (worn unstrapped or single strapped), baseball caps, team sweats and jackets, and Nike basketball shoes (worn unlaced one year, laced the next) have bounded beyond the gangs who first favored them to adolescents who line up to adopt the gangsta look. You aren't a gangster, of course, just because you dress like one, but you may be saying something all the same.

You Say You Want a Revolution

Have you ever felt, for example, that by listening to NWA, Snoop Doggy Dog, Tupac Shakur, Ice-T, and Tha Dogg Pound you're making a statement of defiance against adult authority? Do you find the misspelling of words (especially using the letter *z* instead of *s* for a plural, as in *Boyz*), the adoption of gang fashions, or shaving your head expressive of a particular attitude you wish to express? If you do, you are joining a history of American youth rebellions in which the codes of the outcast have been appropriated by the middle class to signify its own discontents. But as has been so often the case in American popular cultural history, what begins as rebellion ends as consumption. The symbols of disaffection become fashion symbols. Images of social despair return as dollar signs in a commercial cornucopia.

It is thus significant that it is the black gang that has supplied most of the imagery of commercial gangsterism. Although Hispanic gangs make up more than half of L.A.'s street gangs, for example, the cholo style sets fewer trends. Suburban gangsta wannabes (even the word *gangsta* originated in the ghetto) emulate not only the prison-inspired styles of Latino East L.A. (for instance, below-the-knee cutoffs and close-cropped hair) but also the professional sports-inspired styles of the black gangs, designs that send them running to the Raiders and Reebok and Nike. While Latino rappers do hit the charts, the sound that can claim that it's "straight outta Compton" gets all the attention. When Edward James Olmos made a film about Latino gangs in L.A., *American Me*, the movie received local press attention but nothing like the national media stakeouts that occur every time a new film about black gangs appears.

Thus, one of the enduring ironies of American race relations makes its way into the semiotics of the street. From generation to generation, black America has provided young white America with metaphors of oppression, with symbols and analogies to use in their own struggles. You might want to begin your thinking about gang culture with this phenomenon. Do you believe that it is valid for white middle-class youths to adopt the symbols of the underclass to express themselves? Does it in any way trivialize the social conditions behind the growth of gangs to turn street gangs into fashion plates?

The "Other" as Victim and the Victim as Hero

The popularity of the street-gang subculture can be seen as a facet of a larger cultural fascination with "otherness" that has become apparent in recent years. In America's past, conformity was valued more than difference—a value that was reflected in the desires of immigrant groups to assimilate as quickly as possible to the codes of the dominant culture. But increasingly, the dominant culture is being viewed as an oppressive force in the lives of anyone who differs from it. This is perfectly understandable in the context of an America that is becoming more and more racially and culturally diverse, as those who have historically been the victims of the dominant culture are achieving their voice and beginning to be heard. What is interesting, then, is not the fact that so many

---

Discussing the Signs of the "Other"

In class, discuss the attractions that people with marginal or victim status have for Americans with relatively mainstream backgrounds. Why have so many celebrities taken to discussing publicly the abuse they suffered as children? What is it about the "victim" that engages the American imagination?

Americans who have been historically marginalized are drawing attention to, and protesting, their victimization by the dominant culture. No, that's only to be expected. What is less expected is that so many Americans who belong to the dominant culture seem to want to see themselves as victims, too. We can see signs of this in the talk-show circuit, where otherwise "ordinary"-looking guests flaunt their differences and gain sympathy for the way the dominant culture has victimized them, say, for being engaged to three pregnant women at once. But it is also visible in the literally explosive emergence of schoolyard groups like Columbine High School's so-called Trenchcoat Mafia (made up of affluent white kids who thought of themselves as the victims of their school's athletic hierarchy), as well as in the appearance of a certain kind of movie that has become quite popular in recent years.

Did you see *Braveheart*? Chances are that you did because it was quite a success when it appeared. It was not the only movie of its kind, however, for the 1990s saw a good number of movies about Celtic resistance to English tyranny, including such modern-era true-life films as *Michael Collins*. What these films shared was the way they depicted the victimization of Celtic peoples (the Irish and the Highland Scots are Celtic in origin) by English overlords. But their appeal went far beyond that of Scottish or Irish audiences, so the question is, why? Why did historical films about the travails of the Celts become so popular in the 1990s?

A brief look at *Braveheart* can help answer this question. First, who are the heroes of *Braveheart*—with whom, that is, are we expected to identify? *Braveheart*'s Scottish tribesmen, of course. And what do they look like, with their painted faces? A bit like Indians, do they not? Now, who are the villains? The English, of course, and they look, well, English. What can we make of this?

Consider how in racial terms both the Scottish tribesmen and English overlords in *Braveheart* are both white but how in the coding of the movie the "white" Scotsmen resemble nonwhite American Indians while the English represent whiteness (indeed, in America the word *Anglo,* which literally refers to the English, is now used to refer to any white person). What we have is a kind of Western translated to Scotland, with *Braveheart*'s Scotsmen standing in for the Indian victims of white aggression. Since the movie invites a largely white audience to identify with the Scottish tribesmen rather than their English oppressors, an interesting racial reversal is being metaphorically enacted here: that is, white audiences are invited to root against the symbols of whiteness. Now, why would this be popular?

Does *Braveheart* signify a white rejection of whiteness in America? We think not. Rather, the movie (and movies and stories like it) reflects a desire on the part of white audiences *to see themselves as victims.* Why? Because in the current discourse of "otherness" in America, not to be a victim is often held to be equivalent to being a victimizer (or as Eldridge

||||||||||||||||||||||||||||||||||||||||||||||||||||||||||||||||||||||||||||||||||||||||||||||||||||||||||||||||||||||||||||||

> ### Reading the "Other" on the Net
>
> Use the Internet to explore how socially marginalized groups, such as the disabled, AIDS patients, and the homeless, perceive their place in American society. You might visit sites sponsored by such groups as Disability Rights Advocates (**http://www.dralegal.org**), the National Coalition for the Homeless (**http://nch.ari.net/**), or the People with AIDS Coalition (**http://www.jaxadnet.com/pwaca/**).

Cleaver once put it, "if you're not a part of the solution, you're a part of the problem"). Conversely, victimage signifies innocence. And since, as young Americans are often taught in school these days, the great victimizer in American history has generally been the dominant white culture that, among other things, imported African slaves and destroyed the Indians, to be white is often equated with being an oppressor.

But as we have seen, American youth frequently identify with the oppressed, with the marginalized "other," not with oppressors. They see themselves as victims, not as victimizers. And movies like *Braveheart* give them a chance to be victims by giving them *white* victims with which to identify, with the white victims being subtly coded as nonwhite (with all that war paint) and the white oppressors being coded as ultrawhite in their Angloness.

Thus, through cinematic magic, white audiences can be relieved of traces of racial guilt by seeing themselves metaphorically as the victims of racial oppression. At a time when "otherness" and victimization are so often seen to go hand in hand, this is no small service, for in an ironic reversal of most of human history, the "other," traditionally history's victim, is becoming popular culture's hero.

The Readings

Our first selection in this chapter, "Signs of the Street: A Conversation," presents an interview conducted by the authors of this book with a group of former gang members attending classes at the West Valley Occupational Center in Los Angeles. Here, the students speak of the styles and signaling systems current among gangsters, describe what gang membership means to them, and offer their opinions of the suburban wannabes who copy them. Peter Doskoch's examination of "The Mind of the Militias" provides some sobering insights into the ideology of the militia movement in the United States. Evelynn Hammonds next argues that AIDS has become a disease of the racially and sexually marginalized in America, an affliction of an alien "other" that has been left to die by a society that views the disease as someone else's problem. A profile of Heather Whitestone, the first deaf Miss America, follows, focusing on the controversy within the deaf community over Whitestone's preference for oral communication over American Sign Language. The following selection, a personal narrative, traces Kevin Jennings's evolution from seeing himself as an "other" to embracing fully his identity as a gay man. Andrew Calcutt next offers a critique of the culture of victimage he sees growing in England and America. Concluding the chapter is Bernard Lefkowitz's reflection on how the omnipresent cliques in American youth culture—the ultimate insiders—may have led two boys who felt very much like outsiders to commit the terrible massacre at Columbine High School.

SONIA MAASIK AND JACK SOLOMON
Signs of the Street: A Conversation

Too often, gangs are interpreted by adults — especially white middle-class professionals — who have no personal experience of gang life or direct knowledge of the social conditions in which youth gangs flourish. One of the best ways to learn about gangs, however, is to speak with those who are associated with them. To see what the kids themselves had to say, the authors of this book visited a Los Angeles high school that offers former gang members an opportunity to complete their secondary school education. The following conversation reveals what a group of some twenty-five students at the West Valley Occupational Center school think about such issues as gang fashion, suburban wannabes, and the value that gang membership holds for those who belong to them. All names of students have been changed to protect their identity.

Can you describe for us what sorts of clothing you see on the streets these days?

JORGE: Baggy pants, skate clothes, stuff like that. Look around, and everybody wears baggy pants.

Do you know when people started wearing baggy pants? About?

JORGE: Well, early you know, like maybe in the forties or back in the thirties.

LUIS: It came out with the zoot suits.

OSCAR: Well, gang members had to like the same thing, you know. Gangsters still stay the same.

JORGE: Designers are wearing baggy pants, just like gangs. Recently, everybody's started wearing them within probably the past what? Maybe year, two, three years.

MIKE: It started getting really crazy around two years ago.

JORGE: You know about sagging? Where they used to sag a long time ago?

LUIS: Oh, that started about, like, forty years ago. I think sagging came out with the black people first. It started with the brothers.

HANK: It was rappers that came first. Remember that song about saggin' pants? It was Ice-T.

RUDY: And colors. You know, a guy may wear like red, mustard colors. And other guys wear dark colors. Everyone belongs in a group, and you can tell him by the way he dresses.

How are Nikes these days? A few years ago Nikes were just the *shoe. What's going on now?*

HANK: They're gangbanger shoes.

OSCAR: A lot of crooks wore 'em. And the Bloods would wear the all-   15
red ones with a little red stripe, but now they're trying to get conservative and they wear black and then have just a little red somewhere. They like dressing down, but they'll let you know where they're from.

Any sneakers that you just wouldn't be seen dead in?

TONY: Crow Wings! They're just cheap, you know, you can get 'em at Penney's for like 10 bucks.

RUDY: Reeboks are cool. Everybody wears Reeboks.

OSCAR: Converse. Converse, man. Converse.

HANK: Converse are gangbanger shoes.   20

LATISHA: Some taggers like the versatile Converse. They have lowtops, hightops, different colors, suede, you know, like that.

Is there anything that you wouldn't wear at school, but would wear at home or in your neighborhood?

OSCAR: Pajamas!

LUIS: You wouldn't wear clothes with your gang on it. You can't wear that in school 'cuz you get in trouble. Or clothes in remembrance of a friend that died.

BRIAN: You can't even wear a hat to school, 'cuz they think it's gang-   25
related.

Two guys here are wearing shorts: one pair are blue denim cutoffs and the other are plaid cutoffs. Do you read those two guys differently?

JORGE: Geeks, geeks! That's a skater.

And the plaid is what?

GARY: Surfer.

TERESA: And gangsters wear cutoff Dickies.   30

What do cutoffs say to guys on the street?

JORGE: You're a gang member. And they have to be Dickies. The make is important. The brand style.

TERESA: And they're ironed. All the gang members iron. They can't be all wrinkled. They want to show their respect, that they care for themselves.

LUIS: Gangsters are the ones that crease it, even their boxer shorts, man! It's the respect they have when they go on the street. They want people to see that they try to look good for other people.

TERESA: Well, you're not going to see a gang member going in the street   35
with wrinkled clothes, you know? They just don't look right.

Is there anything else that they do to show respect?

ALICIA: Short haircuts. It's got to be clean cut. It shows they respect
themselves and they want respect for their gang.
OSCAR: And bald people. Bald means that they're gangbangers.

Bald is a code word. Do you really mean shaven head?

MIKE: Well, it means two different things. One's a gangbanger. But my   40
head's shaved all the way around, all the way under and I have hair
on top. When I shaved my head, I shaved it clean. Because I'm not
Hispanic or I'm not black, I immediately looked skinhead. So it has
something to do with the color you are. I have a goatee and a full
shaved head. I was fully labeled a skinhead, right off.

*I don't think there are any skinheads in the room now. That way nobody needs
to feel defensive. What about the skinheads? What do you think about them?*

TONY: They're mostly all white power.
MIKE: That's bull, dude. They're not.
BRIAN: You're so wrong, dude. You guys have such a misconception of
the skinheads. There are so many skinhead groups that are totally
against racism and stuff like that. Like shark skinheads.
MIKE: There's a lot of groups like that, you know, there's groups like   45
Ghost Town Skinheads and there're Nazi skinheads and stuff like
that.
BRIAN: But there's Peace Punk, stuff like that. And they won't wear
leather and stuff like that or do things like killing animals or hurting
the environment. And people just have misconceptions and think
that if you're white and got a shaved head, you're like a Nazi, you're
a skinhead and you're a racist toward everyone. But that's not the
way it is.
LATISHA: Don't you think that that's the image they project to us? And
that image is what most of the skinheads are about?
BRIAN: That's what you see, that's what you see on the media. That's
what you see on TV.
LATISHA: Okay, so what makes the difference if I see a white guy walking down the street and he just bald-headed? I have never met one
skinhead who ain't racist toward a black person.
MIKE: I think everyone pretty much has a little bit of racism in them.   50
Everybody's against every race.
BRIAN: But there's a lot of different groups, I'm telling you. See, the
media makes it seem like skinheads are, you know, the epitome of
racist people. The majority of skinheads are probably racist, but a lot

of them are not. People give skinheads bad names and that's not cool.

Is it useful to you to be able to figure people out by the way they dress?

TONY: On the street, yeah. If you're walking by yourself, and you see a bunch of people, you just don't want to get involved.

MIKE: You know that people mess with each other out on the streets. Me and him, we were just skating at a parking lot and a car full of guys drives up and they scream out some names. They scream out these nicknames, and if we start talking back, then that's how things happen, you know. Just by their appearance you can see stuff coming. Their cars even tell you.

JORGE: Yeah, Impalas and Regals, '65 Impalas.   55

You can read a car real quick?

MANY: Yeah.

What are the cars?

HANK: Cadillacs, Regals, Impalas, older cars.

LUIS: In the olden days, they used to drive old cars. Now they're trying   60 to keep the tradition of those old cars. All you see today is pure *raza*,[1] just driving old cars so they look good.

How do you and your friends in your neighborhoods feel when you see in movies or on television or on the streets obviously rich, generally white kids trying to dress up like gangsters? What do you think when you see that?

TERESA: Stupid!

JORGE: We laugh at them. We laugh.

OSCAR: They try to dress like us, they're trying to make a statement, like they are like we are. But if somebody approach 'em or something, they'd be the first one to back down and run away or something like that. And that ain't cool.

TERESA: They're trying to be like everybody else, trying to fit in.   65

TONY: They're just wannabes.

When I ask you where you're from, what does that question really mean?

JORGE: What gang we're from, what neighborhood.

LUIS: You know what? They can dress like gangs, but they have to show it. They have to prove themselves.

So it's something more than just the clothing?   70

LUIS: You gotta have heart for it.

-----

1. **raza**   Refers to *la raza*, the race or Hispanic people. —EDS.

JORGE: A lot of people that dress up like that, they're starting in rich, rich areas, they're starting to like get their own little gangs and they're starting to tag up the walls there, and they're starting to do the same stuff that's going on out here.

RUDY: They imitate everybody else, they try to dress the same way.

So if it's your own style, it's cool, but, if you try to take somebody else's style that you haven't earned, that's kind of dumb?

TERESA: There's a lot of people, just to fit in they'll dress like gangsters, but they ain't about shit. They're punks. It's true, man. Say my brother or my cousin sees someone dressed like a gangster and they ask, "Where were you from?" He says, "I'm not from nowhere, I just like the way I dress." He straight out says it. He acts like he's from somewhere, but he's just scared to say he's afraid, but that's stupid. Why you gonna dress like that if you're not gonna be down for your group?

I've heard that some guys like to wear tattoos and those tattoos mean something. Why do people tattoo?

OSCAR: Most Chicanos, they like getting tattoos, like naked girls, Aztec warriors. It has to do with *la raza,* to do with their race. See, other guys, other races, they can get other kinds of tattoos, like cats, like lions.

BRIAN: That's like a totally different thing.

I notice the letters. Why'd you pick those letters (points to Gothic lettering on one student's tattoo)?

LUIS: Because that's like gang letters. It's the old style.

LATISHA: I think the Hispanics started it, but black people like it too, you know.

What about the three dots on the hand? Is that where they go?

ALICIA: Um, like about right here (*points*), between my thumb and my first finger. You can put them anywhere else too. You could put 'em on the elbow or the wrist.

What if you saw somebody from the suburbs with three dots that obviously weren't really tattoos, but just kind of a wash-off tattoo, with three dots on their wrist, what would you think?

JORGE: I'd ask 'em why it's there and what kind of life do you have?

TERESA: A fake tattoo! Like, what are they trying to prove? To make it look hard?

BRIAN: If you can't take the ink, don't draw on yourself. If you're not down to getting drawn on, then, you know, don't start playing with pens drawing things.

TERESA: I know, but what are they trying to prove? If they get one, then get a real one.

OSCAR: One thing I want to point out, see, it doesn't really matter the way you dress.

LUIS: Yeah. Because you can dress the dorkiest-assed person on the 90 planet, but you could be still a gang member, and if you're that gang member and dress so dorky you could have a lot of heart for that gang that you're from. It doesn't really matter how you dress. You could dress like some different type of style, but still you have heart for that neighborhood that you got jumped in to. It doesn't matter the way you dress. It doesn't.

OSCAR: It's how people perceive you, how people look at you. All that matters is what you have inside your heart.

MIKE: It's what society puts on teens. It's the way society says, "This is how these people dress, this is how these people dress, this is how these people dress." No questions. And it's fucked up. It sucks.

TERESA: But you know what? The media puts everything so wrong when they talk about kids, but it's not the story.

Can you think of something that's really dead wrong that the media do?

LUIS: Oh, yeah. Like in the news or in radio, when they talk about 95 gangs, like Hispanic gangs. They make us look bad. They always talk about the things we do bad, like, "Oh, another drive-by," but they never talk about when one of us Hispanics graduates or does something good, become a doctor or something like that. They only talk about the bad about us and that's one thing I don't really understand. Why do they have to talk about things that are bad about us? I think there's good stuff and there's bad stuff here. Like us, you know, everybody in this class, we're *raza,* they're black, they're white, but we go to this school, we can learn and try to make something of our lives.

JORGE: Man, I'm a gang member, but I don't go up against society. I'm gonna be up there on top of everybody else, we can do it too, you know. It don't matter the way that you dress. I could be a gang member, but hey, I'm smart too. I could do the same thing other people could do.

LUIS: Yeah, I could go to college.

OSCAR: Last night, I was listening to the radio and they were talkin' about gangs, and I didn't like it, 'cuz they were talkin' about just the bad part: We kill people and we shank.

JORGE: Well, you don't?

OSCAR: No . . . all gang members don't. Most gang members get into a 100 gang because they're scared of other people, you know. They need somebody to be around, they need a base, like a family, 'cuz see, most gang members don't have love at home so they join the neighborhood. They want the love your family can't give you.

LUIS: It's like, say your mom and your dad are ignoring you or something, you go to your neighborhood, and they pay attention to you, you know, they cheer you up. They're there for you, they give you love.

OSCAR: Let's say if I got kicked outta my house, I could go with my homeboy right here, I could go to his house and kick back as long as I want. You know, they'd take care of me.

LUIS: We're always there for each other. No matter what. Thick and thin. We're family.

OSCAR: I'm gonna show you guys. You guys want to hear a rap about love?

TONY: All right! Listen, listen.   105

OSCAR: All right, here we go . . . (*rapping*) This is a story about a young kid, about his life and things he did. Young kid, he wants to join a gang. He wanta live his life in the fast lane. Hold out with the troubles in the neighborhood, doing little things that he never should. Robbing, stealing, beating up *gente*,[2] rocking around saying things like these. Dressed down, khakis and a white T-shirt standing proud and tall. *Todos vatos, todos vatos*[3] they jump me in. I want to gangbang with you, my friends, and todos step to the *calle*,[4] rock it down to L.A. from the *valle*.[5] It was accomplished, you did what I said, when he made the promise. He promised himself one day he'll be a man. I don't think they truly understand. He gonna grow like one day working, now he's watching his back in order to live, so he tries the gang. For the very first time, first time in his life that he got high. He dropped out of school at the age of twelve. People said he messed up, he said, "Oh, well." He doesn't care about anything, 'cuz now he steps on up to cocaine. He could care less about the things he lost, because this is the story about a rebel without a cause.

(*Applause.*) *What do you guys think when you hear that? Where did rap come from?*

HANK: It's just like nursery rhymes. A nursery rhyme is a rap. All you gotta do is speed it up or slow it down.

LATISHA: Yeah, it's like poetry. Before it was just instinct, it just happened. But now they really rappin' mean stuff.

TERESA: They rap to make a record, but now they're rappin' to mean   110 something. Messages are being sent by rap.

---

2. *gente*   People. — EDS.
3. *todos vatos*   All these guys. — EDS.
4. *calle*   Street. — EDS.
5. *valle*   Valley. — EDS.

We're interested in what you understand when you see graffiti on the wall, how you can know who did it and what it means. There're all sorts of differences, aren't there?

HANK: First of all, you know who it is 'cuz they write their name on the wall. Then you'll basically know what gang they are. Anywhere you go, you can tell if it's a tagger writing or if it's gang writing.

How?

JORGE: By the way they write. Most taggers kinda handwrite, mostly handwriting with a big, big spray can. You know, gangbangers they do block letters, little blocklike letters. They use different kinds of letters, different styles.

LATISHA: There's another thing with taggers. When I used to tag—I 115 don't do it anymore—but when I used to hang with a tagger crew, when we wrote, we used different kinds of ink, like scribe and streaks. Being original, you can cut half of one and cut half of the other and put it in one pen and make it double like it's rainbow color.

What's a scribe?

LATISHA: Scribe is when you carve it on a window. You can carve your name on it.

TERESA: It looks like crayon chalk. You can carve wood and you can carve it in a bus window.

What do you think when you see people in the suburbs becoming taggers?

JORGE: They're trying to prove a point. 120

OSCAR: They're trying to get their space. That's what everybody wants in this whole world, you know, to gain your respect. And writing on the wall is doing it or the way you dress is doing it. There's all kinds of ways of gaining respect. That's what everybody wants. No matter what race you're from, you know, black, white, Hispanic. The point is, everybody just wants respect, okay? Sometimes being in the gangs gets you that respect or being a tagger gets you that respect from other taggers. You know, it depends where you're coming from.

LATISHA: That's true, because when I was in junior high I used to gang-bang with a Mexican gang, me and another black girl. I tried to go with them because I used to get picked on by a lot of girls, because I came from a small town, I used to be like a school girl. Everybody used to pick on me and then I was talking with one of my friends and she was in the gang and she was like, "Well, you can come kick it with us." But after a while, kicking it became more. I started dressing like them and doing my hair like them, everything. And I just changed completely. Then I got picked on again for acting like a Mexican girl wannabe. But when I walked with them and we all walked around that junior high, we all had respect and they all looked at me like, you know, "I ain't gonna mess with her." But then, after that, I went to taggers because I found out that the Mexicans didn't really want to hang with me. The taggers I went to were an all-black gang in L.A., and then I had respect with them too.

LUIS: You see, in the old days, the way we, *la raza,* used to get respect was by throwing one on one. Fighting. But now, no one don't throw no blows at each other, they just pull out a gun and bam, right there. One minute just takes your life away.

ALICIA: Another thing about the imitation is that I know a lot of gangsters think taggers try to imitate them by carrying a gun or something.

TERESA: Actually there's a lot of real gangsters who are older, like in   125
their twenties and stuff, they always say that the taggers are trying to copy them. When they see them, they chase them out of their 'hood.

Any other stories you want to tell?

TONY: Sometimes you're going down the street, and you see a gang member by the way he's dressed. But sometimes he's not even a gang member, you know, his clothes don't necessarily mean he's in a gang. He wears it for his race. They just want to get their own respect by themselves.

OSCAR: Many people think that, when gang members go to a white party, everybody treats 'em different. Just like about two weeks ago, I went to some white party and I asked for something to drink, and people just gave it to me and they wanted to open it up for me. They gave me respect. I swear to God, man, he opened it for me and he said, "Here you go, would you like anything else?"

TONY: That's what they do in the stores, they try to just hurry up and give you what you want before you get mad and you tear up something.

HANK: I know if I get mad I'm gonna tear up something and then leave.   130
Somebody say I can't have something and I ask politely and they look at you like you got shit on your face. And you be ready to swing on somebody, real quick. And that's what they trying not to have. They don't want to get in a fight with you 'cuz they know you kick ass.

OSCAR: Yeah, when you go to the store, the first thing they say is, "Do you need something?"

HANK: I get sweat all the time. Every time I walk through a store, I get sweat, I get followed, I get asked questions. Every time.

Reading the Text

1. How is clothing used as a signaling system on the street?
2. What is the value of gang membership, in the students' views?
3. What attitudes do the students have toward suburban gang wannabes?
4. How do the students feel about skinheads?

Reading the Signs

1. Gang culture is often depicted in the media as a counterculture. Basing your discussion on the students' comments, write an essay in which you explore the extent to which this depiction is valid. Why do you think, for instance, that Luis so frequently refers to tradition and *la raza*?
2. In class, have one student sing Oscar's rap, and discuss your responses to it.
3. What role does gang membership have in forming a teen's identity, especially a teen living in the inner city? Write an essay in which you formulate your own argument.
4. "Respect" frequently surfaces as an issue in the students' conversation. In your journal, compare what respect means to the students with what it means to you. Do you define respect in similar ways, and if so, how? If not, how do you define it? What might you say to the students about their notions of respect?

PETER DOSKOCH

The Mind of the Militias

‖‖‖‖‖‖‖‖‖‖‖‖‖‖‖‖‖‖‖‖‖‖‖‖‖‖‖‖‖‖‖‖‖‖‖‖‖‖‖

They're out there. Mysterious black helicopters watching your every move. Ghurka troops under U.N. command ready to cross the border and seize your weapons. A cadre of international financiers plotting to construct a New World Order. Such is the belief of a small but growing number of Americans who have banded together to assert their rights to bear arms and to resist the federal government in every way. In this selection, Peter Doskoch (b. 1965) offers both an historical background of militias and an analysis of their fears and aims, concluding with some recommendations on what to do, and not to do, about them. A former senior editor with Psychology Today, *Doskoch specializes in psychology, biology, and neuroscience.*

Edward L. Brown, spokesman for New Hampshire's Constitutional Defense Militia, is patiently explaining to me how the United States government masterminded the Oklahoma City bombing, how the United Nations is taking over America, how a small consortium of international power brokers orchestrated the breakup of the Soviet Union. And what's most striking is how normal he sounds.

Not his words: His constant reference to "they" and "them" are the calling cards of a conspiracy hound. So are his repeated mentions of "Marxist socialist puke"—meaning Bill and Hillary, journalists like myself, and the Jews who purportedly control the world's economy.

What's shockingly ordinary, rather, is his friendly, low-key demeanor. Much of the time Brown comes across like a grumpy but beloved uncle. When I confess that I just don't buy the conspiracy theories he's spewing, Brown doesn't rant—he gently growls, "Awwww, Peter," the way he might at a nephew's mischievous but harmless antics. And he dismisses any thought of militiamen as paranoid or dangerous. "We're kind of backwoods bubbas up here. We're a bunch of harmless old folks. We'll take you fishing, have you over for dinner, and put you up for the night. That's the kind of folks we are."

But the Norman Rockwell image forming in my brain shatters as Brown's homespun chitchat turns into advice on which foods I should be stockpiling in my basement just in case "these guys orchestrate this thing" and the world economy collapses.

In barely two years, thousands of "harmless old folks" like Brown have transformed the word "militia" from a quaint anachronism into an armed threat. They've altered the political landscape as well, creating a chasm across which rational dialogue has ceased and liberals and conservatives now only point accusatory fingers. President Clinton has taken swipes at right-wing talk show hosts like Rush Limbaugh, claiming that their rhetoric incites militia violence. Conservatives, for their part, attribute the rise of militias to anti-government backlash.

But in talking with psychologists, psychiatrists, sociologists, local sheriffs, and militia members themselves, a far more complex picture emerges. Denouncing paramilitary groups as terrorists—or hailing them as patriots—ignores the often-subtle interplay of forces that have led to their rebirth some two centuries after Lexington and Concord. The psychological and cultural dynamics behind this resurrection can't be reduced to a catchy sound bite. But either we understand them—or we risk more Oklahoma City conflagrations.

Apocalypse Now

There's a huge overlap between militias and Christian fundamentalists, contends Charles Strozier, Ph.D., of John Jay College's Center on Violence and Human Survival, and the end of the millennium "is the shadow on everyone's mind on the Christian right." That shadow, he says, is galvanizing militia members who truly think apocalypse is at hand.

A key concern is the timing of the period of tribulation. That's when, believers say, Christ will return to claim his people amid earthly destruction. Most ordinary fundamentalists are "pre-tribbers"—they think Jesus will come before Armageddon occurs. But fundamentalist militia members, Strozier says, tend to be mid- or post-tribbers: they believe Christ will return only *after* violent apocalypse.

"That's an arcane point of theology, but it has enormous psychological significance because they want to be there during tribulation. They want to be there when the rivers run red. They want to take their Uzis and fight it out with the Beast. God needs their help."

Hence the gun controls that militias so vigorously oppose are a threat   10 not just to their constitutional rights but to the Lord. The 1993 raid on the Branch Davidian compound in Waco, Texas, strikes a sinister chord with fundamentalist militias because it's tangible evidence that the Bureau of Alcohol, Tobacco, and Firearms is trying to prevent them "from rising up in revolution to keep the seed of Satan from destroying us," argues sociologist Brent L. Smith, Ph.D., chairman of the department of criminal justice at the University of Alabama in Birmingham and author of *Terrorism in America*.

Impending apocalypse might even tug at nonreligious militia members. For those motivated by idealism, violence "can take on a kind of transcendence," reports psychiatrist Robert Jay Lifton, M.D., director of John Jay's Center for Violence and Human Survival in New York. "People involved in it can see themselves as moving into a heroic domain, a higher purpose." And millennium fever intensifies the urge toward transcendent violence.

Paranoia

Political pundits interpreted last November's election as proof that voters want government off their backs. But militias believe the Feds are not only on their backs but up their pant legs, in their pockets, and—as some claim—ready to implant computer chips in their buttocks.

"The leaders of the group may be sincere in their complaints about federal intrusion into people's lives," says Theodore Feldmann, M.D., a consultant to the FBI and psychiatry professor at the University of Louisville. "But there's an excessive nature to their concern."

As a result, nearly any government law, any gathering of the rich and powerful, becomes damning proof of conspiracy. In the rhetoric of militia groups, gun control laws aren't a strategy to curb violence; they're part of a plan to enslave us. Secret societies like Yale's Skull and Bones aren't elitist fraternal groups but part of a plot to form a single world gov-

ernment, the New World Order. Reports of mysterious black helicopters over Montana, of foreign troops training in the Rockies, buzz
across the Internet unencumbered by such nuisances as confirmation.

Outside the realm of political rhetoric, this paranoia seems more sad   15
than frightening. When California State University sociologist James
William Gibson, Ph.D., author of *Warrior Dreams: Paramilitary Culture in
Post-Vietnam America,* enrolled in combat pistol training as part of his research, he learned "how warriors should go to the bathroom." Urinals
leave you vulnerable to rear attack, so the proper technique is to sit on
the toilet with the pistol between your legs, ready to fire on any who invade your stall.

Despite their pervasive fears, most militia members are psychologically healthy, Feldmann believes. But many "are on the fringes of mental
health." They're the ones he thinks most likely to commit violence.

Our Uzis, Our Selves

There's more to militias than weapons training and scampering
around in the woods in camouflage get-up. They also give members a
place to fit in. "For many members, the political belief that the group es-
pouses may be less important than the sense of belonging and identification from being a part of it," reports Feldmann. Of course, people also
get that sense of belonging from the Elks. But militia members may have
a particular need to find social acceptance.

"Militias seem to attract people who have trouble fitting in anywhere else," Feldmann says. In that regard they resemble leftist terrorist
groups of the 1970s, like the Symbionese Liberation Army. "Only a
handful of people in that group had any real commitment to the group's
cause. The rest were drawn by a sense of alienation and a need to find
people they could identify with."

The militias's emphasis on guns further feeds that sense of self. "The
act of violence can create a sense of vitality where that had been waning," notes Lifton. Wielding a powerful weapon instills a sense of purpose or invincibility, particularly for the economically or socially disenfranchised. That goes double for militia members who have achieved
notoriety. Shortwave radio guru "Mark from Michigan" works as a jani-
tor in a society that doesn't value manual labor. "His life as Militiaman
Mark is far more meaningful than cleaning up a dorm," notes Gibson.

The Post–Cold War Blues

The United States, notes Lifton, is going through a period of   20
"post–Cold War confusion." The collapse of the Soviet Union has left us
adrift. We may have won the Cold War, but we've lost a purpose. As a

result, Lifton says, "a sense of frustration and anger pervades the whole society."

It's no coincidence that this frustration is felt most deeply by the same socioeconomic group that has embraced militias: young to middle-aged white males in rural areas. "Worker bees in the movement tend to be much lower-educated than the general population," reports Alabama's Smith. And with jobs for unskilled workers drying up, they are unlikely to attain middle-class status—or have much of a stake in the status quo.

No wonder, then, that militias long for an earlier, more inno-cent America. But instead of waxing nostalgic about the 1950s, as did Reagan-era Republicans, militias look as far back as you can go: the Minutemen. Indeed, the very name of the Patriots—a broader move-ment that shares the militias's fears of a "suspended" constitution and a single world government—conjures images of Jefferson, Hamilton, and Washington. Some groups form self-sufficient communities that would resemble 18th-century villages were it not for modern amenities like computers. Danny Hashimoto, of the Boulder Patriots, even advocates the barter system, exchanging goods and services with others directly. (It also helps him avoid income taxes.)

Weapon Obsession

However concerned they may be about defending the Bill of Rights, militias aren't running through the woods waving copies of the Consti-tution.

"They want access to weapons," says Greg Moffat, Sheriff of Idaho's Madison County, "and I'm not talking about small arms: tanks, missiles, high explosives." Some groups acquire special equipment like night-vision goggles; the Florida State Militia is allegedly capable of defending themselves against chemical and biological warfare.

Extreme as it sounds, experts say it's just an extension of America's 25 love affair with guns. And it has less to do with our frontier past—after all, Canada was founded in a similar fashion—than with a cultural vac-uum. "The American obsession with guns and violence is a partial substi-tute for a traditional cultural base," Lifton says. If you're living in a re-mote region of Montana, visiting the local museum—or even checking out what's on cable—simply isn't an option. So why not shoot beer cans off a rock with a .22?

And throw in Rambo fantasies as well. The U.S. withdrawal from Vietnam was a crushing blow to men who equated American military might with their own masculine identity, says Gibson. Blaming defeat on bureaucrats and politicians, they rejected the John Wayne model of sol-diering in favor of a new American warrior: one who fights outside a corrupt political system. Thus was born the American paramilitary movement, laying the foundation for the militias who would adopt the anti-government rhetoric intact.

But while a fondness for firearms and warrior fantasies might be a prerequisite for militiahood, it's by no means sufficient. "I think a lot of people joined thinking, 'Let's grab rifles, go out in the trees, and play games,'" says Moffat. "Then they found out it's a bit more than that, that they'd have to support theories that they didn't want to support."

The Enemy Within

One reason so many of those theories involve Orwellian visions of government, says America's premier cult expert, Margaret Thaler Singer, Ph.D., is that for militia members, many of whom operate in remote regions, the Federal government lacks a human face. Since it's far away — in Washington, D.C., or in a large city elsewhere in the state — they see little evidence in their daily lives of the good that government does — or of the people who do it.

As a result of this psychic distance, "militias have dehumanized and demonized the government," notes Frank M. Ochberg, M.D., a psychiatrist who's served on the National Task Force on Terrorism. The implications are truly frightening. Several militia leaders claim that civil war is imminent. And turning brother against brother is far easier psychologically when you believe that "these people no longer belong to the same nation," says Ochberg. "It's rationalized as attacking an enemy — an enemy within."

Adding to the geographical distance between militia and government   30
is a striking information gap. Militias tend to shun mainstream media, relying instead on their own newsletters, radio broadcasts, pamphlets, and the Internet for news of political and world affairs. So they rarely tap into information or perspectives that might moderate their views. And the Internet's cloak of anonymity further allows extreme views to fester uncensured.

Racism

When the media reported ties between militias and white supremacists, militias in Michigan and elsewhere scurried to prove themselves equal-opportunity organizations. True, the movement is not entirely homogenous: Patriot radio personality Norm Resnick is a bespectacled Jew with a Ph.D. in psychology. (Resnick declined to talk with PT.) But in pointing frantically to one or two black or Jewish members, most militias succeed only in emphasizing how white and Christian the movement actually is.

Even so, only a minority of militia groups are explicitly racist. But their hatred is of a particularly virulent strain. Klan-watch researcher Tawanda Shaw says that 45 militias in 22 states have ties to white supremacists, including the neo-Nazi Aryan Nations. An even greater threat may be the Christian Identity movement, which believes that whites are God's chosen people and Jews are the children of Satan. Theology, more than politics, is central to these militias: many have resident pastors. But whereas religion may moderate the violent impulses of most Christians, the highly combustible mix of extreme religious, social, and political views makes Identity groups particularly dangerous.

The Future

So what should we do about the militia movement? Gibson says that it's crucial "not to demonize the demonizers." By expressing strong disapproval toward militia members, but not ostracizing them, we may be able to pull back toward the mainstream those who have one foot in the warrior world and the other in the world of job and family. The horror of the Oklahoma bombing may also bring some back: "Dead babies and social security clerks is not an image of heroic violence."

And if millennium fever and social upheaval are indeed major forces, the militia movement may lose steam once the new century begins — provided the government does not overreact in the interim. Most experts agree that given the militias's fears, cracking down or infiltrating them is the *worst* thing to do.

"If Congress makes militias illegal, if they pass more gun control   35
laws, we could see these groups grow more in size and scope," warns Smith. "It's important that the government not overreact. We need to prosecute terrorist incidents, but we don't need to expand the ATF so that it becomes the Bureau of Alcohol, Tobacco, Firearms, and Fertilizer."

Reading the Text

1. What limitation does Doskoch see in labeling militia members "terrorists" (para. 6)?
2. According to Doskoch, what connections have scholars drawn between the militia movement and Christian fundamentalism?
3. What is the New World Order conspiracy theory, according to militia ideology?
4. What, according to Doskoch, is the typical socioeconomic profile of a militia member?
5. What role do guns play in militia culture, in Doskoch's description?

Reading the Signs

1. Experts on militias suggest that "cracking down [on] or infiltrating them is the *worst* thing to do" (para. 34). In an essay, support, challenge, or modify this contention.
2. In class, discuss the extent to which the militia mentality contributes to school shootings such as the one at Colorado's Columbine High School in 1999. Then write your own argumentative essay on the appeal militias hold for some young people. To develop your ideas, consult Bernard Lefkowitz, "Don't Further Empower Cliques" (p. 653).
3. Research popular media coverage of militias, focusing perhaps on coverage of the Oklahoma City bombing in magazines such as *Newsweek*. Then write an analysis of the coverage. To what extent does the coverage condemn or glamorize the militia movement?
4. Read through a pro-gun magazine such as *Soldiers of Fortune* or *American Rifle,* studying both the articles and the advertising. Then write an essay in which you analyze the ideology implicit in the magazine. To what extent does the publication's ideology match that of the militia groups described by Doskoch?
5. In your journal, write a response to Charles Strozier's contention that militias are closely related to Christian fundamentalism.

EVELYNN HAMMONDS

Race, Sex, AIDS: The Construction of "Other"

Like all highly stigmatized diseases, AIDS turns the world into "us" and "them." "They"—those with AIDS—are perceived as different and alien by those who do not have it. In this essay, Evelynn Hammonds analyzes the role that difference plays in the AIDS epidemic, especially racial and sexual difference, and how those differences have contributed to the social marginalization of people with AIDS. Would AIDS have been neglected as long as it was if its first victims were Boy Scouts or any other group considered part of mainstream society? Or did the fact that the first people with AIDS hailed from the gay community and the black underclass contribute to a national policy of indifference? Hammonds, who writes on the intersection of science, medicine, and feminism, is currently associate professor of the history of science at Massachusetts Institute of Technology. She is the author of Childhood's Deadly Scourge: The Campaigns to Control Diphtheria in New York City, 1880–1930 *(1999) and coeditor of* Gender and Scientific Authority *(1996).*

In March of this year [1987] when Richard Goldstein's article, "AIDS and Race—the Hidden Epidemic" appeared in the *Village Voice,* the following statement in the lead paragraph jumped out at me: "a black woman is thirteen times more likely than a white woman to contract AIDS, says the Centers for Disease Control; a Hispanic woman is at eleven times the risk. Ninety-one percent of infants with AIDS are non-white." My first reaction was shock. I was stunned to discover the extent and rate of spread of AIDS in the black community, especially given the lack of public mobilization either inside or outside the community. My second reaction was anger. AIDS is a disease that for the time being signals a death notice. I am angry because too many people have died and are going to die of this disease. The gay male community over these last several years has been transformed and mobilized to halt transmission and gay men (at least white gay men) with AIDS have been able to live and die with some dignity and self-esteem. People of color need the opportunity to establish programs and interventions to provide education so that the spread of this disease in our communities can be halted, and to provide care so that people of color with AIDS will not live and die as pariahs.

My final reaction was despair. Of course I *knew* why information about AIDS and the black community had been buried—by both the black and white media. The white media, like the dominant power structure, have moved into their phase of "color-blindness" as a mark of progress. This ideology buries racism along with race. In the case of AIDS and race, the problem with "color-blindness" becomes clear. Race remains a reality in this society, including a reality about how perception is structured. On the one hand, race blindness means a failure to develop educational programs and materials that speak in the language of our communities and recognize the position of people of color in relation to the dominant institutions of society: medical, legal, etc. Additionally, we must ask why the vast disproportion of people of color in the AIDS statistics hasn't been seen as a remarkable fact or as worthy of comment. By their silence, the white media fail to challenge the age-old American myth of blacks as carriers of disease, especially sexually transmitted disease. This association has quietly become incorporated into the image of AIDS.

The black community's relative silence about AIDS is in part also a response to this historical association of blacks, disease, and deviance in American society. Revealing that AIDS is prevalent in the black community raises the spectre of blacks being associated with two kinds of deviance: sexually transmitted disease and homosexuality.

As I began to make connections between AIDS and race I slowly began to pull together pieces of information and images of AIDS that I had seen in the media. Immediately I began to think about the forty-year-long Tuskegee syphilis experiment on black men. I thought about the innuendoes in media reports about AIDS in Africa and Haiti that hinted at bizarre sexual practices among black people in those countries; I remembered how a black gay man had been portrayed as sexually irresponsible in a PBS documentary on AIDS; I thought about how little I had seen in the black press about AIDS and black gay men; I began to notice the thinly veiled hostility toward the increasing number of IV drug users with AIDS. Goldstein's article revealed dramatically the deafening silence about who was now actually contracting and dying from AIDS—gay/bisexual black and Hispanic men (now about 50% of black and Hispanic men with AIDS); many black and Hispanic IV drug users; black and Hispanic women, and black and Hispanic babies born to these women.

In this culture, how we think about disease determines who lives and who dies. The history of black people in this country is riddled with episodes displaying how concepts of sickness, disease, health, behavior and sexuality, and race have been entwined in the definition of normalcy and deviance. The power to define disease and normality makes AIDS a political issue.

The average black person on the street may not know the specifics of concepts of disease and race but our legacy as victims of this construction means that we know what it means to have a disease cast as the result of the immoral behavior of a group of people. Black people and other people of color notice, pay attention to what diseases are cast upon us and why. As the saying goes—"when white people get a cold, black people get pneumonia."

In this article I want to address the issues raised by the white media's silence on the connections between AIDS and race; the black media's silence on the connections between AIDS and sexuality/sexual politics, the failure of white gay men's AIDS organizations to reach the communities of people of color, and finally the implications for gay activists, progressives, and feminists.

It is very important to outline the historical context in which the AIDS epidemic occurs in regards to race. The dominant media portrayals of AIDS and scientists' assertions about its origins and modes of transmission have everything to do with the history of racial groups and sexually transmitted diseases.

The Social Construction of Disease

A standard feature of the vast majority of medical articles on the health of blacks was a sociomedical profile of a race whose members were rapidly becoming diseased, debilitated, and debauched and had only themselves to blame.[1]

---

1. James H. Jones, *Bad Blood: The Tuskegee Syphilis Experiment* (New York: Free Press, 1981), p. 21.

One of the first things that white southern doctors noted about blacks imported from Africa as slaves was that they seemed to respond differently than whites to certain diseases. Primarily they observed that some of the diseases that were epidemic in the South seemed to affect blacks less severely than whites—specifically, fevers (e.g., yellow fever). Since in the eighteenth and nineteenth centuries there was little agreement about the nature of various illnesses and the causes of many common diseases were unknown, physicians tended to attribute the differences they noted simply to race.

In the nineteenth century when challenges were made to the institution of slavery, white southern physicians were all too willing to provide medical evidence to justify slavery.

> They justified slavery and, after its abolition, second-class citizenship, by insisting that blacks were incapable of assuming any higher station in life. . . . Thus, medical discourses on the peculiarities of blacks offered, among other things, a pseudoscientific rationale for keeping blacks in their places.[2]

If, as these physicians maintained, blacks were less susceptible to fevers than whites, then it seemed fitting that they and not whites should provide most of the labor in the hot, swampy lowlands where southern agriculture was centered. Southern physicians marshalled other "scientific" evidence, such as measurement of brain sizes and other body organs to prove that blacks constituted an inferior race. For many whites these arguments were persuasive because "objective" science offered validity to their personal "observations," prejudices, and fears.

The history of sexually transmitted diseases, in particular syphilis, indicates the pervasiveness of racial/sexual stereotyping. The history of syphilis in America is complex, as Allan Brandt discloses in his book *No Magic Bullet*. According to Brandt, "venereal disease has historically been assumed to be the disease of the 'other.'" Obviously the complicated interaction of sexuality and disease has deep implications for the current portrayal of AIDS.

Like AIDS, the prevailing nineteenth century view of syphilis was characterized early on in moral terms—and when it became apparent that a high rate of syphilis occurred among blacks in the South, the morality issue heightened considerably. Diseases that are acquired through immoral behavior were considered in many parts of the culture as punishment from God, the wages of sin. Anyone with such a disease was stigmatized. A white person could avoid this sin by a change in behavior. But for blacks it was different. It was noted that one of the primary differences that separated the races was that blacks were more flagrant and loose in their sexual behavior—behaviors they could not control.

---

2. Ibid., p. 17.

Moreover, personal restraints on self-indulgence did not exist, physicians insisted, because the smaller brain of the Negro had failed to develop a center for inhibiting sexual behavior.[3]

Therefore blacks deserved to have syphilis, since they couldn't control their behavior ... the Tuskegee experiment carried that logic to [the] extreme—blacks also deserved to die from syphilis.

[B]lacks suffered from venereal diseases because they would not, or could not, refrain from sexual promiscuity. Social hygiene for whites rested on the assumption that attitudinal changes could produce behavioral changes. A single standard of high moral behavior could be produced by molding sexual attitudes through moral education. For blacks, however, a change in their very *nature* seemed to be required.[4]

If in the above quotation, you change blacks to homosexuals and whites to heterosexuals then the parallel to the media portrayal of people with AIDS is obvious.

The black community's response to the historical construction of sexually transmitted diseases as the result of bad, inherently uncontrollable behavior of blacks—is sexual conservatism. To avoid the stigma of being cast with diseases of the "other," the black media, as well as other institutions in the community, avoid public discussion of sexual behavior and other "deviant" behavior like drug use. The white media on the other hand is often quick to cast blacks and people of color as "other" either overtly or covertly.

Black Community Response to AIDS

Of 38,435 diagnosed cases of AIDS as of July 20, 1987, black and Hispanic people make up 39% of all cases even though they account for only 17 percent of the adult population.[5] Eighty percent of the pediatric cases are black and Hispanic. The average life expectancy after diagnosis of a white person with AIDS in the United States is two years; of a person of color, nineteen weeks.[6]

The leading magazines in the black community, *Ebony* and *Essence,* carried no articles on AIDS until the spring of this year. The journal of the National Medical Association, the professional organization of black physicians, carried a short guest editorial article in late 1986 and to date

3. Ibid., p. 23.

4. Ibid., p. 48.

5. "High AIDS Rate Spurring Efforts for Minorities," *New York Times,* Sunday, August 2, 1987.

6. *Mother Jones,* Vol. 12, May 1987.

has not published any extensive article on AIDS. The official magazines of the NAACP and the National Urban League make no mention of AIDS throughout 1986 nor to date this year. Only the Atlanta-based SCLC (Southern Christian Leadership Conference) has established an ongoing educational program to address AIDS in the black community.

When I examined the few articles that have been written about AIDS in the national black press, several themes emerged. Almost all the articles I saw tried to indicate that the black people are at risk while simultaneously trying to avoid any implication that AIDS is a "black" disease. The black media has underemphasized, though recognized, that there are significant socioeconomic cofactors in terms of the impact of AIDS in the black community. The high rate of drug use and abuse in the black community is in part a result of many other social factors—high unemployment, poor schools, inadequate housing, and limited access to health care, all factors in the spread of AIDS. These affect specifically the fact that people of color with AIDS are diagnosed at more advanced stages of the disease and are dying faster. The national black media have so far also failed to deal with any larger public policy issue that the AIDS crisis will precipitate for the community; and most importantly homosexuality and bisexuality were dealt with in a very conservative and problematic fashion.

Testing

In terms of testing *Ebony* encourages more opportunity for people to be tested anonymously; *Essence* recommends testing for women thinking of getting pregnant. Both articles mention that exposure of test results could result in discrimination in housing and employment but neither publication discusses the issue at any length. There is no mention of testing that is going on in the military and how those results are being used nor is there mention of testing in prison. It is clear from the sketchy discussion of testing that the political issues around testing are not being faced.

Sexuality

The most disappointing aspect of these articles is that by focusing on individual behavior as the cause of AIDS and by setting up bisexuals, homosexuals, and drug users as "other" in the black community, and as "bad," the national black media falls into the trap of reproducing exactly how white society has defined the issue. But unlike the situation for whites, what happens to these groups within the black community will affect the community as a whole. Repressive practices around AIDS in prisons will affect all black men in prison with or without AIDS and their families outside and any other black person facing the criminal justice system; the identification of significant numbers of people of color in the military with AIDS will affect all people of color in the military. Quarantine, suspension of civil liberties for drug users in the black community with AIDS, will affect everyone in the community. Health care and housing access will be restricted for all of us. If people with AIDS are set off as "bad" or "other," no change in individual behavior in relation to them will save any of us. There can be no "us" or "them" in our communities.

The *Ebony* article entitled "The Truth about AIDS: Dread Disease Is   20 Spreading Rapidly through Heterosexual Population," while highlighting the increase of AIDS among heterosexuals in the black community, makes several comments about black homosexuals. The author notes that there is generally a negative attitude toward homosexuals in the community and quotes several physicians who emphasize that the reticence on this issue is a hindrance to AIDS education efforts in the community. It does not emphasize that, because of this "reticence," only now as AIDS is being recognized as striking heterosexuals, is it beginning to be talked about in the black community.

> One of the greatest problems in the black community, other than ignorance about the disease, is the large number of black men who engage in sex acts with other men but who don't consider themselves homosexuals.[7]

The point is then that since AIDS was initially characterized as a "gay disease" and many black men don't consider themselves gay in spite of their sexual practices, the black community did not acknowledge the presence of AIDS.

The association of AIDS with "bad" behavior is prominent in this article. Homosexuals and drug users are described as a "physiologically and economically depressed subgroup of the black community."[8]

The message is that to deal with this disease the individual behavior of a deviant subgroup must be changed. Additionally, the recommendation to heterosexuals is to "not have sex" with bisexuals and drug users. There are no recommendations about how the community can find a way to deal with the silence around the issues of homosexuality/bisexuality, sexual practices in general, and drug use. The article fails to say what the implications of the sexual practices of black men are for the community.

The *Essence* article, entitled "Nobody's Safe," avoids the issue as

---

7. *Ebony*, April 1987, p. 128, quoting a Los Angeles AIDS expert.
8. Ibid., p. 130.

well.[9] The authors describe a scenario of a thirty-eight-year-old middle-class professional woman who is suddenly found to have AIDS. Her husband had died two years earlier due to a rare form of pneumonia. After testing positive for AIDS she is told by one of her husband's relatives that he had been bisexual. The text following this scenario goes on to describe how most women contract AIDS; it gives a general sketch of the origins of the disease and discusses the latency period and defines asymptomatic carriers of the virus. There is no mention of bisexuality or homosexuality. The implication is again—just don't have sex with those people if you want to avoid AIDS. It avoids discussion of the prevalence of bisexuality among black men, and consequently the way that AIDS will ultimately change sexual relationships in the black community.

The Mainstream (White) Press

In general the mainstream media have been silent on the rise of AIDS in the black and Hispanic communities. Until very recently, with the exception of a few special reports, such as a quite excellent one on the PBS *MacNeil-Lehrer Report,* most media reports on AIDS continue to speak of the disease without mention of its effects on people of color. In recent months specific attention has been paid to the "new" phenomenon of heterosexuals with AIDS or "heterosexual AIDS." This terminology is used without the slightest mention that among Haitians and extensively in Africa, AIDS was never a disease confined to homosexuals.

The assumption in reports about the spread of AIDS to heterosexuals   25 is that these heterosexuals are white—read that as white, middle-class, non-drug-using, sexually active people. The facts are that there are very few cases of AIDS among this group. As many as 90 percent of the cases of AIDS among heterosexuals are black and Hispanic. In many media reports blacks and Hispanics with AIDS are lumped in the IV drug users group. What the media has picked up on is that heterosexual transmission in the United States now endangers middle-class whites.

A good example of the mainstream media approach is an article by Kate Leishman in the February 1987 issue of *Atlantic Monthly.* She writes that most Americans, even liberals, have the attitude that AIDS is the result of immoral behavior. Leishman lists the statistics on heterosexual transmission of AIDS at the beginning of her article. Fifteen pages later the following information appears:

> In the case of sexually active gay men [AIDS] is a tragedy—as it is for poor black and Hispanic youths, among whom there is a nationwide epidemic of venereal disease, which is a certain cofactor in

---

9. *Essence,* June 1987.

facilitating transmission of HIV. This combination with the pervasive use of drugs among blacks and Hispanics ensures that the epidemic will hit them hardest next.[10]

Her first explicit mention of people of color describes them as a group that uses drugs extensively, and as also riddled with venereal disease (a fact she does not support with any data). The image is one of the "unregenerate young street tough" that causes all the trouble in our cities, in short the conventional racist stereotype of black and Hispanic youth displayed in the press almost every day. Her use of the word "tragedy" because of the risk to blacks, Hispanics, and gays is gratuitous at best. The main focus of the article is the risk of AIDS to white heterosexuals and the need for them to face their fears of AIDS so they can effectively change their behavior.

In a passage reminiscent of nineteenth-century physicians' moral advice she notes the problems associated with changing people's behavior and promoting safe sex, and wonders if one can draw any lessons for heterosexual behavior from the gay male experience.

> Many people believe that the intensity or quality of homosexual drives is unique, while others argue that the ability to control sexual impulses varies extraordinarily within groups of any sexual preference.[11]

What I find striking in this passage is that there is still debate over whether certain "groups" of people have the same ability to exercise control over their sexual behavior and drives as "normal" white heterosexuals do. The passage also suggests that white heterosexuals are still the only group who have the strength, the moral fortitude, the inherent ability if educated, to control their sexual and other behavior. After all, this is a disease about behavior and not viruses, right? Leishman doesn't interview any blacks or Hispanics about their fears of AIDS, or how they want to deal with it with respect to sexual practice or other behavior.

Two months later in May several letters to the editors of *Atlantic Monthly* appeared in response to Leishman's article. In particular one reader observed her omission of statistics about the risk of AIDS to blacks and Hispanics. She responded in a fairly defensive manner:

> My article and many others have commented on the high risk of exposure to AIDS among blacks and Hispanics. Mr. Patrick's observations that blacks and Hispanics already account for ninety percent of the case load seems oddly to suggest that AIDS is on its way to becoming a disease of minorities. But the Centers for Disease Control has stressed that the overrepresentation of blacks and Hispanics in

---

10. *Atlantic Monthly,* February 1987, p. 54.
11. Ibid., p. 40.

AIDS statistics is related not to race per se but to underlying risk factors.[12]

The risk factor she mentions is intravenous drug use. Leishman fails to deal with the "overrepresentation" of blacks and Hispanics in AIDS statistics. To mention our higher risk only implies that AIDS is a disease of minorities if you believe minorities are inherently different or behave differently in the face of the disease or if you believe that the disease will be confined to the minority community.

So pervasive is the association of race and IV drug use that the fact that a majority of black and Hispanic men who have AIDS are gay or bisexual, and *non*-IV drug users, has remained buried in statistics.[13] In the face of the statistics, the *New York Times* continues to identify IV drug use as the distinguishing mode of transmission among black and Hispanic men, by focusing not on the percentage of black and Hispanic AIDS cases that are drug related, but on the percentage of drug-related AIDS cases that are black or Hispanic, which is 94%. This framework, besides blocking information that the black and Hispanic communities need, also functions to keep the white community's image "clean."

30

Conclusion

As this article goes to press, media coverage of the extent of AIDS in the black and Hispanic communities is increasing daily. These latest articles are covering the efforts in the black and Hispanic communities both to raise consciousness in these communities with respect to AIDS and to increase government funding to support culturally specific educational programs. Within the black community, the traditional source of leadership, black ministers, are now publicly expressing the reasons for their previous reluctance to speak out about AIDS. The reasons expressed tend to fall into the areas I have tried to discuss in this article, as indicated by the following comments that recently appeared in the *Boston Globe:*

> Although some black ministers described gays as the children of God and AIDS as just another virus, many more talked about homosexuality as sinful, including some who referred to AIDS as a God-sent plague to punish the sexually deviant.[14]

> There's a lot of fear of stigmatization when you stand up. . . . How does this label your church or the people who go to your church? said Rev. Bruce Wall, assistant pastor of Twelfth Baptist Church in Roxbury. Rev. Wall said ministers may also fear that an

---

12. *Atlantic Monthly,* May 1987, p. 13.
13. *New York Times,* Sunday, August 2, 1987.
14. *Boston Globe,* Sunday, August 9, 1987, p. 1.

activist role on AIDS could prompt another question: "Maybe that pastor is gay."[15]

The arguments I have made as to the background of these kinds of comments continue to come out in the public discourse on AIDS and race in the national media. As the public discussion and press coverage have increased, one shift is apparent. The media is now focusing on why the black and Hispanic communities have not responded to AIDS before as a "problem" specific to these communities, while there is no acknowledgment that part of the problem is the way the media, the CDC, and the Public Health Service prevented race-specific information about AIDS from being widely disseminated. Or, to say it differently, there is no recognition of how the medical and media construction of AIDS as a "gay disease" or a disease of Haitians has affected the black and Hispanic communities.

Finally, as the black and Hispanic communities mobilize against AIDS, coalitions with established gay groups will be critical. To date, some in the black community have noted the lack of culturally specific educational material produced by these groups. Some gay groups are responding to that criticism. For progressives, feminists and gay activists, the AIDS crisis represents a crucial time when the work we have done on sexuality and sexual politics will be most needed to frame the fight against AIDS in political terms that move the politics of sexuality out of the background and challenge the repressive policies and morality that threaten not only the people with this disease but all of us.

Reading the Text

1. Why does Hammonds consider the ideology of "color-blindness" (para. 2) in the media to be a problem?
2. Why, according to Hammonds, has the black community remained silent about the AIDS epidemic?
3. What relationship does Hammonds see between syphilis and other sexually transmitted diseases and the stereotyping of blacks?
4. What is Hammonds's explanation for the relative lack of media coverage of the AIDS epidemic in the black and Hispanic communities?

Reading the Signs

1. Compare and contrast the coverage of AIDS in the black press and in the white, or mainstream, press. To develop your essay, both refer to

---

15. Ibid., p. 12.

Hammonds's evidence, and generate your own by analyzing current coverage of AIDS in popular magazines.

2. Go to the library, research the Tuskegee syphilis experiment that Hammonds describes, and then write an essay in which you explore her claim that "'objective' science" (para. 11) has been used to support racist stereotypes.

3. Compare and contrast Evelynn Hammonds's understanding of the social forces that make one an "other" with that of Melissa Algranati in "Being an Other" (p. 570). How can you account for differences that you observe?

4. Write an essay in which you defend, refute, or modify the contention that the mass media play a major role in defining what counts as "mainstream" or as "other" in our culture. To develop your ideas, consult any of the selections in this chapter and Michael Omi, "In Living Color: Race and American Culture" (p. 526).

GIGI ANDERS AND THE EDITORS OF *DEAF LIFE*

Beauty and the Battle

‖‖‖‖‖‖‖‖‖‖‖‖‖‖‖‖‖‖‖‖‖‖‖‖‖‖‖‖‖‖‖‖‖‖‖‖‖

Among the most invisible communities on the American margins is the community of the deaf—those people who, though coming from every race, religion, ethnicity, gender, and age group, share a silent secret and a culture unknown to most hearing Americans. That culture is contained, and conveyed, in a language that the deaf themselves have developed over many years, a language whose American variant is called ASL (American Sign Language). ASL is not simply English cast into signs: it is an independent language with its own cultural tradition. So when in 1994 Heather Whitestone became the first deaf woman to be crowned Miss America, deaf Americans were faced with a dilemma because Whitestone does not know ASL and communicates instead in spoken English. Could such a person really be a true representative of the deaf? In the following article, the editorial staff at Deaf Life, in a revision of an article by Gigi Anders, pursues that question.

When Heather Whitestone was crowned Miss America on September 17, 1994, waves of surprise, delight, and other less enthusiastic reactions reverberated through the Deaf community.

She got front-page coverage—and plenty of it. As reporters noted, even those who sneer at beauty pageants were moved by Whitestone. There was something irresistible about the story of a young woman, profoundly deafened in infancy, taking the coveted prize—the Miss America title, scholarship, prestige, glamour, glitz, and accompanying perks.

Not that she's had a tranquil time of it.

Whitestone broke the "disability barrier." But could ASL-Deaf people claim her as "one of their own"? No.

After she'd begun her year-long "tour of service," Deaf advocates   5
were trying to explain to the media why she didn't, and couldn't, represent the Deaf community. (Can *any* deaf person justly do that?) Deaf people expressed concern that her atypical success as an oralist might prejudice parents against allowing their deaf children to learn sign and go to a residential-school, and learning to sign themselves. It didn't help that statements were attributed to her (particularly that notorious remark about sign language limiting one's dreams) that she denies having made.

An essential ingredient of Whitestone's success story is the choice her mother made—a choice that many Deaf people disapprove of. Articles like the one by Kathy Kemp of Scripps Howard News Service in the *Journal* (Washington, D.C.) described how Daphne Gray, a tough-minded math teacher, tried and rejected signing in favor of a strict oral/aural approach because she wanted Heather to be "a part of the hearing world"—and provoked angry reactions:

> Tests revealed that Heather was profoundly deaf. Doctors told her parents to teach her sign language and not to expect much for the little girl's future.
>
> "They said it's typical for a lot of hearing-impaired kids to end up with a third- to sixth-grade education, because academically, they tend to have some problems," Gray says.
>
> Not knowing what else to do, she bought a sign-language book, and Heather began lessons. "But it just didn't feel right," the mother recalls.
>
> Heather, who had been trying to speak, stopped using her voice when the signing lessons began. Alarmed, Gray consulted a Florida specialist, who suggested she explore all of Heather's options before deciding what to do.
>
> Gray learned of the Doreen Pollack Acoupedics Center at Denver's Porter Memorial Hospital. She visited and was impressed with the youngsters who, though deaf, had learned to speak and read lips and were living seemingly normal lives. In acoupedics, students do not learn or use sign language.
>
> So Gray, along with Heather's speech therapist, enrolled at the center, where they learned how to teach Heather. Back home, they began working with the little girl, who became increasingly proficient at lipreading and speaking. As part of her therapy, she began ballet lessons, which helped her learn to recognize faint sounds and pitch.
>
> At age 11, Heather began three years of study at the Central Institute for the Deaf in St. Louis, which focuses on preparing hearing-impaired children to function in the mainstream.

Certain details of Heather's story are distressingly familiar. Too many doctors—i.e., the ones who break the news to anxious parents that their child is deaf—not only have criminally negative, stereotypical ideas about deaf people, but succeed in convincing parents not to set their goals too high.

Unanswered questions: why didn't Ms. Gray send Heather to the Alabama School for the Deaf and Blind in Talladega? Surely she visited it? If so, why wasn't she as "impressed" as she was by the Pollack Center? Was there something "alien" about the sight of kids using ASL? Was it a question of comparatively lower academic standards? But if she didn't approve of ASDB, why not a local public-school program for deaf children? Why go through all that?

As for her tentative use and rejection of sign language, we note that it is a very bad idea to learn and teach signing skills from a book. Of course "it just didn't feel right." It wasn't natural to her, because she had no background in it. Signing is best learned through exposure and practice. Immersion is best. Deaf children in residential schools pick it up from other deaf children immediately and quickly become fluent. They don't learn it from a book. The acquisition of sign language need not interfere with developing good speech skills, and can even enhance them. Native-ASL users often develop superior speech skills to those in strict oral/aural programs, whether or not they choose to rely on them. The point is to get access to language, to communication, as early as possible.

Too many hearing parents of deaf children make little or no attempt to communicate with them. This creates a debilitating language gap— and this, we maintain, is the cause of deaf students' failing to achieve a level of English skills equal to that of their hearing peers. It is the language gap, and not sign language as such, that causes "academic problems." Had Ms. Gray treated Heather as far too many other parents treat *their* deaf children, we wouldn't be reading about her today.   10

Possibly it was her determination to work with Heather (more than the actual method used) that tipped the balance. We will never know.

Whitestone has said publicly that she supports her mother's choice, and appreciates her fight to get the best possible education for her. The two have always been close—a bond that is often lacking between hearing mothers and deaf daughters.

Other basic details of Whitestone's story are familiar, too, and moving—the academic struggle ("having to work twice as hard as the others"), the fight to get interpreters, how she began entering the pageants to raise needed scholarship money.

She's told her audiences how she lost her first beauty pageant (Miss St. Clair, Alabama) because she bungled the interview. The officials asked her questions that she couldn't understand, and she was too embarrassed to ask them to please repeat so she could understand. "Instead, she guessed at what they were saying, answered questions incorrectly, and blew her shot at the crown."

"Know your problems, but don't let them master you," she said at 15
the University of New Hampshire. "I thought I didn't win Miss St. Clair
because of my deafness," she said in Florida. "But my family watched the
videotape of that interview and said I didn't win because I didn't master
the situation."[1] At the next pageant—Miss Jacksonville State University—she was upfront about being deaf. She asked the judges to speak
slowly. They accommodated her, and she won the title.

Needless to say, Whitestone has been asked the same questions over
and over again. All this is very tiring. She quickly learned that to take a
stance that pleases one faction is automatically to alienate the other fac-
tions. Her terse answers to our interview questions indicate this weariness—burnout, even.

When a member of an ethnic minority rises to the top of her profession, the rest of the community is supposed to cheer. "This represents a
victory for all of us," they say. When an oral-deaf person achieves
renown, Deaf people are concerned; some of us even feel threatened.
But there's another factor involved: crab theory. Deaf people resent it
when another deaf person achieves unusual success, especially in a nontraditional field. It matters little whether this deaf person signs or speaks.
S/he *must* be pulled down. The very fact of success condemns her (or
him) to becoming a target for all sorts of abuse: malicious gossip, back-
stabbing, slander, falsehoods. And worse. So far, Whitestone has managed
to cope. But there are indications that it's gotten to be a bit much.

While we're worried about the bonanza of free publicity for oralists,
we're likewise concerned about the hostile feelings Whitestone has unwittingly aroused in the Deaf community, and what this could mean to
other deaf women who might also like to compete for the crown.
Whitestone is not the first deaf competitor, or even the first one to
achieve finalist status. But will crab theory make it harder for those who
follow? We're pretty sure that Whitestone will survive the criticism, the
controversy, and the burnout. But will others be scared off?

Reading the Text

1. Why did some members of the Deaf community feel betrayed by Heather
   Whitestone when she was selected as Miss America in 1994?
2. What is the difference between oral/aural instruction for the deaf and
   American Sign Language?
3. Why did Heather Whitestone's mother choose oral/aural education, and
   not American Sign Language, for her daughter?
4. Describe in your own words the term "crab theory" (para. 17).

---

1. Karen Kaplan, "Kids Urged to Battle Obstacles: Try to Be Positive, Miss
America Says," *The Herald* (Broward edition of *The Miami Herald*), December 3, 1994.

Reading the Signs

1. In class, form teams and debate whether Heather Whitestone owed it to the Deaf community to learn or support ASL.
2. As the selection notes, successful members of minority groups—social "others"—frequently find themselves held as representatives of their group. Write an essay in which you offer your explanation for this common pattern.
3. The selection outlines the ways in which Heather Whitestone became an "other" within the Deaf community. Research other disabilities or illnesses, and write an essay in which you examine the conflicting attitudes that may divide the group into insiders or outsiders. You may wish to consult Evelynn Hammonds, "Race, Sex, AIDS: The Construction of 'Other'" (p. 625).
4. In an essay, reflect on the reasons behind "crab theory" (para. 17) in any minority group. To develop your evidence, you might interview members of a minority group and ask them about their experiences with intragroup criticism. To what extent does the mass media play a role in encouraging crab theory?
5. Research the history of ASL, and write an essay in which you chart changing attitudes toward deafness as a disability.

KEVIN JENNINGS

American Dreams

||||||||||||||||||||||||||||||||||||||||||||||||||||

When Ellen DeGeneres became the first television star to come out of the closet on prime-time TV, gay men and lesbians around the country celebrated what appeared to be a major step forward for America's most marginalized community. But the firestorm of protest that also attended Ellen's coming out equally demonstrated just how far homosexuals have to go before winning full acceptance into American society. In this personal narrative of what it means to grow up gay in America, Kevin Jennings (b. 1963) reveals the torment endured by a child forced to conceal his difference from everyone around him, especially his own parents. With years of self-denial and one suicide attempt behind him, Jennings shows how he eventually came to accept himself as he was and in so doing achieved his own version of the American dream.

When I was little, I honestly thought I would grow up to be the President. After all, I lived in a land of opportunity where anyone, with enough determination and hard work, could aspire to the highest office in the land. I planned to live out the American Dream.

I realized, however, that something was amiss from an early age. I grew up in the rural community of Lewisville, North Carolina, just outside the city of Winston-Salem. As you might guess from the city's name, Winston-Salem, Winston-Salem makes its living from the tobacco industry: it was cigarettes that propelled local conglomerate RJR-Nabisco to its status as one of the world's largest multinational corporations. Somehow this rising tide of prosperity never lapped at our doors, and the Jennings family was a bitter family indeed. Poor whites descended from Confederate veterans, we eagerly sought out scapegoats for our inexplicable failure to "make it" in the land of opportunity. My uncles and cousins joined the Ku Klux Klan, while my father, a fundamentalist minister, used religion to excuse his prejudices—against blacks, against Jews, against Catholics, against Yankees, against Communists and liberals (basically the same thing, as far as he was concerned), and, of course, against gays. Somehow the golden rule of "Do unto others as you would have them do unto you" never made it into his gospel. Instead, I remember church services filled with outbursts of paranoia, as we were warned about the evils of those whom we (incorrectly) held responsible for our very real oppression. I grew up believing that there was a Communist plot undermining our nation, a Jewish conspiracy controlling the banks and the media, and that black men—whom I unselfconsciously referred to as "niggers"—spent their days plotting to rape white women. In case this seems like a history lesson on the Stone Age, please consider that I was born in 1963 and graduated from high school in 1981. Hardly the ancient past!

My father's profession as a traveling minister never left much money for luxuries like college tuition. Nevertheless, my mother was determined that I, her last chance, was going to make good on the Dream that had been denied to her and to my four older siblings. Not that it was going to be easy: my father died when I was eight, and my mother went to work at McDonald's (the only job she could get with her limited credentials). Every penny was watched carefully; dinner was often leftover Quarter-pounders that she didn't have to pay for. I'm the only person I know who sees the Golden Arches, takes a bite, and thinks, "Mmm, just like Mom used to make!"

Throughout high school, I was determined to make it, determined to show my mother—and myself—that the American Dream really could come true. I worked hard and got ahead, earning a scholarship to Harvard after I had remade myself into the image of what I was told a successful person was like. Little did I realize at that point the price I was paying to fit in.

The first thing to go was any sign of my Southern heritage. As I came into contact with mainstream America, through high school "gifted and talented" programs and, later, at college in Massachusetts, I began to realize that we Southerners were different. Our home-cooked meals—grits, turnip greens, red-eye gravy—never seemed to show up in frozen dinners, and if a character on television spoke with a Southern accent, that immediately identified him or her as stupid or as comic relief. As the lesbian writer Blanche Boyd put it:

> When television programs appeared, a dreadful truth came clear to me: Southerners were not normal people. We did not sound like normal people . . . [and] what we chose to talk about seemed peculiarly different also. I began to realize we were hicks. Television took away my faith in my surroundings. I didn't want to be a hick. I decided to go North, where people talked fast, walked fast, and acted cool. I practiced talking like the people on television. . . . I became desperate to leave the South.

Like Blanche Boyd, I deliberately erased my accent and aped the false monotone of television newscasters. I never invited college friends home to North Carolina for fear they might meet my family and realize they were worthless, ignorant hicks—which is how I'd come to view those whom I loved. I applied to colleges on the sole criterion that they not be in the South. I ran as far from Lewisville, North Carolina, as I could.

But there were some things about myself I could not escape from or change, no matter how hard I tried—among them the fact that I am gay.

I had always known I was gay, even before I had heard the word or knew what it meant. I remember that at age six or seven, the "adult" magazines that so fascinated my older brothers simply didn't interest me at all, and I somehow knew that I'd better hide this feeling from them. As I grew older and began to understand what my feelings meant, I recoiled in horror from myself. After all, my religious upbringing as a Southern Baptist had taught me that gay people were twisted perverts destined for a lifetime of eternal damnation.

Being as set as I was on achieving the American Dream, I was not about to accept the fact that I was gay. Here is where I paid the heaviest price for my Dream. I pursued what I thought was "normal" with a vengeance in high school, determined that, if the spirit was weak, the flesh would be more willing at the prospect of heterosexuality. I dated every girl I could literally get my hands on, earning a well-deserved reputation as a jerk who tried to see how far he could get on the first date. I attacked anyone who suggested that gay people might be entitled to some rights, too, and was the biggest teller of fag jokes at Radford High. But what I really hated was myself, and this I couldn't escape from, no matter how drunk or stoned I got, which I was doing on an almost daily basis by senior year.

That was also the year I fell in love for the first time, with another boy in my class. It turned out he was gay, too, and we made love one night in late May. I woke up the next morning and realized that it was true—I really was a fag after all. I spent that day trying to figure out how I was going to live the American Dream, which seemed impossible if I was homosexual. By nightfall I decided it *was* impossible, and without my Dream I couldn't see a reason why I'd want to be alive at all. I went to my family's medicine cabinet, took the new bottle of aspirin out, and proceeded to wash down 140 pills with a glass of gin. I remember the exact number—140—because I figured I could only get down about ten at one swallow, so I carefully counted out fourteen little stacks before I began. Thanks to a friend who got to me in time, I didn't die that night. My story has a happy ending—but a lot of them don't. Those moments of desperation helped me understand why one out of every three gay teens tries to commit suicide.

At Harvard, the most important lessons I learned had little to do with   10
Latin American or European history, which were my majors. Instead, I learned the importance of taking control of my own destiny. I met a great professor who taught me that as long as I stayed in the closet, I was accepting the idea that there was something wrong with me, something that I needed to hide. After all, as my favorite bisexual, Eleanor Roosevelt, once said, "No one can make you feel inferior without your consent." By staying closeted, I was consenting to my own inferiority. I realized that for years, I had let a Dream—a beautiful, seductive, but ultimately false Dream—rule my life. I had agreed to pay its price, which was the rejection of my family, my culture, and eventually myself. I came to understand that the costs of the Dream far outweighed its rewards. I learned that true freedom would be mine only when I was able to make my own decisions about what I wanted out of life instead of accepting those thrust upon me by the Dream. Since I made that realization, I have followed my own path instead of the one I had been taught was "right" all my life.

Once I started down this new path, I began to make some discoveries about the society in which I was raised, and about its notions of right and wrong. I began to ask many questions, and the answers to these questions were not always pleasant. Why, for example, did my mother always earn less than men who did the same exact work? Why did I learn as a child that to cheat someone was to "Jew" them? Why was my brother ostracized when he fell in love with and later married a black woman? Why did everyone in my family work so hard and yet have so little? I realized that these inequalities were part of the game, the rules of which were such that gays, blacks, poor people, women, and many others would always lose to the wealthy white heterosexual Christian men who have won the Presidency forty-two out of forty-two times. Those odds—100 percent—are pretty good ones to bet on. No, I discovered that true freedom could not be achieved by a Dream that calls on us to give up who we are in order to fit in and become "worthy" of power.

Holding power means little if women have to become masculine "iron ladies" to get it, if Jews have to "Americanize" their names, if blacks have to learn to speak so-called Standard English (though we never acknowledge *whose* standard it is), or if gays and lesbians have to hide what everyone else gets to celebrate — the loves of their lives.

Real freedom will be ours when the people around us — and when we ourselves — accept that we, too, are "real" Americans, and that we shouldn't have to change to meet anyone else's standards. In 1924, at age twenty-two, the gay African-American poet Langston Hughes said it best, in his poem "I, Too":

> Tomorrow,
> I'll be at the table
> When company comes.
> Nobody'll dare
> Say to me,
> "Eat in the kitchen,"
> Then.
>
> Besides,
> They'll see how beautiful I am
> And be ashamed —
>
> I, too, am America.

By coming out as a gay man and demanding my freedom, I realize that I have done the most American thing of all. And while I have come a long way since the days when I dreamed of living in the White House, I have discovered that what I'm fighting for now is the very thing I thought I'd be fighting for if I ever became President — "liberty and justice for all."

Reading the Text

1. According to Jennings, how did his Southern upbringing influence his goals for the future?
2. Why did Jennings feel he had to eschew his Southern heritage?
3. In what ways did Jennings deny to himself his sexual orientation, and why did he do so?
4. In your own words, trace the evolution of Jennings's understanding of the American dream as he grew up.
5. What is the relationship between the excerpt from Langston Hughes's "I, Too" and Jennings's story?

Reading the Signs

1. In your journal, write your own account of how you responded to social and cultural expectations as a high school student. To what extent did you

feel pressure to conform or to renounce those expectations—or to do both?

2. Jennings describes his early attempts to deny his sexual orientation. In class, discuss how other minority or underprivileged groups—ethnic minorities, women, the disabled—sometimes try to erase their own identity. What social and cultural forces motivate such self-denial? Use the discussion as the basis for an essay in which you explore why one might be motivated to treat oneself as an "other."

3. Write an essay supporting, modifying, or challenging Jennings's assertion that "the costs of the [American] Dream far outweighed its rewards" (para. 10).

4. Jennings explains how a geographical region, the South, can be seen as "other." Write an essay explaining which regions most members of your own community would consider "other" or different. To develop your ideas, consult Lucy R. Lippard, "Alternating Currents" (p. 778) or Camilo José Vergara, "The Ghetto Cityscape" (p. 784).

5. Compare and contrast Jennings's arrival at a confident sense of identity with that of Melissa Algranati ("Being an Other," p. 570). How do you explain any differences you observe?

ANDREW CALCUTT

The End of Adulthood?

||||||||||||||||||||||||||||||||||||||||||||||||||||||||||||||||||||

Though the point is rarely raised explicitly, Americans today seem obsessed with victimage: everyone seems to want to claim victim status, from the guests on Oprah *to the men who believe they are the victims of feminism and join the Promise Keepers in response. Andrew Calcutt, for his part, thinks that things have gone far enough, and in this excerpt from* Arrested Development: Pop Culture and the Erosion of Adulthood *(1998), he charts the development of "victim culture" and offers his own diagnosis: we are becoming a culture of children in retreat from adulthood. And his provocative solution? Grow up. Andrew Calcutt is a writer and journalist whose books include* White Noise: An A–Z of the Contradictions in Cyberculture *(1999) and* Beat: The Iconography of Victimhood from the Beat Generation to Princess Diana *(1998).*

A new political order has emerged in which the victim is supreme, and adults are treated more like children. Meanwhile, many adults are more likely to think of themselves as victims, or to identify with the motif of the authentic, innocent child. The result is a convergence between on the one hand the spontaneous development of a cultural personality which is victimized and childlike, and on the other hand the remoulding of the individual's relationship to the state in accordance with his supposed immaturity. The convergence of these trends is facilitated by the already existing non–adult language provided by the counterculture and the pop culture which succeeded it.

The key question in such circumstances is whether adulthood will go into abeyance; or whether the end of adulthood can be resisted by a critique of infantilism and the reclamation of subjectivity.

"I draw most strength from the victims for they represent America to me . . . You are my heroes and heroines. You are but little lower than the angels."[1] So said Janet Reno, attorney general of the United States of America, as part of her address to a victims' rights conference in August 1996. Reno's near-worship of victims ("little lower than the angels") demonstrates the drastic change that has occurred in the *mores* of the most powerful country in the world, which, as American critic James Hillman has pointed out, used to be famous for its "heroic culture."[2] The effusive praise for victims on the part of one of the most senior officers appointed by the federal government also suggests that the Clinton administration has adopted the victim as a model persona—the kind of person it can do business with.

A small number of American critics have noted and protested against the elevation of victimhood. "The victim," observed Christopher Lasch, "has come to enjoy a certain moral superiority in our society," to the point where competing interest groups now "vie for the privileged status of victims."[3] The conservative critic C. J. Sykes was equally unimpressed by the elevation of victimhood, which he correlated with "the decay of American character." Sykes was concerned that "the claim that one is a victim has become one of the few currencies of intellectual exchange,"[4] to the extent that the invocation of victim status is often sufficient to close down debate and prevent further interrogation of almost any controversial topic.

We're All Victims Now

Victims are everywhere; and, by the same token, it seems that everyone is involved in a relationship of victimization. In 1995 Channel 4 broadcast *Battered Britain,* an extensive season of programs, most of them

---

1. Janet Reno, quoted by Bruce Shapiro, *The Nation,* February 10, 1997.
2. James Hillman, *The Soul's Code* (New York: Random House, 1997), quoted in *Utne Reader,* January-February 1997, pp. 53–5.
3. Christopher Lasch, *The Minimal Self* (London: Picador, 1985), p. 67.
4. C. J. Sykes, *A Nation of Victims: The Decay of the American Character* (New York: St. Martin's Press, 1992), pp. 16–17.

documentaries, which depicted British society as a nexus of abusive relationships. Writing in the *Observer* in the summer of 1996, Nicci Gerrard wrote a feature article entitled "The Monster Inside Us All" in which she claimed that "some people are born bullies—others are born victims. Each of us has been one or the other."[5] Gerrard's categorization of the general population into bullies and victims is now commonplace, with the added complication that bullies are often said to be responding in kind to an earlier phase of their lives in which they themselves were victimized. Experience of victimhood has come to be regarded as the common denominator which defines our humanity.

In *The Face,* meanwhile, Damon Albarn (the lead singer in the band Blur) saw through the perceptions of victimhood which Gerrard et al. seem to take at face value. Albarn recognized that our self-image has been re-oriented to the point where there is a tendency for all of us to see ourselves as victims, regardless of whether or not such an image is justified: "If there's going to be an epitaph for the nineties, it will be 'by the end, we all felt like victims.'"[6]

This is the era in which celebrities from footballers to princesses, cannot hope to retain their celebrity unless they come up with a story in which they play the role of the victim. . . .

Just as Adam Smith's *homo oeconomicus* (economic man) was the predominant self-image of the individual during the progressive phase of capitalism, so nowadays the victim is among the top personae in today's society. Moreover, it seems that the greasy pole which brought the victim to this position was none other than the axis which runs through pop culture all the way back to the counterculture which preceded it.

In the mid-1990s the figure of the pop star as self-made victim was updated by Richey Edwards, the lead singer of The Manic Street Preachers, who disappeared on the morning of January 31, 1995, never (yet) to be seen again. Before his unexpected exit, Edwards's lyrics had proclaimed that "everyone's a victim," and he sang of "the beautiful dignity in self-abuse."[7] Edwards first made a name for himself when, in front of a journalist, he carved "4REAL" in his arm with a razor, and a photograph of him, bleeding but impassive, went to the *NME* [*New Musical Express*]. Edwards's enigmatic retreat from pop life provides an equally powerful image of victimhood, on which his current reputation now rests.

It would be fanciful to suggest that either Nicci Gerrard or Janet Reno is devoted to The Manic Street Preachers and the memory of missing band member Richey Edwards. Nevertheless both of them will undoubtedly have been touched by the pop sensibility to which Edwards is now a prominent contributor, and which itself contributed to the

---

5. Nicci Gerrard, "The Monster Inside Us All," *Observer,* June 16, 1996.

6. Damon Albarn, "End of a Century," *The Face,* January 1997, p. 169.

7. Richey Edwards's lyrics, quoted by Andy Beckett, "Missing Street Preacher," *Independent on Sunday,* March 2, 1997, p. 21.

notion that everyone is a victim (Edwards/Gerrard) and to the image of
the beautiful dignity of victims (Edwards/Reno).

Pre-adult

In today's society the other, equally powerful self-image is that of the
child. Apart from the victim, pre-adulthood is the only other universal
unit of cultural currency, while adulthood itself is about as welcome as
negative equity. Hence the statement by William Eccleshare, chief executive of the leading advertising agency Amnirati Puris Lintas to the effect
that contemporary advertising constantly utilizes images of the pre-adult
in the knowledge that over-twenty-ones will identify with them: "If all
advertising seems to be directed at the young it's because we've found
the most effective way to appeal to everyone is to make commercials
which embody attitudes associated with youth."[8] . . .

The victim and the child are the two leading cultural personalities in   10
today's society. Moreover they complement each other, in that they are
joined together by the common element of powerlessness. Abused and
defenseless, the victim and the child are attractive personae in that they
represent life beyond the discredited struggle for power between competing, self-interested adults. How ironic, therefore, that the motifs of
the victim and the child have been adopted by a new ruling elite in its
pursuit of more power over individuals and society. . . .

Children's Rights? — Wrong

As well as through the promotion of the victim, adulthood is being
attacked from another direction. The growing demand for "children's
rights" may do little to improve the lives of children. But it serves to undermine parents and their rights, while extending the authority of state-
sponsored professionals.

With the Children Act 1989 the Conservative government put children's rights at the center of social policy, and the New Labour government has followed suit. At first sight, the bipartisan emphasis on
children's rights might seem progressive; comparable, perhaps, to the
emancipation of women or blacks. But this very comparison is indicative
of the fallacious character of "children's rights."

Women and blacks are adults who are denied equal rights in so far as
they belong to specific social groups which are oppressed in society.
Were it not for the fact that their rights have been withheld, they would
be capable of exercising them fully. Children, on the other hand, are by

---

8. William Eccleshare, quoted by Alasdair Palmer, *Sunday Telegraph,* February 2,
1997.

definition not adults. They are still learning to be adults, hence they are incapable of exercising rights on an equal footing with already existing adults. Children are necessarily immature, in a way that women and black people are not. In this respect they can have no claim to equal rights.

Official emphasis on "children's rights" cannot succeed in raising children to the same level of capability as adults, any more than you can legislate to put the amoeba and the monkey at the same point on the evolutionary scale. But the cause of "children's rights" does have the effect of bringing adults, in official eyes, down to the level of children. It does this by putting children on a par with adults, as if they were no more and no less capable than adults in their dealings with society. The corollary is that adults are no more and no less capable than children. As a result we are all officially infantilized by means of the progressive-sounding language of "children's rights."

While adults are pulled back to the same level as minors who by definition cannot yet exercise rights for themselves, various state-sponsored professionals have raised themselves up to new heights of super-adult authority by promising to exercise rights on behalf of children. Under the Children Act 1989, for example, the state acts on behalf of the child to protect it from abuse. According to the libertarian commentator James Heartfield, "it is not the child that exercises the rights, but the state. The state steps in as a kind of super-parent, to lord it over those parents deemed to have failed in their responsibility to children."[9] 15

The events at Waco, Texas, in April 1993 provide a graphic illustration of how the state's role as super-parent can go tragically wrong. Janet Reno, the aforementioned Attorney-General of the United States of America, was persuaded that the children in the compound of the Branch Davidian cult were at risk of abuse. As a lawyer who made her name in child-abuse cases, Reno may have been particularly sympathetic to such claims. In any case, she gave the FBI permission to move in. The authorities mounted a military-style operation which resulted in the death of eighty-six people, who were either gunned down or killed in the ensuing fire. Of these seventeen were children, of whom Heartfield says they were "apparently killed in defense of their own rights."[10] . . .

Beyond Left and Right

If politics today has gone beyond left and right, then the transcendent motifs of the new politics are the victim and the child. These motifs are now as significant throughout pop culture and mainstream politics as they were in the minority counterculture of thirty or forty years ago.

---

9. James Heartfield, "Why Children's Rights Are Wrong," *Living Marxism,* October 1993, pp. 13–14.

10. Ibid., p. 14.

The authoritarian consequences of the transfer of such icons from the counterculture to the new political order has attracted the attention of a handful of commentators. Andrew Sinclair, for example, observed the "trend" of the 1960s being "stood on its head," and becoming "the thought-police of the politically correct academics and politicians who would rise to govern America."[11] Jeff Nuttall noted that "Political Correctness comes straight out of the old sixties Underground."[12] At the beginning of the 1980s Bernice Martin sensed that the sensibility of the 1960s would outlive the left-wing politics with which it was originally associated, and that it would give shape to the times to come: "Underneath the red clothing was a beast of a different color, or perhaps a chameleon able to take on *any* political coloring . . . a specialist and exaggerated form of a phenomenon which is affecting all spheres of society."[13]

The radical sociologist Stanley Cohen recognized that the 1960s notion that "the personal is political" has come to unexpected fruition in victim culture, where it also has the effect of undermining democratic rights:

> For victims, if not for deviants (as we thought in the sixties), the personal has indeed become political. This culture of victimization emerges from identity politics: groups defining themselves only in terms of their claims to special identity and suffering. And this trend is given a spurious epistemological dignity by the ethic of multiculturalism. The result of all this is to actually subvert the . . . politics based on such old fashioned Enlightenment meta-narratives as common citizenship and universal rights.[14]

Cohen seems to be suggesting that, by coming down to the level of the personal, politics has been reduced in scale. But instead of thereby expanding the scope of the individual, as was the hope in the 1960s, this has served only to reduce the range of humanity. . . .

It is hardly surprising, therefore, that politics should now be redolent with the iconography of powerlessness. This has come about not least because politics, as the implementation, "magically," of "imaginary" solutions, is at one and the same time the fantastic and the fetishized expression of powerlessness at the programmatic level. If politics today focuses on the image of the child, that is entirely in keeping with the

20

11. Andrew Sinclair, *In Love and Anger* (London: Sinclair Stevenson, 1994), p. 168.

12. Jeff Nuttall, interviewed by Roger Hutchinson, in *High Sixties* (Edinburgh: Mainstream, 1992), p. 192.

13. Bernice Martin, *A Sociology of Contemporary Cultural Change* (Oxford: Blackwell, 1981), p. 21.

14. Stanley Cohen, "Crime and Politics," *British Journal of Sociology,* vol. 47, no. 1 (March 1996), p. 15.

advent of a new generation of politicians who in the face of adversity, and their own programmatic bankruptcy, liken themselves to children in their powerlessness and vulnerability. Nor are they alone in their self-image. The sense of powerlessness is widely shared throughout society; and it is through the common language of pop culture (née counterculture) that the elite and the rest of society are able to communicate their shared sense of powerlessness and victimization.

New Adulthood?

From this it can be seen that the erosion of adulthood, and the absence of a plausible image of history-making activity, cannot be remedied merely by the invention of a new self-image or the re-presentation of an old one. Indeed, when the outward form of adulthood is re-presented in today's context, its content is usually turned inside out. Thus the donning of suits and bow ties by followers of the black separatist leader Louis Farrakhan does not express the progressive but by no means perfect culture of universalism and democracy which was originally presented in the anonymity of the man's dark suit; rather it is a loud demonstration of particularism, in this case on the part of blacks—a response to the failure of bourgeois universalism which re-presents that failure all the more intensely.

In short there are no cultural solutions to the problems posed by victim culture. The latter can be addressed, not by the desire to look like adults but only by our attempts to act as adults. How can we succeed in our attempts? Firstly, by resisting any further incursion into what little adult autonomy we have left. For example, if Jack Straw, the Home Secretary, proceeds to act *in loco parentis* by imposing a curfew on under-sixteens, parents should resist any such measure on the grounds that it makes children out of them too, and inform the relevant authorities that they are perfectly capable of fixing their own children's bedtimes, thank you very much.

Generally speaking, if those in authority insist on issuing lists of instructions on how we should bring up our children, we can make it clear that we have no need of such "advice" (for to accept it, and hence to become dependent on it, is the equivalent of wearing L plates for the rest of our lives). Furthermore, we should encourage those around us to reject the self-image of victims. On different occasions, the rejection of this self-image might mean issuing a challenge to the current preeminence of identity politics, or it might involve campaigning for free speech, and opposing the authorities' patronizing assumption that the rest of us are not adult enough to cope with offensive remarks.

However, resisting the new power generation in our day-to-day lives will make sense only if it is connected to a broader critique of society and its current impasse—otherwise the new mode of infantilized existence will never be revealed as the creature of authoritarianism and the obstacle to human development which it most certainly is. When such a critique becomes something like common knowledge, the absence of history-making subjectivity will have been recognized as a consequence of the essential but none the less not immovable character of today's society; and, having demystified the dearth of subjectivity, we will once more be able to envisage ourselves making history. It is this last which is the ultimate rejoinder to the insidious process of infantilization.

Reading the Text

1. How, in Calcutt's opinion, has "the victim" (para. 1) come to replace the hero as a cultural icon?
2. Why does Calcutt see the focus on children's rights as an assault on adulthood?
3. What link does Calcutt make between "politically correct" (para. 17) thinking and the "culture of victimization" (para. 19)?
4. What recommendations does Calcutt make to solve "the problems posed by victim culture" (para. 22)?

Reading the Signs

1. In a critical essay, support, complicate, or refute Calcutt's claim that victim culture stems from political correctness.
2. Calcutt observes that the category of "victim" is expanding. In an essay, argue whether or not you believe the expansion of this category is fair to groups, such as African Americans and Jews, who have been victimized in history because of who they are.
3. In class, form teams, and debate Calcutt's contention that children should not have the same rights as adults.
4. Brainstorm examples of mass entertainment that celebrate the victim or the child. Then write an essay in which you respond to Calcutt's position that victim culture represents "The End of Adulthood."

BERNARD LEFKOWITZ

Don't Further Empower Cliques

Every American high school has its in-groups and out-groups, the pop-
ular crowd and the kids pushed out onto the margins. This has never
been particularly fair nor pleasant, but in the late 1990s it turned
deadly with a spate of campus killings that culminated in the massacre
at Columbine High School in Littleton, Colorado. In the aftermath of
the shootings, commentators around the country sought to explain how
such a thing could happen — pointing their fingers at such culprits as
easy gun access and violent video games — but in this op-ed piece
Bernard Lefkowitz identifies yet another factor in the killings: "the
power of high school cliques to make life miserable for many adoles-
cents." Without excusing the killers, Lefkowitz thus illuminates one of
America's most pernicious, yet largely invisible, forms of social margin-
alization. Lefkowitz is a writer who specializes in youth issues and
whose books include Our Guys: The Glen Ridge Rape and the
Secret Life of the Perfect Suburb *(1997) and* Breaktime: Living
without Work in a Nine to Five World *(1979).*

While it's difficult to generate sympathy for a couple of teenagers
who decided to vent their grievances through the barrel of a gun, the
carnage at Columbine High School should not eclipse an important part
of this story: the power of high school cliques to make life miserable for
many adolescents.

When I heard that the two young murderers in Littleton, Colorado,
had targeted athletes who, they said, had ridiculed them, it sounded a lot
like what young people told me ten years ago when I was researching the
rape of a retarded young woman by a group of teenage athletes at Glen
Ridge High School.

In that attractive upper-middle-class New Jersey suburb, thirteen
jocks were present in the basement where the young woman's body was
penetrated by a baseball bat and a broomstick. The country was sickened
by the inhumanity of a bunch of guys who were among the most admired and envied young men in their community and high school.

After the rape, they came to school and openly boasted about what
they had done. Weren't they afraid of being punished? Later, many
people who knew them concluded that they had come to feel omnipotent after being treated like big-time celebrities for years by their school
and by many parents in town.

And why shouldn't they feel omnipotent? When you walked into   5
the high school the first thing you saw were halls lined with trophy cases

celebrating the exploits of the athletes. The school held two-hour assemblies to honor the jocks. But assemblies to honor the best students rarely lasted more than twenty minutes. The school yearbook displayed ten photographs of the most mediocre football player. But the outstanding scholar was lucky to get one grainy photo.

The message the school sent to its impressionable students was: You don't count unless you're part of this clique or at least pay homage to it. Instead of celebrating the individuality and diversity of all its students, it chose to honor this one type of youngster—aggressive, arrogant, and intensely competitive—above all the others. This left many kids feeling alienated and isolated, and not only during this brief passage into adulthood. Ten years later, I still hear from Glen Ridge graduates who remain enraged, not only by how they were mistreated by the athletes but by the school's unqualified adulation of them.

After my book was published, I received hundreds of letters from people, some in their 70s and 80s, who recalled how excluded they felt when their schools anointed one group of guys as leaders. Educators are reluctant to discourage the formation of cliques because that may be considered interference in the students' "private" lives. They are disinclined to challenge parents who are proud of their child's membership in a popular group. Then, too, some educators tolerate cliques because they think they are just a passing phenomenon.

That's unfortunate because there is much that schools can do to demonstrate that all students, rather than the few members of favored cliques, have value. They can promote activities and projects that bring together students with diverse interests and skills. They can celebrate achievements that are intellectual and artistic as well as athletic. And they can demonstrate that there's a single standard of acceptable conduct that is applied to everyone. In Glen Ridge, as in many other schools, the athletes got away with behavior for which others were punished.

We don't know much about how Columbine High School responded to student cliques. But I do know that schools are not passive entities. Educators make collective judgments about which students are valuable and which aren't. Often, educators are quick to venerate kids who are superficially attractive—who are handsome, who are athletic, who come from wealthy families. And too often they marginalize youngsters who are awkward or unsocial or iconoclastic.

Kids with supportive families and friends may ultimately succeed in   10
life although they were treated like outcasts in school. But even they will not easily recover from the wounds they suffered as adolescents. For youngsters who already feel abandoned, the power granted to cliques by school authorities, and the inevitable abuse of that power, may be potentially devastating.

This doesn't explain the pathological behavior of two kids turned killers at Columbine High School. That will require a calmer and more thoughtful investigation into how they grew up and their school lives than is possible in the heat of the moment. But we should take the opportunity that the catastrophe in Littleton offers to reflect on the damage that cliques can inflict on youngsters when they are most vulnerable.

Reading the Text

1. What relationship does Lefkowitz see between the shooting at Columbine High School and the gang rape of a teenage girl in Glen Ridge, New Jersey?
2. According to Lefkowitz, why do schools do harm when they celebrate the accomplishments of athletes?
3. In your own words, describe the reasons Lefkowitz considers cliques problematic.

Reading the Signs

1. In your journal, reflect on the power of cliques in your life, either in high school or in college. To what extent did (or do) they shape your sense of identity, either as an insider or as an outsider?
2. In an argumentative essay, respond to Lefkowitz's charge that a school celebration of athletes' accomplishments can "honor this one type of youngster—aggressive, arrogant, and intensely competitive—above all others" (para. 6).
3. Read or reread Peter Doskoch's "The Mind of the Militias" (p. 618), and write an essay in which you explain whether the militia movement is really a clique or something more.
4. In class, discuss whether cliques do indeed inflict damage on young people, as Lefkowitz argues, or whether they can be beneficial. Then write your own essay in which you demonstrate your own position.

CHAPTER NINE

AMERICAN ICONS

The Mythic Characters of Popular Culture

Air Jordan

When Michael Jordan announced his retirement (his second) from the NBA in 1999, the whole world was watching. Chicago Bulls fans wondered if life without Jordan would ever be the same, while others wondered if the NBA (which had just settled a bruising strike) could ever be the same. Meanwhile, companies from across the consumer spectrum lined up to sign Jordan as their pitchman, even as Nike stock, which had risen with Air Jordan's own rise to king of the hoops, fell off a cliff.

All in all, it was a remarkable event—most remarkable, we would suggest, because most people found all this fuss over the retirement of a professional athlete to be expected. But then, why shouldn't we expect all this fuss? Jordan, after all, was no ordinary athlete; he was a reigning cultural icon, a distinctly American character who had become a symbol of much that America—and the world as well—had come to value and desire.

In this chapter, you will read about America's cultural icons, about those figures—some entirely fictional and others quite real—who have been mythologized into larger-than-life symbols that capture the American imagination. An icon is not simply a popular figure or celebrity; an icon is someone, or something, that has a *meaning,* a cultural significance that goes beyond any particular qualities he, she, or it might have. Kareem Abdul Jabbar, for example, was certainly the greatest basketball player of his era (and, arguably, of all time), but he never quite made it to icon status. Celebrated, yes, and rewarded but not mythologized. Michael "Air" Jordan, on the other hand, is more than a man and more than a basketball player; he's a cultural myth.

Interpreting the Mythic Characters of American Culture

So how might you go about interpreting the myth of Air Jordan? As with any semiotic analysis, you will want to construct the systems in which Jordan signifies and determine the differences that distinguish him from others within the system with whom he might otherwise be associated. So let's start with some basic questions centered on some fundamental facts—the fact, for instance, that in the space of a few years, Michael Jordan rocketed from impoverished obscurity to almost incalculable wealth and fame through the exercise of his own talents. Now, what fundamental American belief does this fact exemplify?

That one's easy: the American dream, of course. And indeed, part of the mythic significance of Michael Jordan lies precisely in the way his life seems to demonstrate the truth of one of America's most cherished beliefs: that anyone in America can make it if he or she simply tries hard enough. Many of our most beloved cultural icons—from Ben Franklin to Bruce Springsteen—signify in this way, and though it is not always true that mere effort will guarantee success in this country, we lavish devotion on those relatively few figures whose lives say that it will.

But as with most cultural icons, the meaning of Michael Jordan goes beyond his significance as an exemplar of the American dream. To pursue that meaning further, we might consider what makes Jordan *different* from many other Americans who have accomplished the dream. The most obvious difference, in historical terms, is the fact that Jordan is black, for until recently, few African Americans figured as exemplars of the American dream. So a racial angle must be added to our interpretation.

But what difference does Jordan's racial status make? Here we need to consider the social context in which Michael Jordan has become meaningful. From the 1980s through the 1990s—the period of Jordan's ascendancy—the successes of the civil rights movement began to come into question. On the one hand, more and more African Americans were entering the middle class as the country became less segregated, both demographically and ideologically. Some racial progress, in short, had been made. But on the other hand, even as a third of the black population was rising to middle-class status and beyond, about two-thirds was falling below the working class into a hopeless underclass. Such a social and economic set of circumstances contradicted the widespread American belief that we had finally overcome the injustices of the past to arrive

||||||||||||||||||||||||||||||||||||||||||||||||||||||||||||||||||||||||||||||||||||||||||||||||||||||||||||||||||||||||||||||||||

Exploring the Signs of American Characters

Children's television is filled with characters, from Winnie the Pooh to G.I. Joe, from the Muppets to the Mighty Morphin Power Rangers. Choose a character with whom you grew up, and explore in your journal what role that character played in your life. Did you simply watch the character on TV, or did you play-act games with it? Did you ever buy—or want to buy—any products related to that character? Why? Does that character mean anything to you today?

at a racially equitable society. As societies often do when faced with a cultural contradiction, Americans invented a mythology to resolve it by constructing national symbols whose iconic status would reinforce the belief that everything was OK after all. Michael Jordan was one of those symbols.

To see how Michael Jordan figures as a symbol of racial equality, we can *associate* him with those African Americans who also rose to superstar status in the 1980s and 1990s, figures like Bill Cosby, Oprah Winfrey, and Michael Jackson. Now, aside from being astoundingly successful and black, what do these figures have in common? First, they are all entertainers; and second, they all enjoyed massive "crossover" appeal, being just as popular among white, Latino, and Asian audiences as among black. So what do these two facts tell us?

Let's begin with the fact that most of the African American icons of the 1980s and 1990s have come from the entertainment and sports worlds, a realm that has grown exponentially with the growth of the mass media. Indeed, thanks to such mass media as television, cinema, and the recording industry, most of America's cultural icons now come from the sports and entertainment worlds, and so in this sense race really isn't an issue. Popular cultural icons like Garth Brooks, Bruce Springsteen, Tom Hanks, Mark McGwire, and Madonna reflect America's preoccupation with mass media entertainment in exactly the same way Cosby, Winfrey, or Jordan do. You might not find this reliance on the media to be remarkable, but it is historically unprecedented. In the past, most societies found their heroes in the realm of politics and the military. America's first major cultural icon, George Washington, was both a politician and a general, as was Dwight D. Eisenhower, a major icon of the 1950s. But aside from Colin Powell, no cultural icons have come from the military recently, and politicians, far from standing as potential heroes, are dropping to the lowest levels of cultural esteem in American history. So the fact that most of America's icons, black or white, are coming from popular media reflects a major shift from a traditional value system to a new one centered on popular entertainment. Americans highly value entertainment and reward their mass media heroes with iconic adoration.

That message is race neutral. But the special iconic status of "crossover" icons is not. To see how race plays a part in the appeal of the crossover artist, consider how such figures are able to make their race more or less invisible and certainly inconsequential. Everyone knows, for example, that Bill Cosby is black, but that's not the way people respond to him. He's gotten beyond race to become one of America's most lovable father figures. Michael Jackson, for his part, has made his effort to transcend race an explicit part of his appeal, while Oprah Winfrey has managed to do so without any apparent effort. This transcendence results not only in enormous popularity for the artist but also mythic status because of the way that he or she is able to resolve symbolically the contradiction between America's desire to be a colorblind society and the fact that it is not. (Interestingly, the media pay far less attention to these celebrities' activities, such as Cosby's long-standing financial support of black colleges, that emphasize racial identity.) By watching Cosby or Oprah, audiences of any ethnic background can see enormously successful African Americans who seem to demonstrate the truth of a colorblind society: after all, that is what appears on the screen, and seeing, as they say, is believing. Everyone goes away satisfied.

Michael Jordan's iconic status, then, is similar to that of Cosby, Oprah, and Michael Jackson. Everyone knows he's black, but Jordan's race is never an issue (indeed, Jordan has been careful not to make it an issue). Instead, Jordan signifies as an immensely successful *winner*, someone with almost supernatural athletic abilities.

But Jordan is not simply a winner. The sports world is filled with winners. What made him special (though not unique, as players like Magic Johnson functioned in a similar fashion) was the way he was able to neutralize the race issue at a time when the NBA was otherwise being racked with racial tensions that finally exploded to the surface in the late 1990s. First there was the notorious Latrell Sprewell incident, in which a black player had his contract annulled after he allegedly attacked his white coach. In the legal flap that followed, Sprewell eventually was represented by Johnnie Cochran—the black attorney most famous for his successful defense of O. J. Simpson—and his case became a cause célèbre in inner cities around the country as "Free Spre" tee shirts became a hot item. And then there was the strike that knocked out half of the 1998 to 1999 NBA season, a strike that many commentators attributed to the racial divide between the mostly black players' union and the white team owners. By coming into the open, the NBA's racial subtext threatened to undo the cherished American belief that the world of professional sports offers a colorblind arena in which all the races can play and to which black youth, in particular, can aspire to achieve their portion of the

American dream. So players like Michael Jordan who erase race, so to speak, are particularly cherished as supporting props to a crumbling mythology. As long as they are around, the myth can be maintained, but with enough episodes like the Latrell Sprewell incident, America may rewrite its athletic mythology.

Which raises a final point. The myth of black athletic success (as exemplified by icons like Michael Jordan), which continues to be promulgated among young African Americans, itself conceals a contradiction. While it may be true that most of the players in the NBA are black and that most professional sports in America are dominated by black athletes, a sports career is not a realistic goal for most kids. There just aren't enough "jobs" of that sort to go around, even if one has the athletic ability. It would be a more realistic goal to aspire to those professions that require a good education. But America is not constructing very many icons of that sort. For every Colin Powell, Toni Morrison, or Maya Angelou (who are all, in their way, cultural icons), there are a hundred iconic sports stars or entertainers, and little in America's popular culture is encouraging black kids to become writers or generals. While there's nothing intrinsically wrong with encouraging talented young people to improve their lives through sports or entertainment, very few will successfully enter these fields, and a lot will be disappointed. In the end, the goal of racial harmony that the mythic stature of the Michael Jordans of America is supposed to exemplify may be subverted.

Disappointed people can be discontented people, and discontent can breed conflict (as Langston Hughes asked, "What happens to a raisin in the sun?"). So, paradoxically enough, icons like Michael Jordan, howsoever they may personally try to avoid it, actually serve a racial status quo in which a relatively small number of people are able to soar high above the boards, while the rest remain firmly planted on the ground.

Forever Elvis

Not all cultural icons are constructed on such serious social contradictions, but if you look closely enough, a surprising number are. Since it is often the purpose of a cultural icon to conceal such contradictions, they are rarely apparent, but a close analysis can reveal some real paradoxes. Take Elvis (we presume you know which Elvis we mean): now there's a paradox.

One of America's most popular and enduring cultural icons, Elvis Presley is yet another exemplar of the American dream (truck driver goes to Graceland). No paradox there. But how did he *get* to Graceland? By becoming a rock 'n' roll star, of course—which is where the paradox lies.

Because at the time Elvis began his meteoric rise, rock 'n' roll was not only still quite new; it was also socially marginalized due to its origins in African American culture. Invented, as many popular cultural historians agree, by Chuck Berry, who blended such black musical forms as gospel, the blues, and bop with country music, rock 'n' roll in the early 1950s was frequently denounced as the devil's music, especially in the southern states where Elvis got his start. White musicians like Carl Perkins and Bill Halley adopted, and adapted, the new music, but when they did, black rock got reclassified as rhythm and blues, which then became code for "black" music. In this way, rock 'n' roll was largely taken away from the people who originated it.

First contradiction: a musical form on its way to becoming the most explosively popular music in American history originates in a people who are despised for creating it. The paradox of Elvis Presley stems precisely from this contradiction, for as has been often related in the history of rock 'n' roll, white southern disk jockeys in the mid-1950s who were aware of the growing appeal of rock music were on the lookout for a "white boy who sounded black." And Elvis was the boy. Himself a child of the segregated South, Elvis Presley could appeal to a white audience hungry for the new music but not for its creators.

But why were white teenagers so hungry for rock music? To answer this, let's consider some other well-known facts from the Elvis files—that is, the fact that his performances were so sexually suggestive that when he first appeared on *The Ed Sullivan Show* he was filmed from the waist up. Sex was a big part of Elvis's appeal at a time when teenagers were being offered the likes of such squeeky clean performers as Pat Boone, Ricky Nelson, and Connie Francis. In short, official popular culture was still offering up sexually sanitized entertainers at a time when American teens were gearing up for a sexual revolution. There was plenty of sexual expression in rock 'n' roll, but in the still segregated America of the 1950s, a black performer could not deliver it. Elvis could, and the rest is history.

By releasing the sexual energies of a generation, Elvis became a kind of modern Dionysus. The mythic center of a cult that swept through Greece over two thousand years ago, Dionysus was a godlike figure—usually depicted as a young man—whose rituals included the violent release of sexual energies that ordinary Greek life repressed. Dionysus has since become an enduring symbol of sexual expression, an archetypal figure whose popular appeal has been reflected in such male sex symbols as Rudolph Valentino and Elvis Presley, men who are not simply good looking or sexy but who seem to embody sexuality itself.

Indeed, Dionysus offers us a clue into the significance of all those stories about Elvis's "survival." That is, part of the cult of Dionysus included his ritual murder, but he always came back to life, refusing to die. Now think of Elvis's death, and all those funny denials, the rumors: that he did not really die, that he is working as a grocery checkout clerk in Minneapolis, that he was just spotted at the 7 Eleven down the street. Refusing to stay dead, Elvis completes his mythic circuit, becoming ar-

||||||||||||||||||||||||||||||||||||||||||||||||||||||||||||||||||||||||||||||||||||||||||||||||||||||||||||||||||||||||||||||||||||||||||||||||||||||

> ### Discussing the Signs of American Characters
>
> In class, brainstorm a list of your favorite pop cultural icons. Then
> analyze your list. What mythological significance can you attach
> to the characters on your list? Do any rival the stature of an Elvis
> or a Marilyn? If so, what's their appeal; if not, why do you think
> they don't? What does the list say about the class's collective in-
> terests, concerns, and values?

chetypal through the never-dying, ever-potent figure of Dionysus. Such
a man can never die.

Like a Candle in the Wind

If all this sounds like a lot for one man to symbolize, don't worry,
Elvis isn't America's only sex symbol. For one thing, there's Marilyn.
You know the one we mean.

In many ways, the iconic significance of Marilyn Monroe resembles
that of Elvis. The rise of Norma Jean to superstardom, for example, also
exemplifies the American dream in its gaudiest aspects. And like Elvis,
Marilyn functions as a potent sex symbol in a society ever on the lookout
for sex symbols. Again like Elvis, Marilyn died young and thus enjoys the
legendary status of those other popular American characters who died
early (have you seen her with Elvis and James Dean in that poster where
they are all sitting together at a fifties-style coffee shop counter?). And, of
course, like Elvis Marilyn has her own postage stamp. But still Marilyn
Monroe is different. She's no female Dionysus, for example. Her appeal
is more subtle than that, less violent and ecstatic. But it has proven just as
enduring.

So what does Marilyn Monroe mean to you? Is she just another sex
symbol? But then, why do some women still identify with her today,
women who can hardly be said to be sexists in their response to her? And
men too: Is the enduring popularity of Marilyn Monroe among American men simply a sexual thing? Is there more to it than that?

As you ponder such questions, you might consider the system of
American sex symbols to which Marilyn Monroe belongs. Each decade
seems to have its dominant figure. In the 1930s, for example, there was
Jean Harlow, a platinum blonde sex goddess who is best remembered
through a photograph in which she is posed lying seductively on a bear
skin rug. In the 1940s, there was Rita Hayworth, whose most famous
image shows her posed crouching in her lingerie on a bed. But then
there's Monroe in *The Seven Year Itch*, playing a gentle if air-headed sex

toy who displays her sexuality without fully being aware of it. Probably her most famous image comes from that film, when an updraft of air blows her skirts around her waist as she walks over a subway vent. She laughs as she tries to hold her skirts down. And that's how she's most often remembered, laughing and innocent, even vulnerable.

Now consider the difference between these three images: Harlow's and Hayworth's seductive, challenging poses, and Monroe's childlike laughter and vulnerability. It's that laughter and that innocence that sets Monroe apart, the vulnerability that distinguishes her from the other sex goddesses of American popular culture. As the song goes, Marilyn is remembered "like a candle in the wind," as a fragile flame unable to endure the gales of popular attention. What can you make of that vulnerability, of the way that Marilyn signifies today more as a victim of her own fame than as a sex symbol? Does this indicate any uneasiness on America's part about its tendency to worship, and so sometimes destroy, its entertainers?

Pitching the Product

By analyzing such cultural icons as Michael Jordan, Elvis Presley, and Marilyn Monroe—real people who came to embody their society's most basic desires and contradictions—we can thus learn a great deal about American culture. But there are many other kinds of American icons—from social heroes like Martin Luther King Jr. to scientific icons like Albert Einstein—who represent the best in a culture. By analyzing heroes of that kind you can uncover an American idealism that could be used to build a better society, if just given the chance. The trouble is that such heroes are getting harder to find. For one thing, many of them—like Thomas Jefferson, and, to a lesser extent, George Washington and Abraham Lincoln—are being pulled off their pedestals. And for another, they are getting crowded out by another kind of cultural character, one that is constructed not from the stuff of America's social and political history but from its nature as a consumer culture. For these icons, whether they are real-life people or pure inventions, are constructed for one purpose: to pitch the product.

Note how whenever anyone achieves widespread popularity, or even notoriety, in America, the measure of their success is made by how many product endorsements they get. Michael Jordan, whom we have already analyzed, is the current king of the endorsers, but consider how one gymnastic leap in the 1996 Summer Olympics turned into a multi-million dollar endorsement bonanza for Keri Strug, while Tiger Woods is now selling everything from golf shoes to fancy watches. And when the heretofore shy and unmediagenic Mark McGwire shattered baseball's single-season home-run record in 1998, everyone started talking about

||||||||||||||||||||||||||||||||||||||||||||||||||||||||||||||||||||||||||||||||||||||||||||||||||||||||||||||||||||||||||||||||||||||||||||||||||||||||||||||

Reading Characters on the Net

One important component in American popular culture is the cult of the celebrity. What role has the Internet played in fostering a celebrity's status? Select a celebrity who interests you, and visit the websites, both offical and fan-sponsored, associated with that person. (You'll find superstars have many sites; you can find well over a dozen sites just for *Ally McBeal*'s Calista Flockhart, for instance, with several even devoted to the dancing baby.) How does the official site construct an image for the celebrity, and how does it create a community of fans? In what ways are the fan-generated sites responses to the celebrity's image?

the endorsements he would soon be lining up. Indeed, sometimes it seems that no American success story is complete without a product endorsement.

Wherever you look, you can find such commercial icons, and some of them aren't even real. How much beer has Louie the Lizard sold, and what were Joe Camel's sales figures before antismoking legislation forced him to "retire"? How many flashlights has the Energizer Bunny lit up? And how's the Taco Bell chihuahua doing? Advertisers are constantly creating such figures in order to appeal to specifically targeted markets (Joe Camel, for instance, was accused of being created to sell cigarettes to children), and they often become much admired in their own right (Spuds MacKenzie was quite a hero in the late 1980s).

That so many of America's cultural icons have been subsumed, or even created, to serve commercial interests is a sign of just how profoundly America has embraced the values of a consumer culture. And few icons have been left out of the consumer stampede. Martin Luther King, Jr. (as far as we know) has never yet been used to pitch a product, but Albert Einstein has, and so have George Washington and Abraham Lincoln (indeed, President's Day is now more a pretext for holding a storewide sale than for remembering Washington's and Lincoln's birthdays). Very little, it seems, is too sacred not to be used for commercial purposes. Or is it that consumerism itself has become sacred?

The Readings

The readings in this chapter analyze a range of American characters, some of whom have been used for marketing purposes and others who function as American heroes, real and fictional. Michael Eric Dyson starts

things off with an interpretation of the cultural significance of Michael
Jordan, a reading of a real-world superman that complements the interpretation offered in the introduction to this chapter. Gary Engle follows
with an analysis of the original Superman, a cartoon hero who, Engle argues, is very much a symbol of the American Way. Andy Medhurst's interpretation of Batman from a gay perspective provides some clues as to
why Robin was excluded from Tim Burton's *Batman*, while N'Gai Croal
and Jane Hughes provide a profile of the hottest superhero on the market
today, Lara Croft, an icon of the cyberset who doesn't even wear tights.
Emily Prager and Gary Cross come next with analyses of two of America's favorite characters, Barbie and G.I. Joe—iconic toys who continue
to shape American childhoods. Roy Rivenburg's playful survey of the
characters that have populated American advertising shows just how entrenched fictional characters are in our consumer economy. And Jenny
Lyn Bader concludes the readings with a nostalgic essay on the place of
heroes within her own generation, twentysomethings who have seen the
old heroes topple and wonder whether America had any room for heroes
as the 1990s wound to an end.

MICHAEL ERIC DYSON

*Be Like Mike? Michael Jordan
and the Pedagogy of Desire*

*It's hard to keep up with Michael Jordan. Not only is it impossible to
beat him on the court, but you can't even figure out what to call him
these days. A former NBA megastar? Well, he's retired twice and may
be coming back for the second time, which would be an appropriate addition to the legend that Michael Eric Dyson (b. 1958) analyzes in
this selection. Situating Jordan within the context of American social
and cultural history, Dyson shows what basketball, and everything
that goes with it, means in America, especially for African American
youth. And it isn't just air time. A professor of African and Afro-
American studies at the University of North Carolina at Chapel
Hill, Michael Eric Dyson is author of* Reflecting Black: African-
American Cultural Criticism *(1995), from which this essay is
taken,* Making Malcolm: The Myth and Meaning of Malcolm X *(1995), and* Between God and Gangsta Rap: Bearing
Witness to Black Culture *(1996).*

Michael Jordan is perhaps the best, and best-known, athlete in the
world today. He has attained unparalleled cultural status because of his
extraordinary physical gifts, his marketing as an icon of race-transcending
American athletic and moral excellence, and his mastery of a sport that
has become the metaphoric center of black cultural imagination. But the
Olympian sum of Jordan's cultural meaning is greater than the fluent
parts of his persona as athlete, family man, and marketing creation. There
is hardly cultural precedence for the character of his unique fame, which
has blurred the line between private and public, between personality and
celebrity, and between substance and symbol. Michael Jordan stands at
the breach between perception and intuition, his cultural meaning
perennially deferred from closure because his career symbolizes possibility
itself, gathering into its unfolding narrative the shattered remnants of previous incarnations of fame and yet transcending their reach.

Jordan has been called "the new DiMaggio" (Boers 1990, 30) and
"Elvis in high-tops," indications of the herculean cultural heroism he has
come to embody. There is even a religious element to the near worship
of Jordan as a cultural icon of invincibility, as he has been called a "savior
of sorts," "basketball's high priest" (Bradley 1991–92, 60), and "more
popular than Jesus," except with "better endorsement deals" (Vancil
1992, 51). But the quickly developing cultural canonization of Michael

Jordan provokes reflection about the contradictory uses to which Jordan's body is put as a seminal cultural text and ambiguous symbol of fantasy, and the avenues of agency and resistance available especially to black youth who make symbolic investment in Jordan's body as a means of cultural and personal possibility, creativity, and desire.

I understand Jordan in the broadest sense of the term to be a public pedagogue, a figure of estimable public moral authority whose career educates us about productive and disenabling forms of knowledge, desire, interest, consumption, and culture in three spheres: the culture of athletics that thrives on skill and performance, the specific expression of elements of African American culture, and the market forces and processes of commodification expressed by, and produced in, advanced capitalism. By probing these dimensions of Jordan's cultural importance, we may gain a clearer understanding of his function in American society.

Athletic activity has shaped and reflected important sectors of American society. First, it produced communities of common athletic interest organized around the development of highly skilled performance. The development of norms of athletic excellence evidenced in sports activities cemented communities of participants who valorized rigorous sorts of physical discipline in preparation for athletic competition and in expressing the highest degree of athletic skill. Second, it produced potent subcultures that inculcated in their participants norms of individual and team accomplishment. Such norms tapped into the bipolar structures of competition and cooperation that pervade American culture. Third, it provided a means of reinscribing Western frontier myths of exploration and discovery-as-conquest onto a vital sphere of American culture. Sports activities can be viewed in part as the attempt to symbolically ritualize and metaphorically extend the ongoing quest for mastery of environment and vanquishing of opponents within the limits of physical contest.

Fourth, athletic activity has served to reinforce habits and virtues 5 centered in collective pursuit of communal goals that are intimately connected to the common good, usually characterized within athletic circles as "team spirit." The culture of sport has physically captured and athletically articulated the mores, folkways, and dominant visions of American society, and at its best it has been conceived as a means of symbolically embracing and equitably pursuing the just, the good, the true, and the beautiful. And finally, the culture of athletics has provided an acceptable and widely accessible means of white male bonding. For much of its history, American sports activity has reflected white patriarchal privilege, and it has been rigidly defined and socially shaped by rules that restricted the equitable participation of women and people of color.

Black participation in sports in mainstream society, therefore, is a relatively recent phenomenon. Of course, there have existed venerable traditions of black sports, such as the Negro (baseball) Leagues, which countered the exclusion of black bodies from white sports. The prohibition of athletic activity by black men in mainstream society severely limited publicly acceptable forms of displaying black physical prowess, an issue that had been politicized during slavery and whose legacy extended into the middle of the twentieth century. Hence, the potentially superior physical prowess of black men, validated for many by the long tradition of slave labor that built American society, helped reinforce racist arguments about the racial regimentation of social space and the denigration of the black body as an inappropriate presence in traditions of American sport.

Coupled with this fear of superior black physical prowess was the notion that inferior black intelligence limited the ability of blacks to perform excellently in those sports activities that required mental concentration and agility. These two forces—the presumed lack of sophisticated black cognitive skills and the fear of superior black physical prowess—restricted black sports participation to thriving but financially handicapped subcultures of black athletic activity. Later, of course, the physical prowess of the black body would be acknowledged and exploited as a supremely fertile zone of profit as mainstream athletic society literally cashed in on the symbolic danger of black sports excellence.

Because of its marginalized status within the regime of American sports, black athletic activity often acquired a social significance that transcended the internal dimensions of game, sport, and skill. Black sport became an arena not only for testing the limits of physical endurance and forms of athletic excellence—while reproducing or repudiating ideals of American justice, goodness, truth, and beauty—but it also became a way of ritualizing racial achievement against socially imposed barriers to cultural performance.

In short, black sport activity often acquired a heroic dimension, as viewed in the careers of figures such as Joe Louis, Jackie Robinson, Althea Gibson, Wilma Rudolph, Muhammad Ali, and Arthur Ashe. Black sports heroes transcended the narrow boundaries of specific sports activities and garnered importance as icons of cultural excellence, symbolic figures who embodied social possibilities of success denied to other people of color. But they also captured and catalyzed the black cultural fetishization of sport as a means of expressing black cultural style, as a means of valorizing craft as a marker of racial and self-expression, and as a means of pursuing social and economic mobility.

It is this culture of black athletics, created against the background of   10 social and historical forces that shaped American athletic activity, that helped produce Jordan and help explain the craft that he practices. Craft is the honing of skill by the application of discipline, time, talent, and energy toward the realization of a particular cultural or personal goal. American folk cultures are pervaded by craft, from the production of cultural artifacts that express particular ethnic histories and traditions to the development of styles of life and work that reflect and symbolize a community's values, virtues, and goals. Michael Jordan's skills within basketball are clearly phenomenal, but his game can only be sufficiently explained by understanding its link to the fusion of African American cultural norms and practices, and the idealization of skill and performance that characterize important aspects of American sport. I will identify three defining characteristics of Jordan's game that reflect the influence of African American culture on his style of play.

First, Jordan's style of basketball reflects the *will to spontaneity*. I mean here the way in which historical accidence is transformed into cultural advantage, and the way acts of apparently random occurrence are spontaneously and imaginatively employed by Africans and African Americans in a variety of forms of cultural expression. When examining Jordan's game, this feature of African American culture clearly functions in his unpredictable eruptions of basketball creativity. It was apparent, for instance, during game two of the National Basketball Association 1991 championship series between Jordan's Chicago Bulls and the Los Angeles Lakers, in a shot that even Jordan ranked in his all-time top ten (McCallum 1991, 32). Jordan made a drive toward the lane, gesturing with his hands and body that he was about to complete a patent Jordan dunk shot with his right hand. But when he spied defender Sam Perkins slipping over to oppose his shot, he switched the ball in midair to his left hand to make an underhanded scoop shot instead, which immediately became known as the "levitation" shot. Such improvisation, a staple of the will to spontaneity, allows Jordan to expand his vocabulary of athletic spectacle, which is the stimulation of a desire to bear witness to the revelation of truth and beauty compressed into acts of athletic creativity.

Second, Jordan's game reflects the *stylization of the performed self*. This is the creation and projection of a sport persona that is an identifying mark of diverse African American creative enterprises, from the complexly layered jazz experimentation of John Coltrane, the trickstering and signifying comedic routines of Richard Pryor, and the rhetorical ripostes and oral significations of rapper Kool Moe Dee. Jordan's whole game persona is a graphic depiction of the performed self as flying acrobat, resulting in his famous moniker "Air Jordan." Jordan's performed self is rife with the language of physical expressiveness: head moving, arms extending, hands waving, tongue wagging, and legs spreading.

He has also developed a resourceful repertoire of dazzling dunk shots that further express his performed self and that have garnered him a special niche within the folklore of the game: the cradle jam, rock-a-baby, kiss the rim, lean in, and the tomahawk. In Jordan's game, the stylization of a performed self has allowed him to create a distinct sports persona that has athletic as well as economic consequences, while mastering sophisticated levels of physical expression and redefining the possibilities of athletic achievement within basketball.

Finally, there is the subversion of perceived limits through the use of *edifying deception,* which in Jordan's case centers around the space/time continuum. This moment in African American cultural practice is the ability to flout widely understood boundaries through mesmerization and alchemy, a subversion of common perceptions of the culturally or physically possible through the creative and deceptive manipulation of appearance. Jordan is perhaps most famous for his alleged "hang time," the uncanny ability to remain suspended in midair longer than other basketball players while executing his stunning array of improvised moves. But Jordan's "hang time" is technically a misnomer and can be more accurately attributed to Jordan's skillful athletic deception, his acrobatic leaping ability, and his intellectual toughness in projecting an aura of uniqueness around his craft than to his defiance of gravity and the laws of physics.

No human being, including Michael Jordan, can successfully defy   15
the law of gravity and achieve relatively sustained altitude without the benefit of machines. As Douglas Kirkpatrick points out, the equation for altitude is $1/2g \times t2 = VO \times t$ ("How Does Michael Fly?"). However, Jordan appears to hang by *stylistically* relativizing the fixed coordinates of space and time through the skillful management and manipulation of his body in midair. For basketball players, hang time is the velocity and speed with which a player takes off combined with the path the player's center of gravity follows on the way up. At the peak of a player's vertical jump, the velocity and speed is close to, or at, zero; hanging motionless in the air is the work of masterful skill and illusion ("How Does Michael Fly?"). Michael Jordan, through the consummate skill and style of his game, only appears to be hanging in space for more than the one second that human beings are capable of remaining airborne.

But the African American aspects of Jordan's game are indissolubly linked to the culture of consumption and the commodification of black culture.[1] Because of Jordan's supreme mastery of basketball, his squeaky-clean image, and his youthful vigor in pursuit of the American Dream, he has become, along with Bill Cosby, the quintessential pitchman in American society. Even his highly publicized troubles with gambling, his refusal to visit the White House after the Bulls' championship season, and a book that purports to expose the underside of his heroic myth have barely tarnished his All-American image.[2] Jordan eats Wheaties, drives Chevrolets, wears Hanes, drinks Coca-Cola, consumes McDonald's,

---

1. I do not mean here a theory of commodification that does not accentuate the forms of agency that can function even within restrictive and hegemonic cultural practices. Rather, I think that, contrary to elitist and overly pessimistic Frankfurt School readings of the spectacle of commodity within mass cultures, common people can exercise "everyday forms of resistance" to hegemonic forms of cultural knowledge and practice. For an explication of the function of everyday forms of resistance, see Scott, *Domination and the Arts of Resistance.*

2. For a critical look at Jordan behind the myth, see Smith, *The Jordan Rules.*

guzzles Gatorade, and, of course, wears Nikes. He and his shrewd handlers have successfully produced, packaged, marketed, and distributed his image and commodified his symbolic worth, transforming cultural capital into cash, influence, prestige, status, and wealth. To that degree, at least, Jordan repudiates the sorry tradition of the black athlete as the naif who loses his money to piranha-like financial wizards, investors, and hangers-on. He represents the new-age athletic entrepreneur who understands that American sport is ensconced in the cultural practices associated with business, and that it demands particular forms of intelligence, perception, and representation to prevent abuse and maximize profit.

From the very beginning of his professional career, Jordan was consciously marketed by his agency Pro-Serv as a peripatetic vehicle of American fantasies of capital accumulation and material consumption tied to Jordan's personal modesty and moral probity. In so doing, they skillfully avoided attaching to Jordan the image of questionable ethics and lethal excess that plagued inside traders and corporate raiders on Wall Street during the mid-eighties, as Jordan began to emerge as a cultural icon. But Jordan is also the symbol of the spectacle-laden black athletic body as the site of commodified black cultural imagination. Ironically, the black male body, which has been historically viewed as threatening and inappropriate in American society (and remains so outside of sports and entertainment), is made an object of white desires to domesticate and dilute its more ominous and subversive uses, even symbolically reducing Jordan's body to dead meat (McDonald's McJordan hamburger), which can be consumed and expelled as waste.

Jordan's body is also the screen upon which is projected black desires to emulate his athletic excellence and replicate his entry into reaches of unimaginable wealth and fame. But there is more than vicarious substitution and the projection of fantasy onto Jordan's body that is occurring in the circulation and reproduction of black cultural desire. There is also the creative use of desire and fantasy by young blacks to counter, and capitulate to, the forces of cultural dominance that attempt to reduce the black body to a commodity and text that is employed for entertainment, titillation, or financial gain. Simply said, there is no easy correlation between the commodification of black youth culture and the evidences of a completely dominated consciousness.

Even within the dominant cultural practices that seek to turn the black body into pure profit, disruptions of capital are embodied, for instance, in messages circulated in black communities by public moralists who criticize the exploitation of black cultural creativity by casual footwear companies. In short, there are instances of both black complicity and resistance in the commodification of black cultural imagination, and the ideological criticism of exploitative cultural practices must always be linked to the language of possibility and agency in rendering a complex picture of the black cultural situation. As Henry Giroux observes:

> The power of complicity and the complicity of power are not ex-
> hausted simply by registering how people are positioned and located
> through the production of particular ideologies structured through
> particular discourses. . . . It is important to see that an overreliance on
> ideology critique has limited our ability to understand how people
> actively participate in the dominant culture through processes of
> accommodation, negotiation, and even resistance. (Giroux 1992,
> 194–95)

In making judgments about the various uses of the black body, especially
Jordan's symbolic corporeality, we must specify how both consent and
opposition to exploitation are often signaled in expressions of cultural
creativity.

In examining his reactions to the racial ordering of athletic and cul-   20
tural life, the ominous specificity of the black body creates anxieties for
Jordan. His encounters with the limits of culturally mediated symbols of
race and racial identity have occasionally mocked his desire to live beyond race, to be "neither black nor white" (Patton 1986, 52), to be
"viewed as a person" (Vancil 1992, 57). While Jordan chafes under indictment by black critics who claim that he is not "black enough," he has
perhaps not clearly understood the differences between enabling versions
of human experience that transcend the exclusive gaze of race and disenabling visions of human community that seek race neutrality.

The former is the attempt to expand the perimeters of human experience beyond racial determinism, to nuance and deepen our understanding of the constituent elements of racial identity, and to understand how
race, along with class, gender, geography, and sexual preference, shape
and constrain human experience. The latter is the belief in an intangible,
amorphous, nonhistorical, and raceless category of "person," existing in a
zone beyond not simply the negative consequences of race, but beyond
the specific patterns of cultural and racial identity that constitute and help
shape human experience. Jordan's unclarity is consequential, weighing
heavily on his apolitical bearing and his refusal to acknowledge the public
character of his private beliefs about American society and the responsibility of his role as a public pedagogue.

Indeed it is the potency of black cultural expressions that not only
have helped influence his style of play, but have also made the sneaker
industry he lucratively participates in a multi-billion-dollar business.
Michael Jordan has helped seize upon the commercial consequences of
black cultural preoccupation with style and the commodification of the
black juvenile imagination at the site of the sneaker. At the juncture of
the sneaker, a host of cultural, political, and economic forces and meanings meet, collide, shatter, and are reassembled to symbolize the situation
of contemporary black culture.

The sneaker reflects at once the projection and stylization of black
urban realities linked in our contemporary historical moment to rap

culture and the underground political economy of crack, and reigns as the universal icon for the culture of consumption. The sneaker symbolizes the ingenious manner in which black cultural nuances of cool, hip, and chic have influenced the broader American cultural landscape. It was black street culture that influenced sneaker companies' aggressive invasion of the black juvenile market in taking advantage of the increasing amounts of disposable income of young black men as a result of legitimate and illegitimate forms of work.

Problematically, though, the sneaker also epitomizes the worst features of the social production of desire and represents the ways in which moral energies of social conscience about material values are drained by the messages of undisciplined acquisitiveness promoted by corporate dimensions of the culture of consumption. These messages, of rapacious consumerism supported by cultural and personal narcissism, are articulated on Wall Street and are related to the expanding inner-city juvenocracy, where young black men rule over black urban space in the culture of crack and illicit criminal activity, fed by desires to "live large" and to reproduce capitalism's excesses on their own terrain. Also, sneaker companies make significant sums of money from the illicit gains of drug dealers.

Moreover, while sneaker companies have exploited black cultural   25
expressions of cool, hip, chic, and style, they rarely benefit the people who both consume the largest quantity of products and whose culture redefined the sneaker companies' raison d'être. This situation is more severely compounded by the presence of spokespeople like Jordan, Spike Lee, and Bo Jackson, who are either ineffectual or defensive about or indifferent to the lethal consequences (especially in urban black-on-black violence over sneaker company products) of black juvenile acquisition of products that these figures have helped make culturally desirable and economically marketable.

Basketball is the metaphoric center of black juvenile culture, a major means by which even temporary forms of cultural and personal transcendence of personal limits are experienced. Michael Jordan is at the center of this black athletic culture, the supreme symbol of black cultural creativity in a society of diminishing tolerance for the black youth whose fascination with Jordan has helped sustain him. But Jordan is also the iconic fixture of broader segments of American society, who see in him the ideal figure: a black man of extraordinary genius on the court and before the cameras, who by virtue of his magical skills and godlike talents symbolizes the meaning of human possibility, while refusing to root it in the specific forms of culture and race in which it must inevitably make sense or fade to ultimate irrelevance.

Jordan also represents the contradictory impulses of the contemporary culture of consumption, where the black athletic body is deified, reified, and rearticulated within the narrow meanings of capital and commodity. But there is both resistance and consent to the exploitation of black bodies in Jordan's explicit cultural symbolism, as he provides brilliant glimpses of black culture's ingenuity of improvisation as a means of cultural expression and survival. It is also partially this element of black culture that has created in American society a desire to dream Jordan, to "be like Mike."

This pedagogy of desire that Jordan embodies, although at points immobilized by its depoliticized cultural contexts, is nevertheless a remarkable achievement in contemporary American culture: a six-foot-six American man of obvious African descent is the dominant presence and central cause of athletic fantasy in a sport that twenty years ago was denigrated as a black man's game and hence deemed unworthy of wide attention or support. Jordan is therefore the bearer of meanings about black culture larger than his individual life, the symbol of a pedagogy of style, presence, and desire that is immediately communicated by the sight of his black body before it can be contravened by reflection.

In the final analysis, his big black body — graceful and powerful, elegant and dark — symbolizes the possibilities of other black bodies to remain safe long enough to survive within the limited but significant sphere of sport, since Jordan's achievements have furthered the cultural acceptance of at least the athletic black body. In that sense, Jordan's powerful cultural capital has not been exhausted by narrow understandings of his symbolic absorption by the demands of capital and consumption. His body is still the symbolic carrier of racial and cultural desires to fly beyond limits and obstacles, a fluid metaphor of mobility and ascent to heights of excellence secured by genius and industry. It is this power to embody the often conflicting desires of so many that makes Michael Jordan a supremely instructive figure for our times.

WORKS CITED

Boers, Terry. "Getting Better All the Time." *Inside Sports,* May 1990, pp. 30–33.
Bradley, Michael. "Air Everything." *Basketball Forecast,* 1991–92, pp. 60–67.
Giroux, Henry. *Border Crossings: Cultural Workers and the Politics of Education.* New York: Routledge, 1992.
"How Does Michael Fly?" *Chicago Tribune,* February 27, 1990, p. 28.
McCallum, Jack. "His Highness." *Sports Illustrated,* June 17, 1991, pp. 28–33.
Patton, Paul. "The Selling of Michael Jordan." *New York Times Magazine,* November 9, 1986, pp. 48–58.
Scott, James. *Domination and the Arts of Resistance.* New Haven, Conn.: Yale University Press, 1990.
Smith, Sam. *The Jordan Rules.* New York: Simon and Schuster, 1992.
Vancil, Mark. "*Playboy* Interview: Michael Jordan." *Playboy,* May 1992, pp. 51–164.

Reading the Text

1. What does Dyson mean by the term "public pedagogue" (para. 3)?
2. What social forces have caused black athletes to assume "a heroic dimension" (para. 9) in American life, according to Dyson?
3. What evidence does Dyson provide to show that Jordan's skills express African American "cultural norms and practices" (para. 10)?
4. What connection does Dyson make between Jordan's athletic skills and America's "culture of consumption" (para. 16)?
5. Why, in Dyson's view, was Jordan especially effective in promoting the sneaker industry?

Reading the Signs

1. Compare and contrast Dyson's interpretation of Michael Jordan with that offered in the introduction to this chapter. Which do you find more persuasive, and why?
2. Dyson observes that some critics have complained that Jordan is not "black enough" (para. 20). Write an essay in which you support or repudiate this criticism, being sure to discuss the underlying assumptions about the role of a hero or role model.
3. Write an argumentative essay in response to the proposition that basketball is primarily a black form of cultural expression. To develop your ideas, read Paul C. Taylor's "Funky White Boys and Honorary Soul Sisters" (p. 549).
4. In class, brainstorm athletic heroes, both male and female. Then discuss the reasons these athletes appeal to the public. Use the class discussion as a basis for an essay in which you analyze why Americans so often turn to athletes for heroes and role models.
5. Write an essay in which you support or refute Dyson's contention that "the culture of athletics has provided an acceptable and widely accessible means of white male bonding" (para. 5). To develop your ideas, consult Michael A. Messner, "Power at Play: Sport and Gender Relations" (p. 460).

GARY ENGLE

What Makes Superman So Darned American?

*In 1992 Superman died—at least for a while. In bookstores and su-
permarkets across the nation, a special edition of D.C. Comics appeared, complete with a tableau of a dying Superman bleeding in Lois
Lane's arms. In this semiotic analysis of the enduring appeal of Superman, Gary Engle (b. 1947) argues why the Man of Steel—whom
Engle views as the ultimate immigrant—has dominated the pantheon
of American characters for so many years. Of all our heroes, Engle
claims, Superman alone "achieves truly mythic stature, interweaving a
pattern of beliefs, literary conventions, and cultural traditions of the
American people more powerfully and more accessibly than any other
cultural symbol of the twentieth century, perhaps of any period in our
history." A specialist in popular culture, Engle is an associate professor
of English at Cleveland State University. In addition to over two hundred magazine and journal articles, he has written* The Grotesque
Essence: Plays from American Minstrel Style *(1978).*

When I was young I spent a lot of time arguing with myself about
who would win in a fight between John Wayne and Superman. On days
when I wore my cowboy hat and cap guns, I knew the Duke would win
because of his pronounced superiority in the all-important matter of
swagger. There were days, though, when a frayed army blanket tied
cape-fashion around my neck signalled a young man's need to believe
there could be no end to the potency of his being. Then the Man of
Steel was the odds-on favorite to knock the Duke for a cosmic loop. My
greatest childhood problem was that the question could never be resolved because no such battle could ever take place. I mean, how would
a fight start between the only two Americans who never started anything, who always fought only to defend their rights and the American way?

Now that I'm older and able to look with reason on the mysteries of
childhood, I've finally resolved the dilemma. John Wayne was the best
older brother any kid could ever hope to have, but he was no Superman.

Superman is *the* great American hero. We are a nation rich with legendary figures. But among the Davy Crocketts and Paul Bunyans and
Mike Finks and Pecos Bills and all the rest who speak for various regional
identities in the pantheon of American folklore, only Superman achieves
truly mythic stature, interweaving a pattern of beliefs, literary conventions, and cultural traditions of the American people more powerfully

and more accessibly than any other cultural symbol of the twentieth century, perhaps of any period in our history.

The core of the American myth in *Superman* consists of a few basic facts that remain unchanged throughout the infinitely varied ways in which the myth is told—facts with which everyone is familiar, however marginal their knowledge of the story. Superman is an orphan rocketed to Earth when his native planet Krypton explodes; he lands near Smallville and is adopted by Jonathan and Martha Kent, who inculcate in him their American middle-class ethic; as an adult he migrates to Metropolis where he defends America—no, the world! no, the Universe!—from all evil and harm while playing a romantic game in which, as Clark Kent, he hopelessly pursues Lois Lane, who hopelessly pursues Superman, who remains aloof until such time as Lois proves worthy of him by falling in love with his feigned identity as a weakling. That's it. Every narrative thread in the mythology, each one of the thousands of plots in the fifty-year stream of comics and films and TV shows, all the tales involving the demigods of the Superman pantheon—Superboy, Supergirl, even Krypto the Superdog—every single one reinforces by never contradicting this basic set of facts. That's the myth, and that's where one looks to understand America.

It is impossible to imagine Superman being as popular as he is and   5 speaking as deeply to the American character were he not an immigrant and an orphan. Immigration, of course, is the overwhelming fact in American history. Except for the Indians, all Americans have an immediate sense of their origins elsewhere. No nation on Earth has so deeply embedded in its social consciousness the imagery of passage from one social identity to another: the Mayflower of the New England separatists, the slave ships from Africa and the subsequent underground railroads toward freedom in the North, the sailing ships and steamers running shuttles across two oceans in the nineteenth century, the freedom airlifts in the twentieth. Somehow the picture just isn't complete without Superman's rocketship.

Like the peoples of the nation whose values he defends, Superman is an alien, but not just any alien. He's the consummate and totally uncompromised alien, an immigrant whose visible difference from the norm is underscored by his decision to wear a costume of bold primary colors so tight as to be his very skin. Moreover, Superman the alien is real. He stands out among the hosts of comic book characters (Batman is a good example) for whom the superhero role is like a mask assumed when needed, a costume worn over their real identities as normal Americans. Superman's powers—strength, mobility, x-ray vision and the like—are the comic-book equivalents of ethnic characteristics, and they protect and preserve the vitality of the foster community in which he lives in the same way that immigrant ethnicity has sustained American culture linguistically, artistically, economically, politically, and spiritually. The myth of Superman asserts with total confidence and a childlike innocence the value of the immigrant in American culture.

From this nation's beginnings Americans have looked for ways of coming to terms with the immigrant experience. This is why, for example, so much of American literature and popular culture deals with the theme of dislocation, generally focused in characters devoted or doomed to constant physical movement. Daniel Boone became an American legend in part as a result of apocryphal stories that he moved every time his neighbors got close enough for him to see the smoke of their cabin fires. James Fenimore Cooper's Natty Bumppo spent the five long novels of the Leatherstocking saga drifting ever westward, like the pioneers who were his spiritual offspring, from the Mohawk valley of upstate New York to the Great Plains where he died. Huck Finn sailed through the moral heart of America on a raft. Melville's Ishmael, Wister's Virginian, Shane, Gatsby, the entire Lost Generation, Steinbeck's Okies, Little Orphan Annie, a thousand fiddlefooted cowboy heroes of dime novels and films and television — all in motion, searching for the American dream or stubbornly refusing to give up their innocence by growing old, all symptomatic of a national sense of rootlessness stemming from an identity founded on the experience of immigration.

Individual mobility is an integral part of America's dreamwork. Is it any wonder, then, that our greatest hero can take to the air at will? Superman's ability to fly does more than place him in a tradition of mythic figures going back to the Greek messenger god Hermes or Zetes the flying Argonaut. It makes him an exemplar in the American dream. Take away a young man's wheels and you take away his manhood. Jack Kerouac and Charles Kurault go on the road; William Least Heat Moon looks for himself in a van exploring the veins of America in its system of blue highways; legions of gray-haired retirees turn Air Stream trailers and Winnebagos into proof positive that you can, in the end, take it with you. On a human scale, the American need to keep moving suggests a neurotic aimlessness under the surface of adventure. But take the human restraints off, let Superman fly unencumbered when and wherever he will, and the meaning of mobility in the American consciousness begins to reveal itself. Superman's incredible speed allows him to be as close to everywhere at once as it is physically possible to be. Displacement is, therefore, impossible. His sense of self is not dispersed by his life's migration but rather enhanced by all the universe that he is able to occupy. What American, whether an immigrant in spirit or in fact, could resist the appeal of one with such an ironclad immunity to the anxiety of dislocation?

In America, physical dislocation serves as a symbol of social and psychological movement. When our immigrant ancestors arrived on America's shores they hit the ground running, some to homestead on the Great Plains, others to claw their way up the socioeconomic ladder in

coastal ghettos. Upward mobility, westward migration, Sunbelt relocation—the wisdom in America is that people don't, can't, mustn't end up
where they begin. This belief has the moral force of religious doctrine.
Thus the American identity is ordered around the psychological experience of forsaking or losing the past for the opportunity of reinventing
oneself in the future. This makes the orphan a potent symbol of the
American character. Orphans aren't merely free to reinvent themselves.
They are obliged to do so.

When Superman reinvents himself, he becomes the bumbling Clark   10
Kent, a figure as immobile as Superman is mobile, as weak as his alter
ego is strong. Over the years commentators have been fond of stressing
how Clark Kent provides an illusory image of wimpiness onto which
children can project their insecurities about their own potential (and,
hopefully, equally illusory) weaknesses. But I think the role of Clark
Kent is far more complex than that.

During my childhood, Kent contributed nothing to my love for the
Man of Steel. If left to contemplate him for too long, I found myself
changing from cape back into cowboy hat and guns. John Wayne, at
least, was no sissy that I could ever see. Of course, in all the Westerns
that the Duke came to stand for in my mind, there were elements that
left me as confused as the paradox between Kent and Superman. For example, I could never seem to figure out why cowboys so often fell in
love when there were obviously better options: horses to ride, guns to
shoot, outlaws to chase, and savages to kill. Even on the days when I became John Wayne, I could fall victim to a never-articulated anxiety
about the potential for poor judgment in my cowboy heroes. Then, I
generally drifted back into a worship of Superman. With him, at least,
the mysterious communion of opposites was honest and on the surface of
things.

What disturbed me as a child is what I now think makes the myth of
Superman so appealing to an immigrant sensibility. The shape-shifting
between Clark Kent and Superman is the means by which this mid-
twentieth-century, urban story—like the pastoral, nineteenth-century
Western before it—addresses in dramatic terms the theme of cultural assimilation.

At its most basic level, the Western was an imaginative record of the
American experience of westward migration and settlement. By bringing
the forces of civilization and savagery together on a mythical frontier, the
Western addressed the problem of conflict between apparently mutually
exclusive identities and explored options for negotiating between them.
In terms that a boy could comprehend, the myth explored the dilemma
of assimilation—marry the school marm and start wearing Eastern
clothes or saddle up and drift further westward with the boys.

The Western was never a myth of stark moral simplicity. Pioneers
fled civilization by migrating west, but their purpose in the wilderness

was to rebuild civilization. So civilization was both good and bad, what Americans fled from and journeyed toward. A similar moral ambiguity rested at the heart of the wilderness. It was an Eden in which innocence could be achieved through spiritual rebirth, but it was also the anarchic force that most directly threatened the civilized values America wanted to impose on the frontier. So the dilemma arose: In negotiating between civilization and the wilderness, between the old order and the new, between the identity the pioneers carried with them from wherever they came and the identity they sought to invent, Americans faced an impossible choice. Either they pushed into the New World wilderness and forsook the ideals that motivated them or they clung to their origins and polluted Eden.

The myth of the Western responded to this dilemma by inventing 15 the idea of the frontier in which civilized ideals embodied in the institutions of family, church, law, and education are revitalized by the virtues of savagery: independence, self-reliance, personal honor, sympathy with nature, and ethical uses of violence. In effect, the mythical frontier represented an attempt to embody the perfect degree of assimilation in which both the old and new identities came together, if not in a single self-image, then at least in idealized relationships, like the symbolic marriage of reformed cowboy and displaced school marm that ended Owen Wister's prototypical *The Virginian,* or the mystical masculine bonding between representatives of an ascendant and a vanishing America— Natty Bumppo and Chingachgook, the Lone Ranger and Tonto. On the Western frontier, both the old and new identities equally mattered.

As powerful a myth as the Western was, however, there were certain limits to its ability to speak directly to an increasingly common twentieth-century immigrant sensibility. First, it was pastoral. Its imagery of dusty frontier towns and breathtaking mountainous desolation spoke most affectingly to those who conceived of the American dream in terms of the nineteenth-century immigrant experience of rural settlement. As the twentieth century wore on, more immigrants were, like Superman, moving from rural or small-town backgrounds to metropolitan environments. Moreover, the Western was historical, often elegiacally so. Underlying the air of celebration in even the most epic and romantic of Westerns—the films of John Ford, say, in which John Wayne stood tall for all that any good American boy could ever want to be—was an awareness that the frontier was less a place than a state of mind represented in historic terms by a fleeting moment glimpsed imperfectly in the rapid wave of westward migration and settlement. Implicitly, then, whatever balance of past and future identities the frontier could offer was itself tenuous or illusory.

Twentieth-century immigrants, particularly the Eastern European Jews who came to America after 1880 and who settled in the industrial and mercantile centers of the Northeast—cities like Cleveland where

Jerry Siegel and Joe Shuster grew up and created Superman—could be entertained by the Western, but they developed a separate literary tradition that addressed the theme of assimilation in terms closer to their personal experience. In this tradition issues were clear-cut: Clinging to an Old World identity meant isolation in ghettos, confrontation with a prejudiced mainstream culture, second-class social status, and impoverishment. On the other hand, forsaking the past in favor of total absorption into the mainstream, while it could result in socioeconomic progress, meant a loss of the religious, linguistic, even culinary traditions that provided a foundation for psychological well-being. Such loss was particularly tragic for the Jews because of the fundamental role played by history in Jewish culture.

Writers who worked in this tradition—Abraham Cahan, Daniel Fuchs, Henry Roth, and Delmore Schwarz, among others—generally found little reason to view the experience of assimilation with joy or optimism. Typical of the tradition was Cahan's early novel *Yekl,* on which Joan Micklin Silver's film *Hester Street* was based. A young married couple, Jake and Gitl, clash over his need to be absorbed as quickly as possible into the American mainstream and her obsessive preservation of their Russian-Jewish heritage. In symbolic terms, their confrontation is as simple as their choice of headgear—a derby for him, a babushka for her. That the story ends with their divorce, even in the context of their gradual movement toward mutual understanding of one another's point of view, suggests the divisive nature of the pressures at work in the immigrant communities.

Where the pressures were perhaps most keenly felt was in the schools. Educational theory of the period stressed the benefits of rapid assimilation. In the first decades of this century, for example, New York schools flatly rejected bilingual education—a common response to the plight of non–English-speaking immigrants even today—and there were conscientious efforts to indoctrinate the children of immigrants with American values, often at the expense of traditions within the ethnic community. What resulted was a generational rift in which children were openly embarrassed by and even contemptuous of their parents' values, setting a pattern in American life in which second-generation immigrants migrate psychologically if not physically from their parents, leaving it up to the third generation and beyond to rediscover their ethnic roots.

Under such circumstances, finding a believable and inspiring balance   20 between the old identity and the new, like that implicit in the myth of the frontier, was next to impossible. The images and characters that did emerge from the immigrant communities were often comic. Seen over and over in the fiction and popular theater of the day was the figure of the *yiddische Yankee,* a jingoistic optimist who spoke heavily accented American slang, talked baseball like an addict without understanding the game, and dressed like a Broadway dandy on a budget—in short, one who didn't understand America well enough to distinguish between image and substance and who paid for the mistake by becoming the butt of a style of comedy bordering on pathos. So engrained was this stereotype in popular culture that it echoes today in TV situation comedy. . . .

Throughout American popular culture between 1880 and the Second World War the story was the same. Oxlike Swedish farmers, German brewers, Jewish merchants, corrupt Irish ward healers, Italian gangsters — there was a parade of images that reflected in terms often comic, sometimes tragic, the humiliation, pain, and cultural insecurity of people in a state of transition. Even in the comics, a medium intimately connected with immigrant culture, there simply was no image that presented a blending of identities in the assimilation process in a way that stressed pride, self-confidence, integrity, and psychological well-being. None, that is, until Superman.

The brilliant stroke in the conception of Superman — the sine qua non that makes the whole myth work — is the fact that he has two identities. The myth simply wouldn't work without Clark Kent, mild-mannered newspaper reporter and later, as the myth evolved, bland TV newsman. Adopting the white-bread image of a wimp is first and foremost a moral act for the Man of Steel. He does it to protect his parents from nefarious sorts who might use them to gain an edge over the powerful alien. Moreover, Kent adds to Superman's powers the moral guidance of a Smallville upbringing. It is Jonathan Kent, fans remember, who instructs the alien that his powers must always be used for good. Thus does the myth add a mainstream white Anglo-Saxon Protestant ingredient to the American stew. Clark Kent is the clearest stereotype of a self-effacing, hesitant, doubting, middle-class weakling ever invented. He is the epitome of visible invisibility, someone whose extraordinary ordinariness makes him disappear in a crowd. In a phrase, he is the consummate figure of total cultural assimilation, and significantly, he is not real. Implicit in this is the notion that mainstream cultural norms, however useful, are illusions.

Though a disguise, Kent is necessary for the myth to work. This uniquely American hero has two identities, one based on where he comes from in life's journey, one on where he is going. One is real, one an illusion, and both are necessary for the myth of balance in the assimilation process to be complete. Superman's powers make the hero capable of saving humanity; Kent's total immersion in the American heartland makes him want to do it. The result is an improvement on the Western: an optimistic myth of assimilation but with an urban, technocratic setting.

One must never underestimate the importance to a myth of the most minute elements which do not change over time and by which we recognize the story. Take Superman's cape, for example. When Joe Shuster inked the first Superman stories, in the early thirties when he was still a student at Cleveland's Glenville High School, Superman was strictly beefcake in tights, looking more like a circus acrobat than the ultimate Man of Steel. By June of 1938 when *Action Comics* no. 1 was issued, the image had been altered to include a cape, ostensibly to make flight easier to render in the pictures. But it wasn't the cape of Victorian melodrama and adventure fiction, the kind worn with a clasp around the neck. In fact, one is hard-pressed to find any precedent in popular culture for the kind of cape Superman wears. His emerges in a seamless line from either side of the front yoke of his tunic. It is a veritable growth from behind his pectorals and hangs, when he stands at ease, in a line that doesn't so much drape his shoulders as stand apart from them and echo their curve, like an angel's wings.

In light of this graphic detail, it seems hardly coincidental that Super- 25
man's real, Kryptonic name is Kal-El, an apparent neologism by George Lowther, the author who novelized the comic strip in 1942. In Hebrew, *el* can be both root and affix. As a root, it is the masculine singular word for God. Angels in Hebrew mythology are called *benei Elohim* (literally, sons of the Gods), or *Elyonim* (higher beings). As an affix, *el* is most often translated as "of God," as in the plenitude of Old Testament given names: Ishma-el, Dani-el, Ezeki-el, Samu-el, etc. It is also a common form for named angels in most Semitic mythologies: Israf-el, Aza-el, Uri-el, Yo-el, Rapha-el, Gabri-el and—the one perhaps most like Superman—Micha-el, the warrior angel and Satan's principal adversary.

The morpheme *Kal* bears a linguistic relation to two Hebrew roots. The first, *kal,* means "with lightness" or "swiftness" (faster than a speeding bullet in Hebrew?). It also bears a connection to the root *hal,* where *h* is the guttural *ch* of *chutzpah. Hal* translates roughly as "everything" or "all." *Kal-el,* then, can be read as "all that is God," or perhaps more in the spirit of the myth of Superman, "all that God is." And while we're at it, *Kent* is a form of the Hebrew *kana.* In its *k-n-t* form, the word appears in the Bible, meaning "I have found a son."

I'm suggesting that Superman raises the American immigrant experience to the level of religious myth. And why not? He's not just some immigrant from across the waters like all our ancestors, but a real alien, an extraterrestrial, a visitor from heaven if you will, which fact lends an element of the supernatural to the myth. America has no national religious icons nor any pilgrimage shrines. The idea of a patron saint is ludicrous in a nation whose Founding Fathers wrote into the founding documents the fundamental if not eternal separation of church and state. America, though, is pretty much as religious as other industrialized countries. It's just that our tradition of religious diversity precludes the nation's religious character from being embodied in objects or persons recognizably religious, for such are immediately identified by their attachment to specific sectarian traditions and thus contradict the eclecticism of the American religious spirit.

In America, cultural icons that manage to tap the national religious spirit are of necessity secular on the surface and sufficiently generalized to incorporate the diversity of American religious traditions. Superman doesn't have to be seen as an angel to be appreciated, but in the absence of a tradition of national religious iconography, he can serve as a safe, nonsectarian focus for essentially religious sentiments, particularly among the young.

In the last analysis, Superman is like nothing so much as an American boy's fantasy of a messiah. He is the male, heroic match for the Statue of Liberty, come like an immigrant from heaven to deliver humankind by sacrificing himself in the service of others. He protects the weak and defends truth and justice and all the other moral virtues inherent in the Judeo-Christian tradition, remaining ever vigilant and ever chaste. What purer or stronger vision could there possibly be for a child? Now that I put my mind to it, I see that John Wayne never had a chance.

Reading the Text

1. Why does Superman's status as "an immigrant and an orphan" (para. 5) make him deeply American, according to Engle?
2. What is the significance of Superman's ability to fly?
3. Why does Engle see physical dislocation as being so typically American?
4. What is the significance of Superman's two identities, according to Engle?

Reading the Signs

1. Interview three classmates or friends whose families are immigrants to this country. Then compare their experience with that of the mythological character, Superman. To what extent does the Superman character reflect real-life immigrant experience? What does his story leave out? Try to account for any differences you may find.
2. Do you agree with Engle's suggestion "that Superman raises the American immigrant experience to the level of religious myth" (para. 27)?
3. How would Superman fit the definitions of hero that Robert B. Ray ("The Thematic Paradigm," p. 299) outlines?
4. Engle claims that Superman is a more authentically American hero than is John Wayne. Write an argument supporting or refuting this claim, basing your argument on specific roles that Wayne has played in film.
5. Engle only briefly discusses the fact that Superman happens to be both male and Caucasian. What is the significance of his gender and race? How do you think they may have influenced his status as an American mythological hero? For a discussion of race and gender, consult Michael Omi's "In Living Color: Race and American Culture" (p. 526) and Holly Devor's "Gender Role Behaviors and Attitudes" (p. 447).
6. Rent a videotape of one of the *Superman* movies, and write an essay in which you explore whether the cinematic depiction of this character either perpetuates or alters his mythological status.

ANDY MEDHURST

Batman, Deviance, and Camp

ꞮꞮꞮ

Have you ever wondered what happened to Robin in the recent Bat-man movies? In this analysis of the history of the Batman, excerpted from The Many Lives of the Batman *(1991), Andy Medhurst (b. 1959) explains why Robin had to disappear. Arguing that Batman has been "reheterosexualized" in the wake of the insinuatingly homo-erotic TV series of the 1960s, Medhurst indicts the homophobia of Batfans whose "Bat-Platonic Ideal of how Batman should really be" holds no place for the "camped crusader." Andy Medhurst teaches media studies, popular culture, and lesbian and gay studies at the University of Sussex, England. His current research interests include popular film and television and lesbian and gay studies.*

Only someone ignorant of the fundamentals of psychiatry and of the psychopathology of sex can fail to realize a subtle atmosphere of ho-moeroticism which pervades the adventure of the mature "Batman" and his young friend "Robin."

—FREDRIC WERTHAM[1]

It's embarrassing to be solemn and treatise-like about Camp. One runs the risk of having, oneself, produced a very inferior piece of Camp.

—SUSAN SONTAG[2]

I'm not sure how qualified I am to write this essay. Batman hasn't been particularly important in my life since I was seven years old. Back then he was crucial, paramount, unmissable as I sat twice weekly to watch the latest episode on TV. Pure pleasure, except for the annoying fact that my parents didn't seem to appreciate the thrills on offer. Worse than that, they actually laughed. How could anyone laugh when the Dynamic Duo were about to be turned into Frostie Freezies (pineapple for the Caped Crusader, lime for his chum) by the evil Mr. Freeze?

Batman and I drifted apart after those early days. Every now and then I'd see a repeated episode and I soon began to understand and share that once infuriating parental hilarity, but this aside I hardly thought about the man in the cape at all. I knew about the subculture of comic freaks,

---

1. Fredric Wertham, *Seduction of the Innocent* (London: Museum Press, 1955), p. 190.

2. Susan Sontag, "Notes on Camp," in *A Susan Sontag Reader* (Harmondsworth: Penguin Books), p. 106.

and the new and alarmingly pretentious phrase "graphic novel" made itself known to me, but I still regarded (with the confidence of distant ignorance) such texts as violent, macho, adolescent and, well, silly.

That's when the warning bells rang. The word "silly" reeks of the complacent condescension that has at various times been bestowed on all the cultural forms that matter most to me (Hollywood musicals, British melodramas, pop music, soap operas), so what right had I to apply it to someone else's part of the popular cultural playground? I had to rethink my disdain, and 1989 has been a very good year in which to do so, because in terms of popular culture 1989 has been the Year of the Bat.

This essay, then, is not written by a devotee of Batman, someone steeped in every last twist of the mythology. I come to these texts as an interested outsider, armed with a particular perspective. That perspective is homosexuality, and what I want to try and do here is to offer a gay reading of the whole Bat-business. It has no pretension to definitiveness, I don't presume to speak for all gay people everywhere. I'm male, white, British, thirty years old (at the time of writing) and all of those factors need to be taken into account. Nonetheless, I'd argue that Batman is especially interesting to gay audiences for three reasons.

Firstly, he was one of the first fictional characters to be attacked on   5
the grounds of presumed homosexuality, by Fredric Wertham in his book *Seduction of the Innocent*. Secondly, the 1960s TV series was and remains a touchstone of camp (a banal attempt to define the meaning of camp might well start with "like the sixties' *Batman* series"). Thirdly, as a recurring hero figure for the last fifty years, Batman merits analysis as a notably successful construction of masculinity.

Nightmare on Psychiatry Street: Freddy's Obsession

Seduction of the Innocent is an extraordinary book. It is a gripping, flamboyant melodrama masquerading as social psychology. Fredric Wertham is, like Senator McCarthy,[3] like Batman, a crusader, a man with a mission, an evangelist. He wants to save the youth of America from its own worst impulses, from its id, from comic books. His attack on comic books is founded on an astonishingly crude stimulus-and-response model of reading, in which the child (the child, for Wertham, seems an unusually innocent, blank slate waiting to be written on) reads, absorbs, and feels compelled to copy, if only in fantasy terms, the content of the comics. It is a model, in other words, which takes for granted extreme audience passivity.

---

3. **Senator McCarthy**   United States Senator Joseph R. McCarthy (1908–1957), who in the 1950s hunted and persecuted suspected Communists and Communist sympathizers. — EDS.

This is not the place to go into a detailed refutation of Wertham's work, besides which such a refutation has already been done in Martin Barker's excellent *A Haunt of Fears*.[4] The central point of audience passivity needs stressing, however, because it is crucial to the celebrated passage where Wertham points his shrill, witch-hunting finger at the Dynamic Duo and cries "queer."

Such language is not present on the page, of course, but in some ways *Seduction of the Innocent* (a film title crying out for either D. W. Griffith or Cecil B. DeMille) would be easier to stomach if it were. Instead, Wertham writes with anguished concern about the potential harm that Batman might do to vulnerable children, innocents who might be turned into deviants. He employs what was then conventional psychiatric wisdom about the idea of homosexuality as a "phase":

> Many pre-adolescent boys pass through a phase of disdain for girls. Some comic books tend to fix that attitude and instill the idea that girls are only good for being banged around or used as decoys. A homoerotic attitude is also suggested by the presentation of masculine, bad, witch-like or violent women. In such comics women are depicted in a definitely anti-erotic light, while the young male heroes have pronounced erotic overtones. The muscular male supertype, whose primary sex characteristics are usually well emphasized, is in the setting of certain stories the object of homoerotic sexual curiosity and stimulation.[5]

The implications of this are breathtaking. Homosexuality, for Wertham, is synonymous with misogyny. Men love other men because they hate women. The sight of women being "banged around" is liable to appeal to repressed homoerotic desires (this, I think, would be news to the thousands of women who are systematically physically abused by heterosexual men). Women who do not conform to existing stereotypes of femininity are another incitement to homosexuality.

Having mapped out his terms of reference, Wertham goes on to peel the lid from Wayne Manor:

> Sometimes Batman ends up in bed injured and young Robin is shown sitting next to him. At home they lead an idyllic life. They are Bruce Wayne and "Dick" Grayson. Bruce Wayne is described as a "socialite" and the official relationship is that Dick is Bruce's ward. They live in sumptuous quarters, with beautiful flowers in large vases, and have a butler, Alfred. Batman is sometimes shown in a dressing gown. . . . It is like a wish dream of two homosexuals living together. Sometimes they are shown on a couch, Bruce reclining and Dick sitting next to him, jacket off, collar open, and his hand on his friend's arm.[6]

---

4. Martin Barker, *A Haunt of Fears* (London: Pluto Press, 1984).

5. Wertham, p. 188.

6. Wertham, p. 190.

So, Wertham's assumptions of homosexuality are fabricated out of his interpretation of certain visual signs. To avoid being thought queer by Wertham, Bruce and Dick should have done the following: Never show concern if the other is hurt, live in a shack, only have ugly flowers in small vases, call the butler "Chip" or "Joe" if you have to have one at all, never share a couch, keep your collar buttoned up, keep your jacket on, and never, ever wear a dressing gown. After all, didn't Noel Coward[7] wear a dressing gown?

Wertham is easy to mock, but the identification of homosexuals through dress codes has a long history.[8] Moreover, such codes originate as semiotic systems adopted by gay people themselves, as a way of signalling the otherwise invisible fact of sexual preference. There is a difference, though, between sporting the secret symbols of a subculture if you form part of that subculture and the elephantine spot-the-homo routine that Wertham performs.

Bat-fans have always responded angrily to Wertham's accusation. One calls it "one of the most incredible charges . . . unfounded rumours . . . sly sneers"[9] and the general response has been to reassert the masculinity of the two heroes, mixed with a little indignation: "If they had been actual men they could have won a libel suit."[10] This seems to me not only to miss the point, but also to *reinforce* Wertham's homophobia — it is only possible to win a libel suit over an "accusation" of homosexuality in a culture where homosexuality is deemed categorically inferior to heterosexuality.

Thus the rush to "protect" Batman and Robin from Wertham is simply the other side to the coin of his bigotry. It may reject Wertham, cast him in the role of dirty-minded old man, but its view of homosexuality is identical. Mark Cotta Vaz thus describes the imputed homosexual relationship as "licentious" while claiming that in fact Bruce Wayne "regularly squired the most beautiful women in Gotham City and presumably had a healthy sex life."[11] Licentious versus healthy — Dr. Wertham himself could not have bettered this homophobic opposition.

Despite the passions aroused on both sides (or rather the two facets   15
of the same side), there is something comic at the heart of this dispute. It

---

7. **Noel Coward** (1899–1973)   British playwright, actor, and composer known for witty, sophisticated comedies. —EDS.

8. See, for example, the newspaper stories on "how to spot" homosexuals printed in Britain in the fifties and sixties, and discussed in Jeffrey Weeks, *Coming Out: Homosexual Politics in Britain* (London: Quartet, 1979).

9. Phrases taken from Chapters 5 and 6 of Mark Cotta Vaz, *Tales of the Dark Knight: Batman's First Fifty Years* (London: Futura, 1989).

10. Les Daniels, *Comix: A History of Comic Books in America* (New York: Bonanza Books, 1971), p. 87.

11. Cotta Vaz, pp. 47 and 53.

is, simply, that Bruce and Dick are *not* real people but fictional constructions, and hence to squabble over their "real" sex life is to take things a little too far. What is at stake here is the question of reading, of what readers do with the raw material that they are given. Readers are at liberty to construct whatever fantasy lives they like with the characters of the fiction they read (within the limits of generic and narrative credibility, that is). This returns us to the unfortunate patients of Dr. Wertham:

> One young homosexual during psychotherapy brought us a copy of *Detective* comic, with a Batman story. He pointed out a picture of "The Home of Bruce and Dick," a house beautifully landscaped, warmly lighted and showing the devoted pair side by side, looking out a picture window. When he was eight this boy had realized from fantasies about comic book pictures that he was aroused by men. At the age of ten or eleven, "I found my liking, my sexual desires, in comic books. I think I put myself in the position of Robin. I did want to have relations with Batman . . . I remember the first time I came across the page mentioning the 'secret batcave.' The thought of Batman and Robin living together and possibly having sex relations came to my mind. . . ."[12]

Wertham quotes this to shock us, to impel us to tear the pages of *Detective* away before little Tommy grows up and moves to Greenwich Village, but reading it as a gay man today I find it rather moving and also highly recognizable.

What this anonymous gay man did was to practice that form of bricolage[13] which Richard Dyer has identified as a characteristic reading strategy of gay audiences.[14] Denied even the remotest possibility of supportive images of homosexuality within the dominant heterosexual culture, gay people have had to fashion what we could out of the imageries of dominance, to snatch illicit meanings from the fabric of normality, to undertake a corrupt decoding for the purposes of satisfying marginalized desires.[15] This may not be as necessary as it once was, given the greater visibility of gay representations, but it is still an important practice. Wertham's patient evokes in me an admiration, that in a period of American history even more homophobic than most, there he was, raiding the citadels of masculinity, weaving fantasies of oppositional desire. What ef-

---

12. Wertham, p. 192.

13. **bricolage**   A new object created by reassembling bits and pieces of other objects; here, gay-identified readings produced from classic texts. — EDS.

14. Richard Dyer, ed., *Gays and Film,* 2nd edition (New York: Zoetrope, 1984), p. 1.

15. See Richard Dyer, "Judy Garland and Gay Men," in Dyer, *Heavenly Bodies* (London: BFI, 1987), and Claire Whitaker, "Hollywood Transformed: Interviews with Lesbian Viewers," in Peter Steven, ed., *Jump Cut: Hollywood, Politics and Counter-Cinema* (Toronto: Between the Lines, 1985).

fect the dread Wertham had on him is hard to predict, but I profoundly hope that he wasn't "cured."

It wasn't only Batman who was subjected to Dr. Doom's bizarre ideas about human sexuality. Hence:

> The homosexual connotation of the Wonder Woman type of story is psychologically unmistakable.... For boys, Wonder Woman is a frightening image. For girls she is a morbid ideal. Where Batman is anti-feminine, the attractive Wonder Woman and her counterparts are definitely anti-masculine. Wonder Woman has her own female following.... Her followers are the "Holiday girls," i.e. the holiday girls, the gay party girls, the gay girls.[16]

Just how much elision can be covered with one "i.e."? Wertham's view of homosexuality is not, at least, inconsistent. Strong, admirable women will turn little girls into dykes—such a heroine can only be seen as a "morbid ideal."

Crazed as Wertham's ideas were, their effectiveness is not in doubt. The mid-fifties saw a moral panic about the assumed dangers of comic books. In the United States companies were driven out of business, careers wrecked, and the Comics Code introduced. This had distinct shades of the Hays Code[17] that had been brought in to clamp down on Hollywood in the 1930s, and under its jurisdiction comics opted for the bland, the safe, and the reactionary. In Britain there was government legislation to prohibit the importing of American comics, as the comics panic slotted neatly into a whole series of anxieties about the effects on British youth of American popular culture.[18]

And in all of this, what happened to Batman? He turned into Fred MacMurray from *My Three Sons*. He lost any remaining edge of the shadowy vigilante of his earliest years, and became an upholder of the most stifling small-town American values. Batwoman and Batgirl appeared (June Allyson and Bat-Gidget) to take away any lingering doubts about the Dynamic Duo's sex lives. A 1963 story called "The Great Clayface-Joker Feud" has some especially choice examples of the new, squeaky-clean sexuality of the assembled Bats.

Batgirl says to Robin, "I can hardly wait to get into my Batgirl costume again! Won't it be terrific if we could go on a crime case together like the last time? (sigh)." Robin replies, "It sure would, Betty (sigh)." The elder Bats look on approvingly. Batgirl is Batwoman's niece—to make her a daughter would have implied that Batwoman had had (gulp) sexual intercourse, and that would never do. This is the era of Troy

20

---

16. Wertham, pp. 192–93.
17. **Hays Code**   The 1930 Motion Picture Production Code, which described in detail what was morally acceptable in films.—EDS.
18. See Barker.

Donohue and Pat Boone,[19] and Batman as ever serves as a cultural ther-
mometer, taking the temperature of the times.

The Clayface/Joker business is wrapped up (the villains of this period
are wacky conjurors, nothing more, with no menace or violence about
them) and the episode concludes with another tableau of terrifying heterosexual contentment. "Oh Robin," simpers Batgirl, "I'm afraid you'll
just have to hold me! I'm still so shaky after fighting Clayface . . . and
you're so strong!" Robin: "Gosh Batgirl, it was swell of you to calm me
down when I was worried about Batman tackling Clayface alone." (One
feels a distinct Wertham influence here: If Robin shows concern about
Batman, wheel on a supportive female, the very opposite of a "morbid
ideal," to minister in a suitably self-effacing way.) Batwoman here seizes
her chance and tackles Batman: "You look worried about Clayface, Batman . . . so why don't you follow Robin's example and let me soothe
you?" Batman can only reply "Gulp."

Gulp indeed. While it's easy simply to laugh at strips like these,
knowing as we do the way in which such straight-faced material would
be mercilessly shredded by the sixties' TV series, they do reveal the retreat into coziness forced on comics by the Wertham onslaught and its
repercussions. There no doubt were still subversive readers of *Batman*,
erasing Batgirl on her every preposterous appearance and reworking the
Duo's capers to leave some room for homoerotic speculation, but such a
reading would have had to work so much harder than before. The *Batman* of this era was such a closed text, so immune to polysemic interpretation, that its interest today is only as a symptom—or, more productively, as camp. "The Great Clayface-Joker Feud" may have been
published in 1963, but in every other respect it is a fifties' text. If the
1960s began for the world in general with the Beatles, the 1960s for Batman began with the TV series in 1966. If the Caped Crusader had been
all but Werthamed out of existence, he was about to be camped back
into life.

The Camped Crusader and the Boys Wondered

Trying to define "camp" is like attempting to sit in the corner of a
circular room. It can't be done, which only adds to the quixotic appeal of
the attempt. Try these:

> To be camp is to present oneself as being committed to the marginal
> with a commitment greater than the marginal merits.[20]

---

19. **Troy Donohue and Pat Boone**   Clean-cut, all-American-boy stars from
the 1950s and 1960s.—EDS.

20. Mark Booth, *Camp* (London: Quartet, 1983), p. 18.

> Camp sees everything in quotation marks. It's not a lamp but a "lamp"; not a woman but a "woman." . . . It is the farthest extension, in sensibility, of the metaphor of life as theatre.[21]

> Camp is . . . a way of poking fun at the whole cosmology of restrictive sex roles and sexual identifications which our society uses to oppress its women and repress its men.[22]

> Camp was and is a way for gay men to re-imagine the world around them . . . by exaggerating, stylizing and remaking what is usually thought to be average or normal.[23]

> Camp was a prison for an illegal minority; now it is a holiday for consenting adults.[24]

All true, in their way, but all inadequate. The problem with camp is   25
that it is primarily an experiential rather than an analytical discourse. Camp is a set of attitudes, a gallery of snapshots, an inventory of postures, a modus vivendi, a shop-full of frocks, an arch of eyebrows, a great big pink butterfly that just won't be pinned down. Camp is primarily an adjective, occasionally a verb, but never anything as prosaic, as earthbound, as a noun.

Yet if I propose to use this adjective as a way of describing one or more of the guises of Batman, I need to arrive at some sort of working definition. So, for the purposes of this analysis, I intend the term "camp" to refer to a playful, knowing, self-reflexive theatricality. *Batman,* the sixties' TV series, was nothing if not knowing. It employed the codes of camp in an unusually public and heavily signaled way. This makes it different from those people or texts who are taken up by camp audiences without ever consciously putting camp into practice. The difference may be very briefly spelled out by reference to Hollywood films. If *Mildred Pierce*[25] and *The Letter*[26] were taken up *as* camp, teased by primarily gay male audiences into yielding meaning not intended by their makers, then *Whatever Happened to Baby Jane?*[27] is a piece of self-conscious camp, capitalizing on certain attitudinal and stylistic tendencies known to exist in audiences. *Baby Jane* is also, significantly, a 1960s' film, and the 1960s

---

21. Sontag, p. 109.
22. Jack Babuscio, "Camp and the Gay Sensibility," in Dyer, ed., *Gays and Film,* p. 46.
23. Michael Bronski, *Culture Clash: The Making of Gay Sensibility* (Boston: South End Press), p. 42.
24. Philip Core, *Camp: The Lie That Tells the Truth* (London: Plexus), p. 7.
25. **Mildred Pierce**   1945 murder mystery film that traces the fortunes of a homemaker who breaks with her husband. — EDS.
26. **The Letter**   1940 murder movie whose ending was changed to satisfy moral standards of the time. — EDS.
27. **Whatever Happened to Baby Jane?**   Macabre 1962 film about a former child movie star living in an old Hollywood mansion. — EDS.

were the decade in which camp swished out of the ghetto and up into the scarcely prepared mainstream.

A number of key events and texts reinforced this. Susan Sontag wrote her *Notes on Camp,* which remains the starting point for researchers even now. Pop Art[28] was in vogue (and in *Vogue*) and whatever the more elevated claims of Lichtenstein,[29] Warhol,[30] and the rest, their artworks were on one level a new inflection of camp. The growing intellectual respectability of pop music displayed very clearly that the old barriers that once rigidly separated high and low culture were no longer in force. The James Bond films, and even more so their successors like *Modesty Blaise,* popularized a dry, self-mocking wit that makes up one part of the multifaceted diamond of camp. And on television there were *The Avengers, The Man from UNCLE, Thunderbirds,* and *Batman.*

To quote the inevitable Sontag, "The whole point of Camp is to dethrone the serious. . . . More precisely, Camp involves a new, more complex relation to 'the serious.' One can be serious about the frivolous, frivolous about the serious."[31]

The problem with Batman in those terms is that there was never anything truly serious to begin with (unless one swallows that whole portentous Dark Knight charade, more of which in the next section). Batman in its comic book form had, unwittingly, always been camp—it was serious (the tone, the moral homilies) about the frivolous (a man in a stupid suit). He was camp in the way that classic Hollywood was camp, but what the sixties' TV series and film did was to overlay this "innocent" camp with a thick layer of ironic distance, the self-mockery version of camp. And given the long associations of camp with the homosexual male subculture, Batman was a particular gift on the grounds of his relationship with Robin. As George Melly put it, "The real Batman series were beautiful because of their unselfconscious absurdity. The remakes, too, at first worked on a double level. Over the absorbed children's heads we winked and nudged, but in the end what were we laughing at? The fact they didn't know that Batman had it off with Robin."[32]

It was as if Wertham's fears were being vindicated at last, but his 1950s' bigot's anguish had been supplanted by a self-consciously hip

---

28. **Pop Art**   Art movement, begun in the 1950s, that borrowed images and symbols from popular culture, particularly from commercial products and mass media, as a critique of traditional fine art. — EDS.

29. **Lichtenstein**   Roy Lichtenstein (1923–1997), American artist at the center of the Pop Art movement, best known for melodramatic comic-book scenes. — EDS.

30. **Warhol**   Andy Warhol (1930?–1987), pioneering Pop artist known for reproducing stereotyped images of famous people, such as Marilyn Monroe, and of commercial products, such as Campbell's Soup cans. — EDS.

31. Sontag, p. 116.

32. George Melly, *Revolt into Style: The Pop Arts in the 50s and 60s* (Oxford: Oxford University Press, 1989 [first published 1970]), p. 193.

Batman and Robin from the 1960s TV series.

1960s' playfulness. What adult audiences laughed at in the sixties' *Batman* was a camped-up version of the fifties they had just left behind.

Batman's lessons in good citizenship ("We'd like to feel that our efforts may help every youngster to grow up into an honest, useful citizen"[33]) were another part of the character ripe for ridiculing deconstruction — "Let's go, Robin, we've set another youth on the road to a brighter tomorrow" (the episode "It's How You Play the Game"). Everything the Adam West Batman said was a parody of seriousness, and how could it be otherwise? How could anyone take genuinely seriously the words of a man dressed like that?

The Batman/Robin relationship is never referred to directly; more fun can be had by presenting it "straight," in other words, screamingly camp. Wertham's reading of the Dubious Duo had been so extensively aired as to pass into the general consciousness (in George Melly's words, "We all knew Robin and Batman were pouves"[34]), it was part of the fabric of *Batman,* and the makers of the TV series proceeded accordingly.

Consider the Duo's encounter with Marsha, Queen of Diamonds. The threat she embodies is nothing less than heterosexuality itself, the

---

33. "The Batman Says," *Batman* #3 (1940), quoted in Cotta Vaz, p. 15.
34. Melly, p. 192.

deadliest threat to the domestic bliss of the Bat-couple. She is even about to marry Batman before Albert intervenes to save the day. He and Batman flee the church, but have to do so in the already decorated Batmobile, festooned with wedding paraphernalia including a large "Just Married" sign. "We'll have to drive it as it is," says Batman, while somewhere in the audience a Dr. Wertham takes feverish notes. Robin, Commissioner Gordon, and Chief O'Hara have all been drugged with Marsha's "Cupid Dart," but it is of course the Boy Wonder who Batman saves first. The dart, he tells Robin, "contains some secret ingredient by which your sense and your will were affected," and it isn't hard to read that ingredient as heterosexual desire, since its result, seen in the previous episode, was to turn Robin into Marsha's slobbering slave.

We can tell with relief now, though, as Robin is "back in fighting form" (with impeccable timing, Batman clasps Robin's shoulder on the word "fighting"). Marsha has one last attempt to destroy the duo, but naturally she fails. The female temptress, the seductress, the enchantress must be vanquished. None of this is in the least subtle (Marsha's cat, for example, is called Circe) but this type of mass-market camp can't afford the luxury of subtlety. The threat of heterosexuality is similarly mobilized in the 1966 feature film, where it is Bruce Wayne's infatuation with Kitka (Catwoman in disguise) that causes all manner of problems.

A more interesting employment of camp comes in the episodes where the Duo battle the Black Widow, played by Tallulah Bankhead. The major camp coup here, of course, is the casting. Bankhead was one of the supreme icons of camp, one of its goddesses: "Too intelligent not to be self-conscious, too ambitious to bother about her self-consciousness, too insecure ever to be content, but too arrogant ever to admit insecurity, Tallulah personified camp."[35]

A heady claim, but perhaps justified, because the Black Widow episodes are, against stiff competition, the campiest slices of Batman of them all. The stories about Bankhead are legendary—the time when on finding no toilet paper in her cubicle she slipped a ten dollar bill under the partition and asked the woman next door for two fives, or her whispered remark to a priest conducting a particularly elaborate service and swinging a censor of smoking incense, "Darling, I love the drag, but your purse is on fire"—and casting her in Batman was the final demonstration of the series' commitment to camp.

The plot is unremarkable, the usual Bat-shenanigans; the pleasure lies in the detail. Details like the elderly Bankhead crammed into her Super-Villainess costume, or like the way in which (through a plot detail I won't go into) she impersonates Robin, so we see Burt Ward miming to Bankhead's voice, giving the unforgettable image of Robin flirting with

---

35. Core, p. 25.

burly traffic cops. Best of all, and Bankhead isn't even in this scene but the thrill of having her involved clearly spurred the writer to new heights of camp, Batman has to sing a song to break free of the Black Widow's spell. Does he choose to sing "God Bless America"? Nothing so rugged. He clutches a flower to his Bat chest and sings Gilbert and Sullivan's "I'm Just a Little Buttercup." It is this single image, more than any other, that prevents me from taking the post–Adam West Dark Knight at all seriously.

The fundamental camp trick which the series pulls is to make the comics speak. What was acceptable on the page, in speech balloons, stands revealed as ridiculous once given audible voice. The famous visualized sound effects (URKKK! KA-SPLOOSH!) that are for many the fondest memory of the series work along similar lines. Camp often makes its point by transposing the codes of one cultural form into the inappropriate codes of another. It thrives on mischievous incongruity.

The incongruities, the absurdities, the sheer ludicrousness of Batman were brought out so well by the sixties' version that for some audiences there will never be another credible approach. I have to include myself here. I've recently read widely in postsixties Bat-lore, and I can appreciate what the writers and artists are trying to do, but my Batman will always be Adam West. It's impossible to be somber or pompous about Batman because if you try the ghost of West will come Bat-climbing into your mind, fortune cookie wisdom on his lips and keen young Dick by his side. It's significant, I think, that the letters I received from the editors of this book began "Dear Bat-Contributor."[36] Writers preparing chapters about James Joyce or Ingmar Bergman do not, I suspect, receive analogous greetings. To deny the large camp component of Batman is to blind oneself to one of the richest parts of his history.

Is There Bat-Life after Bat-Camp?

The international success of the Adam West incarnation left Batman   40
high and dry. The camping around had been fun while it lasted, but it hadn't lasted very long. Most camp humor has a relatively short life span, new targets are always needed, and the camp aspect of Batman had been squeezed dry. The mass public had moved on to other heroes, other genres, other acres of merchandising, but there was still a hard Bat-core of fans to satisfy. Where could the Bat go next? Clearly there was no possibility of returning to the caped Eisenhower, the benevolent patriarch of the 1950s. That option had been well and truly closed down by the TV

---

36. This essay originally appeared in an anthology, *The Many Lives of the Batman: Critical Approaches to a Superhero and His Media.* —EDS.

show. Batman needed to be given his dignity back, and this entailed a return to his roots.

This, in any case, is the official version. For the unreconstructed devotee of the Batman (that is, people who insist on giving him the definite article before the name), the West years had been hell—a tricksy travesty, an effeminizing of the cowled avenger. There's a scene in *Midnight Cowboy* where Dustin Hoffman tells Jon Voight that the only audience liable to be receptive to his cowboy clothes are gay men looking for rough trade. Voight is appalled—"You mean to tell me John Wayne was a fag?" (quoted, roughly, from memory). This outrage, this horror at shattered illusions, comes close to encapsulating the loathing and dread the campy Batman has received from the old guard of Gotham City and the younger born-again Bat-fans.

So what has happened since the 1960s has been the painstaking reheterosexualization of Batman. I apologize for coining such a clumsy word, but no other quite gets the sense that I mean. This strategy has worked, too, for large audiences, reaching its peak with the 1989 film. To watch this and then come home to see a video of the 1966 movie is to grasp how complete the transformation has been. What I want to do in this section is to trace some of the crucial moments in that change, written from the standpoint of someone still unashamedly committed to Bat-camp.

If one wants to take Batman as a Real Man, the biggest stumbling block has always been Robin. There have been disingenuous claims that "Batman and Robin had a blood-brother closeness. Theirs was a spiritual intimacy forged from the stress of countless battles fought side by side"[37] (one can imagine what Tallulah Bankhead might say to *that*), but we know otherwise. The Wertham lobby and the acolytes of camp alike have ensured that any Batman/Robin relationship is guaranteed to bring on the sniggers. Besides which, in the late 1960s, Robin was getting to be a big boy, too big for any shreds of credibility to attach themselves to all that father-son smokescreen. So in 1969 Dick Grayson was packed off to college and the Bat was solitary once more.

This was a shrewd move. It's impossible to conceive of the recent, obsessive, sturm-und-drang Batman with a chirpy little Robin getting in the way.[38] A text of the disturbing power of *The Killing Joke*[39] could not have functioned with Robin to rupture the grim dualism of its

---

37. Cotta Vaz, p. 53.

38. A female Robin is introduced in the *Dark Knight Returns* series, which, while raising interesting questions about the sexuality of Batman, which I don't here have the space to address, seems significant in that the Dark Knight cannot run the risk of reader speculation that a traditionally male Robin might provoke.

39. ***The Killing Joke*** Graphic novel by Alan Moore, Brian Bolland, and John Higgins (New York: DC Comics 1988). —EDS.

Batman/Joker struggle. There was, however, a post-Dick Robin, but he was killed off by fans in that infamous telephone poll.[40]

It's intriguing to speculate how much latent (or blatant) homophobia   45
lay behind that vote. Did the fans decide to kill off Jason Todd so as to redeem Batman for unproblematic heterosexuality? Impossible to say. There are other factors to take into account, such as Jason's apparent failure to live up to the expectations of what a Robin should be like. The sequence of issues in which Jason/Robin died, *A Death in the Family,* is worth looking at in some detail, however, in order to see whether the camp connotations of Bruce and Dick had been fully purged.

The depressing answer is that they had. This is very much the Batman of the 1980s, his endless feud with the Joker this time uneasily stretched over a framework involving the Middle East and Ethiopia. Little to be camp about there, though the presence of the Joker guarantees a quota of sick jokes. The sickest of all is the introduction of the Ayatollah Khomeini, a real and important political figure, into this fantasy world of THUNK! and THER-ACKK! and grown men dressed as bats. (As someone who lived in the part of England from which Reagan's planes took off on their murderous mission to bomb Libya, I fail to see the humor in this cartoon version of American foreign policy: It's too near the real thing.)

Jason dies at the Joker's hands because he becomes involved in a search for his own origins, a clear parallel to Batman's endless returns to *his* Oedipal scenario. Families, in the Bat-mythology, are dark and troubled things, one more reason why the introduction of the fifties versions of Batwoman and Batgirl seemed so inappropriate. This applies only to real, biological families, though; the true familial bond is between Batman and Robin, hence the title of these issues. Whether one chooses to read Robin as Batman's ward (official version), son (approved fantasy), or lover (forbidden fantasy), the sense of loss at his death is bound to be devastating. Batman finds Robin's body and, in the time-honored tradition of Hollywood cinema, is at least able to give him a loving embrace. Good guys hug their dead buddies, only queers smooch when still alive.

If the word "camp" is applied at all to the eighties' Batman, it is a label for the Joker. This sly displacement is the cleverest method yet devised of preserving Bat-heterosexuality. The play that the texts regularly make with the concept of Batman and the Joker as mirror images now takes a new twist. The Joker is Batman's "bad twin," and part of that badness is, increasingly, an implied homosexuality. This is certainly present in the 1989 film, a generally glum and portentous affair except for Jack Nicholson's Joker, a characterization enacted with venomous camp.

---

40. **telephone poll**   In a 1988 issue of the *Batman* comic, a "post-Dick Robin," Jason Todd, was badly injured in an explosion, and readers were allowed to phone the publisher to vote on whether he should be allowed to survive. —EDS.

The only moment when this dour film comes to life is when the Joker and his gang raid the Art Gallery, spraying the paintings and generally camping up a storm.

The film strives and strains to make us forget the Adam West Batman, to the point of giving us Vicki Vale as Bruce Wayne's lover, and certainly Michael Keaton's existential agonizing (variations on the theme of why-did-I-have-to-be-a-Bat) is a world away from West's gleeful subversion of truth, justice and the American Way. This is the same species of Batman celebrated by Frank Miller: "If your only memory of Batman is that of Adam West and Burt Ward exchanging camped-out quips while clobbering slumming guest-stars Vincent Price and Cesar Romero, I hope this book will come as a surprise. . . . For me, Batman was never funny. . . ."[41]

The most recent linkage of the Joker with homosexuality comes in   50
Arkham Asylum, the darkest image of the Bat-world yet. Here the Joker has become a parody of a screaming queen, calling Batman "honey pie," given to exclamations like "oooh!" (one of the oldest homophobic clichés in the book), and pinching Batman's behind with the advice, "Loosen up, tight ass." He also, having no doubt read his Wertham, follows the pinching by asking, "What's the matter? Have I touched a nerve? How is the Boy Wonder? Started shaving yet?" The Bat-response is unequivocal: "Take your filthy hands off me . . . Filthy degenerate!"

Arkham Asylum is a highly complex reworking of certain key aspects of the mythology, of which the sexual tension between Batman and the Joker is only one small part. Nonetheless the Joker's question "Have I touched a nerve?" seems a crucial one, as revealed by the homophobic ferocity of Batman's reply. After all, the dominant cultural construction of gay men at the end of the 1980s is as plague carriers, and the word "degenerate" is not far removed from some of the labels affixed to us in the age of AIDS.

Batman: Is He or Isn't He?

The one constant factor through all of the transformations of Batman has been the devotion of his admirers. They will defend him against what they see as negative interpretations, and they carry around in their heads a kind of essence of batness, a Bat-Platonic Ideal of how Batman should really be. The Titan Books reissue of key comics from the 1970s each carry a preface by a noted fan, and most of them contain claims such as "This, I feel, is Batman as he was meant to be."[42]

---

41. Frank Miller, "Introduction," *Batman: Year One* (London: Titan, 1988).
42. Kim Newman, "Introduction," *Batman: The Demon Awakes* (London: Titan, 1989).

Where a negative construction is specifically targeted, no prizes for guessing which one it is: "you . . . are probably also fond of the TV show he appeared in. But then maybe you prefer Elvis Presley's Vegas years or the later Jerry Lewis movies over their early stuff . . . for me, the definitive Batman was then and always will be the one portrayed in these pages."[43]

The sixties' TV show remains anathema to the serious Bat-fan precisely because it heaps ridicule on the very notion of a serious Batman. *Batman* the series revealed the man in the cape as a pompous fool, an embodiment of superseded ethics, and a closet queen. As Marsha, Queen of Diamonds, put it, "Oh Batman, darling, you're so divinely square." Perhaps the enormous success of the 1989 film will help to advance the cause of the rival Bat-archetype, the grim, vengeful Dark Knight whose heterosexuality is rarely called into question (his humorlessness, fondness for violence, and obsessive monomania seem to me exemplary qualities for a heterosexual man). The answer, surely, is that they needn't be mutually exclusive.

If I might be permitted a rather camp comparison, each generation 55 has its definitive Hamlet, so why not the same for Batman? I'm prepared to admit the validity, for some people, of the swooping eighties' vigilante, so why are they so concerned to trash my sixties' camped crusader? Why do they insist so vehemently that Adam West was a faggy aberration, a blot on the otherwise impeccably butch Bat-landscape? What *are* they trying to hide?

If I had a suspicious frame of mind, I might think that they were protesting too much, that maybe Dr. Wertham was on to something when he targeted these narratives as incitements to homosexual fantasy. And if I want Batman to be gay, then, for me, he is. After all, outside of the minds of his writers and readers, he doesn't really exist.

Reading the Text

1. Summarize the objections Fredric Wertham makes to Batman in *Seduction of the Innocent*.
2. In a paragraph, write your own explanation of what Medhurst means by "camp" (para. 24).
3. What evidence does Medhurst supply to demonstrate that Batman is a gay character?
4. Explain what Medhurst means by his closing comment: "And if I want Batman to be gay, then, for me, he is. After all, outside of the minds of his writers and readers, he doesn't really exist" (para. 56).

---

43. Jonathan Ross, "Introduction," *Batman: Vow from the Grave* (London: Titan, 1989).

Reading the Signs

1. Do you agree with Medhurst's argument that the Batman and Robin duo were really a covert homosexual couple? Write an essay arguing for or challenging his position, being sure to study his evidence closely. You may want to visit your campus's media library to see if they have file tapes of old *Batman* shows, or read contemporary reviews of *Batman,* to gather evidence for your own essay.
2. Check your college library for a copy of Fredric Wertham's *Seduction of the Innocent.* Then write your own critique of Wertham's attack on Batman.
3. Buy a few copies of the current *Batman* comic book, and write an essay in which you explain Batman's current sexual orientation.
4. Visit your college library, and obtain a copy of Susan Sontag's "Notes on Camp" (included in Sontag's collections *Against Interpretation* and *The Susan Sontag Reader*). How would Sontag interpret the character of Batman?

N'GAI CROAL AND JANE HUGHES
Lara Croft, the Bit Girl

She's toured with U2, modeled for Gucci, recorded her own single, and been called "the perfect fantasy girl for the digital generation." No, we're not talking about Courtney Love; this is the profile of Lara Croft, the Tomb Raider star who has taken virtual celebrity into a dimension that Max Headroom could only dream of. The center of a multimillion dollar videogame empire, Croft is a sort of evolutionary successor to the "toon," an icon of virtual reality who may only be the harbinger of things to come. Will there someday be an Oscar award for Best Virtual Actress? Virtual celebs fleeing virtual paparazzi on the pages of a virtual Enquirer? *Virtual minds want to know. N'Gai Croal and Jane Hughes write for* Newsweek, *where this selection originally appeared.*

It's not easy being Lara Croft. After the British aristocrat and adventure-seeking archeologist starred in last year's hit Tomb Raider, she appeared on the cover of 40 magazines, toured with U2, modeled Gucci fashions, and recorded a single with ex-Eurythmics guitarist Dave Stewart. All the while, she's been in China, Tibet, and Venice working on the sequel. But you won't hear Lara whine about her hectic schedule. When you're a woman made of more than 540 polygons, part of your job is making it all look easy.

Equal parts Pamela Anderson and Indiana Jones with a dash of *La Femme Nikita,* Lara Croft is the computer-generated action heroine at the center of one of the hottest PC and console videogames on the market. To date nearly 8 million copies have been sold worldwide, putting it in the same company as the best-selling adventure game Myst.

Along the way, Lara became an icon as recognizable to gamers as Mario and Sonic the Hedgehog. U2 got the game makers at Core Design in England to create custom footage of Lara for the video wall in its current PopMart world tour. Some fans, convinced or praying that she's real, have bombarded Core with e-mail requesting info on her boyfriends and favorite pop bands. There are more than 100 Web sites devoted to her glory, ranging from nice, like the well-written *Croft Times* newsletter **www.cubeit.com/ctimes,** to naughty, like *Nude Raider,* for fans who think Lara's a bit overdressed in her skintight vest and Daisy Duke shorts.

Like Lara, the folks at Core haven't had much time to enjoy their success; plans for a sequel were underway two months before the first game came out. Since then it's been nothing but takeout food and catnaps on inflatable beds at the company's funky offices in a converted mansion on the outskirts of the northern English town of Derby for the designers as they scramble to get Tomb Raider 2 in stores.

The folks at Core are still a bit surprised at the Tomb Raider phe-   5
nomenon. "Lara has had an awful lot more media attention than the game itself because people like to lead on the sex angle, the size of her chest, and whether she takes her clothes off," says Core managing director Jeremy Smith. Yet he's shocked, shocked, to hear that U.S. parent company Eidos is pushing the pinup angle by listing her measurements as 38-24-34. Core insists that, in Lara's native England at least, she is a more modest 34D. "We have never really got hung up on that sort of thing," Smith sniffs. "When people ask what she would be like if you took her clothes off, the team simply says she would be a wire mesh. I am sure a lot of people enjoy ogling her, but she was never designed with the marketing in mind."

J. C. Herz, the author of *Joystick Nation,* a book on the history of videogames, isn't buying it. "Female characters are the rage because boys like to look at them. They're the pinup girls of the 21st century." But she thinks it was smart of Eidos to build the game around Lara. "If you can create a great character, what you've got is a franchise. It's like making a blockbuster movie and knowing that before anyone says a word you can make $100 million."

There's so much software on store shelves these days that simply creating a good game isn't enough to break out of the pack. With Lara, Eidos has created a star. "And the character belongs to you," Herz adds. "It doesn't pout in a trailer or ask you for $20 million for its next videogame. You own it. It's like minting money."

It all seems obvious now that Tomb Raider would go over big with lads of all ages, but when Core prodigy Toby Gard who later left to start his own company created a game around his vision of the perfect woman, he was violating several unspoken rules of 3-D gaming. Unlike with popular first-person-perspective games like Doom and Duke Nukem, players see the action over Lara's shoulder, like a movie. It's a single-player game with no options for Internet play. And, as Core's reps in France and Germany warned, who's going to play a game where the hero is a girl?

They shouldn't have worried. When the first version hit the stores in November 1996, it sold 500,000 copies in two months. Any good videogame is as much about the experience of watching as it is playing, and it was quite a corneal treat for players to see Lara run fluidly through caves and tunnels, turning cartwheels like Dominique Dawes and diving off ledges like Fu Mingxia. But unlike most action games, TR balances shooting and butt-kicking with exploration and puzzle-solving. So a female character—smart, strong, and supadupa fly—fit in perfectly with Core's vision for the game.

"A man," says designer Adrian Smith, "would have changed what   10
the game's about. But it wouldn't have mattered how gorgeous Lara was if the game itself wasn't any good." When Lara caps her foes, both guns blazing like Chow-Yun Fat in a John Woo action flick, Lara takes the slogan "Girl Power" to the next level. Call her Shotgun Spice; right in front of you, yet always just out of reach, she's the perfect fantasy girl for the digital generation.

Tomb Raider 2 is more ambitious and complex than its predecessor, so there are also more opportunities for error. At Core HQ, six testers play the game over and over—each runthrough takes about 11 hours— hunting down stray bugs. Smith was playing the game an hour before the PlayStation version went to Sony, when Lara fell off a ledge, and he couldn't get her back up. "If Sony found a bug, it would be nuclear here, but we're almost there." Then they found that they'd sent out thousands of demo CD-ROMs with the copy-protection timers already expired, making them unplayable. Then they went nuclear. Fortunately, someone came up with a patch, and they recalled the discs to make the fix. That's par for the course in the high-stakes world of game design, says Adrian's brother and managing director Jeremy Smith. "You're working under pressure to meet deadlines, and somehow you forget to take out one line of code. Still, it could have been worse. It could have gone out to the whole game," he laughs.

Core hasn't changed the formula much for the sequel, but the team of four artists and three programmers have crammed in a bunch of ideas that they didn't have time to put in the original. Gameplay is smoother and more detailed, with impressive lighting effects, such as flares illuminating a corridor as they fly through the air. Where the first game had mostly animal opponents, the sequel has several human villains as well as new beasties. There are new puzzles, new locations, outdoor as well as indoor, new weapons, new moves. See Lara climb. See Lara drive. And Lara herself has had a digital make-over to give her what Eidos calls "a more shapely and life-like look," including 46 polygons alone for her fully animated ponytail. But what fans really want are new form-fitting outfits, and Core has obliged with a wet suit, a flight jacket and, for those who finish the game, a nightie.

How long Tomb Raider will be able to preserve its unique qualities remains to be seen. Eidos CEO Mike McGarvey acknowledges that there's tremendous pressure to bring multiplayer and Internet play to the Tomb Raider franchise. The designers at Core aren't convinced that they should go that route. "We know from the success of Tomb Raider that the combination of different elements—exploration, puzzles, and combat—works really well as it stands," says Adrian Smith. "The inter-action is between the player and Lara; it's a very personal experience. Having seven or eight Laras running around on screen would detract from the whole atmosphere of the game."

Eidos is now the house that Lara built; sales of Tomb Raider helped turn a 1996 pretax loss of $2.6 million into a $14.5 million profit. So the company is proceeding aggressively in its efforts to leverage her appeal into other areas. The action figure is already in stores, and you can order jackets at the Web site **www.tombraider.com.** The single performed by Rhona Mitra, who serves as Lara's flesh-and-flesh incarnation at trade shows, has been postponed so it won't interfere with the movie deal that Eidos hopes to finalize [soon]. The designers—and most fans—hope that it will be a computer-animated movie, but McGarvey says it will probably be live action. For now, fans will have to content themselves with the ad blitz on MTV, ESPN, and the syndicated show *Xena: Warrior Princess.* The tag line? "Lara's Back. Where the Boys Are."

Reading the Text

1. Why did some Core employees believe at first that the Tomb Raider video game would be a commercial failure?
2. According to Croal and Hughes, what are the reasons for the extraordinary success of Tomb Raider?
3. Why did Lara Croft become a 1990s cultural icon, according to the authors?

Reading the Signs

1. In your journal, reflect on the success of Lara Croft. If you play video games, are you a fan of Lara, and if so, why? If you are not a fan, what is your explanation for her appeal?

2. This selection originally was published in *Newsweek*'s Focus on Technology section. In what ways do the style and content reflect the article's journalistic origins?

3. As an independent and powerful female character, Lara Croft could be seen as a potentially feminist icon, but her physical appearance could be seen as sexist. Write an essay arguing whether Lara Croft is a feminist or counterfeminist character.

4. Select a male video game character, and write a semiotic analysis of him. In what ways does he embody traditional male gender codes? To develop your ideas, consult Holly Devor's "Gender Role Behaviors and Attitudes" (p. 447) or James William Gibson's "Warrior Dreams" (p. 496).

EMILY PRAGER
Our Barbies, Ourselves

IIIIIIIIIIIIIIIIIIIIIIIIIIIIIIIIIIIIIIIIIIIIIIIIII

Little girls throughout America should know that Barbie is not drawn to scale. In this tongue-in-cheek essay on the role Barbie has played in her life, Emily Prager (b. 1952) reveals the damaging effect of a doll that establishes such an impossible standard of physical perfection for little girls — and for little boys who grow up expecting their girlfriends to look like Barbie. When not contemplating what Barbie has done to her, Emily Prager is a columnist with the New York Times *and an essayist and fiction writer who has published for* The National Lampoon, *the* Village Voice, *and* Penthouse, *among other magazines. Her books include a work of historical fiction for children,* World War II Resistance Stories; *a book of humor,* The Official I Hate Videogames Handbook; *and works of fiction such as* Eve's Tattoo *(1991) and* Clea and Zeus Divorce *(1987).*

I read an astounding obituary in the *New York Times* not too long ago. It concerned the death of one Jack Ryan. A former husband of Zsa Zsa Gabor, it said, Mr. Ryan had been an inventor and designer during his lifetime. A man of eclectic creativity, he designed Sparrow and Hawk missiles when he worked for the Raytheon Company, and, the notice said, when he consulted for Mattel he designed Barbie.

If Barbie was designed by a man, suddenly a lot of things made sense to me, things I'd wondered about for years. I used to look at Barbie and wonder, What's wrong with this picture? What kind of woman designed this doll? Let's be honest: Barbie looks like someone who got her start at the Playboy Mansion. She could be a regular guest on *The Howard Stern*

Show. It is a fact of Barbie's design that her breasts are so out of proportion to the rest of her body that if she were a human woman, she'd fall flat on her face.

If it's true that a woman didn't design Barbie, you don't know how much saner that makes me feel. Of course, that doesn't ameliorate the damage. There are millions of women who are subliminally sure that a thirty-nine-inch bust and a twenty-three-inch waist are the epitome of lovability. Could this account for the popularity of breast implant surgery?

I don't mean to step on anyone's toes here. I loved my Barbie. Secretly, I still believe that neon pink and turquoise blue are the only colors in which to decorate a duplex condo. And like many others of my generation, I've never married, simply because I cannot find a man who looks as good in clam diggers as Ken.

The question that comes to mind is, of course, Did Mr. Ryan design   5
Barbie as a weapon? Because it *is* odd that Barbie appeared about the
same time in my consciousness as the feminist movement—a time when
women sought equality and small breasts were king. Or is Barbie the
dream date of weapons designers? Or perhaps it's simpler than that: Perhaps Barbie is Zsa Zsa if she were eleven inches tall. No matter what, my
discovery of Jack Ryan confirms what I have always felt: There is something indescribably masculine about Barbie—dare I say it, phallic. For all
her giant breasts and high-heeled feet, she lacks a certain softness. If you
asked a little girl what kind of doll she wanted for Christmas, I just don't
think she'd reply, "Please, Santa, I want a hard-body."

On the other hand, you could say that Barbie, in feminist terms, is
definitely her own person. With her condos and fashion plazas and pools
and beauty salons, she is definitely a liberated woman, a gal on the move.
And she has always been sexual, even totemic. Before Barbie, American
dolls were flat-footed and breastless, and ineffably dignified. They were
created in the image of little girls or babies. Madame Alexander was the
queen of doll makers in the fifties, and her dollies looked like Elizabeth
Taylor in *National Velvet*. They represented the kind of girls who looked
perfect in jodhpurs, whose hair was never out of place, who grew up to
be Jackie Kennedy—before she married Onassis. Her dolls' boyfriends
were figments of the imagination, figments with large portfolios and
three-piece suits and presidential aspirations, figments who could keep
dolly in the style to which little girls of the fifties were programmed to
become accustomed, a style that spasm-ed with the sixties and the appearance of Barbie. And perhaps what accounts for Barbie's vast popularity is that she was also a sixties woman: into free love and fun colors,
anticlass, and possessed of real, molded boyfriend, Ken, with whom she
could chant a mantra.

But there were problems with Ken. I always felt weird about him.
He had no genitals, and, even at age ten, I found that ominous. I mean,
here was Barbie with these humongous breasts, and that was OK with
the toy company. And then, there was Ken with that truncated, uniden-
tifiable lump at his groin. I sensed injustice at work. Why, I wondered,
was Barbie designed with such obvious sexual equipment and Ken not?
Why was his treated as if it were more mysterious than hers? Did the fact
that it was treated as such indicate that somehow his equipment, his essential maleness, was considered more powerful than hers, more worthy
of the dignity of concealment? And if the issue in the mind of the toy
company was obscenity and its possible damage to children, I still object.
How do they think I felt, knowing that no matter how many water beds
they slept in, or hot tubs they romped in, or swimming pools they
lounged by under the stars, Barbie and Ken could never make love? No
matter how much sexuality Barbie possessed, she would never turn Ken
on. He would be forever withholding, forever detached. There was a

loneliness about Barbie's situation that was always disturbing. And twenty-five years later, movies and videos are still filled with topless women and covered men. As if we're all trapped in Barbie's world and can never escape.

God, it certainly has cheered me up to think that Barbie was designed by Jack Ryan. . . .

Reading the Text

1. Why does Prager say "a lot of things made sense" (para. 2) to her after she learned Barbie was designed by a man?
2. What is Prager's attitude toward Ken?
3. How do Madame Alexander dolls differ from Barbies?

Reading the Signs

1. Bring a toy to class, and, in same-sex groups, discuss its semiotic significance; you may want to focus particularly on how the toys may be intended for one gender or another. Then have each group select one toy and present your interpretation of it to the whole class. What gender-related patterns do you find in the presentations?
2. Think of a toy you played with as a child, and write a semiotic interpretation of it, using Prager's essay as a model. Be sure to consider differences between your childhood response to the toy and your current response.
3. Did you have a Barbie doll when you were a child? If so, write a journal entry in which you explore what the doll meant to you when you were young and how Prager's essay has caused you to rethink your attitudes.
4. Consider how Jack Ryan, the creator of Barbie, would defend his design. Write a letter, as if you were Ryan, addressed to Prager in which you justify Barbie's appearance and refute Prager's analysis.
5. Barbie can be seen as embodying not only America's traditional gender roles but also its consumerist ethos. Visit a toy store to learn what "accessories" one can buy for Barbie, and then write an essay in which you explore the extent to which she illustrates the "hunger for more" described by Laurence Shames ("The More Factor," p. 55).

GARY CROSS

Barbie, G.I. Joe, and Play in the 1960s

Toys aren't only toys. For as Gary Cross observes in this excerpt from
Kid's Stuff: Toys and the Changing World of American Childhood *(1997), toys are signifiers of the shifting terrain of American
culture and belief. So it is revealing that Barbie, who was designed to
be the ultimate consumer, has stayed that way for more than forty
years, while G.I. Joe mutated from an ordinary infantryman into a
high-tech action-adventure hero and finally disappeared. Consumption,
it seems, never goes out of style, but not everything we consume stays
in fashion. So who says that toys aren't signs of our times? Gary
Cross is a professor of history at Pennsylvania State University who
specializes in analyzing the roles that toys play in the shaping of
American childhood.*

Television and the new business climate in the toy industry alone did
not transform the meaning of play. Toys were changing because American society was changing. By looking at the two most important trend-
setting toys we can find clues to these changes. Much has been written
about Barbie and G.I. Joe as icons of popular culture. But Barbie and
G.I. Joe were also toys, and like other toys they were mostly given to
children by adults.

Barbie began her career as a stiff plastic dress-up figure. Ruth
Handler often claimed that she invented Barbie to fill a void in girls' play.
Girls wanted a less cumbersome and more fun version of the fashion
paper doll. In using paper dolls as a model Mattel was in effect redirect-
ing doll play away from the friendship and nurturing themes of the companion and baby dolls that had predominated since the 1900s. In the
nineteenth century paper dolls were used to display the latest styles and
to portray royalty and famous actresses, especially in magazines devoted
to fashion. They were associated with an adult world of quasi-aristocratic
consumption. They had little to do with domestic or friendship themes.
Paper dolls and their focus on fashion were an important part of girls'
play in the first half of the twentieth century, but they were only a minor
part of the toy business.[1]

---

1. Ruth Handler, *Dream Doll* (Stamford, Conn.: Longmeadow Press, 1994), chs.
4–5; Rebecca Harnmell, "To Educate and Amuse: Paper Dolls and Toys, 1640–1900"
(M.A. thesis, University of Delaware, 1988, University Microforms International, Ann
Arbor, 1989).

Mattel, however, put fashion doll play at the center of the industry. The idea of making the paper fashion doll three dimensional was hardly new. Even the association of doll play with consumption was not innovative. It had been built into the concepts of dolls from Patsy to Toni. But Barbie was not a child doll dressed in children's fashions. Rather Barbie was in the shape of a young woman with very long legs and an exaggerated hourglass figure. She looked neither like the little girl who owned her nor like the little girls' mother. She was neither a baby, a child, nor a mother but a liberated teenager, almost a young woman. Handler admitted that even in this her creation was not so original. She "borrowed" the look from a German dress-up doll she and her daughter Barbara had noticed on a vacation in Switzerland. But she marketed it on a grand scale at a perfect point in the history of American childhood: at the end of the 1950s.[2]

Barbie was an early rebel against the domesticity that dominated the lives of baby-boom mothers. It may not be surprising that some of the first generation of Barbie owners became feminists in the late 1960s and 1970s. The revolt against at least the momism of the feminine mystique was played out with Barbie, who never cared for babies or children. But Mattel's doll was also an autonomous teenager with no visible ties to parents in a time when the earliest of the baby-boom generation were just entering their teens. This crop of teenagers, coming of age in a more affluent United States, had more choices than their parents had had and were freer of adult control. To the eight-year-old of 1960, Barbie represented a hoped-for future of teenage freedom. It was this attraction of Barbie that long survived the maturation of the baby-boom generation. It is also not surprising that when Mattel market-tested Barbie it found that mothers were not nearly so positive about the doll as were their daughters. Mothers recognized that this doll was a break from the tradition of nurturing and companion play and that girls apparently welcomed it.

Despite all this, Barbie hardly "taught" girls to shed female stereotypes. Rather she prompted them to associate the freedom of being an adult with carefree consumption. With her breasts and slender waist, Barbie came literally to embody the little girl's image of what it meant to be grown up. At the same time, in her contemporary fashions, she represented the up-to-date. Barbie did not invite children to be Mommy, nor was she the child's friend in a secret garden of caring and sharing. She was what the little girl was not and, even more important, what her mother was not. She was a fashion model with a large wardrobe designed

5

2. Handler, *Dream Doll;* A. Glen Mandeville, *Doll Fashion Anthology and Price Guide,* 4th ed. (Cumberland, Md.: Hobby House, 1993), 1–33; K. Westenhouser, *The Story of Barbie* (Paducah, Ky.: Collector Books, 1994), 5–15; Billy Boy, *Barbie: Her Life and Times* (New York: Crown, 1987), 17–28, 40–44.

to attract attention. Instead of teaching girls how to diaper a baby or use floor cleaners, Barbie play was an education in consumption—going to the hairdresser and shopping for that perfect evening gown for the big dance. Even when she had a job (model, stewardess, or later even a doctor), her work and life had nothing to do with the jobs of most women. Barbie was never a cashier at Wal-Mart or a homemaker.

If Barbie taught that freedom meant consumption, the Barbie line was designed to maximize parents' real spending. Playing consumer required that Barbie have a constantly changing wardrobe of coordinated clothing and accessories. Clothing sets were often much more expensive than the "hook," the doll itself. The first Barbie advertising brochure featured, for example, a Barbie-Q Outfit, Suburban Shopper, Picnic Set (with fishing pole), Evening Splendor (complete with strapless sheath), and even a Wedding Day Set. By the early 1960s Barbie had play environments, for example the Barbie Fashion Shop and Barbie's Dream House.[3]

Barbie's glamour required constant purchases of dolls and accessories. Playing grown up meant that Barbie had to have a boy friend, Ken (introduced in 1961). Because Barbie seemed to be six to seven years older than her owners, Mattel introduced in 1964 a little sister, Skipper, with whom the children could identify. Naturally Skipper developed her own entourage of "friends." In 1975 Mattel carried the transition doll to its logical conclusion with "Growing Up Skipper." Six-year-olds could mechanically reenact their growing-up fantasy: when her arm was rotated, Skipper grew taller and developed breasts.

Barbie also needed "friends" to shop and have fun with. Mattel manufactured an endless array of Midge, Francie, and Stacey dolls, all "sold separately." Like Barbie's clothing, they changed with the times. While Midge (1963) was the "freckled-faced and impish" girl next door, Francie (1966) and Stacey (1968) reflected the impact of English styles and music in the age of the Beatles. In 1968 Christie, a black friend for Barbie, was introduced, reflecting changing American race relations. Ken vanished suddenly in 1969 (apparently too stodgy an image to fit the long-haired Vietnam era) only to reappear two years later looking much more husky and hip.[4]

Mattel tapped into a young girl's fantasy life to create a demand for possessions. Company researchers watched girls play and noted that they enjoyed hair and dress-up games as well as acting out shopping, travel, and dating. They designed accessories to provide props for these play ac-

---

3. Mattel, "Barbie, Teen-Age Fashion Model," "Barbie, Teen-Age Fashion Model, and Ken, Barbie's Boy Friend (He's a Doll)," "Exclusive Fashions by Mattel," book 3 (Hawthorne, Calif.: Mattel, 1958, 1960, 1963). All in the Strong Museum.

4. "The Origins of the Barbie Doll (and Her 'Family')," Mattel Press Kit, Please Touch Museum, Toy Fair Collection (hereafter TFC), Box 5.

tivities. And if the child did not immediately know what the story lines were to be, Mattel provided them on the back of the packages.

Barbie's impact on the traditional doll industry was enormous. Only 60 doll companies remained in 1969 of the more than 200 that existed when Barbie appeared in 1959. Barbie helped reduce the share of baby dolls from 80 percent of dolls in 1959 to only 38 percent in 1975. Barbie's success inevitably prompted much imitation. Ideal produced Tammy (who conceded the existence of parents with Mom and Dad dolls). American Character offered Tressy, with "hair that really grows." Topper's Penny Brite and the "perfectly proportioned" Tina of Ross Products were others. None survived long in a field dominated by Barbie.[5]

Mattel succeeded [in] keeping successive generations of little girls wanting Barbie and not some other fashion doll. Ruth Handler resisted the temptation to give Barbie a fixed personality or even a "look." Handler liked to say this allowed girls to imagine what Barbie was really like. But from a marketing standpoint this made Barbie a fixture, even a "clothes hanger," upon which accessories could be draped. Partly because she came first, Barbie became the trademark fashion doll. All others were imitations. And Barbie never grew old or out of date as did the dolls made in the image of ephemeral glamour queens like Farah Fawcett-Majors. Barbie was the eternal star — despite her changeable hair and skin color. Barbie was still Barbie.

Mattel even succeeded in persuading little girls to "trade in" their old Barbies for a discount on a new look in 1967. Adults found this strange — voluntarily parting with a "loved" doll. But the girls saw it differently: they were simply trading in an old model for a new, much as their parents traded in their flashy 1959 Chevys for the more sedate look of 1960s models. Barbie's environment — clothes, hair, playsets, and friends — changed with adult fashion. But Barbie's face and shape remained a constant symbol of growing up. Thus Mattel created that elusive and contradictory prize — an ephemeral classic — and in doing so reshaped the play of American girls. A doll that mothers at first disliked became the doll that mothers had to give to their daughters.[6]

Hasbro's G.I. Joe mirrored the success of Barbie by becoming a perennial fad. It achieved this feat, at first, not by challenging expectations of fathers as Barbie broke with the doll culture of mothers, but by affirming the values and experiences of many fathers. Like so many other contemporary toys, G.I. Joe was inspired by a TV series, an action-adventure show, *The Lieutenant* (1963), that was supposed to appeal to

10

5. "Inside the Doll Market," *Toys,* March 1975, 23–25.

6. Billy Boy, *Barbie,* 92; Mandeville, *Fashion Anthology,* 41–43, 69–71; Ron Goulart, *The Assault on Childhood* (Los Angeles: Sherbourne, 1969), 26.

adult men. But the program failed even before the toy appeared. G.I. Joe was not tied to any specific media personality or story. He represented the average soldier, evoking memories of fathers' experience in World War II and the Korean War. The original G.I. Joe of 1964 shared with Barbie the critical feature of being a dress-up doll, although marketed as "America's Moveable Fighting Man." At twelve inches, half an inch taller than Barbie, G.I. Joe was suitable for costuming in the uniforms of the four American military services (sold separately). Again like Barbie, G.I. Joe was accessorized. Hasbro adopted what was often called the "razor and razor blade" principle of marketing. Once the boy had the doll he needed accessories—multiple sets of uniforms, jeeps, tents, and weaponry.[7]

Still, Joe was not simply a boy's version of Barbie. The obvious historical precedent was the cast-metal soldier, very different from the paper doll. Miniature soldiers had been part of boy's play for centuries. The object was to reenact the drama of present and past battles. G.I. Joe added to this traditional game by giving boys articulated figures with a man's shape and musculature. The Joes were a major improvement over cheap and impersonal plastic soldiers that stood on bases. Joe took the play beyond the traditional deployment of infantry, cannon, and cavalry. Detailed "Manuals," accompanying the doll, marched "Joe through basic training up to combat readiness," showing the boy how to pose his toy to crouch in a trench or throw a grenade. Joe changed war games from the pleasure of acting the general—arranging soldiers and weapons on a field of battle—to playing the soldier, the G.I. whom the boy dressed and posed. This probably made war play far more appealing to young children because they could identify with the individual soldier. Joe may have contributed to the decline of other forms of boys' play, at least temporarily, insofar as erector sets almost disappeared and Tinkertoys and Lincoln Logs were relegated to preschoolers in the G.I. Joe era.[8]

Nevertheless, the early G.I. Joe did not challenge traditional war play as Barbie displaced baby doll and companion doll play. G.I. Joe's success was based on a boy's identity with the all-male world of heroic action aided by modern military equipment and gadgetry. The play was conventional, featuring males bonding in adventure. This was a womanless world. Boys rejected the idea of a female nurse when it was introduced to the G.I. Joe line in 1965. These boys could play war the way their fathers might have fought it in World War II or in Korea. And they could

7. "Fact Sheet: Hasbro's G.I. Joe, A Real American Hero," Hasbro Press Kit, Feb. 1993, TFC, Box 3; Susan Manos and Paris Manos, *Collectible Male Action Figures* (Paducah, Ky.: Collector Books, 1990), 8–9.

8. "G.I. Joe, Action Soldiers: America's Moveable Fighting Man" (Pawtucket, R.I.: Hasbro, 1964), Strong Museum.

dress their Joes in battle gear similar to that worn by conscripted uncles or older brothers serving their two-year stints in the army of the mid-1960s. The object was not the clash of enemies (as would be the case with later action figures). Even though boys made their Joe dolls fight each other, Hasbro offered soldiers from only one side. The point was to imitate the real world of adults in the military. G.I. Joe still connected fathers with sons.

Again in contrast to Barbie, G.I. Joe went through major changes. By 1967 as the Vietnam war heated up and adults such as Benjamin Spock attacked war toys, sales decreased. Beginning in 1970 Hasbro responded by transforming the "fighting" Joes into an "Adventure Team." Joes searched for sunken treasure and captured wild animals. As the Vietnam war wound down to its bitter end in 1975, it was awkward to sell military toys glorifying contemporary jungle warfare. While veterans of World War II and even Korea might enjoy giving their sons toys that memorialized their own youth, the situation for fathers who had reached manhood during the Vietnam era was very different. Most of these men wanted to forget the Vietnam war (whether they fought in it or opposed it), not to give their sons toys recalling this military disaster or any real war.

In 1976, with the Vietnam War in the past, G.I. Joe became "Super Joe" and shrunk to eight inches (because of higher costs for plastic). He no longer could be dressed. He returned to the role of a fighter, but he did not rejoin the ranks of enlisted men. He no longer was part of a world that fathers, uncles, or older brothers had ever experienced. Instead he was a high-tech hero, no longer connected to a troublesome reality. His laser beams and rocket command vehicles helped him fight off aliens, the Intruders. Added to his team was Bullet Man, the first of a long line of superhumans. The object of play was to pit good guys against bad guys, not to imitate real military life. But even these changes could not save Joe. From 1978 to 1981 the "Great American Hero" disappeared from store shelves to be pushed aside by an even more fantasyful line of toys based on George Lucas's *Star Wars*.[9]

With Barbie little girls combined growing up with feminine consumerism. This gave Barbie a permanent aisle of hot-pink packages in every serious toy store. G.I. Joe began as a celebration of an all-male world of realistic combat. But Joe encountered deeper contradictions in the 1960s than did Barbie and was forced to flee into fantasy. Still, both toys became models for toy play and consumption that still prevail today. They did so by breaking away from the worlds of parents.

---

9. Manos and Manos, *Male Action Figures,* 20–33, 38–43; Vincent Santelmo, *The Official 30th Anniversary Salute to G.I. Joe* (Iola, Wis.: Kreuse, 1994), 17–18, 66–72, 75–97, 325, 343, 412–413.

Reading the Text

1. According to Cross, how was the creation of Barbie related to the fashion paper doll?
2. How did Barbie assist, in Cross's words, in the "revolt against . . . the momism of the feminine mystique" (para. 4)?
3. Why did the G.I. Joe doll undergo more profound design changes in its history than did Barbie?
4. In Cross's view, what were the ingredients for the G.I. Joe doll's success?

Reading the Signs

1. What sort of doll would you design for girls or boys? Sketch your proposed doll, and write an essay explaining the rationale for your design. Share your sketch with your class.
2. Visit a toy store, and study the action-adventure dolls that now share shelf space with G.I. Joe. Then write an essay in which you analyze the extent to which the dolls reflect the "warrior dreams" that James William Gibson describes ("Warrior Dreams," p. 496).
3. Write an essay in which you explain your own view of how toys and games socialize children to cultural norms and expectations. To develop your ideas, read or reread Jennifer Scanlon ("Boys-R-Us: Board Games and the Socialization of Young Adolescent Girls," p. 472), bell hooks ("Baby," p. 568), and Emily Prager ("Our Barbies, Ourselves," p. 706).
4. Divide the blackboard into two sections: male and female. Have the class write on the board, in the gender-appropriate section, the name of a favorite childhood toy. Then study the results. Do you find any gender patterns? How many of the toys could be classified as "gender-neutral"?

ROY RIVENBURG

Snap! Crackle! Plot!

In this age of insatiable curiosity about the private lives of American celebrities, why don't we know more about the love life of Tony the Tiger or the Energizer Bunny? After all, these product mascots, and dozens like them, both human and humanoid, are as familiar to us, thanks to advertising, as most Hollywood stars. So in this tongue-in-cheek feature that originally appeared in the Los Angeles Times *in 1999, Roy Rivenburg sets out on a journalistic mission to find out whatever he can about the personal "lives" of the commercial characters who sell us everything from toilet paper to green beans. And while*

Rivenburg's article is meant to be a joke, the fact that the product mascots he "researches" are so well known to us is not, signifying just how ad-saturated a culture we are. Rivenburg is a staff writer for the Los Angeles Times *who specializes in humorous features and columns.*

Now that it's open season on the warped personal lives of presidents and politicians, we decided to investigate a few other American icons, such as the Pillsbury Doughboy, Betty Crocker, and Count Chocula.

What we uncovered is shocking.

For example, when the Jolly Green Giant first appeared in 1925, he was neither green nor jolly. He wore a bearskin outfit and scowled. It wasn't until the 1930s that someone in marketing apparently realized that "Angry White Endocrine Freak" probably wouldn't sell very many frozen peas. So the giant donned a suit of leaves, started reading Dale Carnegie, and had his skin surgically altered to green (which also came in handy for affirmative-action programs).

And that's just the beginning.

Consider the case of Mrs. Butterworth and Mrs. Paul. When we   5
phoned Aurora Foods for biographical information on the mascots' husbands, a spokesman confessed that both characters had never been married. He acknowledged that the "Mrs." title is misleading but said it is legally accurate and not impeachable.

Next we called Quaker Oats to ask about Aunt Jemima. Whose aunt is she, exactly? Answer: nobody's. Corporate genealogists could produce no evidence of nephews, nieces, or relatives of any kind.

In fact, someone should open a dating service for product mascots because none seems to have a spouse. A few possible exceptions are at General Mills, home of the Trix rabbit, the Lucky Charms leprechaun, Betty Crocker, Frankenberry, Count Chocula, and Sonny the CooCoo for Cocoa Puffs bird. When asked about the marital status of those characters, spokeswoman Pam Becker said, "I don't know. We don't delve into their personal lives."

But nearly every other mascot we scrutinized—from the Ty-D-Bol man to Charlie the Tuna (sorry, Charlie)—is single. The Energizer bunny's official biography, for example, says he is "interested in a long-term relationship but too busy at the moment." No wonder the divorce rate in this country is so high, with role models like these. About the closest we came to a nuclear family was 46-year-old Tony the Tiger and his son, Tony Jr.

Is there a Mrs. Tony?

"Uh, no," admitted a Kellogg publicist.   10

Wait. How can that be?

Good point, said the publicist. "We can't have Tony fathering children out of wedlock. Let me look into this." About a week later,

Kellogg called back to report that Tony Jr.'s mother, who has no name, once appeared in a TV commercial on an unspecified date. The publicist also discovered that in 1974, which was the Chinese year of the tiger, Tony briefly had a daughter, Antoinette.

Another suspicious family history involves Jack in the Box's clown mascot, Jack, who had a near-death experience in 1980 (when his own company blew him up) and remained in hiding until 1995. The new Jack, who lives in La Jolla and wears Armani suits, has a look-alike son and a human wife. Company officials say Jack Jr.'s physique "proves that the gene for large white plastic heads is passed on the male side of the family." Maybe so, but it's still a biological miracle. That's because Jack Jr. is actually older than his mother, who wasn't created by the company's ad agency until July 31. Perhaps that also explains why Jack's corporate associates are tight-lipped about the woman's background, identifying her only as "Mrs. Box."

Of course, being related to a product mascot can be hazardous.

The Chicken of the Sea mermaid originally had an older sister, but   15
the sibling must've been rammed by a Russian fishing trawler or something because company officials cannot account for her whereabouts now. Nor can they provide a name or exact birth date for the mermaid herself. "She's a very mysterious person," a company spokesman said. "We think she's about 45 years old."

Likewise, the Pillsbury Doughboy—who has been poked in the gut an estimated 57,000 times during his 33 years of existence—once fraternized with a doughgirl and a doughdog, but they also vanished quickly and mysteriously. (Perhaps in a baking accident?)

Even Toucan Sam's innocent young nephews were given the Jimmy Hoffa treatment shortly after they hatched.

Sam must have known too much about that incident because, in the early 1970s, he underwent a Witness Protection Program-style identity change. He had a "beak job" to shorten his nose, cosmetic surgery to brighten his feathers, and he was ordered to stop speaking Toucanese (a variation of Pig Latin) and dump the towering Carmen Miranda–style fruit hat worn in his 1963 debut.

Other mascot make-overs include the Brawny paper towel man (who recently moved the part in his hair and discarded his Lizzie Borden-esque ax), the smiling Kool-Aid pitcher (which in 1975 inexplicably sprouted legs, arms, and a torso) and Kellogg's Snap, Crackle, and Pop (who began life as gnomes with huge noses, floppy ears, and oversized hats but in 1949 adopted boyish haircuts, new uniforms, and smaller facial features).

But sometimes cosmetic surgery can backfire. According to the *Wall*   20
Street Journal, Kellogg is so convinced that the Exxon tiger is becoming a Tony the Tiger copycat that it recently sued for trademark infringement, alleging in court papers that Exxon's "whimsical tiger" illegally emulates

Tony because he "walks or runs on his two hind legs and acts in a friendly manner."

Other mascot facts and figures:

- Little Sprout is no relation to the Jolly Green Giant.

- The Keebler elves insist they are "not leprechauns, gnomes, dryads, shoemakers, fairies, or sprites. We're American elves, and our job is to bake uncommonly good cookies and crackers."

- The name of the Kellogg's Corn Flakes mascot is Cornelius. Although he is mute, company officials describe him as "a happy-go-lucky, confident rooster."

- The diameter of Jack in the Box's plastic head is 2 feet. There's also a fan inside it, according to *Restaurant and Institutions* magazine.

- Mr. Clean is not gay, despite the earring. Also, his full name is Mr. Veritably Clean.

- Cap'n Crunch's Crunchberry Beast was developed by Jay Ward and Bill Scott, who also created Rocky and Bullwinkle. Ditto for Quisp, the pink-fleshed space alien whose cereal vanished in the 1970s but is staging a comeback. Quisp also recently broke up with his human girlfriend, Sandy Rosenbaum, citing "cross-species dating obstacles."

- The filmstrip character who appears in previews at AMC movie theaters is named Clip. He is 7 years old.

- Mr. Goodwrench, the Ty-D-Bol man, the Ajax white knight, the politically incorrect Frito Bandito, Quisp's muscleman rival Quake, and Mr. Whipple are described by their corporate slave masters as "no longer active," a euphemism for comatose or deceased.

- The oldest mascots in our survey are Aunt Jemima and the Michelin tire man, who are 109 and 100, respectively. Perhaps they'd make a good couple if someone ever starts a mascot matchmaker service.

Reading the Text

1. In Rivenburg's view, why are "the warped personal lives of presidents and politicians" (para. 1) a context for interpreting advertising characters?
2. What evidence does Rivenburg advance for his statement that "someone should open a dating service for product mascots" (para. 7)?
3. Explain in your own words why "being related to a product mascot can be hazardous" (para. 14).
4. Characterize Rivenburg's tone in this selection: To what audience do you think he is appealing?

Reading the Signs

1. In class, brainstorm on the blackboard as many advertising characters as you can, drawing both from Rivenburg's essay and your own experience. With your class, categorize the characters, perhaps according to gender, ethnicity, or profession. Then discuss the significance of your categories. How do the different groups appeal to consumers to buy their products? What do they reveal about American values?
2. Visit your college library and research the controversy surrounding Joe Camel. What was his appeal, and to whom and why? Do you believe that this character's influence was as great as cigarette-industry critics claimed?
3. Select one of the products from the "Portfolio of Ads" (p. 210) and sketch a new character that could serve as an advertising representative of that product. Then write an essay in which you explain how your character would act as a sign. How would it sell the product? What values would it project?
4. In recent years, athletic shoe companies have transformed real athletes into characters to sell their products (for instance, Nike's Bo Jackson "Bo knows" campaign). Analyze the appeal of one such campaign, basing your analysis on specific examples of ads (you might watch some sports shows on television for broadcast ads, or study an issue of *Sports Illustrated* for print ads).

JENNY LYN BADER
Larger Than Life

‖‖‖‖‖‖‖‖‖‖‖‖‖‖‖‖‖‖‖‖‖‖‖‖‖‖‖‖‖‖‖‖‖‖‖‖‖‖

Do you have any heroes? Or does the very concept of heroism seem passé in today's irony-rich, self-conscious era? In this essay that first appeared in Next: Young American Writers on the New Generation *(1994), Jenny Lyn Bader (b. 1968) surveys the role of heroes for her generation, comparing her point of view with those of past generations. Maybe heroes are obsolete, Bader suggests; maybe we'd just be better off with role models who, while not providing the commanding presence of the full-fledged hero, can at least provide some guidance to an often confused Generation X. A New York–based playwright, Bader has published numerous essays on language and culture, specializing in artistic, spiritual, and moral issues. She is coauthor of* He Meant, She Meant: The Definitive Male-Female Dictionary.

When my grandmother was young, she would sometimes spot the emperor Franz Josef riding down the cobbled roads of the Austro-Hungarian Empire.

She came of age so long ago that the few surviving photographs are colored cream and chestnut. Early on, she saw cars replace horses and carriages. When she got older, she marveled at the first televisions. Near the end of her life, she grew accustomed to remote control and could spot prime ministers on color TV. By the time she died, the world was freshly populated by gadgetry and myth. Her generation bore witness to the rise of new machinery created by visionaries. My generation has seen machinery break down and visionaries come under fire.

As children, we enjoyed collecting visionaries, the way we collected toys or baseball cards. When I was a kid, I first met Patrick Henry and Eleanor Roosevelt, Abraham Lincoln and Albert Einstein. They could always be summoned by the imagination and so were never late for play dates. I thought heroes figured in any decent childhood. I knew their stats.

Nathan Hale. Nelson Mandela. Heroes have guts.

Michelangelo. Shakespeare. Heroes have imagination.   5

They fight. Alexander the Great. Joan of Arc.

They fight for what they believe in. Susan B. Anthony. Martin Luther King.

Heroes overcome massive obstacles. Beethoven, while deaf, still managed to carry an unforgettable tune. Homer, while blind, never failed to give an excellent description. Helen Keller, both deaf and blind, still spoke to the world. FDR, despite his polio, became president. Moses, despite his speech impediment, held productive discussions with God.

They inspire three-hour movies. They make us weepy. They do the right thing while enduring attractive amounts of suffering. They tend to be self-employed. They are often killed off. They sense the future. They lead lives that make us question our own. They are our ideals, but not our friends.

They don't have to be real. Some of them live in books and legends. 10 They don't have to be famous. There are lower-profile heroes who get resurrected by ambitious biographers. There are collective heroes: firefighters and astronauts, unsung homemakers, persecuted peoples. There are those whose names we can't remember, only their deeds: "you know, that woman who swam the English Channel," "the guy who died running the first marathon," "the student who threw himself in front of the tank at Tiananmen Square." There are those whose names we'll never find out: the anonymous benefactor, the masked man, the undercover agent, the inventor of the wheel, the unknown soldier. The one who did the thing so gutsy and terrific that no one will ever know what it was.

Unlike icons (Marilyn, Elvis) heroes are not only sexy but noble, too. Unlike idols (Gretzky, Streisand), who vary from fan to fan, they are almost universally beloved. Unlike icons and idols, heroes lack irony. And unlike icons and idols, heroes are no longer in style.

As centuries end, so do visions of faith—maybe because the faithful get nervous as the double zeroes approach and question what they've been worshipping. Kings and queens got roughed up at the end of the eighteenth century; God took a beating at the end of the nineteenth; and as the twentieth century draws to a close, outstanding human beings are the casualties of the moment. In the 1970s and 1980s, Americans started feeling queasy about heroism. Those of us born in the sixties found ourselves on the cusp of that change. A sweep of new beliefs, priorities, and headlines has conspired to take our pantheon away from us.

Members of my generation believed in heroes when they were younger but now find themselves grasping for them. Even the word *hero* sounds awkward. I find myself embarrassed to ask people who their heroes are, because the word just doesn't trip off the tongue. My friend Katrin sounded irritated when I asked for hers. She said, "Oh, Jesus . . . Do people still have heroes?"

We don't. Certainly not in the traditional sense of adoring perfect people. Frequently not at all. "I'm sort of intrigued by the fact that I don't have heroes right off the top of my head," said a colleague, Peter. "Can I get back to you?"

Some of us are more upset about this than others. It's easy to tell   15 which of us miss the heroic age. We are moved by schmaltzy political speeches, we warm up to stories of pets saving their owners, we even get misty-eyed watching the Olympics. We mope when model citizens fail us. My college roommate, Linda, remembers a seventh-grade class called "Heroes and She-roes." The first assignment was to write about a personal hero or she-ro. "I came home," Linda told me, "and cried and cried because I didn't have one. . . . Carter had screwed up in Iran and given the malaise speech. Gerald Ford was a nothing and Nixon was evil. My parents told me to write about Jane Fonda the political activist and I just kept crying."

Not everyone feels sentimental about it. A twentyish émigré raised in the former Soviet Union told me: "It's kind of anticlimactic to look for heroes when you've been brought up in a culture that insists on so many heroes. . . . What do you want me to say? Lenin? Trotsky?" Even though I grew up in the relatively propaganda-free United States, I understood. The America of my childhood insisted on heroes, too.

Of all the myths I happily ate for breakfast, the most powerful one was our story of revolution. I sang about it as early as kindergarten and read about it long after. The story goes, a few guys in wigs skipped town on some grumpy church leaders and spurned a loopy king to branch out on their own. The children who hear the story realize they don't have to believe in oldfangled clergy or a rusty crown—but they had better believe in those guys with the wigs.

I sure did. I loved a set of books known as the "Meet" series: *Meet George Washington, Meet Andrew Jackson, Meet the Men Who Sailed the Seas,* and many more. I remember one picture of an inspired Thomas Jefferson, his auburn ponytail tied in a black ribbon, penning words with a feather as a battle of banners and cannon fire raged behind him.

A favorite "Meet" book starred Christopher Columbus. His resistance to the flat-earth society of his day was engrossing, especially to a kid like me who had trouble trying new foods let alone seeking new land masses. I identified with his yearning for a new world and his difficulty with finding investors. Standing up to the king and queen of Spain was like convincing your parents to let you do stuff they thought was idiotic. Now, my allowance was only thirty-five cents a week, but that didn't mean I wasn't going to ask for three ships at some later date.

This is pretty embarrassing: I adored those guys. The ones in the   20
white powder and ponytails, the voluptuous hats, the little breeches and cuffs. They were funny-looking, but lovable. They did outrageous things without asking for permission. They invented the pursuit of happiness.

I had a special fondness for Ben Franklin, statesman and eccentric inventor. Inventions, like heroes, made me feel as though I lived in a dull era. If I'd grown up at the end of the nineteenth century, I could have spoken on early telephones. A few decades later, I could have heard the new sounds of radio. In the sixties, I could have watched black-and-white TVs graduate to color.

Instead, I saw my colorful heroes demoted to black and white. Mostly white. By the time I finished high school, it was no longer hip to look up to the paternalistic dead white males who launched our country, kept slaves and mistresses, and massacred native peoples. Suddenly they weren't visionaries but oppressors, or worse—objects. Samuel Adams became a beer, John Hancock became a building, and the rest of the guys in wigs were knocked off one by one, in a whodunit that couldn't be explained away by the fact of growing up.

The flag-waving of my youth, epitomized by America's bicentennial, was a more loving homage than I know today. The year 1976 rolled in while Washington was still reeling from Saigon, but the irony was lost on me and my second-grade classmates. The idea of losing seemed miles away. We celebrated July fourth with wide eyes and patriotic parties. Grown-ups had yet to tell themselves (so why should they tell us?) that the young nation on its birthday had suffered a tragic defeat.

Historians soon filled us in about that loss, and of others. Discovering America was nothing compared to discovering the flaws of its discoverers, now cast as imperialist sleaze, racist and sexist and genocidal. All things heroic—human potential, spiritual fervor, moral resplendence— soon became suspect. With the possible exception of bodybuilding, epic qualities went out of fashion. Some will remember 1992 as the year Superman died. Literally, the writers and illustrators at D.C. Comics decided the guy was too old to keep leaping buildings and rescuing an aging damsel in distress. When rumors circulated that he would be resurrected, readers protested via calls to radio shows, letters to editors, and complaints to stores that they were in no mood for such an event.

A monster named Doomsday killed Superman, overcoming him not with Kryptonite but with brute force. Who killed the others? I blame improved modes of character assassination, media hype artists, and scholars. The experts told me that Columbus had destroyed cultures and ravaged the environment. They also broke the news that the cowboys had brazenly taken land that wasn't theirs. In a way, I'm glad I didn't know that earlier; dressing up as a cowgirl for Halloween wouldn't have felt right. In a more urgent way, I wish I had known it then so I wouldn't have had to learn it later.

Just fifteen years after America's bicentennial came Columbus's quincentennial, when several towns canceled their annual parades in protest of his sins. Soon other festivities started to feel funny. When my aunt served corn pudding last Thanksgiving, my cousin took a spoonful, then said drily that the dish was made in honor of the Indians who taught us to use corn before we eliminated them. Uncomfortable chuckles followed. Actually, neither "we" nor my personal ancestors had come to America in time to kill any Native Americans. Yet the holiday put us in the same boat with the pilgrims and anchored us in the white man's domain.

I am fascinated by how we become "we" and "they." It's as if siding with the establishment is the Alka-Seltzer that helps us stomach the past. To swallow history lessons, we turn into "we": one nation under God of proud but remorseful Indian killers. We also identify with people who look like us. For example, white northerners studying the Civil War identify both with white slaveholders and with northern abolitionists, aligning with both race and place. Transsexuals empathize with men and women. Immigrants identify with their homeland and their adopted country. Historians proposing a black Athena and a black Jesus have inspired more of such bonding.

I'll admit that these empathies can be empowering. I always understood the idea of feeling stranded by unlikely role models but never emotionally grasped it until I watched Penny Marshall's movie *A League of Their Own*. For the first time, I appreciated why so many women complain that sports bore them. I had enjoyed baseball before but never as intensely as I enjoyed the games in that film. The players were people like me. Lori Petty, petite, chirpy, wearing a skirt, commanded the pitcher's mound with such aplomb that I was moved. There's something to be said for identifying with people who remind us of ourselves, though Thomas Jefferson and Lori Petty look more like each other than either of them looks like me. I'll never know if I would've read the "Meet" books with more zeal if they'd described our founding mothers. I liked them as they were.

Despite the thrill of dames batting something on the big screen besides their eyelashes, the fixation on look-alike idols is disturbing for those who get left out. In the movie *White Men Can't Jump,* Wesley Snipes tells Woody Harrelson not to listen to Jimi Hendrix, because "White people can't hear Jimi." Does this joke imply that black people can't hear Mozart? That I can admire Geena Davis's batting but never appreciate Carlton Fisk? Besides dividing us from one another, these emotional allegiances divide us from potential heroes too, causing us to empathize with, say, General Custer and his last stand instead of with Sitting Bull and the victorious Sioux.

Rejecting heroes for having the wrong ethnic credentials or sex organs says less about our multicultural vision than our lack of imagination. By focusing on what we are instead of who we can become, by typecasting and miscasting our ideals—that's how we become "we" and "they." If heroes are those we'd like to emulate, it does make sense that they resemble us. But the focus on physical resemblance seems limited and racist. 30

Heroes should be judged on their deeds, and there are those with plenty in common heroically but not much in terms of ethnicity, nationality, or gender. Just look at Harriet Tubman and Moses; George Washington and Simón Bolívar; Mahatma Gandhi and Martin Luther King; Murasaki and Milton; Cicero and Ann Richards. Real paragons transcend nationality. It didn't matter to me that Robin Hood was English—as long as he did good, he was as American as a barbecue. It didn't matter to Queen Isabella that Columbus was Italian as long as he sailed for Spain and sprinkled her flags about. The British epic warrior Beowulf was actually Swedish. Both the German hero Etzel and the Scandinavian hero Atli were really Attila, king of the Huns. With all this borrowing going on, we shouldn't have to check the passports of our luminaries; the idea that we can be like them not literally but spiritually is what's uplifting in the first place.

The idea that we can never be like them has led to what I call jealousy journalism. You know, we're not remotely heroic so let's tear down anyone who is. It's become hard to remember which papers are tabloids. Tell-all articles promise us the "real story"—implying that greatness can't be real. The safe thing about *Meet George Washington* was that you couldn't actually meet him. Today's stories and pictures bring us closer. And actually meeting your heroes isn't the best idea. Who wants to learn that a favorite saint is really just an egomaniac with a publicist?

Media maestros have not only knocked public figures off their pedestals, they've also lowered heroism standards by idealizing just about everyone. Oprah, Geraldo, and the rest turn their guests into heroes of the afternoon because they overcame abusive roommates, childhood disfigurement, deranged spouses, multiple genitalia, cheerleading practice, or zany sexual predilections. In under an hour, a studio audience can hear their epic sagas told.

While TV and magazine producers helped lead heroes to their graves, the academic community gave the final push. Just as my peers and I made our way through college, curriculum reformers were promoting "P.C." agendas at the expense of humanistic absolutes. Scholars invented their own tabloidism, investigating and maligning both dead professors and trusty historical figures. Even literary theory helped, when deconstructionists made it trendy to look for questions instead of answers, for circular logic instead of linear sense, for defects, contradictions, and the ironic instead of meaning, absolutes, and the heroic.

It was the generations that preceded ours who killed off our heroes.   35 And like everyone who crucified a superstar, these people thought they were doing a good thing. The professors and journalists consciously moved in a positive direction—toward greater tolerance, openness, and realism—eliminating our inspirations in the process. The death of an era of hero worship was not the result of the cynical, clinical materialism too often identified with my generation. It was the side effect of a complicated cultural surgery, of an operation that may have been necessary and that many prescribed.

So with the best of intentions, these storytellers destroyed bedtime stories. Which is too bad for the kids, because stories make great teachers. Children glean by example. You can't tell a child "Be ingenious," or "Do productive things." You can tell them, "This Paul Revere person jumped on a horse at midnight, rode wildly through the dark, figured out where the mean British troops were coming to attack the warm, fuzzy, sweet, great-looking colonists, and sent messages by code, igniting our fight for freedom," and they'll get the idea. America's rugged values come gift wrapped in the frontier tales of Paul Bunyan, Daniel Boone, Davy Crockett—fables of independence and natural resources. Kids understand that Johnny Appleseed or Laura Ingalls Wilder would never need a Cuisinart. Pioneer and prairie stories convey the fun of roughing it, showing kids how to be self-reliant, or at least less spoiled.

Children catch on to the idea of imitating qualities, not literal feats. After returning his storybook to the shelf, little Billy doesn't look around for a dragon to slay. Far-off stories capture the imagination in an abstract but compelling way, different from, say, the more immediate action-adventure flick. After watching a James Bond film festival, I might fantasize about killing the five people in front of me on line at the supermarket, while legends are remote enough that Columbus might inspire one to be original, but not necessarily to study Portuguese or enlist in the navy. In tales about conquerors and cavaliers, I first flirted with the idea of ideas.

Even Saturday-morning cartoons served me as parables, when I woke up early enough to watch the classy Superfriends do good deeds.

Sure, the gender ratio between Wonder Woman and the gaggle of men in capes seemed unfair, but I was rapt. I wonder whether I glued myself to my television and my high expectations with too much trust, and helped to set my own heroes up for a fall.

Some heroes have literally been sentenced to death by their own followers. *Batman* subscribers, for example, were responsible for getting rid of Batman's sidekick, Robin. At the end of one issue, the Joker threatened to kill the Boy Wonder, and readers could decide whether Robin lived or died by calling one of two "900" numbers. The public voted overwhelmingly for his murder. I understand the impulse of those who dialed for death. At a certain point, eternal invincibility grows as dull and predictable as wearing a yellow cape and red tights every day of the year. It's not human. We get fed up.

My generation helped to kill off heroism as teenagers, with our language. We used heroic words that once described brave deeds — *excellent, amazing, awesome* — to describe a good slice of pizza or a sunny day. In our everyday speech, *bad* meant good. *Hot* meant cool. In the sarcastic slang of street gangs in Los Angeles, *hero* currently means traitor, specifically someone who snitches on a graffiti artist.   40

Even those of us who lived by them helped shatter our own myths, which wasn't all negative. We discovered that even the superhero meets his match. Every Achilles needs a podiatrist. Every rhapsodically handsome leader has a mistress or a moment of moral ambiguity. We injected a dose of reality into our expectations. We even saw a viable presidential candidate under a heap of slung mud, a few imperfections, an alleged tryst or two.

We're used to trysts in a way our elders aren't. Our parents and grandparents behave as if they miss the good old days when adulterers wore letter sweaters. They feign shock at the extramarital exploits of Thomas Jefferson, Frank Sinatra, JFK, Princess Di. Their hero worship is a romance that falters when beloved knights end up unfaithful to their own spouses. People my age aren't amazed by betrayal. We are suspicious of shining armor. Even so, tabloid sales escalate when a Lancelot gives in to temptation — maybe because the jerk who cheats on you somehow becomes more attractive. Other generations have gossiped many of our heroes into philanderers. The presumptuous hero who breaks your heart is the most compelling reason not to get involved in the first place.

Seeing your legends discredited is like ending a romance with someone you loved but ultimately didn't like. However much you longed to trust that person, it just makes more sense not to. Why pine away for an aloof godlet who proves unstable, erratic, and a rotten lover besides? It's sad to give up fantasies but mature to trade them in for healthier relationships grounded in reality.

We require a new pantheon: a set of heroes upon whom we can

rely, who will not desert us when the winds change, and whom we will not desert. It's unsettling, if not downright depressing, to go through life embarrassed about the identity of one's childhood idols.

Maybe we should stick to role models instead. Heroes have become   45 quaint, as old-fashioned as gas-guzzlers — and as unwieldy, requiring too much investment and energy. Role models are more like compact cars, less glam and roomy but easier to handle. They take up less parking space in the imagination. Role models have a certain degree of consciousness about their job. The cast members of *Beverly Hills 90210,* for example, have acknowledged that they serve as role models for adolescents, and their characters behave accordingly: they refrain from committing major crimes; they overcome inclinations toward substance abuse; they see through adult hypocrisy; and any misdemeanors they do perpetrate are punished. For moral mediators we could do better, but at least the prime-time writing staff is aware of the burden of having teen groupies.

Heroes don't have the luxury of staff writers or the opportunity to endorse designer jeans. Hercules can't go on *Nightline* and pledge to stop taking steroids. Prometheus can't get a presidential pardon. Columbus won't have a chance to weep to Barbara Walters that he didn't mean to endanger leatherback turtles or monk seals or the tribes of the Lucayas. Elizabeth I never wrote a best-seller about how she did it her way.

Role models can go on talk shows, or even host them. Role models may live next door. While a hero might be a courageous head of state, a saint, a leader of armies, a role model might be someone who put in a three-day presidential bid, your local minister, your boss. They don't need their planes to go down in flames to earn respect. Role models have a job, accomplishment, or hairstyle worth emulating.

Rather than encompassing that vast kit and caboodle of ideals, role models can perform a little neat division of labor. One could wish to give orders like Norman Schwarzkopf but perform psychoanalysis like Lucy Van Pelt, to chair a round-table meeting as well as King Arthur but negotiate as well as Queen Esther[1], to eat like Orson Welles but look like Helen of Troy, and so forth. It was General Schwarzkopf, the most tangible military hero for anyone my age, who vied instead for role-model status by claiming on the cover of his book: *It Doesn't Take a Hero.* With this title he modestly implies that anyone with some smarts and élan could strategize and storm as well as he has.

Role models are admirable individuals who haven't given up their lives or livelihoods and may even have a few hangups. They don't have to be prone to excessive self-sacrifice. They don't go on hunger strikes;

---

1. **Queen Esther**   Jewish heroine of the biblical *Book of Esther.* — EDS.

they diet. They are therefore more likely than heroes to be free for lunch, and they are oftener still alive.

Heroism is a living thing for many of my contemporaries. In my informal poll, I not only heard sob stories about the decline of heroes, I also discovered something surprising: the ascent of parents. While the founding fathers may be passé, actual mothers, fathers, grands, and great-grands are undeniably "in." An overwhelming number of those I polled named their household forebears as those they most admired. By choosing their own relatives as ideals, people in their twenties have replaced impersonal heroes with the most personal role models of all. Members of my purportedly lost generation have not only realized that it's time to stop believing in Santa Claus, they have chosen to believe instead in their families—the actual tooth fairy, the real Mr. and Mrs. Claus. They have stopped needing the folks from the North Pole, the guys with the wigs, the studs and studettes in tights and capes.

In a way it bodes well that Superman and the rest could be killed or reported missing. They were needed to quash the most villainous folks of all: insane communists bearing nuclear weapons, heinous war criminals, monsters named Doomsday. The good news about Superman bleeding to death was that Doomsday died in the struggle.

If the good guys are gone, so is the world that divides down the middle into good guys and bad guys. A world without heroes is a rigorous, demanding place, where things don't boil down to black and white but are rich with shades of gray; where faith in lofty, dead personages can be replaced by faith in ourselves and one another; where we must summon the strength to imagine a five-dimensional future in colors not yet invented. My generation grew up to see our world shift, so it's up to us to steer a course between naïveté and nihilism, to reshape vintage stories, to create stories of spirit without apologies.

I've heard a few. There was one about the woman who taught Shakespeare to inner-city fourth graders in Chicago who were previously thought to be retarded or hopeless. There was a college groundskeeper and night watchman, a black man with a seventh-grade education, who became a contracts expert, wrote poetry and memoirs, and invested his salary so wisely that he bequeathed 450 acres of mountainous parkland to the university when he died. There was the motorcyclist who slid under an eighteen-wheeler at full speed, survived his physical therapy only to wind up in a plane crash, recovered, and as a disfigured quadriplegic started a business, got happily married, and ran for public office; his campaign button bore a caption that said "Send me to Congress and I won't be just another pretty face. . . ."

When asked for her heroes, a colleague of mine spoke of her great-grandmother, a woman whose husband left her with three kids in Galicia, near Poland, and went to the United States. He meant to send

50

for her, but the First World War broke out. When she made it to America, her husband soon died, and she supported her family; at one point she even ran a nightclub. According to the great-granddaughter, "When she was ninety she would tell me she was going to volunteer at the hospital. I would ask how and she'd say, 'Oh, I just go over there to read to the old folks.' The 'old folks' were probably seventy. She was a great lady."

My grandmother saved her family, too, in the next great war. She   55
did not live to see the age of the fax, but she did see something remarkable in her time, more remarkable even than the emperor riding down the street: she saw him walking down the street. I used to ask her, "Did you really see the emperor Franz Josef walking down the street?"

She would say, "Ya. Walking down the street." I would laugh, and though she'd repeat it to amuse me, she did not see what was so funny. To me, the emperor was someone you met in history books, not on the streets of Vienna. He was larger than life, a surprising pedestrian. He was probably just getting some air, but he was also laying the groundwork for my nostalgia of that time when it would be natural for him to take an evening stroll, when those who were larger than life roamed cobblestones.

Today, life is larger.

Reading the Text

1. Why do you think Bader begins and ends her essay with an anecdote regarding her grandmother, and what effect does that anecdote have on the reader?
2. How does Bader define *hero, icon,* and *role model,* and what is her attitude toward each?
3. What are the heroes and myths that Bader grew up with, and how does she feel about them now?
4. In your own words, explain Bader's attitude toward political correctness.
5. How does Bader characterize her generation of twentysomethings?

Reading the Signs

1. In your journal, brainstorm a list of heroes that you admired as a child, and then compare your list with the traditional heroes whom Bader mentions. How do you account for any differences or similarities?
2. Write an argumentative essay that supports, challenges, or modifies Bader's central contention that her generation needs role models, not heroes.

3. In class, discuss how a writer might, as Bader suggests, "reshape vintage stories, . . . create stories of spirit without apologies" (para. 52). Then, in a creative essay, write your own "story of spirit."
4. In class, brainstorm a list of traditional American heroes, and then discuss whether they have lost their luster and, if so, why.
5. Assume Bader's perspective on heroes, and write an analytic essay in which you explain why Michael Jordan remains so admired by today's twentysomething generation. To develop your ideas, read or reread Michael Eric Dyson's "Be Like Mike? Michael Jordan and the Pedagogy of Desire" (p. 667).

POPULAR SPACES

Interpreting the Built Environment

The Territorial Imperative

Space. When most of us think about it, if we think about it at all, we think of emptiness, of the nowhere through which we must pass to get somewhere, of sheer distance, or of the starlit reaches of the universe. Time may be money, but space is, well, nothingness or little more than the empty hollow in which we find ourselves.

And yet, in spite of its apparent blankness, space isn't empty at all because the spaces in which we conduct our everyday lives are filled with meanings, with visible and invisible codes that govern the way we move and that tell us, quite literally, where we may and may not go and what we may do when we get there. Consider an ordinary street. You may walk down it, but you need to stick to the margins (or sidewalk if there is one), and it's best to stay to the right if there's any oncoming foot traffic. If private houses are on the street, you may approach the front door, but you're not supposed to cut through the yard, and you're certainly not allowed to enter without permission. You *may* enter the public space of a store, shopping center, or post office, but you might need to pay to enter a museum, and you will need to pass through a security checkpoint if you are entering a courthouse or an airline terminal.

The spaces created by the built environment are not the only ones shot through with written and unwritten rules. Take your personal space: What rules govern it? Ask yourself: How close will you allow someone to get to you? It depends on who it is, doesn't it? Friends can get close, and lovers closer indeed, but what happens when someone who is neither intrudes into those spaces that are reserved only for your closest acquaintances? How does your home signal to others the rules you wish to set for maintaining your personal space?

The spaces of everyday life, both public and private, personal and architectural, in short, are packed with complex codes that we violate or ignore at our peril. These codes all originate in the way that human beings define their *territories*. A territory is a space that has been given meaning through having been claimed by an individual or group of individuals. Unclaimed, unmarked space is socially meaningless, but put up a building or a fence, and the uncircumscribed landscape becomes a bounded territory, a human habitat with its own rules for permitted and unpermitted behavior. Anyone unaware of those rules can't survive for long in human society.

Human beings, of course, are not alone in living under the territorial imperative. Many animal species mark their territories and so transform empty space into codified environments. Where humans are different is in the complexity of their territorial codes and, more profoundly, in the way that culture has intervened to produce them. To put this another way, the territorial imperative is ours by nature, but the actual codes that govern our territories are socially constructed and thus differ from culture to culture.

To see this, one need only look at the varied ways in which different cultures inscribe space with rules for behavior. Take the way we define the permitted distance between two people who are speaking to one another. The spatial codes of Mediterranean culture, for example, allow you to get very close to the person you are talking to, while those of traditional English society call for quite a generous setback—which is why the English seem cold and stand-offish to Italians and why Italians look "pushy" to the English. Or consider the codes that govern the way you should enter a private home. In traditional Japanese society, the polite move is to take off your shoes first. But how would that look if you do so as you enter a typical American home?

Because the human environment is socially constructed, it is semiotic through and through and thus open to cultural interpretation. By interpreting the spatial rules that govern a culture, you can learn a great deal about that culture. Sometimes what you will learn is not especially earthshaking (that Italians and the English differ on the rules for proper speaking distance, for instance). But often interpreting spatial codes, especially of the built environment, can be quite eye opening, particularly because public spaces can reflect, and reinforce, a culture's political ideology and power structure. It is no accident, for example, that the distinctive architecture of imperial Rome was designed to reflect and convey the massive power of a society that thrived through military conquest. Buildings like the Roman Coliseum and Forum expressed the might of an empire that stretched from North Africa to Britain. While Americans have copied

Roman design in their own political architecture (the Capitol Building in Washington, D.C., is Roman in essence), twentieth-century America's major contributions to architectural history include the shopping mall and the office tower, buildings that reflect the values of a capitalist society devoted to business and consumption rather than military conquest and empire building.

A culture's spatial codes can reflect its gender codes as well. Consider how in America we tend to regard the private, domestic space of the home as being essentially feminine (if you think not, consider how Martha Stewart targets female consumers or how magazines like *Better Homes and Gardens* are still largely women's publications), while the more public space of a business office is considered to be essentially masculine. Such a division reproduces a cultural ideology that still, after some thirty years of feminist activism, sees the domestic realm as primarily a woman's environment, while men belong in the "jungle," fighting it out with other men for supremacy and power.

The organization of a business office reflects such an ideology of power relations through its distribution of space. Hierarchically patriarchal in its spatial organization, the business office rewards the winner of the fight — the company CEO — with the largest office, the biggest desk, and the best views. Ordinary office workers have to make due with cubicles — nonoffices that spatially communicate their subordinate status in the corporate hierarchy.

The home, in contrast, is considered a matriarchal space and so reflects the essentially nonhierarchical nature of traditional women's culture (though patriarchal privilege intrudes into the domestic space of the home by way of the "master" bedroom, which, as the space where the man of the house sleeps, is usually larger and more luxurious than the other bedrooms in the house). And perhaps no other room in the modern American home better exemplifies the nonhierarchical nature of matriarchal space than the kitchen. Once a place reserved almost exclusively for women or servants, the contemporary kitchen is a space where the whole family can gather together more or less as equals. It is significant, then, that modern homebuyers often regard the size of a home's kitchen as a crucial factor in deciding whether to purchase a house — the bigger, the better. Could this be a sign of a cultural desire, among men as well as women, for a space that is marked by cooperation rather than competition? Or is the size of one's kitchen just another status symbol? Think it over. We'll let you decide.

Home, Home on the Range

Space is of particular importance to Americans, who have made it a part of their national character. From the very beginning of the European settlement of what would become the United States, the availability of land, of open space ("open," of course, to Europeans: the Native Americans living on the territory didn't consider the land open), has been a crucial factor in the shaping of American identity. Whether officially inscribed in the nineteenth-century notion of manifest destiny or simply reflected in a national tendency for itchy-footedness, the restless need to pull up stakes now and then and go on the road—the American desire for an open frontier—has never ceased. Indeed, the "open road," which has been celebrated in such literary classics as Walt Whitman's "Song of the Open Road" and Jack Kerouac's *On the Road*, is one of America's most evocative public symbols. Now that the real frontier has long been settled and closed to further free wandering, Americans have turned to a new electronic "frontier" that is often called, not coincidentally, the "information superhighway."

The American attitude toward space is especially reflected in our preferred housing patterns. Middle-class Europeans tend to live in urban apartments. If they can afford one, a European family may own a country villa, but most have their primary residences in cities. Americans, on the other hand, prefer to live in single-family homes, usually situated in residential suburbs, complete with their own yards and grounds. Those yards, especially when covered with a lawn, are essentially symbolic remnants of the pastures and prairies that once beckoned to restless Americans from the frontier. The frontier has long since disappeared, but its ghost still lingers on the suburban lawn, crabgrass and all.

So important to Americans is the notion of frontier spaciousness that we even give it a moral value. City dwellers are still considered less American than country folk (note how we speak of the agricultural Midwest as the American "heartland": this refers not only to the geographic location of the Midwestern states but to its national significance as the moral center of the nation), and the city itself is still often regarded as a place of sin where you work but from which you flee at the end of the day on long commutes back to the more open spaces of a residential sub-

Exploring the Signs of Public Space

In your journal, reflect on your use of public space for recreational or entertainment purposes. Where do you spend most of your time? In fully public parks (include both urban and wilderness parks in your consideration)? Or in commercial spaces such as theme parks or shopping malls? Do you spend time in public libraries or in bookstores such as Borders or Barnes and Noble? In which sort of public spaces do you feel more comfortable, and what is it about the spaces that make you feel this way?

urb. This national moral preference for rural open space over the tighter spaces of the city was made explicit in Thomas Jefferson's stated hope that America would remain a nation of small farmers and would not repeat the urban experience of Europe, and it continues today in populist political movements (such as the "militia" movement) that demonize the city (and those who live in it) while celebrating the virtues of country life. Thus, while today America is, despite Jefferson's hopes, largely an urban nation, our ideology is still essentially rural, tied to a vanished frontier that lingers on in our dreams and desires.

Interpreting Popular Spaces: The Social Meaning of a Shopping Mall

Let's say that your assignment is to write a paper in which you are to analyze the cultural significance of a public space of your choosing and you decide to interpret a shopping mall. How would you go about it? You might well begin by visiting one. Once there, look around you: What do you see, and who do you see? You will want to answer both of these questions carefully because the answers you come up with will comprise the heart of your analysis.

Let's begin with who you see. Do you see a lot of teenagers? It will be likely that you do. Now ask yourself what they are doing. Are they shopping, or are they walking around in groups and generally hanging out? Some of the teens will be shopping (we'll get back to them, and other shoppers, in a moment), but many, if not most, will probably be hanging out. Your next question is, "Why here?"

To answer that question, you need to consider some alternatives, some *different* places where teens can hang out. There are many such places, and we'll leave most of them to you to identify and consider, but for the moment we'll look at one alternative: a public park. That would be different, and, what is more, public parks are designed for relaxation, recreation, and socializing. But if you ever hung out in shopping malls yourself, did you ever consider a park instead?

It is likely that you didn't. Now ask yourself why. Most probably your answer would include one or more of the following responses, depending on where you grew up. If it was in a large city, you may have considered the local parks to be too dangerous (New York's Central Park, a popular teen hangout, may be an exception here), or there may not have been any parks convenient for the purpose. If you grew up in a suburb, there probably weren't any public parks anyway, beyond a few rather sterile squares of lawn with play equipment designed for young children. And if your hanging-out years were spent in a small town or village, the town center was probably too dull.

All of these possible responses (and any other ones that you may come up with) point to larger cultural issues. Let's look at them one by one. Say that the parks in your city are simply too dangerous for hanging out—that they have been allowed to decay and are now the territories of street gangs, drug dealers, and the homeless. That, of course, isn't what they were built for. America's urban parks are supposed to provide a kind of public garden for city dwellers who otherwise would have little or no access to the pleasures of nature. They are spaces in which all classes of society can gather on terms of relative equality and were once the sites of such public entertainments as band and orchestral concerts. To some extent, urban parks are still used for such purposes, but less and less so in America's most hard-pressed cities, where the public gardens are becoming public nuisances. At the same time, few, if any, parks are being built today on the scale of such urban gardens as San Francisco's Golden Gate Park, the Boston Common, or New York's Central Park, as whatever land is still left for development is reserved for office towers, shopping centers, and condominiums. When new public spaces are developed, as in Baltimore's Harbor Place, they are often tied to commercial projects that favor upscale consumers over the inner-city residents that they frequently displace. Now ask yourself: What shift in values does this neglect of public park construction in favor of commercial development reflect?

But maybe you live in a suburb, and the state of the local park isn't an issue. There might not even be any public parks in your neighborhood. So you will have a different set of questions to ask. First, why do you (or your family) live in a suburb? After answering that, ask why your suburb has so few public parks, if any. Are there any substitutes for a park? Does your apartment or condominium complex have recreational facilities, including swimming pools and gyms, reserved for the residents? Do your parents belong to a country club, or do you live in a gated community that has its own exclusive park? Or is your family's yard all the park you need?

The answers to these questions all point to a cultural meaning, from the reasons America has changed from being an urban society (as it was in the 1930s and 1940s) to a suburban society (as it increasingly has been since World War II), to the ways in which spaces tied to private property rights are replacing public parks as places of recreation. These are facts that can be *associated* with some of your conclusions about America's current attitude toward its urban centers because there is a relation between suburbanization, commercialization, and privatization, on the one hand, and the decay of such public spaces as the urban park, on the other. Can you articulate that relation?

Maybe you don't think any of this applies to you because you come from a small town that is neither urban nor suburban. Fine, so ask where teens hang out in your community. Do they choose the town center if a nice new mall has gone up on the interstate? If they are at all typical, it is likely they will prefer the new mall. Why?

The answer seems obvious—because there's more to do at the mall. And there is. A lot more. The same answer could be given by someone from the city or the suburbs. But let's continue to look at what teens are doing at the mall, and, while we're at it, let's now include another group that tends to hang out in modern shopping malls, spending more time sitting and strolling than actually shopping: senior citizens.

Whether teen or senior, we can observe that a lot of people at the mall are using it *as if it was a public park*. Just look at the place. See any park benches, sidewalk-style cafes, trees (artificial or real), even running water? If your local mall is at all like most contemporary malls, it will include some, if not all, of these amenities, as well as others that make it resemble, well, what? A public park, right? Which is exactly the way that many of its patrons, who are not, incidentally, spending a lot of money, treat it. It would seem, then, that Americans have not lost the knack of enjoying public parks; it's just that they are looking elsewhere for them and finding them simulated at the local shopping mall. Now, ask yourself what this might mean.

To answer that question, you should consider what the mall is there for in the first place. It isn't there for the public good, you know. And it isn't owned by the public. Shopping malls are designed and built by corporate interests whose purpose is to make money. Though they resemble, or even actively simulate, nonprofit public spaces like parks, they are not really public; rather, they are quasi-public commercial spaces that wish to attract people into them as potential consumers. And one way of doing that is to offer the kind of park experience that the public sector is increasingly failing to offer.

Do you see a pattern emerging here? How might you characterize a society that is investing fewer and fewer of its resources in public parks and more and more in what are essentially private parks under corporate control? What does such a society value? What is it losing interest in?

But, you may object, you don't have to spend any money at the mall, and, since anyone can enter and use the facilities, isn't this awfully generous on the part of the private companies that own the malls? Doesn't it save the public sector a lot of money on park construction? A fair enough objection, but consider: Is it true that anyone at all can really use the mall? Private security patrols are hired to discourage some entrants. And while people are allowed to visit the mall without spending any money, malls are not really designed with generosity in mind. As we've just mentioned, the simulated parks found in many modern shopping malls were constructed with the intention of drawing people into the mall. After all, you can't sell anything without having foot traffic. But that's only the beginning because simulating parks is only the tip of the iceberg when it comes to ways in which shopping malls are designed to encourage consumption. For while the mall does offer a parklike experience to the nonshopping public, the whole structure of the contemporary shopping center—from its spatial arrangement to the "themes" around which modern malls are designed—is addressed to the shopper.

To "read" this address, you can turn from asking *who* you see at the mall to *what*. We've already considered the parklike settings, so let's turn to some other features likely to appear in modern malls.

In the past two decades, two "thematic" styles have tended to dominate mall construction and design. The first, which was especially popular in the 1980s, is the so-called birdcage or atrium mall—like Chicago's Water Tower Place, Houston's Galleria, and Toronto's Eaton Centre (or probably a mall near you). The second, which became popular in the 1990s, especially in large urban areas, is the streetwalk, like Santa Monica's Third Street Promenade. An analysis of these two kinds of mall can

---

Discussing the Signs of Public Space

Discuss in class the spatial organization of your college or university campus. In what ways does your campus environment encourage—or discourage—communal relations among students, both for socializing and for studying? What styles of learning does classroom space encourage? For instance, are most classrooms large lecture halls or small seminar rooms? Can chairs and desks be moved to facilitate small group work? What message does the campus's architectural style send? Is it monumental and imposing? Cozy and supportive? Sterile and impersonal? Boastful?

reveal a great deal about the ways in which malls are designed to stimulate consumption and so, in effect, pay for themselves. Let's start with the birdcage mall.

Birdcage malls tend to be towers of glass and steel, with vaulting skylights, rocketing glassed-in elevators, cascading stairways, and aerial sidewalks. Though they are often set in urban centers and feature parklike attractions, they tend to shut out the real city by providing no views to the outside except what can be seen of the sky through the skylights. Indeed, with their sprawling foodcourts and parklike plazas—often filled (especially at Christmastime) with carnival-like attractions—they can look like a mixture of urban park and theme park all rolled into one. So, as always in a semiotic analysis, we need to ask why.

To answer this, consider why birdcage malls would want to shut out any view of the city streets on which they are set. That's not too hard to answer: Many cities today are pretty rundown and so can be threatening to the kind of shoppers malls want to attract—middle-class consumers with money to spend. So the birdcage mall insulates them from the grittier realities of the street while offering some of the pleasures of an urban park in a simulated, and sanitized, form. That's why you're likely to find trees and park benches, fountains and sidewalk cafes, in a birdcage mall. Now, what about the theme-park ambience?

To answer this question, just ask yourself how you feel when you enter a real theme park, such as Disneyworld. Don't you feel like you're happily suspended from the cares of everyday life? Now ask how you spend money in a theme park. Won't you pick up some otherwise useless object that in any other circumstances you would regard as badly overpriced just as a souvenir? Or a snack whose cost might equal the price of several dinners at home? That at least is what most people do when visiting theme parks because the whole point of the visit is to stop worrying about things like money and just have fun, something that usually translates into a bout of free spending.

How does that explain why birdcage malls are designed to look like theme parks? Are those products you're buying or souvenirs?

The spatial design of a birdcage mall not only makes you want to spend money, it also controls your itinerary as you walk from one shop to another. Have you ever wondered why it is so difficult to find a stairway that will take you where you want to go in a birdcage mall? That's because the stairways aren't designed to take you where you want: they're designed to take you where the mall designers want, which means past as many shops as possible before you get to your destination. This effect is especially pronounced in the layout of an IKEA furniture warehouse: visit one if there's one nearby, and check it out. Isn't it almost impossible to get out of the store once you've entered it without having to walk past every display in the place? And there's so much nice stuff: Won't you be likely to end up buying something you weren't even looking for?

Streetwalks are different. For one thing, they aren't enclosed. For another, they tend to be as linear as the streets they are set on. And they don't resemble theme parks. But that doesn't make them innocent; streetwalks simply work a different strategy in getting you to buy.

To decode a streetwalk mall, it is useful to consider where it is situated. Usually a streetwalk is located in an area that has been reclaimed from urban blight. Ironically, streetwalk malls often rise on the same streets that once were part of a city's central business district but that decayed as middle-class consumers drifted to the suburbs (and to outlying shopping malls), leaving empty and boarded-up storefronts in their wake, along with a few struggling businesses catering mostly to the poor. As the street is resurrected (or, rather, gentrified) in a streetwalk development, the original look and feel of an urban business district is often simulated—complete with turn-of-the-century style streetlamps and brownstone shopfronts—but the resulting experience is not authentically urban. For one thing, to make room for the upscale emporia and cappuccino bars that streetwalk malls feature, the lingering businesses that served the poor have to be forced out—usually through the agency of rapidly rising rents. At the same time, to make certain that the clientele that the streetwalk wants to attract—usually younger, affluent consumers—don't feel threatened, private security patrols are hired to keep out the sorts of people who might make the streetwalk experience, well, a little too genuine, people like the homeless and street gang members who are very much a part of authentic urban experience these days.

So there's something a little ironic about the streetwalk, isn't there? Designed to recreate an authentic urban shopping experience, and so at-

---

Reading the Signs of Virtual Space on the Net

With the much-celebrated invention of "virtual space," the Internet has the potential to alter our conceptions and experience of space. Visiting a library, for example, once meant traveling to a large public building; now, with the Internet, you can visit most public and university libraries without leaving your home. Test the effect of this change by visiting online several libraries from around the world, perhaps by conducting a search for information related to a current assignment, and then visit in person your campus library. Then, in a reflective essay, consider the effect that the Internet has on your behavior as a student and on your sense of space. Does the Internet expand your sense of the world or, conversely, shrink it?

tract shoppers who are tired of the simulations of birdcage and other enclosed malls, the streetwalk creates its own set of simulations. Indeed, as
has been made explicit at Universal City's City Walk shopping mall,
which you pay to enter after parking your car underground so you can
shop on a "city street" that has no cars on it, the streetwalk is essentially
an urban theme park.

You're now ready to write your analysis. After sifting through all of
your observations, and all of the questions and answers that stem from
them, you can construct a thesis around the patterns you have discovered.
We have seen how the modern shopping mall has replaced the public
park as a place to gather and socialize in in America, and we have also
seen how two contemporary mall styles seek to simulate an urban shopping experience by taking the city out of the city and so, essentially, turn
that experience into a commodity itself that can be consumed as the entertainments at a theme park are consumed. These patterns can be further
related to America's traditional preference for rural space over urban
space—hinting, perhaps, at a certain reversal, or at least modification, of
our past attitudes toward the city in the 1980s and 1990s. Which of the
two styles of mall characterizes the mall you plan to analyze? Or does your
mall use different architectural codes to prompt consumers to buy? We'll
leave it to you to put all the pieces together to see what they might mean.

The Readings

Susan Willis begins this chapter with a visit to one of America's most
famous, and most often interpreted, cultural spaces: the synthetic utopia
of Disney World. Malcolm Gladwell next reveals the elaborate research
behind the design of retail spaces, showing how the most innocent-
looking display may be designed in response to detailed studies of the behavior and psychology of the shopping public. Aaron Betsky and Daphne
Spain offer analyses of the way that gender codes influence everything
from the layout of a city street to the organization of office space, with
Betsky comparing the masculine spaces of city streets and public architecture to more feminine spaces like shopping malls and homes and Spain
focusing on the workplace. Lucy R. Lippard's analysis of the "alternating
current" in the American psyche between the city and the country that
pulls in both directions as we choose our places in which to dwell and
work is followed by Camilo José Vergara's exploration of an environment that offers its inhabitants little choice for either work or habitation,
the urban ghetto. The chapter concludes with two selections that address
the road as a public space: Megan Shaw and Rick Prelinger discuss the
mythologies inherent in the freeway, and Cecelia Tichi offers a reflection
on the "open road"—its place both within American cultural history
and contemporary country music.

SUSAN WILLIS

Disney World: Public Use/Private State

||||||||||||||||||||||||||||||||||||||||||||||||||

If your idea of heaven is a place where you need only relax and wait for someone to take care of your every comfort and amusement, and where no unexpected surprises can crop up and destroy your enjoyment, then Disney World is for you. For Susan Willis (b. 1946), on the other hand, such a thoroughly programmed environment falls a good deal short of paradise. In this essay, she explains why: Could it be that Disney World is just another "brave new world"? A professor of English at Duke University, Willis specializes in minority literature and cultural studies and is the author of Specifying: Black Women Writing the American Experience *(1987),* A Primer for Daily Life *(1991), and* Inside the Mouse *(1995).*

At Disney World, the erasure of spontaneity is so great that spontaneity itself has been programmed. On the "Jungle Cruise" khaki-clad tour guides teasingly engage the visitors with their banter, whose apparent spontaneity has been carefully scripted and painstakingly rehearsed. Nothing is left to the imagination or the unforeseen. Even the paths and walkways represent the programmed assimilation of the spontaneous. According to published reports, there were no established walkways laid down for the opening-day crowds at Disneyland.[1] Rather, the Disney Imagineers waited to see where people would walk, then paved over their spontaneous footpaths to make prescribed routes.

The erasure of spontaneity has largely to do with the totality of the built and themed environment. Visitors are inducted into the park's program, their every need predefined and presented to them as a packaged routine and set of choices. "I'm not used to having everything done for me." This is how my companion at Disney World reacted when she checked into a Disney resort hotel and found that she, her suitcase, and her credit card had been turned into the scripted components of a highly orchestrated program. My companion later remarked that while she found it odd not to have to take care of everything herself (as she normally does in order to accomplish her daily tasks), she found it "liberating" to just fall into the proper pattern, knowing that nothing could arise that hadn't already been factored into the system. I have heard my companion's remarks reiterated by many visitors to the park with whom I've

---

1. Scott Bukatman, "There's Always Tomorrowland: Disney and the Hypercine-matic Experience," *October* 57 (Summer 1991), pp. 55–78.

talked. Most describe feeling "freed up" ("I didn't have to worry about my kids," "I didn't have to think about anything") by the experience of relinquishing control over the complex problem-solving thoughts and operations that otherwise define their lives. Many visitors suspend daily perceptions and judgments altogether, and treat the wonderland environment as more real than real. I saw this happen one morning when walking to breakfast at my Disney resort hotel. Two small children were stooped over a small snake that had crawled out onto the sun-warmed path. "Don't worry, it's rubber," remarked their mother. Clearly only Audio-Animatronic simulacra of the real world can inhabit Disney World. A real snake is an impossibility.

In fact, the entire natural world is subsumed by the primacy of the artificial. The next morning I stepped outside at the end of an early morning shower. The humid atmosphere held the combination of sun and rain. "Oh! Did they turn the sprinklers on?" This is the way my next-door neighbor greeted the day as she emerged from her hotel room. The Disney environment puts visitors inside the world that Philip K. Dick depicted in *Do Androids Dream of Electric Sheep?*—where all animal life has been exterminated, but replaced by the production of simulacra, so real in appearance that people have difficulty recalling that real animals no longer exist. The marvelous effect of science fiction is produced out of a dislocation between two worlds, which the reader apprehends as an estrangement, but the characters inside the novel cannot grasp because they have only the one world: the world of simulacra. The effect of the marvelous cannot be achieved unless the artificial environment is perceived through the retained memory of everyday reality. Total absorption into the Disney environment cancels the possibility for the marvelous and leaves the visitor with the banality of a park-wide sprinkler system. No muggers, no rain, no ants, and no snakes.

Amusement is the commodified negation of play. What is play but the spontaneous coming together of activity and imagination, rendered more pleasurable by the addition of friends? At Disney World, the world's most highly developed private property "state" devoted to amusement, play is all but eliminated by the absolute domination of program over spontaneity. Every ride runs to computerized schedule. There is no possibility of an awful thrill, like being stuck at the top of a ferris wheel. Order prevails particularly in the queues for the rides that zigzag dutifully on a prescribed path created out of stanchions and ropes; and the visitor's assimilation into the queue does not catapult him or her into another universe, as it would if Jorge Luis Borges fabricated the program. The Disney labyrinth is a banal extension of the ride's point of embarkation, which extends into the ride as a hyper-themed continuation of the queue. The "Backstage Movie Tour" has done away with the distinction between the ride and its queue by condemning the visitor to a two-and-a-half-hour-long pedagogical queue that preaches the process of movie production. Guests are mercilessly herded through sound stages and conveyed across endless back lots where one sees the ranch-style houses used in TV commercials and a few wrecked cars from movie chase scenes. Happily, there are a few discreet exit doors, bail-out points for parents with bored children. Even Main Street dictates programmed amusement because it is not a street but a conduit, albeit laden with commodity distractions, that conveys the visitor to the Magic Kingdom's other zones where more queues, rides, and commodities distinguish themselves on the basis of their themes. All historical and cultural references are merely ingredients for decor. Every expectation is met programmatically and in conformity with theme. Mickey as Sorcerer's Apprentice does not appear in the Wild West or the exotic worlds of Jungle and Adventure, the niches for Davey Crockett and Indiana Jones. Just imagine the chaos, a park-wide short circuit, that the mixing of themed ingredients might produce. Amusement areas are identified by a "look," by characters in costume, by the goods on sale: What place—i.e., product—is Snow White promoting if she's arm in arm with an astronaut? The utopian intermingling of thematic opportunities such as occurred at the finale of the movie *Who Framed Roger Rabbit?*, with Warner and Disney "toons" breaking their copyrighted species separation to cavort with each other and the human actors, will not happen at Disney World.

However, now that the costumed embodiment of Roger Rabbit has   5 taken up residence at Disney World, he, too, can expect to have a properly assigned niche in the spectacular Disney parade of characters. These have been augmented with a host of other Disney/Lucas/Spielberg creations, including Michael Jackson of "Captain EO" and C3PO and R2D2 of *Star Wars,* as well as Disney buyouts such as Jim Henson's Muppets and the Saturday morning cartoon heroes, the Teenage Mutant Ninja Turtles. The Disney Corporation's acquisition of the stock-in-trade of popular culture icons facilitates a belief commonly held by young children that every popular childhood figure "lives" at Disney World. In the utopian imagination of children, Disney World may well be a never-ending version of the finale to *Roger Rabbit* where every product of the imagination lives in community. In reality, the products (of adult imaginations) live to sell, to be consumed, to multiply.

What's most interesting about Disney World is what's not there. Intimacy is not in the program even though the architecture includes several secluded nooks, gazebos, and patios. During my five-day stay, I saw only one kiss—and this a husbandly peck on the cheek. Eruptions of imaginative play are just as rare. During the same five-day visit, I observed only one such incident even though there were probably fifty thousand children in the park. What's curious about what's not at Disney is that there is no way of knowing what's not there until an aberrant event occurs and provokes the remembrance of the social forms and behaviors that have been left out. This was the case with the episode of spontaneous play. Until I saw real play, I didn't realize that it was missing. The incident stood out against a humdrum background of uniform amusement: hundreds of kids being pushed from attraction to attraction in their strollers, hundreds more waiting dutifully in the queues or marching about in family groups—all of them abstaining from the loud, jostling, teasing, and rivalrous behaviors that would otherwise characterize many of their activities. Out of this homogenous "amused" mass, two kids snagged a huge sombrero each from an open-air stall at the foot of the Mexico Pavilion's Aztec temple stairway and began their impromptu version of the Mexican hat dance up and down the steps. Their play was clearly counterproductive as it took up most of the stairway, making it difficult for visitors to enter the pavilion. Play negated the function of the stairs as conduit into the attraction. The kids abandoned themselves to their fun, while all around them, the great mass of visitors purposefully kept their activities in line with Disney World's prescribed functions. Everyone but the dancers seemed to have accepted the park's unwritten motto: "If you pay, you shouldn't play." To get your money's worth, you have to do everything and do it in the prescribed manner. Free play is gratuitous and therefore a waste of the family's leisure time expenditure.

Conformity with the park's program upholds the Disney value system. Purposeful consumption—while it costs the consumer a great deal—affirms the value of the consumer. "Don't forget, we drove twenty hours to get here." This is how one father admonished his young son who was squirming about on the floor of EPCOT's Independence Hall, waiting for the amusement to begin. The child's wanton and impatient waste of time was seen as a waste of the family's investment in its amusement. If a family is to realize the value of its leisure time consumptions, then every member must function as a proper consumer.

The success of Disney World as an amusement park has largely to do with the way its use of programming meshes with the economics of consumption as a value system. In a world wholly predicated on consumption, the dominant order need not proscribe those activities that run counter to consumption, such as free play and squirming, because the consuming public largely polices itself against gratuitous acts which would interfere with the production of consumption as a value. Conformity with the practice of consumption is so widespread and deep at Disney World that occasional manifestations of boredom or spontaneity do not influence the compulsively correct behavior of others. Independence Hall did not give way to a seething mass of squirming youngsters even though all had to sit through a twenty-minute wait. Nor did other children on the margins of the hat dance fling themselves into the fun. Such infectious behavior would have indicated communally defined social relations or the desire for such social relations. Outside of Disney World in places of public use, infectious behavior is common. One child squirming about on the library floor breeds others; siblings chasing each other around in a supermarket draw others; one child mischievously poking at a public fountain attracts others; kids freeloading rides on a department store escalator can draw a crowd. These playful, impertinent acts indicate an imperfect mesh between programmed environment and the value system of consumption. Consumers may occasionally reclaim the social, particularly the child consumer who has not yet been fully and properly socialized to accept individuation as the bottom line in the consumer system of value. As an economic factor, the individual exists to maximize consumption—and therefore profits—across the broad mass of consumers. This is the economic maxim most cherished by the fast-food industry, where every burger and order of fries is individually packaged and consumed to preclude consumer pooling and sharing.

At Disney World the basic social unit is the family. This was made particularly clear to me because as a single visitor conducting research, I presented a problem at the point of embarkation for each of the rides. "How many in your group?" "One." The lone occupant of a conveyance invariably constructed to hold the various numerical breakdowns of the nuclear family (two, three, or four) is an anomaly. Perhaps the most family-affirming aspect of Disney World is the way the queues serve as a place where family members negotiate who will ride with whom. Will Mom and Dad separate themselves so as to accompany their two kids on a two-person ride? Will an older sibling assume the responsibility for a younger brother or sister? Every ride asks the family to evaluate each of its member's needs for security and independence. This is probably the only situation in a family's visit to Disney World where the social relations of family materialize as practice. Otherwise and throughout a family's stay, the family as nexus for social relations is subsumed by the primary definition of family as the basic unit of consumption. In consumer society at large, each of us is an atomized consumer. Families are composed of autonomous, individuated consumers, each satisfying his or her age- and gender-differentiated taste in the music, video, food, and pleasure marketplace. In contrast, Disney World puts the family back together. Even teens are integrated in their families and are seldom seen roaming the park in teen groups as they might in shopping malls.

Families at Disney World present themselves as families, like the one I saw one morning on my way to breakfast at a Disney resort hotel: father, mother, and three children small to large, each wearing identical blue Mickey Mouse T-shirts and shorts. As I walked past them, I overheard the middle child say, "We looked better yesterday—in white." Immediately, I envisioned the family in yesterday's matching outfits, and wondered if they had bought identical ensembles for every day of their stay.

All expressions of mass culture include contradictory utopian impulses, which may be buried or depicted in distorted form, but nevertheless generate much of the satisfaction of mass cultural commodities (whether the consumer recognizes them as utopian or not). While the ideology of the family has long functioned to promote conservative—even reactionary—political and social agendas, the structure of the family as a social unit signifies communality rather than individuality and can give impetus to utopian longings for communally defined relations in society at large. However, when the family buys into the look of a family, and appraises itself on the basis of its look ("We looked better yesterday"), it becomes a walking, talking commodity, a packaged unit of consumption stamped with the Mickey logo of approval. The theoretical question that this family poses for me is not whether its representation of itself as family includes utopian possibilities (because it does), but whether such impulses can be expressed and communicated in ways not accessible to commodification.

In its identical dress, the family represents itself as capitalism's version of a democratized unit of consumption. Differences and inequalities among family members are reduced to distinctions in age and size. We have all had occasion to experience the doppelgänger effect in the presence of identical twins who choose (or whose families enforce) identical dress. Whether chosen or imposed, identical twins who practice the art of same dress have the possibility of confounding or subverting social order. In contrast, the heterogeneous family whose members choose to dress identically affirms conformity with social order. The family has cloned itself as a multiple, but identical consumer, thus enabling the maximization of consumption. It is a microcosmic representation of free market democracy where the range of choices is restricted to the series of objects already on the shelf. In this system there is no radical choice. Even the minority of visitors who choose to wear their Rolling Stones and Grateful Dead T-shirts give the impression of having felt constrained not to wear a Disney logo.

Actually, Disney has invented a category of negative consumer choices for those individuals who wish to express nonconformity. This I discovered as I prepared to depart for my Disney research trip, when my daughter Cassie (fifteen years old and "cool" to the max) warned me, "Don't buy me any of that Disney paraphernalia." As it turned out, she was happy to get a pair of boxer shorts emblazoned with the leering images of Disney's villains: two evil queens, the Big Bad Wolf, and Captain Hook. Every area of Disney World includes a Disney Villains Shop, a chain store for bad-guy merchandise. Visitors who harbor anti-Disney sentiments can express their cultural politics by consuming the negative Disney line. There is no possibility of an anticonsumption at Disney World. All visitors are, by definition, consumers, their status conferred with the price of admission.

At Disney World even memories are commodities. How the visitor will remember his or her experience of the park has been programmed and indicated by the thousands of "Kodak Picture Spot" signposts. These position the photographer so as to capture the best views of each and every attraction, so that even the most inept family members can bring home perfect postcard-like photos. To return home from a trip to Disney World with a collection of haphazardly photographed environments or idiosyncratic family shots is tantamount to collecting bad memories. A family album comprised of picture-perfect photo-site images, on the other hand, constitutes the grand narrative of the family's trip to Disney World, the one that can be offered as testimony to money well spent. Meanwhile, all those embarrassing photos, the ones not programmed by the "Picture Spots," that depict babies with ice cream all over their faces or toddlers who burst into tears rather than smiles at the sight of those big-headed costumed characters that crop up all over the park—these are the images that are best left forgotten.

The other commodified form of memory is the souvenir. As long as   15
there has been tourism there have also been souvenirs: objects marketed to concretize the visitor's experience of another place. From a certain point of view, religious pilgrimage includes aspects of tourism, particularly when the culmination of pilgrimage is the acquisition of a transportable relic. Indeed, secular mass culture often imitates the forms and practices of popular religious culture. For many Americans today who make pilgrimages to Graceland and bring home a mass-produced piece of Presley memorabilia, culture and religion collide and mesh.

Of course, the desire to translate meaningful moments into concrete objects need not take commodified form. In Toni Morrison's *Song of Solomon,* Pilate, a larger-than-life earth mother if there ever was one, spent her early vagabondage gathering a stone from every place she visited. Similarly, I know of mountain climbers who mark their ascents by bringing a rock back from each peak they climb. Like Pilate's stones, these tend to be nondescript and embody personal remembrances available only to the collector. In contrast, the commodity souvenir enunciates a single meaning to everyone: "I was there. I bought something." Unlike the souvenirs I remember having seen as a child, seashells painted with seascapes and the name of some picturesque resort town, most souvenirs today are printed with logos (like the Hard Rock Cafe T-shirt), or renderings of copyrighted material (all the Disney merchandise). The purchase of such a souvenir allows the consumer the illusion of participating in the enterprise as a whole, attaining a piece of the action. This is the consumerist version of small-time buying on the stock exchange. We all trade in logos—buy them, wear them, eat them, and make them the containers of our dreams and memories. Similarly, we may all buy into capital with the purchase of public stock. These consumerist activities give the illusion of democratic participation while denying access to real corporate control which remains intact and autonomous, notwithstanding the mass diffusion of its logos and stock on the public market. Indeed the manipulation of public stock initiated during the Reagan administration, which has facilitated one leveraged buyout after another, gives the lie to whatever wistful remnants of democratic ownership one might once have attached to the notion of "public" stocks.

Disney World is logoland. The merchandise, the costumes, the scenery—all is either stamped with the Disney logo or covered by copyright legislation. In fact, it is impossible to photograph at Disney World without running the risk of infringing a Disney copyright. A family photo in front of Sleeping Beauty's Castle is apt to include dozens of infringements: the castle itself, Uncle Harry's "Goofy" T-shirt, the kids' Donald and Mickey hats, maybe a costumed Chip 'n Dale in the background. The only thing that saves the average family from a lawsuit is that most don't use their vacation photos as a means for making profit. I suspect the staff of "America's Funniest Home Videos" systematically eliminates all family videos shot at Disney World; otherwise prize winners might find themselves having to negotiate the legal difference between prize and profit, and in a larger sense, public use versus private property. As an interesting note, Michael Sorkin, in a recent essay on Disneyland, chose a photo of "[t]he sky above Disney World [as a] substitute for an image of the place itself." Calling Disney World "the first copyrighted urban environment," Sorkin goes on to stress the "litigiousness" of the Disney Corporation.[2] It may be that *Design Quarterly,* where Sorkin published his essay, pays its contributors, thus disqualifying them from "fair use" interpretations of copyright policy.

Logos have become so much a part of our cultural baggage that we hardly notice them. Actually they are the cultural capital of corporations. Pierre Bourdieu invented the notion of cultural capital with reference to individuals. In a nutshell, cultural capital represents the sum total of a person's ability to buy into and trade in the culture. This is circumscribed by the economics of class and, in turn, functions as a means for designating an individual's social standing. Hence people with higher levels of education who distinguish themselves with upscale or trendy consumptions have more cultural capital and can command greater privilege and authority than those who, as Bourdieu put it, are stuck defining themselves by the consumption of necessity. There are no cultural objects or practices that do not constitute capital, no reserves of culture that escape value. Everything that constitutes one's cultural life is a commodity and can be reckoned in terms of capital logic.

In the United States today there is little difference between persons

---

2. Michael Sorkin, "See You in Disneyland," *Design Quarterly* (Winter 1992), pp. 5–13.

and corporations. Indeed, corporations enjoy many of the legal rights extended to individuals. The market system and its private property state are "peopled" by corporations, which trade in, accumulate, and hoard up logos. These are the cultural signifiers produced by corporations, the impoverished imagery of a wholly rationalized entity. Logos are commodities in the abstract, but they are not so abstracted as to have transcended value. Corporations with lots of logos, particularly upscale, high-tech logos, command more cultural capital than corporations with fewer, more humble logos.

In late twentieth-century America, the cultural capital of corporations has replaced many of the human forms of cultural capital. As we buy, wear, and eat logos, we become the henchmen and admen of the corporations, defining ourselves with respect to the social standing of the various corporations. Some would say that this is a new form of tribalism, that in sporting corporate logos we ritualize and humanize them, we redefine the cultural capital of the corporations in human social terms. I would say that a state where culture is indistinguishable from logo and where the practice of culture risks infringement of private property is a state that values the corporate over the human.

While at Disney World, I managed to stow away on the behind-the-scenes tour reserved for groups of corporate conventioneers. I had heard about this tour from a friend who is also researching Disney and whose account of underground passageways, conduits for armies of workers and all the necessary materials and services that enable the park to function, had elevated the tour to mythic proportions in my imagination.

But very little of the behind-the-scenes tour was surprising. There was no magic, just a highly rational system built on the compartmentalization of all productive functions and its ensuing division of labor, both aimed at the creation of maximum efficiency. However, instances do arise when the rational infrastructure comes into contradiction with the onstage (park-wide) theatricalized image that the visitor expects to consume. Such is the case with the system that sucks trash collected at street level through unseen pneumatic tubes that transect the backstage area, finally depositing the trash in Disney's own giant compactor site. To the consumer's eyes, trash is never a problem at Disney World. After all, everyone dutifully uses the containers marked "trash," and what little manages to fall to the ground (generally popcorn) is immediately swept up by the French Foreign Legion trash brigade. For the consumer, there is no trash beyond its onstage collection. But there will soon be a problem as environmental pressure groups press Disney to recycle. As my companion on the backstage tour put it, "Why is there no recycling at Disney World—after all, many of the middle-class visitors to the park are already sorting and recycling trash in their homes?" To this the Disney guide pointed out that there is recycling, backstage: bins for workers to toss their Coke cans and other bins for office workers to deposit papers.

But recycling onstage would break the magic of themed authenticity. After all, the "real" Cinderella's Castle was not equipped with recycling bins, nor did the denizens of Main Street, U.S.A., circa 1910, foresee the problem of trash. To maintain the image, Disney problem solvers are discussing hiring a minimum-wage workforce to rake, sort, and recycle the trash on back lots that the environmentally aware visitor will never see.

While I have been describing the backstage area as banal, the tour through it was not uneventful. Indeed there was one incident that underscored for me the dramatic collision between people's expectations of public use and the highly controlled nature of Disney's private domain. As I mentioned, the backstage tour took us to the behind-the-scenes staging area for the minute-by-minute servicing of the park and hoopla of its mass spectacles such as firework displays, light shows, and parades. We happened to be in the backstage area just as the parade down Main Street was coming to an end. Elaborate floats and costumed characters descended a ramp behind Cinderella's Castle and began to disassemble before our eyes. The floats were alive with big-headed characters, clambering off the superstructures and out of their heavy, perspiration-drenched costumes. Several "beheaded" characters revealed stocky young men gulping down Gatorade. They walked toward our tour group, bloated Donald and bandy-legged Chip from the neck down, carrying their huge costume heads, while their real heads emerged pea-sized and aberrantly human.

We had been warned *not* to take pictures during the backstage tour, but one of our group, apparently carried away by the spectacle, could not resist. She managed to shoot a couple of photos of the disassembled characters before being approached by one of the tour guides. As if caught in a spy movie, the would-be photographer pried open her camera and ripped out the whole roll of film. The entire tour group stood in stunned amazement; not, I think, at the immediate presence of surveillance, but at the woman's dramatic response. In a situation where control is so omnipresent and conformity with control is taken for granted, any sudden gesture or dramatic response is a surprise.

At the close of the tour, my companion and I lingered behind the rest of the group to talk with our tour guides. As a professional photographer, my companion wanted to know if there is a "normal" procedure for disarming behind-the-scenes photographic spies. The guide explained that the prescribed practice is to impound the cameras, process the film, remove the illicit photos, and return the camera, remaining photos, and complimentary film to the perpetrator. When questioned further, the guide went on to elaborate the Disney rationale for control over the image: the "magic" would be broken if photos of disassembled characters circulated in the public sphere; children might suffer irreparable psychic trauma at the sight of a "beheaded" Mickey; Disney exercises control over the image to safeguard childhood fantasies.

25

What Disney employees refer to as the "magic" of Disney World has actually to do with the ability to produce fetishized consumptions. The unbroken seamlessness of Disney World, its totality as a consumable artifact, cannot tolerate the revelation of the real work that produces the commodity. There would be no magic if the public should see the entire cast of magicians in various stages of disassembly and fatigue. That selected individuals are permitted to witness the backstage labor facilitates the word-of-mouth affirmation of the tremendous organizational feat that produces Disney World. The interdiction against photography eliminates the possibility of discontinuity at the level of image. There are no images to compete with the copyright-perfect onstage images displayed for public consumption. It's not accidental that our tour guide underscored the fact that Disney costumes are tightly controlled. The character costumes are made at only one production site and this site supplies the costumes used at Tokyo's Disneyland and EuroDisney. There can be no culturally influenced variations on the Disney models. Control over the image ensures the replication of Disney worldwide. The prohibition against photographing disassembled characters is motivated by the same phobia of industrial espionage that runs rampant throughout the high-tech information industry. The woman in our tour group who ripped open her camera and destroyed her film may not have been wrong in acting out a spy melodrama. Her photos of the disassembled costumes might have revealed the manner of their production—rendering them accessible to non-Disney replication. At Disney World, the magic that resides in the integrity of childhood fantasy is inextricably linked to the fetishism of the commodity and the absolute control over private property as it is registered in the copyrighted image.

As I see it, the individual's right to imagine and to give expression to unique ways of seeing is at stake in struggles against private property. Mickey Mouse, notwithstanding his corporate copyright, exists in our common culture. He is the site for the enactment of childhood wishes and fantasies, for early conceptualizations and renderings of the body, a being who can be imagined as both self and other. If culture is held as private property, then there can be only one correct version of Mickey Mouse, whose logo-like image is the cancellation of creativity. But the multiplicity of quirky versions of Mickey Mouse that children draw can stand as a graphic question to us as adults: Who, indeed, owns Mickey Mouse?

What most distinguishes Disney World from any other amusement park is the way its spatial organization, defined by autonomous "worlds" and wholly themed environments, combines with the homogeneity of its visitors (predominantly white, middle-class families) to produce a sense of community. While Disney World includes an underlying utopian impulse, this is articulated with nostalgia for a small-town, small-business America (Main Street, U.S.A.), and the fantasy of a controllable corporatist world (EPCOT). The illusion of community is enhanced by the longing for community that many visitors bring to the park, which they may feel is unavailable to them in their own careers, daily lives, and neighborhoods, thanks in large part to the systematic erosion of the public sector throughout the Reagan and Bush administrations. In the last decade the inroads of private, for-profit enterprise in areas previously defined by public control, and the hostile aggression of tax backlash coupled with "me first" attitudes have largely defeated the possibility of community in our homes and cities.

Whenever I visit Disney World, I invariably overhear other visitors making comparisons between Disney World and their home towns. They stare out over EPCOT's lake and wonder why developers back home don't produce similar aesthetic spectacles. They talk about botched, abandoned, and misconceived development projects that have wrecked their local landscapes. Others see Disney World as an oasis of social tranquility and security in comparison to their patrolled, but nonetheless deteriorating, maybe even perilous neighborhoods. A recent essay in *Time* captured some of these sentiments: "Do you see anybody [at Disney World] lying on the street or begging for money? Do you see anyone jumping on your car and wanting to clean your windshield—and when you say no, they get abusive?"[3]

Comments such as these do more than betray the class anxiety of the middle strata. They poignantly express the inability of this group to make distinctions between what necessarily constitutes the public and the private sectors. Do visitors forget that they pay a daily use fee (upwards of $150 for a four-day stay) just to be a citizen of Disney World (not to mention the $100 per night hotel bill)? Maybe so—and maybe it's precisely *forgetting* that visitors pay for.

If there is any distinction to be made between Disney World and our local shopping malls, it would have to do with Disney's successful exclusion of all factors that might put the lie to its uniform social fabric. The occasional Hispanic mother who arrives with extended family and illegal bologna sandwiches is an anomaly. So too is the first-generation Cubana who buys a year-round pass to Disney's nightspot, Pleasure Island, in hopes of meeting a rich and marriageable British tourist. These women testify to the presence of Orlando, Disney World's marginalized "Sister City," whose overflowing cheap labor force and overcrowded and under-funded public institutions are the unseen real world upon which Disney's world depends.

30

---

3. "Fantasy's Reality," *Time*, 27 May 1991, p. 54.

Reading the Text

1. In Willis's view, how does Disney World create an artificial, programmed environment, and why does it do this?
2. What does Willis mean when she claims that "Amusement is the commodified negation of play" (para. 4)?
3. Why does Willis believe that a theme park such as Disney World "puts the family back together" (para. 9)?
4. How does Disney World appeal to nonconformists?
5. What does Willis mean by saying that "Disney World is logoland" (para. 17)?
6. Summarize in your own words Willis's interpretation of the "magic" of Disney World.

Reading the Signs

1. In class, brainstorm a list of Disney products, characters, and movies, and then discuss the impact of the Disney corporation on American consumer life.
2. In an essay, write an argument that defends, refutes, or modifies Willis's assumption that Disney World is too controlling in its "processing" of visitors. If you prefer, you can focus your essay on any other Disney park you may have visited. You may want to refresh your memory of the park by visiting the Disney website at **http://www.disney.go.com.**
3. Visit a local theme park, and study whether it controls the consumer habits of its visitors as Willis claims Disney World does. Then write an essay in which you analyze your park's control over consumer behavior.
4. Write an essay in which you describe how you would design a theme park for the twenty-first century. What themes would you emphasize? What activities and amenities would you provide, and what would they look like? Be sure to explain your choices and what messages you communicate to visitors.
5. At the close of her essay, Willis suggests a comparison between Disney World and shopping malls. In an essay, compare and contrast the ways that Disney World and a local mall you have visited control consumer spending habits. To develop your ideas, consult Anne Norton's "The Signs of Shopping" (p. 62), or Malcolm Gladwell's "The Science of Shopping" (p. 757).

MALCOLM   GLADWELL

The Science of Shopping

|||||||||||||||||||||||||||||||||||||||||||||||||||||||||||

*Ever wonder why the season's hottest new styles at stores like the Gap
are usually displayed on the right at least fifteen paces in from the front
entrance? It's because that's where shoppers are most likely to see them
as they enter the store, gear down from the walking pace of a mall corridor, and adjust to the shop's spatial environment. Ever wonder how
shop managers know this sort of thing? It's because, as Malcolm Gladwell reports here, they hire consultants like Paco Underhill, a "retail
anthropologist" and "urban geographer" whose studies (often aided by
hidden cameras) of shopping behavior have become valuable guides to
store managers looking for the best ways to move the goods. Does this
feel just a little Orwellian? Read on. A regular writer for the* New
Yorker, *in which this selection first appeared, Gladwell has also written* The Tipping Point *(forthcoming).*

Human beings walk the way they drive, which is to say that Americans tend to keep to the right when they stroll down shopping-mall con-
courses or city sidewalks. This is why in a well-designed airport travellers
drifting toward their gate will always find the fast-food restaurants on
their left and the gift shops on their right: people will readily cross a lane
of pedestrian traffic to satisfy their hunger but rarely to make an impulse
buy of a T-shirt or a magazine. This is also why Paco Underhill tells his
retail clients to make sure that their window displays are canted, preferably to both sides but especially to the left, so that a potential shopper approaching the store on the inside of the sidewalk—the shopper, that is,
with the least impeded view of the store window—can see the display
from at least twenty-five feet away.

Of course, a lot depends on how fast the potential shopper is walking. Paco, in his previous life, as an urban geographer in Manhattan,
spent a great deal of time thinking about walking speeds as he listened in
on the great debates of the nineteen-seventies over whether the traffic
lights in midtown should be timed to facilitate the movement of cars or
to facilitate the movement of pedestrians and so break up the big pla-
toons that move down Manhattan sidewalks. He knows that the faster
you walk the more your peripheral vision narrows, so you become unable to pick up visual cues as quickly as someone who is just ambling
along. He knows, too, that people who walk fast take a surprising
amount of time to slow down—just as it takes a good stretch of road to
change gears with a stick-shift automobile. On the basis of his research,

Paco estimates the human downshift period to be anywhere from twelve to twenty-five feet, so if you own a store, he says, you never want to be next door to a bank: potential shoppers speed up when they walk past a bank (since there's nothing to look at), and by the time they slow down they've walked right past your business. The downshift factor also means that when potential shoppers enter a store it's going to take them from five to fifteen paces to adjust to the light and refocus and gear down from walking speed to shopping speed—particularly if they've just had to navigate a treacherous parking lot or hurry to make the light at Fifty-seventh and Fifth.

Paco calls that area inside the door the Decompression Zone, and something he tells clients over and over again is never, *ever* put anything of value in that zone—not shopping baskets or tie racks or big promotional displays—because no one is going to see it. Paco believes that, as a rule of thumb, customer interaction with any product or promotional display in the Decompression Zone will increase at least thirty per cent once it's moved to the back edge of the zone, and even more if it's placed to the right, because another of the fundamental rules of how human beings shop is that upon entering a store—whether it's Nordstrom or K Mart, Tiffany or the Gap—the shopper invariably and reflexively turns to the right. Paco believes in the existence of the Invariant Right because he has actually verified it. He has put cameras in stores trained directly on the doorway, and if you go to his office, just above Union Square, where videocassettes and boxes of Super-eight film from all his work over the years are stacked in plastic Tupperware containers practically up to the ceiling, he can show you reel upon reel of grainy entryway video—customers striding in the door, downshifting, refocusing, and then, again and again, making that little half turn.

Paco Underhill is a tall man in his mid-forties, partly bald, with a neatly trimmed beard and an engaging, almost goofy manner. He wears baggy khakis and shirts open at the collar, and generally looks like the academic he might have been if he hadn't been captivated, twenty years ago, by the ideas of the urban anthropologist William Whyte. It was Whyte who pioneered the use of time-lapse photography as a tool of urban planning, putting cameras in parks and the plazas in front of office buildings in midtown Manhattan, in order to determine what distinguished a public space that worked from one that didn't. As a Columbia undergraduate, in 1974, Paco heard a lecture on Whyte's work and, he recalls, left the room "walking on air." He immediately read everything Whyte had written. He emptied his bank account to buy cameras and film and make his own home movie, about a pedestrian mall in Poughkeepsie. He took his "little exercise" to Whyte's advocacy group, the Project for Public Spaces, and was offered a job. Soon, however, it dawned on Paco that Whyte's ideas could be taken a step further—that the same techniques he used to establish why a plaza worked or didn't work could also be used to determine why a store worked or didn't work. Thus was born the field of retail anthropology, and, not long afterward, Paco founded Envirosell, which in just over fifteen years has counselled some of the most familiar names in American retailing, from Levi Strauss to Kinney, Starbucks, McDonald's, Blockbuster, Apple Computer, A.T.&T., and a number of upscale retailers that Paco would rather not name.

When Paco gets an assignment, he and his staff set up a series of   5
videocameras throughout the test store and then back the cameras up with Envirosell staffers—trackers, as they're known—armed with clipboards. Where the cameras go and how many trackers Paco deploys depends on exactly what the store wants to know about its shoppers. Typically, though, he might use six cameras and two or three trackers, and let the study run for two or three days, so that at the end he would have pages and pages of carefully annotated tracking sheets and anywhere from a hundred to five hundred hours of film. These days, given the expansion of his business, he might tape fifteen thousand hours in a year, and, given that he has been in operation since the late seventies, he now has well over a hundred thousand hours of tape in his library.

Even in the best of times, this would be a valuable archive. But today, with the retail business in crisis, it is a gold mine. The time per visit that the average American spends in a shopping mall was sixty-six minutes last year—down from seventy-two minutes in 1992—and is the lowest number ever recorded. The amount of selling space per American shopper is now more than double what it was in the mid-seventies, meaning that profit margins have never been narrower, and the costs of starting a retail business—and of failing—have never been higher. In the past few years, countless dazzling new retailing temples have been built along Fifth and Madison Avenues—Barneys, Calvin Klein, Armani, Valentino, Banana Republic, Prada, Chanel, Nike Town, and on and on—but it is an explosion of growth based on no more than a hunch, a hopeful multimillion-dollar gamble that the way to break through is to provide the shopper with spectacle and more spectacle. "The arrogance is gone," Millard Drexler, the president and C.E.O. of the Gap, told me. "Arrogance makes failure. Once you think you know the answer, it's almost always over." In such a competitive environment, retailers don't just want to know how shoppers behave in their stores. They *have* to know. And who better to ask than Paco Underhill, who in the past decade and a half has analyzed tens of thousands of hours of shopping videotape and, as a result, probably knows more about the strange habits and quirks of the species *Emptor americanus* than anyone else alive?

Paco is considered the originator, for example, of what is known in the trade as the butt-brush theory—or, as Paco calls it, more delicately, *le facteur bousculade*—which holds that the likelihood of a woman's being converted from a browser to a buyer is inversely proportional to the likelihood of her being brushed on her behind while she's examining merchandise. Touch—or brush or bump or jostle—a woman on the behind when she has stopped to look at an item, and she will bolt. Actually, calling this a theory is something of a misnomer, because Paco doesn't offer any explanation for why women react that way, aside from venturing that they are "more sensitive back there." It's really an observation, based on repeated and close analysis of his videotape library, that Paco has transformed into a retailing commandment: a women's product that requires extensive examination should never be placed in a narrow aisle.

Paco approaches the problem of the Invariant Right the same way. Some retail thinkers see this as a subject crying out for interpretation and speculation. The design guru Joseph Weishar, for example, argues, in his magisterial *Design for Effective Selling Space,* that the Invariant Right is a function of the fact that we "absorb and digest information in the left part of the brain" and "assimilate and logically use this information in the right half," the result being that we scan the store from left to right and then fix on an object to the right "essentially at a 45 degree angle from the point that we enter." When I asked Paco about this interpretation, he shrugged, and said he thought the reason was simply that most people are right-handed. Uncovering the fundamentals of "why" is clearly not a pursuit that engages him much. He is not a theoretician but an empiricist, and for him the important thing is that in amassing his huge library of in-store time-lapse photography he has gained enough hard evidence to know how often and under what circumstances the Invariant Right is expressed and how to take advantage of it.

What Paco likes are facts. They come tumbling out when he talks, and, because he speaks with a slight hesitation—lingering over the first syllable in, for example, "re-tail" or "de-sign"—he draws you in, and you find yourself truly hanging on his words. "We have reached a historic point in American history," he told me in our very first conversation. "Men, for the first time, have begun to buy their own underwear." He then paused to let the comment sink in, so that I could absorb its implications, before he elaborated: "Which means that we have to *totally* rethink the way we sell that product." In the parlance of Hollywood scriptwriters, the best endings must be surprising and yet inevitable; and the best of Paco's pronouncements take the same shape. It would never have occurred to me to wonder about the increasingly critical role played by touching—or, as Paco calls it, petting—clothes in the course of making the decision to buy them. But then I went to the Gap and to Banana Republic and saw people touching, and fondling and, one after another, buying shirts and sweaters laid out on big wooden tables, and what Paco told me—which was no doubt based on what he had seen on his videotapes—made perfect sense: that the reason the Gap and Banana Republic have tables is not merely that sweaters and shirts look better there, or that tables fit into the warm and relaxing residential feeling that the Gap and Banana Republic are trying to create in their stores, but that tables invite—indeed, symbolize—touching. "Where do we eat?" Paco asks. "We eat, we pick up food, on tables."

Paco produces for his clients a series of carefully detailed studies, to-   10
talling forty to a hundred and fifty pages, filled with product-by-product breakdowns and bright-colored charts and graphs. In one recent case, he was asked by a major clothing retailer to analyze the first of a new chain of stores that the firm planned to open. One of the things the client wanted to know was how successful the store was in drawing people into its depths, since the chances that shoppers will buy something are directly related to how long they spend shopping, and how long they spend shopping is directly related to how deep they get pulled into the store. For this reason, a supermarket will often put dairy products on one side, meat at the back, and fresh produce on the other side, so that the typical shopper can't just do a drive-by but has to make an entire circuit of the store, and be tempted by everything the supermarket has to offer. In the case of the new clothing store, Paco found that ninety-one per cent of all shoppers penetrated as deep as what he called Zone 4, meaning more than three-quarters of the way in, well past the accessories and shirt racks and belts in the front, and little short of the far wall, with the changing rooms and the pants stacked on shelves. Paco regarded this as an extraordinary figure, particularly for a long, narrow store like this one, where it is not unusual for the rate of penetration past, say, Zone 3 to be under fifty per cent. But that didn't mean the store was perfect—far from it. For Paco, all kinds of questions remained.

Purchasers, for example, spent an average of eleven minutes and twenty-seven seconds in the store, nonpurchasers two minutes and thirty-six seconds. It wasn't that the nonpurchasers just cruised in and out: in those two minutes and thirty-six seconds, they went deep into the store and examined an average of 3.42 items. So why didn't they buy? What, exactly, happened to cause some browsers to buy and other browsers to walk out the door?

Then, there was the issue of the number of products examined. The purchasers were looking at an average of 4.81 items but buying only 1.33 items. Paco found this statistic deeply disturbing. As the retail market grows more cutthroat, store owners have come to realize that it's all but impossible to increase the number of customers coming in, and have concentrated instead on getting the customers they do have to buy more. Paco thinks that if you can sell someone a pair of pants you must also be able to sell that person a belt, or a pair of socks, or a pair of underpants, or even do what the Gap does so well: sell a person a complete outfit. To Paco, the figure 1.33 suggested that the store was doing something very wrong, and one day when I visited him in his office he sat me down in front of one of his many VCRs to see how he looked for the 1.33 culprit.

It should be said that sitting next to Paco is a rather strange experience. "My mother says that I'm the best-paid spy in America," he told me. He laughed, but he wasn't entirely joking. As a child, Paco had a nearly debilitating stammer, and, he says, "since I was never that comfortable talking I always relied on my eyes to understand things." That much is obvious from the first moment you meet him: Paco is one of those people who look right at you, soaking up every nuance and detail. It isn't a hostile gaze, because Paco isn't hostile at all. He has a big smile, and he'll call you "chief" and use your first name a lot and generally act as if he knew you well. But that's the awkward thing: he has looked at you so closely that you're sure he does know you well, and you, meanwhile, hardly know him at all.

This kind of asymmetry is even more pronounced when you watch his shopping videos with him, because every movement or gesture means something to Paco—he has spent his adult life deconstructing the shopping experience—but nothing to the outsider, or, at least, not at first. Paco had to keep stopping the video to get me to see things through his eyes before I began to understand. In one sequence, for example, a camera mounted high on the wall outside the changing rooms documented a man and a woman shopping for a pair of pants for what appeared to be their daughter, a girl in her midteens. The tapes are soundless, but the basic steps of the shopping dance are so familiar to Paco that, once I'd grasped the general idea, he was able to provide a running commentary on what was being said and thought. There is the girl emerging from the changing room wearing her first pair. There she is glancing at her reflection in the mirror, then turning to see herself from the back. There is the mother looking on. There is the father—or, as fathers are known in the trade, the "wallet carrier"—stepping forward and pulling up the jeans. There's the girl trying on another pair. There's the primp again. The twirl. The mother. The wallet carrier. And then again, with another pair. The full sequence lasted twenty minutes, and at the end came the take-home lesson, for which Paco called in one of his colleagues, Tom Moseman, who had supervised the project.

"This is a very critical moment," Tom, a young, intense man wearing little round glasses, said, and he pulled up a chair next to mine. "She's saying, 'I don't know whether I should wear a belt.' Now here's the salesclerk. The girl says to him, 'I need a belt,' and he says, 'Take mine.' Now there he is taking her back to the full-length mirror." 15

A moment later, the girl returns, clearly happy with the purchase. She wants the jeans. The wallet carrier turns to her, and then gestures to the salesclerk. The wallet carrier is telling his daughter to give back the belt. The girl gives back the belt. Tom stops the tape. He's leaning forward now, a finger jabbing at the screen. Beside me, Paco is shaking his head. I don't get it—at least, not at first—and so Tom replays that last segment. The wallet carrier tells the girl to give back the belt. She gives back the belt. And then, finally, it dawns on me why this store has an average purchase number of only 1.33. "Don't you see?" Tom said. "*She wanted the belt. A great opportunity to make an add-on sale . . . lost!*"

Should we be afraid of Paco Underhill? One of the fundamental anxieties of the American consumer, after all, has always been that beneath the pleasure and the frivolity of the shopping experience runs an undercurrent of manipulation, and that anxiety has rarely seemed more justified than today. The practice of prying into the minds and habits of American consumers is now a multibillion-dollar business. Every time a product is pulled across a supermarket checkout scanner, information is recorded, assembled, and sold to a market-research firm for analysis. There are companies that put tiny cameras inside frozen-food cases in supermarket aisles; market-research firms that feed census data and behavioral statistics into algorithms and come out with complicated maps of the American consumer; anthropologists who sift through the garbage of carefully targeted households to analyze their true consumption patterns; and endless rounds of highly organized focus groups and questionnaire takers and phone surveyors. That some people are now tracking our every shopping move with video cameras seems in many respects the last straw: Paco's movies are, after all, creepy. They look like the surveillance videos taken during convenience-store holdups — hazy and soundless and slightly warped by the angle of the lens. When you watch them, you find yourself waiting for something bad to happen, for someone to shoplift or pull a gun on a cashier.

The more time you spend with Paco's videos, though, the less scary they seem. After an hour or so, it's no longer clear whether simply by watching people shop — and analyzing their every move — you can learn how to control them. The shopper that emerges from the videos is not pliable or manipulable. The screen shows people filtering in and out of stores, petting and moving on, abandoning their merchandise because checkout lines are too long, or leaving a store empty-handed because they couldn't fit their stroller into the aisle between two shirt racks. Paco's shoppers are fickle and headstrong, and are quite unwilling to buy anything unless conditions are perfect — unless the belt is presented at *exactly* the right moment. His theories of the butt-brush and petting and the Decompression Zone and the Invariant Right seek not to make shoppers conform to the desires of sellers but to make sellers conform to the desires of shoppers. What Paco is teaching his clients is a kind of slavish devotion to the shopper's every whim. He is teaching them humility.

Reading the Text

1. Summarize in your own words the ways that retailers use spatial design to affect the behavior and buying habits of consumers.
2. What is Gladwell's tone in this selection, and what does it reveal about his attitude toward the retail industry's manipulation of customers?

3. What is the effect on the reader of Gladwell's description of Paco Underhill's appearance and background?

4. Why does Paco Underhill's mother say that he is "the best-paid spy in America" (para. 13)?

Reading the Signs

1. Write an essay in response to Gladwell's question "Should we be afraid of Paco Underhill?" (para. 17).

2. Visit a local store or supermarket, and study the spatial design. How many of the design strategies that Gladwell describes do you observe, and how do they affect customers' behavior? Use your observations as the basis for an essay interpreting the store's spatial design. To develop your ideas further, consult Anne Norton's "The Signs of Shopping" (p. 62).

3. In class, form teams and debate the proposition that the surveillance of consumers by retail anthropologists is unethical and manipulative.

4. Visit a website of a major retailer (such as http://www.eddiebauer.com or http://www.abercrombieandfitch.com). How is the online "store" designed to encourage consuming behavior?

AARON BETSKY
The Man-Made World

‖‖

Ever notice how the typical urban landscape is dominated by soaring skyscrapers, linear thoroughfares, and massive blocks of brick and concrete construction? Such a "muscular" look, Aaron Betsky argues in this selection from his book Building Sex: Men, Women, Architecture and the Construction of Sexuality *(1995), is part of the whole point of urban architecture, which is designed to express the patriarchal power of men. But women, Betsky notes, have had their "revenge" insofar as "nobody really cares about architecture." What people like are parks, shopping malls, and the domestic spaces of the home, Betsky observes, places that are seen as "the realms of women." Thus buildings, one might say, are from Mars, but homes are from Venus. The author of numerous books on architecture, including* Fabrications *(1998),* Icons: Magnets of Meaning *(1997), and* Violated Perfection: Architecture and the Fragmentation of the Modern *(1991), Betsky has also published in such journals as* Horizon, Progressive Architecture, L.A. Architect, *and* Architectural Record.*

"Why do I always feel out of place when I'm walking down the Champs-Élysées?" a woman asked me when I was waxing enthusiastic about the grandeur of Paris. "Because you are a woman," I responded. The Champs-Élysées, I went on to explain, was designed by men. It represents their power. You might even say that it represents the body of a man. The street starts in front of a very large building (the Louvre) that has two legs reaching out to the street. At the center of each leg is a slightly higher portion that corresponds to the breast. It is rigid and symmetrical, muscular, and festooned with columns. The combination of the geometry, the phallic imagery, and the way in which the building looks like a man in granite armor is intimidating and is meant to be so.

The whole building dominates a large court. It sends out a long line that is the Champs-Élysées. It was constructed with little regard for what had been on the site; it was an erection, symbolized by the obelisk that stands at the beginning of the street. Where the Champs-Élysées ends, it marks its triumph with an arch and a round plaza that sends out many smaller avenues like so many nearly identical but smaller children disseminated across the field of Paris.

On either side of the oldest part of the street were parks. These were places where nature was rebuilt in a domesticated version. Here grand purpose gave way to sensual but contained delights. You could lose yourself within the geometry, rather than be confronted with it as an image. Trees spread their leaves, light was filtered, and a collage of paths and levels made you lose yourself as if in a labyrinth. Here culture reigned, people drifted in and out, wares were once sold, and men could find prostitutes. This was the place of women.

You can "read" the whole situation as a picture of the relationship between men and women in our society. Men dominate space, and women are shunted to the side to sex, nature, and culture. Male body imagery is everywhere, from the phallic constructions of skyscrapers to the "muscular" constructions of our civil buildings. Men rule, and their power is made real through architecture.

Yet women have their revenge. Nobody really cares about architecture. Most people don't even notice the shapes over which architects slaved so much. A building has to be pretty large or strange (like the Louvre or the Sears Tower) to make us realize that it is even there. The world that men have made, the world of the straight streets, proud erections, and rational relationships that make up our cities, is not very popular. Most of us see our world as alien, uncomfortable, and even dangerous. We want to go to shopping malls, to parks, and into our homes. In our society these are the realms of women.

A shopping mall, for instance, is usually not a piece of "good" architecture. It is a blob that contains riches. It has no facade, and it does not propagate anything except entrance signs. Inside, the route you take is often serpentine. It has few edges and seems to be woven together out of all the merchandise on display. Space dissolves; textures emerge. This is a world that we think of as feminine. It is a place where we can delight in what we have made, where real and fantasy mix, where we go to clothe ourselves. It is a place of activities and qualities that, for some reason, in our society are seen as feminine. The shopping mall has become the female temple.

A woman's "real" place, of course, is the home. That is where she cooks, cleans, and takes care of the children. A house might look like something on the outside (though these days our fear of violence is making houses increasingly into just blank boxes), but it is the inside that matters. The most popular image of a dream home is of a rambling, expansive set of rooms, each one connected to another. Their shapes are defined either by use or by such comfort factors as light and air. A dining room should be near the kitchen but also near the living room. It should be large enough to house guests but not too large to overwhelm the family. The table should be well lighted, the chairs should be comfortable, and the whole place should be conducive to conversation.

We fill our houses with objects of memory: photographs, paintings, and mementos. We cover them with fabrics and stake out areas in them with rugs, beds, chairs, and lights. Unless we have decorators, our homes are usually a mess, at least if you try to judge them by the criteria of orderliness we use in looking at the outside world. We feel at home there. We go out only because we have to, unless we are going to another place of pleasure or culture.

This is not something new. Behind the facades that line the Champs-Élysées, women made their salons. Marked by asymmetrical designs and sensual materials, these were sheltered places of culture where the orders made outside there by men could be criticized, evaluated, and domesticated. Women had a role and a place: to make livable the world men made.

We thus live in a strangely and unequally divided world. Our man-   10
made world was made by men. Men founded our cities and designed the buildings in them. Men decided what the world we travel through every day was going to look like, and men decided what the streets would look like. Men planned, designed, built, and ran the towns, suburbs, and cities we live in. Where were women during all this? They were the ones who made this world livable. They made the homes comfortable and the streets places of activity. Women brought up the children and cared for the old. They made the grand plans of men real within a framework that contained and imprisoned them.

The result has been a split in the world we inhabit. Men rule the outside, women the inside. On the one hand, there are the grand structures of men. They are impressive palaces, skyscrapers, and straight streets. They are cold, oppressive, and inhuman. Then there is the interior realm women have carved out within this world. It is warm, sheltering, rich, and comfortable. We are taught that we should aspire to the world of men, which is a world of importance and meaning, but we feel at home in the world created by women.

This distinction is obviously abused. There is no reason why skyscrapers are more important than bedrooms or why women should make places that are more comfortable than those men make. Our culture has assigned these roles and made these places, building on the skills and attributes of our bodies but transforming them into roles that are as oppressive as those we ascribe to wage earners, soldiers, or prostitutes.

The rule of men came first. In a culture dominated by men, it was assumed that men should build and women should decorate. Men were actors in the public realm, while women were passive recipients of their largess. This was so, men thought, because it was decreed in the Bible, because woman was by her nature sinful, or because these roles were biologically determined. After all, women have wombs and men have penises; ergo, women protect and men project. This strange conflation of biological form and social roles goes almost unquestioned to this day. Writers who want to prove that this makes women superior have even given it a feminist twist.

The split between projection and protection is not a fact of nature. It is a fact of man. It is the result of millennia of oppression of women by men. It has resulted in a world of inhuman cities in which we try to carve out places for ourselves. That means that we all are women trying to make ourselves at home in a world of men. It means that we all inhabit two worlds: one of projection that is artificial, abstract, and male; the other of protection that is sensual, informal, and female. . . .

I shall not argue about the "natural" place of men and women. Several recent critics have said that the division between the sexes starts in the womb, where women shelter their babies in the prototype of an interior. All the homes women then make in the world are attempts to rebuild that realm for their infants. Female children copy this activity when they grow up. Men, for some reason that must be hard-wired into their brain (or, and this is the one place where feminists agree with Freud, because they have penises that project out urine and semen), leave these homes and desire their spaces as images of their mothers. They build homes that are versions of themselves to attract women to them and then allow these women to shelter inside. They go out and find resources for the women, defend them, and protect them. They also keep the women, who just want to procreate as much as possible and are thus by nature promiscuous, inside so that they can't get at other men.

This, we are still told, is natural. It is just the way things are. The woman is a virgin and a whore because that is what her body "tells her" to be. Evidence from everything like how male apes shelter females to the behavior of New Guinea natives to the games little children play is used as evidence of the inevitable, natural fact of projection and protection. The big feminist twist is to reverse the usual value judgment about this "fact": Females, these new apologists argue, are in touch with the rhythms and laws of nature because they ovulate and give birth. Men are not, and thus they create an artificial alternative to this world. It is fake, but it is our culture. We should accept the fact that men made our culture and that they made it evil because the very act of suppressing nature is evil. What makes the world of literature, art, and music vital, they say, is the danger or reality of a female nature that always threatens to pervert, to seduce, or even to destroy the clear-cut alternative structure men have created. Thus high art is decadent and delicious, more real and more sensuous than abstract male work. It is the woman's revenge against male order.

I shall leave it to anthropologists to continue their work in figuring out whether these assigned roles are facts. I shall merely point out that these are all interpretations that we lay over observations. The very fact that we go looking for reasons to explain the division between the sexes is a product of our culture. We want to assign roles and tasks and create a truth. We assume that a house should be like our body. We assume that a grid we project over a landscape should be like urine. Somehow, we assume, our brain makes that connection.

Let's look at it the other way around. A house is not a body. Urine is not a street. Why do we make the connection? How do we construct these analogies? What purpose do they serve? The single answer to these questions is that they help us find our way in the world. What is more important, they divide power and resources. They assign qualities and allow us to judge our reality. If a building is like a body, it should have a front, a back, a bottom, a middle, and a top. It should have legs and a face (or facade). If "projection" is a male act, that means we can efficiently ascribe that task to a certain group. Women will stay in their place or, if the feminists "win," will destroy male structures and replace them with female cohousing. In either case, people will know their places and make them. . . .

Culture is the product of making a place. It is only when a species settles down in one particular part of the space of the world and, using tools and language, makes it into a place with boundaries, routes, directions, and dimensions that it constructs a world. Space becomes a place through architecture, and we define ourselves within a certain time and place. We define the space in which we appear, and that act of appearance then defines our roles in society.

In our society the allocation of space and roles seems pretty fixed. For 20 that reason I am fascinated by nomadic cultures. They seem to exist between space and place. Cultures like that of the Australian Aborigines trace lines of connection in the sand that are soon wiped clean by the wind. They create structures out of natural materials that either become part of the baggage they carry with them or are abandoned before new ones are constructed. They do not claim a place but occupy it in a provisional manner. They tell stories about why they are on this earth that do not distinguish between the real and the imaginary, between gods and humans, or between the constructions of man and the structures of nature. They live outside fixed boundaries and laws. Theirs is a mutable world woven together by the textures of language, art, and common agreement.

This is my ideal. It is what I shall call our first home in the world. Architectural theoreticians like to think that it all started when Adam made a home for Eve in paradise or when some unknown man made a house that gave shelter and mimicked the four directions of the winds, the trees or mountains out of which it was made, or the male body. This male construction stands in contrast with the cave, the natural womb out of which man set forth in his quest to conquer the world.

I propose another model: the hut or tepee, woven together by men and women together (though each may have a separate task). It is round, omnidirectional, and flexible. It can be added on to, and it can be demounted. It is somewhere between the cave and the construction, somewhere between a woven cloth put down on the ground and something with walls and a roof. It allows us to be at home in the world.

In many ways we are returning to the world of nomads. Few of us occupy one place, one house, or one job for very long. The average American moves once every other year, for instance. We try to navigate through a man-made world that has become as large and complex as the natural world must have seemed to the first wanderers. We stake a claim to that world by redecorating homes, apartments, or offices that we accept as natural facts, rather than build them for ourselves. We make our own provisional additions, unpacking our belongings piece by piece, memento by memento, book by book, until they cover every surface, change the structures we inhabit, take over more territory, and then, more often than not, we move on.

Who makes these nomadic moments? Men and women together. Are they architecture or interiors, buildings or baggage? It is difficult to say. Partially planned and partially the result of sensual needs, they are, above all else, sensible. In this way we make ourselves at home in the world.

This is not necessarily a bad way to live, except that we feel as if we   25
have to claim or privatize little pieces of an alien environment to accomplish this. We also don't value this activity because we have been taught that permanence and order are the building blocks of society. We *should* . . . dream of weaving together a realm of men and women. We can imagine a world in which interior and exterior flow together, structure dissolves into surface, comfort and abstractions are intertwined. It would be an extension of the small moments of coherence we make every day for ourselves, but it would include others. It would mean a breakdown of law and order and the making of another place.

In a way, this dream stands for a world without men and women, at least as we know them, just as it stands for a world without classes or races and perhaps even a world without human beings. It is a dream that is neither one in which we dissolve back into (feminine) nature nor one in which we continue to build (male) alternatives, but a world where we fold ourselves into a texture of culture, a landscape that gives birth to many different sexes and forms.

This is a nice reverie. In reality, we first need to trace the emergence of the prisons of femininity and the facades of masculinity in order to question them. If we can merely not be so sure about how we are constructed, if we can understand that it is not inevitable that we wander down the mean streets or retreat into our defensible private realms, we can already start to build another sex.

Reading the Text

1. Summarize in your own words Betsky's concepts of male and female space.
2. What is the reasoning behind Betsky's claim that "Men rule the outside, women the inside" (para. 11) in our world?
3. What assumptions about social organization undergird Betsky's choice of a hut or tepee as a model for ideal architecture?
4. According to Betsky, what is the relationship between nature and culture?

Reading the Signs

1. In your journal, describe or sketch what would be your ideal architecture. Would it share the gender-equal values that Betsky prefers, or would it display other ideals?
2. In class, form teams and debate whether human spatial organization is driven by nature or by culture. To prepare for your debate, your team should analyze specific human environments. Consult as well Holly Devor, "Gender Role Behaviors and Attitudes" (p. 447), and Deborah Blum, "The Gender Blur: Where Does Biology End and Society Take Over?" (p. 453).
3. If you live in or near a big city, explore your city and its predominant architectural patterns. Then write an essay that argues the extent to which it has the masculine feel that Betsky ascribes to cities.
4. Write an essay in which you support, refute, or complicate Betsky's central belief that human space is gendered: "Men rule the outside, women the inside" (para. 11).
5. In an essay, support, challenge, or complicate Betsky's assertion that "The shopping mall is the female temple" (para. 6). To develop your ideas, consult Anne Norton, "The Signs of Shopping" (p. 62), and Malcolm Gladwell, "The Science of Shopping" (p. 757).

DAPHNE SPAIN

Spatial Segregation and Gender Stratification
in the Workplace

IIIIIIIIIIIIIIIIIIIIIIIIIIIIIIIIIIIIIIIIIIIIIIIIIIIIIIIIIIIIIII

In the spatial hierarchy of the American workplace, having a private of-
fice all to yourself is one of the most visible signifiers of status within
the organization. But as Daphne Spain reveals, the spatial arrange-
ment of the ordinary workplace is often a marker of gender relations as
well. With most women working in "open-floor" (such as secretarial)
occupations, and most men frequently enjoying "closed-door" (or man-
agerial) positions, a certain level of gender segregation is to be found in
the typical American workplace. Analyzing the social implications of
this stratification of working space, Spain shows how the architecture of
the workplace not only reflects but reinforces existing gender hierarchies.
Daphne Spain teaches in the School of Architecture at the University
of Virginia and is the author of Gendered Spaces *(1992), from*
which this selection is taken.

To what extent do women and men who work in different occupations also work in different spaces? Baran and Teegarden (1987, 206)
propose that occupational segregation in the insurance industry is "tantamount to spatial segregation by gender" since managers are overwhelmingly male and clerical staff are predominantly female. This essay examines the spatial conditions of women's work and men's work and
proposes that working women and men come into daily contact with
one another very infrequently. Further, women's jobs can be classified as
"open floor," but men's jobs are more likely to be "closed door." That
is, women work in a more public environment with less control of their
space than men. This lack of spatial control both reflects and contributes
to women's lower occupational status by limiting opportunities for the
transfer of knowledge from men to women.

It bears repeating that my argument concerning space and status
deals with structural workplace arrangements of women as a group and
men as a group, *not* with occupational mobility for individual men and
women. Extraordinary people always escape the statistical norm and experience upward mobility under a variety of circumstances. The emphasis here is on the ways in which workplaces are structured to provide
different spatial arrangements for the typical working woman and the
typical working man and how those arrangements contribute to gender
stratification. . . .

Typical Women's Work: "Open-Floor Jobs"

A significant proportion of women are employed in just three occupations: teaching, nursing, and secretarial work. In 1990 these three categories alone accounted for 16.5 million women, or 31 percent of all women in the labor force (U.S. Department of Labor 1991, 163, 183). Aside from being concentrated in occupations that bring them primarily into contact with other women, women are also concentrated spatially in jobs that limit their access to knowledge. The work of elementary schoolteachers, for example, brings them into daily contact with children, but with few other adults. When not dealing with patients, nurses spend their time in a lounge separate from the doctors' lounge. Nursing and teaching share common spatial characteristics with the third major "women's job" — that of secretary.

Secretarial/clerical work is the single largest job category for American women. In 1990, 14.9 million women, or more than one of every four employed women, were classified as "administrative support, including clerical"; 98 percent of all secretaries are female (U.S. Department of Labor 1991, 163, 183). Secretarial and clerical occupations account for over three-quarters of this category and epitomize the typical "woman's job." It is similar to teaching and nursing in terms of the spatial context in which it occurs.

Two spatial aspects of secretarial work operate to reduce women's   5
status. One is the concentration of many women together in one place (the secretarial "pool") that removes them from observation of and/or input into the decision-making processes of the organization. Those decisions occur behind the "closed doors" of the managers' offices. Second, paradoxically, is the very public nature of the space in which secretaries work. The lack of privacy, repeated interruptions, and potential for surveillance contribute to an inability to turn valuable knowledge into human capital that might advance careers or improve women's salaries relative to men's.

Like teachers and nurses, secretaries process knowledge, but seldom in a way beneficial to their own status. In fact, secretaries may wield considerable informal power in an organization, because they control the information flow. Management, however, has very clear expectations about how secretaries are to handle office information. Drawing from their successful experience with grid theory, business consultants Robert Blake, Jane Mouton, and Artie Stockton have outlined the ideal boss-secretary relationship for effective office teamwork. In the first chapter of *The Secretary Grid,* an American Management Association publication, the following advice is offered:

> The secretary's position at the center of the information network raises the issue of privileged communications and how best to handle

it. Privileged communication is information the secretary is not free to divulge, no matter how helpful it might be to others. And the key to handling it is the answer to the question "Who owns the information"? The answer is, "The boss does." . . . The secretary's position with regard to this information is that of the hotel desk clerk to the contents of the safety deposit box that stores the guest's valuables. She doesn't own it, but she knows what it is and what is in it. The root of the word *secretary* is, after all, *secret:* something kept from the knowledge of others. (Blake, Mouton, and Stockton 1983, 4–5; emphasis in original)

In other words, secretaries are paid *not* to use their knowledge for personal gain, but only for their employers' gain. The workplace arrangements that separate secretaries from managers within the same office reinforce status differences by exposing the secretary mainly to other secretaries bound by the same rules of confidentiality. Lack of access to and interaction with managers inherently limits the status women can achieve within the organization.

The executive secretary is an exception to the rule of gendered spatial segregation in the workplace. The executive secretary may have her own office, and she has access to more aspects of the managerial process than other secretaries. According to another American Management Association publication titled *The Successful Secretary:* "Probably no person gets to observe and see management principles in operation on a more practical basis than an executive secretary. She is privy to nearly every decision the executive makes. She has the opportunity to witness the gathering of information and the elements that are considered before major decisions are made and implemented" (Belker 1981, 191).

Yet instructions to the successful executive secretary suggest that those with the closest access to power are subject to the strictest guidelines regarding confidentiality. When physical barriers are breached and secretaries spend a great deal of time with the managers, rules governing the secretary's use of information become more important. The executive secretary is cautioned to hide shorthand notes, remove partially typed letters from the typewriter, lock files, and personally deliver interoffice memos to prevent unauthorized persons from gaining confidential information from the boss's office (Belker 1981, 66).

The executive secretary has access to substantial information about   10
the company, but the highest compliment that can be paid her is that she does not divulge it to anyone or use it for personal gain. Comparing the importance of confidentiality to the seal of the confessional, Belker counsels secretaries that "the importance of confidentiality can't be overemphasized. Your company can be involved in some delicate business matters or negotiations, and the wrong thing leaked to the wrong person could have an adverse effect on the result. . . . Years ago, executive secretaries were sometimes referred to as confidential secretaries. It's a shame

that title fell out of popular usage, because it's an accurate description of the job" (Belker 1981, 73–74).

Typical Men's Work: "Closed-Door Jobs"

The largest occupational category for men is that of manager. In 1990, 8.9 million men were classified as "executive, administrative, and managerial." This group constituted 14 percent of all employed men (U.S. Department of Labor 1991, 163, 183). Thus, more than one in ten men works in a supervisory position.

Spatial arrangements in the workplace reinforce these status distinctions, partially by providing more "closed door" potential to managers than to those they supervise. Although sales and production supervisors may circulate among their employees, their higher status within the organization is reflected by the private offices to which they can withdraw. The expectation is that privacy is required for making decisions that affect the organization. Rather than sharing this privacy, the secretary is often in charge of "gate-keeping"—protecting the boss from interruptions.

Just as there are professional manuals for the successful secretary, there are also numerous guidelines for the aspiring manager. Harry Levinson's widely read *Executive* (1981) (a revision of his 1968 *The Exceptional Executive*) stresses the importance of managerial knowledge of the entire organization. A survey of large American companies asking presidents about suitable qualities in their successors revealed the following profile: "A desirable successor is a person with a general knowledge and an understanding of the whole organization, capable of fitting specialized contributions into profitable patterns. . . . The person needs a wide range of liberal arts knowledge together with a fundamental knowledge of business. . . . A leader will be able to view the business in global historical and technical perspective. Such a perspective is itself the basis for the most important requisite, what one might call 'feel'—a certain intuitive sensitivity for the right action and for handling relationships with people" (Levinson 1981, 136).

The importance of knowledge is stressed repeatedly in this description. The successful manager needs knowledge of the organization, of liberal arts, and of business in general. But equally important is the intuitive ability to carry out actions. This "feel" is not truly intuitive, of course, but is developed through observation and emulation of successful executives. Levinson identifies managerial leadership as "an art to be cultivated and developed," which is why it cannot be learned by the book; rather, "it must be learned in a relationship, through identification with a teacher" (Levinson 1981, 145).

Because the transfer of knowledge and the ability to use it are so crucial to leadership, Levinson devotes a chapter to "The Executive as Teacher." He advises that there is no prescription an executive can fol-

15

low in acting as a teacher. The best strategy is the "shine and show them" approach—the manager carries out the duties of office as effectively as possible and thereby demonstrates to subordinates how decisions are made. There are no formal conditions under which teaching takes place; it is incorporated as part of the routine of the business day. In Levinson's words, "The process of example-setting goes on all the time. Executives behave in certain ways, sizing up problems, considering the resources . . . that can be utilized to meet them, and making decisions about procedure. Subordinates, likewise, watch what they are doing and how they do it" (Levinson 1981, 154).

Just as in the ceremonial men's huts of nonindustrial societies, constant contact between elders and initiates is necessary for the transmission of knowledge. Levinson implies that it should be frequent contact to transfer most effectively formal and informal knowledge. Such frequent and significant contact is missing from the interaction between managers and secretaries. Given the spatial distance between the closed doors of managers and the open floors of secretaries, it is highly unlikely that sufficient contact between the two groups could occur for secretaries to alter their positions within the organization.

In addition to giving subordinates an opportunity to learn from the boss, spatial proximity provides opportunities for subordinates to be seen by the boss. This opportunity has been labeled "visiposure" by the author of *Routes to the Executive Suite* (Jennings 1971, 113). A combination of "visibility" and "exposure," visiposure refers to the opportunity to "see and be seen by the right people" (Jennings 1971, 113). Jennings counsels the rising executive that "the abilities to see and copy those who can influence his career and to keep himself in view of those who might promote him are all-important to success." The ultimate form of visiposure is for the subordinate's manager to be seen by the right managers as well. Such "serial visiposure" is the "sine qua non of fast upward mobility" and is facilitated by face-to-face interaction among several levels of managers and subordinates (Jennings 1971, 113–14).

Both Levinson and Jennings acknowledge the importance of physical proximity to achieving power within an organization, yet neither pursues the assumptions underlying the transactions they discuss—that is, the spatial context within which such interactions occur. To the extent women are segregated from men, the transfer of knowledge—with the potential for improving women's status—is limited.

Office Design and Gender Stratification

Contemporary office design clearly reflects the spatial segregation separating women and men. Secretaries (almost all of whom are women) and managers (nearly two-thirds of whom are men) have designated areas assigned within the organization. . . .

Privacy can be a scarce resource in the modern office. Empirical 20
studies have shown that privacy in the office involves "the ability to control access to one's self or group, particularly the ability to *limit others' access to one's workspace*" (Sundstrom 1986, 178; emphasis added). Business
executives commonly define privacy as the ability to control information
and space. In other words, privacy is connected in people's minds with
the spatial reinforcement of secrecy. Studies of executives, managers,
technicians, and clerical employees have found a high correlation between enclosure of the work space (walls and doors) and perceptions of
privacy; the greater the privacy, the greater the satisfaction with work.
Employees perceive spatial control as a resource in the workplace that affects their job satisfaction and performance (Sundstrom, Burt, and Kemp
1980; Sundstrom 1986).

Not surprisingly, higher status within an organization is accompanied
by greater control of space. In the Sundstrom study, most secretaries (75
percent) reported sharing an office; about one-half (55 percent) of book-
keepers and accountants shared an office; and only 18 percent of managers and administrators shared space. Secretaries had the least physical
separation from other workers, while executives had the most (Sundstrom 1986, 184).

Two aspects of the work environment are striking when the spatial
features of the workplaces for secretaries and executives are compared:
the low number of walls or partitions surrounding secretaries (an average
of 2.1), compared with executives (an average of 3.5), and the greater
surveillance that accompanies the public space of secretaries. Three-
quarters of all secretaries were visible to their supervisors, compared with
only one-tenth of executives. As one would expect given the physical
description of their respective offices, executives report the greatest sense
of privacy and secretaries the least (Sundstrom 1986, 185). Doors do not
necessarily have to be closed or locked in order to convey the message of
differential power; they merely have to be available for closing and be
seen as controlled at the executive's discretion (Steele 1986, 46).

The spatial distribution of employees in an office highlights the complex ways in which spatial segregation contributes to gender stratification.
Workers obviously are not assigned space on the basis of sex, but on the
basis of their positions within the organization. Theoretically, managers
have the most complex jobs and secretaries have the least complex, yet
research on secretaries and managers with equal degrees of office enclosure suggests that women's space is still considered more public than
men's space. Sundstrom found that "in the workspaces with equivalent
enclosure—private offices—[respondents] showed differential ratings of
privacy, with lowest ratings by secretaries. This could reflect social
norms. Secretaries have low ranks, and co-workers or visitors may feel
free to walk unannounced into their workspaces. However, they may
knock respectfully at the entrance of the workspaces of managers. . . .
Perhaps a private office is more private when occupied by a manager than when oc-

cupied by a secretary" (Sundstrom 1986, 191; emphasis added). This passage suggests that even walls and a door do not insure privacy for the typical working woman in the same way they do for the typical working man. Features that should allow control of workspace do not operate for secretaries as they do for managers.

WORKS CITED

Baran, Barbara, and Suzanne Teegarden. 1987. "Women's Labor in the Office of the Future: A Case Study of the Insurance Industry." In *Women, Households, and the Economy,* edited by Lourdes Beneria and Catharine R. Stimpson, pp. 201–24. New Brunswick, N.J.: Rutgers University Press.

Belker, Loren. 1981. *The Successful Secretary.* New York: American Management Association.

Blake, Robert, Jane S. Mouton, and Artie Stockton. 1983. *The Secretary Grid.* New York: American Management Association.

Jennings, Eugene Emerson. 1971. *Routes to the Executive Suite.* New York: McGraw-Hill.

Levinson, Harry. 1981. *Executive.* Cambridge: Harvard University Press.

Steele, Fritz. 1986. "The Dynamics of Power and Influence in Workplace Design and Management." In *Behavioral Issues in Office Design,* edited by Jean D. Wineman, pp. 43–64. New York: Van Nostrand Reinhold.

Sundstrom, Eric. 1986. "Privacy in the Office." In *Behavioral Issues in Office Design,* edited by Jean Wineman, pp. 177–202. New York: Van Nostrand Reinhold.

Sundstrom, Eric, Robert Burt, and Douglas Kemp. 1980. "Privacy at Work: Architectural Correlates of Job Satisfaction and Job Performance." *Academy of Management Journal* 23 (March): 101–17.

U.S. Department of Labor. 1991. *Employment and Earnings* 38 (January). Washington, D.C.: Bureau of Labor Statistics.

Reading the Text

1. Summarize in your own words how traditional office design can be considered "tantamount to spatial segregation by gender" (para. 1).
2. Define the differences between "open-floor" and "closed-door" (para. 1) jobs. What are the spatial arrangements that signal those differences?
3. According to Spain, how is the executive secretary "an exception to the rule of gendered spatial segregation in the workplace" (para. 8)?
4. What sort of evidence does Spain present to demonstrate her claim that the workplace exhibits gender segregation?
5. In Spain's view, how does office design restrict or enhance the privacy of employees?

Reading the Signs

1. In class, form small groups, and design an office space that is not hierarchically organized. Have the groups present the design to the class, explaining the reasoning behind their design choices.

2. If you work in an office environment, write an analysis of the spatial design of your workplace. To what extent does it follow the gendered patterns that Spain describes? Alternately, survey the faculty and staff offices at your college or university. Do they reflect Spain's analysis?
3. Interview at least five women about their jobs and work environment. To what extent do their experiences support Spain's claim that "women are . . . concentrated spatially in jobs that limit their access to knowledge" (para. 3)?
4. Write a letter to business consultants Robert Blake, Jane Mouton, and Artie Stockton in which you respond to their description of the ideal boss-secretary relationship, published in the American Management Association's *The Secretary Grid* (para. 6).

LUCY R. LIPPARD
Alternating Currents

||||||||||||||||||||||||||||||||||||||||||||||||||||||

With three-quarters of the population living in cities or suburbs, America is a thoroughly urbanized nation. But as Lucy Lippard (b. 1937) indicates in this excerpt from The Lure of the Local: Senses of Place in a Multicentered Society *(1997), you can take an American out of the country, but you can't take the country out of America. Reflecting on the complex interplay between our urban realities and rural mythologies, Lippard meditates here on the role that space plays in the construction of personal and communal consciousness. An art critic and historian whose many books include* Mixed Blessings: New Art in a Multicultural America, The Pink Glass Swan: Selected Feminist Essays on Art, *and* Get the Message? A Decade of Art for Social Change, *Lippard has written as well for the* Village Voice, In These Times, *and* Z Magazine.

The U.S. population today is 75 percent urban/suburban, but there remains an emotional tension between city and country, an alternating current that pulls at most Americans at various times in their lives. If the city represents the high voltage of the new (or at least the novel) and the country represents the calming tradition of the old, we are always looking for ways to balance our needs for both. I lived in Manhattan for my first nine years and returned at age twenty-one for thirty-seven adult years. While my current addresses are rural, my local knowledge of cities is New York–based and New York–biased.

The city has been seen as a field of indifference to the rest of world, as a triumph of objective over subjective, male over female, culture over nature, materialism over spirituality and idealism.[1] The inherited rural kinship systems of ancient cities were replaced with civil communities, which in turn broke down with industrialization (or perhaps before, with the medieval plagues), when cities became increasingly impersonal. The idealized vision of the Puritans' "City on the Hill" (exposed and exemplary to those living "below") notwithstanding, most positive American mythologies depend on a rural context. During the nineteenth century, as the colonization of the countryside by capital accelerated, the Jeffersonian ideal of a nation of small towns and farmers waned. Ralph Waldo Emerson's ideal "City of the West" was an attempt to reconcile nature and civilization, intended as a human community with open gates and open arms. Instead, cities, aided by absentee landlords and proto-agribusiness, began to suck up country energy and resources. By 1880, urban populations in the western U.S. were already growing at four times the rate of the countryside.

Herbert Gans observed in the late sixties that American society gives its allegiance to two poles—the micro-unit of the family and the macro-unit of the nation, while local community falls through the cracks. Today, one of those poles is collapsing: under half of eligible Americans voted in the 1996 presidential election.[2] This decline in participation in social policymaking can be seen as a product of a dehumanized urban ambience, the loss of a sense of local power in places where "neighborliness is often exhausted by a nod of the head."

The clichéd image of the cold, heartless city and the warm, cuddly heartland of small towns has long since been disproved. There is no Eden. But the sheer size of the metropolis can be intimidating as well as exhilarating and seems to bely communal intimacy. What, then, constitutes the lure of the local in this environment presumed to transcend any such affect? How do cities look and feel to those who live in them? And what are their relationships to the land they are built on, to the land people left to come to them?

Cities are enormously complex palimpsests of communal history and memory, a fact that tends to be obscured by their primary identities as sites of immediacy, money, power, and energy concentrated on the present and future. Many people come to the city to escape the "local," the isolation of rural life, the rigidity and constrictions of smaller towns.

---

1. Yi-Fu Tuan's *Topophilia* was an invaluable source for this section.

2. The League of Women Voters estimates that 49 percent of eligible voters did vote in 1996, some 6 percent less than 1992, but other groups put the figure much lower; I read somewhere that only 39 percent voted in 1992.

> We who live here wear this corner of the city like a comfortable old coat, an extension of our personalities, threadbare yet retaining a beauty of its own. This is the intimacy of cities, made more precious and more secret by our knowledge that it is one of many cells or corners in a great city that is not so much a labyrinth as a web or a shawl. We wrap ourselves in the city as we journey through it. Muffled, we march, "like Juno in a cloud," drawing it around us like a cloak of many colours: a disguise, a refuge, an adventure, a home.
>
> —ELIZABETH WILSON

The urban ego is in fact parochial; New Yorkers (like Parisians or Bostonians) are among the most provincial people in the world. They are often as bound to their own neighborhoods and as ignorant of the rest of the city (aside from midtown) as any small towner. A city is a center plus the sum of its neighborhoods, a collage created by juxtaposing apples and oranges. When I first lived in New York I would sometimes take the subway to a stop I'd never been to and spend hours walking in new territory, foreign countries. It was always interesting even when it was boring. All those people, all those little rooms. What were they doing in there? What lives were being played out so near and yet so far from my own? I loved my own life and didn't envy the women closed behind those doors; but at the same time I pictured an intimacy, a reassuring monotony that I knew I had surrendered forever.

Women in particular come to the city to break away from family expectations, domestic confinement, or to escape boredom and past mistakes. Some thrive on the crowds and new anonymity; others spend the rest of their lives thinking that someday they'll go "home." My own experience reflects Elizabeth Wilson's contention that the disorder of the city is a woman's medium, implying that it allows us to slip through the cracks of order: "The city is 'masculine' in its triumphal scale, its towers and vistas and arid industrial regions; it is 'feminine' in its enclosing embrace, in its indeterminacy and labyrinthine uncentredness. We might even go so far as to claim that urban life is actually based on this perpetual struggle between rigid routinized order and pleasurable anarchy, the male–female dichotomy."

Where the citydweller may revel in her daily anonymity and freedom from self within crowded spaces, she also struggles to find an emotional community that will offer the intimacy for which Americans pine, even after we have made the choices that make it less and less likely. In small towns, if you go to the store, you must be prepared for at least minimal social intercourse. In cities, you can go out and float in your own space for hours, expending no more than an occasional monosyllabic request for food or services. You don't even have to say please and thank you if you're in an area where you don't expect to be seen again or where you just want to burn your bridges. However, spaces take on the aura of your interactions in them. There is a hardwon median between idiotically artificial courtesy and complete, even hostile, disregard.

Urban experience, vast and elusive, epitomizes the multicentered experience that fuels such energies. I'd include the arts among them. "One of the most fascinating aspects of place in recent years is that it has become more homogenous in some ways"—through mass culture—"and more heterogeneous in others" (through specialization and ghettoization), according to Sharon Zukin. The city is a social network, a web that entangles everyone who enters it, even the loneliest. Visually articulated by the syncretic cultures it contains, it is defined by a dialectic between the opinions of locals and of outsiders. Looking around in a city is visual overload (whereas looking around in a suburb tips the opposite end of the scale). Impressions are confused and even chaotic. Longtime residents rushing here and there often forget to look at their surroundings while newcomers and visitors get lost and overwhelmed.

The city is the site of delightful and terrifying encounters that could   10
not happen anywhere else. But each city is different, evoking different feelings in its residents and visitors, attractive to individuals at different moods of their lives. The light, the climate, the style, the materials, the flora and fauna (or lack thereof), the spaces and proportions, not to mention the demography and population, make cities and their neighborhoods unique. Cultural geographers have argued about whether the city is a series of reflections of "reality" held as images in the minds of its observers, or whether it is in itself a concrete representation, a collective work of art, a symbolic creation of those who inhabit it or those who control it.

Anne Spirn describes the city as an "infernal machine" with nobody coordinating it, nobody in charge, nobody taking responsibility or understanding the cumulative ecological effect of all the fragmented construction. Yet the city produces spaces and buildings, and even parks, that share its scale and impersonality. Class stratification is one component; especially in midtown New York, where the range of stores, restaurants, and modes of public transportation serve very different clients. Country estates may be inaccessible, and elite suburban neighborhoods guarded, but in cities, rich and poor occupy the same spaces. The habitats of the powerful and the powerless exist within tighter confines, side by side in sharp contrast. (As a child, I had a sitter who often detoured from our culturally determined route to Central Park; she took me to weddings in Fifth Avenue churches, as well as to a German bar in Yorkville where her boyfriend worked.) So long as we behave ourselves, any of us can loiter briefly outside the Plaza Hotel or Park Avenue apartment houses to glimpse the stomping grounds of the rich and famous, and the rich and famous must now and then drive through the Lower East Side or the South Bronx, or the outwardly colorless byways of Forest Hills or Sunnyside. . . .

Nature is fragmented and isolated in the city. Those who have no urge whatsoever to live in the country have houseplants to recall the existence of "nature," or to reassure themselves that nature can be or has been tamed: they go to parks to see trees. The more affluent have rooftop gardens, tiny designer back yards and bucolic weekend retreats. The less affluent cultivate community gardens. Even those who love the city and can live there comfortably look for ways of escaping it periodically, either by the Fresh Air Fund, vacations or, for the more privileged, weekend homes featuring lawns, trees, and other simulacra of small town life—visited, but not committed to. In 1956, Marshall McLuhan wrote that the city was in fact a return to the simultaneity that governed tribal cultures, in which "all experience and all past lives were *now*." From the Native American historical viewpoint, cities simply replaced civilization. Artist Jimmie Durham decries the deracination of civic centers from their landscapes: "At one time New York was a city *on an island*: it was a city with a location in the physical world. Unlike villages or settlements, cities always establish themselves *against* their environment. . . . Where are we? We are in the European City. The U.S. is a political/cultural construction *against* the American continent. . . . There have been many, but it is hard for us to imagine a 'great sylvanization,' like a 'great civilization.' Civilizations, cities, build signs and monuments by definition and are then recognized by their signs. The sign of forest dwellers is the absence of monuments."

As soon as we move to a city, we search for our own center in it. In the absence of valid communal centers, cities need artificial symbolic centers like Saint Louis's Arch, Washington's Monument, or particularly obtrusive office buildings that function (only) visually as the church spire once did, marking the place where power is abstracted and institutionalized. Landmarks have to be imposing and/or charged with celebrity status to claim attention. New York's Chrysler and Empire State buildings are classic examples. Like earlier skyscrapers, they were probably inspired to some extent by the "stateliness of the American landscape."[3] Now they are outgrown but not outclassed by the bland towers of the World Trade Center. Giant complexes like Battery Park City in Lower Manhattan, created by celebrity architects and usually accompanied by large-scale, expensive public art, are "designer" objects "of quality," veiling the reality of social polarization in "real life." Generating ideological vibes of domination through spectacle, such control centers can be seen, Darrel Crilley observes, "not as signs of enduring vitality, but as enormous and cautionary symbols of changes underway in the relationship between property development and aesthetics."

> I view great cities as pestilential to the morals, the health and the liberties of man. True, they nourish some of the elegant arts, but the useful ones can thrive elsewhere, and less perfection in the others, with more health, virtue and freedom, would be my choice.
> —THOMAS JEFFERSON (in the midst of a yellow-fever epidemic)

---

3. *Cosmopolitan*, 1875, quoted in Gwendolyn Wright.

The city's image remains negative, or Un-American, in opposition to the "family values" purportedly nourished outside of these "dens of iniquity." One reason for this bad press is that cities have traditionally been the homes of the sinful arts. Marxists have noted that in order to maintain its dynamism, capitalism must keep destroying and recreating itself, whether through planned obsolescence or a novelty-driven art market. For economic as well as aesthetic and educational reasons, artists are attracted to change.

The city visibly illustrates the dialectic between the heterogenous   15 market, where everything is for sale, and the homogenous place, where people resist the processes of defamiliarization and change. As new ideas and new money-making schemes pop up each day, the most imposing structures can prove short lived. The social cacophony of a big city multiplies exponentially with its diversity and excess of nervous energy. At the same time, the dissolution of its familiar landscapes has the same effect on its inhabitants as slower changes in the countryside. The rug is pulled out from under our sense of self when stores close or switch functions, when vacant lots appear or disappear, or when buildings are remodeled. Even when the changes are for the better, the ghosts remain.

WORKS CITED

Crilley, Darrel. "Megastructures and Urban Change: Aesthetics, Ideology, and Design." In Paul Knox, ed., *The Restless Urban Landscape*. Englewood Cliffs, N.J.: Prentice Hall, 1993.

Durham, Jimmie. *A Certain Lack of Coherence: Writings on Art and Cultural Politics,* ed. Jean Fisher. London: Kala Press, 1993.

Jefferson, Thomas. *Primary Documents, no.* 4, 1995.

McLuhan, Marshall. "The Media Fit the Battle of Jericho." *Explorations Six,* July 1956.

Spirn, Anne W. *The Granite Garden: Urban Nature and Human Design.* New York: Basic Books, 1984.

Tuan, Yi-Fu. *Topophilia: A Study of Environmental Perception, Attitudes and Values.* Englewood Cliffs, N.J.: Prentice Hall, 1974.

Wilson, Elizabeth. *The Sphinx in the City.* Berkeley: University of California Press, 1991.

Wright, Gwendolyn. *Building the Dream: A Social History of Housing in America.* New York: Pantheon Books, 1981.

Zukin, Sharon. *Landscapes of Power: From Detroit to Disney World.* Berkeley: University of California Press, 1991.

Reading the Text

1. Define in your own words the "alternating current," as Lippard puts it, "that pulls at most Americans at various times in their lives" (para. 1).
2. According to Lippard, what differential mythological significances do urban and rural areas have?
3. What role does nature play in the cityscape, in Lippard's view?

4. What are the assumptions underlying the common image of the city as "negative, or Un-American" (para. 14)?

5. Why does Lippard assert that women especially find freedom in city life?

Reading the Signs

1. Whether you live in a rural or urban environment, reflect in your journal on Lippard's claim that most Americans feel torn between the country and the city at some point in their lives. Have you felt this "alternating current" (para. 1) yourself? Why or why not? If you have, in what way did you resolve the competing desires?

2. Read or reread Aaron Betsky's "The Man-Made World" (p. 764). In an essay, compare and contrast his analysis of the gendered nature of urban space with Lippard's. Which do you find more persuasive, and why?

3. Today many Americans live neither in the city nor the country; they live in suburbs. Using Lippard's discussion of the mythologies of the city and country as a model, write an essay in which you analyze the suburb's mythological significance.

4. If you live in a city, conduct a survey of local residents that addresses the "lure" that the urban environment has for them. Use your results to formulate a response to Lippard's question "What . . . constitutes the lure of the local in this environment presumed to transcend any such effect?" (para. 4).

5. Study the landmarks in a city close to you. To what extent do they bear out Lippard's contention that "Landmarks have to be imposing and/or charged with celebrity status to claim attention" (para. 13)? Alternately, if you do not live near a city, study the landmarks in a small town or village. What messages do they send to the people who observe them?

CAMILO JOSÉ VERGARA

The Ghetto Cityscape

||||||||||||||||||||||||||||||||||||||||||||||||||

What happens when a society abandons its central-city residential districts (better known as urban ghettos) to the forces of poverty and decay? Usually those who take an interest in these matters focus on the people left behind in such neighborhoods, but Camilo José Vergara (b. 1944) feels that something has been left out of the sociology of urban poverty: an examination of the ghetto environment itself and its effects on the people who live there. So packing camera and notebook, Vergara has spent years visiting the places that much of America would like to forget—the "green ghettos," the "institutional ghettos," and the "new immigrant ghettos," as he defines them—that lie beyond the gaze of most Americans. A photographer, Vergara has written for many publications, including the New York Times, *the* Nation, *the* Atlantic, *and* Architectural Record, *and has published* Silent Cities: The Evolution of the American Cemetery *and* The New American Ghetto *(1995), from which this selection was taken.*

If you were among the nearly eleven thousand people who lived in two-story row houses in North Camden in the 1960s, you could walk to work at Esterbrook Pen, at Knox Gelatin, at RCA, or at J. R. Evans Leather. You could shop on Broadway, a busy three-mile-long commercial thoroughfare, nicknamed the "Street of Lights" because of its five first-run movie theaters with their bright neon signs.

After J. R. Evans Leather was abandoned and almost completely demolished, its smokestack stood alone in a vast field by the Delaware River, a symbol of the demise of industry in Camden. Hundreds of row houses—once counted among the best ordinary urban dwellings in America—have been scooped up by bulldozers, their debris carted to a dump in Delaware. Walking along North Camden's narrow streets, one passes entire blocks without a single structure, the empty land crisscrossed by footpaths. The scattered dwellings that remain are faced with iron bars, so that they resemble cages.

With nearly half of its overwhelmingly Latino population on some form of public assistance, this once thriving working-class neighborhood is now the poorest urban community in New Jersey. In 1986, former mayor Alfred Pierce called Camden a reservation for the destitute. The north section of the city has become the drug center for South Jersey, and it hosts a large state prison.

North Camden is not unique. Since the riots of the 1960s, American cities have experienced profound transformations, best revealed in the spatial restructuring of their ghettos and in the emergence of new urban forms. During the past decade, however, the "underclass" and homelessness have dominated the study of urban poverty. Meanwhile, the power of the physical surroundings to shape lives, to mirror people's existence, and to symbolize social relations has been ignored. When scholars from across the political spectrum discuss the factors that account for the persistence of poverty, they fail to consider its living environments. And when prescribing solutions, they overlook the very elements that define the new ghettos: the ruins and the semi-ruins; the medical, warehousing, and behavior-modification institutions; the various NIMBYs, fortresses, and walls; and, not least, the bitterness and anger resulting from living in these places.

Dismissing the value of information received through sight, taste,   5 and smell, or through the emotional overtones in an informant's voice, or from the sensation of moving through the spaces studied, has led to the creation of constructs without character, individuality, or a sense of place. And although the limitations of statistical data—particularly when dealing with very poor populations—are widely acknowledged, our great dependency on numbers is fiercely defended. Other approaches are dismissed as impressionistic, anecdotal, as poetry, or "windshield surveys."

Yet today's ghettos are diverse, rich in public and private responses to the environment, in expressions of cultural identity, and in reminders of history. These communities are uncharted territory; to be understood, their forms need to be identified, described, inventoried, and mapped.

An examination of scores of ghettos across the nation reveals three types: "green ghettos," characterized by depopulation, vacant land overgrown by nature, and ruins; "institutional ghettos," publicly financed places of confinement designed mainly for the native-born; and "new immigrant ghettos," deriving their character from an influx of immigrants, mainly Latino and West Indian. Some of these communities have continued to lose population; others have emerged where a quarter-century ago there were white ethnic blue-collar neighborhoods; and sections of older ghettos have remained stable, working neighborhoods or have been rebuilt.

The Green Ghetto: Return to Wilderness?

Green ghettos, where little has been done to counter the effect of disinvestment, abandonment, depopulation, and dependency, are the leftovers of a society. Best exemplified by North Camden, Detroit's East Side, Chicago's Lawndale, and East St. Louis in Illinois, they are expanding outward to include poor suburbs of large cities such as Robbins, Illinois, and are even found in small cities such as Benton Harbor, Michigan.

Residents, remembering the businesses that moved to suburban malls, the closed factories, the fires, complain of living in a threatening place bereft of jobs and stores and neglected by City Hall. In many sections of these ghettos, pheasants and rabbits have regained the space once occupied by humans, yet these are not wilderness retreats in the heart of the city. "Nothing but weeds are growing there" is a frequent complaint about vacant lots, expressing no mere distaste for the vegetation, but moral outrage at the neglect that produces these anomalies. Plants grow wildly on and around the vestiges of the former International Harvester Component Plant in West Pullman, Chicago. Derelict industrial buildings here and in other ghettos have long ago been stripped of anything of value. Large parcels of land lie unkempt or paved over, subtracted from the life of the city. Contradicting a long-held vision of our country as a place of endless progress, ruins, once unforeseen, are now ignored.

Institutional Ghettos: The New Poorhouses

In New York City, Newark, and Chicago, large and expensive habi-   10
tats—institutional ghettos—have been created for the weakest and most vulnerable members of our society. Institution by institution, facility by facility, these environments have been assembled in the most drug-infested and destitute parts of cities. They are the complex poorhouses of the twenty-first century, places to store a growing marginal population officially certified as "not employable." Residents are selected from the entire population of the municipality for their lack of money or home, for their addictions, for their diseases and other afflictions. Nonresidents come to these institutions to pick up medications, surplus food, used clothes; to get counseling or training; or to do a stint in prison. Other visitors buy drugs and sex.

As Greg Turner, the manager of a day shelter on the Near West Side of Chicago, puts it: "They say, 'Let's get them off the streets and put them together in groups.' It is like the zoo: we are going to put the birds over here; we are going to put the reptiles over there; we are going to put the buffalo over here; we are going to put the seals by the pool. It is doing nothing to work with the root of the problem, just like they do nothing to work with the children, to teach them things so they don't grow up and become more homeless people or substance abusers."

Although the need for individual components—for instance, a homeless shelter or a waste incinerator—may be subject to public debate, the overall consequences of creating such "campuses" of institutions are dismissed. The most important barrier to their growth is the cost to the taxpayers of building and maintaining them.

Such sections of the city are not neighborhoods. The streets surrounding Lincoln Park in south Newark, for example, an area that includes landmark houses, grand public buildings, and a once-elegant hotel, were chosen by two drug treatment programs because six of its large mansions would provide inexpensive housing for a residential treatment program. On the northwest corner of the park, a shelter for battered women just opened in another mansion, and a block north in a former garage is a men's shelter and soup kitchen. The largest structures overlooking the park, the hotel and a former federal office building, house the elderly, who fear going out by themselves. No children play in the park; no parents come home from work. This is a no-man's-land devoted to the contradictory goals selling drugs and getting high, on the one hand, and becoming clean and employed on the other.

Sterling Street, Newark, 1980.

New Immigrant Ghettos: Dynamic and Fluid

In other parts of New York and Chicago a community of recent immigrants is growing up, but this type of ghetto is most visible in South
Central Los Angeles and Compton, where the built environment is more
intimate than in older ghettos, the physical structures are more adaptable,
and it is easier for newcomers to imprint their identity. Here paint goes a
long way to transform the appearance of the street.

The new immigrant ghettos are characterized by tiny offices provid-   15
ing services such as driving instruction, insurance, and immigration assistance; by stores that sell imported beer, produce, and canned goods; and
by restaurants offering home cooking. Notable are the businesses that reflect the busy exchange between the local population and their native
country: money transfers, travel agencies, even funeral homes that ar-
range to have bodies shipped home.

To get by, most residents are forced to resort to exploitative jobs
paying minimum wage or less and usually lacking health benefits. For
housing they crowd together in small, badly maintained apartments, in
cinder-block garages, or in trailers.

Not being eligible for public or city-owned housing may in the long
run prove to be a blessing for the newcomers. Although forced to pay
high rents, immigrants tend to concentrate in neighborhoods that are
part of the urban economy, thus avoiding the extreme social disorganiza-
tion, isolation, and violence that characterize other types of ghettos. Be-

Sterling Street replaced by a parking lot, 1994.

cause of the huge influx of young people with expectations that life will be better for their children and grandchildren, these ghettos are more dynamic and fluid, resembling the foreign-born communities of a century ago.

Reading the Text

1. Why does Vergara see North Camden, New Jersey, as exemplary of city life?
2. According to Vergara, what realities of city life have scholars overlooked, and what explanation does he give for their oversights?
3. Summarize in your own words the three categories of cityscape that Vergara proposes.

Reading the Signs

1. If you live in or near an inner-city area, analyze it in items of the three categories Vergara proposes in this selection. Which category does it best fit, and why? If it doesn't fit any of Vergara's categories, propose one of your own, and explain why it best fits your area.
2. Adopting Vergara's perspective, write a response to Lucy R. Lippard ("Alternating Currents," p. 778) in which you critique her analysis of city life. Consider both her interpretations and the scope of her selection.

3. In a reflective essay, discuss the symbolic meaning of nature in urban life. In addition to Vergara's selection, read or reread Lucy R. Lippard's "Alternating Currents" (p. 778) and Aaron Betsky's "The Man-Made World" (p. 764).

4. In an essay, support, challenge, or modify Vergara's suggestion that "the power of the physical surroundings to shape lives, to mirror people's existence, and to symbolize social relations" (para. 4) is at least equivalent to economic conditions.

MEGAN SHAW AND RICK PRELINGER

Manifest Congestion:
Freeway Landscapes and Timescapes

ǁǁǁ

Americans once got their kicks on Route 66, but they don't have much fun on today's freeways. Though designed to enhance automobility, the modern freeway, as Megan Shaw (b. 1967) and Rick Prelinger (b. 1953) observe here in an essay that originally appeared in Bad Subjects, *is no open road. Rather, it is a site of paradoxes, where frontier-loving SUV owners stand lined up in traffic jams, "looking at concrete soundwalls, and otherwise disengaged from any activity resembling freedom or exploration." With traffic congestion only getting worse every year no matter how many freeways are built to ease the load, who knows what the future holds for American motorists and the landscapes they can no longer see from their cars? Co-director of* Bad Subjects, *Shaw is an independent scholar who writes on American history and culture. Prelinger is a film archivist and author of* Our Secret Century *(1994–96), a CD-ROM anthology of twentieth-century American culture.*

The construction of the U.S. interstate highway system was the largest public works project in human history and has altered our landscape more than any other project. Because Americans value mobility and live in urban sprawls, we spend a lot of time on freeways. Freeway environments invite people to experience landscape in a temporally alienated manner. As a result, people experience time on the freeway very differently than time spent on other highways and streets, as well as time not spent driving. Freeway time, as we see it, develops out of three currents: the historical narratives of which freeways are a contemporary expression, the physical isolation of being on a freeway, and the futures that freeway landscapes project.

Manifest Driving

The historical context that freeways inhabit is the American mythology of the freedom of the open road. Our national mythology of exploring, groundbreaking, and pathfinding is based on the doctrine of manifest destiny, which Europeans used to justify their conquest of North America. By the early twentieth century there wasn't much unexplored land remaining in the continental United States. But there was plenty of land that had been seen by only a few—land that the automobile gave the general population, increasingly concentrated in urban areas, the freedom to explore on their own. The mass availability of the automobile that began in the first quarter of the twentieth century promised that each family would have the American woods and valleys at their feet for exploration, and that the exploration narratives that are central to our country's foundation mythology could be re-enacted by each family on a time scale that would allow those explorations to fit within a summer vacation.

The construction of the interstate highway system in the 1950s was the ultimate public expression of this interpretation of manifest destiny. It was also an expression of the perceived need to decentralize productive resources and open up less-accessible areas in order to strengthen the U.S.'s ability to make war. The dominant relationship that freeways have to the landscape that they inhabit is an inheritance of manifest destiny. Concrete embodies the entitlement felt by the settlers to inhabit the North American landscape. Freeways are therefore a visible history of Americans' love affair with the freedom to explore.

But borrowing from a pre-twentieth-century paradigm for an understanding of the uniquely twentieth-century road-building technology that freeways represent has left us open to the dissonances that arise from the conflict between the lived experience of freeways in the late twentieth century and the remembered experience of free horizons that we were drawing on when we built them. This dissonance is most obvious in urban freeway environments where congestion, frequent reconstruction and re-planning, and mass synchronized work schedules create barriers that break the promises of speed and spontaneous freedom. Urban dwellers spend hundreds of hours a year behind the wheels of vehicles that are going slower than they wish. We navigate this gap between the vision and the reality of freeway driving by building new roads, making existing roads "smarter," and building and buying more commanding vehicles. These are ways that our present-day relationship with the

American roadway is unfolding, leaving us ill-prepared to envision a future in which roadways will continue to satisfy the desires of new generations for speed and freedom.

Lost in a Blur of Speed

If, as J. B. Jackson says, "landscape is history made visible," then   5
looking at freeways as expressions of manifest destiny is one aspect of that
visible history. But Jackson's observation also suggests a parallel question:
what histories do freeways conceal? This second question leads us to look
at what freeways have interrupted, rather than what they have created.

Freeways are newer corridors that are carefully cordoned off by wide
shoulders, guardrails, and soundwalls from the areas through which they
pass. By being so spatially distinct from their environments, they bypass
and conceal the accretion of preexisting historical traces within the landscape, and substitute a carefully limited set of sensory stimuli that has been
edited to minimize distraction and surprise. While driving a two-lane
highway with the windows open, we can hear the calls of animals and
birds, feel different pavements under our tires, smell roadside restaurants
and bodies of water, and see a vast and delightful panorama of nearby visual imagery that illuminates ongoing natural and cultural processes and
offers infinite clues to the history of the place they occupy. Freeways, by
contrast, shift our vision into extreme long shot and confuse the nearby
sensory field with a blur of speed, wind, and noise, pushing us to seek
refuge in the sounds of our car stereos or silences of our daydreams.
Rather than enabling our contemplation, they drive us to distraction, and
condense the richness of the landscape they traverse into a kind of transitional, liminal space. On freeways, people meet without ever quite meeting and interact anonymously, hidden within their vehicles.

Freeways are dramatic monuments to velocity, prosperity, and dispersal but make poor memorials to the human and non-human communities they have displaced. Old city maps and photographs show once-
thriving streets and neighborhoods that were traded in for highways and
"redeveloped" zones, and freeways themselves sit silently where these
communities often flourished, offering few clues as to what previously
existed in the same place. . . .

Freeways to the Future

Freeways as we know them today first emerged in the late 1930s and
early 1940s. The Merritt Parkway was partially opened in 1937 as a scenic
motor route linking affluent Connecticut suburbs with New York City
and soon metamorphosed into a racetrack for speeding commuters. The

Pennsylvania Turnpike opened in October 1940, two months before the first link in the Los Angeles freeway system, the Arroyo Seco Parkway (now the Pasadena Freeway). The interstate system was blueprinted in a 1939 report by the U.S. Bureau of Public Roads, and its visionary equivalent was hyped in Norman Bel Geddes' "Highways and Horizons" or "Futurama" exhibit at the 1939–40 New York World's Fair, General Motors pavilion. The Futurama depicted the "world of 1960," traversed by express highways up to fourteen lanes wide, upon which radio-controlled cars traveled at 50, 70, and 100 miles per hour, separated by high sidewalls for safety. Alone among the many corporate-sponsored utopian visions that came and went prior to World War II, Futurama approached the reality of what actually came to pass. Its vision was dramatically anti-communitarian: a landscape completely organized around facilitating the movement of individual motor vehicles, where freeways replaced "outmoded industrial sections" and "undesirable slum areas."

During World War II, the government stopped most highway construction, attempted to ban pleasure driving, and imposed a national 35 mph speed limit to conserve tires and gasoline. This temporary damper on drivers' freedom was quickly forgotten after the war. Suburbs dramatically expanded, meeting a pent-up demand for new, affordable housing. Demand for passenger cars did not abate: over 40 million were registered in 1950; 61.5 million in 1960; 87 million in 1969; 134 million in 1994. Turnpikes and thruways opened, mostly in the East, enabling rapid access to major cities. In 1956 the Interstate system was finally authorized, and freeways began to appear almost everywhere, enabling sprawl on a dramatically increased scale.

By 1980 the typical U.S. housing unit consisted of a single family   10
living in a single dwelling surrounded by an ornamental yard (57 million out of a total of 86 million housing units). The 1990 census revealed that 73.2 percent of American workers reached their jobs by driving alone. Almost as many people walked (3.9%) as took public transportation (5.3%). Though the census indicated that half of all trips to work took under 22 minutes, many commuters in expensive metropolitan areas commuted two or more hours from remote communities where housing was affordable. In addition, everyday services (shops, child care centers, recreational facilities, schools and colleges, etc.) were also dispersed, and suburban residents found themselves spending more and more time behind the wheel.

Today's Traffic Jam

In the nineties many North Americans were surprised to find themselves regularly inhabiting freeway space. A new and very particular culture has begun to emerge around the roadscape. While it can't any longer be a culture of pure speed, it is beginning to resemble a culture of size, grandiosity, and conspicuous consumption. In the late 1990s, sales figures for SUVs began to approach those for automobiles, and by 1997, almost 37 million "light trucks" (a category that includes SUVs) had been produced in the United States. It is also a culture where aggression and frustration with liminal time expresses itself in violent or threatening encounters that have become known and socially assimilated as "road rage." Though road rage has become a matter of official concern, there has been little, if any, attempt to change driver behavior or address the conditions that lead to violent behavior.

The latest development in freeway technology brings highways and vehicles together with computing and communications technologies. Since 1991, the government has sponsored research into "Intelligent Transportation Systems," known colloquially as "smart highways." In a growing number of cities, intelligent transport systems seek to manage and equalize traffic flow by expediting the transmission of personalized traffic information to drivers so that they can avoid bottlenecks, adjusting traffic signal sequences to manage congestion, and administering "demand pricing" (tolls that vary by time of day and traffic volume) on certain roads. Recently, an experimental smart highway section opened in California. Cars equipped with the proper equipment can navigate this stretch without relying on control by their drivers. What all of these strategies have in common is that none of them depend on changing driver behavior or question the unchallenged primacy of the automobile in our society.

Today, relative prosperity, increased consumption and anticommunitarianism combine to increase traffic congestion. As the number of consuming households and workers in each household increases, so does the number of vehicles: 200 million in all, driven by over 175 million drivers. By joining the fray, people act to create "negative externalities," economics jargon for an individual action whose costs are borne by others. The home remedies for congestion are many, but three seem most significant. Many opt for personal dissociation by acquiring more self-contained, secure vehicles such as SUVs. The trend toward decentralization, which dates back to the 1850s, is in its highest gear ever. Finally, those whose position or skills permit them a high degree of autonomy are beginning to practice the highest form of decentralized living/working: telecommuting.

Telecommuters occupy a highly privileged position, free of vexingly close supervision, close to their families and presumably to nature. Perhaps their greatest privilege is the freedom to withdraw from involuntary participation in the public environment, such as freeways. Presently, the telecommuting model is being dangled tantalizingly in front of all of us, presented as a prototype of the future shape of work. We can't yet know whether this model is sustainable or whether it is adaptable to economic changes, but it's fair to say that the rest of us will have a hard time avoiding backups on the freeway.

A Roadless Future?

The landscape photography that reaches the greatest number of   15
Americans most frequently is doubtless the photography of television
commercials for automobiles. Since the 1950s, when television and freeways concurrently began to affect public consciousness, there has been a
transformation in the way urban and suburban Americans receive information about the "natural landscape." Television advertisements for sport
utility vehicles (SUVs) portray a landscape that is reachable by cars, yet
unmarred by them. In such advertisements, the landscape is identifiably
North American, usually western, depicting either desert or mountain
locations. The natural environment is pristine; it is photographed at sun-
set or sunrise, with alabaster glosses coating windswept rocks that unfold
between stands of soft cliffs or whistling pines. The landscape is born
from the camera, virginal, and then—just as we are wondering which
state tourism department created the ad—the vast and sleek red silhouette of an SUV slices through the center of the calendar-ready picture
and comes to leaden rest upon the rocky breast of the earth.

Conspicuous in their absence from these commercials are roadways.
These landscapes contain no streets or freeways, and the SUV is united
with wilderness in a manner reminiscent of pre-roadway horse-and-
wagon exploration. The vision that is being sold in these commercials ignores all implications of the environmental impact of millions of two-ton
vehicles let loose on roadless spaces, and instead invites the viewer to
imagine a personal freedom to explore uncharted territories—a freedom
that doesn't exist anymore in well-mapped North America.

This advertising works well, and SUVs are purchased right and left
by suburban and urban dwellers. But the roadless vision of a utopian
driving experience invites the question of what has happened to the
American love affair with the promised freedom of the open road. That
this promise should be foregone for a roadless auto-utopia is a startling
disavowal of the particularly American freedom of which the interstate
highway system was an idealized expression. SUVs are marked by their
internal contradictions as creatures that inhabit the same gap between vision and reality that has produced this disavowal. They are supposedly
about access to nature but are environmentally unsustainable machines.
Their functions and accessories have constantly increased in the past ten
years, but are largely unused. They are perceived as safer than small cars
because of their ability to dominate other vehicles, but they are rife with
dangerous design flaws of their own. They are conceived and designed as
"free range" vehicles, but mostly navigate our overcrowded streets and
highways. They are marketed as status symbols but have become a fad.
Their roots lie in trucks, "working vehicles," but they are rarely (at least
in urban areas) used for work: "sport" has replaced "utility." To think of
it another way, "utility" has come to mean "sport." And it's doubt-
ful that they would be as effective status symbols as they are if their

suspensions were lowered closer to the ground. People like to look down on their neighbors.

Most SUV owners experience a kind of driving time that is very different from the radical freedom promised by the advertised roadless frontier. Rather than exploring limitless landscapes, the average SUV owner spends hundreds of hours a year on suburban and urban freeways; caught in traffic, looking at concrete soundwalls, and otherwise disengaged from any activity resembling freedom or exploration. These freeway dwellers are navigating the gap between the millennial promise of the freedom to cruise and the cement-chute reality of urban commuting. Given this gap, a disavowal of freeway mythos is not such a surprise.

Or a Newly Roaded Frontier?

It is not clear what new kinds of relationships will emerge between North Americans and the landscapes they inhabit. The envisioning of a roadless future may say something about our disavowal of the historical weight carried by contemporary freeway sprawl. But it is an imagined future, one that has little to do with the real future of the time commitment that our way of life has made to driving time. As "natural landscapes" become increasingly elusive and scarce, and as sprawl consumes greater territory, there may be more attempts to create "wilderness infills" in the midst of urbanized areas: highly constructed recreational or meditative environments that stand in for what is no longer so accessible. At the same time it also seems likely that authorities in some regions will pioneer the idea of redesigning freeways so that they no longer look like they do today. In the future we may not have a roadless landscape, but instead the next best thing: the well-engineered experience of riding through town in our SUVs along a "smart highway" that has been landscaped to look like a woodland glade.

Reading the Text

1. According to Shaw and Prelinger, how do America's freeways reflect the nation's "open road" and "manifest destiny" (para. 2) mythologies?
2. In the authors' view, how does today's freeway experience contradict the myth of the open road? How have Americans responded to this contradiction?
3. In the authors' analysis, how do the marketing and use of SUVs reflect the end of "the American love affair with the promised freedom of the open road" (para. 17)?
4. How does the statistical information that the authors provide contribute to the persuasiveness of their selection?
5. What are Shaw and Prelinger's predictions for the future meanings of the freeway in America?

Reading the Signs

1. Conduct a survey of the types of automobiles members of the class would prefer to drive if they could have any vehicle they want. Be sure to have students state the reasons for their choices. Then, as a class project, interpret the results. What do they say about your class's attitude toward driving and the mythology of the open road?

2. Read or reread Laurence Shames's "The More Factor" (p. 55), and write an essay that explains the extent to which America's freeway system reflects the "hunger for more."

3. Write an essay that supports, refutes, or modifies Shaw and Prelinger's suggestions that SUVs may represent a "disavowal of [the] freeway mythos" (para. 18). To develop your ideas, consult David Goewey's "'Careful, You May Run Out of Planet': SUVs and the Exploitation of the American Myth" (p. 105).

4. Examine several popular magazines (ranging from *Time* to *Road and Driver*) that contain many advertisements for automobiles. Study the ads semiotically, and then write an essay that interprets the symbolic significance of the car and the road in the ads. To what extent do advertisers promote their vehicles through the myths of the open road and manifest destiny? Do they use other myths as well?

5. In an essay, support, refute, or modify Shaw and Prelinger's contention that "Freeways are dramatic monuments to velocity, prosperity, and dispersal but make poor memorials to the human and nonhuman communities they have displaced" (para. 7).

CECELIA TICHI

Country Music Goes on the Road

|||||||||||||||||||||||||||||||||||||||||||||||||||||||||||||||||

Americans like nothing better than going on the road from time to time, and when they do, they usually turn on their car radios. And what they'll hear, as Cecelia Tichi (b. 1942) notes in this selection from High Lonesome: The American Culture of Country Music *(1994), may depend on where they are. In the Blue Ridge region from Virginia to Tennessee, for instance, there's likely to be a good deal of bluegrass music on the air but even more "country," the Nashville sound, which Americans can now hear from coast to coast and border to border. And listening to that music, Tichi hears a deeper music, an American song of the open road that has been sung from Whitman to Kerouac. Happy trails. Tichi is also the editor of* Reading Country Music: Steel Guitars, Opry Stars, and Honky-Tonk Bars *(1998).*

Suppose you and your family or friends decide to drive cross-country for a summer vacation. You head west from your home in, say, Philadelphia one hot July right after the picnics and fireworks of the Fourth. You plan to cross the United States, the Plains and the Divide, and along the way you listen to a succession of country music stations playing older favorites and current hits at the top of the country charts: songs by Garth Brooks, Alan Jackson, George Jones, Hal Ketchum, Dolly Parton, Reba McEntire, Willie Nelson, Rodney Crowell, the Oak Ridge Boys, Shenandoah, Alabama, Clint Black, Lorrie Morgan, Marty Stuart, k. d. lang, Vern Gosdin, Vince Gill, Tammy Wynette, Dwight Yoakam, K. T. Oslin, Johnny Cash, Randy Travis, Travis Tritt, Emmylou Harris.

Opting for a southerly route down Interstate 81, you cross through southeastern Virginia into Tennessee, perhaps unaware that the beautiful surrounding green mountain ridges and valleys are the cradle of American country music, which "evolved primarily out of the reservoir of folksongs, ballads, dances, and instrumental pieces brought to North America by Anglo-Celtic immigrants" (Malone) who settled in these Appalachian hills and hollows. Passing through this part of Tennessee and Virginia (with Kentucky in hailing distance), your group tunes in to a radio station playing bluegrass, the "high lonesome sound" (Lomax) manifestly expressing this old ballad tradition. Setting the cruise control, you listen to Bill Monroe and his Blue Grass Boys, to the Stanley Brothers or Flatt and Scruggs, and to several bluegrass bands with names like Northern Lights, the Doug Dillard Band, Livewire, Lonesome Standard Time, Alison Krauss and Union Station. At 60 mph, you are speeding through country music's point of origin as you listen to the Nashville Bluegrass Band play and sing the lines, "Sometimes it feels like the highway's my home / The interstate's the street where I live." An apt traveler's tune, you think, noting the title, "When I Get Where I'm Goin' " (*Waiting for the Hard Times to Go*, 1993). It's as if the deejay picked the song just for you.

High on the Cumberland Plateau, heading toward Nashville, by now on I-40, you joke about stopping in Nashville to look up Garth Brooks. Certainly you plan to visit Memphis to see Elvis's Graceland, which you associate solely—and wrongly—with rock 'n' roll, not country. Along Routes 40, 76, and 81, you listen to rock and to rhythm-and-blues, then to National Public Radio's classical programs (Mozart across Missouri) and, late each afternoon, *All Things Considered*.

The odometer clocks miles by the hundreds, then thousands, and you and your group, seeing styles change to Western boots and wide-brimmed hats, increasingly think of yourselves as romantic pioneers of a sort, especially approaching the Rockies, for the mountain ranges look much like pictures of Western landscapes seen all your lives, even down to mountain valleys suggesting the path or roadway leading toward the setting sun. And the cinematic quality is not lost on you, because you've seen numerous "road" movies, including *Thelma and Louise* (1991). Now in the West, you begin thinking of yourselves as a kind of "road" movie, though you might feel a bit embarrassed to say so. It occurs to you that your American vacation is happening right on the road, that your destination is maybe less important than the drive itself—the movement across vast spaces, plains and valleys, hills and mountains. You feel somehow certified or validated by the road trip, which feels quintessentially American. Across Colorado, you sing along with a country song coming over the radio. You try to remember the words to "Rocky Mountain High."

This scenario could end at Denver, but let's push it a bit farther to   5 open up some possibilities. Say two days later you have crossed into California and are visiting San Francisco's North Beach section. You learn from a local resident that the area is famous as a onetime center for the rebellious Beat-generation writers of the 1950s, and that the best-known statement of the Beats relates to your own road travel. Jack Kerouac's *On the Road* (1957) is a picaresque automobile-age adventure. You remember that a 1960s, then 1993, TV series, *Route 66,* was based on a famous American highway and dubbed a "Kerouac-style adventure." If you know country artist Steve Earle's "The Other Kind," you could recall a reference to Kerouac. Neat coincidence, TV and the Beat writer hooked up with the country singer/songwriter and with your group, too—but you don't dwell on it.

Instead, elated to have driven coast to coast, you are claiming a certain fellowship of the road with the postwar Kerouac. One lasagna lunch later, you stop into the North Beach's City Lights Bookstore, shrine of the Beats. Surrounded by books, mindful of classroom days, you notice paperbacks of other American "road" writers like Walt Whitman, who imagined his "right hand pointing to . . . the public road" and whose "Song of the Open Road" (1867) celebrated "the long brown path before me leading wherever I choose."

Back in the car, en route to the motel, you turn once again to a country radio station—the kind of music you have listened to all across the continent—and note that Hank Snow's "I'm Movin' On," Rodney Crowell and Donivan Cowart's "Leaving Louisiana in the Broad Daylight," Ricky Van Shelton singing "Backroads," Willie Nelson's "On the Road Again," and Emmylou Harris singing John C. Fogerty's "Lodi" all have something in common. All are about life on the American road.

At this point, you have a unique opportunity to grasp the extent to which, in this historically mobile nation, country music is virtually a missing puzzle piece in the many representations of the American road. If literature, film, and the visual arts all celebrate the American road as a long-term, important, and prominent part of the national culture, so does country music, contributing extensively to the meanings we attach to the road. They are meanings you vacationers attach to yourselves on this trip:

escape, freedom, adventure, self-discovery, initiation, success, knowledge. Your group, in fact, has been taking part in an American national experience imprinted repeatedly in numerous imaginative forms—and very much present in country music. As a traveler, you find yourself at the center of the music and of the poems and novels and paintings of the road. Most important for this book, your trip suggests the extent to which country music is a crucial and vital part of the American identity. The country songs show a profound understanding of the power of the road—the "open road," as Whitman called it—as form and symbol in the formation of an American self-concept over centuries. As you have discovered, the road is much more than a pass-through, a transportation device, a means from *here* to *there*. Surpassing all these, it is a place in and of itself, a fundamental defining part of an American experience.

So far, this road venture seems mainly jubilant, a celebration of self and space. But there are somber sides to country music, as to American cultural life. Perhaps the national ideology of "the pursuit of happiness" has simply proved too burdensome over the centuries. Once again, your vacation is helpful here. You are traveling, remember, in the month of July, setting off just after the July 4th commemoration of the 1776 signing of the Declaration of Independence. But when Thomas Jefferson wrote that phrase, "the pursuit of happiness," into the Declaration, he could not have imagined the strain it would ultimately impose on the citizenry. A national founding document authorizing not just life and liberty but *the pursuit of happiness* has become especially burdensome in a twentieth-century consumer and media culture, in which images and objects promising "happiness" can only tantalize, and when human relationships so often prove difficult, painful, or impossible.

Emotional life in America, according to our artists and analysts, is   10
much less a storybook conclusion to "the pursuit of happiness" than it
is, all too often, a face-to-face encounter with loneliness. The artists of
country music have confronted this issue directly and in a wide range
of styles over decades, most memorably in Hank Williams's classic
"I'm So Lonesome I Could Cry." But other artists and writers have
also acknowledged this reality up front. Heading back east and approaching the Mississippi, you might slip in a books-on-tape cassette
and listen to Mark Twain's *Adventures of Huckleberry Finn,* hearing that
young Huck, rafting on the river "roadway" of the Mississippi, watches
"the lonesomeness of the river . . . just solid lonesomeness." Stopping
in Chicago for a day or so, you might decide to stroll Michigan
Avenue and visit the Art Institute, where you stand face-to-face with
Edward Hopper's *Nighthawks* (1942), the famous and much-reproduced
twentieth-century painting of figures in a diner at night. Seen through
the plateglass windows of the diner, they look like loneliness itself.
Back on the interstate, you complete the theme by playing some more
country tapes: Roy Orbison singing the up-tempo "Only the Lonely"
or Patsy Cline, Tammy Wynette, or Emmylou Harris singing the
haunting show ballad "Lonely Street." Together, these texts become a
sensory surround of a prominent American trait, loneliness—a part of
the national experience so deeply embedded in the culture that it continues over centuries to insist on its own message in our literature, social commentary, and art, prominent among these the art of country
music.

What, finally, is the point of this marathon road trip? It is to realize
that the "tourists" I invented provide a model by which culture can be
defined in its many connections. When the poetry of Walt Whitman
links up with the country music of Hank Williams, when Dolly Parton
and Ralph Waldo Emerson pair up and Mark Twain and Emmylou
Harris are found to have a common ground, and the vacationing traveler is also involved, then new ideas about cultural relations become
possible.

WORKS CITED

Kerouac, Jack. *On the Road.* 1955. Reprint. New York: Penguin, 1991.
Lomax, Alan. "Bluegrass Background: Folk Music in Overdrive." *Esquire,* October
    1959, 108–9.
Malone, Bill C. *Country Music U.S.A.* Rev. ed. Austin: University of Texas Press,
    1985.
Twain, Mark. *The Adventures of Huckleberry Finn.* Edited by Sculley Bradley, Richard
    Croom Beatty, and E. Hudson Long. New York: Norton, 1961.
Whitman, Walt. "Song of Myself," "Song of the Open Road." In *Leaves of Grass.*
    Edited by Sculley Bradley and Harold W. Blodgett. New York: Norton, 1973.

Reading the Text

1. Summarize the musical and cultural changes that Tichi charts on her imaginary cross-country trip.
2. How do country music, Walt Whitman's poetry, and the writing of Mark Twain and Jack Kerouac relate to the theme of the open road, in Tichi's view?
3. What does Tichi consider the somber side of country music—and of American cultural life?
4. How does Tichi construct a semiotic system of meanings that are associated with the road?

Reading the Signs

1. In your journal, reflect on a road trip that you have taken (either by yourself or with friends or family). What were the symbolic significances of the places you drove through? If you listened to local radio stations, how did they convey a sense of place?
2. In an essay, respond to Tichi's contention that, in country music, "emotional life . . . is much less a storybook conclusion to the 'pursuit of happiness' than it is, all too often, a face-to-face encounter with loneliness" (para. 10).
3. In class, divide the United States into regions and assign each region a characteristic musical form (or forms). Then discuss whether your assignments are more reflective of genuine regional differences or of images and stereotypes associated with each region.
4. Research the audience of country music today. Is it still a regional taste, or has it become mainstream or a mixture of both? Use your findings as the basis of an essay in which you argue for or against Tichi's assumption that the mythologies inherent in country music are, in essence, American mythologies.

GLOSSARY

archetype (n.)   A recurring character type or plot pattern found in literature, mythology, and popular culture. Sea monsters like Jonah's whale and Moby Dick are archetypes, as are stories that involve long sea journeys or descents into the underworld.

canon (n.)   Books or works that are considered essential to a literary tradition, as the plays of Shakespeare are part of the canon of English literature.

class (n.)   A group of related objects or people. Those who share the same economic status in a society are said to be of the same social class: for example, working class, middle class, upper class. Members of a social class tend to share the same interests and political viewpoints.

code (n.)   A system of **signs** or values that assigns meanings to the elements that belong to it. Thus, a traffic code defines a red light as a "stop" signal and a green light as a "go," while a fashion code determines whether an article of clothing is stylish. To *decode* a system is to figure out its meanings, as in interpreting the tattooing and body-piercing fads.

connotation (n.)   The meaning suggested by a word, as opposed to its objective reference, or **denotation.** Thus, the word *flag* might connote (or suggest) feelings of patriotism, while it literally denotes (or refers to) a pennantlike object.

consumption (n.)   The use of products and services, as opposed to their production. A *consumer culture* is one that consumes more than it produces. As a consumer culture, for example, America uses more goods such as TV sets and stereos than it manufactures, which results in a trade deficit with those *producer cultures* (such as Japan) with which America trades.

context (n.)   The environment in which a **sign** can be interpreted. In the context of a college classroom, for example, tee shirts, jeans, and sneakers are interpreted as ordinary casual dress. Wearing the same outfit in the context of a job interview at IBM would be interpreted as meaning that you're not serious about wanting the job.

cultural studies (n.)   The academic study of ordinary, everyday culture rather than **high culture**. See also **culture; culture industry; mass culture; popular culture.**

culture (n.)   The overall system of values and traditions shared by a group of people. Not exactly synonymous with *society,* which can include numerous cultures within its boundaries, a culture encompasses the worldviews of those who belong to it. Thus, the United States, which is a **multicultural** society, includes the differing worldviews of people of African, Asian, Native American, and European descent. See also **cultural studies; culture industry; high culture; mass culture; popular culture.**

culture industry (n.)   The commercial forces behind the production of **mass culture** or entertainment. See also **culture; cultural studies; high culture; mass culture; popular culture.**

denotation (n.)   The particular object or class of objects to which a word refers. Contrast with **connotation.**

discourse (n.)   The words, concepts, and presuppositions that constitute the knowledge and understanding of a particular community, often academic or professional. In the discourse of modern medicine, for example, illness is first presumed to have material causes—for instance, chemical problems or invasive agents—and only secondly hypothesized to have emotional causes.

dominant culture (n.)   The group within a **multicultural** society whose traditions, values, and beliefs are held to be normative, as the European tradition is the dominant culture in the United States.

Eurocentric (adj.)   Related to a worldview founded on the traditions and history of European culture, usually at the expense of non-European cultures.

function (n.)   The utility of an object, as opposed to its cultural meaning. Spandex or lycra shorts, for example, have a functional value for cyclists because they're lightweight and aerodynamic. On the other hand, such shorts have become a general fashion item for both men and women because of their cultural meaning, not their function. Many noncyclists wear Spandex to project an image of hard-bodied fitness, sexiness, or just plain trendiness, for instance.

gender (n.)   One's sexual identity and the roles that follow from it, as determined by the norms of one's culture rather than by biology or genetics. The assumption that women should be foremost in the nurturing of children is a gender norm; the fact that only women can give birth is a biological phenomenon.

hacker (n.)   A person who "breaks into" another person's or an institution's computer system without permission, either for entertainment or criminal purposes.

high culture (n.)   The products of the elite arts, including classical music, literature, drama, opera, painting, and sculpture. See also **cultural studies; culture; culture industry; mass culture; popular culture.**

icon (n.), **iconic** (adj.)   In **semiotics,** a **sign** that visibly resembles its referent, as a photograph looks like the thing it represents. More broadly, an icon is someone (often a celebrity) who enjoys a commanding or representative place in popular culture. Michael Jackson and Madonna are music video icons. Contrast with **symbol.**

ideology (n.)   The beliefs, interests, and values that determine one's interpretations or judgments and that are often associated with one's social class. For example, in the ideology of modern business, a business is designed to produce profits, not social benefits.

image (n.)   Literally, a pictorial representation; more generally, the identity that one projects to others through such things as clothing, grooming, speech, and behavior.

Internet, the (n.)   An electronic network, originally developed for military purposes, that links millions of computers around the world. Also called *the Net, World Wide Web,* or *Web.*

mass culture (n.)   A subset of **popular culture** that includes the popular entertainments that are commercially produced for widespread consumption. See also **cultural studies; culture; culture industry; high culture.**

mass media (n. pl.)   The means of communication, often controlled by the **culture industry,** that include newspapers, popular magazines, radio, television, film, and the Internet.

militia (n.)   A citizen army; often used to refer to a paramilitary group that holds antigovernment views.

multiculturalism (n.), **multicultural** (adj.)   In American education, the movement to incorporate the traditions, history, and beliefs of the United States' non-European cultures into a traditionally *monocultural* (or single-culture) curriculum dominated by European thought and history.

mythology (n.)   The overall framework of values and beliefs incorporated in a given cultural system or worldview. Any given belief within such a structure—like the belief that "a woman's place is in the home"—is called a *myth.*

politics (n.)   Essentially, the practice of promoting one's interests in a competitive social environment. Not restricted to electioneering; there may be office politics, classroom politics, academic politics, and sexual politics.

popular culture (n.)   That segment of a **culture** that incorporates the activities of everyday life, including the consumption of consumer goods and the production and enjoyment of mass-produced entertainments. See also **cultural studies; culture industry; high culture; mass culture.**

postmodernism (n.), **postmodern** (adj.)   The worldview behind contemporary literature, art, music, architecture, and philosophy that rejects traditional attempts to make meaning out of human history and experience. For the *postmodern* artist, art does not attempt to create new explanatory myths or **symbols** but rather recycles or repeats existing images, as does the art of Andy Warhol.

semiotics (n.)   In short, the study of **signs.** Synonymous with *semiology,* semiotics is concerned with both the theory and practice of interpreting linguistic, cultural, and behavioral sign systems. One who practices *semiotic analysis* is called a *semiotician* or *semiologist.*

sign (n.)   Anything that bears a meaning. Words, objects, images, and forms of behavior are all signs whose meanings are determined by the particular **codes,** or **systems,** in which they appear.

symbol (n.), **symbolic** (adj.)   A **sign,** according to semiotician C. S. Peirce, whose significance is arbitrary. The meaning of the word *bear,* for example, is arbitrarily determined by those who use it. Contrast with **icon.**

system (n.)   The **code,** or network, within which a **sign** functions and so achieves its meaning through its associational and differential relations with other signs. The English language is a sign system, as is a fashion code.

text (n.)   A complex of **signs,** which may be linguistic, imagistic, behavioral, or musical, that can be read or interpreted.

virtual reality (n.)   A simulated world that is created using computer technology.

CITING SOURCES

When you write an essay and use another author's work—whether you use the author's exact words or his or her ideas—you need to cite that source for your readers. In most humanities courses, writers use the system of documentation developed by the Modern Language Association (MLA). This system indicates a source in two ways: (1) notations that briefly identify the sources in the body of your essay and (2) notations that give fuller bibliographic information about the sources at the end of your essay. The notations for some commonly used types of sources are illustrated below. For documenting other sources, consult a writing handbook or Joseph Gibaldi's *MLA Handbook for Writers of Research Papers,* fifth edition (New York: Modern Language Association of America, 1999).

In-Text Citations

In the body of your essay, you should signal to your reader that you've used a source and indicate, in parentheses, where your reader can find the source in your list of works cited. You don't need to repeat the author's name in both your writing and in the parenthetical note.

SOURCE WITH ONE AUTHOR:

Patrick Goldstein asserts that "Talk radio has pumped up the volume of our public discourse and created a whole new political language — perhaps the prevailing political language" (16).

SOURCE WITH TWO OR THREE AUTHORS:

Researchers have found it difficult to study biker subcultures because, as one team describes the problem, "it was too dangerous to take issue with outlaws on their own turf" (Hooper and Moore 368).

AN INDIRECT SOURCE:

In discussing the baby mania trend, *Time* claimed that "Career women are opting for pregnancy and they are doing it in style" (qtd. in Faludi 106).

List of Works Cited

At the end of your essay, include a list of all the sources you have cited in parenthetical notations. This list, alphabetized by author, should provide full publishing information for each source; you should indicate the date you accessed any online sources.

The first line of each entry should begin flush left. Subsequent lines should be indented half an inch (or five spaces) from the left margin. Double space the entire list, both between and within entries.

BOOK BY ONE AUTHOR:

Faludi, Susan. *Backlash: The Undeclared War against American Women*. New York: Crown, 1991.

BOOK BY TWO OR MORE AUTHORS:

Collins, Ronald K. L., and David M. Skover. *The Death of Discourse*. New York: Westview Press, 1996.
(Note that only the first author's name is reversed.)

WORK IN AN ANTHOLOGY:

Prager, Emily. "Our Barbies, Ourselves." *Signs of Life in the USA: Readings on Popular Culture for Writers.* 3rd ed. Ed. Sonia Maasik and Jack Solomon. Boston: Bedford/St. Martin's, 2000.

ARTICLE IN A WEEKLY MAGAZINE:

Goldstein, Patrick. "Yakety-Yak, Please Talk Back." *Los Angeles Times Magazine* 16 July 1995: 16+.
(A plus sign is used to indicate that the article is not printed on consecutive pages; otherwise, a page range should be given: 16–25, for example.)

ARTICLE IN A MONTHLY MAGAZINE:

Smith, Gina. "Worlds without End." *Buzz* Sept. 1995: 46–48.

ARTICLE IN A JOURNAL:

Hooper, Columbus B., and Johnny Moore. "Women in Outlaw Motorcycle Gangs." *Journal of Contemporary Ethnography* 18 (1990): 363–87.

FILM OR VIDEOTAPE:

The English Patient. Dir. Anthony Minghella. Perf. Willem Dafoe, Juliette Binoche, Ralph Fiennes, and Kristin Scott Thomas. Miramax, 1996.

TELEVISION PROGRAM:

Ally McBeal. Perf. Calista Flockhart. KBFX, Bakersfield. 2 Aug. 1999.

PERSONAL INTERVIEW:

Chese, Charlie. Personal interview. 28 Sept. 1999.

E-MAIL:

Katt, Susie. "Interpreting Marlowe." E-mail to the author. 29 Sept. 1999.

ARTICLE IN AN ONLINE REFERENCE BOOK:

"Color." *Britannica Online*. Vers. 97.1.1. Mar. 1998. Encyclopaedia Britannica. 30 May 1999 <http://www.eb.com:180>.

ARTICLE IN AN ONLINE JOURNAL:

Schaffer, Scott. "Disney and the Imagineering of History." *Postmodern Culture* 6.3 (1996): 62 pars. 12 Aug. 1999 <http://jefferson.village .virginia.edu/pmc/backissues/contents.596.html>.

ARTICLE IN AN ONLINE MAGAZINE:

Rosenberg, Scott. "Don't Link or I'll Sue!" *Salon* 12 Aug. 1999. 13 Aug. 1999 <http://www.salon.com/tech/col/rose/1999/08/12 /deep_links/index.html>.

ONLINE BOOK:

James, Henry. *The Bostonians*. London and New York, 1886. *The Henry James Scholar's Guide to Web Sites*. Ed. Richard Hathaway. Aug. 1999. SUNY New Paltz. 13 Aug. 1999 <http://www .newpaltz.edu/~hathaway/bostonians1.html>.

ONLINE POEM:

Frost, Robert. "The Road Not Taken." *Mountain Interval*. New York, 1915. *Project Bartleby Archive*. Ed. Steven van Leeuwen. Mar. 1995. 13 Aug. 1999 <http://www.bartleby.com/119/1.html>.

PROFESSIONAL WEB SITE:

National Council of Teachers of English. Urbana, IL. Feb. 1997. 1 May 1997 <http://www.ncte.org>.

PERSONAL HOME PAGE:

Rochelle, James. Home page. May 1999. 13 Aug. 1999 <http://www
.homestead.com/jamestheviking>.

POSTING TO A DISCUSSION LIST:

Diaz, Joanne. "Poetic Expressions." Online posting. 29 Apr. 1999. Conference on College Composition and Communication. 4 Jul. 1999
<http://www.ncte.org/cccc/99>.

ONLINE SCHOLARLY PROJECT:

Corpus Linguistics. Ed. Michael Barlow. Apr. 1998. Rice U. 13 Aug.
1999 <http://www.ruf.rice.edu/~barlow/corpus.html>.

WORK FROM AN ONLINE SUBSCRIPTION SERVICE:

"Pool." *Compton's Encyclopedia Online.* Vers. 2.0. 1997. America Online.
30 Jul. 1999. Keyword: Compton's.

Fred Davis, "Blue Jeans." Originally titled "Of Maids' Uniforms and Blue Jeans: The Drama of Status Ambivalences in Clothing and Fashion." First appeared in *Qualitative Sociology* 12, no. 4 (Winter 1989). Copyright © 1989. Reprinted by permission of Kluwer Academic/Human Sciences Press.

Benjamin DeMott, "Put on a Happy Face." Appeared in the September 1995 issue of *Harper's* magazine. Copyright © 1995 by *Harper's* magazine. All rights reserved. Reproduced by special permission.

Holly Devor, "Gender Role Behaviors and Attitudes," from *Gender Blending* by Holly Devor. Copyright © 1989 by Holly Devor. Reprinted by permission of Indiana University Press.

Philip K. Dick, "Do Androids Dream of Electric Sheep?" from *Blade Runner.* Copyright © 1982 by Philip K. Dick. Reprinted by permission of Ballantine Books, a division of Random House, Inc.

Peter Doskoch, "The Mind of the Militias." Appeared in the July–August 1995 issue of *Psychology Today.* Copyright © 1995 by Sussex Publishers, Inc. Reprinted with permission from *Psychology Today* magazine.

Susan Douglas, "Signs of Intelligent Life on TV." Appeared in the May–June 1995 issue of *Ms.* Copyright © 1995 by *Ms.* Magazine. Reprinted by permission of *Ms.* Magazine.

Michael E. Dyson, "Be Like Mike? Michael Jordan and the Pedagogy of Desire." Originally published in *Cultural Studies*, 1993 (Routledge). Reprinted by Taylor & Francis Ltd.

Gary Engle, "What Makes Superman So Darned American?" from *Superman at Fifty: The Persistence of a Legend*, Gary Engle and Dennis Dooley, eds. Copyright © 1987 by Octavia Press. Reprinted by permission of Octavia Press.

Stuart Ewen, "Hard Bodies," from *All Consuming Images* by Stuart Ewen. Copyright © 1988 by Basic Books, Inc. Reprinted by permission of Basic Books, a division of HarperCollins Publishers, Inc.

James William Gibson, "Post-Vietnam Blues," from *Warrior Dreams: Violence and Manhood in Post-Vietnam America* by James William Gibson. Copyright © 1994 by James William Gibson. Reprinted by permission of Hill and Wang, a division of Farrar, Straus & Giroux, LLC.

Malcolm Gladwell, "The Science of Shopping," from *The New Yorker*, November 4, 1996. Reprinted with permission.

David Goewey, "Careful, You May Run Out of Planet." Copyright © 1999 David Goewey. Used with permission.

Jessica Hagedorn, "Asian Women in Film: No Joy, No Luck." Appeared in the January–February 1994 issue of *Ms.* magazine. Copyright © 1994 by Jessica Hagedorn. Reprinted by permission of the Harold Schmidt Literary Agency.

Evelynn Hammonds, "Race, Sex, AIDS: The Construction of 'Other.'" Originally appeared in *Radical America*, vol. 20. Copyright © 1987 by Evelynn Hammonds. Reprinted with permission of the author.

LynNell Hancock, "The Haves and the Have-Nots," from *Newsweek*, February 27, 1995. Copyright © 1995 by Newsweek, Inc. All rights reserved. Reprinted by permission.

Thomas Hine, "What's in a Package?" from *The Total Package* by Thomas Hine. Copyright © 1995 by Thomas Hine. By permission of Little, Brown and Company (Inc.).

Laura Stempel Mumford, "Plotting Paternity: Looking for Dad on the Daytime Soaps," from *Love and Ideology in the Afternoon: Soap Opera, Women, and Television Genre.* Copyright © 1995 by Laura Stempel Mumford. Reprinted by permission of the Indiana University Press.

K. C. Myers, "Roadside Bones." Published by *Eternity, The Online Journal of the Speculative Imagination,* February 1999. Copyright © 1999 Eternity Press.

Anne Norton, "The Signs of Shopping," from *Republic of Signs* by Anne Norton, pp. 68–75. Copyright © 1993 by The University of Chicago Press. Reprinted with the permission of the University of Chicago Press and the author.

Michael Omi, "In Living Color: Race and American Culture." Reprinted from *Culture Politics in Contemporary America,* edited by Ian Angus and Sut Jhally, Routledge, New York. Copyright © 1989 by the author. Reprinted by permission of the author.

Michael Parenti, "Class and Virtue," from *Make-Believe Media: Politics of Film and Television* by Michael Parenti. Copyright © 1991 by Michael Parenti. Reprinted by permission of St. Martin's Press, Inc.

Emily Prager, "Our Barbies, Ourselves." Originally titled, "Major Barbie." Originally appeared in *Interview,* Brant Publications, Inc., December 1991. Reprinted with permission from *Interview* Magazine.

Robert B. Ray, "The Thematic Paradigm—The Resolution of Incompatible Values," originally titled "Formal and Thematic Paradigms," from *A Certain Tendency of the Hollywood Cinema, 1930–1980* by Robert B. Ray. Copyright © 1985 by Princeton University Press. Reprinted by permission of Princeton University Press.

Jimmie L. Reeves, Mark C. Rodgers, and Michael Epstein, "Rewriting Popularity: The Cult Files," from *Deny All Knowledge: Reading the* X-Files, edited by David Lavery, Angela Hague, and Marla Cartwright. Copyright © 1996 by Syracuse University Press. Reprinted with permission.

Roy Rivenburg, "Snap! Crackle! Plot!" from *The Los Angeles Times,* October 18, 1998. Copyright © 1998 by Roy Rivenburg. Reprinted by permission of *The Los Angeles Times.*

Tricia Rose, "Bad Sistas: Black Women Rappers and Sexual Politics in Rap Music," from *Black Noise.* Copyright © 1994 by Tricia Rose, Wesleyan University Press. By permission of University Press of New England.

Jennifer Scanlon, "Board Games and the Socialization of Young Adolescent Girls," from *Delinquents and Debutantes: Twentieth Century American Girls' Cultures,* edited by Sherrie A. Inness. Copyright © 1998 by New York University. Reprinted by permission of New York University Press and the editor.

Amy E. Schwartz, "The ABCs of Popular Culture," *The Washington Post,* May 9, 1996. Copyright © 1996 by *The Washington Post.* Reprinted with permission.

Linda Seger, "Creating the Myth," from *Making a Good Script Great* by Linda Seger. Copyright © 1987 by Linda Seger. Reprinted by permission of Samuel French, Inc.

Matt Zoller Seitz, "Grisham Succeeds in a Novel Way," from *The Newark Star Ledger.* Copyright © 1996 by Matt Zoller Seitz. Reprinted by permission of *The Newark Star Ledger.*

Susan Willis, "Disney World: Public Use/Private State," *South Atlantic Quarterly*, 92:1 (Winter 1993), pp. 119–38. Copyright © 1993, Duke University Press. All rights reserved. Reprinted with permission.

Naomi Wolf, "The Beauty Myth," from *The Beauty Myth* by Naomi Wolf. Copyright © 1991 by Naomi Wolf. Reprinted by permission of William Morrow and Company, Inc.

Photo Credits

Introduction
Aliens image appears courtesy of the Everett Collection.
Alien with woman appears courtesy of the Everett Collection.

Chapter 1
Mall of America photograph appears courtesy of Steve Woit/NYT Pictures.
Man working out with weights appears by permission of Stock Connection/ Picture Quest.

Chapter 2
Energizer Bunny appears courtesy of the Energizer Battery Company.

Portfolio of Advertisements
Altoids advertisement, "They appear to be dividing." Copyright © 1998 by Callard & Bowser-Suchard, Inc. Appears courtesy of Hunter & Associates.

"Got Milk?" (image of Kermit the Frog) appears courtesy of Bozell Worldwide, Inc. as agent for National Fluid Milk Processor Promotion Board.

"Four minimum wage jobs" is reprinted with courtesy of Duck Head Apparel Co., Inc.

Volkswagen advertisement used by permission of Volkswagen of America, Inc. and Arnold Communications, Inc.

Forever Moschino advertisement is reprinted courtesy of Moda and Company.

Joe Boxer ad appears courtesy of the Joe Boxer Corporation.

"Who Says Guys Are Afraid of Commitment?" reprinted with permission of Eastpak, Inc.

"What would you do? Ask people to judge me by my ability, not my disability" reprinted courtesy of Esprit de Corp.

Gardenburger, Inc., advertisement. Copyright © 1999 by Gardenburger, Inc. Reprinted by permission.

Chapter 3
Stack of TV sets, © John Coletti. Appears by permission of Stock Boston/ Picture Quest.

The crew of *Star Trek* appears by permission of Archive Photos/Picture Quest.

Chapter 4
Hollywood sign photograph appears by permission of Michael J. Howell/ Stock Boston/Picture Quest.

Doris Day photograph appears by permission of Archive Photos/Picture Quest.

Chapter 5
Cover of *Dangerous Passions* by Kat Martin. Reprinted by permission of St. Martin's Press.

Chapter 6

Hennessey advertisement, "appropriately complex." Courtesy of Schiefflin & Somerset Company.

Chapter 7

"I think there's a pretty simple reason Jackie and I are so comfortable with each other" is copyright © 1992 by the Cherokee Group. Reprinted with courtesy of The Cherokee Group.

Chapter 8

Tattoo Man with sunglasses, photograph by Hans Neleman. Appears by permission of Image Bank/Picture Quest.

Chapter 9

Michael Jordan photograph appears by permission of Archive Photos/Picture Quest.

Adam West & Burt Ward, "Batman and Robin," appears by permission of Archive Photos/Picture Quest.

Barbie "Got Milk?" photograph by Greg Mancuso. Appears by permission of Stock Boston/Picture Quest.

Chapter 10

Disneyland photograph by permission of Uniphoto/Picture Quest.

Mall scene photograph by permission of Martin Rogers/Picture Quest.

Camilo José Vergara, "Sterling Street, Newark, 1980." Copyright © 1995 by Camilo José Vergara. By permission of the author.

Camilo José Vergara, "Sterling Street replaced by a parking lot, 1994." Copyright © 1995 by Camilo José Vergara. By permission of the author.

Edward Hopper, "Nighthawks, 1942." Copyright © 1993, The Art Institute of Chicago.

INDEX OF
AUTHORS
AND TITLES